Fodor's '07

P9-BIV-419

NEW ZEALAND

Where to Stay and Eat for All Budgets

Must-See Sights and Local Secrets

Ratings You Can Trust

Fodor's Travel Publications   New York, Toronto, London, Sydney, Auckland
www.fodors.com

FODOR'S NEW ZEALAND 2007
Editors: Sarah Gold, Shannon Kelly

Editorial Production: Aviva Muse-Orlinoff
Editorial Contributors: Sue Farley, Doug Johansen, Alia Levine, Bob Marriott, Toni Mason, Kathy Ombler, Jan Poole, Stephanie Stephens
Maps: David Lindroth, Inc., and Ed Jacobus, *cartographers;* Rebecca Baer and Bob Blake, *map editors*
Design: Fabrizio La Rocca, *creative director;* Guido Caroti, *art director;* Moon Sun Kim, *cover designer;* Melanie Marin, *senior picture editor*
Production/Manufacturing: Angela L. McLean
Cover Photo (Farmland near Blenheim): Rob Suisted/naturespic.com

ISBN-10: 1–4000–1684–3

ISBN-13: 978–1–4000–1684–6

ISSN: 1531–0450

SPECIAL SALES

This book is available for special discounts for bulk purchases for sales promotions or premiums. Special editions, including personalized covers, excerpts of existing books, and corporate imprints, can be created in large quantities for special needs. For more information, write to Special Markets/Premium Sales, 1745 Broadway, MD 6-2, New York, New York 10019, or e-mail specialmarkets@randomhouse.com.

AN IMPORTANT TIP & AN INVITATION

Although all prices, opening times, and other details in this book are based on information supplied to us at press time, changes occur all the time in the travel world, and Fodor's cannot accept responsibility for facts that become outdated or for inadvertent errors or omissions. So **always confirm information when it matters,** especially if you're making a detour to visit a specific place. Your experiences—positive and negative—matter to us. If we have missed or misstated something, **please write to us.** We follow up on all suggestions. Contact the New Zealand editor at editors@fodors.com or c/o Fodor's at 1745 Broadway, New York, New York 10019.

PRINTED IN THE UNITED STATES OF AMERICA

10 9 8 7 6 5 4 3 2 1

Be a Fodor's Correspondent

Your opinion matters. It matters to us. It matters to your fellow Fodor's travelers, too. And we'd like to hear it. In fact, we *need* to hear it.

When you share your experiences and opinions, you become an active member of the Fodor's community. That means we'll not only use your feedback to make our books better, but we'll publish your names and comments whenever possible. Throughout our guides, look for "Word of Mouth," excerpts of your unvarnished feedback.

Here's how you can help improve Fodor's for all of us.

Tell us when we're right. We rely on local writers to give you an insider's perspective. But our writers and staff editors—who are the best in the business—depend on you. Your positive feedback is a vote to renew our recommendations for the next edition.

Tell us when we're wrong. We're proud that we update most of our guides every year. But we're not perfect. Things change. Hotels cut services. Museums change hours. Charming cafés lose charm. If our writer didn't quite capture the essence of a place, tell us how you'd do it differently. If any of our descriptions are inaccurate or inadequate, we'll incorporate your changes in the next edition and will correct factual errors at fodors.com *immediately.*

Tell us what to include. You probably have had fantastic travel experiences that aren't yet in Fodor's. Why not share them with a community of like-minded travelers? Maybe you chanced upon a beach or bistro or B&B that you don't want to keep to yourself. Tell us why we should include it. And share your discoveries and experiences with everyone directly at fodors.com. Your input may lead us to add a new listing or highlight a place we cover with a "Highly Recommended" star or with our highest rating, "Fodor's Choice."

Give us your opinion instantly at our feedback center at www.fodors.com/feedback. You may also e-mail editors@fodors.com with the subject line "New Zealand Editor." Or send your nominations, comments, and complaints by mail to New Zealand Editor, Fodor's, 1745 Broadway, New York, NY 10019.

You and travelers like you are the heart of the Fodor's community. Make our community richer by sharing your experiences. Be a Fodor's correspondent.

Happy Traveling!

Tim Jarrell, Publisher

CONTENTS

Be a Fodor's Correspondent 3
About This Book 7
What's Where 8
Quintessential New Zealand 12
When to Go 15
If You Like .16
Great Itineraries 18
On the Calendar 22

1 AUCKLAND 27
Exploring Auckland 30
Where to Eat 48
Where to Stay 59
Nightlife & the Arts 66
Sports & the Outdoors 70
Shopping 75
Auckland Essentials 77

2 NORTHLAND & THE BAY
OF ISLANDS 84
Northland 88
The Bay of Islands 99
Northland & the Bay
of Islands Essentials 117

3 COROMANDEL PENINSULA &
THE BAY OF PLENTY 119
The Coromandel Peninsula 123
The Bay of Plenty 142

4 EAST COAST &
THE VOLCANIC ZONE 156
The Rotorua Area 160
Lake Taupo & Tongariro
National Park 179
Napier & Hawke's Bay 190
Gisborne & Eastland 202

5 WESTERN NORTH ISLAND 211
The Waikato & Waitomo 215
New Plymouth & Taranaki 229
Wanganui, the Whanganui River &
Palmerston North 246

6 WELLINGTON &
THE WAIRARAPA 259
Wellington 262
The Wairarapa 293

7 UPPER SOUTH ISLAND &
THE WEST COAST 301
Marlborough & Kaikoura 308
Nelson & the Northwest 335
The West Coast 361

8 CHRISTCHURCH &
CANTERBURY 378
Christchurch 382
Arthur's Pass & Canterbury 410

9 THE SOUTHERN ALPS &
FIORDLAND 432
The Southern Alps 436
Fiordland .464

10 OTAGO, INVERCARGILL &
STEWART ISLAND 477
Dunedin 481
Otago Peninsula 493
Invercargill 495
Stewart Island 503

11 ADVENTURE VACATIONS 511
Bicycling 512
Canoeing .514
Cross-Country Skiing 514
Diving 514

CONTENTS

ABOUT THIS BOOK

Our Ratings

Sometimes you find terrific travel experiences and sometimes they just find you. But usually the burden is on you to select the right combination of experiences. That's where our ratings come in.

As travelers we've all discovered a place so wonderful that its worthiness is obvious. And sometimes that place is so experiential that superlatives don't do it justice: you just have to be there to know. These sights, properties, and experiences get our highest rating, **Fodor's Choice,** indicated by orange stars throughout this book.

Black stars highlight sights and properties we deem **Highly Recommended,** places that our writers, editors, and readers praise again and again for consistency and excellence.

By default, there's another category: any place we include in this book is by definition worth your time, unless we say otherwise. And we will.

Disagree with any of our choices? Care to nominate a place or suggest that we rate one more highly? Visit our feedback center at www.fodors.com/feedback.

Budget Well

Hotel and restaurant price categories from ¢ to $$$$ are defined in the opening pages of each chapter. For attractions, we always give standard adult admission fees; reductions are usually available for children, students, and senior citizens. Want to pay with plastic? **AE, D, DC, MC, V** following restaurant and hotel listings indicate if American Express, Discover, Diner's Club, MasterCard, and Visa are accepted.

Restaurants

Unless we state otherwise, restaurants are open for lunch and dinner daily. We mention dress only when there's a specific requirement and reservations only when they're essential or not accepted—it's always best to book ahead.

Hotels

Hotels have private bath, phone, TV, and air-conditioning and operate on the European Plan (a.k.a. EP, meaning without meals), unless we specify that they use the Continental Plan (CP, with a Continental breakfast), Breakfast Plan (BP, with a full breakfast), or Modified American Plan (MAP, with breakfast and dinner) or are all-inclusive (including all meals and most activities). We always list facilities but not whether you'll be charged an extra fee to use them, so when pricing accommodations, find out what's included.

Many Listings

★	Fodor's Choice
★	Highly recommended
⊠	Physical address
↔	Directions
⌂	Mailing address
☎	Telephone
🖷	Fax
⊕	On the Web
✉	E-mail
🖅	Admission fee
☉	Open/closed times
►	Start of walk/itinerary
Ⓜ	Metro stations
⊟	Credit cards

Hotels & Restaurants

🏨	Hotel
🛏	Number of rooms
☖	Facilities
⧖	Meal plans
✕	Restaurant
☝	Reservations
🏛	Dress code
↘	Smoking
⌷⌷	BYOB
✕🏨	Hotel with restaurant that warrants a visit

Outdoors

🏌	Golf
⛺	Camping

Other

☺	Family-friendly
ℹ	Contact information
⇨	See also
⊠	Branch address
☞	Take note

WHAT'S WHERE

New Zealand consists of three main islands: the North Island (44,197 square mi), the South Island (58,170 square mi), and Stewart Island (676 square mi). The country also includes the Subantarctic Islands, composed of five island groups, and the ten Chatham Islands—the first inhabited land in the world to greet the sun. New Zealand is relatively small—if the country were stretched out along the west coast of the United States, it would extend from Los Angeles to Seattle. No point is more than 112 km (70 mi) from the sea, and owing to the narrow, hilly nature of the country, rivers tend to be short, swift, and broad. Much of the country is made up of hilly, expansive, green fields occupied by some 40 million sheep and 5 million cattle.

More than 70% of the total population lives on the North Island, where industry and government are concentrated. The South Island is dominated by the Southern Alps, a spine of mountains running almost two-thirds the length of the island close to the West Coast.

NORTH ISLAND

The revered and mighty 1,200-year-old kauri (*cow*-ree) trees, ferny subtropical forests, and miles of island-strewn coastline of Northland and the Coromandel Peninsula are a perfect foil for the bustle and sprawl of Auckland, New Zealand's largest city. Mid-island is steamy, sulfuric—and accordingly smelly—Rotorua, which oozes with surreal geothermal activity. The city remains a major population center for Māori, New Zealand's pre-European inhabitants. Parklands at Tongariro and Mt. Taranaki offer outstanding hiking (a.k.a. "tramping"), while world-renowned trout-fishing opportunities abound at Lake Taupo (Australasia's largest), and the 30 rivers that feed into it. In the agriculturally bountiful Waikato region, subterranean caves are home to entrancing glowworms. Townies revel in charming, art-deco Napier in the famous wine-producing Hawke's Bay region, while the nation's cosmopolitan capital city, Wellington, remains an arts and culinary haven.

SOUTH ISLAND

Natural wonders never cease—not on the South Island. Nor do the opportunities for adventure: sea-kayaking, glacier hiking, trekking, fishing, mountain biking, rafting, bungy jumping, and rock climbing are all popular in this region that's dubbed itself "The Adventure Capital of the World." Fly over brilliant glaciers and snowy peaks, watch whales from on

North Island

- Cape Reinga
- Kerr Point
- 90 Mile Beach
- Bay of Islands
- Paihia
- Russell
- ① NORTHLAND
- Whangarei
- Great Barrier Island
- Coromandel
- Hauraki Gulf
- Whitianga
- *Coromandel Peninsula*
- Auckland
- Firth of Thames
- Tairua
- Thames
- Whangamata
- ① Tauranga
- Cape Runaway
- Hamilton
- *Bay of Plenty*
- Cambridge
- Whakatone
- Opotiki
- Raglan WAIKATO
- EASTLAND
- Waitomo Caves ③
- Rotorua
- *Tasman Sea*
- *TE UREWERA N.P.*
- Awakino
- *Lake Taupo*
- Gisborne
- *North Taranaki Bight*
- Taupo
- ④
- New Plymouth
- *TONGARIRO N.P.*
- HAWKE'S BAY
- *Hawke Bay*
- Mt. Taranaki
- Cape Egmont
- TARANAKI
- Mt. Ruapehu
- Napier
- ③ WANGANUI
- ⑤⁴
- Wanganui
- ②
- Bulls
- Palmerston North
- MANAWATU
- WAIRARAPA
- *Farewell Spit*
- *Golden Bay*
- Masterton
- Martinborough
- *Tasman Bay*
- Picton
- Cook Strait
- ☆ Wellington
- Nelson
- ⑥ MARLBOROUGH
- ①

KEY
– – – *Ferry routes*

0 _____ 100 miles
0 _____ 150 km

WHAT'S WHERE

deck, or taste the acclaimed vintages of the Marlborough area's numerous wineries. South of gracious Christchurch you'll head straight into "picture-postcard" New Zealand, where the country's tallest mountains, including Mt. Cook, are reflected in crystal-clear lakes, and sheer rock faces tower above silent, awe-inspiring fiords. You can enjoy the dramatic views in peace and quiet, or leap—literally, if you like—from one adrenaline rush to the next. Walk the "Great Walks" of the Milford, Routeburn, Queen Charlotte, Heaphy or Kepler Tracks, or, if you'd rather, look for an elusive kiwi bird on re-mote, pristine Stewart Island.

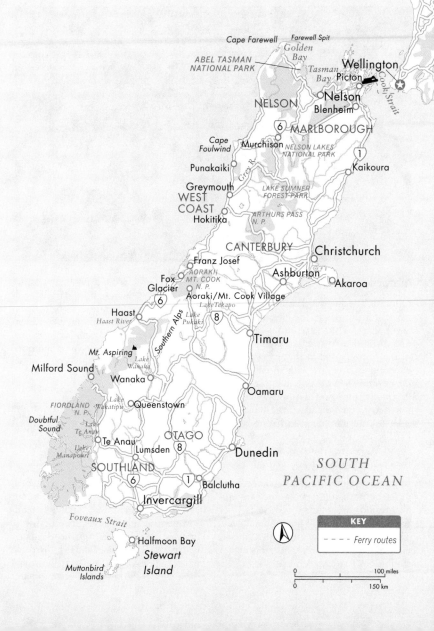

South Island

NORTH ISLAND

Cape Farewell
Farewell Spit
Golden Bay
ABEL TASMAN NATIONAL PARK
Tasman Bay
Wellington
Picton
Cook Strait
⑥
NELSON
Nelson
Blenheim
MARLBOROUGH
Cape Foulwind
Murchison
NELSON LAKES NATIONAL PARK
①
Punakaiki
Greywacke R.
Kaikoura
Greymouth
LAKE SUMNER FOREST PARK
WEST COAST
ARTHURS PASS N. P.
Hokitika
CANTERBURY
Christchurch
Franz Josef
AORAKI MT. COOK N. P.
Ashburton
Akaroa
Fox Glacier
Aoraki/Mt. Cook Village
Lake Tekapo
⑥
Lake Pukaki
⑧
Haast
Haast River
Southern Alps
Timaru
Mt. Aspiring
Lake Wanaka
Milford Sound
Wanaka
Oamaru
FIORDLAND N. P.
Lake Wakatipu
Queenstown
Doubtful Sound
Lake Te Anau
OTAGO
⑧
Te Anau
Lake Manapouri
Lumsden
Dunedin
SOUTHLAND
⑥
①
Balclutha
Invercargill
SOUTH PACIFIC OCEAN
Foveaux Strait
Halfmoon Bay
Muttonbird Islands
Stewart Island

KEY
– – – Ferry routes

0   100 miles
0   150 km

QUINTESSENTIAL NEW ZEALAND

Matariki

"Matariki" is the Māori name for the cluster of stars known as the Pleiades or The Seven Sisters. The term is also used to refer to the Māori New Year, marked by the rise of the constellation in the sky (the event corresponds roughly with the arrival of the new moon in the month of June). Traditionally, the stars' visibility was supposed to portend the success of the coming season's crop; these days, however, Matariki has become a more all-encompassing celebration, where Māori show respect to the land where they live.

Matariki is celebrated at different times by different tribes, but events (which are held all around the country) always fall between the beginning of June and mid-July. These can range from special Matariki dinners, day events, to art and performance exhibitions lasting several weeks.

During the Matariki season many restaurants around New Zealand add traditional Māori dishes to their menus. For example, eateries in the Northland towns of Paihia and Opua offer special Matariki dishes, like lamb and kumara pie or roast muttonbird. Many of the dishes served are baked in a *hāngi*, a traditional Māori earth oven, in which food is baked underground with hot stones.

Wining & Dining, New Zealand-Style

New Zealand is one of the wine world's latest upstarts, and Kiwi grapes and vignerons are producing first-class wine. Sauvignon blanc was the first New Zealand varietal to win an international award—that was Hunter's 1985 vintage, from the Marlborough region. Dry rieslings and rich chardonnays are also excellent, and some *méthode champenoise* sparkling wines are coming

into their own as well. As for reds, pinot noir tends to be the most refined.

New Zealand winemakers—heavily concentrated in the regions of Marlborough, Hawke's Bay, Gisborne–East Cape, Wairarapa-Martinborough, and central Otago—more often than not have food in mind when they create their wine, and you should plan to try sauvignon blanc alongside scallops or crayfish, chardonnay with salmon, or some of the bold reds with lamb or venison. You'll discover just how well those audacious flavors work with local cuisine.

You won't have to go out of your way to try New Zealand wine—licensed restaurants (meaning those with liquor licenses) are extremely loyal to Kiwi wineries—but you might want to. If you've come from Australia or the United Kingdom, chances are you've seen more Kiwi wine back home. Not so for Americans: the California wine in-dustry has acted as a barrier to the importation of New Zealand wine, and New Zealand's production isn't high enough to allow mass distribution in the U.S. market.

Close Encounters with Sealife

There's a reason why dolphin-, whale-, and seal-lovers treasure the coastal and island regions of New Zealand. Every time you're on a boat, it seems, you're likely to spot these beautiful animals frolicking in the waves—sometimes right alongside your ferry. Bottlenose dolphins are the most commonly sighted—you can see them on a day-cruise to Auckland's Hauraki Gulf—but during certain seasons you might be lucky enough to spy an orca, or perhaps even a rare Hector's dolphin (they're the world's smallest) near Kaikoura or off the Banks Peninsula.

If it's an up-close-and-personal encounter you're after, you'll find that many east-coast towns in the North and South Islands offer

QUINTESSENTIAL NEW ZEALAND

day tours, where you're invited jump in the water and swim among seals and dolphins. Paihia (in Northland) Tauranga and Whakatane (in the Bay of Plenty), Kaikoura (in Marlborough Sounds), and Abel Tasman National Park (near Motueka, at the top of the South Island) have such tours. Many of them guarantee at least a sighting of marine mammals, and offer a free trip the next day if the animals are not spotted.

Getting Back to the Land

Aotearoa, the Māori name for New Zealand (it means "The Land of the Long White Cloud") is mostly green, with rural settings never far away from the largest cities. For an authentic taste of Kiwi life, don't confine your stay to tourist spots, towns, and cities. Many farms are open to visitors, either for a day visit or an overnight "farmstay," and owners may welcome you to milk a cow, plant seeds, or pick fruits and vegetables for dinner.

The country is steeped in agriculture. Agricultural and pastoral (A&P) fairs are held at various times of the year by many communities; the best time to see them is during summer. Farmers bring their chickens, cattle, goats, sheep, and other stock into town and compete for ribbons; they'll usually chat amiably about their animals, and let children and loving adults pet them, too. Horse shows, often featuring hunters and jumpers, are often a key part of the fairs, for Kiwis love their equines. Other fair events include wood-chopping contests and sheep-shearing displays, sheep dog trials and crafts exhibits. One tip: Many shows last several days, and some are even declared local holidays so that families in the area can attend. Try to avoid such times and go on quieter days. The Canterbury A&P Show, labeled "the South Island's largest event," is a blue-ribbon winner.

WHEN TO GO

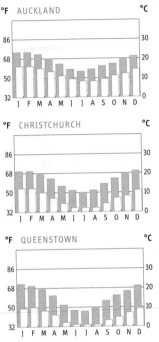

New Zealand is in the southern hemisphere, which means that the seasons are reversed—it's winter Down Under during the American and European summer. The ideal months for comfortable all-round travel are October through April, especially if you want to participate in adventure activities. Avoid school holidays, when highways may be congested and accommodation is likely to be scarce and more expensive. Summer school holidays (the busiest) fall between mid-December and the end of January; other holiday periods are mid-May to the end of May, early July to mid-July, and late August to mid-September.

Climate

Climate in New Zealand varies from subtropical in the north to temperate in the south. Summer (December–March) is generally warm, with an average of seven to eight hours of sunshine per day throughout the country. Winter (June–September) is mild at lower altitudes in South Island, but heavy snowfalls are common, particularly on the peaks of the Southern Alps. Strong southerly winds bring a blast of Antarctica. Rain can pour at any time of the year. (Some areas on the west coast of South Island receive an annual rainfall of more than 100 inches.)

IF YOU LIKE

Beaches

New Zealand's two main islands share over 15,000 km in coastline, which ripples and zigzags to create bays, coves, fjords—and almost countless beaches. These run the gamut from surfing hotspots to quiet, sheltered lagoons to rugged, boulder-studded strands. And though all of them are open to the public, very few of them are crowded, even in the high season. You won't find pollution or dangerous sea life. The greatest hazards are sunburn—the lack of smog and a subequatorial location mean the sun is **strong**—and strong currents.

Many New Zealanders prefer beaches along the East Coast of the North Island. Coromandel's eastern shore and the Bay of Plenty—especially busy **Mount Maunganui**—are perennial favorites during summer "time off." Sand on the West Coast of the North Island is black—called "iron sand"—as a result of volcanic activity; not a negative, for you'll delight in the ruggedness of the scenery. One of the North Island's most beautiful beaches is **Karekare Beach,** west of Auckland; it's the striking, cliff-backed beach that was made famous in Jane Campion's film *The Piano*. The spectacular dunes at **90 Mile Beach,** in Northland (which is actually about 60 miles long) are also not to be missed, and nearby **Doubtless Bay,** also in Northland, has some of the country's loveliest caramel-colored beaches. New Zealand's most famous surf breaks are located west of Hamilton in the laid-back town of **Raglan**; you can "hang-ten" here or at **Piha** near Auckland.

South Island beaches are captivating, particularly in **Abel Tasman National Park** and neighboring **Golden Bay.** The sands are golden, and the water is jade green. Farther south, things are colder and rockier.

Bushwalking

Range upon range of mountains; deep, ice-carved valleys; wilderness areas that have never been farmed, logged, or grazed; and a first-class network of marked trails and tramping huts are just some of the reasons that bushwalking (read: hiking) is a national addiction.

The traditional way to hike in New Zealand is freedom walking. Freedom walkers carry their own provisions, sleeping bags, food, and cooking gear and sleep in basic huts. A more refined alternative—usually available only on more popular trails—is the guided walk, on which you trek with just a light day pack, guides do the cooking, and you sleep in heated lodges.

The most popular walks are in the Southern Alps. The **Milford Track** is a four-day walk through breathtaking scenery to the edge of Milford Sound. The **Queen Charlotte Track** winds along the jagged, gorgeous coast of the Marlborough Sounds region; you can see seals and sometimes orcas from the waterside cliffs.

The North Island has plenty of wonders of its own. The Coromandel Peninsula has tremendous forests of gigantic 1,200-year-old kauri trees, 80-foot-tall tree ferns, a gorgeous coastline, and well-marked tracks. You can hike among active volcanic peaks in **Tongariro National Park.** And on a nub of the west coast formed by volcanic activity hundreds of years ago, the majestic, Fuji-like **Mt. Taranaki** alternately dons cloaks of mist and exposes its brilliant, sunlit snowy cap.

If time is short, at least put aside a few hours for trekking in the **Waitakerei Ranges,** just a short drive from Auckland city.

Boating

New Zealand's long and varied coastlines are a mecca for "boaties." Sailors, kayakers, and anglers all flock to areas like the Bay of Islands, Abel Tasman National Park, and Marlborough Sounds for their sheltered waters, marvelous scenery, and secluded anchorages.

In Auckland, the City of Sails, you can rent a yacht and go out "bareboating" for the day, or, if you're more of a landlubber, hire a skipper and vessel to take you around. Ferries and cruise boats make half- and full-day trips around Hauraki Gulf and its islands.

The Whanganui River, flowing from the western slopes of Mt. Tongariro on the North Island to meet the sea at the west-coast town of Wanganui, is New Zealand's premier canoeing river. The longest navigable waterway in the country, its placid waters wind through native bushland with occasional rapids, cascades, and gorges. The most popular canoe trip begins at Taumarunui, taking four to five days to get downstream to Pipriki. The best times are during warmer months, November to March.

You can travel between the North and South Islands via ferries that run from Wellington to Picton (get where you're going, and soak up scenery, too). You can also tour Marlborough Sounds on a mailboat ride out of Picton—the boats wind around many of the gorgeous inlets and islands that make up this jagged coastal paradise.

For thrills and spills, white-water rafting on the Shotover River near Queenstown is exhilarating. Or, you can push the adventure envelope even further on the North Island's Kaituna River, near Rotorua, which has the highest commercially rafted waterfall (7 m, 21 ft) in the Southern Hemisphere.

Fishing

The trout population in New Zealand's lakes and rivers is phenomenal. One reason for this is that commercial trout fishing is illegal, which means you won't find trout on restaurant menus. You can, however, bring your own catch for a chef to prepare.

On the North Island, trout fishing mainly entails lake fishing, with wet flies or spinners, for rainbow trout. Trolling is popular, too. On the South Island, where brown trout predominate, you'll find outstanding dry-fly fishing, best in the Nelson region and at Lake Wakatipu. Trout season lasts from October through April in most areas, though Lakes Taupo and Rotorua are open all year. "Catch and release" is common practice. On both islands, luxury lodges cater to anglers; among the best are the Huka Lodge and Solitaire Lodge, near Lakes Taupo and Rotorua, and the Lake Brunner Sporting Lodge near Greymouth in the south.

Salmon mainly swim in rivers that drain the eastern slopes of the Southern Alps—especially those that reach the sea between Christchurch and Dunedin. Salmon season also runs from October to April, peaking from January to March.

In the seas off the North Island's East Coast the quarry is big: mako, hammerhead, tiger shark, and marlin—especially striped marlin, which average 250 pounds. For light tackle fishing, bonito and skipjack tuna and *kahawai* (sea trout) offer excellent sport. The big-game fishing towns of Paihia and Russell (the latter was a favorite fishing spot of Zane Grey's) have established charter operators. The season runs from January to May, although smaller game fishing is good year-round.

GREAT ITINERARIES

INTRODUCTION TO NORTH ISLAND
8 TO 9 DAYS

Auckland

2 days. After a long international flight, take it easy on your first day. Stretch your legs and invigorate your circulation with a walk around the city center, with perhaps stops at Auckland Museum and Auckland Domain Park or Albert Park. Head to the harbor (or "harbour") and take a ferry ride round-trip between Auckland and Devenport for a great view of the city from the water. You can also choose to visit Sky Tower Auckland, the tallest tower in the Southern Hemisphere. Have an early dinner and turn in to get over the worst of the jet lag.

On your second day, you'll have more wind in your sails to explore the City of Sails. Depending on your interests, head to Kelly Tarlton's Underwater World and Antarctic Encounter, the New Zealand National Maritime Museum, the Auckland Art Gallery, or the Parnell neighborhood for window-shopping. If you're feeling energetic, you can even do a bit of kayaking (or just sunbathing) at Mission Bay or Karekare Beach.

Waitomo & Rotorua

1 or 2 days. Waitomo is known for what's beneath the surface—intricate limestone caves filled with stalactites, stalagmites, and galaxies of glowworms. If this is up your alley, get an early start from Auckland to arrive here before 11 AM and sign up for a cave tour. Afterward, continue on to Rotorua, which literally seethes with geothermal activity. In the late afternoon you should have time for a walk around the town center, strolling through the Government Gardens and perhaps also Kuirau Park. If you decide to skip the Waitomo worms, you

can zip straight down from Auckland to Rotorua. In addition to the town proper, visit some of the eye-popping thermal areas nearby, such as Waiotapu. At night, be a guest at a *hāngi,* a Māori feast accompanied by a cultural performance. On the next day, you can either see some of the outlying thermal areas if you didn't the previous day, or continue south to Taupo.

Taupo

1 day. Midway between Auckland and Wellington, the resort town of Taupo, on its giant namesake lake, is the perfect base for a day full of aquatic activities. If you're at all interested in trout fishing, this is the place to do it.

Napier

1 day. This small town is an art deco period piece; after a devastating Richter 7.9 earthquake in 1931, the center of town was rebuilt in the distinctive style, and it's been carefully preserved ever since. Take a guided or self-guided walk around the Heritage (historically significant) neighborhood. If you have a car, drive out of town and visit one of the 30-odd wineries around Hawke's Bay. In the afternoon, take a drive to the top of Te Mata Peak, or visit nearby towns Hastings or Havelock North. Otherwise, hang out at the waterfront or visit the aquarium.

Wellington

2 days. New Zealand's capital, Wellington, is a terrific walking city—and there's even a cable car to help you with the hills. The big cultural draw is Te Papa Tongarewa—The Museum of New Zealand, which with five floors and great interac-

tive activities for kids, can take several hours to explore. You may wish to spend the rest of your first day here along the waterfront, winding up with dinner in the area. Be sure to check out the entertainment listings, too; you could be in town during one of the many festivals or catch a cool local band. On your second day, explore more of the urban highlights, like the City Gallery and the Museum of Wellington, City & Sea, followed by a bit of browsing on the main shopping drags or a trip up into the hills to the Botanic Garden. If you'd prefer more time out in the country and have a car, drive up the Kapiti Coast and book to visit Kapiti Island Nature Reserve, or sip acclaimed Pinot Noir in the wine center of Martinborough.

Other Top Options

1 or 2 days. With at least one more day at your disposal, you could squeeze in one of the following destinations. The Tongariro Crossing, a challenging but spectacular day-long hike, could be added to your Taupo stay. You'll "tramp" up-close to three volcanoes: Tongariro, Ngauruhoe, and Ruapehu. If you have two days and are keen on swimming with dolphins or doing some diving, loop up to Paihia, a small seaside town and gateway to the Bay of Islands, after your initial two days in Auckland. You can dip into the mellow, rural Coromandel Peninsula, perhaps the gateway town of Thames, before going south to Rotorua. Most places on the Coromandel are within one to 1.5 hours' drive from the Thames township.

By Public Transportation: Bus service links all major North Island destinations. You'll ride InterCity Coachlines or Newmans Coach Lines. Contact Tranz Scenic for rail tickets on The Overlander, between Auckland and Wellington or the Capital Connection, between Wellington and Palmerston North.

TIPS & LOGISTICS

Summer in New Zealand—winter in North America—is the best time to visit the North Island. From Christmas through January's end, schools are out—it's the "Silly Season"—and you'll be competing for reservations at hotels, so book ahead. During the cold-weather months, rates are cheaper, crowds thin out, and the weather is actually quite mild; there's the frequent rain, but that just means the countryside looks greener than ever.

GREAT ITINERARIES

INTRODUCTION TO SOUTH ISLAND
8 TO 10 DAYS

Picton & Blenheim

2 days. Hop or drive on to the ferry from Wellington to Picton. This small seaside township is the Marlborough region's main commercial port, and the gateway to the gorgeously jagged coastline of Marlborough Sounds. Hop on a mail boat, which makes stops at coves and islands along the Sounds; take a day-walk along the famous Queen Charlotte Track for spectacular water views; or join a kayak tour (you might just see some seals and dolphins as you paddle around). Have dinner along the foreshore and turn in early.

The next morning, head out of town to the Blenheim region, where the rolling hills are covered with grape vines and dotted with scores of wineries. Stop in for tastings at esteemed spots like the Seresin Estate, Cloudy Bay, and Allan Scott Wines; if you've pre-booked, you might also be able to dine at Herzog or Hunter's Vineyard Restaurant. Be sure to pick up a few bottles (of wine and olive oil) to take with you.

Kaikoura

1 day. Get an early start and continue down the South Island's eastern coast to the seaside settlement of Kaikoura, where you can go whale-watching, reef diving, swimming with dolphins or seals, or stay on land and indulge in a big crayfish lunch ("Kaikoura" actually means "meal of crayfish" in the Māori language).

Christchurch

1 or 2 days. Although Christchurch, "The Garden City," is the South Island's largest city, it's still a relaxing place to be. Depending on when you get here from Kaikoura, you can stroll through the city center, visit the Arts Centre (especially fun during the weekend market), the Botanic Gardens, or one of the city's museums or galleries. Overnight here, then for a two-day stay, fit in a couple of hours at the International Antarctic Centre after a ride on the Christchurch Gondola. You might enjoy a cruise to see the endangered Hector's dolphins. The next morning, get an early start to make the push to Queenstown.

Queenstown

2 or 3 days. Depending on your appetite for adventure, Queenstown may be the locus of your South Island trip. Take the plunge with AJ Hackett Bungy, freefall on the Shotover Canyon Swing, try a jet-boat ride, or go rafting. As the town is set on Lake Wakatipu with the jagged peaks of the Remarkables mountains around it, you won't lack for scenic distractions. If you're interested in the area's gold-mining history, detour to nearby Arrowtown and see the Lakes District Museum. If the area looks familiar, you're not dreaming: many scenes from the *Lord of the Rings* film trilogy were shot here.

Fiordland National Park

2 days. Follow your extreme sports adventure with some extremely beautiful landscapes. At Milford and Doubtful sounds in Fiordland National Park, deep green slopes fall steeply down to crystalline waters. Rare species live in the unique underwater environment here, so try to visit the Milford Deep Underwater Observatory. Drink in the views by catamaran, by kayak,

NORTH ISLAND

WELLINGTON
Picton
MARLBOROUGH
Blenheim · Cloudy Bay

Kaikoura

Tasman Sea

Christchurch

Timaru

Milford Sound

Fiordland N.P.

Doubtful Sound

Queenstown
Lake Wakatipu

Lumsden

Foveaux Strait

SOUTH PACIFIC OCEAN

or by flightseeing. Whatever you do, don't forget your rain gear and bug repellent! If pressed, you could make a trip to Milford Sound a long day's trip from Queenstown.

Other Top Options

2 or 3 days. With more time in your schedule, you can build in a couple of low-key days to offset the thrills-and-chills outdoors activities. After you arrive at Picton, you can drive or take a bus to Nelson, a relaxed waterfront town that's a good base for arts and crafts shopping and wine tasting. One fun stop is the World of WearableArt & Collectable Cars Museum. If ice is on your mind and you're willing to brave rainy conditions, push on down the rugged West Coast, stopping at the Pancake Rocks—columns of limestone resembling stacks of pancakes—on your way to the Fox or Franz Josef glaciers in Westland National Park. Their flow rates are up to ten times the speed of most valley glaciers. (To do this, plan on three days, as it's a long drive and you'll want at least one full day at the glaciers.)

By Public Transportation: Buses run between all major South Island destinations, but in the Southern Alps trips can take several hours. You may want to consider a short-hop flight between Christchurch and Queenstown. Consider a couple of train options, too, with the TranzAlpine train linking Christchurch and Greymouth on the West Coast and the TransCoastal train connecting Christchurch with Kaikoura and Picton.

TIPS & LOGISTICS

❶ If you're planning to do some bushwalking on this island—and some of New Zealand's greatest "Great Walks" are here, including the Milford Track and Queen Charlotte Track—it's best to visit in the New Zealand spring, summer, or fall. Most tracks at the northern tip are open all year, while those positioned at higher altitudes—such as Milford, Kepler, and Routeburn—remain open when weather and track conditions permit.

❷ When driving South Island roads, which really are "those less traveled," use caution. Some roads don't have center divider lines, which can make it easy to get disoriented—especially when you're not used to driving on the left-hand side of the road.

ON THE CALENDAR

	Sport features heavily in New Zealand's festival calendar. Horse and boat races, triathlons, and fishing competitions are prominent; although there are also arts festivals, and those celebrating the country's food and wine. Just about every town holds a yearly agricultural and pastoral (A&P) show, and these proud displays of local crafts, produce, livestock, and wood-chopping and sheep-shearing prowess provide a memorable look at rural New Zealand. An annual calendar of New Zealand special events can be found on the web at ⊕ www.newzealand.com.
SUMMER Dec. 25–26	On **Christmas Day** and **Boxing Day** the country virtually closes down.
Jan. 1	**New Year's Day** is a nationwide holiday.
Last Mon. in Jan.	For the **Auckland Anniversary Day Regatta** (☎ 0800/734–2882 ⊕ www.regatta.org.nz), Auckland's birthday party, the City of Sails takes to the water.
Feb. 6	**Waitangi Day**, New Zealand's national day, commemorates the signing of the Treaty of Waitangi between Europeans and Māori in 1840. The focus of the celebration is, naturally enough, the town of Waitangi in the Bay of Islands.
Feb. 9–10	**Speights Coast to Coast** (☎ 03/326–5493 ⊕ www.coasttocoast.co.nz) is the ultimate Ironman challenge—a two-day, 238-km (148-mi) marathon, "World Multisport Championship," of cycling, running, and kayaking that crosses South Island from west to east.
Feb. 17–18	**The Devonport Food & Wine Festival** (☎ 09/353–4026 ⊕ www.devonportwinefestival.co.nz), the first of its kind in New Zealand, showcases some of the country's best restaurants. It is easily reached by a ferry trip from Auckland.
Mid-Feb.	The **Festival of Flowers & Romance** (☎ 03/365–5403 ⊕ www.festivalofflowers.co.nz) is held in Christchurch—the city where lovers can stroll through an old English garden and enjoy a punt ride on the Avon River. Admission is free and you'll see the Christchurch Cathedral Floral Carpet and Wearable Flowers Parade.
	HERO Festival (⊕ www.hero.org.nz) is Auckland's annual GayPride event with big-scale festivities such as the HERO Party.
Feb. 15–19	Napier's **Art Deco Weekend** (☎ 06/835–1191 ⊕ www.artdeconapier.com/weekend/index.htm /) celebrates the city's style with wining, dining, house tours, vintage car displays, and more.

AUTUMN	
1st Thurs.–Sat. of Mar.	Golden Shears International Sheep Shearing and Wool Handling Championships (☎ 06/378–8008 ⊕ www.goldenshears.co.nz) is a three-day event, the world's premier competition, that pits men armed with shears against the fleecy sheep in Masterton, north of Wellington.
2nd Sat. in Mar.	Screw up your courage to try some unusual bush tucker like grubs and "Westcargots" (local snails), possum pies and gorse-flower wine at Hokitika's Wildfoods Festival (☎ 03/755–8321 ⊕ www.wildfoods.co.nz).
Mid-Mar.	Some people take the wine tasting along the route of the Martinborough Round the Vines Fun Walk/Run (☎ 06/306–9330 ⊕ www.roundthevines.org.nz) much more seriously than the running. Fancy dress isn't compulsory, but you'll feel far more a part of the proceedings if you at least wear a funny hat.
	The Pasifika Festival (☎ 09/379–2020 ⊕ www.aucklandcity.govt.nz/whatson/events/pasifika/default.asp) highlights the many Pacific Island cultures found in Auckland with plenty of color, music, and dance. It's the South Pacific's largest Pacific Islands community event, and it's free. The main activity is at Western Springs Lakeside and Stadium near the Auckland Zoo. The festival is extremely popular and crowded, so don't try to find parking. Check local newspapers for special bus services on the day.
Late Mar.	Up, up and away! About 30 hot-air balloons from around the world take part in the Genesis Wairarapa International Balloon Festival (☎ 04/473–8039 ⊕ www.nzballoons.co.nz). The event finishes with a night glow, where balloons are lit to show off their colors, and fireworks in Masterton's Solway Showgrounds.
	Auckland's Round the Bays Run (☎ 09/360–3190 ⊕ www.roundthebays.co.nz) is one of the world's largest 8.4-km (5.2-mi) fun runs. A few people are hardcore but 70,000 participants run or walk the course in their own time. The event starts in the city, follows Tamaki Drive around the waterfront, and finishes in the plush suburb of St. Heliers.
Mar. or Apr.	The Easter holiday weekend lasts from Good Friday through Easter Monday. Dates change each year and generally fall in March or April. The Royal Easter Show (☎ 09/623–7724 ⊕ www.royaleastershow.co.nz) is held at Auckland's Showgrounds over the holiday. It's the country's largest and most varied family festival.

ON THE CALENDAR

Apr. 25	**Anzac Day** honors the soldiers, sailors, and airmen and women who fought and died for the country. This public holiday is marked by dawn parades around the country.
Late Apr.	The **Bluff Oyster and Southland Seafood Festival** (☎ 0800/272–687 ⊕ www.bluffoysterfest.co.nz) stars the local specialty, the Bluff oyster.
Early May	The **Lion Foundation Rotorua Marathon** (☎ 09/570–2222 ⊕ www.rotoruamarathon.co.nz) around Lake Rotorua is New Zealand's premier long-distance event at 42.2 km or 26.2 mi. There's a fun run, too, or you can walk the course.
WINTER Late May–early June	The **Out Takes Gay & Lesbian Film Festival** (☎ 04/972–6775 ⊕ www.outtakes.org.nz) is held in theaters in Auckland, Wellington, Dunedin, and Christchurch. The **Queen's Birthday** is celebrated nationwide on the first Monday in June.
Late July	At the **Queenstown Winter Festival** (☎ 03/441–2453 ⊕ www.winterfestival.co.nz) the winter-sports capital hits the slopes for a week of competition by day and entertainment by night. The Southern Hemisphere's ultimate winter party takes place at Coronet Peak, Earnslaw Park, and Queenstown Bay; there are free and ticketed events.
SPRING Mid-Sept.	The **42 Below Cocktail World Cup** in Queenstown brings cocktail bar staff from top bars worldwide to mix it up in "extreme" cocktail making. Cocktails are stirred and shaken while the mixologists bungy jump, jet boat, and more. (⊕ www.42below.com) Tickets to Wellington's free-spirited **Montana World of WearableArt Awards** (⊕ www.worldofwearableart.com) sell like hotcakes.
Last weekend in Oct.	**Dunedin Rhododendron Festival** (☎ 03/474–5162 ⊕ www.rhododunedin.co.nz) opens the city's gardens for tours and offers lectures and plant sales.
Oct. 23	**Labour Day** is observed throughout the country.
Late Oct.–early Nov.	**Taranaki Rhododendron & Garden Festival** (☎ 0800/746–363 ⊕ www.rhodo.co.nz) showcases gardens approved by the New Zealand Gardens Trust. As many as 45 private gardens are open to the public in cities including New Plymouth and Stratford, plus plant-o-philes can partake of guided walks, seminars, and other related events.
2nd week in Nov.	The **Canterbury Agricultural and Pastoral Show** (☎ 03/343–3033 ⊕ www.theshow.co.nz) spotlights the farmers and graziers of the rich countryside surrounding Christchurch.

| Nov. | **Ellerslie Flower Show** (☎ tickets: 09/309–5000, info: 09/579–6260 ⊕ www.ellerslieflowershow.co.nz) in Auckland is one of the headline events on New Zealand's gardening calendar. It is modeled on London's Chelsea Flower Show. In a confusing twist, the show moved in 1998 from the suburb of Ellerslie to the Botanic Gardens at Manurewa, farther south, while retaining its old name. The city of Blenheim's **Hunter's Garden Marlborough** (☎ 0800/ 627–527 ⊕ www.garden-marlborough.co.nz) six days long, has local garden tours and a Garden Fête with products for sale. Meet gardening luminaries and celebrity chefs, too. |
| | **Toast Martinborough Wine, Food & Music Festival** (☎ 04/473–4838 ⊕ www.toastmartinborough.co.nz) pours new releases and previously sold-out vintages that you pair with gourmet cuisine from the region's finest restaurants. Groove to top-flight music, too. Tickets are held for foreign guests. |

Auckland

WORD OF MOUTH

"Auckland's outsize sprawl mirrors the scope of experience it offers. A vibrant city with a colorful cultural mix, it still retains a relaxed Kiwi attitude. The central city neighborhoods, with their cafés, bars, and restaurants, quickly give way to bays and marinas. A short drive can take you to breathtaking beaches with pounding surf. Standing on one of the city's volcanic cones and looking toward the shimmering harbor, you can take your pick."

—Toni Mason

Updated by
Toni Mason

AS YOU FLY INTO AUCKLAND, New Zealand's gateway city, you might wonder where the city is. Most people arriving for the first time, and even New Zealanders coming home, are impressed by the seascape and green forest that dominate the view on the approach to the airport.

The drive from the airport does little to dispel the clean, green image so many people have of the country. The scenery is commanded by some of the city's 46 volcanic hills, their grass kept closely cropped by those four-legged lawn mowers known as sheep. And reading the highway signs will begin to give you a taste of the unusual and sometimes baffling Māori place-names around the country.

According to Māori tradition, the Auckland isthmus was originally peopled by a race of giants and fairy folk. When Europeans arrived in the early 19th century, however, the Ngāti-Whatua tribe was firmly in control of the region. The British began negotiations with the Ngāti-Whatua in 1840 to purchase the isthmus and establish the colony's first capital. In September of that year the British flag was hoisted to mark the township's foundation, and Auckland remained the capital until 1865, when the seat of government was moved to Wellington. Aucklanders expected to suffer from the shift, but it hurt only their pride, not their pockets. As the terminal for the South Sea shipping routes, Auckland was already an established commercial center. Since then the urban sprawl has made this city of approximately 1.2 million people one of the world's largest geographically.

A couple of days in the city will reveal a level of development and sophistication that belies first impressions. Since the early 1990s, Auckland has grown up in more ways than one. Most shops are open daily, central bars and nightclubs buzz well into the wee hours, and a cosmopolitan mix of Māori, Polynesians, Asians, and Europeans all contribute to the cultural milieu. (In fact, Auckland has the world's largest single population of Pacific Islanders.) Topping things off is the 1,082-foot Sky Tower, dwarfing everything around it and acting as a beacon for the casino, hotel, and restaurant complex that opened early in 1996. This is the newest, if least pervasive, face of modern New Zealand.

In the midst of the city's activity, you'll see knots of cyclists and runners. Like all other New Zealanders, Aucklanders are addicted to the outdoors—especially the water. There are some 70,000 powerboats and sailing craft in the greater Auckland area—about one for every four households. And a total of 102 beaches lie within an hour's drive of the city center. The city has enhanced its greatest asset, Waitemata Harbour—a Māori name meaning "sea of sparkling waters." The city staged its first defense of the America's Cup in the year 2000, and the regatta was a catalyst for major redevelopment of the waterfront. The area is now known as Viaduct Basin or, more commonly, the Viaduct, and has some of the city's most popular bars, cafés, and restaurants. The Cup energized the area again in 2003, as Auckland was host to the Louis Vuitton Challenger Series in October 2002 to determine the challenger to the home team for the America's Cup in February 2003. The Cup was lost but not the Viaduct's attraction for revelers and superyachts.

GREAT ITINERARIES

Numbers in the text correspond to numbers in the margin and on the maps.

IF YOU HAVE 3 DAYS

Consider splitting the Good Tour into a two-day endeavor. On your first day, hit the **Auckland Museum** ❿ to see a stunning collection of Māori artifacts and catch a performance of Māori song and the famous haka dance. From the museum's commanding site in the **Auckland Domain** ⓫ you'll get a good view of the harbor and Rangitoto Island. If you're fresh off a flight, stretch your legs with a walk in the Domain grounds. From here it's a short trip to **Parnell Village** ⓮, with its Victorian villas and boutiques. If you've got the stamina for another museum, you could visit the **Auckland Art Gallery Toi o Tāmaki** ❸ for an introduction to the perspective of the early-European settlers. Or if you're more interested in the city's maritime character, head to the Viaduct, stroll around the marina, and visit the **National Maritime Museum** ❼. To get the greatest overview of the isthmus and surrounding harbors, take a trip up the **Sky Tower** ❺. On the other hand, if jet lag makes this all seem too taxing, have a late lunch or early dinner in one of the city's best restaurant areas—Ponsonby, Parnell, or the Viaduct—and save the sightseeing for another day. On your second day, head west to the Waitakere Ranges and explore the bush or visit the west-coast beaches with their volcanic black sand. (You'll need to rent a car or take one of the wilderness tours to get here.) Or take the day and visit the beaches and vineyards of **Waiheke Island.** On your last day, start off at **Kelly Tarlton's Underwater World and Antarctic Encounter** ❽, then catch up on the other sightseeing or shopping that piques your interest. On either Day 2 or 3, be sure to work in a short foray to charming **Devonport,** taking in the harbor views on the ferry.

IF YOU HAVE 5 OR MORE DAYS

Follow the three-day itinerary described above. Next, go on a kayak trip to **Rangitoto Island,** or perhaps try your hand at sailing with Sail NZ. If you're in town over the weekend, take in some Polynesian flavor by heading out to the Otara Market with its stalls of local arts and crafts. If you haven't already, you should take in some of the city's nightlife and head to Ponsonby Road's myriad bars and restaurants, or the vibrant Viaduct, particularly in summer. Instead of visiting **Waiheke Island** just for the day, you could stay for a night or two in one of the many B&Bs. If you're itching to explore farther afield, take the roughly two-hour drive to Coromandel Peninsula (see Chapter 3), or the longer trip to the Bay of Islands (see Chapter 2).

These days, Auckland is considered too bold and brash for its own good by many Kiwis who live "south of the Bombay Hills," the geographical divide between Auckland and the rest of New Zealand (barring Northland). "Jafa," an acronym for "just another f—ing Aucklander," has entered the local lexicon; there's even a book out called *Way of the Jafa:*

A Guide to Surviving Auckland and Aucklanders. A common complaint is that Auckland absorbs the wealth from the hard work of the rest. Most Aucklanders, on the other hand, shrug and see it as typical envy of the largest city in the country. Whatever the opinion, the glass towers, crawling rush-hour traffic, and cell-phone culture do set the city apart from points north and south. You will likely see beyond all that. Indeed, much of Auckland's charm lies in the fact that you can enjoy a cappuccino in a downtown café watching the city bustle pass you by—knowing that within 30 minutes' driving time you could be cruising the spectacular harbor, playing a round at a public golf course, or even walking in subtropical forest while listening to the song of a native *tūī bird*.

EXPLORING AUCKLAND

Auckland is not easy to explore. Made up of a sprawling array of neighborhoods (Kiwis call them suburbs), the city spreads around both the Waitemata and Manukau harbors. It's best to have a car for getting around between neighborhoods, and even between some city-center sights. What might look like reasonable walking distances on maps can turn out to be 20- to 30-minute treks, and stringing a few of those together can get frustrating. If you want to see the city center close to the harbor, Ponsonby, Devonport, and Parnell, you can get around by walking, busing, and ferrying between places. To explore farther afield, it's best to drive.

If you're nervous about driving on the left, especially when you first arrive, purchase a one-day Link Bus Pass that covers the inner-city neighborhoods or, for a circuit of the main sights, an Explorer Bus Pass, and take a bus to get acquainted with the city layout. One good introduction to the city, particularly if you arrive at the end of a long flight and time is limited, is the commuter ferry that crosses the harbor to the village of Devonport, where you can soak up the charming suburb's atmosphere on a leisurely stroll.

Aucklanders seem to talk as much about what surrounds the city as what's in it: the beaches, the Waitakere Ranges, and the vineyards of Waiheke Island. Again, to get to most of these you will need a car, which you can then use to go farther afield—up to Northland and southeast to the Coromandel Peninsula.

Getting Your Bearings

What Aucklanders consider the city center stretches from the waterfront up around Queen Street, including the Viaduct. The neighborhoods known as Parnell and Ponsonby take their names from their major streets. Parnell, to the east of the center and bounded by Newmarket and Hobson Bay, has a wealth of historic buildings and chic restaurants. Ponsonby's narrow streets are lined with its iconic wooden Victorian villas, and its main strip is lined with cafés, bars, and restaurants. It lies to the west of the center and merges with the desirable north-facing suburbs of St. Mary's Bay and Herne Bay, known as the "northern slopes." Karangahape Road, or K Road, crosses the top of Queen Street and has a colorful mix of shops and cheap eateries, which are now encroaching on

TOP REASONS TO GO

GORGEOUS BEACHES

When the sun comes out, Aucklanders head to the beach. With seas both to the west and the east, few people in the city live more than a 15-minute drive from the coast. The west coast's black-sand beaches are best for surfing, whereas the safest swimming is on the east coast. Beaches that have a reputation for large waves and rips are patrolled in the summer, so play it safe and swim between the flags. The only other danger is from the sun itself. The ozone layer is weak above New Zealand, so slap on the sunscreen and resist the temptation to bake.

BOATING & SAILING

Auckland is dubbed "City of Sails," and for good reason. The population is crazy about boating and any other recreation associated with the sea. A variety of ferries and high-speed catamarans operate on Waitemata Harbour. Even better, go for a leisurely sail on the Pride of Auckland, or experience a genuine match race on America's Cup yachts with Sail NZ.

CUISINE & CAFÉ CULTURE

Some of the finest restaurants in the country reside in Auckland—and not just fine dining. The restaurant scene thrives from top-end down to bistro-cum-bars. In typical New Zealand fashion, many chefs gain a few years' OE (overseas experience), bringing home world-class skills and putting them to work on the excellent local produce. Neighborhoods such as Ponsonby are crammed with vibrant eateries and cafés, their tables spilling onto the pavement, turning out fine fare for the discerning locals.

GOLF YEAR-ROUND

Frank Nobilo's hometown, Auckland has more than 20 golf courses catering to all levels of ability, from informal and easygoing to challenging championship courses designed by the likes of Sir Bob Charles and Alister MacKenzie. Most have beautiful scenery, some with views of the Hauraki Gulf. Golf is played year-round here, and the greens fees are among the cheapest anywhere.

what used to be the seedy area toward the Ponsonby end. Newmarket, south of Parnell, brims with more upscale boutiques.

The Auckland Harbour Bridge spans the Waitemata Harbour, connecting the city with the highway north and the North Shore, where more suburbs sprawl north along a coast of safe swimming beaches.

A dozen "city ambassadors" patrol the city center on weekdays between 8:30 and 5; they can give you directions and field any other questions you might have. They're identified by their yellow and gray uniforms with "ambassador" written on their tops in red.

City Center & Parnell

Auckland's city center includes the port area, much of it reclaimed from the sea in the latter half of the 19th century. City administrators have not been kind to Auckland's older buildings, so Queen Street is a mix of glass tower office buildings shadowing the few remaining gracious buildings. Tucked away in Lorne and High streets, running parallel with Queen Street, you'll find good examples of the city's early architecture, now shop windows for many of New Zealand's leading fashion boutiques. The central business district (CBD) has been energized by a residential surge since the late 1990s, boosted by apartment development and an influx of Asian students. The Auckland Domain and Parnell areas are where you'll find the city's preeminent museum as well as historic homes and shops. Parnell was Auckland's first suburb, established in 1841, and is a good place to look for arts and crafts or sample some of Auckland's most popular cafés, bars, and restaurants.

A GOOD TOUR

Start at the **Civic Theatre,** ❶ a restored mid-city landmark close to most major hotels. Right next door is the **Sky City Metro Centre.** ❷ Step in to check out its futuristic architecture. Walk out of the complex onto Queen Street, face down toward the harbor, and then turn immediately right into Wellesley Street East. A short walk will get you to the two buildings that compose the **Auckland Art Gallery Toi o Tāmaki.** ❸ For historic works, look around the Heritage Gallery, but for more-modern art spend time at the New Gallery. At the main entrance to the gallery you are right on the edge of **Albert Park,** ❹ which divides the city from the university. It's a good place to take a break and watch the students studying and chatting under the trees.

Walk back to the Queen Street edge of the park and make a right onto Kitchener Street. Make your first left onto Victoria Street East. Head downhill toward Queen Street and past a bevy of student-oriented shops and cafés. Continue across Queen Street and up the other side of Victoria Street to the **Sky Tower** ❺ at Sky City. This complex houses the casino, a convention center, a hotel, a theater, restaurants—including the revolving Orbit—and bars. The main Auckland i-Site Visitor Information Centre is in the atrium. Before ascending the tower, take a moment to glance up from the base. It's an awesome experience but nothing compared with the view from the top. And these days you can even take the quick way down on the Sky Jump, a controlled leap from a platform far above ground.

Leave Sky City and double back to Queen Street and turn left, toward the waterfront. Malls, travel agents, and shops line both sides of the road. Walk all the way to the end, cross QEII square, and you'll be at the **Ferry Building.** ❻ Follow the signs to the Devonport Ferry but, instead of buying a ticket for that trip alone ($9 round-trip), spend $1 more on a full-day pass, good on all Stagecoach buses as well. The ferry crosses between Auckland city and Devonport regularly, and the round-trip takes only 20 minutes. It's the best way to get onto the harbor if you're pressed for time and gives great views of the city, the Harbour Bridge, the North Shore, and Rangitoto Island.

Back in Auckland, walk out of the Ferry Building, turn right, and walk a few minutes along Quay Street to the Viaduct, where you'll find the **National Maritime Museum,** ❼ which is dedicated to New Zealand's seafaring past and present.

Next catch an Explorer Bus ($30 for a full day) in front of the museum or at the better-marked stop back at the Ferry Building. Once on the Explorer Bus go to the left side of the top level for the best views. After the bus passes some industrial ports, you'll get excellent views of Devonport, Rangitoto Island, and the Hauraki Gulf. A little farther along is Okahu Bay—the closest swimming beach to the city. The Explorer Bus travels to Mission Bay, a popular swimming and picnic spot, and then stops at **Kelly Tarlton's Underwater World and Antarctic Encounter, ❽** where you can check out sharks, giant stingrays, and other species. Continue by Explorer Bus to the **Parnell Rose Gardens. ❾** You'll have to tell the driver if you want to disembark here, as it is a "request stop." In flowering season (November to March) you should make the effort, but if it's wintertime, you can skip the gardens and continue straight on to the **Auckland Museum ❿** to view the most comprehensive collection of Māori artifacts in the country. The museum is set in the attractive parklands known as **Auckland Domain. ⓫**

Head away from the museum by foot, back down Maunsell Road; then cross the road and turn left on Parnell Road. Take a right onto Ayr Street, where you'll find the historic **Ewelme Cottage ⓬**. Walk back up Ayr Street, turn right into Parnell Road, and you will quickly reach the Cathedral of the Holy Trinity and **St. Mary's Church, ⓭** a Gothic-style church built in 1886. Walk down the hill just a bit and you'll reach charming **Parnell Village. ⓮** The last Explorer Bus passes through Parnell at 4:35 PM, but if you prefer to stay in Parnell for dinner, you can head back downtown later by taxi or on a Link bus. Catch a bus at any Link bus stop on the left-hand side of the road as you face the sea. They run every 10 minutes. A convenient stop is at the corner of Parnell Road and Birdwood Crescent.

TIMING   This tour can be done in a full day, but you'd be restricting your gallery, museum, and Kelly Tarlton's visits to about an hour each. If you have two days, it would make sense to walk the first part of this tour on Day 1 and get off the ferry at Devonport, spending some time in this quaint, seaside suburb. On the second day, you could head to Kelly Tarlton's first and then explore the Auckland Museum and Parnell area in a more leisurely manner. You might want to pack a picnic lunch to eat in the Domain. Most sights are open daily, with the exception of Ewelme Cottage.

What to See

❹ Albert Park. These 15 acres of formal gardens, fountains, and statue-studded lawns are a favorite for Aucklanders who pour out of nearby office buildings and the university and polytechnic to eat lunch on sunny days. The park is built on the site of a garrison from the 1840s and 1850s that was used to protect settlers from neighboring Māori tribes. There are still remnants of its stone walls (with rifle slits) behind university buildings on the east side of the park. ⊠ *Bounded by Wellesley St. W, Kitchener St., Waterloo Quad, city center.*

★ **❸ Auckland Art Gallery Toi o Tāmaki.** The country's finest collection of contemporary art hangs here as well as paintings of New Zealand dating from the time of Captain Cook. The châteaulike main gallery, built in

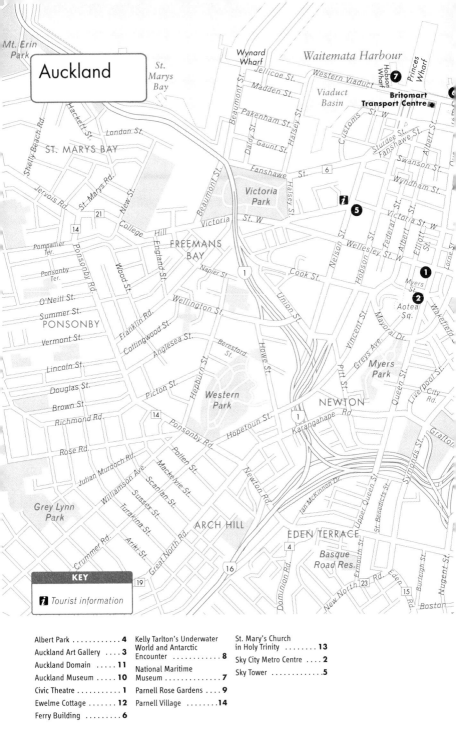

Auckland

Waitemata Harbour

Mt. Erin Park

St. Marys Bay

Wynard Wharf

Hobson Wharf

Princes Wharf

7

Jellicoe St.

Western Viaduct

Madden St.

Viaduct Basin

Britomart Transport Centre

ST. MARYS BAY

Beaumont St.

Pakenham St.

Customs St. W

Sturdee St.

Fanshawe St.

Hackett St.

London St.

Dady St.

Gaunt St.

Halsey St.

Swanson St.

Shelly Beach Rd.

St. Marys Rd.

New St.

Fanshawe St.

6

Wyndham St.

Jervois Rd.

21

College Hill

Victoria Park

Victoria St. W

Albert St.

Elliott St.

Victoria St. W

Pompallier Ter.

FREEMANS BAY

England St.

Nelson St.

Wellesley St.

i

5

Ponsonby Ter.

Wood St.

Napier St.

1

Cook St.

Hobson St.

Federal St.

1

O'Neill St.

Ponsonby Rd.

Franklin Rd.

Wellington St.

Union St.

Myers St.

2

Summer St.

PONSONBY

Collingwood St.

Vincent St.

Greys Ave.

Aotea Sq.

Vermont St.

Anglesea St.

Beresford St.

Mayoral Dr.

Wakefield

Lincoln St.

Hepburn St.

Howe St.

Pitt St.

Myers Park

Queen St.

Liverpool St.

Douglas St.

Picton St.

Western Park

NEWTON

Brown St.

Richmond Rd.

Ponsonby Rd.

Hopetoun St.

1

Karangahape Rd.

Graftor

Rose Rd.

Pollen St.

Newton Rd.

Simonds St.

Julian Murdoch Rd.

Mackelvie St.

14

Williamson Ave.

Scanlan St.

Ian McKinnon Dr.

Upper Queen St.

St. Benedicts St.

Grey Lynn Park

Sussex St.

Turakina St.

ARCH HILL

EDEN TERRACE

Basque Road Res.

Dominion Rd.

Eden Rd.

Burleigh St.

Nugent St.

Crummer Rd.

Ariki St.

Great North Rd.

16

4

New North Rd.

23

15

Boston

KEY

i Tourist information

19

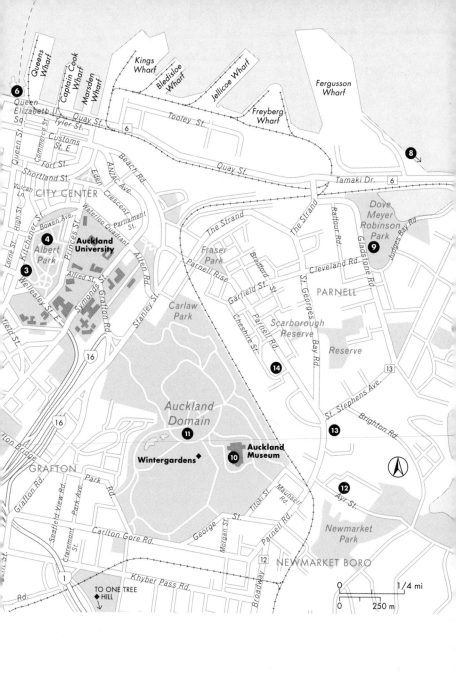

6 Queens Wharf

Captain Cook Wharf

Marsden Wharf

Kings Wharf

Bledisloe Wharf

Jellicoe Wharf

Freyberg Wharf

Fergusson Wharf

6 Queen Elizabeth II Sq.

Tyler St.

Quay St.

Tooley St.

6

Queen St.

Commerce St.

Customs St. E

Fort St.

Beach Rd.

Quay St.

Tamaki Dr. **6**

8

Shortland St.

Vulcan Ln.

CITY CENTER

Eden Crescent

ANZAC Ave.

Waterloo Quadrant

Parliament St.

The Strand

The Strand

Balfour Rd.

Judges Bay Rd.

Dove Meyer Robinson Park

9

High St.

Bowen Ave.

4

Auckland University

Albert Park

Princes St.

Allen Rd.

Fraser Park

Parnell Rise

Bradford St.

St. Georges Bay Rd.

Cleveland Rd.

Gladstone Rd.

PARNELL

3

Kitchener St.

Wellesley St. E

Alfred St.

Symonds St.

Grafton Rd.

Garfield St.

Parnell Rd.

Parnell St.

Scarborough Reserve

Reserve

field St.

Stanley St.

Carlaw Park

Cheshire St.

14

13

16

16

Auckland Domain

11

Wintergardens ♦

10

Auckland Museum

St. Stephens Ave.

Brighton Rd.

13

GRAFTON

Grafton Rd.

Park Ave.

Park Rd.

Carlton Gore Rd.

Seafield View Rd.

Claremont St.

George St.

Titoki St.

Morgan St.

Maunsell Rd.

Parnell Rd.

12

Ayr St.

Newmarket Park

12

NEWMARKET BORO

1

TO ONE TREE
♦ **HILL**

Khyber Pass Rd.

Broadway

Rd.

12

0   1/4 mi

0   250 m

the 1880s, holds many of the historic paintings, whereas the **New Gallery** across the street shows temporary exhibitions. The Mackelvie Gallery on the ground floor of the main gallery gives some insight into how early European settlers saw New Zealand. Portraits of Māori chiefs by C. F. Goldie and Gottfried Lindauer give splendid character studies of a fiercely martial people. Goldie used sitters introduced to him by friends, often using the same sitters repeatedly—odd, considering he aimed to document what he considered a dying race. Keep an eye out for *The Arrival of the Māoris in New Zealand,* which Goldie painted with his teacher, Louis John Steele, basing the work on Theodore Géricault's *Raft of the Medusa.* The painting is full of inaccuracies—the figures are not like Māori and they're in a type of *waka* (war canoe) not built until they settled in New Zealand—but it was a hit at the time and launched Goldie's career. The Grey Gallery, also in the main building, rotates New Zealand art from the 1950s to the present, including works by Frances Hodgkins, the country's best-known artist, and Colin McCahon. Note that the main gallery will close in late 2006 for redevelopment, expected to take around two years. Its collection will be shown in the New Gallery and satellite venues. ⊠ *5 Kitchener St., at Wellesley St. E, city center* ☎ *09/307–7700* ⊕ *www.aucklandartgallery.govt.nz* ⊠ *Heritage Gallery free, except for special exhibits; New Gallery $7. Both galleries free Mon.* ⊙ *Daily 10–5.*

NEED A BREAK? Reflect on your gallery visit from one of the balconies virtually suspended in the treetops at **Reuben** (⊠ New Gallery, Kitchener and Wellesley Sts. ☎ 09/302-0226 ⊙ Closed Sun.). Tuck into a fried-egg sandwich with harissa (Tunisian hot-chili paste) and crispy pancetta, or perhaps the namesake classic Reuben. Glasses of wine, usually of international varietals such as viognier and sangiovese, are very reasonably priced.

⑪ Auckland Domain. Saturday cricketers, Sunday picnickers, and everyday morning runners are three types of Aucklanders you'll see enjoying the rolling, 340-acre park. Watch the local paper for free summer weekend-evening concerts, which usually include opera and fireworks displays. Take a bottle of wine and a basketful of something tasty and join in with the locals—up to 300,000 of them per show. Within the Domain, the domed **Wintergardens** (open daily 10–4) house a collection of tropical plants and palms and seasonally displayed hothouse plants—a good stop for the horticulturally inclined. ⊠ *Entrances at Stanley St., Park Rd., Carlton Gore Rd., and Maunsell Rd.* ⊠ *Free* ⊙ *24 hours.*

★ ⊛ **⑩ Auckland Museum.** Dominating the Domain atop a hill, the Greek Revival museum is known especially for its Māori artifacts, the largest collection of its kind. Be sure to see the *pātaka,* or storehouse; these structures were a fixture in Māori villages, and the pātaka here is one of the finest known examples. Another must-see is "Te Toki a Tapiri," the last great Māori *waka* (canoe). It was carved from a single log, and, at 85 feet long, could carry 100 warriors. The figurehead is a particularly fine example of carving. To delve further into this culture, attend one of the Māori performances held at least three times daily; the show demonstrates Māori song, dance, weaponry, and the *haka* (war dance).

Another particularly good exhibit is "Scars on the Heart," which documents the Pacific theater of World War II with films, memorabilia, weaponry, and uniforms. Other exhibits address natural history, geology, and local history, including a reconstructed streetscape of early Auckland. Also check out the **Discovery Centres,** two interactive displays for kids of all ages. The "Weird and Wonderful" section covers everything from fossils to the water cycle. ⊠ *Auckland Domain, Park Rd.* ☎ *09/ 309–0443* ⊕ *www.aucklandmuseum.com* ▣ *$5; $15 for Māori cultural performance* ⊙ *Daily 10–5.*

NEED A BREAK?

Take in the scenery at **The Pavilion on Domain** (⊠ Wintergarden Pavilion, Domain Dr., Auckland Domain ☎ 09/303-0627). You can have brunch or a light lunch from a table inside the pavilion or on the terrace overlooking the duck ponds. Try the signature smoked fish pie or crispy skinned duck, or take a stab at the Caesar salad.

★ ❶ **Civic Theatre.** This extravagant art nouveau movie theater was the talk of the town when it opened in 1929, but just nine months later the owner, Thomas O'Brien, went bust and fled, taking with him the week's revenues and an usherette. During World War II a cabaret show in the basement was popular with Allied servicemen in transit to the battlefields of the Pacific. One of the entertainers, Freda Stark, is said to have appeared regularly wearing nothing more than a coat of gold paint—now the café at the front of the Civic bears her name. The building reopened in late 1999 after being closed for extensive refurbishment. To see the best of the Civic, don't restrict your visit to standing outside. Sit down to a show or movie, look up to the ceiling, and you'll see a simulated night sky. ⊠ *Queen and Wellesley Sts., city center* ☎ *09/307–5075.*

⓬ **Ewelme Cottage.** Built between 1863 and 1864 by the curiously named Reverend Vicesimus Lush (*vicesimus* is Latin for "20th," his birth order) and inhabited by his descendants for more than a century, this historic cottage stands behind a picket fence. The house was constructed of kauri, a resilient timber highly prized by the Māori for their war canoes and later by Europeans for ship masts. The home contains much of the original furniture and personal effects of the Lush family. You have to duck as you climb the steep, narrow stairs to the small pitched-roof bedrooms, made up as the Lushes might have left them. The drawing room, veranda, and garden appeared in Jane Campion's film *The Piano.* ⊠ *14 Ayr St., Parnell* ☎ *09/379–0202* ▣ *$7.50* ⊙ *Fri.–Sun. 10:30–noon and 1–4:30.*

❻ **Ferry Building.** This magnificent Edwardian building continues to stand out on Auckland's waterfront. The 1912 building is still used for its original purpose, and it's here that you can catch the ferry to Devonport as well as to Waiheke and other Hauraki Gulf islands. The building also houses bars and restaurants—more recent additions. Nearby, and easily seen from the Ferry Building, is Marsden Wharf, where French frogmen bombed and sank the Greenpeace vessel *Rainbow Warrior* in 1985. ⊠ *Quay St., city center.*

Kelly Tarlton

DIVER, DREAMER, explorer, inventor, instigator, worker, storyteller, father, a man who linked us all with his love of the sea." This inscription on the bust of the celebrated figure that stands in the eponymous Kelly Tarlton's Underwater World reveals something of the man whose charisma and vision knit together a team of fellow adventurers.

In 1956 Kelly Tarlton was set to join a climbing expedition to the Andes. When political unrest in Peru canceled the trip, he was left at loose ends. Bored, he went to see the Jacques Cousteau film Silent World and thought diving looked like more fun than climbing, with no politics to worry about. With typical Kiwi No. 8 fencing wire ingenuity (aka a do-it-yourself mentality), he built much of his own diving gear, got an underwater camera, and devised housings for the camera and flash.

In the 1960s, Tarlton focused on photographing marine life. In 1967 a trip to the Three Kings Islands to photograph and collect marine specimens whetted his appetite for treasure hunting. He and companion Wade Doak found the wreck of the Elingamite, which had foundered on the islands in 1902 with thousands of pounds in gold bullion on board, much of which they recovered.

One of Tarlton's most celebrated finds was the jewels of Isodore Rothschild on the Tasmania, which had sunk in 1897. Through his characteristic detailed research, Tarlton pinpointed the whereabouts of the wreck and succeeded in salvaging most of the jewelry in the late 1970s. The treasure was put on display in his now defunct Museum of Shipwrecks in Paihia but was then stolen by a staff member. Though the thief was imprisoned, he has never revealed the jewelry's fate.

Tarlton's interest broadened to marine archaeology. His first major success was finding the first de Surville anchor. Jean François Marie de Surville sailed the St. Jean Baptiste into Doubtless Bay in the Far North in 1769, where three of his anchors were lost in a storm. Tarlton plotted their whereabouts from crew accounts of the ship's dangerous proximity to a "big rock" and its position "a pistol shot" from shore, and by calculating the magnetic variations and wind directions from the original maps. The anchor is now in Wellington's Te Papa Museum.

But Tarlton is perhaps best known for the aquarium he built on Auckland's waterfront. Not having the funds to buy ready-molded acrylic to build his planned transparent viewing tunnels, Kelly said that if he could mold his own camera housings, he could create his own tunnels, too. And do it he did, with a team of skilled and loyal friends, building an "oven" for the molding and inventing a new gluing technique to form the curving tunnels.

Opened in January 1985, the aquarium was a huge success. After only seven weeks Tarlton shook the hand of the 100,000th visitor, an image captured in the last photo of him. Tragically, he died that very night, at the age of 47, of a heart complication.

—Toni Mason

⟳ **8** **Kelly Tarlton's Underwater World and Antarctic Encounter.** The creation of
Fodor'sChoice   New Zealand's most celebrated undersea explorer and treasure hunter
★   (*see the* Kelly Tarlton CloseUp box), this harborside marine park offers
a fish's-eye view of the sea. A transparent tunnel, 120 yards long, makes
a circuit past moray eels, lobsters, sharks, and stingrays. In Antarctic
Encounter, you enter a reproduction of explorer Robert Falcon Scott's
1911 Antarctic hut at McMurdo Sound, then circle around a deep-freeze
environment aboard a heated Sno-Cat (snowmobile) that winds through
a penguin colony and an aquarium exhibiting marine life of the polar
sea. You emerge at Scott Base 2000, where you can see a copy of the
Antarctic Treaty and flags of all the countries involved, as well as some
scientific research equipment currently used in Antarctica. ⊠ *Orakei
Wharf, 23 Tamaki Dr., 5 km (3 mi) east of downtown Auckland* ☎ *09/
528–0603* ⊕ *www.kellytarltons.co.nz* ⊠ *$26* ⊙ *Daily 9–6, last admis-
sion at 5 PM.*

Lionzone. Lion Beer doesn't have the international reputation of brews
such as Guinness or Budweiser, but it's a Kiwi icon all the same. A tour
takes you through the brewing process, recounting the history of Lion
Brewery through interactive computer displays, and the bottling and packaging hall. Of course, there's a chance to taste the company's Lion Red
or Steinlager at the end of the tour. ⊠ *380 Khyber Pass Rd., Newmarket* ☎ *09/358–8366* ⊕ *www.lionzone.co.nz* ⊠ *$15* ⊙ *Tours Mon.–Sat.
at 9:30, 12:15, and 3.*

⟳ **7** **National Maritime Museum.** You can plunge into New Zealand's rich seafaring history in this marina complex on Auckland Harbour. Experience
what it was like to travel steerage class in the 1800s in a simulated rocking cabin, or check out a reproduction of a shipping office from the turn
of the last century. There are detailed exhibits on early whaling and a
collection of yachts, ship models, and Polynesian outriggers—not to
mention *KZ1*, the 133-foot racing sloop built for the America's Cup challenge in 1988. A scow conducts short harbor trips twice a day on Tuesday, Thursday, and weekends. ⊠ *Eastern Viaduct, Quay St., city center*
☎ *09/373–0800* ⊕ *www.nzmaritime.org* ⊠ *$12, harbor trip $15 extra*
⊙ *Oct.–Easter, daily 9–6; Easter–Sept., daily 9–5.*

One Tree Hill. The largest of Auckland's extinct volcanoes and one of
the best lookout points, One Tree Hill, or Maungakiekie, was the site
of three Māori *pā* (fortifications). The hill is not as distinctive as it once
was, though; its signature lone pine was attacked several times by activists who saw it as a symbol of colonialism, and in 2000 it had to be
taken down. Sir John Logan Campbell, founding father of the city, is
buried on the summit. Surrounded by parklands with avenues of oaks,
a kauri plantation, and an old olive grove, the hill is popular for picnics and jogging. ⊠ *Greenlane Rd. W.*

9 **Parnell Rose Gardens.** When you tire of boutiques and cafés, take a 10-
minute stroll to gaze upon and sniff this collection of some 5,000 rose-
bushes. The main beds contain mostly modern hybrids, with new
introductions being planted regularly. The adjacent **Nancy Steen Garden** is the place to admire the antique varieties. And don't miss the garden's incredible trees. There is a 200-year-old *pohutukawa*

(puh-hoo-too-*ka*-wa) whose weighty branches touch the ground and rise up again, and a *kanuka* that is one of Auckland's oldest trees. The Rose Garden Restaurant serves lunch (closed Saturday). ⊠ *Gladstone and Judges Bay Rds., Parnell* ☎ *09/302–1252* 🖃 *Free* ⊙ *Daily dawn–dusk.*

★ ⓮ **Parnell Village.** The pretty Victorian timber villas along the slope of Parnell Road have been transformed into antiques shops, designer boutiques, cafés, and restaurants. Parnell Village is the creation of Les Harvey, who saw the potential of the old, run-down shops and houses and almost single-handedly snatched them from the jaws of the developers' bulldozers in the early 1960s by buying them, renovating them, and leasing them out. The project was completed in 1976. Harvey's vision has paid handsome dividends, and today this village of trim pink-and-white timber facades is one of the most delightful parts of the city. It has a special place in local shoppers' hearts because this was the only part of town where shops were open on Saturday until restrictions on retail hours were repealed in the mid-1980s. At night, the area's restaurants and bars attract Auckland's upmarket set. ⊠ *Parnell Rd. between St. Stephen's Ave. and Augustus Rd., Parnell.*

⓭ **St. Mary's Church in Holy Trinity.** Gothic Revival wooden churches don't get much finer than this one. Built in 1886, it's one of a number of churches commissioned by the early Anglican missionary Bishop Selwyn. The craftsmanship inside the kauri church is remarkable, down to the hand-finished columns. One of the carpenters left his trademark, an owl, sitting in the beams to the right of the pulpit. If you stand in the pulpit and clasp the lectern, you'll feel something lumpy under your left hand—a mouse, the trademark of another of the craftsmen who made the lectern, the so-called Mouse Man of Kilburn. The story of the church's relocation is also remarkable. St. Mary's originally stood on the other side of Parnell Road, and in 1982 the entire structure was moved across the street to be next to the new church, the Cathedral of the Holy Trinity. Photographs inside show the progress of the work. ⊠ *Parnell Rd. and St. Stephen's Ave., Parnell* ⊙ *Daily 8–6.*

❷ **Sky City Metro Centre.** With design concepts that could be from a science-fiction movie (actually, some of them are), the Metro Centre is worth a walk even if you don't intend to partake in its entertainment. Spiral staircases, bridges designed to look like film, and elevators in the shape of rockets regularly attract design and architecture students—as well as hordes of teenagers. The Metro Centre incorporates a 13-screen cineplex (which includes two "gold class" cinemas with reclining armchairs), an international food court, and several bars, including the **Playhouse Pub,** an English-style tavern with a Shakespearean theme. A video arcade, bookstore, and photo developer add to the diverse mix. ⊠ *291–297 Queen St., city center* ⊙ *Daily 9 AM–midnight.*

❺ **Sky Tower.** The joke among Auckland residents is that your property value rises if you *can't* see this 1,082-foot beacon. Yet it's also the first place Aucklanders take friends and relatives visiting from overseas to give them a view of the city. Up at the main observation level, the most outrageous thing is the glass floor panels—looking down at your feet, you see the street hundreds of yards below. Adults usually step gingerly onto the glass, and kids delight in jumping up and down on it. More educational are the audio guides to Auckland and touch-screen computers that you'll find on the deck. There's also an outdoor observation level. Through glass panels in the floor of the elevator you can see the counterweight fly up to pass you. For an adrenaline rush you can even take a controlled leap off **Sky Jump**, a 630-foot observation deck, for a steep $195. For a slightly less heart-stopping experience (and price, at $145), take the **Vertigo Climb.** On this, you can climb up inside the mast to emerge at the crow's nest 1,000 feet up. At that height you're above the weather, and people have reportedly seen rainbows as complete circles. ⊠ *Victoria and Federal Sts., city center* ☎ *09/912–6000* 🎫 *$18* ⊙ *Sun.–Thurs. 8:30 AM–11 PM, last elevator 10:30 PM, Fri. and Sat. 8:30 AM–midnight, last elevator 11:30 PM.*

Western Springs

★ ☺ **Auckland Zoo.** Since the 1990s, this zoo has focused on providing its animals with the most natural habitats possible, as well as on breeding and conservation. The primates area, sea lion and penguin shores, and the Pridelands section, where lions, giraffes, zebra, springbok, rhino, and ostriches range in savannalike grasslands, best exemplify this approach. To catch a glimpse of New Zealand flora and fauna, spend time in the New Zealand Native Aviary, where you walk among the birds, and the Kiwi and Tuatara Nocturnal House, which are at opposite ends of the zoo. In early 2004, an enterprising Asian elephant escaped by dropping a tree on an electric fence and took herself for a walk in the neighboring park. She was coaxed home after 45 minutes, and the zoo's fences are now elephant-proof. By car, take Karangahape Road (which turns into Great North Road) west out of the city, past Western Springs. Take a right onto Motions Road. Buses from the city stop opposite Motions Road. ⊠ *Motions Rd., Western Springs, 6 km (4 mi) west of Auckland* ☎ *09/360–3819* ⊕ *www.aucklandzoo.co.nz* 🎫 *$16* ⊙ *Sept.–May, daily 9:30–5:30, June–Aug., daily 9:30–5.*

☺ **Museum of Transport and Technology.** This fascinating collection of vehicles, telephones, cameras, locomotives, steam engines, and farm equipment is a tribute to Kiwi ingenuity. The aviation collection includes the only surviving Solent flying boat. One of the most intriguing exhibits is the remains of an aircraft built by Robert Pearse. There is a reproduction of another he built in which he made a successful powered flight around the time the Wright brothers first took to the skies. The flight ended inauspiciously when his plane crashed into a hedge. But Pearse, considered a wild eccentric by his farming neighbors, is recognized today as a mechanical genius. MOTAT, as the museum is called, also has the scooter Prime Minister Helen Clark rode to her university. The museum is near the Auckland Zoo; a tram ($2) shuttles between the two. ⊠ *825 Great North Rd., off Northwestern Motorway, Rte. 16, Western Springs, 6 km (4 mi) west of Auckland* ☎ *09/846–0199* ⊕ *www.motat.org.nz* 🎫 *$14* ⊙ *Daily 10–5.*

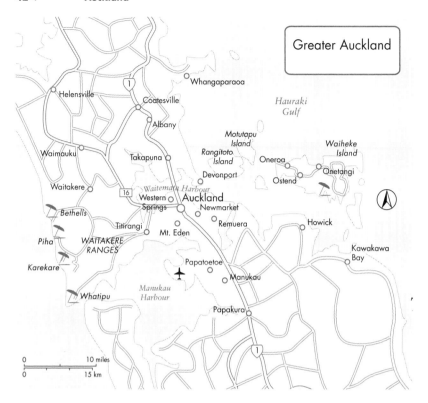

Greater Auckland

Devonport

The 20-minute ferry to Devonport across Waitemata Harbour provides one of the finest views of Auckland. The first harbor ferry service began with whaleboats in 1854. Later in the century the Devonport Steam Ferry Co. began operations, and ferries scuttled back and forth across the harbor until the Harbour Bridge opened in 1959. The bridge now carries the bulk of the commuter traffic, but the ferry still has a small, devoted clientele.

Originally known as Flagstaff, after the signal station on the summit of Mt. Victoria, Devonport was the first settlement on the north side of the harbor. Later the area drew some of the city's wealthiest traders, who built their homes where they could watch their sailing ships arriving with cargoes from Europe. These days, Aucklanders have fixed up and re-populated its great old houses, laying claim to the suburb's relaxed, seaside atmosphere.

The Esplanade Hotel is one of the first things you'll see as you leave the ferry terminal. It stands at the harbor end of Victoria Road, a pleasant street for taking a stroll; stopping at a shop, a bookstore, or a café; or picking up some fish-and-chips to eat next to the giant Moreton Bay fig tree on the green across the street.

Long before the era of European settlement, the ancient volcano of **Mt. Victoria** was the site of a Māori *pā* (fortified village) of the local Kawerau tribe. On the northern and eastern flanks of the hill you can still see traces of the terraces once protected by palisades of sharpened stakes. Don't be put off by its name—this is more molehill than mountain, and the climb isn't much. Mt. Victoria is signposted on Victoria Road, a few minutes' walk from the Esplanade Hotel. ⊠ *Kerr St. off Victoria Rd.*

New Zealand's navy is hardly a menacing global force, but the small **Navy Museum** has interesting exhibits on the early exploration of the country and information on its involvement in various conflicts. Displays of firearms, swords, and memorabilia will likely grab former navy men far more than the uninitiated. The museum is five blocks west of Victoria Wharf. ⊠ *Queens Parade* 🍱 *Small donation* ⊙ *Daily 10–4:30.*

The position of **North Head**, an ancient Māori defense site, jutting out from Devonport into Auckland's harbor, was enough to convince the European settlers that they, too, should use the head for strategic purposes. Rumor has it that veteran aircraft are still stored in the dark, twisting tunnels under North Head, but plenty of curious explorers have not found any. You can still get into most tunnels (they're safe), climb all over the abandoned antiaircraft guns, and get great views of Auckland and the islands to the east. North Head is a 20-minute walk east of the ferry terminal on King Edward Parade, left onto Cheltenham Street, and then out Takarunga Road. ⊠ *Takarunga Rd.*

Hauraki Gulf Islands

More than 50 islands lie in the Hauraki Gulf, forming the Hauraki Gulf Marine Park, managed by the Department of Conservation (DOC). Many of the islands are nature reserves, home to endangered plants and birds, and public access to these is restricted. Others are public reserves that can be reached by ferry, and a few are privately owned. Great Barrier Island, the largest in the gulf, has a population of around 1,100, and is mostly agricultural. Motuihe, a popular swimming spot, was a prisoner-of-war camp during World War I and the scene of a daring escape: Count Felix Von Luckner, known as the "Sea Devil," commandeered the camp commander's boat and got as far as the Kermadec Islands before being recaptured.

You can see rare native birds up close at **Tiritiri Matangi,** a bird sanctuary open to the public. A gentle walk on well-maintained and signposted tracks takes you to the top of the island and the oldest lighthouse in the gulf, still in operation. The island is, of course, free from predators, and the birds are unafraid. Tiritiri is home to at least 18 *takahe,* large blue and green flightless birds with red beaks. You can usually spot them eating grass near the lighthouse. The grave of Mr. Blue, the hand-reared male of the first pair on the island, is marked by a plaque at his favorite spot near the lighthouse.

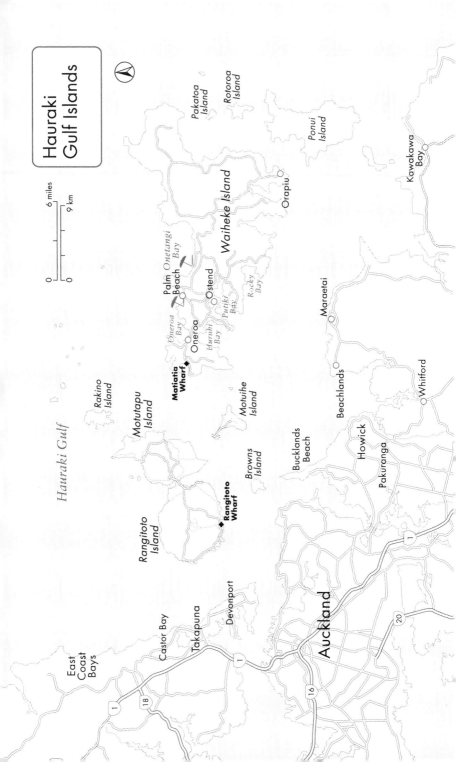

Hauraki
Gulf Islands

6 miles
9 km

Hauraki Gulf

Rakino Island

Motutapu Island

Rangitoto Island

Rangitoto Wharf

Browns Island

Motuihe Island

Matiatia Wharf

Oneroa Bay

Oneroa

Huruhi Bay

Putiki Bay

Ostend

Rocky Bay

Palm Beach

Onetangi Bay

Waiheke Island

Orapiu

Pakatoa Island

Rotoroa Island

Ponui Island

Kawakawa Bay

Maraetai

Beachlands

Whitford

Bucklands Beach

Howick

Pakuranga

East Coast Bays

Castor Bay

Takapuna

Devonport

Auckland

Volcano Views

CLOSE UP

AUCKLAND IS BUILT on and around 48 volcanoes, and the tops of many of them provide sweeping views of the city. **One Tree Hill,** the largest of Auckland's extinct volcanoes, was the site of an early Māori settlement. **Mt. Eden,** the highest volcano on the Auckland isthmus, is probably the most popular, and several bus tours include this central site. **Rangitoto Island** has an even better vista. This volcano emerged from the sea just 600 years ago, no doubt much to the wonder of the Māori people living next door on Motutapu Island. Take a ferry to the island; then either a short ride or an hour's walk to the top will give you a 360-degree view of the city and the Hauraki Gulf islands.

It is thought that Māori settled on the volcanoes beginning in the 14th century, taking advantage of the fertile soils. There's evidence that in the 16th century, the Māori used the cones as defensive *pā* (fortified villages). Evidence of complex earthworks can be seen on Mt. Eden and One Tree Hill where Māori cleared volcanic stone to develop garden plots and form the terraces that are features of *pā*.

To get the full scoop on the various islands, stop by Auckland's **Department of Conservation Visitor Centre** (✉ Ferry Bldg., Quay St. ☎ 09/ 379–6476 ⊕ www.doc.govt.nz).

Rangitoto Island

When Rangitoto Island emerged from the sea in a series of fiery eruptions 600 years ago, it had an audience. Footprints in the ash on its close neighbor Motutapu Island prove that Māori people watched Rangitoto's birth. It is now the largest and youngest of about 50 volcanic cones and craters in the Auckland volcanic field, though scientists are confident that it will not blow again. During the 1920s and 1930s hundreds of prisoners built roads and trails on the island, some of which are still used as walkways. Small beach houses were also erected on the island in the early 20th century. Many were pulled down in the 1970s until their historical significance was recognized. Thirty-two remain, and a few are still used by lease-holders who are allowed to use them during their lifetimes. (Afterward, they'll be relinquished to the DOC.)

Rangitoto is covered with a hardy *pohutukawa* forest. When the flowers bloom around Christmastime, the slopes are a sea of red (hence the tree's popular name, the New Zealand Christmas tree). The most popular activity on the island is the one-hour summit walk, beginning at Rangitoto Wharf and climbing through lava fields and forest to the peak. At the top, walkers are rewarded with panoramic views of Auckland and the Hauraki Gulf. Short detours will lead to lava caves and even to the remnants of a botanical park planned in 1915, and you can walk around the rim of the crater.

GETTING THERE **Fullers Booking Office** (☎ 09/367–9111 ⊕ www.fullers.co.nz) operates ferries year-round to Rangitoto daily at 9:15 and 12:15, departing the island at 12:45 and 3:30. The fare is $18.40 round-trip; boats leave from the Ferry Building. Fullers also arranges Volcanic Explorer tours, which include a guided ride to the summit in a covered carriage. The cost is $29, or $47.40 for the tour and ferry ride, and the trip must be booked in advance.

Waiheke Island

Once a sleepy spot, Waiheke was mainly used as a weekend and summer vacation retreat and hippie haven, with beach houses dotting its edges. In the late 1980s, though, commuters started moving in, attracted by the mellow lifestyle—the island now has a population of around 7,000. Gentrification has hit Waiheke, and many affluent city-dwellers have built large vacation homes, raising housing costs in their wake. The island is earning an international reputation for its vineyards, and local cafés sometimes stock wines that aren't available on the mainland—vintners make them purely for island enjoyment. The annual Waiheke Jazz Festival at Easter is also earning something of a reputation, attracting renowned overseas performers.

From the ferry landing at Matiatia Wharf you can walk five minutes to the small town of **Oneroa,** the island's hub, with its shops, cafés, bars, and real estate agents. Another minute's walk gets you to **Oneroa Beach,** one of the most accessible beaches. The north-facing beaches—sheltered bays with little surf—are the best for swimming. The most popular is **Palm Beach,** 10 minutes by bus from Oneroa. Around the rocks to the left is **Little Palm Beach,** one of Auckland's three nudist beaches. Another great beach on Waiheke is **Onetangi,** on the north side of the island, 20 minutes from Matiatia by bus. **Whakanewha Regional Park,** on the south side of the island, is a lovely bush reserve leading down to a half-moon bay. You can go hiking and picnicking here, and the wetland area is home to rare birds such as the New Zealand dotterel. You can get to the park from Oneroa by shuttle bus.

There are around 35 vineyards on Waiheke Island, but because some are new, only 20-odd are producing wine. First to plant grapes were Kim and Jeanette Goldwater, whose eponymous wines have earned a reputation for excellence. The **Goldwater Estate** (⌧ 18 Causeway Rd., Putiki Bay ☏ 09/372–7493 ⊕ www.goldwaterwine.com) cabernet sauvignon–merlot blend is outstanding, and the Esslin Merlot has been hailed as the best Kiwi interpretation of this popular variety. The winery is open for tastings only in January, daily between 11 AM and 4 PM. It's best to call ahead. **Passage Rock Wines** (⌧ 438 Orapiu Rd., Te Matuku Bay ☏ 09/372–7257 ⊕ www.passagerockwines.co.nz), on the eastern end of the island, is worth the trip for their good-value wines. The Passage Rock Forté, a blend of cabernet franc, merlot, and cabernet sauvignon, is rated highly. The café makes delicious thin-crust pizzas in a wood-fired oven. It's open for tastings on weekends April through November, Wednesday through Sunday in December and March, and daily in January and February. Stephen White's **Stonyridge Vineyard** (⌧ 80 Onetangi Rd., Ostend ☏ 09/372–8822 ⊕ www. stonyridge.com) has the island's highest profile, and the Stonyridge Larose, made from the classic bordeaux varieties, is world class—and priced accordingly. Stephen gets faxed orders months before release and is usually sold out hours later. Call before you visit—he may have nothing left to taste or sell. Reservations for lunch at the Veranda Café, overlooking the vines, are essential; but if it's booked, you may be accommodated with antipasto platters and wine on a blanket in the olive grove. The winery is open for tastings daily December through March and Thursday through Tuesday April through November. The Dunleavy family of **Te Motu Vineyard** (⌧ 76 Onetangi Rd., Onetangi ☎ 09/372–6884 ⊕ www.temotu.co.nz) started planting vines in 1989. Now their Te Motu bordeaux blend is on the wine list at six Michelin-starred restaurants in France—a great endorsement. The restaurant, the Shed, serves wonderful food in a Tuscan setting. The winery is open for tastings Tuesday through Sunday from late October to Easter and Friday through Sunday May through September.

WHERE TO STAY & EAT

$$$$

✕ **Mudbrick Vineyard and Restaurant.** Mudbrick's a good place to try wines that never make it to the mainland. The vineyard produces a small portfolio of whites and reds of its own and serves them and those of other tiny producers, all paired with the menu. Because bordeaux varieties predominate on the island, the food emphasis is on red meat; particular favorites are the rack of lamb and Black Angus eye fillet. The front terrace is the best spot to take in the harbor views. Unlike many places on Waiheke, Mudbrick is open for lunch and dinner daily, year-round. ⌧ *Church Bay Rd., Oneroa* ☎ *09/372–9050* ▭ *AE, DC, MC, V.*

$$$$

Fodor'sChoice ★

✕ **Te Whau Vineyard and Café.** With a wine list of more than 550 of the best New Zealand and international wines, it's no wonder this restaurant has been described as one of the best in the world for wine lovers. Owners Tony and Moira Forsyth have many vintages that are no longer available anywhere else. Spectacularly perched atop a finger of land, the restaurant commands a nearly 360-degree view. Te Whau's own bordeaux blend is much praised; you'll be able to try their chardonnay only here. They specialize in seafood; if the salmon house-smoked over oak and *manuka* (a native tea tree) wood is on the menu, don't miss it. ⌧ *218 Te Whau Dr., Te Whau Point* ☎ *09/372–7191* ▭ *AE, MC, V* ☾ *Closed Tues. Nov.–Easter, and weekdays Easter–late Oct. No dinner.*

$$–$$$

✕ **Vino Vino.** Waiheke's longest-running restaurant perches on Oneroa's main street, with a large all-weather deck overlooking the bay. The platters—Mediterranean, grilled (with Italian sausages and calamari), or seafood—are perennial favorites. Or try something with a North African spin, such as the dry-marinated chicken over a red-pepper-and-tomato salad. ⌧ *3/153 Ocean View Rd., Oneroa* ☎ *09/372–9888* ⊕ *www.vinovino.co.nz* ⌭ *Reservations essential* ▭ *AE, MC, V* ☾ *Closed Mon. No dinner Sun. June–Oct.*

★ **$$$$**

▦ **Boatshed.** An internal spiral staircase leads to the Lighthouse, a two-story suite on the top floor of a turret. The glass doors of the day room fold right open onto a wraparound deck overlooking the golden sands of Oneroa Bay, where boats moor and the swimming is great. From the bedroom on the first floor the view is as spectacular. A long central room, with doors onto the sail-covered deck, divides this boutique hotel and gives onto a cozy sunken lounge. In the Bridge Room, up a flight of stairs, bifold windows off the sunporch frame a view of the bay. If you go for one of the three Boatshed Rooms, leave the louvred doors to your private deck open, for fresh sea air as you sleep. Owner Jonathan Scott, a former chef, prepares dinners by arrangement, served in the Long Room, on the "jetty" outside, or delivered to the Lighthouse suite by dumbwaiter. ⊠ *Tawa and Huia Sts., Little Oneroa* ☎ *09/372–3242* 🗐 *09/372–3262* ⊕ *www.boatshed.co.nz* ⤴ *4 rooms, 1 suite* ⛁ *In-room DVD, Wi-Fi, massage, spa* ⊟ *AE, DC, MC, V* ⏐◯⏐ *BP.*

$$$ 🖼 **The Moorings.** From the bright guest rooms of this L-shape Mediterranean farmhouse-style home, you can look outward or inward: out onto the bay or in to a sheltered courtyard with lavender hedges and lemon trees. Each room has a king-size bed, a spacious seating area, and a small deck. Below the decks a terraced path leads down to the bay—though it's a bit of a climb back up. The roomy bathrooms are equipped with hair dryers and L'Occitane toiletries. ⊠ *9 Oceanview Rd., Oneroa* ☎🗐 *09/372–8283* ⊕ *www.themoorings.gen.nz* ⤴ *2 rooms* ⛁ *Kitchenette, cable TV, in-room data ports* ⊟ *MC, V* ⏐◯⏐ *CP.*

$$ 🖼 **Winemaker's Loft.** From the dining area of this modern apartment-style loft, you can look onto the vines of Cable Bay vineyard and beyond them to Church Bay. Standing a short distance from the owners' home, this is a private retreat, yet it's only five minutes to the relative bustle of Oneroa. In keeping with the wine theme, all the right wineglasses are provided, and you can start with the complimentary bottle of theirs. One-night stays incur a $50 surcharge. ⊠ *20 Nick Johnston Dr., Oneroa* ☎ *09/372–9384* 🗐 *09/372–5869* ⊕ *www.winemakersloft.co.nz* ⤴ *1 suite* ⛁ *Kitchenette, in-room DVD, in-room data port* ⊟ *MC, V* ⏐◯⏐ *CP.*

GETTING THERE & AROUND **Fullers ferries** (☎ 09/367–9111) make the trip between the Ferry Building and Waiheke at least a dozen times a day, even on Sunday. However, it pays to phone first, as crossings can be canceled if the seas are rough. The return fare is $26. Buses meet ferries at the Waiheke terminal and make a loop around the island. You can also take a shuttle to beaches or vineyards; **Waiheke Shuttles** (☎ 09/372–7262) has reliable service. The best way to get to Whakanewha Regional Park is by shuttle.

If you're planning on going farther afield on the island, you can purchase an all-day bus pass from **Fullers Booking Office** (☎ 09/367–9111) at the Ferry Building on Quay Street ($10 for regular service: to Oneroa, Palm Beach, Onetangi, and Rocky Bay). To use the pass, you need to take the 10 AM ferry. Return time is optional. Fullers also offers a couple of tours that include the ferry fee (*see the* Tours section *in* Auckland A to Z). After either tour, on the same day, passengers may use their ticket to travel free on regular island buses to visit additional attractions.

WHERE TO EAT

New Zealand chefs have a reputation for being innovative, unafraid to put ingredients on the same plate that have rarely shared the same kitchen. Because of this approach, their cuisine has often been tagged "Pacific Rim" or "fusion," but this misses the point. Kiwi cooks are most concerned about the best combinations of the freshest ingredients, whatever the influence—and Auckland has some of the country's best home-grown chefs. The city's cosmopolitan mix of cafés, restaurants, brasseries, and bars spreads from the city center to the closest suburbs. Appropriately enough, given the maritime climate, the local style leans to the Mediterranean, with a strong sideways glance toward Asia. Seafood is a strong suit. Don't miss such delicacies as Bluff oysters (in season March–August), salmon from Akaroa or Marlborough, Greenshell mussels (also known as green-lipped or New Zealand green mussels), scallops, crayfish, and two clamlike shellfish, *pipi* and *tuatua.* In spring, many restaurants feature whitebait, known to Māori as *inanga,* which are the juvenile of several fish species. They are eaten whole, usually in an omeletlike fritter. You'll also encounter plenty of opportunities to try *kūmara,* a local sweet potato and staple of the Māori diet.

The downtown waterfront area was extensively rebuilt for the America's Cup yachting series that straddled the millennium changeover. Princes Wharf and adjoining Viaduct Quay, an easy stroll from the city's major thoroughfare, Queen Street, now burst at the seams with dozens of eateries in every style from cheap-and-cheerful to superposh. High Street, running parallel to Queen Street on the Albert Park side of town, has developed into a busy café and restaurant strip over the last few years. You can get between Queen and High streets via Vulcan Lane, which has some attractive bars itself. Asian immigrants have spurred a flock of cheap noodle and sushi bars throughout the inner city.

Away from the city center, the top restaurant areas are Ponsonby and Parnell roads, both a 10-minute bus or cab ride from the city center. Dominion and Mt. Eden roads in the city, as well as Hurstmere Road in the suburb of Takapuna, over the Harbour Bridge, are also worth exploring. The mix is eclectic—Indian, Chinese, Japanese, and Thai eateries sit comfortably alongside casual taverns, pizzerias, and high-end restaurants. At hole-in-the-wall spots in and around the city center a few dollars will buy you anything from fish-and-chips to nachos, noodles, or naan bread. Ponsonby Road leads the field in outdoor dining, but Hurstmere Road is catching up fast.

To the west, out toward the Waitakere Ranges, the suburb of Titirangi has earned a reputation as a dining village, with everything from low-key pizza, Middle Eastern, and Southeast Asian places to wine bars and upscale restaurants with harbor views.

WHAT IT COSTS In New Zealand dollars				
$$$$	**$$$**	**$$**	**$**	**¢**
RESTAURANTS over $30	$20–$30	$15–$20	$10–$15	under $10

Prices are per person for a main course at dinner, or the equivalent.

Know-How

Peak dinnertime in Auckland is between 8 and 9, but most kitchens stay open until at least 10 PM. Many restaurants, particularly in Ponsonby and Parnell, serve food all day, some with a limited menu between 3 and 6 PM; some still close between their lunch and dinner services. On Sunday and Monday, it pays to check whether a place you're interested in is open. Locals dress reasonably casually for a meal out; only in the most formal restaurants do men need to wear a jacket. BYOB policies have become scarce, limited mainly to ethnic restaurants such as Thai and Indian. There's usually a per-person corkage fee of a few dollars. Some restaurants have started charging a 15% surcharge on public holidays, reflecting their need to pay their staff higher holiday wages, but generally they will remind you of this surcharge when you make a reservation.

City Center

$$$$
Fodor'sChoice
★
✕ **The French Café.** It's not really a café, and it's not strictly French, but don't let the inaccurate nomenclature put you off—the food's great and considered by many to be the best in town. Simon Wright has a light touch that translates to clean, focused flavors, harmonizing in dishes such as pot-au-feu of organic chicken and crayfish with spring vegetables, lemon aïoli, and basil bouillon. The menu changes frequently, but you will always find the best ingredients in perfectly executed dishes. The wine list includes a few finds, and the staff can make well-informed recommendations. ✉ *210B Symonds St., near Karangahape Rd., city center* ☎ *09/377–1911* ⊕ *www.thefrenchcafe.co.nz* ▤ *AE, DC, MC, V* ⊘ *Closed Sun. and Mon.*

$$$$
✕ **Harbourside Seafood Bar and Grill.** Overlooking the water from the upper level of the restored ferry building, this sprawling, modish seafood restaurant is great for warm-weather dining. Some of the finest New Zealand fish and shellfish, including tuna, salmon, snapper, pipi, and tuatua, appear on a menu with a fashionably Mediterranean accent. Lobster fresh from the tank is a house specialty. Non-fish-eaters have their choice of lamb, eye fillet (beef tenderloin), and perhaps *cervena* (farmed venison). On warm nights, reserve ahead and request a table outside on the balcony. ✉ *Ferry Bldg., Quay St., city center* ☎ *09/307–0486* ⊕ *www.harboursiderestaurant.co.nz* ▤ *AE, DC, MC, V.*

$$$$
✕ **Number 5 Restaurant.** The sign outside declares, "Life is too short to drink bad wine." Accordingly, the wine list here is designed to prevent such a mishap, with a vast selection by the glass as well as the bottle. Unlike most high-end restaurants, Number 5 is happy to serve just a small dish with a glass of wine if that's all you feel like eating. But you shouldn't pass up the main courses, such as individual beef Wellingtons, or venison steak with mashed kūmara and truffled mushrooms and syrah reduction. ✉ *5 City Rd., city center* ☎ *09/309–9273* ▤ *AE, DC, MC, V* ⊘ *Closed Sun. No lunch.*

$$$$
Fodor'sChoice
★
✕ **White.** Vast windows blur the boundary between the harbor and the alabaster decor of this stylish restaurant. Fittingly, New Zealand seafood dominates the sophisticated contemporary menu, with dishes such as scampi and salmon tortellini served with arugula and caper-butter sauce or *hapuka* (grouper) in a crust of hazelnut and *horopito* (an indigenous pepper) served with baby turnips and pearl onions. If you come for lunch, you may need to bring your sunglasses. ✉ *Hilton Auckland, Princes Wharf, 147 Quay St.* ☎ *09/978–2000* ▤ *AE, DC, MC, V.*

$$$–$$$$
✕ **Cin Cin on Quay.** Auckland's original seaside brasserie is still one of the best. The innovative menu makes good use of local produce, such as creamy Clevedon coast oysters and fried shallots in a champagne vinai-

grette, and Waimarino free-range pork served with kūmara (New Zealand sweet potato), apple syrup, and toasted-fennel jus. The extensive wine list has several vintages of local icons such as Kumeu River. If you're in town on the weekend, reserve an outside table overlooking the harbor for brunch. ⊠ *Ferry Bldg., Quay St., city center* ☎ *09/307–6966* ⊟ *AE, DC, MC, V.*

$$$–$$$$ ✕ **Dine by Peter Gordon.** New Zealand's most celebrated chef and fusion cuisine pioneer, Peter Gordon, opened this signature restaurant— **Fodor's**Choice his first in the country since the 1980s—in 2005, in the city's newest ★ major hotel. He oversees the restaurant from London, where he runs The Providores, and visits regularly. As you would expect from a chef of his standing, the refined food delights with surprises such as the wasabi-*tobiko* (flying-fish roe)–spiked avocado cream served with the truffled yellowfin tuna, or the roast five-spice pork belly and rum-roast pineapple that accompanies sautéed scallops. Classic melds with modern: leather banquettes line the white walls, where enormous mirrors reflect the large ring-shape lights hanging from the high ceilings. This is a place to feel special. ⊠ *Sky City Grand Hotel, 90 Federal St., city center* ☎ *09/363–7030* ⊟ *AE, DC, MC, V.*

$$$–$$$$ ✕ **Kermadec.** This complex's two restaurants are owned by a major fishing company, so naturally, the chefs lean on seafood. Both places have harborside views and dramatic Pacific-theme decor. In the more casual brasserie, seek the kitchen's advice on the best way to enjoy the catch of the day. The adjacent restaurant prepares great sashimi, or you could try orange roughy (a mild fish) steamed and served with sesame-ginger Chinese greens. Can't decide? Share a platter—it will probably include smoked salmon, scallops, prawns, mussels, smoked eel, scampi, John Dory, and snapper. ⊠ *1st fl., Viaduct Quay Bldg., Quay and Lower Hobson Sts., city center* ☎ *09/309–0413 brasserie, 09/309–0412 restaurant* ⊕ *www.kermadec.co.nz* ⊟ *AE, DC, MC, V.*

★ $$$–$$$$ ✕ **O'Connell Street Bistro.** An intimate dining room is not easy to find in Auckland; this one is consistently rated among the top in the city. The former bank vault, on one of the city's fashionable back streets, is chic yet serene, and has a cozy bar from which you can watch passersby through thin venetian blinds. Loyal diners keep coming back for uncomplicated but impressive dishes such as roasted pork piccata on butter-bean cassoulet, or duck two ways—roast duck breast, and confit duck leg on a capsicum-and-red-onion stew with fried *haloumi* (a salty, Middle-Eastern-style sheep's milk cheese) served on tables covered in crisp white linen. On the wine list you will find varieties rarely seen elsewhere, such as Waiheke's sought-after Stonyridge Larose Cabernets. ⊠ *3 O'-Connell St., city center* ☎ *09/377–1884* ⊟ *AE, DC, MC, V* ☺ *Closed Sun. No lunch Mon. and Sat.*

$$$ ✕ **Prime.** Diners can gaze out at the harbor view over lunch in this slick, sparely designed restaurant opposite Princes Wharf. The menu is easygoing. Most dishes are offered at appetizer or entrée sizes, and you're welcome to simply linger over some tapas—as in small dishes, though not particularly Spanish—with a glass of wine. For something more substantial, try the perennial favorite, braised rabbit pappardelle with *rimu* wood–smoked bacon and walnut-watercress pesto. The menu suggests pairing it with the Rabbit Ranch pinot noir from central Otago, a match

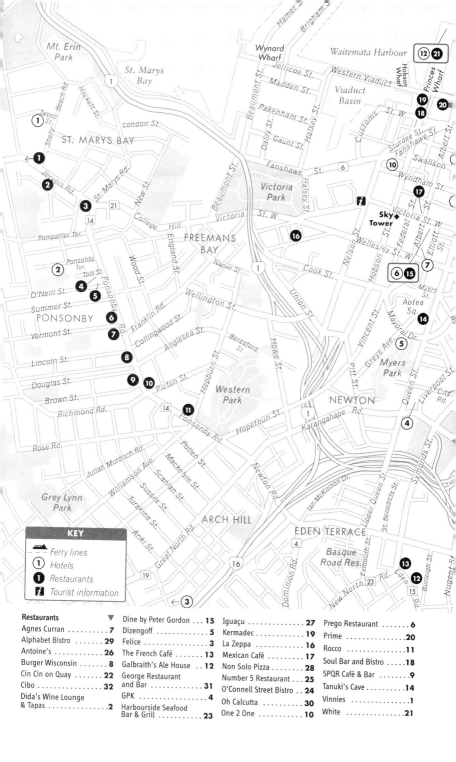

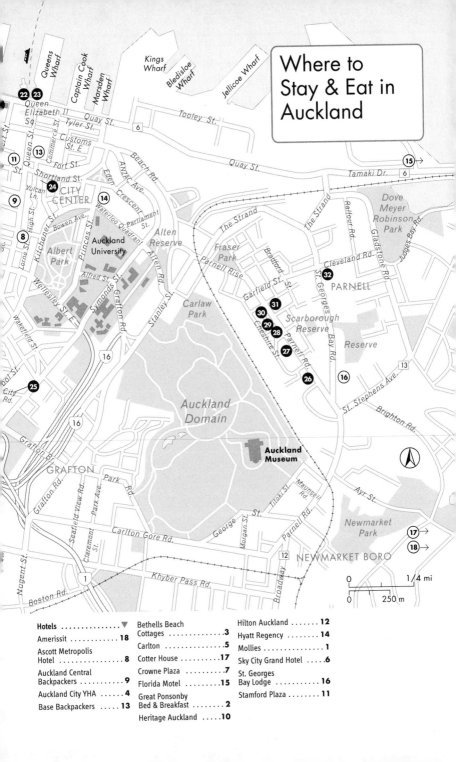

Where to Stay & Eat in Auckland

Queens Wharf
Captain Cook Wharf
Marsden Wharf
Kings Wharf
Bledisloe Wharf
Jellicoe Wharf

22 **23**

Queen Elizabeth II Sq.
Tyler St.
Commerce St.
Customs St. E
Fort St.
Shortland St.
Vulcan Ln.
High St.

Quay St.
Tooley St.
Quay St.
Tamaki Dr. **6**

15 →

11

13

24 CITY CENTER

9

8

Albert Park

Beach Rd.
ANZAC Ave.
Eden Crescent
Waterloo Quadrant
Parliament St.
Princes St.
Bowen Ave.
Kitchener St.
Lorne St.

Alten Reserve

14

Auckland University

Alfred St.
Symonds St.
Grafton Rd.
Stanley St.
Alten Rd.

Wellesley St. E
Waterfield St.

Carlaw Park

The Strand
The Strand
Fraser Park
Parnell Rise
Garfield St.
St. Georges Bay Rd.
Bradford St.
Cleveland Rd.
Gladstone Rd.
Balfour Rd.
Judges Bay Rd.

Dove Meyer Robinson Park

32

PARNELL

31
30
29
28
27
26

Scarborough Reserve

Reserve

16

13

St. Stephens Ave.

Brighton Rd.

25
City Rd.

16

16

Grafton Rd.

GRAFTON

Grafton Rd.
Seafield View Rd.
Park Ave.
Park Rd.
Claremont St.

Auckland Domain

Cheshire St.
Parnell Rd.

Auckland Museum

Maunsell Rd.
Titoki St.
Morgan St.
Parnell Rd.
George St.
Ayr St.

Newmarket Park

17 →
18 →

Carlton Gore Rd.

12

NEWMARKET BORO

1

Nugent St.
Boston Rd.

Khyber Pass Rd.

Broadway

0   1/4 mi
0   250 m

Hotels .... ▼	Bethells Beach Cottages **3**	Hilton Auckland **12**
Amerissit **18**	Carlton **5**	Hyatt Regency **14**
Ascott Metropolis Hotel **8**	Cotter House **17**	Mollies **1**
Auckland Central Backpackers **9**	Crowne Plaza **7**	Sky City Grand Hotel **6**
Auckland City YHA **4**	Florida Motel **15**	St. Georges Bay Lodge **16**
Base Backpackers **13**	Great Ponsonby Bed & Breakfast **2**	Stamford Plaza **11**
	Heritage Auckland **10**	

that's a good one in flavor as well as in name. Tapas only are served from 3 to 6:30. ☒ *188 Quay St.* ☎ *09/357–0188* ▭ *AE, DC, MC, V* ☾ *No dinner. Closed weekends.*

$$$ ✕ **Soul Bar and Bistro.** On the deck at Soul, center stage in the Viaduct, you're close enough to the moorings to study the paintwork on the yachts. Tear your eyes away to study the menu to decide, first, on which type of fish you'd like—perhaps John Dory, snapper, yellowfin tuna, or Chatham Island blue cod—then how to have it prepared. You might go for grilled, with a side of sage-fried potatoes and a coriander-walnut vinaigrette, or blackened served on a parsnip *skordalia* (puréed with garlic, lemon, vinegar, and olive oil) with a broccolini and parsley salad. At night, the bar and outside tables are packed with a polished crowd. ☒ *Viaduct Harbour, city center* ☎ *09/356–7249* ▭ *AE, DC, MC, V.*

$$$–$$$$ ✕ **La Zeppa.** *Zeppa* is Italian for "wedge," but you won't get the thin end here. Tapas-style dishes are served in this cavernous warehouse-type space, an old powerhouse, that despite its size is always abuzz. Mediterranean flavors come in dishes such as porcini-and-Parmesan risotto balls, and espresso-cured lamb loin with *machiatto* dressing—served on sweet-potato salad in a New Zealand twist—but Asian influences abound. Freshly smoked salmon with a lemon glaze and added zing of wasabi caviar is delivered to your table on its individual slab of cedar fresh from the hot plate. And the miso-cured pork on a salad of glass onion and sugar–snap peas is inclined to be fought over. ☒ *33 Drake St., Victoria Park Market, city center* ☎ *09/379–8167* ▭ *AE, DC, MC, V* ☾ *Closed Sun. and Mon. No lunch Sat.*

$$–$$$ ✕ **Mexican Café.** The worn red paint on the steps leading to this lively favorite says it all. Get to this restaurant at least a half hour ahead of time and join the crowds at the bar. Over the years, this spot has grown from 24 seats to 140. People go as much for the noisy, friendly atmosphere as they do for the food—though the dishes aren't chopped liver. The menu is packed with traditional choices such as nachos, tacos, and enchiladas. Don't get tucked away in a corner table unless you want to linger and soak up the atmosphere. ☒ *67 Victoria St. W, city center* ☎ *09/373–2311* ▭ *AE, DC, MC, V.*

$$ ✕ **Galbraith's Ale House.** Brew lovers and Brits craving a taste of home head straight for Keith Galbraith's alehouse. The English-style ales are made on the premises and served at proper cellar temperature (not too cold). Keith learned the art of brewing in the U.K. and sticks religiously to the style. Order a pint and dig into bangers and mash (seriously good sausages made by a local butcher with meat marinated in the Grafton Porter ale atop creamy mashed potatoes). People also come specially for the smoked fish platter—a selection of fish and seafood smoked at the Coromandel smokehouse. ☒ *2 Mt. Eden Rd., near Karangahape Rd., city center* ☎ *09/379–3557* ⊕ *www.alehouse. co.nz* ▭ *AE, DC, MC, V.*

$–$$ ✕ **Tanuki's Cave.** A flight of dimly lighted stairs leads to a buzzing Japanese yakitori and sake bar. The oblong bar is usually jammed with people ordering cheap small plates of skewers before going out for the night. (The place is open until 11:30, so you might be able to snag a late-night snack, too.) Grilled chicken, with or without cheese, and deep-fried fish are popular picks. In addition to more than 20 types of sake by the glass, you'll see large bottles of sake on the "bottle-keep" shelves—these are for people who keep their own bottle to have when they come to eat. ⊠ *319B Queen St., city center* ☎ *09/379–5151* ▤ *AE, DC, MC, V* ☾ *No lunch.*

Devonport

$$$–$$$$ ✕ **Esplanade Hotel.** The cooking in this landmark hotel overlooking the pier is enough to lure citysiders, who are notoriously reluctant to visit the shore. But they can see the city from the conservatorylike dining room before tucking into contemporary dishes with a Mediterranean spin, such as baked chicken stuffed with chervil and ricotta. The Esplanade also has elegant rooms upstairs, befitting its Edwardian heritage. ⊠ *1 Victoria Rd., Devonport* ☎ *09/445–1291* ⊕ *www.esplanadehotel.co.nz* ▤ *AE, DC, MC, V.*

$$–$$$ ✕ **Manuka.** Sitting on a corner on Devonport's main street makes for perfect people-watching, and Manuka is a mighty popular place in which to do it. It's a relaxed spot with bare wooden tables and stacks of newspapers and magazines. Weekend brunch is its busiest time, but tables turn over quickly. Wood-fired pizzas are available all day, with toppings ranging from classic pepperoni to smoked chicken, brie, and roasted cashews. You could also nibble on a delicious salad or slice into a meaty offering such as venison with blueberry-and-onion marmalade. ⊠ *49 Victoria Rd., Devonport* ☎ *09/445–7732* ▤ *AE, DC, MC, V.*

Parnell

$$$$ ✕ **Antoine's.** Owners Tony and Beth Astle have run this stately institu-
Fodor's Choice tion for more than a quarter century, and it still enjoys a reputation as
★ *the* special-occasion spot in town. The decor is old-style stately, the service immaculate, and the food classy—and expensive. Tony is still at the stove, and his "table menu" reads as if it were designed by a chef half his age. On his "nostalgic menu" are classics such as braised duckling with orange and Grand Marnier sauce, along with inventive dishes such as the appetizer of Bloody Mary jelly (just as it sounds: a jelly made from Bloody Mary ingredients) with prosciutto, artichokes, asparagus, and citrus-infused olive oil; or sautéed spiced watermelon, grilled scallops, and wasabi flying-fish roe topped with a lime-and-pink-peppercorn vinaigrette. The wine list is extensive and international. ⊠ *333 Parnell Rd., Parnell* ☎ *09/379–8756* ⊕ *www.antoinesrestaurant.co.nz* ▤ *AE, DC, MC, V* ☾ *Closed Sun. No lunch Sat.*

$$$–$$$$ ✕ **Cibo.** Italian for "good food," *cibo* is an apt name for this restaurant with Mediterranean- and Asian-influenced dishes. The smart crowd have made this a second home, coming for the adventurous cuisine of chef Kate Fay served by slick but relaxed staff. Housed in an old chocolate factory, the restaurant opens onto a quiet courtyard where you can dine by a fishpond lined with rushes. Or take a table in the airy interior where palms grow toward the high skylights. Try the spiced duck leg confit with rocket and mascarpone risotto, or duck parfait with grilled plum. In season, you can't pass up the whitebait fritter, served with lemon

beurre blanc. ⊠ *91 St. Georges Bay Rd., Parnell* ☎ *09/303–9660* 🖃 *AE, DC, MC, V* ☾ *Closed Sun. No lunch Sat.*

$$$–$$$$
Fodor's Choice
★
✕ **George Restaurant and Bar.** Chef Jeremy Schmid won a scholarship to study charcuterie at the prestigious Culinary Institute of America in the Napa Valley and now makes his own range of sausages under the label Little Boys. Check the menu for examples such as the duck and porcini, which you may find served with wood-fired duck leg, apple-and-potato bake, and wilted spinach. Sausages don't dominate, however, and choices may include lamb rump spiced with harissa, or Pacific tuna with white radish. The relaxed, high-ceiling room hums efficiently in the hands of a knowledgeable and friendly staff. ⊠ *144 Parnell Rd., Parnell* ☎ *09/358–2600* ⊕ *www.georgerestaurant.co.nz* 🖃 *AE, DC, MC, V.*

$$$–$$$$ ✕ **Iguaçú.** With flares blazing near the entrance, a terra-cotta tiled floor, enormous mirrors in Mexican metalwork frames, and a pair of chandeliers made from copper tubing, the decor is eclectic and the menu follows suit. The kitchen goes nationalistic with battered fish-and-chips with tartar sauce. Or you might find venison rubbed with *Dukkah* (an Egyptian nut-and-spice blend), topped with a lemongrass-and-tamarind sauce. Locals come to see and be seen as much as to enjoy the food. ⊠ *269 Parnell Rd., Parnell* ☎ *09/309–4124* 🖃 *AE, DC, MC, V.*

★ **$$$–$$$$** ✕ **Non Solo Pizza.** The name means "not only pizza," and that tells it like it is. This uncompromisingly Italian eatery offers pasta as a single serving or in table-sharing bowls that feed four or more. Head for a table in the lush, Italianate courtyard and try the spaghetti with fresh shellfish in chili and white wine, or osso bucco *di cervo:* venison braised in white wine served with creamy truffled polenta. And there's always pizza with traditional toppings followed by a masterfully prepared green salad. The same team runs Toto, on the other side of town, so if you can't get a seat here, ask if the sister restaurant is also full. ⊠ *259 Parnell Rd., Parnell* ☎ *09/379–5358* 🖃 *AE, DC, MC, V.*

★ **$$–$$$** ✕ **Oh Calcutta.** When executive chef Meena Anand moved to New Zealand, she applied her traditional cooking skills to new produce, focusing on fresh seafood and vegetables. The results are fantastic. You'll find plenty of traditional dishes—it would be hard to beat her butter chicken—but her own interpretations, such as prawn *malabari* (fat shelled prawns sautéed with onions, peppers, coriander, and fresh coconut cream), are light and brimming with flavor. Her fish tikka, made with deep-sea kingfish and served with a sharp mint chutney, is another standout. This is widely considered the best Indian restaurant in town, and on Friday and Saturday nights you need to reserve ahead. ⊠ *149–155 Parnell Rd., Parnell* ☎ *09/377–9090* ⊕ *www.ohcalcutta.co.nz* 🖃 *AE, DC, MC, V.*

¢–$$ ✕ **Alphabet Bistro.** Take a table on the sidewalk here for the best breakfast and brunch on the strip. Classics such as eggs Benedict and boiled eggs with "toast soldiers" (strips of toasted bread for dipping) are done just right, and the coffee is great. Bigger appetites might go for the redflannel hash, with two types of sausage (pork-and-fennel, and garlic) or panfried lamb's kidneys. Lunch is good, too, with a small but perfectly formed blackboard menu offering salads, pasta, and steak sandwiches. ⊠ *193 Parnell Rd., Parnell* ☎ *09/307–2223* 🖃 *AE, MC, V* ☾ *No dinner.*

Ponsonby

★ **$$$$** ✕ **Vinnies.** Chef Geoff Scott earned a following with discerning foodies in his time at the Hilton's White, and they have followed him to
this shop-front restaurant. It has a warm, intimate feel, with long filmy
curtains and velvet-covered chairs. Specialty local produce prepared
with elegant flair is Scott's trademark. Start with savory cones filled
with smoked eel pâté, beef *bresaola* (Italian cured and air-dried beef)
and cantaloupe, and ostrich carpaccio. Or perhaps with Clevedon coast
oysters chased with a lemon-and-vodka-sour shooter. If fish is your
thing, try the main course of seared hapuka served with spinach, ruby
grapefruit, Sicilian pasta, crab, and coconut cream. This place is right
on the border of Ponsonby. ⊠ *166 Jervois Rd., Herne Bay* ☎ *09/376–
5597* ⊕ *www.vinnies.co.nz* ⊟ *AE, DC, MC, V* ☉ *Closed Sun. and
Mon. No lunch.*

$$$–$$$$ ✕ **Felice.** Simon Gault, a chef of formidable experience and reputation,
helmed several top restaurants in Auckland but dropped off the public
radar for two years when America's Cup competitor Larry Ellison hired
him as his personal chef. Now Gault is back and delivering subtle, ex-
quisite Italian cuisine to the rest of us. This two-story brick restaurant
has a lively bar downstairs and a smattering of tables, but the serious
business of food takes place upstairs. And Gault takes his food seriously
enough to import from Italy what he can't get at home, so the *insalata
caprese* has the creamiest buffalo mozzarella. He gives a contemporary
spin to traditional dishes, so the veal on polenta with onions, mushroom
truffle mascarpone, and Marsala sauce is like a new classic. ⊠ *70 Jer-
vois Rd., Ponsonby* ☎ *09/376–2049* ⊕ *www.felice.net.nz* ⊟ *AE, MC,
V* ☉ *No lunch Sat.–Mon.*

$$$ ✕ **GPK.** The initials stand for Gourmet Pizza Kitchen or Gourmet Pizza
Konnection—take your pick. This corner eatery was the city's pioneer
posh-pizza place and soon afterward spawned a sister establishment at
234 Dominion Road, Mt. Eden. Some of the toppings would make a
traditionalist squirm (tandoori chicken with banana and yogurt), but
there are plenty of offerings more typically Italian. The wine and beer
list is impressively comprehensive. ⊠ *262 Ponsonby Rd., Ponsonby* ☎ *09/
360–1113* ⌖ *Reservations not accepted* ⊟ *AE, DC, MC, V.*

★ **$$$** ✕ **Rocco.** That it's slightly away from the heaviest foot traffic on Pon-
sonby Road doesn't deter the crowds who come for the glorious con-
temporary Mediterranean food here. Spanish flavors pepper a menu that
lets favorites survive changes, so you'll always find the squid-ink noo-
dles with seafood and the roast pork chop filled with chorizo, pancetta,
and apple, with garlic-and-honey aioli—a fiendish dish that tempts you
to eat beyond capacity. The wine list gives a good sampling of some of
New Zealand's best at reasonable prices. This is not a place for intimate
dining, however; the buoyant crowd sees to that. ⊠ *23 Ponsonby Rd.,
Ponsonby* ☎ *09/360–6262* ⊕ *www.rocco.co.nz* ⌖ *Reservations essen-
tial* ⊟ *AE, DC, MC, V* ☉ *Closed Sun. No lunch Sat.*

★ **$$$** ✕ **SPQR Cafe & Bar.** There's no better vantage point for people-watch-
ing on Ponsonby Road than the tables outside this longtime local fa-
vorite. Should outdoors not be an option, you can sit in the minimalist
concrete interior of what was once a motorcycle shop. (With an eclec-

tic clientele, the people-watching is good inside, too.) The excellent food is largely Italian, and the place is particularly known for its thin-crust pizzas, the best in Auckland. Other seemingly simple dishes shine, too, such as the scampi on linguine with a hint of chili. The bar cranks up as the sun goes down. ⊠ *150 Ponsonby Rd., Ponsonby* ☎ *09/360–1710* ⌂ *Reservations not accepted* ▭ *AE, MC, V.*

$$–$$$
Fodor's Choice
★

✕ **Prego Restaurant.** It's no mean feat being the longest-running restaurant in Ponsonby, a trendy area whose inhabitants count eating out among the necessities of life. The comprehensive Italian menu includes wood-fired pizzas and pasta prepared just as it should be, but many can't go past the fish of the day, usually panfried and served over a risotto with a delicate sauce or zesty salsa. You may strain to hear your companions over the din, unless you sit in the courtyard shaded by the robinia tree. Prego is always full, but the expert staff will usher you to the bar and secure a table within about 20 minutes. ⊠ *226 Ponsonby Rd., Ponsonby* ☎ *09/376–3095* ⌂ *Reservations not accepted* ▭ *AE, DC, MC, V.*

$$
✕ **Dida's Wine Lounge & Tapas.** In 1941 a grocer's shop stood on this site, run by a Croatian, Joseph Jakicevich, who also made his own wine. Today, three generations on, his descendants run this lively and stylish wine and tapas bar in the same building, alongside one of the wineshops in their Glengarry chain. A photo of *Dida*, Croatian for "Grandfather," hangs on the wall in the company of many family photos, and it is likely you'll be served by one of his great-grandchildren. Befitting such wine specialists, more than 100 wines are offered by the glass to accompany a menu of around 18 different tapas, such as chorizo sausage cooked in Merlot and bay leaf, meatballs in sherry tomato sauce, and salt-cod croquets. Locals love it, so you may need to arrive early to get a table. ⊠ *54 Jervois Rd., Ponsonby* ☎ *09/376–2813* ⌂ *Reservations not accepted* ▭ *AE, DC, MC, V.*

★ ¢
✕ **Agnes Curran.** Named after the grandmother of owner Cameron Woodcock, this small café just off Ponsonby Road recalls a time when home baking was served for afternoon tea on plates lined with doilies. You can choose from a counter selection—displayed on cake stands, of course—of classic antipodean homemade cakes and cookies, which are duly served with lashings of thick cream and style. Breakfast is a choice between croissants and brioches, and for lunch, filled rolls and chicken mustard pie. A bank of shelves holds quirky finds for sale: cookware, glassware, and assorted treasures. ⊠ *181 Franklin Rd., Ponsonby* ☎ *09/360–1551* ▭ *MC, V* ⊗ *No dinner.*

¢–$
✕ **Dizengoff.** The food is Jewish, though not strictly kosher, and contemporary. The most popular breakfast dish is scrambled eggs and veal sausages with homemade pesto and French bread. At lunch try the beet salad—baby beets with fava beans in a balsamic dressing, topped with pesto and shaved Parmesan. The coffee is among the best around. ⊠ *256 Ponsonby Rd., Ponsonby* ☎ *09/360–0108* ▭ *AE, DC, MC, V* ⊗ *No dinner.*

¢–$
✕ **One 2 One.** Chris Priestley was a Ponsonby pioneer, and he still runs one of the best coffee bars on the strip. There's food here for vegetarians, vegans, macrobiotics, meat eaters—and even children. Young ones are catered to in the outside courtyard, where scattered toys and other

distractions keep them amused while you nibble on rice bowls or eclectic salads, followed by coffee made from beans roasted on the premises. The decor is bohemian, and the service is supercasual and friendly—though ordering at the counter can be a lengthy affair while the diet-conscious make their choices. ✉ *121 Ponsonby Rd., Ponsonby* ☎ *09/376–4954* ▤ *No credit cards* 🍴 *BYOB* ☻ *No dinner.*

¢ ✕ **Burger Wisconsin.** Traveling Americans consistently rate Wisconsin's five Auckland outlets the best burger joints in town. The bunned delights include chicken breast with cream cheese and apricot sauce, Malaysian satay, bacon and beef with coconut mayonnaise, and a vegetarian soy and sesame-seed burger. At this branch you can order your burger to go, then wander over to nearby Western Park. ✉ *168 Ponsonby Rd., Ponsonby* ☎ *09/360–1894* ▤ *AE, DC, MC, V.*

Other Suburbs

$$–$$$ ✕ **Akdeniz.** "Mediterranean" stretches to its widest sense at this North Shore restaurant. Greek salad and Turkish dishes join the pizzas and pasta. Best of all is the seafood *guvech*: fish, mussels, calamari, and prawns cooked in a clay dish in the wood-fired oven, topped with tomato sauce and grilled mozzarella. If it's a cold night, reserve a table near the open fire. ✉ *34 Anzac St., Takapuna* ☎ *09/486–4900* ▤ *AE, DC, MC, V.*

$$–$$$ ✕ **Takahe.** Perched on a steep hillside overlooking native bush, this restaurant stands out with its corrugated iron and polished timber exterior. The menu undergoes radical changes from time to time, according to the season. In summer you find the likes of seafood pasta, tuna niçoise, and classic Caesar salad, whereas winter brings more rib-sticking fare such as lamb shanks. You don't have far to go if you want to walk it off in the Waitakere Ranges. On Sunday afternoons you may want to forgo the walk and listen to live jazz. ✉ *421 Titirangi Rd., Titirangi* ☎ *09/817–5057* ▤ *AE, MC, V* ☻ *Closed Mon. and Tues.*

WHERE TO STAY

As New Zealand's gateway city, Auckland has all the large international chain hotels you'd expect, but luckily it also has plenty of comfortable bed-and-breakfasts, mom-and-pop motels, and other individually owned places, making for a nicely varied lodging profile. Many of the large flashy hotels cluster around the central business district (CBD), whereas B&Bs tend to congregate in the nearby neighborhoods. Many of the best are found in Devonport and Ponsonby. Because Kiwis are so naturally hospitable, it's hard not to recommend lodgings where you have a chance to talk with your hosts—unless you prefer anonymity.

WHAT IT COSTS In New Zealand dollars				
	$$$$	**$$$**	**$$**	**$**	**¢**
HOTELS	over $300	$200–$300	$125–$200	$75–$125	under $75

Prices are for a standard double room in high season, including 12.5% tax.

Know-How

November to March are the busiest months for Auckland hotels, so it pays to book by August to ensure you get a room in your first choice. Hotel rooms are usually equipped with TVs, hair dryers, ironing boards, and basic toiletries. All the major hotels have parking available, too, at a price. A number of the B&Bs offer parking as well, an especially useful perk since they're usually in narrow city-center streets where the competition for parking is fierce. Better yet, B&Bs generally don't charge for parking. High-speed Internet access is becoming standard in hotels and B&Bs alike, and there's almost always a computer available if you didn't bring a laptop. B&B owners are extremely knowledgeable about their neighborhoods and are keen to supply information about the city. Some will even make reservations and other arrangements for you. One amenity you won't find in many places is air-conditioning; only the major hotels tend to have it. This isn't a problem, though, when you can fling open the windows and let in the sea breeze.

City Center, Parnell & Remuera

★ $$$$ 🏨 **Ascott Metropolis Hotel.** Auckland's old Magistrate's Courthouse was transformed into an elegant lobby with a stunning onyx ceiling, restaurant, and bar for this all-suite hotel. The guest rooms are all in a Manhattan-inspired tower built just behind the court. Though most rooms have decent views, the best sea views are available higher up on the east side of the hotel, at a slightly higher price. On a clear day you'll be able to see right across the harbor to the Coromandel Peninsula. The stylish mushroom-toned apartments are either one- or two-bedroom with sliding doors separating the living area; most have balconies, and all come with a kitchenette, including dishwasher, and washing machine and dryer. ⊠ *1 Courthouse La., city center* ☎ *09/300–8800* 🖨 *09/300–8899* ⊕ *www. the-ascott.com* 🛏 *145 suites* ⚐ *Restaurant, in-room safes, kitchens, cable TV with movies, in-room broadband, indoor pool, health club, 2 hot tubs, sauna, bar, Internet room, parking (fee)* ⊟ *AE, DC, MC, V.*

$$$$ 🏨 **Carlton.** Its proximity to the Aotea Centre performance venue—an underground tunnel runs from the hotel to Aotea Square—and downtown makes the Carlton a favorite with business travelers. The large guest rooms are elegantly furnished, with striped bed linen, sofas, writing desks, and well-equipped bathrooms (custom-made bath pillows are a thoughtful touch). The best views are from the rooms that overlook the parklands and the harbor to the east. Polished granite and warm, earthy tones have been used liberally throughout the building. ⊠ *Mayoral Dr. at Vincent St., city center* ☎ *09/366–3000* 🖨 *09/366–0121* ⊕ *www.carlton-auckland.co.nz* 🛏 *440 rooms, 15 suites* ⚐ *2 restaurants, café, minibars, cable TV, in-room broadband, indoor pool, gym, sauna, bar, Internet room, business services* ⊟ *AE, DC, MC, V* ⊙ *EP.*

$$$$ 🏨 **Cotter House.** This 1847 Regency mansion, the fifth-oldest house in
Fodor'sChoice Auckland, has been refurbished in original style, with classic features
★ such as egg-and-dart molding, recessed arches, and narrow shutters on the high windows. French owner Gloria Poupard-Walbridge says her mission is to spoil people. Pre-dinner drinks are served in the two refined lounges, and she bakes brioches and croissants herself as part of

the four-course breakfast. On a different mission, traveling as a diplomat's wife for two decades, she has amassed a significant collection of antiques that share the space with her modern art throughout the living areas and rooms, which have antique writing desks, vanities, and armoires; the suite has a French scallop-shape bath. Table d'hôte dinners are available by arrangement. In ambassadorial style, Gloria also holds large functions attended by ambassadors and ministers in the vaulted ballroom. ⊠ *4 St. Vincent Ave., Remuera* ☎ *09/529–5156* 🖷 *09/529–5186* ⊕ *www.cotterhouse.com* ➾ *2 rooms, 1 suite* ⌂ *In-room safes, cable TV, in-room DVD, Wi-Fi, massage, spa, Internet room; no a/c* ☰ *AE, DC, MC, V* ⏉❙ *BP.*

$$$$ 🖭 **Heritage Auckland.** Transforming one of Auckland's landmark buildings, the Farmers Department Store, this hotel opened in 1998 and quickly earned a reputation as one of the finest in the city. Since then it has added a tower wing, making it New Zealand's largest hotel as well. The size hasn't detracted from its character—the main building has retained its original 1920s art deco design, including high ceilings, large jarrah-wood columns, and native timber floors. The tower wing is more contemporary and includes New Zealand art especially commissioned for the rooms and public areas. Ask for a harbor-view room. ⊠ *35 Hobson St., city center* ☎ *09/379–8553* 🖷 *09/379–8554* ⊕ *www.heritagehotels.co.nz* ➾ *224 rooms, 243 suites* ⌂ *2 restaurants, café, in-room safes, minibars, in-room broadband, Wi-Fi in some rooms, tennis court, 2 pools (1 indoor), health club, sauna, spa, bar, meeting rooms* ☰ *AE, DC, MC, V.*

$$$$
Fodor'sChoice
★
🖭 **Hilton Auckland.** Perched on the end of Princes Wharf, the Hilton resembles the cruise ships that dock alongside it. White walls and neutral furnishings in the chic, clean-lined rooms let your eyes drift to the view, best in the bow and starboard. Each room has a piece of original art—and a teddy bear. The hallways are painted chocolate on one side and white on the other, presumably to aid navigation. The hotel's restaurant, White, is one of the finest in town. ⊠ *Princes Wharf, 147 Quay St., city center* ☎ *09/978–2000* 🖷 *09/978–2001* ⊕ *www.hilton.com* ➾ *160 room, 6 suites, 35 apartments* ⌂ *Restaurant, in-room safes, cable TV, in-room data ports, pool, gym, bar* ☰ *AE, DC, MC, V.*

$$$$ 🖭 **Hyatt Regency.** This branch of the international chain has been keeping up with the Joneses. In 2003, the Residence tower was added to the original hotel; the rooms there are brighter and larger, and all have balconies and at least partial harbor views. Corner suites have surprisingly large wraparound balconies. Then in 2004, a hushed, luxurious spa opened; among its treatments is a detoxifying wrap in Rotorua mud. For a more energetic pursuit, splash along the 25-meter indoor lap pool, which has a retractable roof. ⊠ *Princes St. and Waterloo Quadrant, city center* ☎ *09/355–1234* 🖷 *09/303–2932* ⊕ *www.auckland.regency.hyatt.com* ➾ *254 rooms, 140 suites* ⌂ *Minibars, cable TV, in-room data ports, indoor pool, gym, sauna, spa, steam room, business services, Internet room* ☰ *AE, DC, MC, V.*

$$$$
Fodor'sChoice
★
🖭 **Sky City Grand Hotel.** The specially commissioned works of top New Zealand artists hanging in the soaring lobby of Auckland's latest major hotel are testimony to the attention to design throughout—even the staff uniforms were designed by local fashion leaders. Rooms are decked in

light, contemporary hues, with rich red bed throws and iconic New Zealand prints by late photographer Robin Morrison. Rooms on the west side have views of the neighboring Sky Tower and beyond to the harbor. On the top floor, the Grand Suite is the size of four standard rooms and even has a butler's pantry. The excellent main restaurant, Dine, is run by acclaimed Kiwi chef Peter Gordon. ⊠ *90 Federal St., city center* ☎ *09/363–7000* 🖷 *09/363–7010* ⊕ *www.skycitygrand. co.nz* 🛏 *296 rooms, 20 suites* ♨ *2 restaurants, cable TV, in-room broadband, indoor pool, gym, hot tub, sauna, spa, bar, babysitting, laundry service, Internet room, business services, convention center* ▭ *AE, DC, MC, V.*

$$$$ 🏨 **Stamford Plaza.** Constant upgrades, noteworthy service, and attention to detail keep this mid-city hotel at the top of its game. Standard rooms are large and furnished extensively with natural fabrics and native woods in an updated art deco style. The best rooms are on the harbor side—the higher the better. Make sure you check out the rooftop area, with its expansive views over Auckland's harbor, or, on a rainy day, take high tea in the lobby. If you've got something to celebrate, head to the Yanrepé champagne bar. ⊠ *Albert St. and Swanson St., city center* ☎ *09/309–8888* 🖷 *09/379–6445* ⊕ *www.stamford.com.au* 🛏 *329 rooms* ♨ *2 restaurants, in-room safes, minibars, in-room broadband, pool, bar* ▭ *AE, DC, MC, V.*

$$$–$$$$ 🏨 **Crowne Plaza.** An escalator connects the atrium of this landmark to the "Atrium on Elliot" shopping complex, a short walk from Queen Street. With 10 conference and banquet rooms, the hotel plays host to many large functions. Guest rooms begin on the 16th floor; all are contemporary, with views across the city. You can choose your pillow preference from the menus on the beds. The suites on the 28th floor have great views and bigger bathrooms for just a slightly higher price. Service is keen and professional. ⊠ *128 Albert St., city center* ☎ *09/302–1111* 🖷 *09/302–3111* ⊕ *www.crowneplaza.co.nz* 🛏 *352 rooms* ♨ *Restaurant, minibars, cable TV, in-room broadband, gym, sauna, bar, Internet room, business services* ▭ *AE, DC, MC, V.*

$$–$$$ 🏨 **Amerissit.** At the end of a quiet cul-de-sac overlooking rooftops and Mt. Hobson, this architecturally modern cedar B&B is a quiet home away from home yet close to the restaurants of Parnell and shops in Newmarket. White walls and bed linen and soft charcoal carpet throughout add to the peacefulness. The two upstairs rooms have private decks, and one has a whirlpool bath. Owner Barbara McKain serves breakfast in the semicircular conservatory-style dining room, and will give you a tour of the city to help you get your bearings. ⊠ *20 Buttle St., Remuera* ☎ *09/522–9297* ⊕ *www.amerissit.co.nz* 🛏 *3 rooms* ♨ *Cable TV, in-room DVD, in-room broadband, free parking; no a/c* ▭ *AE, DC, MC, V* ⦿ *BP.*

$$–$$$ 🏨 **St. Georges Bay Lodge.** Walk around a classical marble statue in an Italianate courtyard to reach the door of this Victorian villa, one of four original villas built on this street. A kauri-floored hallway leads to a large conservatory-style dining area looking over a deck and rooftops, with a peep of Rangitoto in the distance. The two front rooms have bay windows looking onto the courtyard, and original fireplaces. A third upstairs is smaller but elegant with a mosquito net draping the bed. The two rooms downstairs have a private deck that gets the morning sun. Parnell Village is a five-minute walk away, and the Link bus stops at the top of the street. ⊠ *43 St. Georges Bay Rd., Parnell* 🕾 *09/303–1050* 🖷 *09/303–1055* ⊕ *www.stgeorge.co.nz* ᗑ *5 rooms* ⚒ *Cable TV, Internet room, free parking; no a/c* ⊟ *MC, V* ❢❶ *BP.*

★ ¢–$ 🔲 **Auckland Central Backpackers.** The best-equipped budget place in town, this hostel manages to keep the lid on its rates despite a Queen Street locale. It includes features such as air-conditioning and a security system that you would normally expect to pay a lot more for. Accommodation varies from a six-bed bunk room to family rooms with bath. The lounge and Internet-café area act as the hostel's social hub, where you'll also find a travel center and even a New Zealand job-search service should you be compelled to cancel your return flight. ⊠ *229 Queen St., city center* 🕾 *09/358–4877* 🖷 *09/358–4872* ⊕ *www.gobeyond. co.nz* ᗑ *71 rooms, 35 with bath* ⚒ *Restaurant, café, kitchen, bar, laundry facilities, travel services* ⊟ *MC, V.*

★ ¢–$ 🔲 **Base Backpackers.** Just off the harbor end of Queen Street you'll find this popular new arrival on the backpacker circuit. Double rooms come with small bathrooms, security lockers, and an extra single bed. A floral scent signals you've arrived at the women-only Sanctuary floor; this has a few extra frills, including hair dryers in the bathrooms. The rooftop deck looks over office buildings out to the harbor. The café is open in the morning and evening, serving meals such as fish-and-chips, lasagna, and spaghetti Bolognese. A lively bar has happy hour from 5 to 8 every evening. ⊠ *16–20 Fort St., city center* 🕾 *09/300–9999* 🖷 *09/ 302–0065* ⊕ *www.basebackpackers.com* ᗑ *37 rooms, 39 dorm rooms with shared bath* ⚒ *Café, kitchen, cable TV, bar, library, laundry facilities, Internet room, travel services* ⊟ *MC, V.*

¢ 🔲 **Auckland City YHA.** Hotels with much higher room rates must envy this hostel's location just behind upper Queen Street. It's a few minutes' walk to the lively area of Karangahape Road and close to the bus circuit. Most rooms have a view over Auckland toward the harbor, but the best outlook is from the sundeck and common room. All share bathrooms. Bunk rooms take three to six people, and there are single, twin-bed, and double-bed rooms, too. Luggage storage and tour booking are available. ⊠ *City Rd. at Liverpool St., city center* 🕾 *09/309–2802* 🖷 *09/373–5083* ⊕ *www.yha.co.nz* ᗑ *162 beds* ⚒ *Café, Internet room, travel services; no a/c, no room TVs* ⊟ *AE, MC, V.*

Ponsonby

$$$$ 🔲 **Mollies.** Music lovers will have extra reason to admire Auckland's most
Fodor's Choice luxurious and interesting boutique hotel. It's run by Frances Wilson, a
★ former voice coach who taught at New York's Metropolitan Opera. Her husband, Stephen Fitzgerald, was a theater set designer and also renovated grand New York apartments before transforming this two-story 1870 villa. Each individually decorated suite has a mix of antiques and stylish modern furnishings, and may be graced with a harp or a grand piano. After dinner, arranged on request, Frances goes to the Steinway grand piano in the drawing room and a butler reveals himself to be one

of her pupils by joining her for a recital. ✉ *6 Tweed St., St. Mary's Bay* ☎ *09/376–3489* 🖷 *09/378–6592* ⊕ *www.mollies.co.nz* ↪ *12 suites* ⚒ *Minibars, cable TV, in-room broadband, spa, bar, library, Internet room, free parking* ▭ *AE, DC, MC, V.*

★ **$$$–$$$$** 🔲 **Great Ponsonby Bed & Breakfast.** Convivial hosts Gerry and Sally will welcome you into their Pacific-themed villa on a quiet street off Ponsonby Road. Rooms are brightened with colorful, locally made tiles and art, and the windows are sand-blasted with Pacific designs. The cozy lounge is stocked with music, films, books, and magazines, and has an honor bar. Five of the rooms have kitchenettes and open off the courtyard. A few minutes' walk puts you in the thick of the Ponsonby cafés. ✉ *30 Ponsonby Terr., Ponsonby* ☎ *09/376–5989* 🖷 *09/376–5527* ⊕ *www.greatpons.co.nz* ↪ *10 rooms, 1 suite* ⚒ *In-room DVD, in-room VCRs, in-room broadband, library, Internet room, free parking; no a/c* ▭ *AE, MC, V* ⑭ *BP.*

Devonport/North Shore

$$$$ 🔲 **Esplanade Hotel.** Commanding the corner opposite the pier, this turn-of-the-century Edwardian baroque-revival hotel is the first thing you see when approaching Devonport by ferry. Upstairs a wide corridor hung with chandeliers leads to generous rooms with period furnishings, with long drapes hanging from high windows. Harbor views come at a slightly higher rate. The elegant two-bedroom, two-bathroom "Penthouse Suite" is ideal for families (at around twice the standard rate). ✉ *1 Victoria Rd., Devonport* ☎ *09/445–1291* 🖷 *09/445–1999* ⊕ *www.esplanadehotel.co.nz* ↪ *15 rooms, 2 suites* ⚒ *Restaurant, cable TV, in-room data ports, bar, Internet room; no a/c* ▭ *AE, DC, MC, V* ⑭ *BP.*

★ **$$$$** 🔲 **Stafford Villa.** Once a missionary's home, this early-1900s building is now an elegant B&B filled with Asian antiques and other artworks. Each room has a thematic bent, such as Papillon's butterfly-decorated wallpaper and China Blue's Asian inflection. The latter is a honeymoon favorite, with a four-poster bed and an antique Chinese chest. There are plenty of gracious touches, from chocolates and fresh flowers to sherry in the guest rooms and pre-dinner drinks. The ferry to the city leaves regularly from the bottom of the road—a five-minute walk. ✉ *2 Awanui St., Birkenhead Point, North Shore* ☎ *09/418–3022* 🖷 *09/419–8197* ⊕ *www.staffordvilla.co.nz* ↪ *3 rooms* ⚒ *In-room DVD, library, Internet room; no a/c* ▭ *AE, MC, V* ⑭ *BP.*

★ **$$$** 🔲 **Peace and Plenty Inn.** Antiques brought over from England are scattered throughout this lovely B&B. The largest room, the Windsor, has a high antique English pine bed and a small but charming bathroom with a Victorian clawfoot tub. Conversely, the smallest room, decorated in blue and white with a brass bed, has a larger bathroom with a full-size clawfoot bath. For a view of the city, ask for the upstairs Waitemata room. ✉ *6 Flagstaff Terr., Devonport* ☎ *09/445–2925* 🖷 *09/445–2901* ⊕ *www.peaceandplenty.co.nz* ↪ *7 rooms* ⚒ *Dining room, in-room broadband, Internet room; no a/c* ▭ *MC, V* ⑭ *BP.*

Other Suburbs & Auckland Environs

$$$$ **Hotel du Vin.** For an excellent introduction to New Zealand, head south from Auckland to this smart, luxurious hotel, surrounded by native forests, and the grapevines of the hotel's estate, Firstland Vineyards. Standard rooms are palatial, and the newer rooms at the far end of the resort are the best. The decor is crisp and modern; the central restaurant and reception areas glow with honey-color wood and rough stone fireplaces. The restaurant has a strong reputation, though prices are high. If you're not staying overnight, you can still stop over for a wine tasting or dinner—a great way to break the journey between Auckland and the Coromandel region. ⊠ *Lyons Rd., Mangatawhiri Valley, 64 km (40 mi) south of Auckland* ☎ *09/233–6314* ⊟ *09/233–6215* ⊕ *www.hotelduvin. co.nz* ⇆ *48 rooms* ⚴ *Restaurant, tennis court, indoor pool, spa, bicycles, archery, bar; no a/c* ⊟ *AE, DC, MC, V.*

★ **$$$$**   **Rangiwai Lodge.** Numerous additions to what started as a California-style bungalow have created a delightfully rambling lodge, set in the bush at the foot of the Waitakere Ranges. The rooms all have private decks with views of the bush, and some have views of the city and Waitemata Harbour. The clawfoot baths stand on art deco chrome feet in keeping with the 1930s-ish Pacific theme of tapa cloths and local art, mixed with antiques. A large indoor pool overlooks the Manukau Harbour to the south. You can see both harbors from the huge lounge, brimming with vigorous indoor plants and artfully arranged flowers, where drinks are served in the evening. ⊠ *29 Rangiwai Rd., Titirangi* ☎⊟ *09/ 817–8990* ⊕ *www.accommodation-nz.com* ⇆ *4 rooms* ⚴ *Indoor pool, library; no room TVs* ⊟ *MC, V* ⦶⦶ *BP.*

★ **$$$–$$$$**   **Bethells Beach Cottages.** Surrounded by pohutukawa trees and overlooking one of west Auckland's beautiful rugged beaches, these two cottages offer the opportunity for a true Kiwi *bach* (rustic beach house) experience. From the conservatory in Turehu Cottage—a converted brick farm building that sleeps two and a child—you can watch the sun set over the ocean or wander out onto the patio and fire up the barbecue. Te Koinga, the larger of the two, sleeps two couples or a family, and has a deck furnished with a large driftwood table. The view is good from the long dining table inside, too. Both cottages are self-contained, but owner Trude will prepare meals by arrangement. A short stroll on a track through the dunes leads to the patrolled beach. ⊠ *Bethells Rd., Bethells Beach* ☎ *09/810–9581* ⊟ *09/810–8677* ⊕ *www.bethellsbeach. com* ⇆ *2 cottages* ⚴ *BBQs, kitchens, outdoor hot tub, massage, Ping-Pong, volleyball* ⊟ *MC, V.*

$–$$ **Florida Motel.** In a harborside suburb a 15-minute drive east of the city center (and close to a major bus route into the city), this motel offers exceptional value. Rooms come in three versions: studios or one- or two-bedroom units that have a lounge room separate from the bedroom; the two-bedroom units are particularly good for families. All rooms have separate, fully equipped kitchens and a few nice touches, such as wall-mounted hair dryers, French-press coffeemakers, and irons with ironing boards. Because the motel is immaculately maintained and extremely popular, rooms must be booked several months in advance. ⊠ *11*

Speight Rd., Kohimarama ☎ *09/521–4660* 🖷 *09/521–4662* ✈ *8 rooms* 🔥 *Kitchens* ▬ *AE, MC, V.*

NIGHTLIFE & THE ARTS

For the latest information on nightclubs get your hands on *What's On Auckland,* a pocket-size booklet available at all visitor information bureaus. The monthly *Metro* magazine, available at newsstands, has a guide to theater, arts, and music, and can also give you a helpful nightlife scoop. *City Mix* magazine, also published monthly and stocked at newsstands, has a complete guide to what's happening in the city, and the Friday and Saturday editions of the *New Zealand Herald* run a gig guide and full cinema and theater listings.

The Arts

The Auckland arts scene is booming, particularly in the area of visual arts, if the number of new galleries can be taken as a sound indicator. Theater has had a renaissance after a demoralizing slump in the 1990s. More touring exhibitions and performing companies are coming through the city than ever before, and the Auckland Philharmonia Orchestra performs regularly, including at the summer series of free concerts in the park at the Domain, when thousands of music lovers sit with picnics under the stars.

For tickets, **Ticketek** (☎ 09/307–5000 ⊕ www.ticketek.com) is the central agency for all theater, music, and dance performances, as well as for major sporting events.

Art Galleries & Studios

An independent contemporary gallery, **Artspace** (✉ 300 Karangahape Rd. ☎ 09/303–4965) shows both international artists and the best of local artists.

A group of 30 artists living and working in Waitakere, west of Auckland, have set up the **Art Out West Trail,** by which visitors can view and purchase art in artists' private studios. Many of the studios require advance notice, and you'll need a car if you want to really explore the trail. Brochures are available at the Auckland Travel and Information Centre (⇨ Visitor Information *in* Auckland A to Z, *below*).

For a one-stop sample of West Auckland art, visit **Lopdell House Gallery** (✉ Titirangi and S. Titirangi Rds., Titirangi ☎ 09/817–8087). The gallery shows local works but also has regular exhibitions by national and international artists.

In a restored villa, **Masterworks** (✉ 77 Ponsonby Rd., Ponsonby ☎ 09/378–1256) exhibits and sells contemporary New Zealand–made art glass, ceramics, and jewelry. A second gallery can be found in the Viaduct on Customs Street.

Music & Opera

The **Aotea Centre** (✉ Aotea Sq., Queen St., city center ☎ 09/307–5060 ⊕ www.the-edge.co.nz) is Auckland's main venue for the performing arts. The **New Zealand Opera** company performs three annual main-stage opera seasons at the Aotea Centre. These feature international and New Zealand performers, accompanied by either the **Auckland Philharmonia Orchestra** or the **New Zealand Symphony Orchestra**. Both orchestras perform at the Aotea Centre on occasion, but perform more regularly at the **Auckland Town Hall** (✉ 303 Queen St., city center ☎ 09/307–5060 ⊕ www.the-edge.co.nz). The **Civic Theatre** (✉ Queen and Wellesley Sts., city center ☎ 09/307–5060) is host to many of the performances by international touring companies or artists. For general inquiries about all three venues check by the information desk on Level Three of the Aotea Centre. If you haven't booked beforehand, hit the Civic and Auckland Town Hall box offices, which open one hour before performance.

Theater

Theater in Auckland went through a slump in the 1990s when the Mercury Theatre, then the main professional theater, closed down. Aucklanders had to endure accusations of philistinism, mostly from Wellingtonians, for not being able to support even one theater. One of the newly out-of-work actors took up the matter as a personal crusade and formed the **Auckland Theatre Company** (☎ 09/309–0390 ⊕ www.atc.co.nz). Now a vibrant dramatic scene exists once again. The ATC has a mixed repertory that includes New Zealand and international contemporary drama and the classics. The company performs at the Herald Theatre at the Aotea Centre, Sky City Theatre, and the Maidment Theatre at the university.

Nightlife

After sunset the bar action is split across four distinct areas, with the central city a common ground between the largely loyal Parnell and Ponsonby crowds. Parnell has several restaurants and bars frequented by a polished, free-spending crowd. For a more bohemian scene, head to Ponsonby Road, west of the city center, where you'll find street-side dining and packed bars—often at the same establishment. If you prefer to stay in the city center, the place to be for bars is the Viaduct, particularly in summer, or High Street and nearby O'Connell Street, with a sprinkling of bars in between. At the Queen Street end of Karangahape Road (just north of Highway 1) you'll find shops, lively bars, cafés, and nightspots. Nightclubs, meanwhile, are transient animals with names and addresses changing monthly if not weekly.

From Sunday to Tuesday many bars close around midnight, and nightclubs, if open, close about midnight or 1 AM. From Thursday to Saturday, most bars stay open until 2 or 3 AM. Nightclubs keep rocking until at least 4 AM and some for a couple of hours after that. People dress relatively casually, but that said, some doormen or bouncers can be unreasonable sticklers and may refuse entry if you're wearing jeans.

An institution with the central city bar crowd is **The White Lady.** Indecorously towed by a tractor to her permanent spot on the corner of Shortland and Queen streets, this long, slumped trailer is far from genteel. But she's a homing beach for those in need of sustenance between bars, serving up burgers crammed with extras such as fried egg, onion, and beetroot that vanquish the appetite of even the hungriest night owls. She's on duty daily from 8 PM to 4 AM.

Bars & Lounges

At the heart of the city center, the **Civic Tavern** (⊠ 1 Wellesley St., city center ☎ 09/373–3684) houses three bars. The **London Bar** has a vast selection of beer and an impressive variety of Scotch whiskey. The **London Underground Bar** has 8-ball pool tables and casino-style poker machines. For a glass of Irish stout, stay on the ground floor and visit **Murphy's Irish Bar.**

★ Panoramic views of the harbor and Viaduct surround the chic **Coast Bar & Lounge** (⊠ Level 7, Hewlett Packard Bldg., Princes Wharf, city center ☎ 09/300–9966). It's at the top of a building originally designed for the harbormaster. Finding the bathroom can be a challenge, as the door fits seamlessly in the wall.

Wednesday nights are big at **The George** (⊠ 144 Parnell Rd., Parnell ☎ 09/358–2600), the funk house DJs attracting students and assorted young things. On Friday, an older after-work crowd packs in for the old-school soul and R&B. The bar is next to the excellent George restaurant.

You might as well leave your inhibitions at the door when you enter **Lime** (⊠ 167 Ponsonby Rd., Ponsonby ☎ 09/360–7167), because everybody else does. People packed in the narrow bar inevitably end up singing their hearts out to classic tunes from the 1960s and '70s. You'll find a similar scene at its sister bar **Plum** (⊠ 8/85 Customs St. W ☎ 09/357–0980) in the Viaduct, but the slightly more conservative crowd takes longer to warm up, and the music stretches to the 1980s.

Part of the Viaduct Village development, the **Loaded Hog** (⊠ 104 Quay St., city center ☎ 09/366–6491) has a vaguely nautical feel. This popular brewery and bistro has indoor and outdoor dining and drinking and can get crowded late in the week, so try to arrive early. Jazz musicians perform most evenings.

Tables for two line the curved windows of the retro **Match Lounge Bar** (⊠ Hopetoun and Pitt Sts., city center ☎ 09/379–0110). The cocktails—concoctions such as a poached-pear martini or the Malagassy, made with vanilla vodka and fig-cardamom syrup—are dangerously tempting.

Sequencing colored lights cast a warm glow over the couches and the bar at **Metropole Lounge** (⊠ 223 Parnell Rd., Parnell ☎ 09/379–9300). The swank clientele works its way through an extensive cocktail and wines-by-the-glass list.

Vulcan Lane has long been an after-work favorite with the suit-and-tie set of downtown Auckland. The lane has been tidied up in recent years, and the **Occidental Belgian Beer Cafe** (⊠ 6 Vulcan La., city center ☎ 09/300–6226) is one of the places that got a face-lift. Pair a pint of Belgian beer with a deep pot of mussels.

A noble aim of the stylish **Orchid Bar** (⊠ 152B Ponsonby Rd., Ponsonby ☎ 09/378–8186) is to create a place where women can relax. It's not overtly feminine (men are more than welcome here), but the expertly made cocktails come garnished with an orchid. The bar has its own label of Martinborough Pinot Noir, called RGP. There's some uncertainty about what the acronym stands for, but a good guess is "really good plonk."

An atmospheric brewpub, the **Shakespeare Tavern** (✉ Albert and Wyndham Sts., city center ☎ 09/373–5396) has beer with colorful names such as Willpower Stout and Falstaff's Real Ale.

Locals spill onto the street from early evening at **Mea Culpa** (✉ 3/175 Ponsonby Rd., Ponsonby ☎ 09/376–4460), a small, relaxed bar with equally appealing cocktails and wine selections.

★ A sophisticated bar for grown-ups, **Whiskey** (✉ 210 Ponsonby Rd., Ponsonby ☎ 09/361–2666) has cozy leather banquettes where you can talk without competing with the music. For an even more intimate tête-à-tête, you'll find a smaller room through the filmy curtains off the main-bar area.

Wines seldom available by the glass can be found at **The Wine Loft** (✉ 67 Shortland St., city center ☎ 09/379–5070). Jocular lawyers and other suits make up most of the after-work crowd. Quotes from the famous are scrawled on the walls—the whole world could indeed be three drinks behind after you leave here.

Comedy

Classic Comedy & Bar (✉ 321 Queen St., city center ☎ 09/373–4321) is housed in what used to be an X-rated movie theater, so if you get a funny look when you ask for directions, you'll know why. These days it is Auckland's main venue for live comedy. The caliber of the acts varies, and you'll find a mix of well-known Kiwi comedians, new faces, and the occasional international act. The Classic is host to the International Laugh Festival every April.

Live Music & Nightclubs

The live music scene in Auckland is fickle—bands often perform in unexpected locations (a bowling alley isn't unheard of), so it's best to keep an eye on the entertainment guides.

Playing strictly disco and with a dance floor lighted in colored squares, **Boogie Wonderland** (✉ Customs and Queen Sts., city center ☎ 09/361–6093) is stuck in the 1970s. You're encouraged to dress up, bust out your Travolta moves, and have a laugh. There's a $10 cover charge.

Deschlers (✉ 17 High St., city center ☎ 09/379–6811), a 1950s-style cocktail lounge, has live jazz on Thursday and Saturday. Park yourself at the long bar or at a paua shell–top table in one of the booths.

Take three flights of stairs or the rickety elevator to **Khuja Lounge** (✉ Level 3, Westpac Bank Bldg., Queen St. and Karangahape Rd., city center ☎ 09/377–3711), where you'll find live soul, jazz, funk, hip-hop, samba, bossa nova, or DJs. You can hit the dance floor or sink into a couch and watch the Moroccan-style lamps cast stars on the walls.

Rakinos (✉ 35 High St., city center ☎ 09/358–3535) hosts live bands and DJs in an easy-to-miss upstairs location.

Auckland's largest venue dedicated to live music, **Studio** (✉ 340 Karanga-hape Rd., city center ☎ 09/374–4278) has four bars over three levels, and puts on local and international bands.

SPORTS & THE OUTDOORS

Beaches

Auckland's beaches are commonly categorized by area—east, west, or north. The eastern beaches, such as those along Tamaki Drive on the south side of the harbor, are closer to the city and don't have heavy surf. They usually have playgrounds and changing facilities. **Judge's Bay** and **Mission Bay** are particularly recommended for their settings. One of Auckland's first churches, St. Stephen's Chapel, overlooks Judge's Bay, a tidal inlet. You'll get a clear view of Rangitoto Island from the beach at Mission Bay or one of the many nearby cafés. Both beaches are close to the city center and can be reached by bus.

West-coast black-sand beaches are popular in summer. They tend to have bare-bones facilities, but many have changing sheds near the parking areas, and you will need a car to get to them unless you take a tour. The sea at the western beaches is often rough, and sudden rips and holes can trap the unwary. Lifeguard patrol varies among the beaches; don't be tempted in unless they are on duty and safe swimming areas are marked with flags. The most visited of these beaches is **Piha**, some 40 km (25 mi) west of Auckland, which has pounding surf as well as a sheltered lagoon dominated by the reclining mass of Lion Rock. A short, steep climb up the rock rewards you with a dramatic view. **Whatipu**, south of Piha, is a broad sweep of sand offering safe bathing behind the sand-bar that guards Manukau Harbour. **Bethells**, to the north, often has heavy surf. In the vicinity, **Karekare** is the beach where the dramatic opening scenes of Jane Campion's *The Piano* were shot. Steep windswept cliffs surround the beach, and the surf is rugged. Again, swim only when lifeguards are on duty. A short walk from the parking lot is a 200-foot waterfall, feeding a lagoon that is good for swimming. To get to the west-coast beaches, head to Titirangi and take the winding road signposted as THE SCENIC DRIVE. Once you are on that road, the turnoffs to individual beaches are well marked—and, as advertised, there are lots of beautiful harbor views. Across Waitemata Harbour from the city, a chain of magnificent beaches stretches north as far as the Whangaparoa Peninsula, 40 km (25 mi) from Auckland. Taking Highway 1 north and keeping an eye peeled for signs, for instance, you'll reach **Cheltenham**, just north of Devonport.

Fodor'sChoice
★

Biking

Auckland can be good for cycling if you stick to certain areas, such as around the waterfront. There are no designated bike lanes, but **Adventure Cycles** (✉ 2 Commerce St., city center ☎ 09/309–5566) arms you with maps of routes that avoid pitfalls such as traffic. Touring bikes are $15 for a half day, $20 for a full day. Mountain bikes are $25. The rental fee includes helmets.

Bridge Adventures

AJ Hackett Bungy—Auckland Harbour Bridge (⊠ Westhaven Reserve, Curran St. Herne Bay ☎ 09/361–2000 ⊕ www.ajhackett.com) is the only bungy site in Auckland. The company operates bungy jumping off the Harbour Bridge ($85) year-round. You could also sign up for their **Harbour Bridge Experience**, a 1½-hour bridge climb ($65) with commentary on the history of the bridge and the region.

Golf

Chamberlain Park Golf Course (⊠ 46 Linwood Ave., Western Springs ☎ 09/815–4999) is an 18-hole public course in a parkland setting a five-minute drive (off Northwestern Motorway, Route 16) from the city. The club shop rents clubs, shoes, and carts. Greens fees are $25.

Formosa Golf Resort (⊠ 110 Jack Lachland Dr., Beachlands ☎ 09/536–5895 ⊕ www.formosa.co.nz) is about 45 minutes from the city center. The 18-hole course, designed by New Zealand golfing legend Sir Bob Charles, has views of the Hauraki Gulf from most holes. Greens fees are $125.

Titirangi Golf Club (⊠ Links Rd., New Lynn ☎ 09/827–5749), a 15-minute drive south of the city and with the course designed by renowned golf architect Alister MacKenzie, is one of the country's finest 18-hole courses. Nonmembers are welcome to play provided they contact the course's professional in advance and show evidence of membership at an overseas club. Clubs and golf carts can be rented; the greens fee is $120.

Hiking

The scenic **Waitakere Ranges** west of Auckland are a favorite walking and picnic spot for locals. The bush-clad ranges, rising sharply from the west-coast beaches, are threaded by streams and waterfalls. The 20-minute **Arataki Nature Trail** (☎ 09/817–4941) is a great introduction to kauri and other native trees. The highlight of another great trail, **Auckland City Walk**, is Cascade Falls, just off the main track of this easy hour's walk. The **Arataki Visitor Centre** displays modern Māori carvings and has information on the Waitakeres and other Auckland parks. To get to the Waitakeres, head along the Northwestern Motorway, Route 16, from central Auckland, take the Waterview turnoff, and keep heading west to the gateway village of Titirangi. A sculpture depicting fungal growths tells you you're heading in the right direction. From here the best route to follow is Scenic Drive, with spectacular views of Auckland and its two harbors. The visitor center is 5 km (3 mi) along the drive.

For a Māori perspective on Auckland take the **Tāmaki Hikoi** (⊠ Auckland i-Site Visitor Centre, Princes Wharf, 137 Quay St., Viaduct ☎ 09/307–0612 ⊠ Atrium, Sky City, Victoria and Federal Sts. ☎ 09/363–7182), a walking tour with guides from the local Ngati Whatua tribe who tell ancient stories and recount their history on a trek from Mt. Eden through sacred landmarks to the harbor. The three-hour tour

My America's Cup Race

"WELCOME ABOARD THE winning boat," jokes one of the crewmen as I look for a good spot to perch on the deck of former America's Cup yacht NZL 40. Not much of a sailor, I'm eager to keep out of the way during this mock match race.

NZL 40, originally FRA 40, was built by the Antibes Yacht Club for the 1995 America's Cup challenge but wasn't finished in time to compete. The Swiss team FAST 2000 brought it as a trial boat for the 2000 America's Cup in Auckland. We were about to race NZL 41, also built for the 1995 cup. Sailed by the Japanese Nippon Challenge, she was thought to be the fastest boat at the regatta but was beaten in the semifinals by Team New Zealand. The crew call her "The Rocket that Never Won a Race."

Both boats have been minimally modified for the safety of novices such as us. There are 17 on each vessel, including "real" crew, and that's about right for sailing these beasts. As we motor out of the Viaduct Basin, the skipper explains that match racing is all they're good for. "You wouldn't take a Formula One car on the Paris to Dakar Rally." In the harbor, the crew shut off the motor and hoist the mainsail. Eight volunteers are required to be grinders, winding large crank handles to trim the sails, positions enthusiastically filled by frustrated sailors. We sail downwind to where we will lay the course in front of Rangitoto, the site of the 2000 and 2003 America's Cup matches.

We drop a buoy for a marker, and we're to race to another buoy about half a mile away, up and back twice. The dial-up—the maneuvering for first over the line—begins. NZL 41 turns into starting position. Our skipper executes an apparently risky maneuver they call "steel balls" where he crosses their stern and gets the windward position—a complicated business to do with port and starboard and right-of-way rules. But hang the details, it worked, and we're off in the lead.

And that's where we stay. They're close behind us as we tack up the harbor but rarely look a threat. We slice through the water at around 15 knots. It seems a great speed—surely the number should be bigger? America's Cup races are called off when the winds are around 20 knots, but these boats can go out in up to 25.

We jibe around the marker, the volunteer crew coping like champions. Frenetic bouts of grinding accompany the tacking back, and we all have a go. A small yacht gets the fright of its life when it strays onto our "course." Luckily he moves fast. By now we are well in the lead. As we round the marker for the last time, we are pretty confident but looking back anyway to see how NZL 41 will fare. Disaster. Her gennaker is half-mast and trailing in the water. A spectacular failure, our crew say, a shame, because usually the competition is fierce.

With some trepidation, I take the helm when offered a "drive" on the trip home. It's a blast, figuring out just where in the wind to head to maintain a good speed. Wind whipped and exhilarated, I can see what all this sailing fuss is about.

Contact: **Sail NZ** (☎ 09/359-5987 🌐 www.sailnz.co.nz).

–Toni Mason

($80) departs at 9 AM and 1:30 PM from the visitor centers at Princes Wharf and Sky City.

Running

Auckland's favorite running track is **Tamaki Drive,** a 10-km (6-mi) route that heads east from the city along the south shore of Waitemata Harbour and ends at St. Heliers Bay. The **Auckland Domain** is popular with executive lunchtime runners.

Sailing & Kayaking

★ Instead of taking the ferry to Rangitoto, you could paddle. **Ferg's Kayaks** (✉ 12 Tamaki Dr. ☎ 09/529–2230 ⊕ www.fergskayaks.co.nz), run by four-time Olympic gold medal winner Ian Ferguson, takes guided trips ($95) to the island twice daily, leaving at 9 and 4. The round-trip takes about five hours—two to paddle each way and one to climb the volcano. On the later trip you paddle back in the dark toward the city lights. Booking is essential.

No experience is necessary to sail on America's Cup yachts *NZL 40* and *NZL 41* with **Sail NZ** (✉ Viaduct Harbour ☎ 09/359–5987 ⊕ www. sailnz.co.nz). The yachts are crewed, but you can participate. Two-hour trips cost $135. Or you can take part in a match race between the two yachts; these take about three hours and cost $195. An "Experience Sailing" trip ($48) with **Pride of Auckland** (☎ 09/373–4557 ⊕ www. prideofauckland.com) departs at 11 and 2:45 daily. The trip takes about 45 minutes and includes entry to the National Maritime Museum.

Swimming

★ ☺ On the waterfront next to the Parnell Rose Gardens, the **Parnell Baths** (✉ Judges Bay Rd., Parnell ☎ 09/373–3561) has a 60-meter (197-foot) saltwater pool, plus a children's playground pool. The baths are open from November to April. The **Tepid Baths** (✉ 100 Customs St. W, city center ☎ 09/379–4745) has a large indoor swimming pool, hot tub, sauna, steam room, and gym. It's open weekdays 6–9, weekends 7–7; admission is $5.50.

Spectator Sports

Eden Park is the city's major stadium for sporting events. This is the best place in winter to see New Zealand's sporting icon, the rugby team All Blacks, consistently among the world's top three teams. More frequently, it sees the Auckland Blues, a Super 12 rugby team that plays professional franchise opponents from Australia, South Africa, and other parts of New Zealand. Cricket teams arrive in summer. For information on sporting events, check out *What's On Auckland,* a monthly guide available from the Auckland i-Site Visitor Centre (⇨ Visitor Information *in* Auckland A to Z, *below*). Tickets can be booked through **Ticketek** (☎ 09/307–5000 ⊕ www.ticketek.co.nz).

Rugby Madness

WHEN NEW ZEALAND LOST the right to cohost the 2003 Rugby World Cup through what was seen as an administrative blunder, it seemed the whole nation was in an uproar. The resulting debates and inquiries dominated the media. But how did a sport invented half a world away in Europe—which has become popular in few other countries—develop into such an integral part of the nation's culture?

Rugby evolved out of soccer in 19th-century Britain. It was born at the elitist English school of Rugby, where in 1823 a schoolboy by the name of William Webb Ellis became bored with kicking a soccer ball and picked it up and ran with it. Rugby developed among the upper classes of Britain, whereas soccer remained a predominantly working-class game.

However, in colonial New Zealand, a country largely free from the rigid class structure of Britain, the game developed as the nation's number-one sport. One reason for this was undoubtedly the success of New Zealand teams in the late 19th and early 20th centuries. This remote outpost of the British empire, with a population of only 750,000 in 1900, was an impressive force at rugby, and this became a source of great national pride. Today, in a country of 4 million, the national sport is played by 250,000 New Zealanders at club level and embraced by huge numbers with an almost religious fervor.

The top-class rugby season in the Southern Hemisphere kicks off in February with the Super 14, which pits professional teams from provincial franchises in New Zealand, South Africa, and Australia against one another. New Zealand's matches are generally held in main cities, and you should be able to get tickets without too much trouble. The international season runs from June to late August. This is your best chance to see the national team, the All Blacks, and the major cities are again the place to be. National provincial championship games hit towns all over the country from late August to mid-October. A winner-takes-all game decides who will attain the domestic rugby Holy Grail, the Ranfurly Shield. If you can't catch a live game, you can always count on a crowd watching the televised match at the local pubs.

The sport is similar to American football, except players are not allowed to pass the ball forward, and they wear no protective gear. There's a World Cup for the sport every four years since 1987, which New Zealand has won once. The New Zealand team's failure to win the trophy in 1999, despite being the favorite, sparked off a huge bout of introspection about what went wrong. More soul-searching followed during the 2002 hosting debacle, after which most of the union board members were replaced. In the end, the 2003 World Cup left the Southern Hemisphere altogether, crossing the equator for the first time with a British victory.

In 2005, New Zealand's rugby star was back on the rise, with the All Blacks winning every trophy in the cupboard except the World Cup (the next chance comes in 2007), and the country winning the bid to host the 2011 World Cup.

SHOPPING

Ponsonby is known for its design stores and fashion boutiques. Auckland's main shopping precincts for clothes and shoes are Queen Street and Newmarket; Queen Street is particularly good for outdoor gear, duty-free goods, greenstone jewelry, and souvenirs. O'Connell and High streets also have a good smattering of designer boutiques, bookstores, and other specialty shops.

Department Store

Smith and Caughey's Ltd. (⊠ 253–261 Queen St., city center ☎ 09/377-4770) is a good place to see plenty of local brands under one roof. The clothing runs the gamut from homegrown favorites such as Trelise Cooper to international megabrands such as Armani. The lingerie department is known for its large, plush dressing rooms. You'll also find the largest cosmetics hall in the city.

Mall

Dress-Smart (⊠ 151 Arthur St., Onehunga ☎ 09/622–2400) is a whole mall of more than 70 factory outlets and is the place to go for high-quality, low-priced goods. As the name suggests, it started as a clothing mall, but it has recently doubled in size and diversified. You'll find books, records, children's toys, bags, jewelry, and housewares. Expect to pay 30%–70% less than you would regular retail. Take the inexpensive **shuttle service** (☎ 0800/748–885) or, if you're driving, take the Penrose turnoff from the Southern Motorway; then follow the signs to Onehunga. This is the heart of Auckland suburbia, so a detailed road map will help. Dress-Smart is close to Onehunga Mall.

Specialty Stores

Books & Maps
Legendary Hard to Find (but worth the effort) Quality Second-hand Books, Ltd. (⊠ 171–173 The Mall, Onehunga ☎ 09/634–4340 ⊠ **Hard to Find North Shore** ⊠ 81A Victoria St., Devonport ☎ 09/446–0300 ⊠ **Hard to Find Central City** ⊠ 238 Karangahape Rd., city center ☎ 09/303–0555) has a name that pretty much says it all. It's a local favorite and very large. Its smaller sisters in Devonport and K Road are great spots for browsing.

Unity Books (⊠ 19 High St., city center ☎ 09/307–0731) is a general bookstore that specializes in travel, fiction, science, biography, and New Zealand–related books.

Clothing & Accessories
★ Six jewelers started **Fingers** (⊠ 2 Kitchener St., city center ☎ 09/373–3974) in the 1970s as a place to display and sell their work. Now it showcases unique contemporary work by about 45 New Zealand artists, working with fine metals and stones. It's jewelry as art.

Tailored women's clothing that pushes traditional boundaries can be found at **Karen Walker** (⊠ 15 O'Connell St., city center ☎ 09/309–6299), one of New Zealand's most recognized fashion designers. The store also stocks some international labels such as Seven Jeans, Marjan Pejoski, and White Trash Charms accessories.

Kia Kaha (⊠ 1/100 Ponsonby Rd., Ponsonby ☎ 09/360–0260 ⊕ www. kiakaha.co.nz), which means "Be Strong" in Māori, carries distinctive casual and sportswear with Māori designs. The store also stocks the Cambo line of golf shirts, made by Kia Kaha; Michael Campbell was wearing one when he won the 2005 U.S. Open.

Marvel Menswear (⊠ 143 Ponsonby Rd., Ponsonby ☎ 09/376–4204) has an eclectic range, from clothing for men who want to look sharp without a collar and tie to clingy club-gear. It also stocks the "Strangely Normal" label of retro shirts with a twist.

Unique pieces from about 25 small local and international designers sit alongside vintage collectibles at **Superette** (⊠ 18 Drake St., Freemans Bay ☎ 09/913–3664). The café at the store serves lunch and good coffee.

For bohemian glamour with a deconstructed edge go to **Trelise Cooper** (⊠ 147 Quay St., Viaduct ☎ 09/366–1964 ⊠ 536 Parnell Rd., Parnell ☎ 09/366–1962 ⊕ www.trelisecooper.com). Flamboyantly feminine designs, plush fabrics, extravagant use of color, and intricate detailing are the hallmarks of this New Zealand fashion icon.

Fabulously individual **WORLD** (⊠ 57 High St., city center ☎ 09/373–3034 ⊠ 175 Ponsonby Rd., Ponsonby ☎ 09/360–4544) is one of New Zealand's groundbreaking fashion labels, making contemporary clothing with attitude. Find its funky streetwear for men just up the street at **WORLD Man** (⊠ 47 High St. ☎ 09/377–8331).

Fashion label **Zambesi** (⊠ Vulcan La. and O'Connell St., city center ☎ 09/303–1701 ⊠ 169 Ponsonby Rd., Ponsonby ☎ 09/360–7391) eschews trends but is always among the top New Zealand designers. Classic men's and women's styles get a modern kick.

Souvenirs & Gifts

Follow elephant footprints down an alley in Parnell Village to **Elephant House** (⊠ 237 Parnell Rd. ☎ 09/309–8740) for an extensive collection of souvenirs and crafts, many unavailable elsewhere, such as one-off hand-turned bowls, pottery, and glass. The sign hanging above **Pauanesia** (⊠ 35 High St., city center ☎ 09/366–7282) sets the tone for this gift shop—the letters are shaped from paua shell, which resembles abalone. You'll find bags, place mats, picture frames, and many other items.

Sports Gear

Kathmandu (⊠ 151 Queen St., city center ☎ 09/309–4615) stocks New Zealand–made outdoor clothing and equipment, with everything from fleece jackets to sleeping bags to haul-everything packs. The extensive range of gear at **Tisdall's Outdoors** (⊠ 176 Queen St., city center ☎ 09/379–0254) is made especially for New Zealand conditions.

Street Markets

★ Brightly clad South Aucklanders shop for bargains to the sounds of hip-hop beats and island music at **Otara Market** (✉ Newbury St., Otara) starting around 6 on Saturday morning. Vegetable stalls groan with produce such as taro, yams, and coconuts. More Asian food stalls are joining the traditional Polynesian tapa cloths, paua-shell jewelry, greenstone, and bone carvings, reflecting the city's increasingly multicultural profile. Look out for T-shirts bearing puns on famous brands, such as "Mikey." Stalls come down around midday. Exit the Southern Motorway at the East Tamaki off-ramp, turn left, and take the second left.

The beautiful countryside of the Waitakere Ranges has attracted artists seeking an alternative lifestyle, close to a major population (and customer) base but away from the hustle and bustle. Many of their wares are on sale at the **Titirangi Village Market** (✉ Titirangi Memorial Hall, S. Titirangi Rd. ☎ 09/817–3584). It's held on the last Sunday of each month, from 10–2.

Auckland's main bazaar, **Victoria Park Market** (✉ 208 Victoria St. W, city center ☎ 09/309–6911), consists of 2½ acres of clothing, footwear, sportswear, furniture, souvenirs, and crafts at knockdown prices. Be sure to stop by **From N to Z** (☎ 09/377–2447) for Kiwi icons such as plastic tomato-shape ketchup dispensers and hand-carved bone and greenstone pendants. The market is housed in the city's former garbage incinerator, and is open daily from 9–6. On a terrace behind the market, you can recharge your batteries with a coffee at **Caffetteria Allpress** (✉ Adelaide and Drake Sts. ☎ 09/369–5842).

AUCKLAND ESSENTIALS

Transportation

BY AIR

Auckland International Airport (AKL) lies 21 km (13 mi) southwest of the city center, about a 30-minute drive away. It has adopted a "quiet airport" policy, so it doesn't use loudspeakers to announce boarding times. Instead, look for display boards and TV monitors for boarding announcements and other flight info.

A free Interterminal Bus links the international and domestic terminals, with frequent departures in each direction 6 AM–10 PM. Otherwise, the walk between the two terminals takes about 10 minutes along a signposted walkway. Luggage for flights aboard the two major domestic airlines, Air New Zealand and Qantas Airways, can be checked at the international terminal.

Air New Zealand and Qantas are the main domestic carriers serving Auckland. Air New Zealand connects with about 25 domestic cities a day, and makes about 10 flights a day to Australia. Qantas connects with five domestic cities daily and crosses the Tasman 20 to 21 times a day. Air Tahiti Nui stops off in Auckland on its L.A.–and New York–Tahiti flights. Frequent price wars between the two carriers have brought fares down—there was a time when it was more expensive to fly to Queenstown than to Sydney. Now the domestic fares are reasonable, though they've pared down the catering accordingly. Origin Pacific connects daily to most main and regional centers.

🛪 Airport **Auckland International Airport** ✉ Fred Thomas Dr., Manukau ☎ 09/256-8899 ⊕ www.auckland-airport.co.nz.
🛪 Carriers **Air New Zealand** ☎ 09/357-3000 ⊕ www.airnewzealand.co.nz. **Air Tahiti Nui** ☎ 09/308-3360 ⊕ www.airtahitinui.co.nz. **Cathay Pacific** ☎ 09/379-0861 ⊕ www.cathaypacific.com/nz. **Emirates** ☎ 09/968-2200 ⊕ www.emirates.com/nz. **Origin Pacific** ☎ 0800/302-302 ⊕ www.originpacific.co.nz. **Qantas** ☎ 09/357-8900 ⊕ www.qantas.co.nz. **Singapore Airlines** ☎ 09/379-3209 ⊕ www.singaporeair.co.nz.

AIRPORT TRANSFERS
The Airbus costs $15 one-way and $22 round-trip and leaves the international terminal every 20 minutes between 6 AM and 6 PM, then every 30 minutes until 10 PM. The fixed route between the airport and the Ferry Building at 180 Quay Street includes, on request, a stop at any bus stop, hotel, or motel along the way. The trip takes 60 minutes. Returning from the city, the bus leaves the Ferry Building at 20-minute intervals between 5 AM and 6 PM, and every 30 minutes until 8:50 PM.

Hallmark Limousines and Tours operates Ford LTD limousines between the airport and the city for approximately $120, and Lincoln limousines for around $275.

Super Shuttle has service between the airport and any address in the city center. The cost is $22 for a single traveler and $5 extra for each additional person. The Shuttle picks up several parties on the way to the airport, so allow an hour's traveling time.

Taxi fare to the city is around $45 to $50. There are always plenty of taxis waiting at the ranks directly outside the terminal.
🛪 **Airbus** ☎ 0508/247-287 ⊕ www.airbus.co.nz. **Hallmark Limousines and Tours** ☎ 09/629-0940. **Super Shuttle** ☎ 0800/748-885.

BUS TRAVEL AROUND AUCKLAND
The Sky City Coach Terminal is Auckland's hub for the two main bus lines, InterCity Coaches and Newmans Coaches. The terminal has secure storage lockers and a café next door. InterCity links Auckland to most other major cities at least once a day. Newmans goes to Wellington daily via Hamilton and Taupo, and to Rotorua and Napier daily. Auckland is also a jumping-off point for several of InterCity's special travel pass routes, with daily departures for trips such as "Forests, Islands and Geysers" and "New Zealand Pathfinder."

Kiwi Experience goes to many more out-of-the-way destinations such as the East Cape. You can get a "Funky Chicken" round-trip pass that allows you to hop on and off where you please along the route. The buses depart Auckland from the Parnell office.

The Northliner Express goes to both Kaitaia and Kaikohe twice daily. It departs from 172 Quay Street, opposite the Ferry Building.
🛪 Bus Depot **Sky City Coach Terminal** ✉ 102 Hobson St., city center ☎ 09/300-6130.
🛪 Bus Lines **InterCity Coaches** ☎ 09/913-6100 ⊕ www.intercitycoach.co.nz. **Kiwi Experience** ✉ 195-197 Parnell Rd., Parnell ☎ 09/366-9830 ⊕ www.kiwiexperience.co.nz. **Newmans Coaches** ☎ 09/913-6200 ⊕ www.newmanscoach.co.nz. **Northliner Express** ☎ 09/307-5873 ⊕ www.northliner.co.nz.

1

BUS TRAVEL
WITHIN
AUCKLAND
The easily recognizable white Link Buses circle the inner city, including many of the most popular stops for visitors, every 10 minutes between 6 AM and 7 PM weekdays, and then every 15 minutes until about 11:30 PM. The same service applies on weekends but starts at 7 AM and runs to 6 PM. The route includes the Britomart Centre between Customs Street and Quay Street, and buses stop at Queen Street, Parnell, Newmarket (near the Auckland Museum), Ponsonby, and Karangahape Road, among other places. The fare anywhere on the route is $1.50, payable as you get onto the bus; you should have change or small notes. A free red-color bus circuits the inner city between Britomart, the university, and the Sky Tower every 10 minutes between 8 AM and 6 PM daily.

To travel farther afield you'll need to get onto a Stagecoach Bus, which is run by the same company as the Link Buses and has services as far north as Orewa on the Hibiscus Coast and south to Pukekohe. An Auckland Day Pass at $10 for unlimited travel is easily the best value for anyone planning extensive use of the buses (both Link and Stagecoach), particularly because it is also valid for travel on Link ferries between the city and the North Shore. The Discovery Pass ($13) also includes the local trains. You can buy the passes from the ferry office or the bus drivers. The information office at Britomart provides information, maps, and timetables, or you can call Maxx for transit details.

Information Office ⊠ Britomart Transport Centre, Queen Elizabeth Sq., Queen and Quay Sts., city center. **Maxx** ☎ 09/366-6400 ⊕ www.maxx.co.nz.

BY BOAT & FERRY

Various companies serve Waitemata Harbour; one of the best and least expensive is Fullers. The ferry terminal is on the harbor side of the Ferry Building on Quay Street, near the corner of Albert Street. Boats leave here for Devonport Monday–Thursday 6:15 AM–11 PM, Friday and Saturday 6:15 AM–1 AM, and Sunday 7:15 AM–10 PM at half-hour intervals, except for one 45-minute interval between the 9:15 AM and 10 AM sailings. From 8 PM Monday through Thursday and from 7 PM on Sunday they sail on the hour. The cost is $9 round-trip. However, a better deal is to buy the Auckland Day Pass for $10, which gets you a return sailing and unlimited travel on Link buses to boot. Ferries also make the 35-minute run to Waiheke Island from 5:30 AM to 11:45 PM at a cost of $26 round-trip. Return ferries leave every hour on the hour, and every half-hour at peak commuter times. SeaLink runs car and passenger ferries to Waiheke, leaving from Half Moon Bay to the east of the city. The round-trip fare is $113 per car, plus $26.50 for each adult.

Fullers Booking Office ⊠ Ferry Bldg., Quay St. ☎ 09/367-9111 ⊕ www.fullers.co. nz. **SeaLink** ⊠ Ara-Tai Dr., Half Moon Bay ☎ 09/534-5663 ⊕ www.sealink.co.nz.

BY CAR

By the standards of many cities, Auckland traffic is moderate, parking space is inexpensive and readily available, and highways pass close to the heart of the city. Local rush hours last from 7 to 9 AM and 4:30 to 6:30 PM. Getting used to driving on the left, if you'll be traveling by car, can be especially difficult when trying to figure out where to get onto motorways. Take a close look at a city map before you set out. The main motorways all have convenient city turnoffs, but watch the signs to make sure you are in the correct lane. When changing lanes, flick on your indicator promptly, as New Zealanders are not always the most obliging when it comes to merging.

City-center parking meters are cheaper than the covered lots, but make sure you have a wide selection of coins on hand and be aware that the meters are well policed. If you go over the time limit, you'll probably end up paying a fine. Meter time is generally limited to an hour in the city center, two hours in outer areas. For parking lots, a good one to try is the underground Civic lot by the Aotea Centre, Town Hall, Sky City Metro Centre, and the Civic Theatre. Drive in from Greys Avenue or Albert Street, right behind the Aotea Centre. After 5 PM you pay a flat rate of $8; before 5, the rate is approximately $4.50 per hour. The Downtown lot, opposite the Viaduct and Princes Wharf, has the same rates as the Civic (both are administered by the City Council), roughly half the rates for parking over the road at Princes Wharf. The entrance is at Customs Street West.

Avis, Budget, and Hertz have offices inside the Auckland International Airport. They stay open for all incoming flights.

🅿 Parking Lots **Civic Car Park** ✉ Greys Ave. and Mayoral Dr. ☎ 09/379-6035. **Downtown Car Park** ✉ 31 Customs St. W ☎ 09/309-6007.

🅿 Rental Agencies **Avis** ☎ 09/275-7239. **Budget** ☎ 09/256-8451. **Hertz** ☎ 09/256-8692.

BY TAXI

Taxis can be hailed in the street but are more readily available from taxi stands throughout the city. Placards with TAXI SIGN in red letters mark the stands. Auckland taxi rates vary with the company. Most are around $2 per ½ mile, but some charge as much as $4. Flag-fall, when the meters start, is usually $2. The rates are listed on the driver's door. Most taxis will accept major credit cards.

🅿 Taxi Companies **Alert Taxis** ☎ 09/309-2000. **Auckland Co-op Taxis** ☎ 09/300-3000. **Auckland Cooperative Taxi Service** ☎ 09/300-3000. **Corporate Cabs** ☎ 09/377-0773. **Eastern Taxis** ☎ 09/527-7077.

BY TRAIN

The terminal for all intercity train services is the Britomart Transport Centre at Queen Elizabeth Square, on the harbor end of Queen Street. There's a booking office at Britomart. However, train service throughout New Zealand is in flux, and at this writing the only North Island service ran between Auckland and Wellington.

🅿 **Britomart Transport Centre** ✉ Queen Elizabeth Sq., Queen and Quay Sts. ☎ 09/270-5211.

Contacts & Resources

BANKS & EXCHANGE SERVICES

Two Bank of New Zealand branches inside the international terminal of Auckland International Airport are open for all arriving and departing flights. In the city, there are several currency-exchange agencies on Queen Street between Victoria and Customs streets offering the same rate as banks. The cashier's desk on the main gaming floor at Sky City is open 24 hours and exchanges currency.

ATMs are easily found throughout the city's central neighborhoods, and traveler's checks are widely accepted.

📳 **Bank of New Zealand** (Auckland International Airport). **Sky City** ✉ Victoria and Federal Sts. ☎ 09/363-6000. **Travelex** ✉ 32 Queen St. ☎ 09/377-2666.

EMERGENCIES

For off-hours over-the-counter needs, hit the After-Hours Pharmacy, which stays open weekdays from 6 PM to 1 AM and weekends 9 AM to 1 AM.

📳 Emergency Services **Fire, police, and ambulance** ☎ 111.

📳 Hospitals **Auckland Hospital** ✉ Park Rd., Grafton ☎ 09/379-7440. **MercyAscot Hospital** ✉ 90 Greenland Rd. E, Remuera ☎ 09/520-9555 or 09/520-9500.

📳 Late-Night Pharmacy **After-Hours Pharmacy** ✉ 60 Broadway, Newmarket ☎ 09/520-6634.

MAIL, SHIPPING & INTERNET

The Post Shop on Wellesley Street West is the only post office with poste restante (general delivery) services. It's open weekdays from 7:30 AM to 5:30 PM. Auckland has offices of all the major courier companies. New Zealand Post's courier service, Courier Post (at the Auckland Mail Service Centre), covers the country and links with international services.

Central Auckland is littered with Internet cafés; these vary widely in price and facilities. Net Central Cybercafé is open 24 hours daily and has coffee and snacks; it charges $2 per hour. At the Central City Library you can get online after buying an Internet card ($1); you're then charged $1 per half hour.

📳 Internet Access **Auckland Central City Library** ✉ 44–46 Lorne St., city center ☎ 09/377-0209. **Net Central Cybercafé** ✉ 5 Lorne St., city center ☎ 09/373-5186.

📳 Post Office **Post Shop** ✉ 24 Wellesley St., city center ☎ 09/379-6710.

📳 Shipping Services **Auckland Mail Service Centre** ✉ 167 Victoria St. West, city center ☎ 0800/268-7437 ⊕ www.courierpost.co.nz.

DHL Express Service Centre ✉ Unit G, 69 St. Georges Bay Rd., Parnell ☎ 09/309-3111 ⊕ www.dhl.co.nz.

TOURS

BOAT TOURS Fullers has a variety of cruises around the harbor and to the islands of Hauraki Gulf. The 1½-hour Auckland Harbor cruise ($31), with commentary and bar, departs daily at 10:30 and 1:30. There's also a Waiheke Island Explorer tour, for $42, which stops at Onetangi Beach, and a Waiheke Vineyard Explorer trip for $85, daily December through February, Wednesday to Sunday March and November, and weekends only from April through October. Reservations for Waiheke tours are essential during the summer. Boats leave from the Ferry Building.

The Pride of Auckland Company sails for lunch and dinner on the inner harbor. The 1½-hour lunch cruise ($73) departs at 1, and the 2½-hour dinner cruise ($95) departs at 7 and includes a pass to the National Maritime Museum. Boats leave from the Maritime Museum, near Princes Wharf.

📳 **Fullers Booking Office** ☎ 09/367-9111 ⊕ www.fullers.co.nz. **Pride of Auckland Company** ☎ 09/373-4557 ⊕ www.prideofauckland.com.

BUS TOURS An Explorer Bus trip is a convenient introduction to Auckland. The white double-decker bus travels in a circuit, stopping at nine of the city's major attractions; you can leave at any stop and reboard any following Explorer bus. The loop begins at the Ferry Building every half hour between 9 and 4 daily from October to April, and hourly from May 10 to September. Tickets are available from the driver and at the Fullers office in the Ferry Building. A one-day pass is $30.

Scenic Tours operates a three-hour Auckland Highlights guided bus tour, which takes in the main attractions in the city and Parnell, and the view from the lookout on Mt. Eden. Tours leave from Quay Street, just across from the Ferry Building, at 9:15, and tickets are $55.
Explorer Bus ☎ 0800/439-756 ⊕ www.explorerbus.co.nz. **Scenic Tours** ☎ 09/307-7880 ⊕ www.scenictours.co.nz.

WILDERNESS TOURS Auckland Adventures has one half-day ($85) and two day-long tours ($120). All three go to the summit of Mt. Eden, head out west to visit at least one winery (tasting included), then go on to Muriwai beach to see a gannet colony. The full-day tours also take in kauri forests and give you time to relax and swim at the patrolled beach.

Bush and Beach Ltd. runs daily afternoon tours ($110) through the Waitakere Ranges and out to a west-coast beach, such as Karekare Beach, popular with people who want to see where Jane Campion's *The Piano* was filmed. At Karekare you'll see a nearby 200-foot waterfall, and at Piha you'll go on a bushwalk. A day-long tour ($155) spends the morning visiting highlights in Auckland, including the Auckland Domain and Parnell Village, before heading out to the Waitakere Ranges.

Red Feather Expeditions Ltd. is run by expat American Beth Coleman, who has built up a love for the wilderness and culture of New Zealand. Tours are tailor-made and can be restricted to the greater Auckland area (Beth has a special knowledge of the Waitakere Ranges) or extended farther afield. Itineraries can include soft-adventure sports or a focus on ecology, Māori culture, or other topics; all include walking or hiking.
Auckland Adventures ☎ 09/379-4545 or 025/855-856 ⊕ www.aucklandadventures.co.nz. **Bush and Beach Ltd.** ⌂ Box 3479, Shortland St., Auckland ☎ 09/575-1458 ⊕ www.bushandbeach.co.nz. **Red Feather Expeditions Ltd.** ⌂ Box 60243, Titirangi ☎ 09/818-7770 or 021/325-461 ⊕ www.ecotoursnz.com.

WINE TOURS Wine writer Phil Parker is the host of wine-tasting tours to West Auckland and Matakana (an hour north of Auckland). The four-hour West Auckland tour ($139) takes in three wineries and includes a picnic lunch. The Matakana tour ($239) is a full-day trip and includes four wineries, with lunch at the Ascension winery café. Both include free pickup from the city.
Fine Wine Tours ☎ 09/849-4519 or 021/626-529 ⊕ www.insidertouring.co.nz.

VISITOR INFORMATION

The main bureau of Auckland's visitor center is open 8 to 8 daily. The branch in the airport opens daily at 5 AM and stays open until the last flight arrives. The branch at the Viaduct Harbour is open 9 to 5 daily.

The Devonport visitor center is open weekdays 8 to 5, and 8:30 to 5 on weekends.

The Thursday *Auckland Tourist Times* is a free newspaper with the latest information on tours, exhibitions, and shopping. The paper is available from hotels and from the visitor centers.

For information on the Hauraki Gulf islands, marine reserves, and other conservation areas, check in with the Department of Conservation Visitor Centre, open on weekdays from 9:30 to 5.

🚩 Tourist Information **Auckland International Airport Visitor Centre** ✉ Ground fl., International Airport Terminal ☎ 09/275-6467 🖨 09/256-8942. **Auckland i-Site Visitor Centre** ✉ Atrium, Sky City, Victoria and Federal Sts. ☎ 09/363-7182 🖨 09/363-7181 ⊕ www.aucklandnz.com. **Department of Conservation Visitor Centre** ✉ Ferry Bldg., Quay St. ☎ 09/379-6476 ⊕ www.doc.govt.nz. **Devonport Visitor Information Centre** ✉ 3 Victoria Rd. ☎ 09/446-0677 ⊕ www.tourismnorthshore.org.nz.

Northland &
the Bay of Islands

WORD OF MOUTH

"You could go to Northland just for the beautiful beaches. Or the fishing. Or the diving. And the seafood is arguably the best in the country. But the area is also steeped in the history of our early settlers, Māori and European, and standing among towering kauri trees you see a piece of what they first found. It's a special place, and nowhere can you sense that more than at the tip of Cape Reinga, where you'll feel like you're on the edge of the world."

—Toni Mason

Updated by
Toni Mason

NEW ZEALAND STRETCHES A LONG ARM into the South Pacific as you head north of Auckland. This is Northland, an undulating region of farms and forests, marvelous beaches, and plenty of the great open space that defines the country.

The east coast up to the Bay of Islands is the most densely populated part of Northland (though "densely populated" here is a relative term)—the largest city, Whangarei, is about two hours north of Auckland. About an hour's drive farther north, the Bay of Islands is the region's main attraction. It's both beautiful, for its lush forests, splendid beaches, and shimmering harbors, and historic, as the place where Westernized New Zealand came into being with the signing of the Treaty of Waitangi in 1840. Continuing north, the region becomes even more rural; the rolling hills are bordered by stunning coastline scalloped with secluded bays and coves. Here, you can swim, dive, or simply laze on the pristine beaches.

The west coast is more sparsely populated still, and the coastline more rugged and windswept. Here, in the Waipoua Forest, is where you will find New Zealand's most impressive examples of kauri trees—some of the oldest and largest in the country.

Crowning the region is the spiritually significant Cape Reinga, the headland at the top of the vast stretch of 90 Mile Beach, where it is believed Māori souls depart after death. Today Māori make up roughly a quarter of the area's population (compared with the national average of around 15%). The legendary Māori navigator Kupe was said to have landed on the shores of Hokianga Harbour, where the first arrivals then made their home. Many different *iwi* (tribes) lived throughout Northland, including Ngapuhi (the largest), Te Roroa, Ngati Wai, Ngati Kuri, Te Aupouri, Ngaitakoto, Ngati Kahu, and Te Rarawa. Many Māori here can trace their ancestry to the earliest inhabitants.

Note: For information on bicycling, diving, deep-sea fishing, hiking, and sailing in Northland and the Bay of Islands, *see* Chapter 11.

Exploring Northland & the Bay of Islands

By far the best way to explore Northland is by car, because there are so many lovely bays, sandy beaches, and worthwhile sights along the way. You can follow an easy loop from Auckland, driving up the east coast on State Highway 1 and returning down the west coast on Highway 12 (or vice versa). It's worth leaving the main highway and following smaller coastal roads, too. These winding but easy-to-navigate routes offer up stunning coastlines and dramatic island vistas, whether around the eastern coast near Tutukaka, or along the short loop past Matauri Bay, north of Kerikeri, to Whangaroa Harbour.

The Bay of Islands is Northland's main attraction, an island-littered seascape with a mild, subtropical climate and some of the finest game-fishing waters in the country. The main town is Paihia, a strip of motels and restaurants along the waterfront. If you plan to spend more than a day in the area, the town of Russell, just a short ferry trip away, makes for a more atmospheric and attractive base.

In the Far North, above the Bay of Islands, the population thins out, but the distance between sights is short. Turning south and down the west coast, the roads wind through forest, heading for the hamlet of Kohukohu, where you take the car ferry across the serene Hokianga Harbour to Rawene on the southern side.

From the sleepy hamlet of Opononi, closer to the harbor's mouth, you can continue down the Kauri Coast to the Waipoua Forest, some of the last virgin kauri forest—it's a reminder of how the North Island once looked. Once through the forest, Highway 12 runs parallel with the coast, with the odd spur leading to more rugged west coast beaches, to the arty town of Dargaville, and on to Matakohe, site of the renowned Kauri Museum. Another half-hour's drive takes you to Brynderwyn, where you rejoin State Highway 1 about an hour north of Auckland.

About the Restaurants

Heading north from Auckland, you'll find small towns such as Warkworth or the larger Whangarei with cafés and restaurants to keep hunger at bay. In the Bay of Islands, Kerikeri has the best selection of restaurants, though Russell and Paihia have some fine ones, too.

Seafood abounds in the north, with fresh fish always available; scallops are dredged from the harbors and oysters farmed throughout the region. Fish such as snapper and kingfish are available most of the year, and deep-sea boats supply game fish such as marlin and broadbill swordfish, particularly between January and June.

The region prides itself on its fresh local produce, enhanced by skillful chefs in the increasing number of upmarket restaurants. Prices are rising accordingly, but there are still many cafés producing top-quality fare at reasonable prices. Kerikeri, in particular, offers good-value eating, catering more to the local population than to tourists.

People tend to eat a bit earlier in Northland than in the cities, with restaurants filling around 7 PM. In keeping with the relaxed vibe, dress is casual—jeans are acceptable in all but the most upscale lodges.

From May through September, many restaurants close entirely or reduce their opening hours, some to only four nights a week. Most start gradually increasing their hours again in late October.

WHAT IT COSTS In New Zealand dollars				
$$$$	**$$$**	**$$**	**$**	**¢**
RESTAURANTS over $30	$20–$30	$15–$20	$10–$15	under $10

Prices are per person for a main course at dinner, or the equivalent.

About the Hotels

Northland may not be swarming with tourists, but it still has all kinds of accommodations, from basic motels to luxury lodges. Your hosts, par-

GREAT ITINERARIES

Numbers in the text correspond to numbers in the margin and on the maps.

IF YOU HAVE 3 DAYS

From Auckland, head north to the Bay of Islands. En route, stop in **Warkworth ❶** for a look at some great old kauri trees and in **Whangarei ❷**, a good place for a picnic by the harbor or waterfall. When you get to the Bay of Islands, stay in either **Paihia ❹** or **Russell ❺** and spend the next couple of days hitting the beach, visiting the historic Waitangi Treaty House, and perhaps making a day trip to **Kerikeri ❻**, aka "the cradle of the nation." If you're at all interested in fishing or diving, look into the local outfitters as soon as you get to the bay.

IF YOU HAVE 5 OR MORE DAYS

If you've got a diving license, make a beeline for **Whangarei ❷** and spend a day at the Poor Knights Islands, considered one of the world's best diving sites. Continue north and spend a couple of days in the Bay of Islands, staying in **Paihia ❹** or **Russell ❺** as described in the three-day itinerary. Then cut across to the western coast, driving down Highway 12 to reach the **Kauri Coast,** where you can trade beaches for trees and walk in the **Waipoua State Forest ❸** to see the tallest living kauri. On the last day, heading back to Auckland, stop at the **Matakohe Kauri Museum** to learn about the area's incredible native trees. Alternatively, if you'd prefer to get farther off the beaten path, shorten your time in the Bay of Islands and drive the full Northland loop, spending a night in a Far North lodge and taking a 4x4 tour of 90 Mile Beach before going down the western coast.

ticularly in the bed-and-breakfasts, are generally eager to impart their local knowledge and advice, from restaurant recommendations to tips on intriguing area walks—they're a great way to discover less obvious attractions.

Paihia has plenty of vacation apartments and standard motels, most of which lack charm but are handy if you prefer to keep to yourself or prepare your own meals. The larger towns, especially Russell, have a range of B&Bs. Luxury lodges are dotted throughout Northland, some on large swaths of land with private bays, and these also have some of the area's best cuisine. Internet access is available in nearly all lodgings, but high-speed access is not as common as in the cities.

Virtually no lodgings have air-conditioning, but it's usually unnecessary. If you inquire about air-conditioning, your hosts will probably suggest that you simply open the windows to let in the sea breeze.

High season runs from December through March. Some lodges have "shoulder seasons" in April and May, and September and November. Overall, room rates drop between May and October.

WHAT IT COSTS In New Zealand dollars				
$$$$	$$$	$$	$	¢
HOTELS over $300	$200–$300	$125–$200	$75–$125	under $75

Prices are for a standard double room in high season, including 12.5% tax.

When to Visit

Snow doesn't fall on this part of New Zealand, known as the winter-less north, and the weather doesn't exactly get frigid. Still, to see these areas at their finest, mid-November through mid-April are the beautiful months, with December through March being the highest season for tourism. December is also the best time to see the "New Zealand Christmas tree," the *pohutukawa*, in bloom. If you plan to visit around the Christmas holidays, reserve well in advance, especially in beachside towns. The accommodations in the Bay of Islands in particular often fill months in advance. The winter months of July and August can be quite wet, and although things don't completely shut down, the area is very quiet. If game fishing is your object, the best months are from February to June.

NORTHLAND

Although the Bay of Islands is the main tourist magnet, the rest of Northland is dotted with enticing rural communities. Large stretches of green farmland separate the mostly tiny towns. Some areas, particularly in the Far North and Hokianga, have higher-than-average unemployment, and New Zealanders joke that cannabis cultivation fuels a hidden economy (though this is more hearsay than evident). Whatever their occupation, Northland residents are generally good-humored and hospitable, proud of their lifestyles and exceptional scenery.

Europeans began settling in Northland in the 18th century, starting with whalers around the Bay of Islands, Scots who settled at Waipu on the east coast, and Dalmatians who worked the west coast's kauri-gum fields. Anglican missionaries also started arriving in Northland in the early 19th century. The first mission was established at Kerikeri by the Reverend Samuel Marsden of the Church Missionary Society, who went about trying to "civilize" the Māori before conversion. He also planted the first grapevines in New Zealand.

If you're driving up the east coast toward the Bay of Islands in December, you'll see scarlet blossoms blazing along the roadside. These are pohutukawa trees in flower, turning crimson in time for the Kiwi Christmas, hence their *Pākehā* (non-Māori) name: "the New Zealand Christmas tree." To the Māori, the flowers had another meaning: the beginning of shellfish season. Other plants that you might see along Northland roads are clumps of spiky-leaf New Zealand flax (the Māori used the fibers of this plant, the raw material for linen, to weave into clothing) and huge tree ferns known as *punga*.

TOP REASONS TO GO

BOUNTIFUL BEACHES

Nearly all Northland beaches are beautiful and safe for swimming. When driving along the coast, keep an eye out for small signs telling you there is a beach tucked away nearby—it could be a gem. The 90 Mile Beach (which is, in fact, 97 km [60 mi] in length) stretches up the top of the western coast to Cape Reinga, where you can swim in two seas in one day—the Tasman Sea and the Pacific Ocean. Shipwreck Bay at the southern base of 90 Mile Beach can be prone to rips, but it's highly rated by experienced surfers.

BOATING & FISHING

Boat trips take off from all over Northland, particularly in the Bay of Islands. You can simply sightsee your way around rock formations, take a cruise to an island, whale-watch, or get in to swim with dolphins. Game fishing is another major draw, with the Bay of Islands as the hub. The best time to go for big game fish such as marlin and broadbill is January through June.

Yellowfin tuna are most plentiful from December to March, and mako sharks are about from November to May. Closer to shore, kingfish and snapper are plentiful all year-round.

SUPERB DIVING

Diving is extremely popular in Northland, with spectacular sites such as the Poor Knights Islands, known for their huge variety of subtropical fish. You can also dive the wreck of the Greenpeace vessel Rainbow Warrior, sunk by French agents in 1985, or try the Matai Bay Pinnacle in the Far North.

WALKING & HIKING

There is superb bushwalking (hiking) around Northland. The bush is full of impressive ancient kauri trees (a local species of pine) and interesting birds, such as tūī (too-ee), fantails, and wood pigeons. The flightless kiwi is making a comeback; visitors are reporting flashlight sightings, particularly in the north on the Kauri Coast.

Warkworth

❶ *59 km (36 mi) north of Auckland.*

A sleepy town on the banks of the Mahurangi River, Warkworth was established in 1853. With lime mined from the local river, it became the first cement-manufacturing site in the Southern Hemisphere. Today, boatbuilding and refitting are the main industries, and Warkworth also serves as a service town for the surrounding farms and market gardens. It's a convenient stopping point en route to nearby Goat Island or the vineyards at Matakana.

Two giants stand in Warkworth, near the Warkworth Museum—giant kauri trees, that is. The larger one, the **McKinney Kauri**, measures almost 25 feet around its base, yet this 800-year-old colossus is a mere adolescent by kauri standards. Kauri trees, once prolific in this part of the North Island, were highly prized by Māori canoe builders, because a canoe capable of carrying 100 warriors could be made from a single trunk. Un-

Northland

NEW ZEALAND

Karikari Peninsula

Doubtless Bay

Mangonui

CAPE REINGA & 90-MILE BEACH

10

Kaeo

Matauri Bay

Takou Bay

Bay of Islands
4 - 6
see detail map

1

Mangamuka

Mt. Bledisloe ◆

Kerikeri

Bay of Islands

Russell

SOUTH

PACIFIC

OCEAN

Paihia and Waitangi

Rawene

Hokianga Harbour

Kaikohe

12

Opononi

Moerewa

Opua

Kawakawa

1

Towai

Waiotu

Poor Knights Islands

3 Waipoua State Forest

Awarua

NORTHLAND

Otonga

Matapouri

Tutukaka

Kauri River

12

Titoki

Maungatapere

2 Whangarei

14

Portland

Whangarei Harbour

Dargaville

Waiotira

Bream Bay

Parry Channel

Hen and Chickens Group

Te Kopuru

12

Taipuha

Waipu Cove

Paparoa

Brynderwyn

Maungaturoto

Little Barrier Island

1

Jellicoe Channel

Wellsford

Leigh

◆ **Goat Island**

Poutu

Tapora

1 Warkworth

Tasman Sea

Ahuroa

Kawau Island

16

1

Shelly Beach

Hauraki Gulf

Orewa

Helensville

Coatesville

Rangitoto Island

Waiheke Island

Albany

Waimauku

Takapuna

Auckland

Waitakere

0		40 miles

0		60 km

2

fortunately these same characteristics—strength, size, and durability—made kauri timber ideal for ships, furniture, and housing, and the kauri forests were rapidly depleted by early European settlers. Today the trees are protected by law, and infant kauri are appearing in the forests of the North Island, although their growth rate is painfully slow.

The **Warkworth Museum** contains a collection of Māori artifacts and farming and domestic implements from the pioneering days of the Warkworth district, as well as kauri-digging implements and kauri gum. Rotating displays of textiles cover clothing dating back to the late 1700s, with fine examples of petit point and lace. There is also a display of a school dental clinic—what Kiwi children called the "murder house." Outside there is a collection of old buildings, including a bushman's hut and an army hut used by Americans stationed at Warkworth in World War II. ⊠ *Tudor Collins Dr.* ☎ *09/425–7093* ⊕ *www.wwmuseum.orcon.net. nz* ☑ *$6* ⊗ *Oct.–Easter, daily 9–4; Easter–Sept. daily 9–3:30.*

⟳ Head for **SheepWorld** for a taste of life on a typical New Zealand sheep farm. You can watch working farm dogs rounding up sheep, sheep shearing, and presentations on the wool industry. Eel feeding at lunchtime is popular, as is the farm-animal feeding later in the afternoon. An ecotrail takes you through the bush, providing lots of information on native trees, birds (with explanations of different birdcalls), and boxes of *weta*, large ugly insects. On the weekends, you can even catch the farm dogs herding ducks. Children can also take pony rides, and, in August, bottle-feed lambs. ⊠ *324 State Hwy. 1* ☎ *09/425–7444* ⊕ *www. sheepworld.co.nz/farm.htm* ☑ *$7.50, $15 including sheep-and-dog show* ⊗ *Daily 9–5.*

EN
ROUTE For a glimpse of what the New Zealand coast must have been like 200 years ago, take a trip to the **Goat Island** marine reserve. Fishing is prohibited here, and marine life has returned in abundance, with prominent species including blue *maomao* fish, snapper, and cod. You can put on a snorkel and easily glide around the island just a little ways offshore. You can rent a mask, snorkel, and flippers ($12) from **Seafriends** (☎ 09/ 422–6212); their sign is about 1 km (½ mi) before the beach on the main road, Goat Island Road. They also have seawater aquariums (free admission) and a café. **Glass Bottom Boat** (☎ 09/422–6334 ⊕ www. glassbottomboat.co.nz) has—surprise, surprise—a glass-bottom boat that runs around the island ($20). If the weather isn't the best, they do an inner reef trip ($15). But you needn't get even this serious to see plenty of fish. Just walk into the water up to your waist and look around you. To drum up more action, throw some bread or noodles into the sea and watch the fish congregate just inches from you. The beach area is good for a picnic as well.

To get to Goat Island head toward Leigh, 21 km (13 mi) northeast of Warkworth. From Leigh, take a left turn and follow the signs for a couple of miles. The area can get crowded, but if you arrive by 10 AM or earlier, you should avoid the masses. Department of Conservation leaflets detailing Goat Island can be obtained from the Warkworth Visitor Information Centre (⇨ Visitor Information *in* Northland & the Bay of Islands A to Z, *below*).

Whangarei

❷ *127 km (79 mi) north of Warkworth, 196 km (123 mi) north of Auckland.*

The main center in Northland is the Whangarei (*fahng*-ar-ay) District; Whangarei Harbour was traditionally a meeting place for Māori tribes traveling south by *waka* (canoe). The full Māori name of the harbor, Whangarei Terenga Paraoa, means "swimming place of whales," which can be interpreted as "the meeting place of chiefs." Europeans started to settle in the area from the mid-1800s; now it's a bustling town of roughly 45,000 people, rooted in the agriculture, forestry, and fishing industries. Boatbuilding is a traditional business, manufacturing everything from superyachts to charter boats. The mouth of the harbor is dominated by the volcanic peaks of Whangarei Heads, atop Bream Bay (so named by Captain James Cook because of the abundant fish). The drive from town to the Whangarei Heads takes about 20 minutes heading out on Riverside Drive, past mangrove-lined bays. At the Heads are white-sand beaches and coves with safe swimming, and several walks, including a hike up the peaks of Mount Manaia.

People often bypass Whangarei on their way to the Bay of Islands, but it's well worth taking the turnoff from the main highway, especially since the area known as the **Whangarei Town Basin** has been improved. This development on the marina, a haven for traveling yachts, has cafés, restaurants, galleries, and crafts shops. There's parking behind the Basin off Dent Street.

Just about every conceivable method of telling time is represented in the Town Basin's **Claphams Clocks—The National Clock Museum.** The collection of more than 1,500 clocks includes everything from primitive water clocks to ships' chronometers to ornate masterworks from Paris and Vienna. Some of the most intriguing examples were made by the late Mr. Clapham himself, such as his World War II air-force clock. Clockwork also shows up in a selection of music boxes. Ironically, the one thing you won't find here is the correct time. If all the bells, chimes, gongs, and cuckoos went off together, the noise would be deafening, so the clocks are set to different times. ⊠ *Dent St., Town Basin* ☎☎ *09/438–3993* ⊕ *www.claphamsclocks.co.nz* ⊠ *$8* ⊙ *Daily 9–5.*

The oldest kauri villa in Whangarei, **Historical Reyburn House** contains the Northland Society of Arts exhibition gallery, which plays host to changing exhibitions from New Zealand artists, as well as from the permanent collection dating from the 1880s to the present. It is separated from the Town Basin by a playground. ⊠ *Reyburn House La., Town Basin* ☎ *09/438–3074* ⊕ *www.reyburnhouse.co.nz* ⊠ *Donation* ⊙ *Tues.–Fri. 10–4, weekends 1–4.*

There's a lovely picnic spot at **Whangarei Falls** on Ngunguru Road, 5 km (3 mi) northeast of town. There are viewing platforms atop the falls, and there's a short trail through the local bush.

Early settlers eager to farm the rich volcanic land around Whangarei found their efforts constantly thwarted by an abundance of rock in the

2

soil. To make use of the stuff they dug up, they built walls—miles of walls. The current settlers at **Greagh,** George and Yvonne Hull, have carried on this tradition, giving their gardens the Celtic name for "land among the stone." The walls form a handsome framework for perennials and roses, and the plantings, in turn, emphasize the beauty and strength of the stone on terraces and in five separate walled gardens. ⊠ *Three Mile Bush Rd.* ☎ *09/435–1980* ⤳ *$4* ⊙ *Oct.–Easter, daily 9–5; Easter–Oct. by appointment.*

Just minutes out of town, the 61-acre **Heritage Park Whangarei** is home to a nocturnal kiwi house, several Heritage buildings, and the Whangarei Museum. At the Kiwi House you can see Kakama, an active North Island brown kiwi, and Woof-Woof, the talking *tūī* bird. The museum has fine examples of pre-European Māori cloaks, waka (canoes), and tools. You can also check out Glorat, an original 1886 kauri homestead, and the world's smallest consecrated chapel, built in 1859 from a single kauri tree. ⊠ *State Hwy. 14, Maunu* ☎ *09/438–9630* ⊕ *www. whangareimuseum.co.nz* ⤳ *Park free, Kiwi House and Whangarei Museum $8* ⊙ *Daily 10–4.*

Craig Busch is New Zealand's "Lion Man." He specializes in raising big cats at **Zion Wildlife Gardens,** just northwest of Whangarei. At last count there were 29 cats, including 13 Barbary lions and four royal white tigers—both of which are "extinct" in the wild—four orange Bengal tigers, and two African Serval cats. Curiously, there's also a baboon. A local TV documentary raised Craig to celebrity status; now he leads guided tours of the park and offers private tours by arrangement. ⊠ *Gray Rd., Kamo* ☎ *09/435–0110* ⊕ *www.zionwildlifegardens.co.nz* ⤳ *$60.*

Where to Stay & Eat

$$$–$$$$ ✕ **Gybe Restaurant and Bar.** This octagonal building overlooking the marina may be colonial-style on the outside, but the menu is purely modern, with a Mediterranean bent. Ask for a table up on the mezzanine or balcony for the best views. Specialty platters focus on fresh seafood; the seafood platter for two brims with prawns, Pacific oysters, smoked salmon, green-lipped mussels, seared game-fish salad, prawn-bisque shooters, and grilled scampi. ⊠ *Quayside, Town Basin* ☎ *09/430– 0406* ▤ *AE, DC, MC, V.*

★ $$$ ✕ **à Deco.** At this restaurant in a faithfully restored art deco house, chef Brenton Low has become a regional favorite for his clean, pure flavors. He spotlights fresh Northland ingredients; for instance, you might find flounder from Kaipara Harbour served with king prawns and Puy lentils. In lieu of garlic or black pepper, Low might add olive oil infused with *horopito,* an indigenous wild herb, to some dishes. Another good example of his modern approach is his salmon-tasting platter, where the fish stars with soy, mirin, pickled ginger, peanuts, and a tempura California roll. ⊠ *70 Kamo Rd.* ☎ *09/459–4957* ▤ *AE, MC, V.*

$$$ ✕ **Tonic.** Owner-chef Brad O'Connell's seasonal menu can set you up with interesting seafood choices such as fish with truffles, mashed peas, and crab tortellini, or crayfish risotto—all made with fresh local ingredients. If he ever tries to take his roast rump of lamb with herb pota-

toes off the menu, customers demand it anyway. In cooler weather, it's hard to pass up the cured loin of pork with honey-roasted *kūmara* (a local sweet potato) and spiced red cabbage. If you're in luck, the warm blackberry-and-almond crumble tart will be on the dessert list. The service is friendly and helpful. ⊠ *239a Kamo Rd.* ☎ *09/437–5558* ⊟ *AE, DC, MC, V* ⊘ *No lunch.*

$$$ ✕**Vinyl.** A stylishly funky licensed café, Vinyl serves contemporary cuisine to a hip Whangarei crowd. A classic example is the seared venison served on a melon, Brie, and arugula salad with a rustic beetroot salsa. The café is on the opposite side of the marina from the Town Basin, making their al fresco tables the perfect place to enjoy a leisurely brunch of classic dishes such as bubble and squeak (a hash made from fried mashed potato and cabbage), corn fritters, and eggs Benedict. ⊠ *Vale Rd. and Riverside Dr.* ☎ *09/438–8105* ⊟ *AE, DC, MC, V* ⊘ *Closed Mon. No lunch Tues.*

¢–$ ✕**Soda.** This café on the outskirts of town is one of the best places for coffee. The cabinets are full of freshly made panini, sandwiches, and various types of lasagna. The blackboard menu lists more substantial choices such as penne with chorizo, bacon, fresh herbs, and roasted-tomato sauce. Just off the main road north, it's a good place to refuel before heading up to the Bay of Islands. ⊠ *505 Kamo Rd.* ☎ *09/435–1910* ⊟ *MC, V* ⊘ *Closed Sun. No dinner.*

$$ ▥**Parua House.** From this spot on the edge of Parua Bay, you can explore the towering Whangarei Heads. The house dates from 1882 and retains much of its colonial feel, enhanced by antiques brought over from England by the owners. You can take a walk through the nearby bush or even help milk their cow. Three-course dinners with wine are available on request—wholesome New Zealand fare, including vegetables from their garden and their homegrown olives. ⊠ *Whangarei Heads Rd., R.D. 4, Parua Bay, 17 km (11 mi) from Whangarei* ☎ *09/436–5855 or 021/186–5002* ⊕ *www.paruahomestay.homestead.com* ⇗ *3 rooms* ⌂ *Dining room, hot tub, lounge, Internet room; no a/c, no room TVs* ⊟ *MC, V* ◎| *BP.*

$ ▥**Graelyn Villa Bed & Breakfast.** This turn-of-the-20th-century villa was once the main homestead in Tikipunga, an outer suburb about 5 km (3 mi) from Whangarei's town center. Urban sprawl has caught up to it, but it still retains a large spread of land with mature trees and a cottage garden. Two small but comfortable rooms are in a cottage in front of the villa, with a balcony onto the garden set to catch nearly-all-day sun. The third room, in the main villa but with a separate entrance, opens onto an enclosed courtyard with a subtropical garden. The Whangarei Falls are just a few minutes' walk away. ⊠ *166 Kiripaka Rd.* ☎ *09/437–7532* 🖷 *09/437–7533* ⊕ *www.graelynvilla.co.nz* ⇗ *3 rooms* ⌂ *BBQs, Internet room; no a/c* ⊟ *No credit cards* ◎| *CP.*

¢ ▥**Bunkdown Lodge.** A popular backpackers' lodge in a large kauri villa, Bunkdown has clean, bright rooms—two four-bed dorms, one six-bed, a twin, and a double. Individual reading lights over the bunk beds are a thoughtful touch. Linen for the dorms is available for a small fee. The homey lounge has guitars, games, and a piano, as well as a TV; common kitchens are available, too. This isn't a party hostel, but it's very popular with people who want to dive off the Tutukaka coast; dive companies pick up here at 7 AM. Helpful hosts Peter and Noell are knowledgeable about the area. Noell takes guests on tours of the nearby Abbey Caves to see glowworms. ⊠ *23 Otaika Rd.* ☎ *09/438–8886* 🖷 *09/ 438–8826* ⊕ *www.bunkdownlodge.co.nz* 📞 *3 dorms, 4 doubles* ♨ *Kitchens, lounge, laundry facilities; no a/c, no room TVs* ☐ *MC, V.*

Nightlife
Killer Prawn Restaurant and Bar (⊠ 26–28 Bank St. ☎ 09/430–3333) doubles as Whangarei's nightlife hub. It's a good place to start the evening—as the night wears on, just follow the crowd.

Shopping
★ Specializing in contemporary fine glass, ceramics, and jewelry, **Burning Issues Gallery** (⊠ 8 Quayside, Town Basin ☎ 09/438–3108) is one of the best places in Northland to buy locally made arts and crafts. Look for beautifully carved greenstone and bone pendants. From inside the shop, you can watch glassblowers at work in the next-door studio.

A cooperative of local craftspeople, including jewelers, potters, wood turners, and glassblowers, runs the **Quarry Craft Co-op Shop** (⊠ Selwyn Ave. ☎ 09/438–9884). Some of them can be seen working on-site, and whoever is minding the shop will be one of the members. You may be lucky enough to run into Sandy Rhynd, an ex-farmer who will be delighted to explain the venerable craft of stick dressing and show you his wares, such as musterer's sticks (shepherds in New Zealand are called musterers, and their sticks are something like traditional shepherds' crooks) and walking sticks, many inlaid with stag horn, known as "New Zealand ivory."

Hokianga & the Kauri Coast

85 km (53 mi) west of Paihia.

The focus of the Hokianga region is the peaceful harbor that sneaks inland quite a ways. It's a quiet area sparsely sprinkled with small towns, well worth visiting for its unspoiled scenery and proximity to the giant kauri trees on the Kauri Coast, a 20-minute drive south on Highway 12. Here the highway winds through Waipoua State Forest, then stretches south to Kaipara Harbour. Giant golden sand dunes tower over the mouth of Hokianga Harbour, across the water from the twin settlements of Omapere and Opononi. Opononi is the place where Opo, a tame dolphin, came to play with swimmers in the mid-1950s, putting the town on the national map for the first and only time in its history. A statue in front of the pub commemorates the much-loved creature. If you're driving and approaching the town from the south, be sure to check out some of the signposted lookouts en route.

③ **Waipoua State Forest** contains the largest remnant of the kauri forests
Fodor'sChoice that once covered this part of the country. A short path leads from the
★ parking area on the main road through the forest to **Tane Mahuta**, "Lord of the Forest," standing nearly 173 feet high and measuring 45 feet around its base. The largest tree in New Zealand, it's said to be 1,200–2,000-odd years old. The second-largest tree, but older by some 800 years, is **Te Matua Ngahere**. It takes about 20 minutes to walk to it from the road. There are other trees of note in the forest, among them the **Four**

The Poor Knights Islands

IT HAS BEEN SAID that you don't dive at the Poor Knights Islands—among the world's top 10 dive sites—you dive in them. The underwater archways, tunnels, caves, and rocky cliffs provide endless opportunities for exploration. More than 1,500 species of subtropical fish swarm in the warm currents that sweep down from the Coral Sea; soft coral, sponge gardens, gorgonian fields, and forests of kelp add to the marinescape.

At 7.9 million cubic feet, Rikoriko Cave, on the northwest side of the southern island, is one of the largest sea caves in the world. Ferns hang from the roof, and at the rear of the cave, an underwater cup coral grows. (Normally found at depths of 200 meters, the cave light has tricked it into thinking it is deeper.) Normal visibility at the Poor Knights is between 20 and 30 meters, but in Rikoriko Cave it goes up to 35 to 45 meters. The cave is renowned for its acoustics—musicians have even performed inside it.

Two large islands and many islets make up the Poor Knights; all remnants of an ancient volcanic eruption, they lie 12 nautical miles off the Tutukaka coast, a half-hour drive east of Whangarei. The ocean around them is a marine reserve, extending 800 meters (½ mi) from any part of the islands.

The islands themselves are a nature reserve, and landing on them is strictly prohibited. A dense canopy of regenerated pohutukawa covers the islands, flowering in brilliant scarlet around Christmastime. The native Poor Knights lily clings to the exposed cliff faces, producing bright red flowers in October. Species of rare birds, such as the bellbird ((koromiko) and red-crowned parakeet ((kakariki), thrive in the predator-free environment. Between October and May, millions of seabirds flock to the islands to breed, including the Buller's shearwaters that arrive from the Arctic Circle. But possibly the most distinguished resident is the New Zealand native tuatara, a reptile species from the dinosaur age that now survives only on offshore islands.

New Zealand fur seals bask on the rocks and feed on the abundant fish life, mostly from July to October each year, and year-round dolphins, whales, and bronze whaler sharks can be seen in the surrounding waters. In summer you can see minke and Brydes whales, too. In March stingrays stack in the hundreds in the archways for their mating season.

Diving is good year-round at the Poor Knights. In October, the visibility drops to about 18 to 20 meters because of a spring plankton bloom, though this brings the fish and marine life teeming in for food. It's rare for conditions to prevent diving. The best places for novices are Nursery Cove and some shallower parts of the South Harbour.

Dive Tutukaka (⊠ Poor Knights Dive Centre, Marina Rd., Tutukaka ☎ 09/434-3867 🖷 09/434-3884 ⊕ www.diving.co.nz) has trips for $199 with full gear rental. If you're not a diver, you can see the scenery from Cave Rider, a 25-passenger, jet-powered inflatable ($90). Free transfers to and from Whangarei are provided.

—Toni Mason

Sisters, four kauri trees that have grown together in a circular formation. If you have three hours to spare, hike the Yakas Track, which links the Four Sisters to the **Department of Conservation Visitor Centre** (✉ Waipoua River Rd., Waipoua Forest ☎ 09/439–3011). It's possible to camp in the forest, as long as you check at the visitor center before you pitch a tent. Facilities include toilets, hot showers, and a communal cookhouse. The track was closed at this writing for repairs, and it is not certain when it will reopen. When it's wet, you may spot some large kauri snails in the forest. Also, the recent successful eradication of predators such as weasels and stoats has led to a rise in the number of kiwis in the forest. Visitors are beginning to report sightings, but it's still very much a case of being in the right place at the right time. You'll need a flashlight to spot one, because the birds come out only at night.

Sixty-four km (40 mi) south of the Waipoua Forest along the Kaihu River, you'll come to **Dargaville,** once a thriving river port and these days a good place to stock up if you're planning to camp in any of the nearby forests. You can also linger in its few small crafts shops and cafés. The surrounding region is best known for its main cash crop, the purple-skinned sweet potato known as *kūmara.* You'll see field after field dedicated to this root vegetable and plenty of shops selling it cheaper than you'll find anywhere else.

★ Continuing south of Dargaville, you'll reach Matakohe, a pocket-size town with an outstanding attraction: the **Matakohe Kauri Museum,** one of the most intriguing museums in the country. The museum's vast collection of artifacts, tools, photographs, documents, and memorabilia tells the story of the pioneers who settled this part of the country in the second half of the 19th century—a story interwoven with the kauri forests. Here you'll find superb examples of craftsmanship: furniture and a complete kauri house, as well as an early example of an American-built Caterpillar bulldozer, which was used to drag logs from the forest. One of the most fascinating displays is of kauri gum, the transparent lumps of resin that form when the sticky sap of the kauri tree hardens. This gum, which was used to make varnish, can be polished to a warm, lustrous finish that looks remarkably like amber—right down to the insects that are sometimes trapped and preserved inside. At one time collecting this gum was an important rural industry. **Volunteers Hall** contains a huge kauri slab running from one end of the hall to the other, and there is also a Women in the Bush display, a reproduction of a cabinetmaker's shop, a chain-saw exhibit, and an area dedicated to fishing in Kaipara Harbour. The Steam Saw Mill illustrates how the huge kauri logs were cut into timber. The life-size mannequins in the exhibit, like others in the museum, are modeled on living descendants of the actual pioneers of the region. If you like the whirring of engines, the best day to visit is Wednesday, when much of the museum's machinery is started up. ✉ *Church Rd., Matakohe* ☎ *09/431–7417* ⊕ *www.kauri-museum. com* 🖅 *$12* ☉ *Nov.–Apr., daily 8:30–5:30; May–Oct., daily 9–5.*

Where to Stay & Eat

★ **$$$$** ✕🏠 **Waipoua Lodge.** Owners Nicole and Chris Donahoe have fully renovated this 19th-century kauri farmhouse and its former working-farm

CLOSE UP

Twilight Encounter

WHEN OUR SPOTLIGHTS HIT THE tree, lighting it up in the dark forest, I nearly stagger. It's beyond huge, stretching toward the night sky past where our flashlight beams can reach. Straining my head back to gaze at the enormous canopy, I can see why the early Māori settlers named this kauri—mature long before their arrival—Tane Mahuta, or Lord of the Forest.

With a height of around 173 feet and girth of 45 feet, Tane Mahuta is one of the largest and most magnificent trees in the world. Nobody knows exactly how old it is, but estimates range from 1,200 to 2,500 years. Tane Mahuta is sacred to the Māori people. According to their mythology, he pushed apart his mother, Papatuanuku, the earth, and his father, Ranginui, the sky, to let light into the world.

As my eyes adjust to the gloom, I marvel at the moonlit canopy. It's like another planet, a whole ecosystem suspended over the forest. And in fact its massive forked branches are home to more than 30 different species of plant life—predominantly epiphytes.

The trunk stretches straight up for about 58 feet before the first branches appear, its surface marked by a hammered appearance caused by the periodic flaking of the bark. It was this characteristic straightness that attracted the early European settlers to fell heartbreaking numbers of these majestic trees to make masts after Captain James Cook reported, on seeing his first kauri forest in 1769, that it was "the finest timber my eyes have ever seen." The early settlers were also attracted to the kauri gum, or resin, exuded by the mature trees, which they used for varnish and floor coverings.

Tane Mahuta stands in Northland's Waipoua Forest, one of the few surviving remnants of the native rain forest that once clad the top of the North Island. But he doesn't stand alone. A 20-minute walk along easy paths through the subtropical forest takes you past countless kauri—all of which are dwarfed by Te Matua Ngahere, the Father of the Forest. Though shorter than Tane Mahuta, he has an even more impressive girth of 50-odd feet and is thought to be the elder by some 800 years.

The forest echoes with native birdcalls, such as that of the morepork, a native owl whose call sounds like "morepork," or perhaps a kiwi. (A New Zealander who has only ever seen our national bird in the zoo, I hoped for a kiwi; the closest I got was a kiwi probe hole where the bird had been digging for worms!)

On the way home, one of our guides, Joe, of the local iwi (tribe) and a bushman with years of experience working with the Department of Conservation, asks us each for one word to describe the evening's experience. "Magical," I say.

The night tours to see Tane Mahuta and Te Matua Ngahere are led by **Footprints-Waipoua** (✉ State Hwy. 12, Omapere ☎ 09/405-8207 ⊕ www.omapere.co.nz). Tours are led by local Māori guides, experienced bushmen, who enrich your experience with their knowledge of the forest and wildlife and tales from Māori legend. The Twilight Encounter is a four-hour night walk ($65); a shortened version, Meet Tane at Night, takes one and a half hours ($45).

2

buildings and turned them into lovely suites. The names of the rooms record their past lives: the Calf Pen, the Woolshed, the Tack Room, and the Stables. All the rooms are decorated differently, from stylishly modern to more rustic, with plenty of space and natural light. The original farmhouse now houses the restaurant and bar and has retained farm memorabilia such as photographs and saws. After dinner, you can toast marshmallows in the central fireplace. (If you notice any blackened bricks, that's where the fireplace was once hit by lightning.) Meals, available by arrangement, usually focus on venison, lamb, or beef, and garden vegetables. At 2 km (1¼ mi) south of Waipoua Forest, the lodge is handy to the legendary kauri Tane Mahuta and one of the few areas where you can take night walks to view kiwi. ⊠ *State Hwy. 12, Waipoua* ☎ *09/439–0422* 🖶 *09/523–8081* ⊕ *www.waipoualodge.co.nz* 🔌 *4 suites* ♨ *Restaurant, kitchenettes, Wi-Fi, hot tub, bar, Internet room; no a/c* ✉ *AE, MC, V* ☉ *BP.*

$$$ ✕🏨 **Copthorne Hotel and Resort Hokianga.** From the deck of this seaside hotel you look straight out to the mouth of Hokianga Harbor, where the Polynesian navigator Kupe first arrived in New Zealand, according to legend, 1,000 years ago. It would be safe to say that the view has not changed since. The in-house restaurant's specialty is crayfish; you can choose your live cray from their tank or, as some prefer, meet it for the first time on your plate. The hotel is the base for local company Footprints–Waipoua, which takes "Twilight Encounter" tours through the Waipoua Forest to visit New Zealand's largest kauri trees. ⊠ *State Hwy. 12, Omapere* ☎ *09/405–8737* 🖶 *09/405–8801* ⊕ *www.omapere. co.nz* 🔌 *38 rooms, 9 suites* ♨ *Restaurant, kitchenettes, cable TV, pool, bar; no a/c* ✉ *AE, DC, MC, V.*

¢–$ 🏨 **Kauri Coast Top 10 Holiday Park.** With a stream running through its grounds and the Trounson Kauri Park marking its northern boundary, this spot is as close to nature as you can get. Owners Herb and Heather Iles can point you in the right direction for several outdoor activities, but perhaps the biggest draw is after-dark exploration. They give guided tours of the kauri park nightly (reservations essential); guests frequently spot kiwis on the walks. The various lodging configurations—cabins with or without kitchens, and with or without bathrooms, as well as self-contained apartments—are all kept spotless, and there's a camp kitchen and barbecue area. If you are traveling from the north, you'll need to turn left off the state highway and onto Trounson Park Road, 3 km (2 mi) before the small village of Kaihu. The holiday park is clearly signposted. ⊠ *Trounson Park Rd., 70 km (43 mi) south of Opononi* ☎🖶 *09/439–0621* ⊕ *www.kauricoasttop10.co.nz* 🔌 *2 motel units, 3 apartments, 8 cabins, 60 campsites* ♨ *Dining room, grocery, some kitchens, playground, laundry facilities; no a/c, no TV in some rooms* ✉ *MC, V.*

THE BAY OF ISLANDS

The Bay of Islands was a large Māori settlement when Captain James Cook first anchored off Roberton Island in 1769. He noted that "the inhabitants in this bay are far more numerous than in any other part of the country that we had visited." When the English started a convict

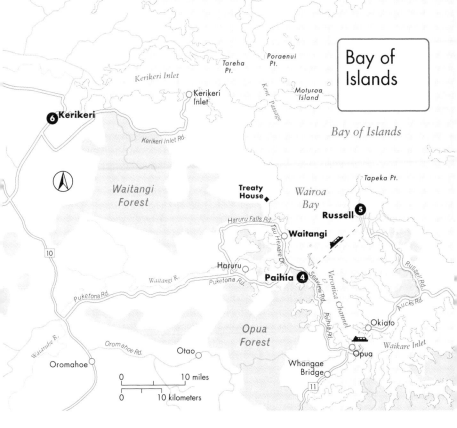

settlement in Australia a couple of decades later, many boats stayed in the South Pacific to go whaling and sealing, and the Bay of Islands became a port of call. Consequently, many of the early European arrivals were sailors and whalers, stopping to blow off steam, have a few drinks, and trade with the local Māori. A missionary, Henry Williams, wrote in 1828 that a whaling captain had told him "all the Europeans were in a state of intoxication, except himself and two others."

It took nearly a century for the Bay of Islands to get some positive reviews. American author Zane Grey visited in the 1920s to fish for marlin and was so impressed that he wrote a book about the bay called *Tales of the Angler's Eldorado*. Game fishing is still one of the bay's many draws, with record catches of marlin and mako shark, along with diving, boating, and swimming with dolphins. Many of the 144 islands were farms, but now only one, Motoroa, is still farmed; most others are now used for vacation homes.

Paihia & Waitangi

4 *69 km (43 mi) north of Whangarei.*

As the main vacation base for the Bay of Islands, Paihia is an unremarkable stretch of motels at odds with the quiet beauty of the island-stud-

CLOSE UP

The Treaty of Waitangi

THE CONTROVERSIAL cornerstone of Māori and Pākehā relations in New Zealand is the 1840 Treaty of Waitangi, the first formal document that bound the Māori to the British crown. This contract became the basis for Britain's claim to the entire country as its colony.

In the mid-1830s, Britain became increasingly concerned about advances by French settlers and the inroads made by the New Zealand Company, a private emigration organization. The British government had an official Resident at Waitangi, James Busby, but no actual means to protect its interests. In 1835, Busby helped orchestrate an alliance between more than 30 North Island Māori chiefs.

In 1840, Captain William Hobson arrived in Waitangi to negotiate a transfer of sovereignty. Hobson and Busby hurriedly drew up a treaty in both English and Māori, and presented it to the Māori confederation on February 5. On the following day, 43 chiefs signed the treaty. But there were significant differences between the Māori and English versions. In the first article, the English version said the Māori would cede sovereignty to the Queen of England. But the Māori translation used the word kāwanatanga (governorship), which did not mean that the Māori were ceding the right to mana (self-determination).

The second article guaranteed the chiefs the "full, exclusive and undisturbed possession of their lands, estates, forests, fisheries and other properties," but granted the right of preemption to the crown. The Māori translation did not convey the crown's exclusive right to buy Māori land, which caused friction over the decades. The third article granted the Māori protection as British citizens—and thus held them accountable to British law.

After the initial wave of signatures at Waitangi, signatures were gathered elsewhere in the North Island and on the South Island. In spring 1840 Hobson claimed all of New Zealand as a British colony. He had not, however, gotten signatures from some of the most powerful Māori chiefs, and this came back to haunt the crown during the Land Wars of 1860.

What wasn't confiscated after the Land Wars was taken by legislation. In 1877 Chief Justice Prendergast ruled that the treaty was "a simple nullity" that lacked legal validity because one could not make a treaty with "barbarians." At first European contact, 66.5 million acres of land was under Māori control, but by 1979 only 3 million remained—of mostly marginal lands.

The battle to have the treaty honored and reinterpreted is ongoing. In 1973, February 6 was proclaimed the official Waitangi Day holiday. From the get-go, the holiday sparked debate, as Māori activists protest the celebration of such a divisive document. The Waitangi Tribunal was established in 1975 to allow Māori to rule on alleged breaches of the treaty, and in 1985 the tribunal's powers were made retrospective to 1840. It has its hands full, as the claims continue to be one of New Zealand's largest socio-political issues. The treaty itself is now in the National Archives in Wellington.

ded seascape and the rounded green hills surrounding it. With its hand-ful of hostels, long, safe swimming beach, and numerous eateries, it's popular with a young backpacker crowd. Most of the boat and fishing tours leave from the central wharf, as do the passenger ferries to the historic village of Russell. The nearby suburb of Waitangi, however, is one of the country's most important historic sites. It was near here on the parklike Treaty Grounds that the Treaty of Waitangi, the founding document for modern New Zealand, was signed.

Fodor'sChoice **Waitangi National Trust Estate** is at the northern end of Paihia. Inside the
★ visitor center a 23-minute video, shown every hour on the hour, sketches the events that led to the Treaty of Waitangi. The center also displays Māori artifacts and weapons, including a musket that belonged to Hone Heke Pokai, the first Māori chief to sign the treaty. After his initial display of enthusiasm for British rule, Hone Heke was quickly disillusioned, and less than five years later he attacked the British in their stronghold at Russell. From the visitor center, follow a short track (trail) through the forest to **Ngatoki Matawhaorua** (ng-ga-to-ki ma-ta-*fa*-oh-*roo*-ah), a Māori war canoe. This huge kauri canoe, capable of carrying 80 paddlers and 55 passengers, is named after the vessel in which Kupe, the Polynesian navigator, is said to have discovered New Zealand. It was built in 1940 to mark the centennial of the signing of the Treaty of Waitangi. It is now used only for the treaty's anniversary celebration on February 6, brought out three days beforehand for the paddlers to practice.

The **Treaty House** in Waitangi Treaty Grounds is a simple white timber cottage that has a remarkable air of dignity despite its size. The interior is fascinating, especially the back, where exposed walls demonstrate the difficulties that early administrators faced—such as an acute shortage of bricks (since an insufficient number had been shipped from New South Wales, as Australia was known at the time) with which to finish the walls.

The Treaty House was prefabricated in New South Wales for British Resident James Busby, who arrived in New Zealand in 1832. Busby had been appointed to protect British commerce and put an end to the brutalities of the whaling captains against the Māori, but he lacked the judicial authority and the force of arms necessary to impose peace. On one occasion, unable to resolve a dispute between Māori tribes, Busby was forced to shelter the wounded of one side in his house. While tattooed warriors screamed war chants outside the windows, one of the Māori sheltered Busby's infant daughter, Sarah, in his cape.

The real significance of the Treaty House lies in the events that took place here on February 6, 1840, the day the Treaty of Waitangi was signed by Māori chiefs and Captain William Hobson, representing the British crown (*see* the Treaty of Waitangi CloseUp box). The Treaty House has not always received the care its significance merits. When Lord Bledisloe, New Zealand's governor-general between 1930 and 1935, bought the house and presented it to the nation in 1932, it was being used as a shelter for sheep.

Whare Runanga (fah-ray roo-nang-ah) is a Māori meetinghouse with an elaborately carved interior. Inside, an audio show briefly explains the

carvings displayed. The house is on the northern
itangi Treaty Grounds. ⊠ *Waitangi Rd., Waitangi*
🖃 *$12* ⊙ *Daily 9–5.*

Trust Estate beyond the Treaty Grounds, **Mt. Bledisloe**
view across Paihia and the Bay of Islands. The hand-
ker at the top showing the distances to major world
Doulton in London and presented by Lord Bledis-
his term as governor-general of New Zealand. The
mi) from the Treaty House, on the other side of the
rse. From a small parking area on the right of Wai-
track rises above a pine forest to the summit.

blic Toilets. On the main street of Kawakawa, a non-
ff State Highway 1 south of Paihia, stand surely the
lic toilets in the country—a must-go even if you
d to. Built by Austrian artist and architect Frederick
7, the toilets are fronted by brightly colored ceramic
n arched portico, which in turn supports a garden
o straight lines in the building, furnished inside with
ctuated with primary colors and set in black grout,
rian after a few drinks. Light filters through a win-
ottles. If you're not satisfied with seeing just one
if you give fair warning and duck into the other.

Eat

and dry on the banks of the Waitangi River sits
ing vessel, which once carried sugar to a sugar re-
finery in Auckland. In its new life, it's a top-end restaurant serving Mediterranean fare. On deck is a cocktail bar; dinner is served below deck on
kauri tables inset with relics that the famous New Zealand diver Kelly
Tarlton salvaged from wrecks. Dishes might include seafood paella
brimming with kingfish, scallops, prawns, calamari, and locally made
chorizo sausage, or leek-and-truffle risotto with seared scallops. ⊠ *Waitangi Bridge, Paihia* ☎ *09/402–7018* 🖃 *AE, DC, MC, V* ⊙ *No lunch.*

$$–$$$ ✕ **The Salty.** If the sea air's given you an appetite, head to this casual
spot to grab a steaming pizza. The Kiwi Pizza, a local favorite, is loaded
with salsa, onions, herbs, and ham. The Greek Pizza with feta cheese,
spinach, and sun-dried tomatoes, and the Meat Lover's, loaded with
salami, ham, bacon, and chicken, are also worth trying. The Salty
moonlights as one of Paihia's liveliest nightspots, with live music and
DJs. ⊠ *Kings Rd., Paihia* ☎ *09/402–6080* 🖃 *AE, DC, MC, V.*

$$–$$$ ✕ **Tides.** The sun streams into this central café in the morning, making
it a great place to enjoy a plate of bacon, eggs, and hash browns. Lunch
and dinner take on more wide-ranging flavors, encompassing North
African, Indian, Mexican, and traditional Kiwi treatments of seafood,
game fish, lamb, and venison. If you're looking for a local wine, go for
something from the Cottle Hill vineyard. ⊠ *Williams Rd., Paihia* ☎ *09/
402–7557* 🖃 *AE, DC, MC, V.*

¢–$$ ✕ **Waikokopu Café.** With a view straight out to sea, this pleasant spot has
a lot going for it. Chunky sandwiches, delicious cakes, and other good-

ies are available throughout the day, many including indigenous foods. For something hot, try the Sweet Corncoction—corn-and-coriander fritters served with guacamole, sour cream, and tomato salsa. ⊠ *Tau Henare Dr., Waitangi Treaty Grounds* ☎ *09/402–6275* ⊟ *MC, V* ☺ *No dinner.*

¢–$ ✕ **Beachhouse Café and Bar.** Great-value casual food is served from 8 AM to midnight at this popular cafe. You can eat outside on the small patio or in surf-style surroundings inside. Breakfast includes classic eggs Benedict, or cereal and yogurt for the more health conscious. Later in the day, gourmet burgers are the staple, with choices such as the Tribal Fish Burger (grilled fish, fried banana, and curry mayonnaise) or the Bacon Hottie (topped with relish, bacon, onion, and the Kiwi burger favorite, beetroot). There's live music nightly. ⊠ *16 Kings Rd., Paihia* ☎ *09/402–7479* ⊟ *DC, MC, V.*

$$$$ ⊞ **Copthorne Hotel and Resort Bay of Islands.** The biggest hotel north of Auckland and a favorite with tour groups, this complex sprawls along a peninsula within walking distance of the Treaty House. Garden-facing rooms are decorated in a French provincial style, with yellows and blues and wrought-iron light fixtures. Most rooms have a terrace or patio, giving them an airier feeling. ⊠ *Tau Henare Dr., Waitangi* ☎ *09/402–7411* 🖷 *09/402–8200* ⊕ *www.copthornewaitangi.co.nz* ↘ *138 rooms, 7 suites* ⌂ *Restaurant, minibars, cable TV, pool, hot tub, bar, laundry facilities; no a/c* ⊟ *AE, DC, MC, V.*

$$$$ ⊞ **Paihia Beach Resort & Spa.** A large *pohutukawa* tree stands next to the heated saltwater pool in front of this resort overlooking the bay. All the rooms have bay views and a deck or patio plus a large whirlpool tub in the bathroom. The larger "superior" rooms have a full kitchen and a flow-through bedroom divided by a louvered wall. You have free private use of the sauna or steam room. The state-of-the-art day spa, which is also open to nonguests, has a full range of treatments, including Vichy showers. ⊠ *116 Marsden Rd., Paihia* ☎ *09/402–6140* 🖷 *09/402–6026* ⊕ *www.paihiabeach.co.nz* ↘ *19 rooms, 2 suites* ⌂ *Restaurant, in-room hot tubs, some kitchens, minibars, cable TV, in-room DVD, pool, spa, bar* ⊟ *AE, DC, MC, V* ⦿ *BP.*

$$$ ⊞ **Abri.** These freestanding studio apartments take advantage of the bush setting just behind the Paihia beachfront, offering lovely sea views across to Russell. The two units have woodwork with indigenous timber, such as *rimu* flooring and *macrocarpa* walls and jet baths; their large living-room areas open onto outside decks. The apartments have their own kitchen facilities, even a small barbecue on the deck, but most guests take the short walk to the restaurants in town for meals. The owners know the little touches that make visitors feel welcome, and you'll find fresh cookies and flowers in your room daily. ⊠ *10–12 Bayview Rd., Paihia* ☎ *09/402–8003* ⊕ *www.abri-accom.co.nz* ↘ *2 studios, 1 suite* ⌂ *In-room hot tubs, kitchens, in-room VCRs; no kids* ⊟ *MC, V.*

$$ ⊞ **Austria Motel.** The large, double-bed rooms here are typical of motel accommodations in the area—clean and moderately comfortable but almost totally devoid of charm. However, all rooms have balconies with patchy sea views, and there is covered off-street parking. The shops and waterfront at Paihia are a two-minute walk away. ⊠ *36 Selwyn Rd., Paihia* ☎🖷 *09/402–7480* ↘ *6 rooms* ⌂ *Kitchenettes, cable TV; no a/c* ⊟ *MC, V.*

★ ¢–$$ 🏠 **Bay Adventurer.** It's hard to imagine a hostel better equipped than this sparkling one. Accommodations range from dorm rooms for just $25 to studio and one-bedroom apartments, which have kitchens, bathrooms, and TVs. Brightly colored linen is supplied in all rooms, even the dorms. Women-only apartments have two bedrooms that each sleep four, a full bathroom (bubble bath supplied), kitchen, lounge, and deck. A subtropical garden surrounds the pool and hot tub, and the beach is about two minutes' walk away. ⊠ *28 Kings Rd., Paihia* ☎ *09/402–5162* 🖷 *09/402–5163* ⊕ *www.bayadventurer.co.nz* ⇌ *15 dorm rooms, 11 doubles, 7 apartments* ⚐ *BBQ, pool, hot tub, lounge, laundry facilities, Internet room, travel services* ☰ *MC, V.*

★ ¢–$ 🏠 **Saltwater Lodge.** This is one of the best spots in Paihia's Kings Road area (the town's hostel corridor), as both cleanliness and comfort are top priorities. The hostel rooms start at $23 a night, and even the cheapest beds have duvets supplied. Bunk-bed dormitories all have en-suite bathrooms with shower, storage facilities, and reading lights over the beds. The second-floor motel units come with king beds and bunks, plus a fridge and a small TV. The communal kitchen is probably the best equipped you'll find in the whole country, with everything from a wok to egg beaters. Even a small gym and bikes can be used at no extra charge. ⊠ *14 Kings Rd., Paihia* ☎ *09/402–7075* 🖷 *09/402–7240* ⊕ *www.saltwaterlodge.co.nz* ⇌ *10 double rooms, 9 dorm rooms* ⚐ *Dining room, BBQ, kitchen, some refrigerators, gym, laundry facilities, Internet room; no a/c, no TV in some rooms* ☰ *MC, V.*

Sports & the Outdoors

BOATING   Paihia is a major boating center. Most tours will take you to—and through—the Hole in the Rock, an archway carved by sea and wind in a rocky outcrop just off Cape Brett.

Carino NZ Sailing and Dolphin Adventures (📪 Box 286, Paihia ☎ 09/402–8040 🖷 09/402–8661 ⊕ www.sailinganddolphin.co.nz) gets as close as practical to sea life such as dolphins (primarily bottlenose) and penguins. Passengers on the 50-foot red catamaran can just relax or pitch in with sailing. This full-day trip ($90) includes a barbecue lunch at one of the islands, weather permitting, and there's a full bar on board.

Fodor'sChoice   **Dolphin Discoveries** (⊠ Marsden and Williams Rds., Paihia ☎ 09/402–
★   8234 🖷 09/402–6058 ⊕ www.dolphinz.co.nz) runs two different trips, both twice a day. "Swim with the Dolphins" is a four-hour trip ($99) in a motorized catamaran to swim with bottlenose dolphins. You might also spot Brydes whales, migrating humpback and orca whales, or groups of tiny blue penguins. The "Discover the Bay" ecotour ($69) is a three-and-a-half-hour trip around the island and to—and through—the Hole in the Rock at the end of Cape Brett Peninsula. This larger jet-powered catamaran is also licensed for viewing dolphins, so if you're not so keen on swimming with them, this is the best choice. On both trips, if you don't get to see any dolphins, you get a voucher that entitles you to come back until you do.

★   **Fullers** (⊠ Maritime Bldg., Marsden Rd., Paihia ☎ 09/402–7421 ⊕ www.fullers-bay-of-islands.co.nz) runs cruises and sea-based adventure trips departing daily from both Paihia and Russell. The most comprehensive and popular sightseeing trip is the Supercruise ($90) aboard a high-speed catamaran. You'll follow about half of what was once called the "Cream Trip" route, but nowadays, instead of picking up cream from farms, the boat delivers mail and supplies to vacation homes. Fullers also visits Urupukapuka Island, once home to a *hapu* (subtribe) of the Ngare Raumati Māori. Little is known about their life, but there are numerous archaeological sites to see. It's also the only one to go to Otehei Bay, one of the most beautiful bays on the island and the one Zane Grey used as his base for fishing expeditions in 1927. The trip also takes in the Hole in the Rock.

A catamaran operated by **Straycat Day Sailing Charters** (⌂ Box 411, Paihia ☎ 09/402–8523 or 0800/101–007) makes one-day sailing trips in the Bay of Islands from Paihia and Russell at $79 per person, which includes a picnic-style lunch and sake or a kiwi-fruit liqueur, stops at two of the islands, bushwalks, swimming, and snorkeling.

DIVING The Bay of Islands has some of the finest scuba diving in the country, particularly around Cape Brett, where the marine life includes moray eels, stingrays, and grouper. The wreck of the Greenpeace vessel *Rainbow Warrior,* sunk by French agents in 1985, is another Bay of Islands underwater highlight. The wreck was transported to the Cavalli Islands in 1987 and is now covered in soft corals and jewel anemones; it's full of fish life. Water temperature at the surface varies from 16°C (62°F) in July to 22°C (71°F) in January. From September through November, underwater visibility can be affected by a plankton bloom.

Paihia Dive Compass Ltd. (⌂ Box 210, Paihia ☎ 09/402–7551 or 0800/107–551 ⊕ www.divenz.com) offers complete equipment rental and regular boat trips for accredited divers for $195 per day; they also run dive courses.

FISHING The Bay of Islands is one of the world's premier game-fishing grounds for marlin and several species of shark.

Marlin Fishing New Zealand (⌂ Box 285, Paihia ☎ 09/402–8189 or 0274/776–604 ⊕ www.marlinfishing.co.nz) goes for the big ones off the Northland coast and around Three Kings Islands. The cost is $2,982 per day for a maximum of four, including all tackle and meals.

A far less-expensive alternative than pricey marlin fishing is to fish for snapper and kingfish within the bay. **Spot-X** (⌂ Box 361, Kerikeri ☎ 09/402–7123 ⊕ www.fish-spot-x.co.nz) runs four-hour snapper-fishing trips for about $85 per person and six-hour kingfish trips for $180, including bait and tackle.

Russell

❺ *4 km (2½ mi) east of Paihia by ferry, 13 km (8 mi) by road and car ferry.*

Russell is regarded as the "second" town in the Bay of Islands, but it is far more interesting, and pleasant, than Paihia. Hard as it is to believe these days, sleepy little Russell was once dubbed the "Hellhole of the Pacific." In the mid- to late 19th century (when it was still known by its Māori name, Kororareka) it was a swashbuckling frontier town, a haven for sealers and whalers who found the east coast of New Zealand to be one of the richest whaling grounds on earth.

Tales of debauchery were probably exaggerated, but British administrators in New South Wales were sufficiently concerned to dispatch a British Resident in 1832 to impose law and order. After the Treaty of Waitangi, Russell was the national capital, until in 1844 the Māori chief Hone Heke, disgruntled with recently imposed harbor dues and his loss of authority, cut down the flagstaff flying the Union Jack above the town three times before attacking the British garrison. Most of the town burned to the ground in what is known as the Sacking of Kororareka. Hone Heke was finally defeated in 1846, but Russell never recovered its former prominence, and the seat of government was shifted first to Auckland, then to Wellington.

Today Russell is a delightful town of timber houses and big trees that hang low over the seafront, framing the yachts and game-fishing boats in the harbor. The atmosphere can best be absorbed in a stroll along the Strand, the path along the waterfront. There are several safe swimming beaches, some in secluded bays, as well as the aptly named Long Beach over the hill from the township.

The road between Russell and Paihia is long and tortuous. The best way to travel between the two is by passenger ferry, which leaves from the Russell Wharf, or by car ferry, which departs from Okiato, about 9 km (5½ mi) southwest of town.

New Zealand's oldest industrial building, the **Pompallier Mission,** at the southern end of the Strand, was named after the first Catholic bishop of the South Pacific. Marist missionaries built the original structure out of rammed earth (a technique known as *pisé-de-terre* in their native France), because they lacked the funds to buy timber. For several years the priests and brothers operated a press here, printing Bibles in the Māori language. You can try your hand at tanning, printing, and bookbinding, which is still done on-site (although these operations are no longer affiliated with the Church). From December through April you can visit independently, but from May to November the mission organizes tours at set times instead. ☒ *The Strand* ☏ *09/403–7861* ⊕ *www. pompallier.co.nz* ☒ *$7.50* ⊘ *Daily 10–5.*

The **Russell Museum** houses a collection of Māori tools and weapons and some fine portraits. The pride of its display is a ⅕-scale reproduction of Captain Cook's ship, HMS *Endeavour,* which entered the bay in 1769. A short video recounts the history of the region. The museum is set back slightly from the waterfront, some 50 yards north of Pompallier House. ☒ *York St.* ☏ *09/403–7701* ☒ *$5* ⊘ *Feb.–Dec. daily 10–4, Jan. daily 10–5.*

★ **Christ Church** is the oldest church in the country. One of the donors to its erection in 1835 was Charles Darwin, at that time a wealthy but unknown young man making his way around the globe on board the HMS *Beagle.* Behind the white picket fence that borders the churchyard, gravestones tell a fascinating and brutal story of life in the early days of the colony. Several graves belong to sailors from the HMS *Hazard* who were killed in this churchyard by Hone Heke's warriors in 1845. Another headstone marks the grave of a Nantucket sailor from the whaler *Mohawk*. As you walk around the church, look for the musket holes made when Hone Heke besieged the church. The interior is simple and charming—embroidered cushions on the pews are examples of a folk-art tradition that is still very much alive. ⊠ *Church and Robertson Sts.* ⊗ *Daily 8–5.*

Where to Stay & Eat

★ $$$–$$$$ ✕ **Gannets.** German chefs Fabian and René may use classic French cuisine as their menu's bedrock, but they also like to play with flavors. You might find such contemporary creations as grilled *cervena* (farm-raised venison) with a cherry-flavored jus reduction, served with kūmara (a native sweet potato), green beans, and feta cheese. Seafood is naturally a focus, too—try the crispy salmon with ginger-and-carrot ragout or the game fish of the day. Be sure to try one of the homemade vodka infusions; the lemongrass version is particularly refreshing when sipped at one of the outdoor tables on a balmy evening. ⊠ *York and Chapel Sts.* ☎ *09/403–7990* ▭ *MC, V* ⊗ *No lunch.*

$$$–$$$$ ✕ **Kamakura.** The prime dining spot in Russell, this minimalist waterfront restaurant combines subtly prepared yet flavorsome cuisine with
FodorśChoice arguably the best restaurant view in town—especially if you can nab a
★ table at the front. If the local Orongo Bay oysters are available, snap them up as an appetizer. You can't go wrong with the seafood entrées either, such as tempura prawns with avocado-and-tomato salsa and a tomato-and-fig dressing. You may swoon over the char-grilled game fish, often blue marlin, served with a Thai coconut broth, jasmine rice, and kūmara gnocchi. ⊠ *The Strand* ☎ *09/403–7761* ▭ *AE, DC, MC, V.*

★ $$$ ✕ **Sally's.** Overlooking Kororareka Bay from the pretty cream-and-green timber Bay of Islands Swordfish Club building, this restaurant aims to please seafood lovers. Sally's seafood chowder, packed with fresh mussels, shrimp, and fish, is the most popular dish—despite numerous requests, the chef refuses to divulge his recipe—followed by fish of the day, which could be *hapuka* (grouper) on a basil risotto topped with a butter lemon sauce. Ask for a window table, or dine outdoors when it's sunny. ⊠ *The Strand* ☎ *09/403–7652* ▭ *AE, MC, V* 🍷 *Licensed and BYOB.*

★ $$$$ ✕🛏 **Omata Retreat.** Nestled in a private bay on the end of Omata Estate's peninsula on the grounds of a vineyard, the main accommodation, a schist (stone) homestead, looks out onto golden sands and over the bay to Paihia. The homestead has four large double bedrooms and a large living area dominated by a kauri–wood bar, with a fireplace to boot. In the boathouse, there's a beach-style apartment with whitewashed wood and doors opening out onto the bay, and above the garage is a loft apartment. You can add a fresh spin to breakfast by having it out on the private jetty. The highly regarded restaurant has spectacular views over the vines to the bay. Seafood platters are lunchtime favorites, and the dinner menu has dishes such as rosemary-crusted rack of lamb on apricot couscous with a syrah-merlot jus and sautéed grapes. ⊠ *Aucks Rd., between the car ferry and Russell* ☎ *09/403–8007* 🖷 *09/403–8005* ⊕ *www.omata.co.nz* ⤴ *4 rooms, 2 apartments* ⌂ *Restaurant,* *kitchens, cable TV, in-room DVD, tennis court, boating, waterskiing, croquet, library, Internet room, helipad* ☰ *AE, DC, MC, V.*

$$$$ ⊞ **Eagle's Nest.** The setting (a private peninsula) feels utterly secluded, and the villas here are pure luxury. Sacred Space, which sleeps eight, is topped by a pitched glass roof, framing spectacular views of sea and sky. It also has a 22-meter infinity pool and hot tub, plus a projector screen that drops at the touch of switch, creating a home theater. The First Light Temple villa likewise makes the most of the views, with floor-to-ceiling windows in the living area and kitchen. From the bed on the mezzanine floor, you can look up at the night sky through the electronic louvered skylight above. Two smaller villas started life as 1950s beach houses; winningly refurbished, they're sleekly modern but still retain the friendly ghost of Kiwi bach style. Both have infinity lap pools, hot tubs, and plasma-screen TVs. Chefs do meals on request. The newest, top-shelf (and over-the-top-dollar) villa, Sanandaloka, commands a near-360-degree view of the bay and has five luxury bedrooms, butler service, and a Porsche for your use. ⊠ *60 Tapeka Rd.* ☎ *09/403–8333* 📠 *09/403–8880* ⊕ *www.eaglesnest.co.nz* 🛏 *5 villas* ♦ *In-room hot tubs, cable TV, in-room broadband, pools, massage, spa, mountain bikes, Internet room, helipad* ☰ *AE, DC, MC, V* ⊞◐ *BP.*

FodorsChoice ★

$$$$ ⊞ **Flagstaff Lodge.** Photos of this 1912 villa in its original state line the central kauri hallway. Its outside appearance has changed little, but inside it has been restored with all modern conveniences. The light, airy, high-ceiling rooms all have Italian-tiled bathrooms and French doors onto the wraparound veranda from where you can see a peep of the bay, only a minute's walk away. Two French bathtubs stand behind a screen off a small courtyard where you can soak in essential oils and rose petals and contemplate the schist water feature. A separate room houses the spa offering massage and beauty treatments, and the large lounge has a fireplace and wide flat-screen TV. ⊠ *17 Wellington St.* ☎ *09/403–7117* 📠 *09/403–7817* ⊕ *www.flagstafflodge.co.nz* 🛏 *4 rooms* ♦ *Cable TV, in-room broadband, spa; no room TVs* ☰ *AE, DC, MC, V* ⊞◐ *BP.*

★ $$$$ ⊞ **The Homestead at Orongo Bay.** Tucked away in gardens off the road between the car-ferry landing and Russell, this historic lodge, built in 1865, soothes with peace and quiet. The two rooms in the main homestead have kauri ceilings and paneling built in a New England colonial style, with large tiled bathrooms. A pair of bi-level barn rooms, set back from the main building and almost over a pond, are more contemporary, with angled roofs and skylights. Sumptuous multi-course dinners are cooked (by prior arrangement) by chef and co-owner Michael Hooper, a nationally known food critic who grows many of his organic ingredients on the property's grounds. ⊠ *Aucks Rd., R.D. 1* ☎ *09/403–7527* 📠 *09/403–7675* ⊕ *www.thehomestead.co.nz* 🛏 *4 rooms* ♦ *Dining room, cable TV, in-room DVD, Wi-Fi, croquet, lounge, piano, Internet room* ☰ *AE, DC, MC, V* ⊞◐ *BP.*

$$$$ ⊞ **Okiato Lodge.** Okiato is high up on Okiato Point, looking out on Opua, Paihia, and other Bay of Islands locales—on Wednesday evening, you may even see vessels from the local yacht club sailing by below. Spacious rooms include step-down lounge areas, with high-vaulted ceilings and large windows with great views. Rates include drinks and a four-course dinner, which emphasizes New Zealand favorites such as scallops, venison, and lamb. ✉ *James Clendon Pl., Okiato Point (R.D. 1)* ☎ *09/403–7948* 🖷 *09/ 403–7515* ⊕ *www.okiato.co.nz* ⤳ *9 rooms* ♿ *Dining room, minibars, in-room data ports, pool, bar, lounge* ▭ *AE, DC, MC, V* ⏐◯⏐ *MAP.*

$$$–$$$$ 🖾 **Te Pa Helios.** Leave the drapes open when you go to sleep in this cliff-top B&B, and the sun rising over the glistening bay may gently wake you. An old Māori *pā* (hilltop fortification) site and a small bay frame a view of islands dotting the clear blue sea. The property evokes Greece with its angular whitewashed buildings. In the main villa are the Island Suite, with a balcony on the cliff edge, and the spacious Russell Room, with a small terrace also set on the cliff. The self-catering Little Villa has two bedrooms. Colorful Hundertwasser prints are hanging in most of the rooms. ✉ *44 Du Fresne Pl., Tapeka Point* ☎🖷 *09/403–7229* ⊕ *www. tepahelios.com* ⤳ *1 room, 1 suite, 1 villa* ♿ *No a/c* ▭ *MC, V* ⏐◯⏐ *CP.*

$$–$$$ 🖾 **Arcadia Lodge.** Rumor had it that this bed-and-breakfast, perched over Matauwhi Bay, a few minutes' walk from town, had been supported for more than 100 years by whale vertebrae. Sure enough, when new owners repiled the foundations of the turn-of-the-century home in 2005, they found that that was virtually the only thing holding it up. One of the "backbones" of the house now sits in the lounge. Two spacious suites off the large guest lounge and dining area both have brass beds, sunrooms, and their own decks. Another three rooms are upstairs. The Tautoru Room has its own entrance, with a deck and a view of the bay where you can watch the boats coming and going from the Russell Boat Club (the club's bar is a good place to meet locals). ✉ *10 Florance Ave.* ☎ *09/ 403–7756* 🖷 *09/403–7657* ⊕ *www.arcadialodge.co.nz* ⤳ *4 rooms, 2 with bath, 2 suites* ♿ *Dining room, piano; no room TVs* ▭ *MC, V* ⏐◯⏐ *BP.*

$$–$$$ 🖾 **Duke of Marlborough Hotel.** An ex-convict built this historic waterfront hotel, the first in New Zealand to gain a pub license. It's a favorite with the yachting fraternity, for whom ready access to the harbor and the bar downstairs are the most important considerations. Antiques and contemporary art add character; in the stairwell up to the bright and cheerful rooms, there's a 1780s clock and a family coat of arms on a stained-glass window. If you like more space, opt for one of the waterfront suites with large whirlpool baths. ✉ *The Strand* ☎ *09/403–7829* 🖷 *09/403–7828* ⊕ *www.theduke.co.nz* ⤳ *19 rooms, 6 suites* ♿ *Restaurant, cable TV, bar; no a/c* ▭ *MC, V* ⏐◯⏐ *CP.*

¢–$ 🖾 **Sheltered Waters Backpackers.** The hominess++CE: homeliness?++ of this small hostel, a leisurely 10-minute walk from town, brings guests back for repeat visits. There are two dorm rooms—one sleeps eight, the other four, and a double room with a bunk can take four as well. Palms circle the large garden, home to a little aviary (with a resident pair of lovebirds). Seafood chowder made with local oysters and mussels is some of the fare offered on request. ✉ *18 Florance Ave.* ☎ *09/403–8818* 🖷 *09/ 403 8461* ⊕ *www.russellbackpackers.co.nz* ⤳ *2 dorm rooms, 1 double room* ♿ *BBQ, kitchen, outdoor hot tub, bicycles, lounge, laundry facilities, Internet room, some pets allowed* ▭ *No credit cards.*

Sports & the Outdoors

Fernz EcoTours (⇨ Northland & the Bay of Islands Essentials, *below*) has ecotours in the Russell area.

FISHING **Major Tom Charters** (☎ 09/403–8553 or 0274/377–844) chases game fish such as marlin, broadbill, and tuna. A full day, with a maximum of four anglers, is $1,195. **Triple B Boat Charters** (✉ 2 Robertson Rd. ☎ 09/403–7200 or 0274/972–177 🖷 09/403–7537) runs saltwater fly-fishing and light-tackle trips at $125 per hour (minimum four hours). All tackle is supplied.

HIKING There are several pleasant walks around the Russell area; the most challenging—and spectacular—is the **Cape Brett Tramping Track** out to the lighthouse. It takes about eight hours round-trip, and you need to be fit. You can stay in a hut for $10 per night. For information, check with the Russell Information Center on the wharf (⇨ Visitor Information *in* Northland & the Bay of Islands A to Z, *below*). **Cape Brett Walkways** (☎ 09/403–8823 ⊕ www.capebrettwalks.co.nz) has guided walks with historical and cultural commentary to Cape Brett lighthouse, via a boat trip to the Hole in the Rock ($175), and to the Whangamumu whaling station ($225). For a shorter jaunt (just an hour each way), you can follow the **Whangamumu Walking Track** to the remnants of a whaling station. Many relics such as an old boiler and vats are still left at the station.

Kerikeri

❻ *20 km (12 mi) north of Paihia.*

Kerikeri is often referred to as the cradle of the nation because so much of New Zealand's earliest history, especially in terms of interaction between Māori and Europeans, took place here. The main town itself is small but gaining a reputation for its crafts and specialty shops. A major citrus-growing area, it was once principally a service town for the whole mid-north region. In a way, it still is, as in recent years newcomers have flocked to Kerikeri for its low-key lifestyle. It still feels like a small town, though, with its homes shaded by trees or dotted about the surrounding countryside.

The **Historic Kerikeri Basin,** just northeast of the modern town on the Kerikeri Inlet, is where most of the interest lies. Anglican missionaries arrived in this area in 1819, having been invited to Kerikeri by its most famous historical figure, the great Māori chief Hongi Hika. The chief visited England in 1820, where he was showered with gifts. On his way back to New Zealand, during a stop in Sydney, he traded many of these presents for muskets. Having the advantage of these prized weapons, he set in motion plans to conquer other Māori tribes, enemies of his own Ngapuhi people. The return of his raiding parties over five years, with many slaves and gruesome trophies of conquest, put considerable strain between Hongi Hika and the missionaries. Eventually his warring ways were Hongi's undoing. He was shot in 1827 and died as a result of complications from the wound a year later.

The 1821 **Kemp House,** otherwise known as Mission House, has gone through many changes since 1821, but ironically, a major flood in 1981 inspired its "authentic" restoration. The flood washed away the garden and damaged the lower floor, and during repair much information about the original structure of the house was revealed. As a result, its ground floor and garden have been restored to the style of missionary days, and the upper floor, which remained unharmed by the flood, is still presented with its Victorian decoration. ⊠ *Kerikeri Historic Basin, Kerikeri Rd.* ☎ *09/407–9236* 🖅*$5* ⊙ *Nov.–Apr., daily 10–5; May–Oct., Sat.–Wed. 10–5.*

Rewa's Village museum re-creates a *kāinga* (unfortified fishing village) where local Māori would have lived in peaceful times. (In times of siege they would have taken refuge in nearby Kororipo Pā.) The village-museum was built in 1969, when the local community wanted to save the area from threatened urban development. A video plays near the entrance, with a history of chief Hongi Hika. In the village itself are reproductions of the chief's house, the weapons store, and the family enclosure, as well as two original canoes dug up from local swamps and original *hāngi* stones (used to cook traditional Māori feasts) found on-site. ⊠ *Kerikeri Historic Basin, Kerikeri Rd.* ☎ *09/407–6454* 🖅 *$3* ⊙ *Nov.–Apr., daily 9–5; May–Oct., daily 10–4.*

The **Stone Store** is Kerikeri's most picturesque attraction and the most striking building in the historic basin. Built between 1832 and 1836, it is New Zealand's oldest existing stone building. It was part of the Kerikeri Mission Station and was built to hold stores for the whole New Zealand mission of the time. It's now open to the public in what is close to its original state, displaying typical wares such as red Hudson Bay blankets, which were sought after by Māori from the *pā* (hilltop fortification).Upstairs are the old steel flour mill, original ledgers from the store, and displays of tools and flintlock muskets—also prized by local Māori. The shop is more interesting than the average tourist trap, with historical items such as iron cooking pots, musket flint, slash hooks, and old English felling axes for sale. ⊠ *Kerikeri Historic Basin, Kerikeri Rd.* ☎*09/407–9236* 🖅*$5* ⊙ *Nov.–Apr., daily 10–5; May–Oct., Sat.–Wed. 10–5.*

Across the road from the Basin's Stone Store is a path leading to the historic site of **Kororipo Pā**, the fortified headquarters of chief Hongi Hika. Untrained eyes will have a bit of difficulty figuring out exactly where the pā was, as there are no structures left. Information boards and drawings aid the imagination. The pā was built on a steep-sided promontory between the Kerikeri River and the Wairoa Stream. You'll still get a fine view over both.

Where to Stay & Eat

$$$ ✕ **Kina Kitchen.** Named after the New Zealand sea urchin, this restaurant tucked down a cobbled mall specializes in seafood with a modern twist. The seafood antipasto of mussels, prawns, calamari, and local oysters is a great starter for two or main dish for one (and an excellent value at $20). Otherwise, begin with the seared scallops with a rosemary, garlic, and anchovy sauce served with crispy polenta strips. There are always three different fish of the day: salmon, a game fish, and a whitefish, perhaps served with a chili-lime salsa. The adjoining bar fills up with the after-work crowd. ⊠ *Cobblestone Mall, 95 Kerikeri Rd.* ☎ *09/407–7669* 🖃 *AE, DC, MC, V* ⊙ *Closed Sun. and Mon. No lunch.*

$$$ ✕ **Pure Tastes.** Chef Paul Jobin brought fine dining to this café town with his classy but approachable modern restaurant. There's a strong Asian influence at work, seen in such dishes as his Penang fish curry with udon noodles, mango-and-lychee relish, and coriander oil. Mediterranean flavors make an appearance, too, as in the slow-roasted leg of lamb with fennel purée. The service is polished but the atmosphere is relaxed—you're welcome to come in just for dessert and coffee. You can also perch at the chef's bar and watch the chefs at work in the open kitchen while you eat. ⊠ *Fairway Dr.* ☎ *09/407–6510* ▤ *MC, V* ⊘ *Closed Tues.*

★ **$$-$$$** ✕ **Marsden Estate Winery and Restaurant.** Named after the missionary Samuel Marsden, who planted New Zealand's first grapevines in Kerikeri in 1819, this winery is a popular place for lunch. If the weather co-operates, ask for a table on the terrace and gaze down at the vines. The seasonal menu is eclectic but leans toward the Mediterranean. The seared squid with lime aioli served in a bowl-shape *pappadam* (paper-thin Indian bread) couldn't be more tender. Of the winery's small but notable output, try the full-bodied Black Rocks Chardonnay. ⊠ *Wiroa Rd.* ☎☎ *09/407–9398* ⊕ *www.marsdenestate.co.nz* ▤ *MC, V* ⊘ *Closed Mon. and June and July. No dinner.*

¢–$ ✕ **Fishbone Café.** Silvery tin fish bones line the walls here. The locals come for the great coffee and the thick sandwiches, panini, and frittatas. You'll also be joining them as they study the extensive blackboard menu, where you'll find the smoked-chicken salad with crispy noodles and a light curry mayonnaise (so popular that it's impossible for the chef to sneak it off the list). ⊠ *88 Kerikeri Rd.* ☎ *09/407–6065* ▤ *AE, DC, MC, V* ⊘ *No dinner.*

$$$ ▥ **The Summer House.** Hosts Christine and Rod Brown both come from artistic families, a background that infuses this B&B. The downstairs room, slightly detached from the house, is done in a South Pacific style, pairing tapa cloth with browns and creams. It has the most space, a kitchenette, and a higher room rate. The two upstairs rooms in the main house share a guest lounge. One room has an 1860 French bed with furniture to match, and the other has a Victorian brass bedstead. Christine's breakfasts are wonderful, including fresh or poached fruits, Greek yogurt, homemade muesli, and free-range eggs cooked as requested. The landscaped subtropical garden surrounding the house attracts native birds, doves, and monarch butterflies. ⊠ *424 Kerikeri Rd.* ☎ *09/407–4294* 🖷 *09/407–4297* ⊕ *www.thesummerhouse.co.nz* ⇆ *3 rooms* ᗭ *Lounge, Internet room; no a/c, no TV in some rooms* ▤ *MC, V* ▯◀ *BP.*

$–$$ ▥ **Kauri Park.** This small cluster of chalets is a notch above the usual, with modern decor and a beautiful setting among fruit trees adjacent to farmland. Friendly hosts Dallas and Delphine Eves display the usual Kiwi warmth with a free drink on arrival in the guest lounge. Each unit has a veranda and colorful furnishings. Kauri Park is a little bit out of town, which gives it a rural feeling, but it's still only a few minutes' drive from the historic sights. ⊠ *512 Kerikeri Rd. (south end)* ☎☎ *09/407–7629* ⊕ *www.kauripark.co.nz* ⇆ *9 rooms* ᗭ *Cable TV, in-room data ports, lounge; no a/c* ▤ *AE, DC, MC, V.*

$–$$ ▥ **Paheke.** An enormous cedar of Lebanon stands in front of this gracious 1864 kauri homestead; both the tree and the house are listed with

CLOSE UP

The Far North

ABOVE THE BAY OF ISLANDS

Northland quickly slides into a series of hypnotically quiet small communities.

The main draw up here is **90 Mile Beach,** which is actually about 60 mi long, a clear stretch of golden sand running up to the tip of the North Island. To visit the beach you should take a tour. Don't roll your eyes—a tour is not only convenient, but the safest bet, as driving on the beach is very risky. What with the quicksand, the incoming tides, and the fact that rental-car-insurance policies won't cover you here, the beach is virtually off-limits for independent drivers.

Cape Reinga, at the end of the peninsula, is a sacred Māori area. They believe that their spirits depart for the underworld by sliding down the roots of the gnarled pohutukawa tree on the headland (reputed to be 800 years old) and into the sea below. A much-photographed solitary lighthouse stands here.

You can easily drive into the Far North, barring 90 Mile Beach. From the Bay of Islands on State Highway 10 you'll reach Mangonui, a charming former whaling port on the southeast side of **Doubtless Bay.** Beach lovers should head for the beautiful sands along the Karikari Peninsula, a finger of land that forms Doubtless Bay's northwestern side. From Doubtless Bay it's less than a half-hour's drive west to Awanui, near the service town of Kaitaia. Be sure to fill up your gas tank in one of these two towns, then head north along Highway 1. The last few miles of the road to Cape Reinga aren't paved, but if you drive carefully, you should be able to get through it relatively easily.

WHAT TO DO

The half-moon Matai Bay is good for diving novices: it's very safe and goes to a maximum depth of 13 meters (43 feet). More experienced divers should try the Matai Bay Pinnacle site, which descends to 39 meters (130 feet). The water's clear and the odds are good you'll see blue maomao, demoiselles, and kingfish. **A to Z Diving** (✉ Whatuwhiwhi, Karikari Peninsula ☎🖷 09/408-7077 ⊕ www. atozdiving.co.nz) takes guided dives, starting at around $85 or $135 with full gear included.

Dune-Rider 4x4 Tours (✉ Maritime Bldg., Marsden Rd., Paihia ☎ 09/ 402-8681 ⊕ www.dunerider.co.nz) goes to Cape Reinga via the vast strip of 90 Mile Beach. The company makes a few special stops, such as a visit to the "world-famous" Mangonui fish-and-chips shop. Trips cost $95.

You couldn't wish for a better guide than Phil Cross of **Far North Outback Adventures** (🖂 Box 668, Kaitaia ☎ 09/408-0927 ⊕ www. farnorthtours.co.nz) for a day trip up 90 Mile Beach to Cape Reinga. Phil takes small groups (up to five people) in his 4x4 vehicle. He knows an impressive amount of pre- and early European history and gives an excellent commentary. He also supplies toboggans for dune sledding and visits Māori archaeological sites. And he's the only operator who can take a vehicle to Great Exhibition Bay. It costs $120 per person, with a minimum of $350 per trip, but it's worth it.

WHERE TO STAY & EAT

✕ **Waterfront Café** ($$$). This relaxed harbor café is a local favorite for its seafood chowder made with fresh

CLOSE UP

The Far North

local fish and oysters. Regulars also rely on the great pizzas served day and night—try the meat-lover's pie served with Kaitaia Fire, Northland's answer to Tabasco sauce. ✉ Beach Rd., Mangonui ☎ 09/406-0850 ⊟ AE, MC, V.

✕⛱ **Carrington Club ($$$$).** Carrington overlooks a sweeping white-sand beach. The spacious rooms in the lodge open onto a wraparound veranda with views of the bay and the resort's par-72 tournament-quality golf course. Chef Mark Oliver puts European and Asian spins on regional produce; chefs from around the world do guest spots. The resort even has its own vineyard, Karikari Estate. ✉ Matai Bay Rd., Karikari Peninsula ☎ 09/408-7222 🖷 09/408-7414 ⊕ www.carrington. co.nz ⤳ 10 rooms, 14 villas ⌂ Restaurant, cable TV, in-room broadband, golf, tennis court, pool, gym, hot tub, beach, fishing, horseback riding, bar, library, Internet room ⊟ AE, DC, MC, V ⫫ BP, MAP.

⛱ **Cavalli Beach House Retreat ($$$$).** Curving down a cliff face like a spinnaker in full sail, this secluded retreat overlooks a private horseshoe-shape bay. Guest rooms are decorated with tapa cloths and local artworks; the king-size beds are made up with cream linen and faux fur throws. A landscaped path leads up the hill behind the house to a hot tub with a private lookout. Dinners are available on request. ✉ Mahinepua Rd., Mahinepua ☎ 09/405-1049 🖷 09/405-1043 ⊕ www.cavallibeachhouse. com ⤳ 1 suite, 2 rooms ⌂ Cable TV, in-room DVD, hot tub, fishing, helipad ⊟ AE, MC, V ⫫ BP.

⛱ **Kauri Cliffs ($$$$).** Several holes of a manicured par-72 championship

golf course sweep past this cliff-top plantation-style lodge. The ocean views stretch out to the Cavalli Islands; you also overlook the lodge's three private beaches—one shimmering pink. The guest rooms' muted blue-and-cream color scheme lets the vistas dominate. ✉ Matauri Bay Rd., Matauri Bay ☎ 09/407-0010 🖷 09/407-0061 ⊕ www.kauricliffs. com ⤳ 22 suites ⌂ Dining room, minibars, cable TV, in-room DVD, golf, tennis court, pool, gym, hot tub, spa, beach, fishing, Internet room; helipad; no a/c ⊟ AE, DC, MC, V ⫫ MAP.

⛱ **Shipwreck Lodge ($$$–$$$$).** Owners Roger and Laura Raduenz are Americans who sailed into New Zealand in the late 1990s, the first stop on a round-the-world voyage. They never left. From the balconies of their contemporary seafront lodge you can look up the sweep of 90 Mile Beach. Dinners are available on request. ✉ 70 Foreshore Rd., Ahipara ☎ 09/409-4929 🖷 09/409-4928 ⊕ www.shipwrecklodge.co.nz ⤳ 3 rooms ⌂ Cable TV, in-room data ports, lounge, laundry facilities; no kids under 16, no smoking ⊟ MC, V ⫫ BP.

⛱ **Mangonui Hotel (¢–$).** This classic wooden two-story pub with front verandas sits just a few feet from Mangonui's harbor. The upstairs guest rooms are smallish but well fitted out in keeping with the style of the early-1900s hotel. The restaurant serves breakfast and Mediterranean-style dinners. ✉ Beach Rd., Mangonui ☎ 09/406-0003 🖷 09/406-0015 ⤳ 14 rooms ⌂ Restaurant, cable TV, 2 bars ⊟ AE, MC, V.

the Historic Places Trust. The restored home has one modern wing, but it's sensitively designed to blend with the original building. Two airy rooms with wooden floors and private baths are in the new wing; one has a chaise longue and balconies looking over the gardens. The rooms in the older wing are smaller but elegantly furnished with antiques. They share a bath, as does another petite room—Jack's Room, named for the hosts' grandson—which has a single bed and is geared for children. Dinner and picnic lunches are available on request. Paheke is about 15 minutes' drive southwest of Kerikieri. ⌧ *State Hwy. 1, Ohaeawai* ☎ *09/ 405–9623* 🖷 *09/405–9628* ⊕ *www.paheke.co.nz* ⇶ *5 rooms, 2 with bath* ⚿ *BBQ, cable TV, croquet, lounge, library, laundry facilities, Internet room* ▤ *MC, V* ⫪⚭ *BP.*

Sports & the Outdoors

FISHING John Gregory of **Primetime Charters & Gamefishing** (⌧ Conifer La., Kerik-eri ☎🖷 09/407–1299 ⊕ www.primetimecharters.co.nz) has more than 25 years' experience at sea. The company, which holds the New Zealand record for most marlin caught, goes after all sport fish, specializing in broadbill swordfish. Prices start at $3,350 per day, with most trips between February and June taking five to seven days.

GOLF The spectacular par-72 championship course at **Kauri Cliffs** (⌧ Matauri Bay Rd., Matauri Bay ☎ 09/407–0010 ⊕ www.kauricliffs.com) was de-signed and built by David Harman. It has four sets of tees to challenge every skill level. Fifteen holes have views of the Pacific, and six are played alongside the cliffs. The inland holes wind through marsh, forest, and farmland. Callaway clubs are available to rent from the pro shop ($75). Greens fees are $400 per person. Kauri Cliffs is approximately 45 minutes' drive from Kerikeri.

Shopping

While you're watching the goodies being made at **Makana Confections** (⌧ Kerikeri Rd. ☎ 09/407–6800), you might be interrupted by an offer of a tempting taste of something fresh from the kitchen. It's nigh impossible to leave without a bagful of, say, chocolate-coated, locally grown macadamias or liqueur truffles.

For locally made arts and crafts, stop at the **Origin Art and Craft Co-op** (⌧ State Hwy. 10 ☎ 09/407–1133), 450 yards south of the Kerik-eri turnoff. The shop stocks plenty of great gift options, such as place mats made from local timber such as rimu, kauri, and *matai;* stained-glass lamp shades and trinket boxes; and beautifully made calf- and doeskin bags.

Andrew and Robyn Leary of **Scopes NZ** (⌧ 265 Waipapa Rd. ☎ 09/407–4415) produce kaleidoscopes out of kauri wood that was buried in swamps for thousands of years. They also make "bubble scopes" (their own inventions), which view colored liquid in a transparent ball. Prices start at around $100 for small kauri scopes produced with materials such as *paua* (abalone shell), shards of glass, or bits of fishing tackle.

NORTHLAND & THE BAY OF ISLANDS ESSENTIALS

Transportation

BY BUS

InterCity, Newmans, and Northliner Express buses run several times daily between Auckland and the Bay of Islands and connect to the other Northland centers at least once a day. As long as you're not too pressed for time, bus travel is an easy way to get around the north—buses serve most towns. There are at least four daily buses between Paihia and Kerikeri, for instance, and at least one daily bus even to whistle-stop towns such as Dargaville. The trip from Auckland to Paihia takes about 4½ hours and costs $45. The Auckland–Kerikeri trip takes about 5½ hours ($50).

🚏 Bus Depots **Paihia** ✉ Paihia Travel Centre, Maritime Bldg. ☎ 09/402-7857. **Whangarei** ✉ Northland Coach and Travel Bldg., 11 Rose St. ☎ 09/438-2653.
🚏 Bus Lines **InterCity** ☎ 09/358-4085 ⊕ www.intercitycoach.co.nz. **Newmans** ☎ 09/913-6200 ⊕ www.newmanscoach.co.nz. **Northliner Express** ☎ 09/307-5873 ⊕ www.northliner.co.nz.

BY CAR

Taking your own car is the most convenient way to explore most of Northland. The main route from Auckland is State Highway 1. Leave the city by the Harbour Bridge and follow signs to Whangarei. Driving time for the 250-km (150-mi) journey to Paihia is about 3½ hours. Highway 12, which goes up the west coast, is longer and more winding than Highway 1, but it's more scenic.

Between Russell and Paihia, take the car ferry instead of bothering with the long, twisty road between the two towns. If you're on the east coast and would like to head to the west coast without going all the way to the Far North, take Highway 12 across the peninsula from Kawakawa, just south of Paihia. If you do drive up to Cape Reinga, don't take your car onto 90 Mile Beach—you can be caught by the tides or quicksands (*see the* Far North CloseUp box).

Northland roads are generally just two lanes wide; you may need to be patient to find a place to pass. Traffic cops police the roads fairly thoroughly, and drivers coming toward you may flash their lights to indicate that one is hiding ahead.

BY FERRY

You can drive all the way between Russell and Paihia, but the road is long and winding—hard driving, and thus not recommended. The quickest and most convenient route is by ferry. Three passenger boats make the crossing between Paihia and Russell, with departures at least once every 30 minutes in each direction from 7:20 AM to 10:30 PM from Paihia, and 7 AM to 10 PM from Russell. The one-way fare is $5. It's also easy to take the short drive to Opua, about 5 km (3 mi) south of Paihia, to join the car ferry. This ferry operates from 6:40 AM to 10 PM, with departures at approximately 10-minute intervals from either shore.

The last boat leaves from Okiato on the Russell side at 9:50 PM. The one-way fare is $9 for car and driver plus $1 for each adult passenger. Buy your tickets on board (cash only).

🚩 **Fullers** ☎ 09/402-7421 ⊕ www.fullers-bay-of-islands.co.nz.

Contacts & Resources

EMERGENCIES

There are no late-night pharmacies in the Northland towns; the main medical center is in Whangarei.

🚩 Emergency Services **Fire, police, and ambulance** ☎ 111.

🚩 Hospital **Whangarei Hospital** ⊠ Maunu Rd., Whangarei ☎ 09/430-4100.

MAIL & INTERNET

🚩 Internet Cafés **Bootsoff** ⊠ 13 Selwyn Rd., Paihia ☎ 09/402-8262. **Hackers** ⊠ 84 Commerce St., Kaitaia ☎ 09/408-4999. **Surf in the City** ⊠ 25 Bank St., Whangarei ☎ 09/430-3540.

🚩 Post Offices **Kaitaia Post Shop** ⊠ 104 Commerce St., Kaitaia ☎ 09/408-6411. **Kerikeri Books and More** ⊠ 6 Hobson Ave., Kerikeri ☎ 09/407-9721. **Mangonui Post Shop** ⊠ Beach Rd. Mangonui ☎ 09/406-0007. **Paihia Post Shop** ⊠ 2 Williams Rd., Paihia ☎ 09/402-7800. **Whangarei Central Post Shop** ⊠ 16-20 Rathbone St., Whangarei ☎ 09/430-2761.

TOURS

SIGHTSEEING TOURS Great Sights, based out of Auckland, leads one-, two-, and three-day trips to the Bay of Islands. The one-day tour stops at Warkworth for morning tea and goes on to visit the Waitangi Treaty House and to cruise out to the Hole in the Rock. You can opt for a tour of historic Russell instead of the cruise. Taking the two-day tour allows you both to cruise and visit Russell, and the three-day itinerary adds a trip along 90 Mile Beach to Cape Reinga, where the Tasman Sea and Pacific Ocean meet. Rates start at $219 for the one-day trip.

ECOTOURS Fernz EcoTours takes tours in and around Russell. Most popular is the Coast and Kauri tour, which starts with a short excursion around the historic sights of Russell, then a trip to the Orongo Bay oyster farm, followed by a visit to Ngaiotonga Forest for a walk among the kauri. A half-day tour is $110, or you can add a trip to the glowworm caves and the Hundertwasser Public Toilets ($195).

🚩 **Fernz EcoTours** ⊠ Kingfisher Rd., Jack's Bary, Russell ☎ 09/403-7887 or 027/280-9600 ⊕ www.fernzecotours.co.nz. **Great Sights** ⊠ Discover New Zealand Centre, 180 Quay St., Auckland ☎ 09/375-4700 ⊕ www.greatsights.co.nz.

VISITOR INFORMATION

🚩 Tourist Information **Bay of Islands Visitor Information Centre Paihia** ⊠ Marsden Rd., Paihia ☎ 09/402-7345 ⊕ www.bay-of-islands.co.nz. **Kaitaia Visitor Information Centre** ⊠ Jaycee Park, South Rd., Kaitaia ☎ 09/408-0879 🖷 09/408-2546. **Russell Information Centre** ⊠ Russell Wharf, Russell ☎ 09/403-8020. **Warkworth Visitor Information Centre** ⊠ 1 Baxter St., Warkworth ☎ 09/425-9081 🖷 09/425-7584 ⊕ www.warkworth-information.co.nz. **Whangarei Visitor Information Centre** ⊠ 92 Otaika Rd., Whangarei ☎ 09/438-1079 🖷 09/438-2943.

Coromandel Peninsula & the Bay of Plenty

WORD OF MOUTH

"Postcard-worthy beaches and lush native forest aside, these regions' impressive geothermal activity is not to be overlooked . . .[T]he underground hot water springs on the coast south of Hahei lie close to the surface of the sand so that you can dig your own hot tub at low tide. With so many beaches and hiking trails around here, not to mention the little-known attractions recommended by the locals, having your own transport is really the best way to take advantage of these areas."

—Alia Levine

Updated by
Alia Levine

ABOUT THREE HOURS SOUTHEAST OF AUCKLAND is the rugged and exhilarating Coromandel Peninsula, with mountains stretching the length of its middle and a pohutukawa-tree-lined Pacific coastline rimmed with islands. Farther south, the coastal highway takes you to some of the great open space that defines New Zealand, the Bay of Plenty, which—if you love seafood—truly lives up to its name.

Postcard-worthy beaches, lush native forests, and steamy geothermal activity make both the Coromandel Peninsula and Bay of Plenty tempting contrasts to concrete-bound Auckland. Most residents here live in fishing villages or small rural towns, with the occasional artsy community or alternative-lifestyle commune thrown in (particularly in the Coromandel). Both areas bask in more than their fair share of sun for much of the year, so avocado, citrus, kiwifruit, nuts, and even subtropical fruits flourish here. Keep an eye out for the ubiquitous unmanned fruit stands and accompanying "honesty boxes"; drop your money in the box and help yourself as you explore this fertile area.

These regions are well loved for their beaches; prepare for a population explosion in peak season (October–February). Although the climate is temperate from March through September, and most hotels and tourist operations function year-round, people flock to the area in summer and the otherwise sleepy seaside towns get a major wake-up call. Fortunately, there are enough obscure coves and sandy stretches to accommodate the masses, and it's not too difficult to stake out your own turf.

The Coromandel coastline alternates between steep rocky cliffs studded with tenaciously clinging pohutukawa trees and white sandy coves and inlets. The coastal road borders a craggy spine of volcanic peaks that rises sharply to a height of almost 3,000 feet. From the peninsula's east coast, the road stretches out to the coastal plains and forests of the Bay of Plenty. From the Bay of Plenty's northern gateway of Katikati as far as Whakatane, the coastline consists of huge stretches of sand, interrupted by rivers, estuaries, and sandbars. Inland, the soil is rich and fertile; this is farming territory. You'll also see sprawling canopies of kiwifruit vines and pockets of dense native forest.

The Bay of Plenty is also one of the country's first areas to be settled by Māori, and the descendants of these earliest arrivals moved north to the Coromandel Peninsula as well. Although intertribal fighting and European-introduced diseases took a heavy toll on the Coromandel communities, the Bay of Plenty still has a strong Māori presence, particularly around Mount Maunganui.

Exploring Coromandel Peninsula & the Bay of Plenty

If you have only a few days to spend in this neck of the woods, choose to visit either the Coromandel or the Bay of Plenty—otherwise, you'll spend much of your time in transit. With at least five days, though, you can start at one end of the region (in either Thames or Whakatane) and work your way comfortably along the coast.

Although buses connect many of the towns and villages, the best way to explore the region is by car. Most roads are well maintained and clearly

GREAT ITINERARIES

IF YOU HAVE 3 DAYS

With just a few days, make the most of your trip to this part of the North Island by choosing to visit either the Coromandel Peninsula or the Bay of Plenty. Although these areas aren't far apart, the twisty roads (and many worthwhile attractions en route) mean that exploring here takes time.

The Coromandel Peninsula is an easy two-hour drive south and east of Auckland. Start in the historic town of **Thames** ❶ with a short self-guided tour of the museums and old buildings. After a bite to eat, head for the peninsula's east coast. Drive over the unpaved **Tapu–Coroglen Road** and spend the night in **Hahei** or **Whitianga** ❹.

Spend your second day on the water; you could dig yourself an open-air hot tub at **Hot Water Beach** ❺ or you could kayak, fish, or swim with the dolphins. In the late afternoon, return to the peninsula's west side; if you're up to it, bump along over the scenic (but unpaved) **309 Road,** pausing for a dip at Waiau Falls. Overnight in **Coromandel** ❷, a good base for exploring the upper peninsula. In the morning, take the hour-long trip on the Driving Creek Railway through the native forest and sculpture gardens to the summit lookout. Spend the afternoon browsing in Coromandel's art shops.

If you're visiting the Bay of Plenty, spend your first day enjoying the beach at **Mount Maunganui** and climbing the namesake mountain. Take an evening soak in the hot saltwater pools at the base of the Mount before spending the night here or in nearby **Tauranga** ❾. The next day, meander down the coast to **Ohope** for a late lunch of local seafood on the beach. Check in for the night in **Whakatane** ❿. The next morning, take a boat trip to White Island, New Zealand's only active marine volcano. If you're returning to Auckland, stop off in **Katikati** ❽ to see the town's distinctive murals.

IF YOU HAVE 5 OR MORE DAYS

With at least five days, you can explore both the Coromandel Peninsula and the Bay of Plenty. Historic **Thames** ❶ is a logical first stop; then wind your way up the Firth of Thames coast to the town of **Coromandel** ❷ and beyond, to explore the upper peninsula. Turning to the east coast, you'll find some of the best Coromandel beaches—**Hot Water Beach** ❺, with a combination of thermal activity and surf, and the beautiful **Cathedral Cove.** You can overnight in nearby **Hahei.** To the south are the popular surf beaches of **Whangamata** ❼ and Waihi.

From there, you can continue south toward the Bay of Plenty, stopping in **Katikati** ❽ for some wine tasting at local vineyards. **Mount Maunganui** and **Tauranga** ❾—both good bases for exploring the mount and surrounding beaches—are a short drive farther south. En route to **Whakatane** ❿, there are plenty of beaches to explore. Leave time for a dolphin- or whale-watch trip and for an excursion to White Island.

3

signposted, and a car gives you the freedom to explore hot pools and waterfalls tucked down obscure side roads. The Pacific Coast Highway is also popular with cyclists, particularly during the summer.

About the Restaurants

Dining options in the Coromandel and Bay of Plenty run the gamut from roadside seafood shacks and take-out fish-and-chips joints, to cafés offering muffins, sandwiches, and city-strength lattés, right through to white-linen affairs—although even when restaurants are formal in appearance, both diners and hosts tend toward country-style casualness. Restaurant owners take pride in the region's abundant resources: the fish on your plate may have been caught that morning from a nearby bay, and shellfish will likely come from local mussel and oyster farms. Paintings by local artists often adorn restaurant walls, and your hosts are likely to sit down and have a yarn with you if you express interest in the area.

Dinner service begins about 6:30 PM in the winter and around 7 PM during the summer months. In peak season most places keep serving until around 9 PM, but otherwise, kitchens generally close before 8 PM. Year-round, though, you'll find a relaxed pace once you've been seated—people here don't rush their meals. Make reservations whenever possible, particularly in the Coromandel; during the summer, restaurants can be packed, and in winter, reservations are essential to let the staff know they should stay open. During the quiet May to September months, many restaurants close early if they think no one is likely to stop by.

WHAT IT COSTS In New Zealand dollars				
$$$$	**$$$**	**$$**	**$**	**¢**
RESTAURANTS over $30	$20–$30	$15–$20	$10–$15	under $10

Prices are per person for a main course at dinner, or the equivalent.

About the Hotels

As you might expect in such mellow towns, you'll find plenty of comfortable bed-and-breakfasts and mom-and-pop motels, but both the Coromandel and the Bay of Plenty also have a sprinkling of luxe boutique lodges tucked away in the forest or along coastal coves. In peak season, from October through February, advance booking is essential across the board. You'll rarely find air-conditioning in lodgings here, but you'll rarely need it either.

WHAT IT COSTS In New Zealand dollars				
$$$$	**$$$**	**$$**	**$**	**¢**
HOTELS over $300	$200–$300	$125–$200	$75–$125	under $75

Prices are for a standard double room in high season, including 12.5% tax.

When to Visit

Summer's the most popular time to travel here, when the weather is mild enough to swim in the ocean, take a late-night stroll along the beach, and otherwise enjoy the outdoors. The peak season runs from October

TOP REASONS TO GO

BOUNTIFUL BEACHES

The eastern shores of the Coromandel and Bay of Plenty are major draws for beach-seeking North Islanders. The coastline has so many inlets and coves that it rarely feels overrun, even during the high season—so slather on the sunscreen, swim between the safety flags, and break out the hokey pokey (honeyed-toffee) ice cream.

VOLCANOES & VISTAS

From the mountainous spine and coastal cliffs of the Coromandel Peninsula to the Bay of Plenty's extinct volcano Mt. Maunganui, this region offers hypnotic views at every turn. The peak of the Pinnacles in Kauaeranga Valley Forest Park is surrounded by sweeping vistas; at White Island, the country's only live marine volcano, the steaming fissures are a dramatic sight by sea, air . . . or from the deck of a local café.

WALKING & HIKING

There is superb bushwalking (hiking) around the Coromandel Peninsula. Inland from Tauranga are stream-side forest walks to McLaren and Kaiate Falls, and the Coromandel bush is full of ancient kauri trees (a local species of pine) and interesting birds, such as *tūī* (*too*-ee), fantails, and wood pigeons.

WATERY WONDERS

Whether you're in the mood for a day of deep-sea fishing or kayaking, a spot of snorkeling, or a swim with the dolphins, this region delivers. White Island provides some of the richest snorkeling and diving in the region. Surfers come from all over the country to ride the waves at Mount Maunganui, and the underground hot springs at Hot Water Beach are a one-of-a-kind attraction.

to April, with a massive tourist surge during the week between Christmas and the New Year. Don't overlook the off-season, though; the weather's usually sunny, prices are lower, and locals have more time to chat during the quieter months. Businesspeople tend to let the weather dictate their peak season, rather than any hard-and-fast dates.

THE COROMANDEL PENINSULA

New Zealand has countless pockets of beauty that are not included in standard itineraries. One of the most accessible is the Coromandel Peninsula, which juts out like a hitchhiker's thumb east of Auckland. As with so many other lands "discovered" by Europeans, the peninsula was looted for its valuable resources: kauri trees, then kauri gum, and finally gold in the 1870s. Relative quiet since the 1930s has allowed the region to recover, and, without question, natural beauty abounds.

In the 1960s and '70s, dairy farms and orchards sprang up, as did communes, spiritual retreats, and artists' communities. There is still a strong "alternative" presence (responsible, in part, for the prevalence of organic

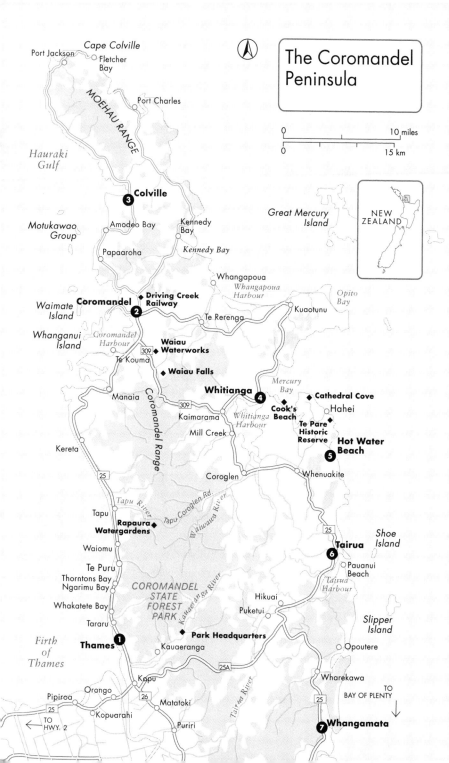

The Coromandel Peninsula

NEW ZEALAND

Cape Colville
Port Jackson
Fletcher Bay
MOEHAU RANGE
Port Charles
Hauraki Gulf
❸ Colville
Motukawao Group
Amodeo Bay
Kennedy Bay
Papaaroha
Kennedy Bay
Whangapoua
Whangapoua Harbour
Opito Bay
Waimate Island
Coromandel ❷
Driving Creek Railway
Te Rerenga
Kuaotunu
Great Mercury Island
Whanganui Island
Coromandel Harbour
309
Waiau Waterworks
Te Kouma
Waiau Falls
Whitianga ❹
Mercury Bay
Cathedral Cove
Hahei
Manaia
309
Cook's Beach
Te Pare Historic Reserve
Kaimarama
Whitianga Harbour
Coromandel Range
Mill Creek
Hot Water Beach ❺
Kereta
Coroglen
Whenuakite
25
Tapu River
Tapu
Tapu Coroglen Rd.
Waiwawa River
25
Tairua ❻
Shoe Island
Rapaura Watergardens
Waiomu
Pauanui Beach
Te Puru
Tairua Harbour
Thorntons Bay
Ngarimu Bay
COROMANDEL STATE FOREST PARK
Hikuai
Slipper Island
Whakatete Bay
Kauaeranga River
Puketui
Tararu
Firth of Thames
Thames ❶
Park Headquarters
Kauaeranga
Opoutere
Kopu
25A
Pipiroa
Orongo
26
Matatoki
Tairua River
Wharekawa
TO BAY OF PLENTY
25
TO HWY. 2
Kopuarahi
Puriri
Whangamata ❼

0   10 miles
0   15 km

food on area menus), but the population increasingly includes Auck-landers looking for a weekend or retirement home.

A craggy spine of volcanic peaks that rises sharply to a height of almost 3,000 feet dominates the center of the peninsula. The west coast cradles the Firth of Thames, and along the east coast the Pacific has carved out a succession of beaches and inlets separated by rearing headlands. Because of its rich volcanic soil, the peninsula has many spectacular gardens, several of which are open to the public. From the town of Thames, the gateway to the region, State Highway 25 and the 309 Road circle the lower two-thirds of the peninsula—an exhilarating drive with the sea on one side and great forested peaks on the other. Especially considering the Coromandel's proximity to Auckland, it would be difficult to find a finer introduction to the wonders of New Zealand.

Thames

❶ *120 km (75 mi) southeast of Auckland.*

The peninsula's oldest town, Thames has evolved from a gold-mining hotbed in the 1920s to a center for local agriculture. Locals have a saying that when the gold ran out, "Thames went to sleep awaiting the kiss of a golden prince—and instead it awoke to the warm breath of a cow." The main street used to be lined with nearly 100 hotels (bars); gold mining and logging was thirsty work. Only five of these hotels still operate, but the town and environs still offer glimpses of the mining era. Thames today is also the gateway to the Kauaeranga Valley Forest Park, home to waterfalls, ancient kauri groves, and the Pinnacles, the peninsula's highest accessible point.

At the **Historical Museum,** you can look into earlier ways of life in the town. The museum contains photographic displays of the gold-rush and logging industries, re-creations of period rooms from the 1800s, and info on the original Māori inhabitants and early European settlers. The garden, with period roses and other flora that settlers commonly planted, is a particularly nice place to take a break. ⊠ *Pollen and Cochrane Sts.* ☎ *07/868–8509* 🖃 *$4* ⊙ *Daily 1–4.*

The **Thames School of Mines Mineralogical Museum** gives a geologic take on the area's history. The School of Mines provided practical instruction to the gold miners of the mid-1880s; the museum was established in 1900 to exhibit geological samples. The school closed decades ago, but the museum's still kicking, displaying those turn-of-the-20th-century rock specimens along with scales, models of stamper batteries, and other gold-mining paraphernalia. ⊠ *Brown and Cochrane Sts.* ☎ *07/ 868–6227* 🖃 *$4* ⊙ *Wed.–Sun. 11–3.*

If you want to learn more about early gold-mining efforts in the Coromandel, stop in at the **Goldmine Experience,** north on the way out of town, and take a brief underground tour of the old Golden Crown Claim, which was first worked in 1868. Five hundred feet below this site, the Caledonia strike was one of the richest in the world. Guides describe the mine's geological and historical interest. ⊠ *State Hwy. 25, north of Waiotahi*

Creek Rd. ☎ *07/862–6733* ⊕ *www.goldmine-experience.co.nz* ✉ *$10* ⊙ *Call to book a tour.*

To soak up a bit of gold-mining atmosphere, head to the 1868 **Brian Boru Hotel.** Stop for a cold drink and check out the mining paraphernalia and historic photographs on the walls of the bar, reception, and dining area. ⊠ *200 Richmond St.* ☎ *07/868–6523.*

St. George's Anglican Church is worth a quick look for its gorgeous kauri-wood interior. ⊠ *Willoughby and MacKay Sts.* ☎ *07/868–6123* ⊙ *Tues–Fri. 9 AM–2 PM.*

Meonstoke is probably New Zealand's most unusual garden. Since 1954, Pam Gwynne has been working every square inch of her ¼-acre lot. Numerous paths wind through a junglelike space; there are no lookouts or vistas to distract you from the lush surroundings. Pam collects found objects and ingeniously incorporates them into surreal and often humorous tableaux with the plantings. On one path, a row of ceramic pitchers is suspended from a rod, and elsewhere, tiny winking porcelain Asian figures festoon bonsai plants. Although the garden is small, allow yourself plenty of time to peer at the details. The small entry fee goes to local charities. ⊠ *305 Kuranui St.* ☎ *07/868–6560 or 07/868–6850* ⊙ *1st 2 weekends in Oct. 10 AM–4 PM, otherwise by appointment only* ✉ *$4.*

☺ The **Tropical Butterfly Garden** is a few minutes' drive north on the way out of Thames, but it's easy to miss unless you're specifically looking for the signs. Owners Roger and Sabine Gass have brought some color to the Coromandel with a flock of butterflies from Australia. Now, up to 20 species and 400 butterflies from all over the world may be on view at any time, including large birdwing butterflies. Exotic birds such as finches, doves, and quails join the butterflies, plus about 100 different plant species. The heliconia and orchids are particularly stunning. Special butterfly and plant exhibits change throughout the year. ⊠ *Dickson Holiday Park, Victoria St.* ☎ *07/868–8080* ⊕ *www.butterfly.co.nz* ✉ *$9* ⊙ *Late Aug.–mid-July, daily 10–4.*

Where to Stay & Eat

★ ¢–$$ ✕ **Sola Café.** Sola isn't your everyday vegetarian health bar; the kitchen is one of the best in town. The counter displays risotto cakes; florentines; and apple, pear, apricot, and fig shortbread. On the dinner menu you might find *strozzapriti* (spinach and Parmesan dumplings) or polenta with smoked field mushrooms and roasted garlic cream. It's also the hippest place in Thames for coffee. ⊠ *720b Pollen St.* ☎ *07/868–8781* ▭ *AE, DC, MC, V* ⊙ *No dinner Sun.–Wed. in summer; no dinner Sat.–Thurs. Feb.–Nov.* ⌕ *BYOB.*

¢ ✕ **Pipiroa Country Kitchen.** Sweet treats have made this café's reputation for the last 15 years. You'll be tempted by brownies and lemon cookies, but best of all is the raspberry tart with a dollop of yogurt. For lunch, try one of the burgers—the most spectacular is the Mountain, topped with cheese, onion, egg, ham, tomato, apricot, and lettuce. Add to all this a sauce of your choice: peanut, plum, spicy tomato, or just plain ketchup. ⊠ *1492 State Hwy. 25, Pipiroa, 15 km (9 mi) southwest of Thames* ☎ *07/867–7599* ▭ *MC, V* ⊙ *No dinner Mon.–Thurs. and Sat.*

$–$$ 🏨 **Tuscany on Thames.** The first owners of this restaurant fell in love with Tuscany on a visit to Italy and decided to bring a bit of its style back to their motel. The details—flowers in the rooms, custom-made pottery cups—haven't changed since, and make this stand out from other area lodgings. For extra space, ask for Room 1, a two-bedroom suite with access to a small courtyard. Two rooms have showers only. ✉ *Jellicoe Crescent at Bank St.* ☎ *07/868–5099* 📠 *07/868–5080* ⊕ *www. tuscanyonthames.co.nz* 🛏 *14 rooms* ⚐ *In-room data ports, pool; no a/c* ⊟ *AE, DC, MC, V.*

$ 🏨 **Brookby Motel.** In this low row of units backed by a tree-lined stream, the off-white brick rooms are small but clean, with wooden balconies overlooking the stream. The best deal is the studio that's attached to the office/owners' home, a turn-of-the-20th-century pioneer cottage. This studio has wooden floors and furnishings, as well as stained-glass windows, but it costs no more than the standard rooms. ✉ *102 Redwood La.* ☎ *07/868–6663* 📠 *07/868–6663* 🛏 *4 rooms, 2 studios* ⚐ *Picnic area, kitchenettes, microwaves, refrigerators, cable TV, in-room data ports, no-smoking rooms; no a/c* ⊟ *AE, DC, MC, V.*

$ 🏨 **Brunton House.** Built by a local draper in the 1870s and later owned by three Thames mayors, this two-story colonial villa is built entirely from kauri wood. All but one bedroom open out onto the upstairs wraparound veranda, and although there are only two bathrooms to share between four bedrooms, the clawfoot bathtub makes up for it. Breakfast, which is included in the price, is a true Kiwi fry-up of bacon, eggs, sausages, and hash browns; if you have other requirements, let your hosts know the night before. ✉ *210 Parawai Rd.* ☎ *07/868–5160* 📠 *07/868–5160* ⊕ *www.bruntonhouse.co.nz* 🛏 *4 rooms with shared bath* ⚐ *Tennis court, pool, hot tub; no a/c, no room phones, no room TVs* ⊟ *AE, DC, MC, V* 🍴 *BP.*

Sports & the Outdoors

★ **Kauaeranga Valley Forest Park** has 22 walking trails that offer anything from a 30-minute stroll to a three-day trek, overnighting in huts equipped with bunks. The most accessible starting point is the delightful Kauaeranga Valley Road, where the **Department of Conservation Visitors Center** (☎ 07/867–9080 ⊕ www.doc.govt.nz) provides maps and information.

The hike to the Pinnacles is the most popular walk on the peninsula; the trek from the trailhead to the Pinnacles hut takes three hours one-way. From the hut you can continue to the peak itself (another hour one-way) for a view that spans both coasts. An overnight in the Pinnacles hut costs $15; you'll need to reserve through the DOC center. You can hike back via the three-hour-long Webb Creek trail or come down the longer (four-hour) alternative route, the Billy Goat track.

Keep in mind that the park can be very busy from late December to mid-January. If you're traveling then, plan to visit the park midweek. To reach the Kauaeranga Valley, head south from Thames and on the outskirts of the town turn left on Banks Street, then right on Parawai Road, which becomes Kauaeranga Valley Road.

┌──────────
│ **EN**
│ **ROUTE**

The Coromandel Ranges drop right down to the seafront **State Highway 25** as it winds up the west coast of the peninsula. When you top the hills north of Kereta on the way to Coromandel, mountains, pastures, and islands in the Firth of Thames open out before you—stunning.

Tapu–Coroglen Road

25 km (16 mi) north of Thames.

The unpaved Tapu–Coroglen Road turns off State Highway 25 in the hamlet of Tapu to wind into the mountains. It's a breathtaking route where massive tree ferns grow out of the roadside hills. About 6½ km (4 mi) from Tapu you come to the magical Rapaura Watergardens. Travel another 3½ km (2 mi) along the road and pull over to climb the 178 steps up to the huge, 1,200-year-old **Square Kauri,** so named for the shape that a cross section of its trunk would have. At 133 feet tall and 30 feet around, this is only the 15th-largest kauri in New Zealand. From a tree-side platform there is a splendid view across the valley to Mau Mau Paki, one of the peaks along the Coromandel Ranges. Continuing east across the peninsula, the road passes through forests and sheep paddocks—a shimmeringly beautiful ride in sun or mist.

Rapaura Watergardens, full of native and exotic flowering species, has been sculpted from the wilderness in a 65-acre sheltered valley in the Coromandel Ranges. Rapaura (running water) is a wonderful example of water's use in New Zealand gardens. In the garden's various streams, waterfalls, fountains, and 14 ponds, fish and ducks swim among colorful water lilies and other bog plants while songbirds lilt overhead. Paths wind through collections of grasses, flaxes, gunneras, rhododendrons, and camellias—all organically gardened. (The camellias and rhododendrons usually flower between late June and October.) Giant tree ferns and rimu, *rata* (related to the pohutukawa, it too has bright red flowers), and kauri trees form a lush canopy overhead. The combination of delicacy and rugged grandeur may have been what inspired the philosophic messages that you'll find painted on signs around the garden, such as KEEP YOUR VALUES IN BALANCE AND YOU WILL ALWAYS FIND HAPPINESS. There is a café on the property, and there's also a wood cottage and a two-story lodge for those who wish to stay longer to explore the walks and waterfalls ($145 and $250 per night, respectively, which includes breakfast). ✉ *Tapu–Coroglen Rd., 6 km (4 mi) east of Tapu* ☎ *07/868–4821* ⊕ *www.rapaurawatergardens.co.nz* 💰 *$10* ⊙ *Daily 9–5.*

Coromandel

❷ *60 km (38 mi) north of Thames, 29 km (18 mi) northwest of Whitianga.*

Coromandel became the site of New Zealand's first gold strike in 1852 when sawmill worker Charles Ring found gold-bearing quartz at Driving Creek, just north of town. The find was important for New Zealand, because the country's workforce had been severely depleted by the gold rushes in California and Australia. Ring hurried to Auckland to claim the reward that had been offered to anyone finding "payable" gold. The town's population soared, but the reef gold could be mined only by heavy and expensive machinery. Within a few months Coromandel resumed its former sleepy existence as a timber town—and Charles Ring was refused the reward. Nowadays, Coromandel is touristy in a low-key way, with 19th-century buildings lining both sides of its single main street, an artists' collective, and the requisite fish-and-chips shop at either end. The local mussel farm means that you can find mussels served every which way on every menu in town, from smoked-mussel pies to chowder.

Driving Creek Railway is one man's magnificent folly. Barry Brickell is a local potter who discovered that clay on his land was perfect for his work. The problem was that the deposit lay in a remote area at the top of a steep slope, so he hacked a path through the forest and built his own miniature railroad to haul the stuff. Visitors to his studio began asking if they could go along for a ride, and Brickell now takes passengers on daily tours aboard his toy train. The diesel-powered, narrow-gauge locomotive's route incorporates a double-decker bridge, three tunnels, a spiral, and a switchback through native forest and sculpture gardens, all the way to Barry's "Eyeful Tower," an old-style railway refreshment room and viewing platform. On a clear day you can see all the way to Auckland. The railway also funds a reforestation program (an attempt to rectify the colonial destruction of land over the last century); to date 15,000 native trees have been planted, and a wildlife sanctuary is also being built. The railway's round-trip takes about 50 minutes. The "station" is 3 km (2 mi) north of Coromandel township. ⊠ *410 Kennedy's Bay Rd.* ☎ *07/866–8703* ⊕ *www.drivingcreekrailway.co.nz* ⬚ *$17* ⊙ *Dec.–Apr., daily 10–evening, with trains running every 1¼ hours; May–mid-Oct., daily 10–5, with trains at 10:15 and 2.*

Opened around 1900, the **Coromandel Goldfield Center and Stamper Battery** was New Zealand's last functional gold-processing plant. You can take a guided tour of the old plant, do some gold panning, or stroll through the bush to a lookout. The huge working waterwheel out front claims to be New Zealand's largest. The Stamper Battery is 2 km (1 mi) north of Coromandel township. ⊠ *410 Buffalo Rd.* ☎ *07/866–7933* ⬚ *$10* ⊙ *Daily 10–4; closed Wed. June–Sept.*

Where to Stay & Eat

¢–$$$$ ✕ **UMU Café.** The trendy UMU Café does a mean pizza, with asparagus, feta, olives, pepperoni, and anchovies. Both the restaurant menu and café counter offer largely organic produce, lots of seafood, and good vegetarian options. Even if you're not planning to eat, stop in to look at the art by Dean Buchanan; he did the locally famous *No Mining* Coromandel protest painting, which you'll see on postcards in many of the town's shops. ⊠ *22 Wharf Rd.* ☎ *07/866–8618* ⊟ *AE, DC, MC, V.*

$$–$$$ ✕ **Pepper Tree Restaurant and Bar.** Coromandel seafood takes precedence on the menu here. Locally farmed oysters are served simply on the half shell, and Greenshell mussels are steamed open and piled into bowls, or turned into fritters. Organic produce, including meat, is used whenever possible. Nachos, potato wedges, and other easygoing nibbles dominate the all-day menu, but things get more serious after sundown, with dishes such as raw fish marinated in vodka and citrus with spiced coconut cream. ⊠ *31 Kapanga Rd.* ☎ *07/866–8211* ⊟ *AE, DC, MC, V.*

¢ ✕ **Coromandel Cafe.** Seek out the best breakfast in town at this main-street café. The menu may not be extensive or adventurous, but the substantial servings of tried-and-true choices such as pancakes with maple syrup or bacon and eggs come piping hot. What's more, you won't miss out if you sleep in, as breakfast runs right through the afternoon. ⊠ *Kapanga Rd.* ☎ *07/866–8495* ⊟ *AE, MC, V* ☉ *No dinner.*

★ $$$ ✕🖬 **Buffalo Lodge.** Perched on a hillside and surrounded by bush just out of Coromandel town, this lodge looks across the Hauraki Gulf toward Auckland. The owner's own artwork hangs at the lodge's entrance and in guest rooms, and wood is used lavishly in the ceilings, floors, and furnishings. Bedrooms and bathrooms are modern and minimalist in design, with huge windows and balconies with spectacular views of the surrounding native trees and countryside. The restaurant's prix-fixe dinner ($90) homes in on New Zealand specialties such as king salmon, venison, and locally caught fish. ⊠ *Buffalo Rd.* ☎🖷 *07/866–8960* ⊕ *www.buffalolodge.co.nz* ⟲ *4 rooms* ⚓ *Restaurant; no a/c, no room TVs, no kids under 12* ⊟ *AE, DC, MC, V* ☉ *Closed May–Sept.* 🍴 *BP.*

$$ 🖬 **Karamana Homestead.** It's not hard to imagine a distinguished family occupying this 1872 home, built for Jerome Cadman, a prominent Auckland contractor. From the gentlemen's smoking lounge to the huge canopy bed of English oak to the stone well out back, the house is a well-kept piece of Coromandel history. Rooms are furnished with antiques; the adjacent 1850 kauri cottage, with its high-beamed ceilings, wrought-iron bed, and kitchenette, is wonderfully private. Breakfast, included in the price, is a silver-service affair. ⊠ *84 Whangapoua Rd.* ☎🖷 *07/866–7138* ⊕ *www.karamanahomestead.com* ⟲ *3 rooms, 1 cottage* ⚓ *Library, piano, no-smoking rooms; no a/c, no room phones, no room TVs* ⊟ *MC, V* 🍴 *BP.*

★ $–$$ 🖬 **Coromandel Colonial Cottages.** These eight immaculate timber cottages offer spacious and comfortable self-contained accommodations for about the same price as a standard motel room. Six of the units have two bedrooms; a living room with convertible beds; a large, well-equipped kitchen; and a dining area. The other two have only one bedroom but still feel spacious. Arranged with military precision in two ranks, the cottages face one another across a tailored lawn surrounded by green hills on the northern outskirts of Coromandel. For vacation periods book several months in advance. ⊠ *Rings Rd.* ☎ *07/866–8857* ⊕ *www.corocottagesmotel.co.nz* ⟲ *8 cottages* ⚓ *Some kitchens, pool, playground; no a/c* ⊟ *AE, DC, MC, V.*

$–$$ 🖬 **Coromandel Court Motel.** Tucked behind the Coromandel Information Centre, these clean units are newer and more spacious than those of the area's average motel. You'll get a friendly welcome at reception, and guest rooms are well equipped with kitchenettes and dining-room tables. All have showers instead of full baths. ⊠ *365 Kapanga Rd.* ☎ *07/866–8402* 🖷 *07/866–8403* ⊕ *www.coromandelcourtmotel.co.nz* ⟲ *9 units* ⚓ *Kitchenettes, microwaves; no a/c* ⊟ *AE, DC, MC, V.*

$ 🖬 **Te Kouma Harbour Farmstay.** A little off the beaten track, these single-story wooden chalets set on a deer farm are excellent for families. There are plenty of activities to keep you busy for a couple of days: kayaking, soccer, *pétanque* (the French game similar to boccie), and swimming in the pool. Large, bright multiroom cabins have contemporary furniture and kitchen areas. You can arrange for breakfast, but most guests cook for themselves. The cabins are down a long drive that is well signposted from State Highway 25 north out of Thames. ⊠ *Te Kouma Harbour* 📞 *07/ 866–8747* ⊕ *www.tekouma.co.nz* 🛏 *9 cabins* ⚭ *Picnic area, kitchens, pool, boating, recreation room; no a/c* ▭ *No credit cards.*

EN ROUTE About 2 km (1 mi) out of Coromandel township heading north on the main road to Colville, look for **Taraire Grove Gardens** (⊠ 2569 Rings Rd. 📞 07/866–8053 🎫 $5 🕙 Daily 10 AM–dusk). Named for the 13 ancient native taraire trees on the property, the gardens gleam with streams, creeks, and water-lily ponds. There are grassy picnic spots and a swimming hole.

Once a grassy cow pasture, **Waitati Gardens** (⊠ 485 Buffalo Rd. 📞 07/ 866–8659 🎫 $5 🕙 Daily 10 AM–dusk) is now landscaped to include a native-plants area and swarms of unusual flowers. Flower-bordered glades and shady spots make for perfect picnic settings.

The 309 Road

The 309 Road is the shortest route between Coromandel and Whitianga; it cuts right across the peninsula. The mostly unpaved road is very winding and narrow in places and takes about 35–40 minutes to cross. The stunning scenery, however, is well worth the drive. The surrounding landscape alternates between farmland, pine trees, and native forest, with numerous reasons to stop along the way.

Five kilometers (3 mi) from Coromandel, the **Waiau Waterworks** is a quirky playground in a series of grassy clearings surrounded by bush, ponds, streams, and a river with a swimming hole. There are sculpture gardens, a number of water-powered artworks, and some unusual takes on playground equipment. ⊠ *309 Rd.* 📞 *07/866–7191* ⊕ *www. waiauwaterworks.co.nz* 🎫 *$10* 🕙 *Daily 9–dusk.*

About 7½ km (4½ mi) from Coromandel, stop for a swim at **Waiau Falls,** a forest-fringed waterfall lagoon that's just a short signposted walk from the road. Additional walking tracks lead farther into the woods.

Less than 2 km (1 mi) east of Waiau Falls, a series of easy, clearly marked gravel paths and wooden walkways takes you through lush forest to a protected giant kauri grove. Continuing along the 309, the road winds through more forest and farmland, past the **309 Manuka Honey Shop,** and eventually comes out on State Highway 25, about 20 minutes south of Whitianga.

Colville & Beyond

30 km (19 mi) north of Coromandel.

To reach land's end in the wilds of the Coromandel Peninsula—with rugged coastline, beautiful coves, and pastures—take the 30-minute drive from Coromandel up to **Colville.** The town isn't much more than a grocery store/gas station, post office, and café, but it's the gateway to some of the peninsula's most untamed landscape, as well as some long-established communes. Maps of the area are available in Coromandel at the Visitor Information Centre and in Colville at the General Store.

Colville's classic counterculture **General Store** (☎ 07/866–6805) sells food-stuffs (there's a well-stocked organic section), wine, and gasoline. It is the northernmost supplier on the peninsula, so don't forget to fill up before you move on. The **Colville Café** (☎ 07/866–6690), right next door, is open every day for lunch, and Fridays for dinner (during December and January it is open for dinner every night). With a focus on locally sourced organic food and fair-trade coffee, this is a good place to stop and pick up fixings for a picnic, or a morning coffee and cake before you head off for the day.

Beyond Colville, a twisty, gravel (but well-maintained) road continues north, coming to a T-junction about 5 km (3 mi) out of town. It is impossible to fully circumnavigate the peninsula; at the junction, the road to your left follows the west coast to the sandy beach at Port Jackson. It continues along the cliff top to **Fletcher Bay**, a smaller, sandy cove banked by green pasture rolling down to the beach. Fletcher Bay is the end of the road, at 60 km (38 mi) from Coromandel—a 1¼-hour drive. From Fletcher Bay, hikers can follow the well-signposted **Coastal Walkway** to Stony Bay; it's about a three-hour walk each way. If you want to hike the Coastal Walkway but don't fancy driving yourself there, **Strongman Coachlines** (☎☎ 07/866–8175 ⊕ www.coromandeldiscoverytours.co.nz) will pick you up either in Colville or in Coromandel and drive you up to Fletcher Bay. From there you can walk to Stony Bay, where you will be met and driven back to your hotel. The full-day trip ($85) includes stops along the way, including one at Colville's General Store, where you can pick up lunch for the hike.

The peninsula's east-coast road runs between Stony Bay and Colville, through the other side of the T-junction. **Mt. Moehau**, the peninsula's highest point (2,923 feet), is in the center of this northernmost tip. If you've got the itch to climb, you'll have to look elsewhere, though; there are no hiking trails open here.

Where to Stay

¢–$ ⊡ **Anglers Lodge Motel and Holiday Park.** Tucked in a valley off the main road between Coromandel and Colville, these wooden motel units are flanked by forest and face the Motukawa Islands of Amodeo Bay. The small rooms have 1970s-style plaid upholstery and Formica tabletops, but the owners are very friendly. You can head out into the bay for a three-hour fishing trip ($50 per person, $150 minimum). The motel is 7 km (4½ mi) south of Colville. ⊠ *Amodeo Bay, Coromandel* ☎ *07/866–8584* 🖷 *07/866–7352* ⊕ *www.anglers.co.nz* ⤶ *8 rooms* ⟡ *Grocery, picnic area, BBQs, kitchenettes, microwaves, refrigerators, cable TV, tennis court, pool, hot tub, boating, fishing, hiking, recreation room, playground, laundry facilities, no-smoking rooms; no a/c, no room phones* ▭ *MC, V.*

Whitianga

❹ *46 km (29 mi) southeast of Coromandel.*

As you descend from the hills on the east coast of the Coromandel, you'll come to the long stretch of Buffalo Beach, lined with motels and hostels. Just past this beach is Whitianga, the main township on this side of the peninsula. Most people use the town as a base for fishing or boating trips, and others stock up for camping at nearby beaches.

Where to Stay & Eat

$$$ ✕ **On the Rocks.** Decked out with a nautical theme, including a bar built from an old Boston Whaler, this restaurant has expansive views of Mercury Bay and the Whitianga River and estuary. In keeping with the seafaring setting, the menu is heavy on Coromandel seafood, such as beer-battered fish-and-chips and Mercury Bay chowder. ✉ *20 The Esplanade* ☎ *07/866–4833* ▭ *AE, DC, MC, V.*

¢–$ ✕ **Café Nina.** Locals gravitate here for both breakfast and lunch, every day of the week. Breakfast might bring corn-and-bacon fritters with tamarillo chutney; at lunch you'll find simple dishes such as roasted root vegetables with dips and bread, or seafood chowder, a staple for regulars. Jasmine vines cloak the front porch of this charming 1890 miner's cottage. ✉ *20 Victoria St.* ☎ *07/866–5440* ▭ *AE, DC, MC, V.*

$$$ ▦ **Mercury Bay Beachfront Resort.** Stepping out of this family-run resort's garden takes you straight onto a beautiful beach. The downstairs rooms claim the best beach access, but upstairs you'll have great views and the most sun. Either way, seven of the eight rooms have beach views. The hosts keep things comfortable and casual, and there's plenty of sports equipment, including kayaks, fishing gear, and body boards, available for use at no extra charge. Note that only one room has a full bath; the rest have showers. ✉ *111–113 Buffalo Beach Rd.* ☎ *07/866–5637* 🖷 *07/866–4524* ⊕ *www.beachfrontresort.co.nz* ➬ *8 rooms* ⌂ *BBQs, spa; no a/c* ▭ *AE, DC, MC, V.*

$–$$$ ▦ **Oceanside Motel.** The views of Mercury Bay are the best assets of this motel, which sits across the street from the beach. Rooms are small and simply furnished in pastels, but each has floor-to-ceiling sliding-glass doors, giving you unobstructed views of the bay. Many have their own front patio. ✉ *32 Buffalo Beach Rd.* ☎ *07/866–5766* 🖷 *07/866–4803* ⊕ *www.oceansidemotel.co.nz* ➬ *12 rooms* ⌂ *Room service, BBQs, some in-room hot tubs, kitchens, microwaves, refrigerators, cable TV, babysitting, laundry facilities; no a/c* ▭ *AE, DC, MC, V* ⦿ *BP, CP.*

$$ ▦ **Baytime Bed & Breakfast.** In this blue-and-white two-story house, 2 km (1 mi) mile from the town marina, you'll have a tight nautical connection; your host Kevin Rintoul is also the skipper of Blue Boat Cruises. As you'd expect from a seafaring man, the home has plenty of marine artwork. The high-ceilinged rooms are much larger than average, with wicker furnishings and decks overlooking the Whitianga River. ✉ *15 Robinson Rd.* ☎ *07/866–4904* 🖷 *07/866–4990* ⊕ *www.baytime.co.nz* ➬ *2 rooms* ⌂ *BBQs, kitchenettes, microwaves, refrigerators, pool, boating, bicycles, no-smoking rooms; no a/c, no room phones* ▭ *AE, DC, MC, V* ⦿ *BP.*

Sports & the Outdoors

BOATING, FISHING & DIVING There are a number of reputable fishing, cruising, and diving operators in the Whitianga area. You can rent diving and fishing gear from the **Whitianga Sports Center** (✉ *32 Albert St., Whitianga* ☎ *07/866–5295*).

The Cave Cruzer (☎ 07/866–2574 or 0800/427–893 ⊕ www.cavecruzer. co.nz) gives you an unusual spin on a boat tour to Cathedral Cove. At one point, you'll head into a sea cave where the guides demonstrate the acoustics by playing a Spanish guitar and African drums. **Blue Boat Cruises** (✉ Whitianga Marina ☎ 027/439–8819 ⊕ www.whitianga.co. nz/blueboat) leaves Whitianga Marina twice a day for two-hour cruises around Cathedral Cove and Mercury Bay's islands. If you're interested in fishing, contact **Water's Edge Charters** (☎ 07/866–5760 ⊕ www. watersedgecharters.net.nz).

Around Hahei

57 km (35 mi) southeast of Coromandel, 64 km (40 mi) northeast of Thames.

The beaches, coves, and seaside villages around Hahei make for a great day of exploring—or lounging. If you're day-tripping from Whitianga, take the five-minute ferry ride (which leaves every hour, $4 round-trip) across to Flaxmill Bay and explore the area by foot. Alternatively, follow State Highway 25 south from Whitianga. The road takes you past the Wilderlands roadside stand (selling organic produce and delicious honey from a local commune) and on to Flaxmill Bay, Cook's Beach, and Hahei. If you're craving a true beach vacation, consider basing yourself in Hahei, rather than in Whitianga. From Hahei, you can easily explore Cathedral Cove, the Purangi Estuary, and Flaxmill Bay; the famous Hot Water Beach is only minutes away.

Past Hahei on Pa Road, **Te Pare Historic Reserve** is the site of a Māori *pā* (fortified village), though no trace remains of the defensive terraces and wooden spikes that ringed the hill. (A much larger pā was on the hilltop overlooking this site.) At high tide, the blowhole at the foot of the cliffs adds its booming bass note to the sound of waves and the sighing of the wind in the grass. To reach the actual pā site, follow the red arrow down the hill from the parking area. After some 50 yards take the right fork through a grove of giant pohutukawa trees, then through a gate and across an open, grassy hillside. The trail is steep in places and becomes increasingly overgrown as you climb, but persist until you reach the summit, and then head toward more pohutukawas off to your right at the south end of the headland. There's no entry fee.

★ **Cathedral Cove** is a beautiful white-sand crescent with a rock arch. The water is usually extremely calm and clear, good for swimming and snorkeling. The beach is accessible only at low tide, however, about a 45-minute walk each way. To get there, travel along Hahei Beach Road, turn right toward town and the sea, and then, just past the shops, turn left onto Grange Road and follow the signs.

Cook's Beach lies along Mercury Bay, so named for Captain James Cook's observation of the transit of the planet Mercury in November 1769. The beach is notable because of the captain's landfall here—it was the first by a European, and it is commemorated by a beachside plaque. Because of the surrounding suburban sprawl, the beach itself is less attractive than its more secluded neighbors.

NEED A BREAK?

Purangi Winery and Café may not make prizewinning wines, but the home-made feijoa liquor is good with club soda, and the café—with its tables made from wine barrels and set under the kiwifruit vines—is worth a stop en route to Cook's Beach. Danny Evans, the owners' son, has a wealth of knowledge about the peninsula's Māori, European, and ecological history; the shelves behind the counter are stacked with kauri gum and other locally found fossils. ⊠ *501 Purangi Rd., Whitianga* ☎ *07/866-3724* ⊗ *Daily 9–5.*

★ ❺ The popular **Hot Water Beach** is a delightful thermal oddity. A warm spring seeps beneath the beach, and by scooping a shallow hole in the sand, you can create a pool of warm water; the deeper you dig, the hotter the water becomes. The phenomenon occurs only at low to mid-tide, so time your trip accordingly. Hot Water Beach is well signposted off Hahei Beach Road from Whenuakite (fen-oo-ah-*kye*-tee). However, nearby, at the end of Hahei Beach Road, you'll find one of the finest protected coves on the coast, with sands tinted pink from crushed shells; it's safe to swim here.

NEED A BREAK?

Colenso Orchard and Herb Garden (⊠ Main Rd., Whenuakite ☎ 07/866-3725), on State Highway 25 just south of the Hahei turnoff, is a relaxed cottage café that you might find yourself wishing would franchise across rural New Zealand. Set in a garden full of lavender and kitchen herbs, Colenso serves fresh juices, daily soups, focaccia sandwiches, addictive chocolate fudge biscuits (also called slices), and Devonshire teas. Colenso is open from 10 to 5 daily, September through July.

Where to Stay & Eat

★ ¢–$$$ ✕ **Eggsentric Café.** Energetic owner Dave Fowell (hence the "egg" references) has created something of a community hub in his popular restaurant. There are nightly live music and jam sessions (instruments provided), periodic ceramics workshops, and poetry and film nights—and that's before you even get to the food. The menu reaches beyond the standards with dishes such as calamari smoked with tea and *manuka* (a native tree) wood or sticky date pudding with warm caramel sauce. Don't think white linen—the decor's rough around the edges, but that's part of the Eggsentric charm. To get here, drive just beyond Cook's Beach on Purangi Road or take the ferry from Whitianga to Flaxmill Bay. The café is about 2 km (1 mi) from the ferry landing. ⊠ *1049 Purangi Rd., Flaxmill Bay* ☎ *07/866-0307* ▤ *MC, V* ⊗ *Call to check opening hours.*

¢–$$$ ✕ **Grange Road Café.** With its roster of seafood and vegetarian dishes paired with New Zealand wines from small boutique vineyards, this restaurant becomes a magnet in summer. However, the potbellied stove brewing complimentary mulled wine and the live music performances are reasons enough to visit in the winter. ⊠ *7 Grange Rd., Hahei* ☎ *07/866-3502* ▤ *AE, DC, MC, V* ⊗ *Closed June and July.*

¢–$$$ ✕ **Luna Café.** There's no doubt you're at the beach here: scallop-shell leis, woven baskets, and cowrie shells hang on the purple walls. The menu sticks to such tried-and-true favorites as roast rack of lamb with *kūmara* (native sweet potato) and ginger slice (shortbread with ginger frosting). You can also get muffins or sandwiches, or stop in for brunch.

In winter, dinner is served only on Friday and Saturday. ⊠ *1 Grange Ct., Grange Rd., Hahei* ☎ *07/866–3303* ▭ *MC, V* ⊗ *Closed Tues. and Wed., Apr.–Nov.*

$–$$ ✕⊡ **The Church.** Originally a 1916 Methodist church, the Church is worth a visit even if you're not planning to stay the night. The church itself, on the main road heading into Hahei, is now a gracious upmarket restaurant ($$–$$$$). Travelers and locals alike mull over choices such as grilled venison with cherry sauce or house-smoked salmon. Though it's a white-linen place, it maintains a relaxed country atmosphere; you don't have to pull out your Sunday best. Behind the building are wooden studios and cottages connected by winding garden paths, each decorated with stained glass and small arched windows. The rooms are small but bright, and each has a back porch overlooking the gardens. ⊠ *87 Hahei Beach Rd., Hahei* ☎ *07/866–3533* 🖷 *07/866–3055* ⊕ *www.thechurchhahei.co.nz* ⤴ *4 studios, 7 cottages* △ *Restaurant, BBQs, some kitchens, some kitchenettes, some microwaves, refrigerators, laundry facilities, no-smoking rooms; no a/c, no room phones, no TV in some rooms* ▭ *AE, DC, MC, V* ⊗ *Closed Aug.* ⦿⃝ *BP.*

$–$$ ⊡ **Purangi Gardens Accommodation.** As you open the door to your wood
Fodor'sChoice cottage nestled in 100 acres of protected park on the shores of the Pu-
★ rangi Estuary, expect to find a loaf of still-warm home-baked bread, a bowl of fruit from the garden, homemade granola and yogurt, and some fresh-laid eggs. Hosts Rod McLaren and Susan Grierson offer plenty of homegrown hospitality here. They're happy to lend you a kayak and send you down the river, but you might prefer to sit on your veranda and enjoy the views. The wood-raftered rooms in each of the cottages are cozy and compact, with wood furnishings, warm apricot or yellow walls, and mermaid- and fish-framed mirrors in the bathrooms. If you're traveling *en masse,* or simply wish to spread out, there are also three spacious houses that sleep up to 10 people. Set apart from the cottages (two of them are nestled amid orchards) they're fully furnished and have well-equipped kitchens. ⊠ *321 Lees Rd., Hahei* ☎ *07/866–4036* 🖷 *07/ 866–4038* ⊕*www.purangigarden.co.nz* ⤴*2 cottages, 3 houses* △ *BBQs, some kitchens, some kitchenettes, some microwaves, refrigerators, in-room VCRs, pond, beach, snorkeling, boating, fishing, hiking, library, laundry facilities, Internet room, no-smoking rooms; no a/c, no room phones* ▭ *MC, V* ⦿⃝ *CP.*

¢–$$ ⊡ **Tatahi Lodge.** In the center of Hahei and across the street from the beach, this lodge comprises a number of low-lying wooden buildings, surrounded by trees. Accommodations range from doubles and studios to dorms (there's a big price range, too), but the cozy rooms have wood-paneled floors, ceilings, and walls, giving the place a rustic country feel. ⊠ *Grange Rd., Hahei* ☎ *07/866–3992* 🖷 *07/866–3993* ⊕ *www.dreamland.co.nz/tatahilodge* ⤴ *5 double rooms, 2 studios, 1 2-bedroom cottage, 2 6-bed dorms, 1 4-bed dorm* △ *Dining room, BBQs, some kitchens, boating, library, recreation room, babysitting, Internet room, no-smoking rooms; no a/c* ▭ *AE, DC, MC, V.*

Sports & the Outdoors

BOATING & Several operators run cruising and diving trips from around Hahei.
DIVING You can go on a sea-kayaking tour with **Cathedral Cove Sea Kayaks** (⊠ 88

Hahei Beach Rd., Hahei ☎ 07/866–3877 ⊕ www.seakayaktours.co.nz); prices start at $65 for a half-day trip, and they're happy to work with beginners. **Cathedral Cove Dive & Snorkel Hahei** (✉ Shop 2, Grange Ct., Hahei ☎ 07/866–3955 ⊕ www.hahei.co.nz/diving) offers beginner, advanced, and dive-master courses, as well as daily dive trips.

Tairua

❻ *28 km (18 mi) south of Hahei, 37 km (23 mi) north of Whangamata.* **3**

A town that you'll actually notice when you pass through it, Tairua is one of the larger communities along the coast. Because State Highway 25 is also the town's main road, it's easy to stop off for a bite to eat en route to the prettier seaside spots around Whitianga and Hahei. In Tairua, the twin volcanic peaks of Paku rise up beside the harbor. The short ferry ride from Tairua across the harbor to Pauanui will take you to the immediate area's best beach; the ferry runs continually October through April, and six times a day during the rest of the year ($4 round-trip).

Where to Stay & Eat

¢–$$$ ✗ **Manaia Café & Bar.** With a large fireplace to get you through the winter and a wraparound deck for the warmer months, this centrally located restaurant is perennially welcoming. Sit at one of the locally hewn wooden tables, eye the art on the walls, and try a contemporary dish such as venison served with roast cumin and pumpkin. If you arrive during the day, pop into the adjacent Manaia Gallery, which sells jewelry, art, and crafts. ✉ *228 Main Rd.* ☎ *07/864–9050* ▭ *MC, V* ☻ *Closed Tues. and Wed., Feb.–Dec.*

¢ ✗ **Surf and Sand.** For a quintessential Kiwi-style beachside lunch of kūmara chips, Coromandel mussels, and fresh fish, washed down with a bottle of Lemon & Paeroa (the iconic Kiwiana soda), this is your spot. The chips are crisp (they're fried in vegetable oil), and the service is friendly. Come early for dinner, though—they close at 8 PM. ✉ *Shop 7, Main Rd.* ☎ *07/864–8617.*

$$–$$$$ ✗⬚ **Puka Park Resort Mercure Grand.** This stylish hillside hideaway, which attracts a largely European clientele, lies in native bushland on Pauanui Beach, at the seaward end of Tairua Harbor. Timber chalets are smartly furnished with black cane tables and wooden Venetian blinds. Sliding-glass doors lead to a balcony perched among the treetops. The restaurant's sophisticated daily menu merits perusal; keep an eye out for the seafood ragout on braised leeks with kūmara (native sweet potato) crisp. The turnoff from State Highway 25 is about 6 km (4 mi) south of Tairua. ✉ *Mount Ave., Pauanui Beach* ☎ *07/864–8088* 🖶 *07/ 864–8112* ⊕ *www.mercure.co.nz* ⤴ *48 rooms* ♻ *Restaurant, tennis court, pool, spa, bicycles, bar; no a/c* ▭ *AE, DC, MC, V.*

$$–$$$ ⬚ **Pauanui Pines.** The light, bright decor of this modern motor lodge suits a beach vacation; even the crockery fits into the color scheme. The units are self-contained, with French-press coffeemakers—a nice extra. You can arrange for a Continental breakfast, but for other meals guests cook their own or wander into town. Portable gas barbecues are available as well. ✉ *168 Vista Paku, Pauanui Beach* ☎ *07/864–8086* 🖶 *07/ 864–7122* ⊕ *www.pauanuipines.co.nz* ⤴ *15 1-bedroom units, 3 2-bed-*

room units ♿ Kitchenettes, putting green, tennis court, pool; no a/c ▭ AE, DC, MC, V.

$–$$ ⊡ **Blue Water Motel.** These bright blue-and-white units are at the southern end of Tairua, across the street from a small sandy beach. Each unit mimics a simple beach cottage, with a deck overlooking the harbor. A pleasant terraced garden surrounds the buildings. ⊠ 213 Main Rd. ☏☏ 07/864–8537 ⊕ www.coromandelmotel.co.nz ⤴ 8 1-bedroom units, 2 2-bedroom units, 1 3-bedroom house ♿ Picnic area, BBQs, kitchenettes, microwaves, refrigerators, in-room data ports, hot tub, laundry facilities, no-smoking rooms; no a/c ▭ MC, V.

EN ROUTE You can also stop at Opoutere Beach and the **Wharekawa Wildlife Refuge** for a 15-minute stroll through the forest to another great stretch of white sand. The long beach is bounded at either end by headlands, and there are stunning views of Slipper Island. An estuary near the parking lot is a breeding ground for shorebirds. In the late afternoon waterfowl are often present as the sun slants across the Coromandel Ranges to the west. A handsome bridge arches over the river to the forest walk. For information and maps about the Wharekawa (fah-ray-ka-wa) Wildlife Refuge, ask at the Tairua or Whangamata Visitor Information Centers. Another good info source is the **YHA Opoutere Hostel** (⊠ 389 Opoutere Rd., Opoutere ☎ 07/865–9072 ⊕ www.stayyha.com), an exceptional hostel that is set in 2 acres of native bush, fruit trees, and an herb garden, across the road from the estuary. A notice board marks a number of walking trails, including those to the wildlife refuge, the beach, and a glowworm grotto. Aside from the dormitories in an old schoolhouse, there is also a self-contained cabin, and double units are scattered throughout the grounds; costs range from $40 to $66 a night.

Whangamata

❼ 37 km (23 mi) south of Tairua, 60 km (38 mi) east of Thames.

The Coromandel Ranges back Whangamata (fahng-a-ma-ta), another harborside village. Although the modest houses and main strip of this town of 4,000 won't exactly bowl you over, its harbor, surf beaches, mangroves, and coastal islands are glorious. It is a great spot for deep-sea fishing, and its bar break brings in some of the best waves in New Zealand. Around the Christmas holidays and into January, it's a favorite for throngs of surfers.

Where to Stay & Eat

$$$–$$$$ ✕ **Oceana's Restaurant.** With its white-linen tablecloths, candles, and atmosphere of "fine dining," Oceana's may not be what you'd expect in this small, seaside town. But that hasn't stopped locals and tourists alike from flocking to the restaurant for traditional New Zealand cuisine. The restaurant's two signature dishes—the seafood platter for two (which lists almost every type of fish and shellfish imaginable and a range of dipping sauces) and the oven-baked lamb loin rubbed with mustard and roasted garlic—are always popular, or you could go easy and have a bowl of seafood chowder and finish up with some old-fashioned bread-and-butter pudding. ⊠ 328 Ocean Rd. ☎ 07/865–7157 ▭ AE, DC, MC, V ⊙ Closed Mon. Apr.–Nov. No lunch.

$$$ ✕ **Coast.** With its white walls, white furnishings, and backlighted modern art, this sharp-looking restaurant is a surprise find in such a mellow seaside town. The kitchen sends out some casual dishes, such as beer-battered fish-and-chips, but it also whips up more sophisticated choices such as roasted pumpkin, mushroom, and asparagus ravioli, or beef with baby leeks and garlic mashed potatoes. ⊠ *501 Port Rd.* ☎ *07/865–6999* ▭ *AE, MC, V* ⊗ *Closed Mar.–Nov. No lunch.*

★ **¢–$**   ✕ **Vibes Café.** This café boasts of being the friendliest place in town, and the daylong crowds support the claim. Paintings by local artists cover the walls (not surprisingly, a beach theme predominates), and magazines and newspapers are on hand for a quick read over your espresso. Of the light meals, the vegetarian dishes are the most exciting, with choices such as kūmara stuffed with pesto and sun-dried tomatoes. ⊠ *638 Port Rd.* ☎ *07/865–7121* ▭ *AE, DC, MC, V* ⊗ *No dinner.*

$$$$ 🏨 **Brenton Lodge.** Looking out over Whangamata and the islands in its harbor from your hillside suite, you'll have no trouble settling into a luxurious mood. Fresh flowers and a tray of fruit and muffins greet you on arrival, as do cheerful furnishings and comforts such as terry robes. The lodge's only rooms are two suites on the second floors of attractive outbuildings, plus another in the main house. Stroll around the garden, peep at the birds in the aviary, and in springtime breathe in the scent of orange and jasmine blossoms. ⊠ *1 Brenton Pl., Box 216* ☎ *07/865–8400* ⊕ *www.brentonlodge.co.nz* ⇱ *3 suites* ⚒ *Pool, laundry service; no a/c, no room phones, no smoking* ▭ *AE, MC, V* ℺ *BP.*

$$$ 🏨 **The Estuary.** On the banks of the Otahu River Estuary, a short walk from Whangamata Beach, is this sprawling, window-filled two-story house. The guest rooms are spacious and modern, with simply designed wooden and wicker furnishings and balconies overlooking the estuary. Kayaks and fishing gear are available if you have a hankering to get out on the water. ⊠ *125 Patuwai Dr.* ☎ *07/865–8841* 🖶 *07/865–7246* ⊕ *www.the-estuary.co.nz* ⇱ *2 rooms* ⚒ *BBQs, laundry service; no room phones, no smoking* ▭ *MC, V.*

$–$$ 🏨 **Pipinui Motel.** Located just out of town, a two-minute walk to Whangamata harbor and a 10-minute walk to the beach, this motel has simple, modern units, with plain white walls, tiled floors, and dark, stylishly utilitarian furniture. ⊠ *805 Martyn Rd.* ☎🖶 *07/865–6796* ⊕ *www.pipinuimotel.co.nz* ⇱ *4 suites* ⚒ *Some kitchens, some kitchenettes, microwaves, refrigerators, cable TV, in-room data ports, no-smoking rooms; no a/c* ▭ *AE, DC, MC, V.*

Sports & the Outdoors

FISHING   **Go Deep Sea** (⊠ 114B Durrant Dr., Whangamata ☎ 0800/118–845 ⊕ www.godeepsea.com) is equipped to fish the deep waters off the coast and around Mayor Island; they'll take you out for a full day of "bottom fishing" for *hapuka, terakihi,* and snapper. The minimum trip is a full day, starting at $195. **Te Ra** (⊠ 120 Moana Anu Anu Ave., Whangamata ☎ 07/865–8681) is licensed for marine-mammal-watching and can incorporate it into a day's fishing or cruising around the bays. Half-day fishing trips start at $35.

MOUNTAIN
BIKING

If you're interested in mountain biking through the forest around Whangamata, **Whangamata Mowers and Cycles** (✉ 652 Port Rd. ☎ 07/865–8096) will rent you a bicycle for the day. Rates start at $10 an hour, $60 for a full day.

SURFING

In the center of town, the **Whangamata Surf Shop** (✉ 634 Port Rd. ☎ 07/865–8252), easily recognized by its bright orange exterior and wooden veranda, has surfboards and Boogie boards for rent, as well as wet suits. If you want a surfing lesson, $40 will cover surfboard rental and an instructor for an hour.

THE COROMANDEL PENINSULA ESSENTIALS

Transportation

BY BOAT & FERRY

To get to Coromandel from Auckland by boat, the *Kawau Kat* is a 150-seat catamaran that runs from Auckland's Pier 3 to Hannaford's Wharf, Coromandel Harbour, in Te Kouma, just outside of Coromandel (a waiting shuttle will bring you to Coromandel). The two-hour trip costs $45 one-way or $75 round-trip. Departures from Auckland leave Sunday and Tuesday at 9 AM, and Friday at 6 PM; the boat also leaves from Te Kouma on Sunday and Tuesday at 3:30 PM, and on Friday at 8:30 PM.

🛈 *Kawau Kat* Cruises ☎ 0800/888-006 ⊕ www.kawaukat.co.nz.

BY BUS

InterCity Coachlines and Go Kiwi Shuttles link Whitianga and Thames with Auckland daily; the trip is just over two hours from Auckland to Thames and just over three hours to Whitianga. The fare to Thames costs $23–$32; to Whitianga, it's $56–$60. Bus travel within the region is reliable, although less frequent in winter. Both InterCity and Go Kiwi travel once daily between Coromandel and Thames; the one-hour trip costs $16. Daily buses connect Coromandel and Whitianga as well; the trip takes about 1½ hours and costs $26.

Both InterCity and Go Kiwi have special Coromandel passes. InterCity offers a one-day, $30 ticket that connects Coromandel with Whitianga and Thames, with 45-minute stops at each destination. Go Kiwi offers a round-trip from Auckland through Whitianga and Coromandel for $105, with an additional $10–$12 charge for side trips to Hot Water Beach, Hahei, and Cook's Beach. Both passes allow you to get on and off at your leisure; the Go Kiwi pass is good for a month, and the InterCity pass is valid for up to three months.

🛈 Bus Depots **Coromandel** ✉ Coromandel Visitor Information Centre, 355 Kapanga Rd. ☎ 07/866-8598. **Thames** ✉ Thames Information Centre, 206 Pollen St. ☎ 07/868-7284. **Whitianga** ✉ Whitianga Visitor Information Centre, 66 Albert St. ☎ 07/866-5555.
🛈 Bus Lines **Go Kiwi Shuttles** ☎ 07/866-0336 or 0800/446-549 ⊕ www.go-kiwi.co.nz. **InterCity** ☎ 07/868-7251 or 0508/353-947 ⊕ www.intercitycoach.co.nz.

BY CAR

It's easiest to get around this area by car. From Auckland take the Southern Motorway, following signs to Hamilton. Just as you get over the Bombay Hills, turn left onto Highway 2; then take the turnoff to State Highway 25, signposted between the small towns of Maramarua and Mangatarata. Follow the signs to Thames. Allow 1½ to 2½ hours for the 118-km (73-mi) journey.

State Highway 25 is the peninsula's main loop, and though the road is winding, it's in good condition. The 309 Road (33 km [21 mi]), which crosses the peninsula between Coromandel and the east coast, and the Tapu–Coroglen Road (20 km [11½ mi]), which begins just north of Thames and crosses the peninsula toward Whitianga, can be challenging. Both are narrow, winding, and unpaved for most of the road. Despite the challenge, the views of the coast and the peninsula's lush native forest—with numerous stopping-off points for short bushwalks—make both roads well worthwhile.

The well-maintained, paved Highway 25A, to the south, is a quicker way to reach the east coast from Auckland. You'll miss Thames and Coromandel, but will get to the east-coast beaches of Cathedral Cove, Buffalo, Whangamata, and Waihi much more quickly.

Even the peninsula's unpaved roads are generally well maintained. Off the main highway, take care on the corners, as there are a lot of sharp turns.

If you plan on driving a rental car north of Colville to the tip of the peninsula, check your rental policy's insurance coverage; some companies restrict coverage in this area (*see* Car Rental *in* Smart Travel Tips).

Contacts & Resources

BANKS & EXCHANGE SERVICES
Banks and ATMs are common in Coromandel, Whitianga, and Thames. Most gas stations and grocery stores in the smaller districts between these towns have EFT-POS, which allows you to pay with credit or bank cards; most places let you get cash back if you're purchasing something.

EMERGENCIES
Thames has the best-equipped medical facilities on the peninsula. Whitianga and Coromandel both have smaller medical centers.
🆘 Emergency Services **Fire, police, and ambulance** ☎ 111.
🆘 Hospitals **Coromandel Medical Center** ✉ 80 Kapanga Rd., Coromandel ☎ 07/866-8200. **Mercury Bay Medical Center** ✉ 87 Albert St., Whitianga ☎ 07/866-5911. **Thames Hospital** ✉ Mackay St., Thames ☎ 07/868-6550. **Thames Medical Center** ✉ 817 Rolleston St., Thames ☎ 07/868-9444.

MAIL, SHIPPING & THE INTERNET
Each town in the peninsula has facilities for posting letters and shipping packages. These are either individual NZ Post "Post Shops" or NZ Post facilities within independent stationery stores. Most of the visitor information centers also sell stamps. To find your nearest post office facilities, call the countrywide NZ Post information line (0800/501–501).

Unless your hotel provides Internet services, the Coromandel's best bets for online access are in the towns of Coromandel, Thames, and Whitianga. Rates are $7–$9 per hour.

🔢 Internet Cafés **Coromandel Visitor Information Centre** ✉ 355 Kapanga Rd., Coromandel ☎ 07/866-8598. **Inter-Earth** ✉ Shop 14, Blacksmith La., Whitianga ☎ 07/866-5991. **World Wide Wash Internet Laundromat** ✉ 740 Pollen St., Thames ☎ 07/868-7912.

🔢 Mail & Shipping ☎ 0800/501-501.

Coromandel Post Shop ✉ Kapanga Rd. and Woolams Ave., Coromandel ☎ 07/866-8865.

Tairua Stationers ✉ 37 Main Rd., Tairua ☎ 07/864-7045.

Thames Post Shop ✉ 517 Pollen St., Thames ☎ 07/868-7850.

Whitianga Post Shop ✉ 72 Albert St., Whitianga ☎ 07/866-4006.

TOURS

BOAT TOURS   Mercury Bay Seafaris has a glass-bottom boat trip, which includes a snorkeling option ($65), and a journey around islands in the area ($75). Trips last about 2½ hours; departures from Whitianga Wharf are subject to weather conditions.

🔢 **Mercury Bay Seafaris** ✉ Whitianga Visitor Information Centre, Whitianga ☎ 07/866-5555 🖨 07/866-2205.

WILDERNESS   A trip to New Zealand really wouldn't be complete without a day or
TOURS   more with Doug Johansen and Jan Poole or one of their expert associate guides from Kiwi Dundee Adventures. Their total enthusiasm for the region inevitably rubs off on anyone who takes a Kiwi Dundee tour. There are one- to five-day or longer experiences of the majesty of the Coromandel, or all of New Zealand if you'd like. The spectacular natural phenomena that they know intimately and respect deeply and the odd bits of history and bush lore are all rolled into their hikes and walks.

🔢 **Kiwi Dundee Adventures** 🎫 Box 198, Whangamata ☎🖨 07/865-8809 🌐 www.kiwidundee.co.nz.

VISITOR INFORMATION

The peninsula's visitor centers are all open daily, though from spring through fall Whitianga's bureau has half days on weekends. For tidal information, check the back page of the *New Zealand Herald* newspaper. *Tait's Fun Maps* of Coromandel, Thames, and Whitianga are not at all drawn to scale, but they clearly mark roads and main attractions. You can pick up a copy at almost any place you overnight, as well as most tour operator offices, and of course, visitor-info centers.

🔢 **Coromandel Visitor Information Centre** ✉ 355 Kapanga Rd. ☎ 07/866-8598 🖨 07/866-7285 🌐 www.coromandeltown.co.nz. **Thames Visitor Information Centre** ✉ 206 Pollen St., Thames ☎ 07/868-7284 🌐 www.thamesinfo.co.nz. **Tairua Visitor Information Centre** ✉ Main Rd. ☎ 07/864-7575 🖨 07/864-7575 🌐 www.tairua.info. **Whangamata Information Centre** ✉ 616 Port Rd. ☎🖨 07/865-8340. **Whitianga Visitor Information Centre** ✉ 66 Albert St. ☎ 07/866-5555 🌐 www.visitor.net.nz.

THE BAY OF PLENTY

Explorer Captain James Cook gave the Bay of Plenty its name for the abundant sources of food he found here; these days it is best known for its plentiful supply of beaches. Places such as Mount Maunganui and Whakatane overflow with sunseekers during peak summer-vacation periods, but even at the busiest times you need to travel only a few miles to find a secluded stretch of beach.

The Bay of Plenty has a strong Māori population; traditional lore (and common belief) has it that this is the first landing place of *Takitimu, Tainui, Arawa,* and *Mataatua,* four of the seven Māori *waka* (canoes) that arrived in New Zealand from Hawaiki. These first arrivals formed the ancestral base for the Māori tribes of the Tauranga region: Ngati Ranginui, Ngai Te Rangi, and Ngati Pukenga.

The gateway to the region is the small country town of Katikati, but the central base for the area is Tauranga, which has managed to retain its relaxed vacation-town atmosphere despite recent spurts of development. From Tauranga you can take day trips to beaches, the nearby bush, and offshore attractions such as volcanic White Island.

Katikati

❽ *62 km (39 mi) southeast of Thames, 35 km (22 mi) northwest of Tauranga.*

In its early days, the Katikati area was heavily populated by Māori, and many pā (fortified village) sites have been found—an indication of frequent tribal warfare. These days, fruit growing keeps the economy afloat. Katikati's most noticeable features are the 35 murals that locals have painted on buildings around town. Look for the Returned Servicemen's Association's *Those Who Served* murals and those that depict the arrival of the Māori by waka. Another unusual attraction is the **Haiku Pathway,** a walking trail studded with haiku-etched boulders. The path starts at the Katikati Bus Company on Katikati's Main Street and follows a path down to the river. You can pick up a map of the route at the visitor information center.

Waihi Beach, 19 km (12 mi) north of Katikati, is ideal for swimming and surfing and has access to numerous walkways. At low tide, people dig in the sand looking for *tuatua* and *pipi*—delicious shellfish that you boil until they open. Don't miss the drive to the top of the Bowentown heads at the southern end of Waihi Beach. This is an old Māori pā with stunning views. A short but steep walk from here leads to Cave Bay directly below the view point.

You'll find great views over the Bay of Plenty at the **Lindemann Road Lookout** a couple of minutes north of Katikati on State Highway 2. The only sign pointing to the lookout is right at the turnoff, so you might come upon it fairly suddenly. The road is good but narrow in parts. Once at the lookout (where the road ends) you'll find a map embedded in rock to help orient you. Look for Mayor Island just to the north and Mt. Maunganui to the south.

Just south of Katikati on Highway 2 you'll spot the Cape Dutch design of the **Morton Estate** winery building. Winemaker Evan Ward produces a large range and has won a stack of awards over the years. He has also talked the company's accountants into letting him hold some bottles back until he thinks they're drinking at their best, so you are likely to find

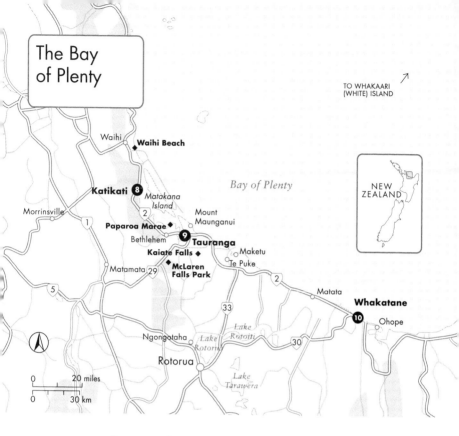

TO WHAKAARI (WHITE) ISLAND

The Bay of Plenty

Waihi
Waihi Beach
Bay of Plenty
Katikati ❽
Matakana Island
Morrinsville
Mount Maunganui
Paparoa Marae ◆
Bethlehem
Kaiate Falls ◆
Matamata
McLaren Falls Park ◆
Tauranga ❾
Maketu
Te Puke
Matata
Whakatane ❿
Ohope
Ngongotaha
Lake Rotoiti
Lake Rotorua
Rotorua
Lake Tarawera

NEW ZEALAND

0   20 miles
0   30 km

earlier vintages here than you would in most wineries. Most of the grapes come from Hawke's Bay, but Evan also occasionally uses Marlborough fruit. The top-of-the-line Black Label Chardonnay is particularly recommended. With its views of the vines and elegant white-linen service, **Morton's,** the winery's on-site restaurant, is also a charming place to stop for lunch or dinner. Start off with steamed Coromandel mussels, followed by the pork grilled with fresh ginger and palm sugar—and don't forget to try a glass of the 2004 pinot gris. ⊠ *Main Rd., Katikati* ☎ *0800/667–866* ⊕ *www.mortonestatewines.co.nz* ☺ *Winery, weekdays 10–5; restaurant, no dinner Sun.–Wed.*

Where to Stay & Eat

¢–$$$ ✕ **the landing.** Hit Katikati's main drag to find this contemporary restaurant in the 1876 Talisman Hotel. Sit down for a quick bowl of seafood chowder and a salad, or tuck into something more substantial, such as the fillet steak served with scallops in a white-wine-and-cream sauce. ⊠ *7–9 Main Rd., State Hwy. 2* ☎ *07/549–3218* ⊟ *AE, DC, MC, V.*

$$$$ ▦ **Fantail Lodge.** Expat Harrie Geraerts has brought some European flair to the region with his lodge's Bavarian-style exterior. His friendships with local landowners mean he can get you places (such as a nearby glowworm grotto) that you wouldn't find alone. Rooms in the main lodge are all done in natural colors with timber ceilings. Fresh fruit and flow-

ers in your room on arrival usually come from the lodge's garden. The lodge sits on 40 acres filled with kiwifruit and citrus orchards, bird-of-paradise flowers, ponds, and courtyards. Breakfast and dinner are included in the price. ✉ *117 Rea Rd.* ☎ *07/549–1581* 🖷 *07/549–1417* ⊕ *www.fantaillodge.co.nz* 🛏 *12 rooms, 2 2-bedroom villas* △ *Restaurant, some kitchenettes, tennis court, pool, spa, bar; no a/c* 🟰 *AE, DC, MC, V* ⦿ *MAP.*

$$$$ 🏠 **Matahui Lodge.** You're in well-connected company at this lodge, a prime example of the boutique hotels that the area is becoming known for. The lodge's neighbors can host you for a tour in a kiwifruit orchard, send you up on a flightseeing trip, or take you clay bird shooting. The lodge's harbor views and outdoor stone fireplace, however, may tempt you to stay on the patio all afternoon. The bedrooms are spacious and uncluttered, with simple wooden furniture, olive-and-taupe walls, and wide windows that look out onto the grounds and harbor. ✉ *187 Matahui Rd., 9 km (5½ mi) south of Katikati* ☎ *07/571–8121* ⊕ *www.matahui-lodge. co.nz* 🛏 *3 suites* △ *Dining room, room service, BBQs, kitchenettes, minibars, in-room data ports, driving range, pond, gym, hot tub, boating, fishing, library, recreation room, laundry service, airstrip, helipad, travel services, no-smoking rooms; no a/c* 🟰 *AE, DC, MC, V* ⦿ *BP.*

$$–$$$ 🏠 **The Point.** If it's total seclusion you're after, the Point delivers. Built from local river stones and untreated timber, the lodge looks half stone cottage and half sprawling barn. The guest rooms have beamed ceilings and four-poster beds; one turreted suite overlooks a small vineyard and the harbor. For an extra charge, hosts Kerry and Anne Guy will prepare dinner with wine from their own vineyard or a picnic hamper to take away for a day's exploring. ✉ *444 Tuapiro Rd., Tuapiro Point, 8 km (5 mi) north of Katikati* ☎ *07/549–3604* 🖷 *07/549–3515* ⊕ *www. thepointlodge.co.nz* 🛏 *3 suites* △ *Room service, BBQs, some fans, some kitchens, some minibars, some microwaves, some refrigerators, putting green, beach, boating, fishing, mountain bikes, library, laundry service, Internet room, travel services, free parking, no-smoking rooms; no a/c, no phones in some rooms, no kids* 🟰 *AE, DC, MC, V* ⦿ *BP.*

$ 🏠 **Kaimai View Motel.** The whitewashed rooms in these low green-and-white buildings are simply furnished, but they have views of the Kaimai Ranges. The motel is right on Katikati's main strip, and its proximity to the area's activities, combined with a good-value rate, makes this a handy base. ✉ *78 Main Rd. (State Hwy. 2)* ☎ *07/549–0398* 🖷 *07/549–3684* ⊕ *www.kaimaiview.co.nz* 🛏 *7 rooms, 7 suites* △ *Some kitchens, some kitchenettes, microwaves, refrigerators, cable TV, in-room data ports, pool, laundry facilities, business services, meeting rooms, free parking, no-smoking rooms; no a/c* 🟰 *AE, DC, MC, V.*

Tauranga

❾ *216 km (134 mi) southeast of Auckland.*

The population center of the Bay of Plenty, Tauranga is one of New Zealand's fastest-growing cities, thanks in large part to retirees and young families escaping the bustle of Auckland. Along with its neighbor, Whakatane, this seaside city claims to be one of the country's sunniest towns. Unlike most local towns, Tauranga doesn't grind to a halt in the off-season. Not only does it have the country's largest export port, but the excellent waves at neighboring Mount Maunganui always draw surfers and there's a fun café scene. To explore the town center, start at the **Strand,** a pretty tree-lined street that separates the shops from the sea. Bars, restaurants, and cafés line the Strand and nearby side streets.

The 1847 **Elms Mission House** was the first Christian missionary station built in the Bay of Plenty. The late-Georgian house, named for the 50 elms that grew on the property, was home to descendants of pioneer missionaries until the mid-1990s. You can explore the lush grounds, but the real appeal lies in the main house, the small wooden chapel, and the collection of furniture, crockery, and other period items. ⊠ *15 Mission St.* ☎ *07/577–9772* ⊕ *www.theelms.org.nz* ✉ *$5* ☽ *House Wed., Sat., and Sun. 2–4; grounds daily 9–5.*

The **Compass Community Foundation** is an early-1900s cobbled-street village that now houses a couple of crafts shops and a café. It's pleasant to wander among the well-maintained buildings, but the main reason to visit is the **House of Bottles Wood Museum,** where Keith Godwin takes old fenceposts originally used in New Zealand's pioneering farms and turns them into handcrafted bottles. They make unusual and attractive souvenirs. ⊠ *17th Ave. W* ☎ *07/571–3700* ✉ *Free* ☽ *Daily 10–3.*

One of the quirkier spots of local color in Tauranga is the open-only-occasionally **Mount Surf Museum,** which displays nearly 350 surfboards and other surf memorabilia—reportedly the largest collection in New Zealand. ⊠ *Unit 5, 15 Portside Dr., Mount Maunganui* ☎ *07/572–4420* ⊕ *www.surfmuseum.org.nz* ☽ *Call for hours and admission.*

★ The formerly volcanic **Mt. Maunganui** is the region's geological icon, with its conical, rocky outline rising 761 feet above sea level. White-sand beaches with clear water stretch from "the Mount" mile after idyllic mile—this is one of the best swimming and surfing areas in New Zealand. One of the early Māori canoes, *Takitimu,* landed at the base of the mountain. A system of trails around Mauao—Maunganui's Māori name—includes an easy walk around its base and the more strenuous Summit Road from the campground by the Pilot Bay boat ramp. The trails are clearly signposted and heavily used, so no bushwhacking is necessary. All roads lead to the Mount, as they say; to get here from Tauranga, follow any of the roads running parallel to the beach. The Mount gets quite crowded around Christmas and New Year's Eve; to see it at its best, come in November, early December, or between mid-January and late March.

McLaren Falls Park is a 15-minute drive south of Tauranga off State Highway 29. You can take the 10-minute easy bushwalk to the falls, or tackle the more strenuous walks to Pine Tree Knoll or the Ridge, where your efforts will be rewarded with great vistas across the park. ⊠ *State Hwy. 29* ☎ *07/578–8103.*

Kaiate Falls (Te Rerekawau) is a little off the beaten track but well worth the trip. About 15 minutes southeast of Tauranga, just off Welcome Bay Road, the Kaiate Stream drops over bluffs in a series of waterfalls and rocky lagoons, culminating in a deep green lagoon flanked by moss- and fern-fringed cliffs. A 20- to 30-minute loop trail takes you down to the main lagoon and through lush greenery, and the falls' summit (and the parking lot) affords views over Tauranga and the coast. ⊠ *Upper Papamoa Rd.* ☎ *07/578–8103.*

Owner–winemaker Paddy Preston of **Mills Reef Winery** used to make kiwifruit wine, but he hasn't looked back since he turned to the real thing, winning national and international awards on a regular basis. The 20-acre complex includes pétanque courts, a classy tasting room, and an underground wine cellar. The reliable restaurant is worth a visit in its own right (it's open for lunch, coffee, and dessert year-round); sautéed black tiger prawns, scallops, and salmon with passionfruit, lemongrass, and pink grapefruit are fabulous with a glass of sauvignon blanc. Although open all year for brunch and lunch, the restaurant is open only occasionally for dinner; it's best to call in advance. ⊠ *143 Moffat Rd., Bethlehem, about 5 km (3 mi) north of Tauranga* ☎ *07/576–8800* ⊕ *www.millsreef.co.nz* ☉ *Daily 10–5.*

OFF THE BEATEN PATH

PAPAROA MARAE – The *whanau* (family) of Paparoa Marae offer a marae experience that is a lot less flashy than the marae package tours offered in Rotorua. Along with a traditional marae welcome and cultural performance, Māori elders explain the marae, Māori carvings, and other aspects of Māori history, culture, and protocol. You're also invited to share in a *hāngi* (the traditional method of Māori cooking) meal. Paparoa Marae is involved with a number of regular international school trips and charter trips; call ahead to see if you can join one of these group events. A marae visit costs around $25–$55, including the hāngi. It's about 20 minutes out of Tauranga, just off State Highway 2 in the village of Te Puna. ⊠ *Paparoa Rd., Te Puna, Tauranga* ☎ *07/552–5796.*

KIWI360 – A four-story-tall slice of kiwifruit in the front yard makes this horticultural theme park impossible to miss. The park offers 40-minute tours (in kiwi carriages) of the kiwifruit sorting and packing factory and through acres of kiwi orchards. Don't worry about getting your daily fruit quota—there are plenty of opportunities for tastings. The inevitable shop sells everything from kiwi candy to kiwi wines. ⊠ *Main Tauranga–Rotorua Hwy., State Hwy. 2, 36 km (22 mi) south of Tauranga Te Puke* ☎ *07/573–6340, 0/800 KIWI–360* ⊕ *www.kiwi360.com* ☉ *Daily 9–5* ⊡ *Free, tours $20.*

Where to Stay & Eat

$$–$$$$ ✕ **Somerset Cottage.** The name says it all—Somerset is a genuine country cottage, and many locals consider it the region's best restaurant. The menu is modern and eclectic, with dishes such as panfried squid with tamarind-lime dressing, or roast duck on vanilla-coconut kūmara (native sweet potato) with orange sauce. The wine list is moderately comprehensive, but you're welcome to take your own bottle as well. ⊠ *30 Bethlehem Rd., 5 km (3 mi) north of Tauranga center on State Hwy. 2* ☎ *07/576–6889* ⊟ *AE, DC, MC, V* ⏛ *Licensed and BYOB* ⌔ *Reservations essential* ☉ *No lunch Sat.–Tues.; no dinner Mon.*

$$–$$$ ✕ **Bella Mia.** The Roman owner succeeded in re-creating a little piece of home in this cozy, central eatery. The decor hits the classic notes, with red-and-white checked tablecloths and grapes hanging from the ceiling.

The food is equally traditional; much of the pasta is homemade—the tortellini is prepared every afternoon—and the flavorful pizzas are thin-crusted. Be sure to leave room for dessert—Bella Mia makes its own gelato, sorbets, and tiramisu. ⊠ *73A Devonport Rd.* ☎ *07/578–4996* ▭ *MC, V* 🍴 *Licensed and BYOB* ⊘ *Closed Sun. and Mon.*

\$\$–\$\$\$ ✕ **Harbourside Brasserie and Bar.** The Oregon timber floor of this Tauranga institution is supported by piles sunk into the seabed. The building began as a yacht club back in the 1930s, but it has been better known as a restaurant for much of its life. The menu keeps things simple and tasty; for a delicious spin on fish-and-chips, try the terakihi in crispy beer batter. ⊠ *Strand Extension* ☎ *07/571–0520* ▭ *AE, DC, MC, V.*

\$\$–\$\$\$ ✕ **Spinnaker's.** This pleasant indoor-outdoor restaurant has great views of Mt. Maunganui across a sea of pleasure craft in one direction and Tauranga township in the other. The emphasis is on seafood, with at least three fish-of-the-day options. The panfried bluenose (that's a fish) with kūmara (native sweet potato) is a popular choice, but you could also go for the apple-and-cinnamon-glazed roast pork—which, like the fish, is sourced locally. From Tauranga, head over the Harbour Bridge toward Mount Maunganui and take the first left turn into the marina. ⊠ *Tauranga Bridge Marina* ☎ *07/574–4147* ▭ *AE, DC, MC, V.*

¢–\$\$\$ ✕ **Bravo.** With jazz and tables spilling out onto the sidewalk patio, this airy, contemporary restaurant is most popular during brunch, when you can sip a strong latté and tuck into a dish of smoked salmon with scallion, fried potatoes, poached eggs, and hollandaise sauce. The pizza's a good choice, too, with unusual toppings such as salmon, scallops, capers, and avocado. ⊠ *Red Sq.* ☎ *07/578–4700* ▭ *AE, DC, MC, V* ⊘ *No dinner Sun. or Mon.*

¢–\$ ✕ **Sidetrack Cafe Pacifica.** Nestled at the base of Mt. Maunganui and across the street from the beach, this bustling café is a great place for breakfast or lunch after a Mount climb. Grab a table (there are more outside than in) for a plate of coconut toast, a salad, or a dense chocolate brownie. You could also get one of the huge sandwiches and a smoothie to go. ⊠ *Shop 3, Marine Parade, Mount Maunganui* ☎ *07/575–2145* ▭ *DC, MC, V* ⊘ *No dinner.*

¢–\$ ✕ **Zeytin.** The brightly painted, mismatched wooden chairs bring out the colors from the Turkish tapestries and artifacts on the terra-cotta walls of this Middle Eastern café. The fresh, well-seasoned food arrives in a snap, and portions are generous. The mixed vegetarian pita—falafel, zucchini fritters, marinated red cabbage, tabouleh, and hummus with a garlicky sauce, all wrapped in a chewy flatbread—is a highlight. ⊠ *83 The Strand* ☎ *07/579–0099* ▭ *No credit cards.*

\$\$\$\$ 🏨 **Ridge Country Retreat.** If money's no object, look to this lodge for priceless views and pampering. Set on 35 acres—a short drive from town—the lodge overlooks a brilliant green valley, all the way to Mt. Maunganui and the ocean. You'll have stellar views everywhere from the outdoor pool and the in-room hot tubs. Suites have private balconies and thoughtful touches such as heated bathroom floors, but the best room in the house is the dining room, with its huge stone fireplace, a wall of windows, and a 22-foot-high Douglas fir–beamed ceiling. Dinner is a six-course affair, and breakfast is whatever you want it to be; hosts Penny and Joanne pull out all the stops. ⊠ *300 Rocky Cutting Rd.* ☎ *07/542–*

FodorsChoice ★

1301 🖶 *07/542–2116* ⊕ *www.rcr.co.nz* ↩ *11 suites* ⚲ *Dining room, room service, BBQs, in-room hot tubs, minibars, refrigerators, cable TV, in-room broadband, in-room data ports, putting green, pool, gym, hot tub, spa, boccie, croquet, lounge, library, business services, meeting rooms, convention center, helipad, free parking, no-smoking rooms; no a/c, no kids under 12* ▤ *AE, DC, MC, V* ⦿ *AI.*

$$–$$$ 🖼 **Hotel on Devonport.** This is the most central hotel in Tauranga, and each earth-toned room has a balcony looking over the city, the harbor, or the port. In the winter, you'll be greeted with a huge fire in the tiled foyer (along with a complimentary drink). The hotel has a "charge-back" arrangement with many of the restaurants in town. ✉ *72 Devonport Rd.* ☎ *07/578–2668* 🖶 *07/578–2669* ⊕ *www.hotelondevonport. nz* ↩ *38 suites* ⚲ *Room service, in-room safes, some in-room hot tubs, kitchenettes, minibars, microwaves, refrigerators, cable TV, in-room broadband, in-room data ports, babysitting, dry cleaning, laundry service, concierge, business services, convention center, meeting rooms, free parking; no a/c, no smoking* ▤ *AE, DC, MC, V* ⦿ *BP.*

★ **$$–$$$** 🖼 **Papamoa Beach Top 10 Holiday Resort.** This resort complex has the widest range of accommodations in the area, and it's all on the beach, about five minutes down the road from the madding Mount Maunganui crowd. If you feel like roughing it, campsites are $15. There are also spartan cabins, where you'll need to bring your own bed linens and bathrooms and kitchen are shared. Or you can stretch out in one of the private rooms, or the spacious, light-filled, cedar-wood suites; most of the walls are windows, and the decks are built onto the sand dunes, just a couple of feet from the water. ✉ *535 Papamoa Beach Rd.* ☎ *07/572–0816* 🖶 *07/572–0816* ⊕ *www.papamoabeach.co.nz* ↩ *260 campsites, 9 cabins, 13 rooms, 13 suites* ⚲ *Fans, some in-room hot tubs, kitchenettes, microwaves, refrigerators, some cable TV, tennis courts, hot tub, beach, soccer, library, babysitting, playground, laundry facilities, Internet room, business services, free parking, some pets allowed, no-smoking rooms; no a/c, no room phones, no TV in some rooms* ▤ *MC, V.*

$$ 🖼 **Puriri Park Boutique Hotel.** In the mass of Tauranga's central hotels, this one is a cut above. It's priced just above the nearby motels but is still less expensive than its location and facilities would suggest. The spacious rooms have private balconies and solid oak work tables. Breakfast can be provided, and for lunch and dinner, guests can walk to a selection of nearby restaurants that have a "charge-back" arrangement with the hotel. ✉ *32 Cameron Rd.* ☎ *07/577–1480 or 0800/478–7474* 🖶 *07/577–1490* ⊕ *www.puriripark.co.nz* ↩ *21 suites* ⚲ *Dining room, room service, in-room hot tubs, kitchens, microwaves, refrigerators, cable TV, in-room data ports, pool, hot tub, bar, dry cleaning, laundry service, car rental, free parking; no a/c* ▤ *AE, DC, MC, V.*

¢ 🖼 **Harbourside City Backpackers.** If you're not camping, this is the cheapest lodging option in Tauranga. The blue-and-white rooms are basic and clean, with shared dorms and a few private twins. The balcony on the third floor overlooking the harbor is a good place for breakfast or a drink at the end of the day. There is a shared kitchen. ✉ *105 The Strand* ☎ *07/579–4066* 🖶 *07/579–4067* ⊕ *www.backpacktauranga.co.nz* ↩ *6 dorm rooms, 18 suites* ⚲ *BBQs, bar, lounge, laundry facilities; no a/c, no room phones, no room TVs, no smoking.*

Sports & the Outdoors

BOATING &
FISHING
Blue Ocean Charters operates three vessels and offers both half- and full-day trips, plus overnight excursions. A half day of reef fishing will cost about $60, but if you want to get serious and go for a large hapuka, the cost will increase to more than $100. Equipment is provided. ⊠ *Coronation Pier, Wharf St., Box 13–100, Tauranga* ☎ *07/578–9685* ⊕ *www. blueoceancharters.co.nz.*

SWIMMING WITH
DOLPHINS
Swimming with dolphins is a big summer activity in the Bay of Plenty, especially off Mount Maunganui. The Department of Conservation licenses and regularly inspects operators and sets limits on the number of boats allowed around any pod of dolphins. You'll likely see bottlenose and common dolphins in these waters.

Dolphin Seafaris will take you out for a dolphin encounter. Wet suits, dive gear, and towels are included in the $100 price tag. Phone ahead for daily departure times from the Bridge Marina. ⊠ *90 Maunganui Rd., Mount Maunganui* ☎ *07/575–4620* ⊕ *www.nzdolphin.com.*

Graeme Butler of **Butler's Swim with Dolphins** has been running dolphin-swimming and whale-watching voyages on the *Gemini Galaxsea* since the early 1990s. Bring your bathing suit and lunch. Trips leave at 9 AM from Tauranga and 9:30 AM from Mount Maunganui, any day that weather allows. Cost is $110. ☎ *07/578–3197 or 0508/288–538* ⊕ *www. swimwithdolphins.co.nz.*

The South Sea Sailing Company will take you out for a full day of sailing on a 60-foot custom-built catamaran around the islands off the coast of Tauranga. With two kayaks on board, as well as snorkels and wet suits, you can either jump in for a swim or paddle among the dolphins. You may also see the odd shark or whale—no swimming with those guys, though. Trips are daily (weather-dependent), cost $100, and depart at 10:30 AM (returning around 4:30 PM). Be sure to bring your own lunch. ⊠ *Mirrielees Rd. (dock).* ☎ *07/579–6376* ⊕ *www. southseasailing.com.*

The **Mt. Maunganui Hot Pools** include a cool pool with marked lanes for anyone who wants some serious exercise, but most visitors prefer to soak in the hotter saltwater pools. ⊠ *Adams Way* ☎ *07/575–0868* 🖅 *$5* ⊗ *Mon.–Sat. 6 AM–10 PM, Sun. 8 AM–10 PM.*

SURFING
The **New Zealand Surf School, Mount Maunganui** offers lessons mid-November through March at 10 AM, noon, and 2 PM every day, starting at $80, which includes all the gear. They also rent surfboards and wet suits by the hour or day. ⊠ *Marine Parade and Tay St., Mount Maunganui* ☎ *07/825–0064 or 021/477–873* ⊕ *www.nzsurfschools.co.nz.*

Whakatane

 100 km (62 mi) southeast of Tauranga.

For yet another chance to laze on the beach, **Whakatane** (fah-kah-*tah*-nee) claims to be the North Island's sunniest town. This was landfall on New Zealand for the first migratory Māori canoes, and the fertile hinterland was the first part of the country to be farmed.

The most popular and safest swimming beach in the area is the 11-km-long (7 mi-long) **Ohope Beach,** in Ohope, a 10-minute drive east of Whakatane. Take the well-signposted Ohope Road out of Whakatane's town center and over the hills to the beach. Pohutukawa Avenue, Ohope's main road, runs parallel to the beach, flanked by lush native forest, citrus trees, and grazing cows, as well as private residences. The beach is far less developed than others along the bay.

NEED A BREAK?

Just beyond Ohope, it's not uncommon to see locals out on the Ohiwa Harbor mudflats harvesting dinner. If you don't want to "pick your own," head for **Ohiwa Oyster Farm.** This roadside oyster shack is the place for oysters by the basket, burger, or sack. You can also get fish-and-chips, Māori *rewena* (a traditional leavened bread), and other local foods such as whitebait fritters, crayfish, and *kina* (akin to a sea urchin). Take your catch to one of the picnic tables alongside the harbor or down to the beach.

The native forest reserves around Whakatane provide a range of bushwalks and hiking trails. The 6-km (4-mi) walkway called **Nga Tapuwae o Toi** ("the footprints of Toi") is named for a descendant of Tiwakawaka, one of the first Māori to settle in New Zealand. It's divided into eight shorter walks that take you past historic pā sites, along the coastline and the Whakatane River, around Kohi Point (which separates Whakatane from Ohope), and through the Ohope and Makaroa Bush Scenic Reserves. Walks range from one to three hours. No guide is necessary, and most tourist operators and information centers in Whakatane stock free trail maps. The trailhead is on Canning Place, behind the Whakatane Hotel on the corner of George Street and the Strand. Follow the steps up the cliff and you'll be at the beginning of the trail.

OFF THE BEATEN PATH

MAKETU – About halfway between Tauranga and Whakatane is the small seaside village of Maketu, one of the least developed places in the area and one of the first points of Māori landfall. Be sure to stop in the **MĀORI EXHIBITION** (✉ Maketu Rd. Village roundabout ☎ 07/533–2176 or 07/533–2375) – gallery and shop. It's the first building you see as you come into Maketu, next to the gas station. The shop isn't open often, and even when it is, the hours are unpredictable (you might want to call before stopping by), but if you're lucky, you'll find Googie Tapsell, a highly regarded local *kuia* (elder Māori woman), weaving *harekeke* (flax). The store has well-priced Māori art for sale, including *piu piu* (traditional Māori clothing), wooden carvings, jewelry, and *kete* (baskets). If Googie or the other kuia have time to spare, they may teach you to weave a small item, in exchange for *koha* (a donation).

Where to Stay & Eat

$$–$$$ ✕ **The Wharf Shed.** At this restaurant on the Whakatane marina, the dinner menu focuses on seafood, bought that day from the quay outside the kitchen door, but also features local beef and lamb. The "Admiral's Beef" is one of the more popular dishes on the menu: a tender beef fillet wrapped in smoky bacon, accompanied by whipped sweet potatoes. The marine theme continues in the decor, with models of yachts, maps, and tools of the fishing trade, and large windows look out over the water.

CLOSE UP

Whakaari (White) Island

WITH ITS BILLOWING PLUMES OF steam, the active volcano of Whakaari (White) Island makes for an awesome geothermal experience. Forty-nine kilometers (29 mi) off the coast of Whakatane, the island is New Zealand's only active marine volcano. Although the last major eruption was in 2000, steam issues continuously from the many fumeroles (vents) and from the central crater, and the area reeks of sulfur. The island itself is eerie but beautiful, with fluorescent sulfuric crystal formations and boiling mud pools.

The least expensive way to see the island is by boat, and as a bonus, you might see dolphins, seals, and even a whale en route. Peter and Jenny Tait, the official guardians of White Island,

operate **White Island Tours** (☎ 0800/ 733–529 ⊕ www.whiteisland.co.nz). Upon arrival, you are issued a hard hat and gas mask and taken for a walk around the volcano and through the remains of a sulfur mine. The cost is $150 and includes lunch. Bring your bathing suit in summer.

Alternatively, you can get a bird's-eye view of the steaming hulk. **Vulcan Helicopters** (☎ 0800/804–354 ⊕ www.vulcanheli.co.nz) has a four-seat and a six-seat helicopter; pilot-owner Robert Fleming is also an authority on the island. Two-hour flights cost $395 and include a landing. **Air Discovery** (☎ 07/308–7760) has a four-seater aircraft that flies over the island's crater; 55-minute trips cost $175.

There are tables outside on the quay, too—a good spot for a bowl of chowder, or for coffee and dessert. Try the "Berry White Island," the restaurant's signature dish, a meringue and custard stack topped by an "eruption" of berries. ⊠ *Whakatane Wharf, The Strand E* ☎ *07/308–5698* ▭ *AE, DC, MC, V.*

$ ✕ **Peejays Coffee House.** Although it's attached to the White Island Rendezvous Motel, Peejays is usually filled at lunchtime with Whakatane locals, ordering favorites such as the venison-and-Guinness pie. If you're preparing for a trip out to the island, nab a table on the deck to get an eyeful of your destination, then fuel up with a traditional Kiwi fry-up of sausages, bacon, eggs, and toast. ⊠ *15 The Strand E* ☎ *07/308–9588 or 0800/242–299* ▭ *AE, MC, V* ☉ *No dinner.*

$$ ▥ **Blue Tides Bed and Breakfast.** At this traditional New Zealand B&B, rooms are modest, but the beds have crisp white cotton sheets and the views from the balcony are terrific, stretching from nearby islands all the way to the Coromandel. The hearty breakfast includes homemade jams as well as a Kiwi fry-up of fresh fish or bacon and eggs. If you wish, the host will take you flounder fishing, at night out on the estuary with spears and lights—guests have even been known to catch a few. ⊠ *7 Awhe Rd., Maketu Beach* ☎ *07/533–2023 or 0800/35–9191* ☎ *07/533–2023* ⊕ *www.bluetides.co.nz* ↩ *3 suites, 1 cottage* ⚙ *No a/c, no room phones, no room TVs, no kids, no smoking* ▭ *MC, V* ⦿ *BP.*

$–$$ ▥ **White Island Rendezvous.** Convenient if you're heading out to White Island, this motel run by the owners of White Island Tours is across the road from the marina and within walking distance of town. Rooms have a somewhat nautical cream-and-blue color scheme and fish-theme art on the walls. ✉ *15 The Strand E* ☎ *07/308–9500 or 0800/242–299* 📠 *07/308–0303* ⊕ *www.whiteisland.co.nz* ➱ *22 studios, 2 suites* ♿ *Café, kitchenettes, microwaves, refrigerators, cable TV, shop, laundry facilities; no a/c* ⊟ *AE, DC, MC, V.*

¢ 🏨 **Awakeri Hot Springs and Holiday Park.** The best reason to stay at this vacation park, about 15 minutes northwest of Whakatane along the Rotorua-Whakatane Highway, is to soak in the hot-spring-fed swimming pool and hot tubs. A steaming stream runs through the property, too, and the forested grounds surrounding the pool and motel units host an ongoing chorus of birdsong. Rooms are basic but comfortable, and there are also camper-van and tent sites. If you're not staying here, you can still stop for a dip ($4); pool hours are 8 AM–9:30 PM. ✉ *Rotorua-Whakatane Highway (State Hwy. 30)* ☎ *07/304–9117* 📠 *07/304–9290* ⊕ *www.awakerisprings.co.nz* ➱ *25 rooms* ♿ *Grocery, ice-cream parlor, picnic area, BBQs, kitchens, kitchenettes, microwaves, refrigerators, 2 pools, 5 outdoor hot tubs, badminton, paddle tennis, soccer, volleyball, playground, laundry facilities, business services, free parking, nosmoking rooms; no a/c, no TV in some rooms* ⊟ *AE, MC, V.*

Sports & the Outdoors

Fishing, diving, and swimming with dolphins are popular activities in the Whakatane area. In particular, the water surrounding White Island has some extremely warm pockets, with abundant, colorful marine life.

DOLPHIN- & WHALE-WATCHING For closer aqueous encounters of the mammalian kind, **Dolphins Down Under** (✉ 2 The Strand E ☎ 0800/354–7737 ⊕ www.dolphinswim.co.nz) has four-hour cruises during which you can swim with or simply view dolphins. Wet suits and snorkels are provided. Cruises leave at 7:30 AM and cost $100.

Whales and Dolphin Watch (✉ The Strand E ☎ 07/308–2001 📠 07/308–2028 ⊕ www.whalesanddolphinwatch.co.nz) has three- to four-hour cruises. Wet suits and snorkels are provided. Cruises leave daily at 8:30 AM year-round, except during the busy summer months, when they leave at 7:30 AM, 9:30 AM, 11:30 AM, and 1 PM. Costs range from $80 to $115.

FISHING & DIVING **John Baker** (✉ 15A James St. ☎ 07/307–0015 ⊕ www.divenfish.co.nz) is one of the area's best-known dive masters. For $1,000, he'll take up to six people out to White Island and some of the smaller nearby islands for a day of fishing and/or diving on his 40-foot boat. Wet-suit and fishing-rod rentals are available, as are $500 half-day trips.

A certified diving instructor and local character with stints as a Māori All Black and a radio announcer in his past, **Val Baker** (✉ Matata ☎ 07/322–2340) has been diving for more than 30 years. He can take you to some of the smaller islands in the bay in his 18-foot "fizzboat." Wet suits and snorkels are provided, and if you want to take a break from diving and fish off the boat, he'll also provide gear for that. Costs begin at around $100 for a half day. He also offers a four-day intensive diving course for beginners.

THE BAY OF PLENTY ESSENTIALS

Transportation

BY BUS

InterCity and Go Kiwi Shuttles offer useful "flexi-pass" packages for touring the area. Both follow the Pacific Coast Highway tourist route from Auckland, allow for stops throughout the Coromandel and the Bay of Plenty, and link up with Rotorua.

Go Kiwi has a door-to-door round-trip service between a number of points in the area; a one-way "flexi-pass" from Auckland through the Coromandel and Tauranga, ending in Rotorua, costs $105. The InterCity "flexi-pass" is a little more expensive but offers more flexibility. Instead of purchasing tickets by destination, you pay for blocks of hours, which you can then apply to any InterCity (or Newmans Coach Lines) bus trip in the country. A 15-hour ticket costs $150, and a trip from Auckland through the Coromandel and Tauranga to Rotorua will use up about 12 of those hours.

🚍 Bus Depots **InterCity Tauranga Depot** ⊠ 95 Willow St. ☎ 07/578-8103. **InterCity Whakatane Depot** ⊠ The Strand ☎ 07/308-6058.

🚍 Bus Lines **Go Kiwi Shuttles** ☎ 07/866-0336 or 0800/446-549 ⊕ www.go-kiwi.co. nz. **InterCity** ☎ 09/913-6100 ⊕ www.intercitycoach.co.nz.

BY CAR

Car travel is the easiest way to get around the area; roads are generally well maintained and many follow the coast, winding in and out of forested areas. State Highway 30 from Rotorua to Whakatane is one of the most scenic; the road winds through lush native forest, playing hide-and-seek with the many lakes in the district, until finally reaching the coast. State Highway 25, which borders the entire Coromandel and Bay of Plenty, is well marked; look for the frequent blue signposts with the image of a wave to check that you're on the right track. To get to Coromandel from Auckland, use State Highway 2.

To reach the Bay of Plenty area from Auckland, take the Southern Motorway, following signs to Hamilton. Just past the narrowing of the motorway, turn left onto State Highway 2, and travel through Paeroa. Stay on Highway 2 all the way to Tauranga, driving through Waihi and Katikati on the way. The driving time between Auckland and Katikati is around 2 hours, 40 minutes. Between Auckland and Tauranga, it's at least 3 hours, 15 minutes.

Contacts & Resources

BANKS & EXCHANGE SERVICES

Banks and ATMs are fairly easy to find in Whakatane, Te Puke (in between Whakatane and Tauranga on State Highway 2), and Tauranga. Most gas stations and grocery stores have EFT-POS, which allows you to pay with credit or debit cards; you can usually withdraw cash if you're buying something at the same time.

3

EMERGENCIES

As the area's largest city, Tauranga has a well-equipped hospital and a medical center. Whakatane also has a hospital, and Mount Maunganui has a local medical center. You won't find a truly late-night pharmacy in this neck of the woods, but a couple of pharmacies in Whakatane do take turns staying open until 7 PM on weekends.

🛈 Emergency Services **Fire, police, and ambulance** ☎ 111.

🛈 Hospitals **Mount Medical Centre** ✉ 257 Maunganui Rd., Mount Maunganui ☎ 07/575-3073.

South City Medical Centre ✉ 454 Cameron Rd., Tauranga ☎ 07/578-6808. **Tauranga Hospital** ✉ 375 Cameron Rd., Tauranga ☎ 07/579-8000. **Whakatane Hospital** ✉ Stewart St., Whakatane ☎ 07/306-0999.

🛈 Pharmacies **Care Chemist** ✉ 42 Girven Rd., Mt. Maunganui ☎ 07/574-8645.

John's Photo-Pharmacy ✉ 292 Cameron Rd., Tauranga ☎ 07/578-3566. **Phoenix Pharmacy** ✉ Pyne St., Whakatane ☎ 07/307-1409. **Total Health Chemist** ✉ 252 The Strand, Whakatane ☎ 07/308-9009.

MAIL, SHIPPING & THE INTERNET

Each town along the Bay of Plenty has facilities for posting letters and shipping packages, whether in individual NZ Post "Post Shops," or through NZ Post facilities within independent stationery stores. Most of the visitor information centers also sell stamps. To find your nearest post office facilities, call the countrywide NZ Post information line (0800/501–501).

Internet cafés are fairly easy to find in the larger towns but rare in the smaller communities (though some accommodations provide Internet access). Rates range from $6 to $10 per hour. Also try local libraries to get online.

🛈 Internet Access **The Gateway Cyber Café Ltd.** ✉ 176 Devonport Rd., Tauranga ☎ 07/571-1112 ⊕ www.thegateway.co.nz.

Mount Maunganui Library ✉ 398 Maunganui Rd., Mount Maunganui ☎ 07/577-7177. **Tauranga Library** ✉ Willow and Wharf Rds., Library Arcade, Tauranga ☎ 07/577-7177. 🛈 Mail & Shipping **NZ Post** ☎ 0800/501-501.

Tauranga Post Shop ✉ 11th Ave. and Cameron St., Tauranga ☎ 07/571-1690. **Whakatane Post Shop** ✉ Commerce St. and the Strand, Whakatane ☎ 07/307-1155.

VISITOR INFORMATION

The Katikati, Tauranga, and Whakatane visitor centers are all open daily; the Mount Maunganui bureau opens on weekdays only.

🛈 **Katikati Visitor Information** ✉ 36 Centre Main Rd. ☎ 07/549-1658 ⊕ www.katikati.co.nz. **Mount Maunganui Visitor Information Centre** ✉ Salisbury Ave. ☎ 07/575-5099 ⊕ www.bayofplentynz.com. **Tauranga Visitor Information Centre** ✉ 95 Willow St. ☎ 07/578-8103 ⊕ www.bayofplentynz.com. **Whakatane Visitor Information Centre** ✉ Quay and Kakahoroa Sts., on the Strand ☎ 07/308-6058 ⊕ www.whakatane.com.

East Coast &
the Volcanic Zone

4

WORD OF MOUTH

"Everything below the surface comes to meet you when you hot-foot it around the geysers and mud pools [of Rotorua], and the Sulphur City's Māori culture is guaranteed to warm your spirits. Napier is a great place to journey back in time for colorful art deco. At Taupo, anglers don't shoot a line, they cast a line and drag huge trout out of New Zealand's largest lake. And Eastland is a type of paradise that's getting as rare as hen's teeth on our crowded planet. Its peace and quiet are addictive. . . . You can learn to surf, or laze on uncrowded beaches where the harshest sound is the seagulls' cry."

—Bob Marriott

Updated by
Bob Marriott

FORTY SHADES OF GREEN is an apt description for large stretches of the North Island's countryside, where startlingly beautiful lakes, forests, and mountains stretch for mile after mile. In such surroundings, it's easy to get lulled into thinking such lushness is a matter of course. Yet this region has peerless geographic amazements. When you get to Rotorua after a trip through the rolling sheep-speckled fields of the Waikato and the wild Mamaku Ranges, the aptly named "Sulphur City," with its mud pots, geysers, and stinky air, comes as a complete surprise.

Rotorua, the mid-island's major city and a longtime Māori hub, has been a tourist magnet since the 19th century, when Europeans first heard of the healing powers of local hot springs. All around the town you'll find surreal wonders that include limestone caverns, volcanic wastelands, steaming geysers, and bubbling, hissing ponds.

South of Rotorua lies Lake Taupo, the country's largest lake and the geographical bull's-eye of the North Island. From the lake, you'll have a clear shot at Ruapehu, the island's tallest peak and a top ski area, and its symmetrically cone-shape neighbor, Ngauruhoe. Ruapehu dominates Tongariro National Park, a haunting landscape of craters, volcanoes, and lava flows that ran with molten rock as recently as 1988. As part of the Pacific Ring of Fire (a zone that's earthquake- and volcanic eruption–prone), the area's thermal features remain an ever-present hazard—and a thrilling attraction.

Southeast of Lake Taupo, on the shores of Hawke Bay, you'll find a fabulous architectural anomaly: the town of Napier, a time capsule of colorful art deco architecture. The Hawke's Bay countryside is thick with vineyards, as this is one of the country's major wine-producing areas.

To truly get off the beaten path, head to isolated Eastland, the thick thumb of land that's east of Rotorua. Gisborne, where Captain James Cook first landed in New Zealand, is the area's largest town. Above it juts the largely agricultural East Cape, a sparsely populated area ringed with stunning beaches, and inland lies the haunting beauty of Te Urewera National Park.

Note: For more information on bicycling, fishing, hiking, kayaking, and rafting in central North Island, *see* Chapter 11.

Exploring the East Coast & the Volcanic Zone

North Island's east coast and volcanic zone include some of the country's most popular attractions, so accordingly there are plenty of excellent tours and bus routes that hit most of the highlights. But driving through this region yourself will give you more flexibility to seek out an untrammeled scenic spot or that lesser-known but outstanding winery. Gisborne and Eastland in particular are far easier to explore by car.

About the Restaurants

The days when you could nearly starve on a journey between Auckland and Wellington have long passed. Virtually all the small towns that dot the eastern half of the North Island's greenscape have someplace to eat, and although some may lack big-city polish, others are of extraordinary merit. From Rotorua out to Hawke's Bay, the restaurant industry has become a major player. And thanks to the generally mild climate, you can expect plenty of outdoor tables. Even small towns have their share of sidewalk cafés dotted with sun umbrellas, where customers hang out with a cell phone in one hand and a cappuccino in the other.

One thing you won't find on any menu in this notable fishing area is fresh trout. Laws prohibit the selling of this particular fish, but if you catch a trout, the chef at most lodging establishments will usually be happy to prepare and cook it for you.

Dressing up for dinner, or any other meal, is a rarity, expected at only the most prestigious lodges and restaurants. Most establishments are happy to see guests wearing smart casual clothing and a smile.

As a tourist hub, Rotorua has the area's most diverse dining scene. You can find anything from Indian to Japanese fare, or try a Māori *hāngi* (meal cooked in an earth oven or over a steam vent). Hawke's Bay is another hot spot; its winery restaurants tend to emphasize sophisticated preparations and food-and-wine pairings. Around Eastland, which is so laid-back it's nearly horizontal, the choices may be simpler, but you'll be treated with the area's characteristic friendliness.

WHAT IT COSTS In New Zealand dollars				
$$$$	**$$$**	**$$**	**$**	**¢**
RESTAURANTS over $30	$20–$30	$15–$20	$10–$15	under $10

Prices are per person for a main course at dinner, or the equivalent.

About the Hotels

Some of the country's best lodges are here in the central North Island—including the most famous, Huka Lodge, which racks up Hollywood celebs and royalty on its guest list. Lodges are ideal if you're keen on fishing, hunting, or other outdoor activities. The best places combine a relaxed country-house atmosphere (perhaps mixing antique furniture and contemporary design), excellent dining, and high-quality, unobtrusive service. If your budget allows, even one night at one of these lodges will be an experience to remember.

Rotorua, meanwhile, has a good cross section of lodgings in all price ranges, including a generous number of motels. If you're willing to stay out of the town center, you can find bargain rates virtually year-round. In both Rotorua and Taupo, many hotels and motels give significant discounts on their standard rates in the off-season, from June through September. The exceptions are the school holidays in December and January, for which you should book well in advance. Also note that peak season in Tongariro National Park and other ski areas is winter (June–September); summer visitors can usually find empty beds and good deals. Many places, even the fanciest lodges, don't have air-conditioning, as the weather doesn't call for it.

TOP REASONS TO GO

WORLD-CLASS FISHING

Central North Island is trout country. You can get out on any of the designated lakes and waterways if you have your own gear and a fishing license—but it's an even better idea to engage a local guide to take you to the right spots. Anglers rarely leave Lake Taupo, the lakes around Rotorua, or the rivers farther south around Turangi disappointed.

MĀORI CEREMONIAL FEASTS

Rotorua may be the best place in New Zealand to try the Māori feast known as a *hāngi*. Traditionally, the meal is made by lining a hāngi pit, or earth oven, with heated stones and wet leaves, and then filling it with lamb, pork, chicken, seafood, potatoes, pumpkin, and *kūmara* (sweet potato). Nowadays, the food may well be prepared above ground, but when it's done well, it doesn't lose much in the translation.

SOAKING

In Rotorua and Taupo, thermal springs are literally on tap. You can soak in your own thermal bath in even the cheapest hotels in Rotorua or take advantage of public facilities such as Polynesian Spa. Many Taupo motels and hotels also have their own thermal baths or pools. Lie back and close your eyes. You'll be amazed at how relaxed you feel afterward.

HIKING & WALKING

The eastern coast of the North Island has several excellent bushwalking trails, including the Tongariro Crossing, which brings you through the alpine areas in Tongariro National Park. Some of the most rugged bush in the country is in Te Urewera National Park southeast of Rotorua, and hiking opportunities abound around Rotorua and Taupo. Just don't tackle the mountain terrain unprepared—the weather in this region can change rapidly.

| WHAT IT COSTS In New Zealand dollars | | | | |
	$$$$	$$$	$$	$	¢
HOTELS	over $300	$200–$300	$125–$200	$75–$125	under $75

Prices are for a standard double room in high season, including 12.5% tax.

When to Visit

Mid-November through mid-April is the best time to visit the central and eastern North Island. The weather is generally balmy, and apart from Christmas Day, New Year's Day, and Easter, everything is open. This is also the season for vineyard festivals, so keep an eye on the local calendars. Try to avoid the school holidays (from early December to late January), when the roads and hotels get clogged with Kiwi vacationers. If you'd like to see the gannet colony at Cape Kidnappers, you'll need to get out there between October and March, when the birds are nesting and raising their young.

Hawke's Bay and Gisborne can be remarkably mild in winter, but Rotorua and Taupo can get very cold, particularly when a southerly wind whips across the snowfields. It's not unusual for the Desert Road—the stretch of State Highway 1 between Waiouru and Turangi—to be closed by snow for short periods. Of course if you want to do some skiing, August is the month to hit the slopes of Tongariro National Park, though the first major snows can fall as early as late June.

THE ROTORUA AREA

One thing that many New Zealanders and visitors share is a love-hate relationship with Rotorua (ro-to-*roo*-ah). It's the spurting geysers, sulfur springs, bubbling mud pools, and other thermal features that set this region apart—but with the sulfurous smell that hangs over the city, some say the farther apart the better. However, this unashamedly touristy town has capitalized on nature's gifts to become not only one of the country's most famous tourist spots but undoubtedly the envy of more sweet-smelling but financially struggling cities.

Rotorua sits smack on top of the most violent segment of the Taupo Volcanic Zone, which runs in a broad belt from White Island in the Bay of Plenty to Tongariro National Park south of Lake Taupo. Wherever you turn in this extraordinary area, the earth bubbles, boils, spits, and oozes. Drainpipes steam, flower beds hiss, jewelry tarnishes, and cars corrode. The rotten-egg smell of hydrogen sulfide hangs in the air, and even the local golf course has its own thermal hot spots where a lost ball stays lost forever. Don't worry too much about the odor, though. Locals advise going outside and taking a deep breath—in no time, you'll be so busy enjoying yourself that you won't even notice it.

The city's well-established Māori community can trace its ancestry to the great Polynesian migration of the 14th century through the Te Arawa tribe, whose ancestral home is Mokoia Island in Lake Rotorua. The whole area is steeped in Māori history and legend—for hundreds of years, the Māori have settled by the lake and harnessed the geological phenomena, cooking and bathing in the hot pools. They also recognized the water's curative powers, knowledge they passed on to European settlers around the mid-19th century. What worked then works now; the lakeside Queen Elizabeth Hospital still specializes in treating arthritis and other joint and muscular diseases.

The countryside near Rotorua includes magnificent untamed territory with lakes and rivers full of some of the largest rainbow and brown trout on earth. Fishing is big business all throughout the area that spreads down through Taupo and on into Tongariro National Park. If you're dreaming of landing the "big one," this is the place to do it.

Exploring the Rotorua Area

Rotorua today is almost entirely a product of the late-19th-century fad for spa towns; its elaborate bathhouses and formal gardens date to this era. The "Great South Seas Spa," as Rotorua was known, was among

Taking in the sunset above Franz Josef Glacier, Westland National Park.

(top left) Counting sheep: ewes in pasture, Athol. (top right) Redwood Forest, Rotorua. (below) Kayaking the Marlborough Sounds.

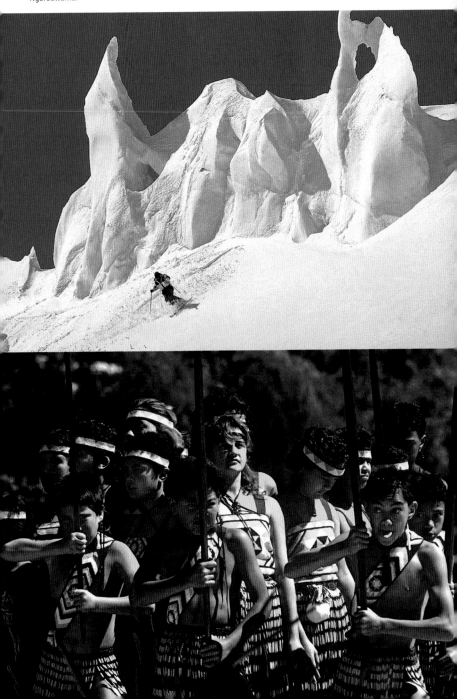

(top) Ski touring, Tasman Glacier, South Island. (bottom) Ngaruawahia *waka* (Maori canoe) regatta, Ngaruawahia.

(top left) Tairua, Coromandel, North Island. (top right) Walking through an ice crevasse on the Franz Josef Glacier. (bottom) *Hongi*—saying "hello," Maori-style.

Giant's Gate Falls, Milford Track, Fiordland.

(top left) Hot-air ballooning, Christchurch, South Island. (top right) Vineyard, Blenheim, Marlborough, South Island. (bottom) Horseback riding past Archway Island, Wharariki Beach, Farewell Spit, Golden Bay.

(top) Split Apple Rock, South Island. (bottom) Young Maori girl with traditional carving, Orakei Marae, Auckland.

Giant kauri tree aptly named Tāne Mahuta (Lord of the Forest), Waipoua Forest, Northland, North Island.

GREAT ITINERARIES

Numbers in the text correspond to numbers in the margin and on the East Coast & Volcanic Zone, Hawke's Bay, and Napier maps.

IF YOU HAVE 3 DAYS

If you have only three days, spend two of them checking out the thermal sights in and around **Rotorua** ❶, then zip to **Taupo** ❷ to fit in some time on the lake with the magnificent mountain views. Alternatively, you could combine a stay in **Napier** ❹–⓬, touring its well-preserved art deco buildings, with two days in the surrounding wine country; fly from there to your next stop.

IF YOU HAVE 6 DAYS

With almost a week, you can put together a more diverse experience. Pick a path for moving from north to south and leave a half day or more for travel between Rotorua and Napier. Start in **Rotorua** ❶, spending two to three days around the bubble and ooze, fishing, and going to a hāngi at night. Then continue east to the art deco city of **Napier** ❹–⓬ and **Hawke's Bay** ⓭–⓮ and the surrounding wine country. Or from Rotorua you could head south to **Taupo** ❷ and **Tongariro National Park** ❸ for serious outdoor activities: fishing, canoeing, rafting, and hiking.

Alternatively, you could spend two days in Rotorua, then head southeast, taking Highway 38 to **Te Urewera National Park** ⓰ and Lake Waikaremoana. It's not an easy road, but the area's pristine beauty makes it a worthwhile drive. Highway 38 continues to Wairoa; from there, you can opt to go north to **Gisborne** ⓯ and spend some time on the truly off-the-beaten-path Eastland beaches or drive south to **Napier** ❹–⓬ and **Hawke's Bay** ⓭–⓮. Either way, the scenery en route is outstanding.

the earliest such ventures in the country—as far back as the 1860s, visitors could tour the geothermal oddities. The modern town has not rested on its laurels, however; its tourist industry thrives year in and year out, and on more than one occasion it has even been voted New Zealand's most beautiful city.

It's an easy place to get around; the streets follow a neat grid pattern, and the walk from the lake to the southern end of town takes only a few minutes. Most of the sights are scattered outside the city area, though, so a car is helpful for sightseeing.

Fenton Street, the straight and wide main drag that comes into town from Taupo and the south, starts around the popular thermal spot of Whakarewarewa. For about 3 km (2 mi), it's lined with motels and hotels until it reaches the lakefront, where it becomes more commercial, with shops, restaurants, and a well-equipped visitor bureau.

Many of the main tourist sites can be reached from State Highway 30, which branches right off Fenton Street at the southern corner of town. Lake Tarawera, the Blue and Green lakes, and the Buried Village are all accessed from Highway 30; farther east, you reach the airport, lakes Ro-

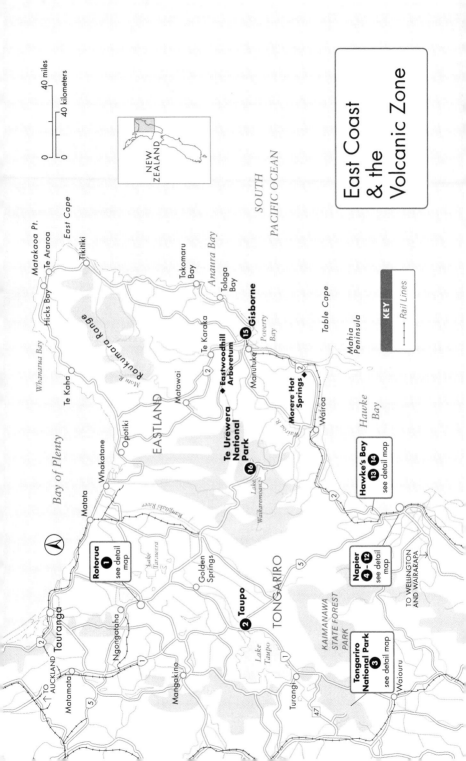

East Coast & the Volcanic Zone

KEY
Rail Lines

Bay of Plenty

Tauranga
← TO AUCKLAND
Matamata
5
2
Ngongotaha
Mangakino
1
Rotorua 1 see detail map
Lake Rotorua
Golden Springs
Kaingaroa River
Taupo 2
Lake Taupo
1
Turangi
47
Waiouru
KAIMANAWA STATE FOREST PARK
Tongariro National Park 3 see detail map
5
Napier 4 – 12 see detail map
TO WELLINGTON AND WAIRARAPA
Hawke's Bay 13 14 see detail map
2
Hawke Bay
Wairoa
Wairoa R.
Morere Hot Springs
2
TONGARIRO

Matata
Whakatane
Opotiki
EASTLAND
Te Kaha
Whanarua Bay
Hicks Bay
Te Araroa
Matakaoa Pt.
East Cape
Tikitiki
Hicks Bay
Raukumara Range
Mata R.
Matawai
2
Te Karaka
Tokomaru Bay
Tolaga Bay
Anaura Bay
Manutuke
Eastwoodhill Arboretum
Gisborne 15
Poverty Bay
Te Urewera National Park 16
Lake Waikaremoana
Table Cape
Mahia Peninsula

SOUTH PACIFIC OCEAN

NEW ZEALAND

0   40 miles
0   40 kilometers

toiti and Rotoma, and Hell's Gate. Keeping on Fenton Street will lead to Lake Road and back onto Highway 5, the road that leads to Paradise Valley, Fairy Springs Road, and farther out of town Ngongataha and the Agrodome. For some stunning scenery and picturesque picnic spots, be sure to drive all around Lake Rotorua.

Central Rotorua

There are plenty of fascinating spots to see within walking distance of the **city center,** but take your time—this is a city for relaxing, particularly along the grassy, tree-lined lakefront. The lakeshore is the berthing place for cruiser boats (there's a helipad, too), and the booking offices for various tours and fishing guides are here as well. Black swans (an Aussie import) and other birds swim around, blissfully unconcerned among the water traffic.

Heading south from the lake takes you to the **Government Gardens,** which occupy a small peninsula that fronts the modern street grid. The Māori call this area Whangapiro (fang-ah-*pee*-ro, "evil-smelling place"), an appropriate name for these gardens, where sulfur pits bubble and fume behind manicured rose beds and bowling lawns. But for all the smell, the gardens look good at any time of the year and are utterly gorgeous around November when the roses are in bloom. The high point is the extraordinary neo-Tudor Bath House. Built as a spa at the turn of the 20th century, it is now the **Rotorua Museum of Art & History.** One room on the ground floor is devoted to the eruption of Mt. Tarawera in 1886. You can see a number of artifacts that were unearthed from the debris and a remarkable collection of photographs of the silica terraces of Rotomahana before they were destroyed in the eruption. Don't miss the old bath rooms, where some of the equipment would be right at home in a torture chamber—one soaking tub even administered electric current to parts of the body. A 20-minute film on the area's volcanic history, included in the cost, should not be missed. Behind the Bath House is a public 9-hole golf course and a driving range. At the southern end of the gardens, you can soak in the **Blue Baths,** a thermally heated swimming pool built in the 1930s. The baths are open weekdays 10–7 and weekends 10–8. ⊠ *Arawa St.* ☎ *07/349–4350* ⊕ *www.rotoruamuseum.co.nz* ✆ *$12* ☉ *Oct.–Apr., daily 9–8; May–Sept., daily 9–5.*

Follow paths of pumice from the Government Gardens to the soothing, naturally heated **Polynesian Spa.** A wide choice of mineral baths is available, from large communal pools to family pools to small, private baths for two. You can also treat yourself to massage or spa treatments, and the Lake Spa has exclusive bathing in four shallow rock pools overlooking Lake Rotorua. ⊠ *Hinemoa St.* ☎ *07/348–1328* ⊕ *www. polynesianspa.co.nz* ✆ *Family or adult pool $12, private pool $12 per ½ hr, lake spa $30* ☉ *Daily 6:30 AM–11 PM.*

A short walk north from the lakefront brings you to the Māori *pā* (fortress) of Ohinemutu. The region's original Māori settlement, it's a still thriving community, centered around its *marae* (meetinghouse) and **St. Faith's,** the lakefront Anglican church. The interior of the church, which

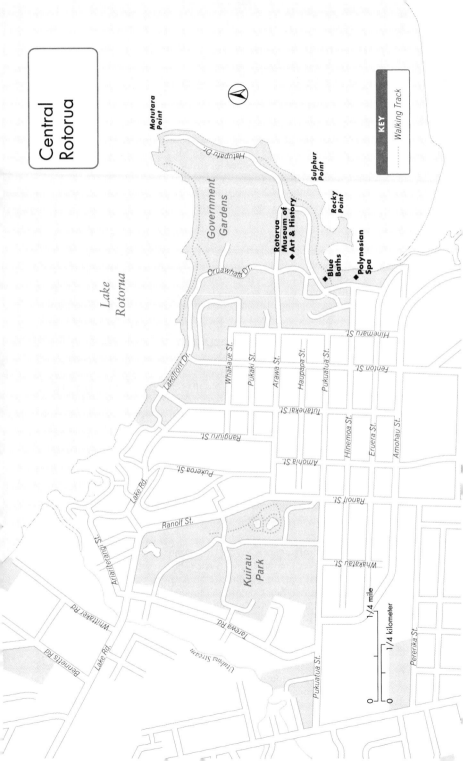

Central Rotorua

KEY

· · · · · · · Walking Track

Lake Rotorua

Motutara Point

Hatupatu Dr.

Government Gardens

Oruawhata Dr.

Sulphur Point

Rocky Point

Rotorua Museum of Art & History ◆

◆ Blue Baths

◆ Polynesian Spa

Lakefront Dr.

Whakaue St.

Pukaki St.

Arawa St.

Haupapa St.

Pukuatua St.

Hinemaru St.

Fenton St.

Tutanekai St.

Amohia St.

Hinemoa St.

Eruera St.

Amohau St.

Rangiuru St.

Pukeroa St.

Lake Rd.

Ranolf St.

Ranolf St.

Whakatau St.

Arianterangi St.

Whittaker Rd.

Kuirau Park

Tarewa Rd.

Bennetts Rd.

Lake Rd.

Utuhina Stream

Pukuatua St.

Peterika St.

0   1/4 mile

0   1/4 kilometer

is richly decorated with carvings inset with mother-of-pearl, deserves attention at any time, but it's at its best during Sunday services, when the sonorous, melodic voices of the Māori choir rise in hymns. The service at 8 AM is in the Māori language; the 10 AM service is in both Māori and English. ⊠ *Memorial Dr.*

From St. Faith's it's a short distance to the popular local hot spot (literally) **Kuirau Park,** a public park that includes an active thermal area. The mud pools and hot springs sit alongside the flower beds, which at times are almost hidden by floating clouds of steam. You can wander around the park or join the locals soaking your weary feet in shallow warm pools. It's easy to strike up a friendly conversation—and best of all, it won't cost you one red cent. This place is very thermally active and can change overnight, so as you stroll around, be sure to stay well outside the fences. ⊠ *Kuirau St., south from Lake Rd.* ☑ *Free.*

Around Rotorua

🐑 At the **Agrodome,** a working sheep-and-cattle farm, you can take a guided tour through the farm and the kiwifruit orchard, but the main attraction is the farm show—it's been going on since 1971 and still pulls in people by the sheep-truckload. Well-trained dogs run across the backs of sheep, and there's a shearing demonstration and a lot of barking, noise, and farmyard smells. You might get to feed newborn lambs who tuck into bottles with much gusto and tail wagging, or you could even find your watch auctioned in exchange for a woolly sweater. Heads-up to the uninitiated: what the shearer is wearing is *not* an undershirt but a shearing vest, a classic Kiwi item worn at some point by every red-blooded male and, yes, a few women, too! Expect plenty of wisecracks about pulling the wool over your eyes and about Whoopi Goldberg (here, a Lincolnshire sheep with dreadlock-style wool). Sure, it's a bit corny, but it's still educational and fun. Shows are at 9:30, 11, and 2:30 daily. ⊠ *Western Rd., Ngongataha, 6 km (4 mi) north of Rotorua* ☎ *07/357–1050* ⊕ *www.agrodome.co.nz* ☑ *Farm tour $28, show $22 (price for both is $45)* ⊘ *Daily 8:30–5.*

Arguably the most active thermal reserve in the Rotorua area, the 50 acres of **Hell's Gate** hiss and bubble with steaming fumaroles and boiling mud pools. Among the attractions here is the Kakahi Falls, reputedly the largest hot waterfall in the Southern Hemisphere, where, according to legend, Māori warriors bathed their wounds after battle. What also sets this reserve apart is the warm mud pools that are available for public bathing; at the Wai Ora Spa, you can soak in a mud bath or try a *mirimiri,* a traditional Māori massage. Spas and mud treatments cost $70–$230. ⊠ *State Hwy. 30, Tikitere, 15 km (9 mi) east of Rotorua* ☎ *07/345–3151* 🖷 *07/345–6481* ⊕ *www.hellsgate.co.nz* ☑ *$25* ⊘ *Daily 8:30 AM–8:30 PM.*

🐑 If you've brought the kids, plan to stop at **Paradise Valley Springs Wildlife Sanctuary,** where you can hand-feed trout and a variety of animals. In the lion enclosure, you can even handle cubs up to six months old, when they're available. ⊠ *Paradise Valley Rd.* ☎ *07/348–9667* ⊕ *www. paradisev.co.nz* ☑ *$20* ⊘ *Daily 8–6.*

The Hinemoa Legend

ONE OF THE GREAT MĀORI love stories has a special local connection, because it takes place on Mokoia Island in Lake Rotorua—and it's a true tale at that. Hinemoa, the daughter of an influential chief, lived on the lakeshore. Because of her father's status she was declared *puhi* (singled out to marry into another chief's family), and her tribal elders planned to choose her husband for her when she reached maturity. Although she had many suitors, none gained the approval of her tribe.

Tutanekai was the youngest son of a family who lived on Mokoia Island. Each of his older brothers had sought the hand of Hinemoa, but none had been accepted. Tutanekai knew that because of his lowly rank he would never win approval from her family. But he was handsome and an excellent athlete—and eventually Hinemoa noticed him and fell in love.

From the lakeshore, Hinemoa would hear Tutanekai play his flute, his longing music drifting across the water. Hinemoa's family, suspicious that their daughter would try to reach the island, beached their canoes so that she could not paddle across to Mokoia. The sound of Tutanekai's flute lured Hinemoa to try to swim to the island. After lashing gourds together to help her float, she slipped into the lake; guided by the music, she reached Mokoia. Cold and naked, she submerged herself in a hot pool, where she was discovered by Tutanekai. Enchanted, he slipped her into his home for the rest of the night. When they were discovered, Tutanekai's family feared an outbreak of war with Hinemoa's tribe, but instead the two tribes were peacefully united.

⟳ Stroll through the bush at **Rainbow Springs Nature Park** to take a close-up look at native birds such as *tūī*, kea, *kereru*, and *kakariki*. You can also eyeball a tuatara (an endangered lizard) and see skinks, geckos, and some mighty trout. ⊠ *Fairy Springs Rd.* ☎ *07/350–0440* ⊕ *www.rainbowsprings.co.nz* ⌂ *$24.70* ☾ *Daily 8–5.*

⟳ **Kiwi Encounter,** Rainbow Springs' neighbor, works with the Department of Conservation by receiving kiwi eggs, then hatching and rearing these endangered birds before returning them to the wild. From September to April you should see eggs or new chicks. ⊠ *Fairy Springs Rd.* ☎ *07/350–0440* ⊕ *www.kiwiencounter.co.nz* ⌂ *$29.50* ☾ *Daily 10–5.*

Whakarewarewa (*fa*-ka-*ree*-wa-*ree*-wa) is one mouthful of a name—locals just call it Whaka. This is the most accessible and popular of the Rotorua region's thermal spots—partly because it's closest to town—but it is also the most varied, as it provides an insight into Māori culture. The reserve is divided between two different groups; both give you some firsthand exposure to the hot pools, boiling mud, and native culture. **The New Zealand Māori Art & Crafts Institute** (⊠Hemo Rd. ☎07/348–9047 ⊕ www.nzMāori.co.nz) has a carving school that hosts workshops and, on the grounds, the Pohutu Geyser and some silica terraces. The Whaka Māori community was founded by people who moved here from around Te Wairoa after the catastrophic eruption in 1886. Don't miss the Nocturnal Kiwi House, where you might spot one of the birds that are the national emblem. Between November and April the institute is open daily from 8 to 6; from May through October it's open from 8 to 5. Entry costs $19.95. For another introduction to Māori traditions, visit the **Whakarewarewa Thermal Village & Reserve** (✉ Tryon St. ☎☎ 07/349–3463 ⊕ www.whakarewarewa.com), an authentic Māori village set in a landscape of geothermal wonders. On the guided tours of this living village you'll see thermal pools where villagers bathe, boiling mineral pools, and natural steam vents where residents do their cooking. Arts and crafts are available at local shops, and nature walks can be booked. The village is open to visitors daily from 8:30 to 5, and entry fees range from $20 to $50. Whakarewarewa is 3 km (2 mi) along Fenton Street from the Rotorua Visitor Centre, heading toward Taupo. If you don't have a car, you can catch one of the sightseeing shuttle buses that leave from the visitor center on Fenton Street.

The **Blue and Green Lakes** are on the road to Te Wairoa and Lake Tarawera. The Green Lake is off-limits except for its viewing area, but the Blue Lake is a popular picnic and swimming area. The best place to view the lakes' vibrant colors is from the isthmus between the two. To get to them, take Highway 30 east (Te Ngae Road) and turn right onto Tarawera Road at the signpost for the lakes and buried village. The road loops through forests and skirts the edge of the lakes.

Skyline Skyrides, which sits alongside the Fairy Springs complex, has a 2,900-foot cable-car system that brings you up to the summit of a mountain—Mount Ngongotaha—for spectacular views over Lake Rotorua. At the summit, 1,600 feet above sea level, there's a café, a restaurant, a souvenir shop, a shooting gallery, and a luge track, where you can take hair-raisingly fast rides on wheeled bobsled-like luges. (If you wish, you can also do the rides slowly; a braking system gives you full control of your speed.) The track runs partway down the mountain, winding through the redwood trees; from the bottom, you can return to the summit on a separate chairlift. ✉ *Fairy Springs Rd.* ☎ *07/347–0027* ☐ *07/348–2163* ⊕ *www.skylineskyrides.co.nz.*

At the end of the 19th century, **Te Wairoa** (tay why-*ro*-ah, "the buried village") was the starting point for expeditions to the pink-and-white terraces of Rotomahana, on the slopes of Mt. Tarawera. As mineral-rich geyser water cascaded down the mountainside, it formed a series of baths, which became progressively cool as they neared the lake. In the latter half of the 19th century these fabulous terraces were the country's major attraction, but they were destroyed when Mt. Tarawera erupted in 1886. The explosion, heard as far away as Auckland, killed 153 people and buried the village of Te Wairoa under a sea of mud and hot ash. The village has been excavated, and of special interest is the *whare* (*fah*-ray, "hut") of the *tohunga* (priest) Tuhoto Ariki, who predicted the destruction of the village. Eleven days before the eruption, two separate tourist parties saw a Māori war canoe emerge from the mists of Lake Tarawera and disappear again—a vision the tohunga interpreted as a sign of impending disaster. Four days after the eruption, the 100-year-

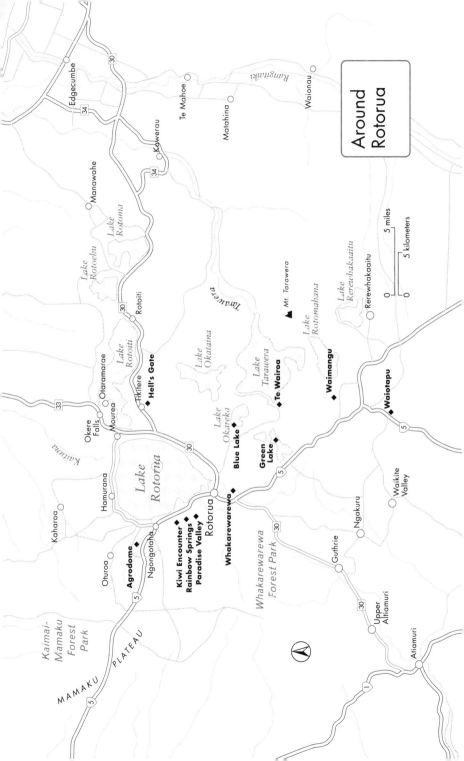

Around Rotorua

5 miles

5 kilometers

old tohunga was dug out of his buried whare still alive, only to die in the hospital a few days later. A small museum contains artifacts and exhibits with photographs and models re-creating the day of the disaster, and a number of small dwellings remain basically undisturbed beneath mud and ash. A path circles the excavated village, then continues on as a delightful trail to the waterfall, the lower section of which is steep and can be slippery in places. Te Wairoa is 14 km (9 mi) southeast of Rotorua, a 20-minute drive. ⊠ *Tarawera Rd.* ☎ *07/362–8287* ⊕ *www. buriedvillage.co.nz* 🖾 *$18* ⊙ *Daily 9–5:30.*

From the shores of Lake Tarawera, the **M.V. *Reremoana,*** a restored lake cruiser, makes regular scenic runs. The 2½-hour cruise is especially recommended; it departs daily at 11, stopping at Te Ariki, the base of Mt. Tarawera, where you can picnic or swim or walk across the isthmus to Lake Rotomahana. Forty-five-minute cruises also depart from the landing at 1:30, 2:30, and 3:30 with a full commentary. The Tarawera landing is on Spencer Road, 2 km (1 mi) beyond the Buried Village. A sign points to LAUNCH CRUISES and the *Reremoana*'s parking lot. ⊠ *Tarawera Launch Cruises* ☎ *07/362–8595* ⊕ *www.purerotorua.com* 🖾 *2½-hr cruise $28.50, 45-min cruise $17.50.*

★ When Mt. Tarawera erupted in 1886, destroying Rotomahana's terraces, not all was lost. A volcanic valley emerged from the ashes—**Waimangu**—extending southwest from Lake Rotomahana. It's consequently one of the world's newest thermal-activity areas, encompassing the boiling water of the massive Inferno Crater, plus steaming cliffs, bubbling springs, and bush-fringed terraces. A path (one–two hours) runs through the valley down to the lake, where a shuttle bus takes you back to the entrance. Or add on a lake cruise as well. Waimangu is 26 km (16 mi) southeast of Rotorua; take Highway 5 south (Taupo direction) and look for the turn after 19 km (12 mi). ⊠ *Waimangu Rd.* ☎ *07/366–6137* ⊕ *www.waimangu.co.nz* 🖾 *$28, including cruise $63* ⊙ *Daily 8:30–5; last entrance times at least 1 hr prior.*

★ If you've got time to visit only one thermal area around Rotorua, make it **Waiotapu** (why-oh-*ta*-pu)—a freakish, fantastic landscape of deep, sulfur-crusted pits; jade-color ponds; silica terraces; and a steaming lake edged with red algae and bubbling with tiny beads of carbon dioxide. Be smart and get here early: the **Lady Knox Geyser** erupts precisely at 10:15 daily—but not through some miracle of Mother Nature. Soap powder is poured into the vent of the geyser, which reduces the surface tension, so that the boiling water below erupts, on schedule, to gasps of delight. Having seen the geyser, which is set apart from the main thermal area, you then drive back to the main entrance for the spectacular one- to two-hour circular walk. Other points of interest include the Devil's Ink Pots, a series of evil-looking, bubbling, plopping mud pools, and the spectacular, gold-edged Champagne Pool, which at 60 meters (195 feet) across and 60 deep, is one of the largest in the area. Birds nest in holes around the aptly named Birds' Nest Crater—the heat presumably allows the adult birds more time away from the eggs. Waiotapu is 30 km (19 mi) southeast of Rotorua—follow Highway 5 south (Taupo direction) and look for the signs. ⊠ *State Hwy. 5* ☎ *07/366–6333* ⊕ *www. geyserland.co.nz* 🖃 *$25* ☉ *Daily 8:30–5, last entry at 3:45.*

A must-see for ornithology fans, the **WINGSPAN Birds of Prey Centre** has a complex of 10 light and roomy aviaries where you can see New Zealand native birds of prey. In Māori mythology, falcons, harriers, and moreporks (little owls) all acted as messengers to the gods; here, you can come nearly face-to-face with them. The aviaries, which are connected by an undercover walkway, echo with the cries of these fierce raptors, and they can be seen flying, feeding, and nesting. Open-air flying and obedience displays take place daily. Some of the birds here have been brought in to recuperate from injury before being released back into the wild. ⊠ *1164 Paradise Valley Rd.* ☎☎ *07/357–4469* ⊕ *www. wingspan.co.nz* 🖃 *$10* ☉ *Daily 9-3.*

Where to Stay & Eat

$$$–$$$$ ╳ **Herbs Licensed Restaurant & Bar.** The oldest licensed restaurant in New Zealand is a family-run business, where pastel-shaded walls and spotless white table linens are complemented by gleaming tableware. Owners Richard and Julie Sewell and their efficient staff serve dishes such as seared South Island salmon fillet garnished with peach-and-pineapple salsa, and desserts such as lemon-passion-fruit tart with whipped cream. ⊠ *Lake End, Tutanekai St.* ☎☎ *07/348–3985* 🖎 *Reservations essential* ▭ *AE, DC, MC, V* ☉ *No dinner Sun. July–Oct.*

$$$–$$$$ ╳ **You and Me.** Chef-owner Hiroyuki Teraoka's cuisine reflects his particular background: Japanese born and French trained, he gives a mainly French style some Japanese input. The menu shifts to take advantage of seasonal vegetables, but tuna and salmon are standards. Look for dishes such as seared yellowfin tuna in a ginger-soy sauce or panfried venison liver with daikon confit and spring onion in a port-wine sauce. ⊠ *1119 Pukuatua St.* ☎ *07/347–6178* ▭ *AE, DC, MC, V* 🍴 *BYOB* ☉ *Closed Sun. No lunch.*

$$–$$$ ╳ **Capers Epicurean.** The pleasing scent of spices may entice you into this large, almost barnlike restaurant that opens early and (on most days) closes late. On the contemporary menu, look for the chicken breast crumbed with basil and Parmesan, served with caponata and spinach. Then wander to the dessert cabinet and choose from a mouthwatering selection that includes peach-and-passion-fruit cheesecake. Half of the space is a delicatessen that sells preserves and specialty foods such as chutney made from *kūmara* (a local sweet potato) and *kawa kawa* (a native herb) rub. ⊠ *1181 Eruera St.* ☎ *07/348–8818* ▭ *AE, DC, MC, V* ☉ *No dinner Sun. and Mon.*

$–$$$ ╳ **The Fat Dog Café and Bar.** The eclectic but homey decor attracts young, old, and everyone in between. Settle in among fish tanks, lots of oak, and a few lounges for a cheap and cheerful meal. On the psychedelic blackboard menu that lights up the place like a rainbow, look for lasagna, Thai curry, or bar favorites such as nachos. ⊠ *69 Arawa St.* ☎ *07/347–7586* ▭ *AE, DC, MC, V* 🍴 *Licensed and BYOB.*

★ **$–$$$** ╳ **Pig & Whistle.** The name winks at this 1940s city landmark's previous incarnation—as a police station. Sip a cold beer in the courtyard

CLOSE UP

Dinner on the Rocks

ROTORUA, THE CULTURAL HOME of the Māori, is the best place to experience a *hāngi*, a traditional Māori feast for which the meal-to-be is cooked over steaming vents. Several local organizations offer the chance to try this slow-cooked treat, paired with a concert—an evening that may remind you of a Hawaiian lu'au. Don't pass it up!

As a *manuhiri* (guest), you'll get the full picture, beginning with a *powhiri*, the awe-inspiring Māori welcome that generally includes the *wero* (challenge), the *karanga* (cries of welcome), and the *hongi*, or pressing together of noses, an age-old Māori gesture that shows friendship. If you're not comfortable bouncing your olfactory organ around on another, don't worry—a simple handshake will suffice.

While the food cooks, a show begins with haunting harmonious singing, foot stamping, and *poi* twirling (rhythmic swinging of balls on strings). The performance might raise the hair on the back of your neck or bring a lump to your throat—but this will be assuaged with food, glorious food. The lifting of the hāngi will produce pork, sometimes lamb and chicken, and kūmara (sweet potato), vegetables, and maybe fish and other seafood, followed by a delicious dessert.

The New Zealand Māori Arts & Crafts Institute (✉ Hemo Rd. ☎ 07/ 348-9047 or 0800/494-252) hosts *Mai Ora*, a premier Māori cultural evening, hāngi, and concert for $70, including pickup at area hotels. **The Park Heritage Hotel** (✉ Froude and Tryon Sts. ☎ 07/348-1189) also has an excellent cultural show and hāngi for $59.

while waiting for tender Moroccan-spiced lamb hot pot (the British pub equivalent of a potpie). After finishing off with chocolate cake served warm with vanilla ice cream, chocolate sauce, and fresh cream, you may be tempted to take a quiet snooze under the enormous elm tree outside. There's live music every Friday and Saturday night. ✉ *Haupapa and Tutanekai Sts.* ☎ *07/347–3025* ▤ *AE, DC, MC, V.*

★ $$ ✕ **Relish.** A boiler-size oven fed on *manuka* wood (from a kind of tea tree) is the heart of the kitchen of this busy modern café. Enhanced by this manuka infusion, twice-cooked lamb shanks on herbed mashed potatoes with beetroot relish are especially delicious, as is the wood-oven-roasted sirloin, served with thick-cut fries and a tomato-and-chili jam. The wine list is limited but high quality; the breakfasts are momentous. On cold evenings, a cheerful fire glows in the firebox. ✉ *1149 Tutanekai St.* ☎ *07/343–9195* ▤ *AE, DC, MC, V* ☉ *No dinner Sun.–Wed.*

$$$ ✕▤ **Royal Lakeside Novotel.** The Royal Lakeside has the handiest position of any of the large downtown hotels—it overlooks the lake and is just a two-minute walk from the restaurants and shops. Furnishings are sleek and contemporary, and the guest rooms are decently sized, though you'll want to specify a lake view when booking. The Atlas Brasserie ($$–$$$) serves dinner daily; you might find a Thai buffet or an all-you-can-eat seafood buffet. The grilled snapper fillet on a leek-and-mussel

risotto with sautéed vegetables might also capture your fancy. ⊠ *Tutanekai St.* ☎ *07/346–3888* 🖷 *07/347–1888* ⊕ *www.novotel.co.nz* ⤵ *199 rooms* ♨ *Restaurant, in-room data ports, pool, sauna, spa, bar, concert hall, no-smoking rooms* ⊟ *AE, DC, MC, V.*

$$–$$$ ✕⬚ **Park Heritage Hotel.** From the massive but welcoming entrance foyer with its comfortable lounge chairs and a vast stone fireplace, to the thermal and lake views from the tower block, this up-to-the-minute hotel spells class. Situated next to the Whakarewarewa reserve, it runs a complimentary shuttle service to town. The superb Pohutu Cultural Theatre inside the hotel, with its carvings and giant statue of the Māori deity Maui, is home to a colorful nightly concert and hāngi feast. At Chapmans Restaurant ($$–$$$), you can choose treats from the menu such as duck confit served on a green-bean-and-potato casserole, or sample the extensive smorgasbord. ⊠ *Froude and Tryon Sts.* ☎ *07/348–1189* 🖷*07/347–1620* ⊕*www.heritagehotels.co.nz* ⤵*200 rooms, 3 suites* ♨ *Restaurant, in-room data ports, pool, gym, sauna, spa, laundry facilities* ⊟ *AE, DC, MC, V.*

$$$$ ⬚ **Solitaire Lodge.** Set high on a peninsula that juts out into Lake
FodorsChoice Tarawera, this plush retreat is surrounded by lakes, forests, and volca-
★ noes. Contemporary furnishings and artwork fill the luxuriously equipped suites; the best room is the Tarawera Suite, which has spectacular 180-degree views. Check out the volcanoes from the telescopes in the library-bar, or settle down in a shaded garden nook and sip a drink. The surroundings are perfect for hiking, boating, and fishing, and the lodge has boats and fishing gear. Smoking is not permitted indoors. ⊠ *Ronald Rd., Lake Tarawera* ☎ *07/362–8208* 🖷 *07/362–8445* ⊕ *www. solitairelodge.com* ⤵ *8 suites, 1 villa* ♨ *Restaurant, spa, boating, fishing, bar; no a/c, no TV* ⊟ *AE, DC, MC, V* ⦿⧘ *MAP.*

★ **$$–$$$$** ⬚ **Regal Palms 5 Star City Resort.** Well-appointed studio, one bedroom and two bedroom suites and apartments are set in spacious grounds here—although they're all walking distance from downtown Rotorua. The resort is handy to shopping, golf, restaurants and the hot pools and there are lots of options for relaxing here. You can also happily lounge on the patio of the outdoor pool, purify in the sauna, or while away the evening in front of the fire in the guest lounge bar. ⊠ *350 Fenton St.* ☎ *07/350–3232* 🖷 *07/350–3233* ⊕ *www.regalpalmsml.co.nz* ⤵ *41 suites, 3 apartments* ♨ *Kitchens, Wi-Fi, miniature golf, tennis court, pool, gym, sauna, spa, bar, playground, laundry facilities; no smoking* ⊟ *AE, DC, MC, V.*

★ **$$$** ⬚ **Country Villa.** Morning sunshine floods through stained-glass windows in Anneke and John Van der Maat's charming and relaxing country home, with its scenic views of the lake and Mt. Tarawera. Colored friezes run at ceiling height around every room; as befits two former professional rose growers, the decor emphasizes flowers. Throughout the house, there are mementos of the hosts' extensive travels—a Buddha figure here, a prayer wheel there, as well as beautiful blue-eyed dolls from Europe. An antique chandelier is suspended over the table in the warm, five-sided breakfast room, where the morning meal includes homemade bread. One room is self-contained, with a separate entrance and a small kitchenette. ⊠ *351 Dalbeth Rd.* ☎🖷 *07/357–5893* ⊕ *www.countryvilla.biz*

⇨ 6 rooms ⌕ No a/c, no room phones, no room TVs, no smoking ☰ MC, V ⌖ BP.

$$ ⌂ **Princes Gate Hotel.** This ornate timber hotel was actually originally built in 1897 on the Coromandel Peninsula; it wasn't transported to its current location until 1920. Inside the elegant lobby, wood-beam ceilings and fancy chandeliers overlook ornate carpets and dark leather furniture. Guest rooms are large and beautifully appointed, and the modern bathrooms all have both tubs and showers, as well as sweet-smelling toiletries. The restaurant has live jazz in the evenings, and there's a deck where you can pull up a chair and gaze at the Government Gardens across the street. ✉ 1057 Arawa St. ☎ 07/348–1179 🖷 07/348–6215 ⊕ www. princesgate.co.nz ⇨ 36 rooms, 2 suites, 12 apartments ⌕ Restaurant, some kitchens, pool, hot tub, massage, sauna, bar; no a/c ☰ AE, DC, MC, V.

$ ⌂ **Ashleigh Court Motel.** Each of the well-maintained modern rooms here has an individual hot tub, which helps distinguish this place from the many other motels on Fenton Street. It's near Whakarewarewa and the golf course, and it's not too far from town, either. ✉ 337 Fenton St. 🖷☎ 07/348–7456 ⊕ www.ashleighcourtrotorua.co.nz ⇨ 13 rooms ⌕ In-room hot tubs, kitchenettes, cable TV; no a/c, no smoking ☰ AE, DC, MC, V.

$ ⌂ **Cedar Lodge Motel.** These spacious, modern, two-story units, about 1 km (½ mi) from the city center, are a good value, especially for families. All have a kitchen and lounge on the lower floor, a bedroom on the mezzanine above, and at least one queen-size and one single bed; some have a queen-size bed and three singles. Every unit has its own hot tub in the private courtyard at the back. Gray-flecked carpet, smoked-glass tables, and recessed lighting give a clean, contemporary look. Request a room at the back, away from Fenton Street. ✉ 296 Fenton St. ☎ 07/349–0300 🖷 07/349–1115 ⇨ 15 rooms ⌕ Kitchens, laundry facilities; no a/c ☰ AE, DC, MC, V.

$ ⌂ **Eaton Hall.** Simplicity's the watchword at this charming historic home in the heart of the city. The rooms—six have private baths and three (with sinks) share baths—are a blast from the past, but the price is right, and the location couldn't be more central. The big English-style breakfast will set you up for the day. ✉ 1255 Hinemaru St. 🖷☎ 07/347–0366 ⊕ www.eatonhallbnb.cjb.net ⇨ 9 rooms ⌕ No a/c, no room phones, no TV in some rooms ☰ MC, V ⌖ BP.

¢ ⌂ **Base Backpackers.** At this central hostel, an easy walk from the visitor center and bus stop, there are 100 beds in a combination of four- to eight-bed dorms, singles, and doubles (including a few with private baths). Women travelers might want to check out the popular "Sanctuary" floor, where the posh-for-a-hostel amenities include hair dryers in the bathrooms, fluffy towels, and a gift package of hair-care products. The friendly staff can share their extensive knowledge of the area. There's even a climbing wall if you'd like to get vertical. ✉ 1140 Hinemoa St. ☎ 07/350–2040 🖷 07/350–3020 ⊕ www.basebackpackers. com ⇨ 100 beds ⌕ No a/c, no room phones, no room TVs, no smoking ☰ MC, V.

¢ ▦ **Hot Rock Backpackers.** A youthful buzz and the on-site Lava Bar give this place a high profile. It's by Kuirau Park, a few minutes' walk from the center of town. The dorm rooms sleep anywhere from 4 to 12 people, but there are also several doubles and a pair of family rooms that have private baths and balconies. If you're sore from hiking or hauling luggage, that's all the more reason to hit the geothermal pools. ⊠ *1286 Arawa St.* ☎ *07/348–8636* 🖷 *07/348–8616* ⊕ *www.gobeyond.co.nz* 🛏 *13 rooms, 18 dorm rooms* ⚲ *Kitchens, 3 pools (2 indoor), bar, lounge, laundry facilities, Internet room; no a/c, no room phones, no room TVs* 🖃 *MC, V.*

¢ ▦ **Kiwi Paka YHA.** A 10-minute walk out of town is this well-maintained lodge overlooking the thermal Kuirau Park. You can take advantage of the area's natural heating by soaking in the thermal pool for free. Rooms range from shares for four or five people to single rooms for $35. Meals at the café are a steal as well. ⊠ *60 Tarewa Rd.* ☎ *07/347–0931* ⊕ *www.kiwipaka-yha.co.nz* 🛏 *83 rooms* ⚲ *Café, pool, bar; no a/c, no room phones, no room TVs* 🖃 *MC, V.*

¢ ▦ **Rotorua Motor Lodge.** This clean and tidy motor lodge is a hands-down great deal: for around $60 you can book a unit with full kitchen facilities, comfortable beds, and a dining area. It's across from a beautiful golf course, just a few minutes from both central Rotorua and Whakarewarewa. ⊠ *418 Fenton St.* ☎ *07/348–9179* 🖷 *07/346–3474* ⊕ *www. rotoruamotorlodge.co.nz* 🛏 *26 rooms* ⚲ *Kitchens, cable TV, 4 pools; no a/c* 🖃 *AE, MC, V.*

Nightlife

Although Rotorua's nightlife may not sizzle like its hot pools, there are a few lively nightspots. Busy until the wee hours, the **Pig & Whistle** (⊠ Haupapa and Tutanekai Sts. ☎ 07/347–3025) shows sports on the big screen in the garden bar and has live music Friday and Saturday nights. **Fuze** (⊠ 1122 Tutanekai St. ☎ 07/349–6306) serves bar food in the early evenings, but when the tables are pushed aside, a noisy disco gets under way. There's plenty of action at the **Lava Bar** (⊠ 1286 Arawa St. ☎ 07/ 348–8618) in the Hot Rock Backpackers complex. A DJ keeps things lively Wednesday through Saturday. Friday night is a theme party night, and Wednesday is extreme games night. If you feel like a quieter evening, there are two big-screen TVs and two pool tables.

Sports & the Outdoors

Biking

Planet Bike (⊠ Waipa Mill Rd. ☎ 07/346–0717 ⊕ www.planetbike. co.nz) runs mountain-bike adventures for everyone from first-timers to experts. You can ride for a couple of hours or several days, and some tours combine biking with rafting, kayaking, indoor climbing, or horseback riding. Prices start at $59 for a two-hour ride; bikes and helmets are provided.

Extreme Adventure

The folks in Rotorua keep coming up with ever more fearsome ways to part adventurers from their money (and their wits). Try white-water sledging with **Kaitiaki Adventures** (☎ 0800/338–736 ⊕ www.kaitiaki.co.nz): $120 gets you up to two hours shooting rapids on a buoyant, plastic water raft the size of a Boogie board. You get a wet suit, helmet, fins, and gloves—you provide the "go for it" attitude.

There's bungy jumping (the New Zealand spelling for bungee jumping), of course, but you would be better off waiting for the spectacular natural sites at Taupo and Queenstown rather than jumping from the 140-foot-high crane in Rotorua. So go Zorbing instead: the "Zorbonaut" (that's you) is strapped into a huge plastic ball and rolled head-over-heels 200 yards down a hill. For the full washing-machine effect, go for a "wet" Zorb, with water sloshing around inside the ball. **Zorb Rotorua** (☎ 07/357–5100 ⊕ www.zorb.com) is outside of town on Western Road, near the Agrodome. Zorbing costs start at $45 a ride.

Rotorua Swoop (☎ 07/357–4747 ⊕ www.swoop.co.nz) sounds innocuous enough—that is, until you're strapped into the hang-gliding harness and raised 120 feet off the ground, and the rip cord is pulled. Is that the Earth whizzing by at 130 kph (80 mph)? It most certainly is. The Swoop takes place out at the Agrodome complex and costs $40 a ride. If you're looking for another thrill, try "body flying," where a 180 kph (108 mph) wind from a giant fan lifts you 3 meters (9 feet) to float in the air.

Fishing

If you want to keep the trout of a lifetime from becoming just another fish story, it pays to have a boat with some expert advice on board. Expect to pay about $80–$90 per hour for a fishing guide and a 20-foot cruiser that will take up to six passengers. The minimum charter period is two hours, and fishing gear and tackle are included in the price. A one-day fishing license costs $17 per person and is available on board the boat. (You'll need a special fishing license to fish in the Rotorua area, and also in Taupo.) For general information about local lake and river conditions, check with the Tourism Rotorua Visitor Information Centre (*see* Visitor Information *in the* Rotorua Area A to Z, *below*).

In Rotorua fishing operators include **Clark Gregor** (☎ 07/347–1123 ⊕ www.troutnz.co.nz), who arranges boat fishing and fly-fishing with up to 10 anglers per trip. With **Bryan Colman** (☎ 07/348–7766 ⊕ www.troutfishingrotorua.com) you can troll Lake Rotorua or try fly-fishing on the region's many streams, including a private-land source. He takes up to five people at a time. A trip with **Gordon Randle** (☎ 07/349–2555, 025/938–733 boat) is a bit less expensive than the usual rates, at about $65 per hour. *See* Chapter 11 for more fishing information.

Rafting & Kayaking

The Rotorua region has a number of rivers with Grade 3 to Grade 5 rapids that make excellent white-water rafting. For scenic beauty—and best for first-timers—the Rangitaiki River (Grades 3–4) is recommended. For experienced rafters who want a challenge, the Wairoa River has exhilarating Grade 5 rapids. The climax of a rafting trip on the Kaituna River is the drop over the 21-foot Okere Falls, among the highest to be rafted by a commercial operator anywhere. The various operators all offer similar trips on a daily schedule, though note that

Spellbound in Middle Earth

SOME OF THE MOST STRIKING elements of the *Lord of the Rings* film trilogy weren't created by special-effects workshops or camera trickery—they were the astonishing views of New Zealand's countryside. The stark and ominous mountains, bucolic fields, and lush forests made a powerful impression on viewers unfamiliar with New Zealand's landscapes. Although the movie sets were cleared in late 2000 after the principal photography was completed on the films, the matchless scenery alone evokes the character of Middle Earth. The film crew traveled all over the country, so there are dozens of locales that could tempt you to stop and dream awhile.

On the North Island, you can visit a handful of hobbit homes in rural Matamata (⊕ www.hobbitontours.com). The volcanic peaks and blasted terrain of Tongariro National Park provided the setting for Mordor. Tackle one of the park's walking trails to see the otherworldly hot springs, lava rocks, and craggy peaks like Ruapehu, the films' Emyn Muil. Take the spectacular Tongariro Crossing trek to pass Ngauruhoe, the volcano the hobbits Frodo and Sam braved as Mount Doom.

Wellington, the film production's home base, is also the hometown of the director, Peter Jackson. Here the orcs, trolls, and the horrible Balrog all came to life. The Mines of Moria, the hellacious bridge of Khazad-dûm, and Cirith Ungol were created by Weta Workshop and the production company Three Foot Six (named for the height of a hobbit). The *Rings* team won an armful of Oscars for its efforts and ever since, Weta's had its hands full with other major films, including Jackson's latest release, *King Kong*. All this activity has spurred local wags to dub the capital "Wellywood."

The Hutt Valley, east of Wellington, saw plenty of hobbit action. During filming a huge polystyrene castle towered over a quarry by the Western Hutt road. Unsuspecting drivers would pass by Minas Tirith and the fortress of Isengard, where the wizard Gandalf was betrayed and imprisoned. Stay on Highway 2 to reach the beautiful Kaitoke Regional Park, used for the elven city of Rivendell and a perfect place to picnic on the riverbank.

On the South Island, Highway 6 unrolls south to glacier country. Stop at Franz Josef and look for Mount Gunn, where the beacon burned. Carving through the magnificent landscape, the road leads on to Wanaka, where the ghastly ringwraiths gave chase to Arwen and Frodo.

The first sight of the White Mountains, or Remarkables, at Queenstown is breathtaking; this gorgeous region was the background for the Ithilien Camp, the giant statues of the Pillars of Argonath, and a host of other scenes. From nearby Glenorchy, you can hire a horse and ride to Paradise, seen as the elven Lothlórien forest. Farther south, near Te Anau, explore the brooding silence of the lake district. This region, shot for the Midgewater Marshes, is also prime trout-fishing territory.

Hungry for more? Then turn to the *"Lord of the Rings" Location Guidebook* by Ian Brodie, which tracks the films up hill and down dale.

–Bob Marriott

different rivers are open at different times of year, depending on water levels. All equipment and instruction is provided, plus transportation to and from the departure points (which can be up to 80 km [50 mi] from Rotorua). Prices start at around $65 for the short (one-hour) Kaituna run; a half day on the Rangitaiki costs from $95. Many operators also offer combination trips. **Kaituna Cascades** (☎ 07/345–4199 or 0800/524–8862 ⊕ www.kaitunacascades.co.nz) organizes one-day or multiday expeditions. **Raftabout** (☎☎ 07/343–9500 ⊕ www.raftabout.co.nz) focuses on day trips, some pairing rafting with other extreme sports such as jet-boating or bungy jumping. **River Rats** (☎ 07/345–6543 or 0800/333–900 ⊕ www.riverrats.co.nz) also offers day trips to the main rivers as well as adventure packages. **Wet 'n' Wild Adventure** (☎ 07/348–3191 or 0800/462–7238 ⊕ www.wetnwildrafting.co.nz) has multiadventure and double-trip options. One-day itineraries cover the Rangitaiki, Wairoa, and Kaituna rivers. *See* Chapter 11 for further rafting information.

Gentler natures should opt for a serene paddle on one of Rotorua's lakes. **Adventure Kayaking** (☎☎ 07/348–9451 ⊕ www.adventurekayaking.co.nz) has a variety of tours, from half a day spent paddling on Lake Rotorua ($65) to a full day on Lake Tarawera ($85) including a swim in a natural hot pool. Especially magical is the twilight paddle ($65) on Lake Rotoiti that incorporates a dip in the Manupirua hot pools (which you can't otherwise reach).

Shopping

At **De Flute Glass Studio & Gallery** (✉ 153 Fairy Springs Rd.), you can watch molten glass being turned into colorful glassware as well as browse the unique wares. It's closed Monday and Tuesday, and all of June and July. See jade carvers at work at the **Jade Factory** (✉ 1280 Fenton St. ☎ 07/349–1828), a bright, spacious shop where handcrafted gifts are for sale. **Madhouse Design Store & Gallery** (✉ 1093 Tutanekai St. ☎☎ 07/347–6066) specializes in art from around the country. Everything from sculpture and pottery to weaving and greeting cards is zany and colorful.

The **New Zealand Māori Arts & Crafts Institute** (✉ Hemo Rd. ☎ 07/348–9047 ⊕ www.nzMāori.co.nz) was established in 1963 to preserve Māori heritage and crafts. At the institute you can watch wood carvers and flax weavers at work and see New Zealand greenstone (jade) being sculpted into jewelry. The gift shop sells fine examples of this work, plus many other items, from small wood-carved kiwis to decorative flax skirts of the kind worn in the Māori cultural shows.

ROTORUA AREA ESSENTIALS

Transportation

BY AIR

Rotorua Airport, with the olfactorily evocative code ROT, is about 10 km (6 mi) from the city center. Taxi fare to the city is approximately

$25. You could also arrange for a ride ($12) with Super Shuttle; call ahead for a reservation.

Air New Zealand has daily flights that link Rotorua with Auckland, Christchurch, and Wellington.

🛪 Airport **Rotorua Airport** ✉ Hwy. 33 ☎ 07/345-6176.
🛪 Carriers **Air New Zealand** ☎ 0800/737-000 ⊕ www.airnewzealand.co.nz.
🛪 Airport Transfers **Rotorua Taxis** ☎ 06/348-1111 or 0800/500-000. **Super Shuttle** ☎ 0800/748-885.

BY BUS

InterCity buses run five times daily between Auckland and Rotorua. The journey takes 4½ hours. Rotorua is something of a transportation hub: it's easy to reach Taupo, Hamilton, Tauranga, Wellington, Gisborne, and Napier by bus. Some of InterCity's routes are done by Newmans buses.

🛪 Bus Depot **Rotorua** ✉ Tourism Rotorua Visitor Information Centre, 1167 Fenton St.
🛪 Bus Information **InterCity** ☎ 09/913-6100 ⊕ www.intercitycoach.co.nz.

BY CAR

Rotorua is about three hours from Auckland. Take Highway 1 south past Hamilton and Cambridge to Tirau, where Highway 5 breaks off to Rotorua. Roads in this region are generally in good condition, and most drivers maintain moderate speeds (perhaps because speeding fines are heavy). In Rotorua proper, traffic slows during the early morning and early evening commutes, but as rush hours go, they're not too bad. If other drivers flash their lights, it often means a traffic cop is in the vicinity.

Avis New Zealand has a branch at Rotorua airport.

🛪 Rental Agency **Avis New Zealand** ☎ 09/526-2847 ⊕ www.avis.com/nz.

Contacts & Resources

EMERGENCIES

For over-the-counter remedies, head to the Lakes Care Pharmacy, which stays open daily 8:30 AM–9:30 PM.

🛪 Emergency Services **Fire, police, and ambulance** ☎ 111.
🛪 Hospital **Rotorua Hospital** ✉ Pukeroa St. ☎ 06/348-1199.
🛪 Pharmacy **Lakes Care Pharmacy** ✉ Arawa St. at Tutanekai St. ☎ 07/348-4385.

MAIL & INTERNET

There are plenty of Internet cafés in Rotorua and in most other decent-size towns in the region as well. Many lodgings now have Internet access, too.

🛪 Internet Cafés **Art Café Rotoruá** ✉ 1195 Fenton St. ☎ 07/348-3288. **Mo's Cafe Bar & Casino** ✉ 1142 Tutanekai St. ☎ 07/349-6930.
🛪 Post Office **Rotorua Books & More** ✉ The Centre, Amohau St. ☎ 06/349-6557.

TOURS

ADVENTURE TOURS Mount Tarawera 4WD Tours has a sensational half-day, four-wheel-drive trip to the edge of the Mt. Tarawera crater. Departures are available at 8 AM and 1 PM; the tour costs $121.

The Waimangu Round Trip is probably the most complete tour of Rotorua. It includes an easy 5-km (3-mi) hike through the Waimangu

Thermal Valley to Lake Rotomahana, where a cruiser takes you past steaming cliffs to the narrow isthmus that divides the lake from Lake Tarawera. After crossing the lake, the tour visits the Buried Village and ends with a dip in the Polynesian Pools in Rotorua. The trip costs $230; reserve a place with the Rotorua visitor center.

🎫 **Mount Tarawera 4WD Tours** ☎ 07/349-3714 ⊕ www.mt-tarawera.co.nz. **Waimangu Round Trip** ☎ 07/366-6137 ⊕ www.waimangu.com.

BOAT TOURS In Rotorua, the Mokoia Island Tours paddle steamer sets off daily from the lakefront piers for cruises on Lake Rotorua. A popular one-hour guided tour goes around Mokoia Island and includes dinner on the boat ($85). Kawarau Jet, a speed boat, takes trips on Lake Rotorua; one option is a 1½-hour trip to Mokoia that includes a guided tour of the island and costs $79.

🎫 **Kawarau Jet** ☎ 07/343-7600 ⊕ www.kjet.co.nz. **Mokoia Island Tours** ☎ 07/348-6634.

BUS TOURS Newmans Coach Lines (working with InterCity) runs a variety of trips around Rotorua. A tour that includes Whakarewarewa, the New Zealand Māori Arts & Crafts Institute, Paradise Valley, and the Agrodome is $88, including all entrance fees.

Paradise Tours and The Connection Bus (owned by the same company) operate various tours around Rotorua plus Taupo and Waitomo. Prices start at $40 for a three-hour tour.

Geyser Link runs several local tours that include attractions such as Rainbow Springs, the Agrodome, and Waiotapu; prices start at $40.

🎫 **Geyser Link** ☎ 0800/000-4321 or 027/544-8820 ⊕ www.geyserlink.co.nz. **Newmans Coach Lines Rotorua** ☎ 07/348-0366 ⊕ www.newmanscoach.co.nz. **Paradise Tours and The Connection Bus** ☎07/378-9955 or 0274/904-944 ⊕www.paradisetours. co.nz.

HELICOPTER Helipro Helicopter Adventures offers a Rotorua city tour for $85, a
TOURS Mokoia trip that includes a tour around the island ($295), and a "Volcanic Adventure" that includes Tarawera for $395.

🎫 **Helipro Helicopter Adventures** ☎ 07/357-2512 ⊕ www.helipro.co.nz.

VISITOR INFORMATION

The Rotorua visitor bureau is open daily 8–5:30. In addition to an information office, it has a café, a film-processing service, a tour-reservation desk, a map shop operated by the Department of Conservation, and a lost-luggage facility.

🎫 **Tourist Information Tourism Rotorua Visitor Information Centre** ✉ 1167 Fenton St., Rotorua ☎ 07/348-5179 ⊕ www.rotoruanz.com.

LAKE TAUPO & TONGARIRO NATIONAL PARK

The largest lake in New Zealand, Lake Taupo is a popular vacation spot for locals and visitors alike. The town of Taupo on the lake's northeastern shore has blossomed into a major outdoor activities center, offering everything from rafting to skydiving. Even if you're not looking for extreme adventures, Taupo is worth a visit to see more examples of the region's geothermal wonders. Within easy traveling distance of Rotorua to the north and the mountainous areas to the south, the town is becoming increasingly developed, but it's still a fairly laid-back place. The abundance of activities here mean that it can get busy, though, particularly during school vacations and the summer holidays. Book late and a bed might be difficult to find.

Fishing is a major lure, both on Lake Taupo and on the rivers to the south. The lake and backcountry rivers are some of the few places where tales of the "big one" can actually be believed. The Tongariro River is particularly famous as an angler's paradise.

Southwest of Lake Taupo rise the three volcanic peaks that make up Tongariro National Park, New Zealand's first national park. This is a year-round magnet for skiers and hikers. Even if you don't have much time, skirting the peaks provides a rewarding route on your way south to Wanganui or Wellington.

Taupo

② *82 km (51 mi) south of Rotorua, 150 km (94 mi) northwest of Napier.*

The tidy town of Taupo is the base for exploring Lake Taupo, the country's largest lake. Its placid shores are backed by volcanic mountains, and in the vicinity is more of the geothermal activity that characterizes this zone (and, unlike Rotorua, most of the natural sites are free to visit). Water sports are popular here—notably sailing, cruising, and waterskiing—but most of all Taupo is known for its fishing. The town is the rainbow-trout capital of the universe: the average Taupo trout weighs in around 4 pounds, and the lake is open year-round. Meanwhile, the backpacker crowd converges upon Taupo for its plethora of adventure activities. The town is celebrated for its skydiving and bungy-jumping opportunities, and white-water rafting and jet-boating are available on the local rivers.

In this easy-to-navigate town, the straight streets are laid out in a grid pattern. Lake Terrace runs along the lakefront; it turns into Tongariro Street as it heads north, crossing the Waikato River and the gates that control the flow of water from the lake. Heu Heu Street is the main shopping street and runs from the traffic lights on Tongariro Street.

At **Huka Falls,** the Waikato River thunders through a narrow chasm and over a 35-foot rock ledge. The fast-flowing river produces almost 50% of the North Island's required power, and its force at this point is extraordinary, with the falls dropping into a seething, milky-white pool 200 feet across. The view from the footbridge is superb, though for an even more impressive look, both the Huka Jet and the Hanna K (⇨ Sports & the Outdoors *and* Taupo & Tongariro National Park A to Z, *below)* get close to the maelstrom. The falls are 3 km (2 mi) north of town; turn right off Highway 1 onto Huka Falls Road.

The construction of the local geothermal project had an impressive—and unforeseen—effect. The underground dynamics were so drastically altered that boiling mud pools, steaming vents, and large craters appeared in an area now known as **Craters of the Moon.** A marked walkway snakes for 2 km (1 mi) through the belching, sulfurous landscape, past boiling pits and hissing crevices. Entrance (during daylight hours) is by donation. The craters are up Karapiti Road, across from the Huka Falls turnoffs on Highway 1, 3 km (2 mi) north of Taupo.

The Waikato River is dammed along its length; the first construction is the **Aratiatia Dam,** 10 km (6 mi) northeast of Taupo (turn right off Highway 5). The river below the dam is virtually dry most of the time, but three times a day (at 10, noon, and 2), and four times a day in summer (Oct.–Mar., also at 4), the dam gates are opened and the gorge is dramatically transformed into a raging torrent. Watch the spectacle from the road bridge over the river or from one of two lookout points a 15-minute walk downriver through the bush. The whole thing lasts 30 minutes, after which the dam gates close, the river subsides, and the gorge returns to serenity.

Even if you think you have seen enough bubbling pools and fuming craters to last a lifetime, the captivating thermal valley of **Orakei Korako** is likely to change your mind. Geyser-fed streams hiss and steam as they flow into the waters of the lake, and there is an impressive cream-and-pink silica terrace, believed to be the largest in the world since the volcanic destruction of the terraces of Rotomahana. At the bottom of Aladdin's Cave, the vent of an ancient volcano, a jade-green pool was once used exclusively by Māori women as a beauty parlor, which is where the name *Orakei Korako* (a place of adorning) originated. The valley is 37 km (23 mi) north of Taupo (take Highway 1 out of town) and takes about 25 minutes to reach by car; you could always see it en route to or from Rotorua, which lies another 68 km (43 mi) northeast of the valley. ☏ *07/378–3131* ⊕ *www.orakeikorako.co.nz* ✉ *$23* ☾ *Oct.–May, daily 8–5:30; June–Sept., daily 8–5.*

OFF THE BEATEN PATH

New Zealand's only **PRAWN FARM –** opened in 1987 with stock imported from Malaysia. Today, you can take a tour around the property, check out the holding tanks where prawns are bred in specially heated river water (in some, baby prawns eat out of your hand). You can also catch your own prawns using a small rod and fishing line, or just buy some onsite; either way, you can have them cooked and served as you like in the adjoining restaurant. ⊠ *Huka Falls Rd. next to the Huka Jet complex, Taupo* ☏ *07/374–8474* ⊕ *www.prawnfarm.co.nz* ✉ *$12* ☾ *Daily 11–4.*

Where to Stay & Eat

$$$$ ✗ **Villino's.** Owners Alex and Carolyn Obel preside over this cozy, wood-beamed eatery, where dishes such as aged beef-eye fillet with wild mushroom gratin and pancetta-wrapped beans are served with a flourish. Desserts include a yummy hazelnut-and-almond pavlova with vanilla mascarpone and berry compote. After your meal, you can relax by the stone fireplace in the adjoining bar and check the rugby scores on the big-screen TV. ⊠ *45 Horomatangi Rd.* ☏ *07/377–4478* ⊕ *www.villino. co.nz* ⊟ *AE, DC, MC, V.*

$$$–$$$$ ✕ **Brantry Restaurant.** The menu is updated seasonally at this low-ceiling, converted 1950s town house—but if you're lucky, chef-owners Prue and Felicity Campbell might be offering a main dish of chocolate-and-licorice-stuffed venison, or vanilla-and-honey panna cotta for dessert. Many of the wines are chosen from emerging and boutique vineyards. ⊠ *45 Rifle Range Rd.* 🖼 *07/378–0484* ⊕ ▭ *MC, V* ⊗ *Closed Mon. No lunch.*

★ **$** ✕ **The Replete Food Company.** There's no wine license, and you have to order your food from display cabinets at the front counter, but a delicious daily menu brings crowds of customers to this casual spot. The panini sandwiches are especially popular at lunch; they come stuffed with various goodies, including eggplant with an Indian-spiced salsa. There are also lots of salads, including a hot calamari salad with fresh herbs and chili-lime dressing. In the morning, try the Complete Replete Breakfast, which consists of honey-cured bacon, tomato relish, poached eggs, and roasted field mushrooms with grilled focaccia. You can choose some tools for your own kitchen from the adjoining shop. ⊠ *45 Heu Heu St.* 🖼 *07/377–3011* ▭ *AE, DC, MC, V* ⊗ *No dinner.*

¢–$ ✕ **Brew.** Place your order over the service counter covered with coffee sacks, then settle into this café with your tea, coffee, or freshly squeezed juice. There's a trendy feel to the interior; the walls vary between patches of plaster and concrete blocks painted bright orange with a touch of purple. Breakfast is served all day—favorites include smoked-salmon bagels and a yummy lemon tart. ⊠ *Marama Arcade* 🖼 *07/378–5779* ⊗ *Closed Tues. No dinner.*

$$$$ ✕⎕ **Huka Lodge.** Secluded in parklike grounds at the edge of the Waikato
Fodor'sChoice River, this lodge is the standard by which New Zealand's other sport-
★ ing lodges are judged. The large, lavish guest rooms, decorated in muted grays and whites, are arranged in blocks of two or three. All have sliding glass doors that open to a view across lawns to the river. In the interest of tranquillity, they're not equipped with phones, TVs, or radios. At dinner, a formal, five-course affair, study the wine list for an extensive view of New Zealand's best vintages—the wine cellar holds more than 20,000 bottles. Meals are served either at a communal dining table or, on request, at one of a dozen private dining areas (including the wine cellar or on the outdoor terrace). The lodge can arrange practically any activity under the sun, including helicopter rides. ⊠ *Huka Falls Rd., Box 95* 🖼 *07/378–5791* 🖼 *07/378–0427* ⊕ *www.hukalodge.co.nz* ↪ *20 rooms, 1 cottage* ⌂ *Restaurant, tennis court, spa, fishing, bar, lounge, library; no a/c, no room phones, no room TVs* ▭ *AE, DC, MC, V* ⫯⚬⫯ *MAP.*

$–$$ ✕⎕ **Caboose Lodge.** The exterior resembles a log cabin, but inside this lakefront lodge the rooms recall luxury rail travel in colonial Africa. Furnishings have an African theme, from the Assegai-style curtain track to the faux-leopard-skin upholstery. The spectacular mountain views recall you to your locale. The Serengeti Restaurant ($$$) serves breakfast for guests and dinner for all comers. Try the roasted ostrich fillet with garlic and red wine jus, followed by the warm apple-and-rhubarb shortcake, and you'll sleep like a well-fed lion. ⊠ *100–102 Lake Terr.* 🖼 *07/ 376–0116* 🖼 *07/377–2055* ⊕ *www.taupo.caboose.co.nz* ↪ *50 rooms*

⌂ *Restaurant, some fans, in-room broadband, pool, gym, spa, bar, laundry facilities* ▤ *AE, DC, MC, V* ⊘ *No lunch.*

$$$–$$$$ ▥ **The Pillars.** All four suites at this modern, Mediterranean-style country manor have private verandas that look out over the expansive park-like grounds. They're individually furnished, but all have voile curtains, comfortable plush furnishings and modern bathrooms. Guests have the use of a large sunny lounge, and breakfast can be taken in the spacious conservatory with stunning views of a lake and the mountains beyond. John and Ruth Boddy are excellent hosts. ⊠ *7 Deborah Rise, Bonshaw Park* ☎ *07/378–1512* 🖷 *07/378–1511* ⊕ *www.pillarshomestay.co.nz* ⇦ *4 suites* ⌂ *In-room data ports, tennis court, pool* ▤ *AE, DC, MC, V* ⊘▯ *BP.*

$$ ▥ **Richlyn Homestay.** Eponymous owners Richard and Lyn are well traveled, charming, and sociable, and they run a tight ship in their modern and comfortable home. The patio area surrounded by well-tended gardens is a peaceful haven, with the silence broken only by birdsong, and inside, the big-screen TV in the spacious lounge delights ardent sports fans. Guest rooms are tastefully furnished and look out onto the gardens, ensuring a stay that is relaxing and restful. Two rooms share a bathroom. ⊠ *1 Mark Wynd, Bonshaw Park, 8 km (5 mi) southeast of Taupo* ☎ *07/378–8023* 🖷 *07/378–7116* ⊕ *www.richlyn.co.nz* ⇦ *5 rooms, 3 with bath* ⌂ *Some fans, spa, laundry facilities, Internet room; no a/c, no room phones, no smoking* ▤ *MC, V* ⊘▯ *BP.*

$–$$ ▥ **Cascades Motor Lodge.** Set on the shores of Lake Taupo, these attractive brick-and-timber rooms are large, comfortable, and smartly decorated. The two-story "luxury" apartments, which sleep up to seven, have a lounge room, bedroom, kitchen, and dining room on the ground floor in an open-plan design, glass doors leading to a large patio, and a second bedroom and bathroom on the upper floor. Studios have one bedroom. All rooms are equipped with a whirlpool bath. Room 1 is closest to the lake and a small beach. ⊠ *Lake Terr., 3 km (2 mi) south of Taupo, just beyond the State Hwy. 5 (Napier) turnoff* ☎ *07/378–3774* 🖷 *07/378–0372* ⊕ *www.cascades.co.nz* ⇦ *22 rooms* ⌂ *Pool, laundry facilities; no a/c* ▤ *AE, DC, MC, V.*

Shopping

K F L. The letters stand for knitwear, fur, and leather, and that's just what you'll find at Louis Pogoni's exclusive store. The clothing and accessories are all top quality, and all are manufactured in New Zealand. ⊠ *20 Heu Heu St.* ☎🖷 *07/377–4676.*

Sports & the Outdoors

BUNGY JUMPING If you're not heading to the South Island and Queenstown—spiritual home of bungy jumping—then Taupo is your best bet. **Taupo Bungy** (⊠ *202 Spa Rd., off Tongariro St., 1 km [½ mi] north of town* ☎ *07/377–1135 or 0800/888–408* ⊕ *www.taupobungy.co.nz*) provides jumps from an awesome cantilevered platform projecting out from a cliff 150 feet above the Waikato River. You can go for the "water touch" or dry versions. Even if you have no intention of "walking the plank," go and watch the jumpers from the nearby lookout point. The jumps cost $135 a shot and are available daily from 9 to 5.

FISHING   There's great fishing in the Taupo area and an attendant number of guides with local expertise. Guides work the Tongariro River as well as the lake. The season's height runs from October to April. Costs are usually $70–$80 per hour, and include all your equipment plus a fishing license (note that you'll need a special license to fish here and in Rotorua). Book at least a day in advance.

Mark Aspinall (☎ 07/378–4453) leads fly-fishing trips for rainbow and brown trout. Gus Te Moana, who runs **Te Moana Charters** (☎ 07/378–4839), also offers fishing trips on his 24-foot boat, who'll quote you a price that includes the trip, all equipment, a license, and usually lunch and beer.

Mark Collins (☎ 07/378–1364) offers fly-fishing with instruction for novices. A luxury cruiser on Lake Taupo costs about $150 per hour; for more information, contact **Chris Jolly Outdoors** (☎ 07/378–0623 ⊕ www.chrisjolly.co.nz). *See* Chapter 11 for more fishing information.

JET-BOATING   For high-speed thrills on the Waikato River take a trip on the **Huka Jet** (☎ 07/374–8572 ⊕ www.hukajet.co.nz), which spins and skips its way between the Aratiatia Dam and Huka Falls. Departures are every 30 minutes from Karetoto Road throughout the day; cost is $79 per person.

RAFTING   The Grade 5 Wairoa and Mohaka rivers are accessible from Taupo, as are the Rangitaiki and more family-friendly Tongariro. Different rivers are open at different times of year, depending on water levels, and operators all run similarly priced trips, starting at around $95 per person. Call **Rapid Sensations** (☎ 07/378–7902 or 0800/353–435 ⊕ www.rapids.co.nz), who provide transportation, wet suits, equipment, and much-needed hot showers at the end. *See* Chapter 11 for more rafting information.

SKYDIVING   On a tandem skydive, you're attached to a professional skydiver for a breathtaking leap. Depending on altitude, free fall can last from a few seconds to close to a minute. **Great Lake Skydive Centre** (☎ 0800/373–335 ⊕ www.freefly.co.nz) is one local operator. **Taupo Tandem Skydiving** (☎ 0800/275–934 ⊕ www.tts.net.nz) is another option. Call at least one day in advance to arrange your jump—which goes ahead weather permitting—and expect to pay around $170–$300 per jump.

SOAKING   Trade in adrenaline for mellowness during a few hours at the **Taupo Hot Springs** (⊠ State Hwy. 5, 3 km [2 mi] southeast of Taupo [Napier Rd.] ☎ 07/377–6502 ⊕ www.taupohotsprings.com), a favored bathing spot for more than a century. In this modern complex, naturally occurring hot springs have been corralled into three interlinked pools and twin hot tubs. There's a waterslide and barbecue and picnic area if you'd like to make a day of it. The pool cost is $9, the waterslide $5; bathing gear and towel rentals are available. The complex is open daily from 7:30 AM until 9:30 PM.

Tongariro National Park

❸ *110 km (69 mi) southwest of Taupo.*

Fodor's Choice
★

Tongariro is the country's first national park, established on sacred land given by the Ngati Tuwharetoa people in 1887. A trio of active volcanoes dominates the park. Tongariro, the shortest and least active, has a heavily truncated cone; Ngauruhoe, a single-vent volcano, has a distinctively smooth cone shape. Ruapehu is the tallest (and at 9,175 feet, the highest mountain on the whole North Island), with a longer, irregular snow-topped profile and a large crater lake. It's also the most active of the three. Ruapehu last erupted in 1995 and 1996, each time giving little warning before spewing forth ash and showers of rocks and unleashing lahars (the water of the crater lake churned with rock). Luckily, no one was hurt, though the eruptions occurred during ski season. Ruapehu's crater lake is filling up again, and there's a risk that another lahar will burst through the crater walls. The last time this happened, in 1953, more than 100 people were killed as the flood destroyed a railway bridge. Now local politicians are debating whether to dig a channel to drain some of the water.

Tongariro's spectacular combination of dense *rimu* pine forests, crater lakes, barren lava fields, and birdlife makes it the most impressive and popular of the island's national parks. It has many hiking trails, the most famous of which is the **Tongariro Crossing,** a 16-km (10-mi) hike that traverses the mountain, passing craters and brilliantly colored lakes, and is generally considered one of the finest walks in the country. You'll need to be reasonably fit to tackle it, because there are some steep inclines and the harsh volcanic terrain can be punishing on a hot day. Other hikes in the park range from multiday circuits to short treks of an hour or two (⇨ Sports & the Outdoors, *below*).

Highway 1 skirts the east side of the park, but the most direct access is from Highway 47, on the north side; Highway 48, which leads to Whakapapa Village, branches off from here, about 10 km (6 mi) before the confusingly named **National Park village,** which sits at the junction of Highways 4 and 47, just outside the park proper. At National Park village you'll find motels, cafés, a gas station, and other services.

Whakapapa Village, on the north side of Ruapehu, is the only settlement within the national park with services and is the jump-off point for the Whakapapa ski slopes. The second ski area is Turoa, and its closest town is **Ohakune,** which is just beyond the southern boundary of the park—take Highway 49, which runs between Highways 1 and 4. Although ski season is the busiest time of year, these towns keep their doors open for hikers and other travelers when the snow melts.

For displays about Tongariro National Park, and helpful hiking and skiing advice, stop off at the **Whakapapa Visitor Centre.** This is also the best place to buy maps and guides, including the very useful Department of Conservation park map—essential for hikers—and individual local-walk leaflets. If you're interested in movers and shakers, check the seismograph in the office that records the activity from the mountain. If it starts trembling, at least you'll have a head start on those stuck on the ski slopes. ⊠ *Whakapapa Visitor Centre, Hwy. 48, Mt. Ruapehu* ☎ *07/892–3729* ⊕ *www.doc.govt.nz* ☉ *Daily 8–5.*

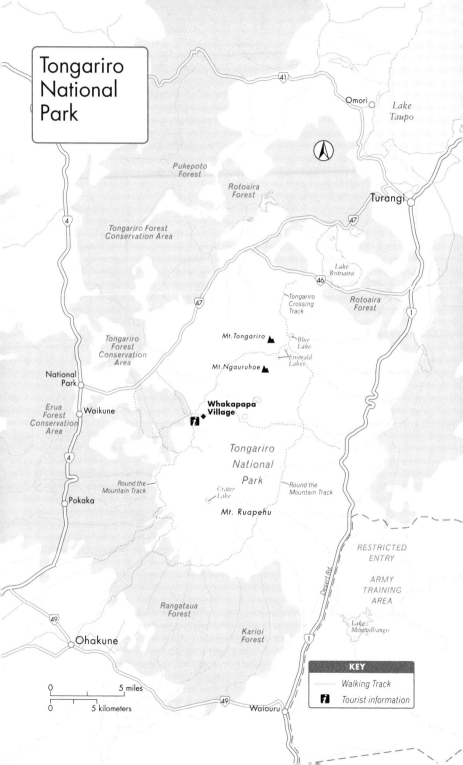

Where to Stay & Eat

\$\$–\$\$\$ ✕ **Eivins Café, Wine Bar, and Restaurant.** This modern diner's trump card is the panoramic mountain views from its front veranda. The pesto-encrusted lamb rack on roasted potato and kūmara (local sweet potato) with julienned vegetables and rosemary jus might go cold if you gaze in awe too long. ⊠ *State Hwy. 4, National Park Village* ☎ *07/892–2844* ☐ *MC, V* ⊗ *No lunch.*

\$\$–\$\$\$ ✕ **Station Cafe.** Modern prints light the dusky pink and wood-panel walls of this bright and breezy café/bar with the tracks of the north–south railway running right outside the door. There's coffee in all shades, and at lunch, the food runs from nachos to potato wedges to ploughman's sarnies (aka thick sandwiches with meat, cheese, and onion). In the evening, you might find more contemporary fare, such as tender venison with juniper-and-tamarillo glaze. Finish up with a pastry shell brimming with rhubarb and custard, topped with berries and crème fraîche, and you're definitely king of the rails. Be prepared for crowds when the train pulls in twice a day. ⊠ *Station Road, National Park Village* ☎ *07/892–2881* ☐ *AE, DC, MC, V.*

\$\$–\$\$\$\$ ✕🔲 **Bayview Chateau Tongariro.** Built in 1929 in a French chateau style, this property really catches the eye as you drive into Whakapapa Village. Most rooms have fine mountain views; be sure to ask for one when booking. Meals are taken in the Ruapehu Restaurant (\$\$\$)—serving traditional New Zealand cuisine with a modern slant—or there's a less formal café. The hotel can arrange guided hikes on all the best-known routes in the park. ⊠ *Hwy. 48* ☎ *07/892–3809 or 0800/242–832* 🖷 *07/892–3704* ⊕ *www.chateau.co.nz* ⤴ *95 rooms, 10 suites* ⚭ *Restaurant, café, cable TV, 9-hole golf course, tennis court, pool, gym, hot tub, bar; no a/c* ☐ *AE, DC, MC, V.*

¢ 🔲 **Discovery Lodge.** The mountain views are dramatic from this friendly complex set in 10 parklike acres, only minutes from the ski slopes. Most of the accommodation is in self-contained motel units and chalets. The rooms are light and airy; the one-bedroom units sleep up to six people. There are also some doubles priced for backpackers, and powered campsites. The restaurant serves breakfast and dinner, and you can request a packed lunch before setting off exploring. The lodge runs its own shuttle to the Tongariro Track, which begins just a 10-minute drive away. ⊠ *State Hwy. 47, Whakapapa Village* ☎ *07/892–2744 or 0800/122–122* ⊕ *www.discovery.net.nz* ⤴ *22 rooms* ⚭ *Restaurant, bar, laundry facilities, Internet room; no a/c, no room phones, no TV in some rooms, no smoking* ☐ *AE, DC, MC, V.*

Sports & the Outdoors

HIKING
FodorsChoice
★

The **Tongariro Crossing** trail grabs the hiking limelight. A one-way track starting in Mangatepopo, the crossing is a spectacular six- to seven-hour hike that follows a 16-km (10-mi) trail up and over the namesake mountain, passing craters, the evocatively named Emerald Lakes, old lava flows, and hot springs. Although children and school groups commonly do the hike, it is not to be taken lightly. Be prepared for rapidly changing weather conditions with warm and waterproof clothing. Wear sturdy footwear, and take food, plenty of water, sunblock, and sunglasses—and don't forget a hat! Also, be careful not to get too close to steam vents; the area around them is scorchingly hot. From late November to May, you'll be sharing the trail with many other hikers. In the colder months, however, it's really only for experienced winter hikers who can deal with snow and ice; some transport companies will take you only if you have an ice ax and crampons.

Tongariro Track Transport (☎ 07/892–3897) runs a bus to the Tongariro Crossing trailhead from the Whakapapa Visitor Centre daily at 8 AM year-round. **Alpine Scenic Tours** (☎ 07/378–7412 ⊕ www.alpinescenictours. co.nz) provides transport to the trailhead from the Taupo visitor information office for $35, with returns from Turangi for $30. In addition, many of the motels and lodges in National Park village can arrange transport to the track for about $15. You'll usually need to make a reservation; they will all pick you up at the end of the track.

The longest hikes in the park are the three-day **Northern Circuit,** which goes over Tongariro and around Ngauruhoe, and the four-day **Round-the-Mountain Track,** which circles Ruapehu. You could also tackle short half-hour to two-hour walks if all you want is a flavor of the region. A 1½-hour round-trip trek to the Tawhai Falls via the **Whakapapanui Track** takes you through the forest, and a two-hour round-trip to Taranaki Falls is in subalpine surroundings. There are trailside huts throughout the park to use on overnight trips. You'll need to buy a hut pass at the visitor center; it costs $10 from mid-June to the beginning of October and $20 the rest of the year. Gas cookers are available in the huts. At this writing, a reservation system was under consideration.

SKIING The **Mt. Ruapehu ski slopes** (⊕ www.mtruapehu.com) add up to New Zealand's most extensive skiing and snowboarding terrain. The **Whakapapa** ski area, on the north side of the mountain, has more than 30 groomed trails, including excellent beginners' slopes. **Turoa,** on the south side, has a half pipe. Ski season generally runs from June through October. Both areas can provide lessons and top-notch rental equipment. Lift passes cost around $68 for access to the whole mountain, but a variety of combination tickets are also available. The area's Web site includes snow reports, trail maps, and other information.

TAUPO & TONGARIRO NATIONAL PARK ESSENTIALS

Transportation

BY BUS

InterCity buses run five times daily from Auckland to Taupo. The trip takes approximately five hours. (Some of InterCity's routes are done by Newmans buses.) From Rotorua to Taupo, four daily buses make the 1-hour-and-20-minute trip.

It's more difficult to reach Tongariro National Park by public transportation, though there is a daily summer InterCity/Newmans bus service (mid-October–April) between Taupo, Whakapapa Village, and the village of National Park; the trip takes around 1½ hours. For information on shuttles to trailheads, *see* Sports & the Outdoors *in* Tongariro National Park.

🚏 Bus Depot **Taupo** ✉ Gasgoine St.
🚏 Bus Information **InterCity** ☎ 09/913-6100 ⊕ www.intercitycoach.co.nz.

BY CAR

Taupo is four hours from Auckland, taking Highway 1 the whole way. It's 70 minutes from Rotorua, also via Highway 1. For Tongariro National Park, the main approach is along Highway 4 on the park's western side; turn off at National Park for Whakapapa and the northern ski slopes, or at Raetihi for Ohakune and the south. From Taupo to the park, follow State Highway 1 south and turn off at Turangi onto State Highway 47.

The roads in this area are generally good, and there are occasional turnouts where you can enjoy the views. Around the national park, snow and ice can be a problem in the winter; at times you may need tire chains.

BY TRAIN

For Tongariro National Park, either the daily Tranz Scenic *Overlander* from Auckland to Wellington or the *Northerner* from Wellington to Auckland stops at National Park village and Ohakune year-round. The journey from Wellington passes over five high viaducts. The train from Auckland goes around the remarkable Raurimu Spiral, where the track rises 200 meters (660 feet) in a stretch only 6 km (3½ mi) long.

There is no train service to Taupo.

🚆 Train Information **Tranz Scenic** ☎ 0800/872-467 ⊕ www.tranzscenic.co.nz.

Contacts & Resources

EMERGENCIES

Pharmacies don't stay open very late here, but the Main Street Pharmacy in Taupo is open from 8 AM to 4 PM.

🆘 Emergency Services **Fire, police, and ambulance** ☎ 111.
🆘 Pharmacy **Main Street Pharmacy** ✉ Tongariro and Heu Heu Sts., Taupo ☎ 07/378-2636.

TOURS

BOAT TOURS & LAKE CRUISES Cruises on Lake Taupo all feature a similar itinerary, usually involving a couple of hours out on the lake visiting local bays and modern Māori rock carvings. The *Barbary* is a 1920s wooden yacht believed to have once been the property of Errol Flynn. Departures are at 10 and 2 and summer evenings at 5 PM ($30). Huka Falls River Cruise runs trips to the falls on the *Hanna K,* leaving from Aratiatia Dam (north of Taupo) at 10:30 AM, 12:30 PM, and 2:30 PM ($30).

🚢 *Barbary* ☎ 07/378-3444. **Huka Falls River Cruise** ✉ Aratiatia Dam Rd. ☎ 0800/278-336.

BUS TOURS Within Taupo, the Hot Bus is a hop-on/hop-off service that takes in all the local sights. Although there's no commentary (they just shuttle people between attractions), it is convenient, because it leaves the visitor center daily on the hour 10–4. Each attraction stop costs $5, or you can get an unlimited pass for $20. Paradise Tours also visits the local attractions in Taupo and travels as far afield as Napier and Hawke's Bay. A three-hour tour costs $40.

Tongariro Expeditions runs trips to Tongariro National Park from the Taupo visitor information center and serves the Tongariro Crossing. It costs $30–$39 in summer and $60 in winter (including ice axes and crampons). It's more of a transport service than a full-blown tour.
🚌 **Hot Bus** ☎ 07/377-1967, 021/468-287 cell. **Paradise Tours** ☎ 07/378-9955 ⊕ www.paradisetours.co.nz. **Tongariro Expeditions** ☎ 07/377-0435 ⊕ www.thetongarirocrossing.co.nz.

VISITOR INFORMATION

Destination Lake Taupo, a regional tourism organization, maintains a helpful Web site, ⊕ www.laketauponz.com. The Department of Conservation's Web site, ⊕ www.doc.govt.nz, includes a good rundown on Tongariro National Park. There's also a Ruapehu promotion site, ⊕ www.ruapehunz.co.nz, with events listings, snow conditions, skiing information, and more.
🚌 Tourist Information **Taupo Visitor Information Centre** ✉ 30 Tongariro St., Taupo ☎ 07/376-0027 ⊕ www.laketauponz.com. **Whakapapa Visitor Centre** ✉ Hwy. 48, Mt. Ruapehu ☎ 07/892-3729.

NAPIER & HAWKE'S BAY

New Zealand prides itself on natural wonders. By that way of thinking, Napier is an exception. This coastal city of 50,000 is best known for its architecture. After an earthquake devastated Napier in 1931, residents rebuilt it in the art deco style of the day. Its well-kept uniformity of style makes it an exceptional period piece. There's a similar aspect to Napier's less-visited twin city, Hastings, just to the south, which was also remodeled after the earthquake. After stretching your legs in either place, you can relax on a brief wine-tasting tour—the region produces some of New Zealand's best wines. In addition, the mild climate and beaches of Hawke Bay make this a popular vacation area for New Zealanders. (*Hawke* Bay is the body of water; *Hawke's* Bay is the region.) You also should make a point of trying to visit the gannet colony at Cape Kidnappers, which you can see only between October and March.

Napier

150 km (94 mi) southeast of Taupo, 345 km (215 mi) northeast of Wellington.

The earthquake that struck Napier at 10:46 AM on February 3, 1931, was—at 7.8 on the Richter scale—the largest quake ever recorded in New Zealand. The force was such that the coastline was wrenched upward several feet. Almost all the town's brick buildings collapsed; many people were killed on the footpaths as they rushed outside. The quake triggered fires throughout town, and with water mains shattered, little could be done to stop the blazes that devoured the remaining wooden structures. One building was destroyed when, as the saying goes, "two buckets of water would have saved it." Only a few buildings survived the double whammy (the Public Service Building with its neoclassical pillars is one), and the death toll was well over 100. Strong aftershocks kept things frighteningly shaky for weeks after the disaster.

The surviving townspeople quickly rallied, first setting up tents and cookhouses in Nelson Park, then tackling the city's reconstruction at a remarkable pace. And in the rush to rebuild, Napier went mad for art deco style, the bold, geometric look that had burst on the global design scene in 1925. The sleek lines pointed to progress and modernity, and the use of concrete made the new buildings more earthquake-resistant. Now a walk through the art deco district, concentrated between Emerson, Herschell, Dalton, and Browning streets, is a stylistic immersion. The decorative elements are often found above the buildings' ground floors, so keep your eyes up.

There's more to Napier than art deco, though. It's a friendly, laid-back place, great for families. The Marine Parade promenade, lined with Norfolk pines, formal gardens, and children's attractions, is backed by pastel-color houses. There's also a town beach, though you should note that the waves and currents here make swimming dangerous.

❹ One of Napier's notable buildings is the **ASB Bank**, at the corner of Hastings and Emerson streets. The Māori theme on the lintels is probably the country's finest example of *kowhaiwhai* (rafter) patterns decorating a European building. The traditional red, white, and black pattern is also continued inside around a coffered ceiling.

❺ The **Criterion Hotel** (✉ 48 Emerson St.) is typical of the Spanish Mission style, which Napier took on because of its success in Santa Barbara, California, where an earthquake had similarly wreaked havoc just a few years before the New Zealand catastrophe. It has smooth plastered concrete walls (in imitation of adobe construction) and tiled parapets. The small square windows and larger round-arched glass doors also re-
❻ flect features of mud-brick construction. Along **Emerson Street** and its pedestrian mall, **Hannahs** and the **Hawke's Bay Chambers** are among the city's finest art deco examples, because they're so well preserved. **Bowmans Building** is a Louis Hay design in brick veneer with the characteristic eyebrow (brick or tiles, often curved, set over a window). Some of Hay's work was influenced by Chicago's Louis Sullivan; his best-known design is the National Tobacco Building in Ahuhiri.

❼ **Dalton Street** has its treasures as well. South of the intersection with Emerson Street, the pink **Countrywide Bank Building,** with its balcony, is one of Napier's masterpieces. **Hildebrand's,** at Tennyson Street, has an excellent frieze, which is best viewed from across Dalton. Hildebrand was a German who migrated to New Zealand—hence the German flag at one end, the New Zealand at the other, and the wavy lines in the middle to symbolize the sea passage between the two countries.

❽ The **Daily Telegraph Building** (✉ Tennyson St. and Church La.) is another Napier classic, used today as a real-estate office. It has almost all the deco style elements, incorporating zigzags, fountain shapes, ziggurats, and a

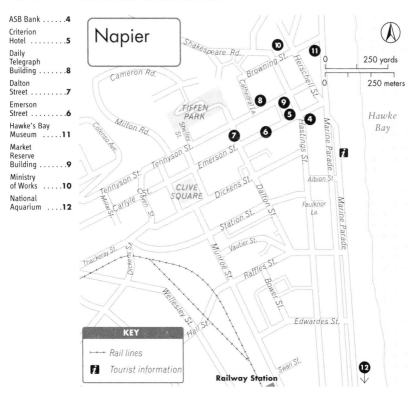

sunburst. If you can turn back the clock in your mind and imagine the
city littered with heaps of rubble, you would see the **Market Reserve
Building** (✉ Tennyson and Hastings Sts.) as the first to rise after the
earthquake. Its steel metal frame was riveted, not welded, so that the construction noise would give residents the message that the city really was
being rebuilt. The bronze storefronts with their "crown of thorns" pat-
terned leaded glass are still original.

The **Ministry of Works** (✉ Browning St.), with its decorative lighthouse
pillar at the front, takes on the almost Gothic menace that art deco architecture sometimes has (like New York's Chrysler Building).

A little over a kilometer (½ mi) north of the central area stands one of
the finest deco buildings, commonly known as the **Rothmans Building**
(✉ Bridge St.). The magnificent 1932 structure has been totally renovated and its original name reinstated: the National Tobacco Company
Building. It has a rose theme on the stained-glass windows and on a magnificent glass dome over the entrance hall. In the foyer, look for the full-
size cigar-store Indian complete with tomahawk but (for security reasons)
minus the musket.

Using newspaper reports, photographs, and audiovisuals, the **Hawke's
Bay Museum** re-creates the suffering caused by the earthquake. It also

houses a unique display of artifacts of the Ngati Kahungunu Māori people of the east coast—including vessels, decorative work, and statues. ⊠ *65 Marine Parade* ☎ *06/835–7781* ⊕ *www.hawkesbaymuseum.co. nz* ⊠ *$7.50* ⊙ *Oct.–Apr., daily 9–6; May–Sept., daily 9–5.*

★ ☺ ⓬ The **National Aquarium** is among the most exciting and informative underwater adventures in the country. Here, you can stand on a moving conveyor that takes you through the world of sharks, rays, turtles, and fish. There are environmental and ecological displays featuring a saltwater crocodile, tropical fish, and other sea creatures. ⊠ *Marine Parade* ☎ *06/834–1404* ⊕ *www.nationalaquarium.co.nz* ⊠ *$14* ⊙ *Feb.–Dec., daily 9–5, Jan., daily 9–7.*

The Seahorse Farm exhibits lobsters, crabs, and fish, but the star attractions are the native New Zealand sea horses, which are bred here in vast numbers. Small but fascinating, sea horses look like tiny pieces of cotton when born, and the mandatory guided tour takes you through the various stages of their development. ⊠ *Main Rd., Awatoto, 5 km (3 mi) south of Napier* ☎ *06/834–0998* ⊕ *www.theseahorsefarm.co.nz* ⊠ *$10* ⊙ *Tours Mon.–Sat. at 10 AM, 1 PM, and 3 PM; Sun. at 1 and 3.*

Where to Stay & Eat

★ $$$ ✕ **Restaurant Indonesia.** The interior of this tiny Hawke's Bay institution may be a bit gloomy, but the food is a revelation. Try a large selection of the Dutch-Indonesian food by sharing a *rijsttafel*, which consists of 13 sampling dishes. Other favorites: marinated prawn *satay* (grilled skewers) and *babi panggang* (grilled pork loin with a sweet-and-sour sauce based on onions, pineapple, and lemon juice). ⊠ *409 Marine Parade* ☎ *06/835–8303* ☰ *AE, DC, MC, V* ⚐ *Reservations essential.*

$$$ ✕ **Toscana.** Despite the name, the menu at this restaurant—it's in a converted old house, with paneled ceilings and polished wood floors—is less Italian than it is pan-European. The lamb shank braised in a Spanish tomato, bean, and herb casserole, and served with chorizo sausage, is prepared while you sip wine by an open fire in the cozy waiting room. ⊠ *112 Tennyson St.* ☎ *06/835–6848* ☰ *AE, MC, V* ⊙ *Closed Mon.*

$$–$$$ ✕ **Caution.** Massive wood-frame mirrors reflect the candles behind the bar in this spot in northern Napier. Try for one of the snug alcove tables and decide whether to go beyond the superb pizzas for something such as the roasted pork fillet served with wild mushrooms, buttered greens, and truffle mash. Caution shares ownership with the attached Shed 2, a wool store built in 1886 that is now a bar. ⊠ *West Quay, Ahuhiri* ☎ *06/835–0028* ☰ *AE, DC.*

★ $$$$ ✕▥ **The County Hotel.** Built in 1909 as the headquarters of the Hawke's Bay County Council, this is one of the few Napier buildings that survived the 1931 earthquake. Wood paneling, chandeliers hanging from ornate ceilings, and clawfoot bathtubs conjure up a more gracious era. The Chambers Restaurant ($$$) shares the overall look, with high ceilings and chandeliers; highlights include the salmon wrapped in prosciutto served with a pea-and-Parmesan risotto, and the pecan pie with *manuka* honey ice cream. Churchill's Bar is decorated with quotes from the great man's speeches, and a cellar room is used for evening wine tastings. ⊠ *12 Browning St.* ☎ *06/835–7800* 📠 *06/835–7797* ⊕ *www.*

countyhotel.co.nz ⤴ *18 rooms* △ *Restaurant, in-room data ports, sauna, spa, bar, library, laundry facilities; no smoking* ⊟ *AE, DC, MC, V.*

$$$$ ⊡ **McHardy House.** The gardens at this colonial mansion, set high on Napier Hill, have panoramic views of the Pacific Ocean and the beautiful Kaweka Ranges. The rooms all have native timber floors, American king-size beds, and elaborate bathrooms. Large verandas open onto landscaped grounds, where you can lounge by the heated swimming pool; there's also a lovely fireplace in the lounge. The four-course set dinners are accompanied by a pre-dinner drink and hors d'oeuvres. ⊠ *11 Bracken St.* ☎ *06/835–0605* 🖷 *06/834–0902* ⊕ *www.mchardyhouse. com* ⤴ *2 rooms, 4 suites* △ *Pool, billiards, bar, laundry facilities; no a/c, no room TVs, no smoking* ⊟ *AE, DC, MC, V* ⊠ *MAP.*

$$ ⊡ **Pebble Beach Motor Inn.** This modern complex trumps the town's other motels by dint of its freshness (it opened in 2003). All the units have balconies facing Marine Parade, overlooking the sea. It's just a short walk to many of the town's sights, restaurants, and cafés. The plush rooms are spacious and finished in soft tones of beige and grey, and all have whirlpool baths. ⊠ *445 Marine Parade* ☎ *06/835–7496* 🖷 *06/835–2409* ⊕ *www.pebblebeach.co.nz* ⤴ *10 rooms, 6 suites* △ *In-room data ports, spa, laundry facilities; no a/c, no smoking* ⊟ *AE, DC, MC, V.*

$$ ⊡ **Mon Logis.** Originally built in the 1860s and one of the few houses that escaped destruction in the 1931 earthquake, this splendid mansion-cum-boutique hotel feels like a little piece of France. Its front windows overlook the ocean and distant Cape Kidnappers; in the guest rooms, white match-board ceilings hover above white bedspreads and lace-trimmed pillowcases. Gallic host Gerard Averous (who speaks Spanish as well as French) is passionate in his desire to ensure his guests are comfortable and enjoy their stay. Breakfast can include freshly baked croissants. ⊠ *415 Marine Parade* ☎ *06/835–2125* 🖷 *06/835–8811* ⊕ *www. babs.co.nz/monlogis* ⤴ *4 rooms* △ *In-room data ports, laundry facilities* ⊟ *AE, DC, MC, V* ⊠ *CP.*

¢ ⊡ **Art Deco Backpackers.** On the top floor of the old Criterion Hotel, one of Napier's central art deco buildings, this hostel offers well-maintained rooms and secure storage. All rooms have washbasins; a few have bunks, but most have regular beds. There's a roomy lounge and a separate TV room. ⊠ *48 Emerson St.* ☎ *06/835–2059* 🖷 *06/835–2370* ⤴ *27 rooms* △ *Café, bar, lounge, laundry facilities, Internet room; no a/c, no room phones, no TV in some rooms, no smoking* ⊟ *MC, V.*

Shopping

Napier's Art Deco Trust maintains an **Art Deco Shop** in town. This beautifully laid-out shop sells everything from table lamps to tiles to ceramics, as well as hats, jewelry, rugs, and wineglasses. You can also pick up booklets outlining self-guided walks through town. ⊠ *163 Tennyson St.* ☎ *06/835–0022* 🖷 *06/835–1912* ⊕ *www.artdeconapier.com.*

Opossum World pairs a shop selling opossum fur products with a mini-museum about the opossum's effects on New Zealand's environment. Wander through a simulated bush and read claims of how opossums consume 21,000 tons of vegetation every night, dramatically altering the forest ecosystem. Products made with opossum fur include hats, gloves, and rugs; a soft blend of merino wool and opossum fur is made into sweaters, scarves, and socks. ✉ *157 Marine Parade* ☎ *06/835–7697* ⊕ *www.opossumworld.co.nz.*

Hawke's Bay

The natural world provides as vital an experience of Hawke's Bay as the human factor does. Not for nothing is this area, bounded by the Kawera and Ruahine Ranges, known as the fruit basket of New Zealand. You can't travel far here without seeing a vineyard or an orchard, and the region produces some of the country's finest wines. Roughly 20 years ago, a dry, barren area known as the **Gimblett Gravels** was about to be mined for gravel. Then an enterprising vine grower took a gamble and purchased the land. The stony soil turned out to be a boon for grapevines because it retains heat, and now several wineries benefit from its toasty conditions. Chardonnay is the most important white variety here; you'll also find sauvignon blanc, Bordeaux varieties, and syrah.

On the coast east of Hawke's Bay is Cape Kidnappers and its colony of gannets, a fascinating area that is home to as many as 15,000 of these large seabirds. To the south, the architecturally notable town of Hastings sits near the charming town of Havelock North, known locally as "the Village," with the Te Mata Peak rising dramatically beyond.

Farther south, a hill near Porangahau is the place with **the longest name in the world.** Take a deep breath and say, "Taumatawhakatangihangakoauauotamateaturipukakapikimaungahoronukupokaiwhehuakitanatahu." Now, that wasn't too hard, was it? Just remember it as "the place where Tamatea, the man with the big knees who slid, climbed, and swallowed mountains, known as landeater, played his flute to his loved one," and it should be no problem at all!

⑬ **Cape Kidnappers** was named by Captain James Cook after local Māori Fodor'sChoice tried to kidnap the servant of Cook's Tahitian interpreter. The cape is ★ the site of a large **gannet colony.** The gannet is a large white seabird with black-tipped flight feathers, a golden crown, and wings that can reach a span of 6 feet. When the birds find a shoal of fish, they fold their wings and plunge straight into the sea at tremendous speed. Their migratory pattern ranges from western Australia to the Chatham Islands, about 800 km (500 mi) east of Christchurch, but they generally nest only on remote islands. The colony at Cape Kidnappers is believed to be the only mainland gannet sanctuary in existence. Between October and March, about 15,000 gannets build their nests here, hatch their young, and prepare them for their long migratory flight.

You can walk to the sanctuary along the beach from Clifton, which is about 24 km (15 mi) south of Napier, but not at high tide. The 8-km (5-mi) walk must begin no earlier than three hours after the high-tide mark, and the return journey must begin no later than four hours before the next high tide. Tidal information is available at Clifton and at Napier Visitor Information Centre. A rest hut with refreshments is available near the colony.

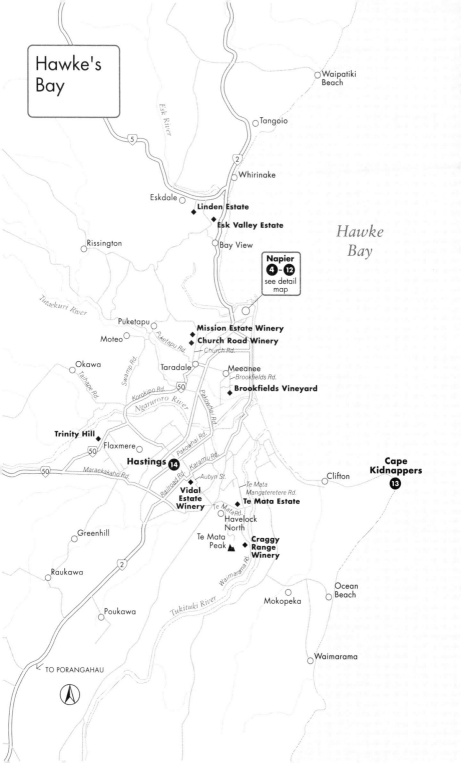

Hawke's Bay

Waipatiki Beach

Esk River

5

Tangoio

2

Whirinake

Eskdale

Linden Estate

Esk Valley Estate

Rissington

Bay View

Hawke Bay

Napier
4 - **12**
see detail map

Tutaekuri River

Puketapu

Mission Estate Winery
Church Road Winery

Moteo

Puketapu Rd.

Church Rd.

Okawa

Taradale

Meeanee

Brookfields Rd.

Taihape Rd.

Swamp Rd.

50

Korokipo Rd.

Ngaruroro River

Pakowhai Rd.

Brookfields Vineyard

Trinity Hill

Flaxmere

50

Pakowhai Rd.

Karamu Rd.

50

Maraekakaho Rd.

Hastings **14**

Railroad Rd.

Clifton

Cape Kidnappers

13

Aubyn St.

Te Mata Mangateretere Rd.

Vidal Estate Winery

Te Mata Rd.

Te Mata Estate

Havelock North

Greenhill

2

Te Mata Peak

Craggy Range Winery

Raukawa

Waimarama Rd.

Ocean Beach

Poukawa

Tukituki River

Mokopeka

Waimarama

TO PORANGAHAU

Because of these tidal restrictions, one easy way to get to the colony is to take a **Gannet Beach Adventures** (☎ 06/875–0898 ⊕ www.gannets. com) tractor-trailer, which is pulled along the beach starting from Clifton Reserve, Clifton Beach. Tractors depart approximately two hours before low tide, and the trip ($30) takes 4–4½ hours. If tides prevent the trip along the beach, the only other access is across private farmland. **Gannet Safaris** (☎ 06/875–0888) runs a four-wheel-drive bus to Cape Kidnappers from Summerlee Station, just past Te Awanga. A minimum of four is required for this tour ($48 each), which takes three hours. Advance booking is essential for all gannet colony tours.

❶❹ **Hastings** is Napier's twin city in Hawke's Bay, and it is worth at least driving through—it's just 18 km (11 mi) south of Napier, down Highway 2. True, the town doesn't have the same concentrated interest of Napier, but buildings in the center exhibit similar art deco flourishes— the 1931 earthquake did a lot of damage here, too. Where Hastings stands out is in its Spanish Mission buildings, a style borrowed from California, which produced such beauties as the **Hawke's Bay Opera House** (✉ Hastings St. and Heretaunga St. E) and the **Westermans Building** (✉ Russell St. and Heretaunga St. E). If you're looking to pick up picnic supplies, or simply ogle the local produce, visit the **Hawke's Bay Farmers' Market** (✉ Kenilworth Rd.) at A&P Showgrounds on Sunday from 8:30 AM to 12:30 PM. Local products include handmade cheese, breads, ice cream, and, of course, fruit.

Out of town, 3 km (2 mi) to the southeast, the village of Havelock North provides access to **Te Mata Peak,** a famed local viewpoint where it's possible to gaze right across the plains to Napier and the rumpled hills behind. The summit is a 15-minute (signposted) drive along Te Mata Peak Road from Havelock North.

Wineries

Esk Valley Estate Winery is terraced on a north-facing hillside, ensuring it full sun. Winemaker Gordon Russell produces chardonnay, sauvignon blanc, merlot, and blends with cabernet sauvignon, merlot, cabernet franc, and malbec in various combinations, including a rare and expensive red simply called The Terraces. Look for the reserve versions of chardonnay and merlot—malbec to find out what he has done with the best grapes from given years. The winery is 12 km (8 mi) north of Napier, just north of the town of Bay View before Highways 2 and 5 split. ✉ *745 Main Rd., Bay View* ☎ *06/836–6411* ⊕ *www.eskvalley.co.nz* ☉ *Daily 10–5, tours by appointment.*

★ Gardens surround the former seminary building of the **Mission Estate Winery** in the Taradale hills overlooking Napier. As the country's oldest winery, dating back to 1851, it should be added to your "must-see" list. Award-winning wines, including the Mission Jewelstone range, can be bought or tasted at the cellar door. Join one of the tours for a look at the underground cellar and a discussion of the mission's history. A gallery sells local handmade pottery and crafts. If you stay for a meal, get a seat on the terrace for a terrific view of the vineyard and Napier. To reach the vineyard, leave Napier by Kennedy Road, heading southwest from the city center toward Taradale. Just past Anderson Park, turn right into Avenue Road and continue to its end at Church Road. ⊠ *198 Church Rd., Taradale* ☎ *06/845-9350* ⊕ *www.missionestate.co.nz* ⊗ *Mon.–Sat. 8:30–5:30, Sun. 11–4.*

The **Church Road Winery** is owned by Montana, the country's largest wine company, but it operates pretty much as a separate entity. The wines are labeled Church Road: their chardonnay is a nationwide restaurant staple, and the many variations on the cabernet sauvignon and merlot themes are all worth sampling. A wine tour of the unique wine museum and beautifully restored cellars (a tasting is included, too) costs $10. Dining can be enjoyed in the indoor-outdoor restaurant. ⊠ *150 Church Rd., Taradale* ☎ *06/845-9137* ⊕ *www.churchroad.co.nz* ⊗ *Daily 9–5; tours at 10, 11, 2, and 3.*

Brookfields Vineyard is one of the most attractive wineries in the area, with its rose gardens and its tasting room overlooking the vines. The gewürztraminer and pinot gris are usually outstanding, but the showpiece is the reserve cabernet sauvignon/merlot, a powerful red that ages well. The winery restaurant is casual and very good, and wine tasting is offered before your meal at no extra cost. From Napier take Marine Parade toward Hastings and turn right on Awatoto Road. Follow it to Brookfields Road and turn left. Signs will point to the winery. ⊠ *376 Brookfields Rd., Meeanee* ☎ *06/834-4615* ⊕ *www.brookfieldsvineyards. co.nz* ⊗ *Daily 10:30–4:30.*

Te Mata Estate is one of New Zealand's top wineries, and Coleraine, a rich but elegant cabernet-merlot blend named after the much-photographed home of the owner, John Buck, is considered the archetypal Hawke's Bay red. Elston Chardonnay and Cape Crest Sauvignon Blanc show similar restraint and balance. If there's any viognier open (it's made only in tiny quantities), try it—it's excellent. From Napier head south on Marine Parade through Clive and turn left at the Mangateretere School. Signs from there will lead you to Te Mata Road and the estate. ⊠ *349 Te Mata Rd.* ⋐ *Box 8335, Havelock North* ☎ *06/877-4399* ⊕ *www. temata.co.nz* ⊗ *Weekdays 9–5, Sat. 10–5, Sun. 11–4; tours mid-Dec.— Jan. daily at 10:30.*

★ Set by a small lake with the towering heights of Te Mata Peak beyond, the **Craggy Range Winery** in the noted Gimblett Gravels district has a stunning setting for wine making—and tasting. The wines include single-varietal chardonnay, merlot, and syrah; a predominantly merlot blend called Sophia; and a cabernet sauvignon blend known as The Quarry. You can sample wines at the cellar, tour the facility by appointment, or enjoy wine with a meal at the Terroir restaurant looking out over the lake. ⊠ *253 Waimarama Rd., Havelock North* ☎ *06/873-0143* ⊗ *Daily 10–6* ⊕ *www.craggyrange.com.*

Vidal Estate Winery, a family-owned winery with a portfolio of award-winning wines, was founded in 1905 and is one of the region's oldest wineries. Its restaurant is a locally popular spot to laze away the afternoon with a glass of sauvignon blanc, chardonnay or syrah. ⊠ *913 St.*

Aubyn St. E, Hastings ☎ *06/876–8105* ⊕ *www.vidal.co.nz* ☉ *Nov.–Apr., Mon.–Sat. 10–6, Sun. 10–5; May–Oct., daily 10–5.*

At **Trinity Hill,** you can taste the fruits of the stony Gimblett Gravels soil, including a notable chardonnay and Bordeaux-style reds. Wines with the Shepherds Croft label are suited for early drinking. Have a glass of wine with a cheese or antipasto platter in the landscaped grounds or by the courtyard fountain. The winery holds periodic art exhibitions. ☒ *2396 State Hwy. 50, Hastings* ☎ *06/879–7778* ☉ *Oct.–Easter, daily 10–5; Easter–Oct., daily 11–4* ⊕ *www.trinityhillwines.com.*

Where to Stay & Eat

★ **$$$–$$$$** ✕ **Terroir Restaurant.** The massive cedar doors and high circular roof give this well-regarded restaurant at Craggy Range Winery a rustic feel. Although the menu is loosely country French, "rustic" here is far from unsophisticated. The open wood fire turns out dishes such as pepper-encrusted beef fillet with herb hollandaise, and spit-roasted chicken with red-wine-radicchio risotto. From the eclectic dessert offerings, thin apple tart with caramel sauce and vanilla ice cream is an appealing choice. On a warm evening, you can dine on the terrace with views of Te Mata Peak. ☒ *253 Waimarama Rd., Havelock North* ☎ *06/ 873–0413* ☐ *AE, DC, MC, V* ☉ *Closed Mon. July and Aug.*

$$$ ✕ **Brookfields Vineyard Restaurant.** Though open only for lunch, this winery restaurant is a winner. The menu is not far-reaching—perhaps three first-course choices and four main dishes—but the contemporary fare is first-rate, particularly when matched with a glass of wine. The beef scotch fillet on asparagus with fried spaetzle, baby spinach, and slow-roasted tomato jus are well matched by the cabernet merlot. ☒ *Brookfields Rd., Meeanee, 5 km (3 mi) south of Napier* ☎ *06/ 834–4615* ⊕ *www.brookfieldsvineyards.co.nz* ☐ *AE, DC, MC, V* ☉ *No dinner.*

$$$ ✕ **Sileni Estates.** More of a culinary compound than a simple winery, this property houses a restaurant, gourmet cellar store, wine discovery center, Wine Discovery Centre, school, and the Village Press Olive Oil press house. Sileni Estates restaurant, specializing in the finest wines and freshest local produce matched with Sileni's extensive range of wines, is open seven days for lunch and Thursday, Friday, and Saturday for dinner. ☒ *2016 Maraekakaho Rd., Bridge Pa, Hastings* ☎ *06/879–8768* ☐ *AE, DC, MC, V.*

$$$ ✕ **Vidal Estate Restaurant.** Chef Kylie Howards emphasizes fresh, organic ingredients at New Zealand's first winery restaurant (it opened in 1979). Her contemporary creations might include a tomato-and-oregano-braised veal shank with a salsa verde, served over soft polenta. If you have a sweet tooth, try the burnt honey and medjool date crème brûlée with peanut wafers. ☒ *913 St. Aubyn St. E, Hastings* ☎ *06/876–8105* ⊕ *www.vidal.co.nz* ☐ *AE, DC, MC, V.*

★ **$$–$$$** ✕ **Corn Exchange.** A large fireplace warms this comfortable restaurant in winter; on sunny days, you can sit outside on the patio. Either way, the service is swift and friendly, and the intriguing fare starts with amazing pizzas and continues to more exotic offerings, such as pork medallions topped with cheddar-whole-grain mustard on a frittata of pumpkin and kūmara (a local sweet potato). ⊠ *118 Maraekakoho Rd., Hastings* ☏ *06/870–8333* ▭ *AE, DC, MC, V.*

$$–$$$ ✕ **Rose & Shamrock.** The developers of this Irish pub were so keen on authenticity, they sent their architect on a three-week tour of Ireland. The result seems to have been spirited over from Dublin. The pints mix with old-fashioned but honest pub fare such as grilled beef sirloin or a generous platter of seafood, much of it battered and deep-fried. ⊠ *Napier Rd., Havelock North* ☏ *06/877–2999* ▭ *AE, DC, MC, V.*

$$–$$$ ✕ **Te Awa Winery.** Profiting from the Gimblett Gravels terrain, this winery produces single-estate wines, which are carefully matched with the restaurant's menu. You might find such pairings such as the Te Awa Boundary 2000 (a merlot blend) with seared lamb's liver on potato purée with crispy pancetta and red-onion jam. ⊠ *2375 State Hwy. 50, Hastings* ☏ *06/879–7602* ▭ *AE, DC, MC, V* ☉ *No dinner.*

★ $$$$ ✕⊡ **Mangapapa Petit Hotel.** This restored lodge, built in 1885, was once the home of the Wattie family, who made their fortune with fruit farming and canning. Reflecting this background, 20 acres of working orchards surround the house. Inside, a dozen guest suites are luxuriously and individually furnished in soft colors and snowy-white damask coverlets. Some rooms have four-posters; all have under-floor heating. The manicured gardens include a grass tennis court, a heated swimming pool, and a sauna. The chefs incorporate local produce into the daily five-course dinner menu, with dishes such as fresh whole baby Aoraki salmon in a creamy champagne-and-mushroom sauce. The thorough wine list includes superb wines from Hawke's Bay wine country. ⊠ *466 Napier Rd., Havelock North* ☏ *06/878–3234* 🖷 *06/878–1214* ⊕ *www.mangapapa.co.nz* ⤶ *12 suites* ↺ *Restaurant, cable TV, in-room data ports, tennis court, pool, sauna, spa, bicycles, croquet, bar* ▭ *AE, DC, MC, V* ⏀ *BP, MAP.*

★ $$$ ⊡ **Hawthorne House.** The guest rooms at this beautiful and recently renovated Edwardian villa all have private verandas, which allow you to look out over 14 acres of lushly landscaped grounds. Each room boasts a high ceiling, antique-style furnishing and fixtures, and embroidered bed linens. There are also tea- and coffee-making facilities, so you can enjoy a quiet morning cuppa before heading off for a sumptuous cooked breakfast (often using eggs laid by the property's free-range chickens). Suppers are also available on request. ⊠ *1420, Railway Rd. South, Hastings South* ☏ *06/878–0035* 🖷 *06/878–0035* ⊕ *www.hawthorne.co.nz* ⤶ *5 rooms* ↺ *No a/c, no room TVs, no smoking* ▭ *MC, V* ⏀ *BP.*

$$ ⊡ **Harvest Lodge.** Set close to the center of Havelock North, this up-to-the-minute motel has spacious studios with original artwork and comfortable king-size beds. All units have bifold windows that open wide onto the lovely courtyard. ⊠ *23 Havelock Rd., Havelock North* ☏ *06/877–9500* 🖷 *06/877–9800* ⊕ *www.harvestlodge.co.nz* ⤶ *19 rooms* ↺ *In-room VCRs, in-room data ports, spa, laundry facilities; no smoking* ▭ *AE, DC, MC, V.*

$–$$ ⊡ **Portmans Motor Lodge.** These 20 modern, light, and airy units surround a spacious courtyard; they're also conveniently near the center of town. Ten rooms have whirlpool baths, and the outdoor swimming pool is heated in the winter. ⊠ *401 Railway Rd., Hastings* ☏ *06/878–8332* 🖷 *06/878–8620* ⊕ *www.portmans.co.nz* ⤶ *20 rooms* ↺ *Kitchenettes, pool, spa, laundry facilities; no a/c, no smoking* ▭ *AE, DC, MC, V.*

NAPIER & HAWKE'S BAY ESSENTIALS

Transportation

BY AIR

The small Hawke's Bay Airport (NPE) is 5 km (3 mi) north of Napier. Shuttle taxis run into town.

Air New Zealand has several flights daily between Napier and Auckland, Wellington, and Christchurch. The flights from Napier to Auckland or Wellington take about an hour; the trip to Christchurch lasts roughly two hours.

🔢 Airport **Hawke's Bay Airport** ✉ Main Rd.
🔢 Carrier **Air New Zealand** ☎ 0800/737-000 ⊕ www.airnewzealand.co.nz.

BY BUS

Newmans and InterCity operate daily bus services between Napier and Auckland, Taupo, Rotorua, and Wellington. The Napier-to-Auckland trip takes 8 hours, Napier–Rotorua is 3½ hours, Napier–Taupo is 2¼ hours, and Napier–Wellington is 6 hours. There are also frequent local services between Napier and Hastings. For tickets and information, go to the Napier Visitor Information Centre; buses stop on Munroe Street.

🔢 Bus Information **InterCity** ☎ 09/913-6100 or 04/499-3261 ⊕ www.intercitycoach.co.nz. **Newmans** ⊕ www.newmanscoach.co.nz.

BY CAR

The main route between Napier and the north is Highway 5. Driving time from Taupo is two hours, five hours if you're coming straight from Auckland. Highway 2 is the main route heading south; it connects Hastings and Napier. Driving time to Wellington is five hours.

Highway 50, the Napier–Hastings road, can help you steer clear of traffic by avoiding central Hastings; it then joins Highway 2 before Napier. Several wineries are on or near the 50, so you may want to designate a driver. Roads here are generally well maintained and easy to drive.

Contacts & Resources

EMERGENCIES

The pharmacy with the most extensive hours is the Chemist Shop Napier Ltd., open daily 8 AM–9 PM.

🔢 Emergency Services **Fire, police, and ambulance** ☎ 111.
🔢 Pharmacy **The Chemist Shop Napier Ltd.** ✉ 32 Munroe St., Napier ☎ 06/834-0884.

TOURS

ARCHITECTURE TOURS The Art Deco Trust has a couple of excellent and informative guided walking tours of Napier. A one-hour walk starts daily at 10 AM from the Napier Visitor Information Centre ($10). A two-hour afternoon walk, starting at the Art Deco Shop at 2 PM, includes slide and video presentations ($15). Both walks end with optional free video screenings and refreshments. Or take the trust's self-guided Art Deco Walk; leaflets ($4) are available at its shop or at the visitor center. There's also the Marewa Meander around Napier's art deco suburb, and the Art Deco Tour

Map, which plots a self-drive route through Napier and Hastings. To really submerge yourself in the 1930s aesthetic, join Bertie in a 1934 Buick for a drive around Napier ($99 for up to four people; book through the Art Deco Shop). For customized half-hour to half-day private tours, contact Art Deco Tours.

⚑ **Art Deco Trust** ⊠ Art Deco Shop, 163 Tennyson St. ☎ 06/835-0022 ⊕ www.artdeconapier.com. **Deco Affair Tours** ⊠ Box 190, Napier ☎ 025/241-5279 🖶 06/835-4491.

WINE TOURS Bay Tours runs a variety of wineries tours, starting around $45, where you can sample some of the boutique wines unavailable to independent travelers. Lunch at one of the winery restaurants is usually available, too (at your own cost).

Vince Picone, at Vince's Vineyard Tours, knows the local wines and vineyards better than most. He manages to combine professionalism with a sense of fun.

On Yer Bike Winery Tours is a great self-guided wine and cycling experience on flat, scenic terrain with some off-road cycling through the vineyards. Bikes, helmets, and a packed lunch are provided; they'll also lend you a cell phone (in case you have a glass too many and need collecting). Rates start at $50.

⚑ **Bay Tours** ⊠ 6 Magdalen Crescent, Napier ☎ 06/843-2046, 027/449-0778 cell ⊕ www.baytours.co.nz. **On Yer Bike Winery Tours** ⊠ 129 Rosser Rd., R.D. 4, Hastings ☎ 06/879-8735, 025/233-3398 cell ⊕ www.onyerbikehb.co.nz. **Vince's Vineyard Tours** ⊠ 9 Thurley Pl., Bay View, Napier ☎ 06/836-6705 or 025/506-658 cell.

VISITOR INFORMATION

Both the Napier and Hastings visitor centers are open from 8:30 to 5 on weekdays. On weekends, Napier's center is open from 9 to 5; in Hastings, the bureau is open from 10 to 3. Hawke's Bay Tourism, a regional organization, puts up the ⊕ www.hawkesbaynz.com Web site.

⚑ Tourist Information **Hastings Visitor Information Centre** ⊠ Russell St. N, Hastings ☎ 06/873-5526. **Napier Visitor Information Centre** ⊠ 100 Marine Parade, Napier ☎ 06/834-1911.

GISBORNE & EASTLAND

Traveling to Eastland takes you well away from the tourist track in the North Island. For some people, that is reason enough to make the trip. Once here, you will find rugged coastline, accessible beaches, dense forests, gentle nature trails, and small, predominantly Māori communities. Eastland provides one of the closest links with the nation's earliest past. Kaiti Beach, near the city of Gisborne, is where the *waka* (long canoe) *Horouta* landed, and nearby Titirangi was named by the first Māori settlers in remembrance of their mountain in Hawaiki, their Polynesian island of origin. Kaiti Beach is also where Captain Cook set foot in 1769—the first European landing in New Zealand. Cook's initial landing was unsuccessful, for even though the natives were friendly, several were killed because of misunderstandings, and when Cook left, he named the place Poverty Bay—"as it afforded us no one thing we wanted." Although

Cook's name stuck to the body of water that hugs the eastern shore, the region is now generally known as Eastland.

Gisborne's warm climate and fertile soil make the region one of New Zealand's top wine areas. Often overshadowed by Hawke's Bay (and its formidable PR machine), Gisborne has about 7,000 acres under vine, and it is the country's largest supplier of chardonnay grapes. It has in fact been dubbed the chardonnay capital of New Zealand, which makes that the variety to concentrate on if you go tasting.

This is an easygoing area, with friendly people and a different pace of life than in other parts of the North Island. It has some of the finest and often almost deserted surfing beaches in the country; the region is also ideal for walking, fishing, horse trekking, and camping. The international spotlight focused briefly on Eastland when scenes for the 2002 hit film *Whale Rider* were shot at Whangara, north of Gisborne, but there have been few changes in what is mainly a quiet, rural place.

Gisborne

⑮ *210 km (130 mi) northeast of Napier, 500 km (310 mi) southeast of Auckland.*

The Māori name for the Gisborne district is Tairawhiti (tye-ra-*fee*-tee), "the coast upon which the sun shines across the water," and, in fact, Gisborne is the first city in New Zealand to see sunrise. Although the city (population 30,000) is hardly large, you will need a day or so to get around town properly. It's a bustling town, proud of its heritage, yet relaxed and friendly. The landmark Town Clock stands in the middle of Gladstone Road; nearby, in a house on Grey Street, Kiri Te Kanawa, New Zealand's world-famous opera diva, was born in 1944 (the house is no longer there).

Europeans settled the Gisborne area early in the 19th century. A plaque on the waterfront commemorates the first official sale—of an acre of land—on June 30, 1831. On that site, the first European house and store was reportedly erected (it, too, is now long gone). Most of the historical sights and other attractions are too spread out to explore them by foot, and you'll need a car to get into the spectacular countryside.

The **Tairawhiti Museum,** with its Māori and Pākehā (non-native) artifacts and an extensive photographic collection, provides a good introduction to the region's history. A maritime gallery covers seafaring matters, and there are changing exhibits of local and national artists' work. The Exhibit Café serves excellent light refreshments. Outside the museum, the colonial-style **Wyllie Cottage,** built in 1872, is the oldest house in town. ⊠ *10 Stout St.* ☎ *06/867–3832* ⊕ *www.tairawhitimuseum.org.nz* 🖾 *Minimum $1 donation* ☉ *Weekdays 10–4, weekends 1:30–4.*

Cook Landing Site National Historic Reserve has deep historical significance for New Zealanders, but not so much to keep an international visitor amused. A statue of Captain James Cook, who first set foot on New Zealand soil here on October 9, 1769, stands on Kaiti Beach, across the river southeast of the city center. The beach itself, at low tide, attracts interesting birdlife. ⊠ *Esplanade on south end of Turanganui River.*

The **Titirangi Domain** on Kaiti Hill has excellent views of Gisborne, Poverty Bay, and the surrounding rural areas. Titirangi was the site of an extensive *pā* (fortified village), the origins of which can be traced back at least 24 Māori generations. The **Titirangi Recreational Reserve,** part of the Domain, is a great place for a picnic or a walk. The Domain is south of Turanganui River. Pass the harbor and turn right onto Esplanade, then left onto Crawford Road, then right onto Queens Drive, and follow it to several lookout points in the Domain.

Te Poho o Rawiri Meeting House is one of the largest Māori marae in New Zealand, and the interior has excellent, complex traditional carving. One example is the *tekoteko,* a kneeling human figure with the right hand raised to challenge those who enter the marae. There are also unusual interior alcoves and a stage framed by carvings; it's essentially a meetinghouse within a meetinghouse. Photography is not allowed inside. On the side of the hill stands the 1930s Toko Toro Tapu Church. You'll need permission to explore either site; contact the **Gisborne-Eastland Visitor Information Centre** (⊠ 209 Grey St. ☎ 06/868–6139). ⊠ *Kaiti Hill* ☎ *06/ 868–5364* ⊠ *Small donation suggested.*

Lindauer Cellars is Gisborne's largest wine outlet. The cellar area has wooden beams and a Nuhaka stone floor, with a large selection of Montana wines on display and available for sale or tasting. Across the courtyard is the dimly lighted and cavernous winery museum featuring the production of *methode traditionelle* wines such as Lindauer, along with the history of wine making in the region. The restaurant provides both indoor and alfresco dining; lunch is available, as are coffee and light refreshments. ⊠ *11 Solander St., Gisborne* ☎ *06/868–2757* ☎ *06/ 868–2758* ⊕ *www.adwnz.com* ⊘ *Daily 10–5.*

Millton Vineyard has an attractive garden area, making it a logical place to sit with a picnic lunch and sip some barrel-fermented chardonnay. The Te Arai vineyard chenin blanc and merlot are top-of-the-line wines, and the award-winning Opou Riesling is also recommended. James and Annie Millton grow their grapes organically and biodynamically, following the precepts of philosopher Rudolf Steiner. The vineyard is signposted off State Highway 2, about 11 km (7 mi) south of Gisborne. ⊠ *Papatu Rd., Manutuke* ☎ *06/862–8680* ⊕ *www.millton.co.nz* ⊘ *Nov.–Apr., Mon.–Sat. 10–5; Mar.–Oct., by appointment.*

**OFF THE
BEATEN
PATH**

EASTWOODHILL ARBORETUM – Inspired by the gardens seen on a trip to England in 1910, William Douglas Cook returned home and began planting 160 acres. His brainchild became a stunning collection of more than 600 genera of trees from around the world. Eastwoodhill is a place of seasonal change seldom seen in New Zealand. In spring and summer daffodils mass yellow, magnolias bloom in clouds of pink and white, and cherries, crab apples, wisteria, and azalea all add to the spectacle. The main tracks in the park can be walked in about 45 minutes. Maps and self-guided tour booklets are available. Drive west from Gisborne center on Highway 2 toward Napier, cross the bridge, and turn at the rotary onto the Ngatapa–Rere Road. Follow it 35 km (22 mi) to the arboretum. ⊠ *Ngatapa–Rere Rd.* ☎ *06/863–9800* ⊕ *www.eastwoodhill. org.nz* ☒ *$8* ⊙ *Daily 9–5.*

MORERE HOT SPRINGS – Set in more than 1,000 acres of native bush, this unique place provides modern bathing facilities in an unusual natural environment. There's a cold outdoor pool alongside a warm indoor pool, and set in the forest a few minutes' walk away are smaller hot or warm pools with a cold plunge pool. Two private hot pools are also available, with all the waters known for their therapeutic value. Following the walking trails through the forest can take 20 minutes or stretch to two to three hours. Morere is roughly halfway between Wairoa and Gisborne, north of the Mahia turnoff. ⊠ *State Hwy. 2, Morere, Gisborne* ☎☎ *06/837–8856* ☒ *$5, private pools $8* ⊙ *June–Oct., daily 10–6; Nov.–May, daily 10–9.*

Where to Stay & Eat

$$$–$$$$ ✕ **Wharf Café Bar Restaurant.** At a former storage shed overlooking the Gisborne Wharf, find a seat at a sunny outdoor table for breakfast or go instead for a lively evening. A standout on the contemporary menu is the fillet of beef served with a caramelized red-onion tart and marinated vegetables. If you have room left, try the Bailey's crème brûlée served with toffee filigree. The wine list leans to local and other New Zealand producers. ⊠ *60 The Esplanade* ☎ *06/868–4876* ☰ *AE, DC, MC, V.*

$$$ ✕ **The Marina Restaurant & Bar.** The high-ceiling dining room of this large colonial house exudes gentility; light filters through stained glass and you can look out toward the river. An upended wooden rowboat serves as an interesting wine rack, and the black napkins on white tablecloths give a dramatic look. Seafood is the specialty; look for the baked salmon on a parsnip-and-cauliflower mash topped with beetroot purée. ⊠ *Marina Park* ☎☎ *06/868–5919* ☰ *AE, DC, MC, V* ⊙ *Closed Sun. No lunch.*

★ **$$$** ✕ **The Works Café & Winery.** Set in a building that was once part of the Gisborne Freezing Works, dating from 1906, this restaurant is delightfully different. The decor harks back to the industrial past, with a large drive shaft and pulleys on the brick walls; the staff is notably friendly and knowledgeable. The menu builds on all kinds of local products, from cheeses to fruit to *kina* (sea urchin). One excellent choice is manuka-smoked rack of lamb, served on a potato-and-feta pancake with baby carrots and a cucumber-and-mint riata. Wrought-iron gates at the back lead to a boutique winery, where you'll find a small range of wines sold here exclusively. ⊠ *Kaiti Beach Rd.* ☎ *06/863–1285* ☰ *AE, DC, MC, V.*

$–$$ ✕ **The Meetings.** For a casual place to hoist a few while nibbling hearty pub fare, you can't beat an Irish pub, and Gisborne now has one of its own. The traditional furnishings include brass chandeliers, dark woodwork, and green leather upholstery, and pretty stained-glass partitions separate the dining alcoves. You could sample from the selection of bar snacks or go for something heartier—perhaps oven-roasted pork finished with an apple-and-brandy sauce. ⊠ *At Reads Quay and Gladstone St.* ☎ *06/863–3733* ☰ *MC, V.*

$–$$ ✕ **Verve Café.** This funky little midtown coffee bar is a popular stop for both locals and travelers from around the world. The decor is eclectic, with an ever-changing display from local artists; the reading matter interesting, and the food honest and generous. Owner-chef Linda Coulston is famous for her chicken and steak sandwiches, and the homemade baked goods and local wines aren't too shabby, either. Best of all, the coffee is terrific; sip a cup while you surf the Net. ⊠ *121 Gladstone Rd.* ☎ *06/868–9095* ☰ *AE, DC, MC, V.*

$$$$ 🏠 **Opou Country House.** This stately 1883 mansion, surrounded by acres
Fodor'sChoice of gardens, is an all-around treasure. Robyn Bickford and Manav Gare-
★ wal, the genial and well-traveled hosts, have given their historic home a fascinating mix of styles, from the European antiques to modern Māori art to the Indian bedspreads. You can relax on the veranda (porches surround three sides of the house) or by the Italian marble fireplace. Robyn is a former diplomat accomplished in Asian and European cooking, and for meals she uses fresh fruits and vegetables that come in daily from the gardens. Afternoon tea and aperitifs are included in the rates; lunch and dinner are extra. ⊠ *95 Whakato Rd., Manutuke, 11 km (7 mi) south of Gisborne off State Hwy. 2* ☎ *06/862–8732* 🖨 *06/862–8042* ⊕ *www.opoucountryhouse.co.nz* 🛏 *4 rooms* △ *Dining room, pool; no a/c, no room phones, no room TVs, no smoking* ☰ *MC, V* ¡○¡ *BP.*

$$$ 🏠 **Tunanui Station Cottages.** On the 5,000-acre Tunanui sheep-and-cattle station, Leslie and Ray Thompson host guests in a 90-year-old restored cottage and an adjacent four-bedroom farmhouse. The cottage has an old-fashioned appeal with its lovely kauri table and rimu wood tongue-and-groove flooring. The farmhouse is more spacious and modern, with a brick fireplace in the comfortable lounge and incredible views of the Mahia peninsula and the sea. Both houses have kitchen facilities and a shared TV—ideal for a longer stay—but you need to bring your own supplies. Ray will take experienced horseback riders out to see the station at work. The station is 5 km (3 mi) off the road, and city slickers may jokingly grumble that the silence can almost hurt your ears. ⊠ *1001 Tunanui Rd., Opoutama, Mahia* ☎ *06/837–5790* 🖨 *06/837–5797* ⊕ *www.tunanui.co.nz* 🛏 *1 cottage, 1 farmhouse* △ *Dining room, kitchenettes, laundry facilities; no a/c* ☰ *No credit cards.*

$$ 🏠 **Captain Cook Motor Lodge.** At this sparkling, up-to-date motel, a stone's throw from Waikanae Beach, all the units are roomy, with clean, modern lines and comfortable furnishings, including king-size beds and kitchen facilities. Three of the rooms have whirlpool tubs. There is a restaurant and bar for in-house guests. ⊠ *31 Awapuni Rd., Waikanae Beach* ☎ *06/867–7002* 🖨 *06/867–7073* ⊕ *www.captaincook.co.nz* 🛏 *21 rooms* △ *Dining room, kitchenettes, in-room VCRs, in-room data ports, bar; no smoking* ☰ *AE, DC, MC, V.*

$ 🏠 **Goldspree Kiwi Fruit Orchard Stay.** This large self-contained cottage, with its windows overlooking 25 acres of grape vines and kiwi-fruit orchards, is ideal for a quiet family holiday. The two bedrooms, the roomy sitting area, the modern bathroom and the fully equipped kitchen are well-furnished and airy. Yummy breakfast supplies are brought to the door every day by the owners, Mark and Marjorie Hayes, and a restaurant is only five minutes away. Gisborne Centre and beaches are close by, as well. ⊠ *37, Bond Rd., Ormond, Gisborne* ☎ *06 862 5688* 🛏 *1 cottage* △ *Kitchen, swimming pool; no smoking* ☰ *Credit cards not accepted* ¡○¡ *BP.*

$ 🖼 **Wairakaia Homestay.** Sandra and Rob Faulkner have taken over this 100-year-old house, where instead of TV you'll be gazing at glorious views from stained-glass bay windows. There's a huge, comfortable sitting room and a conservatory looking out to the ocean. The guest rooms are basic; one has a private bath and the other two share a bathroom. ✉ *Wairakaia Station, State Hwy. 2 (R.D. 2), 24 km (15 mi) south of Gisborne* ☎ *06/862–8655* 📠 *06/862–8677* 🛏 *3 rooms* ♿ *Tennis court; no a/c, no room phones, no room TVs* 🍴 *BP.*

¢   🖼 **Sycamore Lodge Backpackers.** The various room configurations here have some valued common denominators: they're modern and very clean and have washbasins. Special facilities, such as a wheelchair-accessible shower, accommodate travelers with disabilities. You can hang out in one of the lounges, outfitted with cable TV, Internet access, and a pool table, or stake out a bench in the picnic area. Children are welcome. ✉ *690 Gladstone Rd.* ☎ *06/868–1000* 📠 *06/868–4000* 🛏 *5 single rooms, 13 double rooms, 2 dorm rooms* ♿ *2 lounges, Internet room; no a/c, no room phones, no room TVs, no smoking* ☱ *MC.*

Sports & the Outdoors

FISHING   Albacore, yellowfin tuna, mako sharks, and marlin are all prized catches off the East Cape from January to April (and no fishing licenses are needed). Fishing operators include **Dive Tatapouri** (☎ 06/868–5153 ⊕ www.divetatapouri.com), 14 km (9 mi) north of the city off State Highway 35. Dean and Leon of Dive Tatapouri cater for all types of fishing and diving; if you get to the dive shop at the right time, you might be lucky enough to hand-feed string-rays that swim close in to the nearby rocks.

Surfit Boat Charters (☎ 06/867–2970 ⊕ www.surfit.co.nz) is based in Gisborne. Fishing trips start at $110 per person. If you fancy being lowered in a shark cage to come face-to-face with a white pointer shark, aka a "great white," you can take the plunge for $200.

GOLF   The **Poverty Bay Golf Course** (✉ Lytton and Awapuni Rds., Gisborne ☎ 06/867–4402), an 18-hole championship course, ranks among the top-five courses in the country. The greens fee is $30.

SURFING   Gisborne has a number of surfing beaches suitable for both beginners or experienced riders; three good ones are very close to town. Waikanae Beach, a short walk from the visitor information center on Grey Street, usually has good learners' surf, and the Pipe and the Island are for the more experienced. The Pipe is just south of Waikanae; the Island fronts the Titirangi Domain. You can arrange for lessons at the **Gisborne Surf School** (☎ 06/868–3484, 027/482–7873 cell ⊕ www.gisbornesurfschool.co.nz). Rates start at $45 per person for two hours; a private two-hour session costs $60. Surfboard rentals are $25 for a half day or $40 for a full day.

Gisborne–Opotiki Loop

Soak in the beauty and remoteness of Eastland driving the Provincial Highway 35 loop between Gisborne and Opotiki, the northwest anchor of the East Cape. Rolling green hills drop into wide crescent beaches or rock-strewn coves. Small towns appear here and there along the route, only to fade into the surrounding landscape. It is one of the country's ultimate roads less traveled. Some scenic highlights are **Anaura Bay,** with rocky headlands, a long beach favored by surfers, and nearby islands; it is between **Tolaga Bay** and **Tokomaru Bay,** two former shipping towns. Tolaga Bay has an incredibly long wharf stretching over a beach into the sea, and Cooks Cove Walkway is a pleasant amble (two-hour round-trip) through the countryside past a rock arch. In **Tikitiki,** farther up the coast, an Anglican church is full of carved Māori panels and beams. Tikitiki has a gas station.

East of the small town of **Te Araroa,** which has the oldest *pohutukawa* (po-hoo-too-*ka*-wa) tree in the country, the coast is about as remote as you could imagine. At the tip of the cape (21 km [13 mi] from Te Araroa), the East Cape Lighthouse and fantastic views are a long, steep climb from the beach. **Hicks Bay** has another long beach. Back toward Opotiki, **Whanarua** (fahn-ah-*roo*-ah) **Bay** is one of the most beautiful on the East Cape, with isolated beaches ideal for a picnic and a swim. Farther on, there is an intricately carved Māori marae (meetinghouse) called Tukaki in **Te Kaha.**

If you plan to take your time along the way, inquire at the **Gisborne–Eastland Visitor Information Centre** (✉ 209 Grey St., Gisborne ☎ 06/868–6139 🖷 06/868–6138 ⊕ www.gisbornenz.com) about lodging. There are motels at various points on the cape and some superbly sited motor camps and backpackers' lodges, though you'll need to be well stocked with foodstuffs before you set off. Driving time on the loop—about 330 km (205 mi)—is about five hours without stops. You can, of course, drive the loop the other way—from Opotiki around the cape to Gisborne: to get to Opotiki from the north, take Highway 2 from Tauranga and the Bay of Plenty.

Te Urewera National Park

16 *163 km (101 mi) west of Gisborne.*

FodorsChoice
★

Te Urewera National Park is a vast, remote region of forests and lakes straddling the Huiarau Range. The park's outstanding feature is the glorious **Lake Waikaremoana** ("sea of rippling waters"), a forest-girded lake with good swimming, boating, and fishing. The lake is circled by a 50-km (31-mi) walking track; the three- to four-day walk is popular, and in the summer months the lakeside hiking huts are often heavily used. For information about this route, contact the Department of Conservation Visitor Centre at Aniwaniwa, on the eastern arm of Lake Waikaremoana. The visitor center is also the site of a major modern artwork, the *Te Urewera* **triptych** by New Zealand artist Colin McCahon. The painting, done in 1976, shows a creamy column or partial cross shape against a dark landscape, superimposed with English and Māori words and a reference to Te Kooti (*see* "The Elusive Te Kooti" CloseUp box). The painting generated controversy, because a Pākehā (non-Māori) artist had incorporated Māori text, and in 1997 it was stolen (or liberated, depending on your point of view) in protest, resurfacing the following year.

You can pick up walking leaflets and maps and ask advice about the many other shorter walks in the park, such as the one to the **Aniwaniwa Falls**

The Elusive Te Kooti

OF ALL THE MĀORI LEADERS who opposed the early Pākehā settlers in New Zealand, Te Kooti was the most elusive and most awe inspiring. He was born at Matawhero, near Gisborne, in the early 19th century. As a young man he fought with government troops in a local uprising, but he was accused of treachery and deported without trial to the remote Chatham Islands in 1866. While detained on the island, he experienced visions and initiated a new creed he called Ringatu ("raised hand," for the practice of raising the right hand after prayer). Ringatu is still practiced by several thousand people in New Zealand.

With his charismatic personality, Te Kooti became the de facto leader of the island's more than 200 prisoners. After two years he engineered their escape by capturing a ship and forcing the crew to sail them back to Poverty Bay. With arms seized from the ship, Te Kooti led his followers to the Urewera mountains, fighting off government troops as they went. In the years that followed, he was relentlessly hunted but continued to carry out vicious raids on coastal settlements. His last stand (and the last major engagement of the New Zealand wars) was at a fortified position at Te Porere, which you can still see near the road between Turangi and Te Urewera National Park. Te Kooti was defeated but escaped yet again. He eluded capture and spent the late 1870s in Te Kuiti, near Waitomo, under the protection of the Māori king. The government formally pardoned him in 1883; he died a decade later.

(30 minutes round-trip) or to **Lake Waikareiti** (five to six hours round-trip). The motor camp on the lakeshore, not far from the visitor center, has cabins, chalets, and motel units. In summer a launch operates sightseeing and fishing trips from the motor camp. There are areas of private Māori land within the park, so be sure to stay on marked paths. Access to the park is from Wairoa, 100 km (62 mi) southwest of Gisborne down Highway 2. It's then another 63 km (39 mi) from Wairoa along Highway 38 to Lake Waikaremoana. ✉ *Department of Conservation Visitor Centre, Aniwaniwa* ☏ *06/837–3803* ⊕ *www.doc.govt.nz.*

GISBORNE & EASTLAND ESSENTIALS

Transportation

BY AIR

The small, easily navigable Gisborne Airport (GIS) is about 5 km (3 mi) from town. You can catch a taxi to the city center for $18.

Air New Zealand Link flies daily to Gisborne from Auckland and Wellington. Flights on these routes last about an hour.

🛈 Airport **Gisborne Airport** ✉ Aerodrome Rd. ☏ 06/867–1608.
🛈 Carrier **Air New Zealand Link** ☏ 0800/737–000 ⊕ www.airnewzealand.co.nz.

BY BUS

There's one bus service a day to Gisborne with Newmans and InterCity from either Auckland, via Rotorua, or from Wellington, via Napier. These trips take a solid day.

🚏 Bus Depot **Gisborne** ✉ Gisborne–Eastland Visitor Information Centre, Grey St.
🚏 Bus Information **InterCity** ☎ 09/913-6100 in Auckland, 04/472-5111 in Wellington ⊕ www.intercitycoach.co.nz. **Newmans** ⊕ www.newmanscoach.co.nz.

BY CAR

Gisborne is a long way from almost anywhere, though the coastal and bush scenery along the way makes the drive wholly worthwhile. The most direct route from the north is to follow State Highway 2 around the Bay of Plenty to Opotiki, Eastland's northern gateway, then continue to Gisborne through the Waioeka Gorge Scenic Reserve. The drive from Auckland to Gisborne takes seven hours. South from Gisborne, continuing on Highway 2, you will pass through Wairoa, about 90 minutes away, before passing Napier, Hawke's Bay, and Wairarapa on the way to Wellington, about 7½ hours by car.

Some roads in Te Urewera park are gravel. If you're driving the Gisborne–Opotiki loop, keep in mind that there are very few gas stations along the way, and stretches of this road are hilly, winding, and narrow. Keep in mind, too, that if you're driving a rental car, your insurance likely won't cover driving on unpaved roads.

Contacts & Resources

EMERGENCIES

Your best bet for a pharmacy with extended hours is the Pharmacy 53 Limited in Gisborne, open from 8 AM to 8 PM daily.

🚏 Emergency Services **Fire, police, and ambulance** ☎ 111.
🚏 Pharmacy **Pharmacy 53 Limited** ✉ Ballance Street Village, Ballance St., Gisborne ☎ 06/867-3038.

TOURS

Trevor Brown of Trev's Tours leads guided tours throughout Eastland. Trips include a half-day tour of local wineries and half- or full-day excursions through Gisborne and the surrounding area, including visits to Eastwoodhill Arboretum. There are also day trips along the East Coast or inland to Te Urewera National Park and Lake Waikaremoana. Tours start at about $50 per person; call ahead to book.

🚏 Trev's Tours ☎ 06/863-9815 🖷 06/863-9515 ⊕ www.geocities.com/trevstours.

VISITOR INFORMATION

The Gisborne tourist office is open daily from 9 to 5:30. For information on Te Urewera National Park, your best bet is the Department of Conservation office in Aniwaniwa.

🚏 Tourist Information **Department of Conservation** ☎ 06/837-3803 ⊕ www.doc. govt.nz. **Gisborne–Eastland Visitor Information Centre** ✉ 209 Grey St., Gisborne ☎ 06/868-6139 🖷 06/868-6138 ⊕ www.gisbornenz.com.

Western North Island

WORD OF MOUTH

"If you're up for a bit of adventure, take one of the black-water rafting tours at the Waitomo Caves. You'll get to take a short hike through a cave to an underground river, where you float on inner tubes while viewing the glowworms. It was just so gorgeous down there once we turned off our headlights. You just lie back in your tube and look up—it's like seeing the Milky Way on a really clear night."

—Lee-anne

Updated by
Kathy Ombler

SURFING, HIKING, RIVER EXPLORING, CAVING . . . western North Island can keep outdoor enthusiasts busy for days. The region's geography encompasses the majestic, Fuji-like Mt. Taranaki, the gorges and wilderness of the Whanganui River region, the underground wonders of the Waitomo Caves, world-renowned surfing beaches, two national parks, and a host of forest-covered conservation areas, along with some highly fertile farmland.

The lush Taranaki region literally sprang from the ocean floor in a series of volcanic blasts, forming that distinctive curve along the West Coast of the North Island. The symmetrically shaped cone of Mt. Taranaki is the dramatic symbol of the province and the setting for climbing routes and hiking tracks (trails). Agriculture thrives in the area's fertile volcanic soil, and the gardens around Taranaki and New Plymouth city are some of the country's most spectacular. The mythology and historical sites relating to the local people are an integral part of Taranaki.

Note: For more information on hiking, surfing, and kayaking on the North Island's West Coast, *see* Chapter 11.

Exploring Western North Island

To reach the Taranaki region, you could travel south from Auckland, explore the surfer's paradise town of Raglan, and continue south along the remote coast road, or detour inland via Cambridge, then Waitomo and on to New Plymouth. This city is an excellent base for exploring Taranaki/Egmont National Park, the gardens of Taranaki, and the surfing beaches. From there, you can continue southward to the Whanganui River region for kayaking, canoeing, or simply exploring this scenic and historic wilderness. En route to Wellington, Palmerston North—one of New Zealand's leading university towns—and its farming surrounds are worth a quick stopover before you move on to the country's capital city.

About the Restaurants

Throughout western North Island you will find a mix of city restaurants and small, tourist-town cafés with several things in common: wholesome and hearty, fresh and tasty food; good espresso and loose-leaf teas; classy wine lists; and an overall sophistication one might expect to find only in the major centers. All-day breakfast menus are likely to feature standards such as eggs Benedict, homemade muesli with organic yogurt and fruit, corn fritters, and variations of the inevitable "big breakfast" (bacon, eggs, sausages, hash browns, tomatoes, mushrooms, and toast that should set you right for a few hours). Counter food for lunches and snacks will generally be fresh salads, paninis, focaccia, filled rolls, quiche, pies, and, in winter, hearty homemade soups.

Dinner menus in the higher-end restaurants will be a gourmet list of the chef's latest creations using high-quality New Zealand eye fillet of beef (beef tenderloin), fish, salmon, lamb racks, pork fillets, and chicken. The best local chefs take good advantage of fresh regional and seasonal ingredients and specialties, and they're not afraid to use techniques and flavors from other cuisines, particularly from Asia, and make them their own.

GREAT ITINERARIES

Numbers in the text correspond to numbers in the margin and on the Western North Island map.

IF YOU HAVE 3 DAYS

If you have only three days to explore the West Coast region, you could easily spend all of them at **Mt. Taranaki** ⑤, hiking in Egmont National Park and wandering through the area's gardens. Similarly, a canoe or kayak trip down the **Whanganui River** could occupy several days. If you prefer a quick tour of the region's highlights, spend part of a day swimming or surfing near easygoing **Raglan** ①, or strolling among the antiques shops and cafés in **Cambridge** ②. Allow a day to explore one or more of the **Waitomo Caves,** taking in the glowworm spectacle (you can overnight in the pretty village of **Waitomo** ③). Then continue south, basing yourself in **New Plymouth** ④ for a day or two in the Mt. Taranaki region; you can detour off the Surf Highway (Highway 45) to check out one of the top surfing beaches. Alternatively, farther south, you could use **Wanganui** ⑧ as a starting point for exploring the

Whanganui River Road or continue on to **Palmerston North** ⑨ for a brief sojourn in this university town and surrounding farming area.

IF YOU HAVE 6 DAYS

If you have almost a week, you'll have time to combine a more extensive exploration of the **Mt. Taranaki** ⑤ area—hiking and garden touring are its highlights, as are the nearby beaches—with a **Whanganui River** paddling or jet-boat trip through the scenic middle reaches or a drive up the **Whanganui River Road** (set aside at least two full days to see its remote river settlements). If you're heading north toward Auckland, you can stop off to see the glowworms at the **Waitomo Caves** ③, shop and stroll in **Cambridge** ②, or surf near **Raglan** ①. Alternatively, if you're going south to Wellington, you could spend a day or two in **Palmerston North** ⑨, where dining, barhopping, or theatergoing are among its more urban pleasures, or a visit to nearby Feilding will give a taste of New Zealand farming life.

Speaking of other cuisines, New Zealanders are a well-traveled, cosmopolitan lot and embrace other ethnicities, especially when it comes to food. Thus you're likely to find any number of Indian, Thai, Malaysian, Japanese, Mexican, and Italian restaurants, even in smaller provincial centers.

On the other hand, there is still a legacy of the more basic cafés and hotel restaurants, particularly in some smaller towns, where instant coffee, tea-bag tea, and lesser-quality fare is served and service is less than professional, so check the guidebook, and be as selective as you wish.

New Zealanders are fond of worldly cuisines, but when it comes to what they drink, they're apt to support local wines over imported ones, especially because the quality of locally produced wines is so high, and there is usually a good selection of both local and imported beers available.

Though locals have a high standard for what's on their plates, their habits are pretty relaxed when it comes to dress. "Smart-casual" is about as formal as you have to get.

WHAT IT COSTS In New Zealand dollars				
$$$$	**$$$**	**$$**	**$**	**¢**
RESTAURANTS over $30	$20–$30	$15–$20	$10–$15	under $10

Prices are per person for a main course at dinner, or the equivalent.

About the Hotels

You'll find every type of accommodation that can be found in New Zealand on the North Island West Coast, most of it hosted by laid-back, friendly locals. Bed-and-breakfasts are often stylishly converted country houses or custom-built to ensure the best views and comfort standards for guests. Some of New Zealand's finest luxury lodges are found in the region, along with a wonderful range of comfortable self-catering villas and cottages, some on working farms, others with spectacular coastal locations, and a few deep in the forest-covered hinterland. There are mountain lodges and river lodges in the national parks and, for hikers, climbers, and canoeists, basic back-country huts and camping spots managed by the Department of Conservation.

In the small tourist towns and larger cities, there's the full range of boutique hotels (small, personal, and stylish), standard hotels with basic rooms, motels with full kitchen facilities, and backpacker hostels. Although the latter are generally budget options, many with shared facilities, an increasing number of new backpacker properties have private, en suite rooms and modern, state-of-the-art equipment and facilities.

WHAT IT COSTS In New Zealand dollars				
$$$$	**$$$**	**$$**	**$**	**¢**
HOTELS over $300	$200–$300	$125–$200	$75–$125	under $75

Prices are for a standard double room in high season, including 12.5% tax.

When to Visit

Although the months from December through mid-April are the most popular for exploring western North Island, most attractions can be enjoyed any time of the year. Summer is obviously warmer—great for swimming or surfing, hiking the mountains, and paddling the rivers. However, the weather is often more settled during winter, and there will be fewer people. Throughout the year, the exposed coast gets more than its fair share of rain and southerly winds, so even in summer, be prepared for the odd chilly day. The upper slopes of Mt. Taranaki are steep, snow covered in winter, and especially exposed to sudden changing weather; ask advice from park staff about heading up there. The summer school holidays run from December to the end of January, so the beach areas will be busy, especially over the Christmas/New Year's period.

TOP REASONS TO GO

CAVING

Waitomo has an amazing underground landscape of ancient limestone formations, fossils, passages, shafts, hidden streams, and brilliant galaxies of glowworms. You can explore these stunning cave systems by taking underground walks, boat rides, or adrenaline-pumping "black-water" rafting and abseiling tours.

KAYAKING & CANOEING

Whanganui River, the longest navigable waterway in the country, is a prime destination for adventurers; it's also regarded as an ideal beginner's river. A multiday journey by kayak or canoe is a truly historic, as well as scenic, experience: the lower reaches of the river from Pipiriki to Wanganui pass several small, historic Māori settlements.

HIKING & WALKING

There's a plethora of natural features and landscapes to explore on foot in this region of the North Island; steep, rocky alpine terrain, tussock and herb fields, wetlands and dense lowland rain forest. The pick of the longer trails include the three-day Pouakai Circuit on the lower and midslopes of Mt. Taranaki, in Egmont National Park, or the Matemateaonga and Mangaparua Tracks in Whanganui National Park. An outstanding short (30-minute) walk is in Ruakuri Reserve, in Waitomo Cave country. In the Raglan area, a short walk takes you to pretty Bridal Veil Falls, and longer, steeper trails lead up Mt. Karioi.

SURFING

They may have black sand, but the surfing beaches along the North Island West Coast rival any other surfing spots in the world. Manu Bay, near Raglan, is famous for its left-hand break. Just along the road is Whale Bay, another top spot to catch a wave. In Taranaki, "Surf Highway 45" accesses some of New Zealand's premier surfing coastline. Surfing schools, hip cafés, crafts galleries, and a cool laid-back vibe are all part of the scene in the small surfing communities established near these beaches.

THE WAIKATO & WAITOMO

Many think of the Waikato region—a fertile, temperate, agricultural district south of Auckland—as the heartland of the North Island. It is home to New Zealand's largest inland city (Hamilton) and some of its most important pre-European sites.

Polynesian sailors first landed on the region's west coast as early as the mid-14th century; by way of contrast, Europeans didn't settle here until the 1830s. In the 1860s, the Waikato's many tribes united to elect a king in an attempt to resist white encroachment upon their lands. This "King Movement," as it is known, is still a significant cultural and political force within Waikato Māoridom.

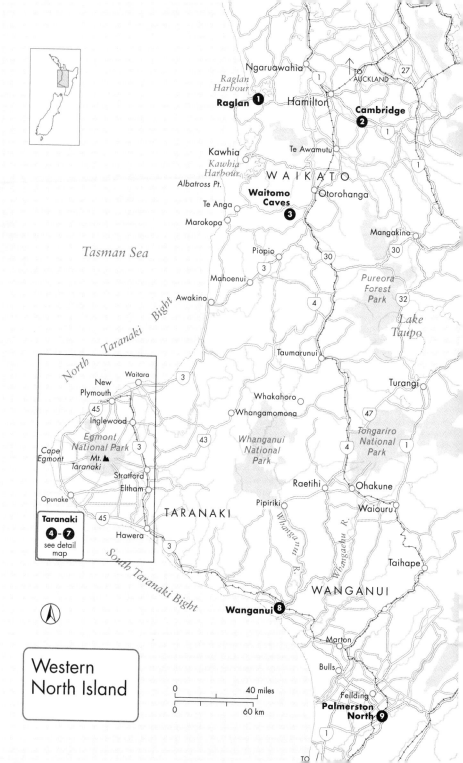

Western
North Island

Hamilton is a city you can afford to miss if time is tight. Instead, pass directly through town to explore and enjoy three nearby attractions: the surfing hot spot of Raglan on the West Coast; attractive Cambridge, an agricultural town renowned as a horse-breeding center; and the extraordinary cave formations at Waitomo.

Raglan

❶ *176 km (110 mi) south of Auckland, 44 km (27 mi) west of Hamilton.*

It's hard to think of a more laid-back town in the country than Raglan. On the drive out there, tune in to radio station Raglan FM 96.6 to catch the local news and grooves. On sheltered Raglan Harbour, and in the lee of Mt. Karioi, the tiny town owes its easygoing ways to the legions of young surfers drawn to the legendary breaks at nearby Manu Bay and Whale Bay, both 8 km (5 mi) southwest of town. The Raglan surf was featured in the 1966 film *Endless Summer.* When the surf's up, drive out to the parking areas above the sweeping bays to see scores of surfers tackling what's reputed to be world's longest left-hand break.

The surfers have made this seaside village cool, and along the tree-lined main street, Bow Street, barefoot dudes in designer shades pad in and out of the few hip café-bars or hang in the smattering of crafts and surf-wear shops. Families vacation here, too, staking out their patch of sand on the beaches on either side of the harbor entrance.

OFF THE BEATEN PATH

KAWHIA – With time on your hands, explore the minor road from Raglan to this isolated, coastal harbor settlement 55 km (34 mi) to the south. It's a fine route, skirting the eastern flank of Mt. Karioi and passing the turnoff for Bridal Veil Falls, though take care, because much of the road is gravel. In 1350 Kawhia was where the Tainui people, the region's earliest Polynesian settlers, first landed after their long sea voyage from Polynesia. Permission is sometimes granted (inquire at the harborside museum) to visit the local *marae* (traditional village). What those in the know come for, however, are the Te Puia hot springs at Ocean Beach, east of town. There's road access to the beach (or it's a two-hour walk from Kawhia). Because you can find the springs only by digging into the sand a couple of hours either side of low tide, you should check the tide tables in Raglan before you set off.

Where to Stay & Eat

$$$ ✕ **Aqua Velvet Kitchen and Ballroom.** There's no dancing, but this spacious, wood-floored minimalistic-style café is plenty big enough to warrant its ballroom moniker, and live music is an occasional treat. Aqua Velvet supports local organic suppliers and carries one of the country's top espresso brands, Havanah organic coffee. All the food is made in-house; there are fresh baked goods, a salad bar, and dishes such as lentil, chickpea, and fresh-herb fritters with spicy tomato relish, organic salad, and minted yogurt. It's open 8 to 3 and occasional evenings in summer. ✉ *17 Bow St.* ☎ *07/825–8588* ▭ *AE, DC, MC, V* ☺ *No dinner in winter; evening hours vary in summer.*

★ **$$–$$$**   ✕**Vinnie's World of Eats.** In this historic kauri cottage, you can tuck into anything from Mexican food to gourmet burgers and pizzas to Thai curries. There's also a lot of seafood and an interesting kids' menu. A full breakfast menu, plus lunches, snacks, summer salads, and nibbles will keep you fed no matter what time of day or night. Vinnie's is fully licensed and also has a full range of smoothies, fresh juices, and espresso. ⊠ *7 Wainui Rd.* ☎ *07/825–7273* ⊕ *www.vinnies.net.nz* ☱ *AE, DC, MC, V.*

$–$$$ ✕**Tongue & Groove.** Popular with the locals, this funky corner café has comfy couches and Formica tables; the walls are lined with surfboards and decorated with Raglan beach scenes—there's even a surfboard for a table. The menu is huge and the meals are hearty, starting at 9 AM with breakfast. Try the stewed fruit and organic yogurt with toasted almonds, or the "hell fry up in chunky pots, mushies, bacon, sausie, eggs, toast, and caramelized onions." All-day snacks come from around the globe: veggie roti, tofu burgers, chicken kebabs, and miso noodles. Evening main courses include a similarly eclectic range, such as organic ramen noodles or lamb shanks. As with neighboring eateries, there's a great selection of beers, wines, espresso, loose-leaf teas, smoothies, and fresh juices. ⊠ *Wainui Rd. and Bow St.* ☎ *07/825–0027* ☱ *AE, DC, MC, V.*

¢   🏠 **Karioi Lodge.** Nestled into the hills above Raglan, this backpackers' lodge is the ultimate off-the-beaten-path place to kick back and unwind— or not. American proprietor Charlie Young and his partner, Erin, may have you "sucking back the fresh air of the native bush" and amped up to ride the waves before you know it. Or, if you'd rather do yoga, meditate in the sun, chill out in the sauna, play pool, or take a *gentle* bushwalk, they'll arrange that, too. Dorm rooms, most with four beds (two bunk beds) per room, are clean and comfy, but they share baths and there are no extras (don't expect plugs for hair dryers, for instance). The staff uses local ingredients to prepare hearty evening meals, including homemade bread, nachos, burgers, and roasts ($12 per person). Whether this remarkably good-value meal is available depends on the number of guests in house, but you can usually count on it in summer. ⊠ *Whaanga Rd., Whale Bay* ☎ *07/825–7873 or 0800/867–873* 🛏 *5 double rooms with shared bath, 15 dorm rooms (58 beds) with shared bath* ♨ *Laundry facilities, Internet room; no a/c* ☱ *MC, V.*

¢   🏠 **Raglan Backpackers & Waterfront Lodge.** Many rate this supremely agreeable, budget-price, harborside lodge the best of its type in the country, and it consistently rates in the top 10 in annual nationwide backpacker surveys. An "outdoor living" ideal, rooms open onto a pretty, wood-decked interior courtyard (complete with hammock). From the lounge you can wander onto the lawn and barbecue area. The shared bathroom facilities are spotless, and there's a well-equipped self-catering kitchen. Linen is provided, and rooms are comfortable and clean, with single or double beds, some with electric blankets and six with sea views. The rooms sleep between two (for a private room) and eight (in dorm rooms). One self-contained house has two double rooms. If you're feeling adventurous, ask for a surfing lesson ($24; includes board and wet suit), or make use of the kayaks ($5 per day) and bikes ($2 per day). ⊠ *6 Wi Neera St.* ☎ *07/825–0515* ⊕ *www.raglanbackpackers.co.nz* 🛏 *8 rooms with shared bath, 1 dorm (8 beds) with shared bath, 1 2-bedroom house* ♨ *Laundry facilities; no a/c* ☱ *No credit cards.*

FodorsChoice ★

Sports & the Outdoors

BOATING Local boatman Don Rangiawha of **Harbour Cruises** (☎🖶 07/825–8153) welcomes you aboard the *Spruce Goose* for a 1½- to 2-hour cruise around the tidal inlets and bays of huge Raglan Harbour. See forest reserves, historic habitation sites, isolated beaches, the "pancakes" limestone outcrops, seabirds, and, if your timing is lucky, the pod of orca that occasionally visits the harbor. Daytime and dinner cruises are available; sailings are weather permitting. Advance reservations are essential and can be made directly with Harbour Cruises or with the **Ranglan Information Centre** (☎ 07/825–0556).

SURFING If you're itching to hit the waves, stop by **Raglan Surf Co.** (⊠ 3 Wainui Rd. ☎ 07/825–8988), a top surfing store. It stocks equipment by all the leading brands and rents surfboards, wet suits, and Boogie boards. It's open daily, and the friendly staff pass along helpful local surf tips.

Raglan Surfing School (⊠ Summer: Whaanga Rd., Whale Bay; Winter: Karioi Lodge ☎ 07/825–7873 ⊕ www.raglansurfingschool.co.nz) has a variety of options for learning to ride the waves. The school was started by local Tim Duff, who spent years following the best surf around the world only to decide that nowhere could beat his hometown. (Duff has since moved on to become co-owner at Raglan Backpackers & Waterfront Lodge.) The school is now in the capable hands of another hometown boy, Eric (Rock) Milroy, and of several present or past national surfing champions who work as instructors. A three-hour session (which includes board and wet suit) is around $79. Surf Adventure Packages run two–five days and include transport, daily surfing lessons, and accommodation, as well as other adventures such as abseiling (rappelling), paragliding, and jet-boating. These packages start at $195.

Fodor$Choice There's no better way to explore huge Raglan Harbour than on nature's ★ terms, with Steve and Candide Reid and their company **Raglan Kayak** (☎ 07/825–8862 ⊕ www.raglankayak.co.nz) Like surfer Tim Duff, local boy Steve searched the world for the perfect place to work on water, then realized it was back home. People of any age and ability are welcome on his shorter kayak trips, where the focus is on paddling with the tide and wind, great scenery, espresso, and home baking. Trips range from two hours ($50) to six hours ($95) and include gorgeous sunset excursions. Kayaks are also available for rent ($15 single, $25 tandem per hour; $35/$55 per half day; $45/$65 per day).

SWIMMING Although the surf looks inviting at most of the West Coast beaches, there can be dangerous rips and undertows, so be careful where you take a dip. The safest spots around Raglan are Te Aro Aro Bay (Wallis and Puriri Sts.), Te Kopua, and at Cox Bay and Lorenzen Bay at high tide. Call 07/825–0556 for tide times. In summer, lifeguards patrol the beach at Ngarunui; to avoid the strong rips, swim between the flags.

WALKING & From Raglan, a number of walks and hikes give you wonderful views HIKING of the coastline and take you through beautiful native bush. **The Department of Conservation** (☎ 07/838–3363 Hamilton) manages these tracks and surrounding conservation land. The Raglan Information Centre (⇨ Visitor Information *in* The Waikato & Waitomo Essentials, *below*) can provide maps. Don't leave valuables in your vehicle while you're away walking.

On hot days, the spectacular **Bridal Veil Falls** make an appealing target. A 10-minute shaded hike from the parking lot leads to a viewing platform above the 150-foot drop; from here, another 10-minute walk down a steep, stepped trail puts you on a wooden platform at the base of the falls. Bring your swimsuit and, if you dare, plunge into the very cold water. The falls are 20 km (12 mi) south of Raglan; take the Kawhia road from town.

A great walk, although somewhat more difficult than the Bridal Veil Falls trail, is up **Mt. Karioi.** Some sections are quite steep, so good walking gear is required, but it's worth the challenge for the fantastic views of the coast. The Te Toto Gorge option is 3½ hours to the summit (one-way); if you leave from Whaanga Road in Kariori, it's 2½ hours to the summit (one-way).

Cambridge

❷ *53 km (33 mi) east of Raglan.*

Because it's on State Highway 1, Cambridge is a handy stopping point for stretching your legs or taking a lunch break on your way elsewhere. But this charming town, with its historic buildings and rural English atmosphere, is worth a closer look.

In summer evenings or weekends, you're likely to find the locals playing cricket in the park in the center of town. Year-round, trees provide an elegant canopy over the streets that are lined with antiques shops and cafés. The best way to check out Cambridge is to park your car and stroll along Victoria, Empire, and Commerce streets.

Cambridge is regarded as New Zealand's Kentucky; the thoroughbred industry has become the most prominent local feature. The surrounding farmland is home to top breeding studs and training stables, including those run by Olympic gold-medal equestrian winner Mark Todd.

Near the center of the town, the 100-year-old **St. Andrew's Anglican Church** is worth a look as you drive or walk past for its beautiful stained-glass windows.

If nature conservation is your thing, take a walk among some of the most ancient forest in the region at the small "mountain" called Maungatautiri, where the **Maungatautiri Ecological Island Trust,** in conjunction with the Department of Conservation, is carrying out one of New Zealand's many successful conservation stories. Through huge community effort, the trust is building a $14 million, 50-km pest-proof fence around 8,400 acres of native forest on Maungatautiri, to create a refuge for some of New Zealand's rarest native species. The project is long term; in the interim there are several short forest walks through smaller fenced enclosures, where animal pests such as rats and stoats have been removed, and birdlife is thriving as a result. Interpretive signs describe the conservation project, and you might see or hear a variety of more common native birds, such as the distinctive *tūī* (*too*-ee), with its tuft of white feathers under its chin and resonant song. The closest walk, 14 km (9 mi) from Cambridge, is Te Ara Tirohia Track. ⊠ *Hicks Rd.* ☎ *07/823–7455* ⊕ *www.maungatrust.org* ⊠ *By donation* ⊙ *Daily dawn–dusk.*

🖑 **New Zealand Horse Magic** at Cambridge Thoroughbred Lodge is a must for anyone interested in horse racing or the thoroughbred industry. Experienced presenters tailor shows for each audience, easily moving from expert-level information to antics for kids. Call ahead for a show reservation and to confirm the show schedule. A minimum of 10 people is required; if there are fewer, a more personal look around the stud might be offered. Numerous breeds of horses can be seen, including a Lippizaner. Two of the most famous horses on show are Rough Habit, the racehorse who was twice named New Zealand Horse of the Year and has won a total of $5.2 million; and Christopher Vance, who has racked up prizes of $2.5 million racing in Australia and New Zealand. Kids can go for a short ride on more placid horses, with the guidance of instructors, while you have a cup of coffee and a muffin. The horse auctions can be interesting to drop in on; call for dates. ⊠ *State Hwy. 1, 6 km (4 mi) south of Cambridge* ☎ *07/827–8118* ⊕ *www.cambridgethoroughbredlodge. co.nz* ⊠ *$12* ⊙ *Stud tours Tues.–Sun. 10-3 (reserve ahead); shows Tues.–Sun. at 10:30* AM *(reserve ahead; min. 10 people).*

Visit the **Cambridge Country Store,** housed in an old pink church, for a good selection of New Zealand–made jewelry, clothing, carvings, and wine. The All Saints Café upstairs sells muffins, pies, quiche, and sandwiches. ⊠ *92 Victoria St.* ☎ *07/827–8715* ⊕ *www.cambridgecountrystore.co.nz.*

Where to Stay & Eat

$$$ ✕ **Rosso's.** This stylish restaurant and bar serves a range of classic, homemade Italian pasta dishes such as spaghetti marinara, along with standard New Zealand fare such as green-lipped mussels, seafood chowder, eye fillet of beef, and salmon dishes. ⊠ *72 Alpha St.* ☎ *07/827–6699* ⊟ *MC, V, DC* ⊙ *Closed Mon. No lunch Tues., Sat., or Sun.*

$–$$ ✕ **Rata Café.** A few doors down the street from Fran's, Rata Cafe is a
Fodor's Choice slightly funky daytime café, with wood floors, redbrick walls, local art-
★ work, and comfy sofas, that serves, arguably, the best coffee in town. Food is made fresh on the premises. The huge breakfast menu (try the organic Greek yogurt–and–berry compote) is available all day, as are tempting premade salads and pastas. ⊠ *64C Victoria St.* ☎ *07/823–0999* ⊟ *AE, D, MC, V* ⊙ *Closes at 5* PM; *open until 8* PM *Fri. in summer.*

¢–$ ✕ **Fran's Café and Continental Cake Kitchen.** Snag a table in the main room, or wander past the kitchen to the courtyard out back. Choose from a big selection of imaginative homemade sandwiches, pasta, quiche, or salads, such as the grilled vegetables with balsamic vinegar. The menu changes regularly. Fran makes her own hummus and falafel. ⊠ *62 Victoria St.* ☎ *07/827–3946* ⊕ *www.franscafe.co.nz* ⊟ *AE, MC, V* ⏳ *BYOB.*

$$ ✕⊡ **Souter House.** If ever a place was worth a detour from the main highway, this has to be it. This beautifully restored Edwardian villa, listed by the New Zealand Historic Places Trust, has superb guest rooms and exceptional dining. The rooms and suites are tastefully furnished with fine paintings and antiques. In the restaurant, choose from New Zealand king salmon and prime-quality aged fillet of beef. The wine list's selection of top New Zealand varieties is reasonably priced. A new bar was added in early 2006. ⊠ *19 Victoria St.* ☎ *07/827–3610* 🖷 *07/827–4885* ⊕ *www.souterhouse.co.nz* ⤚ *7 rooms, 2 suites* ⚘ *Dining room, bar; no smoking* ▭ *AE, MC, V* ﮩﻞ *CP.*

$$$$ 🏨 **Maungatautiri Lodge.** In an idyllic country setting overlooking Lake Karapiro, and just a 10-minute drive from Cambridge, is one of New Zealand's newest and finest luxury lodges. Suites and villas are luxuriously appointed with private balconies, double whirlpool baths, DVD players, and in-room broadband (by 2007). The lodge also has a spacious lounge, sitting room, formal dining room, and sunny conservatory ideal for breakfasts. Arresting shades of terra cotta, coral, and aqua feature throughout. Outside are grass terraces, formal rose and lavender gardens, and an infinity pool. Rates include dinner, predinner canapés and drinks, and breakfast. ⊠ *844 Maungatautiri Rd., Lake Karapiro* ☎ *07/827–2220* 🖷 *07/827–2221* ⊕ *www.malodge.com* ⤚ *4 suites, 3 villas* ⚘ *Dining room, minibars, cable TV, in-room DVD, in-room data ports, lounge* ▭ *AE, D, MC, V* ﮩﻞ *MAP.*

Waitomo

80 km (50 mi) southwest of Hamilton, 65 km (41 mi) southwest of Cambridge, 150 km (95 mi) west of Rotorua.

A short drive from the main highway, Waitomo is a pretty village catering to tourists visiting the region's famous cave systems. The surrounding hills are a mix of native bush and verdant farmland, and everything is within walking distance of the village center, which gives it an easy, relaxed feel.

★ ❸   The **Waitomo Caves** are part of an ancient seabed that was lifted and then spectacularly eroded into a surreal underground landscape of limestone formations, gushing rivers, and contorted caverns. Many of the caves are still unexplored, although an increasing number are accessible on adventurous underground activity trips involving rafting, caving, and rappelling. But you don't need to be Indiana Jones to appreciate the magnificent underground structures.

Since 1889, guided tours through the biggest, best-known caves have been available; today these tours attract thousands of visitors each year, especially in summer, though the caves can be visited—and are spectacular—at any time of year.

Four major cave systems are open for guided tours: Ruakuri, Spellbound, Aranui, and Waitomo Glowworm Cave. Each has its own special characteristics, such as impressive limestone formations, glowworm-lighted "starry skies," spiritual significance for the Māori people, and stories of discovery and intrigue. You won't be disappointed with whichever you choose; try them all if you have the time. Your guides are likely to be descendants of local chief Tane Tinorau (who discovered Waitomo Glowworm Cave) or local caving experts who have spent years exploring the amazing network of shafts and passageways around Waitomo.

Extreme adventure, a sedate guided tour along well-lighted pathways, or anything in between is possible in these amazing subterranean passages. If adventure is your thing, don a wet suit, helmet, and headlamp and take a tour where you can abseil (rappel) through narrow shafts, leap over a waterfall, and go black-water rafting through the dark caves beneath a twinkling roof of glowworms. Bookings for all cave tours and activities can be made with the individual tour operators, or at the Waitomo i-SITE Visitor Centre (⇨ Sports & the Outdoors, *below*).

Waitomo Glowworm Cave takes the first part of its name from the words *wai* (water) and *tomo* (cave), since the Waitomo River vanishes into the hillside here. The second part of the cave's name refers to the larvae of *Arachnocampa luminosa,* measuring between 1 and 2 inches, that live on cave ceilings. They snare prey by dangling sticky filaments, which trap insects attracted to the light the worm emits by a chemical oxidation process. A single glowworm produces far less light than any firefly, but when they are massed in great numbers in the dark, their effect is a bit like looking at the night sky in miniature. The Waitomo Glowworm Cave was first officially explored in 1887 by local Chief Tane Tinorau, accompanied by the English surveyor Fred Mace. They built a raft of flax stems and, with candles as their only light source, floated into the cave where the stream goes underground. Chief Tane continued his exploration over the years and, in 1889, began leading tours. Like those first explorers, you traverse the cave by boat; tours are 45 minutes and groups meet at the cave. ⊠ *Waitomo Caves Rd., entrance to cave about 100 m (300 feet) beyond Waitomo Caves i-SITE Visitor Centre* ☎ *0800/456–922* ⊕ *www.waitomocaves.co.nz* ✉ *Tours $30, $48 combo ticket with Aranui Cave* ☉ *Tours every half hour 9–5; bookings not required.*

Fodor'sChoice
★

Ruakuri Cave was discovered several hundred years ago by a Māori hunting party and takes its name from the pack of wild dogs that used to inhabit the cave entrance—*rua* means "den" or "pit," and *kuri* means "dog." The cave first opened to the public in 1904, then was closed for 18 years while issues of ownership and respect for Māori spirituality were settled. The cave's original entrance was an *urupa* (burial site) for Māori and is now left alone by visitors, who enter through a dramatic new spiral "drum passage." Narrow passages, hidden streams, ancient rockfalls, glowworms, and an amazing variety of limestone formations feature in Ruakuri. The two-hour tours are limited to 15 people. ⊠ *Tour groups meet at Long Black Café, 585 Waitomo Caves Rd.* ☎ *0800/222–323* ⊕ *www.ruakuri.co.nz* ✉ *Tours $49* ☉ *Tours daily at 9, 11, 1, and 3; book in advance.*

On the Spellbound Tour, you visit **Spellbound and Te Ana o te Atua caves.** At Spellbound, a gentle raft ride passes through a magnificent glowworm chamber, one that has been filmed by the BBC with Sir David Attenborough. Te Ana o te Atua (Cave of the Spirit) has been known to the Ngati Kinohaku people for centuries. On the walking tour, the highlights are limestone formations, fossils, and bones. The 3½-hour tours are limited to 12 people. ⊠ *Tours leave from the Waitomo Caves i-SITE Visitor Centre, Waitomo Village* ☎ *0800/773–552* ⊕ *www.waitomospellbound. co.nz* ✉ *Tours $47.50* ☉ *Five tours daily; book in advance.*

At **Aranui Cave,** eons of dripping water have sculpted a delicate garden of pink-and-white limestone. The cave is named after a local, Te Ru-tuku Aranui, who discovered the cave in 1910 when his dog disappeared inside in pursuit of a wild pig. Tours (45 minutes) lead along boardwalks into tall, narrow chambers. Tickets must be purchased from the Wait-omo Glowworm Cave, before meeting at Aranui. ⊠ *Entrance at Ru-akuri Reserve, on Tumutumu Rd., 3 km (2 mi) beyond Waitomo Caves Village* ☎ *0800/773–552* ⊕ *www.waitomocaves.co.nz* ✆ *Tours $28, $48 combo ticket with Waitomo Glowworm Cave* ☼ *Several tours daily; book in advance.*

☺ At the visitor center of Waitomo Caves Village the **Museum of Caves** pro-vides an entertaining and informative look at the formation of the caves and the life cycle of the glowworm, with a number of multimedia and interactive displays designed especially for children. You can also squeeze through models of caves and tunnels. ⊠ *Waitomo i-SITE Visitor Cen-tre, Waitomo Caves Rd., Waitomo Village* ☎ *07/878–7640* ⊕ *www. waitomo-museum.co.nz* ✆ *$5, or entry is included in cost of several cave and adventure tours* ☼ *Jan.–mid-Mar., daily 8–8; mid-Mar.–Dec., daily 8–5:30.*

One of the most interesting short walks in the country is at the **Waitomo Walkway.** The 5-km (3-mi), approximately 2½-hour walk begins across the road from the Museum of Caves and follows the Waitomo River. The track passes through forests and impressive limestone outcrops, and is relatively easy. You have to walk back to Waitomo Caves Village on the same path, or you can follow the road, a distance of just over 2 km (1 mi). For an alternative to the complete walk, take Te Anga Road from the village, turn left onto Tumutumu Road, park at Ruakuri Reserve, and walk the short (about 30-minute) final section of the track. There are two natural rock tunnels on the way and informative signs explaining the natural features. Many people come out here after dusk for a free view of the local glowworms; bring a flashlight to find your way.

OFF THE BEATEN PATH

TE ANGA–MAROKOPA ROAD – This classic backcountry road works its way west out of Waitomo toward the coast. It makes for a spectacu-lar detour—or the scenic long way to Taranaki—winding past stunning vistas. If the weather is clear, **Haggas Lookout,** 7 km (4 mi) from Wait-omo, is worth a stop for the expansive view that extends southward to the volcano mountains of Tongariro National Park. Some 26 km (16 mi) from Waitomo, stop at the **Mangapohue Natural Bridge** (pronounced mang-ah-po-*hoo*-ay). From the parking area, there are two approaches to the bridge. One to the right climbs over a hill, dropping into a val-ley strewn with boulders embedded with oyster fossils—the remains of a seismic shift that thrust up the seabed millions of years ago. The natural bridge rises off to the left of the boulders. The other path fol-lows a stream through a gorge it has carved out. The gorge walls climb ever higher until they meet and form the bridge that closes over the path. The circular walk—going out on one path, returning on the other—takes only 15 to 20 minutes to complete. A note of caution here: carry your valuables such as wallet and passport with you, and keep luggage in your vehicle out of sight.

About 5 km (3 mi) farther along the road from the Mangapohue Bridge to Marokopa, **Piripiri Caves** beckon with their interesting fossil legacy— the marks of giant oysters that resided here during the area's onetime subaqueous existence. The approach and entrance to the caves are steep and slippery, so wear appropriate shoes or boots, and bring a jacket for the cool air and a powerful flashlight to cut through the gloom. There are no guided tours; just follow the trail markers. A few kilometers farther still, you can view the 120-foot **Marokopa Falls** from a viewpoint reached via a pleasant forest trail (about 15 minutes round-trip).

Just beyond Marokopa Falls, **Te Anga Tavern** is a good place to stop for refreshment and to meet the locals. It's open daily 2 to 10:30 for drinks, and serves basic dinners—fish-and-chips, steak and salad—Friday and Saturday nights. Another incentive: pool tables are only 50 cents a game!

The road splits at Te Anga, heading north to Kawhia or southwest for 14 km (9 mi) to the small hamlet of **Marokopa,** where there's a stupendous lookout point over the coast's black-sand beaches. At Marokopa you are 50 km (31 mi) from Waitomo; time either to turn back or keep on south on a more difficult (mostly gravel) but very scenic route to the Taranaki region. If you're in for the duration, fill up your gas tank before turning off State Highway 1 for Waitomo.

An attraction of the non-cave variety, **Billy Black's Kiwi Culture Show** gives an entertaining glimpse into pioneer life, complete with sheep-shearing instructions. It's just a two-minute drive from Waitomo Village. ⊠ *Woodlyn Park, 1177 Waitomo Valley Rd.* ☎ *07/878–6666* ⊕ *www. woodlynpark.co.nz* ✎ *$18* ⊙ *Daily at 1:30.*

Where to Stay

¢–$$ 🏨 **Waitomo Caves Hotel.** High on the hill overlooking the village, this hotel would make a perfect haunted house for a horror film. Built in 1908, it has an elegant, if tired, charm about it. Some consider its down-at-the-heels appearance an embarrassment when New Zealand has such comparatively outstanding hotels. And the restaurant, which aspires to greatness, is off the mark with a hit-or-miss mix of traditional and contemporary New Zealand dishes ($$$–$$$$) and spotty service. However, the hotel is an important historic icon of this small village, and some visitors love the spooky factor. The owners have made a cursory attempt at restoration, starting with the public areas, but the rooms and their decor are still very much of a bygone area. Four of the rooms can accommodate families. Breakfast is also served; lunches are available with advance notice. ⊠ *39 Waitomo Caves Rd., Waitomo Village* ⊕ *RD7, Otorohanga* ☎ *07/878–8204* 🖷 *07/878–8205* ⊕ *www. waitomocaveshotel.co.nz* 🛏 *33 rooms* ☁ *2 restaurants; no a/c, no TV in some rooms* ➦ *AE, DC, MC, V.*

$–$$ 🏨 **Abseil Breakfast Inn.** When hosts John and Helen say they treat you
Fodor'sChoice better than family, they are not joking (though they do have quirky senses
★ of humor). This delightful bed-and-breakfast property overlooks the green Waitomo countryside and resounds with birdsong on the outside and conviviality within. Four rooms, each tastefully decorated to a local theme (Farm, Cave Room, Bush, and Swamp), have super-queen beds and an

entrance from the deck; one has a two-person bathtub. The guest lounge has a great range of DVDs and music, plus a significant library. Some excellent New Zealand wines are available at very reasonable prices in a trusting self-service, pay-later system. The breakfasts are seriously good. The story goes that John bought the inn as a present for Helen. Now he says it was really an excuse for him to augment his beloved wine cellar. ⊠ *Waitomo Caves Rd.* ☎ *07/878–7815* ⊕ *www.abseilinn.co.nz* ⤶ *4 rooms* ♨ *No room TVs* ⊟ *MC, V* ✪ *Closed June* ❤ *BP.*

¢–$ ▥ **Kiwi Paka Youth Hostel.** This relaxed hostel is in the heart of Waitomo village—just a couple of minutes' walk from the Waitomo Glowworm Caves. Drawing on the area's rural vernacular, the design is a deliberate cross between New Zealand's archetypal red corrugated wool sheds (for shearing sheep) and ski chalets. You can either stay in the communal rooms with shared or private bathrooms or opt for a chalet. The rooms and chalets share a well-equipped kitchen. The friendly staff provide gum boots and flashlights for exploring the caves; they can help organize other activities, too. You can easily while away a few hours on the decks overlooking the bush at the on-site Morepork Pizzeria and Café, which serves breakfast, lunch, and dinner. The pizzas are seriously big. ⊠ *School Rd.* ☎ *07/878–3395* 🖷 *07/878–3396* ⊕ *www.kiwipaka-yha.co.nz* ⤶ *22 rooms with shared bath, 2 rooms with private bath, 20 chalets* ♨ *Café, kitchen, billiards, 2 lounges, laundry facilities, Internet room; no room phones, no room TVs* ⊟ *MC, V.*

Sports & the Outdoors

Several companies offer an initially confusing range of adventures. Each company has its own booking office and base, but activities can also be booked through the **Waitomo i-SITE Visitor Information Centre** (☎ 07/878–7640). This free service gives unbiased advice and information about which of the various tours is most suitable.

ATV TOURS **Waitomo Big Red** (☎ 07/878–8393) leads exhilarating and often muddy four-wheel bike adventures through farm and forest for $90 per driver and $25 per passenger.

CAVE
ADVENTURES
Most of Waitomo's subterranean adventure tours contain some element of black-water rafting—that is, floating through the underground caverns on inflated inner tubes, dressed in wet suits and equipped with cavers' helmets. Be prepared for the pitch-black darkness and freezing cold water. Your reward is an exhilarating trip gliding through vast glowworm-lighted caverns, clambering across rocks, and jumping over waterfalls. Some tours involve steep rappelling or tight underground squeezes.

★ Most adventurous types will be able to cope with the basic trip, "Black Labyrinth," offered by one of the longest-standing companies, **The Legendary Black Water Rafting** (⊠ 585 Waitomo Caves Rd. ☎ 07/878–6219 or 0800/228–464 ⊕ www.blackwaterrafting.co.nz). Trips finish with welcome hot showers and a mug of soup back at base. The cost is $90 per person for three hours, $175 per person for "Black Abyss" (five hours), and includes free admission to the Museum of Caves. Departure times vary, depending on demand.

Thrill seekers might prefer to venture out with **Rap, Raft 'n' Rock** (✉ 95 Waitomo Cave Rd. ☎ 0800/228–372 ⊕ www.caveraft.com), which has a 4½-hour combo adventure that includes rappelling, black-water rafting, rock climbing, caving, and checking out the glowworms. The trips cost $99 per person.

HORSEBACK RIDING Take a ride by horseback through the limestone and fossilized country-side with **Waitomo Caves Horse Treks** (☎ 07/878–5065). The price is $60 for two hours, or $150 for a full day (by arrangement).

THE WAIKATO & WAITOMO ESSENTIALS

Transportation

BY BUS

InterCity Coachlines runs buses several times daily between Auckland and Hamilton, with onward services to Cambridge. For Waitomo, take the bus from Auckland to Otorohanga, 50 minutes south of Hamilton, where there is also a train station. From here, the Waitomo Shuttle makes the half-hour trip from Otorohanga to Waitomo five times daily, connecting with all major bus and train arrivals. Book in advance: the shuttle is $9 per person each way, but $30 for those who don't book in advance. One Newmans bus leaves Auckland daily direct to Waitomo for $62. The Waitomo Wanderer bus service makes the two-hour trip between Rotorua and Waitomo once (each way) daily. Fares are $40 one-way or $65 round-trip.

Buses for Raglan ($5.50) run from Hamilton three times daily and return from the Hamilton Transport Centre. They stop at several points in Raglan, including the Raglan Library.

🚌 Bus Depots **Cambridge bus stop** ✉ Lake St., Cambridge. **Hamilton Travel Centre** ✉ Bryce St., Hamilton ☎ 07/834–3457 or 0800/242–645. **Raglan Library** ✉ Bow St., Raglan. **Waitomo depot** ✉ Waitomo i-SITE Visitor Centre, Waitomo Caves Rd., Waitomo Caves Village ☎ 07/878–7640.

🚌 Bus Companies **InterCity** ☎ 09/913–6100 ⊕ www.intercitycoach.co.nz. **Newmans** ☎ 09/913–6200 ⊕ www.newmanscoach.co.nz. **Waitomo Shuttle** ☎ 0800/808–279. **Waitomo Wanderer** ☎ 07/349–2509 or 0508/926–337 ⊕ www.waitomotours.co.nz.

BY CAR

Although regional bus lines serve the main route, traveling by car is generally the most convenient way to see this region. Access to the Waikato region is straight down State Highway 1 from Auckland—count on 90 minutes to Hamilton. Cambridge is another 15 minutes southeast on Highway 1. For Raglan, take Highway 23 west, a 40-minute drive. For Waitomo (one hour from Hamilton), take Highway 3 south and turn off onto Highway 37 past Otorohanga. Some roads are narrow and winding, so you'll need to stay alert.

Contacts & Resources

BANKS & EXCHANGE SERVICES

In Raglan, there are two ATMs, both on Bow Street; one is outside the 4-Square Store, and the other is outside the Westpac Bank. In Cambridge, all the major banks are represented along Victoria Street, and all have ATMs. At Waitomo there is no ATM available; the closest is in Otorohanga, 16 km (10 mi) away.

🖪 Banks Westpac Bank ✉ Bow St., Raglan ☎ 0800/400−600.

Westpac Bank ✉ *Maniapoto St., Otorahanga* ☎ *0800/400−600.*

EMERGENCIES

The hospital for the Waikato and Waitomo region is in Hamilton; Anglesea Accident and Urgent Medical Centre is open 24/7 and serves the region surrounding Hamilton. In Cambridge, four pharmacies take turns at late-night duty; the closest late-night pharmacy to Waitomo is 16 km (10 mi) away in Otorohanga.

🖪 Emergency Services Fire, police, and ambulance ☎ 111.

🖪 Hospitals & Medical Centers Anglesea Accident and Urgent Medical Clinic ✉ Anglesea St., Hamilton ☎ 07/858−0800. **Waikato Hospital** ✉ Pembroke St., Hamilton ☎ 07/839−8899.

🖪 Late-Night Pharmacies Trevor Walters Pharmacy ✉ 44 Maniapoto St., Otorohanga ☎ 07/873−7294.

MAIL & INTERNET

The two main places for Internet access in Raglan are at the Raglan Video & Laser Colour Copy store, which is open daily, and the Waikato District Council Library, which is open weekdays 9 to 5 and Saturday 9 AM to 1 PM.

For mail, head for the Raglan Post Shop, which is open weekdays 9 to 5. In Cambridge, the Cambridge Country Store (Mon.–Sat. 8:30–5, Sun. 9–5) has Internet access, as does the Cambridge Public Library. In Waitomo, the i-SITE Visitor Centre at the Museum of Caves provides Internet access and acts as a postal delivery center.

🖪 Internet Access Cambridge Country Store ✉ 92 Victoria St., Cambridge ☎ 07/827−8715. **Cambridge Public Library** ✉ Wilson St., Cambridge ☎ 07/827−5403. **Raglan Video & Laser Colour Copy** ✉ 9 Bow St., Raglan ☎ 07/825−0008. **Waikato District Council Library** ✉ 7 Bow St., Raglan ☎ 07/825−8929. **Waitomo i-SITE Visitor Centre** ✉ Waitomo Caves Rd., Waitomo Caves Village ☎ 07/878−7640.

🖪 Post Office Raglan Post Shop ✉ 37−39 Bow St., Raglan ☎ 07/825−8007.

TOURS

Newmans has a one-way bus tour from Auckland to the Waitomo Caves and on to Rotorua, or from Rotorua to the Waitomo Caves, ending in Auckland, including a brief stop at a historic battle site, a presentation on warriors, and admission to the Waitomo Caves. You'll be picked up at your Auckland accommodation and dropped at your Rotorua accommodation, or vice versa. The cost is $130 per person. You can also do a one-day round-trip from Auckland for $138.

🖪 Newmans ☎ 09/913-6200 ⊕ www.newmanscoach.co.nz.

VISITOR INFORMATION

Cambridge and Raglan both have visitor centers open weekdays from 9 to 5, and weekends from 10 to 4. The Waitomo Caves i-SITE Visitor Centre visitor bureau has slightly longer daily hours, opening at 8 AM year-round and extending until 8 PM in summer. Tourism Waikato (online only) is a helpful regional resource.

🔲 Tourist Information **Cambridge Information Centre** ✉ Queen and Victoria Sts. ☎ 07/823-3456. **Raglan Information Centre** ✉ 4 Wallis St. ☎ 07/825-0556. **Tourism Waikato** ⊕ www.waikatonz.co.nz. **Waitomo i-SITE Visitor Centre** ✉ Museum of Caves, Waitomo Caves Rd., Waitomo Caves Village ☎ 07/878-7640 ⊕ www. waitomocaves.co.nz.

NEW PLYMOUTH & TARANAKI

On a clear winter day, with a cover of snow, Mt. Taranaki (officially, Mt. Egmont) towers above its flat rural surroundings and seems to draw the sky right down to the sea. No less astonishing in other seasons, the solitary peak is similar in appearance to Japan's Mt. Fuji. It is the icon of the Taranaki region, and the province has shaped itself around the mountain. Northeast of Taranaki, the provincial seat of New Plymouth huddles between the monolith and a rugged coastline, and smaller towns dot the road that circles the mountain's base.

Taranaki is one of New Zealand's fastest-growing tourism destinations, and for many visitors, Mt. Taranaki and surrounding Egmont National Park are the major draw cards. You can climb the mountain (a steep and serious challenge in winter, requiring climbing expertise), hike around the lower slopes, enjoy short forest walks to streams and waterfalls, or even spend the night up here.

The Taranaki region is one of the most successful agricultural areas in the country, because of the layers of volcanic ash that have created superb free-draining topsoil and the mountainous coastal position that ensures abundant rainfall. What serves farmers serves gardeners as well. Some of the country's most magnificent gardens grow in the rich local soil, and the annual Rhododendron Festival, held late in the year, celebrates the area's horticultural excellence.

This festival and other events, such as the Arts Festival, WOMAD (World of Music, Art and Dance), international sporting competitions, and a regular calendar of top international performers who love appearing in the unique Bowl of Brooklands in Pukekura Park, add immensely to the area's attractions.

Taranaki has plenty of other ground-level delights. By the water's edge—along the so-called Surf Highway (Highway 45)—you can surf, swim, and fish. Several museums delve into Taranaki history, which is particularly rich on the subject of the Māori.

You could take in most of the area in a couple of days, but that will keep you on the run. Just getting from place to place around the mountain takes time. Most people use New Plymouth as a base, though Stratford also has comfortable accommodations, and there are B&Bs, motels, and campgrounds spread throughout the region.

The weather is constantly in flux—locals say that if you can't see Mt. Taranaki, it's raining, and if you can, it's going to rain. Day in and day

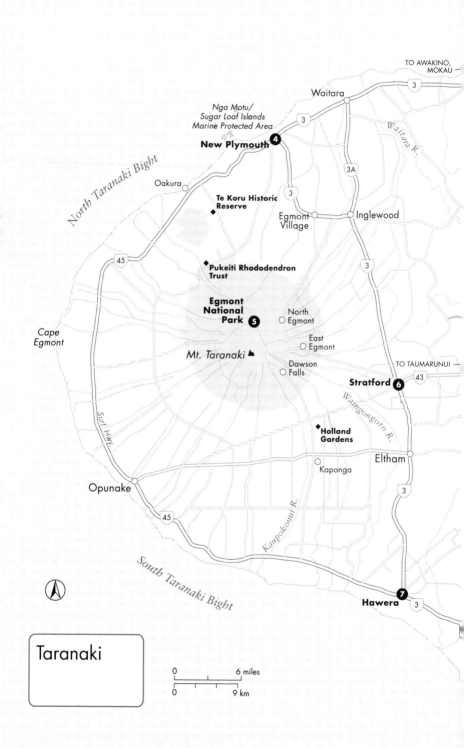

TO AWAKINO,
MOKAU

Waitara

3

Nga Motu/
Sugar Loaf Islands
Marine Protected Area

New Plymouth 4

3

3A

Oakura

Egmont
Village

Inglewood

North Taranaki Bight

Te Koru Historic
Reserve

45

Pukeiti Rhododendron
Trust

3

Cape
Egmont

**Egmont
National
Park** 5

North
Egmont

East
Egmont

Mt. Taranaki ▲

Dawson
Falls

TO TAUMARUNUI

Stratford 6

43

Waingongoro R.

Holland
Gardens

Surf Hwy.

Eltham

Kaponga

Opunake

3

45

Kaupokonui R.

South Taranaki Bight

Hawera 7

3

Taranaki

0   6 miles

0   9 km

out, this meteorological mix makes for stunning contrasts of sun and clouds on and around the mountain.

New Plymouth

❹ *375 km (235 mi) south of Auckland, 190 km (120 mi) southwest of Waitomo, 163 km (102 mi) northwest of Wanganui.*

New Plymouth is a center both for one of New Zealand's most productive dairy regions and the nation's gas and oil industries. This natural wealth means that even when New Zealand's economy is in hard times, the people of New Plymouth retain a sense of optimism. This optimistic outlook is reflected in its healthy arts scene, the abundance of cafés and restaurants, and a lifestyle that maximizes the great outdoors—from Egmont National Park, with Mt. Taranaki at its heart, to the extensive gardens and parklands, to the world-class surf beaches.

Before the arrival of Europeans in 1841, several *pā* (fortified villages) were in the vicinity. In the mid-1800s, European land disputes racked Taranaki. An uneasy formal peace was made between the government and local Māori tribes in 1881, and that was when New Plymouth began to form its current identity. Situated on the edge of the Tasman Sea, today's city is second-best to its surroundings, but its few surviving colonial buildings and extensive parklands merit a half day's exploration. The cafés and stores along the main drag, Devon Street (East and West), provide as cosmopolitan an experience as you'll find this far west.

The jewels of New Plymouth are most definitely **Pukekura Park and Brooklands Park.** Together the valley lawns, lakes, groves, and woodlands of these connected parks make up a tranquil, 121-acre heart of the city. From December through mid-February, **Pukekura Park** comes to life at night with the stunning summer Festival of Lights. There's free entertainment most evenings, and the park takes on a magical feel as different lighting effects transform the gardens and giant trees. Pukekura has water running throughout; hire a rowboat (from near the lakeside teahouse) and explore the small islands and nooks and crannies of the main lake. The park also has a fernery—caverns carved out of the hillside that connect through fern-cloaked tunnels—and botanical display houses, whose flowering-plant collections are some of the most extensive in the country.

Brookland Park, on Brooklands Road, was once a great estate, laid out in 1843 around the house of Captain Henry King, New Plymouth's first magistrate. Today, Brooklands is best known for its amazing variety of trees, mostly planted in the second half of the 19th century. There are giant copper beeches, pines, walnuts, and oaks, and the Monterey pine, magnolia *soulangeana,* ginkgo, and native *karaka* and *kohekohe* are all the largest of their kind in New Zealand. Take a walk along the outskirts of the park on tracks leading through native, subtropical bush. This area has been relatively untouched for the last few thousand years, and 1,500-year-old trees are not uncommon. A *puriri* tree near the Somerset Street entrance—one of 20 in the park—is believed to be more than 2,000 years old.

For a reminder of colonial days, visit Brooklands' former hospital, the **Gables,** built in 1847, which now serves as an art gallery and medical museum. The adjacent zoo is an old-fashioned example of how to keep birds and animals, but it is still a favorite of children. Brooklands has a rhododendron dell and the Brookland Bowl, a stadium used for a variety of shows throughout the year, regarded as a favorite performance venue by many international artists. ✉ *Park entrances on Brooklands Park Dr. and Liardet, Somerset, and Rogan Sts.* ☎ *06/759–6060* ☞ *Free* ☉ *Daily dawn–dusk; teahouse Wed.–Mon. dawn–dusk; display houses daily 8:30–4.*

To get a feel for the city, take a stroll or rent a bike and ride along the **New Plymouth Coastal Walkway.** This path runs for 7 km (4 mi) from Port Taranaki to Lake Rotomanu and leads past four of the city's beaches, three rivers, four playgrounds, a mini-golf course, the Aquatic Centre, a golf course, a skating park, and numerous food vendors. You also pass right under the *Wind Wand,* a sculpture almost as iconic to New Plymouth residents as the *Statue of Liberty* is to New Yorkers. Created by the late New Zealand artist Len Lye, the red fiberglass tube stands 45 meters (147 feet) high and, like a conductor's baton, dances in the wind as Lye's tribute to what he called "tangible motion."

Fodor'sChoice
★

Across the road from the *Wind Wand* is **Puke Ariki,** the region's heritage, research, and information center. Though not as large as Wellington's Museum of New Zealand, Te Papa Tongarewa, its displays tell compelling stories of the region, from the Land Wars, to the discovery of natural oil and gas in 1959, to today's surfing culture. Check out the interactive science exhibits for children in the basement. ✉ *Puke Ariki Landing, St. Aubyn St.* ☎ *06/758–4544* ⊕ *www.pukeariki.com* ☞ *Free* ☉ *Mon., Tues., Thurs., and Fri. 9–6, Wed. 9–9, weekends 9–5.*

If contemporary art is your thing, don't miss the **Govett-Brewster Art Gallery,** one of New Zealand's leading modern art museums. The gallery has a strong collection of New Zealand conceptual art produced in the 1970s, abstract art from the '70s and '80s, and contemporary sculpture. It is also the home of the internationally acclaimed Len Lye collection and has regular visiting exhibitions from abroad. ✉ *42 Queen St., at King St.* ☎ *06 759 6060* ⊕ *www.govettbrewster.com* ☞ *Free* ☉ *Daily 10:30–5; café daily 8–4.*

There are approximately 24 **Gardens of National Significance** in New Zealand, and seven of them are in Taranaki. The rainfall and fertile volcanic-ash soils provide excellent growing conditions, in particular for rhododendrons and azaleas, which are celebrated each year during the Taranaki Rhododendron Festival. During the festival, these splendid gardens are open for the public to enjoy their colorful profusions. Some are open throughout the year, such as Pukerua Park, Pukeiti, and **Hollard Gardens** (⇨ Stratford, *below*). Others are open by appointment outside festival time. Most of these gardens are the labors of love of their private owners, whereas the Taranaki Regional Council supports the development of publicly owned gardens. A brochure listing these gardens is available from i-SITE visitor centers in New Plymouth and Stratford. Or contact the **Taranaki Regional Council** (☎06/765–7127 🖷06/765–5097).

CLOSE UP

Something to Chew On

A POETIC GOURMET once called New Zealand "the little green garden at the bottom of the world." It's an apt description, as all kinds of plate-bound treats thrive in the country's temperate climate.

New Zealand first earned international food fame for its butter and its lamb, but today other local staples such as taro, a root vegetable that is a mainstay of Pacific Islanders' diets, are finding their way to restaurant menus. A popular and exclusively local meat is *cervena* (farmed venison), which has a less gamey taste than its wild counterpart.

Locally reared ostrich and emu, whose flavor is mildly gamey, are also turning up in New Zealand dining rooms. They are relatively expensive compared with other meats, but are virtually fat-free; they are eaten as steaks, casseroles, burgers, and even sausages. Generally speaking, the most popular meats found on a New Zealand restaurant table are locally farmed lamb, chicken, and beef.

Several unique species of shellfish are caught around the coast. *Pipi* and *tuatua* are both similar to clams. Greenshell, the succulent and slightly sweet New Zealand farmed mussel, is larger than its North American counterpart. Oysters are available in several species—look for bivalves from Bluff and Nelson bays. Whitebait, the juvenile of several fish species, are eaten whole, usually mixed into an omelet-like fritter. Another local delicacy from the sea is the roe of the *kina*, or sea egg; it's similar to sea urchin, and you might find it for sale in innovative restaurants.

If you're looking for a good-natured argument with a Kiwi, suggest that it was the Australians who invented that cream-topped, fruit-and-meringue concoction called the Pavlova. Though it was certainly named for Russian ballerina Anna Pavlova, the question of where it originated is a source of ongoing trans-Tasman Sea rivalry.

There's not a lot of Māori influence on mainstream New Zealand cuisine. The best-known Māori meal is a *hāngi*, a traditional method that involves cooking food over heated stones buried in the earth. It's a method that doesn't translate easily to a European-style kitchen; however, there are opportunities to try the real thing in Māori tourism ventures throughout the country, in particular in Rotorua. One vegetable that is a common sight on most New Zealanders' tables is the *kūmara*, or sweet potato. It's eaten boiled, baked, mashed, or whipped into elaborate concoctions. Look for kūmara *rösti*, a sweet-potato fritter, in top urban restaurants.

At the bottom of the South Island and on Stewart Island you might be offered muttonbird, also known as *titi*, eaten by local Māori for centuries and today regarded as a delicacy. It's a young seabird, cured for eating, and is extremely fatty. Kiwi cynics, who quip that the muttonbird tastes like an extremely salty boot sole, remark that the bird is better boiled for several hours with a stone, after which it is a good idea to throw away the bird and suck the stone. As you'll find, the local sense of humor is an essential ingredient in virtually every meal.

5

★ The world-renowned **Pukeiti Rhododendron Trust** spreads over 900 acres of lush native rain forest, surrounded by rich Taranaki farmland. The Pukeiti (poo-ke-*ee*-tee) collection of 2,500 varieties of rhododendrons is the largest in New Zealand. Many of the varieties were first grown here, such as the giant winter-blooming *R. protistum var. giganteum* Pukeiti, collected from seed in 1953 and now standing 15 feet tall—or the beautiful Lemon Lodge and Spring Honey hybrids that bloom in spring. Kyawi, a large red "rhodie," is the very last to bloom, in April (autumn). Rhododendrons aside, there are many other rare and special plants to enjoy at Pukeiti. All winter long the Himalayan daphnes fragrance the pathways. Spring- to summer-growing candelabra primroses can reach up to 4 feet, and for a month around Christmas, spectacular 8-foot Himalayan *cardiocrinum* lilies bear heavenly scented 12-inch white trumpet flowers. This is a wonderful bird habitat, so keep your eyes and ears open for them, too. Pukeiti is 20 km (12½ mi) southwest of New Plymouth's center. ✉ *2290 Carrington Rd.* ☎ *06/752–4141* ⊕ *www. pukeiti.org.nz* ✉ *$8* ☉ *Oct.–Mar., daily 9–5; Apr.–Sept., daily 10–3.*

To get some feeling of the turbulent history in Taranaki, take a drive through the countryside inland from Oakura to **Te Koru Historic Reserve.** A Department of Conservation track leads 500 meters (about ¼ mi) to the site of the pā (fortified village), a former stronghold of the Nga Mahanga a Tairi *hapū* (subtribe). Regenerating native forest has covered part of the site, but still visible is the main defensive ditch and stonewalled terraces that drop a considerable way from the highest part of the pā to the Oakura River. There are no facilities at the reserve, just a pleasant picnic area. Take Highway 45 southwest out of New Plymouth to the beach suburb of Oakura, 17 km (10 mi) away. Just past Oakura turn left onto Wairau Road and follow the signs to the parking lot, which is 3.7 km (2½ mi) from the turnoff. ☎ *06/759–0350 Department of Conservation* ✉ *Free* ☉ *Daily dawn–dusk.*

OFF THE BEATEN PATH

TARANAKI–WAITOMO – Mt. Taranaki is an ever-receding presence in your rearview mirror as you head northeast up the Taranaki coast from New Plymouth on Highway 3. The highway provides the most direct route to Waitomo Caves and Hamilton, turning inland at Awakino, 90 km (56 mi) from New Plymouth. The Awakino Gorge, between Mahoenui and the coast, is particularly appealing. Forest-filled scenic reserves are interspersed with stark, limestone outcrops and verdant farmland, where sheep have worn trails that seem to hang on the sides of precipitous green hills. At the mouth of the Awakino River, little fishing shacks dot the river's edge. **Awakino** is worth a stop, either at the family-oriented country hotel or for a rest at the river mouth. Turn off the main road by the hotel and you'll see a lovely sheltered picnic spot beneath the summer flowering *pohutukawa* trees. A little farther along is **Mokau,** with a couple of little cafés where delicious whitebait fritters might be on the menu September to November, the season for catching these little fish that are a New Zealand delicacy.

From Awakino, you could be in Waitomo within the hour if you stick to the main highway, but a far more enjoyable route is to follow the minor road north, at the turnoff just beyond Awakino. This runs for 58 km (36 mi) to Marokopa (⇨ Waitomo Caves *in* the Waikato and Wait-omo, *above*). It's a gravel road for the most part, but a reasonable trip, provided you take care. The drive is through attractive sheep country, passing through the Manganui Gorge, and with a possible 4-km (2½-mi) detour down the Waikawau Road to the stunningly isolated Waikawau Beach. The sweep of black sand here, backed by high cliffs, is reached through a hand-dug drover's tunnel. Total driving time from Awakino to Marokopa, including a picnic stop, is about three hours, plus another hour from Marokopa to Waitomo.

Where to Stay & Eat

$$$$ ✕ **André L'Escargot Restaurant and Bar.** New Plymouth's oldest commercial building houses what many consider the town's finest restaurant. The menu updates classic southern French cuisine, for example, French burgundy snails stuffed in button mushrooms with herb butter or blue-cheese sauce; or half-cured beef Provencale. The ambience is one of casual elegance, the white linen tableware contrasting pleasingly with dark-wood decor. The intimate dining room seats just 15, and the mezzanine area seats 20. Top French, New Zealand, and Australian wines are available. ⊠ *37–43 Brougham St.* ☎ *06/758–4812* ⊟ *AE, DC, MC, V* ☉ *Lunch by arrangement only. Closed Sun.*

$$$ ✕ **Macfarlane's Caffe.** This lively place energizes the café scene in Inglewood, a town midway between New Plymouth and Stratford. It is
Fodor's Choice   the original outlet of the MacFarlanes Group, which operates several
★   small espresso bars and the Ozone coffee roastery in New Plymouth. All-day breakfasts from 9 AM include the hearty Farmer's Breakfast, with bacon, eggs, smoked-cheese kransky sausage, grilled tomatoes, and homemade hash browns. Lunches include fresh salads, seafood linguine, fettuccine, falafel pita pockets, and the challengingly large Taranaki Burger. The evening dinner menu is international with a New Zealand tweak, such as a pork saltimbocca (tenderloin steaks with sage leaf and parma ham, panfried and served with mozzarella-stuffed risotto balls). ⊠ *Kelly and Matai Sts., Inglewood, 20 km (12½ mi) east of New Plymouth* ☎ *06/756–6665* ⊟ *AE, DC, MC, V* ☉ *No dinner Sun.–Wed. (closes at 5* PM).

$–$$ ✕ **Ultra Lounge.** This hip, funky, and laid-back bar has a retro feel, with orange booths, Formica tables, and '60s-modern-style couches. It's popular with locals throughout the day for its good coffee, hearty brunches, and light meals such as lamb shanks or roast pumpkin with feta cheese. At night, stop in for dinner, cocktails, or dessert and coffee; most weekends a DJ plays downbeat grooves. ⊠ *Devon St. E* ☎ *06/758–8444* ⊟ *AE, DC, MC, V.*

¢–$ ✕ **Empire.** A sedate place to stop and recharge, this café serves good espressos but is best known for its huge range of loose-leaf teas, a heady selection that includes jasmine, rose, sunflowers, and calendula flowers, and mixes such as "Cooletta," a refreshing and fruity blend of rosehip, hibiscus, papaya, blackberry leaves, and mango. Food is all made on the premises and includes a full breakfast menu, bagels served all day, filled rolls, crepes, and salads, and the Empire's signature two-in-a-bowl soup, its flavors changing according to the weather. Vegetarian and

5

gluten-free options are available. ✉ *112 Devon St. W* ☎ *06/758–1148* 🍽 *AE, MC, V* ⊘ *Closed Sun. No dinner.*

$$$
Fodor'sChoice
★
✕🏠 **Nice Hotel & Bistro.** Local entrepreneur and now attentive host Terry Parkes transformed this 19th-century hospital into an opulent city-center retreat. Modern art, including works by leading Taranaki artists such as Don Driver, Tom Kriesler, and Michael Smither, lines the walls, and the chic guest rooms and opulent suites come complete with double whirlpool baths or massage showers. The bistro, Table *($$–$$$$),* has a feel of contemporary elegance and hums with formally and smartly casual–attired diners. It is regarded as one of the city's best, and has been the recipient of many local restaurant awards. The menu changes seasonally to emphasize fresh, local fare but is likely to feature delicious presentations of salmon, duck, eye fillet of beef, and perhaps ostrich or rabbit. Individual tastes are catered to: vegetarian, gluten-free, dairy free, and so on; current menus are on the hotel's Web site. The wine list features New Zealand's best varieties. But before you drink, Terry might let you take a hotel bike for a spin to drink in the city's shoreline. ✉ *71 Brougham St.* ☎ *06/758–6423* 🖷 *06/758–6433* ⊕ *www.nicehotel.co. nz* 🛏 *7 rooms, 2 suites* ⚖ *Restaurant, minibars, in-room broadband, airport shuttle* 🍽 *AE, DC, MC, V.*

$$
✕🏠 **The Waterfront.** Stylish and modern, this aptly named hotel is New Plymouth's only waterfront lodging. It's handily situated right next to the Puke Ariki Museum and the Information Centre. Each room has sea or city views. Configurations range from studios with showers (no tubs), to elite studios with individual whirlpoolbaths, to the Penthouse Suite with separate bedroom, double whirlpool bath, shower, full laundry and kitchen facilities, and other options in between. All rooms have super-king or -queen beds. Salt, the restaurant and bar, feels urbane, almost minimalist, all the better to appreciate the vista across the walkway and the beach. Have a traditional Kiwi breakfast—perhaps baked beans on toast with crispy bacon—as you read the morning paper. For dinner, seafood features high on the menu; a favorite is the pan-seared scallops with a sweet chili-ginger sauce. ✉ *1 Egmont St.* ☎ *06/769–5301* 🖷 *06/769– 5302* ⊕ *www.waterfront.co.nz* 🛏 *42 rooms, 3 suites* ⚖ *Refrigerators, in-room broadband, Wi-Fi; no a/c in some rooms* 🍽 *AE, DC, MC, V.*

$$–$$$
Fodor'sChoice
★
🏠 **Ahu Ahu Beach Villas.** A magical place to stay, on coastal farmland just above the beach, this property with five rustic villas (each sleeps four) has magnificent sea views: you can catch the moon rise over the ocean horizon. The villas are made of recycled materials, including 100-year-old French clay tiles and hardwood wharf piles; the design is inspired by the likes of Hunderwasser and Gaudí. The latest addition, completed in 2006, is a spectacular "underground" villa that's built in against the bank and has a grassed roof and dramatic view. Inside there are two queen-size double beds and enough space to host a small party. For those with laptops, a dial-up Internet connection is shared between villas. The owners can provide breakfast supplies, or you can drive five minutes to Oakura Village (there's also the popular Wunder Café in town), which has a renowned surf beach. The villas are about a 15-minute drive south of New Plymouth. ✉ *321 Ahu Ahu Rd., Surf Hwy. 45, Oakura* ☎ *06/752–7370* ⊕ *www.ahu.co.nz* 🛏 *5 villas* ⚖ *Kitchens, laundry facilities; no a/c* 🍽 *MC, V.*

$–$$ 🏨 **Devon Hotel.** This hotel is easy to find, just a short drive (or 20-minute walk) north of the city center. The standard rooms have bathrooms with showers (no tubs); they are on the small side, but look out over a pretty internal courtyard. The larger, superior rooms are better equipped (with refrigerators, minibars, and whirlpool baths) and have either sea or mountain views, though those at the front face onto a busy main road. Marbles, the hotel's Roman-themed restaurant, serves a buffet breakfast and a la carte dinner. It is popular for local family functions, such as birthdays and anniversaries. There is also a superb heated pool, a hot tub, and a garden, and the hotel is undergoing gradual refurbishment. ✉ *390 Devon St. E* ☎ *06/759–9099* 🖷 *06/758–2229* ⊕ *www.devonhotel.co. nz* 🛏 *110 rooms* ⚿ *Restaurant, some minibars, some refrigerators, in-room data ports, pool, bar, Internet room; no a/c, no smoking* ☰ *AE, DC, MC, V.*

¢ 🏨 **Shoestring Backpackers.** Within walking distance of New Plymouth's main shops and cafés, this lovely old home has spacious rooms and a welcoming staff. Two dorms each sleep four; rooms come with one double bed, two single beds, or one single bed. All rooms share bathrooms, but there are plenty to go around. There's an outdoor veranda to relax on, a communal kitchen, and, in winter, a cozy fire in the lounge. ✉ *48 Lemon St.* ☎🖷 *06/758–0404* ⊕ *www.shoestring.co.nz* 🛏 *13 rooms, 2 dorms (8 beds) with shared bath* ⚿ *Sauna, laundry facilities, Internet room; no a/c, no room phones, no room TVs* ☰ *AE, MC, V.*

Nightlife

The younger (twentysomething), louder set will be happiest at **55** (✉ 55a Egmont St. ☎ 06/759–0997), open until 5 AM Thursday, Friday, and Saturday.

If you fancy good live music in the atmosphere of a full-on Celtic bar, **Peggy Gordon's Celtic Bar** (✉ Egmont and Devon Sts. ☎ 06/758–8561) is the place to go. Wednesday and Thursday are quiz nights; Thursday through Saturday brings live music in a range of genres. Lunch and dinner are served every day: signature dishes are beef-and-Guinness stew with dumplings, Irish seasoned beef, and Flanaghan's fish-and-chips; gourmet pizzas are good, too. Host Bertie Burleigh serves six international beers and local ales on tap. It's open seven days a week.

If a classy cocktail is more your thing, the modern, minimalist **Powder Room** (✉ 108 Devon St. ☎ 07/759–2089) can oblige. It's open Tuesday–Saturday 4 PM–3 AM.

Shopping

Devon Street, which runs from Fitzroy in the east to Blagdon in the west, is New Plymouth's main shopping street.

For beautiful locally made arts and crafts with an edge, visit **Kina** (✉ 101 Devon St. W ☎ 06/759–1201), which exhibits the works of Taranaki artists and stocks contemporary design pieces, from jewelry to sculpture. **Trade Aid** (✉ 82 Devon St. E ☎ 06/758–4228) sells an eclectic mix of gift items from Asia, Africa, South America, and the Pacific.

Boutique shop **Meyer & Prichard** (✉ 38 Devon St. W ☎ 06/769–5459) has the best selection of designer clothing in town, carrying leading New

5

Nga Motu/Sugar Loaf Islands Marine Protected Area

ABOUT 17,000 SEABIRDS nest in the Nga Motu/Sugar Loaf Islands Marine Protected Area. Shearwaters, petrels, terns, penguins, shags, and herons, some of them threatened species (the reef heron is one), nest and feed on and around these little islands. The islands are also a breeding colony and hauling grounds for New Zealand fur seals; during winter more than 400 seals congregate here. Dolphins and orca and pilot whales frequent the waters around the islands, and humpback whales migrate past in August and September.

Beneath the water's surface, caves, crevices, boulder fields, and sand flats, together with the merging of warm and cool sea currents, support a wealth of marine life. More than 80 species of fish have been recorded here, along with jewel and striped anemones, sponges, and rock lobsters.

The diving is fabulous; visibility is best in summer and autumn (up to 20 meters [65 feet]). Contact **New Plymouth Underwater** (✉ 16 Hobson St. ☎ 06/758-3348 ⊕ www. newplymouthunderwater.co.nz).

On land, more than 80 different native plant species survive on the islands. Cook's scurvy grass, almost extinct on the mainland, grows on two of the islands. The palatable species is rich in vitamin C and was sought by early sailors to treat scurvy.

The best way to appreciate these islands is by boat. Landing is restricted, but kayaking and chartered launch trips leave regularly from New Plymouth. Nga Motu/Sugar Loaf Islands are managed by the **Department of Conservation** (✉ 220 Devon St. W, New Plymouth ☎ 06/ 759-0350).

Zealand labels such as Karen Walker, World, and Carlson. If you're after some serious outdoor gear, check out **Taranaki Hardcore Surf Shop** (✉ 454 Devon St. E ☎ 06/758-1757), which stocks surf and snow wear and gear, plus the stylish Taranaki clothing label.

Sports & the Outdoors

BEACHES Some of the coastal waters can be quite wild, so it's wise to swim at patrolled beaches. The beaches all have black sand and rocky outcrops, which make for interesting rock-pool exploring. In summer, *pohutakawa* trees provide shade in some spots; otherwise be sure to take plenty of sunblock. **Fitzroy Beach** has lifeguards in summer and is easily accessible from New Plymouth, just 1½ km (¾ mi) from the city center. The adjoining **East End Beach** also has lifeguards. **Ngamotu Beach,** along Ocean View Parade, is calm and suitable for young children.

BICYCLING Line up a rental bike with **Cycle Inn** (✉ 133 Devon St. ☎ 06/758-7418) to ride the New Plymouth Coastal Walkway. They've got touring bikes with helmets at $10 for a half day, $15 for a full day.

BOATING & A launch with **Happy Chaddy's Charters** (✉ Ocean View Parade ☎ 06/
KAYAKING 758-9133 ⊕ www.windwand.co.nz/chaddiescharters) starts with the guide

announcing, "Hold on to your knickers, because we're about to take off." Then the old English lifeboat rocks back and forth in its shed (with you on board), slides down its rails, and hits the sea with a spray of water. The $25 trip lasts an hour, during which you'll see seals and get a close-up view of the Nga Motu/Sugar Loaf Islands just offshore from New Plymouth. You can also charter a boat for a fishing trip ($60 per person, minimum six people); these start at 7 AM to avoid choppy water.

Canoe & Kayak Taranaki (⌧ 631 Devon Rd., Waikwakiho ☎ 06/769–5506 ⊕ www.canoeandkayak.co.nz) has a range of guided trips, lasting from a couple of hours to a couple of days. One popular kayak tour goes to the Sugar Loaf Islands Marine Park ($45 per person, three hours).

SURFING Not for nothing is the coastal road between New Plymouth and Hawera known as the **Surf Highway.** Virtually any beach en route has consistently good waves. Fitzroy and East End (⇨ Beaches, *above*) are both popular with surfers, as are **Back Beach** and **Bell Block Beach.** The favored surf beach by those in the know is at **Oakura,** a village 17 km (10 mi) southwest of New Plymouth teeming with cafés and crafts shops as well as good surf.

Beach Street Surf Shop (⌧ 30 Beach Rd. ☎ 06/758–0400 ⊕ www. lostinthe60s.com) is run by local legend Wayne Arthur, who'll give you the lowdown on the hot surf spots in Taranaki. The shop rents equipment and organizes lessons for beginners and advanced surfers. **Taranaki Tours** (☎ 06/757–9888 or 0800/886–877 ⊕ www.taranakitours.com) takes experienced surfers on half-day trips to the best breaks of the day.

At Oakura Beach, accredited surf coach Heather Dent runs **Surf School Taranaki** (☎ 06/752–8283). To try riding a wave with a professional surfer on a tandem surfboard ($80), contact **Hang 20—Tandem Surf Taranaki** (⌧ 27 Mace St., Oakura ☎ 06/752–7734).

Egmont National Park

❺ *North Egmont Visitor Centre is 26 km (16 mi) south of New Plymouth; Dawson Falls Visitor Centre is 68 km (42 mi) southwest of New Plymouth.*

Fodor'sChoice **Mt. Taranaki** dominates the landscape and Egmont National Park. In fact, ★ it's the park's raison d'etre. The mountain rises 8,309 feet above sea level; it's difficult not to be drawn toward it. The lower reaches are cloaked in dense and mossy rain forests; above the tree line, lower-growing tussocks and subalpine shrubs cling to spectacularly steep slopes. The mountain's European name is Egmont; James Cook named it in 1770 after the Earl of Egmont, who supported his exploration. Both names are used today.

Mt. Taranaki is notorious for its ever-changing weather conditions, and the peak is often surrounded by a twist of cloud. It may be sunny on the mountain one minute, but the next, rain sweeps in off the West Coast (the mountain is in one of the wettest areas in New Zealand). Be sure to take appropriate gear if you are visiting the national park. On a clear day, you can see the three mountains of Tongariro National Park in the central North Island—and sometimes even as far as the South Island.

The mountain is surrounded and protected by Egmont National Park. The three main roads to the mountain turn off State Highway 3 and are all well signposted. The first mountain turnoff, as you drive south from New Plymouth, is Egmont Road and leads to the start of many walking trails and the **North Egmont Visitor Centre** (☒ Egmont Rd. ☎ 06/756–0990). It's worth dropping in to peruse the excellent displays and to learn something about the mountain's history and the natural features of the park. There's also a café at the visitor center. The second road up the mountain (Pembroke Road) takes you to the Mountain House and, a little farther on, to **Stratford Plateau,** from which there are some stunning views. The third mountain turnoff (Manaia Road) leads to the southernmost visitor center, the **Dawson Falls Visitor Centre** (☒ Manaia Rd. ☎ 06/756–0990). For information on the hiking trails around and up the mountain, *see* Sports & the Outdoors, *below.*

Where to Stay & Eat

$$$ ✕☐ **Dawson Falls Lodge.** This lodge's position on the southern slopes of Mt. Taranaki gives charming views of the coastline and native bush. It's an interesting place, with down-to-earth, New Zealand country hospitality in an old Swiss-style inn where you can unwind in front of a roaring fire or in the sauna or alpine plunge pool. The rooms, each with unique decoration, have wood paneling and carved and painted headboards. The Chalet bar and restaurant is an intimate space for a drink or to enjoy the daily three-course prix-fixe feast ($$$$) of traditional New Zealand country fare: soups, corned silverside, fish, or pork chops, with a host of accompanying vegetables, followed by dessert. Saturday nights are set aside for roast beef and Yorkshire pudding. ☒ *Manaia Rd. off Opunake Rd., Dawson Falls* ☎☐ *06/765–5457* ⊕ *www.dawson-falls.co.nz* ⤵ *12 rooms* ⟁ *Restaurant, gym, sauna, bar, lounge, laundry facilities; no a/c* ⊟ *AE, DC, MC, V* ⍩⊙⧾ *BP, MAP.*

$$ ✕☐ **Mountain House Motor Lodge.** Berta Anderson runs this comfortable hotel, motel, and locally renowned restaurant in one of the best locations in the area, high on Mt. Taranaki. Tracks from the lodge traverse the lower reaches of the mountain, through a mix of subalpine shrublands and dense forest, and the ski slopes are a 10-minute drive away. Six rooms stand apart from the main building and are equipped with kitchenettes. Berta brings her Swiss background to the restaurant ($$$). Although the menu has a good selection of vegetarian options, the signature dishes are roast lamb shank with homemade Swiss spaetzle, tarragon-scented rabbit, and other hearty entrées that make it difficult to finish the Black Forest cake. ☒ *Pembroke Rd., E. Egmont, Stratford* ☎☐ *06/765–6100* ⊕ *www.mountainhouse.co.nz* ⤵ *10 rooms* ⟁ *Restaurant, sauna, bar, laundry facilities; no a/c* ⊟ *AE, DC, MC, V.*

$$–$$$ ☐ **Anderson's Alpine Lodge.** A few minutes' drive down the road from the Mountain House is Berta Anderson's other venture, a modern (built in 1995) Swiss alpine-style B&B. The trio of rooms includes a deluxe Top Room, with glorious mountain views from a separate lounge area. The lodge has a log staircase, wood-burning fire, and wooden deck; the walls are decorated with paintings of Taranaki, talented works by Berta's late husband, Keith Anderson. ☒ *922 Pembroke Rd., Stratford*

☎ *06/765–6620* 🖷 *06/765–6100* ⊕ *www.mountainhouse.co.nz* ⟋ *3 rooms* △ *No a/c, no kids, no smoking* ▭ *AE, DC, MC, V* |◯| *CP.*

Sports & the Outdoors

MOUNTAIN- **EERING**
Mt. Taranaki is a potentially perilous mountain to climb; unpredictable weather and ease of access to the upper slopes, with their sheer bluffs and winter ice, are an extremely dangerous combination. For more adventurous pursuits on the mountain, or for midwinter summit climbs, use a local guide who's familiar with the terrain and conditions.

To the local Māori people, the mountain is sacred, regarded as an ancestor. They ask that climbers respect the spirituality and not clamber over the summit rocks.

Ross Eden, who has been mountaineering since the 1980s, is the head guide for **Top Guides** (☎ 0800/448–433 ⊕ www.topguides.co.nz). His organization guides adventurers in summit climbs, and instructs in everything from abseiling to avalanche awareness and rock climbing. Daily rates start at $250 for one person with one guide (a summit climb can be made in a day trip). Ian MacAlpine of **MacAlpine Guides** (☎ 06/ 751–3542 or 0274/417–042 ⊕ www.macalpineguides.com) has made more than 1,500 ascents of Mt. Taranaki and climbed in Nepal, India, and Antarctica. He guides individual and group climbs, and leads other outdoor pursuits ranging from bushwalking to abseiling to bridge swinging. Summit-climb daily rates are $250.

SKIING
There is one small club-owned and -operated ski run on Mt. Taranaki; **Manganui.** The club operates for up to 30 days each winter (June–October), and nonmembers can buy tow passes for a day. There are limited facilities, and the terrain is best suited for intermediate and advanced skiers. Rent equipment at the **Mountain House Motor Lodge** (☎ 06/ 765–6100), 3 km (2 mi) below the ski slope.

WALKING & HIKING
Egmont National Park is one of the most accessible parks in New Zealand, with more than 300 km (180 mi) of walking trails that take you around the mountain and across to the adjoining Pouakai Range, through dense forests, across the higher subalpine slopes, past waterfalls, across mountain streams, and beneath massive lava bluffs. There are signposted short walks, suitable for all ages and degrees of fitness, from each of the three main park access roads. For a taste of the scenery, the best of these are from the Dawson Falls Visitor Centre, where there are five popular options—each taking 1 to 2½ hours—including the easy walk to the 50-foot-high **Dawson Falls** themselves. In late summer, when there is usually no snow on the mountain, **summit ascents** are a popular challenge. The most straightforward route is from the North Egmont Visitor Centre and takes anywhere from 7 to 10 hours round-trip. You must be properly equipped, keeping in mind that the weather conditions can change extremely quickly, and let the visitor center know in advance of your intentions.

For a multiday hiking trip, consider the **Pouakai Circuit,** which starts from the North Egmont Visitor Centre, climbs above the forest line, and crosses a huge wetland to the Pouakai Range, then returns through the lower, forested slopes of the mountain. The circuit is well signposted, and there are accommodation huts at one-day intervals along the way, the cost for which is usually $10 for adults per night. There are also budget bunkhouses ($20 per person per night) at Dawson Falls and North Egmont. Advance bookings for all hiking accommodation are essential; contact the park visitor centers.

Stratford

❻ *41 km (27 mi) southeast of New Plymouth.*

Stratford is the main town on the eastern side of Mt. Taranaki, and a service town for surrounding farms. Its streets are named after characters from Shakespeare's works, and it has the only glockenspiel in New Zealand, which chimes three times a day. Because the town sits at the junction of Highways 3 and 43, you're more than likely to pass through at some stage during any exploration of Taranaki. In the valley to the east are some of the country's most interesting private gardens.

FodorsChoice   Surrounded by dairy farms, the **Hollard Gardens** were created by dairy
★   farmer Bernard Hollard, who, in 1927, fenced a 14-acre patch of native bush on his farm and started establishing what is now a Garden of National Significance. There are two distinctive sections, one an old woodland garden of mature native and exotic trees, with closely underplanted rhododendrons, azaleas, camellias, and perennials, the other a more recent creation. Broad lawns, paths with mixed borders, and vistas of Mt. Taranaki are features of the new garden, established in 1982. Bernard Hollard gave the garden to the Queen Elizabeth II National Trust in 1982, and in 2002 ownership was transferred to the Taranaki Regional Council, which manages a group of Taranaki's Gardens of National Significance. The gardens are particularly colorful during the rhododendron flowering season from September to late November. Facilities include a shelter with garden information, and toilets. ⊠ *Upper Manaia Rd., off Opunake Rd., Kaponga, 8 km (5 mi) south of Dawson Falls* ☎ *06/ 765–7127 (Taranaki Regional Council)* ☜ *Free* ☉ *Daily 9–5.*

▌ OFF THE
BEATEN
PATH

STRATFORD–TAUMARUNUI – Known as the Forgotten World Highway, Highway 43, heading northeast from Stratford, takes travelers on an intriguing, history-rich tour of Māori and colonial heritage as it winds through rolling farmland and pristine subtropical rain forests to Taumarunui (the northern access point for the Whanganui River region). Highlights on the way include Mt. Damper Falls, the spectacular view from Tahora Saddle, the dramatic Tangarakau Gorge, two road tunnels, and riverboat-landing sites. A must-stop for its fine food and warm, country hospitality is the **Whangamomona Hotel** (⊠ 6018 Ohura Rd. ☎☎ 06/ 762–5823), awarded New Zealand's Country Hotel of the Year in 2005. The 145-km (90-mi) highway is sealed for all but 11 km (7 mi). Allow three hours, at least, and don't rush. Fill up with gas before you leave Stratford. For information contact the **Stratford i-SITE Visitor Centre** (☎ 06/765–6708 or 0800/765–6708 ⊕ www.stratfordnz.co.nz).

Where to Stay

$$ ▦ **Te Popo.** Tucked away on a back road northeast of Stratford, this peaceful homestead is magnificently set in one of Taranaki's Gardens of National Significance. *Tūī* (a native bird with a unique, melodic song), wood

pigeons, bellbirds, and fantails visit the gardens year-round, and glow-worms shine at dusk. The spacious guest rooms have wood-burning fire-places and private garden views. Breakfast is served in a sunny conservatory; dinner can be arranged separately. There is also a kitchen for guest use adjacent to the conservatory. Te Popo is a 15-minute drive from Stratford on good country roads. You can visit the gardens separately by appointment ($8), but it's well worth staying the night. ⌧ *636 Stanley Rd., Stratford ⌂ R.D. 24, Stratford ☎☎ 06/762–8775 ⊕ www. tepopo.co.nz ⌐ 3 rooms, 1 apartment ⌂ In-room data ports; no a/c ⊟ AE, DC, MC, V ⎮⚬⎮ BP.*

Shopping

Opossums, an Australian marsupial, were introduced to New Zealand to generate a fur trade but have had a devastating effect on the native forest and birds. Thus they are regarded as an environmental pest. Nevertheless their fur is known for its softness and warmth. **Envirofur** (⌧ 1103 Opunake Rd., Mahoe ☎ 06/764–6133 ⊕ www.envirofur.co. nz), a small but thriving business near Stratford, is turning this local environmental pest into excellent by-products, producing high-quality opossum fur and leather products such as hats, rugs, coats, and scarves.

Hawera

❼ *29 km (18 mi) south of Stratford.*

This quiet country town, a hub for the farming community, can give you a close look at the local history and way of life. For the more adventurous there is the opportunity to "dam-drop" on the Waingongoro River.

An unlikely find in Hawera is the **Kevin Walsey Elvis Presley Memorial Room,** a private museum devoted to "The King." The unique collection here includes more than 2,000 records and an impressive collection of memorabilia. The museum does not keep regular hours; phone well ahead for an appointment (finding Kevin isn't always easy). ⌧ *51 Argyle St.* ☎ *0274/982–942 ⊕ www.digitalus.co.nz/elvis ⌐ By donation.*

☾ The **Tawhiti Museum** is a labor of love for Nigel Ogle, and an outstand-
Fodor'sChoice ing presentation of regional history. The former schoolteacher-cum-his-
★ torian bought an old cheese factory in 1975 and proceeded to fill it up with life-size figures from Taranaki's past. He creates the fiberglass figures from molds of local people, giving them a far more lifelike look than those in other museums, and sets them in scenes depicting the pioneering days. Nigel is continually adding "stories." The latest dioramas depict huge intertribal wars of the 1830s and European/Māori land wars of the 1860s. More than 800 model warriors, none of them the same, have been created. On the first Sunday of each month, the museum's Tawhiti Bush Railway springs to life, rattling through a variety of outdoor displays that highlight the historical logging operations in Taranaki. **Mr. Badger's Café,** with its delightful *Wind in the Willows* theme, has excellent food and espresso, and is quite simply one of the best cafés in southern Taranaki. To get to the museum, take Tawhiti Road northeast out of Hawera and continue 4 km (2½ mi). ⌧ *401 Ohangai Rd.* ☎ *06/278–6837 ⊕ www.tawhitimuseum.co.nz ⌐ $10 ⊙ Sept.–May, Fri.–Mon. 10–4; June–Aug., Sun. 10–4; Dec. 26–Jan. 31, daily 10–4.*

Where to Stay & Eat

$$ ⬚ **Tairoa Lodge.** The translation for *Tairoa* is "linger, stay longer," and that's what you'll want to do at this relaxing B&B. In this renovated kauri villa, built in 1875, the two spacious guest rooms look out over the woodland garden and swimming pool. Both rooms have fireplaces with carved wooden mantels; one room is done in deep reds, the other in cheery yellows and blues. A separate two-bedroom cottage can accommodate families; it has a full kitchen as well as a home-theater system. To keep busy, you can peruse piles of the latest magazines, play chess or *pétanque* (the French version of boccie), or take a dip in the pool. ⊠ *3 Puawai St.* ☎ *06/278–8603* ⊕ *www.tairoa-lodge.co.nz* ⌁ *2 rooms, 1 cottage* ⌂ *Restaurant, pool, in-room data ports, laundry facilities* ⊟ *AE, DC, MC, V* ⍾ *BP.*

Sports & the Outdoors

White-water sledging (like sledding, but on water) has become one of New Zealand's many zany adventure sports. You'll have your nose nearly to the water as you maneuver your sledge headfirst down the rapids. **Kaitiaki Adventures** (☎ 021/461–110 or 0800/336–376 ⊕ www.damdrop. com) runs daily trips on the Waingongoro River, leaving from the Powerco Aquatic Centre on Waihi Road in Hawera. Bring a swimsuit and towel; you'll be outfitted with a padded wet suit, booties, life jacket, helmet, fins, and a sledge (which resembles a small surfboard). The trips take about three hours and also include a journey around Okahutiti Pā, an old fortification. The cost is $60–$80; advance reservations are required. Kaitiaki Adventures also organizes surfing and mountain-biking tours.

NEW PLYMOUTH & TARANAKI ESSENTIALS

Transportation

BY AIR

New Plymouth Airport (NPL) is about 12 km (7½ mi) from the city center. Taxis wait at the airport; expect to pay about $25 to get into town. Withers Coachlines runs a door-to-door shuttle service for $15 per person; phone ahead to book.

Air New Zealand operates flights eight times daily between Auckland and New Plymouth and five times daily between New Plymouth and Wellington.

🗺 Airport **New Plymouth Airport** ⊠ 192 Airport Dr. ☎ 06/755-0500.
🗺 Carrier **Air New Zealand** ☎ 0800/737-000 ⊕ www.airnewzealand.co.nz.
🗺 Airport Transfers **Withers Coachlines** ☎ 06/751-1777.

BY BUS

New Plymouth is served twice daily by InterCity buses from Auckland, via Hamilton. A daily bus from Wellington, via Wanganui, also stops at Hawera and Stratford on its way to New Plymouth. Buses arrive at and depart from the New Plymouth Travel Centre on Queen Street. There is no regular public transportation to Mt. Taranaki, though shuttle-bus services are available to destinations such as North Egmont Visitor Centre and Stratford's Mountain House—call the New Plymouth Travel

Centre for details. Taranaki Tours has shuttles from New Plymouth to Mt. Taranaki and Egmont National Park, from $40 round-trip.

⃞ InterCity ☎ 09/913-6100 ⊕ www.intercitycoach.co.nz. **New Plymouth Travel Centre** ⊠ 32 Queen St. ☎ 06/759-9039. **Taranaki Tours** ☎ 06/757-9888 or 0800/886-877 ⊕ www.taranakitours.com.

BY CAR

New Plymouth looks well out of the way on the map, but it is only 5 to 6½ hours from Auckland and 5 hours from Wellington. From the north, head to Te Kuiti near Waitomo Caves, and then simply continue on State Highway 3. Leaving Taranaki heading south, take State Highway 3 to Wanganui. Staying on Highway 3, keep traveling to Sanson, where you have the option of heading east—still on Highway 3—through Palmerston North, the Manawatu Gorge, and on to the Hawke's Bay and Wairarapa regions; or following State Highway 1 south to Wellington. The roads in this region are generally in good condition. If you're traveling west on a sunny afternoon, watch out for strong glare from the setting sun.

Contacts & Resources

BANKS & EXCHANGE SERVICES

There are ATMs along Devon Street, the main shopping street in New Plymouth. In several of the region's smaller towns, there are ATMs outside the local banks.

EMERGENCIES

In New Plymouth, the local pharmacies take turns providing late-night service; check the local paper for schedules.

⃞ Emergency Services Fire, police, and ambulance ☎ 111.
⃞ Hospital Taranaki Base Hospital ⊠ David St., New Plymouth ☎ 06/753-6139.

MAIL & INTERNET

The post office in New Plymouth is open during regular business hours. If you're looking to use the Internet in New Plymouth, the best deal is the Puke Ariki Library, which charges $2 per 15 minutes from 9 to 6 on weekdays and 9 to 5 on weekends. There's also the Interplay Taranaki Internet café, open from 9 AM to 10 PM daily, which charges $5 an hour.

⃞ Internet Access Interplay Taranaki ⊠ Ground Floor, Top Town Complex, Devon St. New Plymouth ☎ 06/758-1918. **Puke Ariki Library** ⊠ Puke Ariki Landing, St. Aubyn St., New Plymouth ☎ 06/758-4544.
⃞ Post Office New Plymouth Post Office ⊠ 21 Currie St., New Plymouth ☎ 06/759-8931.

TOURS

BICYCLE TOURS Native bush, surf beaches, lush countryside, and hardly any traffic make rural Taranaki a cyclist's dream. Go at your own pace, with friends or family; Cycle Tours Taranaki can tailor-make a trip through the region's back roads to suit your time, age, and fitness level. Equipment is provided, and they transfer your luggage along the way. Prices for a three-day trip start at about $350 per person; seven-day tours start at $650 per person, plus accommodation and food.

⃞ Cycle Tours Taranaki ☎ 06/756-7727 ⊕ www.cycle-taranaki.co.nz.

FLIGHTSEEING Helicopter and fixed-wing flights are a quick but spectacular way to enjoy views of Taranaki. Not surprisingly, the most popular flight is to the Mt. Taranaki summit (snow covered in winter, steep rocky peaks in summer). Costs with Air New Plymouth are $240 for a three-seater plane ($320 for a four-seater, $480 for a six-seater). Beck Helicopters charges $225 per person for a 30-minute flight. You can also take a fixed-wing plane trip along the coastline ($180 for three, $240 for four, $360 for six). Both Beck Helicopters and Air New Plymouth can be chartered for custom trips.

🏂 **Beck Helicopters** ✉ Mountain Rd. ☎ 0800/336-644. **Air New Plymouth** ✉ New Plymouth Airport ☎ 06/755-0500 ⊕ www.airnewplymouth.co.nz.

SIGHTSEEING There's no better way to gain insight into a place than to hook up with
TOURS a knowledgeable local—and Ann Olsen, who runs Just for You Tours, is just such a person. Ann specializes in private guided tours for individuals or small groups. She'll plan an itinerary to suit your interests and budget, and she can take you well off the beaten track.

Taranaki Tours has an Around Mt. Taranaki Tour ($120/person) that's a splendid introduction to the region. Knowledgeable Māori guides share the history, legend, and culture of Taranaki in this road trip that circumnavigates the mountain. Trips last six to seven hours, lunch included. The company also has garden tours.

🏂 **Just for You Tours** ☎ 06/751-2198 🖶 06/751-2180 ⊕ www.windwand.co.nz/olsen main.htm. **Taranaki Tours** ☎ 06/757-9888 or 0800/886-877 ⊕ www.taranakitours.com.

VISITOR INFORMATION

All of the visitor centers listed below are open daily, with the exception of the Dawson Falls center, which opens only from Wednesday through Sunday (except during summer school holidays, when it opens daily).

The regional tourism organization maintains a Web site, www.taranakinz. org, with plenty of local listings and event information. The site www. windwand.co.nz also has fairly extensive regional listings. For information about Egmont National Park, visit the Department of Conservation's site (⊕ www.doc.govt.nz) and click on "National Parks."

🏂 **Tourist Information Dawson Falls Visitor Centre** ✉ Manaia Rd., Egmont National Park ☎ 027/433-0248. **Hawera Information Centre** ✉ 55 High St., Hawera ☎ 06/278-8599. **New Plymouth i-SITE Visitor Information Centre** ✉ Puke Ariki, 1 Ariki St., New Plymouth ☎ 06/758-4544 🖶 06/758-5485 ⊕ www.newplymouthnz.com. **North Egmont Visitor Centre** ✉ Egmont Rd., Egmont National Park ☎ 06/756-0990. **Stratford i-SITE Visitor Information Centre** ✉ Prospero Pl. ☎ 06/765-6708 or 0800/765-6708 ⊕ www.stratfordnz.co.nz.

WANGANUI, THE WHANGANUI RIVER & PALMERSTON NORTH

The attractive river city of Wanganui marks the starting point of one of the North Island's most distinctive, yet unsung, journeys—following the historic trail that lies along the slow-moving Whanganui River, the longest navigable waterway in the country (as opposed to the Waikato, which is the longest river). You'll need to put aside time to make the trip, since this is not country you can rush through, especially if you plan to kayak along, or hike around, the river's middle reaches, which flow through the forest-covered wilderness of Whanganui National Park. Three days gives you enough leeway to see the best of the river and park, though even with just a day to spare you can visit the historic settlements along the meandering Whanganui River Road, which winds alongside the river's lower reaches from Wanganui.

Note: The city is Wanganui, the river and national park are Whanganui (with an *h*). The name *Whanganui* refers to a legendary story about an ancestral chief, Haunui a Paparangi, who, upon journeying to the river, found it too deep to cross. He therefore settled to wait on the river bank for the tide to turn—a very long (*nui*) wait (*whanga*). The *Wh* of *Whanga* is pronounced as in *when*, or *what*, a subtle sound that was not picked up when committing the Māori language to writing. *Wanganui*, the city, is a misspelled and meaningless but entrenched version of the river name.

South of the Wanganui region is the Manawatu region, where the landscape sweeps from the Ruahine and Tararua Ranges that form part of the mountainous backbone of the North Island, to the coastal plains of Tangimoana and Himatangi. The Rangitikei and Manawatu rivers flow from high in the ranges and meander through fertile and pastoral farmlands to the coast, which is dotted with windswept, unpopulated beaches. At the heart of the Manawatu region is the city of Palmerston North— one of New Zealand's leading university towns and a major service center for the surrounding farms and agricultural industries. Free of major tourist attractions and the attendant tourist hype, it makes for a pleasant stopover en route to Wellington or other points south.

Wanganui

🐟 *163 km (102 mi) southeast of New Plymouth, 193 km (121 mi) north of Wellington, 225 km (141 mi) southwest of Taupo.*

On the banks near the mouth of the Whanganui River, Waanganui's compact city center shows off revitalized streets and Heritage buildings that hark back to colonial times and trading days. A stroll along Victoria Avenue, with its Victorian gaslights, wrought-iron seats, and avenue of palm and plane trees, gives you a pretty good idea of the city's style. Majestic Square, just off Victoria Avenue, is surrounded by galleries and crafts shops, and there are often live performances on the square's small stage. In summer (December to March), a profusion of hanging baskets and window boxes enhances the street appeal.

For hundreds of years, the Māori people have lived along the banks of the Whanganui River, which provided a major access route between the coast and interior. In the 1800s, Wanganui township became established as one of New Zealand's most prosperous early European settlements. Local Māori people trace their occupation of the land around the Whanganui River back as far as the 10th century. European settlers started moving to the area in the 1840s. Subsequent appropriation of land caused conflict with local Māori, and a British garrison was temporarily established in the town. From the 1880s the port and riverboat transport that provided a link to the North Island interior led to a prosperous time for trade and tourism, until completion of the main trunk railway line meant that Wanganui was essentially bypassed. Today, Wanganui has evolved into an attractive provincial city, serving local industry, tourism, and the region's farming community.

Fodor'sChoice For an overview of the region's history, drop into the **Whanganui Regional**
★ **Museum,** by Queens Park, which contains *taonga* (Māori ancestral treasures) of the River people, and is acknowledged as one of the best collections in the country. There are some wonderful *waka* (canoes), as well as carvings, decorative ornaments, kiwi-feather cloaks, greenstone clubs, tools, bone flutes, and ceremonial portraits. The museum also re-creates 19th-century Wanganui in a series of traditional shop windows filled with relics and curios. Another treasure in this museum is Te Pataka Whakaahua (the Lindauer Gallery), with 19th-century paintings of Māori leaders by Gottfried Lindauer. ⊠ *Watt St.* ☎ *06/349–1110* ⊕ *www.wanganui-museum.org.nz* ⊠ *$5* ⊗ *Daily 10–4:30.*

In the domed **Sarjeant Gallery,** the naturally lighted exhibit areas display more than 5,000 artworks, including pieces by leading contemporary New Zealand artists Gretchen Albrecht, Robert McLeod, and Rodney Fumpston. There's a good bookshop, too. ⊠ *Queens Park* ☎ *06/349–0506* ⊕ *www.sarjeant.org.nz* ⊠ *Free* ⊗ *Daily 10:30–4:30.*

For a taste of the old days on the river, catch a ride on the restored paddle steamer, the **Waimarie,** built in 1899 by Yarrow and Company at Toplar London. The steamer worked the river for 50 years before sinking in 1952, but painstaking restoration has made the craft shine like new. Two-hour cruises take you on a stately ride up the Whanganui River from Wanganui. A museum at the River Boat Centre houses a collection of photographs from the days when riverboats were a key form of transport. Also on view are images of the salvage of the *Waimarie,* a great engineering feat by a team of volunteer enthusiasts. ⊠ *Whanganui River Boat Centre, Taupo Quay* ☎ *06/347–1863* ⊕ *www.riverboat.co. nz* ⊠ *Cruise $30, museum by donation* ⊗ *Cruises Oct. 22–May 1 daily at 2, May 2–Oct. 21 weekends at 1. No cruises in Aug. Museum Mon.–Sat. 9–4, Sun. 10–4.*

By day, the formal gardens of **Virginia Lake** are a delight, and at night, the trees and lake fountain are softly illuminated. A gentle 25-minute stroll leads around the lake, through woodlands and gardens and past rose and wisteria pergolas. The lake is just north of Wanganui, off State Highway 3.

Where to Stay & Eat

$$$ ✕ **Vincent's Yellow House Café and Art Gallery.** Spread throughout the veranda, garden, and several rooms of this old yellow villa is a café showing local art (for sale). The menu changes weekly, but expect something nourishing such as seafood chowder chock-full of kingfish, bluenose, mussels, and salmon. Breakfast is served beginning at 7:30. The café is across the road from the river and a two-minute drive from the city center. ⊠ *Pitt St. at Dublin St.* ☎ *06/347–9321* ⊟ *MC, V.*

$$–$$$ × **Stellar.** Giant gourmet pizzas are a specialty at this relaxed eatery that retains the brick-and-stone interior of an 1850s former hotel—try the Funky Fungi or the CCB (chicken, cranberry, and Brie). If you prefer something more substantial, you could opt for a steak, classic surf 'n' turf, or the fish of the day. There's live music some nights. ⊠ 2 Victoria Ave. ☎ 06/345–7278 ▤ AE, MC, V.

$$–$$$ × **Vega.** With its funky, modern interior and French doors open onto the river, this former warehouse is a stylish spot to sample eclectic cuisine with a Mediterranean bent. Although there's a big emphasis on seafood, Vega is also a national Lamb and Beef Award winner, and the wine list and beer selection are probably the best in the region. ⊠ 49 Taupo Quay ☎ 06/345–1082 ⊕ www.vega.net.nz ▤ AE, MC, V ⊗ No lunch Mon.

$–$$ × **Red Eye Café.** This brightly painted, licensed café is a popular haunt
Fodor'sChoice with art students and folks who appreciate the hearty muffins, cakes, veg-
★ etarian food, and renowned Wellington coffee brand Havannah. There's a fire in winter and regular open-mike nights where locals show off their musical talents. ⊠ 96 Guyton St. ☎ 06/345–5646 ▤ AE, MC, V.

$–$$ ×▦ **Rutland Arms.** This renovated Victorian inn in the center of Wanganui is the top choice in town. The guest rooms have comfortable beds, reproduction period furniture, and bright bathrooms, four with whirlpool baths. Downstairs, the restaurant/bar has traditional-English character: a roaring fire (in winter) and a wide choice of imported beers. You can eat here ($$–$$$), surrounded by the horse brasses, other agricultural paraphernalia, and pictures of Old Wanganui, or in the sunny courtyard. Food is generous, interesting, contemporary New Zealand–style cuisine, and the menu changes regularly. ⊠ 48-50 Ridgeway St. ☎ 06/347–7677 ▤ 06/347–7345 ⊕ www.rutland-arms.co.nz ⤺ 8 rooms ⟡ Restaurant, in-room broadband, bar ▤ AE, DC, MC, V ⊙I CP.

$$–$$$ ▦ **Arlesford House.** This elegant country home, an easy 10-minute drive from Wanganui, is built almost entirely of native timber and surrounded by beautifully landscaped gardens. Hosts June and George Loibl prepare delicious, leisurely breakfasts; afterward you can relax by the pool or play tennis or pétanque (similar to boccie). Rooms are large, light, and airy, with king-size beds, inviting armchairs, and either have en-suite bathrooms (some with a stunning garden outlook from the bath), or private bathrooms across the hall. Also on the property is a self-catering, three-bedroom log cabin. ⊠ 202 State Hwy. 3 ⌂ R.D. 4, Westmere ☎ 06/347–7751 ▤ 06/347–7561 ⊕ www.arlesfordhouse.co.nz ⤺ 4 rooms, 1 cottage ⟡ Tennis court, pool; no a/c ▤ MC, V ⊙I BP.

$–$$ ▦ **Anndion Lodge.** One of New Zealand's new brand of high-end back-
Fodor'sChoice packer lodges, Anndion has a range of accommodations that include
★ bunkrooms ($30/person), singles (bed for one), twins (two single beds), and doubles with shared bathrooms—though soaps and shampoos are provided. One larger room has a super-king-size bed and its own bath. The fully equipped and modern shared kitchen has a sandwich press, rice cooker, electric knives, and a cappuccino maker. Outside is a great poolside barbecue area; inside is a comfortable TV lounge with an extensive DVD library. A free shuttle takes you to and from town. The hotel is across the road from the Whanganui River. ⊠ 143 Anzac Parade ☎ 06/ 343–3593 or 0800/343–056 ▤ 06/343–3056 ⊕ www.

anndionlodge.co.nz ♨ *Dining room, BBQ, Wi-Fi, pool, outdoor hot tub, billiards, 3 lounges, laundry facilities, Internet room; no a/c, no room phones* ⊟ *AE, D, MC, V.*

$–$$ ▣ **Bushy Park Forest Reserve.** Activities abound at this bed-and-breakfast in a grand old Heritage homestead, surrounded by ancient forest and prolific native birdlife. The remnant forest is administered by a trust and has been surrounded by an animal predator-proof fence to protect endangered native birds, such as the flightless kiwi. Walking tracks meander through the forest; look for the "Ratanui," the world's biggest rata tree. Back at the homestead are six spacious bedrooms, a formal dining room, several lounges, and a television lounge. The homestead's Category One Heritage status restricts any significant changes, providing a true bygone-era experience. The café is known for its espresso and Devonshire teas. Backpackers can share a bunkhouse ($20/person) that sleeps 11; your own bedding is required, and you will need to bring and cook your own meals. There are campsites and a couple of RV sites as well. ⊠ *Rangitautau East Rd., 24 km (15 mi) northwest of Wanganui* ☎ *06/342–9879* ⊕ *www. bushypark.co.nz* ⤵ *6 rooms, 1 bunkhouse; all with shared bath* ♨ *Dining room, café, 3 lounges, Internet room, travel services* ⊟ *MC, V* ⧉ *BP.*

¢ ▣ **Tamara Backpackers Lodge.** You can sit on the balcony of this Edwardian homestead and look out over the Wanganui River (and toward Mt. Ruapehu in the distance) or chill out in a hammock in the back garden. Either way, this budget lodge is a relaxed base, just a five-minute walk from town. There's a small art gallery, games room with piano and pool table, TV room, dining room, and fully equipped shared kitchen. Or you can head for the café next door. The simple rooms include those with double beds, one or two single beds, and dorms (with four beds each). ⊠ *24 Somme Parade* ☎ *06/347–6300* ⊟ *06/347–6300* ⊕ *www. tamaralodge.com* ⤵ *12 rooms, 3 dorms (12 beds)* ♨ *Dining room, BBQ, lounge, laundry facilities, Internet room* ⊟ *AE, DC, MC, V.*

The Whanganui River

The city of Wanganui sits near the mouth of the Whanganui River, which flows through the heart of Whanganui National Park and is one of New Zealand's most historic and scenic waterways. The Whanganui begins its journey high on the mountains of Tongariro National Park. In its 329-km journey the river flows through sheer-sided gorges, forested wilderness, and isolated pockets of farmland. For several hundred years the *Te Atihau nui a paparangi* tribe of Māoris has lived along the riverbanks, and they still regard the river as their spiritual ancestor. Most have now left the river *kainga* (villages), though some remain in small communities along the lower reaches. For a brief period around 1900, thousands of tourists were drawn to riverboats and steamers that plied the river as far up as Taumarunui, 170 km (106 mi) north of Wanganui.

Today the river is popular for kayaking and jet-boating, with 239 named rapids—though most of them are shallow and suitable for novice paddlers. Guided trips (⇨ Sports & the Outdoors, *below*) generally operate during summer, the most popular time for kayakers; however, a river trip is feasible any time of the year. Winters are mild in the valley, and floods can occur year-round.

An alternative for those without the time or inclination to travel by kayak is to explore the river's lower reaches by following the **Whanganui River Road** from the city of Wanganui. Built in the 1930s to provide access to communities otherwise reliant on the then-less-frequent riverboat services, the road runs for 79 km (49 mi) north, as far as Pipiriki. It's a narrow backcountry road, unpaved in stretches, though perfectly doable ★ with care. Many choose instead to take the early morning **Rural Mail Coach Tour** (☎ 06/347–7534), which gets you to Pipiriki and back in a day and includes sightseeing stops and optional extra tours. The tour is $35, given weekdays only, departing Wanganui between 7:15 and 7:30 AM, returning midafternoon (times vary depending on how much mail he has to deliver).

You'll see the remains of giant, fossilized oyster shells at **Oyster Cliffs** (28 km [17 mi] from Wanganui). You'll call at the tidy village of **Koriniti** (47 km [29 mi]), with its well-kept ceremonial buildings and small Anglican church. The restored **Kawana Flour Mill** (56 km [35 mi]) and colonial miller's cottage is always open, if you'd like a glimpse of bygone pioneer life. At the farming settlement of **Ranana** (60 km [37 mi]), a Roman Catholic church from the 1890s is still used today. And there is the larger St. Joseph's Church and Catholic Mission, established by Home of Compassion founder Mother Aubert, at pretty **Hiruharama** (66 km [41 mi]), better known locally as Jerusalem. Drive up the track to see the carved altar inside the church.

Finally at **Pipiriki** (79 km [49 mi]), the turnaround point, it's possible to arrange a jet-boat tour to the magnificent river gorges farther upriver. A popular trip continues to the Mangapurua Landing, where a short walk leads to the Bridge to Nowhere, a huge concrete bridge in remote forested country that is a remnant of the pioneering Mangapurua farming settlement, abandoned in 1942.

Other things to do along the lower reaches are short **canoe trips,** with Máori cultural experience included, and overnight stays at some of the idiosyncratic lodges and farms in the area (⇨ *below*). For information about canoe trips, contact the **Wanganui i-SITE Visitor Information Centre** (☎ 06/349–0508 ⊕ www.wanganuinz.com).

Where to Stay

$$–$$$ 🏠 **Bridge to Nowhere Lodge.** In a private enclave deep in Whanganui National Park, 21 km (31 mi) upriver from Pipiriki, this lodge can only be reached by jet boat (arranged by the lodge). The payoff for the remote location is magnificent forest vistas, birdsong at dawn, and the chance to bathe under the stars (there's an outdoor tub). Accommodation ranges from doubles in the lodge (meals provided), with bush and river views to self-catering family and bunk rooms, to "The Paddlers Rest," a six-berth dorm-style cabin, also self-catering. There's also a camping area (bring your own tent). In the lodge rooms, you can choose between self-catering, or bed, breakfast, and dinner. Companies associated with the Lodge run jet-boat tours to the Bridge to Nowhere, canoe trips, canoe rental, and hiking trips in the National Park. ✉ *Whanganui River, Box 4203, Wanganui* 📠 *06/348–7122 or 0800/480–308* ⊕ *www. bridgetonowhere-lodge.co.nz* ⊟ *MC, V* ⏣ *EP, MAP.*

★ $ 🖼 **The Flying Fox.** Even the arrival is exceptional at this truly unique lodging. You'll reach it by its namesake Flying Fox—a simple aerial cable car—which deposits you high above the west bank of the Whanganui River. There you'll find a pair of cottages, each accommodating two to four people. They're distinctly eco-friendly, from their construction using recycled materials to their facilities, such as the wood- and gas-fired showers and an outdoor clawfoot tub. Inside, they're warmly comfortable, with rug-covered brick floors, tie-dye throws, carved screens, and wood-burning stoves. Meals (arrange in advance; $110–$120 per day) hinge on mostly organic and homegrown ingredients: avocados from the owner's trees; smoked eel from the river; seasonal produce; and homemade ice cream, bread, and muffins. Or you can bring your own groceries. Camping in a bush clearing is another "lodging" option ($10/person). You can get here from Wanganui on the Rural Mail Coach Tour (⇨ *above*); for those who are driving, there's secure parking on the road side of the river. ⊠ *Whanganui River Rd., Koriniti* 🕾🖥 *06/342–8160* ⊕ *www.theflyingfox.co.nz* ⤵ *2 cottages* 🛁 *Kitchens; no a/c, no room phones, no room TVs* 🖃 *MC, V* 🍴 *MAP.*

Sports & the Outdoors

CANOEING & KAYAKING
The main season for Whanganui River trips is between October and Easter; the busiest period is during the summer holidays (Christmas–January). Winter trips are doable; the weather will be slightly colder, but you'll probably have the river to yourself. In summer, although there can be several hundred travelers on the river at any one time, they are all moving in one direction and so a group can often travel long periods without seeing another soul. The time they do come together is in the evenings, at the huts and campsites.

All forms of craft have been seen on the river; however, transport is generally in open, two-seater, Canadian-style canoes or in kayaks. Tour options range from one-day picnic trips to five-day camping expeditions. Operators can supply all equipment, transfers, and the necessary hut and campsite passes, and trips can either be guided and catered, or independently undertaken (you supply your own food).

Your first call should be to one of the commercial operators or the **Department of Conservation** (🕾 06/348–8475 ⊕ www.doc.govt.nz) to discuss itineraries. No experience is necessary; the Whanganui is considered a beginner's river—it's definitely not "white-water" adventure, though the river should be respected and there are one or two rapids that can play nasty tricks on paddlers. Prices vary considerably according to the length and style of the trip, but you can expect to pay from about $55 for a simple one-day trip and in the $500–$600 range for a fully inclusive three-day excursion.

The **Whanganui Journey,** a canoe journey down the Whanganui River, is regarded as one of nine "Great Walks" in New Zealand's national parks and can be paddled independently or with tour operators (⇨ *below*). There are park huts and campsites along the river. Most tours go from Taumarunui to Pipiriki, a four- to five-day trip, or from Whakahoro to

Pipiriki (three to four days). Whakahoro to Pipiriki is a true wilderness experience; there is no road access. A lower river trip, from Pipiriki to Wanganui, passes through a mix of native forest, farmland, and several small communities. Tour operators offer anything from five-day wilderness experiences to one-day or overnight trips on the lower reaches. Kayaking the river is about getting back to nature, savoring the beauty of the thick forest, and going with the flow of the river.

Fodor'sChoice **Canoe Safaris** (☎ 06/385–9237 ⊕ www.canoesafaris.co.nz) leads two-
★ to five-day trips on the Whanganui; their "big boats," six-person open canoes, are built on the lines of the Canadian fur-trapper boats. The price, which starts at $320 for a two-day safari, covers all equipment, including a waterproof gear bag. **Bridge to Nowhere** (☎ 06/344–2554 ⊕ www. bridgetonowheretours.co.nz) has a range of trips, ranging from all-inclusive, family-friendly overnight trips to four-day excursions. Prices vary depending on whether the trip is self-catered, but are comparable with other river-tour companies. **Blazing Paddles** (☎ 0800/252–946 ⊕ www. blazingpaddles.co.nz) runs the one-day "Splash 'n Dash" kayak or canoe trip ($70 per person), which starts at Taumarunui, finishes at Ohinepane, and passes through 49 rapids en route. The company also arranges trips of two to five days for $130–$220 per person (including kayak rental and transportation) and can help book accommodation at one of the lodges or campsites along the river.

Waka Tours (✉ 17a Balance St., Raetihi ☎🖶 06/385–4811 ⊕ www. wakatours.net) runs one-day, overnight, and three-day guided kayak journeys with a Māori cultural element. Traveling on the lower reaches, local Māori guides share their stories, songs, customs, and love of the river. The tours include visits to or overnight stays on marae (traditional Māori settlements).

JET-BOAT TOURS If you fancy a faster-paced river adventure than a canoe or kayak paddle, consider a jet-boat tour—you'll skim across the rapids, dodge the rocks, and see some fantastic river scenery. One of the most popular trips is from Pipirki to the Mangapurua Landing, then a short walk to the Bridge to Nowhere in the Mangapurua Valley, a Whanganui tributary. The Mangapurua Valley was a farming settlement established and abandoned all between 1918 and 1942, owing to the impossibly remote and rugged country. The old concrete bridge in the bush is a fascinating reminder. Jet-boat companies also transport hikers to two national park hiking trails: the Matemateonga Track and Mangapurua Track.

Ken and Josephine Haworth grew up on the river, now their company **Whanganui River Adventures** (✉R.D. 6 Pipiri ☎🖶06/385–3246 ⊕www. whanganuiriveradventures.co.nz) has a range of tours from Pipiriki to the Bridge to Nowhere, and shorter tours to scenic delights such as the Drop Scene, and Manganui o te ao River. **Bridge to Nowhere Jet-boat Tours** (☎ 0800/480–308 ⊕ www.bridgetonowheretours.co.nz) runs jet-boat trips from Pipiriki to the Bridge to Nowhere (a four-hour trip) and other natural and historic sights.

Palmerston North

📍 *145 km (87 mi) northeast of Wellington, 72 km (45 mi) southeast of Wanganui.*

Palmerston North—or "Palmy" as the locals call it—may not be at the top of the tourist hit list, but it's worth a detour if you want to get a feel for New Zealand urban life without the hype of the usual tourist centers. A six-hour drive south from Auckland and two hours north of Wellington, Palmerston North is one of New Zealand's largest regional cities, with a population of 79,000.

Palmerston North is home to more than 70 major educational and research institutes, including the Institute of Rugby, where the All Blacks often come to train. Thanks to these magnets, one-third of Palmerston's population is between the ages of 15 and 30. The biggest influence on the city, however, is Massey University, one of the country's leading universities. The Massey campus has two Palmerston locations: Turitea, set among huge trees and beautiful gardens, and Hokowhitu, on the city side of the Manawatu River, with modern buildings near the lagoon.

Activity in Palmerston North is centered around The Square. From there, you can easily explore on foot most of the city's cafés, restaurants, shops, art galleries, and museums.

☺ The distinctive **Te Manawa** museum is divided into three sections that weave together the region's history, art, and science. It include artworks and natural history displays, and traces the history of Rangitane, the local Māori people. If traveling with young ones, the Mind Science Centre, with its sometimes quirky interactive science exhibits, is particularly entertaining and educational. ✉ *396 Main St.* ☎ *06/355–5000* ⊕ *www.temanawa.co.nz* ✉ *Life and Art galleries free; Mind Science Centre $6* ⊙ *Daily 10–5.*

The only one of its kind in New Zealand, the small **New Zealand Rugby Museum** is worth a visit whether or not you're a fan of the sport, for an insight into the tradition surrounding a game that many in New Zealand treat like a religion. The collection of rugby memorabilia dates back to the start of this national game in 1870. Look for the historic whistle that is used to open the World Cup every four years. ✉ *87 Cuba St.* ☎ *06/358–6947* ⊕ *www.rugbymuseum.co.nz* ✉ *$5* ⊙ *Mon.–Sat. 10–noon and 1:30–4; Sun. 1:30–4.*

Inside the art deco **Square Edge** building is a center for emerging local artists. Its galleries, boutiques, and gift shops stock unique, locally made artworks. You can also take a break in its café. ✉ *Church St. and The Sq.* ☎ *06/353–3806* ⊙ *Weekdays 10–4:30, Sat. 10–3.*

The **Tararua and Apiti Wind Farms** two of the largest of wind farms in the southern hemisphere, make a dramatic sight on the ranges that overlook the city. A drive up Saddle Road to the largest windmills will reward with fantastic views. There is a car park directly beneath one huge windmill, and the return drive can be a pleasant look via Woodville and the Manawatu Gorge.

OFF THE
BEATEN
PATH
★

FEILDING – For a taste of authentic, farming New Zealand, take a side trip to the township of Feilding, 20 km (12 mi) northwest of Palmerston North. **The Feilding Saleyards,** one of the largest livestock sales in the Southern Hemisphere, are close to the Edwardian town center. At least twice weekly, sheep and cattle farmers buy and sell more than 15,000 sheep and 1,400 head of cattle. The Feilding Saleyards Guided Tour ($5) through the sheep pens and state-of-the-art computerized cattle auction pavilion provides a fascinating glimpse of one of New Zealand's oldest farming traditions. After your tour, visit the rustic Saleyards Café, where the farmers meet for pie and chips, or toasted steak toasted sandwich. If you prefer, there are more modern cafés in town. Other Feilding attractions are the farmers' market (Friday mornings), Kowhai Gardens, the Manawatu Horsedrawn Vehicle Museum, a steam-rail museum, and Manfeild Park (which hosts regular national and international events, from motor sports to the annual garden festival in early May). From Feilding, Kimbolton Road passes through prime sheep-farming country to Kimbolton Village (28 km [17 mi] from Feilding), where there is a café. Close to the village (within a few minutes' drive) are two outstanding gardens with rhododendrons and myriad other plants: Cross Hills ($8 admission) and Heritage Park Garden ($5 admission). For more information, contact the **Feilding & District Information Centre** (✉ 10 Manchester Sq. ☎ 06/323–3318 ⊕ www.feilding.co.nz).

Where to Stay & Eat

$$$–$$$$ ✕ **Déjeuner.** Relaxed and friendly, this well-regarded restaurant in an old bungalow draws on a range of influences—from French to Asian and Pacific. Try the signature Déjeuner lamb shank (slow-cooked lamb atop garlicky mashed potatoes) or the Jack Daniels whiskey-barrel house-smoked venison on kūmara (a native sweet potato) mash and port-and-rhubarb coulis. When you phone for your reservation, inquire about the tasting menu, offered occasionally. ✉ *159 Broadway Ave.* ☎ *06/356–1449* ⊕ *www.dejeuner.co.nz* ▭ *AE, D, MC, V* ⛿ *Licensed and BYOB.*

$$$ ✕ **Bella's Café.** Serving a mix of Italian, Thai, and Pacific Rim dishes, Bella's
Fodor's Choice has been one of the city's favorite eateries for more than a decade. It is
★ smart and cheerful, with friendly and efficient service. Try the poached salmon on arborio risotto, Bella's classic Thai chicken curry, or black-and-white sesame calamari. The café's founders also run the Herb Farm café in nearby Ashhurst. ✉ *2 The Sq.* ☎ *06/357–8616* ▭ *MC, V.*

$$$ ✕ **Café Cuba.** Just off The Square, this café is a funky and popular local haunt for breakfast, brunch, lunch, and dinner. Laid-back jazz plays in the background, and there are plenty of magazines to peruse while you tuck into the Cuba Breakfast—a hearty plate of eggs, bacon, mushrooms, and tomatoes—or later in the day perhaps a Cajun chicken "sarnie" (sandwich) with fried banana, salad greens, and *taziki* (tangy cucumber-yogurt sauce). The kids menu is appealing, too, with more healthful and interesting choices than you usually find. ✉ *Cuba and George Sts.* ☎ *06/356–5750* ▭ *MC, V.*

$$$–$$$$ ▣ **Hiwinui Country Estate.** For a luxurious farm stay, do the short (18-km [11-mi]) drive from Palmerston North to this 1,100-acre working sheep and dairy farm, hosted by the family that has farmed this land for generations. The homestead looks across sweeping lawns and gardens, beyond farm paddocks to the forest-covered Ruahine Ranges. You can take a farm tour, go walking in nearby Ruahine Forest Park, or try fly-fishing or jet-boating in the dramatic Manawatu River gorge. Less-active pursuits include lounging by the roaring stone fireplaces (outdoors or in), having breakfast delivered to your room, or being treated to a gourmet dinner of fresh, local produce, complemented by New Zealand wine (by advance arrangement only). The three rooms open out to gardens, lawns, and rural views; all have underfloor heating and high-quality linens. One room has a whirlpool bath, and one has a double shower. Discreet and considerate hosts Jan and Dave Stewart judge whether guests would like privacy or prefer their delightful company. ⊠ *465 Ashurst–Bunnythorpe Rd.* ☎ *06/329–2838* ⊕ *www.hiwinui.co.nz* ↵ *3 rooms* ⚭ *In-room DVD, in-room data ports, outdoor hot tub, massage; no kids under 10* ⊟ *DC, MC, V* ⏐◎⏐ *BP.*

$$ ⊡ **Novotel Palmerston North.** In a 1927 Heritage building, this city hotel is just minutes by foot from shops, theaters, and cafés. The restaurant, Toast, serves breakfasts and contemporary Pacific Rim cuisine for dinner. There's also an intimate lounge bar with a Cuban theme, Zeeba; and a sports bar popular with the local after-work crowd. Rooms have extra-long queen-size sofa beds, with feather duvets and pillows. In 2005, 75 new rooms were added to the original 20, and older rooms were refurbished for continuity. ⊠ *175 Cuba St.* ☎ *06/355–5895* ⊕ *www.accorhotels.co.nz* ↵ *95 rooms* ⚭ *In-room safes, minibars, cable TV, in-room broadband, Wi-Fi, business facilities, meeting rooms* ⊟ *DC, MC, V.*

$$ ⊡ **Plum Trees Lodge.** A charming inner-city retreat, this lodge was built
Fodor'sChoice in 1999 as a loft over the garage of the 1920s home of hosts Robyn and
★ Robert Anderson. The apartment is spacious but best suited to couples or solo travelers, because it has only one room. It's full of character, with its stained-glass windows and use of aged native timbers and recycled ceramics; it also has a private balcony. Surrounding trees ensure privacy. The sumptuous breakfast basket is stocked with tasty local nibbles and treats. Dial-up Internet access is available for those with laptops. ⊠ *97 Russell St.* ☎ *06/358–7813* ⊕ *www.plumtreeslodge.com* ↵ *1 studio apartment* ⚭ *Kitchen, in-room data ports* ⊟ *MC, V* ⏐◎⏐ *BP.*

Nightlife & the Arts

NIGHTLIFE At **The Fitz** (⊠ Fergusson St. ☎ 06/350–0718), which is legendary among area students, you can have beer delivered to your table by the crate. **The Fat Ladies Arms** (⊠ Church and Linton Sts. 334 Church St. ☎ 06/358–8888) is one of several popular student haunts. The interior is a soothing mix of tapa cloth and warm woods at the **Flying Fish–Pacific Sushi Cocktail Bar** (⊠ Regents Arcade ☎ 06/359–3474), where the bartenders mix drinks with the flair of Tom Cruise in the movie *Cocktail*; the tasty fusion sushi is the perfect accompaniment.

THE ARTS Several theaters in the city center regularly host local and visiting productions. **Centrepoint** (⊠ Pitt and Church Sts. ☎ 06/354–5740 ⊕ www.centrepoint.co.nz), the only professional theater company outside New Zealand's main cities, has performances Tuesday through Sunday. Ballet, traveling musical productions, opera, and rock groups take the stage at the opulent **Regent on Broadway** (⊠ 63 Broadway ☎ 06/350–2100 ⊕ www.regent.co.nz), which was built in 1930.

Shopping

Palmerston North's shopping is centered around The Square; Broadway Avenue and the Plaza shopping centers are all within easy walking distance. George Street, which is also just off The Square, has a number of specialty shops, galleries, and cafés.

Check out **Taylor Jensen Fine Arts** (⊠ 39 George St. ☎ 06/355–4278) for contemporary and traditional New Zealand and international art, sculpture, jewelry, crafts, and furniture. Call into **Art Attack** (⊠ 42 George St. ☎ 06/354–6278) and see resident artist Elizabeth Knapp at work. If you're looking for a good read, while away some time at **Bruce McKenzie Booksellers** (⊠51 George St. ☎06/356–9922), considered to be among New Zealand's leading independent bookstores.

IHI Aotearoa (⊠ 71 George St. ☎ 06/354–0375) sells high-quality, contemporary art and crafts, jewelry and streetwear, much of it made by local artists. You can enjoy gourmet breads and pastries, gluten-free if you prefer, at **Breadworks Artisan Breads** (⊠ 85 The Sq.). Indulge your sweet tooth at **Munchkins** (⊠61 Broadway Ave. ☎06/356–4615), a child's haven of chocolates and homemade fudge. **Rêve** (⊠ The Elm, Fitzherbert Ave. ☎06/353–0570) is a boutique specializing in trousers for women and garments made with local spun wool.

WANGANUI, THE WHANGANUI RIVER & PALMERSTON NORTH ESSENTIALS

Transportation

BY AIR

The Palmerston North International Airport (PMR) is a 10-minute drive from the city center. Currency exchange is available when international flights arrive, and there is an ATM by the escalator. The taxi stand is outside the terminal, and shuttle services are available for roughly $15. The airport also has an Internet kiosk.

Air New Zealand has regular nonstop flights between Palmerston North and Auckland, Hamilton, Wellington, and Christchurch. Freedom Air runs nonstop service from Palmerston North to the Australian destinations Sydney, Melbourne, and Brisbane and also flies to Fiji directly from Palmerston North. Origin Pacific Airways flies nonstop between Palmerston North and Auckland, Wellington, Christchurch, Nelson, and Bleinheim.

🛪 Airport **Palmerston North International Airport** ☎ 06/351–4415 ⊕ www.pnairport.co.nz.

🛪 Carriers **Air New Zealand** ☎ 0800/737–000 ⊕ www.airnewzealand.co.nz. **Freedom Air** ☎ 0800/600–500 ⊕ www.freedomair.co.nz. **Origin Pacific Airways** ☎ 0800/302–302 ⊕ www.originpacific.co.nz.

BY BUS

InterCity buses make four or five daily trips between Wellington and Wanganui ($38; four hours). Several buses a day make the daylong trip between Auckland and Wanganui ($75). There's also daily service to Wanganui from New Plymouth ($33; three hours).

InterCity runs regular buses between Wellington and Palmerston North ($31; two hours). There are daily buses between Auckland and Palmerston North ($80; nine hours). Buses arrive at the Palmerston North Travel Centre, about a five-minute walk from the central business district.

🚌 Bus Companies **InterCity** ☎ 09/913-6100 or 04/472-5111 ⊕ www.intercitycoach.co.nz.
🚌 Bus Depots **New Plymouth bus stop** ✉ 19 Ariki St., city center. **Palmerston North Travel Centre** ✉ Main and Pitt Sts. **Wanganui bus stop** ✉ 156 Ridgeway St.

BY CAR

Wanganui is a three-hour drive from Wellington; take State Highway 1 north to Sanson and Highway 3 west from there. The Whanganui River Road is a minor route—you can expect it to take two hours to drive from Wanganui to Pipiriki, longer if you stop to sightsee on the way. Remember to keep left on the narrow corners. To reach the kayak starting points, take Highway 4 north from Wanganui; it's a three-hour drive to Taumarunui, via Raetihi. A minor road connects Pipiriki to Raetihi, so you could always drive north up the Whanganui River Road, cut east along the minor road to Raetihi, and then return down Highway 4 to Wanganui, a paved though winding road through steep farmland and forest.

Contacts & Resources

BANKS & EXCHANGE SERVICES

In Wanganui and Palmerston North, all the major banks have ATMs in the central business districts.

EMERGENCIES

🚨 Emergency Services **Fire, police, and ambulance** ☎ 111.
🚨 Hopsitals **Palmerston North Hospital** ✉ 50 Ruahine St. ☎ 06/356-9169. **Wanganui Hospital** ✉ Heads Rd. ☎ 06/348-1234.

MAIL & SHIPPING

CourierPost is New Zealand's largest courier service and has a partnership with DHL for shipping international packages. New Zealand Post shops will accept packages for CourierPost, or they can be delivered directly to the CourierPost depot. Alternatively, try TNT Express Worldwide.

🚚 **CourierPost** ✉ 62 Wilson St., Wanganui ✉ McGregor St., Palmerston North ☎ 0800/268-7437 ⊕ www.courierpost.co.nz. **TNT Express Worldwide (NZ)** ✉ Unit 16, 16 Bennett St., Palmerston North ☎ 06/356-8399.

VISITOR INFORMATION

The Wanganui Visitor Information Centre is open weekdays 8:30–5 and weekends 10–2. Its Web site includes information on the Whanganui River. In Palmerston North, the Manawatu Visitor Information Centre is open weekdays 9–5 and weekends 10–3. For information about Whanganui National Park, visit the Department of Conservation's site (⊕ www.doc.govt.nz) and click on "National Parks."

🏛 Tourist Information **Manawatu Visitor Information Centre** ✉ The Sq. ☎ 06/354-6593 or 06/350-1922 ⊕ www.manawatunz.co.nz. **Wanganui Visitor Information Centre** ✉ 101 Guyton St. ☎ 06/349-0508 ⊕ www.wanganuinz.com.

Wellington &
the Wairarapa

WORD OF MOUTH

"I love Windy Wellington, the harbor city where the views aren't the only things that can blow you away. You can walk its busy streets or relax on golden sands. It's a breeze to dine at restaurants on its delightful harborfront or browse around the bookshops. Seat of government it may be, but its nightlife is livelier than the politics. For a change of scenery, drive through green valleys to the Wairarapa to unwind in pristine countryside while sampling world-class wines."

—Bob Marriott

Updated by
Bob Marriott

MORE AND MORE PEOPLE ARE FINDING THEIR WAY TO WELLINGTON, New Zealand's capital, and not merely because it's the sailing point for the ferries heading south. Arguably the country's most cosmopolitan metropolis, this charming city has gained a justifiable reputation for fostering the arts. Its world-class Te Papa Tongarewa–Museum of New Zealand is a don't-miss attraction, and the burgeoning film industry—led, of course, by the *Lord of the Rings* extravaganzas—has injected new life into the local arts scene. Ardent film fans can still visit the many *LOTR* sites around the city, but everyone is benefiting from the lively café scene and the rapidly expanding restaurant culture. Attractive and compact enough to be explored easily on foot, New Zealand's capital is a booming destination.

Wellington and the adjacent Hutt Valley are the southern gateway to the Wairarapa, a region whose name has recently become synonymous with wine. Head out over the hills to meander along the ruler-straight highways or quiet byways from vineyard to vineyard for a day—or two or three—of wine tasting and first-class dining. Even if wine isn't your thing, the Wairarapa is worth an excursion for its gardens, fishing, walks, and even hot-air ballooning. Head for the coast here, too, where waves crash against craggy, windswept beaches, and you can gaze in silent awe at the dramatic sunsets.

Exploring Wellington & the Wairarapa

Whether you enter Wellington from the coastal State Highway 1 or over the hills from the flat rural plain of the Wairarapa, the majestic Tararua Ranges, a natural barrier separating east from west, stand etched like a cardboard cutout against the sky. You don't need a car in the city, but to explore the Wairarapa, where the countryside is dotted with vineyards, it's best to drive. You'll also need to drive if you'd like to head north to the long, sweeping beaches of the Kapiti Coast.

About the Restaurants

If the national sport of New Zealand is rugby, then the national hobbies surely must be eating and drinking. In Wellington, restaurants, cafés, and sports bars have been springing up overnight like mushrooms. Food and wine magazines are flying off the shelves, and the local newspapers and TV stations are focusing more attention on all matters of the palate. This fresh interest translates into a growing number of dining options.

Although there will always be a place for a classic meal of steak, french fries, and cold ale and the humble meat pie is still an iconic Kiwi mouthful, Wellington restaurants are branching out into more adventurous fare. Chinese, Thai, Japanese, Malaysian, Mexican, and Italian cuisine are all increasingly common on the menus, and wine lists are actually being studied (though perhaps not yet with the same intensity as the racing journals and sports pages). Indigenous food, too, is appearing in restaurants around the city—native plants might be paired with traditional seafood or made into sauces to accompany meat or sweet-potato dishes.

GREAT ITINERARIES

IF YOU HAVE 1 DAY

One day will give you enough time for a quick tour of **Wellington**'s city center and waterfront, perhaps stopping for lunch at a harborfront restaurant, as well as a visit to the excellent **Te Papa Tongarewa–Museum of New Zealand** ⓱. Depending on how long you stay at the museum, you could also take a ride on the **Kelburn Cable Car** ❶ and squeeze in a stroll through the **Wellington Botanic Garden** ❷. In the evening, linger over dinner at one of the city's stylish bistros, take in a theater or music performance, or belly up to the bar at a local pub.

IF YOU HAVE 3 DAYS

After getting your bearings on the one-day tour above, spend more time exploring the city's attractions on Day 2. Art lovers should visit **City Gallery** ⓰, or if history is more your thing, take in the **Museum of Wellington, City and Sea** ⓮. You can browse the funky boutiques on **Cuba Street** or make your way there in the evening when the clubs get lively. On Day 3, plan an excursion out of town—you've got plenty of options. You could head for the Wairarapa to tour the vineyards

around **Martinborough** ⓴; do some wine tasting and enjoy a leisurely winery lunch. Alternatively, visit the **Akatarawa Valley** for its gardens, blueberry farms, and the Staglands Wildlife Reserve, a particularly worthwhile stop if you have kids in tow. For coastal scenery or an offshore afternoon, drive up the **Kapiti Coast** and possibly visit Kapiti Island (for this, you'll need to book in advance). Automobile buffs may want to detour en route to the **Southward Car Museum.**

IF YOU HAVE 5 DAYS

Stretch out your time in **Wellington** by including a trip on the harbor ferry and perhaps a visit to **Maori Treasures.** If you spend just one day in the city center, you could hit both the Kapiti Coast and the Akatarawa Valley as day trips. Then spend a night in **Martinborough** ⓴ for a round of wine tasting. On the next day, work the pinot noir out of your system by walking or cycling on the Hutt River Trail before returning to Wellington. Or if you've a taste for windswept scenery, you'll have time to drive out to **Cape Palliser** ㉑.

In rural areas outside Wellington, the wine industry has revolutionized local tables, with excellent dining and wine-tasting spots proving more than a match for the old-fashioned greasy spoons. In the Wairarapa, restaurants equaling anything in the big cities are winning a well-justified reputation for creative cuisine.

Local dining habits have expanded along with the cuisine. It's not unusual to see sidewalk tables in the capital or the suburbs occupied on a fine morning by 10 AM, and late-night spots stay open until the wee hours. Generally, lunch runs from noon until 2, and most restaurants then close for a few hours before opening for dinner around 6. On Monday, many restaurants are shuttered. Dress codes are still very relaxed; jeans would be frowned on only in the top restaurants.

WHAT IT COSTS In New Zealand dollars				
$$$$	$$$	$$	$	¢
RESTAURANTS over $30	$20–$30	$15–$20	$10–$15	under $10

Prices are per person for a main course at dinner, or the equivalent.

About the Hotels

Accommodation in the country's capital ranges from no-frills backpacker hostels and innocuous motel units, to classic bed-and-breakfasts in colonial-era villas, to sleek central hotels. Among these, Wellington has a good sprinkling of truly distinctive places. In the suburb of Island Bay, you can stay in a lighthouse or in a castle's tower, both with magnificent views of Cook Strait and the South Island mountain ranges. A couple of places target women travelers; there's a central hostel with a women-only floor plus a women-only guesthouse in the laid-back suburb of Aro Valley. And on the sunny slopes of Mt. Victoria, a Wellington author has turned her home into a B&B for book lovers.

As more people move into the city, apartments moonlighting as "serviced-apartment" hotels are gaining steam. Rates are significantly more expensive than those of the average motel, but the apartments, such as City Life Wellington, are a good option if you're planning to stay a while. Most of these apartment/hotels have weekend or long-term specials.

Most lodgings generally do not have air-conditioning, but the temperate weather in Wellington rarely warrants it.

WHAT IT COSTS In New Zealand dollars				
$$$$	$$$	$$	$	¢
HOTELS over $300	$200–$300	$125–$200	$75–$125	under $75

Prices are for a standard double room in high season, including 12.5% tax.

When to Visit

November to mid-April are the best months weather-wise in the Wellington area. Most establishments are open (apart from Christmas Day, New Year's Day, and Good Friday). Everything is particularly busy during the summer school holidays from mid-December to the end of January; book well ahead if you're traveling during this holiday period. From February to April, you can expect fewer crowds and many brilliant, warm days. Winters bring more rain, but they're rarely bitterly cold. Do be prepared for unpredictable weather; rain and southerly gales, though they may not linger, are possible even during the summer.

WELLINGTON

The city of Wellington nestles between the sea and the Tararua Ranges, which tower almost 3,000 feet. Colored roofs cascade down the steep hillsides, creating a vibrant collage against a spectacular green backdrop. An old brick monastery peers down on a jigsaw of masts and sails in the marina; alongside the marina is the impressive Te Papa museum. Mod-

TOP REASONS TO GO

ARTS & CULTURE

Even before director Peter Jackson gave the local film industry three shots in the arm with the blockbuster *Lord of the Rings* trilogy—earning Wellington the moniker "Wellywood"—the city offered culture vultures plenty of pickings. The national symphony, ballet, and opera are all headquartered here. And the biennial New Zealand International Arts Festival, with its extensive program of drama, music, dance, and other arts events, attracts visitors both from all over the country and from overseas.

A WEALTH OF WINERIES

You can easily spend a day wine tasting your way through the Wairarapa; this lovely rural area that only a few years ago was predominantly agricultural is now home to more than 30 vineyards.

ECLECTIC CUISINE

It's been said that in Wellington you can visit a different restaurant for every day of the year—and though that is an exaggeration, it's probably a pretty slight one. The city's eateries allow you to sample foods from dozens of different countries, and they also serve down-to-earth Kiwi tucker. Grabbing a table at an outdoor café, and looking out over the beautiful waters of the harbor, only enhances the dining experience.

WATERFRONT RELAXATION

Wandering along the Wellington waterfront is one of the most pleasurable ways to spend a day in this region. You can pay a leisurely visit (for free!) to Te Papa Tongarewa, one of the country's best museums. Or you can walk to Oriental Bay, where on a fine day you can join the local residents in jogging, swimming, riding a bike, or people-watching. In the afternoon, have a seat at one of the many waterfront cafés, order a meal or a glass of local wine, and just drink in the scenery.

6

ern high-rise buildings gaze over Port Nicholson, surely one of the finest natural anchorages in the world. Known to local Māori as The Great Harbor of Tara, its two massive arms form the "jaws of the fish of Maui" (Maui is the name of a god from Māori legend). The interisland and east–west ferries churn patterns on the green water while seabirds preen and survey the scene. On the waterfront, the Westpac Trust Stadium, the place for rugby matches and rock concerts, dominates the skyline.

Sometimes referred to as "the windy city," Wellington has been the seat of government since 1865. The Parliamentary enclave with its distinctive "Beehive" building stands close by a lively city center. Civic Square is the heart of town. Lambton Quay is part of a waterfront constructed on land reclaimed from the waters of Port Nicholson and, with Willis Street and Cuba Street, forms a bustling shopping area. Courtenay Place is the center of the entertainment district. Thorndon, the oldest part of the city—notable for its many historic wooden houses—lies just north of the Parliamentary district. At the southern end of the harbor, Norfolk pines line the broad sweep of Oriental Bay, a suburb with a small beach and a wide promenade, backed by a clutch of fine art deco buildings and some of the most expensive real estate in the city.

Exploring Wellington

Driving around central Wellington can be frustrating, because of the many narrow one-way streets, but it's an easy place to get around on foot. The compact area around Lambton Quay and on to Cuba Street is flat and comfortable for walking. The stroll along the waterfront around toward Oriental Bay and beyond offers outstanding sea views. If you want to head for the hills, take it easy—take the cable car.

A GOOD WALK

Begin at the **Kelburn Cable Car** ❶ terminus in Cable Car Lane off Lambton Quay, opposite Grey Street. Taking the cable car is a good way to get up high to see the city's layout—and end up walking down many of the hills instead of up them.

Leave the Kelburn Terminal and double back on your immediate right through the Uplands Road entrance to the **Wellington Botanic Garden** ❷. Take the farthest right of the three paths and head downhill about 10 minutes, taking in views over the harbor and city. You'll pass a Henry Moore bronze and then reach the **Lady Norwood Rose Garden** ❸, with more than 100 rose cultivars spilling out their blossoms and fragrance between November and the end of April.

Tear yourself away from the roses and walk to the right around the enclosed Anderson Park, following the sign to Bolton Street Memorial Park, site of the city's historic cemeteries. At the end of this short road, turn right to see the **John Seddon Memorial** ❹, dedicated to the remarkable early-20th-century prime minister. Close to the memorial, a track, with three flights of steps, zigzags down the hill. At the bottom, cross Bowen Street, walk downhill, take the path to your left, and climb narrow **Ascot Street** ❺, with its wonderful old city cottages.

Turn right into **Tinakori Road** ❻. Another fact of early life in Wellington is illustrated by No. 306, the pasta shop. Pressed for want of level ground, the residents of early Wellington tended to build tall, narrow houses. This example—one room wide and five stories high—took things to extremes. Just below the house, make a short detour to see the three superbly kept timber houses side by side in Upton Terrace. Behind a green fence a few steps farther down Tinakori Road is **Premier House,** the official residence of the prime minister.

Continue down Tinakori Road. Just beyond the Hobson Street Bridge look for 25 Tinakori Road, the **Katherine Mansfield House** ❼, where the celebrated writer was born (as Kathleen Beauchamp) and lived the first five years of her life.

Turn back along Tinakori Road to the Hobson Street overpass, and on the far side of the motorway, turn right to walk through the elms of Katherine Mansfield Memorial Park. Turn left around the rather stern compound of the U.S. Embassy and walk down Murphy Street, which becomes Mulgrave Street, to **Old St. Paul's Cathedral** ❽, one of the country's wooden Gothic Revival gems. Just next door are the **Archives New Zealand** ⑨, a trove of historic documents. From here, turn right into Aitken Street, where the modern building on the right is another scholarly hot spot, the **National Library** ⑩, housing the nation's largest collection of books. Cross Molesworth Street and walk through the gate to the various **Parliament Buildings** ⑪ on the far side. Left of Parliament House, the **Executive Office Building** ⑫, alias the Beehive, is the strange-looking office space for government officials. Walk down the hill from the Beehive to the tremendous wooden **Original Government Buildings** ⑬.

The wide street curving behind the bronze lions is Lambton Quay. As its name suggests, this was once Wellington's waterfront. All the land between your feet and the present-day shoreline has been reclaimed, and brass markers at intervals on the sidewalk show just how much of downtown Wellington stands on reclaimed land. From this point, the shops of the city center are within easy walking distance along Lambton Quay, and if you cut off to the left down Brandon or Panama street, you'll reach Customhouse Quay and the present-day harborside. At Queens Wharf, the **Museum of Wellington, City and Sea** ⑭ occupies a former warehouse. Walk along and around the wharf and up the steps into Frank Kitts Park, site of many an outdoor concert. Your route continues through the small park, down around the rowing club basin, and across the wooden bridge on Cable Street into **Civic Square** ⑮, an expanse containing the library, town hall, **City Gallery of Wellington** ⑯, cafés, and some thought-provoking public sculptures. From the bridge, you'll have glimpsed the imposing shell of the national museum, **Te Papa Tongarewa–Museum of New Zealand** ⑰; reach it on foot by going back over the bridge and heading across the waterfront. Note the *Hikitia,* the floating crane that's been a familiar harbor sight for more than 70 years. One of her saddest jobs was helping to demolish the wreck of the *Wahine,* a ferry that sank in 1968. Stop for a beer in one of the waterfront pubs and take in the stunning harbor views.

Timing

You could briskly walk the route outlined above in four hours, stopping to take in the views, but this doesn't allow for time in the museums. To spend some time in the Parliament buildings or the main museums—Te Papa and the Museum of City and Sea being the best draws—you should count on a seven-hour day, including a stop for lunch downtown. Better yet, split this walk over two days. In this case, do the cable car, Botanic Gardens, and Parliament area on one day, and save downtown, shopping, and museums for Day 2.

Sights to See

⑨ **Archives New Zealand.** History buffs should make a beeline here, as these national archives offer a treasure trove of documents, photographs, and maps. One highlight, displayed in the Constitution Room, is *Te Tiriti o Waitangi,* the Treaty of Waitangi. This controversial 1840 agreement between the British crown and hundreds of Māori chiefs is considered the founding document of modern New Zealand. (*See* the CloseUp box *in* Chapter 2.) Outside the Constitution Room is a bowl of water called a *wai whakanoa.* Because documents in the Constitution Room are associated with the dead and regarded as *tapu* (taboo),

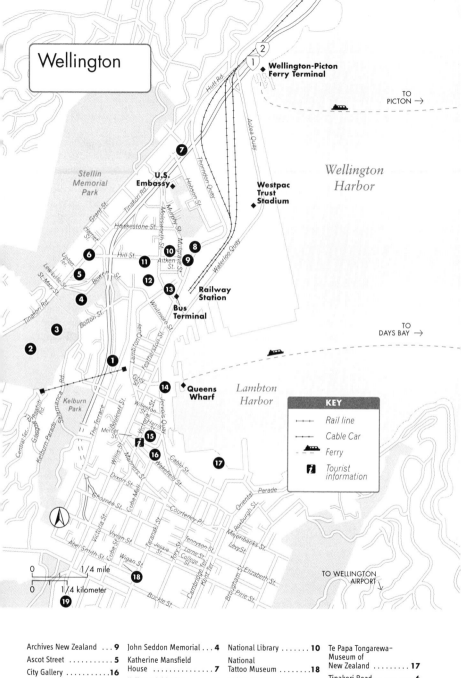

Wellington

Wellington-Picton Ferry Terminal

TO PICTON →

Wellington Harbor

U.S. Embassy

Stellin Memorial Park

Westpac Trust Stadium

Railway Station

Bus Terminal

TO DAYS BAY →

Kelburn Park

Queens Wharf

Lambton Harbor

KEY

Rail line	
Cable Car	
Ferry	
Tourist information	

TO WELLINGTON AIRPORT

0 — 1/4 mile
0 — 1/4 kilometer

visitors are invited to sprinkle a little of the water over themselves after leaving the room to lift the tapu and return to the land of the living.

The oldest document on display is the Declaration of Independence of the Northern Chiefs, signed by 34 northern Māori chiefs on October 28, 1835, a confederation agreement that led up to the Waitangi treaty. Also on view is the 1893 Women's Suffrage Petition, which led to New Zealand becoming the world's first nation to grant women the vote. ⊠ *10 Mulgrave St., Thorndon* ☎ *04/499–5595* ⊕ *www.archives.govt.nz* ⊡ *Free* ⊘ *Weekdays 9–5, Sat. 9–1.*

⑤ Ascot Street. The tiny, doll-like cottages along Ascot were built in the 1870s, and this remains the finest example of a 19th-century streetscape in Wellington. A bench at the top end of the street has been thoughtfully provided in the shady courtyard if you need to catch your breath. ⊠ *Off Glenmore St. and Tinakori Rd. northeast of Wellington Botanic Garden, Thorndon.*

Bolton Street Memorial Park. Soon after its foundation in 1840, the new city needed a cemetery. Burials until 1892 were conducted on this site (now a landscaped park) and divided into Anglican, Roman Catholic, and Jewish plots. The surviving gravestones, now entwined by roses and shrubs, provide a snapshot of early colonial life and death. ⊠ *Bolton St. northeast of Wellington Botanic Garden, Thorndon.*

★ ⑯ City Gallery Wellington. Whether it's the latest exhibition of New Zealand's contemporary artists, an international collection on tour, or just the gallery's café, there are plenty of reasons to put Wellington's eyes-and-ears-on-the-arts on your schedule. City Gallery Wellington is an excellent representation of New Zealand's dynamic contemporary culture—something you won't see much of in the countryside. The gallery has no permanent collection, so its exhibits change constantly; you might be in town during a show by anyone from the major New Zealand painter Colin McCahon to Tracey Emin, one of the hot Young British Artists. Other attractions include the Michael Hirschfeld Gallery, dedicated to showing Wellington artists, and the popular Nikau Café, which serves some of the city's best coffee. In addition to free tours every weekend, City Gallery runs an extensive and engaging events program, including talks by local and international artists, films, and dance performances. ⊠ *Civic Sq., Wakefield St.* ☎ *04/801–3021* ⊕ *www.city-gallery.org.nz* ⊡ *Most exhibitions free; charges for special exhibits vary* ⊘ *Daily 10–5.*

⑮ Civic Square. Wellington's modernist Civic Square is the most visible symbol of the cultural vitality of Wellington. Reminiscent of an Italian piazza, it is both a social hub and a delightful sanctuary from the traffic, with its outdoor cafés, benches, lawns, and harbor viewpoints. The **City Gallery** (see above), perhaps the nation's finest art space, the library, and the Town Hall concert venue are all just steps apart. Architect Ian Athfield's steel sculptures of *nikau* palms are a marvel, and Māori artist Para Matchitt contributed the impressionistic sculptures flanking the wide wooden bridge that connects the square to the harbor. With its sweeping water views, this bridge is a popular spot for picnics or as a place to sit and dream. ⊠ *Wakefield, Victoria, and Harris Sts.*

⑲ The Colonial Cottage Museum. Built in 1858 as a family home by immigrant carpenter William Wallis, this cottage is Wellington's oldest remaining building. With its steep shingled roof and matchboard ceilings, kauri wood paneling and somber Victorian wallpapers, the house has been kept almost completely in its original state. The spinning wheel, smoke-blackened cooking pot, hand-pegged rugs, and oil lamps re-create the atmosphere of those pioneer days. Outside, there's a handmade butter churn and a garden where flowers and herbs bloom in a riot of color and perfume in the summer. ⊠ *68 Nairn St.* ☎ *04/384–9122* ⊕ *www.colonialcottagemuseum.co.nz* ⊡ *$4* ⊙ *Late Dec.–late Apr., daily noon–4; early May–late Dec., Wed.–Sun. noon–4.*

⑫ Executive Office Building. It would be difficult to imagine a more complete contrast in architectural styles than that of the stately Parliament House and the Executive Office Building. Known for obvious reasons as the Beehive, it contains the offices of government ministers and their staffs. Locals are now used to the building, and the initial flurry of jokes such as "What's buzzing in the Beehive?" or "We always knew our politicians spent most of their time going round in circles" has died down. ⊠ *Molesworth St.*

④ John Seddon Memorial. This life-size portrait statue is dedicated to the colorful and popular liberal politician who hailed from the United Kingdom and was New Zealand's longest-serving prime minister—his tenure ran from 1893 to 1906. Under Seddon's leadership, New Zealand became the first country to give women voting rights and to pay its citizens an old-age pension. ⊠ *Bolton Street Memorial Park, northeast end of Wellington Botanic Garden, Thorndon.*

⑦ Katherine Mansfield House. Here the writer, née Kathleen Beauchamp, came into the world (1888) and lived the first five years of her life. Mansfield left to pursue her career in the wider world of Europe when she was 20, but many of her short stories are set in Wellington. A year before her death in 1923, she wrote, "New Zealand is in my very bones. What wouldn't I give to have a look at it!" The house, which has been restored as a typical Victorian family home, contains furnishings, photographs, and videos that elucidate Mansfield's life and times. ⊠ *25 Tinakori Rd., Thorndon* ☎ *04/473–7268* ⊡ *$5.50* ⊙ *Tues.–Sun. 10–4.*

① Kelburn Cable Car. The Swiss-built funicular railway makes a short but sharp climb to Kelburn Terminal, from which there are great views across parks and city buildings to Port Nicholson. Sit on the left side during the six-minute journey for the best scenery. ⊠ *280 Lambton Quay, at Grey St. and Upland Rd.* ☎ *04/472–2199* ⊕ *www.wellingtonnz.com/ cablecar* ⊡ *$1.80 each way* ⊙ *Departures about every 10 min, weekdays 7 AM–10 PM, weekends 9 AM–10 PM.*

NEED A BREAK?
At the airy **Dux Café** (⊠ Level 2, Capital on the Quay ☎ 04/473–0134), sit overlooking Lambton Quay for a light meal, perhaps the chicken-and-apricot frittata or a salmon *ficelle* (sandwich on French bread) with tomato, pesto, and Brie. It's closed Sunday.

★ ❸ **Lady Norwood Rose Garden.** On a fine summer day you couldn't find a better place to go for a sniff and a smile. The rose garden is in fact the most popular part of the ⇨ **Wellington Botanic Garden.** Situated on a plateau, the formal circular layout consists of 106 beds, each planted with a single variety of modern and traditional shrubs. Climbing roses cover a brick-and-timber colonnade on the perimeter. Adjacent to the rose beds, the Begonia House conservatory is filled with tender plants and has a teahouse. ⊠ *North end of Wellington Botanic Garden, Tinakori Rd., for parking lot* ☎ *04/801–3071* ✉ *Donation requested* ⏱ *Begonia House daily 10–4, main gardens daily sunrise–sunset.*

★ ⑭ **Museum of Wellington, City and Sea.** You can smell the hessian sacks, hear the gulls, and see the (mechanical) rats scuttling around in this refurbished 1892 bond store, now a museum that vividly portrays the history of the original Māori tribes and of the European settlers who came here around 1840. Spread over three floors, the displays cover work, leisure, crime, and education in 19th-century Wellington. Holographic effects bring to startling life two Māori legends, and in the Wahine Gallery, exhibits and a short film depict the 1968 *Wahine* ferry sinking that cost 51 lives. The Plimmer's Ark Gallery tells the story of John Plimmer, known as the "Father of Wellington" for his work in developing the city. You can see **Plimmer's Ark,** the excavated remains of the ship *Inconstant,* wrecked in 1849 on Pencarrow Head, in the Old Bank Arcade, a shopping center on Lambton Quay. Plimmer had bought the wreck and intended to turn it into a shop; its remains were discovered in 1997. ⊠ *The Bond Store, Queens Wharf* ☎ *04/472–8904* ⊕ *www. museumofwellington.co.nz* ✉ *Free* ⏱ *Daily 10–5.*

⑩ **National Library.** Opposite the Parliament Buildings you'll find the country's national library, stuffed with rich holdings. The Alexander Turnbull Library, a "library within a library," specializes in documentary materials about New Zealand and the Pacific. Its books, manuscripts, photographs, newspapers, maps, oral history tapes, and more are open for genealogy research. Public exhibitions are regularly held in the National Library Gallery, and murals and contemporary artworks are displayed throughout the building. The Gallery also runs a lively public events program. ⊠ *Molesworth St. at Aitken St., Thorndon* ☎ *04/ 474–3000* ⊕ *www.natlib.govt.nz* ✉ *Free* ⏱ *Weekdays 9–5, Sat. 9–1.*

⑱ **National Tattoo Museum of New Zealand.** You won't miss the entrance here, as it's guarded by massive Māori-style sculptures; inside, this small museum gives a fascinating glimpse of body art, from biceps to buttocks. Tattooing is an important part of Māori culture; like a coat of arms, a traditional *moko* (tattoo) demonstrates a person's heritage. The volunteer-run collection introduces the art with carvings, pictures, and plenty of literature. You might even catch a video of the procedure. One shows a 74-year-old Māori woman having her chin moko renewed the traditional way: her skin is carved with a bone chisel . . . and she doesn't utter a word of complaint. If you're inspired, you can get decorated yourself in one of the three tattoo studios at the rear; the country's only female tattoo artist might picture you in a different light. ⊠ *42 Abel Smith St.* ☎ *04/385– 6444* ⊕ *www.mokomuseum.org.nz* ✉ *$5* ⏱ *Tues.–Sat. noon–5:30.*

8 Old St. Paul's Cathedral. Consecrated in 1866, the church is a splendid example of the English Gothic Revival style executed in native timbers. Even the trusses supporting the roof transcend their mundane function with splendid craftsmanship. ⊠ *Mulgrave St., Thorndon* ☎ *04/473–6722* 🖃 *Free* ⊙ *Daily 10–5.*

NEED A BREAK? **At Stanley Road** (⊠ Aitken and Mulgrave Sts. ☎ 04/499–2898), nab an outdoor table to catch the sun while you refuel with some coffee and a delicious slice of banana-walnut loaf or chocolate ganache cake. It's closed Sunday.

13 Original Government Buildings. This second-largest wooden structure in the world is now home to Victoria University's law faculty. It's an extraordinary conceit—built in 1876 and designed to look like stone, it was instead entirely fashioned from kauri timber. Inside are historic exhibits about the building and a Department of Conservation information center, though it's the exterior that most captivates. ⊠ *15 Lambton Quay* ☎ *04/472–7356* 🖃 *Free* ⊙ *Weekdays 9–4:30, weekends 10–3.*

11 Parliament Buildings. The three structures that compose the Parliament Buildings are open for public tours. The eye-catching pink Gothic Revival structure is the **Parliamentary Library,** a soaring, graceful building compared with the ponderous gray bulk of the **Parliament House** next door. One-hour tours of the buildings explain the parliamentary process in detail. The **Debating Chamber,** where legislation is presented, debated, and voted on, is a copy of that in the British Houses of Parliament at Westminster, right down to the Speaker's mace and the dispatch boxes. There's fine Māori artwork in the **Māori Affairs Select Committee Room,** at the front of Parliament House; and your tour may even step into the Executive Office Building, known popularly as the **Beehive.** ⊠ *Molesworth St.* ☎ *04/471–9999* ⊕ *www.ps.parliament.govt.nz* 🖃 *Free* ⊙ *Tours depart on the hr weekdays 10–4, Sat. 10–3, Sun. noon–3.*

Premier House. The official residence of New Zealand's prime minister was a simple cottage when first erected in 1843, though it has increased in size and grandeur somewhat since then. Prime ministers remained in residence until 1935, when the new Labour government, caught up in its reforming zeal, turned it into a dental clinic. The house had fallen into disrepair by the early 1990s. Since then it has been restored—and the prime minister has moved back in. The house isn't open to the public. ⊠ *260 Tinakori Rd., Thorndon.*

⟳ **17 Te Papa Tongarewa–Museum of New Zealand.** This bright, lively museum
FodorśChoice remains one of New Zealand's major attractions, largely because it
★ provides such a good introduction to the country's people, cultures, landforms, flora, and fauna. Unusual exhibits include a simulated earthquake experience and a visit to a *marae* (Māori meetinghouse), where a *pōwhiri* (Māori greeting involving song and speeches) welcomes you. You can also explore an outdoor forest area with moa (the extinct, ostrichlike native bird) bones and glowworms or delve into the stories of New Zealand's early European migrants. In the Time Warp area, a sort of theme park where most activities have additional fees, you can simulate a bungy jump or leap three generations ahead to Wellington in 2055.

Four discovery centers allow children to weave, hear storytelling, and learn a bit of Māori through song. ⊠ *Cable St.* ☏ *04/381–7000* ⊕ *www. tepapa.govt.nz* ✉ *Free, some exhibits cost up to $8* ⊙ *Fri.–Wed. 10–6, Thurs. 10–9.*

❻ Tinakori Road. The lack of suitable local stone combined with the collapse of most of Wellington's brick buildings in the earthquake of 1848 ensured the almost exclusive use of timber for building here in the second half of the 19th century. Most carpenters of the period had learned their skills as cabinetmakers and shipwrights in Europe, and the sturdy houses in this street are a tribute to their craftsmanship. Two notables are the tall and narrow No. 306 and ⇨ **Premier House.**

★ ❼ Wellington Botanic Garden. In the hills overlooking downtown is a concentration of beautifully varied terrain. Woodland gardens under native and exotic trees fill the valleys, water-loving plants line a pond and mountain streams, and lawns spread over flatter sections with beds of bright seasonal bulbs and annuals. The lovely ⇨ **Lady Norwood Rose Garden** is in the northeast part of the garden. **Carter Observatory and Planetarium,** the only one of its kind in New Zealand, has public displays and programs, including evening telescope viewings, which are great opportunities for those from the Northern Hemisphere to learn about the southern night sky. If you don't want to walk the hill up to the garden, the ⇨ **Kelburn Cable Car** can take you. Or take the No. 12 bus (direction: Karori) from Lambton Quay to the main (Glenmore Street) entrance. ⊠ *Tinakori Rd. for parking lot; main entrances on Upland Rd. (for cable car) and Glenmore St.* ☏ *04/801–3071 gardens, 04/472–8167 observatory and planetarium* ⊕ *www.carterobs.ac.nz* ✉ *Main gardens free, Carter Observatory $7, planetarium $10* ⊙ *Main gardens daily sunrise–sunset; observatory and planetarium Mon., Wed., and Fri. 10–5; Tues., Thurs., and Sat. 10–5 and 6:30–10:30 PM; Sun. noon–5.*

Around Wellington

The Hutt Valley. A 10-minute drive north of Wellington on State Highway 2—with magnificent harbor views all the way—leads you to the Hutt Valley and its namesake river. Attractions in the bustling **Hutt City** include **The Dowse Art Gallery** (⊠ 45 Laings Rd., Hutt City ☏ 04/570–6500), which has a permanent Māori art exhibit plus rotating shows by local craftspeople, and the cosmopolitan area of tempting shops and cafés around Jackson Street. Don't miss the small but interesting **Petone Settlers Museum** (⊠ The Esplanade, Hutt City ☏ 04/568–8373), on the waterfront of Wellington Harbor near the landing site of the first organized European settlement in New Zealand.

The Petone Esplanade on the eastern side of the harbor, overlooked by houses clinging to steep bush-clad hills, winds about 8 km (5 mi) through the suburb of **Eastbourne.** Stop in the tiny shopping area for an al fresco bite before driving on to where the road eventually dies away to become a 4-km (2½-mi) walking track, following the coast to **Pencarrow Head** and its lighthouse, with expansive views across the strait.

Back in Hutt City, the **Hutt River Trail** starts at Hikoikoi Reserve on Petone Marine Parade near the Hutt River mouth. Specifically for walk-

CLOSE UP

Matui Island

A WONDERFUL PLACE to spend a day walking and exploring, the Matui Island Scientific and Historic Reserve lies in Wellington Harbour approximately 8 km (5 mi) from the city. Traveling here by boat is one of the most popular day trips for visitors to the city, especially those with kids; the island has lots of walking tracks, great beaches for swimming, good picnic spots, and opportunities to see whales, dolphins, penguins, and other birds (sharp eyes may also pick out skinks and other small lizards, and giant weta insects along the paths). Because the boats bring only a limited number of passengers to the island at a time, it's never crowded.

Although the 62-acre island was opened as a DOC reserve only in 1995, it has an interesting place in New Zealand's history. From the early 1880s until around 1980, it was used as a quarantine station by early European settlers for both humans and animals—including dogs, cattle, sheep, red deer, llamas, and other livestock—on their way into the country. During the world wars, it was also used as a place of internment for aliens considered a security threat.

In 1981 Matui became a project of the Royal Forest and Bird Protection

Society. Volunteers began planting trees that year, to replace vegetation that had previously been cleared to allow grazing for quarantined animals. Many other native plants that flourished before the arrival of European settlers have also been replanted, and native insects such as wetas have been reintroduced. The island now hosts breeding grounds for a variety of seabird species.

There is no town and no accommodation on the island; it's strictly a place to enjoy natural beauty for a few hours at a time. The few man-made structures on Matui today include the old quarantine station, and gun emplacements from World War II—which were never used, and which remain on the southernmost summit of the island. An automated lighthouse built in 1900 to replace the original structure from 1866 also still sends out its southward beacon to ships traveling from Wellington Harbour.

The island can be reached by the Dominion Post East/West ferry service; there are nine round-trip runs made from Wellington Harbour per day. For more information, see Boat Tours in Wellington Essentials.

---

ers and cyclists, this scenic trail follows the river for more than 32 km (20 mi) between Hutt City and Upper Hutt.

Back on State Highway 2 heading north, the views of the distant Tararua Ranges, snow covered in the winter, might make you think you are in the South Island. If you're a *Lord of the Rings* fan, stop by the **Dry Creek Quarry,** where the scenes of Helms Deep and Minas Tirith were filmed; it's at the bottom of Haywards Hill Road—look for the traffic lights for the turnoff from State Highway 2. Farther into the Hutt Valley on State Highway 2 is the pleasant small city of **Upper Hutt.** Have a coffee at the bright **Expressions Art & Entertainment Centre** (⊠ 836 Fergusson Dr., Upper Hutt ☎ 04/527–2168 ⊕ www.expressions.org.nz), a combination art gallery, theater, and event space.

From Upper Hutt, continuing north on State Highway 2 leads to the Wairarapa region, but just beyond Upper Hutt, look for **Kaitoke Regional Park** (⊠ Waterworks Rd., off State Hwy. 2 ☎ 04/526–7322 for rangers), a great camping and picnic spot with pleasant walks by the river. In the park, *LOTR* fans can check out the bridge, which stood in for Rivendell, the rallying place for elves. Pause by the crystal-clear river, flanked by towering trees and native bush, and listen to the birdsong.

Karori Wildlife Sanctuary. Just minutes from downtown Wellington, these 623 acres of regenerating forest have become a sanctuary for some of New Zealand's endangered species. A predator-proof fence surrounds the haven, where rare wildlife such as the little spotted kiwi, saddleback, bellbird, and *kaka* (an indigenous parrot) have been introduced; stitchbirds also use the refuge as a breeding ground. Two former city reservoirs have been turned into a wetlands area; additional native plants and birds are being introduced there according to a carefully controlled plan. You can walk along bush tracks and stroll around the lakes, or join one of the volunteer-led guided tours. ⊠ *31 Waiapu Rd., Karori* ☎ *04/920–9200* ⊕ *www.sanctuary.org.nz* ▱ *$8* ⊗ *Dec.–Mar., daily 10–5; Apr.–Nov., weekdays 10–4, weekends 10–5.*

★ **Maori Treasures.** A visit to this exceptional Māori enterprise gives you a wonderful, firsthand look at Māori arts and culture. Based on the Waiwhetu marae (meetinghouse) about 21 km (13 mi) from Wellington, the complex showcases artisans at work carving, weaving, or fashioning instruments. You might even hear someone playing the nose flute or get your hands on a woven cloak. There is a traditionally carved *waka* (war canoe) on display; other examples of carving and artwork produced in the studio are for sale in the gift shop. Guided tours can be arranged through Flat Earth New Zealand Experiences (see Tours in Wellington Essentials, below). ⊠ *58 Guthrie St., Hutt City* ☎ *04/939–9630* ⊗ *Daily 9–4; tours as arranged.*

★ **Otari Native Botanic Garden.** Anyone with even the slightest interest in native New Zealand flora should spend an afternoon at Otari, just outside the city. Devoted to gathering and preserving indigenous plants, Otari's collection is the largest of its kind. With clearly marked bushwalks and landscape demonstration gardens, it aims to educate the public and thereby ensure the survival of New Zealand's unique plant life. While in the garden, you'll learn to identify much of the plant life in the forest, from the various *blechnum* ferns underfoot to the tallest trees towering overhead. An aerial walkway crosses high above the bush to offer an unusual vantage point over the gardens. Look and listen for the native birds that flock to this haven: the bellbird (*korimako*), gray duck (*parera*), New Zealand wood pigeon (*kereru*), silvereye (*tauhou*), and *tūī*, among others. Take the No. 14 Wilton bus from downtown (20 minutes) and ask the driver to let you off at the gardens. ⊠ *Wilton Rd., Wilton* ☎ *04/475–3245* ⊕ *www.owb.co.nz* ▱ *Free* ⊗ *Daily dawn–dusk.*

CLOSE UP

The Akatarawa Valley

WINDING THROUGH THE STEEP bush-clad hills north of Wellington, the narrow road to the Akatarawa Valley (which, in the Māori language, means "place of tangled vines"), may require a degree of driving care, but it leads to a number of hidden gems. About 35 minutes out of Wellington on State Highway 2, turn left at the clearly marked Brown Owl turnoff north of Upper Hutt. About two minutes after the turnoff, look for **Harcourt Park,** where a number of scenes for the *Lord of the Rings* movies were filmed. Nearby, **Harcourt Holiday Park** (☎🖵 04/526-7400) has motel units, tourist flats, cabins, and tent sites in lovely bush surroundings.

Half a mile farther on, a bridge at the junction of the Hutt and Akatarawa rivers leads into the Akatarawa Valley proper. Drive over the bridge, go past the cemetery, and then on the left, look for **The Blueberry Farm** (☎ 04/526-6788), where you can pick your own blueberries (January) or go for a swim in the river. Nearby **Bluebank Blueberry and Emu Farm** (☎🖵 04/526-9540) also grows delicious blueberries and raises the large flightless emus. In winter (July–September), you might be able to watch the chicks hatch, provided you phone in advance.

Continue on to **Efil Doog Garden of Art** (☎ 04/526-7924 ⊕ www.efildoog-nz.com), where Shirley and Ernest Cosgrove tend a stunning 11-acre garden and sculpture display. They also have an art gallery exhibiting some fine early New Zealand paintings. The grounds are magnificent at rhododendron time, October–early December. The garden's open October through March, Wednesday–Sunday; entry is $12.

The winding road crosses some wonderful old trestle bridges over the Akatarawa River before reaching **Staglands Wildlife Reserve** (☎ 04/526-7529 ⊕ www.staglands.co.nz), filled with friendly animals and birds that will eat out of your hand. As you wander through these peaceful 25 acres, meet the kea, kune-kune pigs (a native variety), deer, and wallabies, and feed trout in the pools. Stop into the falcon aviary before picnicking by the river or stopping by the log-cabin café. The reserve is open daily and costs $12.

Look on the right for the tiny wooden Church of St. Andrews, then turn right almost immediately for the **Reikorangi Potteries** (☎ 04/293-5146). Here, Wilf and Jan Wright display local handicrafts and paintings, plus their own pottery. Wander around the small animal park to view rabbits, llamas, wallabies, and a host of different birds, or stroll along the riverbank and perhaps take a swim. If you haven't eaten yet, the café here is a delightful stop. The potteries are open November through March, Tuesday through Sunday, and April through October, Wednesday through Sunday. Admission is $5.

The road continues for about 2 mi to join State Highway 1 at the Waikanae traffic lights, where you can head back to Wellington; from here, you're about 45 minutes north of the city. You can get more information on the Akatarawa Valley from the **Upper Hutt Information Centre** (✉ 84–90 Main St., Upper Hutt ☎ 04/527-2141 ⊕ www.upperhuttcity.com).

★ **Southward Car Museum.** The largest collection of vintage cars in the Southern Hemisphere has more than 300 vehicles on display. A Davis three-wheeler, one of only 17 ever made, was used in the inaugural parade of U.S. President Harry Truman. It stands among Cadillacs, Bugattis, and gleaming Rolls Royces. The motorcycle section is a must for two-wheeler buffs. The museum is just off Highway 1, a 45-minute drive north of Wellington. ⊠ *Otaihanga Rd., Paraparaumu* ☎ *04/297–1221* ⊕ *www.southward.org.nz* ☒ *$7* ☉ *Daily 9–4:30.*

> **AKATRACK-WELLINGTON**
>
> Liz and Keith Budd now offer two-day walks through the Akatarawa Valley for active groups of up to six. The walks, which take five-six hours, operate from October to April 30 and include all transport, luggage transfer, and comfortable accommodation. Gardens and wildlife park admissions and meals are also included in the cost of $275. Bookings are essential. (☎ 04/526-4867 🖷 04/526-3872 ⊕ www.akatrack.co.nz)

☺ **Wellington Zoo.** Along with various exotic birds and animals at this small zoo, pleasantly sited on a hillside, look for the native critters such as *tuatara* (an ancient species of reptile), geckos, weta (large, grasshopper-like insects), kiwis, and kea birds. You can also enjoy "open encounters" with giraffes, red pandas, and otters—where you get to feed and touch the animals. It's about 5 km (3 mi) from central Wellington; Buses 10 and 23 run there. ⊠ *200 Daniell St., Newtown* ☎ *04/381–6750* ⊕ *www.wellingtonzoo.com* ☒ *$10* ☉ *Daily 9:30–5.*

OFF THE BEATEN PATH

THE RIMUTAKA INCLINE – The Rimutaka Incline Railway operated from 1878 until 1955, connecting Wellington and the Wairarapa. Special locomotives known as Fell engines that pulled on a center line were needed to haul trains up the steepest grade in the country. In 1955, a tunnel superseded the Rimutaka Incline route, the tracks were torn up, and the former railway route was converted into a path for walking and cycling. The track runs for about 16 km (10 mi) from Kaitoke, just north of Upper Hutt, to a parking area just beyond Cross Creek near Featherston on the Wairarapa side. It takes about five hours to walk the length. The track retains a feel of rail history as it passes through two old tunnels, several bridges, and some wild countryside. The track is mostly compacted gravel, but it can get muddy in bad weather. Beware, also, of high winds on the Wairarapa side; a train was once blown off the tracks here! To arrange transport at both ends of the track, contact Fred Roberts of **Valley Shuttles** (☎ 04/973–8150, 027/248–1745 cell). The only remaining Fell engine is now on display at the Fell Locomotive Museum in the Wairarapa (⇨ Masterton *in* The Wairarapa, *below*).

Where to Eat

$$$$ ✕ **Logan Brown.** Partners Steve Logan and Al Brown have created a winner in this stylishly renovated 1920s bank building. There's an aquarium tank set into the bar top, so that fish swim by under your cocktail. At a table, you could try the *paua* (akin to abalone) ravioli with fresh

Fodor's Choice
★

Kapiti Coast & Kapiti Island

A TRIP UP THE WEST COAST from Wellington is not to be missed if you have a car and a day to spare. State Highway 1 will take you north, and about a half hour out of the city you'll hit the coast at Paremata. From here you can follow South Highway 1 straight up the Kapiti Coast, so called for the view of Kapiti Island. Alternatively, you can take the longer—but infinitely more scenic—drive around the Pauatahanui Inlet and Bird Sanctuary, following the road up and along the ridge of the rugged, winding, and windy Paekakariki Hill. From here you'll have stunning views of the coastline and Kapiti Island. Both routes will take you to **Paekakariki** (pie-*kahk*-a-reeky), a small, artsy beach town.

Paekakariki's draw is the shore, but it's also the main entry point of **Queen Elizabeth Park** (✉ Entrance on Wellington Rd. ☎🖥 04/292–8625), more than 1,000 acres of fields and sand dunes along the coast. The park has a walking trail, horseback riding, mountain biking, and a playground. A little farther up the coast on State Highway 1 is **Lindale Farm** (☎ 04/297–0916), which is home to Kapiti Cheeses and Ice Cream. Along with terrific locally made cheeses, you can try decadent ice cream with Kiwi flavors, such as feijoa or fig and *manuka* honey (manuka is a kind of tea tree). The farm is just past Paekakariki's neighboring town, Paraparaumu.

Paraparaumu is the departure point for one of Wellington's best-kept secrets: **Kapiti Island** (✉ Coastlands Parade ☎ 04/298–8195). The island has been a protected reserve since 1897 and is a fantastic place to hike.

All pests have been eliminated from the island, and birdlife flourishes, including saddlebacks, stitchbirds, and colonies of little spotted and South Island brown kiwi. Don't be surprised if a curious and fearless weka investigates your daypack or unties your shoelaces. Climb to the Tuteremoana lookout point at more than 1,700 feet.

The island's most famous inhabitant was the Ngati Toa chief Te Rauparaha, who took the island by ruse in 1822. From this stronghold, he launched bloodthirsty raids before he was captured in 1846. He died in 1849, but his burial place is a mystery. Old tri-pots (used for melting down whale blubber) on the island bear testimony to the fact that Kapiti was also used as a whaling station in the late 19th century.

The **Department of Conservation** (DOC; ☎ 04/472–7356, www.doc.govt.nz) oversees the island and restricts visitors to 50 a day. You'll need a permit in advance ($9). Book at least three months in advance. Two tour companies provide transportation to the island: **Kapiti Marine Charter** (☎ 0800/433–779) and **Kapiti Island Tours** (☎ 04/472–7356). Boats leave from the beach at Paraparaumu; both companies charge $30 for the round-trip. Once on the island, you'll be taken to the DOC headquarters, where you can get trail maps. For more information about Kapiti Island, contact the Wellington Visitor Information Centre (⇨ Visitor Information *in* Wellington A to Z, *below*) or the **Paraparaumu Visitor Information Center** (☎ 04/298–8195 ⊕ www.naturecoast.co.nz)

basil, followed by wild boar pie with cranberry relish. ⊠ *Cuba St. at Vivian St.* ☎ *04/801–5114* ▦ *AE, DC, MC, V* ☺ *No lunch Sat.*

$$$$ ✕ **White House.** The contemporary menu here is driven by seasonal pro-
Fodor'sChoice duce; you might choose from grilled *cervena* (farmed venison) served
★ with an "orgy" of mushrooms, porcini porridge, and truffle essence. Molten chocolate pudding served with raspberry sorbet and crème fraiche makes for a fine finish. Windows on both floors of the name-sake house, an early-20th-century beach cottage, give stunning views across Oriental Bay and the harbor. ⊠ *232 Oriental Parade* ☎ *04/385–8555* ▦ *AE, DC, MC, V* ☺ *No lunch Sat.–Thurs.*

$$$–$$$$ ✕ **Dockside Restaurant & Bar.** A wooden-beam roof and oiled floor-boards give this former warehouse on the wharf a nautical feel—you can get close to the water, too, outside on the large harborfront deck. Inside or out, it's a lively spot, particularly on Friday nights, when a DJ often spins to a packed house. The menu changes daily but has a seafood bias, with such options as char-grilled Akaroa salmon served with *boc-concini* (small balls of fresh mozzarella). ⊠ *Shed 3, Queens Wharf, Jer-vois Quay* ☎ *04/499–9900* ▦ *AE, DC, MC, V* ⌂ *Reservations essential.*

★ $$$–$$$$ ✕ **Il Casino.** Framed autographs of famous patrons and a gallery of awards point to the lasting popularity of this local dining star. The menu is mainly northern Italian, with lots of pasta choices as well as dishes such as scallops and asparagus sautéed with butter and sage, and rose-mary-roasted rack of lamb. After dinner, you can retire to sit by the fire in the upstairs piano bar. The wine list reads like a brochure for the New Zealand–Italian friendship society, and the service is correct in the old-fashioned way, with a dash of Kiwi warmth. ⊠ *108 Tory St.* ☎ *04/385–7496* ▦ *AE, DC, MC, V.*

$$$–$$$$ ✕ **Shed 5.** Huge windows facing the harbor belie the fact that this his-toric building on the wharf was once a woolshed. Crisp white tablecloths and sparkling tableware gleam under the dark-wood beams in the spa-cious dining room. On the broad-ranging menu, seafood stands out, with choices such as potato-crusted grouper with caramelized pumpkin gnoc-chi. Desserts, such as the banana-and-butterscotch crumble, are rich yet unpretentious. ⊠ *Shed 5, Queens Wharf, Jervois Quay* ☎ *04/499–9069* ▦ *AE, DC, MC, V.*

$–$$$$ ✕ **Great India.** A lengthy menu packs in dozens of authentic Indian dishes, from curries to vegetarian options to meats cooked in the tan-door oven. Specialties include *rogan gosh*, lamb cooked in a thick tomato gravy, and *samba masala*, venison sauced with coconut cream. Sequinned, embroidered wall hangings glint in the soft lighting. The serv-ice is friendly and helpful. ⊠ *141 Manners St.* ☎ *04/384–5755* ▦ *AE, DC, MC, V* ☺ *No lunch weekends.*

$$$ ✕ **Boulcott Street Bistro.** A well-respected institution on the Wellington dining scene, this old colonial-style house conveys both tradition and warmth. Chef Chris Green whips up dishes such as herb-and-pepper-crusted salmon with creamed sweet corn and red pepper. On the dessert list, keep an eye out for the lemon tart with yogurt sorbet. ⊠ *99 Boul-cott St.* ☎ *04/499–4199* ▦ *AE, DC, MC, V* ☺ *No lunch weekends.*

$$$ ✕ **Café Bastille.** This charming French provincial café looks cheery with its lemon walls, plum-color ceilings, and "washing line" hung with posters—and the menu has plenty to cheer about, too. Choices might

include a smoked-eel plate with celeriac remoulade, pickled apples, and horseradish cream. The list of vintages here is written on the mirrors in classic café style. ⊠ *16 Majoribanks St.* ☎ *04/382–9559* ⊟ *AE, DC, MC, V* ⊘ *Closed Sun.*

$$$ ✕ **The Potters Kiln Café.** If you've got weekend wanderlust as well as an appetite, take a drive out to this tiny cottage in the Reikorangi Potteries, 48 km (30 mi) from town. The menu here offers mouthwatering creations such as roasted rack of lamb in a spiced plum sauce, and sticky date pudding topped with hot caramel sauce. Pottery and paintings line the dining room walls, as do interesting curios—an old wooden butter churn stands next to a small accordion. To get here from Wellington, take State Highway 1 north to Waikanae and turn right at the second traffic light. Cross the train tracks, and in about 4½ km (2¾ mi), turn left into the Reikorangi Potteries. Reservations are a good idea. ⊠ *27 Ngatiawa Rd., Reikorangi* ☎ *04/293–5146* ⊟ *MC, V* ⊘ *Closed Mon. and Tues.*

★ **$$–$$$** ✕ **The Back-Bencher Pub & Café.** Right across the way from the Parliament buildings sits this landmark watering hole, where politicians seek out a cold beer after a hot debate. The walls have become a gallery of political cartoons and puppets tweaking government characters and well-known sports figures. The menu is never conservative, and you won't have to "labour" over the prices. The popular vote goes to the fresh steamed mussels tossed in salsa verde. Just don't slurp your soup; you could be sitting next to the prime minister. ⊠ *34 Molesworth St.* ☎ *04/ 474–3065* ⊟ *AE, DC, MC, V.*

★ **$$–$$$** ✕ **The Green Parrot.** Talk about atmosphere: this stalwart, diner-style steak-and-seafood joint, which has been serving meals continuously since 1926, has a grill made from melted-down gun barrels. Kosta Sakoufakis, the welcoming chef and co-owner, makes people feel at home and can talk about American Marines visiting the place during World War II. Celebrities such as Peter Jackson gravitate here, and a mural depicts notable clients ranging from famous writers to two former prime ministers. ⊠ *16 Taranaki St.* ☎ *04/384–6080* ⊟ *AE, DC, MC, V* ⊘ *No lunch.*

$$–$$$ ✕ **Ocean Restaurant & Bar.** With floor-to-ceiling windows giving sweeping views of Evans Bay, this modern restaurant feels a bit like a cruise ship. The menu is varied, and the helpings are generous and well priced. The smoky pork fillet wrapped in Parma ham, served on leek-and-cabbage risotto, is an especially tempting choice. While watching the white horses (whitecaps) gallop across the bay, finish off with banana bread pudding with butterscotch sauce and mango sorbet. ⊠ *301 Evans Bay Parade* ☎ *04/386–1363* ⊟ *DC, MC, V.*

$$ ✕ **Scorpio's Restaurant & Welsh Dragon Bar.** New Zealand's only Welsh restaurant occupies a heritage building with twin domes—it's known locally as the Taj Mahal. A spinning wheel by the open hearth gives a cozy feel to the bar, which serves genuine Welsh beer and mead. In the dining room, you get real home cooking, Welsh-style; try the Cardiff chicken, roasted in honey and lemon and served in a rich red-wine and mushroom gravy. The equally homey desserts include bantaffy pie—bananas in caramel sauce topped with whipped cream. There's live entertainment most nights. This place is literally middle of the road—out on a traffic island between Cambridge and Kent terraces. ⊠ *Cambridge and Kent Terraces* ☎ *04/385–6566* ⊟ *MC, V* ⊘ *Closed Mon.*

Where to Stay & Eat in Wellington

KEY

② Hotels

❶ Restaurants

🛈 Tourist information

Wellington-Picton Ferry Terminal

TO PICTON →

Wellington Harbor

Westpac Trust Stadium

U.S. Embassy

Stellin Memorial Park

Parliament Buildings

Bus Terminal

Railway Station

TO DAYS BAY →

Queens Wharf

Lambton Harbor

Kelburn Park

Civic Square

Te Papa Tongarewa

Oriental Parade

TO WELLINGTON AIRPORT ↓

0   1/4 mile
0   1/4 kilometer

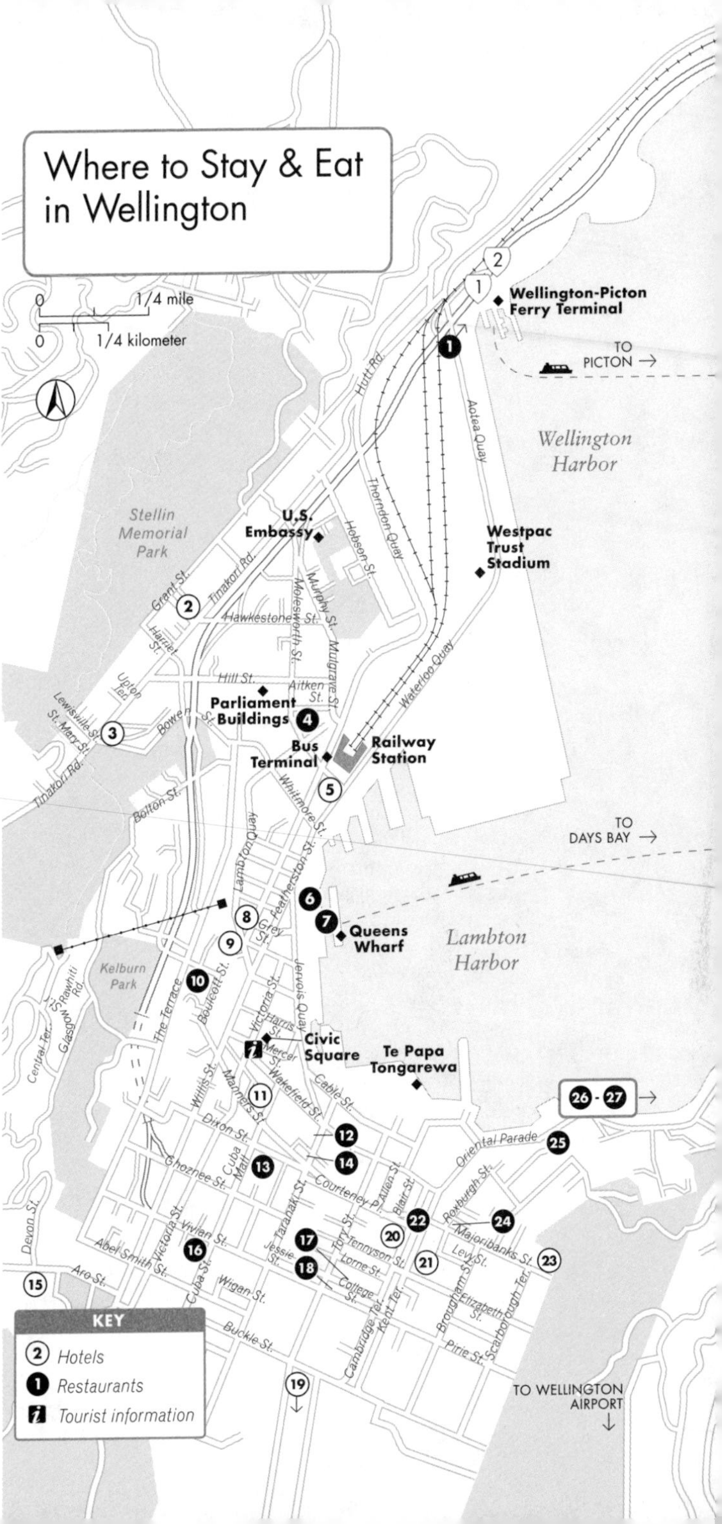

★ $–$$ ✕ **Caffe L'Affare.** The delicious smell of roasting coffee fills the air at this bustling café, where huge steel plates cut from the side of a ship—complete with climbing rungs—cover the walls. Two wooden fans the size of aircraft propellers rotate slowly in the ceiling. The all-day breakfast is popular, and the place is abuzz at lunchtime, too, when your choices might include Vietnamese chicken-and-noodle salad. ⊠ *27 College St.* ☎ *04/385–9748* ▭ *AE, MC, V* ⊗ *No dinner. No lunch Sun.*

★ $–$$ ✕ **Dixon Street Gourmet Deli.** The owner's grandfather opened this establishment in 1920; the friendly staff and excellent pickings have kept it a local favorite ever since. You could snag provisions for a picnic lunch or get a table inside for a bagel with smoked salmon and cream cheese or a tangy slice of lemon cheesecake. ⊠ *45–47 Dixon St.* ☎ *04/384–2436* ▭ *AE, DC, MC, V.*

$–$$ ✕ **Vista.** For a breezy meal and some morning sunshine, grab an outdoor table at this busy café that looks across Oriental Parade to the bustling harbor. Breakfast is available until 4 PM; try the poached eggs on a toasted muffin with hollandaise sauce, to which you can add your choice of ham, spinach, or smoked salmon. In the evening, the fare looks farther afield. You might snare a vegetarian plate—polenta topped with eggplant, peppers, and zucchini and sauced with a green-olive tapenade—or try the char-grilled pork, served on a celeriac puree. ⊠ *106 Oriental Parade* ☎ *04/385–7724* ▭ *AE, DC, MC, V* ⊗ *No dinner Sun.–Tues.*

Where to Stay

$$$$ ▣ **Duxton Hotel Wellington.** Right near the waterfront and Te Papa Tongarewa–Museum of New Zealand, this hotel is also close by the central business district and shopping, with the vibrant entertainment area of Courtney Place literally at the back door. Rooms are decorated in pastel shades, and furnishings include writing desks, tea/coffeemakers, and marble bathrooms with separate bath and shower. Most rooms have stunning views over the harbor or the city. Valet parking is provided, and the hotel is only minutes from the airport. ⊠ *170 Wakefield St.* ☎ *04/473–3900 or 0800/655–555* 🖷 *04/473–3929* ⊕ *www.duxton.com* ↵ *192 rooms ⚒ Restaurant, in-room broadband, bar, laundry facilities* ▭ *AE, DC, MC, V.*

$$–$$$$

FodorsChoice

★

▣ **Hotel InterContinental.** With an ideal location in the heart of the business district, and just a stone's throw from the waterfront, this landmark high-rise gets all the details right. The art deco–inspired foyer is spacious and welcoming, decorated with ferns, orchids, and fruit bowls (help yourself). New Zealand paintings and prints line the walls of the hallways and the guest rooms, which are also done up in a faintly deco style. The basic rooms are small but warmly appointed in russet and gold. The top-end "club rooms" are more modern and stylish; snowy white duvets on the king-size beds stand out against the dark-wood furnishings. The expert staff offer such first-rate touches as a 24-hour car service. ⊠ *Featherston and Grey Sts.* ☎ *04/472–2722* 🖷 *04/472–4724* ⊕ *www.intercontinental.com* ↵ *232 rooms ⚒ Restaurant, café, in-room data ports, indoor pool, gym, sauna, 2 bars, laundry service, convention center, no-smoking floors* ▭ *AE, DC, MC, V.*

$$$ ☒ **CityLife Wellington.** This contemporary all-suite hotel is right in the middle of the city—and if you can snag a suite at a weekend or special summer rate, you've got one of the best-value lodgings in town. Guests have a wide selection of cream-and-white studios and spacious one-, two-, and three-bedroom suites enlivened by Asian-style area rugs. Facilities are similar in all suites and include kitchens, washers, dryers, and dishwashers (though the rooms are also serviced). Despite the central location, you don't get street noise in the rooms. ☒ *300 Lambton Quay* ☎ *04/922–2800 or 0800/368–888* 🖷 *04/922–2803* ⊕ *www.dynasty. co.nz* ⇆ *70 suites* ♿ *Kitchenettes, in-room VCRs, in-room data ports, gym* ▤ *AE, DC, MC, V* ⧗ *BP.*

★ **$$** ☒ **Booklovers B & B.** Residents of the Mount Victoria neighborhood claim to live in the sunniest part of town—the lure of all this sunlight, plus the pretty wooden Victorians and views of the city and harbor, make this one of the most-painted city landscapes. Wellington author Jane Tolerton has set up house in one of these villas and, true to her passion, lined the hallways and many of the rooms with books. Some of the books are free to take away with you (Jane doesn't believe in leaving a book half finished). In addition to books, the big, bright, high-ceilinged rooms are furnished with a hodgepodge of antiques, comfortable sofas, and armchairs. Jane will provide babysitting and long literary chats, as well as a steady supply of homemade oatmeal chocolate-chip cookies. ☒ *123 Pirie St.* ☎ *04/384–2714* ⊕ *www.booklovers.co.nz* ⇆ *2 rooms, 3 suites* ♿ *Babysitting; no a/c* ▤ *AE, DC, MC, V* ⧗ *BP.*

★ **$$** ☒ **The Lighthouse and the Keep.** These two unique properties—a lighthouse and a stone tower—both have stunning views of Cook Strait and the mountain ranges of the South Island. Each three-story building is primarily a one-bedroom accommodation. The Lighthouse has two wraparound balconies, one at the very top of the building, and at the Keep, you can climb through a hatch from the bedroom out onto the roof. The price (on the high end of this category) includes a fully stocked kitchen, including pastries, coffee, and anything you might need to cook your own breakfast. It's always busy here on stormy nights; check the week's weather listings and book quickly. ☒ *326 and 116 The Esplanade, Island Bay, 3 mi (5 km) from central Wellington* ☎🖷 *04/472–4177* ⊕ *www.bnb.co.nz/thelighthouse.html* ⇆ *2 suites* ♿ *Kitchens, microwaves, refrigerators; no a/c, no room phones, no TV at The Keep, no smoking* ▤ *AE, MC, V.*

$–$$ ☒ **Halswell Lodge.** For restaurant, theater, and cinema going, you can't beat this hotel's location, right by the eastern end of Courtenay Place. And you'll find it hard to beat the prices, too. Standard hotel rooms at the front of the building are small and functional. Motel units, with studios or two bedrooms, are set farther back, each with a kitchenette (four of these have whirlpool baths). Finally, there's the restored 1920s villa at the rear of the property; its six superior rooms come with whirlpool baths, cane chairs, burnished wood decor, antique wardrobes, and restored fireplaces. You can use the villa kitchen to prepare light meals. ☒ *21 Kent Terr.* ☎ *04/385–0196* 🖷 *04/385–0503* ⊕ *www.halswell.co. nz* ⇆ *25 rooms, 11 motel units* ♿ *Some kitchenettes, laundry facilities; no a/c* ▤ *AE, DC, MC, V.*

$–$$ 🏠 **The Mermaid Guesthouse for Women.** This turn-of-the-20th-century Vic-
Fodor'sChoice torian villa is in the heart of Aro Valley, one of Wellington's suburbs.
★ Each room has a theme; the midnight-blue ceiling of the "Bengali"
glows with tiny starlike halogen lamps, and the king-bedded "Latino"
is swathed in burgundy, gold, and olive satin and velvet. Rooms look
out onto the hills or to the area's laid-back main street. The self-catering kitchen is stocked with free cereal, although you might prefer heading out to a nearby café or bakery for breakfast. The Mermaid is about
a five-minute stroll from Cuba Street; as the name implies, men (as well
as babies and very young children) are strongly discouraged from staying here. ⊠ *1 Epuni St.* ☎ *04/384–4511* 🖷 *04/976–3525* ⊕ *www.*
mermaid.co.nz ➷ *3 rooms, 1 suite* ⚙ *Kitchen (shared); no a/c, no*
room phones, no TV in some rooms ⊟ *DC.*

$–$$ 🏠 **Shepherd's Arms Speight's Ale House.** New Zealand's oldest hotel, the
Shepherd's Arms has been refurbished to approximate its original 19th-
century state. Two rooms have four-poster beds, all have deep-blue carpets and burgundy curtains, and all are fairly small, especially the three
single rooms, which share a bathroom. You can head down to the bar
to mix with the local after-work crowd; old photos on the wall show
what Wellington looked like in the hotel's early days. ⊠ *285 Tinakori*
Rd., Thorndon ☎ *04/472–1320* 🖷 *04/472–0523* ⊕ *www.shepherds.*
co.nz ➷ *12 rooms, 9 with bath* ⚙ *Restaurant, bar; no a/c, no smok-*
ing ⊟ *AE, DC, MC, V.*

$–$$ 🏠 **Tinakori Lodge.** You can stay on the same road as the prime minis-
ter's residence at this 1868 Victorian timber villa. The rooms have a mix
of antiques and reproductions, with brass beds, quilts, and wicker and
wood furnishings, with a nod to the era and style of the house itself.
Owners Richard and Julene Lennon have done some classy renovating,
but the best room is arguably the sunny glassed-in conservatory, which
looks out onto the "Town Belt," Wellington's sprawling bush reserve.
⊠ *182 Tinakori Rd., Thorndon* ☎ *04/473–3478* 🖷 *04/939–3475*
⊕ *www.tinakorilodge.co.nz* ➷ *4 rooms, 5 suites* ⚙ *In-room broadband;*
no a/c ⊟ *AE, DC, MC, V* ⧆ *BP.*

¢–$ 🏠 **Base Backpackers.** This beautiful Heritage building in a great loca-
tion draws a varied crowd of budget travelers. Rooms here are spacious,
bedding is provided, and all except the double rooms share bathrooms.
The whole establishment is decked out in burgundy and white, with the
exception of the Sanctuary floor, a women-only dorm section where, surprise, rooms are pink and white. Sanctuary guests also get some girly
perks (full-length mirrors, hair dryers, free Aveda hair products, and feather
pillows). The place is kept remarkably clean, the staff is friendly, and
the rates are some of the most competitive in town. ⊠ *21–23 Cambridge*
Terr. ☎ *04/801–5666* 🖷 *04/801–5668* ⊕ *www.basebackpackers.com*
➷ *10 rooms, 10 dorms* ⚙ *Café, bar, laundry facilities, Internet room;*
no a/c, no room phones, no smoking ⊟ *AE, DC, MC, V.*

¢ 🏠 **Downtown Backpackers.** In a classic backpackers' location opposite
the train station, this hostel stands out by virtue of its amenities and its
landmark art deco building. The rooms, which are clean, if small and
a bit worse for wear, range from singles to six-person shares. The extensive communal areas include a café (serving breakfasts that are big
and cheap), kitchen, bar, and pool room; computers are at the ready if

you'd like to jump on the Web. Check out the old Māori carved fireplace surround in the bar; you won't see anything better in the national museum. ⊠ *Bunny St. and Waterloo Quay* ☎ *04/473–8482* 🖨 *04/471–1073* ⊕ *www.downtownbackpackers.co.nz* ⇗ *60 rooms, 54 with bath* ⚿ *Café, kitchen, billiards, bar, laundry facilities, Internet room; no a/c, no room phones, no room TVs* ⊟ *AE, DC, MC, V.*

Nightlife & the Arts

For current listings of cultural events in Wellington, check the entertainment listings in the *Dominion Post,* Wellington's daily newspaper, or the free weekly entertainment newspaper, *Capital Times.* The free booklet *Wellington What's On,* available from the Visitor Information Centre, also has seasonal listings of cultural events, and the Wellington City Council puts out the free monthly "Feeling Great" (⊕ www.feelinggreat. co.nz) brochure, which lists events, exhibits, lectures, and workshops. The Web site for the **Wellington Visitor Information Centre** (⊕ www. wellingtonnz.com) also has up-to-date listings, from movies, to theater and music, to free events. *The Package* (⊕ www.thepackage.co.nz), a free palm-size publication, has a weekly event calendar with listings that tend toward the alternative and edgy; pick up a copy at the Visitor Information Centre or at many cafés, or check it out online. **Ticketek** (☎ 04/384–3840), between the Michael Fowler Center and the Town Hall, sells tickets for local performances.

The Arts

FESTIVALS Wellington's arts scene, traditionally a strong suit, continues to boom. The major arts event in town is the **New Zealand International Arts Festival,** held in March every two years (in even-numbered years) at venues across the city. This event attracts a huge array of international talent in the fields of music, drama, dance, the visual arts, and media. Advance information and a festival program are available from the **Festival Office** (☎ 04/473–0149 ⊕ www.nzfestival.telecom.co.nz). Many events fill up quickly; book a month in advance if you can.

Wellingtonians turn out in droves for the many free festivals that occur from November to April. One of the largest of Wellington's summer fests is the six-week **Summer City,** which includes more than 70 events throughout the city. A highlight is **Whopper Chopper** (⊠ Frank Kitts Park), a hugely popular day of music at a waterside park that runs the gamut from folk to funk to reggae, hip-hop, and soul. Although the music may not be mainstream, this concert lures picnicking families as well as tattooed, pierced, and dreadlocked urban hipsters. At the **Cuba Street Carnival,** for two days in March, food and crafts stalls and music and dance performances sweep the length of Cuba Street, culminating in a nighttime parade (a family-friendly show, not a rowdy Mardi Gras–style blowout).

One of the key Māori occasions in Wellington is **Matariki,** the North Island Māori New Year, which occurs in late May/early June, beginning with the first new moon after the appearance of Matariki (Pleiades). Te Papa Tongarewa–Museum of New Zealand is host of nearly a month of musical, storytelling, and dance performances; the events begin with a ceremony at dawn. Pick up a brochure and calendar of events at the museum. For a unique gift or souvenir, Te Papa Press also publishes a beautifully illustrated Matariki calendar, which runs from June until May and is based on traditional Māori lore of the seasons.

PERFORMING ARTS Wellington is the home of the **Royal New Zealand Ballet,** known as much for contemporary works by New Zealand and international choreographers as for its perennial *Nutcracker* and *Swan Lake* performances. The **NBR New Zealand Opera** and the **New Zealand Symphony Orchestra** both mix equal parts "old favorites" with contemporary works as well. The glass, concrete, and steel Michael Fowler Center and the adjacent, older **Wellington Town Hall** (⊠ Civic Square, Wakefield St. ☎ 04/801–4242) jointly operate as the main venue for the symphony and other classical music performances. The ornate, turn-of-the-20th-century **St. James Theatre** (⊠ 77–83 Courtenay Pl. ☎ 04/802–4060 ⊕ www.stjames.co.nz) hosts dance performances, musicals, and opera. The equally well-preserved **Opera House** (⊠ 111–113 Manners St. ☎ 04/384–3840), with its plush carpets and tiered seats, has a similar lineup. Because the Opera House and the St. James Theatre are under the same ownership, the NBR New Zealand Opera and the Royal New Zealand Ballet use either venue as schedules allow.

Bats Theatre is Wellington's long-standing source for experimental, sometimes off-the-wall theater. Bats hosts the Fringe Festival during the International Arts Festival, as well as a range of performances by different groups throughout the year. ⊠ *1 Kent Terr.* ☎ *04/802–4175* ⊕ *www.bats.co.nz.*

Circa Theatre is a good bet to catch contemporary New Zealand pieces along with established masterworks from Harold Pinter to Oscar Wilde. The theater is cooperatively run, and although it has its own in-house director, the company also plays host to international and traveling shows. It's on the wharf next to the Te Papa museum. ⊠ *1 Taranaki St.* ☎ *04/801–7992* ⊕ *www.circa.co.nz.*

Downstage Theatre holds frequent performances of stage classics, contemporary drama, comedy, and dance. It is host to its own productions as well as other dramatic performances by traveling or independent groups. ⊠ *Hannah Playhouse, Courtenay Pl. and Cambridge Terr.* ☎ *04/801–6946* ⊕ *www.downstage.co.nz.*

Nightlife

Wellington's after-dark scene splits between several main areas. **Cuba Street**'s funky cafés, bars, and clubs, open until around 1 AM during the week and about 3 AM on weekends, are where the "alternative" set spends its time; cocktails are innovative, and the music is not likely to be anything played on Top 20 radio.

Courtenay Place is where most of the traditional drinking action is, with a selection of brash Irish pubs, sports bars, and a few upscale establishments. This area can get packed late on Friday and Saturday nights, especially when there is a rugby game on, when the streets fill with beery couples in their late teens and early twenties (New Zealand's legal drinking age is 18), lining up to get into the pubs.

In the downtown business district—between Lambton Quay and Manners Street—a couple of brewpubs and a few taverns cater to the after-work mob. Down by the harbor, a flashy twenty- to thirtysomething corporate crowd hangs out in several warehouse-style bars, sipping martinis on weeknights and filling the dance floor on weekends.

BARS If beer is your thing, head downtown and make an early start at the **Arizona Bar** (⊠ Grey and Featherston Sts. ☎ 04/495–7867), a Western-theme bar on the ground floor of the Hotel Inter-Continental. The **Malthouse** (⊠ 47 Willis St. ☎ 04/499–4355), upstairs in a renovated historic building, brews its own beers and has conservatory-style seating looking down on the street.

Of Courtenay Place's Irish spots, try **Molly Malone's** (⊠ Taranaki St. and Courtenay Pl. ☎ 04/384–2896), a large, traditional bar with regular live music and a rowdy crowd, particularly on weekends. A restaurant serves pub grub, and the upstairs bar has an outside balcony for people-watching. You can also check out the crowd from **Kitty O'Shea's** (⊠ 28 Courtenay Pl. ☎ 04/384–7392) outside veranda; there is regular traditional live music. The well-lived-in **Shooters Bar** (⊠ 69–71 Courtenay Pl. ☎ 04/801–7800), once a brewery and then a distillery, has exposed brick walls, timber floors, and four levels with everything from a 400-person main bar to a garden bar to a 10-table poolroom.

Wellington's twenty- to thirtysomething hipsters gravitate toward **Motel** (⊠ Forresters La. off Tory St. ☎ 04/384–9084), with its dimly lighted booths and DJ playing funky, down-tempo hip-hop. As an added bonus, you can order food at the bar from the adjacent **Chow**, a hip pan-Asian eatery. Although it's not formal, you'll want to leave the jeans and sneakers behind; legend has it that Motel's bouncers turned away *Lord of the Rings* star Liv Tyler because she wasn't properly attired.

Centrally located **Matterhorn** (⊠ 106 Cuba St. ☎ 04/384–3359), which also has a good restaurant, draws a refreshing mix of urban hipsters and after-work corporate crowds with its indoor and outdoor fireplaces, a laid-back DJ, and a list of inventive cocktails—you can blow $100 on the "Bling Bling," a top-shelf Long Island Ice Tea that comes in a trophy with your name engraved on it. Although it's right on bustling Cuba Street, **Good Luck** (⊠ 126 Cuba St. ☎ 04/801–9950) is a little hard to find. Stairs take you below street level to a club done in the style of a Shanghai opium den, glowing with candles in Chinese teapots. An up-tempo DJ draws crowds onto the dance floor until the wee hours, particularly on Saturday night.

Wellington's only officially gay bar and nightclub is **Pound** (⊠ Level 1, The Oaks Complex, 63 Cuba St. ☎ 04/384–6024), which attracts both men and women. The crowd is mixed every night, and more than a little cruisey. The music's not live, unless you count the drag performances. Friday and Saturday are the busiest nights; it doesn't get jumping until around 11 PM.

On the waterfront, the two big draws are restaurant bars. **Shed Five** (⊠ Shed 5, Queens Wharf, Jervois Quay ☎ 04/499–9069) is an airy, high-beamed space, decked out with lilies, stained-glass windows, and

6

gilded mirrors. **Dockside** (✉ Shed 3, Queens Wharf, Jervois Quay ☏ 04/499–9900), a restaurant and bar with a nautical theme, has antique boats hanging from the ceiling. In good weather, everyone spills outside for the best close-up harbor views in Wellington. Later on, move across to **Chicago** (✉ Jervois Quay ☏ 04/473–4900) on Queens Wharf, a spacious sports bar that sees boisterous post-game parties.

LIVE MUSIC & **Valve** (✉ 154 Vivian St. ☏ 04/385–1630) is one of the best places to
DANCE CLUBS catch live, local rock music. It's a classic hole-in-the-wall: small, dark, and a little seedy, with concrete floors. On nights without music, a pool table takes the stage. Another good bet for local bands is **Bodega** (✉ 103 Ghuznee St. ☏ 04/384–8212), which pulls in a slightly more wholesome crowd than Valve. It's larger, with couches in the front and a dance floor in the back by the stage. Both of these spots attract a predominantly university student crowd; the nights with cheap drink specials are packed. Touring acts sometimes play at the **Starlight Ballroom** (✉ 235 Willis St. ☏ 04/802–1310), a high-ceilinged, no-frills space lined with Speight's beer memorabilia and old concert posters. Bigger international stars tend to play at **Westpac Stadium** (✉ 1 Waterloo Quay ☏ 04/471–0333). The **Queens Wharf Events Centre** (✉ Queen's Wharf, Jervois Quay ☏ 04/470–0190) also gets its share of the bold-face touring acts.

At the bottom end of Courtney Place, **Sandwiches** (✉ Majoribanks St. and Kent Terr. ☏ 04/385–7698) has a stylish bar filled with long, black vinyl couches on one side and a dance floor on the other, where international DJs play soul, funk, disco, and jazz. There is also live jazz on Wednesday and on the last Sunday of every month.

Shopping

The main downtown shopping area, for department stores, clothes, shoes, books, outdoor gear, and souvenirs, is the so-called **Golden Mile**—from Lambton Quay, up Willis, Victoria, and Manners streets. For smaller, funkier boutiques, visit the more alternative **Cuba Street.**

Department Store & Malls

★ For more than a century, **Kirkcaldie & Stains** (✉ 165–177 Lambton Quay ☏ 04/472–5899) has maintained an impeccable standard of customer service; the store is Wellington's version of Harrod's. If you appreciate having the door opened by a top-hatted, liveried doorman as you enter a lovely early-19th-century façade, then this is the place for you. The extensive perfume department is an olfactory delight, and you can relax in either of two modern cafés and listen to live piano music before browsing the racks.

There are a couple of indoor malls on upper Lambton Quay: Harbour City and Capital on the Quay, both with a decent range of jewelry, lingerie, housewares, and clothing boutiques. A better mall bet is the **Old Bank Arcade** (✉ 233–237 Lambton Quay, at Customhouse Quay and Willis St. ☏ 04/922–0600) in the charming historic former Bank of New Zealand building, which is becoming something of a fashion enclave. The Arcade gathers up a slew of well-known designer boutiques, including those of New Zealand designers Andrea Moore and the tempting

Minnie Cooper shoe store. Napoleon Cosmetics does wonderful makeovers, and for the fellas, Rixon Groove are shirt- and tie-makers par excellence.

Markets

For a look at the weekly market of a close-knit ethnic community, catch an early train or take a drive north of Wellington on SH1 to Porirua and hit the morning-only **Porirua Market** (⊠ Cobham Ct.). The stalls here sell everything from eggplants and pineapples to colorful clothing to woven basketry and beadwork. Entertainers and hoarse-voiced evangelists play to the crowd and add to the ambience. If you get hungry, there are lots of food stalls selling curry and roti, chop suey, banana pancakes, and nearly every other treat you can imagine. The stalls open at 5:30 AM but close at 10 AM sharp.

James Smiths Corner (⊠ 55 Cuba St. ☎ 04/801–8812) has a second-floor market area offering fortune-telling and selling Māori art and crafts, jewelry, cheap Asian knickknacks, and gifts; the main floor houses more mainstream stores and a food court. It's open daily 9–5.

Two **outdoor markets** (⊠ Chaffers St., opposite the New World supermarket ⊠ Willis St., between Vivian and Ghuznee Sts.) set up every Sunday between dawn and noon in parking lots at either end of the city. These fruit-and-vegetable markets are fun spots to people-watch, because they're among the most culturally diverse gathering points in the city. If you're looking to picnic, you can pick up supplies.

The **Wellington Market** (⊠ Taranaki and Cable Sts. ☎ 04/801–8991), although a bit shabby these days, still has a good selection of souvenirs and Māori crafts, as well as an underrated Asian food court. It's open Friday–Sunday 10–5:30.

Specialty Stores

BOOKS & MAPS **Arty Bee's Books** (⊠ 17 Courtenay Pl. ☎ 04/385–1819) is a friendly store for secondhand books and sheet music. **Parson's Books & Music** (⊠ 126 Lambton Quay ☎ 04/472–4587) may not be the largest bookstore in town, but it's one of the most intriguing—strong on New Zealand writing and travel, and also featuring comprehensive classical recordings and a small upper-floor café. **Unity Books** (⊠ 57 Willis St. ☎ 04/499–4245) stocks a generous supply of New Zealand and Māori literature.

CLOTHING & ACCESSORIES Wellingtonians are a discerning bunch when it comes to the fashion scene, as evidenced by the numerous designer boutiques throughout the city. The nifty (and free) Wellington **Fashion Map,** which you can pick up at the Visitor Information Centre or any number of stores, divides the city into easily navigable shopping quarters and lists a good cross section of women's and men's designer boutiques throughout the central city. Slightly off-the-beaten-track streets such as Woodward Street, Customhouse Quay, Wakefield Street, and upper Willis Street are home to some uniquely New Zealand designers and are well worth exploring.

Area 51 (⊠ Cuba and Dixon Sts. ☎ 04/385–6590) stocks such street-savvy clothes brands as Diesel, but the real reason to come in is to check out the popular local Huffer label. An "I [huffer logo] NZ" T-shirt is a cool alternative to the usual souvenir Ts. **Gold Ore Silver Mine** (✉ Left Bank, Cuba Mall ☎ 04/801–7019) has one of the city's largest selections of jewelry made from carved *pounamu* (a green stone similar to jade). Prices are reasonable, starting at around $18 for a pendant. The store also sells gold and silver jewelry, crafted on the premises. **Juno** (✉ 148 Willis St. ☎ 04/384–5557) is a small women's clothing boutique owned by designer Rebekah Greig (also one of New Zealand's most prominent accordionists). **Karen Walker** (✉ 126 Wakefield St. ☎ 04/499–3558) has made a name for herself overseas. Her Wellington store carries her own designs and also stocks other hip international labels, such as Bernard Willhem and Viveka Bergstrom. **unity collection** (✉ 101 Customhouse Quay ☎ 04/471–1008) carries clothing from a clutch of New Zealand designers, good for a one-stop view of the local talent. Long-standing New Zealand designer Elisabeth Findlay of **Zambesi** (✉ 107 Customhouse Quay ☎ 04/472–3638) whips up innovative but extremely wearable clothes. They're relatively expensive; keep an eye out for a sale. For elegant, minimalist outfits, browse through **ZFA** (✉ 111 Customhouse Quay ☎ 04/499–0408), another local girl made good.

OUTDOOR EQUIPMENT   Wellington is a fine place to stock up on camping supplies before hitting the great outdoors. **Kathmandu** (✉ 57 Willis St. ☎ 04/472–0113) carries its house brand of clothing and equipment. **Mainly Tramping** (✉ 39 Mercer St. ☎ 04/473–5353) is a good bet for backpacks and other gear. **Ski & Snowboard Centre–Gordons** (✉ Cuba and Wakefield Sts. ☎ 04/499–8894) focuses on snow-sport equipment and clothing.

SOUVENIRS   **Iko-Iko** (✉ 118 Cuba St. ☎ 04/385–0977) is a gift shop specializing in kitsch, particularly all manner of Kiwiana. One of the best bargains in town is the $5 emerald green, plastic tiki-handled salad servers. They make a fun gift and come packaged on a background map of New Zealand. **Kura Contemporary Art and Design** (✉ 19 Allen St. ☎ 04/802–4934) is part gallery, part gift store, with a strong Māori current running through the work. Some of the smaller, less expensive items make unique souvenirs. **Living Nature** (✉ 195 Lambton Quay ☎ 04/499–5060) has a range of beauty, hair, and skin products "made of New Zealand." Most products include *manuka* honey, a richly scented honey from a kind of tea tree native to New Zealand that's known for its health benefits. Preparations are preservative-free. On Lambton Quay, the best bet for souvenirs is **Sommerfields** (✉ 296 Lambton Quay ☎ 04/499–4847). Everything in the store—from jewelry to artwork, scarves, and soaps—has been made in New Zealand.

WELLINGTON ESSENTIALS

Transportation

BY AIR

Wellington International Airport (WLG) lies about 8 km (5 mi) from the city. The airport is small and easy to negotiate.

The domestic carriers serving Wellington are Air New Zealand, Origin Pacific, and Sounds Air. The international carriers are Air New Zealand and Qantas, but here *international* means "over to Australia"; other overseas flights go through Auckland's airport. There are generally a half dozen flights to Australia daily. Air New Zealand, between its Link and national services, connects Wellington to more than 20 other New Zealand cities daily for very reasonable fares. Origin Pacific has flights from Wellington to all major New Zealand cities daily. Sounds Air flies between Wellington and Picton several times a day.

Co-operative Shuttle operates a 10-seater bus between the airport and any address in the city ($15 for one person, $20 for two). The bus meets all incoming flights; tickets are available from the driver. To take the shuttle to the airport you'll definitely need to make a reservation; if you're coming from the airport into town, you can usually catch one without advance arrangements. The Stagecoach Flyer runs between the airport and Upper Hutt Railway Station via Wellington city center. These shuttles run from the airport every 40 minutes from 6:20 AM to 8:20 PM weekdays and from 6:50 AM to 8:50 PM weekends; the cost is $9 for one day's unlimited travel. Taxis are always available at the airport; a taxi ride to central Wellington costs about $25.

🛂 Airport **Wellington International Airport** ✉ Stewart Duff Dr., Rongotai ☎ 04/385-5123.

🛂 Carriers **Air New Zealand** ☎ 0800/737-000 ⊕ www.airnewzealand.co.nz. **Origin Pacific** ☎ 0800/302-302 ⊕ www.originpacific.co.nz. **Qantas** ☎ 0800/808-767 ⊕ www.qantas.com.au. **Sounds Air Ltd** ☎ 0800/505-005 ⊕ www.soundsair.com.

🛂 Transfers **Co-operative Shuttle** ☎ 04/387-8787. **Stagecoach Flyer** ☎ 04/801-7000.

BY BIKE

If the sun is shining and the wind is still, cycling is an ideal way to explore the city and its surrounding bays. There are designated bike lanes in and around Wellington; they're marked with a continuous white line and a white bike image on the pavement. More details about urban cycling are available on the city of Wellington's Web site, ⊕ www.wcc.govt.nz. Penny Farthing Cycles rents out mountain bikes for $35 per day or $100 per week, including helmets.

🛂 Bike Rentals **Penny Farthing Cycles** ✉ 89 Courtenay Pl. ☎ 04/385-2279 ⊕ www.pennyfarthing.co.nz.

BY BOAT & FERRY

The Interisland Line runs a passenger and vehicle ferry service between Wellington and Picton; the Interislander boats take three hours, and fares vary by time of year and range from $39 to $60 one-way per person; for a car and driver, fares are $100-$220. Vehicles exceeding 18 feet in length incur an extra charge. You can book up to six months in advance.

The Interislander ferry terminal is about 3 km (2 mi) from the city. A free bus leaves Platform 9 at the Wellington Railway Station for the ferry terminal 40 minutes before sailings.

The Bluebridge vessel, MV *Santa Regina*, sails twice daily between Wellington to Picton. Fares are $40 one-way per person, $150 for a driver with car up to 20 feet in length, $240-$290 for cars between 20-30 feet. The ferry leaves from the terminal opposite the railway station.

Most car-rental agencies have North Island–South Island transfer programs for their vehicles; you can drop one car off in Wellington and pick up another in Picton on the same contract.

🚩 Boat & Ferry Lines **Interisland Line** ☎ 0800/802-802 or 04/498-3302 ⊕ www. interislandline.co.nz. **MV *Santa Regina*** ☎ 0800/844-844 or 04/471-6188 ⊕ www. bluebridge.co.nz.

BY BUS

InterCity and Newmans buses provide daily departures to all major North Island destinations. They also connect with the Interisland Line that operates the ferries to Picton in the South Island.

🚩 Bus Companies **InterCity** ☎ 04/472-5111 ⊕ www.intercitycoach.co.nz. **Newmans** ☎ 04/499-3261 ⊕ www.newmanscoach.co.nz.

🚩 Bus Depot **Wellington Railway Station** ⊠ Bunny St. and Waterloo Quay ☎ 04/ 498-3000.

BUS TRAVEL
WITHIN
WELLINGTON
Wellington's bus network is operated by several companies, though it's easy to find out information on routes and fares by calling the public-transport-information service known as Metlink. The main terminals for services are at the railway station and from Courtenay Place. The City Circular Bus departs every 10 minutes on a circular loop through the center, passing all the main sights and attractions. For all trips in the inner city, the fare is $2; pay when you board the bus. You don't need exact change, but they probably won't take anything over $5. Bus stops are marked with red-and-white signs.

STARpass tickets ($9) allow a day's unlimited travel on all area buses; a $5 ticket gives you a day's bus travel within the city center. For maps and timetables, go to the Visitor Information Centre at Victoria and Wakefield streets, the railway station on Bunny Street, or the Wellington Regional Council Centre on Wakefield Street.

🚩 **Metlink** ☎ 04/801-7000 or 0800/801-700 ⊕ www.metlink.org.nz.

BY CAR

The main access to the city is via the Wellington Urban Motorway, which starts just after the merging of Highways 1 and 2, a few miles north of the city center. The motorway links the city center with all towns and cities to the north.

You won't need a car to explore Wellington's center, but it's convenient to have one to get out to surrounding areas such as Akatarawa. If you do have a car in the city, keep in mind that central Wellington can be a frustrating place to drive, because it's rife with narrow one-way streets. Rush hours usually last from 7:30 to 9:30 AM and 4 to 6:30 PM.

There's little on-street parking; instead, look for parking lots, which are clearly marked, usually with a white "P" on a blue background. There are several multistory parking lots in the city center; a particularly convenient one is Wilson Parking, with direct elevator access to Lambton Quay. There are also plenty of gas stations in the city center. You'll find stations at the corner of Jervois Quay and Willeston Street, the corner of Customhouse and Whitmore streets, and the corner of Wakefield and Taranaki streets.

Avis, Budget, and Hertz have offices at Wellington airport. Offices are open 6 AM–1 AM daily.

🚩 Parking Wilson Parking ⊠ Level 28, Grand Plimmer Tower, Boulcott St. and Gilmer Terr. ☎ 04/473-2293.

🚩 Rental Agencies Avis ☎ 04/801-8108. **Budget** ☎ 04/802-4548. **Hertz** ☎ 04/384-3809.

BY TAXI

Wellington is only a small city, but a taxi ride can save your legs on the long haul around the harbor or up the steep hills to Kelburn and the Botanic Gardens. Most city rides cost $10–$12; rates are $3 on entry, then $2.30 per km (½ mi). There are taxis outside the railway station, as well as on Dixon Street and along Courtenay Place and Lambton Quay. Stands are marked with a TAXI sign. Taxis have a light on the roof to indicate if they are taken.

Contacts & Resources

BANKS & EXCHANGE SERVICES

Both the National Bank of New Zealand and the ANZ have branches with ATMs in central Wellington. Lambton Quay has a branch of both banks, and there are others on Manners Street and Courtenay Place. Harvey World Travel does currency exchange during regular business hours.

🚩 ANZ ⊠ 49–53 Courtenay Pl. ☎ 0800/269-296.

Harvey World Travel (Travelex Financial Services) ⊠ 358 Lambton Quay ☎ 04/472-2848.

National Bank of NZ ⊠ 188 Lambton Quay ☎ 0800/181-818.

EMERGENCIES

There are no 24-hour pharmacies, but Wellington Urgent Pharmacy has extended hours; it's open weekdays 5 AM–11 PM, weekends and holidays 8 AM–11 PM.

🚩 Emergency Services Fire, police, and ambulance ☎ 111.

🚩 Hospital After-Hours Medical Centre ⊠ 17 Adelaide Rd., Newtown ☎ 04/384-4944, open 24 hours. **Wellington Hospital** ⊠ Riddiford St., Newtown ☎ 04/385-5999.

🚩 Late-Night Pharmacy Wellington Urgent Pharmacy ⊠ 17 Adelaide Rd. ☎ 04/385-8810.

MAIL, SHIPPING & THE INTERNET

In addition to the main post office, which is open weekdays 7:30–5, postal services are available at Books and More outlets around town, which are open daily. The Books and More location at Lambton Quay is open weekdays 7–6, Saturday 9–5:30, and Sunday 10–4:30.

New Zealand Couriers and DHL Express are two of several firms that run an international courier service. Pickups and deliveries are usually made the same day for local packages.

There are several Internet cafés in the city center. Internet access generally costs $3–$4 per hour. iPlay Internet Cafe is open 24 hours.

🚩 Internet Cafés Cyber Spot Internet ⊠ 180 Lambton Quay ☎ 04/473-0098. **iPlay Internet Cafe** ⊠ 49 Manners St. ☎ 04/494-0088. **iWorld** ⊠ Shop 7, 98–110 Victoria St. ☎ 04/472-1144.

☑ Post Offices Books and More ⊠ Cable Car La. and Lambton Quay ☎ 04/472-9694 or 0800/426-657. **Capital Post Shop** ⊠ 7-27 Waterloo Quay ☎ 04/496-4065.
☑ Shipping Services New Zealand Couriers ⊠ 195 Aotea Quay, Wellington ☎ 04/472-9131. **DHL Express** ⊠ Wellington Airport, Stewart Duff Dr. at Freight Dr., Wellington ☎ 04/387-1450.

TOURS

BOAT TOURS East West Ferries runs the *Dominion Post* Ferry, a commuter service between the city and Days Bay, on the east side of Port Nicholson, and it's one of the best-value tours in the city. On the way to Days Bay you can stop at Matiu or Somes Island; this former quarantine station makes an unusual picnic spot on a warm afternoon. Days Bay itself has a seaside village atmosphere, local crafts shops, and great views of Wellington. Weekdays the catamaran departs from Queens Wharf at 6:30 AM, 7:25, 8:15, 10, noon, 2:15, 4:30, 5:30, and 6:30 PM. The return boats leave Days Bay roughly 30 minutes later. The sailing schedule is cut back on weekends and holidays. The one-way fare to Days Bay is $7.50; the cost if you include a Somes Island stop is $16.50 round-trip. You can pick up tickets at the ferry terminal between 8 and 5; otherwise, tickets can be bought on board.
☑ *Dominion Post* Ferry ⊠ Queens Wharf ☎ 04/499-1282 and 04/494-3339 ⊕ www.eastbywest.co.nz.

BUS TOURS Wellington Rover runs local tours that range from a two-hour overview ($35) to a full-day *Lord of the Rings* sites tour, which includes a picnic lunch ($150). Tours leave from the Visitor Information Centre on Wakefield Street. Reservations are essential.
☑ Wellington Rover ☎ 021/426-211 cell ⊕ www.wellingtonrover.co.nz.

PRIVATE GUIDES Wally Hammond, a tour operator with a great anecdotal knowledge about Wellington, offers a 2½-hour minibus tour of the city. This can be combined with a half-day Kapiti Coast Tour, which includes a visit to the Southward Car Museum. The city tour costs $45, the Kapiti Coast tour is $75, and the combined tour is $160. A full-day Palliser Bay and *Lord of the Rings* sites tour is also available ($150).
☑ Wally Hammond ☎ 04/472-0869 ⊕ www.wellingtonsightseeingtours.com.

SIGHTSEEING TOURS Flat Earth–New Zealand Experiences runs a wide range of tours to scenic areas both locally and countrywide.
☑ Flat Earth–New Zealand Experiences ☎ 04/977-5805 or 0800/775-805 ⊕ www.flatearth.co.nz.

TRAIN TRAVEL

The terminal for all TranzScenic train services is Wellington Railway Station on Bunny Street, 1½ km (1 mi) from the city center. The Overlander train connects Auckland and Wellington, going daily once each way on the 11-hour trip.

TranzMetro operates suburban train services to Wellington Railway Station from the Hutt Valley, Palmerston North, and Masterton.
☑ Train Station Wellington Railway Station ⊠ Bunny St. and Waterloo Quay ☎ 04/498-3000.

Train Lines **TranzMetro** ☎ 04/801-7000 ⊕ www.tranzmetro.co.nz. **TranzScenic** ☎ 0800/872-467, 04/495-0775 ⊕ www.tranzscenic.co.nz.

TRAVEL AGENCIES
Local Agent House of Travel ✉ 6 Margaret St., Lower Hutt ☎ 04/569-0950 🖷 04/570-2845.

Lambton Quay Flight Centre ✉ 182 Lambton Quay ☎ 04/471-2995 or 0800/354-448.

VISITOR INFORMATION
The city's visitor bureau is open Monday through Wednesday and Friday 8:30 to 5:30, Thursday 9:30 to 5:30, and weekends 9:30 to 4:30. In addition to its Web site, check out the City Council site, ⊕ www.wcc.govt.nz, for information on Wellington's services, sights, and activities. **Tourist Information Wellington Visitor Information Centre** ✉ Civic Administration Bldg., Victoria and Wakefield Sts. ☎ 04/802-4860 ⊕ www.wellingtonnz.com.

THE WAIRARAPA

To cross the Rimutaka Ranges, which form a natural barrier between Wellington and the Wairarapa, you climb a twisting snake of a road known locally as "The Hill." Near a small plateau at the road's peak, at a height of about 1,800 feet, a footpath leads to even higher ground and some spectacular views on all sides. Heading down from the summit, the road plunges through a series of hairpin bends to reach the plain that the Māori called "Land of Glistening Water."

For some years, the rather daunting access road gave a sense of isolation to the Wairarapa, which was essentially a farming area. More recently, the emergence of the wine industry has triggered a tourism boom in the region. Grapes have been grown in the region for more than 100 years, but the present wine industry dates from 1979. Red grape varieties flourish in the local soil (the pinot noir is particularly notable), and Wairarapa wines, produced in small quantities, are becoming sought after both in New Zealand and overseas. These days, vineyards, wine tasting, olive farms, and the twice-yearly Martinborough Fair are firmly established attractions. Hot-air ballooning, sea- and freshwater fishing, walking, and other outdoor activities have also brought visitors over the hill in droves.

Martinborough

20 *70 km (44 mi) north of Wellington.*

The pleasant town of Martinborough is at the cutting edge of the changes that have taken place in the Wairarapa as a result of the burgeoning wine industry and the associated tourism boom. The town gets its name from its founder, John Martin, who, in 1881, laid out the streets in a Union Jack pattern, radiating from the square that forms the hub. Most restaurants and shops are on or close to the square.

To tap into the Wairarapa wine world, this is the place to come. There are more than 20 vineyards within a few miles of the town—an easy drive or horse-drawn-carriage ride away (*see* Tours, *below*). The **Toast**

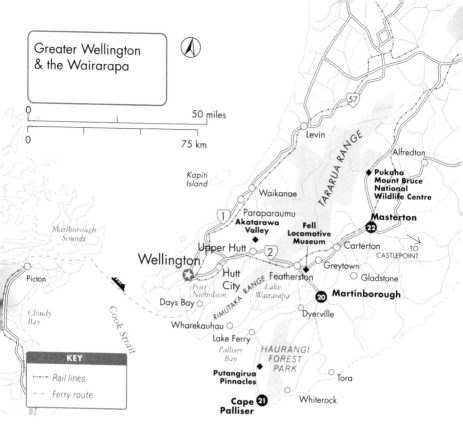

Greater Wellington
& the Wairarapa

0   50 miles

0   75 km

TARARUA RANGE

Levin

Alfredton

Kapiti
Island

Pukaha
Mount Bruce
National
Wildlife Centre

Waikanae

Paraparaumu

Masterton

22

Akatarawa
Valley

Fell
Locomotive
Museum

Marlborough
Sounds

Carterton

TO
CASTLEPOINT

Upper Hutt

2

Greytown

Wellington

Gladstone

Picton

Hutt
City

Featherston

Port
Nicholson

Lake
Wairarapa

Days Bay

Martinborough

20

RIMUTAKA RANGE

Dyerville

Cloudy
Bay

Wharekauhau

Lake Ferry

Palliser
Bay

HAURANGI
FOREST
PARK

KEY

Putangirua
Pinnacles

Tora

Rail lines

Ferry route

Cape
Palliser

21

Whiterock

Cook Strait

Martinborough Wine, Food & Music Festival (☎ 0800/000–575 or 04/
473–4838 ⊕ www.toastmartinborough.co.nz) takes place on the third
Sunday in November; thousands of tickets are typically sold within hours.
You can get tickets ($50) through the Web site. The **Martinborough Fair,**
held on the first Saturday in February and March, also draws thousands
of people; this free event packs the town with crafts stalls.

For an overview of the area's wines, take an oenophile's shortcut and hit
the **Martinborough Wine Centre** (⊠ 6 Kitchener St. ☎ 06/306–9040 ⊕ www.
martinboroughwinecentre.co.nz). The shop stocks a thorough selection
of local vintages for sipping and purchasing, plus books and wine accessories, and ships wines to customers all over the world. It's open daily
9–5. With this introduction under your belt, branch out to the tasting rooms
nearby (see the CloseUp box "Wairarapa's Best Wineries").

Olives are another local crop. For a taste-bud-tickling exercise that
doesn't involve grapes, head to **Olivo** (⊠ Hinakura Rd. ☎ 06/306–
9074 ⊕ http://olivo.co.nz), Helen and John Meehan's olive grove, 3 km
(2 mi) north of Martinborough. You can tour the grove and its 5 acres
of gardens to learn how their oils are produced. Tastings (and sales) of
their extra-virgin and infused olive oils are encouraged. They're open
10–6 Thursday to Sunday and otherwise by appointment.

Wairarapa's Best Wineries

PICK UP A MAP of the area vineyards at Martinborough's visitor center, then hit the road to sip at some of the country's best up-and-coming vineyards. Here are the top local picks.

Ata Rangi Vineyard. This winery makes exceptional chardonnay, pinot noir, and Célèbre (a cabernet-merlot-shiraz blend) in small quantities. ⌧ *Puruatanga Rd.* ☎ *06/306-9570* ⊕ *www.atarangi. co.nz* ☉ *Tastings Oct.–Apr., weekdays 1–3, weekends 11–5.*

Coney Wines. Have lunch here for a view over the vines that produce a terrific pinot noir and pinot gris plus a rosé you can get only on-site. ⌧ *Dry River Rd.* ☎🖷 *06/306-8345* ☉ *Tastings Fri., Sat., and Sun. 11–5.*

Martinborough Vineyard. This fine regional winery was the first to convince the world of the Wairarapa's pinot noir potential. The chardonnay is also exceptional. ⌧ *Princess St.* ☎ *06/306-9955* ⊕ *www.* *martinborough-vineyard.co.nz* ☉ *Tastings daily 11–3.*

Murdoch James Vineyard. This boutique producer of a wide range of Martinborough wines is only a 10-minute scenic drive out of town. Try their smooth 2004 Blue Rock pinot noir in the on-site Riverview Café, paired with a pan-seared sirloin with wild mushrooms on soft polenta. The café keeps the same hours as the tasting room but is closed Wednesday, November through March, and Monday and Tuesday April through October. ⌧ *Dry River Rd.* ☎ *06/306-9165* 🖷 *06/306-9120* ⊕ *www. murdochjames.co.nz* ☉ *Tastings year-round, daily 11–5:30.*

Palliser Estate. Don't miss the whites here—they're some of the best locally. The sauvignon blanc, as well as the pinot noir, are distinguished by their intense flavors. ⌧ *Kitchener St.* ☎ *06/306-9019* ⊕ *www.palliser.co.nz* ☉ *Tastings daily 10–4.*

6

RUAKOKOPATUNA GLOWWORM CAVES – The glowworm display here is not quite as impressive as the one at Waitomo, but the sense of adventure is much greater—nobody will tell you to duck when you're approaching a low-hanging rock, so be careful. You'll walk right through a cave following a freshwater stream: expect to get wet feet, and take a flashlight. Once you have found a cluster of glowworms, turn your flashlight off for the best display, then switch it on again as you walk deeper into the cave. As you stay in the cave longer, your eyes will adjust to the darkness, allowing you to see more lights. Take Jelicoe Street from Martinborough 7 km (4½ mi), turn left at Dry River Road, and drive another 8 km (5 mi) to a sign for the caves. Entrance is free, and it is best to call ahead for permission before you go, because the caves are on private property. ☎ *06/306-9393.*

Where to Stay & Eat

$–$$$ ✕ **The French Bistro.** Like the black-and-white photos of Parisian models that adorn the walls of this compact, trendy bistro, the regional cuisine here is done up with style. Settle into the modern chrome-and-black room for chef-owner Wendy Campbell's similarly contemporary creations. You might find duck confit with porcini mushroom risotto or an apple tart topped with fresh figs. There is an excellent selection of local wines. ✉ *3 Kitchener St.* ☎ *06/306–8862* ⌂ *Reservations essential* ▭ *AE, DC, MC, V* ⊘ *Closed Mon. and Tues. No lunch Wed.–Fri.*

¢–$$$ ✕ **The Village Café.** At this rustic café with a sunny outdoor courtyard, all the food is made from local produce and cooked on the premises. The cooks smoke their own salmon and make their own sausages. Breakfast is served all day, and a typical lunch might be chicken braised in sauvignon blanc, served with Mediterranean vegetables. The café shares a building with Martinborough Wine Centre. ✉ *6 Kitchener St.* ☎ *06/306–8814* ▭ *MC, V* ⊘ *No dinner.*

★ $$$ ✕⌂ **Peppers Martinborough Hotel.** Sitting on a corner of the Martinborough Square, this 1890s hotel has rooms that open onto either the veranda or the garden. The rooms mix antique and contemporary fittings, such as four-poster beds or writing tables, and the classic decorating styles vary from French provincial to Shaker to comfortable country. In the Bistro ($$$), where tables spread out from the veranda onto the pavement, the menu leans toward steak and seafood. The wine list is impressive. Reservations are essential for dinner. ✉ *The Sq.* ☎ *06/306–9350* ⌂ *06/306–9345* ⊕ *www.peppers.co.nz* ⇗ *16 rooms* ⌂ *Restaurant, cable TV, in-room data ports, bar; no a/c* ▭ *AE, DC, MC, V.*

$$ ⌂ **The Claremont.** In a quiet rural area just outside the village center, this motel complex has a variety of stylishly modern, self-contained accommodations to suit a range of budgets. All have decks; the apartments have whirlpool baths. The studios and one- and two-bedroom apartments are in a garden setting with ample parking. ✉ *38 Regent St.* ☎ *06/306–9162* ⌂ *06/306–8289* ⊕ *www.theclaremont.co.nz* ⇗ *16 rooms, 7 apartments* ⌂ *In-room hot tubs, kitchens, bicycles, boccie, laundry facilities; no a/c, no smoking* ▭ *AE, DC, MC, V.*

Palliser Bay & Cape Palliser

Southwest of Martinborough: 25 km (16 mi) to Lake Ferry, 40 km (25 mi) to Putangirua Pinnacles, 60 km (37 mi) to Cape Palliser.

To witness Wairarapa's most remote, blustery scenery—and to see the North Island's southernmost point, Cape Palliser—you need to make the drive southwest from Martinborough. It's 25 km (16 mi) through rolling sheep country to the coast at the little settlement of **Lake Ferry** on Palliser Bay. The lake in question, called Onoke, is a salt lagoon formed by the long sandbank here. Vacation homes, fishing spots, and remarkable sunsets bring in the weekend Wellingtonian crowd.

Just before Lake Ferry, turn left (coming from Martinborough) at the sign for Cape Palliser and drive another 15 km (9 mi) around Palliser Bay to Te Kopi, where the **Putangirua Pinnacles Scenic Reserve** is protected from the hordes by its relative isolation. The spectacular rocks have been formed over the last 120,000 years as rains have washed away an ancient gravel deposit, and pinnacles and towers now soar hundreds of feet into the air on both sides of a stony riverbank. An hour-long round-trip walk from the parking area takes you along the riverbank and close to the base of the pinnacles. If you're feeling adventurous, there is a three-to four-hour bushwalk involving some steep climbs and wonderful vistas of the coast—as far off as the South Island on a clear day. The Pinnacles are an hour's drive from Martinborough. The Martinborough visitor bureau is the best place to check for more information.

The road to Cape Palliser deteriorates after the Pinnacles and is unpaved in places. It's a dramatic, bleak ride, though not particularly hard, provided you take care. After 20 km (12 mi), the road ends at **Cape Palliser** itself, where 250 wooden steps climb up to the candy-striped lighthouse. The views from here, up and down the wild coastline, are terrific. Below the lighthouse, splashing in the surf and basking on the rocks, are members of the North Island's only resident **fur seal colony.** You'll be able to get pretty close for photos, but not too close—these are wild animals and fiercely protective of their young. Best advice: don't get between seals and pups, or seals and the ocean.

Where to Stay & Eat

$$$$ ✕🏠 **Wharekauhau.** This Edwardian-style lodge set on a 5,000-acre
Fodor'sChoice working sheep station has luxury lashed by nature. On a hot summer
★ afternoon this is one of the most peaceful places on earth; on a windy, wet morning it's like something out of *Wuthering Heights*. Self-contained guest cottages are scattered around the main lodge; each has a king-size bed, a small patio, and an open fireplace. On the farm you can watch the workings of the sheep station and walk around the gloriously remote coastline. Trout fishing is also an option, as are tours to the seal colony at Palliser Bay. The dining room's seasonally changing menus ($$$$) highlight the best of local produce—especially lamb and fish—accompanied by fine Martinborough wines. The lodge is a 40-minutes' drive south of Featherston on the rugged coast at the northern end of Palliser Bay. ⊠ *Western Lake Rd., Palliser Bay* 🏠 *R.D. 3, Featherston* 🕾 *06/307–7581* 🖷 *06/307–7799* ⊕*www.wharekauhau.co.nz* ↘*12 cottages* ⟁ *Dining room, in-room data ports, tennis court, pool, gym, lounge; no a/c, no room TVs, no smoking* ☱ *AE, DC, MC, V* ⑩*MAP.*

¢ ✕🏠 **Lake Ferry Hotel.** The North Island's southernmost pub sits almost on the beach, with breathtaking views across Cape Palliser to the South Island's Kaikoura Ranges. The rooms are no-frills (in addition to the doubles, there's a 10-bunk dorm), but having a drink on the deck at sunset is an unbeatable experience. The menu ($$–$$$) focuses on fish; the local classic whitebait fritters are served on mesclun salad greens with tomato salsa. This place is so Kiwi, you get a chocolate fish with your cappuccino. (Chocolate fish are iconic Kiwi candy, chocolate-covered pink marshmallows.) The highlight of the menu is the whole crayfish—and though it costs a whopping $46 and has to be ordered two days in advance, it's guaranteed to have been caught that morning. ⊠ *Lake Ferry* 🕾 *06/307–7831* 🖷 *06/307–7891* ↘ *8 rooms, 1 with bath; 1 10-bunk dorm* ⟁ *Restaurant; no a/c, no room phones, no room TVs, no smoking* ☱ *MC, V* ⑩ *BP.*

Around Masterton

Masterton is 40 km (25 mi) northeast of Martinborough.

State Highway 2 strings together a handful of eye-catching small towns on its way north past the Rimutakas. The tiny town of **Featherston** is worth a stop for its train museum, if nothing else. With its photos, models, and memorabilia, the **Fell Locomotive Museum** (✉ Lyon and Fitzherbert Sts., behind the Information Centre on State Hwy. 2, Featherston ☎ 06/308–9379) is a must-see for railway buffs. It has the last remaining Fell locomotive in the world; built in 1875 and beautifully restored, the engine is one of only six that clawed its way up the notorious Rimutaka Incline on the way to Wellington. The museum's open weekdays 10–4:30 and weekends 10–4; admission is $5.

Roughly 10 km (6.2 mi) farther up the arrow-straight highway is **Greytown**, where well-preserved Victorian buildings (now filled with cafés and boutiques) line the main street. After a few miles more you'll reach **Carterton**, another small town with a handful of tempting crafts and antiques stores—especially the Paua Shell Factory and Shop (⇨ *below*). The tranquil, 6-acre **Awaiti Gardens** (✉ Chester Rd., Carterton ☎☎ 06/379–8478 ⊕ www.awaitigardens.co.nz) are also worth a stop for the aromatic lavender walkways, dovecotes, and waterwheel. The gardens are open September–May, Tuesday–Sunday 10–4, and entry costs $5.

㉒ Masterton is Wairarapa's major population center, and like Martinborough to the south, it's in a developing wine region. There's not much to do in the town itself, but it is a handy gateway for hiking in the nearby parks and at the coast. Popular annual events here include the Hot Air Balloon Festival in the first few days of April and the Golden Shears sheepshearing competition, usually held the first weekend in March.

Queen Elizabeth Park, with its lake, aviaries, fernery, small deer park, and children's playground, is a favorite spot for families.

★ Nearby **Pukaha Mount Bruce** (✉ State Hwy. 2, 30 km [19 mi] north of Masterton ☎ 06/375–8004 ⊕ www.mtbruce.doc.govt.nz) makes a fine introduction to the country's wildlife, particularly its endangered bird species. An easy-to-walk trail (one hour round-trip) through the bush takes you past aviaries containing rare, endangered, or vulnerable birds, including the *takahē*, a flightless bird thought to be extinct until it was rediscovered in 1948. The real highlight, though, is the nocturnal habitat containing foraging kiwis, the country's symbol, which are endearing little bundles of energy. It takes a while for your eyes to adjust to the artificial gloom, but it's worth the wait. The *kaka* (indigenous parrots) are fed daily at 3 PM. Don't miss the eel feeding at 1:30, when the reserve's stream writhes with long-finned eels. The center is open daily 9–4:30; admission costs $8. (⊕ www.mtbruce.org.nz)

An hour's drive east of Masterton along Te Ore-ore Road (which turns into the Masterton-Castlepoint road), **Castlepoint** is perhaps the most spectacular site on the entire Wairarapa coast. Here, Castle Rock rises a sheer 500 feet out of the sea; below, in **Deliverance Cove**, seals sometimes play. There's a fantastic walk to the peninsula lighthouse, and surfers flock to the beach break at Deliverance Cove.

There are enjoyable bushwalks in beautiful forests laced with streams at **Tararua Forest Park** (☎ 06/377–0700 DOC office), which also has picnic facilities. The Mt. Holdsworth area at the east end of the park is particularly popular for tramping. To get there turn off State Highway 2 onto Norfolk Road, 2 km (1 mi) south of Masterton.

Where to Stay & Eat

$$$ ✕ **Café Cecille.** Set in Queen Elizabeth Park, this colonial wooden pavilion has a covered veranda and windows overlooking the grounds and lake. The prints on the wall nod to Paris, but the menu sticks to New Zealand strengths, such as the rack of lamb served with Parmesan polenta. ⊠ *Queen Elizabeth Park, Masterton* ☎ *06/370–1166* ⊟ *AE, DC, MC, V.*

★ $$$ ✕ **Salute.** It's worth a detour to Greytown to eat at this highly regarded bistro—it's among the best in the Wairarapa and is considered by some to be among the best in the country. Chef Travis Clive-Griffin puts a Middle Eastern twist on contemporary Mediterranean dishes. One of his specialties is the Moroccan braised and barbecued pork belly served on *skordalia* (a garlicky Greek sauce) with an aromatic roasted carrot salad. There's a welcoming log fire in winter, and in summer, an outdoor courtyard with oak trees and a fountain beckons. ⊠ *83 Main St., Greytown* ☎ *06/304–9825* ⊟ *AE, MC, V* ⌑ *Reservations essential* ⊙ *Closed Mon.*

$$–$$$ ✕ **Solstone Vineyard & Restaurant.** Wine pairings are the way to go at Seasons, the restaurant at this boutique winery. For instance, you could try fresh fish of the day poached in buttered wine, served with wilted bok choy and ginger *kūmara* (native sweet potato) mash, followed by chocolate-dipped strawberries, alongside a Classic Riesling. The room itself, with its vaulted ceiling, brick fireplace, and expansive view of the Tararuas, is a delight. You can take a winery tour, which includes a wine tasting, for $5. ⊠ *119 Solway Crescent, Masterton* ☎ *06/377–5505* ⊟ *AE, DC, MC, V.*

$$ ✕⊡ **Copthorne Resort Solway Park Wairarapa.** Set in 24 acres of landscaped grounds and gardens on the southern outskirts of Masterton, this is a large complex for this small town. The helpful staff and spacious rooms make this especially good if you're traveling with children. ⊠ *High St. S, Masterton* ☎ *06/3700–500* 🖷 *06/3700–501* ⊕ *www.solway.co.nz* ➷ *93 rooms, 8 apartments* ⌂ *2 restaurants, some kitchens, driving range, tennis court, 2 pools (1 indoor), gym, spa, boccie, squash, bar; no a/c* ⊟ *AE, DC, MC, V* ¶⊙| *BP.*

Sports & the Outdoors

Get a bird's-eye view of the area with a flight with **Ballooning New Zealand Ltd.**; a one-hour trip followed by a champagne breakfast costs $260. ⊠ *54b Kent St., next to the Paua Shell Factory, Carterton* ☎🖷 *06/379–8223.*

Shopping

For a unique souvenir, visit the **Paua Shell Factory and Shop** (✉ 54 Kent St., Carterton ☎ 06/379–6777 ⊕ www.pauashell.co.nz), 15 km (9 mi) south of Masterton. Paua (akin to abalone) has been collected by the Māori for food since ancient times. The rainbow-color shell interiors are highly prized (used by the Māori to represent eyes in their statues) and here are polished and processed, then turned into jewelry and other gifts.

THE WAIRARAPA ESSENTIALS

Transportation

BY CAR

A car is essential for getting around the Wairarapa. State Highway 2 runs through the region from north and south, between Napier and Wellington. From Wellington you'll drive through Upper Hutt, over the hills into the gateway town of Featherston. Highway 53 will take you to Martinborough; turn southwest here on Lake Ferry Road for Lake Ferry and Cape Palliser. Masterton is farther north along State Highway 2, roughly a half hour's drive from Martinborough. The journey from Wellington to Martinborough takes 1½ hours; Masterton is another half hour. From Napier, Masterton is about three hours. Most of the roads are straight two-lane highways in good condition. Unless there's a festival or special event happening, traffic is generally light.

TOURS

The Horse and Carriage Establishment runs tours around the Martinborough-area vineyards. The cost is $45 per person for a two-hour tour; advance booking is essential. The company also has twilight carriage drives, mystery tours, and horse-and-carriage rental for any specific journey.
🚩 **Horse and Carriage Establishment** ✉ Martinborough ☎ 0274/477–852.

VISITOR INFORMATION

There are two main Wairarapa visitor centers. In Martinborough, the visitor center is open daily 10 to 4, and in Masterton the visitor office is open 9 to 5 weekdays and 10 to 5 weekends. There's also a Featherston office, but the hours of operation can be erratic.
🚩 Tourist Information **Featherston Visitor Centre** ✉ The Old Courthouse, State Hwy. 2, Featherston ☎☎ 06/308–8051 ⊕ www.wairarapanz.com. **Martinborough Visitor Information Centre** ✉ 18 Kitchener St., Martinborough ☎ 06/306–9043. **Masterton Visitor Centre** ✉ 316 Queen St., Masterton ☎ 06/370–0911 ⊕ www.wairarapanz.com.

Upper South Island & the West Coast

WORD OF MOUTH

"If you want to see the real South Island, then be prepared to get your feet wet and your trousers a little dirty. Because the essence of this largely untamed, beautiful island lies in the great outdoors. Walk up a few riverbeds, hike a bush path, or paddle a kayak along the coast for a while. Wander along a pounding West Coast surf beach or climb high above an alpine lake. No five-star hotel, art gallery, or restaurant can give you this kind of hands-on experience."

—Sue Farley

Updated by
Sue Farley

THE CLOSE PASSAGE across Cook Strait separates the North Island from the South Island, but the difference between the two is far greater than the distance suggests. Whether you're first seeing the South Island from aboard a ferry as it noses through the rocky entrance to the Marlborough Sounds, or from the window of a plane, the immediate impression is that the landscape has become surreal: the mellow, green beauty of the North Island has given way to jagged snowcapped mountains and rivers that sprawl across vast, rocky shingle beds. The South Island has been carved by ice and water, a process still rapidly occurring. Locals will tell you that you haven't seen rain until you've been drenched by a storm on the West Coast, where annual precipitation is ambitiously measured in meters. Minor earthquakes rattle some part of the island every month—and residents are so used to them they barely notice. But you can still see the scars on the landscape left by some of the stronger ones over the last centuries.

The top half of the South Island is a fair introduction to the contrasts of New Zealand's less populated island. The Marlborough province occupies the northeast corner, where the inlets of the Marlborough Sounds flow around verdant peninsulas and sandy coves. Marlborough is now the largest wine-growing region in New Zealand, with more than 10,000 acres of vineyards. It's a relatively dry and beautifully sunny area, and in summer the inland plains look something like the American West, with mountains rising out of grassy flats. Throughout the upper South Island, you'll notice commercial foresting of the hills—Californian *Pinus radiata* (Monterey pine) mature rapidly in New Zealand soil. Their 25-year harvest cycle is one of the shortest in the world, a fact duly noted by Japanese lumber concerns.

The northwest corner of the island, the Nelson region, is a sporting paradise with a relatively mild climate that allows a year-round array of outdoor activities. Sun-drenched Nelson, a lively town with fine restaurants and a vibrant network of artists and craftspeople, is the gateway to an area surrounded by great national parks and hiking tracks (trails). Abel Tasman National Park, to the west of the city, is ringed with spectacularly blue waters studded with golden beaches and craggy rocks; these outcroppings guard coves and sands that are the stuff of dreams. To the southwest is Kahurangi National Park, home of the Heaphy Track, one of the world's Great Walks, and Nelson Lakes National Park with its alpine lakes and snowcapped peaks lies to the south.

After the gentler climate of Marlborough and Nelson, the wild grandeur of the West Coast comes as a surprise. This is Mother Nature with her hair down, flaying the coastline with huge seas and drenching rains and littering its beaches with pieces of bleached driftwood. When it rains, you'll feel like you're inside a fishbowl; then the sun bursts out, and you'd swear you're in paradise. (With such changeable weather, it's essential to check local conditions before heading out for an excursion.) It's a country that has created a special breed of people, and the rough-hewn and powerfully independent locals—

GREAT ITINERARIES

Numbers in the text correspond to numbers in the margin and on the Upper South Island and West Coast maps.

IF YOU HAVE 4 DAYS

With four days you confront the kind of conundrum that makes trip planning for the upper South Island difficult. You can see the northernmost part of the island: relaxing **Nelson** ❻, the wineries of **Blenheim** ❹, the beautiful beaches and forests of **Abel Tasman National Park** ❽ (if you're dead set on hiking, then all four days hiking the Abel Tasman track, the Heaphy Track on the upper West Coast, or the Queen Charlotte Track in the Marlborough Sounds). Or you can head straight for four days with the glaciers and wildlife of the West Coast.

IF YOU HAVE 7 DAYS

You *could* try to cover three of the major areas in this chapter—Marlborough, Nelson, and the West Coast, or Marlborough, Nelson, and Kaikoura, but allowing three or four days each for two areas is a better

plan. (Keep in mind that it takes at least half a day just to get to the West Coast from Nelson, and a full day from Picton.) Spend a day or two at the wineries, a day or two on the Marlborough Sounds sea kayaking or walking, perhaps swinging through **Havelock** ❸ on the way to or from the beautiful Kenepuru and Pelorus sounds, and then head to **Nelson** ❻ or the West Coast.

Or spend the first three days in and around Nelson, looking at arts and crafts, following a Heritage trail, tasting wine, and taking in **Abel Tasman National Park** ❽ and **Golden Bay–Takaka** ❾ area; then head to the West Coast. On the way down, stop at the town of Punakaiki for the coastal phenomenon called **Pancake Rocks** ⓬. You could overnight at **Greymouth** ⓭ or **Hokitika** ⓮ before continuing to Westland National Park to get yourself on the **Franz Josef Glacier** ⓰ or **Fox Glacier** ⓯. Then head south to Wanaka or Queenstown via the Haast Pass.

7

known to the rest of the country as Coasters—occupy a special place in New Zealand folklore.

Note: For more information on bicycling, fishing, hiking, and sea kayaking in Upper South Island, *see* Chapter 11.

Exploring Upper South Island & the West Coast

Many people arrive in the South Island on the ferry from Wellington to Picton, the northern entrance to the South Island. The trip is quite spectacular in good weather, but Cook Strait can also be a very rough stretch of water in bad weather. The only practical ways to travel through the upper South Island (with one or two exceptions) are by rental vehicle or by bus—but because there are so many scenic spots, you may find bus travel too restrictive. If driving, be conservative in your estimates of how long travel will take. Roads through the countryside's mountain ranges and deep river gorges are sometimes narrow and winding, taking longer to drive than you might think. A 100-mi drive, for instance, can easily take well over two hours. However, the roads are generally of a high standard.

Local tourism organizations have developed a driving route called **The Treasured Pathway** that covers the top of the South Island. A guide to the route, available in local bookshops, details all the significant scenic, cultural, and historic sights along the way.

A long narrow plain stretches from the Marlborough Sounds down the eastern coast of the upper South Island; State Highway 1 runs along this plain, going through Blenheim and Kaikoura on its way down to Canterbury. To the west, a series of high ranges separate Blenheim and Nelson. The side roads up into the Marlborough Sounds are slow and winding and often unpaved, so instead of driving, the best way to explore the sounds is often by boat from either Picton or Havelock.

South of Nelson and along the West Coast, the country becomes very mountainous. The series of high passes and long river gorges is broken only by small settlements. Much of this area is incredibly beautiful parkland, a great buildup to the glaciers and mountains in the South Westland World Heritage Area.

Though driving is the most convenient way to get around, there are two passenger train services worth considering here. One, the Coastal Pacific service, runs along the east coast between Picton and Christchurch, stopping at Blenheim and Kaikoura. The other, the TranzAlpine, crosses the Southern Alps between Christchurch on the east coast and Greymouth on the west. This route is a spectacular "back door" entry to the West Coast as it clambers over mountain passes, crosses high viaducts, and winds down through the heavily forested Taramakau River Valley.

About the Restaurants

The top of the South Island is where you'll find some of the country's best seafood, fruit, and wine. In Marlborough check out at least one winery restaurant—there's no better way to ensure that your meal suits what you're drinking. Salmon and Greenshell mussels are both farmed in the pristine Marlborough Sounds, and local crops—besides grapes—include cherries, wasabi, and garlic. In Kaikoura try crayfish (lobster). The region is named after this delicacy (*kai* means "food" in Māori; *koura* means "lobster"), and you'll find it not only in restaurants but occasionally sold in makeshift vans or roadside sheds. On the West Coast, try whitebait fritters—a sort of omelet starring masses of baby fish.

Some restaurants in this area close down in winter (June through August). Others may open only on weekends, or curtail their weekday hours. In summer, all doors are open, but you may find that there are too many people for the number of eateries. The Christmas and January holiday season is particularly busy, so it's best to make reservations whenever possible. Also, keep in mind that if a restaurant is open on a major hol-

TOP REASONS TO GO

MOUNTAINS & GLACIERS

The South Island is piled high with mountains. The massive Southern Alps mountain chain virtually slices the island lengthwise, and many outlying ranges spring up in the north. Extensive parklands make these mountains tantalizingly accessible—you can walk on and around them, ski them, or catch a helicopter to land on a glacier and hike around. In some places, such as the Kaikoura Coast Track, pioneering farmers have banded together to create farm-to-farm hiking trails. These take you through otherwise inaccessible mountains, bush, and coastal areas.

PUB LIFE

An essential part of the upper South Island experience is time with the locals—and there's no better place to get this than in a small-town pub at night, especially on the West Coast. When the wind is howling outside, or the surf is roaring, the pubs feel even cozier. There's often a big fire in a corner fireplace and local farmers, miners, or tour guides standing around the bar, tall stories flowing with the beer. Blokes and women alike tend to work hard and play hard, and they're keen to share a yarn. Should you blank on a topic of conversation, you can't go wrong with a rugby question.

WILDLIFE

The West Coast is the habitat for some very interesting creatures.

Tuatara, the last reptiles of their kind, live on the protected Stephens Island in Marlborough Sounds. South by Lake Moeraki, you may see fiordland crested penguins, and you'll have an even better chance of spotting New Zealand fur seals. On the other side of the island, along the Kaikoura Coast, you can get very close to whales, dolphins, and seals in the wild. In and around the Marlborough Sounds you're likely to see dolphins on a daily basis and orca whales in season. The Abel Tasman coastline is home to several colonies of fur seals. There's abundant birdlife up and down the coasts as well.

WINE

It took only a couple of decades for Marlborough to establish itself as one of the world's great wine-making regions. The local sunny-day–cool-night climate means grapes come off the vines plump with flavor, and that translates into wines with aromas that positively burst out of the glass. It's an exciting feistiness that some American connoisseurs consider too unbridled—but the wine is delicious, and you should seriously consider bringing a few bottles home. At any of the smaller wineries, it's quite likely you'll share your first taste of their labors with the winemakers themselves.

7

iday, it will likely add a surcharge to your bill to cover the higher rates it must pay its staff.

Year-round, the restaurants and cafés around the glaciers can be quick to close their doors at night. Be there by 8:30 (it's sometimes even earlier in winter), or you might go hungry. Some of the smallest towns, including Punakaiki, settlements in the Marlborough Sounds, and parts of Golden Bay, have few cafés and no general stores, so you may need to bring your own supplies.

WHAT IT COSTS In New Zealand dollars				
$$$$	**$$$**	**$$**	**$**	**¢**
RESTAURANTS Over $30	$20–$30	$15–$20	$10–$15	under $10

Prices are per person for a main course at dinner, or the equivalent.

About the Hotels

North Islanders might disagree, but you may find New Zealand's friendliest people in the rural areas of the South Island. And the best way to get to know them is to stay with them. Bed-and-breakfasts, farm stays, and homestays, all a variation on the same theme, abound in the South Island in some spectacular coastal or mountain settings. Your hosts will feed you great breakfasts and help with advice on where to eat and what to do locally. Other choices include luxury lodges and hotels, or inexpensive motel rooms and backpacker lodges—which are increasingly becoming more "luxurious," with higher-quality standards and more amenities for guests.

Summer (December through February) is the high season here. Locals generally take vacations from Christmas to January, so virtually every remote spot will be full of locals enjoying their summer break. Book early at these times. But from March through November everything settles down again, and in most towns you can book at short notice. The climate means that although heating is standard in virtually every room, air-conditioning is not; very few places have it, or need it.

WHAT IT COSTS In New Zealand dollars				
$$$$	**$$$**	**$$**	**$**	**¢**
HOTELS over $300	$200–$300	$125–$200	$75–$125	under $75

Prices are for a standard double room in high season, including 12.5% tax.

When to Visit

Nelson and Marlborough are pleasant year-round, but beach activities are best from December to mid-April if you plan to actually be *in* the water. December to February is the busiest time on walking tracks, with New Zealanders setting out on their own vacations. (Nelson, the Abel Tasman Track, and Golden Bay get especially crowded.) Snow covers the mountains from June through October, which is a beautiful sight from seaside Kaikoura. The best time to go whale-watching off Kaikoura is between October and August. The pleasures of winter weather around the West Coast glaciers—clear skies and no snow at sea level—are so far a well-kept local secret. Be sure to look into local festival schedules, such as Marlborough's Wine and Food Festival in February, Kaikoura's SeaFest in October, and Hokitika's Wild Foods Festival in March.

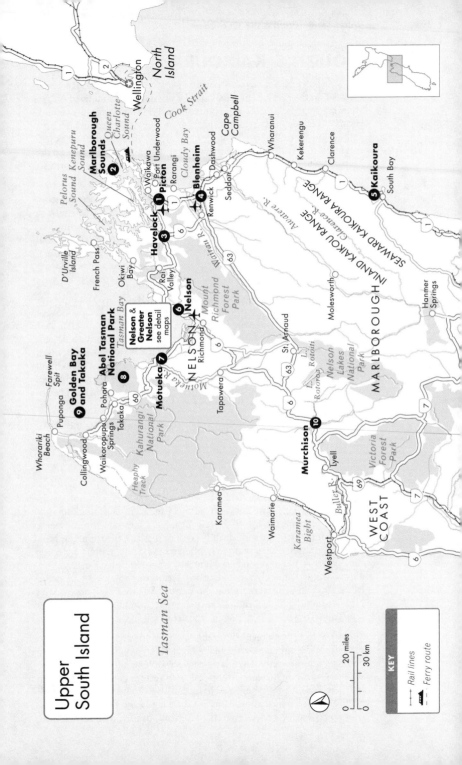

MARLBOROUGH & KAIKOURA

The Marlborough Sounds were originally settled by seafaring Māori people who, in their day, kept mostly to the coastal areas and lived off the abundant marine life. It's no wonder they didn't often venture inland, because these coastal areas are spectacular. The Māori named the area Te Tau Ihu O Te Waka a Māui ("the prow of Maui's canoe"), as legend has it that from his canoe the trickster demigod Maui fished up the North Island with the jawbone of a whale. Consequently the North Island is called Te Ika a Māui—"the fish of Maui."

European settlers first arrived in the early 1800s to hunt whales and seals. By the 1830s the whale and seal population had dropped drastically, so the settlers looked inland to the fertile river plains of the Wairau Valley, where Blenheim now stands. Surveyors were pressured to open more territory, but local Māori were reluctant to part with any more of their land and sabotaged the surveyors' work and equipment.

Outraged European settlers, led by Captain Arthur Wakefield, arrived from Nelson to "talk some sense" into the Māori chiefs. An angry fracas flared up beside the tiny Tuamarina River (now a marked picnic spot on the road between Picton and Blenheim). Captain Wakefield and 21 other Europeans, plus 9 Māori, including chief Te Rauparaha's daughter, were killed in what later became known as the Wairau Incident. Local government officials declared the attack "despicable," and the Nelson settlers were chastised for their actions. The land was later sold reluctantly by the Māori tribes, and by 1850 the Pākehā (non-Māori) began farming.

Thirty years later, the unwittingly prescient Charles Empson and David Herd began planting red muscatel grapes among local sheep and grain farms. Their modest viticultural torch was rekindled in the next century by the Freeth family, and by the 1940s Marlborough wineries were producing port, sherry, and Madeira most successfully.

At the same time, commercial wineries were growing up around Auckland and Hawke's Bay. But the volume of their grape production didn't meet their needs. In 1973 New Zealand's largest wine company, Montana, planted vines in Marlborough to increase the supply of New Zealand grapes. Other vintners followed suit, and within a decade today's major players—such as Hunter's, whose founder, Ernie Hunter, almost single-handedly launched the Marlborough name—had established the region's international reputation. Marlborough now boasts New Zealand's single largest area under vine, and many local growers sell grapes to winemakers outside the area.

Down the coast from Blenheim, Kaikoura is another area that the Māori settled, the predominant tribe being Ngai Tahu. True to their seafaring heritage, they are active in today's whale-watching interests. Ngai Tahu was one of the first major Māori tribes to receive compensation from the New Zealand government—to the tune of $170 million—along with an apology for unjust confiscation of their lands and fishing areas. The tribe today has extensive interests in tourism, fishing, and horticulture.

Picton

❶ *29 km (18 mi) north of Blenheim, 110 km (69 mi) east of Nelson.*

The maritime township of Picton (population 4,000) lies at the head of Queen Charlotte Sound and is the arrival point for ferries from the North Island, as well as a growing number of international cruise ships. It plays a major role in providing services and transport by water taxi to a multitude of remote communities in the vast area of islands, peninsulas, and waterways that make up the Marlborough Sounds Maritime Park. With such an expansive watery environment, it is not surprising that Picton is a yachting mecca and has two sizable marinas, at Picton Harbour and at the adjacent Waikawa Bay. Along with the port of Havelock, these make up the second-largest marina complex in New Zealand.

There's plenty to do in town, with crafts markets in summer, historical sights to see, and walking tracks to scenic lookouts over the sounds. The township wraps around the harbor and is easy to traverse on foot. The main foreshore is lined by London Quay, which looks up Queen Charlotte Sound to the bays beyond. High Street runs down to London Quay from the hills, and between them these two streets make up the center of town.

Take a walk along the waterfront to get a feel for Picton. The **Picton Museum** (✉ London Quay ☎ 03/573–8283 ☉ Daily 10–4 🎫 $4) details much of Picton's early seafaring history. The area was first a key Māori settlement called Waitohi, then an important whaling and sealing location for European immigrants in the early 19th century. Until 1860 there was no road access to Picton, so all trade and travel was done by sea. The restored scow *Echo* (✉ London Quay) is another reminder of the town's maritime past. Built in 1905 of the native hardwoods kauri and *totara,* the ship spent several years exporting frozen meat before joining the Picton-to-Wellington freight run in 1920. After a varied service career, she was decommissioned when the big new Cook Strait ferries made her redundant. Now she's been restored and opened as a gallery and café. (It's closed in winter.)

The preserved hulk of the *Edwin Fox,* now the **Edwin Fox Maritime Museum** (✉ Dunbar Wharf ☎ 03/573–6868), demonstrates how young New Zealand's European settlement is. The ship was used in the Crimean War, transported convicts to Australia, and brought settlers to New Zealand. Now dry-docked and restored, it serves as a museum, bringing to life the conditions the early immigrants faced. Check out the interesting interpretative displays upstairs, which outline the ship's history and service, before walking through the ship, where you can imagine how the settlers felt when shut below decks for months at a time, seasick, homesick, and unsure of what awaited them at landfall. Admission costs $8, and the ship is open daily 9 to 5.

❷ Picton is the base for cruising in the **Marlborough Sounds,** the labyrinth of waterways that was formed when the rising sea invaded a series of river valleys at the northern tip of the South Island. Backed by forested hills that at times rise almost vertically from the water, the sounds are

A Close Encounter with Dolphins

NEAR THE INNER ENTRANCE to Tory Channel, Dan, the boatman, skillfully brought the boat around as six of us slid into the water right beside a pod of playful Dusky dolphins. The 15-minute boat ride from Torea Bay had given us time to change, have a quick biology lesson, and learn a bit more about the dolphins. Although not as big as the common bottlenose dolphins, these beautiful silvery creatures were still at least 6 feet long and very strongly built. As we lay face down in the water, buoyant in our thick wetsuits, the dolphins came blasting up from the depths to swim right past us, time and again. Fins, masks and snorkels made it easier for us to follow them as they swirled and twirled around us. They never touched us, but were definitely interacting with us as they wheeled and turned just inches away. As they swam by, they turned on their sides and looked at us with their dark little eyes, their strong tails pushing them through the water. At other times they leaped from the water and came back down with a resounding splash. This was better than any wildlife documentary.

a wild, majestic place edged with tiny beaches and rocky coves and studded with islands where native wildlife remains undisturbed by introduced species. (Operators run tours to several of these special islands.) Māori legend says the sounds were formed when a great warrior and navigator called Kupe fought with a giant octopus. Its thrashings separated the surrounding mountains, and its tentacles became parts of the sunken valleys. These waterways are one of the country's favorite areas for boating, but for rugged grandeur they are in a class of their own.

Much of the area around Picton is untamed, forest-covered country, broken by sheltered bays and deep waterways, and it has changed little since Captain Cook found refuge here in the 1770s. There are rudimentary roads on the long fingers of land jutting into the sounds, but the most convenient access is invariably by water. Several operators travel the sounds' waterways on a daily basis, taking visitors along for the ride as they deliver the mail, groceries, and farming supplies to isolated residents and farms. Both Beachcomber and Cougar Line run from Picton and travel throughout Queen Charlotte Sound. Or leave from Havelock aboard the Pelorus mail boat, *Pelrous Express*, which delivers mail and supplies to outlying settlements scattered around Pelorus Sound. To get your feet on the ground in and around the sounds, you can take any number of hikes on the Queen Charlotte Track (*see* Sports & the Outdoors, *below*).

Where to Stay & Eat

$$$–$$$$ ✕ **The Chart Room.** True to its name, this smart, central restaurant is hung with copies of Captain Cook's nautical charts and maps—plus a rowing sculler suspended from the ceiling. The kitchen serves local favorites, such as green-lipped mussels, scallops, and venison medallions served with a vegetable ragout and mashed *kūmara* (native sweet potato). ⊠ *Yacht Club Hotel, Waikawa Rd.* ☎ *0800/991–188* ▭ *AE, DC, MC, V.*

$$$ ✕ **Skippers of Waikawa Bay.** The specialty of this laid-back beachfront café is local seafood, which they land off their own trawler. They also do good things with Nelson scallops, which are served with a mornay or garlic-chili sauce. ✉ *Port Underwood Rd., Waikawa Bay* ☎ *03/573–6351* ▤ *MC, V* ⊙ *No dinner Sun; closed Mon. and Tues. Apr.–Dec.*

$–$$$ ✕ **Expresso House.** This sunny, friendly place rapidly established a reputation for both terrific quality and value. The lunch menu includes open sandwiches such a chicken on rye bread with lemon-caper sauce; there are also some great choices that incorporate Thai flavors. At night the restaurant hits a bistro stride, with dishes such as oven-baked local salmon with lime glaze, rare-baked fillet of beef with wasabi cream, or heartier options such as Dutch sausage with *kūmara* (sweet potato) mash. There's a good selection of local wines and outdoor eating in the courtyard if you wish. ✉ *58 Auckland St.* ☎ *03/573–7112* ▤ *MC, V* ⊙ *Closed Wed. and winter.*

$–$$$ ✕ **Le Café.** Sitting outside Le Café you can look right down Queen Charlotte Sound and watch the local boat traffic and the big InterIslander ferries coming and going. While there you can enjoy a coffee or a cuppa from their pleasant selection of teas. Meals are available all day and well into the evening, and as night moves in, the tempo at the bar picks up and live acts appear on a casual basis. ✉ *London Quay* ☎ *03/573–5588* ▤ *MC, V.*

¢–$$$ ✕ **Rumba Café and Bar.** With big folding doors opening out onto the street, this spot is a favorite with locals throughout the summer. Dishes here—such as whitebait, fresh mussels and fish, steaks, and venison—draw on regional produce, and there's also a solid brunch menu and cabinet full of homemade goodies for a snack anytime. The upstairs bar does quick meals day and night and is perfect for enjoying an evening beer or glass of local wine. ✉ *31 High St.* ☎ *03/573–7040* ▤ *MC, V.*

¢–$ ✕ **Seumuss's Irish Nook.** Step inside this super-friendly little pub and you can feel a lilt rise in your throat and your "r"s starting to roll while your eyes adjust to the dim light. Just a short walk from the waterfront, Seumuss's is obviously well loved by locals and visitors alike; Alastair and Liz are very friendly hosts. The menu may be limited, but the dishes, such as the Guinness hot pot and stuffed potatoes, are satisfying and cheap. The full bar stocks eight different Irish whiskeys. The pub's open daily until 1 AM, making it a great spot to wait for the late-night ferry. ✉ *25 Wellington St.* ☎ *03/573–8994* ▤ *MC, V.*

$$–$$$$ ✕▥ **Bay of Many Coves Resort.** This resort is the pick of the spots in the FodorsChoice Sounds, set high on a bluff overlooking a private bay. Designed by the ★ architect who also did the national museum, Te Papa, in Wellington, the resort melts into its surrounding bush and seascape, belying its contemporary construction. The resort café and restaurant, and the modern, beautifully furnished units with their private verandas, all overlook the surrounding bays where yachts bob on their moorings and the sunsets are spectacular. The bathrooms feature open tiled showers, fluffy robes and locally made herbal toiletries. (There are also 6 studios, with shared bathroom facilities, that are only available between May and September.) You'll need to get here by taking a water taxi from Picton. ✉ *Bay of Many Coves, Queen Charlotte Sound* ☎ *03/579–9771, 0800/579–*

9771 🖨 *03/579–9777* ⊕ *www.bayofmanycovesresort.co.nz* ↰ *11 apartments, 6 studios* ⌂ *Restaurant, café, pool, outdoor hot tub, spa, kayaks, diving, tours* ⊟ *AE, DC, MC, V* ⎮◎⎮ *EP, MAP.*

★ **$$$** ✕⊡ **Furneaux Lodge.** This majestic old homestead was built in the early 1900s. Now a major lodge in the Marlborough Sounds, it still holds that feeling of being an oasis in the wilderness with its clipped lawns and sweeping palm trees edged by thick native forest. Recently refurbished, with a string of luxury units added, it offers a full range of accommodation for track walkers, fishermen, and those looking for the ultimate retreat. Meals are available in the restaurant or bar, and the menu ($$$) reflects the setting—lots of fish and venison. Because it's accessible only by water taxi or on foot, the masses are left far behind. ⊠ *Endeavour Inlet, off Queen Charlotte Sound* ☎ *03/579–8259* 🖨 *03/579–8279* ⊕ *www.furneaux.co.nz* ↰ *1 dorm, 26 rooms* ⌂ *Restaurant, bar* ⊟ *MC, V.*

★ **$$$–$$$$** ⊡ **Sennen House.** Just a few minutes' stroll from downtown Picton is this white, peak-roofed 1886 villa, whose verandas overlook 5 acres of lush landscaping and the glittering harbor beyond. The suites and apartments here are furnished with attention to historical detail, with carved wooden bedsteads and fireplace mantels, stained glass, rich upholstery, and brass fixtures. But modern-day luxury is here, too—the spotless bathrooms have heated towel bars and hair dryers, and there's a common high-speed Internet connection for guests to use. Owners Richard and Imogen Fawcett, who live on the property with their young family, bring a yummy breakfast hamper to your door each morning. ⊠ *9 Oxford St.* ☎☎ *03/573–5216* ⊕ *www.sennenhouse.co.nz* ↰ *2 suites, 3 apartments* ⌂ *Kitchens, in-room DVD, library, Internet room; no smoking* ⊟ *AE, MC, V* ⎮◎⎮ *CP.*

¢–$$$$ ⊡ **Punga Cove Resort.** Private chalets are tucked into the bush at this Queen Charlotte Track crossroads, with accommodation ranging from a backpacker lodge to luxury suites. The smaller A-frames have balconies, and several larger, more luxurious studio, one-, and two-bedroom chalets have large private decks with serene vistas of Camp Bay and Endeavour Inlet. You can rent kayaks and dinghies on site, and fishing trips can be arranged. Access is quickest by the *Cougar Line* water taxi, 45 minutes from Picton. Otherwise, a two-hour-plus drive winds along Queen Charlotte Sound Drive to the turnoff at Linkwater, where you come through the spectacular scenery of the Kenepuru Sound via some 5 km (2 mi) of gravel road. ⊠ *Punga Cove, Endeavour Inlet, Queen Charlotte Sound, Rural Bag 408, Picton* ☎ *03/579–8561* 🖨 *03/579–8080* ⊕ *www.pungacove.co.nz* ↰ *3 suites, 12 chalets, 4 lodge rooms, 8 backpacker cabins* ⌂ *Restaurant, café, some kitchens, pool, sauna, boating, 2 bars, shop; no a/c, no TV in some rooms* ⊟ *AE, MC, V.*

$$ ⊡ **The Gables.** You'll find this very centrally located 1924 house, now a B&B, just a short walk from the ferry terminal. Enjoy a predinner drink with hosts Ian and Paula Allen in the lounge, where there's a piano and a TV. The decor suggests a colonial theme without getting too hung up on the idea. For the most space, ask for the Pictonian room, which is bigger and has a large bathroom. Two individual cottages behind the main house are ideal if you'd prefer more privacy. ⊠ *20 Waikawa Rd.* ☎☎ *03/573–6772* ⊕ *www.thegables.co.nz* ↰ *3 rooms, 2 cottages*

⚥ *Lounge; no a/c, no room phones, no TV in some rooms, no smoking* ▭ *MC, V* ⏐❂⏐ *BP, CP.*

$$ 🖵 **Jasmine Court Travellers Inn.** A fresh, well-appointed place to stay, specializing in accommodation for adults, Jasmine Court looks down over the town to the main harbor. The guest rooms are well sized and done in soft pastels, with thoughtful touches such as fans, nonallergenic pillows, and CD and DVD players with a library of discs. Several bathrooms have either a whirlpool tub or a multihead shower. There's a supermarket just opposite the motel, handy for stocking up before hitting the remote areas of the Marlborough Sounds. ✉ *78 Wellington St.* ☎*03/573–7110 or 0800/421–999* 📠*03/573–7211* ⊕*www.jasminecourt. co.nz* 📶 *13 rooms, 1 apartment* ⚥ *Kitchens, in-room data ports, sauna, laundry service, Internet room; no kids under 14, no smoking* ▭ *AE, DC, MC, V.*

$$ 🖵 **Ocean Ridge Holiday Apartment.** From this secluded spot overlooking Port Underwood Sound, you might catch sight of fur seals, penguins, dolphins, or even an orca. Every room in this contemporary, self-catered apartment has a sea view, either across Cloudy Bay to the distant Kaikoura Ranges, up Port Underwood Sound, or across to Robertson Point. The space includes a lounge, dining area, fully equipped kitchen, and three large bedrooms; the basic fee covers the use of one bedroom, and each additional bedroom adds another $95. Bookings guarantee exclusive use of the apartment, whether booking one room or all three. Several hiking trails wind through the 54-acre property. Port Underwood Road is partially unpaved, steep, and winding, and can be rough in wet weather, so allow 45 minutes from Blenheim, turning off at Tuamarina, or from Picton via Waikawa Bay. But the effort to get there will be more than rewarded by the fantastic setting and the warm hospitality of hosts Sara and Ken Roush. Note that you'll need to bring in your own groceries. ✉ *Port Underwood Rd., Ocean Bay* 🖃 *Private Bag, Blenheim* ☎ *03/579–9474* 📠 *03/579–9474* ⊕ *www.nmb.quik.co.nz/roush* 📶 *3 rooms* ⚥ *Outdoor hot tub, beach, hiking; no room TVs, game room, no kids under 10, no smoking* ▭ *MC, V* ⏐❂⏐ *CP.*

$$ 🖵 **Whatamonga Homestay.** From the lounge here you can watch the ferries coming and going and hear fish splash in the clear, green water below. Whatamonga is a sheltered bay just a short drive from Picton, and if you haven't got time to do the full drive around Port Underwood, this is a delightful spot to fill the gap. Each unit has a kitchenette and balcony overlooking the sea. A private jetty, kayaks, and a dinghy are on hand for you to use. The water taxi will bring you here and pick you up from the jetty if you want to do a cruise around the sounds or get transport to the Queen Charlotte Track. Kids are welcome with prior arrangements. ✉ *425 Port Underwood Rd., Waikawa Bay* ☎ *03/573–7192* ⊕ *www.whsl.co.nz* 📶 *3 rooms* ⚥ *No a/c, no room phones, no room TVs, no smoking* ▭ *MC, V* ⏐❂⏐ *BP.*

¢ 🖵 **The Villa.** Like a big, happy tribe, Villa guests fill a small, lovely colonial house. The hostel's central courtyard hums day and night with people relaxing after a day on the water, mountain biking, or walking the Queen Charlotte Track. On rainy days you can lie in front of the fire with a book, play guitar, or curl up in a quiet corner to write letters. A legendarily good apple pie and ice-cream dessert in winter, pickups and drop-offs, a hot tub, use of the gym, and bike usage are included in the price. New kitchens have good space for cooking your own meals. ✉ *34 Auckland St.* 🕾🕾 *03/573–6598* ⊕ *www.thevilla.co.nz* ↩ *7 double rooms, 2 with bath, 50 dorm beds; no room phones* ⚒ *Gym, outdoor hot tub, bicycles, no in-room phones, no in-room TVs* ⊟ *MC, V.*

Sports & the Outdoors

For information on deep-sea fishing out of Picton, *see* Chapter 11.

DIVING The Marlborough Sounds has an excellent dive site in the *Mikhail Lermontov*. In 1986, this Russian cruise ship sank on her side in 30 meters (100 feet) of water in Port Gore. (Only one life was lost.) The 200-meter-long (600-foot) ship is now an exciting dive site for anyone with moderate diving skills. Highlights are the swimming pool in its glass veranda room, the bridge, and the huge funnel. September and October are generally the best months for good visibility.

Dive Marlborough's Brent McFadden takes daily guided trips out to the Mikhail Lermontov (as long as there are at least two people who want to go, and as long as the weather cooperates). The $190 fee includes lunch and all diving gear; it costs a bit less if you have your own wet suit and BC, and a bit more if you want nitrox. ✉ *Waikawa Bay Marina* 🕾 *03/573–9181 or 0800/463–483* ⊕ *www.godive.co.nz.*

DOLPHIN ENCOUNTERS ★ Marine biologists Amy and Dan Engelhaupt, who run **Dolphin Watch,** will take you to where the dolphins are. Often just a 15-minute boat ride out of Picton you can slide into the water and swim with these beautiful creatures ($125), or stay dry and watch them from the boat ($80). If the weather's a bit rough you can visit an island wildlife reserve instead and see rare and protected birds in their natural native forest surroundings. There are certain months when dolphin swims aren't available, either because the dolphins are migrating or breeding, so be sure to call ahead. ✉ *Picton Harbour:* 🕾 *03/573–8040, 0800/9453–5433* 🖷 *03/573–7906* ⊕ *www.dolphinswimming.co.nz.*

HIKING FodorsChoice ★ Starting northwest of Picton, the **Queen Charlotte Track** stretches 67 km (42 mi) south to north, playing hide-and-seek with the Marlborough Sounds along the way. Hike through lush native forests, stopping here and there to swim or to pick up shells on the shore. Unlike other tracks such as the Abel Tasman in Golden Bay, there are no Department of Conservation huts to stay in, just a few points on the way for camping. There are other types of accommodation on the walk, however, from backpacking options to lodges, resorts, and homestays. Boats such as the *Cougar Line* can drop you off at various places for one- to four-day walks (guided or unguided), or you can kayak or bike parts of it.

Though it's relatively easy to access, the track shouldn't be taken lightly. It has steep inclines and long drop-offs, and the weather along it can be unpredictable. In particular, day three, if you're walking north to south, is a 22-km (14-mi) stretch that can test even a good hiker's endurance in bad weather. If you're a novice or not in great shape, it's a good idea to do the track with a guide.

Both the Picton Visitor Information Center and the local **Department of Conservation–Sounds Area Office** (✉ Box 161, Picton ☎ 03/520–3002 ⊕ www.doc.govt.nz) are good sources of track information.

★ One way to get the best of a trip along the Queen Charlotte Track is to do a combination trip, combining a bit of hiking, some arm-flexing in a kayak, and some legwork on a mountain bike. A three-day trip organized by **Marlborough Sounds Adventure Company** (✉ The Waterfront, Picton ☎ 03/573—6078 or 0800/283–283 ⊕ www.marlboroughsounds.co.nz) combines these three activities in a fully guided experience with all the details such as where to eat and sleep taken care of, as well as having your packs ferried ahead each day. Accommodation is bunk-room standard, and you'll need a reasonable level of fitness. The $695 fee includes all water transfers, guide, twin share accommodation, packed lunches, and equipment. The trip kicks off every Wednesday from November through April.

KAYAKING   The best way to experience the Marlborough Sounds is by sea kayak—and the mostly sheltered waters of Queen Charlotte Sound are the perfect place to try your hand at kayaking. **Marlborough Sounds Adventure Company** offers both guided and self-guided kayak trips, with everything from half-day to three-day tours, in either Queen Charlotte or Kenepuru sounds. The bays are ringed by dense native forest, echoing with the trilling calls of native birds; the water around you ripples as dolphins glide past. Costs range from $50 for a half-day kayak rental to $410 for a three-day guided trip. ✉ *The Waterfront, Picton* ☎ *03/573–6078 or 0800/283–283* ⊕ *www.marlboroughsounds.co.nz.*

You can take a one-day guided kayak trip with **Wilderness Guides** for just $80, lunch included. It's an easy option if you're short on time and can't make it into the more remote waterways of Queen Charlotte Sound. They also do multiday trips beside the Queen Charlotte Track, and kayak rentals if you want to do it on your own (as long as a minimum of two people are paddling together). ✉ *Picton Railway Station, 3 Auckland St.* ☎ *03/520–3095 or 0800/266–266* 🖷 *03/520–3096* ⊕ *www.wildernessguidesnz.com.*

Shopping

Latitude 41 (✉ 42 High St. ☎ 03/573–9070 ⊙ Daily 9–8 in summer, 9–5 in winter) has a tasteful selection of affordable New Zealand art, including a good range of iconic artwork by Diana Adams. Wind-tossed cabbage trees, edgy coastal scenes, and deep blue seascapes will provide lasting mementos of your trip Down Under.

EN ROUTE   To take the long way to Blenheim, **Port Underwood Road** is yet another unbelievably scenic route in a country full of unbelievably scenic routes. There are picnic areas north of Waikawa before you reach the eastern coastal bays, and a couple more near Rarangi. Head toward Waikawa Bay just north out of Picton and continue around the bay before heading up the Whatamonga Hill from Karaka Point. You could also pick up the road driving north out of Rarangi from the Blenheim end. Be prepared for a winding, hilly route without any stores, cafés, or gas stations along the way. But you'll be rewarded with far-reaching views out over Port Underwood and Cloudy Bay and a glimpse of some truly New Zealand country. Kakapo Bay is marked as the site of the first whaling station in Port Underwood—it's also the site where the first European child was born in the South Island.

Heading west out of Picton toward the town of Havelock, **Queen Charlotte Drive** rises spectacularly along the edge of Queen Charlotte Sound. It cuts across the base of the peninsula that separates this waterway from Pelorus Sound, then drops onto a small coastal plain before coming to Havelock. Beyond Havelock the road winds through forested river valleys before it rounds the eastern side of Tasman Bay and reaches Nelson. To start the drive from the InterIslander ferry terminal in Picton, turn right after leaving the parking lot and follow the signs. About a third of the way to Havelock, Governor's Bay is a gorgeous spot for a picnic or a stroll along the forested shore. Cullen Point, at the Havelock end of the drive, is a good vantage point to view the inland end of the Pelorus Sound and across the bay to Havelock. A short walk to the lookout is well worth the effort.

Havelock

❸ *35 km (22 mi) west of Picton.*

Known as the Greenshell mussel capital of the world (Greenshells are a variety of green-lipped mussels), Havelock is at the head of Pelorus Sound, and trips around the sounds on the Pelorus Sound mail boat, *Pelorus Express,* depart here. Locals will forgive you for thinking you've seen what the Marlborough Sounds are all about after crossing from the North Island to the South Island on the ferry—that's just a foretaste of better things to come. Small, seaside Havelock (population 400) is a good place to stroll; check out the busy little marina, poke into a few arts and crafts shops, and tuck into some of those mussels.

Where to Stay & Eat

$$$ ✕ **The Clansman.** Built of chunky gray stone and heavy bridge beams, the Clansman will warm the cockles of your heart. In warm weather, ask for a table in the outdoor courtyard; in winter, gather around the big stone fireplace. The menu focuses on local seafood such as mussels and cockles, scallops, and the freshest blue cod cooked in beer batter. ⊠ *72 Main Rd.* ☎ *03/574–1170* ▭ *AE, MC, V.*

$$–$$$ ✕ **Slip Inn.** Down at the marina, the Slip Inn overlooks the main boat ramp and working area—it's a sunny spot to stop for a light lunch or dinner. And a big outdoor fire keeps it warm even on chilly winter days. The chef favors local mussels; one favorite dish is the Kilpatrick, mussels grilled with bacon and cheese. Or try the bivalves steamed and served with a creamy coriander sauce. If you're not a mussel fan, you can choose from options such as the panfried fish with a warm zucchini-and-leek salad. ⊠ *Havelock Marina* ☎ *03/574–2345* ▭ *MC, V.*

$–$$$ ✕ **Mussel Boys Restaurant.** Outside, giant fiberglass mussels play rugby on the roof. Inside, the real things are served two ways—steamed for three minutes in the whole shell (steamers) and on the half shell (flats). Choose a light sauce for both steaming and topping: white wine, garlic, and fresh herbs; coconut, chili, and coriander; or even pesto with tomato and Parmesan cheese. Sauvignon blanc from nearby Marlborough perfectly pairs with almost any dish on the menu. The "Secret Life of Mussels" display on the wall details all the facts you would ever want to know about the creature and its rather ho-hum lifestyle. ⊠ *73 Main Rd.* ☎ *03/574–2824* ⊟ *AE, DC, MC, V.*

¢–$ ✕ **Pelorus Bridge Café.** Fancy a wild pork and kūmara (native sweet potato) pie, some mussel fritters, a piece of carrot cake dripping under a smear of sweet frosting, or just a nice cup of coffee? This spot is one of the better on-the-road cafés you'll find in the area; it even has some special kid-friendly options. The lovely setting beside the rocky, tree-lined Pelorus River is a bonus, especially in summer when you can eat outside under the trees. The café closes at 5 PM. ⊠ *State Hwy. 6, by Pelorus Bridge* ☎ *03/571–6019* ⊟ *No credit cards.*

$$$–$$$$ 🏠 **Glentui Lodge.** A 20-minute boat ride up Pelorus Sound from Havelock, this lodge is a perfect rural getaway. The house is available as a self-catering stay (bring your own food and wines, as there are no stores nearby), but Julie Boys is available to cook if requested beforehand. Accessible only by boat, with big open fires, a woodstove, a selection of local wines, and a veranda overlooking the sea, the lodge is a perfect antidote to the rat race. You can take out a dinghy or slip into the water for a swim. You'll need to bring any necessary supplies from Havelock. The price is a whole-house rate. ⊠ *Rimu Bay, Pelorus Sound* ☎ *03/574–1198* 🖷 *03/574–1197* ✍ *rimubays.glentui@xtra.co.nz* ⚓ *3 rooms* ⚓ *Fishing; no a/c, no room TVs, no smoking* ⊟ *MC, V.*

$$–$$$ 🏠 **Mudbrick Lodge.** The pretty winding road that leads to Mudbrick sets the mood for this charming, welcoming spot, presided over with Kiwi hospitality by owner Tania Lawrence. Cheerful log fires, excellent meals, and fresh espresso all feed the senses while just out the window the rugged Marlborough landscape reminds you that you're almost on the edge of the world here. Experienced guides are available to take you to quiet trout pools, deserted islands, and sunny fishing spots. ⊠ *Carluke, near Rai Valley* ☎ *03/571–6147* ⊕ *www.mudbricklodge.co.nz* ⚓ *2 suites* ⚓ *Outdoor hot tub, fishing, library; no a/c, no room TVs* ⊟ *MC, V* ⋔ *BP.*

★ ¢–$$$ 🏠 **The Portage Resort Hotel.** This hotel's remote location doesn't prevent the staff from offering high-quality, even luxurious accommodations. Lodgings here range from backpacker beds for hikers straight off the Queen Charlotte Track to very comfortable hotel rooms with private deck sand and fabulous views across Kenepuru Sound. Dining at the Te Weka restaurant is as good as any city restaurant; local seafood and mussels, along with excellent local wines, are the highlights. You can access the Portage by boat or car from Havelock; the drive takes about 1½ hours on a paved but winding road. ⊠ *Kenepuru Sound, 19 km (12 mi) off Queen Charlotte Dr.* ☎ *03/573–4309* 🖷 *03/573–4362* ⊕ *www.portage. co.nz* ⚓ *35 rooms, 22 dorm beds* ⚓ *Restaurant, café, pool, hot tub, bar* ⊟ *AE, DC, MC, V* ⋔ *BP.*

EN ROUTE The **Pelorus Bridge Scenic Reserve** is about halfway between both Picton and Nelson and Blenheim and Nelson on State Highway 6. This scenic area is a good example of the native lowland forest—with beech, podocarp, and broadleaf trees—that once covered this whole region.

There's a network of easy walking trails through the reserve, and in summer the river is warm enough to jump in for a refreshing swim (just watch out for the sand flies after the sun goes down). **Kahikatea Flat** (☎ 03/571–6019), a hidden gem of a campground, is part of the reserve; it's in a quiet spot where, most of the year, the loudest noises are made by the bellbirds and the nearby river. A fee of $22 will get you a campsite with access to showers and BBQs.

Blenheim

❹ *29 km (18 mi) south of Picton, 120 km (73 mi) southeast of Nelson, 129 km (80 mi) north of Kaikoura.*

Many people come to Blenheim (pronounced *bleh*-num by the locals) for one reason—wine. There are dozens of wineries around this town, and taste-the-good-life restaurants and hotels are springing up all over, ready for the resulting wave of oenophiles. Blenheim itself is developing fast, though its center still has a small-town veneer, with narrow streets, paved crossings, and low-slung buildings.

Most years, Marlborough has lots of sunshine, and this daytime warmth combines with crisp, cool nights to give local grapes a long, slow ripening period. The smooth river pebbles that cover the best vineyards are a bonus—they reflect heat onto the ripening bunches. All these factors together create grapes with audacious flavors. Whites reign supreme. Cabernet sauvignon has mostly been pulled out after disappointing results, but recent examples of pinot noir have been pretty impressive.

In 1973 the Montana company paid two Californian wine authorities to investigate local grape-growing potential. Both were impressed with what they found. It was the locals who were skeptical—until they tasted the first wines produced. After that, Montana opened the first modern winery in Marlborough in 1977, although there had been fledgling efforts 100 years earlier by pioneering wine growers. The region now has more than 70 vineyards and wineries, and Montana continues to be a market force in the region.

Although Marlborough made its name initially on sauvignon blanc, firmly placing New Zealand on the world map as a high-quality wine producer, it is now as well known for its excellent riesling, pinot noir, chardonnay, gewürztraminer, and pinot gris wines. Medals at international wine competitions are a regular occurrence, and the Marlborough Wine and Food Festival held in mid-February each year celebrates the region's success in suitable style.

Don't bury your nose in a tasting glass entirely, though; the landscape here shouldn't be overlooked. The vineyards sprawl across the large alluvial plains around the Wairau River, ringed by high mountains. On clear days you'll be able to spot **Mt. Tapuaenuku**, which, at 3,000 meters (10,000 feet), is the tallest South Island mountain north of the Mt. Cook area.

The wineries described below are among the country's notables, but you won't go wrong if you stop at any of the vineyards around Blenheim.

CLOSE UP

News from the Grapevine

NEW ZEALAND WINE IS ON A roll. At international competitions all over the world, Kiwi winemakers are becoming a regular presence on awards lists. Despite all the accolades, the history of top-wine production here can be counted in just decades, not generations.

There are more than 500 wineries here, but only six produce more than 2 million liters annually. The total vineyard acreage is just two-thirds the amount of California's Sonoma County alone. Because even the largest companies are small by international standards, management remains close to the wine-making process—with outstanding results.

New Zealand's rugged landscape leads to major differences between the grape-growing regions, even if they're small in scale, and this diversity means that most of Europe's great grapes have found a second home somewhere in the country. Pinot noir in particular is benefiting (and if you've seen the movie *Sideways*, you'll remember how finicky this grape is) as the hardier European varieties are planted at increasingly higher latitudes, especially in the Otago region.

- **Sauvignon blanc,** particularly from Marlborough, is the export star. It's noted for tropical-fruit characters such as passion fruit and pineapple.

- **Chardonnay** grows well all over the country. Left to its own devices, it has a citric, melonlike flavor, but wood-aging gives it spiciness.

- **Riesling** is a gentle variety, with a floral, lightly scented bouquet and fruity taste. Most local versions have at least a touch of sweetness.

- **Gewürztraminer** is the most distinctive grape variety of them all, with a superspicy bouquet reminiscent of litchis and cloves. Many of the best Kiwi examples come from Gisborne, but a couple of exceptional versions have come out of Hawke's Bay and Martinborough.

- **Pinot gris** is an up-and-comer in New Zealand. At its best, it produces wine with delightfully grainy character and loads of honest flavor. Marlborough growers see a lot of potential in this thin-skinned variety.

- **Cabernet sauvignon** is suited to warmer parts of New Zealand. Most years, it performs best in Hawke's Bay and on Waiheke Island. It's often blended with merlot and cabernet franc.

- **Merlot** was first used in blends, but more and more Kiwi winemakers are bottling it on its own. It has leather-coffee-tobacco undertones that are often summed up as "British gentleman's club."

- **Pinot noir,** long considered a stumbling block, has been working well for many winemakers across the country. It's often described in red-fruit terms, with notes of strawberries, cherries, and plums. Central Otago is the top region for this variety, with winemakers rushing to put more acres under vine.

Kiwi vintners don't stand on ceremony—even the ceremony of uncorking a bottle. Frustrated by faulty natural cork, an increasing number of winemakers have made the move to screw caps—so you shouldn't automatically shudder if there's no corkscrew required.

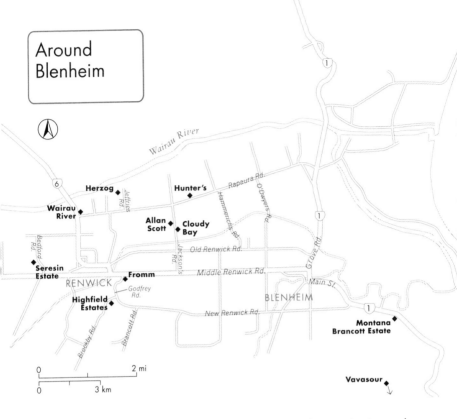

Around
Blenheim

Wairau River

6 Herzog
Wairau
River
Jeffries Rd.

Hunter's
Rapaura Rd.
O'Dwyers Rd.

Allan
Scott Cloudy
Bay
Harmerichs Rd.

Bedford Rd.
Jacksons Rd.
Old Renwick Rd.

Grove Rd.

Seresin
Estate
Fromm
RENWICK
Godfrey Rd.
Middle Renwick Rd.
Main St.

BLENHEIM

Highfield
Estates
Brookby Rd.
Brancott Rd.
New Renwick Rd.

Montana
Brancott Estate

0   2 mi
0   3 km

Vavasour

Tastings are generally free, although more and more wineries are charging a tasting fee, typically around 50 cents per tasting. More than half of the wine bottled here is exported, particularly to the United Kingdom, although a few forward-thinkers are targeting the United States. If you've never tried a Marlborough wine, you have some great discoveries ahead of you.

The roads where most wineries are located are arranged more or less in a grid, which makes getting around relatively straightforward. Rapaura Road is the central artery for vineyard visits; wineries also cluster around Jeffries and Jacksons roads, radiating out from Rapaura Road, the area around Renwick village, and State Highway 1 south of Blenheim. Pick up a map of the Marlborough wine region at the **Marlborough Visitor Information Centre** (⊠ The Old Railway Station, Sinclair St., along State Hwy. 1 ☎ 03/577–8080 🖶 03/577–8089).

If you're hankering for something a little different from vineyard tours and tastings, you can try visiting the **Aviation Heritage Centre** (⊠ Omaka Aerodrome, Aerodrome Rd., off New Renwick Rd. 🖶 03/578–8227 ⊕ www.classicfighters.co.nz). Although it's currently under construction, it will be completed in time to host the two-day Classic Fighters Airshow of April 2007 (the center will also be the showpiece for the Classic Fighters Charitable Trust, which runs the airshow every two years.) A large range of vintage and classic aircraft will be on display, both on the ground and in the sky. Dogfights, war memorabilia, and real-action replays keep the action going.

Wineries

★ **Allan Scott Wines.** Allan Scott helped establish the big-selling Stoneleigh label for Corbans, the country's second-biggest wine company, before launching his own company in 1990. Now he makes well-respected sauvignon blanc, chardonnay, pinot noir, gewürztraminer, and riesling (the last two are particularly good). The winery also makes Marlborough's first beer—a tasty, rather manly brew called Moa. The tasting room is next to a pleasant indoor-outdoor restaurant (open for lunch only) with lavender hedges and tall shade trees. ⊠ *Jackson's Rd., R.D. 3, Blenheim* ☎ *03/572–9054* 🖷 *03/572–9053* ⊕ *www.allanscott.com* ☉ *Daily 9:30–5.*

Cloudy Bay Vineyards. From the start, Kevin Judd produced first-class sauvignon blanc, and an equally impressive chardonnay was added to the portfolio soon afterward. That was the intention of Australia's Cape Mentelle Vineyards when it got Cloudy Bay up and running in 1985. Its sauvignon blancs are consistently highly rated for their notes of citrus, pear, and passion fruit; these are generally ready for immediate drinking. The chardonnay is more complex and can take medium-term cellaring. ⊠ *Jackson's Rd., Blenheim* ☎ *03/520–9140* 🖷 *03/520–9040* ⊕ *www.cloudybay.co.nz* ☉ *Daily 10–4:30; tours by appointment.*

Fromm Winery–La Strada. Although Marlborough is best known for its white wines, Fromm pioneered the local use of pinot noir, which now makes up 50% of their production. Rieslings are another Fromm strength, and they have become well known for their syrah, malbec, and merlot reserves as well. All their wines are produced from handpicked, carefully selected grapes; the intense vintages are made to cellar. ⊠ *Godfrey Rd., Renwick* ☎ *03/572–9355* ⊕ *www.frommwineries.com* ☉ *Oct.–Apr., daily 11–5; May–Sept., Fri.–Sun. 11–4 or by appointment.*

Fodor'sChoice **Herzog.** Therese and Hans Herzog planted their first vines along Jeffries
★ Road back in 1994, while still living much of the year in Europe. Now full-time Kiwis, they produce a superb range of wines off their pesticide- and chemical-free vineyard. Pinot gris, pinot noir, and what may be the area's only montepulciano are standouts, and the tasting area invites you to spend a long sunny afternoon exploring the delights of the cellar. You can enjoy an elegant bistro lunch in the tasting room, or, if you've made reservations and want to really experience gustatory nirvana, you can have a full meal at the adjoining restaurant—widely considered to be one of the best in the country. ⊠ *81 Jeffries Rd., off Rapaura Rd.* ☎ *03/572–8770* ⊕ *www.herzog.co.nz* ☉ *Daily 9–4; variable hours in winter.*

Highfield Estate. This magnificent place sits high on the Brookby Ridge, with spectacular views over the Wairau plains all the way to the North Island. The winery building unabashedly imitates Tuscan style with arches, tiles, and terra-cotta plaster. Highfield specializes in sauvignon blanc, with interesting pinot noir, chardonnay, riesling, and a sparkling wine in its cellars as well. There's an indoor-outdoor restaurant here, too, where bookings are recommended in summer. ⊠ *Brookby Rd., R. D. 2, Blenheim* ☎ *03/572–9244* 🖷 *03/572–9257* ⊕ *www.highfield. co.nz* ⊙ *Daily 10–5.*

★ **Hunter's Wines.** Ernie Hunter's marketing skills pushed Marlborough into the international spotlight; after his tragic death in a car crash, his wife, Jane, with winemaker Gary Duke, forged ahead and expanded the vineyard to 2½ times its original size. They have a reputation for remarkable wines, including an oak-aged sauvignon blanc, and have won dozens of awards. Likewise, the winery's restaurant is worth seeking out (⇨ Where to Stay & Eat, *below*). ⊠ *Rapaura Rd., Blenheim* ☎ *03/ 572–8489* 🖷 *03/572–8457* ⊕ *www.hunters.co.nz* ⊙ *Daily 9:30–4:30.*

Montana Brancott Winery. With plenty of bells and whistles, this impressive center is a new departure for Marlborough. The visitor center includes a tasting area, a restaurant, a theater, and of course, retail. Winery tours are given daily from 10 to 3. Their star vintage is sauvignon blanc; their pinot noir is on the rise as well. Tastings cost a few dollars, and if you plan to come in summer, you may need to reserve in advance. ⊠ *State Hwy. 1, 2½ mi (4 km) south of Blenheim* ☎ *03/578–2099* 🖷 *03/ 578–0463* ⊕ *www.montana.co.nz* ⊙ *Daily 9–5.*

Seresin Estate. Named for owner Michael Seresin, a New Zealand–born filmmaker, this estate stands out by virtue of its organic viticulture. Viticulturalist Bart Arnst and his team pursue high standards of environmentally friendly cultivation while winemaker Brian Bicknell uses wild yeasts and natural methods to produce the wines. Seresin also produces a Tuscan-style extra-virgin olive oil. ⊠ *Bedford Rd., Blenheim* ☎ *03/ 572–9408* 🖷 *03/572–9850* ⊕ *www.seresin.co.nz* ⊙ *Daily 10–4:30.*

Vavasour Wines. An almost instant hit among Marlborough's mid-1980s start-ups, the small, extremely conscientious wine-making operation at Vavasour produces sensitively balanced whites and reds. Based on the quality of a given year's harvest, grapes will be used either for Reserve vintages available in limited quantities or the medium-price-range Dashwood label. Vavasour is in its own microclimate, in the Awatere Valley south of Blenheim. You won't taste as many varieties here, but what you taste will be interesting and very well crafted—for instance, the rosé is definitely worth trying. ⊠ *Redwood Pass Rd., Awatere Valley, 20 km (12 mi) south of Blenheim* ☎ *03/575–7481* 🖷 *03/575–7240* ⊕ *www. vavasour.com* ⊙ *Nov.–Mar., daily 10–5; Apr.–Oct., Sun.–Fri. 10–4; tours by appointment.*

Wairau River Wines. Phil and Chris Rose were the first contract grape growers in Marlborough. Now they produce a very good range of classic Marlborough-grown wines under their own label. The tasting room is made from mud bricks; it also serves as a restaurant, concentrating on local produce, which is open noon–3. Try the multi-award-winning sauvignon blanc and, if it's available, the startlingly good, sweet riesling, made in some years from grapes infected with the mold the French call the "noble rot." ⊠ *Rapaura Rd. and State Hwy. 6, Blenheim* ☎ *03/572–9800* 🖷 *03/572–9885* ⊕ *www.wairauriverwines.com* ⊙ *Daily 10–5.*

Where to Stay & Eat

$$$$ ✕ **Herzog.** Marlborough's finest dining experience is tucked away along
Fodor'sChoice a short side road leading down to the Wairau River. Superb three- and
★ five-course dinner menus pair Herzog wines with innovative dishes; the
set and á la carte menus might include silky yellowfin tuna carpaccio,
seared Nelson scallops with asparagus-ricotta ravioli, or a millefeuille
with mascarpone mousse and rhubarb compote. The legendary degustation dinners ($199 per person) are booked out well in advance. In addition to the wine pairings, you can study the wine list of 500 vintages.
Retire to the lounge after dinner for a cigar and coffee. Herzog also runs
very popular cooking classes from November to March; once again book
ahead. ⊠ *Jeffries Rd., off Rapaura Rd.* ☎ *03/572–8770* ⚒ *Reservations essential* ☰ *AE, D, MC, V* ☉ *Closed Mon. and June–Sept.*

★ **¢–$$$$** ✕ **The Store.** Sue and Richard Macfarlane run a visually stimulating one-stop store and café right by the sea on SH1 heading south toward Kaikoura. The space uses natural wood and displays interesting potted
plants, barrels, and an open fireplace. On this dramatic perch at the edge
of the Pacific, the waves almost reach the open deck. You can choose
lunch from either the cabinet or a blackboard menu; try the fresh
seafood or chicken and avocado salad with a glass of local wine. Dinner bookings are essential in summer; in winter, The Store closes at 7
PM, with the last order taken around 6:30. ⊠ *State Hwy. 1, Kekerengu,
64 km (40 mi) south of Blenheim* ☎ *03/575–8600* 🖷 *03/575–8620*
☰ *MC, V.*

$$$ ✕ **Bacchus.** Marcel Rood has cooked at Michelin-starred restaurants in
Europe and done the rounds of top kitchens in New Zealand. Now he's
settled in wine country—and loving it. His restaurant has a romantic
feel, with rich burgundy walls and lots of brocade. A fountain (in the
shape of Bacchus—who else?) occupies the small courtyard, and inside
an open fire keeps things cozy in winter. Marcel makes good use of New
Zealand produce in dishes such as bacon-wrapped beef fillet on kūmara
(native sweet potato) mash. ⊠ *3 Main St.* ☎☎ *03/578–8099* ☰ *AE,
MC, V* ☉ *No lunch.*

$$$ ✕ **Bellafico Caffé & Wine Bar.** Serving only dinner allows the hosts here
to hold their dishes, which feature local produce and wines, to a very
high standard. The kitchen uses wild venison whenever it can get it, and
if you're a meat lover, you can try the Angus beef served with almond
croquettes potatoes and balsamic jus. The tamarillo and white chocolate cheesecake is also to die for. ⊠ *17 Maxwell Rd.* ☎ *03/577–6072*
☉ *No lunch* ☰ *AE, DC, MC, V.*

$$$ ✕ **Hunter's Vineyard Restaurant.** Dining at a vineyard is a great way to
Fodor'sChoice appreciate how seriously the best New Zealand winemakers have food
★ in mind when they create their wine. Local produce stars at this pleasant indoor-outdoor eatery. Marlborough Greenshell mussels, steamed
open in Hunter's Riesling with wild thyme and garlic, are a great match
for a glass of that same riesling. Dishes such as double-braised lamb shanks
with rosemary potatoes may tempt you to try one of the Hunter's reds.
They're leaner and greener than North Island examples, but they go well
with the local food. The garden here is especially lovely, with native
plants—cabbage trees, tussock grasses, rengarenga lilies—interspersed

with exotic rhododendrons, magnolias, and Australian gums. ✉ *Rapaura Rd.* ☎ *03/572–8803* ⊟ *AE, DC, MC, V* ⊘ *No dinner Sun.–Wed.*

$$$ ✕ **Paysanne.** This bright and breezy central restaurant is a popular meeting place for Blenheimites. The food is modern New Zealand café style, which means you can choose from a simple snack to a full-blown three-courser. The pizzas, fresh out of the wood-fired oven, have a big local following—tandoori lamb is the biggest-selling topping. At night, look for the likes of pan-seared pork roulade, stuffed with roasted pear and mint, and served with sweet potato *rösti* (shredded and fried) and wilted spinach. ✉ *The Forum, Market Pl.* ☎ *03/577–6278* ⊟ *AE, DC, MC, V* ⊘ *Closed most Sun.; call first.*

$$$ ✕ **Rocco's.** Dozens of chianti bottles hang from the roof trusses here, and in winter an open fire with a spit provides both warmth and atmosphere. Try the spaghetti à la marinara, with mussels, prawns, scallops, fish, and garlic butter—the fish is fresh off the boat. Crayfish lovers take note: the crayfish here is some of the cheapest you'll find. The helpings are more than generous, but you're welcome to share dessert. Look for the delicious Marlborough cherries marinated in brandy. The wine list covers most of the local labels and includes several Italian imports. ✉ *5 Dodson St.* ☎ *03/578–6940* ⊟ *AE, DC, MC, V* ⊘ *No lunch. Closed Sun.*

$$ ✕ **The Living Room Café and Lounge Bar.** The sunny corner location right in the heart of Blenheim's shopping area means this café never lacks for action. Surrounded by glass on two sides, the triangular Living Room serves excellent breakfasts, with choices such as coconut-and-orange French toast, toast with cream cheese and honeycomb, and a Big Breakfast with all the usuals plus big field mushrooms and fried potatoes. Come dinnertime, you might find green-lipped mussels, spicy lamb, and local cheeses on the menu. The minimal decor means you can give more attention to your meal. ✉ *Scott St. at Maxwell Rd.* ☎ *03/579–4777.*

$–$$ ✕ **Paddy Barry's Bar and Restaurant.** Locals come here for a chat and a beer, and the menu is casual, straightforward, and very well priced. In other words, it's a good place to come down from traveler's stomach and overenthusiastic gourmandizing—a local peril. Pair a plate of battered and fried seafood with a well-poured Guinness. You'll find Guinness *in* the food, too, in the form of a beef 'n' Guinness hot pot. You can get your sports fix by watching the big screen TV while you tuck in. ✉ *51 Scott St.* ☎ *03/578–7470* ⊟ *AE, DC, MC, V.*

¢–$ ✕ **Mud House Village.** Whether you're craving a light lunch, want to sip a few more local wines, or would simply like to stop for a coffee or ice cream, pop into Mud House Village, on the winery strip along Rapaura Road. Tastings of both Le Grys and Mud House wines are available; the Le Grys chardonnay has developed quite a following over the years. A pleasant gift shop in the complex will answer some of those questions about what to take home for the family. ✉ *197 Rapaura Rd.* ☎ *03/572–7170* ⊘ *No dinner.*

★ **$$$** ✕☐ **Hotel d'Urville.** Every room is unique in this modern boutique hotel in the old Public Trust building. You could choose the Raja Room, with its sari-draped main bed and a carved Javanese daybed; the room with an African theme; or the sensory trip of the Color Room. One room matches the overall travel theme of the hotel and is based on the exploits of Dumont d'Urville, who made voyages to the Pacific and the

Antarctic in the 1820s and 1830s. The excellent restaurant ($$$) serves everything from a cup of coffee to delightful dinners based on local produce. Try the lamb rack, perhaps matched with an offering from Konrad or Cloudy Bay vineyards. ⊠ *52 Queen St., Blenheim* ☎ *03/577–9945* 🖷 *03/577–9946* ⊕ *www.durville.com* ↩ *11 rooms* ⌂ *Restaurant, bar; no smoking* ▭ *AE, DC, MC, V* ⦿ *CP.*

$$$$
Fodor'sChoice
★
Old St. Mary's Convent. This striking turn-of-the-20th-century building really was once a convent, beloved by a small group of local nuns who visit for Christmas cheer even now. The relocated and refurbished structure hardly evokes a nunnery now, though, with its luxuriously decorated rooms, rambling lawns and gardens, and evening glasses of Marlborough wine. The Chapel honeymoon suite is the pick of the rooms, but each has a lovely view. Be quick, because this place books fast every year. ⊠ *Rapaura Rd.* ☎ *03/570–5700* 🖷 *03/507–5703* ⊕ *www.convent. co.nz* ↩ *7 suites* ⌂ *Minibars, some refrigerators, lounge, library, business services; no a/c in some rooms, no smoking* ▭ *MC, V* ⦿ *BP.*

$$$$
✕▥ **Timara Lodge.** This 1923 house is one of Marlborough's original homesteads, and its craftsmanship, skilled used of native timber, and luxurious decor evoke an elegant past. The gardens extend over 25 acres and include a pool, tennis court, and private lake. Chef Louis Schindler prepares sumptuous four-course dinners based on local ingredients. Wine tours, trout fishing, sea kayaking, golf, skiing, even whale-watching (an hour and a half away in Kaikoura) can be arranged for you. The owners also have their own vineyard and winery, producing the very successful Spy Valley label. ⊠ *Dog Point Rd., R.D. 2* ☎ *03/572–8276* 🖷 *03/572–9191* ⊕ *www. timaralodge.co.nz* ↩ *2 rooms, 2 suites* ⌂ *Tennis court, pool, pond; no kids, no smoking* ▭ *AE, DC, MC, V* ⦿ *MAP* ⊘ *Closed June—Aug.*

$$$
▥ **Le Grys Vineyard Cottage.** If wine has brought you to Marlborough, you could truly immerse yourself with a stay in the heart of a vineyard. Waterfall Lodge, a mud-brick cottage, sits next to a brook in the midst of rows of grapevines. Its rooms are light and homey; the main bedroom has a canopied queen-size bed. Le Grys focuses on sauvignon blanc, chardonnay, and pinot noir; naturally, a wine tasting is part of the welcome. Various activities can also be arranged. ⊠ *Conders Bend Rd., Renwick, 12 km (7 mi) west of Blenheim* ☎ *03/572–9490* 🖷 *03/572–9491* ⊕ *www.legrys.co.nz/cottage* ↩ *1 cottage* ⌂ *Indoor pool; no a/c, no room phones, no room TVs, no smoking* ▭ *MC, V* ⦿ *BP.*

★ **$$$**
▥ **Straw Lodge.** Down a quiet lane near the Wairau River, Straw Lodge is about as peaceful as it gets, with the choice of self-catering or B&B accommodation. The buildings are of solid straw bale construction, making them extra-quiet, as well as warm in winter and cool in summer. You can start your day with breakfast under the grape-covered pergola overlooking the lodge's working vineyard (a tasting is included), and end it with a hot tub soak under the stars. ⊠ *Fareham La., off Wairau Valley Rd., Renwick* ☎ *03/572–9767* 🖷 *03/572–9769* ⊕ *www. strawlodge.co.nz* ↩ *3 suites* ⌂ *BBQ, refrigerators, golf privileges, outdoor hot tub, bicycles; no a/c, no smoking* ▭ *MC, V* ⦿ *BP.*

$$$
▥ **Vintners Retreat.** At the heart of Marlborough's wine district, this all-villa resort has balconies that overlook no fewer than six different vineyards. As the different varieties ripen and are harvested and their leaves turn red, the view changes like a technicolor quilt. Each villa is a fully

equipped home away from home and is well suited for family groups. There's a homey restaurant just across the road. ⊠ *55 Rapaura Rd.* ☏ *03/ 572–5094* 🖷 *03/572–5093* ⊕ *www.vintnersretreat.co.nz* ⤵ *14 villas* ⌂ *BBQs, tennis court, pool, boccie* 🖿 *AE, DC, MC, V.*

$$ 🏨 **Chateau Marlborough.** Behind its Camelot-esque turret and peaked gables, this quiet motor inn in central Blenheim is a relaxing and convenient place to crash. The good-size rooms have separate kitchen areas; some have whirlpool baths. Ask for one of the rooms overlooking Seymour Square, with its stone clock tower and memorial gardens. ⊠ *High St. at Henry St.* ☏ *03/578–0064* 🖷 *03/578–2661* ⊕ *www.marlboroughnz. co.nz* ⤵ *24 rooms, 6 suites* ⌂ *Pool, bar, business services; no a/c, no smoking* 🖿 *AE, DC, MC, V.*

Kaikoura

❺ *129 km (81 mi) south of Blenheim, 182 km (114 mi) north of Christchurch.*

The town of Kaikoura sits on a rocky protrusion on the east coast, backed by an impressive mountainous upthrust. There is plenty of local crayfish to be had at roadside stalls, which is an excellent reason to come here, but an even better one is sighting the sperm whales that frequent the coast in greater numbers than anywhere else on earth. The sperm whale, the largest toothed mammal, can reach a length of 60 feet and a weight of 70 tons. The reason for the whales' concentration in this area is the abundance of squid—among other species, the giant squid of seafaring lore— which is their main food. Scientists speculate that the whales use a form of sonar to find the squid, which they then bombard with deep, powerful sound waves generated in the massive cavities in the fronts of their heads. Their hunting is all the more remarkable considering that much of it is done at great depths, in darkness. The whales' food source swims in the trench just off the continental shelf, barely a kilometer (½ mi) off Kaikoura. You are most likely to see the whales between October and August.

Kaikoura's main street straggles along the beach behind a high stony bank, which offers some protection from the often rough weather along this coast. A bit farther south curves South Bay, the docking point for many of the whale-watching operators working out of the town. Kaikoura has undergone a bit of a transformation over the past decade as its whale-watching opportunities have brought thousands of people to its doorstep, gradually turning more of its attention to tourism.

Fyffe House is Kaikoura's oldest surviving building, erected soon after Robert Fyffe's whaling station was established in 1842. Partly built on whale-bone piles high on a hill overlooking the sea, the house provides a look at what life was like when people aimed at whales with harpoons rather than cameras. ⊠ *62 Avoca St.* ☏ *03/319–5835* 🎫 *$7, family $15* ⊙ *Daily 10–6.*

★ At **Lavendyl Lavender Farm,** just off the main highway a few minutes' drive north of the town center, rows of lavender stretch out against the stunning backdrop of Mt. Fyffe and the Seaward Kaikouras. Mike and Maureen Morris run a working 5-acre farm; the blooms are harvested in late January and early February. Walk through the heaven-scented gardens, and then head for the shop, where bunches of lavender hang from the ceiling. If you can't tear yourself away, you can stay overnight (⇨ Dylan's Country Cottages, *below*). ✉ *268 Postmans Rd.* ☎ *03/319–5473* ⊕ *www.lavenderfarm.co.nz* ✉ *$2–$3* ⊙ *Daily 10–4.*

On the first Saturday of October Kaikoura celebrates its annual **Seafest**, during which the best of this coastal area's food, wine, and beer is served while top New Zealand entertainers perform on an outdoor stage. Tickets are available from the town's information center.

Seaward Pottery has been running on this coastal site now since the 1970s, and in that time Juanita Edelmann has refined her ability to catch the colors of the surrounding beach, sea, and snowy mountains in her pottery. (✉ Just off State Hwy. 1, 15 km (9 mi) north of Kaikoura ☎ 03/319–5795 ⊕ www.kaikouranet.co.nz/seaward ⊙ Dawn–dusk.)

Where to Stay & Eat

Crayfish is the big-ticket item here; there are a number of crayfish stalls along the coast, but none stand out especially. Unless you're staying somewhere with a kitchen and can cook up some fresh crayfish yourself, you may prefer to get your crayfish fix at a local café. They tend to be on the expensive side, so even a casual place can have entrées over $30.

$$$–$$$$ ✕ **The Craypot.** This casual and modern café relies strongly, as the name suggests, on the local delicacy. Crayfish isn't cheap, but this kitchen sure knows how to prepare it. Other types of seafood also figure large on the menu, and if you feel like a change, you can choose from several variations on the steak, chicken, and lamb themes. Homemade desserts are worth leaving room for. In summer you can get a table outdoors; in winter an open fire roars at night. ✉ *70 West End Rd.* ☎ *03/319–6027* ▭ *AE, DC, MC, V.*

★ $$$–$$$$ ✕ **White Morph Restaurant.** Crayfish is always on the menu at this elegant eatery (the building once housed the first bank in Kaikoura), but there are plenty of alternatives, such as venison, lamb loin, wild hare, and at least one vegetarian dish. A favorite is Fish of the Bay—usually a roasted grouper fillet, served with walnut-and-parsley pesto and lemon-baked risotto. The desserts are fabulous, too. The décor is stylish and locally made gilded mirrors fill the walls, but the best scenes are the seaside views from the front windows. ✉ *92–94 The Esplanade* ☎ *03/319–5676* ⊙ *No lunch* ▭ *MC, V.*

$$–$$$$ ✕ **Hislops Café.** Homey and wholesome Hislops is a few minutes' walk north of town and well worth the trip. In the morning you'll find tasty eggs and bacon, plus freshly baked, genuinely stone-ground wholegrain bread served with marmalade or their own brand of honey. The imaginative lunch and dinner menus are all based on organic ingredients, and there are wheat- and gluten-free options as well. For instance, you might choose between a kūmara (native sweet potato), bacon, and avocado salad or marinated tofu and falafel. On sunny days, score a table on the veranda. ✉ *33 Beach Rd.* ☎ *03/319–6971* ⊙ *Reduced hours in winter; call ahead* ▭ *AE, DC, MC, V.*

$$ ✕▤ **Donegal House.** The name refers to owner Murray Boyd's home county; life-size statues of his ancestors stud the parklike grounds. The units are all modern and spacious, but the real attraction is the Irish bar and restaurant ($$$), where posters and photographs of "Auld Oireland" cover the paneled walls. Tuck into local crayfish with garlic or fresh lime and caper butter, followed by a Guinness or three while you listen to traditional music. ⊠ *School House Rd.* ☎ *03/319–5083* ⊕ *www.donegalhouse.co.nz* ⇦ *29 rooms* ⌂ *Restaurant, bar, some TVs; no a/c, no room phones, no smoking* ⊟ *AE, MC, V* ¶◦| *BP.*

★ $$–$$$ ⊡ **White Morph Motor Inn.** A waterfront view is hard to ignore—even more so on the rugged Kaikoura coast. This contemporary hotel is in a great spot just opposite the beach, a few minutes' walk from the town center. The suites have double whirlpool baths, as do a few of the other rooms; four units are two stories, well suited for families or larger parties. ⊠ *92–94 The Esplanade* ☎ *03/319–5014* 🖷 *03/319–5015* ⊕ *www. whitemorph.co.nz* ⇦ *19 units, 12 suites* ⌂ *Kitchens, minibars, microwaves, some in-room DVD; no a/c in some rooms, no smoking* ⊟ *AE, DC, MC, V.*

$$ ⊡ **Dylans Country Cottages.** A pair of timber-clad cottages perch at the edge of the Lavendyl Lavender Farm. Both make special use of their gardens; Kowhai's private garden virtually extends its living room, and Mahoe has an open-air bath and shower (in addition to its standard bath). The cottages' upstairs bedrooms have balconies looking onto the Seaward Kaikoura mountains; their living rooms, kitchens, dining areas, and bathrooms are downstairs. Breakfast hampers are delivered to the door each day. ⊠ *Postmans Rd., R.D. 1* ☎ *03/319–5473* 🖷 *03/319–5425* ⊕ *www. dylanscottages.co.nz* ⇦ *2 cottages* ⌂ *Kitchens; no a/c, no room phones, no smoking* ⊟ *MC, V* ¶◦| *BP.*

$–$$ ⊡ **The Old Convent.** It's easy to get into the habit of staying at this former convent. Built in 1911 for French nuns, it's now protected by the Historic Places Trust, and the interiors still reveal its past. The lounge, for instance, used to be a chapel and still has a cathedral ceiling and an ornate wrought-iron stairwell that winds down to a reception area. The Travellers' Bar showcases the owners' souvenirs, including weavings from Bhutan. The lounge in the former chapel is warmed by an open fire. ⊠ *Mt. Fyffe and Mill Rds.* ☎ *03/319–6603 or 0800/365–603* 🖷 *03/319–6660* ⊕ *www.theoldconvent.co.nz* ⇦ *16 rooms, 1 suite* ⌂ *Restaurant, café, pool, bicycles, shop, Internet room; no a/c, no room phones, no room TVs, no smoking* ⊟ *DC, MC, V* ¶◦| *BP.*

¢–$$ ⊡ **69 Beach Road Holiday Park.** A short walk from town, this nicely-laidout site has spotless facilities. There are cabins, studios, and full motel units available; there are also powered camper-van sites and campsites. The view of the Seaward Kaikoura mountains is breathtaking. There are two holiday parks on Beach Road—this one is on the inland side of the road. ⊠ *69 Beach Rd.* ☎ *03/319–6275* ⊕ *www.69holidaypark. co.nz* ⇦ *16 cabins, 4 studio units, 2 2-bedroom units, 50 campsites* ⌂ *BBQs, kitchen, laundry facilities; no a/c, no room phones, some room TVs, no smoking* ⊟ *MC, V.*

Sports & the Outdoors

December and January are the peak months for whale-watching and swimming with dolphins or seals; if you decide to come then, be sure to book well in advance.

BIRD-WATCHING **Albatross Encounter** (✉ 96 The Esplanade ☎ 03/319–6777, 0800/733–365 ⊕ www.oceanwings.co.nz)arranges tours by boat to go out and view the large varieties of seabirds off the Kaikoura Coast, including the mighty albatross. Tours operate up to three times daily and cost $75 for adults and $35 for children.

HIKING The descendants of two Scottish pioneering families—the Caverhills and Macfarlanes, who settled the huge 57,000-acre Hawkswood Range in 1860—have opened up their farms and homes to travelers. The three-day **Kaikoura Coast Track** walk combines uncrowded hiking—10 people at a time maximum—and farm hospitality. Take binoculars to search out sea life such as whales and dolphins.

Warm, clean cottages with kitchens and hot baths or showers are at the end of each day's hike. You can have a meal prepared by your hosts on Monday through Thursday, or buy fresh farm produce to prepare yourself. Breakfasts and lunches are also available daily. The first night is at Hawkswood in the historic sheep station setting of the **The Staging Post,** where host J. D. Macfarlane has a passion for Shakespeare and old stage-coaches. Accommodations are in rustic mud-brick or log cabins. A challenging four- to six-hour walk through native bush and down to the coast the next day will take you to **Ngaroma,** Heather and Bruce Macfarlane's 3,000-acre sheep and cattle farm. The Loft has a large lounge with a log fire and rooms that each sleep as many as four people. The next day's hike is along the beach, passing an ancient buried forest before heading across farmland to an area of regenerating bush to **Medina,** where you'll spend the third night in either Te Whare or The Garden Cottage (better for couples). You might meet David Handyside's father, Miles, who settled the 1,600-acre sheep and cattle farm in 1945. On the final day, a moderate four- to six-hour walk takes you over the 2,000-foot-plus Mt. Wilson, with its breathtaking views of the inland valleys of the Waiau River and the Kaikoura Ranges. The total track length is 40 km (25 mi), about 13 km (8 mi) each day. Bags are transferred to the next night's accommodation daily, so you'll only need to bring a day-pack while you're walking the track.

The fee for walking the track is $150 per person, and a guided walk can be arranged. If you opt to have all meals included and need bedding, the total cost is available on request. Reservations are essential. The start point is a ¾-hour drive south of Kaikoura on State Highway 1. Public transport can drop you at the gate. ✉ *Medina, R.D. 4, Cheviot, North Canterbury* ☎ *03/319–2715* 📠 *03/319–2724* ⊕ *www. kaikouratrack.co.nz* ⊘ *Daily Oct.–Apr.*

The peninsula has two other **walking tracks**—not to be confused with the Kaikoura Coast Track—that are particularly worthwhile, considering the town's spectacular coastal scenery: the cliff-top walk, from which you can look over seal colonies, and the longer shoreline walk, which takes you much closer to the colonies. Consult the town's information center about tides to avoid getting flooded out of certain parts of the walks. ✉ *Walks start at end of Fyffe Quay.*

SWIMMING WITH
DOLPHINS &
SEALS The dolphin- and seal-spotting opportunities here are fantastic. Although operators have led visitors to view and swim with dolphins and seals off the Kaikoura coast for years, and the animals may be familiar with boats, none of the animals is in the least bit tame. Getting so close to them in a natural state is what makes swimming beside a pod of dolphins or near seals so special. Fur seals are common, and you might also spot an octopus or crayfish. Pods of dusky dolphins stay in the area year-round; you may even see them doing aerial jumps and flips.

The offerings vary and operators will explain their expectations before you book. For instance, some boat operators go farther offshore, whereas others hug the coast. The offshore operators prefer their clients to be strong swimmers, because you'd be swimming in the open ocean. If you have any questions about the suitability of a trip, pipe up; these guys are all happy to help. On all trips, guides can prime you with information on the local species. Wet suits and other gear are provided.

Dolphin Encounter (⊠ 96 The Esplanade ☎ 03/319–6777 or 0800/733–365 🖷 03/319–6534 ⊕ www.dolphin.co.nz) arranges dolphin swims two or three times a day through summer and twice a day in winter, for $125 per person. (It's just $60 to watch them from the boat.) Because they operate in the open ocean, you need to be confident in the water, and it is an advantage to have some snorkeling experience. They also offer "Albatross Encounter" tours that take you out to view the seabirds off the Kaikoura coast.

Seal Swim Kaikoura (☎ 03/319–6182 ⊕ www.sealswimkaikoura.co.nz) is New Zealand's original seal swimming experience and has boat and shore-based tours running daily from October to May for $60–$70 per person. The swims are easy because they're behind the shelter of the Kaikoura Peninsula, and you're virtually guaranteed to see fur seals. **Top Spot Seal Swims** (☎ 03/319–5540) has two trips daily November–April, for $60 per person.

WHALE-
WATCHING
Fodor'sChoice
★ **Whale Watch Kaikoura Ltd.** Whale Watch is owned by the Ngai Tahu *iwi* (tribe). Since arriving in the Kaikoura area in AD 850, Ngai Tahu, the predominant South Island Māori *iwi* (tribe), claims to have lived and worked based on a philosophy of sustainable management and sensible use of natural resources. Having worked these waters since 1987, Whale Watch skippers can recognize individual whales and adjust operations, such as the boat's proximity to the whale, accordingly. Allow 3½ hours for the whole experience, 2¼ hours on the water.

Book in advance: 7 to 10 days November–April, 3 to 4 days at other times. Trips depend on the weather, and should your tour miss seeing a whale, which is rare, you will get up to an 80% refund of your fare. Take motion-sickness pills if you suspect you'll need them: even in calm weather, the sea around Kaikoura often has a sizable swell. ⟟ *Whaleway Station, Box 89, Kaikoura* ☎ *03/319–6767 or 0800/655–121* 🖷 *03/319–6545* ⊕ *www.whalewatch.co.nz* 🖃 *$130* 🖃 *AE, MC, V.*

Wings over Whales. If you'd rather get above the action, take a half-hour whale-viewing flight. From a seven-seater Airvan or three-seater Cessna aircraft, you'll have a bird's-eye view of the giant sperm whales' immensity. While searching for other whales' telltale water spouts, the pilot and co-pilot provide informative commentary on the creatures' habits. The trick is to stay glued to your window—which isn't hard, because at least half the time, with the plane banked in an almost perpetual circle, gravity ensures that your face is just about stuck to it. Children's fares are significantly less than the standard fee of $75. ⊠ *Kaikoura Airfield, State Hwy. 1, Kaikoura* ☎ *03/319–6580 or 0800/226–629* 🖷 *03/319–6668* ⊕ *www.whales.co.nz* 🖃 *$135* ☰ *AE, DC, MC, V.*

MARLBOROUGH & KAIKOURA ESSENTIALS

Transportation

BY AIR

Blenheim Airport (BHE) is quite close to town; you can hop a shuttle bus for a roughly 10-minute ride into Blenheim. Soundsair operates Picton's Koromiko Airport (PCN); this is also within 10 minutes of town and has shuttle bus service. Both are small regional airports—Picton's Koromiko airfield is little more than a paved runway in farmland—so you don't have to worry about long check-in or security lines.

The very scenic flight from Wellington to Blenheim takes about a half hour. Air New Zealand Link has at least 10 departures to and from Wellington daily. From Wellington, Soundsair makes the half-hour trip to Picton a few times daily from May to October and at least seven times a day from October through April.

🛪 Airports **Blenheim Airport** ☎ 03/572–9899. **Koromiko Airport** ☎ 0800/505–005.
🛪 Carriers **Air New Zealand Link** ☎ 0800/737–000 ⊕ www.airnewzealand.co.nz.
Soundsair ☎ 03/520–3080 or 0800/505–005 ⊕ www.soundsair.co.nz.

BY BOAT & FERRY

InterIsland Line runs vehicle and passenger ferries between Wellington and Picton. The one-way adult fare ranges from $36 to $60, depending on the time of year. The fare for a medium-size sedan ranges from $118 to $215, which includes one adult fare. The crossing takes about three hours and can be very rough in Cook Strait if the weather is bad. In fair weather, though, it's a fantastic trip. There are several departures in each direction every day, and bookings should be made in advance, particularly during holiday periods. Ferries dock in Picton at the town wharf.
🛥 **InterIsland Line** ☎ 0800/802–802 ⊕ www.interislander.co.nz.

BY BUS

InterCity runs services between Christchurch and Kaikoura, Picton, Blenheim, and Nelson a couple of times a day. The ride between Christchurch and Blenheim takes about 5 hours, from Christchurch to Picton closer to 6 hours, and from Picton to Nelson, about 2½ hours. A trip between Kaikoura and Christchurch runs 2 hours and 40 minutes. Blenheim, Picton, and Kaikoura don't have separate bus depots. At Blenheim, buses stop at the train station; at Picton, they use the ferry terminal as a hub. In Kaikoura, southbound buses stop at the parking lot by the Craypot restaurant, northbound buses at the Sleepy Whale.

Aside from tour buses, the only reliable local alternative is Atomic Shuttles. Atomic operates coaches between the most popular tourist spots and shuttle vans on the lower-profile regional runs. Prices are similar to those of InterCity; Atomic's rates may be cheaper for a single fare, but InterCity offers special discounted fares for longer trips. In the December and January holiday season, you should book at least a couple of days before you plan to travel, but during the rest of the year a day's advance reservation should do the trick.

⊞ Bus Lines **Atomic Shuttles** ☎ 03/322-8883 ⊕ www.atomictravel.co.nz. **InterCity** ☎ 03/365-1113 ⊕ www.intercitycoach.co.nz.

BY CAR
Driving your own car is the most unrestricted way of seeing the area, but you'll need to take extra care on the roads, as even the highways can be quite narrow and locals often tear around at higher speeds than you may be comfortable with. (If you're a bit slower, especially while driving a larger vehicle such as a camper van, it's a good idea to pull over from time to time to let faster traffic pass, especially on the hilly or winding stretches of road.) One-way bridges are common in this area, and occasionally these include railway tracks. You may also find yourself behind a slow-moving sheep truck for a while before finding a place to pass. Allow plenty of time for travel and enjoy the ride—the countryside around the main roads is often beautiful. Blenheim is a 25-minute drive from the ferry terminal in Picton and just less than two hours from Nelson to the west and Kaikoura to the south.

Most car rental agencies have North Island–South Island transfer programs for their vehicles: leave one car in Wellington and pick another one up in Picton on the same contract. It is common practice, quickly and easily done, and saves you the cost of freighting a car across Cook Strait. If you initiate a rental in Picton, Avis, Budget, and Hertz have offices at the ferry terminal; the offices stay open from 8 to 6 daily and are available for call-out (at a charge) if you need to pick up a vehicle after a late-night crossing. Apex Rentals are particularly easy to deal with and are happy for their cars to explore more outlying areas. They give a copy of the 125-page *New Zealand Driving Holidays* booklet with each rental.

Parking is rarely a problem in these smaller towns, as there are plenty of on-street spaces along the main streets. Blenheim has a good-size parking lot on Seymour Street, and Kaikoura has one near the Visitor Information Center along West End.

If you plan to do a wine tasting or two, remember that driving under the influence is not tolerated and generally carries a hefty fine at least.

⊞ Rental Agencies **Apex** ☎ 03/573-7009 or 0800/422-744. **Avis** ☎ 0800/655-111. **Budget** ☎ 0800/283-438. **Hertz** ☎ 0800/654-321.

Contacts & Resources

BANKS & EXCHANGE SERVICES
Almost all towns have ATMs, usually outside a major bank. There is no bank or ATM facility in Havelock, though, and it can be difficult to get cash there, so come prepared. Banks are open weekdays from ap-

proximately 9 to 4:30. Most stores and tour operators accept credit cards, though many will take only Visa or MasterCard.

EMERGENCIES
The main hospital for this region is in Blenheim, although there are small medical centers in Havelock, Picton, and Kaikoura. None of the towns has a late-night pharmacy as such, but local pharmacists act in that capacity on a rotating basis. Call the hospital for information.

🚑 Emergency Services **Fire, police, and ambulance** ☎ 111. **Wairau Hospital** ✉ Hospital Rd., Blenheim ☎ 03/520-9999.

MAIL & INTERNET
Most hotels and motels in this area have Internet access of some kind, and each town has an Internet facility or café. Local libraries also have Internet access, but they sometimes charge more than Internet cafés, and they're open only weekdays and occasional hours on the weekends. In Blenheim, you can hit up the Sagai Restaurant, which has the only Internet facility open after standard business hours.

🖥 Internet Cafés **Internet Outpost** ✉ 19 West End, Kaikoura ☎ 03/319-7970. **I-Site Visitor Centre** ✉ Blenheim Railway Station, State Hwy. 1, Blenheim ☎ 03/577-8080.

United Video ✉ 63 High St., Picton ☎ 03/573-7466.

📮 Post Office **NZ Post Blenheim** ✉ Main St. at Scott St. ☎ 03/578-3904. **NZ Post Kaikoura** ✉ 41 West End ☎ 03/319-6808. **NZ Post Picton** ✉ Mariners Mall, High St. ☎ 03/573-6900.

TOURS
BOAT TOURS The Pelorus mail boat, *Pelorus Express,* a sturdy launch that makes a daylong trip around Pelorus Sound, is one of the best ways to discover the waterway and meet its residents. The boat leaves from Havelock, west of Picton, Tuesday, Thursday, and Friday at 9:30 AM and returns in the late afternoon. The fare is $105.

Beachcomber Cruises can take you to and from any point on the Queen Charlotte Walkway for one-day or longer unguided walks. Boats depart at 9:30 and 10:15 from the Picton waterfront and charge about $35.

The Cougar Line runs scheduled trips from Picton through the Queen Charlotte Sounds three to four times daily, depending on the time of year, dropping passengers (sightseers included) at accommodations, private homes, or other points. A Queen Charlotte drop-off and pickup service costs $75 for multiday hikes, $58 for day hikes that end at Furneaux Lodge. Water-taxi service to area lodges costs from $25 to $45, depending on distances and number of people.

Marlborough Sounds Adventure Company has one- and four-day guided kayak tours of the sounds, leaving from Picton, as well as kayak rentals for experienced paddlers. The cost is $95 for a one-day guided tour and $465 for a three-day guided tour, including water transportation, food, and camping equipment. A kayak rental costs $50 per person per day.

★ Green Shell Mussel Cruises will take you into the largely untouched Kenepuru and Pelorus sounds, which are part of the labyrinth of waterways that make up the Marlborough Sounds. The world's largest production of Greenshell mussels is done in the sounds, and the boat will take you to explore some of the intricate system of waterways where these farms are situated. Try the mussels steamed, with a glass of local sauvignon blanc, while hearing the history of the area. The tour costs $95 per person, and the season runs November through March; you can get more information from the Marlborough Sounds Travel Company.

🄵 **Beachcomber Cruises** ⊠ Beachcomber Pier, Town Wharf ☍ Box 12, Picton ☎ 03/573-6175 🖶 03/573-6176 ⊕ www.beachcombercruises.co.nz. **Cougar Line** ⊠ Picton Wharf ☎03/573-7925 or 0800/504-090 🖶03/573-7926 ⊕www.cougarline.co.nz. **Have-lock Sea Kayaking Company.** ⊠ 77 Main Rd., Havelock ☎ 03/574-1060.

Marlborough Sounds Adventure Company ⊠ The Waterfront, London Quay, Picton ☎ 03/573-6078 🖶 03/573-8827 ⊕ www.marlboroughsounds.co.nz. **Marlborough Travel Company** ☎ 03/577-9997 ⊕ www.marlboroughtravel.co.nz. *Pelorus Express* ☎03/574-1088. **Rutherford Travel** ⊠ 46 Main Rd., Havelock ☎ 03/574-2114 ⊕ www. rutherfordtravel.co.nz.

FISHING TOURS   The Sounds Connection, a family-run tour company, offers regular half-day fishing trips and full-day trips by request. They leave from Picton; a half day runs $69. They'll supply all the necessary gear and fillet your catch.

🄵 **The Sounds Connection** ⊠ 16 Wellington St., Picton ☎ 0800/742-866 ⊕ www. soundsconnection.co.nz.

WALKING &   To see the glorious Marlborough Sounds, try a four- or five-day fully
HIKING TOURS   catered and guided inn-to-inn walk on the Queen Charlotte Track with Southern Wilderness. The four-day walk includes all land and water transport, as well as overnight stays in three sounds resorts: Punga Cove Resort, Furneaux Lodge, and the Portage. Experienced guides give informative talks on the area's rich natural and human history. Advance bookings are essential; trips cost $1,095. Marlborough Sounds Adventure Company guides hikers on the Queen Charlotte Walkway as well, with four-day ($1,095) or five-day ($1,345) trips.

🄵 **Marlborough Sounds Adventure Company** ⊠ The Waterfront, London Quay, Picton ☎ 0800/283-283 🖶 03/573-8827 ⊕ www.marlboroughsounds.co.nz.

WINERY TOURS   The Sounds Connection runs daily tours from October through July to visit a handful of Marlborough's main wineries, including Nautilus Estate, Grove Mill, Cellier Le Brun, and Johanneshof Cellars. Marlborough Wine Trails run half-day trips to eight wineries of your choice. Marlborough Wine Trails runs personalized tours tailored to customer requests. These can include visits to some of the smaller boutique wineries and experiences such as wine and food matching. Marlborough Travel Company runs six-hour personalized trips in a variety of vehicles, depending on party size. Their luxury BMW is a nice vehicle in which to spend a day.

🄵 **Marlborough Wine Trails** ☎ 027/264-4704 ⊕ www.marlboroughwinetrails.co.nz. **The Sounds Connection** ⊠ 16 Wellington St., Picton ☎ 0800/742-866 ⊕ www. soundsconnection.co.nz. **Marlborough Travel Company** ☎ 03/577-9997 ⊕ www. marlboroughtravel.co.nz.

VISITOR INFORMATION

The visitor-information centers in Blenheim, Kaikoura, and Picton are all open daily during standard business hours. Destination Marlborough, a regional organization, puts out a nice visitor guide that covers local accommodation, cafés, and activities, as well as an events calendar.

The Treasured Pathway, ⊕ www.treasuredpathway.co.nz, is an excellent joint regional endeavor with the neighboring Nelson area. Its guide outlines the best of the sights in the "Top of the South."

🗂 Tourist Information **Kaikoura Information and Tourism Centre** ⊠ West End ☎ 03/319-5641 🖶 03/319-6819 ⊕ www.kaikoura.co.nz. **Marlborough Visitor Information Centre** ⊠ The Old Railway Station, State Hwy. 1, Blenheim ☎ 03/577-8080 🖶 03/577-8089 ⊕ www.destinationmarlborough.com. **Picton Visitor Information Centre** ⊠ Picton Foreshore ☎ 03/520-3113 🖶 03/573-5021 ⊕ www.picton.co.nz.

NELSON & THE NORTHWEST

Set on the broad curve of Tasman Bay with views of the Kahurangi mountains on the far side, Nelson makes a strong case for itself as one of the top areas in New Zealand for year-round adventure. To the west beckon the sandy crescents of Abel Tasman National Park and Golden Bay. To the south, mellow river valleys and the peaks and glacial lakes of Nelson Lakes National Park draw hikers, mountaineers, and sightseers. There's a climatic allure as well; Nelson has more hours of sunlight than any other city in the country. New Zealanders are well aware of these attractions, and in December and January the city is swamped with vacationers. Apart from this brief burst of activity, you can expect the roads and beaches to be relatively quiet most of the time.

First settled by Māori hundreds of years ago, the site, then called Whakatu, was chosen for its extremely sheltered harbor and good climate. These enticements later caught the eye of the New Zealand Company, and Nelson became the second town to be developed by that organization, with British immigrants arriving in the 1840s. These days Nelson is the country's chief fishing port and a key forestry area, with vineyards and olive groves developing into another major industry. Because the town is quite isolated geographically, residents tend to be a self-reliant bunch who get down to business without any fuss. The quiet, beautiful setting has attracted creatively minded people, and there's a significant community of artists, craftspeople, and writers in the countryside around Nelson.

Nelson

6 *116 km (73 mi) west of Blenheim.*

Relaxed, hospitable, and easy to explore on foot, Nelson has a way of making you feel as though you should stay longer, no matter how many days you're here. You can make your way around the mostly two-story town in a day, poking into crafts galleries and stopping at cafés, but two days is a practical minimum, especially if you need a respite in the midst of a busy itinerary. Use Nelson as a base for a variety of activities within an hour's drive of the town itself.

French Pass & D'Urville Island

FRENCH PASS AND D'URVILLE island are two of the best-kept secrets in the whole top of the South Island. They're not easy to get to, but if you have an adventurous spirit and don't mind a bit of rough road, set aside a couple of days to visit them.

The **road to French Pass** splits off State Highway 6 at Rai Valley, halfway between Havelock and Nelson. It's winding, rough, and steep in places, but quite passable in a regular vehicle in all weathers. The sign at the start of the road says FRENCH PASS 2 HRS, and although it's only 64 km (40 mi) to the pass, this estimate is true. The road first climbs over the Rongo Saddle and down to Okiwi Bay through beautiful native bush; from here, you'll have spectacular views of D'Urville Island off in the distance. Then the road crosses to the Pelorus Sound catchment and climbs along the ridge separating the waters of that sound from Tasman Bay to the west. Small side roads drop precariously to beautiful, hidden bays such as Te Towaka, Elaine Bay, and Deep Bay.

The last 12 km (7 mi) is a dramatic drop down to sea level, skirting the Current Basin before arriving at the powerful stretch of water separating Tasman Bay from Cook Strait—the French Pass. This narrow stretch of water moves at up to 9 knots during the tidal run and is well respected by hardy local mariners. Both the waterway and the island were named for French explorer Dumont D'Urville, who made a heroic crossing through the pass in the 1820s when it was uncharted and unknown to European navigators. **D'Urville Island** is on the far side of this stretch of water, and it's a fabulous destination if you really want to feel what isolated coastal New Zealand is all about.

D'Urville Island was home to several Māori tribes before Europeans arrived. It was a strategic position on the local war trails, as canoes of marauding tribes moved along the coast. The island also had valuable fish reserves and stone quarries for toolmaking. European settlers arrived in the 1830s and '40s to hunt seals and whales, then to farm. The island is now being returned to native bush by many of the landowners.

Between Okiwi Bay and French Pass there are no facilities—no gas stations, bathrooms, or cafés—so come prepared. There are only limited public facilities at French Pass: a basic toilet, gas pump, and essential supplies during limited hours.

If you want to stay overnight at French Pass, a great choice is **French Pass Sea Safaris and Beachfront Villas** (☎ 03/576-5204 ⊕ www.seasafaris. co.nz), on the shores of Admiralty Bay. The property has comfortable studio apartments and great activities: seal and dolphin swims in season, plus guided tours to some of the protected islands in Cook Strait. Diving and fishing charters can also be arranged.

Once you're on D'Urville Island, the best lodging option is the **D'Urville Island Wilderness Resort $$-$$$**; (☎ 03/576-5268 ⊕ www. durvilleisland.co.nz). The resort is a 30-minute boat ride across French Pass (a water-taxi service picks you up from the French Pass wharf), and overlooks the sheltered waters of Catherine Cove. You can go hiking, mountain biking, and snorkeling here, or just watch the rosy sunrises and the orcas passing the end of the bay.

One of the defining features of the landscape here is the **Boulder Bank,** a 13-km (8-mi) natural stone bank, built up from eroding cliff faces farther north along the coast. In creating a sheltered harbor, the bank is essentially the reason Nelson was settled in the first place. You can easily reach it by car, driving 9 km (5½ mi) north of town and turning into Boulder Bank Drive, then going another mile along a gravel road.

To get your bearings in town, start at the visitor center on the corner of Trafalgar and Halifax streets. The heart of town is farther up **Trafalgar Street,** between Bridge Street and the cathedral steps (this is also now home to the region's newly refurbished museum). This area is fringed with shops, and the block between Hardy Street and the cathedral steps is a sunny spot to enjoy a coffee. A weekend crafts market is held at the Montgomery parking lot. There are a few art stores and galleries in Nile Street, too. For a dose of greenery, the **Queens Gardens** are on Bridge Street between Collingwood and Tasman.

The waterfront area along **Wakefield Quay** has been developing steadily for the past few years, and now has several cafés, along with a promenade that incorporates a historic stone seawall built by 19th-century prisoners. A statue commemorates the arrival of the early European pioneers, and Sunderland Quay features a memorial to local fishermen lost at sea (Nelson is New Zealand's chief fishing port and has a strong tradition of fishing families). It is also the site of the annual Blessing of the Fleet in October. (Visit ⊕ www.seafarerstrust.org.nz/fleet for more information.)

The Suter Te Aratoi o Whakatu exhibits both historical and contemporary art; it's a good place to see a cross section of work from an area that has long attracted painters, potters, woodworkers, and other artists. Many of them come for the scenery, the lifestyle, and the clay, and as a result, Nelson is considered the ceramics center of New Zealand. In recent years the gallery has increased its emphasis on painting and sculpture. A highlight is the area set aside for local artists—a perfect opportunity to see the best work of the region. National touring exhibits come through every three or four weeks, supplementing the permanent collection. A pleasant lunch café in the gallery looks out over neighboring Queen's Gardens. ⊠ *Queens Gardens, Bridge St.* ☎ *03/548–4699* ⊕ *www.thesuter. org.nz* 🖼 *$3* ⊙ *Daily 10:30–4:30.*

Nelson's new regional museum, **Te Pupuri Taonga O Te Tai Ao** (Nelson Provincial Museum), is well worth visiting. Occupying part of the original site of New Zealand's first museum it explores the early settlement of the town, its original Māori inhabitants, and the events that have shaped the region since then. Exhibits include a small but outstanding collection of Māori carvings, plus a number of artifacts relating to the so-called Maungatapu murders, grisly goldfields killings committed near Nelson in 1866. The Town Warp is a multimedia wander through the early central-city streets, highlighting local identities such as Ann Bird the Butcher (a hard-as-nails woman who was one of the town's first European settlers). ⊠ *Hardy St. at Trafalgar St.* ☎ *03/547–9740* ⊙ *Weekdays 9–5, weekends 10–4:30* 🖼 *Free; $5 for special seasonal exhibitions* ⊕ *www. museumnp.org.nz.*

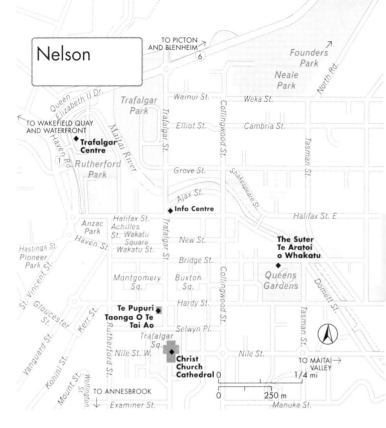

Nelson

TO PICTON AND BLENHEIM
6

Founders Park

Neale Park

North Rd.

Queen Elizabeth II Dr.

Trafalgar Park

Wainui St.

Weka St.

TO WAKEFIELD QUAY AND WATERFRONT

Haven Rd.

Maitai River

Trafalgar Centre

Rutherford Park

Trafalgar St.

Elliot St.

Cambria St.

Collingwood St.

Tasman St.

Grove St.

Shakespeare St.

Ajax St.

Info Centre

Halifax St. E

Anzac Park

Halifax St.

Achilles St.

Wakatu Square

Haven St.

Wakatu St.

Hastings St.
Pioneer Park

Trafalgar St.

New St.

The Suter
Te Aratoi
o Whakatu

St. Vincent St.

Bridge St.

Collingwood St.

Montgomery Sq.

Buxton Sq.

Queens Gardens

Domett St.

Gloucester St.

Kerr St.

Te Pupuri
Taonga O Te
Tai Ao

Hardy St.

Rutherford St.

Trafalgar Sq.

Selwyn Pl.

Tasman St.

Vanguard St.

Nile St. W.

Christ Church Cathedral

Nile St.

TO MAITAI VALLEY

Konini St.

Wellington St.

Mount St.

TO ANNESBROOK

Examiner St.

Manuka St.

0   250 m
0   1/4 mi

★ Wacky and wonderful, the **World of Wearable Art & Collectable Car Museum (WOW)** gives you the chance to see garments from the World of Wearable Art Awards Show, an event long held in Nelson but now presented in Wellington. The theme of the Wearables is to turn art into a garment, something best understood when facing mannequins in their inventive ensembles. Imagine brightly colored, hand-painted silks draped into a giant winged headdress. Or papier-mâché fashioned into dramatic body suits, glittering oceanic creations in the colors of *paua* shell. The elaborate sets, sound, and psychedelic lighting make this gallery a must-see. An adjoining gallery exhibits a superb collection of restored classic cars, ranging from a pink Cadillac to sleek sports tourers. Here, too, the displays are revved up with special effects. All together, the museum more than lives up to its acronym. ✉ *95 Quarantine Rd., Annesbrook* ☏ *03/547–4573* ⊕ *www.wowcars.co.nz* ✉ *$18* ☉ *Easter–late Dec., daily 10–5; late Dec.–Easter, daily 10–6.*

Nelson's boldest architectural "highlight" is **Christ Church Cathedral,** which sits on a hilltop surrounded by gardens. The site itself has played an integral part in Nelson's history, first as a Māori *pā* or fortified village, then as the base for the initial city street survey. It also housed the immigration barracks when the city was first settled by Europeans. A tent church was first erected in 1842, followed by more permanent ones in 1851 and 1887. Work on the current cathedral began in 1925 and dragged on for the next 40 years, with middling results. But the steps running down to Trafalgar Street have become a destination in their own right, a social hub in the city center. ⊠ *Cathedral Sq.* ⌨ *Free, tower $4.*

NEED A BREAK?

Penguino's Ice Cream Cafe (⊠ 85 Montgomery Sq. ☎ 03/545–6450) is a cool source for delicious gelato—particularly their signature creation, the gelato panini. Like a gussied-up version of an ice-cream sandwich, this treat is heated in a panini press and served warm, but with the ice cream still cold inside.

Tucked away in a quiet backstreet, **Rosy Glow Chocolates** (⊠ 20 Harley St. ☎ 03/548–3383) is a must for chocoholics. Their handmade chocolates are decadently rich and sometimes unusually flavored, such as the Lime Sour. It's closed Sunday.

There's mud at **Happy Valley Motorbikes and SkyWire,** and lots of it. But it's also a lot of fun when you hop on a four-wheeled motorbike and career off up into the bush before breaking out 14 bone-jarring km (8½ mi) later to see a wide-reaching view across Delaware Bay. Guides will show you some of the native plants and explain their uses, and also point out some spectacular examples of ancient trees. They also do a Māori Cultural Tour with a local guide who explains the cultural and spiritual aspects of the land you cross, and who also demonstrates ancient crafts. There's a high-wire ride that takes you zooming over the surrounding bush and chattering native birds, and also an on-site café. ⊠ *Cable Bay Rd. (15 min drive north of Nelson)* ☎ *03/545–0304 or 0800/157–300* ⊕ *www.happyvalleyadventures.co.nz.*

Where to Stay & Eat

$$$–$$$$ ✕ **Appelman's.** The paneled walls and beamed ceilings make the dining room in this renovated colonial house particularly inviting. The excellent chef looks to European classics; popular demand ensures that the chateaubriand for two is in no danger of being taken off the menu. The sharp wine list slips some Australian labels in with the local vintages. ⊠ *294 Queen St., Richmond, 6½ km (4 mi) southwest of Nelson* ☎ *03/544–0610* ☱ *AE, DC, MC, V* ☉ *No lunch.*

$$$–$$$$ ✕ **The Boat Shed.** The name is no gimmick: this genuine boat shed perches on wooden piles with the tide lapping below. The restaurant offers what they call an "Aotearoa" menu, showcasing Kiwi cuisine. Freshly harvested crab, crayfish, and green-lipped mussels are all standouts. There's local art on display, and on Wednesday evenings in summer you can watch the local sunset yacht racing from the balcony. ⊠ *350 Wakefield Quay* ☎ *03/546–9783* ⚑ *Reservations essential* ☱ *AE, DC, MC, V.*

$$$–$$$$ ✕ **The Cut.** This may be Nelson's most polished restaurant, with a sophisticated European approach. A menu mainstay is the loin of lamb (you can't beat New Zealand lamb), served with braised Savoy cabbage and garlic mashed potatoes. Reservations are essential in summer. ⊠ *94 Collingwood St.* ☎ *03/548–9874* ☉ *Closed Sun. and Mon. No lunch.*

$$–$$$ ✕**Ma Fish.** This casual waterfront restaurant is superbly located; it sits above the local yacht club with views over the harbor. Although the staff are a little slow on service here, the fish is fresh and delicious, and well worth the wait. The menu lists turbot, gurnard, terakihi, monkfish, blue cod, grouper, and snapper, among others. If there's a wait for a table, have a drink on the balcony. ✉ *322 Wakefield Quay* ☎ *03/539–1307 or 0800/ 623–474* 🍴 *Reservations essential in summer* 🚪 *AE, DC, MC, V.*

★ $–$$$ ✕**Harry's Bar.** This intimate bar and café is a bit hidden down at the river end of Hardy Street, but once inside you'll find that the atmosphere is very upbeat. Asian cuisine is the focus here, but the menu also includes Indian dal and chapatis, as well as pad thai and green papaya salad (and a not-to-be-missed Kaffir lime tart for dessert). There's a hot selection of cocktails, and on Friday night the bar fills with locals who come to celebrate the end of the work week. ✉ *306 Hardy St.* ☎ *03/ 539–0905* 🚪 *AE, DC, MC, V* ⊘ *Closed Sun. and Mon. No lunch* 🍴 *Reservations essential in summer.*

★ ¢–$ ✕**Morrison Street Café.** With its pleasant outdoor courtyard, this café has become a favorite with locals and visitors alike. The baristas here know their stuff, and as a result the coffee here is the best in town. Along with a caffeine fix, come for the bacon and eggs served on fresh *ciabatta* bread with pesto and hollandaise. There's local art on the walls and the menu changes seasonally, as does the wine list. The friendly staff are happy to offer local advice and tips. ✉ *244 Hardy St.* ☎ *03/548–8110* 🚪 *AE, DC, MC, V* ⊘ *No dinner.*

★ $$$ 🛏**Cambria House.** Built for a sea captain, this 1880s house, now a B&B, mixes old and new, from the original kauri doors to the high-speed Internet access. The decor pairs antiques with *rimu*-wood paneling and modern fabrics. Each bedroom has an en-suite bathroom with shower; two have a shower and separate bathtub. You can settle in with coffee or a drink by the wood-burning fireplace or on the garden deck. The house is near the town center. ✉ *7 Cambria St.* ☎ *03/548–4681* 🖶 *03/ 546–6649* ⊕ *www.cambria.co.nz* 🛏 *7 rooms* 🖥 *Internet room; no a/c, no TV in some rooms, no kids, no smoking* 🚪 *AE, MC, V* ❒ *BP.*

$$$ 🛏**Mapledurham.** Deborah Grigg operates this highly rated B&B on the hills overlooking Tasman Bay and out across to the ranges of Kahurangi Park. Both rooms have extensive views (one has its own lounge), and the house is a showcase of her love of all things beautiful. ✉ *12 Windsor Dr., Tasman Heights* ☎ *03/546–5678* ⊕ *www.mapledurham.co.nz* 🛏 *2 rooms* 🖥 *No a/c* 🚪 *MC, V* ❒ *BP.*

$$–$$$ 🛏**Cathedral Inn.** This beautiful old villa began life in 1856 and was once the home of prominent Nelsononian Bishop Suter. In turning the house into a B&B, period details have been matched with modern amenities, from hair dryers to data ports. You can join the other guests around the recycled *matai*-wood table for breakfast. The inn is a short walk through Christ Church Cathedral's garden to shops and restaurants. ✉ *369 Trafalgar St.* ☎ *03/548–7369 or 0800/883–377* ⊕ *www.cathedralinn. co.nz* 🛏 *7 rooms* 🖥 *Outdoor hot tub, Internet room; no a/c, no kids, no smoking* 🚪 *AE, DC, MC, V* ❒ *BP.*

$$–$$$ 🛏**Delorenzo's Studio Apartments.** These reasonably priced apartments are just a short walk from the city center, across the Maitai River bridge. The decor may be bland, but the rooms have plenty of conveniences, includ-

ing CD players and washer-dryers. There's also handy off-street parking. ✉ *43–55 Trafalgar St.* ☎ *03/548–9774* 🖷 *03/548–9775* ⊕ *www. delorenzos.co.nz* ➫ *26 suites, 1 family cottage* ♨ *BBQ, in-room fax, kitchenettes, in-room data ports, pool, laundry facilities* ▭ *AE, DC, MC, V.*

$$–$$$ ⌂ **The Little Manor.** This little historic A-frame home, on land first surveyed in 1864, seems to defy the modern-day neighborhood around it. The place is full of antiques, not to mention the original clawfoot bath and open fire. (Guests share the bathroom.) The sunny upper deck and lower garden are well secluded. There is a pantry full of goodies (such as homemade jams and sauces) that you can use to make your own breakfast, a dining area, and a reading room. The house is just a short walk to cafés, restaurants, art galleries, and pottery studios. ✉ *12 Nile St.* W ☎ *03/545–1411* 🖷 *03/545–1417* ✐ *the.little.manor@xtra.co.nz* ➫ *2 rooms with shared bath* ♨ *Kitchenette, 2 lounges; no smoking* ▭ *AE, DC, MC, V* ❘⊙❘ *BP.*

★ **$$–$$$** ⌂ **Wakefield Quay House.** With just the road running between the front door and the sea, Woodi and John Moore's beautiful old villa has one of the best waterfront locations in town. Overlooking Haulashore Island and the harbor entrance, the rooms have dark rimu-wood ceilings and luxurious furnishings, and are decorated with local artwork and antique maritime memorabilia. Pure wool rugs and carpets warm the floors while heavy cotton duvets warm the beds. When the weather is fine, you can take breakfast (fresh local eggs, juices, salmon and freshly ground coffee) on the veranda. Woodi and John's 30-foot yacht is always on hand for a quiet sail in the evenings ✉ *385 Wakefield Quay* ☎ *03/546–7275* ⊕ *www.wakefieldquay.co.nz* ➫ *2 rooms* ♨ *CD players; no a/c* ▭ *MC, V* ❘⊙❘ *BP.*

$–$$ ⌂ **Aloha Lodge.** A stone's throw from Tahunanui Beach, this modern B&B is a great deal. The design of the lodge is Asian, even in its garden, which is landscaped using the principles of the Chinese design philosophy *feng shui.* An ample breakfast is served in the outer courtyard or the spacious dining room. You can reach Tahunanui on a five-minute drive from Nelson via Haven Road. ✉ *19 Beach Rd., Tahunanui* ☎ *03/546–4000* 🖷 *03/546–4420* ⊕ *www.alohalodgenelson.co.nz* ➫ *17 rooms, 4 suites* ♨ *BBQ, sauna; no a/c, no smoking* ▭ *AE, DC, MC, V* ❘⊙❘ *BP.*

★ **¢–$** ⌂ **Accents on the Park.** This guesthouse and backpackers lodge will spoil you for all others. The grand old house in Trafalgar Square, just off the main street of Nelson, feels more like a boutique hotel than a typical hostel, with its rich brocade fabrics, soundproof rooms, and immaculate bathrooms with high-pressure showers. Room setups vary from doubles with private baths to dorm rooms; linen is provided. The balconies overlook the cathedral and its gardens. ✉ *335 Trafalgar Sq.* ☎ *03/548–4335* 🖷 *03/548–4334* ⊕ *www.accentsonthepark.com* ➫ *18 rooms, 2 with bath* ♨ *Dining room, bar; no a/c, no room phones, no room TVs* ▭ *MC, V.*

Nightlife & the Arts

The **School of Music** (✉ *48 Nile St.* ☎ 03/548–9477 ⊕ www.nsom.ac. nz) hosts music performances, mostly local productions (and surprisingly good ones at that). In July, the school is the site of the annual **Winter Festival,** which brings in excellent musicians from elsewhere in New

Zealand. Another top music event is the **Nelson Arts Festival** in October, likewise a magnet for top-notch Kiwi and international acts. Over the Christmas break, the city rocks to the annual **Jazz Festival,** much of which is held in local cafés and in the streets.

For the younger set, there are several late-night clubs and music spots along **Bridge Street,** which change month by month as venues and acts come and go. Take a wander along the street after 11 PM to check out the options, or grab a copy of the free *Passport* gig guide—it's available in many cafés.

On Tuesday nights the **Maen Fiddler** (⊠ 145 Bridge St. ☎ 03/546–8516) has Irish Music night, which is a quieter, more pleasant affair than the rowdier nightlife offerings along this strip. It also runs at a much earlier hour, starting around 8:30 PM.

Shopping

There are artist's studios and crafts shops in various parts of town (they're not clustered in any particular area). More than 300 artists live around Nelson, working full or part time in various media: ceramics, glassblowing, wood turning, fiber, sculpture, and painting. Not surprisingly there are 16 arts-and-crafts trails to follow, for which there is a brochure at the information center. There is also a colorful Saturday morning crafts market. A very good booklet, *Art in Its Own Place,* available from the visitor center, Nelson's museums and local cafés and shops, details these walks and many local artists.

Walking through the door of the **Bead Gallery** (⊠ 18 Parere St. ☎🖷 03/546–7807 ⊕ www.beads.co.nz), you may be overwhelmed by the sheer number and range of beads around you. The owner gets his beads from all around the world, with a good selection of Pacific and New Zealand beads and pendants as well. *Paua* shell is big, and there are local greenstone beads and shells from distant islands, not to mention ceramic, wood, bone, porcelain, Swarovski crystal, semiprecious, bone, horn, porcelain, and glass beads from far-flung countries. You can put a strand together at a worktable or buy separate beads to take with you.

The skilled craftspeople of the **Jens Hansen Gold & Silversmith Workshop** (⊠ 320 Trafalgar Sq. ☎ 03/548–0640 or 027/208–0687 ⊕ www.jenshansen.com) create lovely gold and silver jewelry. Contemporary pieces are handmade at the workshop-showroom, and many are set with precious stones or *pounamu* (jade) from the West Coast of the South Island. But they may be best known as the jewelers who made the precious "One Ring" used in the *Lord of the Rings* film trilogy. There's an original prototype on display, and you can order a faithful replica for a very reasonable price. They are happy to open by appointment outside regular work hours; you can also preview or order merchandise on their Web site.

★ If you're in Nelson on a Saturday morning, head down to Montgomery Square off Trafalgar Street to the **Nelson Saturday Market,** held from 8 AM to 1 PM. This market is one of the most successful in the country; it gained its reputation from the wealth of artists and craftspeople who sell their wares here. Now locals and visitors can rely on getting some good bargains while wandering through the maze of stalls, browsing the fresh produce, handmade breads and cheeses, clothing, artwork, flowers, ceramics, and more. Grab a coffee and some spicy apple cake as you prowl. If you're here in summer, go early to beat the crowds.

The 19th-century, two-story cottage of the **South Street Gallery** (⊠ 10 Nile St. W ☎ 03/548–8117 ⊕ www.nelsonpottery.co.nz) overflows with ceramic art, sculpture, and housewares. The gallery represents 23 Nelson artisans with a national reputation; some are gaining international recognition. Upstairs a number of West Coast artists display their work.

Around Nelson

Though Nelson's a bustling city, it manages to retain a certain rural feel. With Tasman Bay before it and the foothills of the Bryant and Richmond Ranges behind, open countryside and vineyards are within easy reach of the city center. State Highway 6 south from the city winds through the outlying suburb of Stoke and through to Richmond, a good-size neighboring town. The commercial and civic center of the Tasman District, Richmond has a good library and a modest shopping mall—the only one in the region.

Just south of Richmond, State Highway 60 branches west off State Highway 6, heading toward Mapua, Motueka, and Golden Bay—all friendly rural backwaters. There's a wealth of vineyards along the coastal strip toward Motueka, plus idyllic farms, hop gardens, and crafts galleries tucked into the many valleys that run inland.

★ One of the best galleries in this neck of the woods is the **Hoglund Art Glass Studio & Gallery.** From the collectible family of penguins to the bold platters and vases, the Hoglund style is unmistakable. If you take a guided tour, you can watch the art glass take shape. As they are heated and whirled, blown and shaped, blobs of molten glass are transformed into colorful vases, platters, and ornaments. There are glass-blowing and glass bead-making classes available. ⊠ *Lansdowne Rd., Richmond* ☎ *03/544–6500* ⊗ *Daily 9–5* ☜ *Gallery free, guided tour $15.*

To dip into the local wine scene, drop by the **Grape Escape Complex** for tastings from two top wineries, Te Mania Estate and the organic Richmond Plains. Tastings are free for the wine of the month, and 50 cents for all other wines. The complex also has a crafts gallery, an indoor-outdoor café, and a couple of boutique galleries. ⊠ *State Hwy. 60 and McShanes Rd.* ☎ *03/544–4054* ⊗ *Daily 9–5.*

It's natural that **Creative Tourism New Zealand** should have started in Nelson, a hotbed of the country's arts and crafts. Bringing artisans such as potters, carvers, weavers, and painters together under one umbrella, for visitors interested in the arts to work with these experts in their own field—or studio, as the case may be. The pottery classes held at Macmillans Gallery (⊠ 92 Bateup Rd., Richmond ☎ 03/544–5853 ⊕ www.creativetourism.co.nz) are especially popular; you can learn to throw a pot or a jug, or paint a design onto a ceramic vase.

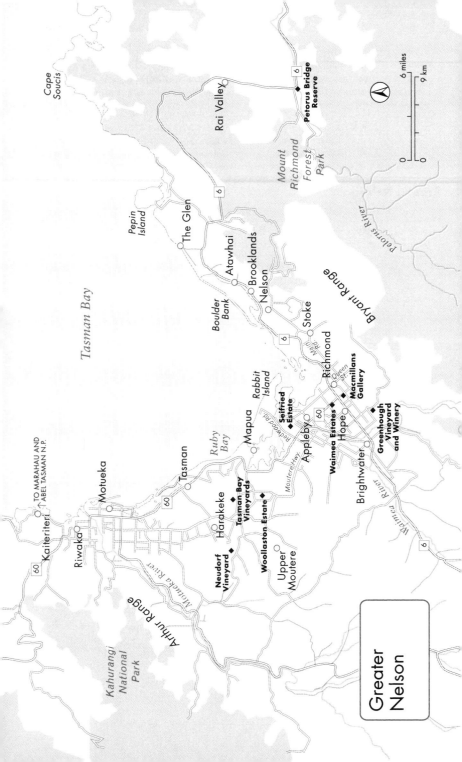

Greater Nelson

Tasman Bay

Cape Soucis

Rai Valley

Mount Richmond Forest Park

Petorus Bridge Reserve

Pelorus River

Bryant Range

Pepin Island

The Glen

Atawhai

Brooklands

Nelson

Boulder Bank

Stoke

Richmond

Queen St.

Macmillans Gallery

Main Rd.

Redwood Rd.

Seifried Estate

Mapua

Rabbit Island

Ruby Bay

Appleby

Waimea Estates

Hope

Greenhough Vineyard and Winery

Brightwater

Moutere Hwy.

Tasman

Motueka

Harakeke

Tasman Bay Vineyards

Woollaston Estate

Neudorf Vineyard

Upper Moutere

Motueka River

Riwaka

Kaiteriteri

TO MARAHAU AND ABEL TASMAN N.P.

Arthur Range

Kahurangi National Park

Waimea River

6 miles

9 km

Stoke

Isel House, in the beautiful tree-filled Isel Park, was built for Thomas Marsden, one of the region's prosperous pioneers. It was Marsden who laid out the magnificent gardens surrounding the house, which include a towering California redwood and a 140-foot Monterey pine. The house itself contains the Marsden family's impressive porcelain and furniture. ✉ *Isel Park, Stoke* ☎ *03/547–1347* 💰 *Donation* ⊙ *Sept.–Apr., daily 11–4, May–Aug. weekends 11–4.*

Broadgreen is a fine example of a Victorian cob house. Cob houses, made from straw and horsehair bonded together with mud and clay, are commonly found in Devon, the southern English home county of many of Nelson's pioneers. The house is furnished as it might have been in the 1850s, with patchwork quilts and kauri furniture. ✉ *276 Nayland Rd., Stoke* ☎ *03/547–0403* 💰 *$3* ⊙ *Daily 10:30–4:30.*

Just about every drinks list in the upper South Island will highlight a McCashin's (Mac for short) beer or two. At **McCashin's Brewery** you can get to the source of these excellent, naturally brewed beers. Because the Nelson area is the heart of New Zealand's hop-growing region, the product here is as fresh as you'll get it. You can tour the plant (reservations essential) and get a free tasting of brews such as the signature Mac's Gold lager. ✉ *660 Main Rd., Stoke* ☎ *03/547–0526* ⊕ *www.macs.co.nz* ⊙ *Tues.–Sat. 10–5, tours at 11 and 2.*

The Vineyards

Since 1997, **Waimea Estates** has been creating award-winning wines. The range includes sauvignon blanc, chardonnay, pinot gris, riesling, rosé, pinot noir, and a cab/merlot blend. Their Café in the Vineyard is open for lunch daily, with a roaring fire in winter and outdoor jazz on sunny summer Sunday afternoons. ✉ *22 Appleby Hwy., Appleby* ☎ *03/544–4963* ⊕ *www.waimeaestates.co.nz* ⊙ *Wine tours and tastings by appointment. Café open daily 11–5 in summer, Wed.–Sun. 11–4 in winter.*

Andrew Greenhough and Jennifer Wheeler's **Greenhough Vineyard and Winery** in the optimistically named suburb of Hope has established a big reputation for quality in a short time. Sauvignon blanc, chardonnay, riesling, pinot noir, and the occasional supersweet dessert wine are all worth trying. They have both single-vineyard and regional-vineyard wines; pinot noir is their flagship wine. In addition to the standard opening hours, you can call ahead for an appointment to visit their European-style winery and showroom, complete with local art. ✉ *Patons Rd., Hope* ☎ *03/542–3868* ⊙ *Late Oct.–Easter, weekends 1–5; Jan., daily 1–5.*

Seifried Estate is a 20-minute drive from Nelson's main center, on the way to Motueka. The winery produces fine sauvignon blanc, rich chardonnay, a very tasty riesling, and a plummy pinot noir. A restaurant next door to the tasting room is open every day for lunch. ✉ *Redwood Rd., Appleby* ☎ *03/544–1555* ⊕ *www.seifried.co.nz* ⊙ *Daily 10–5.*

The literally state-of-the-art, multilevel gravity-fed winery and gallery of **Woollaston Estate** sits on a quiet hillside in Mahana. In an area once known solely for apple production, the wines now being created from this district are maturing superbly. The gallery is part of the tasting area, and features the work of owner Phillip Woollaston's father, Toss, one of the country's best-known artists. Woollaston produces pinot rosé (from 100% pinot noir grapes), sauvignon blanc, riesling, and pinot gris, and their pinot noir has received special accolades. ⊠ *School Rd., Mahana, Turn off coastal State Hwy. 60 at Dominion Road, turn left into Old Coach Road, then right into School Road. The winery is 328 feet up on the right* ☎ *03/543–2817* ⊕ *www.woollaston.co.nz* ☾ *Jan. and Feb. 11–4:30 and by arrangement.*

Expatriate Californian Philip Jones doesn't follow established flavor patterns at his equipment-crammed **Tasman Bay Vineyards.** His best wines have great flavor concentration, and many have won major awards. Fifteen acres of grapes—sauvignon blanc, chardonnay, pinot gris, and pinot noir—surround the winery. Most of the wines are made from their estate vineyards, although some grapes are brought in from Marlborough. Except for the three-month window for tasting, the winery is open only for sales. ⊠ *Best Rd., Upper Moutere* ☎ *03/543–2031* ⊕ *www.tasmanbaywine.com* ☾ *Tastings Dec.–Feb., daily noon–4.*

★ Despite its tiny size, **Neudorf Vineyard** has established an international reputation for its pinot noir and chardonnay, but riesling, pinot gris, and sauvignon blanc are also highly regarded. Owners Tim and Judy Finn are enthusiastic about their region's attributes and will talk at length about local food and wine. The top wines wear the Moutere designation on the label, as the winery is in a valley surrounded by acres of vineyards and hop gardens. ⊠ *Neudorf Rd., Upper Moutere* ☎ *03/543–2643* ⊕ *www.neudorf.co.nz* ☾ *Daily 10:30–4:30.*

Where to Stay & Eat

The little town of Mapua has several nice places to eat, and the area down by the wharf, at the far end of Aranui Street, has some neat cafés. Apart from Mapua and a few outlying wineries, though, there are few restaurants in this area. There are, however, lots of B&Bs and boutique lodges for accommodation.

$$$ ✕ **Flax.** With a fabulous view overlooking the sea where the Waimea Fodor'sChoice Estuary meets Tasman Bay, Flax is one of the nicest spots in the area to ★ enjoy a meal. The building itself retains the airy space and soaring beamed ceilings of the boathouse it once was; there's a lovely outdoor seating area with shade sails to protect you from the sun. Owners Tim Greenhough and Karen Hannan share a fine pedigree as restaurateurs. Their summer mains include salmon with hokkien noodles, comfit of duck thigh, and a beef fillet. There is, naturally, a wonderful selection of local wines, and some spectacular desserts. Try the lemon posset—a velvety custard served with fresh berries and pistachio biscotti. ⊠ *Shed 1, Mapua Wharf* ☎ *03/540–2028* ⌲ *Reservations essential in summer.*

★ $$$ ✕ **Smokehouse Café.** Don't try to resist stopping here. The menu is based around delicately hot-smoked products, not just fish but lamb and chicken as well. There's also a "smoke-free" seasonal menu. You won't find a better lunch than their specialty platter piled with smoked whitefish, smoked salmon, mussels, and a sweet chilli jam and basil pesto dipping sauce, all served with fresh, crusty home-baked bread. There are great views up the estuary from the café and across to the Richmond Ranges, often peaked with snow in winter. You can't miss the big blue corrugated iron building on the wharf. The café has slightly truncated hours from May through October; reservations are recommended in summer. ⊠ *Mapua Wharf* ☎ *03/ 540–2280* ⊕ *www.smokehouse.co.nz* ⊟ *MC, V.*

$$–$$$ ✕ **Flavour.** This restaurant is upstairs in the same building as the Inlet Café and is a great spot to taste vintages from small local producers. The menu focuses on local produce, from the pears in the roasted pear salad to the olive oil drizzled over the vegetables. Lofty timber beams and wooden paneling make for a warmly welcoming look. It's open from 9 AM for breakfast. ⊠ *67 Aranui Rd., Mapua* ☎ *03/540–2526* ⊟ *AE, MC, V.*

¢–$ ✕ **The Naked Bun Patisserie and Café.** You've got to be quick here to beat the locals at lunchtime—it's the best place in Mapua to get a quick meal or fill a paper bag for a picnic. The bagels are bursting with fillings, the Samosas steam with hot spicy veggies, and the coffee is excellent. In good weather, try for one of the outdoor tables (there's also plenty of seating indoors if you want to hide from that hot Mapua sun). ⊠ *66–68 Aranui Rd., Mapua* ☎ *03/540–3656.*

★ $$$$ ▣ **Bronte Lodge.** Perched on the edge of the Waimea Estuary, this lodge gets you right down to the water. At high tide the lawn outside the villas is lapped by the sea, and at low tide you can walk out onto the sandflats to watch migratory wading birds. The villas are decorated with original works by well-known local artists. The garden is draped with flowering wisteria and shaded by tall trees, where breakfast is served in summer. Should you be feeling competitive, you can play a game of *pétanque* (boccie) or tennis or take a swim in the pool. If the tide is right, you can take a small boat across the estuary to Mapua for a coffee. They also have their own small vineyard and winery next door. ⊠ *Bronte Rd. East, off State Hwy. 60* ☎ *03/540–2422* 🖷 *03/540–2637* ⊕ *www. brontelodge.co.nz* ⤻ *4 villas* ⟁ *Kitchenettes, tennis court, pool, boating, bicycles* ⊟ *MC, V* ⦿ *BP.*

Sports & the Outdoors

RAFTING **★ ☾** **Ultimate Descents New Zealand.** This highly experienced company takes rafting trips on the Maruia (Grade III), Clarence (Grade II), Buller (Grade III–IV), and Karamea (Grade V) rivers. They also run inflatable kayaking on the easier rivers, half-day kayaking trips suitable for kids ($95), and half-day ($115), full-day ($195), and multiday wilderness trips ($395–$850). All half-day and day trips have a meal included, and the multiday trips are fully catered. ⊠ *51 Fairfax St., Murchison* ☎ *03/523– 9899 or 0800/748–377* 🖷 *03/523–9811* ⊕ *www.rivers.co.nz.*

Shopping

Built in an old apple cool store (where apples were stored at cool temperatures after being picked; Nelson was famous for its apples long before the grapes arrived), the funky **Cool Store Gallery** has some very reasonably priced art and craftwork. Much of the work has a vibrant Pacific theme, and all is produced by artists from the Nelson and West Coast regions; *paua* shell items, ceramics, glasswork, and jewelry line the walls. It's a great spot to scoop up souvenirs. ⊠ *7 Aranui Rd., Mapua* ☎ *03/540–3778* ⦿ *Daily 10–5 in summer, 11–4 in winter.*

Motueka

➐ *50 km (31 mi) west of Nelson.*

Motueka (mo-too-*eh*-ka) is an agricultural center—tobacco, hops, kiwifruit, and apples are among its staples. The town sits at the seaward end of the Motueka Valley, under the ranges of the Kahurangi National Park. Like Golden Bay, Motueka is a stronghold for the "alternative" communities around Nelson, and every byway seems to have a few artisans and erstwhile hippies living side by side with the traditional farming families. However, most of the good cafés and places to stay are outside the town center, either in the sheltered inland valleys or out along the Abel Tasman coast and nearby bays. South of town, for instance, the Motueka River valley is known for its sporting lodges. Motueka's also a good jumping-off point for Abel Tasman National Park, north of town.

Where to Stay & Eat

¢–$$$ ✕ **The Moorings.** This charming, nautically themed café sits right on the main street of Motueka and offers a nice place to break the drive to Takaka, or just to sit and watch the funky Motueka world go by. Seafood, pizzas, steak, and pastas all please hungry families; the café is very child-friendly. ⊠ *218 High St.* ☎ *03/528–6103* ▭ *AE, DC, MC, V.*

¢–$ ✕ **Hot Mama's Café.** Decorated in a funky Pasifika-kitsch style, Hot Mama's attracts the upbeat and the off-beat. The straightforward menu includes spectacular burgers, pizza, and yummy nachos. They often have live music in the front area opening onto the street, but there's a quiet sunny courtyard out back as well. ⊠ *105 High St.* ☎ *03/528–7039* ▭ *MC, V.*

★ $$$$ 🏠 **Motueka River Lodge.** Tranquillity, marvelous scenery, and a superb standard of comfort are the hallmarks here. Owned and operated by former Londoner Mick Mason, the lodge is on 80 acres bordering the Motueka River, with magnificent mountain views. Its sunny deck, vine-covered archways, and fragrant lavender hedges give the place a Mediterranean feel. The interior of the rustic house is accented with antiques collected from around the world. You can hike the national park nearby, but the lodge's specialty is fishing, especially dry fly-fishing for brown trout in the wild river country. The activities are restricted outside the October to April fishing season. ⊠ *Motueka Valley Hwy. (State Hwy. 61), Motueka* ☎ *03/526–8668* 🖨 *03/526–8669* ⊕ *www.motuekalodge. co.nz* 🛏 *5 rooms* ⚒ *Dining room, tennis court, hot tub, fishing, lounge; no a/c, no room phones, no room TVs, no kids* ▭ *AE, DC, MC, V* ⊙ *BP.*

★ $$ 🏠 **Doone Cottage.** At this charming 140-year-old cottage, hosts Stan and Glen Davenport have welcomed homestay guests for more than 25 years. The villa sits in a leafy garden overlooking the trout-filled Motueka River; five other trout streams are a short drive away. Guest rooms and the private garden chalet are all done in a low-key, rustic style. Glen spins and weaves wool from her own Suffolk sheep; her on-site studio has sweaters, rugs, and wall hangings for sale. ⊠ *Motueka Valley Hwy. (SH61), Motueka* ☎🖨 *03/526–8740* ⊕ *www.doonecottage.co.nz* 🛏 *2 rooms, 1 chalet* ⚒ *Hot tub; no a/c, no room phones, no room TVs, no kids, no smoking* ▭ *MC, V* ⊙ *BP.*

Sports & the Outdoors

You won't lack for places to land some whopping brown trout. Fishing season in this area runs from September to May. **Peter Carty** (✉ Chalgrave St., Murchison ☎☎ 03/523–9525 ⊕ www.browntroutheaven.co.nz) leads fly-fishing excursions to local rivers as well as to remote backcountry areas, which involve hiking or helicopter trips. The cost for one angler starts at $700. Zane Murfin of **Strike Adventure** (☎ 0274/732–483 ⊕ www.strikeadventure.com) also runs trips to both easily accessible and wilderness rivers, starting at $750 per day. He can lead photography expeditions, too.

EN ROUTE If you don't intend to visit the Abel Tasman National Park and Golden Bay and are headed for the West Coast, turn south onto Highway 61 at the Rothmans Clock Tower in Motueka, following the sign to Murchison. The road snakes through the **Motueka Valley** alongside the Motueka River, with the green valley walls pressing close alongside. If this river could talk, it would probably scream, "Trout!" After the town of Tapawera, turn south on State Highway 6 and continue to the West Coast.

Abel Tasman National Park

8 *77 km (48 mi) northwest of Motueka, 110 km (69 mi) northwest of Nelson.*

If all the beautiful scenery you're seeing is tempting you to get out in the wilds, head to Abel Tasman, a stunning yet accessible swath of parkland. Its succession of idyllic beaches is backed by a rugged hinterland of native beech forests, granite gorges, and waterfalls. Unlike many of New Zealand's national parks, Abel Tasman has few serious challenges in its climate or terrain, making it a perfect place for an outdoorsy day trip.

The approach to this park is notably lovely. From the town of Motueka, State Highway 60 passes close to Kaiteriteri Beach, then turns inland to skirt Abel Tasman National Park. The road to Kaiteriteri branches off State Highway 60 a few kilometers after the small village of Riwaka; ★ a drive down the narrow, winding route will reward you with **Kaiteriteri Beach,** arguably one of New Zealand's prettiest beaches, with its curve of golden sand, the rocky islets offshore, and deep, clear water. This place is packed in midsummer as locals enjoy the holiday break, but once the six-week Christmas rush is over, the area returns to its usual quiet. (Take care driving on frosty winter mornings, as some corners stay frozen well into the day.)

The small town of **Marahau** is the gateway to the national park. An interpretation board posted near the park café will give you some information, but you may want to stop by the Department of Conservation (DOC) office in Motueka instead to get maps. (If you're planning to use the DOC huts, you'll need to pick up hut tickets there, too—if you haven't already booked online at www.doc.govt.nz/explore.) The park has excellent hiking, sailing, and sea-kayaking opportunities—and water taxis service the coves (*see* Sports, *below*). Midsummer, from December to February, is the peak tourist season here, so plan ahead if you'll be visiting then.

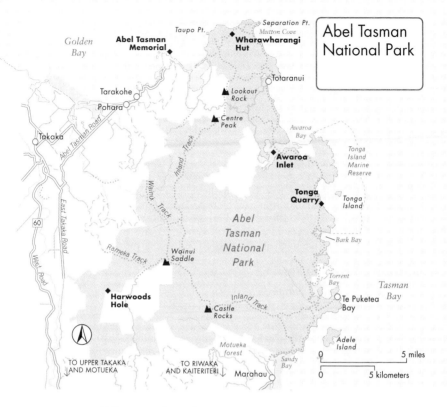

Where to Stay & Eat

$$–$$$ ✕▦ **Kimi Ora Spa Resort.** Kimi Ora means "seek health" in Māori, and here you can do just that. The developer was set on creating an environmentally friendly resort, including a restaurant serving organic food. For all the pampering, though, the overall vibe is low-key. The guest rooms have cozy wood walls and simple furnishings; most have a view of Kaiteriteri Beach. ⊠ *Martins Farm Rd., Kaiteriteri* ☎ *03/527–8027* ⊟ *03/527–8134* ⊕ *www.kimiora.com* ☞ *22 units* ⚷ *2 pools (1 indoor), gym, sauna, steam room, mountain bikes; no a/c, no smoking* ⊟ *MC, V.*

★ $$$–$$$$ ▦ **Awaroa Lodge.** Relax in an idyllic part of the spectacular Abel Tasman National Park, surrounded by native bush, just two minutes' walk to the beach. You can sea-kayak to the lodge or walk, as the Abel Tasman Track passes right through the property. To reach the lodge by boat, contact **Aqua Taxis** (☎ 03/527–8083), which leaves from Marahau daily, or fly direct from Nelson with **Nelson Helicopters** (☎ 03/528–8075). Choose from a luxurious studio, deluxe, or family rooms. The attached restaurant, with its chunky wooden furnishings and open adobe fireplace, serves stylish regional cuisine; most of the produce is grown organically on the property. The restaurant is also open to walkers off the park's Coastal Track and visitors arriving by boat, from 8 AM to 4:30 PM. ⊠ *Awaroa Bay, Abel Tasman National Park, Motueka*

☎ *03/528–8758* 🖷 *03/528–6561* ⊕ *www.awaroalodge.co.nz* 🛏 *26 rooms* ⚭ *Restaurant; no a/c, no room TVs* ▭ *AE, MC, V.*

$$ 🖵 **Abel Tasman Marahau Lodge.** With Abel Tasman National Park 200 yards in one direction and the Marahau beach 200 yards in the other, this location is hard to resist. The boutique lodge has spacious fully self-contained chalets, clustered in groups of two or four with native gardens between them. Units are finished in natural wood and have high cathedral ceilings, clean-lined wooden furniture, New Zealand wool carpets, queen- or king-size beds, and balconies from which to take in the park's natural beauty. Rates do not include breakfast, but room-service breakfasts and a communal kitchen are available. Staff can give information about and make reservations for sea kayaking, water taxis, and hiking options. ✉ *Marahau, R.D. 2, Motueka* ☎*03/527–8250* 🖷*03/527–8258* ⊕ *www.abeltasmanmarahaulodge.co.nz* 🛏 *12 rooms* ⚭ *Kitchen, outdoor hot tub, sauna; no a/c* ▭ *DC, MC, V.*

Sports

HIKING Abel Tasman has a number of walking trails, from both Totaranui at its north end and Marahau in the south. Shuttles are available to take you to the trailheads or pick you up afterward. Pest eradication schemes are markedly improving the native bird population, so you'll get quite a morning chorus on your trek. The tracks and conditions here aren't too grueling, but remember that, as with any outdoor activity, conditions can change quickly, especially in winter. Carry bottled water, as the park sources are not reliably pure, and be sure to have warm clothing, food, and sun and insect protection. The sand flies can be voracious. The **Department of Conservation offices** provide trail maps. ✉ *King Edward and High Sts., Motueka* ☎ *03/528–1810* ✉ *62 Commercial St., Takaka* ☎ *03/525–8026* ⊕ *www.doc.govt.nz.*

The most popular hike is the two- to three-day **Coastal Track,** open year-round. Much of the track's popularity is because of its relatively easy terrain and short distances. Launches from Abel Tasman National Park Experiences will drop off and pick up hikers from several points along the track.

Abel Tasman Wilson's Experiences are the original operators of day excursions to this park. They offer several kinds of bushwalks, trips to beaches, launch cruises, and sea kayaking. They also run one- to five-day hiking or hiking-kayaking treks around the park. ✉ *265 High St., Motueka* ☎ *03/528–2027 or 0800/223–582* 🖷 *03/528–2029* ⊕ *www. abeltasman.co.nz.*

SAILING If you'd like a day in the park without breaking a sweat, call up **Abel ★ Tasman Sailing Adventures.** Their two large catamarans sail daily into the heart of the park from Kaiteriteri Beach and Marahau. On the way you stop at Split Apple Rock before heading off to swim at a gorgeous beach such as Te Pukatea Bay, where the water is a clear translucent green. You can also view a colony of fur seals up close. A day trip costs $135, including lunch and hot and cold drinks, plus pickup. A range of sail and walk options are available from $55. Advance reservations are essential. ☎ *0800/467–245* ⊕ *www.sailingadventures.co.nz.*

CLOSE UP

Farewell Spit

A 35-KM (22-MI) protected sandbar with a 19th-century lighthouse, Farewell Spit is renowned for its tremendous seabird population. The best way to see the sandy, rather barren landscape is on a tour. A trip with **Farewell Spit Eco Tours** (⊠ Tasman St., Collingwood ☎ 03/524–8257 or 0800/808–257 ⊕ www.farewellspit.co.nz) is an absolute must if you are in Golden Bay. Each of the two tour itineraries takes you out along the Farewell Spit; one tour will take you to a gannet colony. (The company is the only one with a DOC license to visit the gannets.) Costs run between $79 and $105; reservations are essential.

You could also saddle up for a trip with **Cape Farewell Horse Treks** (⊠ Wharariki Beach Rd., Puponga ☎ 03/524–8031 ⊕ www.horsetreksnz.com); this outfit offers some of the best horse trekking in the country, with spectacular beaches and wild views. The sturdy, handpicked standardbred horses know exactly where they're going. For the best views, sign up for the Pillar Point Light trek ($45).

SEA KAYAKING **Ocean River Sea Kayaking** specializes in freedom unguided sea-kayaking trips in Abel Tasman National Park, including rental of camping equipment and water-taxi backup. Prices start at $40 per day over five days (a single-day rental is $69). ⊠ *Marahau, Motueka* ☎ *03/527–8266* 🖷 *03/527–8006* ⊕ *www.seakayaking.co.nz.*

The **Sea Kayak Company** offers a range of guided kayaking options through the pristine waters of the national park to beaches and campsites often inaccessible to hikers. These include a one-day discovery tour ($99), a two-day "More than Beaches" tour ($320), and three- and five-day tours ($399 and $950, respectively). All tours are fully catered and all equipment is supplied, down to the Department of Conservation camp passes. ⊠ *506 High St., Motueka* ☎ *03/528–7251 or 0508/252–925* 🖷 *03/528–7221* ⊕ *www.seakayaknz.co.nz.*

Golden Bay & Takaka

❾ *55 km (35 mi) northwest of Motueka, 110 km (70 mi) west of Nelson.*

From the Motueka–Nelson area, a spectacular hill road, State Highway 60, rises up about 2,500 feet before plunging again to sea level to reach the tiny township of **Takaka,** a jumping-off point for Kahurangi National Park. If you enjoy a challenging drive, then you'll likely find this road great fun to traverse. It's a 40-minute climb of twisting corners, steep drop-offs, and occasional passing bays. If you don't have your eyes glued to the road, check out the views back across the plains to Nelson, out over the coast along the Abel Tasman National Park, and, toward the end, across the Upper Takaka valley from Harwoods Lookout to the mountains of Kahurangi National Park.

The gorgeous stretch of coastline that begins at Separation Point and runs westward past Takaka, is known, deservedly, as **Golden Bay.** Alternating sandy and rocky shores curve up to the sands of Farewell Spit, the arcing prong that encloses the bay. Other than a 19th-century lighthouse, the spit is pure, raw nature. Faultlines slash the cliffs, and the area is a favorite for all kinds of birds. In short, it's solitude at its very best. Dutch navigator Abel Tasman anchored here briefly just a few days before Christmas 1642. His visit ended abruptly when four of his crew were killed by the then-resident Māori iwi (tribe), Ngāti Tumata Kokiri. Bitterly disappointed, Tasman named the place Moordenaers, or Murderers' Bay, and sailed away without ever setting foot on New Zealand soil. If you have time to explore it, Golden Bay is a delight—a sunny, 40-km (25-mi) crescent with a relaxed crew of locals who firmly believe they live in paradise.

The lifestyle here has always been considered "alternative"—a hideout for hippies, musicians, and artists. But it's also the center of a rich dairy farming area, and its warm, sheltered climate nurtures crops such as citrus, avocados, and kiwifruit that struggle on the colder, Nelson side of "the hill." Overseas buyers have been snapping up Golden Bay properties to get their own little part-time spot of paradise, but local bylaws are changing to encourage full-time residents back to the bay.

Eight kilometers (5 mi) west of Takaka is **Waikoropupu Springs,** known as Pupu Springs. This is the largest spring system in New Zealand, and clear, cold water bubbles into the Waikoropupu Valley after traveling underground from its source at the nearby Takaka Hill. Dated tourist brochures still available in the area show people swimming in the springs, but this is now frowned upon—alas—because of the effect it has on the delicate flora within the springs. Divers can enter the springs and dive its unbelievably clear, but painfully cold, water so long as they are not part of a commercial trip, have only four divers in the water at any one time, and dive only after midday with a maximum of 15 minutes in the water per dive. At a constant 11°C, nobody stays in for long, but the exuberant plant life and interesting fish make it a fascinating dive. Local dive clubs visit the springs on a regular basis, and if you're here during one of their trips, you'll gain a sense of the springs' impressive scale. If you're not a diver, it's best to leave the bathing suit in the car and take a leisurely stroll around the valley on the 90-minute Pupu Walkway. Take your time and go quietly—the better to spot tūī, bellbirds, wood pigeons, and other birdlife. The turnoff from State Highway 60 at the Waitapu River is signposted.

Rapidly gathering notoriety in Golden Bay, the **Labyrinth** is a system of twisting tunnels and gullies carved into the rocks by long-receded river systems. This karst system of bush-covered limestone pathways curls through a natural maze for 2 km (1 mi), taking about an hour to negotiate. There's also a bridge, a $1 café (everything's a dollar), and a picnic site. ⊠ *Labyrinth La., off Abel Tasman Dr.* ☎ *03/525–8434* 🖃 *$7* ⊙ *Daily noon–dusk.*

After winding through several small farming districts and beach communities such as Paton's Rock, Onekaka, and Tukurua, State Highway

60 arrives at **Collingwood,** a small seaside village at the mouth of the giant Aorere River, 26 km (16 mi) west of Takaka. The earliest European settlers came here in the 1840s to build small ships from the timber lining the beaches and to farm the fertile river plains that spill out of the surrounding mountains. In the 1850s, gold was discovered nearby and Collingwood became a thriving port-of-entry town; at one time it was even under consideration to be the country's capital. Arriving here you'll find that very hard to believe now.

These days Collingwood's main claims to fame are as the northern access point for the Heaphy Track and as a base for trips to the Farewell Spit and the West Coast beaches. The old 1910 council office building houses a small museum with a good photographic record of the area from colonial times. You might also want to make a sweet stop by Rosy Glow Chocolates on Beach Road.

The wild **Kahurangi National Park** (✉ 62 Commercial St., Takaka ☎ 03/525–8026 ⊕ www.doc.govt.nz) is one of New Zealand's newest national parks, opened in 1996. This vast patch of land covers 1.1 million acres of untamed wilderness, covering fern-clad forests, rocky rivers, rolling tussock-covered hills, rugged snowcapped mountains, and wind-blown beaches pounded by West Coast surf. The park is laced with 570 km (353 mi) of hiking tracks of various levels of difficulty; there are also several rafting and kayaking rivers and some serious caving areas, especially toward the West Coast. Of the various entry points to the park, the most convenient is 35 km (21 mi) west of Takaka, south of the town of Collingwood. This is also the northern head of the Heaphy Track (*see* Sports & the Outdoors, *below*). The **Department of Conservation Golden Bay Area Office** provides local trail maps.

OFF THE BEATEN PATH **TOTARANUI –** From Takaka the coast road heading east leads around to the northern entry to the Abel Tasman National Park at Totaranui. This very picturesque road passes through Pohara Beach, which has several cafés and a campground, before winding around to Wainui Bay with its alternative Tui community (a onetime commune which welcomes visitors) and cascading waterfall. From Wainui Bay, the road over the Totaranui Hill is just a hard sand surface and can be treacherous in wet weather. But in good weather, it's a beautiful drive through dense native bush to the coast. Totaranui beach is a long golden-sand beach that is safe for swimming. This area can also be reached by boat from Kaiteriteri and Marahau, on the Motueka side of the Takaka hill. It's a slice of pure beach bliss.

Where to Stay & Eat

$–$$$ ✕ **Totally Roasted.** The little community of Pohara Beach has an ace in the hole with this café. Chef Chris Falconer is a coffee devotee and roasts single-origin organic Cuban beans on-site. Before you get the caffeine jitters, order a sweet treat or light meal to sample on the patio. The contemporary space also doubles as a gallery for local artists. ✉ *Abel Tasman Dr., just before Pohara Beach* ☎ *03/525–9396* ⊟ *No credit cards* ⊗ *No dinner.*

$–$$$ ✕ **Wholemeal Café.** Don't be put off by the laid-back appearance of the staff here—the Wholemeal is a long-standing favorite in Takaka. Not only is the food healthful and delicious, but they also make some of the best coffee in town. Drop by for a thick slice of pizza or quiche at lunch or dig into one of their curries at dinner. Whenever you come, switch to a lower gear; life's set to a slower speed in Golden Bay. ⊠ *60 Commercial St., Takaka* ☎ *03/525–9426* ⊟ *MC, V.*

$$ ✕ **Mussel Inn.** If you want to experience a quintessential slice of Golden Bay life, swing by this place. Locals come for the live music (usually jazz or folk bands, which play on differing evenings starting at about 7), a bowl of mussel chowder, and some of the house-brewed beer. The decor is interestingly described as "Kiwi woolshed meets Aussie farmhouse." We'll take their word for it. ⊠ *State Hwy. 60, Onekaka* ☎ *03/525–9241* ⊟ *MC, V* ⊙ *Closed late July–early Sept.* ⚭ *Reservations not accepted.*

$$–$$$ ⊡ **Westhaven Retreat.** If it's remote luxury you're after, this peninsula retreat is for you. It's set on 1,000 acres of regenerating native forest surrounded by the Tasman Sea and the Whanganui Inlet. Austrian-born Bruno and Monika Stompe literally carved the accommodations out of the environment; access roads were built by Bruno, once an industrial engineer. Rooms in the main house have rimu-wood paneling and a neutral color scheme; the separate cottage is modern, roomy, and bright. Lunch and dinner can be added on. On-site you'll find a menagerie of farm animals, including more than 60 gentle llamas. There's at least 40 km (25 mi) of gravel road between you and the nearest neighbor. If you're leery of the gravel roads, inquire about helicopter access or about being picked up at Nelson Airport, Motueka, or Takaka. At this writing, the retreat was continuing a comprehensive expansion. ⊠ *Te Hapu Rd., Collingwood* ☎ *03/524–8354* 🖷 *03/524–8354* ✍ *westhave@ihug. co.nz* ⊲ *3 rooms, 1 cottage* ⚭ *Beaches, hiking; no a/c, no room phones, no room TVs, no smoking* ⊟ *AE, DC, MC, V* ⊙| *BP.*

$ ⊡ **Anatoki Lodge.** This spacious, contemporary motel is close to Takaka center. Owners Gaye and Garth Prince can help point out the main attractions and best places to eat in the area. The lodge has spacious studios and one- and two-bedroom units; each opens out to a private patio and grass courtyard. ⊠ *87 Commercial St., Takaka* ☎ *03/525–8047* 🖷 *03/525–8433* ✍ *anatoki@xtra.co.nz* ⊲ *5 studios, 6 units* ⚭ *BBQ, indoor pool; no a/c, no smoking* ⊟ *AE, MC, V* ⊙| *CP.*

$ ⊡ **Sans Souci Inn.** Tucked away behind high leafy hedges, Sans Souci is a quiet, mellow, ecofriendly spot just a two-minute walk from Pohara Beach. There's a small restaurant, and you can arrange to take breakfast and dinner here. ⊠ *Richmond Rd., Pohara Beach* ☎🖷 *03/525–8663* ⊕ *www.sanssouciinn.co.nz* ⊲ *7 rooms* ⚭ *Kitchen, restaurant; no a/c, no room phones, no room TVs* ⊙ *Closed July, Aug., and 1st 2 wks of Sept.* ⊙| *BP.*

Sports & the Outdoors

BEACHES Golden Bay has miles of swimming beaches. **Paton's Rock** is one of the best near Takaka. Check the tides before taking the 10-minute drive from town, as swimming is best with a full tide. Farther out, less suitable for swimming but spectacular for its coastal landscapes, is **Wharariki Beach.** You'll find massive sand dunes, and among these you're likely to come across fur seals sunbathing. They are, of course, wild seals, and if you get too close to them, they might charge or even bite, so keep a 15-foot distance, and never get between a seal and the sea. To get here, drive past Collingwood and follow the signs. Go as far as the road will take you, and then walk over farmland on a well-defined track for 20 minutes. Because these are quite remote beaches, there are no lifeguards on duty.

FISHING For information on deep-sea fishing in Golden Bay out of Takaka, *see* Chapter 11.

HIKING The most famous walk in Kahurangi National Park is the one-way, 82-
★ km (51 mi) **Heaphy Track.** The track is one of the Great Walks trails, so you will need to buy a Great Walks Pass for hut stays, although you can carry a tent and be independent of the hut system. Passes range from $10 to $20 per night, depending on the time of year. It is best to purchase these tickets in advance from information centers at Nelson, Motueka, or Takaka or book online at greatwalksbooking£doc.govt. nz. Track-user numbers are limited by the number of beds available on any one night. Tickets in hand, all you really need to do is get to the track and start walking toward Karamea on the West Coast. You'll need a reasonable level of fitness since the conditions can become very challenging in poor weather. Huts along the way have gas cooking and heating facilities, water, and toilets. You'll need to carry your own food and bedding. And be prepared for weather of all kinds at all times of year—bring rain gear and warm clothing even in summer (and insect repellent for the sand flies!). You can get trail maps from the **Department of Conservation Golden Bay Area Office** ⊠ *62 Commercial St., Takaka* ☎ *03/525–8026.*

K Bus (☎03/578–4075 or 0800/881–188 ⊕www.kbus.co.nz) offers transport to the track from Takaka on demand (drop-off and pickup). It also provides general charter services and scheduled services between Golden Bay, Abel Tasman, and Nelson. From Nelson, **InterCity** (☎ 03/548–1538) runs buses at 6:45 AM each day to the trailhead; the ride costs $30. Some routes do not run year-round, so check when booking.

If you'd like some expert company on hikes around the national park, **Kahurangi Guided Walks** (☎ 03/525–7177 ⊕ www.kahurangiwalks. webnz.co.nz) runs easy one-day treks on routes known to locals but virtually untouched by visitors. A more strenuous, three-day walk goes to the rarely visited Boulder Lake, and there's also the five-day hike on the Heaphy Track, and other hikes as well. Prices vary for each customized trip.

Murchison

❿ *125 km (78 mi) south of Nelson, 63 km (40 mi) west of Lake Rotoiti.*

This small town is in the center of some very big country, surrounded by high mountains and roaring rivers. With the Nelson Lakes National Park to the west, the Kahurangi National Park to the north, and the Matakitaki, Buller, Matiri, and Mangles rivers all converging on its doorstep, Murchison has gained the reputation as New Zealand's "white-water capital" and justifiably so. There are 13 rivers within 20 km (12½ mi) of town. Fly-fishers, kayakers, and rafting junkies turn up here at all times of the year, although the summer is much kinder to those who love the water, as in winter the water is cold snowmelt.

Murchison residents still consider their landmark event "the earthquake," a major quake that hit back in June 1929. The epicenter was nearby in the lower Matakitaki Valley, and the quake drastically altered the landscape. Those who remember it still speak of it as a life-changing event. The local **Murchison District Museum** (⊠ 60 Fairfax St. ☎ 03/523–9392) has an excellent exhibit on this disaster and how it affected the area. There's also a good collection of farming and agricultural machinery from the town's colonial era, plus displays on a local gold rush.

Now a stopover town for travelers heading between the West Coast and the northern end of the South Island, and a trout-fishing and white-water destination, Murchison has several good places to stay. The restaurant scene, though, is pretty limited.

Where to Stay

$$$$ ⊡ **Korimako Lodge.** *Korimako* is a Māori word meaning "bellbird," a little native bird with a big song. The namesake trills happily in the forest surrounding this luxurious lodge high above the Matakitaki River Valley, often the only sound to be heard other than the river far below. A contemporary, minimalist decor guides your eye to the vast windows to drink in the views. The hosts can hook you up with a guide for trout fishing on the Buller River. ⊠ *10 km (8 mi) up the Matakitaki Valley* ☎ *03/523–9763* ⊕ *www.korimako.co.nz* ⇨ *3 rooms* ⛬ *Hot tub, bicycles; no a/c, no room phones, no room TVs, no kids under 14, no smoking* ⊟ *MC, V* ⊗ *Closed May–Sept.* ◯| *MAP.*

$$ ⊡ **Murchison Lodge.** Tucked in a tiny back street of Murchison, this rural retreat is within easy walking distance of the mighty Buller River. The guest rooms are comfortably countrified, with strong colors and lots of wood. Breakfast is a big affair, and the barbecue is often fired up. The hosts can put you in touch with a good local guide for trout fishing. ⊠ *15 Grey St.* ☎ *03/523–9196* ⊕ *www.murchisonlodge.co.nz* ⇨ *3 rooms* ⛬ *Massage, bicycles, Internet room; no a/c, no room phones, no room TVs, no smoking* ⊟ *MC, V* ⊗ *Closed May–Sept.* ◯| *BP.*

Nelson Lakes National Park

100 km (62 mi) south of Nelson.

Spread around two stunningly scenic glacial lakes, Rotoroa and Rotoiti, the Nelson Lakes National Park is an alpine zone of soaring mountains, rocky rivers, and bush-lined trails. The native beech forests are especially beautiful as they pour down to the lakeshore. On cloudy days, mist swirls through the trees, wetting the draping mosses and silencing the birds. On sunny days the intense green color comes through and the birds' chorus resumes. Lake Rotoiti is also the site of a kiwi-recovery program; in 2004 several kiwi were released back into the forest after an intense pest-eradication program. (The removal of exotic pests such as stoats, rats, and wasps has allowed the return of a number of bird species that had been threatened by the change in the ecosystem.)

Of the two lakes, Lake Rotoroa is the most pristine, with just a few fishing cottages, a campsite, and a lodge on its shore. The village of St. Arnaud sits at the northern end of Lake Rotoiti; it's the gateway to the park, with a handful of B&Bs, a general store, and the Department of Conservation bureau. The **DOC Headquarters** here is a particularly good one, with plenty of information on the geology and ecology of the area. Maps and details on the hiking trails are available, and a mountain weather forecast is issued daily. ⊠ *View Rd., St. Arnaud* ☎ *03/521–1806* ⊕ *www.doc.govt.nz/explore.*

Where to Stay

$$$$
Fodor'sChoice
★
🏠 **Lake Rotoroa Lodge.** Here's where the rich and famous come, and those who want to remain anonymous. Sheltered beneath tall trees on Lake Rotoroa, this is an elegant and truly private haven. The lodge was built for "gentlemen travelers" back in the days when horse and coach was the only transport through these parts. Now it lures anglers with a combination of old-fashioned charm and newfangled luxury, from the brass beds and hunting trophies to the expert fishing guides and outstanding wine list offered in the dining room. ⊠ *Lake Rotoroa* ☎ *03/523–9121* 🖨 *03/523–9028* ⊕ *www.lakerotoroalodge.com* ↪ *10 rooms* ⌂ *Fishing, hiking; no room TVs* ⊟ *AE, MC, V* ⊙ *Closed June–Oct.* ⦿ *MAP.*

¢–$$
🏠 **Alpine Lodge and Alpine Chalets.** The accommodation here runs the gamut from full suites to backpacker dorms. With the wood paneling and dormer windows, the building may feel somewhat European-alpine, but the view out the window is all Kiwi. The lodge is right up at the national park boundary, a short bushwalk away from Lake Rotoiti. There are a few two-bedroom apartments which are a good fit for families. ⊠ *Main Rd., St. Arnaud* ☎ *03/521–1869* 🖨 *03/521–1868* ⊕ *www.alpinelodge.co.nz* ↪ *24 rooms, 4 suites, 4 apartments, 1 dorm* ⌂ *Restaurant, some minibars, bar, playground, laundry facilities; no a/c, no smoking* ⊟ *AE, D, MC, V.*

Sports

Nelson Lakes park has several half- and full-day trails that can be "freedom walked" (walked without a guide) if you wish. The **Lake Rotoiti Circuit** gets you around the lake in an easy daylong walk. The rather steep **Mt. Robert Track** zigzags up the face of Mt. Robert, giving you a superb view back across the lake toward St. Arnaud village. The return walk can be done by looping down the face of the mountain to meet up with the Lake Rotoiti Circuit track.

If you prefer to be guided, **Nelson Wilderness Guides** can take the work out of finding tracks, gear, and accommodation. They have three- and four-day tours through the park, based at their accommodation, Golden Downs Lodge, and offer multiday wilderness expeditions into the backcountry. ⊠ *Kohatu, Golden Downs* ☎ *03/522–4175* ⊕ *www.goldendowns.co.nz.*

NELSON & THE NORTHWEST ESSENTIALS

Transportation

BY AIR

Nelson Airport (NSN) is 10 km (6 mi) south of the city. It's a small regional airport, so there aren't any major lines to worry about. There are two terminals, the larger one for Air New Zealand flights and the smaller one for local Origin Pacific flights.

Air New Zealand links Nelson with Christchurch, Queenstown, Dunedin, the West Coast town of Hokitika, and all major cities on the North Island.

Super Shuttle buses meet all incoming flights and can take you wherever you need to go in town; the cost is $15 to the city for one passenger, $19 each for two. You don't need to book for incoming flights, but you do need to reserve ahead to go out to the airport. Taxi fare into town is about $25 to $40.

🛪 Airport **Nelson Airport** ✉ Trent Dr. ☎ 03/547-3199.

🛪 Airport Transfers **Super Shuttle** ☎ 03/547-5782.

🛪 Carrier **Air New Zealand** ☎ 03/547-8721 or 0800/737-000 ⊕ www.airnewzealand.co.nz.

BY BUS

InterCity buses leave daily for Nelson from the ferry terminal in Picton. The trip takes about three hours. From Nelson, InterCity runs the length of both the west and east coasts daily. Atomic Shuttles also runs daily services along these main routes. Abel Tasman Coachlines, InterCity, and K Bus run the smaller routes to Motueka, Takaka, and the Abel Tasman and Kahurangi national parks.

Many of the smaller routes cut their service frequency in winter, some stop altogether, and others reduce their route destinations, so if traveling then, be sure to double-check the schedules. Some companies downsize their buses as you get farther from Nelson, so a trip to Totaranui may involve two changes as the bus size decreases along the way.

🚌 Bus Depot **Nelson** ✉ 27 Bridge St. ☎ 03/548-3290.

🚌 Bus Lines **Atomic Shuttles** ☎ 03/322-8883 ⊕ www.atomictravel.co.nz. **InterCity** ☎ 03/548-1538 ⊕ www.nelsoncoaches.co.nz. **K Bus** ☎ 03/578-4075 or 0800/881-188 ⊕ www.kbus.co.nz.

BY CAR

Nelson is about a two-hour drive from the ferry in Picton. The distance is 145 km (90 mi), but the winding roads don't allow for fast open-road driving.

From Nelson, State Highway 6 runs southwest to the West Coast, down the coast to the glaciers, then over the Haast Pass to Wanaka and Queenstown. If you're going to the West Coast, allow at least seven hours for the 458-km (284-mi) journey from Nelson to Franz Josef. The same applies if you plan to drive from Nelson to Christchurch, 424 km (265

7

mi) to the southeast, whether you drive through the mountains of Nelson Lakes National Park or through Blenheim and Kaikoura.

Driving is the most convenient way to get around the region, although even the highways can be narrow and winding. Nelson roads are easily negotiated. There's plenty of parking in the city, with three large lots behind the main shopping area. As with Blenheim, Nelson's shopping zone is crisscrossed with raised-brick crossings. Although these are not legally pedestrian crossings, locals treat them as if they are, so be ready to stop frequently. During the summer peak season, traffic slows, and you should allow extra time if trying to reach the airport. If you plan to do some wine tasting, remember that driving under the influence carries a hefty fine at least.

Highway 60 splits from State Highway 6 about 13 km (8 mi) out of Nelson near Richmond to reach the Abel Tasman area. Keep in mind that towns marked on maps are often tiny—blink and you'll miss them—and it can be a long way between gas stations.

The major car-rental agencies all have branches at Nelson's airport. Rental desks stay open to meet all arrivals and during normal business hours. Apex Rentals are particularly easy to deal with and are happy for their cars to explore more outlying areas. They give a copy of the 125-page *New Zealand Driving Holidays* booklet with each rental.

🛈 Rental Agencies **Apex** ☎ 03/546-9028 or 0800/939-777. **Avis** ☎ 03/547-2727. **Budget** ☎ 03/547-9586 or 0800/283-438. **Hertz** ☎ 03/547-2299 or 0800/654-321.

Contacts & Resources

BANKS & EXCHANGE SERVICES

Nelson, Richmond, Motueka, and Takaka all have ATMs outside the major banks. But don't count on being able to get cash outside of these places. In the smaller towns, some accommodations and retailers will give cash advances on credit cards if they have cash to spare.

EMERGENCIES

The only extended-hours pharmacy in the area is Prices Pharmacy on the corner of Collingwood and Hardy streets in central Nelson. It is open daily, 7 to 7.

🛈 Emergency Services **Fire, police, and ambulance** ☎ 111. **Nelson Base Hospital** ✉ Waimea Rd., Nelson ☎ 03/546-1800.

MAIL & INTERNET

Nelson has several Internet cafés, and with a little scrounging you can find one in several of the smaller towns. In the more remote communities, however, you'll need to rely on whatever access your lodgings might have.

🛈 Internet Cafés **Aurora Tech** ✉ 161 Trafalgar St., Nelson ☎ 03/546-6867. **Bites Café** ✉ 46 Commercial St., Takaka ☎ 03/525-9676. **Cyberworld Internet** ✉ 178 High St., Motueka ☎ 03/528-8090. **Internet Outpost** ✉ 35 Bridge St., Nelson ☎ 03/529-1150.
🛈 Post Offices **NZ Post Nelson** ✉ Halifax and Trafalgar Sts. ☎ 03/546-7818. **NZ Post Motueka** ✉ Books & More, 207 High St. ☎ 03/528-6600. **NZ Post Takaka** ✉ Commercial St. ☎ 03/525-9916.

TOURS

ACTIVITY TOURS Bay Tours Nelson runs daily half- and full-day tours of wine trails, arts-and-crafts tours, and scenic adventure tours by arrangement. Trips include the city and its immediate district and also go farther afield to the wine regions, Motueka and Kaiteriteri Beach and south to Nelson Lakes National Park.

Bay Tours Nelson ✉ 31A Stansell Ave., Nelson ☎ 03/548-6486 or 0800/229-868 🖶 03/548-6481 ⊕ www.baytoursnelson.co.nz.

WALKING TOURS Abel Tasman Wilson's Experiences guides day trips and three- and five-day treks in the beautiful coastal park. Spend nights in comfortable lodges and eat well, without having to carry a big pack. The rates for a five-day kayaking and hiking trip or five-day guided walk are from $1,080, depending on the season; the three-day kayaking and hiking trip or three-day guided walk each start at $720.

Abel Tasman Wilson's Experiences ✉ 265 High St., Motueka ☎ 03/528-7801 or 0800/221-888 🖶 03/528-6087 ⊕ www.abeltasman.co.nz.

VISITOR INFORMATION

The visitor-information centers in Nelson, Motueka, and Takaka are all open daily 9 to 5. The Nelson area is included in **The Treasured Pathway** (⊕ www.treasuredpathway.co.nz), a historically focused trail across the top of the South Island. The *Art in Its Own Place* guidebook, available at visitor centers and local shops, is a good resource for the area's crafts offerings.

The Taste Web site, ⊕ www.thetaste.co.nz, is regularly updated, covering mostly the local wine, food, and arts scenes.

Tourist Information **Golden Bay Visitor Information Centre** ✉ Willow St., Takaka ☎ 03/525-9136 ⊕ www.nelsonnz.com. **Motueka Visitor Information Centre** ✉ Wallace St. ☎ 03/528-6543 🖶 03/528-6563 ⊕ www.abeltasmangreenrush.co.nz. **Nelson Visitor Information Centre** ✉ Trafalgar and Halifax Sts. ☎ 03/548-2304 ⊕ www.nelsonnz.com.

THE WEST COAST

Southwest of Nelson, the wild West Coast region is a land unto itself. The mystical Pancake Rocks and blowholes around Punakaiki (poon-ah-*kye*-kee) set the scene for the gigantic, rugged, sometimes forlorn landscape to the south. Early *Pākehā* (European) settlers carved out a hardscrabble life during the 1860s, digging for gold and farming where they could, constantly washed by the West Coast rains. After the gold rushes, new waves of settlers arrived to mine the vast reserves of coal in the surrounding hills. Farmers and loggers followed; although the gold has gone, the coal mining and farming remain. The towns along this stretch of coastline are generally no-frills rural service centers, but they make good bases for exploring the primeval landscape—as more and more visitors are discovering.

The original Māori inhabitants knew this area to be rich in *kai moana* (seafood), *weka* (bush-hens), and most important, *pounamu* (greenstone or jade). The Māori name for the South Island, Te Wai Pounamu, reflects this treasure. The river beds, beaches, and forested mountains were threaded with walking trails they used to transport pounamu for intertribal trade, and you'll still hear references to "greenstone trails" throughout the area.

At the glacier towns of Franz Josef and Fox, the unique combination of soaring mountains and voluminous precipitation means that the massive valleys of ice descend straight into rain forests—interestingly enough, a combination also found on the southwest coast of South America. South of the glaciers, the road follows the seacoast, where fur seals and fiordland crested penguins inhabit fantastical beaches and forests. On sunny days the Tasman Sea along the stretch between Lake Moeraki and Haast takes on a transcendent shade of blue.

Legal changes in 2000 brought an end to commercial logging of the West Coast's native forests; since then the local communities have been in flux, as residents turn to other jobs and newcomers arrive to take advantage of the relatively low property prices. But it's the environment that continues to determine the lifestyle here. Locals pride themselves on their ability to coexist with the wild landscape and weather. As a visitor, you may well need a sense of adventure—be prepared for rain, swirling mist, and cold winter winds. "The Barber," Greymouth's infamous winter wind, blasts down the Grey River valley to the sea. The meteorological mix can, unfortunately, mean that the glacier flight that you planned at Franz Josef or Fox won't fly the day that you're there. If you do end up here on a rainy day, keep in mind that you might wake up the next morning to have brilliant sunshine lighting up the region's glorious scenery. Because although the coast is well known for its rain, it also has clear, bright days when the mountains shine above the green coastal plains and the surf pounds onto sunny, sandy beaches.

EN ROUTE If you're driving to the West Coast from Nelson or Motueka, State Highway 6 passes through Murchison before turning right at O'Sullivans Bridge and heading down through the Buller Gorge toward the West Coast. This twisting, narrow road parallels the tortuous **Buller River** as it carves a deep gorge below the jagged, earthquake-rocked mountain peaks. Nineteen kilometers (12 mi) south of Murchison, the old **Newtown Hotel** teeters on the brink of the gorge, surrounded by a wild junkyard of obsolete farm machinery. The Buller once carried a fabulous cargo of gold, but you'll have to use your imagination to reconstruct the days when places such as Lyell, 34 km (21 mi) past Murchison, were bustling mining towns. Not far from here is New Zealand's longest swaying footbridge, the **Buller Gorge Swing Bridge.** You'll pass high forest-clad mountains, narrow single-lane bridges, and the sleepy little village of Inangahua along the way. **Hawk's Crag and Fern Arch,** where the highway passes beneath rock overhangs with the river wheeling alongside, is another highlight. At the end of the gorge, turn left to continue along State Highway 6 toward Punakaiki, or carry on straight ahead to Westport and Karamea. Although on a map the distances along the West Coast appear small, it's best to allow plenty of time to explore.

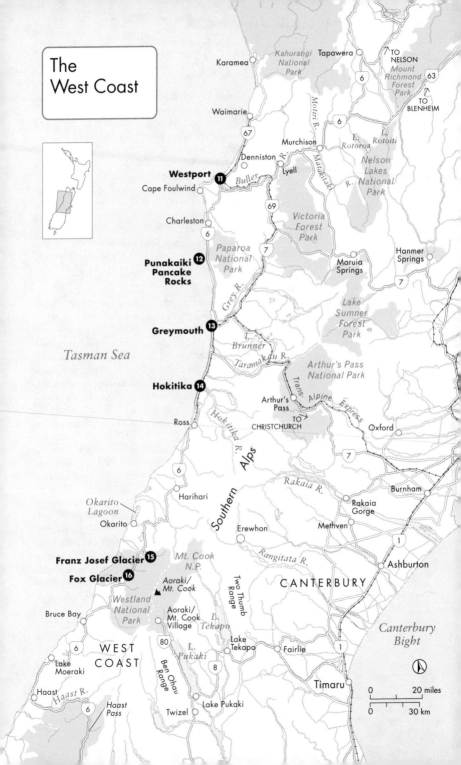

The West Coast

Tasman Sea

Karamea

Kahurangi National Park

Tapawera

TO NELSON

Mount Richmond Forest Park

63

TO BLENHEIM

Waimarie

67

6

Motri R.

Murchison

Denniston

Lyell

L. Rotoroa

L. Rotoiti

Westport 11

Buller R.

Matakitaki R.

Nelson Lakes National Park

Cape Foulwind

Charleston

69

6

Matakitaki R.

7

Punakaiki Pancake Rocks 12

Paparoa National Park

Victoria Forest Park

Maruia Springs

Hanmer Springs

7

Grey R.

Lake Sumner Forest Park

Greymouth 13

L. Brunner

Taramakau R.

Arthur's Pass National Park

Hokitika 14

Trans Alpine Express

Arthur's Pass

TO CHRISTCHURCH

Oxford

Ross

Hokitika R.

Southern Alps

7

6

Rakaia R.

Burnham

Harihari

Erewhon

Rakaia Gorge

Okarito Lagoon

Methven

Okarito

Rangitata R.

1

Ashburton

Franz Josef Glacier 15

Mt. Cook N.P.

Two Thumb Range

CANTERBURY

Fox Glacier 16

Aoraki/ Mt. Cook ▲

Canterbury Bight

Bruce Bay

Westland National Park

Aoraki/ Mt. Cook Village

L. Tekapo

Lake Tekapo

Fairlie

1

6

80

WEST COAST

L. Pukaki

Ben Ohau Range

8

Lake Pukaki

Twizel

Timaru

Lake Moeraki

Haast

Haast R.

6

Haast Pass

0   20 miles

0   30 km

Westport

11 *230 km (144 mi) southeast of Nelson.*

Westport is one of New Zealand's oldest ports, sitting at the mouth of the mighty Buller River. Once a boomtown for two separate gold rushes, it is now a quiet little hub (population 3,100) for the local farming and coal industries, plus the rapidly expanding adventure tourism niche. It's a nice place to stop over before heading south toward Punakaiki and the glaciers. Stop by the **Coaltown Museum** on Queen Street to learn about the port's history and check out an extensive mineral collection. Another museum at **Denniston,** 18 km (11 mi) north of town, details life in this lonely outpost from the late 1800s through the early 1900s. Carving a living from the rich seams of coal found in the surrounding tussock-covered hills, the settlers had to struggle with wild weather, isolation, and primitive conditions. A popular historical novel about these pioneers, *The Denniston Rose,* by New Zealand writer Jenny Pattrick, details the area and the early lifestyle well.

Where to Stay & Eat

$$$ Fodor'sChoice ★ ✕ **Bay House Café.** Tucked amongst flax and manuka bushes beside the wild, foaming surf beach at Tauranga Bay this busy little café serves as fine a menu as you'll get anywhere in the South Island. Owner/chef Luke McCann prepares top-quality local beef, lamb and seafood dishes, like the Whitebait Burger (whitebait are a local fish delicacy) layered with mozzarella, aioli and tomatoes. Or try the pan-fried scallops with black rice, or the West Coast beef fillet served with garlic-roasted mushrooms, chorizo and chive mash. You'll find an extensive, mainly South Island wine list, and their own Bay House–brewed beers. It's well worth the bit of extra driving to get here. ✉ *Tauranga Bay, Cape Foulwind, 5 km (3 mi) west of Westport* ☎ *03/789–7133* 💳 *AE, MC, V.*

$$–$$$ ✕ **Denniston Dog.** This ex-bank building, complete with an old vault, is loaded with local character in its new guise as a cheerful pub and diner spot. Order up a fritter with feta cheese and whitebait (tiny fish eaten whole). ✉ *18 Wakefield St.* ☎ *03/789–5030.*

$$ 🏨 **Riverview Lodge.** High above the lower Buller River, at the seaward end of the Lower Buller Gorge, this B&B can give you a truly rural experience. The house is surrounded by high bush-clad hills and green farmland; each room overlooks the river and gives you a perfect view of the dramatic sunsets. Owner Noeline Biddulph, a human treasure trove of local lore, will serve dinner by arrangement, and keeps a beautiful garden where you can have a stroll after your meal. ✉ *State Hwy. 6, 7 km (4 mi) east of Westport* ☎📠 *03/789–6037* 🌐 *www.rurallodge.co.nz* 🛏 *4 rooms* 👍 *No a/c, no smoking* 💳 *MC, V* 🍽 *BP.*

$–$$ 🏨 **Havenlee Homestay.** A homestay in the best sense of the word—truly welcoming—Havenlee exudes comfort without being flashy. The house is near Westport's town center, and owners Jan and Ian Stevenson have a fast-growing, often international clientele. In warm weather, you can hang out in the barbecue area and the lush garden. Two of the simple, bright guest rooms share a bathroom. ✉ *76 Queen St.* ☎ *03/789–8543* 📠 *03/789–8502* 🌐 *www.havenlee.co.nz* 🛏 *3 rooms* 👍 *BBQ,*

laundry facilities; no a/c, no room phones, no room TVs, no smoking
🖃 *MC, V* ❘◎❘ *BP.*

¢ 🖳 **Trip Inn Hostel.** Backpackers now fill the beds in one of Westport's grandest old 19th-century homes. It's geared for all ages, not just students, and the owners have arranged the rooms for various kinds of travelers, from solos to families. There's a fireplace lounge where people swap stories about their hikes on the Heaphy Track, plus a TV/video common room. Lockers and linens are provided. ✉ *72 Queen St.* 🕾🕾 *03/789–7367* ⊕ *http://home.clear.net.nz/pages/tripinn* ➦ *64 dorm beds* ♨ *BBQ, kitchen, lounge, Internet room; no a/c, no room TVs, no smoking* 🖃 *MC, V.*

Sports & the Outdoors

★ You might actually pray for rain during a tour with **Norwest-Underworld Adventures.** This adventure tour group takes you into the rain forest off the main highway. You can sign up for an open-sided bush-train ride through the dense temperate lowland forest or take a cave walk into one of the giant limestone mountains up the Nile River Valley (a glowworm grotto is a highlight). For something more challenging, go for the daylong caving adventure with abseiling, white-water rafting, and scary squeezes. Prices range from $20 for the train ride to $275 for caving; reservations are essential. ✉ *Charleston Tavern, Main Rd., Charleston* 🕾 *03/789–6686* ⊕ *www.caverafting.com.*

Karamea

98 km (61 mi) north of Westport.

North of Westport, the coastline squeezes between high mountain ranges and pounding surf. Among the sprinkling of tiny settlements is Karamea, known to most people as the southern entry (or exit) to the renowned Heaphy Track, which starts in Golden Bay. But there's a bit more to Karamea; it's also a fine trout-fishing destination, the western entry point to the wild ranges of the Kahurangi National Park (*see above*), and home to the **Oparara cave system.** These caves are a series of huge limestone arches, passages, and caverns, surrounded by lush forests. One of the best is the Honeycomb Cave, an underground system of roughly 13 km (8 mi) of passages. Bones from the extinct moa bird have been found here, and chances are good that you'll see glowworms. Contact the **Karamea Information & Resource Centre** for information on cave tours. ✉ *Market Cross intersection* 🕾 *03/782–6652* ⊕ *www.karameainfo.co.nz.*

Where to Stay

$ 🖳 **The Last Resort.** Karamea is one of those deliciously remote places, so it's only fitting that there be accommodation to match. The Last Resort should be considered the first resort when looking for a place to stay in the area. Its glowing hardwood beams, stylish local artwork, and unusual turf roof make it very much at peace with its setting. The staff can arrange tours, helicopter rides, and shuttles to and from the Heaphy Track. ✉ *71 Waverley St.* 🕾 *03/782–6617 or 0800/505–042* 🖨 *03/782–6820* ⊕ *www.lastresort.co.nz* ➦ *18 self-contained rooms, 6 lodge rooms (shared bath), 3 cottages, 3 dorm rooms* ♨ *Restaurant,*

7

BBQ, massage, spa, bicycles, bar no phones in some rooms, no TV in some rooms.

Punakaiki

269 km (168 mi) southeast of Nelson.

★ ⑫ At first glance, Punakaiki looks like nothing more than a small cluster of beach houses and shops—a blip on the radar without even a gas station or ATM. It's still worth a detour, though, for its nearby maze of limestone stacked high above the sea: the surreal **Pancake Rocks** (☎ 03/731–1895). The huge swells that batter this coast have eroded the limestone cliffs, carving them into fantastic shapes. A paved walkway leads you through the windswept cover of tenacious New Zealand flax and *nikau* palms to see the most dramatic points, including the boiling cauldron called the Surge Pool and the pumping fissure of the Chimney Pot. At high tide, a blowhole spouts a thundering geyser of spray. Aoraki (Mt. Cook) is sometimes visible across the sea to the south. To reach the rocks from town, take the easy 10-minute walk from the visitor center. High tide on a southwest swell under a full moon at midnight is an outstanding time to visit, if you dare. Otherwise, try for high tide or a big westerly swell. The **Department of Conservation Visitors Centre** across the road from the main gate is a handy place to learn more about the formations.

The Pancake Rocks are the star of **Paparoa National Park** (✉ Main Rd. ☎ 03/731–1895 ⊕ www.doc.govt.nz), a reserve based loosely along the Paparoa Range, a long, rugged chain of mountains running parallel to the coast. With craggy summits, serrated ridges, cirques carved out of ancient granite and gneiss, and U-shape glacial valleys, it's a formidable environment. But its sheer cliffs, flood-prone rivers, dense rain forest, and extensive cave systems spell out paradise for hikers. The major entry points—Bullock Creek, Fox River, and Pororari River—open immediately onto an otherworldly zone of jungly green, striking *nikau* palms, rushing streams, and sweeping coastal views. Much of this area is serious outback country, requiring either a guide or considerable bush experience. There are several short day hikes, though; drop by the **DOC Visitors Centre** for maps and information.

Where to Stay & Eat

In the past couple of years, the accommodation options in Punakaiki have taken a big step forward. Unfortunately, the eating options often fall short, especially during the summer high season from December to February. Because there are only a couple of places to eat in town, it's best to reserve a table ahead in summer. If you decide to stay in a self-catering unit, you'll need to bring in all your food, as there are no general stores in town. Some homestays do meals by arrangement.

¢–$$$ ✕ **Wild Coast Café.** This is the only café, as such, in Punakaiki, and it does a roaring trade during the day. It's just opposite the Pancake Rocks—and the signature dish is, of course, stacked pancakes, served with fruit and maple syrup or bacon and sliced bananas. Dinner is served only during the high season. ✉ *Main Rd.* ☎ *03/731–1873* ▭ *MC, V* ☺ *No dinner Apr.–Oct.*

$$–$$$ ⊞ **Hydrangea Cottages.** You'll be lulled by the constant roar of the ocean here, just ½ km (⅓ mi) south of the Pancake Rocks. Three of the apartments—Rata, Mamaku, and Nikau—are done in bright colors with recycled native timbers and contemporary furniture. The smaller studio cottage, Rimu, goes rustic with a cute indoor shower built of river rock and corrugated iron. All are self-catering. ⊠ *Main Rd.* ☎ *03/731–1839* ⊕ *www.pancake-rocks.co.nz* ⊲ *4 studios* ⚐ *Horseback riding; no a/c, no room phones, no room TVs, no smoking* ⊟ *MC, V.*

$$ ⊞ **The Rocks Homestay.** You won't lack for views, real or reproduced, here. All the guest bedrooms have private balconies or conservatory areas looking along the coast, and the walls are hung with striking landscape pictures by the keen photographer-hosts Peg and Kevin Piper. Children are welcome by prior arrangement only. ⊠ *Hartmount Pl.* ☎ *03/731– 1141* ⊟ *03/731–1142* ⊕ *www.therockshomestay.com* ⊲ *3 rooms* ⚐ *Minibars, laundry facilities, Internet room; no room phones, no smoking* ⊟ *MC, V* ⦿ *BP.*

Sports & the Outdoors

Green Kiwi Tours runs guided hiking and ecotours tours into the magical Paparoa National Park. You can add caving to your expedition, too, and the company also provides shuttle access for freedom (unguided) walkers to and from trailheads. ⊠ *Hartmount Pl.* ☎ *0800/474–733* ⊕ *www.greenkiwitours.co.nz.*

Greymouth

🔞 *44 km (28 mi) south of Punakaiki.*

The town of Greymouth (said like the anatomical feature) is aptly named—at first take it's a rather dispirited strip of motels and industrial buildings stretched along a wild beach. It sits, as the name suggests, at the mouth of the Grey River and is thus exposed to a bone-chilling wind in winter. But in warmer weather, its good points come to the fore, and no matter the season it's a handy place to overnight. Many travelers arrive here on the TranzAlpine train from Christchurch and are plopped into the middle of the West Coast without the stunning drives along either the north or the south coasts to set the scene. If you're arriving and returning by train, take a day or two for a trip up to Punakaiki or down to the glaciers, to grasp the scope of the landscape. Although Greymouth is a small town on a big coast, it's also the regional commercial center and so worth using as a base before venturing farther afield.

The land around Greymouth is particularly rich in pounamu, the greenstone that is highly prized by the Māori. You're in a Ngai Tahu iwi (tribe) area, and as part of the tribe's 1997 Treaty of Waitangi settlement, the government recognized Ngai Tahu as having sole rights to collect and sell the precious jade in its natural form. The **Left Bank Art Gallery** on the corner of Tainui Street and Mawhera Quay is a good place to see some contemporary pounamu carvings. Better yet, visit the **Jade Boulder Gallery,** which exhibits the work of Ian Boustridge, one of the country's most accomplished sculptors of greenstone. The gallery is a great place to pick up a distinctive souvenir; earrings start at about $10, pendants generally cost a couple hundred, and sculpture can cost thousands.

The gallery's latest addition, the Jade Boulder Trail, is an interesting interpretative walk-through display detailing the legends and forms of New Zealand greenstone, with displays of carved and raw jade. ⊠ *1 Guinness St.* ☎ *03/768–0700* ⊕ *www.jadeboulder.com* ⊙ *Nov.–Apr., daily 8:30 AM–9 PM; May–Oct., daily 8:30–5.*

On the southern outskirts of Greymouth, **Shantytown** is a lively reenactment of a gold-mining town of the 1880s. This is how the settlers who stayed on after that gold rush would have lived—but without the electricity, running water, and paved entry road. Except for the church and the town hall, most of the buildings are reproductions, including a jail, a blacksmith shop, a railway station, and a barbershop. The gold-digging displays include a water jet for blasting the gold-bearing quartz from the hillside, water sluices, and a stamper—battery-powered by a 30-foot waterwheel—for crushing the ore. You can pan for gold with a good chance of striking "color," as this was the site of the world's last major gold rush. ⊠ *Rutherglen* ☎ *03/762–6634* ⊕ *www.shantytown.co.nz* ⊠ *$15* ⊙ *Daily 8:30–5.*

If your crafts craving hasn't yet been sated, drive a few miles south of Greymouth to Kūmara's **Carey Dillon Woodworker.** The namesake artisan's workshop and gallery is devoted to wood-turning and landscape photography, and Dillon's work is superb. He turns chunks of aged rimu, a native hardwood, into magnificent bowls that glow like amber; each one takes at least a year to create. Because he uses only dead wood, the craft is totally sustainable. His photographs are large and highly scenic and make great mementos to take home. ⊠ *State Hwy. 73, Main Rd., Kūmara* ☎ *03/736–9741* ⊕ *www.careydillon.com.*

Where to Stay & Eat

¢–$$ ✕ **ABC Café.** Restaurants are thin on the ground in Greymouth; this café fills the comfort food niche with heaping plates of bacon-and-egg croissants, steaks, nachos, and whitebait sandwiches. ⊠ *14 Tainui St.* ☎ *03/ 768–5594* ⊙ *No dinner.*

$$$$ 🏨 **Lake Brunner Lodge.** Set on the southern shore of Lake Brunner, a 40-
Fodor'sChoice   minute drive southeast of Greymouth, this lodge, first established in 1868,
★   is an enticing retreat at a price that is relatively low by the standards of New Zealand's elite lodges. Rooms are large and well equipped, with the emphasis on comfort rather than opulence. The best rooms are at the front of the villa, overlooking the lake. Brown trout can easily be seen in the clear waters of the surrounding rivers; fly-fishing is the main sport, but good spin fishing is also available at certain times of the year. (There's a catch-and-release policy.) The lodge is surrounded by untouched forests, which you can explore on a guided environmental tour. Because of its remote setting, it's not on the national grid, and generates power with a hydro plant running off a spectacular waterfall behind the main building. In the evening, the lights glow with a soft candlelike flicker. The kitchen (which runs on bottled gas) turns out seasonal dishes with a local bent, such as roast lamb with ratatouille. Note that children are welcome here only by advance arrangement. ⊠ *Mitchells, R.D. 1, Kūmara* ☎ *03/738–0163* 🖷 *03/738–0713* ⊕ *www.lakebrunner.com*

🛏 *11 rooms* ⚒ *Dining room, Wi-Fi, fishing, mountain bikes, library, no a/c, no room TVs, no smoking* ⊟ *AE, DC, MC, V* ⑩ *MAP.*

$$ 🏠 **Rosewood.** Rhonda and Stephan Palten run this B&B in a restored 1920s home close to the town center. Original oak paneling and stained-glass windows remain, and there are cozy seats in the bay windows. Some rooms are done in a contemporary look; others have period furniture. Stephan's a chef, so expect a very good breakfast of fresh rolls, bacon, pancakes, French toast, and eggs any way you want them. Two rooms share a bathroom. You can get a courtesy pickup at the train station. ✉ *20 High St.* ☎ *03/768–4674* 📠 *03/768–4694* ⊕ *www.rosewoodnz. co.nz* 🛏 *5 rooms, 3 with bath* ⚒ *Lounge, Internet room; no a/c, no smoking* ⊟ *AE, DC, MC, V* ⑩ *BP.*

Hokitika

⑭ *41 km (26 mi) south of Greymouth.*

Hokitika is the pick of the towns running down the West Coast, with the pounding ocean before it and the bush-covered hills behind. It's a place of simple pleasures: scouting the crafts boutiques, taking a bush-walk, enjoying a meal of local fish, or looking for interestingly shaped driftwood on the beach.

In several places along and just off **Tancred Street,** you can check out the work of local artisans, particularly the pounamu carvings the area's known for. For instance, **Westland Greenstone** (✉ 34 Tancred St. ☎ 03/755–8713) has an interesting walk-through workshop where you can watch greenstone being cut, shaped, and polished. At the **Hokitika Craft Gallery Co-operative** (✉ 25 Tancred St. ☎ 03/755–8802) greenstone carvings are joined by pottery, woodwork, and textiles. **Ocean Paua** (✉ 25 Weld St. ☎ 03/755–6128) has a varied range of *paua* shell, greenstone, and bone artworks and jewelry.

For many Kiwis, Hokitika is on the map purely for its annual **Wildfoods Festival,** which celebrates bush tucker (food from the bush) from the West Coast's natural food sources. Bite into such delectables as *huhu* grubs (they look like large maggots), worm sushi, whitebait patties (far more mainstream), and snail caviar, and follow it all with gorse wine, moonshine, or Monteith's bitter beer. The mid-March fest attracts crowds of up to 20,000, six times the local population. Entertainment includes lively performances by members of the Hokitika Live Poets Society at the tree stump by Billy Tea Hut (where else). It can get rowdy at night at the barn dance, which seems to spill through the town. Of course, a good dump of West Coast rain will quiet things down—until the next year. Take your gum boots. ⊕ *www.wildfoods.co.nz.*

Where to Stay & Eat

$$$ ✕ **Café de Paris.** Pronounced "*parr*iss" in these parts, this spot sets the bar for local cafés, and serves French cuisine with a New Zealand accent. The simple decor is in keeping with owner/chef Pierre Esquilat's straightforward approach: unfussy French cooking with fresh local ingredients. Wild boar oven-baked with mushrooms, onion, and red wine is a delicious example, as is local venison seared and finished with a blueberry and port wine glaze. There's a liquor license, but you're also welcome to BYOB. Reservations are essential in summer. ⊠ *19 Tancred St.* ☎ *03/755–8933* ⊟ *AE, D, MC, V.*

$ ✕ **Adz on Tancred.** An enormous collection of teapots marches around the walls here. This isn't the place for dainty finger sandwiches, though; instead, tuck into a generous serving of lasagna, homemade fries, or a huge custard square. ⊠ *39 Tancred St.* ☎ *03/755–8379* ⊟ *MC, V.*

★ $$$$ ⌂ **Kapitea Ridge Lodge.** This modern lodge has a special connection to its setting; its creek is part of an ancient Māori greenstone trail. The spacious guest rooms are all tastefully done, with strong colors playing off the intense blues and greens seen from the windows. The Sunset Room, for instance, has a sunset color scheme and gazes west to the coast, and the Tasman Room (named for its view of the Tasman Sea) borrows the hues of an opalescent paua shell. You can arrange to go fishing or clay bird shooting, or simply play a bit of pétanque (boccie) before dinner (an extra fee). Dinner is available November to March by arrangement. ⊠ *Chesterfield Rd., off State Hwy. 6* ☎ *03/755–6805* 📠 *03/755–6895* ⊕ *www.kapitea.co.nz* ⟿ *6 rooms* ⚴ *Hot tub; no a/c, no kids under 12, no smoking* ⊟ *AE, DC, MC, V* ¶⊙¶ *BP.*

$$ ⌂ **Teichelmann's Bed & Breakfast.** Named for Dr. Ebenezer Teichelmann, the surgeon-mountaineer-conservationist who built the original part of the house, this is the most comfortable place in the center of town. Its warm, friendly atmosphere has a lot to do with hosts Frances Flanagan and Brian Ward, who are happy to make suggestions for local activities. Furnishings are a combination of antique and country-cottage style, using plenty of native wood. The rimu-wood bookcase is full of literature about the area. ⊠ *20 Hamilton St.* ☎ *03/755–8232* 📠 *03/755—8239* ⊕ *www.teichelmanns.co.nz* ⟿ *5 rooms, 1 cottage* ⚴ *No a/c, no room phones, no room TVs, no kids under 10, no smoking* ⊟ *MC, V* ¶⊙¶ *BP.*

☾ ¢–$$ ⌂ **Shining Star.** These oceanfront chalets are about as close to the beach as you'll get; the surf rolls in, the air has a salty tang, and the sky is filled with wheeling seabirds. The various units range from basic cabins to chalets with full kitchens and big fluffy duvets; a few have whirlpool baths. There's a menagerie of sorts, too, including sheep, goats, alpaca, pigs, and an emu, and powered sites for camper vans. ⊠ *11 Richards Dr.* 📠📠 *03/755–8921* ⊕ *www.accommodationwestcoast.co.nz* ⟿ *12 chalets, 8 cabins, 3 suites* ⚴ *Some in-room safes, some in-room broadband; no a/c in some rooms, no smoking* ⊟ *AE, DC, MC, V.*

Westland National Park

Fodor'sChoice
★ *North end 146 km (91 mi) south of Hokitika.*

Westland National Park joins the Fiordland and Mt. Aspiring national parks to form a sweeping World Heritage Area of more than 5 million acres, including some of the best examples of the plants and animals once found on the ancient Gondwanaland supercontinent in its compass. It's a place of extremes, including the extreme precipitation at the top of Westland. Up to 300 inches of snow per annum falls here, feeding Westland's glacier field. The snow is compressed into ice on the névé, or head, of the glaciers (New Zealanders say "glassy-urs"), then flows downhill under its own weight. There are more than 60 glaciers in the park; the most famous and accessible are at Franz Josef and Fox.

16 The **Fox Glacier** is slightly larger and longer than that at Franz Josef, but you'll miss nothing important if you see only one. Both glaciers have
15 separate villages, and if you are spending the night, **Franz Josef Glacier** is marginally preferable. (Both towns have solid tourist infrastructures, but the summer tourist rush means you should make reservations in advance for both lodgings and restaurants if you're visiting in December or January.) There are parking areas outside both towns from which you can walk about 30 minutes to reach the glaciers' terminal faces. Both parking lots are sometimes visited by mischievous keas (*kee*-ahs)— mountain parrots—that take delight in destroying the rubber molding around car windows and eating left-open lunches. Their beaks are like can openers. *Keas* are harmless to humans, but you shouldn't feed them.

Trails from the parking lots wind across the rocky valley floor to the glacier faces, where a tormented chorus of squeaks, creaks, groans, and gurgles can be heard as the glacier creeps down the mountainside at an average rate of up to 3 feet per day. Care must be taken here, because rocks and chunks of ice frequently drop from the melting face.

These being New Zealand glaciers, there is much to do besides admire them. You can fly over them in helicopters or planes and land on the stable névé, or hike on them with guides. Remember that these structures are dynamic and always in motion—an ice cave that was visible yesterday might today be smashed under tons of ice that used to be just uphill of it. Likewise some of the fascinating formations that you see on the surface of the glacier were fairly recently at the very bottom of it higher up in the valley. Danger comes with this unstable territory; guides know the hazardous areas to avoid.

For the most part, flights are best made early in the morning, when visibility tends to be clearest. Seasonal variables around the glaciers are a surprising thing. Summer may be warmer and by far the busiest season, but there is a lot more rain and fog that can scuttle "flightseeing" and hiking plans. There's actually a lot to be said for winter visits. In winter, snow doesn't fall at sea level in Franz Josef or Fox; in fact, in winter this area is a lot warmer than the snow towns farther south. Skies are clearer, which means fewer canceled flights and glacier hikes and more of the dazzling sunshine that makes views of the mountains so spectacular. No matter when you visit, of course, warm clothing is essential on the glaciers, and evenings can be cold any time of year.

Outside the town of Fox Glacier, **Lake Matheson** has one of the country's most famous views. A walking trail winds along the lakeshore, and the snowcapped peaks of Aoraki and Mt. Tasman are reflected in the water. Allow at least an hour for the complete walk from town to the "view of views." The best time is early morning, before the mirrorlike reflections are fractured by the wind. From town, turn and walk toward the sea where a sign points to Gillespies Beach; then turn right again to reach the lake.

Lake Moeraki sits in the midst of Westland National Park, 90 km (56 mi) south of Fox Glacier. There isn't a town here; it's the site of a thoughtfully designed wilderness lodge. Access to the coast is easiest at **Monro Beach.** The 45-minute walk to the beach takes you through spectacular, fern-filled native forest to a truly remarkable beach: rock clusters jut out of incredibly blue waters, and rivers and streams flow over the sand into the Tasman Sea. You might arrive at a time when spunky little fiordland crested penguins are in transit from the sea to their stream or hillside nests. Early morning and late afternoon are when you'll have the best chance of seeing them.

Two kilometers (1 mi) south of the trail entrance on the beach is a seal colony, which you will smell before you see it. If you venture that way, be sure to keep about 15 feet away from the seals (the legal distance), and don't block their path to the sea. A spooked seal will bowl you over on its lurch for the water and may even bite, so be extremely respectful of their space. Sculpted dark gray rocks also litter the beach to the south, and seals like to lie behind and among them, so look carefully before you cross in front of these rocks.

Monro Beach is an utter dream, not least if you collect driftwood or rocks. On the road 2 km (1 mi) or so south of it, there is a lookout over the rock stacks at **Knights Point.** Farther south still, between Moeraki and Haast, the walkways and beach at **Ship Creek** are another stop for ferny forests and rugged coastline. Sand flies here can be voracious, so bring insect repellent and hope for a windy day. (There are far fewer sand flies in winter.)

Where to Stay & Eat

Franz Josef is on the backpacker circuit and is well serviced with hostel accommodation, but it also has a good range of hosted and hotel lodgings.

\$\$–\$\$\$\$ ✕ **Blue Ice Café.** The two levels here can carry you from an early dinner through the wee hours. Go downstairs for a dinner of local standbys such as West Coast whitebait, venison, or lamb, with homemade bread. (It can be a bit chilly in winter, so bring your jacket.) Upstairs there's a bar where you can order a pizza and rack up at the free pool table. Because it has a 3 AM license and regularly hosts DJs, this becomes the town's late-night party spot during the tourist season. ⊠ *South end of Main Rd., Franz Josef* ☎ *03/752–0707* ═ *MC, V* ⊘ *No lunch.*

\$–\$\$\$\$ ✕ **Nevé Café.** A standout along the Fox Glacier's commercial strip, the Nevé sparks up no-nonsense options with fresh local flavors, such as the pizza topped with locally made Blackball salami, field mushrooms, spinach, rosemary, and tomato. Beef, lamb, and seafood also feature, and for a tiny place, the wine list of 150 vintages is impressive. The lunch menu is more varied, with choices such as a feta-and-olive salad or a West Coast whitebait omelet. ⊠ *Main Rd., Fox Glacier* ☎ *03/751–0110* ⌂ *Reservations not accepted* ═ *MC, V.*

\$\$\$ ✕ **The Alice May.** This café and bar is one of those cozy, buzzing places so prevalent on the West Coast. After a busy day hiking the glacier, kayaking, or dropping onto the ice by helicopter, it's the perfect place to refuel. All their pizzas are good, but the vegetarian option is outstanding, with thick chunks of feta, juicy spinach, and cubes of tasty pumpkin, all dripping with mozzarella. ⊠ *Cowan and Cron Sts., Franz Josef* ☎ *03/752–0740* ⊟ *MC, V.*

$$$$
Fodor'sChoice
★
✕⊞ **Wilderness Lodge Lake Moeraki.** A superb setting—in the rain forest on the banks of the Moeraki River—and a team of ecoguides make this lodge an ideal place to get absorbed in the environment. On-site naturalists will take you along while they feed eels, and show you ancient podocarp trees, orchids, fur seals (year-round), and fiordland crested penguins (June to December). On organized night walks, they'll point out glowworms, freshwater crayfish, and the southern constellations. As well as a full breakfast and four-course dinner, rates include the use of canoes and kayaks, plus two short guided activities daily. Longer guided hikes, fishing guides, lunch, and dinner drinks are available for an extra charge. ⊠ *State Hwy. 6, 90 km (56 mi) south of Fox Glacier* ① *Private Bag, Hokitika* ☎ *03/750–0881* 🖷 *03/750–0882* ⊕ *www. wildernesslodge.co.nz* ⮌ *26 rooms* ♨ *In-room hot tubs, boating, fishing, laundry facilities; no room TVs, no smoking* ⊟ *MC, V* ☾ *Closed July and Aug.* ⦿ *MAP.*

$$$–$$$$
✕⊞ **Franz Josef Glacier Hotels.** The largest hotel in the glacier region, this complex is split into two sites about 1 km (½ mi) apart at the north end of Franz Josef village. The rooms are a cut above average in size and furnishings, but be sure to ask for a room with glacier views—particularly stunning as the sun rises over the Southern Alps and lights up the glaciers. Larger suites with upgraded facilities are also available, and the hotel has a choice of three restaurants ($$$), none of which serves lunch. Entrées go beyond the basic lamb with choices such as grilled salmon with bok choy and dill aïoli. ⊠ *State Hwy. 6 Franz Josef* ☎ *03/752–0729 or 0800/100–729* 🖷 *03/752–0709* ⊕ *www.scenic-circle.co.nz* ⮌ *177 rooms* ♨ *3 restaurants, 4 hot tubs, 4 bars, laundry facilities, Internet room; no a/c* ⊟ *AE, DC, MC, V.*

★ **$$$$**
⊞ **Westwood Lodge.** For unpretentious luxury among the glaciers, turn to this spacious, modern wooden lodge with exceptional alpine views. The suites have thoughtful details such as heated bathroom floors and DVD players on request; several have verandas. Check out the huge open fire in the lounge and watch as the sunset turns the snow high above the glaciers to a lovely pink. ⊠ *Main Rd., Franz Josef* ☎ *03/752–0112* 🖷 *03/752–0111* ⊕ *www.westwood-lodge.co.nz* ⮌ *7 suites* ♨ *Billiards, lounge, library; no a/c, no kids under 12, no smoking* ⦿ *MAP, BP* ⊟ *AE, MC, V.*

$$–$$$
⊞ **Holly Homestead.** This 1920s homestead, built in the Arts-and-Crafts era, has found its feet as a B&B. It's a stylish alternative to a backcountry lodge stay, just 1½ km (1 mi) north of Franz Josef village. The bedrooms glow with the warm colors of native rimu timbers, and the breakfast area looks out to the snowcapped mountains above the glacier. ⊠ *Main Rd., State Hwy. 6 Franz Josef* ☎ *03/752–0299* 🖷 *03/752–0298* ⊕ *www.hollyhomestead.co.nz* ⮌ *4 rooms* ♨ *Lounge, laundry facilities, Internet room; no room TVs, no kids under 12* ⊟ *MC, V* ⦿ *BP.*

Sports & the Outdoors

BIRD-WATCHING
★ ☾
Even though the white heron (known to the Māori as *kotuku*) nests only from October to March, a trip with **White Heron Sanctuary Tours** is worth doing at any time of the year. A rollicking jet-boat ride takes you

down the beautiful Waitangiroto River to the sea, passing whitebait fishermen and solitary birds on the swampy banks before winding along a short coastal lagoon and then drifting into a nature reserve. High *kahikatea* and rimu trees arch over the river, and flax bushes droop into the dark brooding water. This is the heart of the southern West Coast's coastal rain forest, somber and silent. In season the elegant *kotuku* nest at their only site in the country, and a bird-watching hide has been set up directly opposite. Trip prices start at $95. ☎ *03/753–4120* ⊕ *www.whiteherontours.co.nz*.

FISHING For information on fishing around Franz Josef and Fox, *see* Chapter 11.

KAYAKING & RAFTING Several mirror-still lakes in the area, plus the large Okarito lagoon out on the coast, offer kayaking opportunities in most weathers. (In good weather, though, you'll get terrific mountain views.) **Okarito Nature Tours** (☎☎ 03/753–4014 ⊕ www.okarito.co.nz) stick to the lagoon, which is a good spot to see white herons away from their nesting grounds. Rates start at $35. **Ferg's Kayaks** (☎0800/423–262) offers guided trips around Lake Mapourika, best paddled in the morning or evening, when the breeze is softer.

Rivers Wild (☎ 0800/469–453 ⊕ www.riverswild.co.nz) takes adventurers and families on rafting and multisport trips throughout the West Coast, from Grade II to the most extreme Grade V. Popular trips include heli-rafting near Franz Josef Glacier and a multiday wilderness experience on the Landsborough River. Full-day trips start around $195. The rafting season runs November to April; reservations are strongly recommended.

ON & ABOVE THE GLACIERS The walks to the glacier heads mentioned above are the easiest way of seeing the glaciers. But joining a guided walk and getting up close to the glaciers' ice formations—the shapes created by the glaciers' movement and the streams of water running through them—is unforgettable.

Flying over the glaciers is also quite thrilling, and that thrill comes at considerable expense. The ultimate combination is to fly by fixed-wing plane or helicopter to the top or middle of the glacier and get out and walk on it. Fixed-wing landings on the snow atop the ice fields are fabulously scenic, but you have only 10 minutes out of the plane. Heli-hikes give you the most time on the ice, two to three hours of snaking up and down right in the middle of a stable part of the glacier. If you've never flown in a helicopter, the experience can be nearly heart-stopping, as the pull of the rotors lifts you up and into the glacial valleys. As you make your way to a landing spot, the pilot banks the helicopter so that the only things between you and the mass of ice below you are a sheet of glass and centrifugal force. It's a wild ride.

☺ **Alpine Guides Fox Glacier** has half- or full-day guided walks on Fox Glacier, the only safe way to experience the ethereal beauty of the ice caves, pinnacles, and crevasses on top of the glaciers. There are trips to suit all fitness levels, budgets, and time frames, and even ones that are good for kids (over the age of eight or so). The 3½- to 4-hour walk travels about 2 km (1 mi) up the glacier. The climb requires some fitness; a half day costs $79, a full day $115. Arguably the best option is to heli-hike, combining a helicopter flight onto and off Fox Glacier and walking for two hours on the ice with a guide ($299). Or try the full-day ice-climbing instruction day with mountaineering equipment provided ($210). Half-day tours depart at 9:15 AM and 1:45 PM. ⊠ *Alpine Guides Building, Main St. Fox Glacier* ☎ *03/751–0825 and 0800/111–600* 🖷 *03/751–0857* ⊕ *www.foxguides.co.nz.*

Mt. Cook Ski Planes has fixed-wing ski planes that fly over the glaciers, landing amid craggy peaks in the high-altitude ski slopes at the head of the glaciers. There are 40-minute ($285) and one-hour ($355) flights. The longer flight includes a circuit of Aoraki/Mt. Cook and lands on the Tasman Glacier. Both flights land for 10 minutes and the engines are shut down so you can hear the natural quiet of the mountains. ⊠ *Main Rd., Franz Josef* ☎ *03/752–0714 or 0800/368–000* 🖷 *03/752–0714* ⊕ *www.mtcookskiplanes.com.*

The Guiding Company provides a comprehensive guide service with a half-day walk ($80), a full-day trip ($135), a three-quarter-day hike ($110) or a heli-hike tour ($320). ⊠ *Main Rd., Franz Josef* ☎ *03/752–0047 and 0800/800–102* 🖷 *03/752–0049* ⊕ *www.nzguides.com.*

The **Helicopter Line** operates several scenic flights over the glaciers from heliports at Franz Josef Glacier and Fox Glacier. The shortest is the 20-minute flight over Franz Josef Glacier ($180 per person); the longest is a 40-minute flight that includes a landing on the head of the glacier and a circuit of Aoraki and Mt. Tasman ($350). Three-hour heli-hikes are yet another option ($320). Reservations are recommended in summer and essential for the heli-hikes. ⊠ *Main Road., Franz Josef* ☎ *03/752–0767 or 0800/807–767* 🖷 *03/752–0769* ⊕ *www.helicopter.co.nz.*

7

THE WEST COAST ESSENTIALS

Transportation

BY BUS

InterCity buses run the length of the West Coast daily; buy tickets at local stations. The trip from Nelson to the glaciers takes about seven hours, but if at all possible you should do that trip with a couple of overnight stops along the way. Atomic Shuttles also run the length of the coast.

🚍 Bus Depots **Franz Josef** ⊠ Franz Josef Hotel, Main Rd.; Franz Josef YHA, 2–4 Cron St; Main Road, opposite the Cheeky Kea Bldg. **Fox Glacier** ⊠ Northbound: Alpine Guides, Main Rd.; Southbound: Fox General Store. **Greymouth** ⊠ Railway Station, Mackay St. **Hokitika** ⊠ Hokitika Travel Centre, Tancred St.

🚍 Bus Lines **Atomic Shuttles** ☎ 03/322–8883 ⊕ www.atomictravel.co.nz. **InterCity Franz Josef** ☎ 03/752–0164 ⊕ www.intercitycoach.co.nz. **InterCity Greymouth** ☎ 03/768–5101 ⊕ www.intercitycoach.co.nz.

BY CAR

Driving is by far the most convenient way to get around this striking, relatively remote region—however, be prepared to drive in rain or other less-than-ideal conditions. The north end of the West Coast is roughly a four-hour trip from Nelson on State Highway 6 or a five- to six-hour drive over Arthur's Pass on Highway 7 from Christchurch, the very top of which is spectacular to say the least. State Highway 7 climbs the steep pass over the backbone of the Southern Alps before winding steeply down through rain forest to the tiny town of Otira and on to the coastal river plains of the mid–West Coast. Be prepared for bad weather at times, ice at night, and snow during winter storms—and take special care if you're driving a camper van in windy weather. Hokitika and Greymouth are about 256 km (166 mi) from Christchurch.

There are several stretches of road where gas stations are few and far between, especially from Westport through to Greymouth and from Fox Glacier through to Haast. Be conservative when estimating driving times, as maps can be deceptive. For instance, although it is only 420 km (262 mi) from Westport to Haast, the drive takes at least six hours, not including breaks or slowdowns caused by poor weather. The West Coast's high rainfall creates the need for a number of bridges, many of which are single lane. All these are signed, with right-of-way generally given to uphill traffic. Roads are closed only in the worst weather, usually heavy rain that causes slips on the hills and at river bridges, or snow and ice in winter. There are several bridges where trains and traffic share the same lane.

To continue south out of the region, beyond Lake Moeraki, take State Highway 6 along the south coast to Haast, where it turns inland to Wanaka and Queenstown. The driving time between Moeraki and Wanaka is about five hours.

BY TRAIN

The West Coast in general is poorly served by the rail network, but one glowing exception is the *TranzAlpine Express,* which ranks as one of the world's great rail journeys. This passenger train crosses the Southern Alps between Christchurch and Greymouth, winding through beech forests and mountains that are covered by snow for most of the year. The five viaducts and 16 tunnels along this line, including the 8-km (5-mi) Otira Tunnel and the 73-meter (237-foot) Staircase viaduct, represent a prodigious feat of engineering. The train is modern and comfortable, with panoramic windows as well as a no-frills dining and bar service. The train departs Christchurch daily at 8:15 AM and arrives in Greymouth at 12:45 PM; the return train departs Greymouth at 1:45 PM and arrives at Christchurch at 6:05 PM. The one-way fare is $81–$116, round-trip $162 if returning on the same day.

🚩 Train Information *TranzAlpine Express* ☎ 04/495-0775 or 0800/872-467 ⊕ www.tranzscenic.co.nz.

Contacts & Resources

BANKS & EXCHANGE SERVICES

Westport, Greymouth, and Hokitika all have ATMs outside branches of major banks. There's also an ATM at the top of the main street in Franz Josef, opposite the DOC headquarters. Outside of these towns, though, don't count on being able to find an ATM, so be prepared with cash. Some hotel managers and retailers will give cash advances on credit cards, in a pinch.

EMERGENCIES

No West Coast towns have a late-night pharmacy, but all have a medical center. Greymouth has the main hospital for the region.

Emergency Services Fire, police, and ambulance ☎ 111. **Greymouth Base Hospital** ⊠ High St. ☎ 03/768-0499. **Westland Medical Centre** ⊠ 54a Sewell St., Hokitika ☎ 03/755-8180.

MAIL & INTERNET

All of the towns with a decent tourist infrastructure have Web resources of some kind—even little Westport. Web cafés usually charge about $1 for 10 minutes.

Internet Cafés Dp:One Café ⊠ 108 Mawhera Quay, Greymouth ☎ 03/768-4005. **FastWeb @ Scott Base Info Centre** ⊠ Cheeky Kea Building, Main St., Franz Josef ☎ 03/752-0288.

Fox FastWeb ⊠ Flat Rd. at State Hwy. 6, Fox Glacier ☎ 03/751-0078.

The Web Shed ⊠ 204 Palmerston St., Westport ☎ 03/788-8002.

Post Offices NZ Post Greymouth ⊠ Tainui St. at Guinness St. ☎ 03/768-0123. **NZ Post Hokitika** ⊠ 93 Revell St. ☎ 03/756-8034. **NZ Post Westport** ⊠ Brougham St. at Palmerston St., Westport ☎ 03/788-8194.

VISITOR INFORMATION

Two regional tourism organizations maintain helpful Web sites: **Tourism West Coast** (⊕ www.west-coast.co.nz) and **Glacier Country Tourism Group** (⊕ www.glaciercountry.co.nz). The visitor-information centers at Franz Josef and Greymouth are both open daily during standard business hours, although the Franz Josef bureau shortens its hours slightly in winter and the Greymouth office has shorter hours on weekends. The Westport visitor center can provide information on Karamea and Kahurangi National Park. The **Department of Conservation** (⊕ www.doc.govt.nz) is always a good source for the various national parks.

Fox Glacier Visitor Centre ⊠ State Hwy. 6, Fox Glacier ☎ 03/751-0807 ⊕ www.glaciercountry.co.nz. **Franz Josef Glacier Visitor Information Centre** ⊠ State Hwy. 6, Franz Josef ☎ 03/752-0796 ⊕ www.glaciercountry.co.nz. **Scott Base Information Centre** ⊠ Cheeky Kea Building, Main St., Franz Josef ☎ 03/752-0288. **Westport Visitor Centre** ⊠ 1 Brougham St. ☎ 03/789-6658 ⊕ www.westport.org.nz.

Christchurch & Canterbury

WORD OF MOUTH

"Don't miss the Christchurch Museum. We had an hour to spare and wandered inside and were enthralled with the exhibits, starting off with early Māori life. We had to drag ourselves away, and it remains one of the 'if onlys' of our trip to NZ. If only we had gone there earlier . . ."

—Jenny

"We liked Christchurch very much . . . . However, we wished we [had] stayed a night in Akaroa. We have to say that this tiny French town was one of the highlights of our trip."

—Portobellob

Updated by
Sue Farley

THE WIDE, FLAT CANTERBURY PLAINS SIT CRADLED BETWEEN A JAGGED ridge of snowy mountains and the remnants of two small conjoined volcanoes pressing out into the Pacific Ocean. A patchwork of fields, crisscrossed by several glacier-fed braided rivers, spreads across the plains until it runs up against the silvery city of Christchurch on the western edge of the Banks Peninsula.

Houses climb higher and higher up the Port Hills, as the western edge of the Banks Peninsula is known, forming a backdrop to the city. This high vantage point offers spectacular views of the Southern Alps in winter, and on a clear day you can sometimes see as far as the Kaikoura mountains to the north and Aoraki/Mt. Cook to the south.

John Robert Godley, whose bronze memorial statue stands in Christchurch's Cathedral Square, would have seen those mountains when he paused for breath at the top of the Port Hills in 1850. The Canterbury Association, a British organization, had sent him to New Zealand to prepare for the arrival of settlers for a planned Church of England community. That year, four ships arrived bearing roughly 800 pioneers, and their new town was named for Godley's college at Oxford.

The Canterbury Association set aside land for Hagley Park and the Botanic Gardens, and the city council planted trees from around the world, a trend continued today with tree-fringed suburban parks. The civic green thumb earned Christchurch the moniker "the Garden City"; each spring numerous public and private gardens are open for viewing.

The association also planted a taste for churchlike public buildings. Built in a Gothic Revival style from the dark gray stone carved out of the Port Hills, civic buildings such as the Arts Centre (built initially as the university) and Canterbury Museum give the city a slightly English feel. This style, plus elements such as punting and cricket, often pegs Christchurch as a little slice of England. But though the city may initially come across as conservative, it has been a nursery for social change. It was here that Kate Sheppard, whose portrait is printed on the $10 note, began organizing a campaign that led to New Zealand being the first country in the world to grant women the vote.

Beyond Christchurch sweep the wide-open Canterbury Plains. This is some of New Zealand's finest pastureland, and the higher reaches are sheep station territory, where life and lore mingle in South Island's cowboy country. This is where young Samuel Butler dreamed up the satirical *Erewhon*—the word is an anagram of *nowhere*. But the towns here are no longer considered the back of beyond; communities such as Hanmer, Timaru, and Geraldine are now favorite day-trip destinations. The Waipara Valley to the north of Christchurch, meanwhile, is quickly becoming one of the country's hot new vineyard areas.

Exploring Christchurch & Canterbury

Canterbury is a long, thin province, with a natural boundary formed by the Main Divide (the peaks of the Southern Alps) in the west and stretching from near Kaikoura in the north down to the Waitaki River in the south. This chapter focuses on the section of Canterbury near the main city of Christchurch, including Banks Peninsula, the Waipara wine country, the ski town of Methven, and the alpine resort town of Hanmer Springs, north and west of the city, plus the towns sprinkled on the plains to the south. The chapter also includes Arthur's Pass National Park, a few hours northwest of Christchurch by car or train and a great day trip from the city. For more information about the Southern Alps themselves, *see* Chapter 9.

Because the population density is so low, and public transport outside the main towns can be patchy, the best way to explore the region is by car. Roads across the Canterbury Plains tend to be straight and flat—they were often based on old sheep-herding tracks. State Highway 1 runs the length of the region's coast, linking all the major towns. State Highway 72 follows the contours of the hills, farther inland. The large braided rivers, such as the Rangitata and Rakaia, can be crossed in only one or two places where they meet state highways.

About the Restaurants

Christchurch's restaurants are becoming increasingly sophisticated and diverse in their decor and menus. There's a growing Asian influence, both in restaurants devoted to a specific country's cuisine and in places that fuse Pan-Asian ingredients or techniques with New Zealand cooking. The newcomers are not all Asian, though: you can find everything from Cajun to Indian. Restaurants in the city are usually open every day; if they do close it is either Sunday or Monday. Busy times are 7 to 9 PM on Friday and Saturday, so it's best to reserve; otherwise, you should be able to get a table without trouble. With the exception of the Casino, which has set rules on what not to wear, dress tends to be informal. Outside Christchurch, restaurants are more likely to close on Monday and sometimes Tuesday as well.

Along with its vineyard boom, the Waipara Valley is seeing a surge in adventurous cooking. Local food producers are broadening their horizons; for example, North Canterbury is now a key producer in the country's fledgling black truffle industry. Locally sourced saffron, hazelnuts, *manuka* (an indigenous kind of tea tree) honey, and ostrich meat are making their way onto area menus in delicious and innovative ways.

WHAT IT COSTS In New Zealand dollars				
$$$$	**$$$**	**$$**	**$**	**¢**
RESTAURANTS over $30	$20–$30	$15–$20	$10–$15	under $10

Prices are per person for a main course at dinner, or the equivalent.

About the Hotels

No matter where you stay in Christchurch, you're sure to find some of the best lodging in New Zealand, from luxury hotels and lodges to very fine bed-and-breakfasts to well-maintained, inexpensive hostels. The two main motel strips are along Papanui Road (the end nearest town) and Riccarton Road, both outside the city center. Most accommodations do

TOP REASONS TO GO

FANTASTIC FESTIVALS
Hardly a month goes by in Christchurch without a festival staged by one organization or another. There are festivals for entertainers, romance, children, cuisine, winter celebrations, the arts, writers, heritage days, and gardens. One of the biggest and best festivals has been run for more than 20 years by the Christchurch City Council: Summertimes, which kicks off with a New Year's Eve party and includes free concerts and cultural events through late February.

PARKS AND GARDENS
The city on the swamp, as it might have been called 150 years ago, blossomed into the Garden City, thanks to the foresight of Christchurch's city fathers. Back in the 1850s they set aside lots of public parkland and planted trees from around the world—you may even find a California redwood.

SUPERB SKIING
With excellent ski areas within two hours' drive of Christchurch, Canterbury is a ski mecca from June until September. Mt. Hutt pulls in

the early birds, as it's perennially the first ski area to open in the country. Heliskiing opens up even more opportunities.

HIKING & TREKKING
Although not the main gateway to the Alps, there are still some excellent places in Canterbury to experience the foothills and the Alps themselves. Arthur's Pass and the Rakaia and Rangitata river gorges in particular offer walking trails, some serious hiking (be meticulous in your preparations before a trek; these mountains can be dangerous), photography, boating, and picnicking.

THE ARTS
Being one of New Zealand's older cities Christchurch has a solid infrastructure of galleries, museums, Heritage buildings, and cultural activities. Many of these are still in their original 19th-century buildings and occupy key sites in the city. There are also several venues such as the Court Theatre and the Westpac Centre, where internationally known musical acts and theater ensembles perform.

not include breakfast in their room rates. Reservations are most necessary in summer (December through March), on public holidays, and during rugby game finals.

Outside Christchurch, it can be hard to find a place to stay in summer, especially over the holidays (late December and January). If you're planning on going to Akaroa, Hanmer Springs, or Waipara during this peak season, be sure to reserve well in advance. Bookings can also be heavy in winter around the ski areas and during school holidays.

WHAT IT COSTS In New Zealand dollars				
$$$$	$$$	$$	$	¢
HOTELS over $300	$200–$300	$125–$200	$75–$125	under $75

Prices are for a standard double room in high season, including 12.5% tax.

Timing

Choosing the best time to come to the Christchurch area depends largely on your tolerance for crowds. In summer, Christchurch is especially busy as its events calendar gets the city buzzing. Christchurch could be called the Festival City of New Zealand. The city council runs the Summertimes program from New Year's until late February, offering free classical music concerts and other activities in Hagley Park. Mid-January brings a World Buskers Festival; the Festival of Flowers & Romance is held in late January or early February. The city's older buildings are celebrated in Heritage Week in October. And in July 2007 the city will be host of the next Arts Festival.

The other main consideration is weather. The song by New Zealand band Crowded House about "four seasons in one day" barely exaggerates the local climate. Summer days can be chilled by a sudden east wind, and the nor'wester can be calm and warm one day and blustery the next. Winter's weather (June–September) is more settled but colder than summer's, and though some activities close down, the lack of crowds can make traveling easier. For skiing, snowboarding, and other winter sports, this is *the* time to come. From the first weekend in June through October you can be assured of snow at Mt. Hutt, the first local ski area to open and often the last to close. Snow in Christchurch, though, is a rarity.

CHRISTCHURCH

Your initial impression of Christchurch will likely be one of a genteel, green city. The drive from the airport into town takes you past tidy wooden villas and brick mansions. Joggers loop through shady Hagley Park, and punters ply the narrow Avon River, which bubbles between banks lined with willows and oaks.

With a population approaching 350,000, Christchurch is the largest South Island city, and the second largest in the country. It is also the forward supply depot for the main U.S. Antarctic base at McMurdo Sound, and if you come in by plane in summer, you are likely to see the giant U.S. Air Force transport planes of Operation Deep Freeze parked on the tarmac at Christchurch International Airport.

The face of Christchurch is changing rapidly, fueled by both internal and international immigration. The Māori community, although still below the national average in size, is growing. Ngai Tahu, the main South Island Māori tribe, settled Treaty of Waitangi claims in 1997 and have been investing in tourism ventures. Old wooden bungalows are making way for town houses, the arts scene is flourishing, and the city's university attracts cutting-edge technology companies. In short, there's plenty of fresh energy percolating underneath the English veneer.

Exploring Christchurch

The inner city is compact and easy to explore by foot; the central sights are easy to reach during an afternoon's walk. Four avenues (Bealey, Fitzger-

GREAT ITINERARIES

Numbers in the text correspond to points of interest on the Christchurch and Canterbury Region maps.

IF YOU HAVE 3 DAYS

Spend at least one day exploring **Christchurch** ❶-⓫, strolling through the beautiful **Christchurch Botanic Gardens** ❼, poking around the **Arts Centre** ❾, and riding the **Christchurch Gondola** for a sweeping view of the region. If you have any interest in the frozen continent, don't miss the **International Antarctic Centre**; if gardens are your thing, head out to **Mona Vale** for afternoon tea. With your remaining time, take a day trip to **Akaroa** ⓮, where you could take a dolphin-spotting cruise, or **Hanmer Springs** ⓰ to soak in the hot springs.

IF YOU HAVE 5 DAYS

Follow the itinerary above, spending a bit more time on the sights in **Christchurch** ❶-⓫, perhaps doing a bit of punting and checking out the **Christchurch Art Gallery—Te Puna O Waiwhetu** ❿. Then branch out into a few day trips; after you've been to Akaroa or Hanmer Springs, consider some vineyard visits in the **Waipara Valley** ⓯ or check out the Southern Alps at **Arthur's Pass** ⓬. If it's ski season, of course, **Methven** ⓱ and Mt. Hutt will be calling.

IF YOU HAVE 7 DAYS

Start with at least a day in **Christchurch** ❶-⓫, taking a guided walk during the morning or visiting the museums, gardens, or galleries that interest you. Next head for **Hanmer Springs** ⓰ to hike and soak in the pools. After an overnight there, head south and stop in the **Waipara Valley** ⓯ for wine tastings and a meal. Next drive over to **Methven** ⓱, where you can either go skiing or jet-boating in season. Spend the night here and make for **Geraldine** ⓲ and **Timaru** ⓳ the next day. Alternatively, head up to **Arthur's Pass** ⓬ and spend a day hiking into the mountains or taking a walk to a nearby waterfall. On Day 6, head back to Christchurch and spend another afternoon sightseeing. Spend your last day spotting dolphins on a cruise from **Akaroa** ⓮ and enjoy the slice-of-paradise feeling of the bays on the Banks Peninsula.

8

ald, Moorhouse, and Rolleston) define the city center. Beyond this core are a number of special-interest museums and activities, about 20 minutes away by car.

Outside the Four Avenues the best way to get around the city is to use the network of buses that radiate from the center. The urban grid pattern collapses outside the city center and streets curve into crescents and cul-de-sacs, particularly in some of the outer suburbs. Although Christchurch was once a series of villages, few of the suburbs retain a distinctive village feel, with the possible exception of Riccarton and the seaside town of Sumner. New suburbs are cropping up, most notably in Halswell and in the developments creeping up the Port Hills.

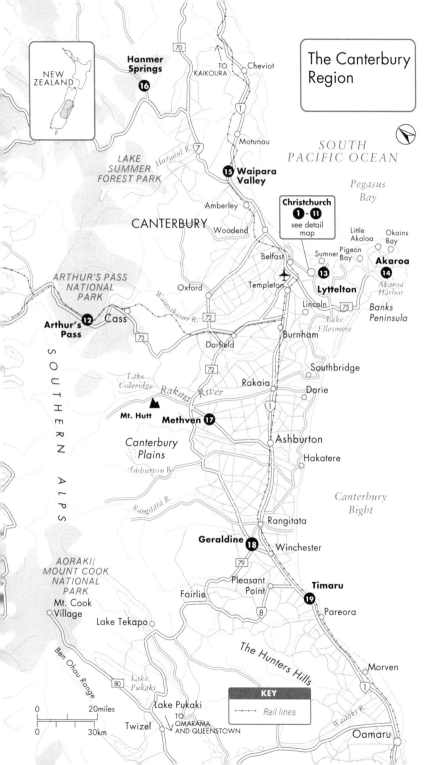

The Canterbury Region

NEW ZEALAND

SOUTH PACIFIC OCEAN

Pegasus Bay

CANTERBURY

Hanmer Springs 16

TO KAIKOURA

Cheviot

Motunau

LAKE SUMMER FOREST PARK

Hurunui R.

15 **Waipara Valley**

Amberley

Woodend

Belfast

Christchurch 1-11 see detail map

Little Akaloa

Okains Bay

Sumner

Pigeon Bay

Akaroa 14

Templeton

13

Lyttelton

Akaroa Harbor

Banks Peninsula

Lincoln

Oxford

Waimakariri R.

ARTHUR'S PASS NATIONAL PARK

Arthur's Pass 12

Cass

Burnham

Lake Ellesmere

Darfield

Southbridge

Rakaia

Dorie

Lake Coleridge

Rakaia River

Mt. Hutt

Methven 17

Ashburton

Hakatere

S O U T H E R N   A L P S

Canterbury Plains

Ashburton R.

Canterbury Bight

Rangitata R.

Rangitata

AORAKI/ MOUNT COOK NATIONAL PARK

Mt. Cook Village

Geraldine 18

Winchester

Fairlie

Pleasant Point

Timaru 19

Lake Tekapo

Pareora

The Hunters Hills

Morven

Ben Ohau Range

Lake Pukaki

Lake Pukaki

TO OMARAMA AND QUEENSTOWN

Twizel

Waitaki R.

Oamaru

KEY

Rail lines

0   20miles
0   30km

A GOOD WALK

Start in Cathedral Square, the city's hub, before the landmark **Christchurch Cathedral** ❶. By climbing up the cathedral's tower, you can survey the city before hitting its streets and parks. Back down in the square, you'll see the statue of Robert Godley, dubbed "the founder of Canterbury," along with the War Memorial and the old post office, built in 1879. You can't miss the tall, conical metal sculpture, the *Chalice*, which commemorates both the new millennium and the 150th anniversary of the founding of Christchurch. Forty-two leaves represent native trees, and complex shapes, intertwined with the leaves, reflect elements of the cathedral's architecture. Take Worcester Boulevard out of the square, passing the **Southern Encounter Aquarium & Kiwi House** ❷ in the Edwardian Regent Theatre building. One block west, you'll pass a statue of Antarctic explorer Robert Falcon Scott, then cross the Avon River on a bridge with ornate iron balustrades. Turn left on Cambridge Terrace to follow the Avon upstream. A hitching post and gas lamp mark one of the city's oldest gentlemen's clubs, the Canterbury Club (now open to women, too). A short distance away, by the Hereford Bridge, is the redbrick Old Library Chambers (1876). The next bridge over the river is the imposing **Bridge of Remembrance** ❸. Trees representing each of Christchurch's sister cities cluster next to the bridge.

The belfry of the Victorian Gothic **St. Michael and All Saints Anglican Church** ❹ rises across the river as you continue along the tree-shaded bank. Crossing Montreal Street, you'll find the **Antigua Boatshed** ❺, which may inspire you to try your hand at punting. If you're working up a thirst, you may want to take a detour down Antigua Street to the **Canterbury Brewery** ❻. Otherwise, you can walk up Rolleston Avenue with the **Christchurch Botanic Gardens** ❼ on your left. These gardens form the eastern side of **Hagley Park**, a magnificent wooded area. The **Canterbury Museum** ❽ juts into the gardens next to a 19th-century boys' school. Across from the park loom the gray Gothic buildings of the **Arts Centre** ❾, a great place to stop for a pick-me-up. Visit the markets there if it's the weekend. Turn right up Worcester Boulevard, and where it crosses Montreal Street you'll find the **Christchurch Art Gallery—Te Puna O Waiwhetu** ❿. You can walk another 10 minutes to Victoria Square by following Montreal Street, then turning right up Gloucester Street, passing the Gothic Revival **Provincial Council Chambers** ⓫, and then taking the footpath along the riverbank.

TIMING   The core of this walk, from Cathedral Square to the Arts Centre and Canterbury Museum area, takes about an hour, not including the time you may spend checking out exhibits, browsing in shops, or punting on the Avon. If you're planning a visit to the Southern Encounter, try to be there for the salmon and trout feeding at 1 PM.

Sights to See

❺ **Antigua Boatshed.** Built for the Christchurch Boating Club in 1882, this green-and-white wooden structure is the last shed standing of a half dozen that once lined the Avon. On sunny days, count on seeing students on punts and families in canoes messing about on the river. Join them by renting a boat and taking a champagne picnic into the Botanic Gardens or punting farther up into the woodlands of Hagley Park, spectacular in autumn. The boat shed also has a café (open for breakfast and lunch) where you can sit outdoors on a deck overlooking the Avon. ⊠ *2 Cambridge Terr.* ☎ *03/366–5885 (boatshed) or 03/366–6768 (café)* ⊕ *www. boatsheds.co.nz* 🖃 *Single canoe $7 per hr, rowboat $20 per hr, punting $16.50 per person (minimum 2 people) per ½ hr* ☉ *Oct.–Mar., daily 9–5:30; Apr.–Sept., daily 9–4.*

❾ **Arts Centre.** By moving to the suburbs in the 1970s, Canterbury University left vacant a fine collection of Gothic Revival stone buildings, which were then transformed into this terrific arts, shopping, and dining complex. Beside the center's information desk in the clock tower you'll find **Rutherford's Den,** where physicist Ernest Rutherford (1871–1937), the university's most illustrious student, conducted experiments in what was then a new field, radioactivity. It was Rutherford who first succeeded in splitting the atom, a crucial step in the harnessing of atomic power. In 1908 Rutherford's work earned him the Nobel Prize—not for physics but for chemistry. Now a dynamic multimedia presentation depicts Rutherford and daily life in the 1890s at Canterbury College, as the campus was known then.

Fodor'sChoice
★
☾

The Arts Centre houses more than 40 specialty shops and studios, as well as art galleries, theaters, and art-house cinemas. It is also an excellent place to stop for food, coffee, or a glass of wine—there are several cafés and a wine bar. At the **Saturday and Sunday Market** you'll find jewelry, prints, bric-a-brac, and handmade clothing and crafts as well as food stalls (*see also* Shopping, *below*). This market is a seeding ground for talented artisans: many former stall holders are now resident in the center or running successful businesses in other parts of the city or country. Free live entertainment kicks off at noon on weekends and goes until 2 PM. Stop by the information desk to join one of the free guided tours, offered daily from 10 to 3:30. ⊠ *Worcester Blvd. between Montreal St. and Rolleston Ave.* ☎ *03/366–0989, 03/363–2836 tours, 03/366–0980* ⊕ *www. artscentre.org.nz* ☉ *Shops and galleries daily 10–5.*

NEED A BREAK?

The Arts Centre has several eateries in its stone buildings and quadrangles. **Dux de Lux** (☎ 03/366–6919) is a sprawling, upbeat, popular cafeteria-style restaurant in a mock-Tudor building that once was the student common room. The blackboard menu offers vegetarian items and seafood: quiches, crepes, sandwiches, breads and dips, pizzas, and a range of crisp salads. The courtyard is a great spot on a sunny day, especially with a beer from the on-site boutique brewery. The **Backstage Bakery** (☎ 03/377–7948) turns out specialty breads daily. Just follow your nose—it's right in the center of the complex. **Annies Wine Bar** (⊠ 41 Hereford St. ☎ 03/365–0566) is the most refined option, a very pleasant place to taste New Zealand wine alongside bistro fare.

❸ **Bridge of Remembrance.** Arching over Cashel Street, this Oamaru limestone memorial arch was built in memory of the soldiers who crossed the river here from King Edward Barracks (demolished a few years ago to build a parking lot) on their way to the battlefields of Europe during World War I. ⊠ *Avon River at Cashel St.*

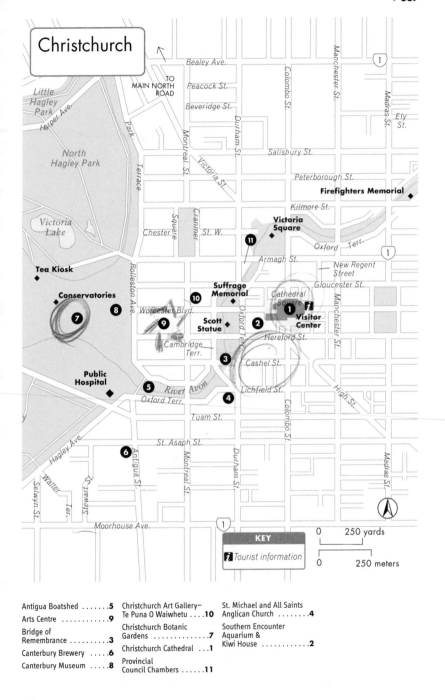

Christchurch

TO
MAIN NORTH
ROAD

Bealey Ave.

Peacock St.

Beveridge St.

Little Hagley Park

Harper Ave.

North Hagley Park

Victoria Lake

Tea Kiosk

Conservatories

Salisbury St.

Peterborough St.

Firefighters Memorial

Kilmore St.

Victoria Square

Oxford Terr.

Chester St. W.

Armagh St.

New Regent Street

Gloucester St.

Suffrage Memorial

Scott Statue

Worcester Blvd.

Cambridge Terr.

Cashel St.

Public Hospital

River Avon

Oxford Terr.

Lichfield St.

Tuam St.

St. Asaph St.

Moorhouse Ave.

Cathedral Square

Visitor Center

Hereford St.

Bealey Ave. — Colombo St. — Manchester St. — Madras St. — Ely St.

Durham St. — Victoria St. — Montreal St.

Square — Cranmer

Rolleston Ave.

Terrace

park

Hagley Ave. — Walter — Selwyn St. — Stewart St. — Ter. — Antigua St. — Montreal St. — Durham St. — Colombo St. — High St. — Madras St.

KEY		
🏛 Tourist information		

0   250 yards

0   250 meters

❻ Canterbury Brewery. Christchurch has been brewing beer since 1854, when Hamilton Ward bottled his first batch. More than a century and several mergers later, the Canterbury Brewery, home of the beer known as Canterbury Draught, celebrates the history of brewing with a museum and 90-minute tours, including a sample in the Heritage Bar afterward. Advance reservations for all tours are essential. ⊠ *36 St. Asaph St.* ☎ *03/ 371–3290* 🔳 *$12* ⊙ *Tours weekdays at 10 and 12:30; Sat. tour at 1 by arrangement.*

❽ Canterbury Museum. When this museum was founded in 1867, its trading power with national and international museums was in moa bones. These Jurassic birds roamed the plains of Canterbury and are believed to have been hunted to extinction by early Māori. The museum still houses one of the largest collections of artifacts from the moa hunting period. You'll also find a reconstruction of an early Christchurch streetscape and a natural-history discovery center where kids get to handle bones and fossils. The Hall of Antarctic Discovery charts the links between the city and Antarctica, from the days when Captain Cook's ship skirted the continent in a small wooden ship. Among the 20th-century explorers celebrated here are the Norwegian Roald Admundsen, who was first to visit the South Pole, and Captain Robert Falcon Scott, who died on his way back from the continent. (Follow local tradition and rub the nose of the bronze sculpture of Scott's head for good luck.) Several vehicles, from a dogsled to a bright-orange Tucker snowcat, trace the methods of transport on the ice. There's a café on-site with a nice outlook over the Botanic Gardens if you plan to stay a while. ⊠ *Rolleston Ave.* ☎ *03/366–5000* 🔳 *Donation requested; Discovery exhibition $2* ⊙ *Oct.–Mar., daily 9–5:30; Apr.–Sept., daily 9–5.*

Captain Robert Falcon Scott statue. *Scott of the Antarctic* (1868–1912), who stayed in Christchurch while preparing for his two Antarctic expeditions, is memorialized by this unfinished white marble statue sculpted by his widow, Kathleen. It's inscribed DO NOT REGRET THIS JOURNEY, WHICH SHOWS THAT ENGLISHMEN CAN ENDURE HARDSHIPS, HELP ONE ANOTHER AND MEET DEATH WITH AS GREAT FORTITUDE AS EVER IN THE PAST. Scott wrote these words in his diary as he and his party lay dying in a blizzard on their return journey from the South Pole. ⊠ *Worcester Blvd. and Oxford Terr.*

❿ Christchurch Art Gallery—Te Puna O Waiwhetu. The city's art gallery has been wowing visitors since it first opened in May 2003, as much for its architecture and facilities as for its artwork. Its tall, wavy glass facade was inspired by Christchurch's Avon River and the shape of the native *koru* fern. Outside the building is a growing collection of sculpture, and the downstairs galleries hold touring national and international exhibitions. Up the wide staircase are galleries for permanent exhibits, including one on Canterbury artists. Look into the lectures and floor talks, most of which are free; there are also audio guides for rent. An in-house crafts gallery sells stunning glasswork, ceramics, and jewelry. There is also a café, and an auditorium that's a popular film festival venue. The museum's Māori name, given by Ngai Tuahuriri, the Māori tribe of this area, refers to an artesian spring on the site and means "the well-spring of star-reflecting waters." ✉ *Worcester Blvd. and Montreal St.* 📞 *03/941–7300* ⊕ *www.christchurchartgallery.org.nz* 🎫 *Free; $8–$15 for special lectures* ⊙ *Wed. 10–9, Thurs.–Tues. 10–5.*

★ ☺ ❼ **Christchurch Botanic Gardens.** Think big. These superb gardens are known for the magnificent trees that were planted in the 19th century. Many are the largest specimens found in the country—or even in their native lands. Pick up the Historic Tree Walk brochure from the information center for a self-guided Who's Who tour of the tree world. The garden kiosk near the information center serves lunches and snacks, and there's a children's playground and swimming pool. Spend time in the conservatories to discover tropical plants, cacti, and ferns on days when you'd rather not be outside. Any time of the year, be sure to go to the New Zealand plants area, where you can see plant life that you won't find in other countries. ✉ *Rolleston Ave.* 📞 *03/366–1701* 🎫 *Free* ⊙ *Daily 7 AM–dusk, conservatories daily 10:15–4.*

❶ **Christchurch Cathedral** (✉ The Sq. 📞 03/366–0046 🎫 Tower $4, tour $3 ⊙ Oct.–Mar., daily 8:30–7; Apr.–Sept., daily 9–5 ⊕ www.christchurchcathedral.co.nz). The city's dominating landmark was begun in 1864, 14 years after the arrival of the Canterbury Pilgrims. Though consecrated in 1881, it wasn't completed until 1904. Carvings inside commemorate the work of the Anglican missionaries, including Tamihana Te Rauparaha, the son of a fierce and, for the settlers, troublesome Māori chief. Free guided tours begin daily at 11 and 2. For a view across the city to the Southern Alps, climb the 133 steps to the top of the bell tower. The cathedral is known for its boys' choir, which can be heard singing evensong at 5:15 on Tuesday and Wednesday and at 4:30 on Friday. Men's Evensong happens every Thursday at 5:15. **Cathedral Square,** the city's focal point, buzzes with an arts-and-crafts market on Thursday and Friday, complete with food stalls and street musicians. Gradual upgrades of the Square have been pursued since 1991, including a giant chessboard and the huge, shiny *Chalice* sculpture, created by local artist Neil Dawson.

Firefighters Memorial. A little piece of New York City has found its way to Christchurch. Local artist Graham Bennett used crooked girders from the collapsed World Trade Center in this memorial sculpture. The work is dedicated not only to the firefighters who died in New York on September 11, 2001, but also to other firefighters who have died in the course of duty. You can reach the memorial along the riverside path; sit awhile in the small park beside the Avon, not far from the central fire station. ✉ *Kilmore and Madras Sts.*

☺ **Hagley Park.** Once cultivated Māori land, Hagley Park was developed by Pākehā settlers in the mid-1800s, with imported plants given trial runs in what would become the Botanic Gardens (⇨ Christchurch Botanic Gardens, *above*). Now the park is divided into four sections, which together include walking and jogging tracks, cycling paths, and self-guided historic tours. Hagley Park North draws people to its tennis and *pétanque* (boccie) courts; Little Hagley Park is classified as a Heritage area. Hagley Park South is another good spot for sports, and the Botanic Gardens are perfect for strolling. ⊠ *Main entrance: Armagh St. at Rolleston Ave.*

⓫ **Provincial Council Chambers.** This complex of Gothic Revival stone buildings beside the Avon River was once the seat of Canterbury's government, which ran from 1853 to 1876. The wooden buildings date from 1859. In 1865 the stone chamber was built and was notable in its day for its underfloor heating and hot-air-extraction system (a third chimney). The elaborate decorations include a painted ceiling, stone carvings, and stained-glass windows. It now houses a small museum devoted to the building's history. A large clock intended for the tower proved too big and stands a few blocks away, at the intersection of Victoria, Salisbury, and Montreal streets. ⊠ *Durham St. at Gloucester St.* ☏ *03/941–7680* ⊡ *Free* ⊘ *Mon.–Sat. 10:30–3:30.*

❹ **St. Michael and All Saints Anglican Church.** One of the bells in this church's belfry came out with the Canterbury Pilgrims on one of the first four ships and was rung hourly to indicate time for early settlers. The white-timber church was built in 1872. ⊠ *Oxford Terr. at Durham St.* ☏ *03/379–5236* ⊘ *Daily noon–2.*

☾ ❷ **Southern Encounter Aquarium & Kiwi House.** Fish and rare kiwi birds in the heart of Christchurch? The giant aquarium has an enormous variety of New Zealand fish species—from rocky tidal-pool creatures to those from lakes, rivers, and the briny deep. You can actually touch some of these critters if you want to in the Touch Tank. Watch divers feed giant eels or carpet sharks, cod, skates, and other rarely seen deepwater fish. Move on to get a glimpse of the kiwi; the shy, nocturnal national symbol is now hard to see in the wild, but here you can watch them foraging in a natural setting. The entrance is through the visitor center. ⊠ *Cathedral Sq.* ☏ *03/359–0581* ⊕ *www.southernencounter.co.nz* ⊡ *$12* ⊘ *Daily 9–5, last entry at 4:30.*

Suffrage Memorial. Unveiled in 1993, this bronze memorial wall commemorates 100 years of votes for women. New Zealand was the first country in the world to grant women the vote, and Christchurch resident Kate Sheppard played a key role in petitioning Parliament for this essential right. The vote for all women over 21, including Māori women, was granted on September 19, 1893; the work of Sheppard and other activists is celebrated each year on that date at the memorial. ⊠ *Oxford Terr.*

Victoria Square. Once the business center of Christchurch, this square was named for Queen Victoria in her Jubilee year. On its north side sits the modern Town Hall, with its auditorium, theater, and conference spaces. Nearby stands a *poupou,* a tall carved wood column, acknowledging the site's history as a trading point between Māori and the European settlers. Keep an eye out for the ice-cream van—it has been parking in the square and selling treats for decades. The stone ramp sloping from the square down to the river was used for watering horses. You'll also see Christchurch's oldest iron bridge, a floral clock, two fountains, including one that's illuminated with colored lights at night, and statues of Queen Victoria and Captain Cook. ⊠ *Armagh and Colombo Sts.*

Beyond Central Christchurch

Air Force Museum. Starting in 1916, New Zealand pilots learned how to fly at Wigram Airport. The airport's old hangars now hold exhibits on aviation history, flight simulators, and 28 classic aircraft, with more being restored behind the scenes in other hangars. To get here by bus, take the number 5, 81, or 82 and walk from the Main South Road, just south of the Sockburn Overbridge. ✉ *Main South Rd., Wigram* ☎ *03/343–9532* ⊕ *www.airforcemuseum.co.nz* 🖅 *$15* ⊗ *Daily 10–5.*

★ **Christchurch Gondola.** East of the city in the Port Hills, the gondola is the best vantage point from which to overlook Christchurch, the Canterbury Plains, and Lyttleton Harbour. At the top, you can wander through the **Time Tunnel,** which gives a brief audiovisual history of the region. Best of all, sit with a glass of local wine at the Summit Café and watch the sunset. Ride the gondola with your back to the Port Hills for the best views of the Southern Alps. The adventurous can walk or mountain-bike back down (*see* Sports & the Outdoors, *below*). The Bridle Path track from Lyttelton to Ferrymead, used by the early settlers in the 1850s, crosses nearby. If you don't have a car, you can hop a number 28 bus from the city center; the Best Attractions Direct bus also includes the gondola on its run. ✉ *10 Bridle Path Rd., Heathcote* ☎ *03/384–0700* ⊕ *www.gondola.co.nz* 🖅 *$18* ⊗ *Daily 10–9.*

Ferrymead Heritage Park. Ferrymead is the site of the country's first railway (it was built in 1863) and is now home to an Edwardian township. While exploring the shops and cottages, you can taste homemade scones or an old-fashioned lamington (chocolate-covered sponge cake dipped in coconut). You can watch an old-time movie at the Arcadia, see some knees-up dancing at the tiny theater opposite, or check out displays of fire engines, farming tools, and printing equipment. The park is home to 20 societies, particularly train and tram enthusiasts, who maintain their collections here, so trams and trains run on weekends and public holidays. A steam train operates on the first Sunday of each month and every Sunday in January. On the weekend closest to July Fourth, a Stars and Stripes event is usually held for an American touch. To get to Ferrymead by public transit, take the number 35 bus to Sumner, getting off at Bridle Path Road. ✉ *Ferrymead Park Rd.* ☎ *03/384–1970* ⊕ *www.ferrymead.org.nz* 🖅 *$10* ⊗ *Daily 10–4:30.*

Gethsemane Gardens. As you might guess from the name, this suburban spot is a Christian-themed garden, where lush plants form religious symbols or texts. As you approach, take note of the 90-foot-long trellis fences and rock walls that spell GETHSEMANE. Inside, four meticulous knot gardens shape a Star of David, a Star of Bethlehem, and two parallel Jerusalem crosses. The path through a fragrant, rose-filled maze spells JESUS, and the Prayer Garden includes the Lord's Prayer written in box hedging. A recent addition, a substantial ark made of rolled logs, is mainly used for weddings. The garden is a 20-minute drive east of central Christchurch along Ferry Road out to Sumner. Opposite Sumner Beach, turn up Clifton Terrace, which leads to Revelation Dr. ✉ *27 Revelation Dr., at top of Clifton Terr., Sumner* ☎ *03/326–5848* 🖅 *$5* ⊗ *Daily 9–5.*

★ ☺ **International Antarctic Centre.** Ever since Scott wintered his dogs at nearby Quail Island in preparation for his ill-fated South Pole expedition of 1912, Christchurch has maintained a close connection with the frozen continent. You can get a small taste of the polar experience through this complex's interactive displays. For instance, bundle up in extra clothing and brave a simulated storm, in which a bitingly cold wind chills the room to 25 degrees below for a few minutes. Or you could take a ride on the Hägglund vehicle used to get around the ice. (The 15-minute trip leaves from the front of the complex daily, every 20 minutes from 9:40 AM on.) Back inside the center, take a look at the four thick layers of clothing worn in summer by polar scientists, or the aquarium where the fish stay so still they look like plastic models. The audiovisual show of life at New Zealand's Scott Base is superb. The center focuses on recent expeditions (fittingly, as it's also the base for a number of Antarctic research organizations), so if you want to know more historic explorers, visit the Canterbury Museum. It's roughly 20 minutes from central Christchurch by car or on the Best Attractions bus. There's even a free shuttle directly from the airport. ⊠ *Orchard Rd., Harewood* ☎ *03/358–9896* ⊕ *www. iceberg.co.nz* ⊠ *$25, Hägglund tour ride $12, joint ticket $35* ☉ *Oct.–Mar., daily 9–7; Apr.–Sept., daily 9–5:30.*

Mona Vale. One of Christchurch's great historic homesteads, the riverside Mona Vale makes for a lovely outing from the city. Built in 1899, the house and garden have been part of the city since 1967—when threatened with demolition, the estate was "sold" to individual Christchurch residents for $10 per square foot. Come for lunch or Devonshire tea, and you can make believe that you're strolling your own grounds along the Avon as you wander under the stately trees and through the well-tended rose, fuchsia, dahlia, herb, and iris gardens. If the mood really takes you, go for a punt ride. Catch a number 9 bus from the city; there's a stop outside the front gate near the gingerbread gatehouse (which is not open to the public). ⊠ *63 Fendalton Rd., Fendalton, 2 km (1 mi) from city center* ☎ *03/348–9659* ⊠ *Free* ☉ *Grounds Oct.–Mar., daily 7 AM–9 PM; Apr.–Sept., daily 7 AM to 6 PM; gates open 24 hrs to pedestrians, only vehicle access closes. Café hours—Summer (mid-Sept to mid-Mar.) 9:30 AM to 4 PM every day. Winter (mid-Mar. to mid-Sept.) Wed to Sun 9 AM to 3 PM. Closed Mon–Tues in winter.*

Ngā Hau e Whā national marae. The "marae of the four winds" is the largest urban *marae* (cultural center and meetinghouse) in New Zealand. You can book a tour during the day to see the striking carvings on the gateway, two meetinghouses, and flagpole. Better yet, sign up for the evening "Night of Māori Magic," starting at 6:45, which includes a tour, cultural performance, and *hāngi* (earth-oven) dinner. You'll have a chance to see a *powhiri* (welcome ceremony), action songs, *poi* (balls rhythmically swung on strings), and the *haka* (war dance) This is not a hands-off experience; you'll be encouraged to join in and to take photos. The marae is a 10-minute drive northeast of central Christchurch; to get here by bus take the number 5 to Southshore or New Brighton and ask for the marae stop. All bookings are subject to minimum numbers. ⊠ *250 Pages Rd., Aranui* ☎ *03/388–7685* ⊕ *www.nationalmarae.*

co.nz ✉ *"Night of Māori Magic" $85; tour and concert only $45; day-time tour $10* ☉ *Weekdays 9–4:30.*

🐾 **Orana Park.** This is the place to come to glimpse endangered animals, both native (kiwi and tuatara, a kind of reptile) and exotic (rare species of antelope and zebras). You can also feed the giraffes and come within a meter of a rhino and its horn. A zebra-striped Safari Shuttle loops around the park with commentary, and there are guided walks twice a day. It takes about a half hour to drive here from town, or you could take the Best Attractions bus. ✉ *McLeans Island Rd., Harewood* ☎ *03/359–7109* ⊕ *www.oranawildlifepark.co.nz* ✉ *$16* ☉ *Daily 10–5, last entry at 4:30.*

Riccarton House and Bush. The Deans, a Scottish family, beat even the Canterbury Association settlers to this region. Riccarton Bush, their home, is now run by a trust. You can view the small wooden cottage (built 1843) that was their first house. The larger wooden house, started in 1856, is being redone in Edwardian style; for instance, the kitchen is outfitted with period iron weights and measures, spice tins, and breakfast plates. The large drawing room at the front of the house is now a restaurant, open for lunch and morning and afternoon teas (from 10 to 4). Guided one-hour tours are given weekdays and on Sundays at 2. You can also amble in the last remnant of the original native forest still standing in Christchurch, with its 600-year-old *kahikatea* trees. ✉ *16 Kahu Rd., Riccarton* ☎ *03/341–1018* ⊕ *www.riccartonhouse.co.nz* ✉ *Free, tours $10* ☉ *Dawn to dusk.*

🐾 **Willowbank.** In addition to familiar farm animals and other zoo regulars, Willowbank has a section devoted to New Zealand animals. Here you can have a close encounter with the cheeky mountain parrot, the *kea,* which usually does not venture far out of its alpine habitat. Kiwi can be viewed in an artificially darkened area after 11 AM. You can get a special viewing of the native animals on the Māori cultural tour given from **Ko Tane,** a reproduction Māori village. You'll be greeted with a *wero,* a traditional welcome, and you can try your hand at swinging poi, flaxen balls on long strings used in traditional Māori dances (it's not as easy as it looks). The tour starts at $36 and goes up to $82 if you include a hāngi (earth-oven) dinner. There are guided tours through the "New Zealand Natural Area"—where the native animals are—at 11, 2:30, and 5:30. To get here without a car, use the Best Attractions bus. ✉ *60 Hussey Rd., Harewood* ☎ *03/359–6226* ⊕ *www.willowbank.co.nz* ✉ *$20* ☉ *Daily 10–dusk.*

Where to Eat

For bargain eats around Christchurch, look to the buffet restaurants such as the Cabbage Tree, three-course prix-fixe meals from the Chancery Restaurant opposite the Christchurch Public Library in Gloucester Street, or pizza or pasta from the Spagalimis chain. For a really cheap take-out meal, you can't beat the price of fish-and-chips eaten from paper wrapping.

★ **$$$$** ✕ **Pescatore.** Some of the dishes that sail out of this kitchen pose a challenge: once you've admired their architectural presentation, how do you take them apart to eat them? Portions are small, so don't skimp on the entrée. Fish dishes dominate the menu, with New Zealand specialties such as Akaroa salmon and Kaikoura crayfish; there are also a few starters such as scallops and oysters. The "Fang au chocolat" dessert exemplifies the theatrical factor, with its foot-long biscuit spikes firing out of a chocolate cylinder filled with two-toned chocolate mousse. ☒ *50 Park Terr.* ☎ *03/371–0257* ⊟ *AE, DC, MC, V* ⊘ *No lunch.*

$$$–$$$$ ✕ **Cook'n with Gas.** This restaurant aims to give new life to provincial South Island cuisine, so look for dishes such as roasted lamb with olive and *kūmara* (a native sweet potato), minted peas, peppers, and aioli, or West Coast whitebait fritters with native parsley and spinach. To go truly local, try some James Cook spruce beer (a modified version of the beer first brewed by the captain in Dusky Sound in 1773, from *rimu* and *manuka* tree twigs). It is just one of more than 40 beers they have here. ☒ *23 Worcester Blvd.* ☎ *03/377–9166* ⊟ *AE, DC, MC, V* ⊘ *Closed Sun. No lunch.*

$$$–$$$$ ✕ **Curator's House.** Here you can dine in a 1920s house, looking out on the Botanic Gardens' flowers and the Peacock Fountain. The menu has a heavy Spanish influence, with tapas selections and a good variety of seafood. The garden out the back is a model of sustainability, supplying herbs, berries, and vegetables to the restaurant. ☒ *7 Rolleston Ave.* ☎ *03/379–2252* ⊟ *AE, MC, V.*

$$$–$$$$ ✕ **50 on Park.** Don't miss the breakfasts at this light and airy restaurant
Fodor'sChoice in the George Hotel, where you can look out at early morning joggers
★ in Hagley Park. Start with the likes of grouper-and-potato hash cakes or spicy petite doughnuts and blueberry compote. Move on to chive waffles with roasted tomatoes and smoked bacon or French-toast-style brioche with vanilla and maple-glazed bananas. Later in the day you can choose from dishes such as tenderloin of Canterbury lamb, roasted pork roulade, or grilled poussin with a tropical fruit salsa and red curry sauce. ☒ *50 Park Terr.* ☎ *03/371–0250* ⊟ *AE, DC, MC, V.*

★ **$$$–$$$$** ✕ **Saggio di vino.** As the name suggests, wine is the raison d'être for this long-established Christchurch vinotheque, but it's also being sought out for its truffles in season, from Gisborne and north Canterbury. Truffles are fairly new to New Zealand restaurants, and here you can indulge in a special menu that uses the famous fungi in nearly every dish. The short daily menu could include rack of lamb, fettuccine with pesto, or antipasto, according to season. The restaurant draws an older crowd who appreciate the extensive wine list that includes around 300 choices, both local and imported. ☒ *185 Victoria St.* ☎ *03/379–4006* ⊟ *AE, DC, MC, V* ⊘ *No lunch.*

$$$–$$$$ ✕ **Sala Sala.** Generally considered to be Christchurch's top Japanese restaurant, Sala Sala wins praise for its ability to pair wines (including sake) with its dishes. Diners can choose from sushi, sashimi, teriyaki, tempura, teppanyaki, or traditional kaiseki set meals. The teppanyaki bar gives the chefs the opportunity to demonstrate their considerable skills with flames and flashing utensils brightening the night scene. You might not recognize all the ingredients, but you can rest assured they will be fresh and delicious. ☒ *184–186 Oxford Terr.* ☎ *03/366–6755* ⊟ *AE, DC, MC, V* ⊘ *No lunch weekends.*

$$$–$$$$ ✕ **Zydeco.** Cajun fans suffering chili withdrawal will find a pretty good facsimile of what they're missing here. The menu is chock-full of New Orleans classics such as gumbo, jambalaya, and prawns (okay, they're not crawfish, but they're close) with wild-venison ragout giving the menu a New Zealand touch. Feel free to mix and match the sauces on many of the dishes. ✉ *57 Victoria St.* ☎ *03/365–4556* ▭ *AE, DC, MC, V.*

$$–$$$$ ✕ **Trilogy Restaurant & Bar.** Some say the lamb served here is the best in New Zealand—cooked rare, with an intriguing juniper-berry sauce. The filet mignon, venison medallions, and chicken Parmesan, though, are also favorites. Though it's about a 10-minute drive from the city center, lots of locals make the trip, especially on the weekends, when pancake stacks and lamb wraps are dished up for brunch. Reservations are recommended. ✉ *705 Gloucester St.* ☎ *03/381–2496* ▭ *AE, MC, V* ☉ *Closed 1st 2 wks in Jan.*

$–$$$$ ✕ **Sign of the Takahe.** From this dining room halfway up the Port Hills, you'll have superb views over Christchurch and the Canterbury Plains to the Southern Alps. The castlelike structure was part of an early-1900s plan to build a series of inns along the Summit Road, all the way to Akaroa. The plan was only partially realized, and now the building is a long-standing local favorite restaurant for its silver-service style and reinterpretations of classic Kiwi dishes. Try the beef fillet Takahe, marinated in soy and sake, or the seared scallops with oysters, spinach, exotic mushrooms, and lemon soy. There's also spiced duo of lamb served with garlic and chicken-liver rice and a coconut-cream-and-chili sauce. Between courses, you can admire the display of the coats-of-arms of many of the earliest European families to settle in Canterbury, and also of some early NZ leaders—it's the largest such exhibit in the Southern Hemisphere. ✉ *200 Hackthorne Rd., Cashmere* ☎ *03/332–4052* ▭ *AE, DC, MC, V.*

$$$ ✕ **Indochine.** Cross the threshold of this mysterious black box and you'll

Fodor's Choice ★ be welcomed by a glass bowl of floating yellow chrysanthemums and candles. The space is an intriguing mix of Christchurch and Asia—clearly, the interior designer had fun creating various intimate corners, large group spaces, and a leafy back courtyard. The menu also stretches between the two cultures; nowhere else would you find *sung choi bao* (a dish made with minced pork and finely diced vegetables) done quite like this. Finish with a latte and something unexpected: a little "fullstop," a marble-size orange-and-chocolate candy. If it's cool out, book later in the evening to give the restaurant time to warm up. ✉ *209 Cambridge Terr.* ☎ *03/365–7323* ⚃ *Reservations essential* ▭ *AE, MC, V* ☉ *No lunch.*

$$–$$$ ✕ **Dux de Lux.** An Arts Centre mainstay, this vegetarian and seafood restaurant inhabits a mock Tudor-style building that was once the student center of the university. You'll usually find Akaroa salmon on the menu, along with vegetarian picks such as pasta or quesadillas. The courtyard is popular for dining in summer, particularly on weekends during the market and live music performances. The Dux complex also has a boutique brewery, cocktail lounge, and live bands four nights a week. ✉ *Hereford and Montreal Sts.* ☎ *03/366–6919 or 03/366–6918* ▭ *AE, MC, V.*

$$–$$$ ✕ **Jolly Poacher Rock Cafe.** Calling themselves "Christchurch's Original Late Night Rock Café," the Jolly Poacher serves a hearty menu. Mains from the plains, which include Canterbury rib eye and rosemary lamb,

8

are available from 5 PM until midnight; lunch is lighter, with pizzas and snacks. Although the cuisine is contemporary, the decor is a cross between an English tavern and a Wild West saloon. Live musicians often play to a wine- and beer-drinking late-night crowd. ⊠ *31 Victoria St.* 🕿 *03/379–5635* ▭ *AE, MC, V.*

$$–$$$ ✕ **Megawatt–Urban Food Kitchen.** The Kitchen combines a European-style coffeehouse with an à la carte restaurant. Seasonal dishes sometimes get a German or French spin. Insider tip: the chef encourages his regular guests and those in the know to cross the road to the City Seafood Market and pick out a piece of fish they'd like cooked. The reasonably priced desserts ($7.50) are scrumptious—you don't need a food allergy to enjoy the gluten-free dark "chocolate thrill." Megawatt is aptly named, as you can see just how much power the South Island is using at any given time on the meter near the front counter. The space is lighted by early-20th-century street lamps to boot. ⊠ *218 Manchester St.* 🕿 *03/363–9680* ▭ *MC, V* ⊙ *Closed early Jan. No dinner Sat.–Tues.*

$–$$$ ✕ **Raj Mahal.** With its regionally structured menu, the Raj Mahal invites you on a virtual gastronomic tour of India; you can try tandoori from the Punjab, fish masala from Goa, or a vegetarian curry that's mild, medium, or strong according to your preference. The restaurant uses contemporary as well as traditional Indian methods, so there's no pork, no beef, and no fusion cooking. Of the dozens of Indian restaurants in Christchurch, this is the best for its quality, its sheer variety of dishes, and its uncluttered decor. ⊠ *Manchester St. at Worcester St.* 🕿 *03/366–0521* ▭ *D, MC, V* ⊙ *Closed Mon. No lunch.*

¢–$$ ✕ **Mainstreet Café.** If you lived in Christchurch and liked hearty vegetarian cooking, you'd probably end up at this bohemian storefront haunt once a week. (The menu also caters to vegans and has gluten-free options.) The rich pumpkin-and-kūmara balls with peanut sauce or a choice of salads with a piece of homemade bread will help you get out of a vacation-food rut. The espresso's great, the desserts are delicious, and there's a good selection of international beers. ⊠ *840 Colombo St.* 🕿 *03/365–0421* ▭ *AE, MC, V.*

Fodor'sChoice
★

Where to Stay

$$$$ 🏨 **Crowne Plaza.** This plush hotel is set in a prime location overlooking Victoria Square and the river. The luxurious, contemporary rooms are decorated in tones of burgundy and gold. In summer the best views are from rooms overlooking Victoria Square, but in the winter popularity switches to those with views of the snowcapped Alps to the west. The hotel is especially well equipped with restaurants and bars, including Yamagen, a Japanese teppanyaki restaurant. A pianist plays in the glass-roof atrium—the heart of this hotel—at lunch or in the evening. Breakfasts are definitely worth getting out of bed for. ⊠ *Kilmore and Durham Sts.* 🕿 *03/365–7799* 🖷 *03/365–0082* ⊕ *www.ichotelsgroup. com* ⇨ *298 rooms* ⬧ *3 restaurants, gym, bicycles, 2 bars, car rental* ▭ *AE, DC, MC, V.*

★ **$$$$** 🏨 **The George.** The adage that great things come in small packages holds true for the George. In the spacious, modern guest rooms a crisp, monochromatic color scheme weaves through everything, from the bed-

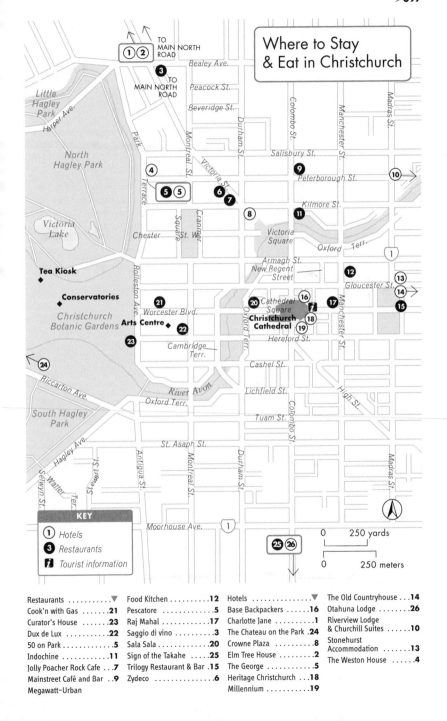

> Where to Stay
> & Eat in Christchurch

KEY
1 Hotels
3 Restaurants
i Tourist information

0   250 yards
0   250 meters

side notepads to the luxe bathroom products. Lovely details continually crop up, such as the magnificent brass handles on the entrance door and the verdigris brass banister. Adjacent to the Avon River and Hagley Park, it's just a short walk to the Arts Centre and downtown shopping. The two on-site restaurants are top-notch. ⊠ *50 Park Terr.* ☎ *03/379–4560* 🖷 *03/366–6747* ⊕ *www.thegeorge.com* ⌦ *55 rooms* ♨ *2 restaurants, tennis court, health club, massage, laundry facilities, laundry service, free parking* ⊟ *AE, DC, MC, V.*

$$$$ 🏨 **Heritage Christchurch.** You can go either modern or old-fashioned in your choice of rooms here. The Tower Building's rooms are contemporary, whereas the adjacent Old Government Building has suites in an Italian Renaissance style, complete with stained glass and dark-wood paneling. The rooms in both blocks have recently been refurbished. The OGB also has the sports facilities, heated pool, spa, and sauna in the basement, and Maddison's Restaurant on the ground floor. Watch out for international rugby players, as this is where some of them stay when there's an All Blacks match on at Jade Stadium. ⊠ *28–30 Cathedral Sq.* ☎ *03/377–9722 or 0800/936–936* 🖷 *03/377–9881* ⊕ *www.heritagehotels.co.nz* ⌦ *135 rooms, 40 suites* ♨ *Restaurant, pool, gym, sauna, spa, bar, lounge* ⊟ *AE, D, MC, V.*

$$$$ 🏨 **Otahuna Lodge.** Just 20 minutes from Christchurch and almost hidden by glorious century-old gardens is one of New Zealand's most important historic homes and best-kept secrets. Built in 1895 for Sir Heaton Rhodes, the three-story homestead has been lovingly restored to its former grandeur, yet has all the modern amenities you would expect in an exclusive luxury lodge. Each of Otahuna's six suites (there's also a lodge room) has a distinctive character and reveals a different element of the Otahuna story. Original fireplaces complement the rooms. Be sure to spend some time wandering the 30 acres of original gardens or taking a dip in the heated pool. ⊠ *224 Rhodes Rd., 17 km (10 mi) from Christchurch, Tai Tapu* ☎ *03/329–6333* 🖷 *03/329–6336* ⊕ *www.otahuna.co.nz* ⌦ *1 room, 6 suites* ♨ *Tennis court, pool, spa, horseback riding, library* ⊟ *AE, MC, V* ⊠ *MAP.*

$$$$ 🏨 **The Weston House.** Paintings, books, prints, flowers, and objets d'art decorate this carefully restored redbrick Georgian-style house opposite Hagley Park. The pair of spacious suites have private access; there's also a guest lounge, dining area, and secluded garden where you can take breakfast or just relax. The city center is a 10-minute walk away. ⊠ *62 Park Terr.* ☎ *03/366–0234* 🖷 *03/366–5454* ⊕ *www.westonhouse.co.nz* ⌦ *2 suites* ♨ *In-room broadband, lounge, laundry service, airport shuttle; no a/c* ⊟ *AE, DC, MC, V* ⊠ *BP.*

$$$$ 🏨 **Charlotte Jane.** Once a girls' school, this magnificent 1891 villa now
Fodor'sChoice sees pampered guests instead of disciplined students. The centrally lo-
★ cated house brims with beautiful elements: the Victorian veranda, a stained-glassed window above the entrance depicting the *Charlotte Jane* (one of the first four ships to bring settlers to Christchurch), a native kauri- and rimu-wood staircase, a rimu-paneled dining room, and period furniture throughout the 10 beautiful guest rooms. Just across the courtyard, a converted 1930s house holds two more suites, a rimu-lined bar, and a restaurant. Delicious breakfasts are served until 11 AM. ⊠ *110 Papanui Rd., Merivale* ☎ *03/355–1028* 🖷 *03/355–8882* ⊕ *www.*

charlotte-jane.co.nz 📞 *12 rooms* ⅄ *Restaurant, in-room VCRs, bar, library, laundry service, no-smoking rooms; no a/c* 🖃 *AE, MC, V* ❄ *BP.*

$$$-$$$$ 🏠 **Elm Tree House.** If you'd prefer a friendly experience away from the city center, this B&B should fill the bill. The 1920s historic house takes its name from the large tree in the front garden. Most of the rooms are upstairs, and each has a distinctive look, from the wood-paneled honeymoon suite to the ground-floor garden room with its French doors opening onto the garden. Restaurants are four minutes away. Papanui Road can be busy, but double-glazed windows keep things quiet. Sun streams into the enormous lounge through leaded glass windows, and you can pop an old favorite on the Wurlitzer jukebox. 🖂 *236 Papanui Rd., Merivale* ☎ *03/355-9731* 🖷 *03/355-9753* ⊕ *www.elmtreehouse.co.nz* 📞 *6 rooms* ⅄ *In-room data ports, lounge, laundry service* 🖃 *AE, MC, V* ☾ *Closed 2 wks in midwinter* ❄ *BP, CP.*

$$ 🏠 **The Chateau on the Park.** Surrounded by 5 acres of landscaped gardens, this Kiwi take on a French chateau even has its own boutique vineyard that will soon produce its own wine. The main building has an indoor water garden that wraps around the main entrance and foyer. Rooms are spacious, and all have a view of part of the greenery. Honeymooners gravitate to a special turret suite. Free golf rounds are offered at the Hagley Park golf course across the road. 🖂 *189 Deans Ave.* ☎ *03/348-8999* 🖷 *03/348-8990* ⊕ *www.chateau-park.co.nz* 📞 *190 rooms, 6 suites* ⅄ *Restaurant, minibars, pool, bar, golf privileges, laundry service* 🖃 *AE, DC, MC, V.*

$$ 🏠 **Millennium.** Right at the city's heart, on Cathedral Square, this glossy complex blends European and Asian touches. In the tasteful blue-and-gold rooms, for instance, Italian lamps stand beside Asian ginger jars. The Cathedral suites have the best views, overlooking the Cathedral and the Square. Have a cappuccino or a cocktail in Bar Santé and watch the goings-on in the busy square. 🖂 *14 Cathedral Sq.* ☎ *03/365-1111 or 0800/245-888* 🖷 *03/365-7676* ⊕ *www.millenniumchristchurch.co.nz* 📞 *162 rooms, 17 suites* ⅄ *Restaurant, café, minibars, in-room data ports, health club, sauna, bar, business services* 🖃 *AE, DC, MC, V.*

★ $$ 🏠 **Riverview Lodge & Churchill Suites.** This grand Edwardian house overlooking the Avon is one of the finest historic B&Bs in Christchurch. Native timber is used throughout the house, such as the solid kauri stairs and doors. All rooms are upstairs, and the three front rooms provide great views of the river. In an adjacent two-story Edwardian town house are two sunny, spacious suites, each with a lounge and kitchen. The lower-floor suite has one bedroom and French doors that open out to a secluded garden. 🖂 *361 Cambridge Terr.* ☎ *03/365-2860* 🖷 *03/365-2845* ⊕ *www.riverview.net.nz* 📞 *4 rooms, 2 suites* ⅄ *Boating, bicycles; no a/c* 🖃 *MC, V* ❄ *BP.*

$ 🏠 **Stonehurst Accommodation.** A cluster of 11 yellow buildings near the city center offers various room setups, from powered camper-van sites and backpacker rooms to apartments. The clientele is nicely varied. Be careful going up the driveway, as it's a bit rough. 🖂 *241 Gloucester St.* ☎ *03/379-4620 or 0508/786-633* 🖷 *03/379-4647* ⊕ *www.stonehurst.co.nz* 📞 *16 rooms, 7 singles, 11 dorm rooms* ⅄ *BBQ, some in-room broadband, pool, bar, 3 lounges, free parking* 🖃 *AE, DC, MC, V.*

¢–$ 🏨 **Base Backpackers.** You can't get any closer to the city center than this upmarket hostel—it's right in Cathedral Square in the former *Christchurch Star* newspaper building. Women travelers score with a special female-only wing called Sanctuary, where rooms come with a bit of pampering: fluffy pillows, skin-care products, and hair dryers in the bathroom. They keep the fun in-house with the Saints and Sinners bar. ✉ *56 Cathedral Sq.* ☎ *03/982–2225 or 0800/227–369* 🖷 *03/982–2226* ⊕ *www.basebackpackers.com* ⤵ *7 rooms, 45 dorm rooms* ♨ *BBQ, kitchen, bar, lounge, Internet room, travel services; no TV in some rooms* ▭ *AE, MC, V.*

¢ 🏨 **The Old Countryhouse.** This old house is actually two colorful restored villas, both with polished wooden floors and handmade, native-wood furniture. You can whip up breakfast in one of the two large, cheery communal kitchens. The dorm rooms have three to seven beds apiece. The courtyard between the villas catches the sun. It's a 15-minute walk from town but on a bus route. ✉ *437 Gloucester St.* ☎ *03/381–5504* ⊕ *www.oldcountryhousenz.com* ⤵ *16 rooms* ♨ *BBQ, 2 kitchens, lounge, library, Internet room* ▭ *MC, V.*

Nightlife & the Arts

The *Christchurch Press* newspaper is a reliable source on the city's arts and entertainment scenes. The Wednesday edition's special arts section lists events and venues, and Thursday's edition has a gig guide on shows and more. You could also check out the Web sites ⊕ www.bethere.org.nz for arts and entertainment listings and ⊕ www.jagg.co.nz for information on live music. Tickets for many performance venues and concerts are sold through **Ticketek** (☎ 03/377–8899). You can find Ticketek outlets in shopping malls. If you're out late on a weekend and looking for a cheap way back to your room, try the Midnight Express bus (*see* Bus Travel *in* Christchurch A to Z, *below*), which runs until 4 AM.

The Arts

Christchurch has a buzzing arts scene, with choirs, orchestras, and theater, not to mention dozens of art galleries. Every two years the city is host of a midwinter **Arts Festival** (⊕ www.artsfestival.co.nz). And in alternate years, another biennial arts festival called **SCAPE** (⊕ www.artandindustry.org.nz) focuses on urban arts. The next Arts Festival will be in winter 2007; the next SCAPE will be in spring 2008.

ART GALLERIES Although the Christchurch Art Gallery—Te Puna O Waiwhetu is the main magnet for the city's visual arts, there are plenty of smaller galleries to check out as well. For more information, pick up the annually published *Canterbury Arts Trail* booklet at the visitor bureau.

Centre of Contemporary Art (COCA). This gallery actually has six galleries showing 60 exhibitions a year, with a long history of showing contemporary works by Canterbury artists—in fact, it was founded as the Canterbury Society of Arts back in 1880. Now their shows mix established names with up-and-comers and Kiwi artists. One gallery, Artzone, exhibits work by children and runs art classes. ✉ *66 Gloucester St.* ☎ *03/366–7261* ⊕ *www.coca.org.nz* 🏷 *Donation requested* ⊗ *Weekdays 10–5, weekends noon–4.*

Physics Room. In rooms high above Alice in Videoland, the Physics Room shows contemporary art (video works, installations, and so on) and occasionally puts on performances, talks, and other public programs. ✉ *209 Tuam St., 2nd fl.* ☎ *03/379–5583* ⊕ *www.physicsroom.org.nz* ⊙ *Tues.–Fri. 10–5, Sat. 11–4.*

Te Toi Mana. Māori artist Riki Manuel often carves in this Arts Centre space. The gallery focuses on traditional and contemporary Māori art and is a good place to find creative souvenirs. ✉ *Arts Centre, Hereford St.* ☎ *03/366–4943* ⊙ *Daily 10–5.*

FILMS Short film festivals have become very popular, particularly in the Christchurch Art Gallery auditorium. Each year in the second half of July there is an international film festival with showings at the Rialto cinema, and it often includes a homegrown section. The independent **Academy Theatre** (✉ 25 Hereford St. ☎ 03/366–0167 ⊕ www.artfilms. co.nz) in the Arts Centre is the place to hit for indie and foreign flicks.

MUSIC If you're here in summer, be sure to check out the schedule for the city-sponsored **Summertimes Festival** (⊕ www.summertimes.org.nz), which includes several free concerts in Hagley Park. The festival kicks off with a New Year's Eve party in Cathedral Square and culminates in "Classical Sparks," music punctuated with fireworks, usually held in late February or early March.

Town Hall (✉ 86 Kilmore St.) is host to many performances of the classical persuasion, including those by the **Canterbury Opera** (☎ 03/366–9932 ⊕ www.canterburyopera.com), the **Christchurch City Choir** (☎ 03/366–6927 ⊕ www.christchurchcitychoir.co.nz), and the **Christchurch Symphony Orchestra** (☎ 03/379–3886 ⊕ www.chsymph.co.nz).

THEATER The **Court Theatre** (✉ Arts Centre, 20 Worcester Blvd. ☎ 03/963–0870 ⊕ www.courttheatre.org.nz) is New Zealand's leading theater company. In its two auditoriums the company performs everything from Shakespeare to contemporary plays by New Zealand playwrights. The Court also offers children's plays during the holidays; the Court Jesters run the hilarious Scared Scriptless improv-comedy sessions on Friday night.

Nightlife

Christchurch's after-dark action has picked up over the years, particularly as more bars open up along Lichfield Street and Manchester Street, two drags popular with students and young pros.

For concentrated action, your best bet is to head to the bars and cafés along the area known as **the Strip.** This is a small section of Oxford Terrace, one of the streets that follows the curves of the Avon River, between Cashel Street and Worcester Boulevard. The end of the Strip near the Bridge of Remembrance has the younger, rowdier crowds. People often spill out onto the footpath, but be sure to do all your drinking indoors, as there's a ban on drinking in public places in certain parts of the city. The **Coyote** (✉ 126 Oxford Terr. ☎ 03/366–6055) serves good food during the day and then transforms into a popular bar, with partying until the break of dawn. With its old-fashioned decor, the **Boulevard Restaurant** (✉ Oxford Terr. and Hereford St. ☎ 03/374–6676) caters to those looking for a more refined late-night experience at weekends. **Sticky Fingers** (⊠ Clarendon Towers ☎ 03/366–6451) has some intimate booths where you can sip a quiet cocktail.

For some natural suds in the city center try the **Loaded Hog Bar & Restaurant** (⊠ Manchester and Cashel Sts. ☎ 03/366–6674). This brewery produces excellent beers such as Hogs Dark and Hogs Gold. Check out the amusing caricatures of pop culture icons. If you just want to kick back over a coffee or a glass of wine, try **Bar Santé in the Square** at the Millenium Hotel (⊠ 14 Cathedral Sq. ☎ 03/365–1111).

For live music head over to the Arts Centre to **Dux de Lux** (⊠ Hereford and Montreal Sts. ☎ 03/366–6919), a standby on the local-band circuit. Sometimes there's a cover charge. Live jazz starts at 7:30 Tuesday to Saturday at **Sammy's Jazz Review** (⊠ 14 Bedford Row ☎ 03/377–8618). If folk music is more your speed, try the **Canterbury Folk Club** at (⊠ Cokers Hotel, 52 Manchester St. ☎ 03/388–8478), which takes over the bar on Sunday evening.

When all else has closed, you could always make your way to the 24-hour **Christchurch Casino** (⊠ 30 Victoria St. ☎ 03/365–9999) for blackjack, American roulette, baccarat, gaming machines, and other ways to try your luck. Dress is smart-casual or better; you will be turned away at the door if you arrive in jeans. There are free shuttles to and from local hotels and motels.

Sports & the Outdoors

Beaches

There are three main beaches around Christchurch: Sumner Beach, New Brighton Beach, and Taylor's Mistake. **Sumner Beach** is a pleasant place for a long, relaxing walk between Shag Rock and Scarborough Hill. Walk the first section along the sand to Cave Rock, which you can climb or walk through at low tide—it has wonderful acoustics. Walk the rest of the way along the esplanade, as the beach is fairly rocky. Sumner Village is based around the Cave Rock area, and there are a number of restaurants, including one right on the beach. You can catch a number 30 bus here if you don't have a car.

New Brighton Beach, about 8 km (5 mi) from the city center, is popular with surfers and fishers. A long pier goes well out into the surf, a great place to stroll whether the sea is calm or rough. The number 5 bus goes here. Experienced surfers prefer **Taylor's Mistake** because the waves are higher. You can drive there over the Scarborough Hill or walk over a track, but there is no public transport.

Bicycling

Christchurch's relative flatness makes for easy biking, and the city has cultivated good resources for cyclists. White lines, and sometimes red-colored tarmac, denote cycling lanes on city streets, and holding bays are at the ready near intersections. You can pick up a route map from the city council; there's a particularly nice paved pedestrian and cycling path along the Avon running from the Bridge of Remembrance.

Cycles can be rented from **Cyclone Cycles** (✉ 245 Colombo St. ☎ 03/332–9588) for around $30 for half a day, including helmet, and $80 a week. **City Cycle Hire** (✉ 73 Wrights Rd., Addington ☎ 03/339–4020 or 0800/343–848 ⊕ www.cyclehire-tours.co.nz) has mountain, touring, and tandem bikes. Rentals include helmets and cost about $25 for a half day and $35 for a full day; they'll deliver your bike to your accommodation.

The **Mountain Bike Adventure Company** (☎ 03/339–4020 or 0800/424–534 ⊕ www.cyclehire-tours.co.nz) offers a $60 package including a Gondola ticket to the summit station and all the equipment needed for a safe ride down. There's the choice of an off-road mountain-bike trail or a scenic road route down to the beach and back to base.

Golf

With views of Mt. Hutt and Rakaia Gorge, the 18-hole **Terrace Downs High Country Resort** course has to be one of the most scenic in the South Island. You can rent equipment, and if you truly can't tear yourself away, you can book a villa for the night. The luxurious suites and chalets overlook the golf course and the mighty Southern Alps. Greens fees start at $65 per person. ✉ *Coleridge Rd.* ☎ *03/318–6943 or 0800/465–373* ⊕ *www.terracedowns.co.nz.*

The 18-hole championship golf course at the **Clearwater Golf Club** was built on the old Waimakariri riverbed near Christchurch Airport. Home to the NZPGA Championship, it is playable year-round and offers a choice of five tee positions. The greens fee is $125; rental equipment is on hand. ✉ *Clearwater Ave.* ☎ *03/360–1103* ⊕ *www.clearwaternz.com.*

Horse Trekking

Horse whisperer Kate Tapley and her team guide gentle rides with **Otahuna Horse Riding** (✉ Rhodes Rd., Tai Tapu ☎ 03/329–0160 ⊕ www.otahunariding.co.nz), set on a historic estate up around the Port Hills. Emphasis is on connection with your horse using natural horsemanship, and each session begins with a partnering session. You'll have stunning views of the Canterbury Plains and the encircling mountain ranges from your saddle. Guided rides start at $90.

Rugby

Canterbury fans are as rugby-mad as the rest of the country, but this is hardly surprising when the first match ever played in New Zealand took place in 1862 in Cranmer Square, in central Christchurch. Every Saturday in winter you can catch little All-Blacks-in-the-making playing games in Hagley Park and suburban parks. Then cheer the Crusaders, the Canterbury rugby team, on their home turf at **Jade Stadium** (✉ 30 Stevens St., Phillipstown ☎ 03/379–1765 ⊕ www.jadestadium.co.nz). The stadium also is host to All Blacks games and international cricket matches.

Walking

There are many good walking routes in the city, including the path along the Avon River in the inner city. You can pick up a free brochure on routes at the visitor center. The track around the edge of Hagley Park is especially popular with walkers and joggers.

To get some literary history with your stroll, follow the city center's Christchurch Writers Trail. More than 30 buildings with connections to celebrated writers have been designated with plaques, and you can follow a route between them. Writers so honored include crime writer Dame Ngaio Marsh, children's writer Margaret Mahy, and Booker Prize winner Keri Hulme.

Shopping

Markets

The **Arts Centre Saturday and Sunday Market** is awash in Kiwi goods, such as handmade sweaters and woolens. Inside the Arts Centre buildings, the **Boulevard** consists of more than two dozen shops and studios for artisans and crafts workers, from potters to weavers to some very good jewelry makers. The quality of work varies considerably from shop to shop, but this is one of the few places where many crafts workers are represented under one roof. Other boutiques dot the complex as well; all are open daily. ✉ *Worcester Blvd.* ☎ *03/363–2836.*

On Sunday from 8 to 2, the parking lot of the Riccarton Racecourse fills with hundreds of stalls for the **Riccarton Market.** Soak up the atmosphere and rummage through everything from secondhand books lying on rolls of carpet to carpentry tools to sheepskin slippers. ✉ *Racecourse Rd., Riccarton* ☎ *No phone.*

Shopping Streets

The **City Mall** area around Cashel and High streets has been out of bounds to cars since the early 1980s. Major branches of music and clothing chains make up most of the frontage here, but there are some one-offs worth stopping at, such as Ballantyne's cashmere, the Vault craft boutique, and Wild Places for souvenirs.

Graduates from the polytech fashion school only have to cross the road to show their wares on **High Street,** a shopping strip lined with early-20th-century buildings. Places such as Quadrata and Tango display cutting-edge clothes; more conservative shoppers seeking local designers should visit Panache in **Tuam Street.** Secondhand booksellers, antiques and decor stores, and the overflowing Globe café keep things busy.

Distinctive blue-and-yellow art deco–era facades line the pedestrian zone of **New Regent Street** between Gloucester and Armagh streets. The buildings are now filled with cafés, restaurants, and boutiques, and New Regent buzzes constantly with window-shoppers and strollers. Some of the best stops are Tolaga Bay for cashmere, Boxes for jewelry and floaty scarves, and Cubana for Cuban cigars and coffee. Look up to the upper stories for more: Shoezies, for instance, stocks embroidered boots, and Canterbury Fare bursts with wines and cheeses. Pause for a smoothie at the Daily Grind or some ice cream at Six Chairs Missing. Do watch out for traffic, though—the tram runs right through the sidewalk cafés on its way to the city's newest shopping center, Cathedral Junction. This colorful street merits a photo op even if your plastic has no credit left.

Victoria Street, which cuts diagonally across the city center's usual grid pattern out from Bealey Avenue, has a good mix of clothing and decor shops interspersed with cafés. Two standouts are Frogmore, for gifts such as beaded jewelry cases and candelabra, and Redcurrent, for table decorations and baskets. If you need a hat for a wedding or the horse races in November, the Hat Shop has a good range, even for men.

Specialty Shops

de Spa Chocolaterie. Their delicious sweets pair Belgian chocolate with Kiwi ingredients (fruit for certain fillings, for instance). For a behind-the-scenes look, visit the factory at 1013 Ferry Road. ✉ *663 Colombo St.* ☎ *03/379–2203.*

Johnsons Grocery. The shelves groan with international treats in this throwback to an earlier era. If you can't find *irn bru* (a Scottish drink) or English toffee in the supermarket, you should find it in this shop. ✉ *797 Colombo St.* ☎ *03/366–3027.*

Kathmandu. Started by a Melbourne medical student 30 years ago, this company sells a colorful range of well-priced outdoor clothing, backpacks, and tents. Base camp for the whole global operation is in Christchurch. There's another branch at 124 Riccarton Road. ✉ *36–46 Lichfield St.* ☎ *03/366–7148.*

Scorpio Bookshop. Don't be surprised if the owner's dog wanders in and out of this independent bookstore. Started in the early 1970s, the shop stocks a wide range of self-help/spiritualism books as well as design studies, philosophy tomes, and travelogues. ✉ *79 Hereford St.* ☎ *03/379–2882 or 0800/726–774.*

Untouched World. All things hip and natural in New Zealand meet up here. Apart from the store's own line of stylish, outdoorsy clothing made from merino mink (a mixture of possum fur and merino wool), organic cotton, and merino silk (100% merino wool), you'll find New Zealand handcrafted jewelry, natural skin-care products, and great gift ideas. The attached restaurant serves fresh food in its native garden setting. There's also a branch in the Arts Centre in the central city. ✉ *155 Roydvale Ave., Burnside* ☎ *03/357–9399.*

CHRISTCHURCH ESSENTIALS

Transportation

BY AIR

Christchurch Airport (CHC) is 10 km (6 mi) northwest of the city. The domestic terminal is at the left-hand end of the complex (the entrance is under the clock), and the international terminal is at the other end. Shops and cafés linking the two sections close after the last flight. The banks can be found at the international end (they keep flight hours), and the travel center is at the domestic end.

International flights to Christchurch are on the rise. Air New Zealand flies direct from Los Angeles to Christchurch four days a week, and the addition of Freedom Air and Pacific Blue (Virgin Air) to the skies alongside Air New Zealand and Qantas has boosted the flight options between Christchurch and Australia.

Origin Pacific, Qantas, and Air New Zealand all link Christchurch with domestic cities on both North and South islands. Flying time between Christchurch and Auckland is an hour and 20 minutes; the flight to Queenstown takes just over an hour.

🛈 **Airport Christchurch International Airport** ⊠ Memorial Ave., Harewood ☎ 03/358-5029 ⊕ www.christchurch-airport.co.nz.

🛈 **Carriers Air New Zealand** ☎ 03/374-7100 or 0800/737-000 ⊕ www.airnewzealand.com. **Freedom Air** ☎ 0800/600-500 ⊕ www.freedomair.com. **Origin Pacific** ☎ 03/547-2020 or 0800/302-302 ⊕ www.originpacific.co.nz. **Pacific Blue Airlines** ☎ 0800/670-000 ⊕ www.flypacificblue.com. **Qantas** ☎ 0800/808-767 ⊕ www.qantas.com.au.

AIRPORT
TRANSFERS
A never-ending line of taxis queues up at the airport to offer $32 fares to city hotels. A less-expensive option is the Super Shuttle (reservations recommended). The van and its trailer often wait outside for incoming flights or can be called once your flight has landed. They charge about $15 per passenger to city hotels and depending on the number of people traveling, the fare is reduced. The cheapest transit between the city and airport are two $5 options: Sunshine Shuttle runs a transfer service, and Metro buses go between the airport and Cathedral Square from 6 AM to 11:35 PM daily.

🛈 **Blue Star Taxis** ☎ 03/379-9799. **Metro** ⊠ Lichfield and Colombo Sts. ☎ 03/366-8855 ⊕ www.metroinfo.org.nz. **Sunshine Shuttle** ☎ 03/379-1699. **Super Shuttle** ☎ 03/357-9950.

BY BUS TO & FROM CHRISTCHURCH

InterCity runs New Zealand's most extensive bus network. There's daily service between Christchurch and other major South Island destinations; affiliated companies link to smaller places such as Akaroa and Hanmer Springs. The InterCity Travel Centre can sort out bookings for InterCity, Newmans, and Hanmer Connection buses. The Coast to Coast Shuttle bus goes to Arthur's Pass Village from Christchurch.

🛈 **Coast to Coast Shuttle** ☎ 0800/800-847. **InterCity Coachlines Christchurch Travel Centre** ⊠ 123 Worcester St. ☎ 03/377-0951 ⊕ www.intercitycoach.co.nz.

BY BUS WITHIN CHRISTCHURCH

Christchurch's city bus system may look confusing because it is run by more than one company, but luckily it has a thorough Web site and a helpful hotline. Tickets cost $2.50 a trip and can be used for one transfer fare if traveling on another bus within a two-hour period. The easiest place to catch a bus is the Bus Exchange, as most buses go through it. Major bus routes have electronically enabled bus stops that indicate how long the bus is away from the stop.

Yellow buses (and some specially signed red buses) are free shuttles, running circuits every 10 minutes during the day through the city center, linking the Casino with Moorhouse Avenue. Look for marked bus stops. There are yet more bus lines, such as the Metrostar and Orbiter, that don't come into the city center at all, but instead link shopping centers and other suburban facilities.

The Red Bus line offers MetroPasses, or pre-paid travel cards; $1.90 will get you 2 hours of unlimited travel, $3.80 gives unlimited travel for a day and $19 gives unlimited travel for a week. Red Bus also runs the Midnight Express, a bus that follows four set routes on the hour from midnight to 4 AM on Friday and Saturday night.

The Christchurch Best Attractions bus service provides transport (and this can be combined with the entry fees) for several attractions: Willowbank, the Gondola, and the Antarctic Centre for $5 per attraction. Tickets can be booked at the Information Centre; the bus stop is opposite the main entrance to the visitor bureau.

🚹 **Christchurch Best Attractions** ☎ 0800/484–485 ⊕ www.chchattractions.co.nz. **Christchurch Metro Services** ☎ 03/366-8855 ⊕ www.metroinfo.org.nz. **Red Bus** ☎ 0800/733-287 ⊕ www.redbus.co.nz.

🚹 Bus Depot **Bus Exchange** ✉ 237–239 Lichfield St.

BY CAR

Getting in and out of Christchurch is quite easy, as a clear lattice of streets leads to the city center. However, central Christchurch is a warren of one-way streets; it's best to leave your car in a parking lot while exploring this area. The city council has a number of parking buildings, marked with a blue "P" sign. Some of these, notably two in Lichfield Street, one above Farmers, in Oxford Terrace and the building on the corner of Manchester and Gloucester streets, offer free parking for the first hour and charge $1 per half hour thereafter. Gas stations are mostly on roads leading out of the city, such as Cranford, Blenheim, Lincoln, and Riccarton roads. Peak traffic times here run from 7:30 to 9 AM and 3 to 6:30 PM.

Arthur's Pass is a 2½- to 3-hour drive southwest out of Christchurch on Highway 73. The pass is the main artery to the West Coast; be aware that its western side is extremely steep and quite unnerving for the uninitiated.

All the major car-rental companies have desks at the Christchurch International Airport. An increasingly popular way to see the South Island is by motor home; the rental prices for these halve in winter. Apex Rentals are particularly easy to deal with and are happy for their cars to explore more outlying areas. They give a copy of the 125-page *New Zealand Driving Holidays* booklet with each rental.

🚹 Rental Agencies **Apex** ✉ Christchurch International Airport ☎ 03/357-4536 or 0800/ 400-121. **Avis** ✉ Christchurch International Airport ☎ 03/358-9661 or 0800/655-111. **Budget** ✉ 15 Lichfield St. ☎ 03/357-0231 or 0800/-652-227. **Hertz** ✉ 46 Lichfield St. ☎ 03/366-0549 or 0800/654-321. **Maui Motorhomes** ✉ 530 Memorial Ave. ☎ 03/ 358-4159 or 0800/651-080.

BY TRAIN

One of the greatest little train journeys in the world, the *TranzAlpine Express*, travels through the Southern Alps to the West Coast, weaving through gorgeous scenery, from the tawny fields of the Canterbury Plains through rugged gorges and high mountains to the jade green, wild West Coast bush. One daily train each way goes between Christchurch and Greymouth; the one-way trip takes 4½ hours, leaving Christchurch at 8:15 AM and Greymouth at 12:45 PM.

The *TranzAlpine* and the *TransCoastal* (to Kaikoura and Picton) are all that remains of the South Island's once-extensive train network. The *Tranz-Alpine Express* heads daily from Christchurch to Arthur's Pass Village at 8:15 AM. The train carries on from there to Greymouth, returning later in the day to Christchurch. The *TransCoastal* to Kaikoura and Picton leaves daily at 7 AM.

🚆 Train Station **Christchurch Railway Station** ✉ Troup Dr. ☎ 0800/872-468.

🚆 Train Information **TranzAlpine** ☎ 0800/872-467 ⊕ www.tranzscenic.co.nz.

Tranz Scenic ☎ 0800/872-467 ⊕ www.tranzscenic.co.nz.

BY TRAM

Christchurch's Tramway serves as an attraction in its own right and doubles as a way to get around when those feet tire. A city circuit takes in Cathedral Square, Worcester Boulevard, Rolleston Avenue, Armagh Street, and New Regent Street and the Cathedral Junction mall complex. It stops close to all major attractions, including the Arts Centre, Botanic Gardens, and Canterbury Museum. A full-day pass costs $12.50 and is valid for 48 hours.

🚆 **Christchurch Tramway** ☎ 03/366-7830 ⊕ www.tram.co.nz.

Contacts & Resources

BANKS & EXCHANGE SERVICES

Banks have been steadily extending their hours of operation; some branches are even open on Saturday as well as weekdays. ATMs are easily found in the city center and suburban shopping areas. Some hotels will do cash advances on credit cards with a bit of warning.

EMERGENCIES

Although Christchurch does not have an all-night pharmacy, Urgent Pharmacy stays open from 9 AM to 11 PM. For minor health problems and shorter waiting times, visit the 24-hour clinic on Colombo Street.

🚑 Emergency Services **Christchurch Hospital** ✉ Riccarton and Deans Aves. ☎ 03/364-0640. **Fire, police, and ambulance** ☎ 111. **24 Hour Surgery** ✉ Bealey Ave. and Colombo St. ☎ 03/365-7777. **Urgent Pharmacy** ✉ Bealey Ave. and Colombo St. ☎ 03/365-7777.

MAIL & INTERNET

The main post office is near the Arts Centre, but it's not the most central. A particularly convenient post office is next to the ANZ Bank in Cathedral Square, open Monday through Saturday. Like all other areas of New Zealand, packages can be mailed or freighted from the local NZ Post center (see above). Christchurch, however, is the only city in the South Island with a FedEx office, situated at the airport; it's open weekdays from 8 to 5.

For e-mail, hit one of the Internet cafés that have blossomed all over the city (although the coffee is often instant if it's offered at all). Prices vary between $3 and $5 per hour, and other services could include burning photos onto CDs or calling internationally via the Internet. New Zealand's largest Internet café is in a former cinema: eBlahBlah Internet Centre has more than 100 computers and offers video conferencing, faxes, cell-phone rentals, Webcams, and even luggage storage. For something smaller try the eCafe in the New Registry building in the Arts Centre. Or you might appreciate the real coffee and the candy-colored Apple iBooks in the High Street Cafe.

Internet Cafés **eBlahBlah Internet Centre** ⊠ 77 Cathedral Sq. ☎ 03/377-2381 ⊕ www.vadal.net. **eCafe** ⊠ New Registry Bldg., Arts Centre ☎ 03/365-6480. **High Street Cafe** ⊠ High St. at Manchester St. ☎ 03/379-4023.

Post Office **Cathedral Square NZ Post** ⊠ 3 Cathedral Sq. ☎ 03/377-5411 or 0800/501-501 ⊕ www.nzpost.co.nz.

Shipping Services **FedEx** ⊠ Christchurch International Airport ☎ 0800/733-339

TOURS

BICYCLE TOURS Christchurch Bike Tours organizes two-hour guided bicycle tours ($25), offered daily from November to March. The route goes through the city center and Hagley Park, then out to Mona Vale and Riccarton Bush before heading back into the city center. Cycles and helmets are provided. Meet outside the visitor center at 10 AM.

Christchurch Bike Tours ☎ 03/366-0337 ⊕ www.chchbiketours.co.nz.

BOAT TOURS Punting on the Avon is perfectly suited to the pace of Christchurch. You can hire punts with expert boatmen, who also point out the sights along the way, at the Worcester Street Bridge, near the corner of Oxford Terrace, daily from 9 AM–10 PM in summer and from 9 to 4 the rest of the year. A 20-minute trip costs $12.

Punting on the Avon ⊠ Worcester Blvd. bridge landing ☎ 03/353-5994.

PRIVATE GUIDES Jack Tregear, descendant of a pre-Adamite (pre-1850) settler, provides a personal historic tour of Christchurch. It covers Lyttleton, Sumner, and the Canterbury Provincial Council buildings and takes just over three hours. The tour includes an elegant morning tea and entry to the Timeball Station at Lyttleton. Jack also takes trips to Akaroa.

Jack Tregear ☎ 03/344-5588 or 0800/344-5588 ⊕ www.jtnztours.co.nz.

SIGHTSEEING TOURS Christchurch Sightseeing Tours has three routes: one including major town sights plus the beaches at Sumner and the Lyttelton harbor, one for Heritage homes, and another that gives you access to private gardens. Each costs between $35 and $39.

Christchurch Sightseeing Tours ☎ 03/366-9660 ⊕ www.christchurchtours.co.nz.

WALKING TOURS Guided walking tours ($10) of the city by members of the **Christchurch Personal Guiding Service** depart daily at 10 and 1 from the red-and-black kiosk in Cathedral Square. (There is no morning walk from May to September.) The tours take about two hours.

Personal Guiding Service ☎ 03/389-6475.

VISITOR INFORMATION

The visitor information center is open daily from 8:30 to 6. Its Web site is a great resource where you can find out about everything from lodging to bike rentals. The visitor center also distributes a monthly brochure called *Canterbury Today/Tonight*, covering sights, events, and more.

Another good local Web site is ⊕ www.localeye.info, which has anything and everything about Christchurch both from a visiting and a local perspective. *See* Nightlife & the Arts, *above,* for sites with entertainment listings. *Avenues,* a local magazine with events listings and reviews, is also worth a browse.

🚩**Arthur's Pass Visitor Centre** ⊠ SH8, Arthur's Pass 🕾 03/318-9211. **Christchurch–Canterbury i-Site Visitor Information Centre** ⊠ Old Post Office Bldg., Cathedral Sq. 🕾 03/379-9629 ⊕ www.christchurchnz.net.

ARTHUR'S PASS & CANTERBURY

If you have more than a day or two to spend in the Christchurch area, head out to the countryside for a change of pace. East of the city, you can explore the wonderful coastline of the Banks Peninsula. The peninsula's two harbors, Lyttelton and Akaroa, were formed from the remnants of two ancient volcanoes; their steep, grassy walls drop dramatically to the sea. Looking north, consider stopping in Waipara and its wineries if you're en route to or from Kaikoura or Hanmer. Hanmer Springs' thermal baths are good for a relaxing soak. Or head south or west of town into the Canterbury Plains countryside, perhaps to do some skiing at Mt. Hutt or to drive the scenic highway to Geraldine and Timaru. Thanks to irrigation and investment, the plains are changing just as rapidly as the city. Where once sheep and cattle grazed, you're now just as likely to spot deer and ostriches. And if you're heading to the West Coast by either road or rail, then Arthur's Pass is worth investigating. The train only stops there a short time, but a road trip will allow time for a meal and a hike in the mountains. You should set an entire day aside for any of these side trips, or, better still, go overnight.

Arthur's Pass

🕑 *153 km (96 mi) northwest of Christchurch.*

Arthur's Pass National Park, a spectacular alpine region, is a favorite hiking destination. On the way to the pass, along State Highway 73 from Christchurch, you'll pass the **Castle Hill Conservation Area,** which is littered with interesting rock formations. The gray limestone rocks range in height from 3 to 164 feet and in spring and fall they're tackled by climbers keen to go bouldering. Nearby **Craigieburn Conservation Park** has wonderful beech and fern forests. Sheltered as they are by the Southern Alps, these parklands get far less precipitation than the western side of the mountains. Still, the area is subject to heavy snowfalls in winter and dramatic changes in the weather year-round.

Arthur's Pass straddles the Main Divide (the midline of the Alps) and is the major mid-island corridor to the West Coast. The route was first surveyed by Arthur Dudley Dobson during the 1860s as European settlers looked for a quick way through the mountains. The discovery of gold on the West Coast spurred the construction of a road, which was built in 1865. When the railway arrived, in 1923, the pass's skiing and hiking opportunities came to the fore, and the TranzAlpine train service now offers a supreme way to see this rugged area without getting your shoes dirty.

The setting is undeniably gorgeous: waterfalls, gorges, alpine herbs and flowers, grasslands, and stunning snowcapped peaks. The landscape and vegetation change dramatically according to the altitude and rainfall, from the drier beech forests and tussock grasslands on the eastern side to the dense forestation on the steep western slopes, which get five times more rain. Above the tree line you'll find snowfields and, between November and March, masses of wildflowers, including giant buttercups. Around the summit you'll also have a good chance of seeing *kea,* the South Island's particularly intelligent and curious birds. More information on the park is available on the **Department of Conservation's Web site** (⊕ www.doc.govt.nz).

The west side of the pass has had a bad reputation for its steep, winding, narrow road. The good news is that the highway has been upgraded and a viaduct now eliminates the need to drive through the main slip-prone area. At this writing, more upgrades were on the way. **Arthur's Pass Village,** at 737 meters (2,395 feet), isn't much to speak of, and in bad weather it looks rather forlorn, surrounded by cloud-covered peaks and dark valleys. A restaurant and a store provide basic food supplies, and there are several places to stay as well as a Department of Conservation visitor center.

Where to Stay & Eat

$$$$
Fodor's Choice
★

Wilderness Lodge Arthur's Pass. That pot of gold at the end of the rainbow is in fact a Southern Alps lodge surrounded by spectacular peaks, beech forests, and serene lakes. This back-to-nature lodge shares 6,000 acres with a sheep farm and nature reserve in a valley called Te Ko Awa a Aniwaniwa (Valley of the Mother of Rainbows) by its first Māori visitors. From a hillside perch it overlooks the Waimakariri River, which has carved a gaping swath through the pass. Rooms have balcony views of this incredible area. Sheep farming is the order of the day here: every second day guests get to muster sheep with border collies and can also help blade-shear the sheep. By taking advantage of the walks and guided nature day trips included in the rate, staying here also gives you an education in rare high-country ecology. Longer, guided trips in the region can take you to limestone caves, a glacier basin, or rare alpine plants. ⊠ *130 km (81 mi) west of Christchurch on State Hwy. 73 Arthur's Pass* ☎ *03/318–9246* ⊕ *www.wildernesslodge.co.nz* ⇆ *20 rooms, 4 suites* ⚓ *Boating, fishing, lounge, library, laundry service; no a/c* ☐ *AE, DC, MC, V* ⊙ *MAP.*

¢–$
Mountain House Backpackers and Cottages. If you're looking for a bargain, this is the place to come. You can sign up for one of the bedrooms in the cottages, reserve an entire cottage, or choose a bed in the four- or eight-person dorm rooms in the main lodge. The decor may be plain, but you can't argue with the impressive peaks right outside your window. ⊠ *State Hwy. 73* ☎ *03/318–9258* ☎ *03/318–9058* ⊕ *www. trampers.co.nz* ⇆ *4 cottages, 1 dorm room, 5 rooms* ⚓ *BBQ, some kitchens, lounge, laundry facilities, Internet room* ☐ *MC, V.*

Sports & the Outdoors

HIKING Arthur's Pass National Park has plenty of half- and full-day hikes and 11 backcountry tracks with overnight huts for backpacking. A popular short walk near Arthur's Pass Village is the Dobson Walk, which crosses the summit. It's a good introduction to subalpine and alpine plants; the alpine flowers are in bloom from November to February. It takes roughly

1½ hours to do the circuit. For a full-day hike, trails leading to the summits of various mountains are found all along State Highway 73. You'll need to be prepared for variable weather conditions. Two of the most popular challenging overnight treks are the Cass Saddle trip and the Minga/Deception route over Goat Pass. For these, you'll need an experienced leader and full gear. The **Department of Conservation Visitor Centre** (☎ 03/318–9211 ⊕ www.doc.govt.nz) has up-to-date information on weather and trail conditions. Fill out an intention form, and remember to let them know when you have completed your trip. The site ⊕ www.softrock.co.nz is another good source for information on mountaineering conditions.

Lyttelton

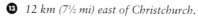 *12 km (7½ mi) east of Christchurch.*

Lyttelton, a busy port town, was the arrival point for many of the early Canterbury settlers. The Canterbury Pilgrims' landing place is marked by a rock near the road entrance to the port. Those who came off the ships in the early 1850s walked up the Bridle Path to Ferrymead while their belongings were brought around Godley Heads and across the Sumner Bar by boat, a perilous journey.

Because of its relative isolation from Christchurch—the road tunnel connecting the two was built only in 1964—Lyttelton has developed its own distinctive feel, attracting creative types who like the small-town atmosphere. Although the tunnel road is a convenient way to get here, the best way to explore the area is to drive from Christchurch to Sumner, where you can take a quick walk on the beach, then head over Evans Pass and down into Lyttelton. Another very scenic route is to follow the main street, Colombo, east out of the city, up the Port Hills, and over Dyers Pass to Governors Bay. Then turn left and head back along the harbor edge to Lyttelton.

Renovated wooden villas now rise halfway up what was once a volcanic crater. There's a small maritime museum on Gladstone Quay, but the main local sight is the castlelike **Timeball Station.** In the days before GPS and atomic clocks, ships would make sure their chronometers were accurate by checking them when the large ball at the Timeball Station was lowered. (Clocks were used to calculate longitude while ships were at sea, and an inaccurate timepiece could result in disaster.) Though it's no longer needed, the Historic Places Trust maintains the station and keeps the ball dropping. The ball is raised above the tower five minutes before 1 PM and then dropped exactly on the hour. ⊠ *2 Reserve Terr.* ☎ *03/328–7311* ⊗ *Daily 10–5.*

Out in Lyttelton Harbour sits **Quail Island,** which was used by the early European settlers as a quarantine zone and leper colony and was named after the now extinct native quail. It was once a significant area for collecting birds eggs by local Māori. To protect the new community from disease, later settlers could find themselves quarantined on this island if there was an outbreak of cholera or other disease on their ships. Animals were quarantined here, too; Antarctic explorer Robert Falcon Scott's dogs and donkeys ended up wintering on the island. These days Quail

Thematic Trails

ENTERPRISING LOCAL TOURIST offices have sketched out thematically linked self-driven sightseeing trails throughout the region. You can pick up pamphlets for these touring routes at the pertinent visitor bureaus. The following are the best of the bunch:

Alpine Pacific Triangle. This links three of the most popular getaways in Canterbury: Waipara, Hanmer Springs, and Kaikoura.

The Peninsula Pioneers. Pick up a brochure from the Akaroa visitor center for information on five different routes through the Banks Peninsula bays. Keep in mind that some of the bay roads may be unpaved or steep.

Pioneer Trail. Connecting several historic sights between Timaru and Geraldine, this trail includes the Richard Pearse Memorial, dedicated to a local aviation innovator.

Scenic Highway 72. Scenic Highway 72 runs from Amberley, north of Christchurch, along the foothills of the Southern Alps through two spectacular gorges, past Geraldine to Winchester. You can join up with it at various points along the way.

Island, also known as Otamahua, is being restored as an ecological reserve. The *Black Cat* ferry from Lyttelton can zip you out here for a hike; stop by the interpretive center near the wharf. Allow for at least three hours on the island. ⊠ *Jetty B, 17 Norwich Quay* ☎ *03/328–9078* 🖃 *$15* ⊙ *Dec–Feb., daily ferries at 10:20 and 12:20; Sept. and Oct., weekends only; Mar–Aug. by charter only.*

Where to Eat

$$$ ✕ **Volcano Café and Lava Bar.** The Lyttelton volcano is long since extinct, but this bright-yellow restaurant and its bright-blue neighbor, the Lava Bar, are very much alive. Toys, rainbow-color lamp shades, Frida Kahlo posters, and Kiwi paintings decorate the former grocery store. Nab one of the 1960s Formica tables and order a great big steak, fresh fish, spicy enchiladas, nachos, or a curry. A good range of wines and beers is available, as well as margaritas by the pitcher. ⊠ *42 London St.* ☎ *03/328–7077* 🖃 *AE, D, MC, V* ⊙ *No lunch.*

Nightlife

Only nice people can enter **Wunderbar.** Or so says the sign at the start of the trek to the Wunderbar. Down some steps, along the back of the building and back up another set of steps takes you to this funky bar with its magnificent harbor views. This place prides itself on weirdness, such as its collection of dolls' heads. The Back Room is a live-performance venue that attracts nice, weird people from Christchurch and the Plains. ⊠ *19 London St.* ☎ *03/328–8818* ⊕ *www.wunderbar.co.nz.*

Sports & the Outdoors

Diamond Harbour. Diamond Harbour is the largest township on the other side of Lyttelton Harbour. Its main feature is Godley House ☎ 03/329–8450, a large house with a restaurant, bar, and accommodations that's popular with weekend visitors and for weddings. You can drive to Diamond Harbour or take a 10-minute journey on the Black Diamond ferry from Jetty B at Norwich Quay ($8 return). Sailings are frequent.

DOLPHIN-
WATCHING
To see some of the small, endangered Hector's dolphins, sign up for a cruise with **Canterbury Cat.** During a tour of the outer harbor you'll likely see some of these playful dolphins; the staff will also point out old shipwrecks, defensive fortifications, and the seabirds that nest in the cliffs. ⊠ *Jetty B, 17 Norwich Quay* ☎ *03/328–9078 or 0800/436–574* ⊕ *www.blackcat.co.nz* ⊠ *$49.*

HIKING
Quail Island (*see above*) is a good option, but if you'd rather stay on the mainland, you could instead follow in the trail of the early settlers by taking the **Bridle Path.** Take the steep zigzag track that leads from Cunningham Street up to the crater rim. You can walk to the Gondola Summit Station, a few minutes' walk farther, to see the Canterbury Plains view from the site of the memorial to the pioneer women, or walk down the rest of the trail to finish near the Christchurch Gondola base station. A number 28 bus will take you to Lyttelton, and the same bus will pick you up on the other side. Allow an hour and a half for the walk (some of which is quite steep).

Akaroa & the Banks Peninsula

82 km (50 mi) east of Christchurch.

Sheep graze almost to the water's edge in the many small bays indenting the coastline of the Banks Peninsula, the nub that juts into the Pacific southeast of Christchurch. On the southern side of the peninsula, in a harbor created when the crater wall of an extinct volcano collapsed into the sea, nestles the fishing village of Akaroa (Māori for "long harbor"). The port is a favorite day trip for Christchurch residents on Sunday drives and over the summer holidays (December to February).

EN
ROUTE
State Highway 75 leads from Christchurch out onto the peninsula, curving along the southern portion past Lake Ellesmere. There are plenty of interesting stops on your way out to Akaroa. The small town of **Little River** used to be the end of the line for a now-defunct railway line from Christchurch; the route is now a walkway and bicycle trail. The old wooden train station now houses a crafts gallery and information office, and there's a pleasant café next door in the grocery store Pick up the *Peninsula Pioneers* brochure of the area which details the Heritage drive from Little River to Akaroa. When you reach **Hilltop,** pause for your first glimpse of Akaroa Harbour; on a sunny day it's magnificent. (At Hilltop the highway crosses the Summit Road, the other major route through the peninsula.) And if you're hungry after the drive over the hill, swing by **Barry's Bay Cheese Factory** (☎ 03/304–5809) and taste the local product.

⓮ Although **Akaroa** was chosen as the site for a French colony in 1838, the first French settlers arrived in 1840 only to find that the British had already established sovereignty over New Zealand by the Treaty of Waitangi. Less than 10 years later, the French abandoned their attempt at colonization, but the settlers remained and gradually intermarried with the local English community. Apart from the *rue* (street) names, a few family surnames, and architectural touches, there is little sign of a French connection anymore, but the village has a splendid setting. A day trip will get you to and from Akaroa, including a drive along the Summit Road on the edge of the former volcanic dome, but take an overnight trip if you want to explore the peninsula bays as well as the town. By the time you've checked out a winery, taken a harbor cruise, driven around a few bays, and stopped for a meal, you'll be right in the mood to kick back overnight in this quiet spot.

The Akaroa Historic Area Walk ambles along the narrow streets past quaint little cottages and historic buildings which reflect the area's multi-cultural background. A free map is available from the information center which outlines the walk and points of interest. A more detailed book is available for $9, which includes information on the historic homes and buildings you'll see along the way. You can start this easy two-hour walk at the information center. **Akaroa Information Centre** (✉ 80 Rue Lavaud ☎ 03/304–8600).

Get the feel of Akaroa with a stroll along the waterfront from the Garden of Tane to Jubilee Park. The focus of historic interest is the **Akaroa Museum,** which has a display of Māori *pounamu* (greenstone) and embroidery dating from the days of the French settlement. The museum complex includes the Old Courthouse and Langlois-Eteveneaux House, the two-room cottage of an early French settler, which bears the slight imprint of his homeland in its architecture with its wooden window panels. ✉ *Rue Lavaud at Rue Balguerie* ☎ *03/304–1013* 🖂 *$4* ⊘ *Daily 10:30–4:30.*

The **French Farm Winery** is the only winery on Banks Peninsula and occupies a stunning site overlooking Akaroa Harbour. Surrounded by groves of native manuka and coastal bush the 20-acre vineyard produces sauvignon blanc, chardonnay and pinot noir. The cellar door also has Akaroa Harbour merlot, cabernet sauvignon, rosé and riesling, so there's something for everyone. The on-site restaurant is hailed for its rack of lamb and Akaroa salmon–main courses cost $10 to $27 and the massive fireplace makes it a cozy spot in winter. ✉ *Just off Wainui Bay Rd., turn off towards the coast at Barry's Bay Cheeses* ☎ *03/304–5784* ⊕ *www.frenchfarm.co.nz.*

The contrast of the rim of the old volcanic cone and the coves below is striking—and when you drop into one of the coves, you'll likely feel like you've found your own little corner of the world. One of the easiest bays to access is **Okains Bay.** Take the Summit Road at Hilltop if approaching from Christchurch or Ngaio Point Road behind Duvauchelles if approaching from Akaroa. It's about 24 km (15 mi) from Akaroa and takes about a half hour to drive. The small settlement lies at the bottom of Okains Bay Road, which ends at a beach sheltered by tall headlands.

The **Okains Bay Māori and Colonial Museum** is a collection of buildings containing 20,000 Māori and 19th-century colonial artifacts, including *waka* (canoes) used in Waitangi Day celebrations and displays such as a smithy and print shop. ✉ *Main Rd.* ☎ *03/304–8611* 🖂 *$6* ⊘ *Daily 10–5.*

OFF THE
BEATEN
PATH

EASTERN BAYS SCENIC MAIL RUN – For a quirky way of seeing nearly a dozen hideaway bays, sign up to ride with the mailman while he delivers the rural mail on the Eastern Bays Mail Run. The trip starts from Akaroa at 9 AM and finishes its circuit around 1:30. In summer the van stops for morning tea by the beach. Reservations are essential, and it's not a suitable trip for young children. ⊠ *80 Rue Lavaud* ☎ *03/304–8600* 🖾 *$45* �}️ *Weekdays Sept.–June.*

Where to Stay & Eat

$$$$ ✕ **Harbour 71.** Eclectic spins on New Zealand produce, meat, and seafood, along with a seaside location, make for sought-after reservations here. Seafood is a highlight, and the grouper comes straight from the fishing boat. Try the Fish Trio—a flavorsome mix of squid, salmon, and oysters. Look through the New Zealand wines on the list to find some Canterbury labels such as Akaroa Harbour, Giesen, or Pegasus Bay. ⊠ *71 Beach Rd.* ☎ *03/304–7656* ▭ *AE, MC, V* �}️ *Closed Wed. and Thurs. Mar.–June and Aug.–Nov. Closed July.*

$$$–$$$$ ✕ **C'est la vie au bout du monde.** Loitering with intent on the steps of this little wooden bungalow "at the end of the world" is encouraged, because it's the only way to study the blackboard menu. There are only a handful of tables, so sharing space is encouraged. Two sittings, at 6 and 8:30 PM, help get around this. The walls, the window frames, and even the ceiling are covered in graffiti left by happy diners. Your dish—whether it's venison à la diana, a salmon steak, the filet de boeuf served with blue vein cheese and blueberries, or the ever popular escargots—will come to the table in copper dishes for serving yourself. Don't miss the crème caramel, or the dame blanche—homemade ice cream served with a hot chocolate sauce. ⊠ *33 Rue Lavaud, Akaroa* ☎ *03/304–7314* ▭ *MC, V* �}️ *Closed June–Aug.*

★ $$–$$$ 🏠 **Linton.** Nicknamed the Giant's House, because it looked like one to a visiting child, Linton is full of art in unexpected places, starting at the funky letterbox topped with a teapot. Up the steep driveway hides a large garden crisscrossed by paths, larger-than-life mosaics, and colorful, welded sculptures. One of the guest rooms has a boat-shape bed, another a conservatory. The 1880 house and garden are open for tours from 2 to 4 PM daily, October to June ($10–$12). The house is also the venue for parties and art workshops run by the owner, artist Josie Martin. ⊠ *68 Rue Balguerie, Akaroa* ☎ *03/304–7501* ⊕ *www.linton.co.nz* 🛏 *4 rooms* ♨ *Lounge; no room TVs* ▭ *MC, V* �}️ *Closed July–Sept.* ⏅ *BP.*

$$–$$$ 🏠 **Oinako Lodge.** Surrounded by a tranquil garden, and just a two-minute walk from the town and harbor of Akaroa, this charming Victorian manor house still has its original ornate plaster ceilings and marble fireplaces. You'll find fresh flowers in the spacious and pleasantly decorated rooms; four have whirlpool baths. Luxurious feather duvets and pillows are a nice touch. ⊠ *99 Beach Rd.* ☎☎ *03/304–8787* ⊕ *www.oinako.co.nz* 🛏 *6 rooms* ♨ *Dining room, lounge; no a/c, no room TVs* ▭ *AE, DC, MC, V* ⏅ *BP.*

¢–$ 🏠 **Chez la Mer.** This comfortable hostel fills a charming 1871 building. There's no TV here; the preferred form of entertainment is sharing travelers' tales in the kitchen or over the BBQ in the sunny courtyard garden. The hosts offer helpful travel advice and free bicycles for exploring

Akaroa. ✉ *50 Rue Lavaud, Akaroa* ☎ *03/304–7024* ⊕ *www.chezlamer. co.nz* ⇆ *6 rooms, 3 dorm rooms* ♿ *BBQ, kitchen, bicycles, lounge, laundry facilities* ▭ *No credit cards.*

Sports & the Outdoors

The 35-km (22-mi) **Banks Peninsula Track** crosses beautiful coastal terrain. From Akaroa you hike over headlands and past several bays, waterfalls, and seal and penguin colonies, and you might see Hector's dolphins at sea. Two-day ($125) and four-day ($200) hikes are available between October and April. Overnight in cabins with fully equipped kitchens, which you might share with other hikers. Rates include lodging, transport from Akaroa to the first hut, landowners' fees, and a booklet describing the features of the trail. No fear of overcrowding here—the track is limited to accommodate 16 people at a time, and booking well ahead is essential. ☎ *03/304–7612* ⊕ *www.bankstrack.co.nz.*

The *Black Cat* catamaran runs two **Akaroa Harbour cruises.** You'll pull in beside waterfalls and bob around in the harbor entrance while tiny Hector's dolphins play in the wake of the boat. (The Hector's dolphins are an endangered and quite adorable species of dolphin; their rounded dorsal fins look like Mickey Mouse ears stuck on their backs.) If you take your swimsuit, you can swim among them. Trips cost $49–$99, and advance reservations are essential. ✉ *Main Wharf* ☎ *03/304–7641 or 0800/436–574* ⊕ *www.blackcat.co.nz.*

Waipara Valley

⓯ *65 km (40 mi) north of Christchurch.*

Once known for its hot, dry summers and sheep ranches, the Waipara Valley is now an established vineyard area. The local riesling, chardonnay, and sauvignon blanc are particularly good thanks to ideal growing conditions. Sheltered from the cool easterly wind by the Teviotdale hills, the valley records hotter temperatures than the rest of Canterbury, and warm, dry autumns ensure a longer time for the grapes to mature. Winemakers are also exploiting the area's limestone soil to grow pinots—pinot noir, pinot gris, and pinotage. Two dozen labels have sprouted up, with more to come, and the area produces more than 100,000 cases of wine a year. All this has happened in less than 30 years, and the sheep are being quickly outnumbered by grapevines.

There is no specified wine trail through the valley, but a good place to start your visit is the **Pukeko Junction Regional Wine Centre** at Leithfield, 10 km (6 mi) south of Waipara. The center is a café, wineshop, information bureau, and gallery rolled into one. With the free regional map, brochures, and posters on the wineries and growing conditions, Pukeko Junction trumps the Waipara visitor bureau as the oenophile's regional gateway. You can also check out the stock of local wines, including some from wineries not open to the public. Some of the larger wineries such Pegasus Bay and Canterbury House are open daily for tastings and lunch; others are open only by appointment. ✉ *458 Ashworths Rd., Leithfield* ☎ *03/314–8834* ⊙ *Daily 10:30–5:30.*

Waipara's wines are celebrated each year at the Waipara Wine and Food Celebration. Held in late March, it fills (ironically enough) the grounds of the local Glenmark Church.

The huge, cathedral-like **Canterbury House Winery** is visible clear across the plain, and although less than 10 years old, it looks like it's been there a lot longer. It's open for lunch and tastings. The main dining hall, which is just three years old, has a medieval-hall feel about it. Try the sauvignon blanc and pinot gris; their pinot noir is also highly regarded. ⊠ *780 Glasnevin Rd. (part of State Hwy 1), Waipara* ☎ *03/314–6900* ⊕ *www.canterburyhouse.com.*

Family-run **Pegasus Bay** has one of the region's best reputations for both wine and food. Taste the riesling while you look through a window at floor-to-ceiling stacks of oak aging casks. In good weather, you can dine outdoors in the garden or picnic in a natural auditorium overlooking a small man-made lake. ⊠ *Stockgrove Rd., Waipara* ☎ *03/314–6869* 🖷 *03/314–6861* ⊕ *www.pegasus.com* ☽ *Tasting room 10:30–5, restaurant noon–4.*

Daniel Schuster is one of Canterbury's pioneering winemakers, with a strong history of success both in New Zealand and California. His vines are grown in a traditional manner, without irrigation, and his wines are crafted by hand—a little from this barrel and a little from that. He is a master to watch at work, and his wines are some of the best coming out of Canterbury. ⊠ *Reeces Rd., Omihi, Waipara* ☎ *03/314–5901* ⊕ *www.danielschusterwines.com.*

🔁 Waipara is also a departure point for the **Weka Pass Railway,** which winds through farmlands and interesting rock formations as far as the township of Waikari in a train pulled by a vintage locomotive. It runs twice a day on the first and third Sunday of each month and on public holidays, leaving at 11:30 and 2. A steam locomotive is used whenever possible, but during summer a fire ban in the region often requires that a diesel be used instead. ⊠ *McKenzies Rd.* ☎ *03/962–2999* ⊕ *www. wekapassrailway.co.nz* 🖾 *$18.*

Where to Stay & Eat

★ **$$–$$$** ✕ **Nor'Wester Café & Bar.** Sophisticated dining in rural places is one of life's great pleasures, especially when it involves the best regional produce. Here you can enjoy a meal inside the mellow 1928 bungalow with its fireplace or outside on the palm-shaded veranda. Lunch offers an eclectic mix of both casual and stylish dishes, and evening is formalized with the Classic After 5 menu. Be sure to try some of Rachel Scott's locally made seaweed-flavored bread or the fruit patés. Ostrich is another specialty. The espresso is superb, and you can complement your meal with one of the fabulous local wines. ⊠ *95 Main North Rd., Amberley, 7 km (4½ mi) south of Waipara* ☎ *03/314–9411* ▭ *AE, DC, MC, V.*

★ **$$** ✕ **Waipara Springs Winery.** At one of the valley's oldest wineries, you can stop for lunch along with a wine tasting. The café, in converted farm buildings, serves tasty dishes made with local foods such as salmon, lamb, cheese, and asparagus. These match well with the vineyard's sauvignon blanc, pinot noir, botrytised riesling, gewürztraminer, and barrique chardonnay. ⊠ *State Hwy. 1* ☎ *03/314–6777* ⊕ *www.waiparasprings. co.nz* ⊟ *AE, DC, MC, V.*

$$$$ 🏨 **Claremont Country Estate.** Watch where you walk on this estate—that

Fodor'sChoice   white stone you see might turn out to be a marine dinosaur fossil. This

★   spectacular deer and sheep station is up the Waipara Gorge, a 10-minute drive inland from Amberley; its luxurious homestead was built from limestone quarried on the property in the late 1860s. The five lodge rooms are furnished with antiques, so families with children under 14 are encouraged to stay in the nearby self-contained cottage. A four-wheel-drive tour is thrown in with the price if you're staying two or more nights. Room TVs are available on request. ⊠ *828 Ram Paddock Rd.* ☎ *03/314–7557* ⊕ *www.claremont-estate.com* ➥ *1 room, 4 suites* ♿ *2 dining rooms, minibars, tennis court, pool, sauna, spa, croquet, 2 lounges; no a/c (except in cottage), no in-room TVs* ⊟ *AE, MC, V* ⊗ *Closed July–Sept.* ⏏️ *MAP.*

$–$$ 🏨 **Bredon Downs.** Stay on an ostrich farm in a renovated 100-year-old farmhouse while you explore wineries farther north. A three-course dinner with local wines is available by arrangement. ⊠ *233 Carters Rd., on State Hwy. 1 Amberley* ☎ *03/314–9356* 📠 *03/314–8994* ➥ *3 rooms* ♿ *Tennis court, pool, laundry facilities* ⊟ *MC, V* ⏏️ *BP, CP.*

¢   🏨 **Waipara Sleepers.** Wake up to fresh-baked bread and newly laid eggs every morning at this unusual backpackers lodge housed in old railway carriages and huts. It's first come, first served for breakfast in the station waiting room, which now does duty as the communal kitchen. Some of the carriages retain old leather seating and travel posters. ⊠ *10–12 Glenmark Dr.* ☎ *03/314–6002* 📠 *03/314–6003* ⊕ *www.inet.net. nz/~waipara.sleepers* ➥ *4 rooms, 2 dorms* ♿ *BBQ, lounge, laundry facilities; no TVs in some rooms* ⊟ *MC, V.*

EN ROUTE   Built from limestone blocks, the **Hurunui Hotel,** New Zealand's oldest continually licensed hotel (since 1860), refreshed weary drovers bringing sheep down from Marlborough. It is still a welcoming place to take a break. A bed for the night is relatively cheap ($40 per person, including a cooked breakfast), and the restaurant with its old-fashioned pub serves à la carte dinners from $17 and an all-day menu from $15. Get a drink from the bar (perhaps a glass of wine from the small vineyard out back) and enjoy it out in the garden. ⊠ *State Hwy. 7, about 20 mins drive from the Waipara turnoff.* ☎ *03/314–4207.*

Hanmer Springs

🔟⑥ *120 km (75 mi) northwest of Christchurch.*

Long before Europeans arrived in New Zealand, Māori travelers knew the Hanmer Springs area as Waitapu (sacred water). Legends tell of how the springs were created to warm the great Māori chief Tamatea and his people as they made their way back to the North Island, after their waka (canoe) sank off the Otago coast. Early European settlers didn't take long to discover these thermal springs, and the first bathing shed, a tiny corrugated iron hut, was built in 1879.

The tranquil alpine village has long been a healthful place, so it's not surprising that the now-closed Queen Mary hospital was host to recovering soldiers, tuberculosis patients, and recovering drug addicts. People still come to Hanmer to chill out with quiet soaks in the hot pools and forest walks, but things have been changing fast in the last few years. The number of boutiques and restaurants has doubled, and an increasing number of off-road and backcountry activities are turning Hanmer into Canterbury's adventure sports hub. The Amuri Ski Field, a small ski area in the mountains behind town, attracts a dedicated following of local skiers. Mountain biking is especially big, and Hanmer is now the end point for several long-distance mountain-bike and endurance races through the backcountry. Weekends and holidays are particularly busy, so visit midweek if you want a quiet stay.

EN ROUTE To see some Māori rock drawings, take the **Weka Pass Walkway** from behind the Star and Garter hotel along a disused railway line before turning away and following the fenceline. The drawings are under limestone overhangs. It is also limestone that creates the strange formations in Weka Pass, including Frog Rock, so named for its shape. A map is available from the Hurunui Information Centre.

The scenic gravel drive along **Jacks Pass,** to the north of the village, crosses the lower slopes of Mt. Isobel before dropping into the upper Clarence River Valley, a particularly alpine area just 10 minutes from Hanmer. This is the beginning of some serious backcountry. The tiny stream trickling past the road at the end of the pass eventually reaches the coast north of Kaikoura as the rough and rumbling Clarence River—a favorite for rafters and kayakers.

The **Hanmer Springs Thermal Reserve** remains the number-one reason to visit the area and consists of nine thermal pools, three sulfur pools, one freshwater pool, a family activity pool, and two waterslides. There are also four private thermal pools, as well as sauna and steam rooms. Massage and beauty treatments are available, too, and even more new spa facilities are planned for the near future. ⊠ *Amuri Ave.* ☎ *03/315–7511* ⊕ *www.hanmersprings.co.nz* ✑ *$10; private pool, steam, or sauna $34 per ½ hr (minimum 2 people), hydroslide $5* ⊙ *Daily 10–9.*

The **Wisteria Cottage Day Spa** is one of the newest day spas in Hanmer, catering to those who don't want or need to soak in a hot pool for their entire stay. Specialty treatments are available, including hot-stone massage, Vichy showers, holistic facials, and massage. ⊠ *34 Conical Hill Rd.* ☎ *03/315–7026* ⊕ *www.nzhotsprings.com/dayspa.*

Where to Stay & Eat

$$$–$$$$ ✕ **Malabar Restaurant.** Indian and Asian food presented with Kiwi flair: Asian duck confit and Chinese dishes sit on the menu alongside a Thai green curry or an Indian tandoori. ⊠ *Alpine Pacific Centre, 5 Conical Hill Rd.* ☎ *03/315–7745* ✑ *Reservations essential in summer* ⊟ *AE, DC, MC, V* ⊙ *No lunch.*

$$$–$$$$ ✕ **The Old Post Office.** Any message posted here will make it only as far as the kitchen. This old wooden building serves elegant meals such as seared venison with kūmara-and-walnut mash (kūmara is a native sweet potato). In winter a fireplace keeps the L-shape dining room warm; on a warm evening, ask for a terrace table. ⊠ *2 Jacks Pass Rd.* ☎ *03/315– 7461* ⊟ *AE, DC, MC, V* ⊙ *No lunch.*

★ **$$–$$$** 🖼 **Albergo Hanmer Lodge.** Postcard views of the mountains (even from the showers) and fresh, eclectic interior design make this place stand out. Stay in the alpine villa with its private Jacuzzi, or in the lodge; either way, you can fall asleep at night listening to the nearby river rushing over the rocks. The delicious three-course breakfast is notably good, with 10 meal choices, homemade mini-loaves, and fresh Italian coffee. Spa-treatment and cuisine packages are available; Swiss–Kiwi cuisine is a specialty. ⊠ *88 Rippingale Rd.* ☎ *03/315–7428 or 0800/342–313* ⊕ *www. albergohanmer.com* 🛏 *5 suites* ⚹ *In-room DVD, spa, lounge* ▤ *AE, DC, MC, V* ⦿ *BP.*

★ **$$–$$$** 🖼 **Heritage Hanmer Springs.** This getaway opened in 1932 as the Hanmer Lodge, when it was the largest hotel in Australasia. Stay in rooms inside the hotel or take a garden suite in among the pine trees on Jollies Pass Road; there are also villas on the rise above the hotel, around a man-made pond. The thermal springs are just a short walk away. ⊠ *1 Conical Hill Rd.* ☎ *03/315–7021* 🖷 *03/315–7023* ⊕ *www.heritagehanmer. nz-hotels.com* 🛏 *38 rooms, 11 villas, 16 singles* ⚹ *Restaurant, tennis court, pool, boccie, piano bar* ▤ *AE, DC, MC, V* ⦿ *BP, CP.*

$–$$$ 🖼 **Settlers Inn Motel.** This property offers peaceful apartments and studios set back off Amuri drive, the main street into Hanmer. Upstairs rooms have balconies with views of Mt. Isobel, and two apartments have private courtyards. Handcrafted slat beds and furniture have been installed in all the rooms. ⊠ *6 Leamington St.* ☎ *03/315–7343 or 0800/ 587–873* 🖷 *03/315–7071* ⊕ *www.settlersinnmotel.co.nz* ⚹ *BBQ, kitchen, in-room data ports, laundry facilities, Internet room* ▤ *AE, DC, MC, V* ⦿ *BP, CP.*

¢–$ 🖼 **Kakapo Lodge.** You reach this lodge where State Highway 7 ends and the tree-divided Amuri Avenue begins. A short walk from the hot pools, this two-story building has underfloor heating and offers various options to the budget conscious, from dorm rooms and double rooms to motel accommodation. The sunny hostel also doubles as the Hanmer YHA. ⊠ *14 Amuri Ave.* ☎🖷 *03/315–7472* ⊕ *www.kakapolodge.co. nz* 🛏 *12 rooms, 5 dorm rooms* ⚹ *BBQ, kitchen, lounge* ▤ *MC, V.*

Nightlife

Saints Cafe can claim to be Hanmer Spring's first nightclub. It's open until 3 AM, except on Monday during the winter school term. It has a dance floor and pool table, keeps the carbs going with pizzas and pasta, and puts on a live band on Saturday night. ⊠ *6 Jacks Pass Rd.* ☎ *03/ 315–5262.*

Sports & the Outdoors

ADVENTURE SPORTS With **Alpine Pacific Adventures,** you can kayak on a lake with snow down to the water's edge, or if you want to really brush away the cobwebs, opt for a seat on an argo, an eight-wheel all-terrain vehicle that goes hell for leather into riverbeds and up steep hillsides. Trips start at $49 and take off from the visitor bureau. ☎ *03/315–7387* ⊕ *www. adventuresnz.com.*

Hanmer Springs Adventure Centre rents ski gear, mountain bikes, and other equipment. For $79 you can take the two-to-four-hour Twin Passes mountain-bike ride, which heads out of town over Jacks Pass and returns over Jollies Pass—a very scenic route. ⊠ *20 Conical Hill Rd.* ☎ *03/315–7233.*

Thrillseekers Canyon Adventure Centre organizes 35-meter (115-foot) bungy jumps off the 19th-century Waiau Ferry Bridge ($114) if you dare. You can also choose to raft or take a ride on a jet-boat through the Waiau Gorge, let the kids ride their own mini-quad bikes, do a kart safari, or take a ride in an ATV. Be sure to book at least one day in advance for any of these activities. ⊠ *839 Main Rd.* ☎ *03/315–7046 or 0800/661–538* ⊕ *www.thrillseekerscanyon.co.nz.*

HIKING   The forest around Hanmer Springs, planted by prison labor in the early 1900s, has a distinctly European look. You'll find European larch, Austrian pine, European alder, and other varieties. The Hurunui Visitor Information Centre (*see* Visitor Information, *below*) has maps and fact sheets detailing several walks.

HORSE TREKKING   **Hanmer Horse Trekking** takes beginner and advanced riders on guided rides through forestry, farmland, and native bush. Be prepared for river crossings and spectacular views. Rides last from 1 to 2½ hours, and prices range from $35 to $90. ⊠ *187 Rogerson Track* ☎ *03/315–7444* ⊕ *www. hanmerhorses.co.nz* ⊗ *Sept.–Apr. rides leave at 10, noon, 2, and 4. May–Aug. rides leave at 11, 1, and 3.*

Methven

🔞 *95 km (59 mi) southwest of Christchurch.*

Methven's main claim to fame is as a ski town—it's the closest town to Mt. Hutt, which does not allow accommodation on its slopes. Peak season here means winter, so if you happen to be traveling here in summer, there are some bargains to be had, the crowds have gone, and you can take advantage of the other activities, such as walking, jet-boating, and hot-air ballooning.

The best way to get to Methven by car is by way of the underused Scenic Highway 72, which you can join near Darfield, or via Hororata (but be wary of icy spots in the shade and hidden speed cameras on these straight roads). You could also travel down the busy State Highway 1 to Rakaia and take Thompson's Track (clearly signposted and paved) to Methven.

Where to Stay & Eat

Methven may not be a culinary hotbed, but it has several good casual places for a meal. Cafe Chill on Macmillan Street is reasonably priced and is known for its comfort food and homemade pies. The Blue Pub and the older-style Brown Pub, opposite each other on Main Street in the center of town, do reasonably priced bar- or bistro-style meals. For something more sophisticated head to Lisah's, also on Main Street.

$$$$ 🏨 **Terrace Downs Resort.** Although not strictly in Methven, Terrace Downs is a 20-minute drive away, with spectacular views of the Rakaia Gorge and the looming presence of Mt. Hutt. Set on a golf course, this resort is a good place to base yourself for a vacation away from the crowds.

Accommodation is in a series of timber-and-stone villas perched on a ridge above the clubhouse and restaurant, with views over the golf course and the mountains from their balconies. ⊠ *Coleridge Rd., Rakaia Gorge* ☎ *03/318–6943 or 0800/465–373* 🖨 *03/317–9372* ⊕ *www. terracedowns.co.nz* ⇨ *50 suites* ⚴ *Restaurant, minibars, in-room broadband, 18-hole golf course, 2 tennis courts, spa, horseback riding, helipad* ▭ *AE, MC, V* ⏉ *BP.*

$ 🖵 **Abisko.** Popular with visiting ski teams and families looking for somewhere central, Abisko caters to two essential needs: skiing (with mountain transfers and ski tuning) and warming up (with a fireplace in the lounge and an on-site sauna). The apartments next door in the old granary building can cater up to 10 people. The lodge rooms are all well appointed, and there are 17 powered camper-van sites for those hardy souls who go camping in winter. ⊠ *74 Main St.* ☎ *03/302–8875 or 0508/ 224–756* 🖨 *03/302–8795* ⊕ *www.abisko.co.nz* ⇨ *12 lodge rooms, 2 apartments* ⚴ *Restaurant, kitchen, sauna, spa, bar, laundry facilities, Internet room* ▭ *MC, V.*

¢ 🖵 **Alpenhorn Chalet.** The hosts of this not-particularly-Swiss-looking chalet are mountaineers and outdoor enthusiasts, and generous with friendly advice about enjoying the area. The house is an old wooden villa from the early 1900s. A log fire in the huge kitchen helps keep the place warm; the bedrooms are centrally heated. At the end of the day, relax in the hot tub or simply sit in the sun (even in winter it can be intense) to bask and read. The Alpenhorn's particularly popular with skiers, fishers, and "flashpackers" (a term used to describe well-off travelers who choose backpacker hostels, saving their money for other experiences rather than lodging). ⊠ *44 Allen St.* ☎ *03/302–8779* 🖨 *03/302–8789* ⇨ *4 rooms, 1 with bath, 2 dorm rooms* ⚴ *Kitchen, spa, laundry facilities, Internet room* ▭ *No credit cards.*

Sports & the Outdoors

BALLOONING On a clear morning you might catch a glimpse of a rainbow-color balloon floating high above—chances are it's **Aoraki Balloon Safaris.** From their balloons, you'll have an incredible view of the patchwork pattern of farm paddocks, the braided branches of the Rakaia River, and a full 300-km (190-mi) panorama of the Canterbury Plains and Aoraki/Mt. Cook, the "cloud piercer." On landing, you'll be served a champagne breakfast. Flights start at daybreak, and you'll be pitching in to help with the launch. The actual time in the air is about one hour, but the whole experience takes at least four hours. Rates for Premier flights—which include a champagne breakfast in a meadow after landing—go up to $295. ☎ *03/302–8172 or 0800/256–837* 🖨 *03/302–8162* ⊕ *www. nzballooning.com.*

JET-BOATING Zoom along the glacier-fed Rakaia River with **Rakaia Gorge Scenic Jet**; the 20-minute jet-boat ride costs $40, 30 minutes costs $50, and 40 minutes costs $60. The Rakaia's jewel-like aqua water contrasts beautifully with the white limestone cliffs. You'll usually find the jet-boat down at the river's edge for most of the day, just below the Rakaia Gorge bridge on State Highway 72. ☎ *03/318–6515 or 0800/435–453* ⊕ *www. rakaiagorgescenicjet.co.nz.*

SKIING Methven is the gateway to a number of ski slopes (or as Kiwis say, ski fields). Thanks to its altitude and snowmaking machines, **Mt. Hutt** is usually the first ski area in Australasia to open, as access begins in early June. Its wide basin and a vertical drop of 655 meters (2,148 feet) ensures a 2-km (1-mi) run. From the chairlifts you'll have terrific views of the mountains and the Canterbury Plains below. Shuttles to the slopes run from Methven and Christchurch, often as part of a package offer (including lift fees and equipment rental). You can also drive yourself if you've got tire chains, but the road isn't paved and it has a number of hairpin turns. Lift tickets start at $74. Rental equipment is available, and there's a ski school. Mt. Hutt is occasionally closed by high winds; beginning daily at 7 AM, up-to-date ski conditions are available on the Web site. ☎ *03/302–8811* ⊕ *www.nzski.com.*

Intermediate and advanced skiers can sign up for **heliskiing** on Mt. Hutt, flying in to slopes where no one else may have skied that day. North Peak Run, the most popular, offers an 800-vertical-meter run (2,600 vertical feet). Costs start at roughly $155 for one run; other options include a full day to the Arrowsmiths Range with gourmet lunch provided. Scenic flights are also available. ☎ *03/302–8401 or 0800/443–547* ⊕ *www. mthuttheli.co.nz.*

Geraldine

⓲ *138 km (85½ mi) southwest of Christchurch.*

For years, this pretty town has been a favorite stop on the road to Aoraki/Mt. Cook; these days, it's becoming a magnet in southern Canterbury for art mavens and foodies. State Highway 1 is the fastest route there from Christchurch; just after crossing the Rangitata River, turn inland for about 10 minutes on State Highway 79. State Highway 72— known as the Inland Scenic Route—gives you closer views of the mountains and river gorges. The rolling downs around Geraldine are especially beautiful in the late afternoon, when the sun turns them golden.

Geraldine's main drag is **Talbot Street,** where you'll find plenty of stores and galleries to browse. Check out Māori portraits and carvings in the **Peter Caley Art Gallery** (⊠ 3 Talbot St. ☎ 03/693–7278). Chocaholics may find it difficult to pass by the pralines in **Chocolate Fellman** (⊠ 10 Talbot St. ☎ 03/693–9982), a small shop run by Swiss chocolatiers. For more treats, stop by **Barker's Berry Barn** (⊠ 76 Talbot St. ☎ 0800/227–537) to try fruit chutneys, juices and cordials, sauces, and glory (an intense spread, better than jam, and often made with locally grown black currants). Over at the **Geraldine Vintage Car and Machinery Museum** (⊠ 178 Talbot St. ☎ 03/693–1006), more than 100 tractors (some of which date back to 1912) and other farm machinery share space with vintage cars. Admission is $5 and the museum is open daily 10–4 between early October and late June.

Where to Stay

★ $$$$ 🏠 **Four Peaks Lodge.** Designed in the 1920s by Christchurch architect Heathcote Helmore, this elegantly renovated farmhouse offers peaceful, secluded accommodation 18 km (11 mi) from Geraldine. The large front lawn doubles as a helipad—the summerhouse light guides helicopters in. Because the home's surrounded by old roses, rhododendrons, English beeches, limes, and oaks, you might feel you're somewhere in New England—that is, until you hear the trill of a native bellbird. The last mile into Four Peaks is on gravel. ⊠ *414 Four Peaks Rd.* ☎ *03/693–8587* 🖷 *03/693–8572* ⊕ *www.fourpeakslodge.co.nz* ⤵ *4 rooms* ♨ *Dining room, hot tub, lounge* ⊟ *AE, MC, V* ⦿⦿ *MAP.*

$$–$$$$ ⊡ **Kavanagh Lodge.** Less than 10 minutes' drive from Geraldine, Kavanagh House makes a good base from which to explore South Canterbury. It's a lovely old neo-Tudor brick-and-stucco mansion. One of the upstairs bedrooms has a bath in the middle of the polished floor of the bedroom, where you might expect an armchair. The creamy "New York" room is huge, with a four-poster bed at one end and a fireplace at the other. Enjoy lunch or afternoon tea out in the garden on a hot summer's day or in front of a real fire in winter. A glass of bubbly and a fruit platter await you upon arrival. ⊠ *State Hwy. 1, five minutes' drive north of Temuka, Winchester* ☎ *03/615–6150* 🖷 *03/615–9694* ⊕ *www.kavanaghhouse.co.nz* ⤵ *3 rooms* ♨ *Restaurant, some in-room hot tubs* ⊟ *AE, DC, MC, V* ⦿⦿ *BP.*

$$ ⊡ **The Crossing.** This 1908 manor house has been turned into a quaint boutique hotel on the edge of Geraldine. The bedrooms are up the slightly threadbare stairs and have had considerable work done on them lately. One of the two lounges has a baby grand piano. Work by local and national artists is displayed in the bedrooms, and a fine garden is yours to enjoy. A three-course à la carte dinner can be arranged for an extra fee; make sure you book on or before arrival for that. ⊠ *124 Woodbury Rd.* ☎ *03/693–9689* 🖷 *03/693–9789* ⊕ *www.thecrossingbnb. co.nz* ⤵ *3 suites* ♨ *Restaurant, 2 lounges, laundry service, Internet room; no kids under 12, no smoking,* ⊟ *MC, V* ⦿⦿ *CP, BP.*

Sports & the Outdoors
The Unimog vehicles used by **Wilderness Adventures 4x4 New Zealand** can go just about anywhere, including riverbeds, making this a good way to visit the backcountry of South Canterbury. You can get to the upper reaches of the Rangitata River, seen in the *Lord of the Rings* film trilogy. Trips range from half a day to more than a week long; rates start at $80. Reservations are essential, and the trips are weather-dependent. ☎ *03/693–8847* ⊕ *www.4x4newzealand.co.nz.*

Rangitata Rafts runs white-water rafting trips on the Grade 5 Rangitata River from September through May. If you can't face the Grade 5 section (the last part of the trip), you can walk around with the photographer. The $162 price includes pickup from Geraldine or Christchurch and lunch, hot showers, and an evening barbecue. Reservations are essential. ☎ *03/696–3534 or 0800/251–251* ⊕ *www.rafts.co.nz.*

Timaru

❶⑨ *162 km (101 mi) south of Christchurch.*

Timaru, whose name comes from the Māori Te Maru (shelter), began life as two towns, one called Government Town and the other

Rhodestown. The two towns met at George Street and merged in 1868. As Timaru's harbor was developed and its foreshore reclaimed, the Caroline Bay beach took shape and became a popular summer venue for its concerts and sideshows. These days, Timaru is the urban hub for South Canterbury and is a two-hour drive south of Christchurch—close enough for a weekend trip but far enough away to have its own strong identity.

Once a harborside office, the **Landing Service Building** is now set back from the port because of the foreshore's land reclamation. The restored bluestone building houses the information center, a restaurant, and a small maritime museum. Just outside the building sits *Captain Cain,* cast in bronze. This harbormaster was at the center of a 19th-century scandal when it was revealed that he had been poisoned by his son-in-law. ✉ *2 George St.* ☎ *03/688–6163.*

Pronounced "egg and tie," the **Aigantighe Art Gallery** is one of the largest museums in the South Island. It mounts rotating exhibitions as well as permanent displays, including works by internationally acclaimed painter Colin McCahon (a Timaru native) and other Canterbury artists. Out in the gardens of the historic mansion, sculptures carved from Mt. Somers stone make themselves at home. ✉ *49 Wai-iti Rd.* ☎ *03/688–4424* 🖃 *Free* 🕐 *Tues.–Fri. 10–4, weekends noon–4.*

Anything to do with South Canterbury's past gets covered in the **South Canterbury Museum,** from Māori artifacts to 19th-century shipwrecks to Richard Pearse's aviation antics. ✉ *Perth St.* ☎ *03/684–2212* ⊕ *www. timaru.govt.nz/museum* 🖃 *Free* 🕐 *Tues.–Fri. 10–4:30, weekends 1:30–4:30.*

A 20-minute drive northwest from Timaru is Pleasant Point, an area known for its role in aviation history. Some months before the Wright brothers took flight in America, a local farmer nicknamed "Bamboo Dick" took bicycle wheels somewhere they'd never been before, launching the first powered flight in New Zealand out in the fields a few miles outside town. The **Richard Pearse Memorial,** a reproduction of his plane, marks the spot where Pearse crashed into a hedge on March 31, 1903. To get here, take the Waitohi–Pleasant Point Road, then take a left on Opihi Terrace Road, and another left onto Main Waitohi Road. ✉ *Main Waitohi Rd.*

The area is also known for its Māori rock art, some of which can be seen in situ at the **Raincliff Historical Reserve.** South Canterbury has one of the country's highest concentrations of Māori rock art paintings, which are being documented by the Ngai Tahu Māori Rock Art Trust. Six hundred years ago or more, Māori moa hunters in the region made drawings of animals, birds, and people in black charcoal or red ocher on stone walls created by limestone overhangs. Although many works are on private land, the Raincliff reserve is open to the public. Faint drawings are visible here, particularly on the small overhang. To reach the reserve, follow the signpost in Pleasant Point that points to Raincliff bridge. Allow an hour for the trip. ✉ *Middle Valley Rd., off State Hwy. 79* 🖃 *Free.*

If you want to look like a true "Southern Man," you'll need to make

The Chatham Islands

ALTHOUGH OFFICIALLY PART OF New Zealand, the Chatham Islands, 800 km (500 mi) east of the South Island, are a land apart. Locals here refer to the mainland as New Zealand, as though it were an entirely separate country. And considering the uniqueness of the terrain and culture here, it might as well be.

Bearing the full force of the open Southern Ocean, the islands are wild and weather-beaten, with a rugged beauty rarely seen anywhere else in the country. The air has a salty taste to it, the colors of the landscapes are softer and more muted, and the vegetation is stunted and gnarly. There are many unusual plants and birds to be seen—including the very rare black robin—and the empty beaches invite fishing and diving (although the presence of sharks makes the latter inadvisable).

Just 2 of the 10 islands are inhabited—the main island and tiny, neighboring Pitt Island. Most residents are either farmers or fishermen, but tourism is steadily increasing here, and bringing

new jobs with it. The Chathams were first settled by the Moriori, a race of Polynesian descent, about 800–1,000 years ago, although there are no full-blooded Moriori left. Māori and Europeans followed, and conflicts broke out between the separate populations throughout the 1800s. By the end of the 19th century, however, tensions had died down after the Native Land Court intervened in key disputes, and the new settlers were able to stay and establish the strong maritime culture that still prevails on the islands today.

When booking to fly to the Chathams it's imperative that you make lodging reservations in advance, as there are limited accommodations available. There are two round-trip flights a week from Christchurch. Check out ⊕ www.newzealandnz.co.nz/chatham-islands for details on travel, accommodation, and activities. Allow at least four days if you really want to get a feel for the islands; you'll rarely get the chance to visit anywhere this remote. And don't forget to try the crayfish (lobsters) while you're there.

8

sure you have a "Swanni," or Swanndri bush shirt. This item, as iconic to Kiwis as the Akubra hat is to Australians, can be found in many versions at the **Swanndri Factory Store.** Swanndri has been diversifying by carrying more urban gear, as well as rugs and scarves. ⊠ *24a Church St.* ☎ *03/684–9037* ⊕ *www.swanndri.co.nz* ⊙ *Weekdays 10–5:30, Sat. 10–4.*

Where to Stay & Eat

$$$–$$$$ ✕ **Ginger & Garlic Café.** This classy spot is considered one of Timaru's best eateries, and owner Jason Cleverly hopes that every visitor here will get to feel a real touch of New Zealand. In winter there's a nice big fire to warm up by, and in summer there are fabulous sunsets to watch from a window table. The view also overlooks Caroline Bay and the port—where the chef gets her seafood fresh each day. The seared lamb with roasted kūmara, served with a walnut and spinach salad, is a menu standout. ⊠ *335 Stafford St.* ☎ *03/688–3981* ⊟ *AE, DC, MC, V* ⊙ *No lunch weekends.*

$$$$ 🏠 **Tighnafeile House.** You never know who you'll share your breakfast with at this inn's large polished dining table—famous authors and royal representatives have had their morning coffee here. Gaelic for "house of welcome," Tighnafeile (*tyne*-a-faylee) was built in 1911. The rooms exude warmth with their choice antiques, navy fleur-de-lis carpet, and honey-colored timbered fireplaces (mostly for show). The house, which has a large garden, is almost opposite the Aigantighe Art Gallery. ✉ 62 *Wai-iti Rd.* ☎ *03/684–3333* 🖷 *03/684–3328* ⊕ *www.tighnafeile.com* 🛏 *4 rooms, 3 with bath* ⚒ *Dining room, in-room broadband, lounge, library; no kids under 12* ▭ *DC, MC, V* ⊖ *BP, CP.*

$ 🏠 **Panorama Motor Lodge.** Perched up on the Bay Hill, the Panorama has a wide view of the Pacific Ocean from the front units on the Bay Wing, and views of Mt. Cook from the Alpine Wing units. Each self-contained unit has a kitchen. ✉ *52 The Bay Hill* ☎ *03/688–0097* 🖷 *03/688–0096* ⊕ *www.panorama.net.nz* 🛏 *19 units* ⚒ *Gym, hot tub, sauna* ▭ *AE, MC, V* ⊖ *CP.*

¢ 🏠 **Wanderer Backpackers.** This 1873 house is named for a ship called the *Wanderer* that sank near Timaru. Because it's close to Timaru's main road, it can be quite noisy, but it has a homey atmosphere. The large kitchen-lounge has a fireplace, and the upstairs rooms facing the street catch the morning and late-afternoon sun. ✉ *24 Evans St.* ☎🖷 *03/688–8795* 🛏 *5 rooms, 1 dorm room, 1 single, 1 trailer home, tent sites* ⚒ *Kitchen, lounge, Internet room* ▭ *No credit cards.*

ARTHUR'S PASS & CANTERBURY ESSENTIALS

Transportation

BY BUS

InterCity buses serve most of the Canterbury destinations covered in this section. In addition, a number of shuttle companies with minicoaches and small buses run services between the Canterbury communities.

The Akaroa Shuttle has daily service between Christchurch and Akaroa: three trips a day in high season (December–April) ranging from a direct shuttle to a scenic tour along the way, but only once a day otherwise. Direct shuttles run twice a day in summer from Christchurch, with an extra run on Friday night, and there are three runs a day from Akaroa. The cost is $15 one-way or $20 round-trip. The Akaroa French Connection also runs a shuttle and day tour out to the peninsula.

The Hanmer Connection is the main bus between Hanmer Springs and Christchurch. Two buses leave Christchurch in the morning, and two leave Hanmer in the afternoon. They stop in Waipara and elsewhere en route in the Waipara Valley, making it a useful way to get to the vineyard area. There's also daily round-trip service direct to Kaikoura from Hanmer.

There are plenty of buses from Christchurch to Methven and Mt. Hutt in ski season, but the options drop off in summer. Leopard Coachlines run from Methven to Mt. Hutt during the ski season.

Because Geraldine is between Christchurch and the popular draws of Aoraki/Mt. Cook and Queenstown, it's served by several bus companies, including InterCity and Newmans. Buses to Dunedin and Invercargill pass through Timaru on the coast.

📋 Bus Companies **Akaroa French Connection** ☎ 0800/800-575. **Akaroa Shuttle** ☎ 0800/500-929 ⊕ www.akaroashuttle.co.nz. **Hanmer Connection** ☎ 0800/377-378. **InterCity Coachline** ☎ 03/365-1113 or 0800/222-146 ⊕ www.intercitycoach.co.nz. **Leopard Coachlines** ☎ 03/332-5000. **Newmans Coachlines** ☎ 03/365-1114 ⊕ www.newmanscoach.co.nz.By Car

Driving is the most convenient way to get around outside of Christchurch. Road conditions are generally good, and if you've got your own wheels, you can stop at whatever village or scenic spot (and there are many) catches your eye.

Lyttelton can be reached by driving down Ferry Road from Christchurch, heading toward Sumner and then taking the road tunnel. To take the scenic route, drive all the way to Sumner and then head up the crater rim via Evans Pass. You can also follow Colombo Street east to the Port Hills and take Dyers Pass Road over the hill to Governors Bay.

The main route to Akaroa is State Highway 75, which leaves the southwest corner of Christchurch as Lincoln Road. The 82-km (50-mi) drive takes about 90 minutes.

To reach the towns north of the city, including Waipara and Hanmer Springs, take State Highway 1 north. Waipara's about 45 minutes away, where State Highway 7 turns left off the main road. From here, you can continue driving through the small town of Culverden and the foothills for another 45 minutes on State Highway 7, before turning onto Highway 7A toward Hanmer Springs (this is well signposted).

There are several ways of driving to Methven, see the Methven section above for details. State Highway 1 will take you to the other points south, including Geraldine and Timaru. An alternate route to Geraldine is by taking Scenic Highway 72; the route is technically longer than the State Highway 1, but it's less trafficked and the scenery's more beautiful. Either way the journey takes nearly two hours. Timaru is about a half hour from Geraldine. State Highway 1 can get very busy, especially in summer. If you take this highway, be prepared to share the lanes with long-haul trucks, sheep trucks, and logging vehicles.

Canterbury roads are mostly paved and flat, making for easy driving. They're often straight for long stretches, making it tempting to speed . . . but resist. Be sure to keep an eye out for cyclists. Most highways are a single lane of traffic in each direction, but because these are a problem for impatient drivers and traffic jams, passing lanes have been added every now and again. Bridges in the country tend to be one lane only; signs will tell you which side has to make way. If driving in cold weather, watch out for paddocks with tall trees or hedges, because the roads past them can get icy. The roads in colder spots tend to be well marked with temporary orange signs warning of ice or grit. Bridges can also be slippery in cold weather. The road to Mt. Hutt has hairpin turns and sharp drops, as does the road to Akaroa.

Contacts & Resources

BANKS & EXCHANGE SERVICES

Some of the smaller Canterbury towns have no bank or ATM. You might be able to find a Kiwi Bank in a post office or a Superbank in a supermarket.

EMERGENCIES

For any emergencies call the national hotline number, 111. There are no 24-hour pharmacies in Canterbury, but some may have extended hours. Smaller towns have been losing their hospital services, but there is usually a roster of doctors on duty for the area. The hospital closest to Hanmer Springs and Waipara, for instance, is at Waikari.

🚹 **Akaroa Hospital** ⊠ Onuku Rd. ☎ 03/304-7023. **Akaroa Medical Centre** ☎ 03/304-7004. **Methven Medical Centre** ☎ 03/302-8105. **Timaru Hospital** ⊠ Queen St. ☎ 03/684-4000. **Waikari Hospital** ⊠ 16 Littles Dr. ☎ 03/314-4005.

MAIL & INTERNET

In the small towns of this region, Internet and post-office facilities are usually part of either a local store, accommodation, or library. Most have limited hours, especially in winter and evenings, so it's a good idea to call ahead.

🚹 **Internet Access Crown Hotel and Village Inn Complex** ⊠ Talbot St., Geraldine ☎ 03/693-8458. **Email Shop** ⊠ The Mall, Methven ☎ 03/302-8982. **Planet Rojo** ⊠ 47 Amuri Ave., Hanmer ☎ 03/315-7999. **Public Library** ⊠ Sophia St. at Church St., Timaru ☎ 03/684-2202. **Turenne Dairy & Coffee Shop** ⊠ 74 Rue Lavaud, Akaroa ☎ 03/304-7005.

🚹 **Post Offices Akaroa Information Centre** ⊠ 80 Rue Lavaud ☎ 03/304-8600. **Books & More** ⊠ 21 Strathallan St., Timaru ☎ 03/686-6040. **Gifts Galore Postal Agency** ⊠ Main Rd., Methven ☎ 03/302-8463. **NZ Post** ⊠ 26 Talbot St., Geraldine ☎ 03/693-8647. **Postal Agency, 4 Square Supermaket** ⊠ Conical Hill Rd., Hanmer ☎ 03/315-7190.

TOURS

ADVENTURE TOURS Taking the TranzAlpine & High Country Explorer is definitely one of the best and most action-packed ways of getting into the Canterbury Plains and the Southern Alps, and experiencing the world-famous TranzAlpine train journey. The full-day trip starts with a hotel pickup for a two-hour trip on the TranzAlpine train, then a 65-km (40-mi) four-wheel-drive safari through the vast 35,000-acre Flock Hill sheep station (filming location for Disney's *The Lion, The Witch and the Wardrobe*), a 15-km (9-mi) jet-boat cruise, and a one-hour bus trip back to your Christchurch hotel. The scenery is spectacular, the boat ride a thrill, and your safari guide will discuss the region's human and natural history, flora and fauna, and geography and geology. A full-day trip is $325 per person.

🚹 **TranzAlpine & High Country Explorer** ☎ 03/377-1391 or 0800/863-975 🖨 03/313-6494 ⊕ www.high-country.co.nz.

SIGHTSEEING TOURS Canterbury Leisure Tours runs day trips to Hanmer Springs and Akaroa. In addition to its Christchurch tours, it also offers a range of half-day tours and activities, including wine trails, horse trekking, night tours, sheep-farm visits, and golfing excursions.

Using luxury four-wheel-drive minicoaches, Canterbury Trails can go off the beaten track on its personally guided tours. Among its itineraries is a full-day tour to Akaroa and the Banks Peninsula, which includes a dolphin-sighting cruise. Other day trips visit Arthur's Pass, Kaikoura, and Hanmer.

Canterbury Leisure Tours ⊠ 260d Port Hills Rd., Christchurch ☎ 03/384-0999 or 0800/484-485 ⊕ www.leisuretours.co.nz. **Canterbury Trails, Ltd.** ☎ 03/337-1185 🖷 03/337-5085 ⊕ www.canterburytrails.co.nz.

SPECIAL-
INTEREST TOURS

On Diana's Garden Tours, the passionate gardener and local garden writer Diana Madgin takes you around some of Christchurch and Canterbury's gardens.

New Zealand food writer Mavis Airey of Taste Canterbury will guide you to the best local food and wine in Waipara and Akaroa, where adventurous cooking is taking off.

As its name suggests, Vin de Pays does tours of the Waipara wine district, but it also organizes garden tours, a Taste of New Zealand tour, and trips to Akaroa and back via Lyttelton Harbour.

Diana's Garden Tours ☎ 03/385-3559. **Taste Canterbury** ☎ 03/326-6753 ⊕ www.goodthings.co.nz. **Vin de Pays** ☎ 03/357-8262 ⊕ www.vindepays.co.nz.

VISITOR INFORMATION

Most information centers are open from around 9 until 4:30, depending on the season. For the best information on the Waipara wineries, stop at the Pukeko Junction Regional Wine Centre (*see the* Waipara Valley, *above*).

Tourist Information Akaroa Information Centre ⊠ 80 Rue Lavaud ☎ 03/304-8600 ⊕ www.akaroa.com. **Geraldine Visitor Information Centre** ⊠ 32 Talbot St. ☎ 03/693-1006 ⊕ www.southisland.org.nz. **Hurunui Visitor Information Centre** ⊠ Amuri Ave. Hanmer ☎ 03/315-7128 ⊕ www.hurunui.com. **Lyttelton** ⊠ 20 Oxford St. ☎ 03/328-9093 ⊕ www.lytteltonharbour.co.nz. **Methven Visitor Centre** ⊠ 93 Main St. ☎ 03/302-8955 ⊕ www.methven.net.nz. **Timaru Visitor Centre** ⊠ 2 George St. ☎ 03/688-6163 ⊕ www.southisland.org.nz.

8

The Southern Alps & Fiordland

WORD OF MOUTH

"I like to travel around fast, but we stayed in Queenstown for four nights and could have stayed longer. This was a highlight of our trip. Beautiful scenery, amazing adventure activities, and just a great place to relax for a few days."

—travelersusan

"Though Milford is certainly more popular, Doubtful Sound was much more spectacular in my mind. The sound is longer than Milford and more peaceful, as there seem to be fewer companies that operate there."

—cbegbie

Updated by
Sue Farley

AS THE KEA FLIES, it's only 130 km (80 mi) from the eastern shores of the South Island to its highest peak, Aoraki, or Mt. Cook. And it's only a quarter of that to the wild beaches of the West Coast. Mt. Cook, 12,283 feet, is New Zealand's highest mountain, yet 27 other peaks in this alpine chain are more than 9,750 feet in height. As many as 60 glaciers are locked in the Southern Alps, slowly grinding their way down to lower altitudes, where they melt into running rivers of uncanny blue-green hues. Aoraki/Mount Cook National Park is a UNESCO World Heritage Area, and the alpine region around it contains the Tasman Glacier, at 27 km (17 mi), New Zealand's longest.

Much of the region was used in shooting the *Lord of the Rings* film trilogy, and floods of tourists have since come to see the otherworldly landscape for themselves. (The vastness of the region, however, has kept it from feeling crowded, even with all the new visitors.) Queenstown, often billed as an adventure-sports hot spot, is perhaps the best-known destination in the Southern Lakes district. It, and the nearby town of Wanaka, are steeped in gold-rush history and surrounded by stunning mountain scenery.

Hiking is one of the things the Southern Alps region does best. Terrain varies here from high alpine tundra to snow-covered peaks, heavily forested mountains, and wide, braided river valleys. Much of it is serious alpine territory, and requires skill and good preparation to explore. There is a good network of trails and marked routes throughout the mountains, but it is vital to be well informed before venturing into them. Always make your intentions known to the local Department of Conservation (DOC) sign-in office before leaving, and check in with them after returning.

Luckily there are also many easier options for exploring the foothills and less arduous parts of the Southern Alps. The southwest corner of the island, where glaciers over millennia have cut the Alps into stone walls dropping into fjords, is laced with walking trails that take you into the heart of wild Fiordland National Park. The Milford Track is the best known—it has been called the finest walk in the world since a headline to that effect appeared in the London *Spectator* in 1908. If you're not keen on walking all the way to Milford Sound, drive in and hop on a boat and take in the sights and sounds from on deck. Most river valleys with road access have well-marked walking trails, and many of these lead to scenic spots such as waterfalls, gorges, and lookout points.

Note: For more information on outdoor activities in lower South Island, *see* Chapter 11.

Exploring the Southern Alps & Fiordland

The Southern Alps start in the northern end of the South Island around Kaikoura and stretch through the provinces of Canterbury, inland Otago, Westland, and Southland. Exploring the region is best done by car on the state highways that weave their way through the vast mountain ranges, skirting several major lakes and rivers. Some of the smaller roads are not paved, so unless you're experienced in driving on gravel roads, they should be avoided. That said, an ideal way to see the Alps is to "tiki-tour"(wander around) by car, as the main network of roads is well formed, paved, and easy to negotiate. Most towns and many of the settlements and villages have accommodation and places to eat, even if it's just a motel or a bed-and-breakfast and a low-key café in the local pub. Other places such as Queenstown, Wanaka, Te Anau, and Mt. Cook village have a variety of options to suit all price ranges.

Although the Southern Alps and Fiordland have four distinct seasons, it's not unusual for the mountains to get snow even in summer. If you're traveling in winter, be sure to check the weather forecasts and road conditions regularly. Mountain passes can close for short periods because of snow and ice and, even when they are open, can be very dangerous. The road into Milford Sound can sometimes be closed for days at a time because of either snow or avalanche risk.

About the Restaurants

Queenstown, as the main regional resort, has the widest range of restaurants. Throughout the area you'll find menus focused on local produce, seafood, lamb, and venison. Wine lists often highlight South Island wines, especially those from central Otago and Gibbston Valley. The cafés and restaurants in some towns that are driven by the summer tourist trade, such as Te Anau, tend to shorten their hours in winter or close entirely. Dress standards are generally relaxed, with jeans or khakis acceptable almost everywhere. Still, at high-end places, particularly in Queenstown, you'll need to reserve a table at least a day in advance. The staff at your hotel will be able to give you a better idea about this.

Outside of Queenstown and Wanaka the options for dining can be a little limited. During summer, meals of some sort are available almost everywhere, but outside the high season, options in the smaller settlements can be minimal.

WHAT IT COSTS In New Zealand dollars				
	$$$$	$$$	$$	$	¢
RESTAURANTS	over $30	$20–$30	$15–$20	$10–$15	under $10

Prices are per person for a main course at dinner, or the equivalent.

About the Hotels

Lodgings in the Southern Alps and Fiordland take advantage of their fantastic surroundings and milk the views for all they're worth. You'll almost always be able to find a room with a view over a lake, river, or rugged mountain range. Queenstown and Wanaka get busy in both the summer (January through March) and winter (July through September), so you should reserve in advance in those peak seasons. There are plenty of award-winning luxury options in Queenstown in particular, and costs are correspondingly high. Other towns, such as Aoraki/Mount Cook Village, have very limited options, so you should plan ahead there, too. Air-conditioning is an exception rather than the norm, since it rarely gets hot enough to warrant it. Heating, though, is standard, and essential in winter.

TOP REASONS TO GO

BUNGY JUMPING

Don't worry, New Zealanders aren't going to pressure you into jumping off a bridge with an elastic cord tied to your ankles. But if you have an overwhelming desire to bungy (the Kiwi spelling for "bungee"), this is the place to do it. The cost of the jump usually includes a "been there–done that" T-shirt and even a video of your daredevil act.

FLY-FISHING

The Southern Alps' lakes and rivers are some of the country's (and therefore, the world's) best fly-fishing spots—and that's before you even consider the eye-popping scenery. The waters are so clear, half the challenge is hiding from your target. Plenty of lodges from Lake Wanaka to Queenstown offer guiding services and/or advice. Most guides follow the catch-and-release policy.

HIKING

South Island's southwestern wilderness areas are the stuff of legendary tramping. The Milford Track, the Kepler, the Routeburn, the Hollyford–it doesn't get any better than these. The variety on these treks is astonishing; you'll see mountains, fjords, waterfalls, and rain forests. You'll need to plan ahead, though, as the DOC keeps a close eye on trail traffic. The upside is that, once on a track, you'll have the exhilarating sense of being alone in the wilderness.

SCENIC FLIGHTS

With high mountain peaks, deep fiords, rambling glaciers, thick forest, and open tussock lands all in close proximity, a scenic flight in either a fixed-wing plane or helicopter is money well spent. If you think the Southern Alps are spectacular from the ground, wait until you see them from above!

9

WHAT IT COSTS In New Zealand dollars				
$$$$	$$$	$$	$	¢
HOTELS	over $300	$200–$300	$125–$200	$75–$125	under $75

Prices are for a standard double room in high season, including 12.5% tax.

When to Visit

This is the part of New Zealand that gets cold with a capital C in winter, so if you're coming for warm weather, stay away between May and November. For skiing, snowboarding, and other winter sports, this is *the* time to come. From July through September you can be assured of snow around Queenstown and Wanaka, where the ski scene is very lively and ushered in by the Queenstown Winter Festival. In the height of summer— from January to March—both resort towns are crowded with Kiwi holiday makers. To avoid the crowds, hold off until March or April, when the leaves start turning. If you're planning on hiking one of the major trails, such as the Milford Track, summer or early autumn are the best times (you'll need to book ahead). This is also the best time to visit Fiordland National Park. Fiordland is soaked with rain year-round (it's the wettest place in the country), so there's little use trying to avoid the rainy season.

THE SOUTHERN ALPS

The Canterbury Plains, which ring Christchurch and act as a brief transition between the South Pacific and the soaring New Zealand Alps, are the country's finest sheep pastures, as well as its largest area of flat land. But although this may be sheep- and horse-trekking heaven, the drive south along the plain is mundane by New Zealand standards until you leave State Highway 1 and head toward the Southern Alps.

Taking the route south, along the eastern flank of the Alps, can leave you breathless. The mountain ranges are reflected in the many lakes and rivers that shimmer among the peaks. No matter how absorbing your activities may be—fishing, hiking, skiing—be sure to take some time to just sit back and gaze at this astonishing landscape. Head through Lindis Pass by traveling inland to Fairlie and Tekapo, then south to Omarama; you'll be entering the country's adventure-sports playground, where Wanaka and Queenstown offer at least a dozen ways to get your adrenaline pumping. A handful of notable vineyards is icing on the cake.

Mackenzie Country & Lake Tekapo

227 km (141 mi) west of Christchurch.

You will know you have reached the **Mackenzie Country** after you cross Burkes Pass and the woodland is suddenly replaced by high-country tussock grassland, which is dotted with lupines in the summer months. The area is named for James ("Jock") McKenzie, one of the most intriguing and enigmatic figures in New Zealand history. McKenzie was a Scot who may or may not have stolen the thousand sheep that were found with him in these secluded upland pastures in 1855. Arrested, tried, and convicted, he made several escapes from jail before he was granted a pardon nine months after his trial—and disappeared from the pages of history. Regardless of his innocence or guilt, there can be no doubt that McKenzie was a master bushman and herdsman. A commemorative obelisk marks Mackenzie Pass, 30 km (18 mi) off the main highway if you turn off at Burkes Pass.

❶ The long, narrow expanse of **Lake Tekapo** anchors the area—it's one of the most photographed sights in New Zealand. Its extraordinary milky-turquoise color comes from rock flour, rock ground by glacial action and held in a soupy suspension. Tekapo, the country's highest large lake, has good fly-fishing both in the lake and in the surrounding rivers and canals.

Kiwis also know the lake as the site of hydroelectric power. On the east side of the lakeside power station is the tiny **Church of the Good Shepherd,** which strikes a dignified note of piety in these majestic surroundings. A nearby memorial commemorates the sheepdogs of the area, who made farming this vast countryside possible in the early pioneering days and still do so today. As you drive into the small town, you'll notice a knot of restaurants with tour buses parked outside. It's rather

GREAT ITINERARIES

Touring the lower half of South Island requires making difficult choices. Do you want to walk the Milford Track or bungy off a bridge? Will you go away disappointed if you miss Queenstown, the adventure capital, or would you rather find a quiet lodge in sight of majestic Aoraki/Mt. Cook? Then there's the choice of waking up with views of mountains, lakes, or both.

To see it all would take a good three weeks, if you intend to do it justice and stay sane. Short of that, treat each of these areas as two- to three-day segments, mix them up to suit your fancy, and take into account travel time of three to five hours between each.

Numbers in the text correspond to points of interest on the Southern Alps & Fiordland map.

IF YOU HAVE 3 DAYS
Spend at least one day and night in **Queenstown** ❻, starting with a ride on the Skyline Gondola to catch a bird's-eye view of the town, Lake Wakatipu, and the Remarkables mountains. Once you've whet your appetite for adventure, either brave a bungy jump or just watch one for a vicarious thrill. A scenic flight over **Milford Sound** ❾ will give you a peek at Fiordland, to the south.

The next day, you could head to **Wanaka** ❺ for some fishing, rafting, or wine tasting. Alternatively, head to **Aoraki (Mt. Cook)** ❷ (a longer drive) to take a flight onto **Tasman Glacier** ❹.

IF YOU HAVE 6 OR 7 DAYS
Spend two or three days in **Queenstown** ❻. Depending on how active you are, you could easily spend three days here throwing yourself off a bridge, heliskiing, jet-boat riding, or wine tasting. During one of your afternoons, head to Queenstown's gold-rush neighbor, **Arrowtown** ❼. If you've booked a stint on one of the multiday trails in Fiordland, such as the Milford Track, spend just two days in Queenstown and head south from there. Otherwise, next head to **Te Anau** ❽, the base for Fiordland National Park. Here you can take a boat or flightseeing tour of **Milford Sound** ❾, work in a day hike, and perhaps see the less-crowded Doubtful Sound as well. Wherever you go in Fiordland, don't forget your bug repellent! After a couple of days here, you can double back for a day at **Wanaka** ❺. If you have a day left, you could try to push on toward **Aoraki (Mt. Cook)** ❷ on your way to Christchurch, or drive over to the West Coast via the Haast Pass.

an off-putting image if you've come for peace and quiet, but it's relatively easy to keep the township at your back and your eyes turned on the lake and mountains—and get a tasty meal. If you're not planning to stay at Mt. Cook, then Tekapo is the best place in the Mackenzie Basin to stop for the night. And once the buses have passed through for the day, it's a quiet spot—at least until the hordes of Cantabrians arrive for the summer break. A pleasant lakefront recreation area separates the town retail area from the lakeshore. It's a nice spot to break the day's drive with a take-out coffee and sandwich, and so avoid the rush of bus passengers who descend on Tekapo at midday.

Southern Alps & Fiordland

KEY
⊢⊣ Rail lines

Hokitika

Arthur's Pass National Park

Arthur's Pass

Trans-Alpine Express

7

6

Southern Alps

Rakaia R.

Okarito Lagoon

Okarito

Mt. Cook N.P.

Erewhon

Rangitata R.

Franz Josef Glacier

Fox Glacier

Aoraki/ Mt. Cook ②

Tasman Glacier ④

Two Thumb Range

① **Lake Tekapo**

Westland National Park

③

Tasman R.

Lake Tekapo

WEST COAST

Aoraki/ Mt. Cook Village

Ben Ohau Range

L. Pukaki

Haast

Haast R.

Southern Alps

Hunter R.

Twizel

Lake Pukaki

CANTERBURY

L. Ohau

Omarama

Mt. Aspiring National Park

6

L. Dingle R.

Lindis Pass

8

Mt. Aspiring ▲

L. Wanaka

L. Hawea

Oamaru

Motatapu R.

⑤ ✈

Lake Hawea

6

8

Milford Sound

Dart R.

Shotover R.

Wanaka

Kyeburn

85

85

Mitre Pk. ▲ ⑨

Paradise

Cardrona

Karawau R.

Cromwell

Palmerston

Milford Sound

Glenorchy ✈

Arrowtown ⑦

Gibbston

Alexandra

OTAGO

Knob Flat

L. Wakatipu

87

Dunedin

94

L. Te Anau

Queenstown ⑥ *see detail map*

8

Raes Junction

1

Milton

Te Anau Downs

Murchison Mts.

Te Anau ⑧

94

Lumsden

8

Balclutha

Doubtful Sound

L. Manapouri

Manapouri

6

SOUTHLAND

Gore

1

Breaksea Sound

Fiordland National Park

1

Dusky Sound

CATLINS COAST

Te Waewae Bay

Invercargill

Toetoes Bay

Stewart Island

1

Bluff

0 ——— 40 miles

0 ——— 60 km

BULLOCK WAGON TRAIL – This 268-km (167-mi) heritage highway, which stretches from Timaru to Twizel via Mt. Cook, recognizes the long, arduous journeys early settlers in the region made by bullock wagon when heading into the high country. Leaving the Canterbury Plains at Geraldine or Pleasant Point (depending on whether you are coming directly from Christchurch or through from Timaru), you'll find that the highways join at Fairlie and very quickly climb toward the first of the alpine passes—Burkes Pass—along the Bullock Wagon Trail. The Three Springs Woolshed, a short distance inland of Fairlie, offers an interesting glimpse into the early pastoral life of the area. The Burkes Pass monument marks the division between the high and low country, and from there the country immediately dries out and takes on the look of high-country tussocklands. To learn more about the trail and the history of the region, you can stop in at one of two information centers along the way. **Lake Tekapo Information** (⊠ Main Rd., Lake Tekapo ☎🖷 03/680–6686). **The Resource Centre** (⊠ 64 Main St., Fairlie ☎🖷 03/685–8496 ⊕ www. southisland.org.nz/heritagetrails/bullockwagon.html).

Where to Stay & Eat

$$$–$$$$ ✕ **Reflections Café.** You'll have great views of the lake from almost every table at this rustically decorated restaurant. Red meat is treated well; Reflections consistently wins awards for its beef and lamb dishes, and salmon from a nearby hatchery is also notably delicious. As many ingredients as possible are obtained locally to maintain freshness in the meals. ⊠ *Lake Tekapo Scenic Resort, State Hwy. 8* ☎🖷 *03/680–6234* ▭ *MC, V.*

$$–$$$$ ✕ **The Garden Courtyard.** An impressive buffet appears three times a day in this pleasant dining room. Lunch and dinner selections always include six entrées and another half-dozen vegetable dishes, as well as soups, salads, and several desserts. The salmon is reliably good, and if you've caught your own, the restaurant kitchen will cook it for you. Between lunch and dinner, a snack menu offers paninis, soup, mussels, warm chicken salad, and the like, all for less than $12. ⊠ *The Godley Hotel, State Hwy. 8* ☎ *03/680–6848* ▭ *AE, MC, V.*

¢–$$$$ ✕ **Kohan Japanese Restaurant.** Masato Itoh runs the only Japanese restaurant in town, which gives him guaranteed access to busloads of tourists from his home country. Sushi, sashimi, and tempura are all on the menu. The restaurant has some of the best views over Lake Tekapo, but unfortunately it lacks atmosphere. The food, however, is a refreshing change from the more traditional lunch options in town. It's open for lunch from 11 to 2 and for dinner from 6 PM on. ⊠ *State Hwy. 8* ☎ *03/ 680–6688* ▭ *AE, DC, MC, V* ☾ *No dinner Sun.*

¢–$$$ ✕ **Observatory Café.** Although this place is obviously built for the tour-bus trade, it's big enough to accommodate lots of people and feed them relatively well. The indoor dining area has a nice view over the lake, and on warm days the outdoor seating is very popular. Food is standard café fare of salads and fries, burgers, quiche, sandwiches, salmon, and a roast of the day. Open 8 AM–8:30 PM, the property has Internet facilities and clean restrooms. ⊠ *Main St., State Hwy. 8* ☎ *03/680–6886 or 0800/806–886* ▭ *AE, MC, V.*

¢ $ ✕ **Doughboys.** In a town where most of the dining options are found along the main drag of souvenir shops and cafés, it's nice to escape with

9

a sandwich, a pastry, or a pie and eat down at the lakefront. Dough-boys does several different breads, croissants, and 10 different kinds of pies. Sandwiches have yummy fillings such as seafood, chicken and mayonnaise, or bacon and eggs, and the scones are legendary. Just in case that's not enough, you can grab a sit-down breakfast (bacon, two eggs, tomato), for about $12. ⊠ *State Hwy. 8* ☎ *03/680–6655* 🖃 *No credit cards* ⊘ *No dinner.*

$$$–$$$$ 🖼 **Lake Tekapo Luxury Lodge.** Top New Zealand craftsmen created this luxurious, earth-brick complex, whose arresting decor competes for attention with the stunning views of Lake Tekapo and the Southern Alps. Arched, studded antique church doors open into a beamed entrance area where fine art mixes with farming paraphernalia. Wrought-iron embellishments run throughout the building, with most furnishings made of oak or elm. The front rooms open out to a covered veranda, the garden, and the best views. ⊠ *24 Aorangi Crescent* ☎ *03/680–6566* 🖷 *03/680–6599* ⊕ *www.laketekapolodge.co.nz* 🖙 *4 rooms* ♤ *Dining room, in-room broadband, lounge; no a/c* 🖃 *AE, DC, MC, V* ⏹ *BP.*

$$–$$$ 🖼 **The Chalet.** The Chalet's six fully self-contained apartments stretch beside the turquoise waters of Lake Tekapo. All units have refreshing color schemes, along with an individual thematic streak, and range from studio size to a two-bedroom cottage apartment. The best are those with spacious living rooms and lake views; two of the rooms open onto a small patio area and lovely alpine gardens. You can arrange a customized local expedition with the host, an experienced hunting, fishing, and nature guide. Tekapo township is a scenic five-minute walk away. ⊠ *14 Pioneer Dr.* ☎ *03/680–6774* 🖷 *03/680–6713* ⊕ *www.thechalet.co.nz* 🖙 *6 units* ♤ *Fishing, hiking, laundry service; no a/c* 🖃 *AE, MC, V.*

$$–$$$ 🖼 **Lake Tekapo Scenic Resort.** A nice mid-range alternative with good family-style facilities, this resort is right in the center of town. Still, it opens out to the lakefront area, and many units have lake views. There's a big three-bedroom upstairs apartment available if you're traveling with the family and want to spread out for a night or two. Meals are available at Reflections restaurant next door on a charge-back basis. ⊠ *State Hwy. 8* ☎ *03/680–6808 or 0800/118–666* 🖷 *03/680–6806* ⊕ *www.laketekapo.com* 🖙 *6 family units, 12 studios, 1 3-bedroom apartment* ♤ *Some in-room hot-tubs, laundry facilities* 🖃 *DC, MC, V.*

¢ 🖼 **Tailor-Made-Tekapo Backpackers.** The beautiful garden here is made for sunbathing in warm weather. In winter, there's a cozy lounge with a fireplace to curl up in front of. There are various room arrangements, from singles to four- and six-bed dorm rooms; all, including the dorms, have regular beds (no bunks). It's a very kid-friendly spot. ⊠ *9–11 Aorangi Crescent* ☎ *03/680–6700* ⊕ *www.tailor-made-backpackers.co.nz* 🖙 *13 rooms, 10 with shared bath, 3 dorms* ♤ *BBQ, tennis court, bicycles; no room TVs* 🖃 *MC, V.*

Sports & the Outdoors

FISHING **Barry Clark Fly-Fishing & Small Game Hunting Guide** (⊠ 1 Esther-Hope St., Lake Tekapo ☎ 03/680–6513 ⊕ www.fredadufaur.co.nz) will take you fly-fishing or spinning, whatever your preference, to the most suitable lake or river spot of the day (Barry's knowledge of the local spots is exhaustive).

HIKING   At the Tekapo Information Centre you can pick up a walking-trail map and then take off to hike the **Domain to Mt. John Lookout track.** In a couple of hours you can be well above the township, enjoying extensive views of the Mackenzie Basin, Southern Alps, and Lake Tekapo.

STARGAZING   There are two options available for stargazing under this region's painfully clear southern night skies. **Star Watching** (⊠ Main St., State Hwy. 8, Lake Tekapo ☎ 03/680–6565 ⊕ www.stargazing.co.nz) sets up telescopes at a spot in Mt. Cook National Park, where astronomer Hideyuki Ozawa expertly interprets the night sky while you await a shooting star to make a wish upon. The trips, which leave at 10 PM in summer and 8 PM in winter, cost $48 and are, obviously, weather-dependent. Dress warmly. **Earth and Sky** (⊠ Main St., State Hwy. 8, Lake Tekapo ☎ 03/680–6960 ⊕ www.earthandsky.co.nz) operates from the Mt. John Observatory and studies the skies above Lake Tekapo. Trips cost $40, and reservations are essential.

Aoraki (Mt. Cook)

❷ *99 km (62 mi) from Lake Tekapo.*

Fodor'sChoice
★

Above the grassy Mackenzie Basin towers **Aoraki (Mt. Cook)**, the tallest of the 22 peaks over 10,000 feet in **Aoraki/Mount Cook National Park.** At approximately 12,283 feet, it is the highest peak between Papua New Guinea and the Andes. The mountain's Māori name is Aoraki (Aorangi to North Island Māori), after one of three brothers who were the sons of Rakinui, the sky father. Legend has it that their canoe was caught on a reef and frozen, forming the South Island. In these parts, South Island's oldest Māori name is Te Waka O Aoraki (Aoraki's canoe) and the highest peak is Aoraki, himself frozen by the south wind, then turned to stone. Māori see these mountains as their ancestors. The officially recognized names of this mountain, the national park, and many other South Island places have been changed to their original Māori names as part of a 1998 settlement between the government and the major South Island Māori tribe, Ngai Tahu.

Aoraki was dramatically first scaled in 1894 by three New Zealanders—Tom Fyfe, George Graham, and Jack Clarke—just after it was announced that an English climber and an Italian mountain guide were about to attempt the summit. In a frantic surge of national pride, the New Zealand trio resolved to beat them to it, which they did on Christmas Day. The mountain is still considered a difficult ascent. In the summer of 1991 a chunk of it broke away, but fortunately there were no climbers in the path of the massive avalanches. High Peak, the summit, is now about 66 feet lower, but its altered form makes for a much more difficult ascent.

At 439 square km (270 square mi), the park is a formidable area of ice and rock, with very little forest cover and glaciers covering 40% of the land, and is part of the greater South West New Zealand World Heritage Area. Unfortunately, the high altitude of this area also attracts its fair share of bad weather. Visitors can often stand at the end of Lake Tekapo or Lake Pukaki, looking westward, and not know that the country's highest mountain is just a few miles away. But that shouldn't prevent you from taking the 40-km (25-mi) paved road up to Mt. Cook village. And stay the night while you're there—nowhere else in the region compares for a true alpine experience. Accommodation and food options range from luxury rooms with silver-service dining to backpackers' lodges and campsites. If the clouds lift and the mountains loom clear, you'll be glad you stayed: the vistas are beyond spectacular.

❸ The national park surrounds **Aoraki/Mount Cook Village** (population 300), which consists of a visitor center, a grocery store, an airfield, a pub, a little school, a hotel/motel complex, and several hostels. Walking is always an option, and in winter there's heliskiing. If the weather is clear, a scenic flight around the Mt. Cook area and across to the West Coast can be the highlight of your stay in New Zealand.

Contact the **Aoraki/Mount Cook National Park Visitor Centre** (☎ 03/435–1186) or the **weather phone** (☎ 03/435–1171) to check conditions before setting out on an unguided excursion. A network of hiking trails radiates from the Aoraki/Mount Cook National Park Visitor Centre, offering everything from easy walking paths to full-day challenges. There are some especially lovely wildflowers to search out, such as the Mount Cook lily, really the world's largest buttercup. A cairn just a few minutes along the track up the Hooker Valley remembers 40 of the more than 180 people who have died in the park since climbing began there. Be sure to fill your car's gas tank before leaving Twizel or Tekapo if you can; although there is limited fuel available at the Hermitage hotel, there are no credit card facilities at the pumps and they run limited hours.

A unique hands-on educational experience is to take a half-hour hike to the fast-growing 2-square-km (1-square-mi) **Terminus Lake of the Tasman Glacier.** Fed by the glacier and the Murchison River, the lake was formed only in the past couple of decades, because of the glacier's retreat. Rock flour, a powdery white residue, gives the water a milky color (farther downstream, it also creates the unusual turquoise-blue color of Lake Pukaki). From Terminus Lake, which is officially growing by a foot a week, you can examine up close the terminal face of the glacier, which is 3 km (2 mi) wide. A trip with Glacier Explorers (⇨ Tours *in* The Southern Alps & Fiordland Essentials, *below*) can take you by boat to explore some of the large floating icebergs that have calved (fallen away) from the Tasman Glacier. It's an eerie experience skimming across the milky-white water and closing in on icebergs—even riding *through* where they have melted—to touch rocks caught in the ice.

❹ Another main activity is "flightseeing." From the airfield at Mount Cook Village, helicopters and fixed-wing aircraft make spectacular scenic flights across the Southern Alps. One of the most exciting is the one-hour trip aboard the ski planes that touch down on the **Tasman Glacier** after a gorgeous scenic flight. The 10-minute stop on the glacier doesn't allow time for much more than a snapshot, but the sensation is tremendous. The moving tongue of ice beneath your feet—one of the largest glaciers outside the Himalayas—is 27 km (17 mi) long and up to 2,000 feet thick in places. The intensity of light on the glacier can be dazzling, and sunglasses are a must. During winter the planes drop skiers on the glacier at 10,000 feet, and they ski down through 13 km (8 mi) of pow-

Safety in the High Country

NEW ZEALANDERS ARE WELL known for their extreme love of the outdoors—which makes sense, given the extreme beauty of the country's landscapes. Although there are many safe, moderately adventurous ways to enjoy these landscapes, the Fiordland region's remoteness and changeable weather make it necessary to take some sensible precautions. So, before you head out on that trek or boat trip, keep the following in mind:

• Be sure to wear, or bring, the right protective clothing: sturdy hiking boots, a waterproof jacket, and a warm layer such as a fleece or wool pullover. Weather in this region, especially at high altitude, can change dramatically in a short time.

• Watch out for sunburn—take sunscreen and a hat with you. It's also a good idea to bring bug repellent for sand flies, which are impossible to avoid in this region unless you're traveling offshore by boat.

• If you're heading off without a guide for more than an hour or two, let someone know where and when you're going and when you've returned. DOC visitor centers have sign-in books and issue regular weather and trail updates.

• Use extreme caution when crossing rivers. Especially after rain, mountain runoff can quickly turn a gentle stream into an angry torrent, and drowning is a major hazard. If you do get trapped on one side of a quickly rising river, wait for the water to recede rather than risk crossing.

• For longer treks into serious country always carry a map and compass, first-aid gear, bottled water, high-energy foods, warm clothes and tent, and a mountain radio or EPIRB (locator beacon—these can be rented locally). Cell phones don't work in the mountains.

der snow and fantastic ice formations. With guides, this run is suitable even for intermediate skiers.

Where to Stay & Eat

$$$–$$$$ ✕⊞ **The Hermitage.** Famed for its stupendous mountain vistas, this rambling hotel has been substantially revamped over the past few years. The improved layout now gives most of the rooms, as well as the lobby, terrific views over Aoraki and a beautiful nearby mountain, Mt. Sefton. (Some accommodations, such as the motel rooms and self-contained chalets, are separate from the main lodge and the views aren't as spectacular; but the prices and space are good for families.) As the name suggests, the Panorama Room ($$$–$$$$) restaurant takes in the scenery, too. Its menu leans toward both the Pacific Rim and Europe; you could try panfried monkfish or a char-grilled beef tenderloin. The Alpine Restaurant ($$$–$$$$) serves a huge buffet-style meal for lunch and dinner. If you're traveling out of the high season, there are excellent discounts available on room rates. Be sure to keep your car in the hotel's parking, safe from the beaks of the cheeky local keas. ⊠ *Aoraki/Mount Cook Village* ☎ *03/435–1809 or 0800/686–800* 🖷 *03/435–1879*

⊕ *www.mount-cook.com* ➥ *221 rooms, 19 chalets, 32 motel units* ᗌ *2 restaurants, café, sauna, bar, shops, Internet room; some a/c* ⊟ *AE, DC, MC, V* ⍒ *BP, CP.*

$–$$ ▦ **Aoraki/Mt. Cook Alpine Lodge.** This comfortable new lodge, run by a young local family, has accommodations ranging from dorm rooms to twin, triple, and family rooms, many with private bathrooms. All rooms have great mountain views (although some are greater than others). The alpine-style decor features lots of native timber and glass, and there's a huge stone fireplace in the lobby. ⊠ *Bowen Dr. Mount Cook Village* ☎ *03/435–1860 or 0800/680–680* ⊕ *www.aorakialpinelodge.co.nz* ➥ *15 rooms* ᗌ *Kitchen, shop, lounge, laundry facilities, Internet room* ⊟ *MC, V.*

$–$$ ▦ **Lake View Homestay.** The name suggests only part of the scenery here—in addition to views of Lake Pukaki, you'll spy Aoraki/Mt. Cook and the Ben Ohau mountains through the floor-to-ceiling windows or from the porch. The peaks of the roofline mirror the toothy ranges beyond; timber walls inside give a warm glow. If you'd like to see a working shepherd-dog demonstration, go fishing, or take a helicopter trip, just say the word to your hosts. ⊠ *Mt. Cook Rd., State Hwy. 80, Lake Pukaki* ☎ *03/435–0567* 🖷 *3/435–0568* ⊕ *www.lakeviewhomestay.co.nz* ➥ *4 rooms, 3 with bath* ᗌ *No a/c, no room TVs, no kids under 12* ⊟ *No credit cards* ⍒ *BP, CP.*

¢ ⛺ **White Horse Hill Campground.** Although this DOC-managed campsite is really just a grassy basin surrounded by massive mountains and a rumbling glacier, its basic facilities and closeness to trails make it an ideal spot to park a camper van or pitch a tent. (Once again, make sure those keas don't steal your lunch or rip the rubber off your windshield wipers!) You can pay at the DOC Visitors Centre before setting up camp or in the honesty box down at the campsite. Running water is available, although it needs to be boiled for three minutes before you drink it; you can grab a shower back at the Day Shelter in the village for $1. No reservations are taken here, so it's first come, first served. ⊠ *Hooker Valley Rd., end of Rd.* ☎ *03/435–1186* 🖷 *03/435–1080* ⊕ *www.doc.govt.nz.*

Sports & the Outdoors

CLIMBING & The Aoraki/Mount Cook National Park area is ideal for rock climbing;
MOUNTAINEERING summer is the best climbing season. **Adventure Consultants** (☎ 03/443–8711 ⊕ www.adventure.co.nz), a group specializing in the world's top peaks, guides ascents of Aoraki as well as the challenging climbs up Mount Tasman. They also give multiday mountaineering, alpine-climbing, and ice-climbing courses. (Because the company is based in Wanaka, they work Mt. Cook only in good weather, so be sure to call and reserve ahead.) Experienced climbers and beginners alike can sign up for the appropriate level of **Alpine Guides'** (⊠ Bowen Dr., Mt. Cook Village ☎ 03/435–1834 ⊕ www.alpineguides.co.nz) 6- to 10-day mountaineering courses, which begin around $2,350. They also offer half-day rock-climbing trips costing $150, including equipment. From July to September they also run heliski trips, ski tours, ice climbing, and ski mountaineering.

FLIGHTSEEING Flightseeing gives you an unparalleled view of the mountains, with the added thrill of landing on a glacier for a short walk. The light can be intensely bright in such dazzlingly white surroundings, so be sure to bring sunglasses. Generally, the best time for flights is early morning. **Mount Cook Ski Planes** (☎ 03/430–8034 or 0800/800–702 ⊕ www.mtcookskiplanes. com) has four options, including a 25-minute flight over two glaciers ($220) or a 55-minute flight with a glacier landing ($430). Or take a breathtaking 50-minute scenic flight to see Aoraki, the Tasman, Murchison, Fox, and Franz Josef glaciers, and the rain forests on the west side of the Main Divide with **Air Safaris** (☎ 03/680–6545 ⊕ www.airsafaris.co.nz). Flights start at $260 per adult. **The Helicopter Line** runs 20-minute and 45-minute flights from Glentanner Station, about 20 km (12 mi) toward Pukaki from the Hermitage. You can land on the glaciers or high snowfields, depending on the weather. ⊠ *Glentanner Station, State Hwy. 80* ☎ *03/435–1801 or 0800/650–651* ⊕ *www.helicopter.co.nz.*

HIKING The hiking trails spooling out from the visitor center range in difficulty and length, from the 10-minute Bowen Track to the 5½-hour climb to the 4,818-foot summit of Mt. Sebastopol. Seven tracks can be done in running shoes and don't require hiking experience; the rest of the park's trails require some hiking experience, and the higher routes require serious mountaineering experience. The Mueller Hut route is a popular climb, taking about three hours; a new 30-bed hut provides overnight accommodation. The rewarding Hooker Valley walk, a four-hour round-trip, will take you across a couple of swingbridges to the Hooker Glacier terminus lake, and the Tasman Glacier Lake walk gives an intimate view of New Zealand's longest glacier.

Twizel

65 km (40 mi) from Lake Tekapo, 40 km (25 mi) from Aoraki/Mt. Cook.

A service town to its core, Twizel was purpose-built in 1968 as a base for workers constructing a major hydroelectric power plant. When the hydroelectric scheme wrapped up, the residents fought to keep their town intact, rather than bulldoze it and move on. Now it's a handy place for tourist overflow in the Aoraki/Mt. Cook area. During filming for the *Lord of the Rings,* almost every local was involved, employed either as an extra or as a service provider. Birders should check with the visitor center about tours to the *kakī* aviary to see these striking, endangered, red-legged birds.

Although there are few reasons to spend time at Twizel when you have the glory of the Mt. Cook area just an hour along the road, it is close to five good-size boating and leisure lakes. Having already passed Tekapo and Pukaki, you'll find Lake Ruataniwha a little tame, but it is a premium rowing venue and has a salmon farm. Lake Ohau is a little off the main road, but is another high-country fishing gem. A ski slope, Ohau Snow Fields, is open starting in July each winter, and there are a number of walks in the nearby Ohau Forest Range.

Where to Stay

$$$$ **Matuka Lodge.** If fly-fishing's your game, this lodge is ideal. You can arrange for a guide to the nearby rivers to go after rainbow and brown trout, or do a bit of angling on the lodge's private pond. Scenery buffs will have plenty to gaze at; each room has a veranda with mountain views.

Your room rate includes dinner and wines. ⊠ *Old Station Rd.* ☎ *03/ 435–0144* ⊕ *www.matukalodge.co.nz* ⤳ *3 suites* ⚭ *Dining room, Internet room; no room TVs, no kids* ▭ *AE, DC, MC, V* ⑩ *MAP.*

$$ 🏨 **MacKenzie Country Inn.** If you decide to stay in Twizel, this well-priced place is your best bet. Its imposing stone-and-timber buildings make an impression in this otherwise nondescript town. Filled mainly by busloads of package tourists, its comfortable rooms and large lounges, complete with welcoming fires, are often full to capacity. Rooms range from standard to deluxe, and the prices are reasonable. ⊠ *Ostler Rd. at Wairepo Rd.* ☎ *03/435–0869 or 0800/500–869* 🖷 *03/435–0857* ⊕ *www. mountcookcollection.co.nz* ⤳ *108 rooms* ⚭ *Restaurant, bar* ▭ *AE, DC, MC, V.*

Wanaka

❺ *70 km (44 mi) northeast of Queenstown, 140 km (87 mi) southwest of Twizel.*

Set on the southern shore of Lake Wanaka, with some of New Zealand's most impressive mountains stretched out behind it, Wanaka is the welcome mat for Mt. Aspiring National Park. It is a favorite of Kiwis on vacation, an alternative of sorts to Queenstown. The region has numerous trekking and river-sports opportunities, but should you arrive on a rainy day, you can hit a couple of unusual cultural attractions instead.

These good points have not gone unnoticed, and Wanaka is one of the fastest-growing towns in New Zealand, with new housing popping up in record time. More cafés and bars are opening, too, to absorb the increasing numbers of tourists.

A short but pleasant drive around to the western side of the lake brings you to Glendhu Bay. With nothing there but a campground and fabulous mountain and lake views, the real charm in this drive lies in the unspoiled atmosphere and surreal quiet (except in midsummer, when it is packed full of vacationing locals). This road also leads on to the Aspiring region and the Treble Cone ski area.

Up in the Crown Range, the Snow Park in the Cardrona Valley is the country's only dedicated snowboard park and offers a real off-season alternative for Northern Hemisphere boarders looking for a fix over the northern summer. The 60-acre property has more than 30 rails and kickers, a super pipe, a half pipe, and a quarter pipe as well as a bar and restaurant.

Spectacularly sited on the shores of Lake Wanaka, **Rippon Vineyard** is one of the most photographed in the country. The vineyard's portfolio includes sparkling wine, riesling, gewürztraminer, chardonnay, sauvignon blanc, and fine (but expensive) pinot noir. Head west from Wanaka along the lake on Mt. Aspiring Road for 4 km (2½ mi). ⊠ *Mt. Aspiring Rd.* ☎ *03/443–8084* ⊕ *www.rippon.co.nz* ⊗ *Dec.–Apr., daily 11–5; July–Nov., daily 1:30–4:30.*

On your way into town on State Highway 6 you'll pass the **New Zealand Fighter Pilots Museum.** The museum is a tribute to New Zealand fighter pilots, of whom the country contributed more per capita than any other nation in World Wars I and II. The collection of planes includes aircraft used during the two world wars, such as the British Spitfire and rarities such as the Russian Polikarpov I–16. If you're visiting around Easter 2008, check out the biennial international air show Warbirds over Wanaka, where you can see some of these magnificent aircraft in flight. ⊠ *State Hwy. 6* ☎ *03/443–7010* ⊕ *www.nzfpm.co.nz* ⊠ *$8* ☉ *Daily 9–4.*

☺ **Stuart Landsborough's Puzzling World** features a number of puzzling life-size brainteasers, including the amazing Tumbling Towers and the Tilted House, which is on a 15-degree angle (is the water really running up-hill?), as well as the Leaning Tower of Wanaka. The Great Maze can be as demanding as you want to make it by setting individual challenges. Most people spend from 30 minutes to an hour in the maze, but if you really get stuck in the passages, there are emergency exit doors. In the Following Faces room it's an eerie feeling to have so many famous people watch your every move. But the place to really take your time is the popular Puzzle Centre. Just take on the puzzle of your choice, order a cup of coffee, and work yourself into a puzzled frenzy. The place is 2 km (1 mi) east of town—just look for the cartoonlike houses on funny angles. ⊠ *Hwy. 84* ☎ *03/443–7489* ⊕ *www.puzzlingworld.co.nz* ⊠ *$10* ☉ *Nov.–Apr., daily 8:30–5:30, May–Oct., daily 8:30–5.*

Where to Stay & Eat

$–$$$$ ✕ **Missy's Kitchen.** A local favorite, Missy's pulls in an after-ski crowd to its bar as well as to its dining room. (They've got a sophisticated cocktail list, as well as dozens of beers and wines.) In summer the balcony is a favored spot for dinner or just a glass of wine. If the Lake Wanaka view has you thinking of shellfish, lap up some Marlborough mussels flavored with lemongrass, lime, and chili jam. You can also try the beef sirloin or the escalope of salmon and choose from a list of yummy desserts. ⊠ *Ardmore St. and Lakefront Dr.* ☎ *03/443–5099* ☉ *Dinner only* ▤ *AE, DC, MC, V.*

$–$$$ ✕ **Kai Whaka Pai.** There's no better place to stop for breakfast on a crisp, sunny morning than this café, which has more tables outside than in. It's set just across the road from the lake, so the views range from pretty nice on a cloudy day to fantastic on a fine one. Meanwhile, the menu ranges from simple breakfast and lunch choices (coffee and croissants, salads, nachos, and kebabs), to more formal plates such as beef ribs or rump roast. Although reservations aren't mandatory, they're a good idea, since this place stays busy year-round. At sundown, things get lively in the upstairs Pa Runga Wine Bar, and dinner is available. ⊠ *Helwick and Ardmore Sts.* ☎ *03/443–7795* ▤ *AE, DC, MC, V.*

$$ ✕ **Thai Siam.** Directly under Missy's Kitchen this contemporary Thai restaurant has some interesting alternatives if you prefer a vegetarian or less meat-based cuisine—although they also run the full range of meat-lovers' options such as local salmon, steak, and Nelson Bay scallops. Still using a Thai method, they manage to incorporate some good South Island vegetables into their dishes rather than the usual Asian vegetables. ⊠ *Ardmore St. and Lakefront Dr.* ☎ *03/443–5010* ▤ *AE, DC, MC, V* ☉ *No lunch.*

¢–$$ ✕ **Relishes Cafe.** You could hit this lakeside spot for every meal of the day, starting with breakfast—perhaps some homemade muesli with a

9

side of toast and jam (Vegemite for homesick Aussies), or the bacon or salmon eggs Benedict. At lunch and dinner, you'll find fresh spins on Kiwi flavors, such as a grilled portobello mushroom–and-mozzarella sandwich with sun-dried tomato and salad. ✉ *99 Ardmore St.* ☎ *03/443–9018* ▭ *AE, DC, MC, V* ⊘ *Closed 1 wk in June.*

$$$$ ⊞ **Minaret Lodge.** This luxury retreat is just a 10-minute walk from town and offers ecofriendly accommodations. Materials used in the rooms, including a themed Lord of the Rings room, are all nontoxic, and peace and quiet is high on the priority list. Although the rooms don't look over the lake, they do have mountain views and are surrounded by trees and gardens (where there's an outdoor chess board). Rates include regional wine tastings and hors d'oeuvres; you can also arrange for dinner. ✉ *34 Eely Point Rd.* ☎ *03/443–1856* 🖷 *03/443–1846* ⊕ *www.minaretlodge. co.nz* ↩ *5 rooms* ♿ *Refrigerators, in-room data ports, tennis court, sauna, bicycles, lounge, recreation room, no kids under 10, no smoking* ▭ *AE, MC, V* ❚⊙❘ *BP.*

$$$$ ⊞ **Whare Kea Lodge.** Location is everything at this spectacular luxury lodge, overlooking the western shores of Lake Wanaka and the mountains beyond. The rooms are decorated in muted, neutral tones—the better to focus on the floor-to-ceiling windows that make you feel as though you could reach out and touch the lake. The lodge table d'hôte menu focuses on New Zealand produce and wines. Whare Kea guests also have the option of staying at a separate and remote mountain lodge, way up in the national park and accessible only by helicopter. Additional costs apply for this; contact the main lodge for more information. ✉ *Mt. Aspiring Rd.* ☎ *03/443–1400* 🖷 *03/443–9200* ⊕ *www.wharekealodge.com* ↩ *2 suites, 4 rooms* ♿ *Dining room, spa, lounge, bar, library* ▭ *AE, MC, V* ❚⊙❘ *MAP.*

$$$–$$$$ ⊞ **Lakeside Apartments.** Although a little on the pricey side, these modern apartments offer nice family-size accommodation in a very central location. Many units have wide-ranging views across the lake to the mountains beyond. Each of the apartments (which have between one and three bedrooms) has a wide balcony, a full kitchen, and laundry facilities; some have spa baths. ✉ *9 Lakeside Rd.* ☎ *03/443–0188 or 0800/002–211* 🖷 *03/443–0189* ⊕ *www.lakesidewanaka.co.nz* ↩ *20 apartments* ♿ *BBQ, pool* ▭ *AE, DC, MC, V.*

$$–$$$ ⊞ **Oakridge Pool & Spa Resort.** With its refreshing, contemporary design, this rather expansive resort is a departure from the usual alpine stone-and-timber lodgings in the region. Opened in 2005, Oakridge has modern but homey units scattered among lawns and a pool complex. The whole property looks across an open valley to the peaks of Aspiring National Park. Two heated swimming pools and a series of warm spas are set in a rock-lined amphitheater, overlooked by the resort restaurant (which has an outdoor patio for good weather and a cozy fireplace for bad). Enjoying a glass of local wine while soaking in the spa is hard to beat after a day on the road. ✉ *Cardrona Valley Rd. at Studholme Rd.* ☎ *03/443–7707 or 0800/869–262* 🖷 *03/443–7750* ⊕ *www.oakridge.co.nz* ↩ *46 rooms, 19 studios, 27 1- and 2-bedroom apartments* ♿ *Restaurant, bar, 2 pools, 7 hot tubs, spa* ▭ *AE, DC, MC, V.*

$$–$$$ ⊞ **Wanaka Homestead Lodge and Cottages.** This relative newcomer balances luxury with ecofriendliness. Roger and Shonagh North used local schist and timber from the farm buildings that once stood here to build their solar-powered lakeshore lodge. In the evening, central Otago wines and snacks are served in the lounge; the room exemplifies the overall aesthetic with its stone fireplace, high ceiling, and plasma flat-screen TV. Cottages have extra pluses such as DVD players and kitchens. Children are accepted for cottage stays but not always in the main lodge. ☒ *1 Homestead Close* ☎ *03/443–5022* 🖷 *03/443–5023* ⊕ *www. wanakahomestead.co.nz* ⊶ *5 rooms, 2 cottages* ⚙ *BBQ, Wi-Fi, outdoor hot tub, bicycles, lounge, laundry facilities, Internet room; no smoking* ⊟ *AE, MC, V* ⏐◉⏐ *BP.*

$$ 🏨 **Glen Dene Station.** You can feel the freedom of space, staying in your own comfortable self-contained unit here, looking out over Lake Hawea and the mountains beyond, or enjoy it as a B&B. Surrounded by trout-filled lakes, this is a busy high-country farm close to skiing areas, so there's something to keep you busy any time of the year. You also get the chance to join in the farmwork, whistle to a few dogs, help muster some sheep, watch them get shorn, or just walk the hills. Activities depend entirely on what is happening on the farm each day. Dinner can be arranged if you wish, and breakfast is included. ☒ *20 mins north of Wanaka, State Hwy. 6, Lake Hawea* ☎ *03/443–1391* 🖷 *03/443–1008* ⊕ *www. glendenestation.co.nz* ⊶ *2 units* ⚙ *Kitchenettes* ⊟ *No credit cards* ⏐◉⏐ *CP.*

$ 🏨 **Wanaka Hotel.** This once rather imposing hotel has been resurrected as a budget travelers' stop. It's nothing fancy—rooms are on the small side, and the décor and facilities are comfortable but basic. Still, it's a good value in this otherwise pricey resort town. ☒ *71 Ardmore St.* ☎ *03/ 443–7826* 🖷 *03/443–9069* ⊕ *www.wanakahotel.co.nz* ⊶ *25 rooms, 1 suite* ⚙ *Restaurant, kitchen, lounge, laundry facilities, Internet room* ⊟ *AE, DC, MC, V.*

¢ 🏨 **Wanaka Bakpaka.** Off a quiet street, this hostel is a mellow one, with a TV-free fireplace lounge and a watchcat on patrol. The lakefront view from the lounge is superb. Among the various room setups (doubles, a single, three- to five-bed dorms) is a women-only dorm room. ☒ *117 Lakeside Rd.* ☎🖷 *03/443–7837* ⊕ *www.wanakabakpaka.co.nz* ⊶ *7 rooms, 1 single, 9 dorms* ⚙ *BBQ, kitchen, bicycles, lounge, laundry facilities, Internet room; no a/c, no room phones, no room TVs* ⊟ *MC, V.*

Nightlife

Shooters Bar (☒ 145 Ardmore St. ☎ 03/443–4345) is the place for twentysomethings who still have energy after a day on the rivers or slopes. It can be really busy here, even during the daylight hours; it's open from 11 AM until 2:30 AM. **Apartment One Lounge Bar** (☒ 99 Ardmore St. ☎ 03/ 443–4911) is more laid-back and popular with locals. It's open from 6 PM to 4:30 AM every night, except in winter, when it shuts Sunday and Monday nights. Upstairs above Kai Whaka Pai, the **Pa Runga Wine Bar** (☒ Ardmore St. at Helwick St. ☎ 03/443–7795) comes alive at sunset. Bar meals are available, and there's a lounge bar, a nice cozy fire, and a balcony overlooking the lake.

★ The local institution **Cinema Paradiso** cinema, cafe and bar (☒ 1 Ardmore St. ☎ 03/443–1505 ⊕ www.paradiso.net.nz) is not your usual movie house—its seating includes couches, recliners, and even cars. During intermission you can snack on homemade ice cream, warm cookies, or dinner with a glass of wine. Try to get here early to get the pick of seats. The shows include all the latest releases.

Sports & the Outdoors

CANYONING With the steep rugged waterways of the Matukituki and Wilkin Valleys within easy reach, Wanaka is a key spot in the country for canyoning. **Deep Canyon** leads expeditions down the Niger Stream, Wai Rata Canyon, and the Leaping Burn; trips start at $195 for a full day. ☎ *03/443–7922* ⊕ *www.deepcanyon.co.nz* ☽ *Nov.–Mar./Apr.*

FISHING Locals will tell you that fishing on Lake Wanaka and nearby Lake Hawea is better than at the more famed Taupo area. You won't want to enter that argument, but chances are good you'll catch fish if you have the right guide. The fishing season here is year-round. **Harry Urquhart** (☎ 03/443–1535) has trolling excursions for rainbow trout, brown trout, and quinnat salmon on Lake Hawea. **Gerald Telford** (☎ 03/443–9257 ⊕ www.flyfishhunt.co.nz) will take you fly-fishing, including night-fishing and multiday Otago/Southland fishing expeditions. **Wanaka Fly Fishing** provides instruction, guided trips, and wilderness fishing safaris, including a heli-fishing option. ☎ *03/443–9072* ⊕ *www.fly-fishing-guide-wanaka-new-zealand.co.nz*.

For more information on trout fishing around Wanaka, *see* Chapter 11.

RAFTING & KAYAKING At **Pioneer Rafting** you can finally do some white-water rafting at a calm pace. Lewis Verduyn is New Zealand's leading ecorafting specialist, with many years' experience as a white-water rafter. Lewis had his share of adrenaline-pumping high-grade trips and then got tired of missing out on what he sees as the real adventure: the environment he was tearing past. His highly informative ecorafting adventure, suitable for most ages, retraces a historic pioneer log-raft route. Both full-day ($165) and half-day ($115) trips are available, and leave from the Visitor Information Centre in Wanaka. ☎ *03/443–1246 or 027/295–0418.*

Exploring this beautiful region's rivers with **Alpine Kayak Guides'** Geoff Deacon is a must while in Wanaka. Unlike many of the large-scale operations of neighboring Queenstown, this company caters to smaller groups, which means a lot of attention for beginners. You'll learn how to glide into a calm eddy, to wave surf, and to safely charge down the center of the white water. You *will* spill, and for this reason all your gear, right down to the polypropylene underwear, is provided. The full-day trip costs $200 per person and a half day is $125. If you're looking for something mellower, sign up for the half-day "relaxed" float, which is rapids-free ($75). ✉ *70 Main Rd., Luggate* ☎ *03/443–9023* ⊕ *www.alpinekayaks.co.nz.*

SCENIC FLIGHTS The weather around Wanaka is clear much of the time, which has allowed it to become a scenic-flight base for both fixed-wing planes and helicopters. Flights take in a variety of sights, including Mt. Cook and the West Coast glaciers, the Mt. Aspiring area, Queenstown, and Fiordland. **WanakaFlightseeing** runs small Cessna aircraft to all the hot spots. ✉ *Wanaka Airport* ☎ *03/443–8787 or 0800/105–105* ⊕ *www. flightseeing.co.nz.* **Aspiring Helicopters** does trips ranging from a 25-minute local flight for $155 to a half-day trip to Milford Sound, where you join a boat cruise on the fjord before heading back to Wanaka (from

$770). There's also a Mt. Aspiring trip where you can land up on the snowfields (for $375 per person). ☎ *03/443–1454 or 027/432–3121* ⊕ *www.aspiringhelicopters.co.nz.* **Alpine Helicopters** offers heliskiing options in season, as well as heli-fishing excursions in Fiordland. ☎ *03/ 443–4000* ⊕ *www.alpineheli.co.nz.*

SKIING With its reliable snow and dry powder, Wanaka offers some of the best skiing and snowboarding in New Zealand. Cardrona and Treble Cone are the two biggest winter-sports resorts. **Cardrona** (☎ 03/443–7341 ⊕ www.cardrona.com)34 km (21 mi) southwest of Wanaka, has especially good offerings for children, with a kids' ski school and activity center, plus three kid- and beginner-friendly "Magic Carpet" lifts and five food out- lets. A special "heavy metal" trail pours on the rails and jumps. Two quad chairlifts and a detachable high-speed lift are available. The season is roughly June–October and a day's lift pass costs $71. A bonus at Cardrona is the accommodation up on the mountain—12 apartments ranging from stu- dios to self-contained three-bedroom units (rates range from $180 to $475 a night). **Treble Cone** (☎ 03/443–7443 ⊕ www.treblecone.com), 19 km (11.5 mi) west of Wanaka, is the South Island's largest ski area, with lots of advanced trails and off-piste skiing. At this writing, a new quad lift and expanded trails were under way. A day's lift pass costs $89. For snowboarders, the **Snow Park** supplies a huge selection of rails, jumps, pipes, and terrain features. ⊠ *Cardrona Valley, 20 km (12 mi) southwest of Wanaka* ☎ *03/443–9991* ⊕ *www.snowparknz.com.*

For more information about skiing and snowboarding in the area, check out the Web site ⊕ www.skilakewanaka.com.

SKYDIVING New Zealand is definitely the place to experiment with wild adventures, and with **Tandem Skydive Lake Wanaka** (⊠ Wanaka Airport, Hwy. 6, Wanaka ☎ 03/443–7207 or 0800/786–877 ⊕ www.skydivenz.com) you're in capable hands. The 9,000-foot jump over gorgeous scenery is $245, with photos or a DVD to save your exploit for posterity for an extra fee. You can also choose to jump from 12,000 and 15,000 feet ($295 and $395, respectively).

WALKING & TREKKING You could stay for a week in Wanaka, take a different walk into the bush and mountains each day, and still come nowhere near exhausting all the options. If you have time for only one walk, **Mt. Iron**, which rises 780 feet above the lake, is relatively short and rewarding. A rocky hump carved by glaciers, its summit provides panoramic views of Lakes Wanaka and Hawea, plus the peaks of the Harris Mountains and Mt. Aspiring Na- tional Park. The access track begins 2 km (1 mi) from Wanaka, and the walk to the top takes 45 minutes. To avoid going over old ground, de- scend on the alternative route down the steep eastern face.

Trekking **Roys Peak,** at 5,120 feet, is a daylong commitment. The track starts at the base of the mountain, 6 km (4 mi) from Wanaka on the road to Glendhu Bay. The round-trip journey takes about six hours and can be done in conjunction with the much longer Skyline Track. It is closed from early October to mid-November for lambing.

The complete **Diamond Lake Track** takes only three hours and starts 25 km (15.5 mi) west of Wanaka, also on the Glendhu Bay/Mt. Aspiring

9

road. The track rises to 2,518 feet at Rocky Peak, passing Diamond Lake along the way. If you've got time for only a short walk, take the one that heads to the lake; it takes only 20 minutes. The Diamond Lake area is also popular with mountain bikers and rock climbers.

The Mt. Aspiring National Park offers some far more serious hiking and mountaineering opportunities, including Wilkins Valley, Makarora River, and Mt. Aspiring tracks and trails. Many of these require previous experience and excellent fitness and should be done either as guided walks or in full communication with the local DOC office.

Siberia Experience (☎ 0800/345–666 ⊕ www.siberiaexperience.co.nz) offers guided walks through Siberia Valley in Mt. Aspiring National Park. **Wild Walks** (☎ 03/443–4476 ⊕ www.wildwalks.co.nz) also leads treks through Mt. Aspiring National Park, including Rabbit Pass, considered one of the most strenuous trails in the country.

For maps and information on these and other local walks, contact the **Department of Conservation** (✉ Ardmore St. ☎ 03/477–0677).

Queenstown

⑥ *103 km (64 mi) southeast of Wanaka, 480 km (300 mi) southwest of*
Fodor'sChoice *Christchurch.*
★

Set on the edge of the glacial Lake Wakatipu, with stunning views of the sawtooth peaks of the Remarkables mountain range, Queenstown is the most popular tourist stop in the South Island. Once prized by the Māori as a source of greenstone, the town boomed when gold was discovered in the Shotover River during the 1860s; the Shotover quickly became famous as "the richest river in the world." Queenstown could easily have become a ghost town when gold gave out in the early 1900s—except for its location. By the 1950s it had become the center of a substantial farming area, and with ready access to mountains, lakes, and rivers, the town has since become the adventure capital of New Zealand. Its shop windows are crammed with skis, Polartec, Asolo walking boots, and Marin mountain bikes. Along Shotover Street, travel agents tout white-water rafting, jet-boating, caving, trekking, heliskiing, parachuting, and parapenting (paragliding). New Zealanders' penchant for bizarre adventure sports culminates in Queenstown; it was here that the sport of leaping off a bridge with a giant rubber band wrapped around the ankles—bungy jumping—took root as a commercial enterprise. In late June and early July, the 10-day Queenstown Winter Festival brings the winter-sport frenzy to a climax, with musical performers, ski-slope antics and races, and serious partying.

As the town's popularity has increased, so have real estate prices and development. These days, there's constantly some form of rebuilding and construction work going on, with fancy houses edging out the old, modest bachs and vacation homes. At the height of the summer season, December and January, every hotel and apartment is full to bursting. Though you'll hear plenty of different accents and languages on the street, Queenstown is still a favorite for Kiwi vacationers as well.

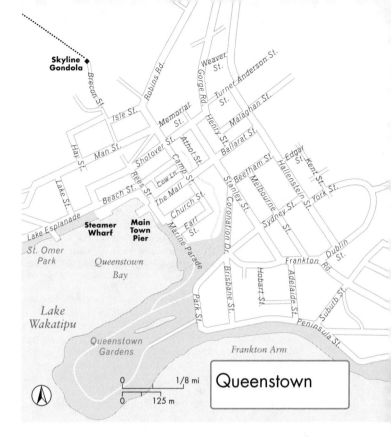

Queenstown

Get the lay of the land by taking the **Skyline Gondola** up to the heights of Bob's Peak, 1,425 feet above the lake, for a smashing panoramic view of the town and the Remarkables. You can also walk to the top on the **One Mile Creek Trail** and watch the paragliders jump off the summit for their slow cruise back down to lake level. There are restaurants at the summit, plus a *haka* show (Māori song and dance) in the evening. For something a little faster, there's a luge ride, weather permitting—start with the scenic track, and then work your way up to the advanced track. If even that isn't exciting enough, you can bungy jump from the summit terminal (⇨ AJ Hackett Bungy *in* Sports & the Outdoors, *below*). ✉ *Brecon St.* ☎ *03/441–0101* ⊕ *www.skyline.co.nz* ✉ *Gondola $19, $26 for gondola and basic luge package* ☉ *Daily 9 AM–9:30 PM.*

☙ The steamship *T.S.S Earnslaw* runs across Lake Wakatipu to Walter Peak Station every day of the year on a 1½-hour cruise. Additional options allow a stopover for several hours at **Walter Peak High Country Farm** to see how a high-country sheep station works, and to get a good farmhouse morning or afternoon tea. The steamship boilers are still stoked by hand, and the steam engines still chuff noisily away just as they did 90 years ago. ☎ *03/442–7500 or 0800/656–503* ✉ *Steamer Wharf* ⊕ *www.realjourneys.co.nz* ✉ *$40 cruise, $60 with farm visit.*

One of the enduring attractions in the area is the drive up **Skippers Canyon.** Harking back to the days when the hills around Queenstown were filled with gold diggers seeking their fortunes, the Skippers Road was hand carved out of rock and reaches into the deep recesses of the Shotover Valley. **Nomad Safaris** (☎ 03/442–6699 or 0800/688–222 ⊕ www.queenstown4wd. com) runs two trips a day up the Skippers Canyon in specialized four-wheel-drive vehicles. **Queenstown Heritage Tours** (☎ 03/442–5949 ⊕ www.queenstown-holiday.co.nz) gives historical tours with the comforts of air-conditioned vehicles, gourmet snacks, and local wines.

Some of the best views of the town, lake, and mountains are from the **Deer Park.** Not only will you have outstanding views, some of which you may recognize from the *Lord of the Rings* films, but you'll also find yourself an object of attention from the resident goats and deer. The animals are used to being fed by people, so they're not skittish. Bring some $1 coins for the food dispensers and wear something you won't mind getting nuzzled. ⊠ *Peninsula Rd.* ☎ *0800/843–333* ⊕ *www.thedeerpark. co.nz* ✍ *$20 self-drive tour, $59 guided tour* ⊙ *Daily 9–dark.*

There are vineyards across Central Otago and into the Queenstown and Wanaka areas, constituting the world's southernmost wine region. Specifically, Bannockburn, Gibbston Valley, and Lowburn are home to big plantings. There are more than 75 wineries in the region. The 177 local vineyards have 2,250 acres in production, producing more than 3,500 tons of grapes each year. The predominant variety is pinot noir. Each year, in February, the region showcases its prowess at the Central Otago Wine & Food Festival, held in the Queenstown Gardens down by the lake. Check ⊕ www.winetastes.com for details and ticket sales.

Amisfield Winery & Bistro is the latest hot-shot winery to join the Queenstown scene. Both the wines and the restaurant, which serves French Basque cuisine, have quickly earned a strong reputation. The restaurant, set in a huge stone-and-timber building with a sunny courtyard and reflection pool, is open for early dinners as well as lunch, although it closes around 8 PM. Pinot noir, aromatic whites such as riesling and pinot gris, and the methode traditionelle are all worth sampling. ⊠ *10 Lake Hayes Rd.* ☎ *03/442–0556* ⊕ *www.amisfield.co.nz* ⊙ *Bistro closed Mon.*

At **Gibbston Valley Wines,** the best-known vineyard in central Otago, you can taste wines in a cool, barrel-lined cave. The showcase wine here is pinot noir, but there are rieslings and a pinot gris to sip as well. At the cheesery, you can watch sheep's-milk and goat's-milk cheeses being made. The attached restaurant offers tempting preparations of mostly local produce and plenty of wines by the glass. ⊠ *State Hwy. 6, Gibbston, 20-min drive east of Queenstown on SH6* ☎ *03/442–6910* ⊕ *www. gvwines.co.nz* ✍ *Wine-cave tour and tasting $9.50, less for larger groups* ⊙ *Tasting room daily 10–5, cave tours on the hr daily 10–4, restaurant daily noon–3.*

The **Chard Farm** vineyard perches on a rare flat spot on the edge of the Kawarau Gorge, not far from Gibbston Valley. The portfolio includes a couple of excellent chardonnays, sauvignon blancs, gewürztraminers, pinot gris, and three variations of pinot noir. They're also venturing into the champagne method. ✉ *Chard Rd.* ⌂ *R.D. 1, Gibbston* ☎ *03/442–6110* ⊕ *www.chardfarm.co.nz* ☉ *Weekdays 10–5, weekends 11–5.*

The public **Queenstown Gardens** on the waterfront peninsula are always worth a quiet stroll. It is one of the few places in Queenstown that hasn't changed over the years. Autumn is especially nice when the leaves turn, and spring arrives with a nice leafy cover as the warm weather unfolds. There's an easy path to wander along to wear off some of those calories you've consumed during your stay.

Where to Stay & Eat

With more than 120 restaurants, cafés, and bars, Queenstown is literally full of places to eat, drink, and enjoy. At first glance the little side streets seem to be full of party bars and pizza joints, but that's because all the really great spots are hidden away, or down at Steamer Wharf (which juts out into Lake Wakatipu). Some places aren't that easy to find, so ask if you can't find what you're looking for.

★ $$$$ ╳ **The Boardwalk.** You might want to eat here just for the view, as the restaurant looks over Lake Wakatipu toward the Remarkables from the second floor of the Steamer Wharf building. Nothing can quite beat that, but the menu makes a good attempt. Seafood is the strong suit; try the fillet of grouper or the wonderful seafood platter with whole crayfish, blue cod, salmon, prawns, scallops, mussels, and oysters. There's also a good selection of dishes made with lamb, beef, and venison. ✉ *Steamer Wharf* ☎ *03/442–5630* ⊟ *AE, DC, MC, V* ☉ *No lunch* ⟁ *Reservations essential.*

★ $$$$ ╳ **The Bunker.** Log fires, leather armchairs, and a clubby atmosphere make the Bunker especially cozy. Whet your appetite with an aperitif at the bar before heading downstairs for a meal that will likely include some of the finest lamb, venison, scampi, duck, and quail you'll find in Queenstown. The wine list is equally impressive. The Bunker stays open very late and is often booked days in advance for dinner. ✉ *Cow La.* ☎ *03/441–8030* ⊕ *www.thebunker.co.nz* ⟁ *Reservations essential* ⊟ *AE, DC, MC, V.*

$$$$ ╳ **The Coronation Café & Bathhouse.** Originally, it was exactly that—a 1911 Victorian bathhouse, right on the beach, built to commemorate the coronation of Britain's King George V. Now, it's a casual café in the mornings and afternoons, and a full-fledged restaurant for dinner. The surroundings remain Victorian, but the kitchen is up-to-date, offering starters such as a mille-feuille of wild rabbit ragout and mains such as the sea-run salmon and the wild Blenheim hare. The waterfront location is superb. ✉ *28 Marine Parade* ☎ *03/442–5625* ⊟ *AE, DC, MC, V* ☉ *Closed Mon. in winter, 6 wks in May/June.*

$$$–$$$$ ╳ **The 19th.** This bright and breezy eatery sits at the town end of Steamer Wharf. The regularly changing and ambitious menu might include river-run salmon with colcannon (a traditional Irish mash made with leek, potato, and kale), or char-grilled Denver leg of venison. Reservations are recommended during high season. ✉ *Steamer Wharf* ☎ *03/442–4006* ⊟ *AE, DC, MC, V.*

$$$–$$$$ ╳ **Wai.** Occupying a corner spot on Steamer Wharf, Wai has one of the best views, and reputations, in town. The fillet of grouper, oven roasted and wrapped in prosciutto, is a standout. But you also can't miss by or-

dering the rack of lamb, venison, salmon, or veal. The degustation menu and the fabulous oyster menu are worth a second visit. It's a good idea to reserve a table during the busy season. ⊠ *Steamer Wharf* ☎ *03/442–5969* ▭ *AE, DC, MC, V.*

¢–$$$ ✕**Gourmet Express.** Reminiscent of a 1960s diner, complete with jukebox, this sunny spot at the front of a shopping center is popular for breakfast. You can get pancakes with maple syrup, eggs any way you want, and heart-starting coffee; later in the day, choose from sandwiches, hamburgers, and a huge selection of salads and omelets—a good number incorporating chili in some shape or form. The wine list emphasizes local bottles. ⊠ *Bay Centre, Shotover St.* ☎ *03/442–9619* ▭ *AE, DC, MC, V.*

¢–$$$ ✕**Vudu Café.** One of the best spots to go for breakfast in Queenstown, the petite Vudu is up and running early when everyone is still sleeping off the party from the night before. The specially roasted coffee is a treat, and the breakfast choices include lots of home-baked goodies. Later in the day they transform into a dinner restaurant and carry on until late. Reservations aren't accepted, so come early to snag a table. ⊠ *23 Beach St.* ☎ *03/442–5357* ▭ *DC, MC, V.*

¢–$$ ✕**Naff Caff.** If all the adventure activities here have you racing, you can get a delicious breakfast egg-and-bacon panini to go here, along with some great coffee (it opens at 6:30 AM). At lunch, look for tasty comfort food such as pasta, veggie rolls, bagels, and burgers. Salads are imaginative, and muffins and cakes are baked daily. ⊠ *1/66 Shotover St.* ☎ *03/442–8211* ▭ *AE, DC, MC, V* ⊘ *No dinner.*

$ ✕**Joe's Garage.** Don't be fooled by appearances; although this place looks like a garage—and in fact it once *was* a garage—it's now one of the country's best cafés. The all-day menu includes simple pleasures such as bacon and eggs, pancakes, and paninis. But it's the trifecta of a laid-back atmosphere, quick and friendly service, and outstanding coffee that really put Joe on the map. The place is super-popular with locals, but it's worth the wait for a table. ⊠ *15 Camp St.* ☎ *03/442–5282* ▭ *AE, MC, V* ⊘ *No dinner.*

¢ ✕**PJ's Fish & Chips.** If it's good, old-fashioned crispy fish wrapped in newspaper you're after, this is the place to go. Brits flock here, as do Aussies, and the locals love it, too. The $10 meal with a big chunk of fresh fish, some chips, and salad or mushy peas is hard to beat, but there are also burgers, hot dogs, and other delightfully unhealthful choices offered on the blackboard menu. ⊠ *37 Camp St.* ☎ *03/442–6080* ▭ *AE, MC, V.*

$$$$ ✕⌂ **Eichardt's Private Hotel.** Once patronized by miners during the 1860s

Fodor'sChoice gold rush, Eichardt's now welcomes travelers drawn by the rush of adventure sports. Guest rooms are done in rich cocoa brown and cream; all have sitting areas with fireplaces, dressing rooms, and bathrooms with heated floors and double vanities. (You can request a lake or mountain view.) The staff is exceptionally helpful and can arrange anything from a massage to a helicopter ride. The House Bar, open to the public for lunch, has delicious takes on lamb and salmon, along with an impressive selection of Otago and other New Zealand wines. ⊠ *Marine Parade* ☎ *03/441–0450* 🖷 *03/441–0440* ⊕ *www.eichardtshotel.co.nz* ⬐ *5 rooms* ⌂ *Minibars, in-room data ports, bar, lounge* ▭ *AE, DC, MC, V* ⦿❘ *BP.*

$$$$ 🏠 **Blanket Bay.** This imposing schist lodge faces Lake Wakatipu and is surrounded by thousands of acres of sheep-station land. At the heart of the lodge is the Great Room, with a grand fireplace, vaulted wharf-timber beams, and antique wooden floors. Floor-to-ceiling windows open out to breathtaking views of the lake and Humboldt Mountains. All five lakeside rooms have a private balcony or terrace. The three suites have stone fireplaces and large bathrooms with a steam shower and a separate tub. The two chalets echo the main lodge's structure and luxuries. The decor throughout is sumptuous; hues of maroon and gold complement native timbers and stone. Blanket Bay is a 35-minute drive from Queenstown. ✉ *Blanket Bay, 3 km (2 mi) south of Glenorchy* ☎ *03/442–9442* 📠 *03/442–9441* ⊕ *www.blanketbay.com* 🛏 *5 rooms, 3 suites, 4 chalet suites* ♿ *Dining room, in-room data ports, pool, gym, hot tub, steam room, boating, fishing, bar, Internet room; no kids under 13, no smoking* ⊟ *AE, DC, MC, V* ⏐◎⏐ *MAP.*

★ $$$$ 🏠 **Nugget Point Boutique Hotel.** Be sure to check out the open-air whirlpool here, perched on the edge of Shotover Valley—it's perfect with a glass of champagne. Rooms are luxuriously large, and each has a balcony and a separate seating area. The lodge is a 10-minute drive from Queenstown on the road to Coronet Peak, one of the top ski areas in the country. The bright glassed-in public rooms give it an especially cheerful atmosphere, even if the weather outside is less than gorgeous. And the views up and down the Shotover River are to die for. ✉ *146 Arthur's Point Rd.* ☎ *03/441–0288* 📠 *03/442–7308* ⊕ *www.nuggetpoint.co.nz* 🛏 *35 rooms* ♿ *Restaurant, kitchenettes, minibars, tennis court, pool, outdoor hot tub, sauna, spa, pool, squash, bar* ⊟ *AE, DC, MC, V.*

★ $$$$ 🏠 **Pencarrow.** It's not just the hillside setting by Lake Wakatipu, or the gardens, or the spacious guest rooms—the friendliness and professionalism of the hosts, Bill and Kari Moers, set this place apart. Less expensive than many lodges in this neck of the woods, Pencarrow has all kinds of thoughtful details, from a special "concierge" room, stocked with information on local attractions, to the welcoming teddy bears on the beds. You can have breakfast in the dining room or on a tray in your room. You can also arrange to go gold panning in a local river, if you're feeling lucky. ✉ *678 Frankton Rd.* ☎ *03/442–8938* 📠 *03/442–8974* ⊕ *www.pencarrow.net* 🛏 *4 suites* ♿ *Dining room, minibars, in-room VCRs, hot tub, bar, lounge, laundry service* ⊟ *AE, DC, MC, V* ⏐◎⏐ *BP.*

★ $$$$ 🏠 **Remarkables Lodge.** After a few years of relative quiet, this lodge has undergone an extensive refurburbishment and is back to its beautiful best— only better. Sitting almost right under the mountains, it has extensive views of the jagged grandeur of the Remarkables Range. Out the windows deer wander in the nearby paddocks, and the silence is deafening. A splendid evening meal is included in the rate, and may include prawn ravioli for a starter, Moroccan rack of lamb, and poached pears for dessert. The Remarkables ski area is nearby, and if you can drag yourself away from the outdoor fireplace in the garden, there's the usual stimulating range of Queenstown activities available just a 10-minute drive away. ✉ *595 Kingston Rd., about 6 km (3.5 mi) south of Queenstown toward Invercargill* ☎ *03/442–2720* 📠 *03/442–2730* ⊕ *www.remarkables.co.nz* 🛏 *3 rooms, 4 suites* ♿ *Pool, sauna, spa, lounge* ⊟ *AE, MC, V* ⏐◎⏐ *MAP.*

$$$–$$$$ ☺ **Aurum Hotel and Suites.** Wide, floor-to-ceiling windows with views over the town, lake, and across to the mountains are the best part of these modern, spacious rooms. It's a short walk downhill to the town center (though a rather steep one on the way back). The neighboring A-Line, a more modestly priced sister hotel, shares the reception area, restaurant, and bar. ⊠ *27 Stanley St.* ☎ *03/442–4718* 🖷 *03/442–4715* ⊕ *www.scenic-circle.co.nz* ↴ *42 rooms, 42 suites* ⚑ *Restaurant, some kitchens, minibars, sauna, bar* ▭ *AE, MC, V.*

$$$–$$$$ ☷ **Sofitel.** Opened in late 2005, the Sofitel is Queenstown's first five-star hotel. With a commanding position in the center of town overlooking the lake, it embodies luxury. The rooms have every comfort—even in-room espresso machines (although they make a bit of a mess if you're not a natural barista). Rooms also have private, but tiny, balconies and TVs over the bathtub to help you keep current with world happenings or the latest rugby score. Downstairs the Nue Bar is a classy place for predinner drinks and canapés. ⊠ *8 Duke St.* ☎ *03/450–0045* 🖷 *03/450–0046* ⊕ *www.sofitelqueenstown.com* ↴ *70 rooms, 10 suites* ⚑ *Restaurant, in-room hot tubs, in-room broadband, bar.*

$$$ ☷ **Stone House.** On the hillside overlooking Queenstown and the mountains beyond, this handsome, historic 1874 cottage has been reinvigorated by its enthusiastic owners. The guest lounge has a large, welcoming open fire, and there is an outdoor hot tub where you can appreciate the alpine night sky. The rooms run to country florals, with feather duvets on the beds; three have a shower only. ⊠ *47 Hallenstein St.* ☎ *03/442–9812* 🖷 *03/441–8293* ⊕ *www.stonehouse.co.nz* ↴ *4 rooms* ⚑ *Outdoor hot tub, lounge, laundry service; no room TVs, no kids, no smoking* ▭ *MC, V* ⊙| *BP.*

$$–$$$ ☷ **Heritage Queenstown.** On Fernhill, just a few minutes from the town center, the Heritage is more peaceful than other local hotels and has great views of the Remarkables and Lake Wakatipu. The hotel was built almost entirely out of South Island materials, including central Otago schist and wooden beams from old local railway bridges. Rooms are notably spacious and are fitted with writing tables and comfortable sitting areas. ⊠ *91 Fernhill Rd.* ☎ *03/442–4988* 🖷 *03/442–4989* ⊕ *www.heritagehotels. co.nz* ↴ *137 rooms, 41 suites, 36 3-bedroom villas* ⚑ *Restaurant, minibars, pool, gym, hot tub, sauna, bar* ▭ *AE, DC, MC, V.*

$–$$ ☷ **Lakeside Motel.** Down at the economy end of the spectrum this homey motel has a premium lakefront location, reflecting the fact that it is one of the earlier-built accommodations in this part of town. The interior décor is a little plain, but there are some nice amenities for the price. There are two two-bedroom family units with full cooking and laundry facilities, but you'll need to book well in advance for these. ⊠ *18 Lake Esplanade* ☎ *03/442–8976* 🖷 *03/442–8930* ⊕ *www.queenstownaccommodation. co.nz* ↴ *13 studios, 2 family units* ⚑ *Some kitchens, laundry facilities* ▭ *AE, DC, MC, V.*

$ ☷ **Queenstown Lakeview Holiday Park.** With everything from spick-and-span, fully equipped apartments to studios, cabins, and campsites, this park is a helpfully varied budget pick. It's right near the Skyline Gondola terminal, with good views of the Remarkables. The staff can help you get good deals on tours and activities. ⊠ *Brecon St.* ☎ *03/442–7252*

⊕ *www.holidaypark.net.nz* ↜ *16 rooms, 22 lodges, 8 cabins* ⚖ *Some kitchens, Internet room* ☰ *AE, MC, V.*

Nightlife

Queenstown gets another boost of energy as darkness falls; after days spent testing limits, visitors cram the clubs and bars to party. There's not much local flavor, diluted as residents are with people from all over the world and all walks of life. All the popular venues are in the center of town, within easy walking distance of one another. Grab a copy of *The Source* weekly gig guide to get an idea of what's on; it's available in most cafés and bars.

Bardeux (⊠ The Mall ☎ 03/442–8284) is a stylish wine bar, good for an intimate, subdued evening. **Chicos** (⊠ The Mall ☎ 03/442–8439) pulls in a young–twenties, somewhat rowdy crowd for late-night dancing. **Surreal** (⊠ Rees St. ☎ 03/441–8492) goes for anything as long as it's not pop music—they'll spin trance, techno, reggae, house, or drum 'n' bass. The upstairs **Winnies** (⊠ The Mall ☎ 03/442–8635) slings pizza, that tried-and-true drinking base, before transforming into a popular nightspot. **Minus 5°** (⊠ Steamer Wharf ☎ 03/442–6050) is literally a place for chilling out—with ice chairs, an ice bar, and ice glasses, it really is only -5 degrees inside. However, warm gear—boots, big Eskimo-style jackets, and gloves—is supplied for you. Then go next door to warm up in the cozy, intimate **Boiler Room** (⊠ Steamer Wharf ☎ 03/441–8066).

Sports & the Outdoors

BUNGY JUMPING   **AJ Hackett Bungy,** the pioneer in the sport, offers a variety of jumps in the area. Kawarau Bridge is the original jump site, 23 km (14 mi) from Queenstown on State Highway 6 and offers a "Secrets of Bungy" tour, an interactive guided tour designed for those who are fascinated by bungy but just can't face the leap. Daredevils who graduate from the 142-foot plunge might like to test themselves on the 230-foot Skippers Canyon Bridge. Top that with the Nevis Highwire Bungy, suspended 440 feet above the Nevis River. With 8.5 seconds of freefall it's said to be the wildest bungy jump in the world. If you're short on time, head to the Ledge Urban Bungy and Ledge Urban Sky Swing, the jumping point by the Skyline Gondola; from April through September you can jump or swing by moonlight. Prices start at $140 for the Kawarau or Ledge jump, $199 for Nevis Highwire Bungy (all three include a T-shirt) and $75 for the Urban Sky Swing. Extra fees apply for DVDs of your exploits. Be sure to check the age, height, and weight requirements. Hours vary seasonally at each site. ⊠ *The Station, Camp and Shotover Sts.* ☎ *03/442–4007 or 0800/286–495* ⊕ *www.ajhackett.com.*

FISHING   For information on trout-fishing guides around Queenstown, *see* Chapter 11.

HIKING   Several scenic walks branch out from town. For a history lesson with your ramble, head to the **Time Walk**, entering through an iron gateway on the Queenstown Hill trail. Narrative panels line the route; it takes about two hours. The **Ben Lomond Track** takes you to one of the highest peaks in the basin. Take the gondola to the summit, then follow signs to the saddle and the steep climb to the peak (5,730 feet). This can be a full-day walk, so make sure you bring all the necessary supplies.

9

HORSE TREKKING **Moonlight Stables** has a choice of full- or half-day rides with spectacular views of the mountains and rivers around the Wakatipu-Arrow Basin. Ride across its 800-acre deer farm. Both novice and experienced riders are welcome. Transportation from Queenstown is provided. The company operates a clay-bird shooting range, and you can shoot in combination with the ride. ⌂ *Morven Ferry Rd., Arrow Junction Queenstown* ☎ *03/442–1229* ⊕ *www.moonlightcountry.co.nz* ✉ *½-day trip $95 per person.*

JET-BOAT RIDES With **Dart River Safaris** you can get a nonpareil look at rugged Mt. Aspiring National Park, one of the most spectacular parts of South Island. The Safari route includes jet-boating on the upper and lower Dart River, along with a bit of walking. The longer Heritage Trail takes private charters on a jet-boat and walking trip with a historic focus. The Funyak option has you travel upstream by jet-boat, then paddle gently downstream, exploring the Rockburn Chasm on the way. Shuttle buses depart daily from Queenstown for the 45-minute ride to the boats. Costs range from $179 plus transfer to $255 plus transfer. ⌂ *27 Shotover St., Queenstown* ☎ *03/442–9992* ⊕ *www.dartriver.co.nz.*

Shotover Jet leads high-speed, heart-stopping rides in the Shotover River canyons; it's got exclusive rights to operate in these waters. The boat pirouettes within inches of canyon walls around full 360-degree spins. If you want to stay relatively dry, sit in the middle, and be prepared for lots of noise and cold wind. The boats are based at the Shotover Jet Beach beneath the historic Edith Cavell Bridge, a 10-minute drive from Queenstown. If you don't have transport, a free shuttle makes frequent daily runs. Reservations are essential. Costs start at $99. ✉ *Shotover River Canyon, Queenstown* ☎ *03/442–8570* ⊕ *www.shotoverjet.co.nz.*

RAFTING Rafting is an adult thrill; children must be at least 13 to participate. You'll need your swimsuit and a towel, but all other gear, including wet suit, life jacket, helmet, and wet-suit booties, are provided by the rafting companies. Instructors spend quite a bit of time on safety issues and paddling techniques before you launch.

Queenstown Rafting runs various half-, full-, and three-day white-water rafting trips in the Queenstown area year-round. The Kawerau River is ideal for first-timers, but you can also brave the Shotover; rapids with names such as Pinball and Jaws should give you a hint of what you're in for. Or go all out with the Nevis Triple Challenge, which includes a jet-boat ride, a helicopter trip, rafting on the Shotover, and a bungy jump, all in one day. Rates start at $145 and go above $1,000 for the multi-activity trips. ✉ *35 Shotover St., Queenstown* ☎ *03/442–9792 or 0800/442–9792* ⊕ *www.rafting.co.nz.*

SAILING Lake Wakatipu can get very windy, and sailing is a popular pastime. **Sail Queenstown** (☎ *03/442–7517* ⊕ www.sailqueenstown.co.nz) runs a two-hour cruise on the lake on *NZL 14,* an America's Cup–class boat that was built for the 1992 challenge in San Diego and sailed by Russell Coutts. The boat is fitted with full safety gear and gives a very comfortable ride on these almost-waveless waters. It's a great way to feel the alpine environment as you tack up the lake then run back down before the wind. Trips leave from the Convelle Wharf in central Queenstown every day at 2 PM—more often in summer, if necessary.

SCENIC FLIGHTS There are several ways to enjoy scenic flights around the spectacular landscapes of this region. You can take a fixed-wing or helicopter flight, you can jump off a high peak and glide down to the town below by paragliding, or you can strap yourself into a wire-bound rocket and experience the view at high speed. **Over the Top Helicopters** (☎ 03/442–2233 or 0800/123–359 ⊕ www.flynz.co.nz) run a diverse selection of flights, including glacier and alpine snowfield landings, and scenic tours above Queenstown, the Remarkables, Fiordland, and both Milford and Doubtful sounds. They'll also deliver you to undreamed-of fly-fishing spots absolutely miles from anywhere, or take you heliskiing or on ecotours as far away as Stewart Island.

Jumping off a mountain isn't everyone's idea of fun, but it's a fantastic way to see Queenstown. These huge sails swoop down over the town like pterodactyls, whirling out over the lake and back in to a gentle landing in a nearby park. **Paraglide** (☎ 03/441–8581 or 0800/759–688 ⊕ www.paraglide.co.nz) leads jumps from the peak above the top of the gondola every day that weather permits. For the adrenaline hooked, **Fly By Wire** (☎ 03/442–2116 ⊕ www.flybywire-queenstown.co.nz) runs a six-minute flight through a deep canyon just out of town. You're strapped into a motorized machine that looks like something between a projectile and a fighter jet that looks like a rocket, and then off you go—at speeds that can reach 106 mi per hour!

SKIING An increasing number of visitors to Queenstown come for the snow. **Coronet Peak** (☎ 03/442–4620 ⊕ www.nzski.com), just 10 minutes from Queenstown along Gorge Road, rocks day and night to a ski and snowboard crowd that returns year after year, many of them using the area as an off-season ski slope during the northern summer. Once Queenstown's original ski resort, it now has a skiable area of 700 acres, a vertical drop of 1,360 feet, and six tows and chairlifts, including a quad lift. The season usually runs June to October, and night skiing is available from mid-July to mid-September. Adult day passes cost $84. Just across the valley **The Remarkables** (☎ 03/442–615 ⊕ www.nzski.com) is a newer ski area that has built a solid reputation for both beginner and intermediate skiing, and also hard-core off-piste runs. The vertical drop here is 1,160 feet, there are five tows and chairlifts, and 30% of the terrain is classified advanced. It's a 45-minute drive from Queenstown to the ski area parking lot on State Highway 6. Adult day passes cost $79.

Arrowtown

❼ *22 km (14 mi) northeast of Queenstown, 105 km (66 mi) south of Wanaka.*

Another gold-mining town, Arrowtown lies northeast of Queenstown. Jack Tewa, or Māori Jack, as he was known, first found gold along the Arrow River in 1861, and when William Fox, an American, was seen selling large quantities of the precious metal in nearby Clyde shortly afterward, the hunt was on. Others attempted to follow the wily Fox back to his diggings, but he kept giving his pursuers the slip, on one occasion even abandoning his tent and provisions in the middle of the night. Eventually a large party of prospectors stumbled on Fox and his team of 40 miners. The secret was out, miners rushed to stake their claims, and Arrowtown was born. At the height of the rush there were more than 30,000 hardy souls in this tiny settlement.

After the gold rush ended in 1865, the place was just another sleepy rural town until tourism created a new boom. This village at the foot of the steep Crown Range, with weathered timber shop fronts and white stone churches shaded by ancient sycamores, was simply too gorgeous to escape the attention of the tour buses. These days it has become a tourist trap, but a highly photogenic one, especially when autumn gilds the hillsides. Each April, Arrowtown celebrates the Autumn Festival when the trees are at their most spectacular. On a stroll along the main street, **Buckingham Street,** you can stop in the old post and telegraph office, still open for business. Take time to explore some of the lanes and arcades, filled with cafés and boutiques.

There are several walks—**Tobin's Track, the Loop, Sawpit Gully** and the **Lake Hayes Walk**—to raise the fitness levels and give you a feeling for where you are. Some investigate the old gold history, but others give nice views. You can get details on all of them from the Lakes District Museum Information Centre.

To get the full story, stop by the **Lakes District Museum,** which has artifacts of the gold-rush days plus hands-on exhibits. (It also doubles as an information center and has a small bookstore and gallery attached.) You can even rent pans and get gold-panning tips to try your luck in the Arrow River. ⊠ *Buckingham St.* ☎ *03/442–1824* ⊕ *www. museumqueenstown.com* ⊡ *$5* ☉ *Daily 8:30–5.*

In a less-visited part of the town is the former **Chinese settlement.** Chinese miners were common on the goldfields, brought in to raise a flagging local economy after the gold rush abated, but local prejudice from resident Europeans forced them to live in their own separate enclave. Some of their tiny 19th-century buildings, which have been restored, were built of sod, which endures well in the dry climate; others were built of layered schist stone, with roofs of corrugated iron or tussock thatch. Ah Lum's store (also now restored) was built in a style typical of the Canton delta region of China and operated until 1972. ⊠ *Bush Creek, west end of town* ⊡ *Free* ☉ *Daily 9–5.*

Where to Stay & Eat

★ ¢–$$$$ ✕ **Saffron.** With its dark wood and elegant atmosphere, this place is much more chichi than you'd expect to find in the heart of rural New Zealand. The evening menu features the best of local foods—venison, lamb, snapper, pheasant, beef, local wines, and beautiful fresh vegetables. The rack of Southland lamb with mint-and-onion sauce is heavenly. Lunch takes a lighter spin with omelets, stir-fries, and egg dishes. Reserving a table in advance is a good idea when heading here. ⊠ *18 Buckingham St.* ☎ *03/442–0131* ⊟ *AE, DC, MC, V.*

$$$ ✕ **Cafe Mondo.** Tucked into a sheltered courtyard off the main street, this is the place for a refreshing, slightly quirky cold drink such as the

Mondo Combo, a blend of orange, carrot, and apple juices with a hint of ginger. You could also dig into a substantial lunch or dinner of salmon or chicken with couscous. There's a kids' menu as well. ✉ *4 Ballarat Arcade* ☎ *03/442–0227* ⊟ *AE, DC, MC, V.*

¢–$ ✕ **Joe's Garage.** If you missed Joe's Garage in Queenstown, or you found it and fell in love, there's another treat for you. Sitting above Blue Moon in The Mall, this branch of the café provides a sunny, quiet spot away from the tour-bus crowd. The menu of casual sandwiches and great coffee is the same as in the main branch. ✉ *Arrow Ln.* ☎ *03/442–1116* ⊟ *AE, MC, V* ☺ *No dinner.*

★ $$$$ ☷ **Millbrook Resort.** A 20-minute drive from Queenstown, this glamorous resort has a special appeal for golfers: an 18-hole championship golf course that was designed by New Zealand professional Bob Charles. A luxurious spa pampers you whether or not you've taken advantage of the extensive exercise options. Accommodations range from rooms in the resort's main hotel to villas and multibedroom cottages. Standard rooms have private balconies and fireplaces. The villas, done in cream and cornflower blue, have kitchens, laundry facilities, and large lounge–dining rooms. ✉ *Malaghans Rd.* ☎ *03/441–7000 or 0800/800–604* ⊟ *03/441–7007* ⊕ *www.millbrook.co.nz* ⬥ *13 villas, 70 villa suites, 51 rooms, 24 cottage apartments* ⬥ *2 restaurants, café, some kitchens, 18-hole golf course, tennis court, indoor pool, health club, outdoor hot tubs, massage, sauna, spa, mountain bikes, hiking, bar, babysitting; no a/c* ⊟ *AE, DC, MC, V* ⍢ *BP, CP.*

$$$ ☷ **Arrowtown Lodge.** Designed to blend in with Arrowtown's historic buildings, these four cottage-style suites are just a two-minute walk from the center of town. All have views toward the Arrow River gorge, which ideally will inspire you to go on a day hike, the hosts' area of expertise. ✉ *7 Anglesea St.* ☎ *03/442–1101 or 0800/258–802* ⊟ *03/442–1108* ⊕ *www.arrowtownlodge.co.nz* ⬥ *4 rooms* ⬥ *In-room data ports, laundry facilities, Internet room* ⊟ *AE, MC, V* ⍢ *BP.*

Nightlife

★   It may not have a flashy marquee, but **Dorothy Brown's Boutique Cinema and Bar** is a truly memorable movie house. The theater doesn't seat many people, but the chairs are cushy and there's plenty of legroom. Better yet, you can get a glass of New Zealand wine or a snack at the fireplace bar and bring it with you. The schedule mixes Hollywood releases with art and international films; in true community spirit, they even take film requests via the Web site. ✉ *Off Buckingham St., upstairs* ☎ *03/442–1968 or 03/442–1964* ⊕ *www.dorothybrowns.com.*

Shopping

Destination Art (✉31 Ramshaw La. ☎03/442–1772 ⊕www.destinationart.co.nz). If you're not an outdoorsy sort of person the Queenstown area could be a little overwhelming. But while he's away playing golf, duck into this little shop in central Arrowtown. It's the one with skeins of colored merino wool, bags of soft possum fur and felting materials, and soft, flowing fabrics outside. Inside is a treasure trove of fabric and wool art materials—enough to keep you going for days. Lessons on various craft forms are available so check with Stephanie when you're there.

FIORDLAND

Fiordland, the name generally given to the southwest coast, is a majestic wilderness of rocks, ice, and beech forest, where glaciers have carved mile-deep notches into the coast. Rivers, sounds, and lakes eat away at the land, and it rains hard and often, so that the area seems to strike a tenuous balance between earth and water. Most of this terrain is officially designated Fiordland National Park, and in conjunction with South Westland National Park, is a designated UNESCO Te Wahipounamu World Heritage Area. Parts of the park are so remote that they have never been explored, and visitor activities are mostly confined to a few of the sounds and the walking trails. Te Anau serves as the base, with lodgings and sports outfitters. The most accessible scenic highlight of this area—and perhaps of the whole country—is Milford Sound, where tremendous green slopes plunge into the sea, and rare species of coral wait just below the water's surface.

The park is exceptional from a naturalist's point of view. More than 700 plants are found only here, and several rare birds as well. The flightless, blue-green takahē, for instance, was long thought to be extinct until one was found in Fiordland's Murchison Mountains in 1948. The last of the kākāpo, flightless nocturnal parrots, were also found in the park. The Department of Conservation steadily works to boost the populations of these endangered birds; you can see the takahē in its local wildlife center.

The winged creature you're far more likely to encounter is the pernicious sand fly. The swarms of sand flies never let up, and they've become the groaning punch line of many a Fiordland tale. Bring tons of insect repellent and just keep slathering it on. Interestingly the flies don't usually make it offshore to boats—one more reason why cruises have definite appeal.

The extreme landscape and the soggy climate have prevented much development; neither the first Māori, the early European explorers, sealers and whalers, nor modern arrivals have made many inroads here. If you really want to take in the raw grandeur of Fiordland, hike one of the many trails in the area, among them the famous four-day Milford Track, long considered one of the finest walks in the world.

Te Anau

❽ *175 km (109 mi) southwest of Queenstown.*

Lake Te Anau (tay-*ah*-no), which is 53 km (33 mi) long and up to 10 km (6 mi) wide, is the second-largest lake in New Zealand after Lake Taupo. The town of Te Anau, on the southern shores of the lake, serves as a base for a wide range of local activities in Fiordland National Park. From Te Anau, you can set out on sightseeing trips by bus, boat, or plane to Milford and Doubtful sounds, or take off on one of the park's world-class hiking trails. (Of these, the most accessible to town is the Kepler Track.) The town itself is not much to write home about, but it does have a few attractions worth checking out if you've got some spare time. It gets busiest in summer; in winter, some cafés and shops close or reduce their hours.

At **Te Anau Caves,** boats and walkways take you through a maze of caves containing underground whirlpools, waterfalls, and gushing streams. On the cave walls, glowworms shine like constellations in a clear night sky. The caves can be reached only by water, and the entire trip takes 2½ hours. There are three trips per day during summer and two per day the rest of the year. ⊠ *Real Journeys, Lake Front Dr.* ☎ *03/249–7416 or 0800/656–502* ⊕ *www.realjourneys.co.nz* ✆ *$50.*

The lakeshore **Te Anau Wildlife Centre** gives you the chance to preview some of the wildlife you're likely to encounter when hiking in Fiordland. The center houses one of New Zealand's rare flightless birds, the takahē, which at one time was thought to be extinct. The lakeside walk to the center makes for a pleasant one-hour afternoon or evening stroll. ⊠ *Manapouri Rd., 1 km (½ mi) west of Te Anau* ☎ *03/249–7921* ✆ *Donation requested* ☉ *Daily dawn–dusk.*

Where to Stay & Eat

$$$–$$$$ ✕ **Redcliff Café & Bar.** Te Anau might not strike you as a crème brûlée kind of place, but Redcliff pulls it off. Among the simple yet sophisticated entrées served in this cottage setting, the Fiordland crayfish and the wild venison on the Fiordland platter are excellent. There's occasionally live music, and reservations aren't accepted—so during the peak summer season, try to arrive by 6 if you don't want to join the wait list. ⊠ *12 Mokonui St.* ☎ *03/249–7431* ▭ *MC, V* ☉ *No lunch. Closed July and Aug.*

$$$–$$$$ ✕ **Settlers Steakhouse.** A carnivore's friend, Settlers revolves around red meat. Choose your own steak, perhaps porterhouse steak or a T-bone, and the chef will cook it just the way you want it. It's not all beef, though— you can also choose from grilled lamb, venison, local salmon, or blue cod. The all-you-can-eat salad bar provides a nice counterpoint. ⊠ *Town Centre* ☎ *03/249–8454* ▭ *AE, DC, MC, V* ☉ *No lunch. Reduced hours June and July.*

$$–$$$$ ✕ **Keplers Restaurant.** The ambience is relaxing, the view is magnificent, and the lamb, venison, and seafood are fantastic at this popular eatery. Tandoori prawns are the standout starter, and the beef Wellington, orange roughy, and blue cod mains are always in demand. Crayfish arrives live in season and is offered simply grilled or with Mornay sauce (these dishes, though delicious, cost $65). As night falls, candles add a romantic air. ⊠ *23 Town Centre* ☎ *03/249–7909* ▭ *AE, MC, V* ☉ *No lunch. Closed June–late Aug.*

$–$$ ✕ **La Toscana.** The wine-color walls in this cheap-and-cheerful café put you in the mood for the well-priced selection of Tuscan soups, pastas, and pizzas. Starters are typically Italian breads or antipasti. Sensibly, both pastas and pizzas are available in medium or large sizes, but remember to keep dessert in mind—the *torta di cioccolata* (chocolate cake smothered in hot fudge sauce) is a local legend. Takeout is available as well. ⊠ *Uptown arcade, 108 Town Centre* ☎ *03/249–7756* ▭ *AE, MC, V* ☉ *No lunch.*

$$$$ ▤ **Fiordland Lodge.** Just a few kilometers out of Te Anau on the road to Milford Sound, this elegant lodge looks right at home in its massive World Heritage setting. Glass, stone, and timber blend together in a contemporary design, making for a stylish place to spend a few days. Each room

Lake Manapouri & Doubtful Sound

JUST 20 MINUTES SOUTH OF Te Anau, Lake Manapouri has long had the reputation as one of New Zealand's prettiest lakes. The subject of contentious debate back in the 1970s when hydroelectricity producers wanted to raise the level of the lake and submerge the town, it is now a very down-to-earth spot that moves at a pace not easily found these days. The lake itself is unspoiled, hemmed by high mountains and studded by many bush-covered islands. Cruises run several times a day to the head of the lake, where you can join a tour of the West Arm hydro-station, deep underground. West Arm is also the departure point for those traveling on to Doubtful Sound, a stunning stretch of water, largely untouched by visitors. A connecting bus crosses you over the 2,177-foot, gradient 1:5 Wilmot Pass before dropping steeply down to sea level at Deep Arm, the head of Doubtful Sound.

Real Journeys (✉ Pearl Harbour, Manapouri ☎ 03/249-660 or 0800/ 656-502 ⊕ www.realjourneys.co.nz) runs daily cruise options on Lake Manapouri, providing scenic cruises, a visit to the power station, or connections to their Doubtful Sound cruises. Costs for these tours start at $59 per person.

Fiordland Expeditions (✉ Deep Cove, Doubtful Sound ☎ 03/442-2996 ⊕ www.fiordlandexpeditions.co.nz) offers a truly New Zealand experience on their great little boat, *Tutuko*. Skipper Richard Abernethy is totally at home on these waters and will take you to the most inaccessible reaches of Doubtful Sound, or out and around the coast, weather permitting (which doesn't happen often). This is the tour to do if you want to do a bit of fishing, dive some of the world-class water beneath the boat, or just soak up the scenery, of which there is plenty. Tours are run by arrangement, rather than on a set schedule, so you'll need to make a group, or join one.

---

has a wide-ranging lake view, and there are also two B&B log cabins, especially well suited for families. ✉ *State Hwy. 94, 472 Te Anau–Milford Hwy.* ☎ *03/249-7832* ☐ *03/249-7449* ⊕ *www.fiordlandlodge.co. nz* ⟲ *10 lodge rooms, 2 cabins* ♿ *Restaurant, in-room data ports, fishing, bar, library* ⦿| *BP, MAP.*

$$$–$$$$ 🏨 **Te Anau Hotel and Villas.** This lakefront spot is popular with hikers who need a bit of pampering on their way to or from the Milford Track. Accommodation is in hotel rooms with views to the lake or the gardens, or in the villa suites, which are surrounded by rose gardens. The heated pool, sauna, or spa will help ease those joints and muscles if you've just finished one of the big walks. ✉ *64 Lake Front Dr.* ☎ *03/249-9700* ☐ *03/249-7947* ⊕ *www.teanauhotel.co.nz* ⟲ *95 rooms, 17 suites* ♿ *Restaurant, BBQ, refrigerators, some in-room data ports, pool, sauna, spa, bar, laundry service* ▭ *AE, DC, MC, V.*

$$–$$$ 🏨 **The Village Inn.** Close to the lake and the town's central shopping area, this inn looks like a carefully reconstructed pioneer village. But behind these shop and business fronts are thoroughly modern hotel rooms and suites, including some family-size units. ✉ *Mokoroa St.* ☎ *03/249-7911* *or 0800/249–791* 🖷 *03/249–7003* ⊕ *www.thevillageinn.co.nz* ⬐ *34 rooms, 16 suites, 6 family units* ⌂ *Restaurant, minibars, bar, laundry facilities* ⊟ *AE, DC, MC, V.*

$$ 🖳 **Cats Whiskers.** Hosts Anne Marie and Lindsay Bernstone keep things homey at their modern lakefront B&B, complete with, you guessed it, a resident cat (there's also a small dog). Each room has pluses such as tea-making facilities and hair dryers; ask for the one with a lake view. The house is a 10-minute walk from the town center and is opposite the National Park Visitor Centre. A courtesy car can take you to any of the local restaurants. ⊠ *2 Lakefront Dr.* 🖷🖷 *03/249–8112* ⊕ *www.catswhiskers. co.nz* ⬐ *4 rooms* ⌂ *Laundry facilities, Internet room* ⊟ *MC, V* ⫴⊙⫴ *BP.*

¢–$$ 🖳 **Te Anau Top 10 Holiday Park Mountain View.** Ideally set across from the lakefront and just a couple of blocks from the town's commercial strip, this well-serviced park offers motel rooms, cabins, and camper van and camping sites. (For the cabins, you'll need to rent linens for a small extra cost.) The Matai Lodge, opened in 2005, also offers basic rooms with private baths. Their architecture is reminiscent of up-market tramping huts, with exposed ceiling beams. ⊠ *Te Anau Terr.* 🖷 *03/249–7462 or 0800/ 249–746* 🖷 *03/249–7262* ⊕ *www.teanautop10.co.nz* ⌂ *BBQ, kitchens (communal), bicycles, playground, laundry facilities, Internet room.*

Sports & the Outdoors

CRUISING   Peaceful Doubtful Sound is three times as long as Milford Sound and sees far fewer visitors. **Real Journeys** (⊠ Lake Front Dr. 🖷 03/249–7416 or 0800-656–502 ⊕ www.realjourneys.co.nz) runs a range of combined bus and boat trips there. Tours include a 2-km (1-mi) bus trip down a spiral tunnel to the Lake Manapouri Power Station machine hall, an extraordinary engineering feat built deep beneath the mountain. On the sound itself, you may see bottlenose dolphins or fur seals. Most people take an eight-hour day trip from Lake Manapouri; there are bus connections from Te Anau and Queenstown. Between October and May you can overnight on the sound, aboard the *Fiordland Navigator*. Rates for the day excursion are $225 per person, and for the overnight cruise, $325 (for a quad share) to $499 (twin share).

HIKING   Information, transport options, and maps for the plethora of hikes near Te Anau, including the Kepler Track, can be obtained from the **Fiordland National Park Visitor Centre.** ⊠ *Lake Front Dr.* 🖷 *03/249–7924* 🖷 *03/ 249–7613* ⊕ *www.doc.govt.nz.*

★   The 60-km (37-mi) **Kepler Track** loops from the south end of Lake Te Anau, starting just 4 km (2½ mi) from Te Anau township. It skirts the lakeshore, climbs up to the bush line, passing limestone bluffs and going through extensive beech forest, and has incredible views of the South Fiord and Te Anau Basin. An alpine crossing takes you to the high point near the peak of Mt. Luxmore. It's a moderate walking trail that takes three to four days to complete. If you're on a tight schedule, it's possible to take day hikes to the Luxmore and Moturau huts.

The track was opened in 1988 as a new alternative for the increasing numbers of people walking the Routeburn and Milford trails. It has some very good-quality trails, three huts, and two camps, and is relatively easy, with only one steep climb to the alpine section up Mt. Luxmore. Hikers should beware, however, of high wind gusts while crossing the exposed saddle above the bush line. During winter and spring the alpine section may be impassable because of snow. Although the trail can be walked in either direction, most people walk it counterclockwise.

In summer, from late October through late April, the three huts are serviced (which means they have gas for cooking and heating, toilets that are cleaned daily, and daily visits from a warden) and cost $40 per night for adults. During winter, when huts are unserviceable, this charge drops to $10. Reservations are required for the huts and the campsites. You can make a reservation with the **Great Walks Booking Office** (☎ 03/249–8514 ⊕ www.doc.govt.nz). See Chapter 11 for more information.

JET-BOATING **Luxmore Jet** zips you up the Upper Waiau River, where the forest comes right down to the river's edge. Once on lovely Lake Manapouri, you'll stop to experience the serene quiet. The company also pairs its jet-boat rides with flights by Wings and Water (*see above*) or Southern Helicopters Heli-jet. Once you reach Manapouri, you could take off on a floatplane to see Doubtful Sound or Lake Te Anau by air, or be whisked back to base by helicopter. Costs start at $85 for the jet-boat, $205 for the jet-boat-and-flight option, and $395 for jet-boat-and-helicopter option. ☎ *03/249–6951 or 0800/253–826* ⊕ *www.luxmorejet.co.nz.*

KAYAKING **Fiordland Wilderness Experiences** runs kayaking day trips and multiday tours on Milford and Doubtful sounds and on Lakes Te Anau and Manapouri. Beginners are welcome. They operate from September to May, with some differences according to location, so call ahead; costs start around $100. ✉ *66 Quintin Dr.* ☎ *03/249–7700* ⊕ *www. fiordlandseakayak.co.nz.*

SCENIC FLIGHTS **Air Fiordland** offers a range of scenic flights on its fixed-wing aircraft to Milford Sound and Doubtful Sound, with prices hovering around $195–$299. It also has combined packages offering the option of flying to Milford Sound and then taking a cruise boat or kayaking before returning to either Te Anau or Queenstown ($335–$375). ⊕ *Ticket Centre, 70 Town Centre* ☎ *03/442–3404 or 0800/107–505* ⊕ *www. airfiordland.co.nz.*

Wings and Water Te Anau Ltd. offers scenic flights with a floatplane that takes travelers to some of the region's most inaccessible areas, including a 10-minute trip over Lake Te Anau, Lake Manapouri, and the Kepler Track and longer flights over Doubtful, Dusky, and Milford sounds. Costs range from $65 for a 10-minute flight to $135 for 20 minutes. ✉ *Lakefront Dr.* ☎ *03/249–7405* 🖷 *03/249–7939.*

EN ROUTE
The **Milford Road,** from Te Anau to Milford Sound, winds through deep, stony valleys where waterfalls cascade into mossy beech forests. It's a spectacular route, but if you're making the trip between May and November, be sure to check local information for avalanche warnings and come equipped with tire chains. (You can rent these in any of the Te Anau service stations.) The road is narrow and winding at times, so allow yourself plenty of time—at least 2½ hours.

The 120-km (75-mi) road starts with a fast 29-km (18-mi) stretch along the shores of Lake Te Anau to Te Anau Downs. This is where the ferry leaves for those wishing to hike the Milford Track. Past Te Anau Downs, the road cuts away from the lake and after 20 km (12½ mi) enters Fiordland National Park. You'll pass some great photo ops at Mirror Lakes, Knobs Flat, and Lake Gunn before reaching the Divide, a watershed between rivers flowing both east and west and the starting point for the Routeburn Track. A few miles farther on, you'll come to the **Homer Tunnel.** Work on the tunnel started in 1935 as a Depression-era government work project. After the lengthy tunnel, the road descends sharply in hairpin bends down the Cleddau Valley for 16 km (10 mi) before reaching the small settlement at Milford Sound.

Milford Sound

⑨ *120 km (75 mi) northwest of Te Anau, 290 km (180 mi) west of Queenstown.*

Fodor'sChoice ★ Fiordland National Park's most accessible and busiest attraction is **Milford Sound,** the sort of overpowering place where poets run out of words and photographers out of film or memory card. Hemmed in by walls of rock that rise from the waterline sheer up to 4,000 feet, the 13-km-long (18-mi-long) fiord was carved by a succession of glaciers as they gouged a track to the sea. Its dominant feature is the 5,560-foot pinnacle of **Mitre Peak,** which is capped with snow for all but the warmest months of the year. Opposite the peak, Bowen Falls tumbles 520 feet before exploding into the sea. On a clear day or after rain this is a spectacular place. Luxuriant rain forest clings to the sheer precipices washed with waterfalls. You'll often see seals on rocks soaking up the sun; dolphins sometimes flirt with the boats. But Milford Sound is also spectacularly wet: the average annual rainfall is around 20 feet, and it rains an average of 183 days a year. In addition to a raincoat you'll need insect repellent—the sound is renowned for its voracious sand flies.

Still, even in heavy rain and storms Milford Sound is magical. Rainfall is so excessive that a coat of up to 20 feet of fresh water floats on the surface of the saltwater fjord. This creates a unique underwater environment similar to that found at a much greater depth in the open ocean. You can observe this at the **Milford Deep Underwater Observatory,** a 15-minute boat ride from the wharf in Milford at Harrison Cove. From the underwater windowed gallery you'll see rare red and black corals and a range of deepwater species. The 30-minute visit and round-trip shuttle boat trip from Milford takes about one hour. Several boating companies, such as Real Journeys and Mitre Peak Cruises, make regular trips to the observatory. ⊠ *Milford Sound* ☎ *03/249–9442 or 0800/ 329–969* ⊕ *www.milforddeep.co.nz* ☽ *Daily 8:30–5.*

Where to Stay & Eat

Accommodations are scant at Milford Sound, and it's best to stay in Te Anau and make your visit a long day trip.

$$–$$$ ✕ **Blue Duck Café & Bar.** The view out the front window, across Milford Sound to Mitre Peak and the mountains beyond, is amazing—and the food's

9

not bad, either. Lunch choices include wraps, rolls, and sandwiches, as well as a full buffet; there are even options for various dietary requirements and vegetarians. Dinner goes à la carte, and the restaurant and bar stay open until late. And if you're brave and don't mind a few sand flies, you can even eat outside. ⊠ *Milford Sound* ☎ *03/249–7982* ⊟ *MC, V*.

¢ ⊡ **Milford Sound Lodge.** Just 1 km (½ mi) out of the Milford settlement, on the banks of the Cleddau River, this backpacker hostel offers basic but relatively fresh accommodations. A few years ago the guest rooms were completely revamped, from the heating system to the mattresses and curtains. The range of rooms includes twin and double units with linen for $67 per person, four-person bunk rooms at $27 per bed, and dormitories for six people also at $27 a bed. All bathrooms are shared. The lodge serves inexpensive breakfast, or people can cook for themselves in the on-site kitchen. There are also powered and nonpowered campsites available. ⊠ *Milford Sound* ☎ *03/249–8071* ⊟ *03/249–8075* ⊕ *www.milfordlodge.com* ⇝ *23 rooms with shared bath* ⌂ *Café, bar, laundry facilities, Internet room; no room TVs* ⊟ *MC, V*.

Sports & the Outdoors

CRUISING The view from the water is mind-bendingly beautiful, which accounts for the popularity of cruising here. It's essential to book ahead between mid-December and March. Some include a visit to the Milford Sound Underwater Observatory (⇨ *above*). All boats leave from the Milford wharf area. If you can, avoid the midday sailings, as they link with tour buses and are most crowded. Milford Sound Red Boat Cruises and Real Journeys run more than a dozen cruises a day between them, with extra options in summer.

Real Journeys (⊠ Lake Front Dr., Te Anau ☎ 03/249–7416 or 0800/656–501 ⊕ www.realjourneys.co.nz) offers daily cruises on the *Milford Monarch* and its companion the *Milford Haven*. These trips cruise the full length of Milford Sound to the Tasman Sea, with views of waterfalls, rain forest, mountains, and wildlife. There's a choice of 1½-hour scenic cruises and 2½-hour nature cruises, at $60 and $80 respectively. To have the most intense Sound experience, sign up for one of the three overnight cruise options that are offered from October to April. The cruises differ in terms of accommodation; the *Milford Mariner* sleeps 60 passengers in private cabins with bathrooms ($350 per person twin share, September–May), the *Milford Wanderer* has bunk-style accommodation for 61 passengers ($210 per person quad share, October–April), and the M. V. *Friendship* has bunks for just 12 passengers ($210 per person (multishare, November–March).

Milford Sound Red Boat Cruises (⊠ Milford Sound Wharf ☎ 03/441–1137 ⊕ www.redboats.co.nz) offers frequent daily scenic cruises on its catamarans to Milford Sound or to the Milford Deep Underwater Observatory. The basic tour, which lasts less than two hours, loops through the sound to the Tasman Sea; the fare starts at $50 and goes up to $79 if you include a stop at the observatory.

HIKING If you plan to walk the **Milford Track**—a wholly rewarding, four-day Fodor'sChoice bushwalk through Fiordland National Park—understand that it is one ★ of New Zealand's most popular hikes. The 53½-km (33-mi) track is strictly one-way, and because park authorities control access, you can feel as though you have the wilderness more or less to yourself. Independent and guided groups stay in different overnight huts. Be prepared for rain and snow, but also for what many call the finest walk in the world. This is still wild country, largely untouched by humanity. Mountains rise vertically for several thousand feet out of valleys carved by glaciers. Forests tower above you, and myriad cascading waterfalls plunge into angry, fast-flowing rivers.

The trailheads for the track are remote. Both guided and unguided walks begin with a two-hour ferry ride to Glade Wharf on Lake Te Anau and end with a ferry taking you from Sandfly Point over to the Milford Sound wharf. Because of the good condition of the track, the walk is rarely demanding. But because the trail is often blocked by snow in winter, there is a restricted hiking season from late April until late October. Reservations are essential through the season, and there are no camping sites winter or summer. You can make a reservation with the **Great Walks Booking Office** (☎ 03/249–8514 ⊕ www.doc.govt.nz). See Chapter 11 for more information. If you don't have enough time for the whole Milford Track, try a day trip with **Real Journeys** (☎ 03/219–7416 or 0800/656–501 ⊕ www.realjourneys.co.nz), which includes a Lake Te Anau cruise and a guided day walk on the Milford Track.

The 33-km (20½-mi) **Routeburn Track,** like the Milford Track, is designated one of the country's Great Walks. Routeburn goes between Lake Wakatipu, near Glenorchy, and the road between Milford and Te Anau; it takes about three days to hike. The alpine landscape is stunning, and once you're above the tree line, the sand flies back off. As on the Milford, be prepared for rain and mud.

To hike independently of a tour group for either the Milford, Kepler, or Routeburn tracks, call the **Great Walks Booking Desk** at the **Fiordland National Park Visitor Centre** (✉ Lake Front Dr., Te Anau ☎ 03/249–8514 🖷 03/249–8515 ⊕ www.doc.govt.nz) or book online through the Web site. Reservations for the coming season can be made starting on the first of July every year. You'll need to book well in advance—especially if you plan to go in December or January. Independent walking, without a guide, requires that you bring your own food, utensils, bedding, and other equipment. You stay in clean, basic Department of Conservation huts. The hut cost from October to April, the prime-booking time, runs $40 per person per night. Campsites on the Routeburn and Kepler tracks are $15 and must also be reserved in advance. For more details on these tracks, see Chapter 11.

If you're itching to see some coastline during your hike, consider the **Hollyford Track** (✉ Lake Front Dr., Te Anau ☎ 03/249–8514 🖷 03/249–8515 ⊕ www.doc.govt.nz). At 56 km (35 mi), it's a four-day endeavor, taking you from the Hollyford Road down to Martins Bay by roughly following the Hollyford River. You'll pass a couple of lakes and waterfalls on your way; at the coastline you'll likely spy seals and penguins. Be particularly careful of flooded creek crossings. There are six DOC huts on the track; at this writing, two were being replaced. Book in advance through the **Fiordland National Park Visitor Centre.**

Going with a guide from **Ultimate Hikes** requires deep pockets but provides comfortable beds and someone to do the cooking. For the Milford Track, it'll cost $1,750 in high season (in multishare accommodation), $1,590 in low season, including a cruise on Milford Sound and transport to and from Queenstown; the Routeburn is a bit cheaper at $1,090 for high season, $950 in low. If you're not up for a multiday trek, you can still get a sense of what all the fuss is about by taking a single-day "encounter" hike on either the Milford or Routeburn tracks for $135. ✉ *1st fl., AJ Hackett Station Bldg., Camp St. at Duke St., Queenstown* ☎ *03/441–1138 or 0800/659–255* 📠 *03/441–1124* ⊕ *www.ultimatehikes.co.nz.*

KAYAKING **Milford Sound Sea Kayaks** (✉ Milford Sound ☎ 03/249–8500, 0800/476–726 in New Zealand ⊕ www.kayakmilford.co.nz) offers guided double kayaking on the sound that includes a hike along part of the Milford track. Prices range from $69 to $169 per person. No experience is required.

SCENIC FLIGHTS If time is limited and you don't want to face the long trip from Queenstown to Milford, consider "flightseeing." This combines a round-trip flight from Queenstown to Milford with a scenic cruise. Flights are weather-dependent. **Milford Sound Scenic Flights** (☎ 03/442–3065 or 0800/207–206 ⊕ www.milfordflights.co.nz) start with one-hour flights for $275. The **Glacier Southern Lakes Helicopters Ltd.** (☎ 03/442–3016 ⊕ www.heli-flights.co.nz) will get you buzzing over Milford Sound; the Milford Sound Fantastic trip has at least two landings and costs $610.

THE SOUTHERN ALPS & FIORDLAND ESSENTIALS

Transportation

BY AIR

Queenstown Airport (ZQN) is 9 km (5½ mi) east of town. Mount Cook Airport is a short distance from the village and is used just for scenic and charter flights. Wanaka Airport (WKA) is 10 km (6 mi) east of the town.

Queenstown is linked directly with Auckland by Air New Zealand and to Christchurch by Air New Zealand Link. Air New Zealand Link also offers a daily service between Christchurch and Wanaka. Qantas and Origin Pacific also offer code-share flights (where two or three airlines share the same plane–very common here, even on international flights in this part of the world). On a clear day, the views are spectacular; in winter, snow sometimes closes the airport.

Super Shuttle Queenstown meets all incoming flights and charges $12 for one person (and increasingly less, depending on the number of people in a group) to hotels in Queenstown. Taxis wait outside the arrivals area; the fare into town is about $20. A Shopper bus ($5) departs to and from Queenstown Airport every hour. You can be picked up by the Shopper bus from some Queenstown hotels.

🚹 **Airports Mount Cook Airport** ☎ 03/430–8034 or 0800/800–702. **Queenstown Airport** ✉ Frankton Rd. Queenstown ☎ 03/442–2670 ⊕ www.queenstownairport.co.nz.

▣ Carriers **Air New Zealand** ☎ 03/441-1900 or 0800/737-000 ⊕ www.airnewzealand. co.nz. **Origin Pacific Airways** ☎ 03/547-2020 or 0800/302-302 ⊕ originpacific.co. nz. **Qantas** ☎ 0800/808-767 ⊕ www.qantas.com.au.

▣ Airport Transfers **Alpine Taxi** ☎ 03/442-6666 or 0800/442-6666. **Queenstown Taxis** ☎ 03/442-7788 or 0800/788-294. **Super Shuttle Queenstown** ☎ 03/442-3639 or 0800/748-8853.

BY BUS

InterCity operates a daily bus service between Christchurch and Queenstown via Mount Cook Village, with a one-hour stop at the Hermitage Hotel for lunch. Fares for the 8- to 10-hour journey range from $60 to $118.

It may take a full day, but you can take buses to and from the major towns in the Southern Alps and Fiordland area. InterCity coaches make daily trips from the Franz Josef and Fox glaciers through Wanaka to Queenstown. Buses run between Queenstown and Wanaka in just under two hours ($26). InterCity also goes down the South Island's eastern flank from Christchurch to Queenstown via Dunedin.

Newmans, meanwhile, runs a daily bus service from Christchurch through Mount Cook to Queenstown for about $148, as well as a daily bus round-trip from Queenstown to Milford Sound for $189, or Te Anau to Milford Sound round-trip for $157.

Wanaka Connections sends buses between Wanaka and Queenstown several times a day for $25 each way. They also run to Christchurch, Te Anau, Dunedin, and Invercargill.

▣ Bus Companies **InterCity** ☎ 03/443-7885 in Wanaka, 03/249-7559 in Te Anau, 03/ 442-8238 in Queenstown ⊕ www.intercitycoach.co.nz. **Newmans** ☎ 09/913-6188 or 0508/353-947 ⊕ www.newmanscoach.co.nz. **Wanaka Connections** ☎ 03/443-9122 ⊕ www.wanakaconnexions.co.nz.

▣ Bus Depots **Queenstown** ✉ Athol St. **Te Anau** ✉ Miro St. **Wanaka** ✉ Edgewater Adventures, 59a Brownston St.

BY CAR

Driving is certainly the best way to get around this region, but be prepared for rugged, quickly changing terrain, ice in winter, and frequent downpours, particularly around Milford Sound. Keep an eye on the weather and the forecast. Rental-car companies may discourage driving on some of the tougher rural roads.

The 330-km (205-mi) drive from Christchurch straight through to Aoraki/Mount Cook Village takes four hours. Take Highway 1 south out of Christchurch. At the tiny town of Rangitata turn right onto Highway 79 to Lake Tekapo. Pass through Lake Tekapo and look on the right for Highway 80 to Aoraki/Mount Cook Village.

Highway 6 enters Queenstown from the West Coast; driving time for the 400-km (250-mi) journey from Franz Josef is eight hours. It takes approximately an hour and a half to drive between Queenstown and Wanaka; the drive between Queenstown and Te Anau generally lasts a little over two hours.

Even on highways, there are few passing lanes, so it's best to allow plenty of driving time. There are rest stops signposted along most major roads, although these usually consist of a cleared area, trash bin, and picnic table (no bathrooms). In winter, watch for icy patches on the road, especially in shaded areas. If you think you'll hit snow, rent tire chains at one of the local garages.

You can pick up a car at the Queenstown Airport if you're not driving in to the region; the rental office is open daily. Apex Rentals are particularly easy to deal with and are happy for their cars to explore more outlying areas. They give a copy of the 125-page booklet *New Zealand Driving Holidays* with each rental.

⊡ Car-Rental Agencies **Apex** ⊠ Terminal Bldg., Queenstown Airport ☎ 03/442-8040 or 0800/531-111.
Avis ⊠ Terminal Bldg., Queenstown Airport ☎ 03/442-7280.

Contacts & Resources

BANKS & EXCHANGE SERVICES

Some smaller towns don't have banks, but most have at least one ATM. When in doubt, make sure you have enough cash on you for necessities.

EMERGENCIES

Queenstown has a late-night pharmacy, Wilkinson's Pharmacy, which stays open until 10 PM, but otherwise, you may need to turn to a local medical center.

⊡ Emergency Services **Fire, police, and ambulance** ☎ 111. **Aspiring Medical Centre** ⊠ 28 Dungarvon St. ☎ 03/443-1226. **Lakes District Hospital** ⊠ Douglas St., Frankton, near Queenstown ☎ 03/441-0015. **Queenstown Medical Centre** ⊠ 9 Isle St. ☎ 03/441-0500. **Wilkinson's Pharmacy** ⊠ The Mall at Rees St., Queenstown ☎ 03/442-7313.

MAIL & INTERNET

Queenstown has the most extensive post office; it stays open weekdays 8:30 to 8, Saturday 9 to 8, and Sunday 9 to 6. Behooving its status as an international hot spot, it has plenty of Internet cafés, and many lodgings offer free or inexpensive Web access. The Wanaka post office is open weekdays 8:30 to 5:30 and on Saturday from 9 to noon.

⊡ Internet Cafes **Bits N Bytes** ⊠ 46 Helwick St., Wanaka ☎ 03/443-7078.
e-Stop Internet ⊠ Jailhouse Mall, Town Centre, Te Anau ☎ 03/249-9461.
Internet Outpost Queenstown ⊠ 27 Shotover St. ☎ 03/441-3018.
⊡ Post Offices **Queenstown** ⊠ 15-19 Camp St. ☎ 03/442-7670. **Te Anau** ⊠ 102-104 Town Centre ☎ 03/249-7348.
Wanaka ⊠ 39 Ardmore St. ☎ 03/443-8211.

TOURS

ADVENTURE TOURS Mid Southern Tracks organizes and provides experienced guides for fishing trips and nature tours both locally and to destinations all over New Zealand.

Nomad Safaris offers four-wheel-drive "safari" trips to old gold-rush settlements (or their remains), such as Skippers Canyon and Macetown. Another off-roading trip takes you to see some of the areas filmed for the *Lord of the Rings* trilogy. Costs start at $110.

Real Journeys has a wide choice of fly-drive-cruise tour options to Milford and Doubtful sounds from Queenstown, Te Anau, and Milford.

Mid Southern Tracks ⊠ 14 Pioneer Dr., Lake Tekapo ☎ 03/680-6774.

Nomad Safaris ⊠ 19 Shotover St., Queenstown ☎ 03/442-6699 or 0800/688-222 ⊕ www.queenstown4wd.com.

Real Journeys ⊠ Lake Front Dr., Te Anau ☎ 03/249-7416 or 0800/656-501 🖷 03/249-7022 ⊠ Steamer Wharf, Queenstown ☎ 03/442-4846 or 0800/656-503 ⊕ www.realjourneys.co.nz.

BOAT TOURS   Glacier Explorers leave from the Hermitage Hotel, the visitor center, or the Mount Cook YHA for guided boat trips on the Tasman Glacier Lake ($105) Tours run at 10 AM and 2 PM, October–April, and last three hours.

Glacier Explorers ⊠ Aoraki/Mt. Cook Village ☎ 03/435-1077 ⊕ www.glacierexplorers.com.

BUS TOURS   The Double Decker is an original London bus that makes a three-hour circuit from Queenstown to Arrowtown and the bungy-jumping platform on the Karawau River. Leaving Queenstown, it goes via Frankton, Lake Hayes, and Gibbston Valley Wines before heading for a break at Arrowtown. The return trip to Queenstown goes by the Shotover River valley. Tours (about $38) depart Queenstown daily at 9:30 AM and 1:30 PM from The Mall outside McDonald's.

Double Decker ☎ 0800/668-888.

SCENIC FLIGHTS   *See* Sports & the Outdoors *in* Aoraki (Mt. Cook), Te Anau, and Milford Sound for information on flightseeing.

VISITOR INFORMATION

All of the regional visitor bureaus are open daily year-round, with slightly longer hours in summer. Some of the smaller offices, such as those in Tekapo and Twizel, may curtail their hours if necessary. The Fiordland National Park's visitor bureau hours vary a bit seasonally; summer hours are 8:30–6 and winter hours are 8:30–4:30. Queenstown's visitor center opens daily from 7 AM to 7 PM.

In addition to the visitor centers listed below, there are some local tourism organizations whose Web sites can be helpful. A Lake Wanaka site (www.lakewanaka.co.nz) provides information on local businesses, events, and attractions. Destination Fiordland (www.fiordland.org.nz) covers Te Anau, Milford, and Doubtful sounds and more. A special site focuses on winter sports in the Mackenzie Country: ⊕ www.mackenziewinter.co.nz.

Tourist Information Aoraki/Mount Cook National Park Visitor Centre ⊠ Aoraki/Mount Cook Village ☎ 03/435-1186 ⊕ www.doc.govt.nz. **Fiordland National Park Visitor Centre** ⊠ Lakefront Dr., Te Anau ☎ 03/249-7924. **Lake Pukaki Visitor Information Centre** ⊠ State Hwy. 8, Twizel ☎ 03/435-3280 ⊕ www.mtcook.org.nz. **Lake Tekapo Information** ⊠ Main Rd., Lake Tekapo ☎🖷 03/680-6686. **Queenstown Visitor Information Centre** ⊠ Clocktower Centre, Shotover St. at Camp St. ☎ 03/442-4100 or 0800/668-888 ⊕ www.queenstown-nz.co.nz. **Twizel Information Centre** ⊠ 61 Mackenzie Dr. ☎ 03/435-3124 ⊕ www.twizel.com. **Wanaka Visitor Information Centre** ⊠ The Log Cabin, Ardmore St. ☎ 03/443-1233 🖷 03/443-1290.

9

Otago, Invercargill & Stewart Island

WORD OF MOUTH

"Dunedin is arguably the culture capital of the South Island, thanks to the university, live music, and arts scene. If it's too sunny to be indoors, there are the wildlife of Otago Peninsula and the surf at St. Clair beach to enjoy. Swooping south, the dusty roads of the Catlins lead to Invercargill and Bluff, the departure points for the walking tracks and birdlife on remote Stewart Island."

—Joseph Gelfer

Updated by
Sue Farley

THE PROVINCE OF OTAGO occupies much of the southeast quadrant of the South Island. Geographically diverse, it's lined with the snowcapped Southern Alps to the west and a string of golden (albeit chilly) beaches to the east. The north is met by the wide Canterbury Plains and the south by the timeless Catlins region.

During the first three decades of the 1800s, European whaling ships cruised its coast and ventured ashore, yielding a mixed response from the local Māori, who had been living in relative harmony here for hundreds of years. In 1848 Dunedin was settled, and with it the purchasing from the Māori of all the land from the top of the Otago Peninsula south to the Clutha River, and also substantial sections farther inland. By the mid-1860s Dunedin was the economic hub of the Otago gold rush and therefore the hub of the whole country. Dunedin's historical wealth endures in such institutions as the University of Otago, the oldest in the country.

Invercargill, to the south, was born out of different economic imperatives. After the Dunedin settlers bought swaths of the Southland flats for their sheep, they needed a local port to bring in more stock from Australia. The town of Bluff, already familiar to sealers sailing the seas since the late 1700s, was selected as an ideal location. Invercargill became the administrative center to the port and then the whole region. Until recent years, the town's economic focus remained that of raising sheep and other livestock and crops; it has begun establishing itself as a more diverse metropolis.

Hanging off the bottom of South Island, Stewart Island is a study in remoteness. Commercial-fishing settlements give way to bushland that the kiwi bird—so rare elsewhere in the country—still haunts. (At night, the birds can be seen wandering on the beaches in many areas.) Expansive views across the Foveaux Strait from time to time are lighted up here with the aurora australis, the spectacular Southern Hemisphere equivalent of the northern lights.

Note: For more information on outdoor activities in lower South Island, *see* Chapter 11.

Exploring Otago, Invercargill & Stewart Island

The best way to explore this region is via car, although a good network of buses serves most places of interest. There are no trains in the region, except for the occasional sightseeing operation. Most people will probably find themselves starting in Dunedin and migrating south via State Highway 1. Once you reach Balclutha, there are two options for continuing south: either stay on the highway and head straight for Invercargill or turn off and go via the Catlins on the Southern Scenic Route. The highway offers an easy though perhaps uninspiring drive. The Catlins route is more demanding—but also more rewarding, scenery-wise. Whichever route you take, by the time you hit the Southland border all roads are wide, flat, and point to Invercargill.

You can reach Stewart Island by either boat or plane (one local described the choices as "either 60 minutes of fear or 20 minutes of terror," but

GREAT ITINERARIES

One real benefit of this region is that apart from Stewart Island you can get anywhere you want to go easily and relatively quickly.

Numbers in the text correspond to points of interest on the Otago & Invercargill and Stewart Island maps.

IF YOU HAVE 3 DAYS

Make your home base **Dunedin** ❶, then acquaint yourself with Otago history at the **Settlers Museum** or the **Otago Museum.** Pretend to be an Oompa Loompa at the **Cadbury World** chocolate factory or a Southern Man at the **Speight's Heritage Centre.** Wind down with dinner and perhaps a nightcap at one of the city's mellower bars. On Day 2, clear your head out on the peninsula with a visit to the **Royal Albatross Centre** and **Yellow-Eyed Penguin Reserve** in the morning and **Larnach Castle** in the afternoon. On Day 3 you could take a trip on the **Taieri Gorge Railway,** take a drive down along the Catlins coast, or just spend the day shopping.

IF YOU HAVE 6 DAYS

Follow the first two days of the three-day itinerary above, then head south via the Catlins, perhaps spreading the drive over two days. Once in **Invercargill** ❹, be sure to visit the **Southland Museum** and **Queens Park.** Stretch your legs with a walk on **Oreti Beach,** and after dinner on one of your nights here, catch a band at Tillermans. If you don't want the 2½-hour drive from Dunedin, fly to Invercargill and then connect on to **Stewart Island** and spend a couple of days exploring the walking trails and spotting kiwi.

IF YOU HAVE 8 DAYS

Follow the six-day itinerary above, with maybe an extra day in Dunedin, and add on a couple of nights on **Stewart Island,** perhaps even undertaking the **Rakiura Track.** Spend the evening over a few drinks in the **South Sea Hotel** bar, leaving your muddy boots on to show you mean business. On the last day or two, continue along the **Southern Scenic Route** and head out west toward Tuatapere to experience the rural heartland of New Zealand as it meets the Southern Ocean.

10

that's true only on a bad day). Once on Stewart Island, it's mainly a case of walking and catching the occasional water taxi to a neighboring island.

About the Restaurants

Dunedin has the area's highest concentration of good restaurants. Many chefs emphasize contemporary cuisine, or what used to be called fusion. Seafood is a big player, in part because of Dunedin's coastal location but also because of its proximity to Bluff, the home of New Zealand's great delicacy, the Bluff oyster. Many of the least-expensive options are café-like Asian restaurants; these tend to close early, around 9 PM. Locals don't usually dress up or make reservations for anything other than the most exclusive establishments.

Invercargill has a more limited selection of restaurants, most of which are moderately priced. Stewart Island has a reasonable selection of places to eat considering its location, but the ranks thin out in winter, when some places limit their hours and others close for the season.

WHAT IT COSTS In New Zealand dollars					
	$$$$	**$$$**	**$$**	**$**	**¢**
AT DINNER	over $30	$20–$30	$15–$20	$10–$15	under $10

Prices are per person for a main course at dinner, or the equivalent.

About the Hotels

Dunedin has a full range of accommodations, from modest hostels up to luxury hotels, whereas Invercargill has more motels than anything else. (Local motels generally offer clean rooms with kitchens and TVs.) Stewart Island's lodging options tend to be smaller, boutique establishments, and because of their situation they're usually on the expensive side.

Throughout the region, air-conditioning is a rarity, but given the cool climate, this isn't a problem. Heating, on the other hand, is standard in most places.

As always, it's a good idea to make a reservation in advance, especially during the summer high season. In Dunedin, rooms can be scarce around the time of special events, such as graduation ceremonies and high-profile rugby games.

WHAT IT COSTS In New Zealand dollars					
	$$$$	**$$$**	**$$**	**$**	**¢**
HOTELS	over $300	$200–$300	$125–$200	$75–$125	under $75

Prices are for a standard double room in high season, including 12.5% tax.

When to Visit

This is the part of New Zealand that gets cold with a capital C in winter, so if you're coming for warm weather, avoid the time between May and September. However, if you're combining your trip with skiing or snowboarding in other regions, this is *the* time to come.

Dunedin gets more visitors in summer, but remember that during the university vacations the city is quieter, which brings with it pros and cons. Inland Otago remains dry year-round, and you can expect crisp, sunny days in winter, but the coast gets its share of rain, and Dunedin in particular can have day after day of clouds and showers. Southland in winter isn't any colder, but it is wetter, and this can put a significant damper on things.

It's often said of New Zealand that you experience all four seasons in one day—but on Stewart Island you may experience all of them in an hour. Even in summer you can expect blustery and wet periods, but that is part of what the island is all about. Most visitors don't let the weather

TOP REASONS TO GO

FABULOUS BIRD-WATCHING

If any region can bring out the bird-watcher in you, this is it. The entire Otago coastline is peppered with scenic reserves full of people wielding binoculars and ornithological guidebooks. The reality of seeing a yellow-eyed penguin or an albatross out on the peninsula, or a kiwi on Stewart Island, *is* undeniably special, even for hardened cynics.

THE SOUTHERN SEA

The lower coast of the South Island is a wild and woolly coast, bordering as it does on the great Southern Ocean that swirls around the base of the globe. Head south along the Catlins section of the Southern Scenic Route, and you'll see ocean views, diving seabirds, and sandy beaches that you can explore. At Bluff, you can watch fishermen unloading their catches of oysters, cod, and lobsters—and then sample the catch yourself, in a local restaurant.

PUBS & CLUBS

With its resident population of 20,000 university students during the academic year the city of Dunedin is full of funky bars, late-night pubs, value-for-the-money cafés, and rocking music venues. The Speight's Ale House, which serves a never-ending stream of the eponymous beer, is a particular local favorite.

TERRIFIC TEAM SPORTS

Sports are the lifeblood of Otago and Southland. Dunedin's Carisbrook Rugby Stadium is home to the Highlanders team, and they're the reason for the swaths of blue and yellow team colors around town. International games, held at the stadium throughout the year, draw near-rabid crowds of fans. In Invercargill, Southland Stadium is home to the Southern Sting, one of New Zealand's best netball teams (netball is akin to outdoor basketball, and almost always played by women). Hence the *Go Sting!* slogans you'll see everywhere.

spoil their enjoyment—indeed, the weather might be part of their enjoyment. In winter, you'll have a better chance of seeing the aurora australis, but keep in mind that some of the island's walking trails may be closed.

DUNEDIN

❶ *280 km (175 mi) east of Queenstown, 362 km (226 mi) south of Christchurch.*

Clinging to the walls of the natural amphitheater at the west end of Otago Harbour, the South Island's second-largest city is enriched with inspiring nearby seascapes and wildlife. Because Dunedin's a university town, floods of students give the city a vitality far greater than its population of 122,000 might suggest. Its manageable size makes it easy to explore on foot—with the possible exception of Baldwin Street, the world's steepest residential street and home to the annual "gutbuster" race, in which people run up it, and the "Jaffa" race, in which people roll the namesake spherical chocolate candy down it.

Otago &
Invercargill

Dunedin, the Gaelic name for Edinburgh, was founded in 1848 by settlers of the Free Church of Scotland, a breakaway group from the Presbyterian Church. The city's Scottish roots are still visible; here you'll find the only kilt shop in the country, the first and only (legal) whiskey distillery, and a statue of Scottish poet Robert Burns, whose nephew was a founding member of the Free Church in Dunedin. The Scottish settlers and local Māori came together in relative peace, but this wasn't true of the European whalers who were here three decades before: place names such as Murdering Beach bear witness to this more volatile history.

During the gold rush of the 1860s, the city boomed, attracting tens of thousands of immigrants. In 1862 the first shipment of gold went back to England, and for a time Dunedin was the largest city in the country. The riches of the Otago goldfields are reflected in the bricks and mortar of Dunedin's handsome Victorian townscape, most notably in the Italianate Municipal Chambers building in the Octagon.

Dunedin has always had a creative history and a reputation for the eccentric. Wearing no shoes and a big beard here, for instance, marks a man as bohemian rather than destitute, and the residents wouldn't have it any other way. The University of Otago was the country's first university and has been drawing writers ever since its founding in 1871, most notably Janet Frame and the poet James K. Baxter. Dunedin also has a musical heritage, one that blossomed into the "Dunedin Sound" of the 1970s and '80s. The movement, which included such bands as the Chills and the Verlaines, is making a comeback.

A town square that happens to have eight sides, the **Octagon** is the city's hub. It's lined with several imposing buildings, as well as a smattering of market stalls, cafés, and bars with tables spilling out onto the pavement. In summer it's something of a meeting place, and it's also the site for the occasional student demonstration. A **statue of Robert Burns** sits in front of **St. Paul's Cathedral,** a part–Victorian Gothic, part-modern building with an imposing marble staircase leading up to a towering facade of Oamaru stone. On Stuart Street at the corner of Dunbar, check out the late-Victorian **Law Courts.** Their figure of Justice stands with scales in hand but without her customary blindfold (the low helmet she wears probably has the same effect).

The **Dunedin Public Art Gallery,** opened in 1996, has notably lovely display spaces. The shell of an original municipal building has been paired with a sweeping, modern glass facade. Natural light streams into the glass-ceiling foyer, and the galleries have native-wood parquet flooring and ironwork decoration. The collection includes European masters such as Monet, Turner, and Gainsborough, as well as New Zealand and Otago artists. A special gallery highlights Dunedin native Frances Hodgkins, whose work won acclaim in the 1930s and '40s. Hodgkins's style changed through her career, but some of her most distinctive works are post-impressionist watercolors. The museum also regularly mounts innovative contemporary exhibits. ✉ *30 The Octagon* ☎ *03/474–3240* ⊕ *www.dunedin.art.museum* ✉ *Free* ☉ *Daily 10–5.*

The **Otago Settlers Museum** dates back to 1898, when it was established to celebrate the 50th anniversary of the settlement of Dunedin. It tells the stories of all Otago settlers, from Māori and early European and Chinese to later Pacific Islanders and Asians. The many artifacts on display include documents, works of art, technological items, and forms of transport. The museum also has other changing exhibits and events, as well as organized walking tours of the city that highlight its history. ⊠ *31 Queens Gardens* ☎ *03/477–5052* ⊕ *www.otago.settlers.museum* ☞ *$4* ⊙ *Daily 10–5.*

☼ A trip to the 70-acre **Botanic Gardens** provides a fine opportunity to examine both international and native flora (or simply to relax and enjoy the birdsong). In addition to the seasonal gardens with their 6,800 species of plants there are year-round attractions: an aviary, a winter garden hothouse, a native plant collection, and a rhododendron garden. There's also a visitor center and a good café as well as a playground—just be sure to keep an eye out for duck droppings. Parking at the lower part of the gardens, off Cumberland Street, has easier access than the Opoho end, which is steeper, but both parts of the park are worth visiting. ⊠ *Great King St. at Opoho Rd.* ☎ *03/477–4000* ☞ *Free* ⊙ *Gardens dawn–dusk, buildings 10–4.*

The 1906 **Dunedin Railway Station**, a cathedral to the power of steam, is a massive bluestone structure in Flemish Renaissance style, lavishly decorated with heraldic beasts, coats of arms, nymphs, scrolls, a mosaic floor, and even stained-glass windows of steaming locomotives. This extravagant building earned its architect, George Troup, a knighthood from the king—and the nickname Gingerbread George from the people of Dunedin. The station has long outlived the life of the steam engine, and for all its magnificence it receives few trains these days. The station is also home to the **Sports Hall of Fame** (☎ 03/477–7775 ⊕ www.nzhalloffame.co.nz ☞ $5 ⊙ Daily 10–4), a tribute to more than 150 athletes from more than 30 sports. It is the country's only sports museum. ⊠ *Anzac Ave. at Stuart St.* ☎ *03/477–4449* ⊙ *Daily 7–6.*

The **First Presbyterian Church** on the south side of Moray Place may be the finest example of a Norman Gothic building in the country. Although the church is not vast, it's still impressive, with a base of Oamaru stone topped by a delicate 200-foot spire. Equally impressive are the leaf patterns, dragon, and other carved details placed around the windows. ⊠ *415 Moray Pl.*

☼ The **Otago Museum** will help you see what galleries and museums were like in Victorian times. In the 19th century, displays were lighted with natural light, so museums often had huge skylight windows. In this museum's 1877 building, you can visit the "Animal Attic," a restored, magnificent skylighted gallery. The museum's first curator was a zoologist, and many of the original animals collected from 1868 are still on display. "Southern Land, Southern People" explores the cultural heritage of this region, and other galleries focus on Māori and Pacific Island artifacts, animal and insect specimens, and nautical items, including ship models and a whale skeleton. "Discovery World" adds a hands-on element for kids. ⊠ *419 Great King St.* ☎ *03/474–7474* ⊕ *www.*

otagomuseum.govt.nz ✉ *Free, Discovery World $6, special galleries and visiting exhibitions $10* ☉ *Daily 10–5.*

The 35-room Jacobean-style **Olveston** mansion was built between 1904 and 1906 for David Theomin, a wealthy businessman and patron of the arts who amassed a handsome collection of antiques and contemporary furnishings. The house and its furnishings are undoubtedly a treasure from an elegant age, but, apart from some paintings collected by Theomin's daughter, there is very little in it to suggest that it's in New Zealand. Even the oak staircase and balustrade were prefabricated in England. The one-hour guided tour is recommended. ✉ *42 Royal Terr.* ☎ *03/477–3320* ⊕ *www.olveston.co.nz* ✉ *$14.50* ☉ *Daily 9–5; tours daily at 9:30, 10:45, noon, 1:30, 2:45, and 4.*

If you're a Willy Wonka fan, you might not be able to resist the tantalizing aroma that wafts from central Dunedin's favorite institution: the Cadbury chocolate factory, which produces most New Zealand–made chocolate. At **Cadbury World** you can watch chocolate candy in the making; keep an eye out for the chocolate waterfall. It's a good idea to pre-book your spot for a factory tour; they're very popular. ✉ *280 Cumberland St.* ☎ *03/467–7967 or 0800/223–287* ⊕ *www.cadburyworld. co.nz* ✉ *$15* ☉ *Daily 9–4, 9–7 in summer.*

For more tasty indulgences, head to the **Speight's Brewery Heritage Centre** for a tour of the South's top brewery, which dates back to 1876. Here you can see the various stages of the gravity-driven brewing process and learn the trade's lingo such as *wort* and *grist*. You can also taste the results. Speight's makes several traditional beers, the most common being its Gold Medal Ale. The company claims that this is the drink of choice for every "Southern Man," which isn't far from the truth. ✉ *200 Rattray St.* ☎ *03/477–7697* ✉ *$15* ☉ *Weekend tours at 10, noon, and 2 (sometimes an additional 4 PM tour at is added on busy days); weekday tours at 10, noon, 2, and 7. Reservations are essential.*

The **Taieri Gorge Railway** tourist train runs from Dunedin through the now closed Otago Central Railway to Pukerangi and Middlemarch. Also available is a seasonal *Seasider* route from Dunedin up the coast to Palmerston. The train is made of modern or vintage wooden-and-steel carriages, a treat in themselves. It runs every day to either Pukerangi, Middlemarch, or Palmerston, but check the timetable for differing options. Reservations are essential. ✉ *Dunedin Railway Station* ☎ *03/477–4449* ⊕ *www. taieri.co.nz* ✉ *$53–$71.*

Where to Stay & Eat

★ **$$$–$$$$** ✕ **Bell Pepper Blues.** Inside a converted historic hotel, this casual, attractive restaurant with its mullioned bay windows and dark-wood interior is where Michael Coughlin, one of the country's most respected chefs, brings an inventive flair to his dishes. His lamb, beef, and *cervena* (farmed venison) dishes are well known; the pan-seared beef sirloin with a spring roll of slow-braised veal shin and aromatic Asian vegetables is a particular standout. Pre- and postdinner drinks can be had next door

The Northern Otago Coast & Oamaru

DRIVING SOUTH FROM TIMARU, **Oamaru** is the first stop of any interest. Described as the best example of Victorian architecture still in use in New Zealand today, the white Oamaru stone (limestone) facades of the ornate buildings in the Port precinct gleam in the southern sun. Each year during the second week of November, the town celebrates with the **Victorian Heritage Celebrations.** Festivities include the New Zealand Penny Farthing Championships, a Heritage Golf Classic, a Heritage Ball, and a Victorian Garden Party. Many local galleries and businesses join the theme and open their doors with various themed events. The town's visitor center has information about the festival and about the Victorian buildings themselves. ⊠ *Oamaru I-Site Info Centre, 1 Thames St., Oamaru* ☎ *03/434-1656* ⊕ *www. tourismwaitaki.co.nz.*

Oamaru's other claim to fame is penguins. Each evening, enthusiastic little blue penguins—the world's smallest penguin breed—emerge from the sea and waddle up the beach, wings outstretched, to their nests up in the bushes off the beach. The **Oamaru Blue Penguin Colony** (⊠ Waterfront Rd. ☎ 03/433-1195 ⊕ www.penguins.co.nz ☜ Tour $15) can be visited any time of the year, and providing penguins are resident at the time, tours and viewing opportunities run day and evening. Evening viewing times vary with the seasons and daylight hours. **Pen-y-bryn Lodge** (⊠ 41 Towey St. ☎ 03/434-7939 ⊕ www.penybryn.co.nz) offers entry to the penguin colony as part of the hotel's room rate. Each night, between the appetizer and the main course in the dining room,

guests are encouraged to leave the table and head down to the ocean to watch the penguins come in, before returning to their meal and a quiet port afterward.

An even more significant population of **yellow-eyed penguins,** or *hoiho* come ashore south of Oamaru. The best places to view them are Bushy Beach and Katiki Point, where hides (camouflaged viewing huts) have been constructed. These penguins are one of the world's rarest breeds, and they are considered an endangered species. Ask at the **local information office** (☎ 03/434-1656 ⊕ www. tourismwaitaki.co.nz) for details on viewing them.

If you're driving along the coast north of Dunedin, you can stop to see the striking **Moeraki Boulders.** These giant spherical rocks are concretions, formed by a gradual buildup of minerals around a central core. Some boulders have sprung open, revealing—no, not alien life forms—but interesting calcite crystals. The boulders stud the beach north of the town of Moeraki and south as well at Katiki Beach off Highway 1, about 60 km (37 mi) above Dunedin, or 40 km (25 mi) south of Oamaru. Unfortunately the boulders at Moeraki Beach have become a bit of a tourist item, and there are often whole busloads of people wandering the beach. Watch for little dolphins jumping in the surf just offshore; they're as interesting as the boulders. If you're feeling a bit peckish after the sea air, pop into **Fleurs Place** (⊠ 169 Haven St., Moeraki ☎ 03/439-5980) out on the old jetty. Here you can enjoy fish straight out of the sea, which is the highlight of the lunch and dinner menus.

at the restaurant's Chilé Club Bar. ⊠ *474 Princes St.* ☎ *03/474–0973* ⊟ *AE, DC, MC, V* ☺ *Closed Sun. No lunch.*

$$$–$$$$ ✕ **Palms Restaurant.** The watchful eye of a statue of Queen Victoria guards this casually elegant eatery, which occupies a historic building. The pleasantly simple menu includes lamb, seafood, beef, and vegetarian options; the mushroom soup starter is locally famous, as is the $10 special lunch offered on Thursday and Friday. Vintages from central Otago lead the mostly New Zealand–based wine list (although there are a few notable Aussie reds as well). ⊠ *18 Queens Gardens* ☎ *03/477–6534* ⊟ *AE, DC, MC, V* ☺ *No lunch Sat.–Wed.*

$$$–$$$$ ✕ **The Reef.** Seafood is the highlight at this relaxed and contemporary restaurant, which is open for lunch and dinner. You can choose among individually crafted main dishes or opt for the seafood platter (an array of deep-fried, grilled, smoked, and steamed prawns and shellfish). All can be paired with a New Zealand bottle selected from the impressive wine list. Reasonable lunches (there's a $10 special) are also available, and there are a few nonseafood dishes, too. ⊠ *333 George St.* ☎ *03/ 471–7185* ⊟ *AE, DC, MC, V.*

$$$–$$$$ ✕ **Two Chefs.** With terra-cotta walls and an often-lighted fireplace, this restaurant is cozy and intimate. The tempting menu, which could be described as Mediterranean with a New Zealand twist, might include smoked salmon with roasted Jerusalem artichokes, steamed scallops, and a chili-and-tomato compote. The well-chosen wine list features some notable Central Otago pinot noirs. ⊠ *428 George St.* ☎ *03/477–9117* ⌕ *Reservations essential* ⊟ *AE, DC, MC, V* ☺ *Closed Sun. No lunch.*

$$–$$$ ✕ **The Esplanade.** With one of the best locations in Dunedin, this place serves terrific pizzas as well as great water views. The pizza choices are traditional, although there are some unusual extras such as artichokes and capers. About a third of the space is given over to a bar, with the rest devoted to tables next to the pizza oven and, in winter, a roaring open fire. The long hours (9 AM to midnight daily) mean you can even have pizza for breakfast if you like. One large pie is enough for two people. ⊠ *5/250 Forbury Rd.* ☎ *03/456–2544* ⊟ *AE, DC, MC, V.*

★ ¢–$$$ ✕ **The Ale House Bar & Restaurant.** A rugged interior with heavy wood furniture, old brewing equipment, and a huge schist fireplace makes the Speight's brewery restaurant feel homey and welcoming. Its hub, naturally, is the bar, whose brass footrest invites you to pull up a stool and relax. The menu includes a "drunken" steak (steak marinated in dark, malty porter) and beer-battered fish. Of course, you also get recommendations for the best Speight's ale to match your meal. Several special seasonal beers are released each year; in the past, these have included Harvest (an apricot beer), Chocolate, and Samradh (a ginger-and-pimiento beer). ⊠ *200 Rattray St.* ☎ *03/471–9050* ⊟ *AE, DC, MC, V.*

$–$$ ✕ **Thai Hanoi.** This popular Thai restaurant has a little bit of a Vietnamese influence. Try one of the green or red Thai curries, or a yellow or jungle (hot) Vietnamese curry. Because it's opposite the Rialto Cinema, Thai Hanoi makes for a convenient pre- or postmovie dinner spot—but reserving a table is a good idea, especially if there's a popular film showing across the road. ⊠ *24 Moray Pl.* ☎ *03/471–9500* ⊟ *AE, DC, MC, V* ☺ *No lunch.*

10

¢–$$ ✕ **Ananda.** The authentic Indian vegetarian *thalis* (meals made up of several small individual servings) here are served on traditional metal platters. You can choose from (in order of ascending size) the Prince, Rani, Raja, or Maharaja thali. A casual restaurant, Ananda is best suited for lunches and early dinners. Although it has a liquor license, you're also welcome to bring your own bottle. ⊠ *365 George St.* ☎ *03/477–1120* ☰ *MC, V* ☉ *Closed Sun.*

¢–$ ✕ **Cafe Tokyo.** Possibly the freshest and most affordable sushi in town can be found at this restaurant. It isn't the place for a quiet or leisurely meal, but then, sushi lends itself to a certain bustle. (There are also a few hot dishes offered if you prefer your food cooked.) Weekday lunchtimes are often very busy, so arrive early or late to guarantee a seat. Cafe Tokyo's also a good option for an early dinner (the restaurant closes at 8 PM). ⊠ *103 George St.* ☎ *03/477–7631* ☰ *MC, V* ☉ *Closed Sun.*

$$$$ ✕🖿 **Corstorphine House.** This restored Edwardian mansion, surrounded
Fodor'sChoice by private gardens, exudes luxurious gentility. The interior's lavishness
★ extends from the public areas, with their carved fireplaces and custom-made furniture, to the themed rooms, which include the Egyptian Room and the French Room. Bathrooms have up-to-date pluses such as demisting mirrors and heated floors. Organic produce grown on the property appears in the conservatory restaurant's contemporary dishes, such as polenta with sage, walnuts, and artichokes and the roasted pork loin with pumpkin-and-fig gnocchi. The higher room rate includes a full breakfast. ⊠ *23 Milburn St.* ☎ *03/487–1000* 🖷 *03/487–6672* ⊕ *www. corstorphine.co.nz* ➷ *7 rooms* ☾ *Restaurant, some in-room VCRs, in-room data ports, Wi-Fi* ☰ *AE, DC, MC, V* ᵀᴼᴵ *BP, EP.*

★ **$$–$$$** ✕🖿 **Lisburn House.** Listed with the Historic Trust, this Victorian-Gothic inn is a romantic retreat set amid lovingly tended gardens. Many of its 1865 details are intact, including decorative Irish brickwork and fishtail slate roof tiles. Inside are high molded plaster ceilings, an impressive turn-of-the-20th-century stained-glass entrance, and a welcoming fireplace. The three sumptuous bedrooms each have four-poster queen beds. At the Claddagh Restaurant ($$$), with its extensive wine list and plush interior and chandeliers, you may have the rare opportunity to try wild venison with a port-and-juniper jus—it's exquisite. The restaurant's seafood chowder, a 27-year-old recipe, is also still drawing compliments. Dining reservations (Claddagh is open Tuesday–Saturday) are essential. ⊠ *15 Lisburn Ave.* ☎ *03/455–8888* 🖷 *03/455–6788* ⊕ *www. lisburnhouse.co.nz* ➷ *3 rooms* ☾ *Dining room, in-room VCRs, lounge* ☰ *AE, DC, MC, V* ᵀᴼᴵ *BP.*

$$$ 🖿 **Southern Cross Hotel.** Named the Grand Hotel when it was built in 1883, this central hotel was then considered one of the finest guesthouses in the Southern Hemisphere. Although it has been completely modernized, much of the ornate Victorian architecture and detail is still in evidence, not least in the casino. Even if you don't want to try your luck, it's worth walking up the sweeping staircase to ogle the chandeliers and the ornate plaster ceilings. The rooms themselves are unexceptional. ⊠ *Princess St. at High St.* ☎ *03/477–0752* 🖷 *03/477–5776* ⊕ *www.scenic-circle.co. nz/SouthernCross* ➷ *178 rooms, 8 suites* ☾ *3 restaurants, in-room data ports, health club, 2 bars, casino* ☰ *AE, DC, MC, V.*

$$ 🏠 **Hulmes Court Bed & Breakfast.** In an 1860 house built for one of the founders of the Otago Medical School, this friendly bed-and-breakfast maintains its scholarly ties: the host, Norman Wood, employs University of Otago students and graduates. The complex includes a 1907 house next door. Rooms are characterized by their architectural elements, such as large bay windows. From Hulmes Court it's a short walk to the center of town. Children are welcome here; note that there's a resident cat named Solstice. ⊠ *52 Tennyson St.* ☎ *03/477–5319* 🖷 *03/477–5310* ⊕ *www.hulmes.co.nz* 🛏 *14 rooms, 8 with bath* ⚿ *In-room VCRs, some in-room broadband, mountain bikes, lounge, Internet room* ☰ *AE, DC, MC, V* ⑩ *CP.*

$–$$ 🏠 **526 George Street.** The building, an old doctor's office built in 1907, is full of character and close to the heart of town. The hotel itself is a good midrange choice, halfway between the anonymity of a motel unit and the higher prices of an exclusive hotel. Most of the comfortable and quiet rooms face away from the street. ⊠ *526 George St.* ☎ *03/477–1261* 🖷 *03/477–1268* ⊕ *www.hotel526.co.nz* 🛏 *14 rooms* ⚿ *Restaurant, bar, laundry service, free parking* ☰ *AE, DC, MC, V.*

¢ 🏠 **Next Stop Backpackers.** A short walk from the Octagon, Next Stop Backpackers provides double rooms as well as dorms, all with shared bathrooms and a typically friendly backpacker vibe. In summer you can head to the rooftop balcony, which has views across the city; in winter there's a sizable log fire. ⊠ *2 View St.* ☎ *03/477–0447* 🖷 *03/477–0430* ⊕ *www.nextstop.co.nz* 🛏 *9 rooms, 4 dorms without bath* ⚿ *TV room, Kitchen, lounge, Internet room; no room TVs* ☰ *DC, MC, V.*

Nightlife & the Arts

Being a student town, Dunedin is a good spot for nightlife and cultural events. Many venues are on or near George and Princes streets, often down dark alleys with no signs, so follow the crowd. Expect things to be quiet until around 10 PM, when it starts to heat up. Information about what's going on can be found on ⊕ www.fink.net.nz, Radio One (91 FM), and the student paper, *The Critic*.

The Arts

ART GALLERIES The **Marshall Seifert Gallery** (⊠ 1 Dowling St. ☎ 03/477–5260) is in a turn-of-the-20th-century, triangular-shape building with a dizzying spiral staircase. It's overflowing with rare and collectible fine art, antiques, prints, and contemporary New Zealand art. It's open Monday–Friday 11–5:30, and Saturday 11–2.

Milford Galleries (⊠ 18 Dowling St. ☎ 03/477–7727 ⊕ www. milfordgalleries.co.nz), a major fine-art dealer on the New Zealand scene, presents solo and group exhibitions of New Zealand paintings, drawings, sculpture, glasswork, ceramic art, and photography. Among the major New Zealand artists represented are Neil Frazer (who does large-scale abstract expressionist paintings) and Elizabeth Rees (whose oil studies explore New Zealand machismo).

THEATER The **Fortune Theatre** (⊠ 231 Stuart St. ☎ 03/477–8323 ⊕ www. fortunetheatre.co.nz) inhabits what was once the neo-Gothic Trinity Methodist Church, made of Oamaru stone. The theater mounts con-

10

temporary plays by both New Zealand and international playwrights, as well as classical works.

Since 1961, the **Globe Theatre** (✉ 104 London St. ☎ 03/477–3274) has been producing high-quality plays, beginning with its early collaborative work with local author James K. Baxter. It now is host to contemporary and classic theater as well as the occasional film.

The **Regent Theatre** (✉ 17 The Octagon ☎ 03/477–6481, ticket reservations 03/477–8597 ⊕ www.regenttheatre.co.nz), in a historic building, holds large-scale musicals, dance, and theater performances, as well as the Royal New Zealand Ballet, the New Zealand Film Festival, and the World Cinema Showcase each year. The highly rated **Bean Scené** café, in the same building, is a nice place to stop for dinner (don't be fooled by the tired décor—the food is excellent).

Nightlife

The **Arc Café** (✉ 135 High St. ☎ 03/474–1135), something of an institution, is a bar, performance venue, café, and gallery all rolled into one. You can often catch local and national bands here. This very informal and affordable joint is probably the only place in town you can ask for a cognac with your morning coffee without raising an eyebrow, which has to be a good thing.

The Duke of Wellington (✉ 1 Queens Garden ☎ 03/479–2870) makes the mistake of keeping the place scrupulously clean—but otherwise, it's one of the country's better reproductions of an English pub, set in an authentic 1870s Victorian building. A good selection of British ales and beers are available, although they're served a little overchilled. Let that pint of Old Speckled Hen sit for 10 minutes, though, and it'll taste like the warm, yummy treacle it really is.

Bath Street Nightclub (✉ 1 Bath St. ☎ 03/477–6750) has DJs playing every night between Tuesday and Saturday, from 10 PM to late. There's an ongoing $2 special on tap beer Tuesday, Wednesday, and Thursday nights, which draws big crowds.

★ Possibly the snuggest bar in Dunedin, **Pequeno** (✉ Savoy Bldg., Lower Ground Floor, 50 Princes St. ☎ 03/477–7830), came to notoriety as the hangout of choice for Gwyneth Paltrow and Chris Martin (of the band Cold Play) during the Dunedin shoot of the film *Sylvia*. The bar is dark, with a low ceiling, comfy club chairs, a roaring fire, and a charming staff. The wine list is good, if pricey, and there's live jazz on Thursday evenings.

There are three good options for viewing art-house movies in town. In descending order of size and ascending order of program obscurity: **The Rialto** (✉ 11 Moray Pl. ☎ 03/474–2200), **The Metro** (✉ Town Hall Building, Moray Pl. ☎ 03/474–3350), and **The Academy** (✉ 50 Dundas St., Dunedin North ☎ 03/479–2980).

Refuel (✉ 640 Cumberland St. ☎ 03/479–5309 ⊕ www.dunedinmusic. com), in the heart of the university campus, has a predominantly student clientele, though everyone is welcome. Nights are split between local or national (or even international) live rock acts and DJ-driven nights of '80s hits, hip-hop, house, and drum 'n' bass music. Their Web site gives a good run-down of what's on when; the club is open during semester breaks as well as when classes are in session.

Sports & the Outdoors

Rugby is followed with cultish devotion in Dunedin, and **Carisbrook Stadium** (⊠ Burns St. ☎ 03/466–4010 or 0800/227–472 ⊕ www.orfu.co. nz), also known as the "House of Pain," is where fans go to worship. (Fans of the local Super 14 team, the Highlanders, paint themselves blue and yellow on match days.) Games are played on many weekends, and you might even catch an international competition. Those used to the ticket prices of places such as Twickenham in England will be delighted at how cheap and available a game can be in Dunedin; terrace tickets start at $12, and the main stand is just $27.

☺ If you're up for a swim, one option is the heated **Saltwater Pool** (⊠ The Esplanade, St. Clair ☎ 03/455–6352). However, if you're brave, you may want to take a swim on **St. Clair beach** instead. To get here, either drive south on State Highway 1 or hop on the Normanby–St. Clair bus from George Street or the Octagon. The sea at Dunedin can be a little wild; during summer there is an area between flags that's patrolled by lifeguards. St. Clair has some good surfing; it plays host to some prestigious competitions. Don't be too spooked by the shark bell on the Esplanade: there hasn't been a fatal attack for 30 years, just the occasional leg nibble.

Signal Hill, to the northeast, with good views of the city below and the hills surrounding it, is a popular walking destination and an excellent mountain-biking venue. At the opposite end of town, Saddle Hill looks southward to Mosgiel and the Taieri Plain. Also south of town is the **Tunnel Beach walk,** which heads through a sandstone tunnel to a secluded beach (note that this walk is closed from August through October for lambing). Information about these and many other walks can be found at the Visitor Information Centre.

Shopping

10

Nearly all the good shopping places in Dunedin are clustered around George Street and Moray Place. The town's an especially good place to stock up on Kiwiana and sharp, chic clothes.

Koru (⊠ Lower Stuart St., opposite Dunedin Railway Station ☎ 03/477–2138 ⊕ www.nzartandjade.co.nz) is a local artists' co-op gallery and interactive studio, which sells crafts made of *punamu* (New Zealand greenstone), *paua* (abalone shell), and wood, as well as weaving and pottery. The artisans are happy to talk to you as they work.

More Kiwi spirit can be found at **Outré** (⊠ 380 Great King St., opposite the University Bookshop ☎ 03/471–7005), where all New Zealand–made crafts are mixed in with clothing, trinkets, and ecofriendly goods (possibly inspired by the Green Party offices across the street).

Plume (⊠ 310 George St. ☎ 03/477–9358) carries major international and New Zealand designer clothes. The stock is focused on women's clothes, but there are also some for men and children. Great New Zealand labels abound, such as Nom D, Zambesi, Kate Sylvester, and Workshop.

The Southern Scenic Route–Catlins Section

THE SOUTHERN SCENIC ROUTE, 440 km (273 mi) long, follows the coast south of Dunedin, picks up the highway to Balcutha, and swings around the Catlins coast before pushing on through Invercargill to Milford Sound in Fiordland. The Catlins stretch (approximately 200 km, or 125 mi) is a particular treat, although some of the roads are unpaved and rough.

If you're driving from Dunedin to Invercargill in one day, you can see many of the sights, but it would be better to split your journey over two days to take better advantage of the area. An excellent *Southern Scenic Route* brochure, available at the Dunedin visitor center, describes the sights; the attractions are signposted as well.

When you leave the highway at Balclutha, you'll notice that the native bush is dense and relatively untouched. This, coupled with the rich song of native birds, gives the countryside an almost tropical feel, contrasting with the actual climate.

The first stop is **Nugget Point.** Its Māori name, Tokatā, means "rocks standing up out of water." Wildlife abounds here, including yellow-eyed penguins, fur and elephant seals, and sea lions. Take a walk to the lighthouse; it's about 20 minutes round-trip.

Heading back inland is **Owaka,** the Catlins' only town. With a population of roughly 400 residents, Owaka has a cluster of shops, a Department of Conservation Field Centre, a small museum, and various basic services.

At the settlement of **Papatowai** there's a convenient picnic spot

tucked behind a tidal inlet. Here you can enjoy rock pools with the bush on one side and open coastline on the other. Just south of here, you'll want to take time for a stop at the **Florence Hill Lookout.** The view down to Tautuku Bay is one of the best coastal views in New Zealand, with more native bush stretching into the west and waves lining up in tight sets on the beach. There's a 30-minute loop walk out on to the estuary at Tautuku Bay if you like silent, wide-open spaces.

Farther on is **Curio Bay,** home to a petrified forest that's easily visible at low tide. These fossilized trees, dating from the mid-Jurassic period, are astonishing (be careful on your way down the cliff steps to the fossils). This is one of the best examples of Jurassic-fossilized forest in the world.

From Curio Bay a back road runs over to **Slope Point.** Heavy rains or unusually high tides can make this road impassable, in which case just return to the main road. Slope Point, mainland New Zealand's southernmost point, is something of a disappointment—just some farmland sloping down to the sea. However, its symbolic value is real enough, and it gets plenty of visitors. There is no access during the lambing season in September and October.

By now the rugged Catlins landscape smoothes out into gentle hills of unusually lush greens. From the township of Fortrose the roads are straight once more across the wide flats of Southland; before you know it, you've reached Invercargill.

If you're under 25 or just feeling brave, head to **Void** (⊠ 8 Albion Pl. ☎ 03/474–1110) for übercool clothes, shoes, and accessories. The items will result in either much respect or much ridicule, depending on where you wear them. Among the trendy labels are Diesel, Sorted, Mossimo, Stüssy, and Lee.

OTAGO PENINSULA

The main items of interest along the claw-shape peninsula that extends northeast from Dunedin are an albatross colony and Larnach Castle. The road along the west side of the peninsula consists of 15 km (9½ mi) of tight curves along the harbor, so be careful while driving, or you could find yourself having an impromptu marine adventure. Along the road are a handful of settlements; these get progressively more rustic as you near the peninsula's tip. On the east side of the peninsula there's a string of rugged beaches, some of which are accessible via walking paths. On the journey back to Dunedin, the Highcliff Road, which turns inland at the village of Portobello, is a scenic alternative to the coastal Portobello Road and gives easiest access to Larnach Castle. Allow an hour to drive from the city.

★ ❷ High on a hilltop with commanding views from its battlements, **Larnach Castle** is the grand baronial fantasy of William Larnach, an Australian-born businessman and politician. The castle, built in the mid-1870s, was a vast extravagance even in the free-spending days of the gold rush. Larnach imported an English craftsman to carve the ceilings, which took 12 years to complete. The solid marble bath, marble fireplaces, tiles, glass, and even much of the wood came from Europe. The mosaic in the foyer depicts Larnach's family crest and the modest name he gave to his stately home: the Camp. Larnach rose to a prominent position in the New Zealand government of the late 1800s, but in 1898, beset by a series of financial disasters and possible marital problems, he committed suicide in Parliament House. (According to one version of the story, Larnach's third wife, whom he married at an advanced age, ran off with his youngest son; devastated, Larnach shot himself.) The 35 acres of grounds around the castle include lodging; a rhododendron garden; a rain-forest garden with kauri, *rimu,* and *totara* trees; statues of *Alice in Wonderland* characters; a herbaceous walk; and a South Seas Walkway lined with palms and aloe plants. During a visit you have access to almost all of the castle and its grounds, and are guided by a pamphlet and a video. ⊠ *Camp Rd.* ☎ *03/476–1616* 🖷 *03/476–1574* ⊕ *www.larnachcastle.co.nz* 🖃 *$20* ☉ *Daily 9–5.*

❸ **Taiaroa Head,** the wild and exposed eastern tip of the Otago Peninsula, is the site of a breeding colony of royal albatrosses. Among the largest birds in the world, with a wingspan of up to 10 feet, they can take off only from steep slopes with the help of a strong breeze. With the exception of this colony and those in the Chatham Islands to the east, the birds are found only on windswept islands deep in southern latitudes, far from human habitation. Under the auspices of the **Royal Albatross Centre,** the colony is open for viewing all year, except during a two-month break between mid-September and mid-November when the birds lay their eggs;

Fodor's Choice ★

10

the visitor center is open year-round. The greatest number of birds are present shortly after the young albatrosses hatch near the end of January. Between March and September parents leave the fledglings in their nests while they gather food for them. In September, the young birds fly away, returning about eight years later to start their own breeding cycle. Access to the colony is strictly controlled, and you must book in advance. From the visitor center you go in groups up a steep trail to the Albatross Observatory, from which you can see the birds through narrow windows. They are magnificent when seen in flight, which is an option even when the observatory is closed.

Overlooking the albatross colony is the **"Disappearing" Gun at Fort Taiaroa,** a 6-inch artillery piece installed during the Russian Scare of 1886, when Russia was making hostile maneuvers through the Pacific. When the gun was fired, the recoil would propel it back into its pit, where it could be reloaded out of line of enemy fire. The gun has been used in anger only once, during World War II, when it was fired across the bow of a fishing boat that failed to observe correct procedures before entering the harbor. Tours range from 30 to 90 minutes and can include albatross viewing, Fort Taiaroa, and an Albatross Insight presentation; you should allow a half day to enjoy the full experience. ⊠ *Taiaroa Head* ☎ *03/478–0499* ⊕ *www.albatross.org.nz* ✉ *Prices range from $8 for the Insight presentation to $33 for the Unique Taiaroa Tour* ☉ *Royal Albatross Centre opens at 8:30; tours run 9* AM*–dusk in summer, 10* AM*–dusk in winter.*

☺ If you'd like to observe the world's most endangered penguin in its natural habitat, visit the **Yellow-Eyed Penguin Reserve,** also called the **Penguin Place,** where a network of tunnels has been disguised so that you can get up close to this rare and protected species. Experienced guides will interpret the birds' behavior and seasonal habits as you creep through the tunnels. The penguins, also known as *hoiho,* are characterized by their yellow irises and headbands. This conservation program has been a success; starting in 1984 with 8 breeding pairs they now have 36 pairs. Reservations are essential. ⊠ *Harrington Point* ☎ *03/478–0286* 🖷 *03/478—0257* ⊕ *www.penguin-place.co.nz* ✉ *$33* ☉ *Daily 9–5.*

☺ To learn about the Southland's underwater species, check out the aquarium at the **New Zealand Marine Studies Centre.** You can spot octopi, sea horses, and sharks in the viewing tanks, or get your hands on a starfish in the touch tanks. There are also displays on marine conservation and current research, as well as guided tours. The center is run by the University of Otago Marine Sciences Department; the enthusiastic guides can regale you with locally specific information. ⊠ *Hatchery Rd., Portobello* ☎ *03/479–5826* ⊕ *www.marine.ac.nz* ✉ *$8; guided tour $16* ☉ *Daily noon–4:30; tours at 10:30.*

OFF THE BEATEN PATH

ARAMOANA ROAD – Taking this road to Carey's Bay, Port Chalmers, and Aramoana, on the northern side of Otago Harbour, is a worthwhile excursion. You can stop at the historic **Carey's Bay Hotel** (⊠ 17 Macandrew Rd., Carey's Bay) for lunch on your way around the harbor drive. And you'll pass Dunedin's port, Port Chalmers, on the way. **The Mole,** at the end of the Aramoana peninsula, is a 1-km- (1/2-mi-) long breakwater protecting the entrance to Otago Harbour. A dozen or so small ships were also sunk between 1920 and 1950 to protect the breakwater from the relentless Southern Ocean that hammers against it every day. You can check these ships out, and the tall kelp forest that protects them, with **Dive Otago** (⊠ 2 Wharf St. Dunedin ☎ 03/466–4370 ⊕ www. diveotago.co.nz), which run trips whenever the weather allows.

Where to Stay & Eat

$$$ ✕ **Bay Café and Bar.** In the first settlement you reach on the peninsula, this well-known café has fine views across the harbor. Seafood choices such as scallops, prawns, blue cod, and mussels are popular, as are the tasty gourmet pizzas with interesting toppings such as smoked salmon and prawns. The brunch menu is served between 11 and 3, and the dinner menu kicks in at 5. In summertime, reservations are essential. ⊠ *494 Portobello Rd.* ☎ *03/476–1357* ▭ *MC, V.*

$$–$$$ ✕ **1908 Café & Bar.** There are good views from this converted post office located "where the high road meets the low road." The interior still feels Edwardian, and classic seafood dishes and steaks lead the menu. Hours can be changeable in winter, and crowds come in summer—so it's a good idea to call ahead. ⊠ *7 Harrington Point Rd.* ☎ *03/478–0801* ▭ *AE, DC, MC, V.*

★ $$$ ▦ **Larnach Lodge.** It's hard to beat the setting—panoramic sea views, 35 acres of gardens, the Larnach Castle next door, and luxury themed suites. The Scottish Room, for instance, has classic tartan bedcovers and curtains, heavy brass bedsteads, and a Robbie Burns rug; the Enchanted Forest Room has 19th-century William Morris wallpaper. More affordable rooms with shared bathrooms are available in a converted 1870 coach house for about half the regular rate. Entry to the castle is included in the room rate. ⊠ *Camp Rd.* ☎ *03/476–1616* 🖷 *03/476–1574* ⊕ *www.larnachcastle.co.nz* ⬎ *12 rooms* ♨ *Restaurant* ▭ *MC, V* ⊚❘ *BP.*

INVERCARGILL

10

❹ *182 km (113 mi) south of Queenstown, 217 km (135 mi) southwest of Dunedin.*

Originally settled by Scottish immigrants, Invercargill has retained much of its turn-of-the-20th-century character, with broad main avenues (Tay Street and Dee Street) and streetscapes with richly embellished buildings. You'll find Italian and English Renaissance styles, Gothic stone tracery, and Romanesque designs in a number of its well-preserved buildings.

In recent history Invercargill has suffered from something of a PR problem. Its significant distance from the rest of New Zealand has led to an "us versus them" syndrome. Rightly or wrongly, Invercargill was often perceived as a geographical and cultural backwater.

However, things are on the move. There are two main catalysts in the Invercargill renaissance. First, Tim Shadbolt, the former mayor of Waitemata City in Auckland, was elected as Invercargill's mayor in 1993 and

The Southern Man

THE LACONIC "SOUTHERN MAN" has a special niche in the Kiwi mind—the typical specimen lives in the country, has a trusty dog by his side, is a rabid rugby fan, and adheres to a rugged lifestyle of farmwork, fixing the ute (pickup truck), and hitting the bars for pool and beer. Speight's beer has gotten a lot of mileage from this icon, using it for a successful Southern Man ad campaign, complete with a Southern Man theme song. ("Cuz here we just know/what makes a Southern boy tick/and it ain't margaritas/with some fruit on a stick . . ."). But this stereotype is rooted in reality. There are plenty of good, hardy blokes in Otago and Southland who dress in shorts and Swannies (Swanndri woolen bush shirts), drink Speight's beer, and work on farms. Before long some visitors may develop similar traits. If you find yourself saying things like "She's a hard road" and "She'll be right" when the going gets tough, then the process is well under way. To help the Southern Man find the right lady there is an annual Perfect Woman competition, with challenges such as digging in a fence post, backing a trailer loaded with hay, fitting snow chains, tipping a 242-pound ram, and opening a bottle of Speight's without a bottle opener. As the ad says, "It's a hard road to find the perfect woman."

—Joseph Gelfer & Sue Farley

brought a tremendous blast of energy to town. Second, a "Zero Fees Scheme" operated at the Southern Institute of Technology has encouraged many young folk wanting to minimize student loans to follow the "lifestyle with attitude," bringing their energy with them. The rest of Invercargill seems happy to join the ride.

The **Southland Museum and Art Gallery,** housed in the Southern Hemisphere's largest pyramid, contains the largest public display of live *tuatara,* New Zealand's extremely rare and ancient lizards, which are kept within several glass enclosures. The museum has also established the world's most successful captive-breeding program for the creatures. It's usually easy to spot these mini-dinosaurs, but they will do a successful job of hiding themselves if it gets too noisy. Southland also contains fine displays of Māori and settler artifacts. Another exhibit, "The Roaring Forties," is particularly interesting: it examines the attempted settlement of the sub-Antarctic Auckland and Campbell Islands. The gallery has both older and modern New Zealand art on permanent display as well as temporary exhibits. Set in Queens Park, with an on-site café and information center, the museum makes a good place to begin your visit to Invercargill. ⊠ *108 Gala St.* ☎ *03/218–9753* ⊕ *www.southlandmuseum.com* ✉ *Donation suggested; Tuatara and Gallery tours* $3 ⊙ *Daily 10–5.*

The **Anderson Park Art Gallery** is set in a splendid 1925 Georgian-style house. The 60 acres of surrounding gardens and lawns are laid out like a public park; they include a traditionally carved Māori house and short bushwalks. The gallery displays notable New Zealand art, sculpture, and pottery. ⊠ *McIver Rd.* ☎ *03/215–7432* ⊿ *Donation* ☉ *Daily 10:30–5.*

Shearing South gives you an insider's look into the sheep-shearing profession and a chance to see the industry that's led New Zealand's agricultural development for the past 150 years. On display are a collection of shearing artifacts, an exhibit of a wool shed along with DVD presentations (including "150 Years of Pain, Sweat and Shears"), a shearers' Hall of Fame (New Zealand consistently wins international shearing competitions) and even a collection of shearing-inspired art. Guided tours are available. ⊠ *Arcade 55, Dee St.* ☎ *03/214–9155* ⊕ *www. shearingsouth.co.nz* ⊿ *$12* ☉ *Weekdays 10–4, weekends 1–4.*

★ ☉ The 200 acres in the center of town that make up **Queens Park** create a fine layout of public gardens by any standards. The numerous different sub-gardens here include two rose gardens (with both modern and "antique" rose varieties), a Japanese garden (complete with meditation area), and an impressive hothouse, which acts as a sanctuary on a wet day. The park also has miles of gentle walking paths and waterways, an 18-hole golf course, and a decent café. There's also a small zoo area and an aviary with a walk-through section that children love. The main entrance is next to the Southland Museum. ⊠ *Queens Dr. at Gala St.* ☎ *03/217–7368.*

Where to Stay & Eat

Many of Invercargill's motels are on Tay Street, handy if you're coming from Dunedin, and North Road, convenient if you're arriving from Queenstown.

$$$–$$$$ ✕ **Cabbage Tree.** For his ideal restaurant, owner Neville Kidd completely revamped this old store on the way to Oreti Beach. The inside is spacious and lined with wood and brick, making it resemble a vineyard restaurant. Popular dishes on the menu are Stewart Island blue cod, lamb shanks, prawns, and pan-seared venison. The broad wine list includes mostly New Zealand wines, with the occasional European bottle for the stubborn. The outdoor garden bar is a perfect place to enjoy the Southland sun while having a glass of wine. ⊠ *379 Dunns Rd.* ☎ *03/ 213–1443* ▭ *AE, DC, MC, V.*

$$–$$$$ ✕ **The Rocks Café.** An urban-chic-meets-Tuscany ambience is achieved at this eatery, where the décor features terra-cotta, brick, and river stone. The kitchen employs local seasonal ingredients in dishes such as the flaming-hot Southland squid starter and the yummy although unfortunately named "Beef Ron Jeremy" with Tuscan potatoes. As chef and owner Mark Elder says, the restaurant likes to do "everything that's good about Southland." ⊠ *101 Dee St., at Courtville Arcade* ☎ *03/ 218–7597* ▭ *AE, DC, MC, V* ☉ *Closed Sun. No lunch Sat.*

$$$ ✕ **Flannagans.** In one of the half-dozen dining rooms in this restored Edwardian house, you can try many different seafood dishes. Oysters are presented in five different styles, and there's also a fresh catch of the day to try. A signature dish of prawns, salmon, scallops, and mussels is a good option for two. Some meaty entrées are available as well. ⊠ *Queens Dr./Bainfield Rd. roundabout* ☎ *03/215–8156* ▭ *AE, DC, MC, V* ☉ *No lunch; no dinner Sun.*

10

$–$$$ ✕ **Zookeepers.** The slightly wacky animal theme and a loud color scheme have helped give this place a reputation of being fun and bustling. There are good brunch-style meals and snacks such as toasted sandwiches, steaks, and nachos to be had from morning to late at night, when you can also enjoy the bar and live music. ✉ *50 Tay St.* ☎ *03/218–3373* ▭ *AE, DC, MC, V.*

$$ ✕ **Sopranos Wood Fired Pizzeria.** The tasty pizzas here are named after various fictional and nonfictional mobsters and gangsters. It makes sense that "Meadow" is the vegetarian option and that "Dr. Melfi" is the smoked salmon, but how "Tony" became a Thai green curry–chicken topping we'll never know. There's a good local wine list. ✉ *33 Tay St.* ☎ *03/218–3464* ▭ *MC, V.*

$–$$ ✕ **Tillermans.** More of a café-bar than a formal restaurant, Tillermans serves well-presented light meals such as lasagna. If you show up late, you can catch one of the numerous live bands that play into the night. The kitchen keeps serving until 10 PM. ✉ *16 Don St.* ☎ *03/218–9240* ▭ *MC, V.*

¢–$ ✕ **Thai Dee.** A central location, affordable prices, and consistent quality all makes this a popular spot for Thai food. Try the red or green Thai curry, or the Panang if you want a little extra heat. Next to a cinema, it's convenient for pre- and postmovie meals. ✉ *9 Dee St.* ☎ *03/214–5112* ▭ *AE, DC, MC, V* ⊙ *Closed Sun.*

$–$$$$ 🏨 **Ascot Park Hotel.** This rambling complex is a welcome sight if you've just battled the rugged gravel roads of the Catlins. The hotel is the largest in town, and just a five-minute drive from the town center. The spacious, modern rooms come with small balconies. An on-site restaurant serves traditional and contemporary New Zealand fare. ✉ *Tay St. at Racecourse Rd.* ☎ *03/217–6195* 🖷 *03/217–7002* ⤵ *64 rooms, 24 motel rooms, 2 suites, 4 studio rooms* ⚭ *Restaurant, minibars, pool, gym, hot tub, sauna, bar; no a/c* ▭ *AE, DC, MC, V.*

$$ 🏨 **Kelvin Hotel.** The big advantage of this modern, rather bland hotel is that it's very central, and just about ideal if you're not driving. There is a choice of rooms facing the street, where you can see all the action. The rooms facing the back are quieter. ✉ *16 Kelvin St.* ☎ *03/218–2829* 🖷 *03/218–2287* ⤵ *58 rooms, 2 suites* ⚭ *Restaurant, minibars, bar, casino, laundry facilities; no a/c* ▭ *AE, DC, MC, V.*

$$ 🏨 **Kereru Cottage.** If you're traveling to Invercargill via the Southern Scenic Route, and want to break your stay in the middle, this one-bedroom self-catering cottage is a good choice. It's lovely to look over the wild coastal views from the outdoor hot tub, with a glass of wine in hand. (Just remember, though, that you'll have to bring your own bottle with you.) ✉ *5 Mirren St. Papatowai* ☎ *03/415–8613 or 0800/228–5467* 🖷 *03/415–8613* ⊕ *www.catlins-ecotours.co.nz/kereru.htm* ⤵ *1 cottage* ⚭ *Kitchen, outdoor hot tub* ▭ *MC, V.*

$ 🏨 **Homestead Villa Motel.** The Homestead's large, self-contained units have contemporary furnishings, and they all have whirlpools. The U-shape motor lodge is a 10-minute walk from the city center, and 5 minutes away from the Southland Museum and Art Gallery. ✉ *Avenal St. at Dee St.* ☎ *03/214–0408 or 0800/488–588* 🖷 *03/214–0478* ⤵ *35 units* ⚭ *Kitchens; some room service; no a/c* ▭ *AE, DC, MC, V.*

¢–$ ☒ **Tuatara Backpackers Lodge.** The world's southernmost YHA hostel is in the center of Invercargill. Friendly and clean, the Tuatara has the usual group of bunks, twins, and double rooms, along with a couple of "executive suites" (with private bathrooms, TVs, and DVD players). There's a communal kitchen, a TV lounge, and a café with visitor information that's open to all. Upstairs there are four computers for guests' use. ☒ *30–32 Dee St.* ☎ *03/214–0954 or 0800/488–282* 🖷 *03/214–0956* 🛏 *23 rooms, 3 suites* ⚐ *Laundry facilities, Internet room* ▭ *MC, V.*

Sports & the Outdoors

Oreti Beach, 11 km (7 mi) southeast of town, is a popular spot for locals to blow away the cobwebs. It would be a brave person who swims here, but people do surf and windsurf, taking advantage of the wind and swells that whip the coast on an almost constant basis. At low tide people drive their cars onto the beach, but be aware that breakdown coverage probably won't cover you for getting stuck in sand.

Another good spot for a walk is **Sandy Point,** which can be reached by taking a left after crossing the Oreti River on the way out to Oreti Beach. A 13-km (8-mi) network of easygoing trails covers the riverbanks, estuary, and the bush. A leaflet detailing the paths is available from the visitor information center in town.

On the western side of the Southern Scenic Route, the **Tuatapere Hump Ridge Track** (☎ 03/226–6739 or 0800/486–774 🖷 03/226–6739 ⊕ www.humpridgetrack.co.nz) is a challenging circular three-day/two-night walk that combines beach, bush, and sub-alpine environments in its 53 km (33 mi). The track starts near Tuatapere, about two hours' drive west of Invercargill and right on the edge of the Fiordland National Park. It's no amble; you'll spend about nine hours walking each day, but there are two good huts sleeping about 40 people each to rest in during the night. This walk has been open only a few years but is already very popular with Kiwis and international visitors. You will need to buy hut tickets in advance.

If you want to experience a bit of what rural New Zealand is all about, then **Waiau Downs Farm Adventures** (☒ 1609 Tuatapere–Orepuki Rd. Tuatapere ☎ 03/226–6622 ⊕ www.farmadventures.co.nz), on the western side of the Southern Scenic Route, is worth getting your gum boots out for. Working dogs Perk and Dan will demonstrate how to "head" or "back" sheep, or you can "throw" a fleece, "handle" some wool—or just learn what all that jargon actually means. Tours start at $15.

EN ROUTE In the tiny township of **Bluff,** you can taste its coveted namesake oysters. An annual festival, held in late April at the town's wharf, wallows in seafood delicacies; oyster-opening and oyster-eating competitions and cook-offs are part of the fun. If you miss the festival, the most spectacular place for oysters, in season, is **Lands End Restaurant** (☒ 10 Ward Parade ☎ 03/212–7575) overlooking the sea. Also here is that odd Kiwi icon, the **Paua Shell House** (☒ 258 Marine Parade ☎ 03/212—8262). Paua is a kind of abalone; the home's walls gleam with the iridescent shells. The family of the original owners, Fred and Myrtle Flutey, keep the house open most days; a donation is requested to tour

10

it. Bluff is also home to the **The Stirling Point** signpost, at the southern end of State Highway 1, which gives directions to places all over the world, including the South Pole. The town is also the main jumping-off point for Stewart Island. It's about 30 km (19 mi) from Invercargill to Bluff, an easy ½-hour drive south on State Highway 1.

OTAGO & INVERCARGILL ESSENTIALS

Transportation

BY AIR

Dunedin Airport, with the rather unfortunate code of DUD, lies 20 km (13 mi) south of the city. Invercargill's airport (IVC) is 3 km (2 mi) from city center. Both are small and easy to navigate.

Both Qantas and Air New Zealand link Dunedin and Christchurch; the flight takes just under an hour. Air New Zealand also flies regularly from Dunedin to Auckland and Wellington. From Invercargill, Air New Zealand offers direct flights to Christchurch, and Stewart Island Flights makes the hop over to Stewart Island.

Taxi fare from Dunedin's airport to the city center is about $60. Kiwi Shuttles and similar companies charge about $20 for a trip between the city and the airport. Reservations are appreciated but not essential.

Taxis from Invercargill Airport into town cost $8–$9. The Spitfire Shuttle costs $6 per person, and there's usually a shuttle waiting for each flight.
🖪 Airports **Dunedin International Airport** ✉ 25 Miller Rd., Momona ☎ 03/486-2879 ⊕ www.dnairport.co.nz. **Invercargill Airport** ✉ 106 Airport Ave. ☎ 03/218-6920 ⊕ www.invercargillairport.co.nz.
🖪 Carriers **Air New Zealand** ☎ 03/479-6594 (Dunedin), 03/215-0000 (Invercargill) or 0800/737-000 ⊕ www.airnewzealand.com. **Qantas** ☎ 0800/808-767 ⊕ www.qantas. com.au. **Stewart Island Flights** ☎ 03/218-9129 ⊕ www.stewartislandflights.com.
🖪 Transfers **Blue Star Taxis—Invercargill** ☎ 03/218-6079. **City Taxis** ☎ 03/477-1771 or 0800/771-771. **Kiwi Shuttles** ☎ 03/473-7017 ⊕ www.kiwishuttles.co.nz. **Spitfire Shuttle** ☎ 03/214-1851.

BY BUS

InterCity's two daily runs between Christchurch and Dunedin take about five to six hours. The company makes an extra run on Friday and Sunday. One daily InterCity bus continues on from Dunedin to Invercargill; this takes another four hours. Other bus companies operating in the region include Atomic Shuttles, Citibus, and Bottom Bus. In Dunedin, local buses to the peninsula depart from Stand 5, Cumberland Street. Stewart Island Experience operates buses to Bluff, which connect with the ferry. They pick up at the Southland Museum and at accommodations. The fare to Bluff is $15.
🖪 Bus Depots **Dunedin** ✉ 205 St. Andrew St. **Invercargill** ✉ Queens Park, 108 Gala St.
🖪 Bus Information **Atomic Shuttles** ☎ 03/477-4449 ⊕ www.atomictravel.co.nz. **Bottom Bus** ☎ 03/434-7370 ⊕ www.bottombus.co.nz. **Citibus** ☎ 03/477-5577 ⊕ www. citibus.co.nz. **InterCity** ☎ 03/471-7143 ⊕ www.intercitycoach.co.nz.

Stewart Island Experience ☎ 03/212-7660 or 0800/000-511 ⊕ www. stewartislandexperience.co.nz.

BY CAR
It takes four hours to drive the 280 km (175 mi) between Queenstown and Dunedin (via highways 6 and 1). The main route between Dunedin and Invercargill is State Highway 1, a 3½-hour drive. A slower, scenic alternative is a journey along the Catlins coast, which takes a full day (unless you choose to overnight along the way). (*See* "The Southern Scenic Route" box *above* for more information.)

Much of the driving around Otago and Southland is easygoing, with good signage and little traffic. Other drivers are mostly well behaved; police are active in patrolling and ticketing people who break the law. If someone flashes you with their headlights, it's probably a warning about something ahead.

Most main roads are paved, and all but the most obscure unpaved roads are drivable in a regular car in good weather. In winter, watch out for roads at altitudes above several hundred feet. Most such roads can get icy, and they'll have signs indicating any danger.

Driving in Dunedin can be challenging; there are some confusing one-way roads and twisting hills in the suburbs. Parking on the street is limited, so it's best to find one of the numerous parking lots. Invercargill's central streets are easier to navigate. Most are flat and open, and there's more on-street parking.

Most major car rentals have offices or agents in Dunedin and Invercargill as well as at the local airports.
🚗 Car-Rental Agencies **Budget** ☎ 03/474-0428 ⊕ www.budget.co.nz. **National** ☎ 03/477-8801 or 0800/800-115 ⊕ www.nationalcar.co.nz. **Thrifty** ☎ 03/477-7087 or 0800/737-070 ⊕ www.thrifty.co.nz.

Contacts & Resources

BANKS & EXCHANGE SERVICES
ATMs are plentiful in Dunedin and Invercargill but not in the countryside (including on the Otago Peninsula). It's wise to carry some cash, but most establishments will take credit cards. Banks are usually open only on weekdays, but other places that change money are open on weekends.

10

EMERGENCIES
Dunedin's Urgent Pharmacy is open until 10 PM; Donna Kerr Unichem Pharmacy in Invercargill is open until 8 during the week and 6 on weekends.
🚨 Emergency Services **Fire, police, and ambulance** ☎ 111. **Donna Kerr Unichem Pharmacy** ✉ 172 Tay St., Countdown Arcade, Invercargill. **Dunedin Hospital** ✉ 201 Great King St., Dunedin ☎ 03/474-7930. **Southland Hospital** ✉ Kew Rd., Invercargill ☎ 03/218-1949. **Urgent Pharmacy** ✉ 95 Hanover St., Dunedin ☎ 03/477-6344.

Urgent Doctor Service ✉ 103 Don St., Invercargill ☎ 03/218-8821.

MAIL & INTERNET
There are post offices and Internet facilities in the center of both Dunedin and Invercargill. Post offices are usually open weekdays 8:30–5:30 and Saturday 10–12:30. Internet points and cafés tend to stay open later;

they charge about $4 per hour. Public libraries generally have Internet access, but the fees they charge may be slightly higher.

🖪 Internet Cafés **Com-Zone.net** ⊠ 45 Dee St., Invercargill 🕿 03/214-0007. **Dunedin I-Site Info Centre** ⊠ 48 The Octagon, Dunedin 🕿 03/474-3300. **Internet Depot** ⊠ 18 George St., Dunedin 🕿 03/470-1730. 🖪 Post Offices **PostShop** ⊠ 233 Moray Pl., Dunedin 🕿 03/474-0932. **PostShop** ⊠ 1 Don St., Invercargill 🕿 03/214-7700.

TOURS

SIGHTSEEING TOURS
One way to see Dunedin is via the Double Decker Bus Tour, which takes in numerous historic buildings in central Dunedin, the hillside suburbs, and the university. The one-hour tour costs $18.

Lynette Jack, an outstanding personal guide and driver, draws on an extensive knowledge of Invercargill and the surrounding area to illuminate local history during an exploration of gardens, beaches, historic houses, and even a smeltery. A two-hour tour costs $59 per person.

🖪 **Double Decker Bus Tour** ⊠ 630 Princes St., Dunedin 🕿 03/477-5577 ⊕ www. citibus.co.nz.

Lynette Jack Scenic Sights ⊠ 22 Willis St., Invercargill 🕿 025/338-370 or 03/215-7741.

WILDLIFE TOURS
Natures Wonders Naturally, a family-run company based at a working farm, uses an all-terrain vehicle to get you to hard-to-reach parts of the Otago Peninsula. Tours include visits to colonies of shags (cormorants), seals, and blue penguins, and you may even catch up with some yellow-eyed penguins coming ashore. The one-hour trip starts at $40.

Twilight Tours organizes minibus tours of Dunedin and its surroundings, including a daily tour that focuses on the albatrosses, penguins, and seals of the Otago Peninsula. This is a good way to see the rare yellow-eyed and little blue penguins if you don't have a car. The tour costs $65 but doesn't include admission to the albatross Observatory. (You can still see albatrosses flying free without entering the observation area.)

Another way to get to know about the prolific wildlife of this area is to take a boat trip to Taiaroa Head with **Monarch Wildlife Cruises.** A guided hour-long cruise includes visits to the breeding sites of the northern royal albatross, New Zealand fur seals, and up to 20 species of coastal and pelagic birds. Very likely, an albatross will fly over your boat—their huge wingspan makes it a spectacular sight. Other trips include landing stops at the yellow-eyed penguin reserve or the Taiaroa visitor center. The basic cruise costs $32.

Earl Matheson at **Catlins Natural Wonders** provides day trips encompassing Catlins flora and fauna. Tours departing from Dunedin cost $140 (including lunch and refreshments), with lower prices for trips departing from Balclutha and Owaka. For a more immersive experience, try **Catlins Wildlife Trackers Ecotours,** operated by Fergus and Mary Sutherland. The two- and four-night tours include day and night walks and conservation activities. Tours cost $345 for two nights and $690 for four nights. Their Catlins Traverse Walk is $395.

🖪 **Catlins Natural Wonders** 🕿 0800/353-941 ⊕ www.catlinsnatural.co.nz. **Catlins Wildlife Trackers Ecotours** ⊠ 5 Mirren St., Papatowai 🕿 03/415-8613 ⊕ www.catlins-ecotours.co.nz. **Monarch Wildlife Cruises** ✉ Wharf St. at Fryatt St., Dunedin ☎ 03/477-4276 ⊕ www.wildlife.co.nz. **Natures Wonders Naturally** ✉ Harrington Point, Portobello ☎ 03/478-1150 🖷 03/478-0714 ⊕ www.natureswondersnaturally.com. **Twilight Tours** ✉ 25 Coolock St., Dunedin ☎ 03/474-3300 ⊕ www.wilddunedin.co.nz.

VISITOR INFORMATION

In addition to the tourist bureau Web sites listed below, you may want to check out the following: ⊕ www.dunedinnz.com for information on Dunedin; ⊕ www.southernscenicroute.co.nz for information on the spectacular drive; ⊕ www.southland.org.nz maintained by a regional tourism group; and Bluff's ⊕ www.bluff.co.nz.

The Dunedin visitor center keeps regular business hours daily, with extended hours in summer. This is also where you can find information about the Otago Peninsula. The Invercargill visitor bureau is open weekdays 9 to 5 and weekends 10 to 5, extending until 6 PM in summer.

🚩 Tourist Information **Dunedin Visitor Information Centre** ✉ 48 The Octagon ☎ 03/474-3300 🖷 03/474-3311 ⊕ www.cityofdunedin.com. **Invercargill Visitor Information Centre** ✉ Southland Museum and Art Gallery, Victoria Ave., Queens Park. ☎ 03/214-6243 🖷 03/218-4415 ⊕ www.invercargill.org.nz.

STEWART ISLAND

The third and most southerly of New Zealand's main islands, Stewart Island is separated from the South Island by the 24-km (15-mi) Foveaux Strait. Its original Māori name, Te Punga O Te Waka a Maui, means "the anchor stone of Maui's canoe." Māori mythology says the island's landmass held the god Maui's canoe secure while he and his crew raised the great fish—the North Island. Today the island is more commonly referred to by its other Māori name, Rakiura, which means "the land of the glowing skies." This refers both to the spectacular sunrises and sunsets and to the southern sky's equivalent of the northern lights—the southern lights, or aurora australis. The European name of Stewart Island dates back to 1809. It memorializes an officer on an early sealing vessel, the *Pegasus*, who was the first to chart the island.

10

The island covers some 1,700 square km (650 square mi). It measures about 75 km (46 mi) from north to south and about the same distance across at its widest point. On the coastline, sharp cliffs rise from a succession of sheltered bays and beaches. In the interior, forested hills rise gradually toward the west side of the island. Seals and penguins frequent the coast, and the island's prolific birdlife includes a number of species rarely seen in any other part of the country. In fact, this is the surest place to see a kiwi. The Stewart Island brown kiwi, or *tokoeka*, is the largest species of this kind of bird. Unlike their mainland cousins, these kiwis can be seen during the day as well as at night. It's a rare and amusing experience to watch these pear-shape birds scampering on a remote beach as they feed on sand hoppers and grubs.

Māori have visited Stewart Island for centuries. Archaeologists' studies of 13th-century Māori middens (refuse heaps) indicate that the island was once a rich, seasonal resource for hunting, fishing, and gathering

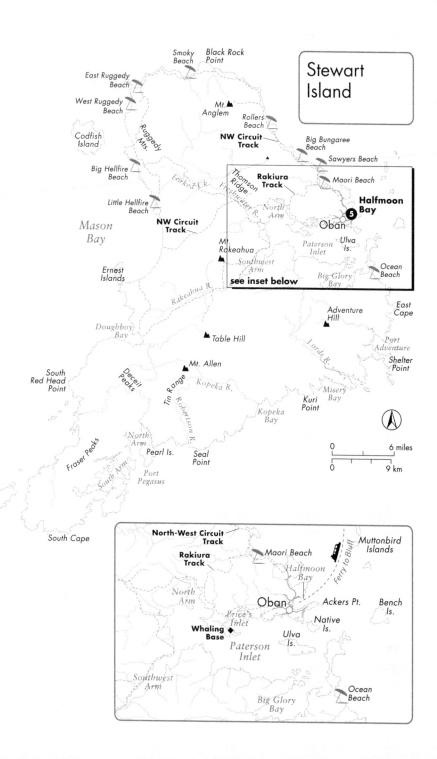

seafood. A commonly eaten delicacy at that time, the *titi,* also known as the mutton bird, still occasionally appears on menus.

In the early 19th century, explorers, sealers, missionaries, and miners settled the island. They were followed by fishermen and sawmillers who established settlements around the edges of Paterson Inlet and Halfmoon and Horseshoe bays. In the 1920s Norwegians set up a whaling enterprise, and many descendants of these seafaring people remain. Fishing, aquaculture, and tourism are now the mainstays of the island's economy.

In this tight-knit island community, many of the residents have family connections dating back for generations; being local means being born here. Despite this there is a healthy mutual respect between the island and mainland New Zealand.

Even by New Zealand standards, Stewart Island is remote, raw, and untouched. Roads total about 20 km (13 mi). The appeal is its seclusion, its relaxed way of life, and—despite the once-busy whaling and lumber-milling industry—its untouched quality. In spring 2002, about 85% of Stewart Island was designated as **Rakiura National Park.** The park encompasses areas that were formerly nature reserves and the like. More than 200 walking trails thread through the park, and a dozen huts give shelter for overnight stays. For information on Rakiura as well as the rest of Stewart Island, contact the **Department of Conservation Stewart Island Visitor Center** (⊠ Main Rd., Oban ☎ 03/219–0002 ⊕ www.doc.govt.nz).

⑤ Apart from the tiny township of **Oban** at **Halfmoon Bay** on Paterson Inlet, Stewart Island is practically uninhabited. Directly behind Oban's waterfront is a short main street with a small collection of establishments. A handful of roads head off up the surrounding hills. The hills are mostly thick bush, with houses poking their heads out for a view of the bay. Everywhere there is birdsong.

One of the best places for bird-watching is **Ulva Island,** 620 acres of thick native bush. The rare birds that live here have no predators, so they have an excellent survival rate. Among the resident species are the *weka,* the saddleback (a kind of gull), *kaka* (a parrot), and kiwi. The forest, which has walking paths accessible to the public, is made up primarily of *rimu, rata,* and *kamahi* trees. To get here, take a boat or water taxi from Halfmoon or Golden Bay. You can also join a **Paterson Inlet Cruise** and spend an hour with a nature guide on the island ($69). ⊠ *Main Rd., Oban* ☎ *03/212–7660 or 0800/000–511* ⊕ *www.stewartislandexperience.co.nz.* ⊠ *Department of Conservation Visitor Centre, Main Rd., Oban* ☎ *03/219–0002* ⊕ *www.stewartisland.co.nz.*

Where to Stay & Eat

$$$–$$$$ ✕ **Church Hill Cafe Bar & Restaurant.** Chef Deanne McPherson specializes in preparing tantalizing cuisine from the sea's bounty, as well as local favorites such as roasted mutton bird. The wine list has some great New Zealand choices. Dining outdoors is recommended (the view is stunning);

10

reservations are also recommended. ⊠ *36 Kamahi Rd., Oban* ☎ *03/ 219–1323* ▭ *MC, V.*

$$–$$$$ ✕ **Empress Restaurant.** This establishment, right on the beach in the Empress Visitor Centre, has some fine sea views. The simple menu includes battered or baked cod, satay chicken, and rib-eye steak. Lunch and dinner are served Wednesday–Sunday; light snacks during the day on Monday and Tuesday. In winter the owners cut back the business hours, so call ahead. ⊠ *45 Elgin Terr., Oban* ☎ *03/219–1123* ▭ *MC, V.*

¢–$$$ ✕ **Wharfside Café.** Located upstairs in the ferry terminal, this spot is perfect for grabbing breakfast or some tasty homemade baked goods before setting out to tackle the island (it's also a cozy spot for watching the boats when the weather is bad). Lunch and dinner dishes include local seafood, pastas, and salads. ⊠ *Main Wharf, Halfmoon Bay, Oban* ☎ *03/219–0070* ▭ *MC, V.*

¢–$ ✕ **Justcafé.** American Britt Moore has set up her cybercafé in this faraway outpost. Stop in for great coffee, muffins, quiche, and cold smoked-salmon sandwiches—and surf the Net while you nibble and sip. ⊠ *Main Rd., Oban* ☎ *03/219–1422* ▭ *No credit cards* ☉ *Closed June–Sept. No dinner.*

$–$$ ✕▥ **South Sea Hotel.** This handsome building dominates the main road in Oban. Containing the only real bar on the island, it bustles with both visitors and locals. Next to the main bar is a café that turns into a restaurant at night, serving seafood, meats, and vegetarian dishes ($$–$$$). The hotel rooms are comfortable, and the three at the front of the building have sea views. ⊠ *Main Rd., Oban* ☎ *03/219–1059* ▤ *03/219–1120* ⊕ *www.stewart-island.co.nz* ⤵ *9 studios, 8 rooms* ▭ *MC, V.*

$$$ ▥ **The Bach.** This secluded house works well for couples, and there's a loft for extra visitors. The place is thoroughly supplied, from beach towels to a CD player. There are plenty of nice design touches, too, such as the paua-shell inlay in the bathroom. The open-plan design makes the most of the sea views, and there's a deck with a barbecue, suited for alfresco meals. If you don't feel like cooking, the owners are nearby and can shuttle you into town. ⊠ *Leask Bay Rd., Halfmoon Bay* ☎ *03/219– 1394* ⤵ *1 house* ▭ *MC, V* ♨ *BBQ, kitchen* ⦿ *EP, CP.*

$$$ ▥ **Port of Call.** Philippa Fraser-Wilson and Ian Wilson are sixth-generation Stewart Islanders who have opened the doors of their house to visitors (they also own the Bach). This modern B&B, overlooking Halfmoon Bay and the Foveaux Strait, is a few minutes' drive from Oban. If you stay here, you can check out the historic 1840 stone house on the property, the second oldest of its kind in New Zealand. Ian and Philippa also own and operate Stewart Island Water Taxi & Eco-guiding, which offers guided and nonguided trips around the island. ⊠ *Leask Bay Rd., Halfmoon Bay* ☎▤ *03/219–1394* ⊕ *www.portofcall.co.nz* ⤵ *1 room* ♨ *Lounge* ▭ *MC, V* ⦿ *CP.*

$$ ▥ **Glendaruel.** At this B&B a short walk from town, you can have private views over Golden Bay. The owners fell in love with the island years ago and couldn't bring themselves to leave; they bring that enthusiasm to those who stay here. The upstairs room is the larger of the two doubles, but both are perfectly comfortable; there's also a single. Most rooms throughout the house have good views of either Paterson Inlet or the surrounding native bush, which is thick with native birds. Kaka (parrots) are frequent visitors to the deck, and the garden is nice for strolling. Continental or cooked breakfasts are available, as is dinner by arrangement. ✉ *38 Golden Bay Rd., Oban* 🕾 *03/219–1092* ⊕ *www.glendaruel.co.nz* ◔ *3 rooms* ♿ *Kitchenette, lounge* ▭ *MC, V* ⏐◉⏐ *BP, CP.*

$$ 🗖 **Turner Cottage.** Tucked away in a secluded bush setting just a few minutes from the sea, this self-contained one-bedroom bungalow is especially nice for couples. It has big doors opening onto the deck, and a cozy woodstove to give you that rustic, isolated island feel. Good restaurants are just down the road, though, if you don't want to cook. ✉ *7 Golden Bay Rd., Oban* 🕾 *03/219–1394* ⊕ *www.portofcall.co.nz* ▭ *MC, V* ♿ *Kitchen.*

Sports & the Outdoors

If you're feeling restless on a bad-weather day, you can use the island's gym in the **community center** (✉ Ayr St., Oban 🕾 03/219–1477) for a small fee.

Fishing

For information on deep-sea fishing out of Halfmoon Bay, *see* Chapter 11.

Hiking

There are numerous day walks departing from the Department of Conservation (DOC) office. Some, such as the Observation Rock and Fuchsia walks, are measured in minutes; others, such as the walks to Fern Gully, Ryan's Creek, and Horseshoe Point, are measured in hours. There are also some outstanding multiday treks.

The **Rakiura Track,** one of New Zealand's Great Walks, takes three days. Day one goes from Halfmoon Bay to Port William Hut via Horseshoe and Lee bays. Day two heads inland through native bush and wood across the ridge, allowing for good views of Paterson Inlet and the Tin Range. Day three connects back to Halfmoon Bay via *rimu* and *kamahi* forest. The huts accommodate up to 30 people on a first-come, first-served basis. They come with mattresses, a wood-burning stove, running water, and toilets. Another popular trek, a step up in both distance and difficulty, is the **North West Circuit**, a 9- to 11-day walk from Halfmoon Bay that circles the north coast and then cuts through the interior to return to its starting point. If that's not enough for you, five days can be tacked on by including the Southern Circuit. Stewart Island's climate is notoriously changeable, so be prepared for sun, wind, rain, and mud. Take the usual safety precautions for these hikes: bring suitable boots, clothing, food, and a portable stove; complete an intentions form at the DOC office before setting out; and, ideally, bring along with you a locater beacon and/or a guide who knows the trails. For information on these walks, contact the **Department of Conservation Visitor Centre** (✉ Main Rd., Oban 🕾 03/219–0002 ⊕ www.doc.govt.nz).

Scuba Diving

With a warm current running down from Australia's Great Barrier Reef, the waters around Stewart Island are often warmer and clearer than in the rest of the South Island (although this still doesn't mean they're especially warm). Underwater life is prolific, and the impossibly long ropes of bladder kelp that rise from rocky reefs to the surface are well worth the trip. Unfortunately, few travelers know this, and so there is no one on the island running scheduled dive trips. But if you want a dive, especially if there are several of you, then Peter Tait of **Talisker Charters** (⊠ 11 View St. Oban ☎ 03/219–1151 or 027/201–6851 ⊕ www. sailsashore.co.nz) is the man to see. He works on an hourly rate of $135, regardless of diver numbers, and tanks are extra. Other gear can be rented in Invercargill before leaving the mainland.

Sea Kayaking

Some of the best and most remote sea kayaking in the country can be done around Stewart Island. The mostly uninhabited Paterson Inlet is 100 square km (38 square mi) of bush-clad, sheltered waterways. It has 20 islands, four DOC huts, and two navigable rivers. You can kayak year-round. There are plenty of good days in winter, but the best months are October through May. Kayak rentals available from **Stewart Island Kayaks** (⊠ Argyle St., Oban ☎☎ 03/219–1080) start at $30 for a half-day rental to $90 for two days. Guided trips are also available; prices start at $60 for a half day. Camping gear and tents are available for rent.

STEWART ISLAND ESSENTIALS

Transportation

BY AIR

The island's bare-bones but paved Ryan's Creek Airstrip is about 2 km (1 mi) from Oban. You can't drive out to the airstrip, but the cost of the shuttle that meets each flight is included in the airfare.

Stewart Island Flights has three scheduled flights daily between Invercargill and Halfmoon Bay. The scenic 20-minute flight costs $155 round-trip; for the best views ask to sit up front with the pilot.

🚩 Carrier **Stewart Island Flights** ☎ 03/218–9129 ⊕ www.stewartislandflights.com.

BY BOAT

Stewart Island Experience runs the *Foveaux Express* and the *Southern Express* between the island and Bluff. The fare is $49 each way, and the crossing lasts one hour. There are three departures daily October to April, and two during the low season. Tea and coffee are served on board, and the skipper will point out various points of interest and the birdlife and mammals encountered. Foveaux Strait can be rough, so if you're prone to motion sickness, sit well back in the boat and consider bringing some medicine along. Even if it's rough, it's still very safe, and worth a few minutes of discomfort to get to such an untouched island. Secure car parking is available at the Bluff terminal, and coach connections to and from Bluff run from Invercargill year-round, and from Queenstown and Te Anau in summer.

🚩 **Stewart Island Experience** ⊠ Stewart Island Visitor Terminal, Main Wharf, Halfmoon Bay ☎ 03/212–7660 or 0800/000–511 🖨 03/212–8377 ⊕ www.stewartislandexperience.co.nz.

Contacts & Resources

BANKS & EXCHANGE SERVICES

There are no banks or ATMs on Stewart Island, and because some establishments don't accept credit cards, you should be sure to have enough cash on hand. Some larger businesses will cash traveler's checks.

EMERGENCIES

⚡ Emergency Services Although there is no hospital on the island, the Health Centre is open every day, and staff members can be paged around the clock. If need be, air evacuations can be arranged to Invercargill.

Fire, police, and ambulance 🕿 111. Stewart Island Health Centre ✉ Argyle St. 🕿 03/219-1098 or 0800/100-776.

TOURS

ADVENTURE
TOURS
Stewart Island Flights and Seaview Enterprises jointly offer a flying, hiking, and boating adventure called Coast to Coast. For $155 per person (with a three-person minimum) you can view the east and west coasts of the island, including Paterson Inlet and Mason Bay. The trip includes an easy four-hour hike on the North West Circuit and a water-taxi ride on the meandering Freshwater River. There's also an exciting plane landing on the beach and the chance to see kiwi birds wandering the beaches. It's an interchangeable trip, so you can fly-hike-boat or boat-hike-fly. There is also the option of an overnight at Mason Bay in a DOC hut.
⚡ Seaview Enterprises 🕿🕿 03/219-1014. Stewart Island Flights 🕿 03/218-9129 ⊕ www.stewartislandflights.com.

BOAT TOURS
Want to learn more about aquaculture, visit salmon and mussel farms, or just get a better idea of the marine life in Stewart Island's waters? The Seabuzzz Experience offers two-hour trips in a glass-bottom boat for $60, and trips to Ulva Island for $25.

The skipper at Thorfinn Charters has an excellent knowledge of the area's natural and human history. Five-hour "superscenic" trips aboard their launch will show you the loveliest parts of Paterson Inlet, and there's a good chance of spotting rare seabirds. Tours run $85 per person.

10

Talisker Charters gives you the opportunity to sail around Stewart Island up to Fiordland in a motor-sailing ketch. The live-aboard cruises cost $180 per day. Peter Tait's extensive knowledge of the southern waters is rivaled only by his wife, Iris's, familiarity with the local ecology—and by her cooking. (They also do dive charters—see Scuba Diving, above.)

Stewart Island Experience's Paterson Inlet Cruise is a 2½-hour trip of the beautiful inlet. The highlight is a one-hour guided stop on the wildlife sanctuary of Ulva Island. There are two departures per day in summer, one in winter; the price is $69.

Stewart Island Experience also runs Underwater Explorer Cruises with semisubmersible craft. The large viewing windows give you a close-up look at kelp forests and dozens of fish species, some of which are really unusual. There are several departures daily, and the 45-minute cruise costs $37.

For information and bookings on shuttles, water taxis, and boat trips around Paterson Inlet, contact the Department of Conservation Visitor Centre or Stewart Island Experience.

Department of Conservation Visitor Centre ⊠ Main Rd. Oban ☎ 03/219-0002. **Seabuzzz Experience** ⊠ 5 Argyle St. Oban ☎ 03/219-1282 ⊕ www.seabuzzz.co.nz. **Stewart Island Experience** ⊠ Main Wharf, Halfmoon Bay Oban ☎ 03/212-7660 or 0800/000-511 ⊕ www.stewartislandexperience.co.nz. **Talisker Charters** ⊠ 11 View St. Oban ☎ 03/219-1151 ⊕ www.sailsashore.co.nz. **Thorfinn Charters** ☎ 03/219-1210 ⊕ www.thorfinn.co.nz.

BUS TOURS Village and Bay Tours provides entertaining insight into the community, history, and environment of Stewart Island. It's $32 for the 1½-hour tour, which takes in Horseshoe Bay and Observation Rock.

Village & Bay Tours ⊠ Oban Visitor Centre, Main Rd. ☎ 03/219-0034.

WALKING TOURS Kiwi Wilderness Walks leads all-inclusive hiking and kayaking trips from the mainland. The four-day guided trips around Stewart Island cost $1,495 and are usually held between November and April. The combination of walks, water-taxi rides, and sea-kayaking excursions will give you ample opportunities to see kiwi birds.

For a unique Rakiura Māori interpretation of Ulva Island's flora and fauna, contact Ulva's Guided Walks. Ulva Goodwillie gives half-day and full-day tours of the island she was named after; the cost, including water-taxi fare, starts at $85.

Kiwi Wilderness Walks ☎ 03/226-6739 ☎ 03/442-8342 ⊕ www.nzwalk.com. **Ulva's Guided Walks** ⊠ Elgin Terr., Oban ☎ 03/219-1216 ⊕ www.ulva.co.nz.

WILDLIFE TOURS Thorfinn Charters arranges half- and full-day nature tours, which include a cruise to the Titi Islands and a guided walk on Ulva Island. You'll have the chance to see several kinds of rare birds, as well as three kinds of penguins. Half- and full-day trips cost $60 and $85.

See also Ulva's Guided Walks *in* Walking Tours, *above*.

Thorfinn Charters ☎ 03/219-1210 ⊕ www.thorfinn.co.nz.

VISITOR INFORMATION

The Department of Conservation Visitor Centre and Stewart Island Experience (See Boat Tours, above) are open daily November through April with extended hours from Christmas to the end of March. Business hours are reduced in winter.

Adventure Vacations

Bicycling

Canoeing

Cross-Country Skiing

Diving

Fishing

Hiking

Horse Trekking

Rafting

Sailing

Sea-Kayaking

Updated by
Doug Johansen
and Jan Poole

FOR SOME OF THE MOST VIBRANT experiences in New Zealand, head out to explore the magnificent outdoors. The mountains and forests in this clean, green land are made for hiking and climbing, the rivers for rafting, and the low-traffic roads for bicycling. The rugged coastline looks wonderful from the deck of a small vessel or, even closer to the water, a sea kayak. And this is the country that invented jet-boating.

These activities are commonly split into soft and hard adventures. Hard adventure requires some physical stamina, although you usually don't have to be perfectly fit; in a few cases, prior experience is a prerequisite. In soft adventures the destination is often the adventurous element—you can sit back and enjoy the ride.

With most adventure-tour companies, the guides' knowledge of flora and fauna—and love of the bush—is matched by a level of competence that ensures your safety even in dangerous situations. The safety record of adventure operators is very good. Be aware, however, that most adventure-tour operators require you to sign waivers absolving the company of responsibility in the event of an accident or a problem. Courts normally uphold such waivers except in cases of significant negligence.

You can always choose to travel without a guide, but in unfamiliar territory you'll learn more about what's around you by having a knowledgeable local by your side. The material in this chapter complements information in the rest of the book on what to do in different parts of the country. If you're interested in a multiday excursion, such as a fishing tour or hike, you'll often need to book at least several weeks in advance. For a day's shot at an extreme-sport activity, such as bungy jumping or jet-boating, you'll generally need to make a reservation only a day in advance, or even on the same day.

Bicycling

New Zealand's combination of spectacular scenery and quiet roads is ideal for cycling. Cycling rates as hard adventure because of the amount of exercise you get. On multiday trips, the average daily riding distance is about 60 km (37 mi), and support vehicles are on hand. These back-up vehicles are large enough to accommodate all riders and bikes if circumstances so demand. Some tours combine cycling with kayaking, hiking, or other outdoor pursuits. For information on day trips or urban bike rentals, see the Sports & the Outdoors sections in the appropriate destination chapters. Wherever you cycle, remember to ride on the left.

Traditionally, the South Island, with its central alpine spine, has been the most popular cycling destination. Rides in the South Island extend from the ferry port of Picton to Queenstown, the center of a thriving adventure day-trip industry. From Picton southward, the eastern route takes you through Kaikoura, with its dramatic mountain backdrop, then into the flat Canterbury Plains. From there, you can either cross the Alps at Arthur's Pass or head through the dry, barren, but beautiful Mackenzie Country to Aoraki/Mt. Cook, New Zealand's highest mountain, before reaching Queenstown. From Queenstown, rides run down to Fiordland with lakes and glacier-formed valleys.

The western route through the South Island takes you through the Marlborough and Nelson wine regions, then follows the Buller River to the West Coast. Continuing southward, you're in for some spectacular mountain and coastal scenery as you head for the Franz Josef and Fox Glaciers. Further south, you cross the Alps over the rugged Haast Pass and then travel from the rain forest to the parched Otago interior within just a few miles. From there, you can cycle past blue-green lakes and on into Queenstown.

But the North Island has plenty of terrific biking terrain as well. The stunning Coromandel Peninsula is easily accessible from Auckland, where most travelers arrive. The areas around the Waitomo Caves and around the hot mud pools of sulfurous Rotorua are other highlights.

Season: October–March.
Best Locations: Countrywide.
Cost: Multiday tours start around $1,500 per person, including food, lodging, and guide services. Supplemental fees are commonly charged for single riders.

Tour Operators

One advantage of touring New Zealand with a biking company is that you'll travel with a knowledgeable guide who can tell you about the terrain, flora, and fauna that you see along the way. Some trips include en route visits to wineries, but taste in moderation—remember that you have to cycle afterward! Depending on the route and type of trip, accommodations can range from camping to farm stays, motels, or lodges. Serious riders may wish to bring their own bikes, but bikes are typically available for rent; if you prefer, you can bring your own seats and/or pedals. Trip operators generally provide helmets and safety flags (to attach to the bikes). Most trips don't have minimum or maximum age limits—just be realistic about your cycling abilities. Most tours are limited to between 10 and 14 people.

Adventure South trips get you onto the quiet South Island back roads for 5 to 21 days. Tours are offered for all levels of cyclist and might include detours for wine tastings, hikes, or lake excursions. Accommodations are generally in comfortable inns and lodges. *Box 33153, Christchurch* *03/942–1222* *03/942–4030* *www.advsouth.co.nz.*

New Zealand Pedaltours operates on both islands, with tours of 4 to 22 days catering to a range of abilities. Tour options include the Coromandel Peninsula, the Southern Alps, and the Banks Peninsula. *Box 37–575, Parnell, Auckland* *0800/3020–968 in N.Z., 888/222–9187 in U.S.* *09/585–1339* *www.pedaltours.co.nz.*

Pacific Cycle Tours operate road- and mountain-bike trips that include Christchurch-to-Queenstown tours, as well as a three-week trip across both islands. They also offer a weeklong bike-and-ski combination trip and a four-day independent ride through the Marlborough wine region. Accommodations include hotels, inns, or farm stays. ✉ *17 Bay Heights, Governor's Bay* *R.D. 1, Lyttelton* *03/329–9913* *09/329–9914* *www.bike-nz.com.*

Canoeing

There are many rivers where you can go canoeing in New Zealand, but one of the most popular rivers for day- and multiday canoeing trips is the Whanganui River, which journeys through some of the most isolated and rugged parts of the North Island. The river starts 180 miles above the small city of Wanganui, on the flanks of Mt. Ruapehu [approximately 9,500 feet] in Tongariro National Park, and then winds through the 700-square-km (270-square-mi) Whanganui National Park—one of New Zealand's newest, with 249 named rapids to traverse on its descent to the Tasman sea.

Season: Year-round.
Best Locations: Whanganui River, North Island.
Cost: From $70 per person for single-day tours to $220 per person for 5-day trips. Tents, sleeping bags, and bedrolls can be rented for an additional fee.

Tour Operator
Blazing Paddles Canoe Adventures runs 1- to 5-day trips on the Whanganui River, during which you can ride mild rapids, and see waterfalls, pristine forests, and bird life. Overnight stays are spent camping or in huts, depending on the trip. ✉ *1033 State Highway 4, Taumarunui* ☎ *07/895–5261 or 0800/252–946* 🖷 *07/895–5263* ⊕ *www.blazingpaddles. co.nz.*

Cross-Country Skiing

Cross-country skiing is arguably the best way to appreciate the winter landscape here. Going cross-country, you'll get away from the downhill hordes and feel like you have the mountains to yourself. Cross-country skiing is hard adventure—the joy of leaving the first tracks across new snow and the pleasure afforded by the unique scenery of the ski slopes is tempered by your fatigue at the end of the day. Multiday tours are arranged so that you stay in lodges every night.

Season: July–September.
Best Location: Aoraki (Mt. Cook), South Island.
Cost: Around $480 for two days, $1,150 for 5 days and $1,500 for five days high on Mt. Cook alpine skiing, which includes equipment, meals, hut accommodation, a guide, and transport.

Tour Operator
Alpine Recreation Canterbury runs multiday cross-country skiing trips on Aoraki (Mt. Cook) and its attendant Murchison and Tasman glaciers, with terrains to suit all reasonably fit skiers. Tours typically start with a flight to the alpine hut that becomes your base; from there the group sets out each day for skiing and instruction. ✉ *Box 75, Lake Tekapo* ☎ *03/680–6736* 🖷 *03/680–6765* ⊕ *www.alpinerecreation.com.*

Diving

The Bay of Islands, in the Northland arm of the North Island, is perhaps New Zealand's best diving location. In the waters around Cape

Brett, you can encounter moray eels, stingrays, grouper, and other marine life. Surface-water temperatures rarely dip below 15°C (60°F). One of the highlights of Bay of Islands diving is the wreck of the Greenpeace vessel *Rainbow Warrior,* which French agents sank in 1985. It is about two hours from Paihia by dive boat. Note that from September through November, a plankton bloom cuts down on underwater visibility.

Another top diving destination is the Poor Knights Islands Marine Reserve, a World Heritage area with crystal clear waters approximately 15 km (9 mi) off the Northland coast. Among the highlights are Rikiora Cave, the world's largest sea cave; the northern arch, where you sometimes see manta rays; and bubble caves, air pockets 45 feet down, where you can remove your regulator and breathe air. The small town of Tutukaka is the main jumping-off point for the Poor Knights reserve.

The clear waters around New Zealand make for good diving in other areas as well, such as Whangamata, with three islands just off the coast. While diving these waters, you are liable to encounter schools of snapper, giant kingfish, tuna, marlin, dolphins, and even sharks.

Remember that you cannot fly within 24 hours of scuba diving.

Season: Year-round.
Best Locations: Bay of Islands and the Coromandel Peninsula, North Island.
Cost: A two-dive day trip without rental gear runs about $90, with gear around $160.

Tour Operators

Cathedral Cove Dive brings groups to dive in the Cathedral Cove Marine Reserve of the Coromandel Peninsula; PADI courses are available. ⊠ *3 Margaret Pl., Hahei* ⟐ *R.D. 1, Whitianga* ☎ *07/866–3955* 🖷 *07/ 866–3053* ⊕ *www.hahei.co.nz/diving.*

Dive Tutukaka runs trips to the Poor Knights Islands Marine Reserve off the Northland coast. Their comfortable dive boats have hot showers on board. ⊠ *Poor Knights Dive Centre, Marina Rd., Tutukaka* ⟐ *R.D. 3, Whangarei* ☎ *09/434–3867* 🖷 *09/434–3884* ⊕ *www.diving.co.nz.*

Knight Diver Tours makes the rounds at the Poor Knights Islands Marine Reserve, which is a great place to see colorful subtropical fish and underwater caves and tunnels. Although the outfit does not give PADI training courses, it can take noncertified people on guided dives. ⊠ *30 Whangarei Heads Rd., Whangarei* ☎ *09/436–2584 or 0800/766–756* 🖷 *09/436–2758* ⊕ *www.poorknights.co.nz.*

Pacific Hideaway Charters runs dives at the Poor Knights Islands, Mokohinau Islands, and the coastal regions around Tutukaka—all of which are home to Manta rays, large Kingfish, and lots of other sealife. Day trips include tea, coffee, and snacks, as well as kayaks to borrow if you want to stay on the surface. ⊠ *Tutukaka Marina, R.D.3, Whangarei* ☎ *09/434–3762 or 0800/693–483* ⊕ *www.divenz.co.nz.*

Paihia Dive Hire and Charter organizes Bay of Islands dives to the wreck of the *Rainbow Warrior,* now an artificial reef; it also offers PADI courses. ⓘ *Box 210, Paihia* ☎ *09/402–7551* 🖷 *09/402–7110* ⊕ *www. divenz.com.*

Tairua Dive & Fishinn dives around the Aldermen Islands 19 km (12 mi) off the coast from Tairua, including Slipper, Shoe, Penguin, and Rabbit Islands. Expect to see a large variety of fish, scallops, seals, black coral, and nudibranchs (sea slugs). ⊠ *The Esplanade, Paku Boat Ramp, Tairua* 🖷🖷 *07/864–8054* ⊕ *www.divetairua.co.nz.*

Fishing

Fishing in New Zealand is as good as it gets. Don't pass up an opportunity to drop a line in the water, whether you're looking for the joy of being away from it all in some remote spot, the simplicity of sitting on a wharf or a rock in the sun with a line in hand, or the adrenaline rush when a big one strikes and the reel starts screaming.

Most harbor towns have reasonably priced fishing charters available. They are generally very good at finding fish, and most carry fishing gear you can use if you do not have your own. Inland areas usually have streams, rivers, or lakes with great trout fishing, where guides provide their knowledge of local conditions and techniques. With the aid of a helicopter, you can get into places few people have ever seen. Catch-and-release practices are becoming more prevalent, especially in wilderness areas. As for equipment, visitors can bring their own gear into the country except for flies, which are forbidden. Equipment can also be rented or provided by a guiding company once you're there.

Licenses and Limits: Different districts in New Zealand require different licenses when fishing for trout, so it pays to check at the local tackle store; for example, Rotorua, is not in the same license area as nearby Lake Taupo. Fees are approximately $60 per year, but at most tackle shops, you can purchase a daily or weekly license. No license is needed for saltwater fishing, but there are limits on the size and numbers of fish that you are allowed to take daily.

Publications: *How to Catch Fish and Where,* by Bill Hohepa, and *New Zealand Fishing News Map Guide,* edited by Sam Mossman—both have good information on salt- and freshwater fishing countrywide. A useful book on trout fishing is *New Zealand's Top Trout Fishing Waters,* by John Kent.

Season: Generally October–June in streams and rivers; year-round in lakes and at sea.

Best Locations: Countrywide.

Cost: Big-game fishing: $275 per person, per day. Heli-fishing: from $545 per person, per day. Trolling and fly-fishing for lake trout: from $75 per hour (one–four people), on rivers and streams from $75 per hour. Costs for fishing charters vary widely; contact operators for specifics.

Freshwater Fishing

Trout and salmon, natives in the northern hemisphere, were introduced into New Zealand in the 1860s and 1880s. Rainbow and brown trout in particular have thrived in the rivers and lakes, providing arguably the best trout fishing in the world. Salmon do not grow to the size that they do in their native habitat, but they still make for good fishing. There is free access to all water. You may have to cross private land to fish certain areas, but a courteous request is normally well received.

The three methods of catching trout allowed in New Zealand are fly-fishing, spinning or threadlining, and trolling. In certain parts of the South Island using small fish, insects, and worms as bait is also allowed. Deep trolling using leader lines and large-capacity reels on short spinning rods is widely done on Lakes Rotoma, Okataina, and Tarawera around Rotorua and on Lake Taupo, with the most popular lures being tobies, flatfish, and cobras. Streamer flies used for trolling are normally late spring patterns: Taupo tiger, green smelt, ginger mick, Jack Sprat, Parsons glory, and others. Flies, spoons, or wobblers used in conjunction with monofilament and light fly lines on either glass fly rods or spinning rods are popular on all the other lakes.

The lakes in the Rotorua district—Rotorua, Rotoiti, and Tarawera are the largest—produce some of the biggest rainbow trout in the world, which get to trophy size because of an excellent food supply, the absence of competition, and a careful and selective breeding program. In Lake Tarawera, fish from 2.7 to 4.5 kg (6 to 10 lbs.) can be taken, especially in the autumn and winter, when bigger trout move into stream mouths before spawning.

The season around Rotorua runs from October 1 to June 30. In the period between April and June, just before the season closes, flies work very well on beautiful Lake Rotoiti. From December to March, fly-fishing is good around the stream mouths on Lake Rotorua. The two best areas are the Ngongotaha Stream and the Kaituna River, using nymph, dry fly, and wet fly. Lake Rotorua remains open for fishing when the streams and rivers surrounding the lake are closed.

Lake Taupo and the surrounding rivers and streams are world renowned for rainbow trout—the lake has the largest yields of trout in New Zealand, an estimated 500 tons. Trolling on Taupo and fishing the rivers flowing into it with a guide are almost surefire ways of catching fish. Wind and weather on the lake, which can change quickly, will determine where you can fish—and going with local knowledge of the conditions on Taupo is essential. The streams and rivers flowing into the lake are open for fly-fishing from October 1 to May 31. The lower reaches of the Tongariro, Tauranga-Taupo, and Waitahanui rivers, and the lake itself, remain open year-round. Lake Waikaremoana in Urewera National Park southeast of Rotorua, is arguably the North Island's most scenic lake, and its fly-fishing and trolling are excellent. As it's well off the beaten track, though, it's not frequented by guides.

The South Island has excellent rivers with very clear water. Some of them hardly ever see anglers, and that untouched quality is particularly satisfying. South Island's best areas for trout are Marlborough, Westland, Fiordland, Southland, and Otago. Good trout fishing can also be found on Lake Dunstan east of Queenstown, Lake Poerua on the West Coast, and near Wanaka on Lake Hawea, the Hunter River, and the Timaru and Dingle creeks, all of which branch out from Lake Hawea. The rivers in the Motueka and Buller Gorge areas in northern South Island produce outstanding brown trout, too. The fishing season for the South Island runs from October 1 through April 30 for rivers going out of lakes, and from November 1 through April 30 for rivers going into lakes.

The Canterbury district has some productive waters for both trout and salmon—along with the West Coast it is the only part of New Zealand where you can fish for salmon, the quinnat or Pacific chinook salmon introduced from North America. Anglers use large metal spoons and wobblers on long, strong rods with spinning outfits to fish the rivers around Christchurch, often catching salmon of 9 to 13.5 kg (20 to 30 lbs.). In particular, top fishing spots include the Waimakariri and Hurunui rivers, both north of Christchurch, for excellent salmon and trout fishing; and the Rangitata River, south of Christchurch, for its sparkling rapids, oily glides, smooth pools, and clean gravel with good stocks of trout and salmon.

Trout fishing is normally tougher than in the North Island, with trout being a little smaller on average. You can catch brown and rainbow trout in South Island lakes using flies or by wading and spinning around lake edges or at stream mouths.

NORTH ISLAND FRESHWATER FISHING OPERATORS

Brett Cameron Lake and River Guides offers wilderness fly-fishing trips to rivers and streams often accessible only with 4x4 vehicles (or, in some cases, helicopters). There are single- and multiday packages available, for both beginners and seasoned anglers. ✉ *21 Glen Mohr, Acacia Bay, Taupo* ☎ *07/378–8192 or 027/681–4134.*

Bryan Colman Trout Fishing fishes for trout in the Rotorua district's lakes and in the streams feeding these lakes. ✉ *32 Kiwi St., Rotorua* ☎ *07/ 348–7766* 🖷 *07/348–0832* ⊕ *www.troutfishingrotorua.com.*

Chris Jolly Outdoors has been in business since the mid-1980s, taking clients trout fishing on the lakes and rivers in the Taupo region. The company also runs hunting trips for deer, boar, goats, and turkeys. 🖃 *Box 1020, Taupo* ☎ *07/378–0623* 🖷 *07/378–9458* ⊕ *www.chrisjolly.co.nz.*

Clark Gregor Trout Fishing specializes in fishing on Lake Rotorua and surrounding lakes for rainbow and brown trout. ✉ *33 Haumoana St., Rotorua* ☎ *07/347–1123* 🖷 *07/347–1313* ⊕ *www.troutnz.co.nz.*

Lake Tarawera Launch Services will take you out on Lake Tarawera for trout fishing (or just sightseeing). They'll drop you off at a remote shore where you can fish, and they'll pick you up later in the day. ✉ *The Landing, Lake Tarawera* ☎ *07/362–8595* 🖷 *07/362–8883.*

SOUTH ISLAND FRESHWATER FISHING OPERATORS

Brown Trout Heaven has been leading guided fishing trips since 1980. They fish for brown trout on local and wilderness rivers in the Nelson region and also run heli-fishing trips. 🖃 *Box 1619, Nelson* ☎ *03/541–0020* 🖷 *03/544–4565* ⊕ *www.browntroutheaven.co.nz.*

Dave Hetherington fly-fishes the rivers near the glaciers for trout and salmon and also does trolling for brown trout on Lake Mapourika. Heli-fishing is also available. ✉ *Alpine Adventure Centre, Main Rd., Franz Josef Glacier* ☎ *03/751–0856 or 03/752–0793* 🖷 *03/752–0764.*

Dean Harrison leads fishing trips in the Canterbury and West Coast regions. ⌂ *Box 21192, Christchurch* ☎☎ *03/385–9631 or 021/324–229* ⊕ *www.flyfishingadventures.co.nz.*

Fish Fiordland specializes in fly-fishing for trout on Fiordland's many stunning lakes and rivers. ⌂ *Box 31, Manapouri* ☎ *03/249–8070* 🖨 *03/249–8470* ⊕ *www.fishfiordland.co.nz.*

Fishing & Hunting Amongst Friends takes you fishing for brown and rainbow trout in the rivers, streams, and lakes in central Otago and Southland. ⌂ *Box 312, Wanaka* ☎☎ *03/443–9257* ⊕ *www.flyfishhunt.co.nz.*

The guides at **Fly Fishing New Zealand Ltd.** will take you fly-fishing, lake trolling, drift-boat fishing, and heli-fishing on the rivers, streams, and lakes in the Lake Wakatipu basin. ⌂ *Box 1061, Queenstown* ☎ *03/442–5363* 🖨 *03/442–2734* ⊕ *www.wakatipu.co.nz.*

Based in Queenstown, **Harvey Maguire** fishes the rivers, lakes, and streams of the central Otago and Southland regions. ✉ *334 Littles Rd., Queenstown* ☎ *03/442–7061* ⊕ *www.flyfishing.net.nz.*

Saltwater Fishing

No country in the world is better suited than New Zealand for ocean fishing. Its coastline—approximately as long as that of the mainland United States—has an incredible variety of locations, whether you like fishing off rocks, on reefs, surf beaches, islands, or harbors. Kiwi anglers have taken many world records over the years. All the big names are here—black, blue, and striped marlin, both yellowfin and bluefin tuna, and sharks like mako, thresher, hammerhead, and bronze whaler.

The most sought-after fish around the North Island are snapper (sea bream), kingfish, *hapuka* (grouper), *tarakihi,* John Dory, *trevally, maomao,* and *kahawai,* to name a few. Many of these also exist around the top of the South Island. Otherwise, the South Island's main catches are blue cod, butterfish, hake, *hoki,* ling, *moki,* parrot fish, pigfish, and trumpeter, which are all excellent eating fish.

Perhaps the most famous angler to fish New Zealand's waters was adventure novelist Zane Grey, who had his base on Urupukapuka Island in the Bay of Islands. On the North Island, the top areas are the Bay of Islands, the nearby Poor Knights Islands, Whangaroa in Northland, the Coromandel Peninsula and its islands, and the Bay of Plenty and White Island off its coast. The South Island does not have a well-established deep-sea game-fishing industry as yet, but places to fish include the Marlborough and Pelorus sounds at the northern tip.

NORTH ISLAND
SALTWATER
FISHING
OPERATORS

Baker Marine Charters is based in Whakatane in the Bay of Plenty, 1½ hours from Rotorua. Skipper John Baker, who has been charter fishing since the 1970s, targets marlin, tuna, sharks, and kingfish, and he bottom fishes for snapper and tereki. An experienced diver, John also runs dive trips to White Island. ⌂ *Box 473, Whakatane* ☎ *07/307–0015 or 0800/494–0324* 🖨 *07/307–1364* ⊕ *www.divenfish.co.nz.*

Blue Ocean Charters run half- or full-day fishing trips in the Bay of Plenty, as well as overnight reef-fishing excursions for snapper, trevalli, kingfish, and kahawhai. ✉ *The Coronation Pier, Wharf St.* 🖂 *Box 13–100, Tauranga* ☎ *07/578–9685* 🖷 *07/578–3499* ⊕ *www. blueoceancharters.co.nz.*

Based in the Bay of Islands, **Earl Grey Fishing Charters** specializes in saltwater fly-fishing and light tackle fishing for a wide range of species. Fishing guide and captain Steve Butler particularly enjoys live-baiting for yellowtail kingfish. ✉ *23 Mission Rd., Kerikeri* ☎ *09/407–7165* 🖷 *09/ 407–5465* ⊕ *www.earlgreyfishing.co.nz.*

Tairua Dive & Fishinn fish the waters off the East Coast of the Coromandel Peninsula—Slipper and Shoe Islands and the Aldermen Islands. You're liable to pull in snapper, kingfish, grouper, trevalli, tereki, or kahawhai. ✉ *The Esplanade, Paku Boat Ramp, Tairua* ☎🖷 *07/864–8054* ⊕ *www.divetairua.co.nz.*

From its Coromandel Peninsula base, **Te Ra–The Sun** fishes the waters around Slipper and Mayor Islands as well as the offshore reefs for snapper, kingfish, tereki, trevalli, and kahawhai. ✉ *120 Moanuanu Ave., Whangamata* ☎ *07/865–8681* ⊕ *tera.whangamata.co.nz.*

SOUTH ISLAND
SALTWATER
FISHING
OPERATORS **Anaru Accommodation and Charters** fish the waters around French Pass, D'Urville Island, and the outer Marlborough Sounds. They target blue cod, groper, snapper, terakihi, sea perch; at times, you may catch kahawai, kingfish, or barracuda as well. They also have backpacker-style accommodation in a comfortable lodge. ✉ *French Pass, R.D. 3, Rai Valley, Nelson* ☎ *03/576–5260* 🖷 *03/576–5090.*

Chris Hobbs Snapper Fishing Charters targets large snapper in Pelorus Sound at the top of the South Island. Expect catches to average 4.5 kg (10 lbs.); up to 9 kg (20 lbs.) is not unheard of. 🖂 *Box 21, Havelock* ☎ *03/574–2911 or 025/397–178* 🖷 *03/574–914* ⊕ *www.tsuribaka-fishing.co. nzpchrishobbs.*

Takapu Charters fish Preservation and Chalky Inlets in Fiordland for blue cod, groper, and trumpeter, all great eating fish. A trip here takes you to an especially wild and beautiful part of New Zealand. 🖂 *Box 2013, Washdyke* ☎🖷 *03/615–7574* ⊕ *www.takapucharters.co.nz.*

Thorfinn Charters targets blue cod, which abound in the waters around Stewart Island. 🖂 *Box 43, Halfmoon Bay, Stewart Island* ☎🖷 *03/ 219–1210* ⊕ *www.thorfinn.co.nz.*

Toa Tai Charters offers day- and multiday fishing trips to the Queen Charlotte, Pelorus and Keneperu Sounds, D'Urville Island, Port Underwood, Cook Straight and Nelson areas. Up to 50 people can be accommodated for day trips; fewer spots are available for overnight trips. ✉ *30 Buller St., Picton* ☎ *03/573–7883* 🖷 *03/573–7882* ⊕ *www. soundsfishing.co.nz.*

Hiking

There isn't a better place on earth for hiking—called tramping here—than New Zealand. If you're looking for short tramps, you may want to head off on your own. "Freedom walking" means that you tramp without a guide and carry all your own food and equipment. For long treks, however, it can be a big help to go with a guide. With their knowledge of the native bush, guides can point out and discuss the country's fascinating flora and fauna. (They often have great senses of humor, too.) Although it varies by operator, most group hiking trips are limited to about 12 people. Book trips at least three weeks in advance.

Particularly in the peak months of January and February, trails can be crowded enough to detract from the natural experience. One advantage of a guided walk is that companies have their own tent camps or huts, with such luxuries as hot showers and cooks. For the phobic, it's worth mentioning one very positive feature: New Zealand has no snakes or predatory animals, no poison ivy, poison oak, leeches, or ticks. In the South Island, especially on the West Coast and in Fiordland, be prepared for voracious sand flies—some call it the state "bird." Pick up insect repellent in New Zealand; their repellent fends off their insects.

New Zealand's Department of Conservation (DOC) oversees a group of nine routes called Great Walks, which are outstanding both for their facilities and their incredible scenery. These routes are the Abel Tasman Coastal Track; the Heaphy Track; the Kepler Track; the Lake Waikaremoana Track; the Milford Track; the Rakiura Track; the Routeburn Track; the Tongariro Northern Circuit; and the Whanganui Journey. (The Whanganui Journey, while technically a Great Walk, traces a canoeing trip.) Most of the Great Walks are moderately difficult and take at least three days to complete. To overnight in a hut on a Great Walk route, you'll need to purchase a Great Walks pass from the local DOC office (*see the* Great Walks chart).

There are also more than 50 routes the DOC dubs "major tracks," many of which go through national parks. These range from day hikes to challenging multiday tramps. At the start of each track, DOC signs outline a map of the route, as well as the track's degree of difficulty, distances, and estimated walking times. Most trail intersections are marked with informational signs as well. Other route markings for the Great Walks and major tracks vary from park to park. The DOC has a four-tier system grading track difficulty, as follows.

Grade 1: For well-formed, clearly marked, and graded tracks. This grade applies to many short walks as well as to longer walks that are suitable to a wide range of people.

Grade 2: For partly formed and marked tracks that are generally easy to follow. These may include bridge crossings and are often rough underfoot, requiring some tramping experience.

Grade 3: For marked, cairned, or poled routes with little or no cut or formed trail. For these you'll need reasonably advanced skill in route-finding and bush skills.

Grade 4: For unmarked or rarely marked routes crossing alpine passes or through deep bush. These are suitable only for experienced trampers with advanced bush and route-finding skills.

One of the top areas in the North Island for hiking and walking is the rugged Coromandel Peninsula, with 3,000-foot volcanic peaks clothed with semitropical rain forest and some of the best stands of the giant kauri tree and giant tree ferns. There is also gold-mining history on the peninsula, though the flicker of miners' lamps has given way to the steady green-blue light of millions of glowworms in the mines.

Tongariro National Park in central North Island has hiking with a difference—on and around active volcanoes rising to heights over 9,000 feet, the highest elevation on the island. It is a beautiful region of contrasts: deserts, forests, lakes, mountains, and snow.

The South Island, meanwhile, claims the most famous New Zealand walk—the Milford Track, a three- to four-day trek through Fiordland National Park. This track covers a wide variety of terrains, lakes, a glowworm grotto, and the spectacle of Milford Sound itself. As the track is strictly one-way (south to north), you rarely encounter other groups and so have the impression that your group is alone in the wild. Independent and escorted walkers stay in different huts about a half-day's walk apart. Escorted walkers' huts are serviced and very comfortable; independent walkers' huts are basic, with few facilities.

Elsewhere in the South Island, standouts are the three- to six-day routes on the beaches and in the forests of the Marlborough Sounds' Queen Charlotte Walkway and in Abel Tasman National Park. These are very popular, relatively easy, and well suited to family groups: your pack is carried for you, and you stay in lodges.

If you want to get up close and personal with a mountain, Alpine Guides has a renowned seven-day course on the basics of mountaineering around Aoraki (Mt. Cook), the highest point in the New Zealand Alps. There is also a 10-day technical course for experienced climbers.

Season: October–March for high-altitude walks, year-round for others.
Best Locations: Coromandel Peninsula and Tongariro National Park in North Island; Aoraki, Westland, Abel Tasman, and Fiordland national parks in South Island.
Cost: One- to three-day guided hikes range from $150 to $1,050. Prices for longer hikes and day tours vary widely; contact outfitters for specifics.

Huts

New Zealand parks have an extensive range of huts for overnight use—they vary from well-equipped multiroom huts to small rough huts with only a few bunks and no facilities to speak of. You might hear of huts graded into categories; they're sometimes rated on a system of 1 (with heating and other facilities) to 4 (freebies with nothing much more than a roof over your head). Normally, backcountry huts work on a "first come, first served" system. However, on the more well-known tracks, you need to prebook. During the peak season, the huts can be full so you need to bring a small tent just in case things get overcrowded.

To pay for hut accommodations, purchase tickets in advance from DOC regional offices or at selected outlets (the DOC can direct you). You then deposit your ticket at each hut. During the high season there may be a hut warden who will take your fees, or you simply put the ticket into an envelope.

When using backcountry huts, ensure that you leave them clean and tidy. Use gas, coal, or wood provided sparingly, and before leaving, replace any firewood you have used. Be sure to sign the hut book and include your planned itinerary; if anything goes amiss, the hut book will help locate you.

Tour Operators

Pioneers of tourism in the South Island's Abel Tasman National Park, **Abel Tasman Wilson's Experiences** run independent or guided walks ranging from a few hours to five days. "Cruise and walk" trips combine a boat tour with hiking, and sea-kayaking excursions are available as well. ✉ *265 High St.* ✇ *Box 351, Motueka* ☎ *0800/221–888 or 03/528–2027* 🖷 *03/528–2029* ⊕ *www.abeltasmannz.com.*

Alpine Guides Ltd. lead 6- to 10-day ascents of New Zealand's highest peaks: Mt. Cook/Aoraki, Mt. Tasman, and Mt. Aspiring. You can also get private climbing instruction winter or summer. ✇ *Box 20, Mt. Cook* ☎ *03/435–1834* 🖷 *03/435–1898* ⊕ *www.alpineguides.co.nz.*

Alpine Recreation runs a 15-day minibus tour of the South Island, with two- to six-hour walks daily along the way. This scenic trip includes visits to six national parks; guides discuss the area's natural history. The company also leads guided ascents of Mt. Cook and Mt. Tasman for experienced climbers. ✇ *Box 75, Lake Tekapo* ☎ *03/680–6736* 🖷 *03/680–6765* ⊕ *www.alpinerecreation.com.*

Bush & Beach operates half-day and overnight tours to the Waitakere Ranges and surrounding black-sand beaches, about a 30-minute drive from Auckland. These trips pair easy walks in the native rain forest and along the beach, with an optional overnight at a comfortable forest lodge. ✉ *Shortland St.* ✇ *Box 121007, Henderson* ☎ *09/837–4130* 🖷 *09/837–4193* ⊕ *www.bushandbeach.co.nz.*

Guided Walks New Zealand Ltd. leads a variety of half- and full-day nature walks in the central Otago region that are designed for travelers of any age and ability. ✇ *Box 347, Queenstown* ☎ *03/442–7126* 🖷 *03/442–7128* ⊕ *www.nzwalks.com.*

Hike New Zealand runs five- to ten-day hiking and camping tours in both the North and South Islands for groups of up to 12. Tours include a trek to Franz Josef Glacier and the river country around the South Island's west coast; and trip through the volcanic region of Tongariro National Park. ✉ *PO Box 93, Lyttelton 8033* ☎ *0274/360–268 or 0800/697–232* 🖷 *03/376–6483* ⊕ *www.nzhike.com.*

Hollyford Track leads guided three-day walks on the wild and stunning Fiordland track of the same name. The track follows the Hollyford River to the Tasman Sea. The tours leave from Queensland and include lodge accommodations en route. ✇ *Box 360, Queenstown* ☎ *03/442–7789* 🖷 *03/442–7781* ⊕ *www.hollyfordtrack.com.*

TRACK	LOCATION	LENGTH	DIFFICULTY	TERRAIN
Abel Tasman Coastal Track	Near Nelson at top of South Island	50 km (31 mi) 3–5 days	Moderate fitness.	Beaches, rocks, forest. (Note tide schedules when crossing inlets.)
Heaphy Track	Northwest tip of South Island	78 km (48 mi) 4–6 days	Moderate fitness. Most difficult section from Brown hut to Perry Saddle hut.	Track begins in dense beech and podocarp forest in north; continues to high-level snow tussock plateaus midway; descends into palm-studded forests, rugged West Coast beaches.
Kepler Track	Near Te Anau, Fiordland, South Island	67 km (41.5 mi) 3–4 days	Moderate fitness. Day one is steep climb from lake to tops.	Varies from beech forests to sometimes snow-covered tussock tops. Wonderful views in clear weather.

*unless otherwise indicated, prices are per person per night.

DOC HUTS	CONDITIONS	SPECIAL ASPECTS	TRACK SAVVY	DOC INFO (www.doc.govt.nz)
4 huts; $25; toilets, bunks, mattresses, heating, filtered water. Bring cooking equipment. 20 campsites; $10.	Possible flooding at river and creek crossings in heavy rain.	Regenerating rainforest with nikau palms, ferns, forest giants; granite rocks; golden-sand beaches. May see seals and penguins.	Hut/camping passes required. In summer, bunks must be booked in advance with DOC. Pack sunscreen. In autumn and winter, walking and weather conditions are good; fewer people.	DOC Nelson Regional Visitor Centre, Tel. 03/546–9339
7 huts; $20. 6 huts: toilets, bunks, mattresses, gas stoves. Gouland Downs hut: bunks, open fire. 3 shelters. 9 campsites; $10	Normally a drier area, but be prepared for rain, especially on western slopes. Primarily a summer route; snow can block track in winter.	One of New Zealand's finest routes. Forests, limestone caves, snow tussock tops, nikau palms, many birds (including kiwis, rare pipits).	Nearest centers are Collingwood in north and Karamea in southwest. Several shuttles serve each end. Hut tickets required; carry a tent during Oct.–Apr. peak season.	DOC Nelson Regional Visitor Centre, Tel. 03/546–9339
3 huts; $40; bunks, mattresses, running water, flush toilets, heating, gas stoves. 2 campsites; $10.	Be prepared for rain. Watch weather on exposed mountain tops; snow is possible. Sand flies at lower altitude.	Lovely forest scenery; may spot kea and other birds. Good for geology buffs, especially Mt. Luxmore. Detour to Iris Burn waterfall, 20-minute walk from Iris Burn hut.	Book huts in advance. Coal supplied to huts between Oct. and April; other times, bring cooking gear. Pack insect repellent.	*Peak Season:* DOC Great Walks Booking Desk, Tel: 03/249–8514 *Off-Peak Season:* Fiordland National Park Visitor Centre, Tel: 03/249–7294

TRACK	LOCATION	LENGTH	DIFFICULTY	TERRAIN
Lake Waikaremoana Track	In Te Urewera National Park, southeast of Rotorua, North Island	46 km (28.5 mi) 3–4 days	Moderate fitness required. Climb from lake edge to Panekiri Bluffs is toughest.	Much of track runs through podocarp forest. Generally in good condition.
Milford Track	Near Te Anau, South Island	54 km (33.5 mi) 4–5 days	Moderately difficult; two strenuous climbs, one very steep descent.	Track follows Clinton River (gets muddy), crosses Mackinnon Pass, goes through alpine meadows, passes waterfalls. Thick forest at beginning and end.
Northwest Rakiura Track	Stewart Island	125 km (77.5 mi, full circuit); 102 km (63 mi) if you catch boat at Freshwater Landing. 10–12 days for full circuit	Difficult; requires good fitness, good equipment, bushcraft and survival skills.	Much of track is in dense forest, but it follows part of western coastline with some steep short climbs. Often muddy.

*unless otherwise indicated, prices are per person per night.

DOC HUTS	CONDITIONS	SPECIAL ASPECTS	TRACK SAVVY	DOC INFO (www.doc.govt.nz)
5 huts; $20; bunks, mattresses, heating. Bring cooking gear. 5 campsites; $10.	Can get very heavy rain at times. Bring repellent for mosquitoes and sand flies.	Great views from Panekiri Bluffs. Great birding: *kaka*, parakeets, paradise ducks, whiteheads, fantails, silvereyes, *morepork* (native owl), kiwi.	Advance booking advised. Don't miss short uphill side trip to Korokoro waterfall. Bus transport available from major centers, including Rotorua and Wairoa.	Aniwaniwa Visitors Centre, Tel: 06/837-3900
3 huts; $120 for all; ranger staff, gas stoves, cold running water, flush toilets.	Frequent rain. Sand flies below tree line. Beware of avalanche conditions at Mackinnon Pass in winter.	Sutherland Falls, country's highest waterfall. Lots of kea (mountain parrots).	New Zealand's most popular track; book at least 4 months ahead. Can only hike south to north); no backtracking allowed. Insect repellent a must.	*Peak Season:* DOC Great Walks Booking Desk, Tel: 03/249-8514 *Off-Peak Season:* Fiordland National Park Visitor Centre, Tel: 03/249-7294
10 huts; $10; toilets (long drops), fireplaces. Bring your own cooking gear.	Wet weather, several river crossings—be prepared to get muddy. Lots of mosquitoes and sand flies.	Wild remote beaches and coastline; could see penguin and seals. Wonderful views from Mt. Anglem, a 3-4 hour side trip (one-way). Great birding; could see bellbirds, *tūī*, fantails, tomtits and parakeets.	Hut tickets required; some camping possible. Regular flights from Invercargil (magical in good weather); also ferry service from Bluff. Pack extra food and insect repellent.	Stewart Island Visitors Centre, Tel: 03/219-0002

TRACK	LOCATION	LENGTH	DIFFICULTY	TERRAIN
Routeburn Track	Western end of Lake Wakatipu, near Glenorchy, South Island	32 km (20 mi) 2–3 days	Moderate fitness required. Mountainous terrain, open tops; good equipment needed.	Track can be done in either direction. Either way runs through beech forest onto exposed mountain tops.
Tongariro Northern Circuit	Tongariro National Park, central North Island.	49 km (30 mi) 3–4 days	Moderate fitness and good gear. Toughest section is "Staircase."	Most of track is out in open. Wonderful alpine and volcanic vistas.
Whanganui Journey	Near Taumarunui on Whanganui River, central North Island.	145 km (90 mi, full trip) 5 days, on average 88 km (54.5 mi, shorter trip) 3 days	Moderate fitness; swimming, canoeing, kayaking skills.	Although a river journey, Whanganui is part of "Great Walks" network. A 3-day journey from Whakahoro to Pipiriki is also possible.

*unless otherwise indicated, prices are per person per night.

DOC HUTS	CONDITIONS	SPECIAL ASPECTS	TRACK SAVVY	DOC INFO (www.doc.govt.nz)
4 huts; $40; bunks, mattresses, gas stoves, heating. 2 campsites; $10	Heavy rain, clouds, snow, ice can be factors. On mountain tops, avalanche danger in winter.	Spectacular mountain scenery. In summer alpine slopes covered with flowers, many unique to New Zealand.	Book in advance, especially during Oct.–Apr. high season. Outside those months, you must pack cooking gear. Good transport services to and from track.	*Peak Season:* DOC Great Walks Booking Desk, Tel: 03/249-8514 *Off-Peak Season:* Fiordland National Park Visitor Centre, Tel: 03/249-7294
4 huts; $20; bunks, heating, water, toilets. Pack cooking gear. 4 campsites; $15.	Mountains often in heavy clouds. Monitor weather conditions—it can rain, snow, or even erupt at any time.	One of New Zealand's best walks. A volcanic area with warm blue-green lakes, steam vents. Goes around Mt. Ngauruhoe— Mt. Doom in *Lord of the Rings.*	Don't attempt track in bad weather. Stay back from steam vents. Must book in advance. Shuttle services can be arranged from Whakapapa.	Whakapapa Field Centre, Tel: 07/892-3729
3 huts; water, bunks, mattresses, stoves, cooking facilities. 11 campsites; water, tables, benches for cooking. $45 for trip.	Be prepared for rain and floods.	Whanganui takes a twisting path to sea; en route, expect narrow gorges, high cliffs, waterfalls, glowworm grottos.	Tieke Marae has good huts and facilities, but must follow Māori protocol; koha (a gift of money) will be expected. Book trip and hire kayaks in advance.	Wanganui Conservancy Ingestre Chambers, Tel. 06/348-8475

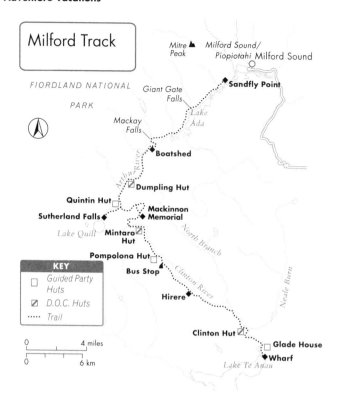

Milford Track

FIORDLAND NATIONAL PARK

Mitre Peak

Milford Sound/ Piopiotahi

Milford Sound

Sandfly Point

Giant Gate Falls

Lake Ada

Mackay Falls

Boatshed

Arthur River

Dumpling Hut

Quintin Hut

Mackinnon Memorial

Sutherland Falls

Lake Quill

Mintaro Hut

North Branch

Pompolona Hut

Bus Stop

Clinton River

Neale Burn

Hirere

Clinton Hut

Glade House

Wharf

Lake Te Anau

KEY
☐ Guided Party Huts
☑ D.O.C. Huts
····· Trail

0   4 miles
0   6 km

Kapiti Island Alive tours include a boat trip to Kapiti Island, a bird sanctuary off the West Coast (north of Wellington). On these guided walks, you may see such rare birds as the kokako, kaka, saddleback, takahe, whitehead, weka, bellbird, tūī, and many sea birds. ✆ *Box 28, Otaki* ☎ *06/364–8818* 📠 *06/364–5828.*

A pioneer of nature tourism in New Zealand, **Kiwi Dundee Adventures, Ltd.** has been running guided walks and hikes since 1975. Their walking, touring, and hiking trips cover all aspects of the Coromandel Peninsula and New Zealand, from its history, flora, fauna, to its rugged mountains, glowworm caves, rain forests, and coastline and suit any age, fitness, and interests. They also lead multiday ecowalks in both the North and South Islands away from the usual tourist spots. ✆ *Box 198, Whangamata* ☎📠 *07/865–8809* ⊕ *www.kiwidundee.co.nz.*

Marlborough Sounds Adventure Company runs four- to five-day guided and "freedom" (unguided but prearranged) walks on the 71-km (43-mi) Queen Charlotte walkway at the top of the South Island. The walkway, which follows a long, narrow ridge of mountains separating Queen Charlotte Sound from Kenepuru Sound, leads through lovely forests with magnificent views through the trees out over the water. The company does sea-kayaking and mountain-biking trips as well. ⊠ *The Waterfront*

Box 195, Picton ☎ *03/573–6078 or 0800/283–283* 🖷 *03/573–8827* ⊕ *www.marlboroughsounds.co.nz.*

Ultimate Hikes leads guided trips of two of New Zealand's best-known treks: the Milford Track and the Routeburn Track. The spectacular **Milford Track,** frequently dubbed one of the world's greatest hikes, is a four-day walk that passes through Clinton Canyon's huge glacier-carved valleys before climbing over the McKinnon Pass and following the river out to Milford Sound. *Box 259, Queenstown* ☎ *03/441–1138 or 0800/659–255* 🖷 *03/441–1124* ⊕ *www.ultimatehikes.co.nz.* The **Routeburn Track,** a three- or four-day hike, takes you through lovely beech forest and river valleys before climbing over the main divide of the Southern Alps past waterfalls and small glacier-fed lakes. *Box 568, Queenstown* ☎ *03/442–8200 or 0800/768–832* 🖷 *03/442–6072* ⊕ *www. ultimatehikes.co.nz.*

Wild West Adventure Co. operates wilderness hikes and guided walks through the rain forests and valleys of the South Island's West Coast. Hikes range from two to five days, with accommodations in hotels, hostels, track lodges, or camp sites. ✉ *8 Whall St., Greymouth* ☎ *03/768–6649 or 0508/286–877* 🖷 *03/768–9149* ⊕ *www.nzholidayheaven.com.*

Horse Trekking

Operators all over New Zealand take people horseback riding along beaches, in native forests, on mountains, and up rivers through pine plantations. One of the best areas to explore on horseback is the sweep of the Canterbury Plains around Christchurch in the South Island—the surrounding mountain ranges create some of New Zealand's most dramatic scenery. The top of the South Island with its *nikau* palms, limestone cliffs, and sandy beaches also has some beautiful spots to ride. On the North Island, the rugged Coromandel Ranges and the Northland's vast stretches of white-sand beaches are popular riding territory as well. Horse treks qualify as soft or hard adventure, depending on the itinerary. All of the outfitters listed here offer trips for inexperienced riders, and all provide the required protective headgear. Some companies will also supply suitable heeled footwear, but be sure to check with the outfitter about what you'll need to bring. On longer trips, you'll likely be expected to help with the horses and equipment.

Season: October–March.
Best Locations: Northland and the Coromandel Peninsula in the North Island, Nelson and Canterbury high country in the South Island.
Cost: Prices range from about $115 for 2 hours to $225 for a day trip, or $495 for overnight; contact outfitters for specifics on shorter or multiday trips.

Tour Operators
Cape Farewell Horse Treks operates a variety of horse treks from Puponga in Golden Bay at the northwest tip of the South Island, taking in beautiful beach scenery with giant limestone rocks and caves and lush palm-studded forests. They also lead four- to five-day treks down the isolated

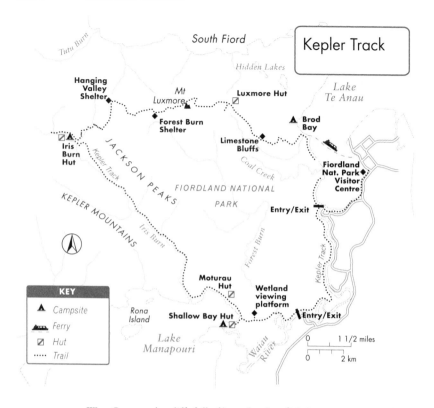

West Coast under cliffs full of huge fossils. ⌂ *R.D. 1, Puponga, Colling-wood* ☎🖥 *03/524–8031* ⊕ *www.horsetreksnz.com.*

Dart Stables Glenorchy, based near Queenstown, takes small groups out on trips ranging from two hours to three days; some of this South Island territory is *Lord of the Rings* country, where a lot of the filming was done. There are rides suitable for beginners and more advanced equestrians. ⌂ *Box 47, Glenorchy* ☎ *03/442–5688 or 0800/474–3464* 🖨 *03/442–6045* ⊕ *www.dartstables.com.*

Hurunui Horse Treks has a variety of rides, including 8- and 10-day horse treks into remote backcountry, where the terrain varies from dense scrub to open meadows to alpine passes. Accommodation options include rustic huts (without electricity, showers, or flush toilets) or more comfortable farm stays; groups are generally limited to six or fewer. ✉ *757 The Peaks Rd.* ⌂ *R.D., Hawarden, North Canterbury* ☎🖥 *03/314–4204* ⊕ *www.hurunui.co.nz.*

Pakiri Beach Horse Rides, north of Auckland, runs trips from several hours to several days, all incorporating a ride on the namesake white-sand beach. You might ride through groves of pohutukawa—known as New Zealand's Christmas tree—which are ablaze with red flowers in the summer, or across the sand dunes with inspiring views of islands on the horizon. ✉ *Taurere Park, Rahuikiri Rd., Pakiri, Wellsford* ☎ *09/422–6275* 📠 *09/422–6277* ⊕ *www.horseride-nz.co.nz.*

Halfway between Whitianga and Tairua on the Coromandel Peninsula, **Rangihau Ranch** leads short rides of an hour or two; the routes follow pack-horse trails from the 1800s with wonderful views of the bush-clad Coromandel mountains, Mercury Bay, and the Pacific Ocean. They specialize in working with inexperienced riders. ✉ *Rangihau Rd., Coroglen* ☎ *07/866–3875* 📠 *07/866–3837.*

With **Stonehurst Farm Horse Treks,** trek through 1,000 acres of a working farm near Nelson with panoramic views over the mountains and Golden Bay. Their treks, for riders of all abilities, run from one hour to a half day. ✉ *Stonehurst Farm, Clover Rd.* ✒ *R.D. 1, Richmond, Nelson* ☎ *03/542–4121 or 0800/487–357* 📠 *03/542–3823* ⊕ *www.stonehurstfarm.co.nz.*

Rafting

The exhilaration of sweeping down into the foam-filled jaws of a rapid is always tinged with fear—white-water rafting is, after all, rather like being tossed into a washing machine. As you drift downriver during the lulls between the white water, it's wonderful to sit back and watch the wilderness unfold, whether it's stately *rimu* or *rata* trees overhanging the stream or towering cliffs with rain forest on the surrounding slopes. Rafting means camping by the river at night, drinking tea brewed over a fire, and going to sleep with the sound of the stream in the background. The juxtaposition of action and serenity gives rafting an enduring appeal that leads most who try it to seek out more rivers with more challenges. Rivers here are smaller and trickier than the ones used for commercial rafting in North America, and rafts usually hold only four to six people. Rafting companies provide all equipment—you only need clothing that won't be damaged by water (cameras are carried in waterproof barrels), a sleeping bag (in some cases), and sunscreen. Rafting qualifies as hard adventure.

In the North Island, near Rotorua, the Rangitaiki offers exciting Grade-IV rapids and some good scenery. Nearby, the Wairoa offers Grade V— the highest before a river becomes unraftable—and the Kaituna River has the highest raftable waterfall in the world: a 21-foot free fall. The Tongariro River flows from between the active 10,000-foot volcanic peaks of Tongariro National Park into the south end of Lake Taupo, New Zealand's largest lake. The Tongariro (Grade III), as well as the mighty Motu River out toward the East Cape (Grade V), is great for rafting.

In the South Island, the great majority of activity centers on Queenstown. The most popular spot here is the upper reaches of the Shotover River beyond tortuous Skippers Canyon. In winter, the put-in site for the Shotover is accessible only by helicopter, and wet suits are essential year-round, as the water is very cold. Some of the rapids are Grade V. The Rangitata River south of Christchurch is fed by an enormous catchment basin, and rafting is serious at all water levels.

Season: Mainly October–May.

Best Locations: Rotorua and Taupo in the North Island, Canterbury and Queenstown in the South Island.

Cost: From $115 for 2 hours to $130 per person for three-hour trips; heli-rafting from $220 per person, three-day trips from $690 per person.

Tour Operators

Challenge Rafting operates half-day white-water raft and raft-combo trips on the South Island's Kawarau and Shotover Rivers; the combo trips mix rafting with jet-boating or bungy jumping. The Kawarau offers exhilarating rafting for first timers, and the Shotover serves up extra excitement for the more experienced. Trips depart twice daily. The company also offers a heli-rafting option on the Shotover, which includes a helicopter flight to the Skipper Canyon launch site. ✆ *Box 634, Shotover and Camp Sts., Queenstown* ☎ *03/442–7318 or 0800/423–836* 🖷 *03/441–2983* ⊕ *www.raft.co.nz.*

Kaituna Cascades does several rafting runs daily down the North Island's Kaituna River, with its 21-foot waterfall. They also raft the Rangitaiki (good for beginners) and Wairoa rivers (for the excitement seekers). ✉ *Trout Pool Rd., Okere Falls, Rotorua* ☎ *07/345–4199 or 0800/ 524–8862* 🖷 *07/345–9533* ⊕ *www.kaitunacascades.co.nz.*

Queenstown Rafting runs raft trips on the South Island's Shotover and Kawarau rivers. Combo trips, pairing rafting with jet-boating, helicopter flights, or bungy jumping, also available. ✉ *35 Shotover St., Queenstown* ☎ *03/ 442–9792 or 0800/723–8464* 🖷 *03/442–4609* ⊕ *www.rafting.co.nz.*

Rangitata Rafts guides day trips through the Grade-V rapids of the spectacular Rangitata Gorge on the South Island. Trips, which run September to May, include round-trip transport from Christchurch (about two hours each way) and finish up with hot showers and a traditional BBQ. ✉ *Rangitata Gorge Rd., Peel Forest, Geraldine, South Canterbury* ☎ *0800/251–251* 🖷🖷 *03/696–3534* ⊕ *www.rafts.co.nz.*

Wet 'n' Wild Rafting Company rafts several of the North Island's rivers: the Rangitaiki (Grade II–III, great for first timers), Kaituna (Grade IV–V, with the 21-foot waterfall), Wairoa (Grade IV–V, an ultimate white-water playground), Motu (Grade III–V, with wilderness camping for two to four days), and Mohaka (Grade III–V, with two to four days camping and fishing). ✉ *2 White St.* ✆ *Box 601, Rotorua* ☎ *07/348–3191 or 0800/462–7238* 🖷 *07/349–6567* ⊕ *www.wetnwildrafting.co.nz.*

Wild West Adventure Co. operates wilderness white-water-raft trips on several of the rivers on the South Island's West Coast. Another intriguing option is blackwater-cave rafting—these half-day trips take you through glowworm caves and down underground waterfalls. ✉ *8 Whall St., Greymouth* ☎ *03/768–6649 or 0508/286–877* 🖷 *03/768–9149* ⊕ *www.nzholidayheaven.com.*

Sailing

Varied coastline and splendid waters have made sailing extremely popular in New Zealand. Admittedly, your role as a passenger on a commercial sailing vessel is hardly strenuous. You are likely to participate in the sailing of the vessel more than you would on a regular cruise line, but for all intents and purposes this is a soft adventure in paradise. The best sailing areas in New Zealand are undoubtedly from the Bay of Islands south to the Coromandel Peninsula and the Bay of Plenty. This coastline has many islands and a wrinkled shoreline that make for wonderful, sheltered sailing.

The rugged Marlborough Sounds at the north end of the South Island are particularly beautiful when seen from the water. The islands and coves make ideal overnight moorings; it's easy to understand why Captain James Cook felt this was his favorite part of the country.

Season: Year-round.
Best Locations: Bay of Islands in the North Island, upper and lower South Island.
Cost: Bay of Islands from $75 for a day trip to $690 to $830 per night depending on the craft; Doubtful Sound from $1,725 for five days; Fiordland National Park area from $3,510 for eight days; sub-Antarctic islands of Australia and New Zealand from USD $2,875 for 7 days.

Tour Operators

Abel Tasman Sailing Adventures based at Kaiteriteri beach, between Motueka and Abel Tasman National Park, runs half-day, one-day, and two-day sailing tours with optional walks along the stunning beaches and islands of Abel Tasman National Park. Fur seals, native birds, penguins, and dolphins are usually visible. ⊠ *Sandy Bay/Marahau Rd., R.D. Motueka* ☎ *0800/467–245 or 06/527–8375* ⊕ *www.sailingadventures.co.nz.*

Catamaran Sailing Charters, based in Nelson, arranges sailing trips around Abel Tasman National Park, D'Urville Island, and the Marlborough Sounds. They specialize in skippered cruises, but experienced sailors can also hire their own boats. Short sails, day trips, and multiday trips are all available. ⊠ *46 Martin St., Nelson* ☎ *03/547–6666* 🖷 *03/547–6663* ⊕ *www.sailingcharters.co.nz.*

Heritage Expeditions runs voyages to the remote sub-Antarctic islands, to the Kermedec Islands (1,000 km [620 mi] northeast of New Zealand), and to Antarctica. Their trips are wonderful for wildlife viewing—you may see royal albatross, sea lions, elephant seals, and several penguin species. ◇ *Box 7218, Christchurch* ☎ *03/365–3500* 🖷 *03/365–1300* ⊕ *www.heritage-expeditions.com.*

From their Opua base, **Sunsail New Zealand** hires out a full range of yachts for multiday trips in the Bay of Islands. You can travel with a captain or arrange a bareboat charter. ◇ *Box 33729, Takapuna* ☎ *09/378–7900* 🖷 *09/378–8363* ⊕ *www.sunsail.co.nz.*

Tauranga Sailing School and Yacht Charters sails to some of the islands in the Bay of Plenty. You can take a piloted launch or, if you have the experience, captain a sailboat yourself. They also operate a sailing school. ⊠ *70 Omokoroa Rd., Tauranga* ☎ *07/548–0689.*

Sea-Kayaking

Unlike rafting, where much of the thrill comes from negotiating white water, sea kayaking is soft adventure. The best places for it are in Northland and the Bay of Islands, the Coromandel Peninsula, the Whanganui River area, the top of South Island, Kaikoura, and as far south as Stewart Island. In the Bay of Islands and the Coromandel, you can kayak along stunning beaches in sheltered waters, whereas kayaking the sometimes mysterious Whanganui River takes you among deep forested gorges. On the South Island, the vast quiet waters and bush-lined bays of the Marlborough Sounds are another popular kayaking spot. If you opt to kayak the remote waters around Stewart Island, you may spot whales, dolphins, penguins, and seals.

Kayaking outfitters usually take out small groups of no more than five kayaks at a time. Usually at least an hour and a half of each excursion is spent going through paddling techniques and safety drills. The level of difficulty depends very much on the weather, so it's always best to talk to the operator to gauge the challenge.

Season: December–May.
Best Locations: Northland, the Coromandel Peninsula, and Whanganui River in the North Island; Marlborough Sounds, Kaikoura, Abel Tasman National Park, and the Southland in the South Island.
Cost: From $60 for a half-day excursion; contact kayaking outfitters for price information for longer trips.

Tour Operators

Cathedral Cove Kayaks offers beginner-friendly half-day guided kayak tours along the spectacular volcanic coast of the North Island's Hahei marine reserve. Explore offshore islands and sea caves, then wrap up the day with a cappuccino. On the sunset kayaking trip, the rock formations look especially gorgeous. ⊠ *88 Hahei Beach Rd., Hahei* ☎☎ *07/866–3877* ⊕ *www.seakayaktours.co.nz.*

Coastal Kayakers runs sea-kayaking excursions in the Bay of Islands, from four- to six-hour guided trips to Waitangi or Haruru Falls, to more leisurely three-day expeditions. On the overnight trips, you might camp on a deserted island after exploring lagoons, sea caves, and sandy beaches; you'll have time to swim, snorkel, or fish along the way. ⊅ *Box 325, Paihia* ☎ *09/402–8105* 🖷 *09/403–8550* ⊕ *www.coastalkayakers.co.nz.*

Fiordland Wilderness Experience provides one-day guided sea-kayaking tours in Milford Sound, departing daily. Other trips include two- to five-day tours in Doubtful Sound and one (or more) days kayaking on Lakes Manapouri and Te Anau. Combination trips pair sea kayaking with hiking or diving. ⊠ *66 Quintin Dr., Te Anau* ☎ *03/249–7700 or 0800/200–434* 🖷 *03/249–7768* ⊕ *www.fiordlandseakayak.co.nz.*

The one- to three-day kayaking trips with the **Marlborough Sounds Adventure Company** explore the deeply indented, bush-clad coastline of the Marlborough Sounds. There is also a three-hour twilight excursion. ⊠ *The Waterfront* ⊅ *Box 195, Picton* ☎ *03/573–6078 or 0800/283–283* 🖷 *03/573–8827* ⊕ *www.marlboroughsounds.co.nz.*

New Zealand Sea Kayaking Adventures offers fully provisioned 3-, 6-, and 10-day guided sea-kayaking/camping trips in the Bay of Islands. The company, which has been running trips since 1986, can provide instruction for novice and more advanced paddlers. ⌂ *Box 454, Paihia* ☎ *09/402–8596* ⊕ *www.nzkayaktours.com.*

Ocean River Adventure Company trips explore the Abel Tasman National Park by water. Their one- to three-day kayak trips follow the granite coastline bordered by native forest, golden-sand beaches, and spectacular tidal lagoons. One tour visits the thriving seal colony in the Tonga Island Marine Reserve. ✉ *Abel Tasman National Park, Marahau* ⌂ *R.D. 2, Motueka* ☎ *03/527–8022, 03/527–8266, or 0800/732–529* 🖷 *03/527–8006* ⊕ *www.seakayaking.co.nz.*

With **Oceanix Sea Kayaking Expeditionz,** you can kayak day or night in the Bay of Plenty. Tours typically last two or three hours. On daytime trips, you explore the offshore islands or kayak the McLaren Falls waterway near Tauranga. On the nighttime trips, you can see glowworms in their natural environment. Trips typically wrap up with a BBQ. ⌂ *Box 4460, Mount Maunganui South* ☎ *07/572–2226 or 0274/942–677* ⊕ *www.oceanix.co.nz.*

Ross Adventures, based at Matiatia Bay on Waiheke Island—just a 35-minute ferry ride from downtown Auckland, runs guided half-day, evening, full-day, and overnight kayaking trips with options for beginners and more advanced paddlers. Day trips explore the northwestern corner of Waiheke and its rock channels, archways, and sea caves. On their nighttime trips, you'll look for phosphorescence, where the water glows along your paddles or hands. ✉ *Matiatia Bay, Waiheke* ⌂ *Box 106037, Auckland* ☎ *09/372–2211* 🖷 *09/357–0550* ⊕ *www.kayakwaiheke.co.nz.*

Stewart Island Sea Kayak Adventures gives you a chance to kayak in New Zealand's newest national park. The sheltered waters of Patterson Inlet here include hundreds of bays with forest extending right to the water's edge; on Ulva Island, kiwi birds sometimes come out during the day. You might also see seals and penguins in this beautiful part of the world. ⌂ *Box 32, Stewart Island* ☎🖷 *03/219–1080.*

UNDERSTANDING NEW ZEALAND

MĀORITANGA:
AN INSIDER'S PERSPECTIVE

Ko au te whenua, ko te whenua, ko au.

I am the land, the land is me. (Māori proverb)

As I write this, there is talk around New Zealand about the definition of the word *indigenous*. The argument concerns whether *Pākehā* New Zealanders, (non-Māori, generally of European extraction) are as indigenous as Māori are to this country. After all, Pākehā New Zealanders' ancestors have been here for centuries—perhaps not quite as long as the Māori, but in some cases, as much as seven generations. Arriving in *waka* (canoes) or tall ships, 900 years ago or 90—we're all immigrants, aren't we? Why is *Māoritanga* ("things Māori" or Māori culture) considered the only indigenous culture?

In fact, the concept of Māoritanga most likely took shape after the 1840 Treaty of Waitangi. Pretreaty, we identified ourselves tribally. Moreover, it's fairly certain that we did not use the word *Māori* to describe ourselves as a people. The term did exist, but as an adjective, meaning "normal, usual, ordinary," or "unadulterated." *Wai māori*, for example, meant "fresh water," as opposed to *wai tai*, "sea or salt water." It's possible that when Pākehā first encountered Māori and asked the inevitable question, who are you? our ancestors may have replied, "*he tangata māori*," meaning "just a person." These days, there's a strong move back to tribal identification rather than the generic term *Māori*. Young people often refer to themselves as "T. W." or "Tee Dub," short for *tangata whenua* (people of the land), or they use their tribal names. (Ngāti Raukawa and Ngāi Tahu, for example, are two of my tribes.) But Māoritanga is still a common term, as it encompasses so many different activities and aspects of our lives.

Taonga tuku iho/
Treasures handed down

Our customs were, and are, based on certain life-sustaining philosophies and practices (*tikanga*), such as *utu* (a principle of reply or return, related to keeping things in balance) and *muru* (a concept related to forgiveness, literally meaning "to wipe out"). Two other important tikanga are *tapu* and its counterpart, *noa*. Although only our *tohunga* (experts, priests) can approach a thorough knowledge of these esoteric principles, the tikanga shape our daily lives.

Tapu is often translated as "sacred" or "set apart." One way in which I explain tapu to myself is this: if something or someone is "tapu," they are capable of invoking strong emotions. The body of someone who has died, for example, is considered very tapu.

Another way to understand the concepts of tapu and noa is to consider the potential something possesses. For instance, a tree growing in a forest may have a different kind of tapu, or potential, than a *waka* (canoe) made from that tree. If the tree is made into a waka, its potential has been reduced, as it can no longer become a *koauau* (traditional flute) or *maihi* (bargeboards for a meetinghouse). Noa has been enacted on the tree to reduce its potential.

The head of any person, particularly someone with great *mana* (status and/or sacred power), is considered the most tapu part of the body, perhaps because of the unlimited potential of the mind and the imagination. Food is ritually used to counter or lift the tapu of many activities, people, places, or objects. This kind of ritual is rooted in centuries of spiritual knowledge and practice, entrusted to those who know what they're doing, the tohunga.

Ko tā te manuhiri/ The role of the visitor

So how do these tikanga apply in everyday life? There are a few basic concepts worth remembering when visiting Māori homes or a community center or village, called a *marae*. (To many Māori, there is little difference between these two places.)

I often summarize a key issue this way: head, food, backside . . . think about it. This point determines the way *kai* (food) and dining utensils are handled. Avoid passing kai or plates over people's heads. Don't put your hat on the table or on a chair. Don't sit on tables, or on any surface on which food has or will be placed. Don't sit on pillows in the *whare nui* (the meetinghouse) or wherever people lay their heads. Walk around people's outstretched legs rather than over them.

Anything to do with food, even tea towels, will likely be treated differently from what you're used to. Most marae, for example, don't wash their kitchen linen with bed linen—often, not even in the same washing machine. In kitchens, there are sometimes separate towels for drying your hands; don't dry your hands on towels reserved only for dishes.

He whare, he tupuna/ Our house is our ancestor

The area in front of the whare nui is known as the *marae ātea* and is considered the domain of the Tū Matāuenga, the Māori divinity of war. Out there, anything goes. This is where problems are thrashed out, debates are held, and disagreements can be resolved. Inside the whare nui, however, is the realm of Rongomā-Tane, the God of Peace. In recognition of this division, we leave our shoes at the door of the house so that the dust of the marae ātea is left outside.

The *whare whakāiro* (carved house) is the physical embodiment of a *tupuna* (ancestor) and as such commands respect. This connection echoes in the vocabulary of the house; the word for *veranda* (*roro*), for example, is the same as the word for *brain*.

The *maihi* (bargeboards) are the outstretched arms of our loved one. The *heke* (rafters) in the ceiling are the ribs, descending from the spine, the *tāhuhu* (ridgepole of the ceiling).

Ngā kōrero o neherā/ Ancient stories

The structure of the carved house incorporates the Māori genesis story. In the beginning was Te Kore, the void, from which arose Te Pō, the night. In this darkness lived Papatūānuku, the Earth Mother, and Ranginui, the Sky Father. Their children were cramped in their embrace and plotted their freedom. One of the sons, Tāne Mahuta (the divinity of the forest and its creatures), finally separated his parents by lying on his back and pushing Ranginui upward with his legs. In carved houses, the roof represents Ranginui, and the *poupou* (posts) represent the children, pushing him upward.

When Tāne separated his parents, he created the World of Light, Te Ao Mārama, the world of human beings. The first human being is also said to have been created by Tāne, when he sneezed life into Hine-ahu-one, the Woman Made of Earth. From this story comes the common blessing "Tihei mauri ora!" or "Behold the breath [or sneeze] of life!"

The descendants of Tāne and Hine-ahu-one increased generation by generation. Among their notable progeny is Hine-tītama, the Woman of the Dawn, who became Hine-nui-te-Pō, the Goddess of Death. She is the ancestor into whose embrace we deliver the spirits of our dead.

Māui is another major figure in our histories. Māui had humble beginnings as an aborted child, set adrift on the sea by his mother, wrapped in her topknot. Māui was saved by a favorable wind and a clump of seaweed, and became the legendary heroic figure who fished up the North Island (Te Ika a Māui, the Fish of Māui) from his canoe, the South Island (Te Waka a Māui). Māui was also a trickster with a penchant for playing practical jokes on his elders. He obtained the secret of fire, for example, by tricking his grandmother into giving up all the flames in her fingernails and toenails. I must mention here that every tribe and subtribe among us will have its own variations, big or small, on these stories.

Ko ngā mahi toi/The arts

In the Māori worldview, all objects have a *mauri* (spiritual essence), including those made by *tohunga toi* (expert artists). Objects were made to be beautiful, but also to serve a practical or symbolic function.

During your trip, you'll see all kinds of crafts made of indigenous materials, from *paua* (abalone) shell earrings and *pounamu* (greenstone) pendants to *kete whakairo* (finely woven flax bags). Perhaps the best known Māori visual art is **carving.** Carving was traditionally lavished on everything wooden, from massive poles in meetinghouses to waka paddles. Surfaces teem with stylized or organic forms such as spirals or waves. The human figure is also highly stylized. Pounamu carving is another major form; now artists use diamond-tipped instruments to carve the extremely hard jadelike stone. *Tā moko* is a variant of traditional carving as well: inked skin carving, or tattooing. These carvings historically indicated one's heritage or status.

A particularly high-profile Māori art form is the **haka,** now world famous thanks to our New Zealand All Blacks rugby team, as the players perform it before their opponents. The so-called "All Blacks haka" was actually composed by a Ngāti Toa Rangatira chief, Te Rauparaha. The opening words, "*ka mate, ka mate, ka ora ka ora*" ("I die, I die, I live, I live") refer to his imminent death at the hands of an enemy, searching for him as he hid in a kūmara (sweet potato) pit. The search was in vain and Te Rauparaha lived to fight—and haka—another day. To haka is simply to dance. Ka mate is often wrongly called a war dance, but it's really more of a short free-form style.

There are many other movement-based art forms; at a cultural performance you might see *poi* dances (poi are balls on string swung in unison to music or rhythms). The *wero* (challenge), with its accompanying ritual choreography, is sometimes included in a *pōwhiri* (welcoming ceremony) for important guests.

Raranga (**weaving**) is a long-established craft that continues to flourish. The primary material is *harakeke* (flax); its fiber can be worked into *kete* (baskets), latticework wall panels, fine mats, ropes, string, nets, and even sandals and clothing. You might spot some harakeke sunhats and woven flowers in your browsings.

He aroha ki te tangata/ Be sensitive

Māori are a colonized people, and many of us are unaware of our own tikanga. As a visitor, remember that Māori will more happily share what they know of their language and culture when they're approached without assumptions. Someone of Māori descent may not know their own tribal connections. We may not be able to tell you the "real" meaning of the greenstone pendant you've just bought. Rather than make the first move to *hongi*, the traditional greeting of pressing noses and foreheads, accept it if it is offered.

Another interesting point: not all of us are dark-skinned with dark eyes and black, curly hair. Some of us are fair-skinned with blue eyes and blonde hair. This is not only because of intermarriage, but because, as in so many countries, there are physical differences characteristic of certain regions.

It is safe to generalize, though, that Māori are extremely good at *manaakitanga* (hospitality). Looking after visitors, particularly *manuhiri tūārangi*, those who have come from far away, is a key part of our traditions.

Ko au te whenua/
I am the land

Far back on one side of my *whakapapa* (genealogy), my roots stretch to England, Germany, and maybe even Holland (we're still working on that one). On the other side, too, my ancestry takes me offshore—to Hawaiiki, ancestral homeland in the Pacific. But the further back I trace my Māori whakapapa, the closer I get to the earth itself. On my Māori side, my grandmother is the earth under my feet. My grandfather is the sky above me. They are, literally, in my family tree. I am the land—as much as I am my Bavarian ancestors, as much as I am my mother and my father.

Tihei mauri ora, behold the breath of life.

—Hinemoana Baker

FLORA & FAUNA

NEW ZEALAND IS A FASCINATING evolutionary case. Its islands are a chip off the one-time Gondwanaland supercontinent—a vast landmass that consisted of current-day South America, Africa, and Australia that started breaking up some 100 million years ago, well before the evolution of mammals. Since then, floating on its own some 1,920 km (1,200 mi) southeast of Australia, this cluster of islands might seem to have developed quietly on its own, away from the hungry, predatory jaws of the rest of the world.

But powerful forces of change have been constantly working on New Zealand. Plate tectonics created the rugged, 12,000-plus-foot mountains of the South Island. And the Pacific Rim's wild geothermal eruptions left their mark on the North Island. For eons volcanic activity has built mountainous cones and laid carpets of ash, making tremendously rich soil for the plant kingdom. The great, rumbling Mt. Ruapehu near Lake Taupo is a living reminder of this subterranean fury.

Global climatic variations haven't spared the islands, either, and on numerous occasions the Antarctic ice cap has edged north from the pole. In those times, glaciers covered the South Island and much of the North Island, significantly affecting the character of plant life. Some plants adapted, and some couldn't survive. Except for the northern portions of the North Island that weren't iced over—interestingly enough the rough extent of New Zealand's glorious kauri trees—after each glacial retreat the country's flora has recolonized the areas previously covered by ice in different ways.

Animals on the islands were, at least until the arrival of humans, almost like living fossils. The only mammal was a tiny bat, and there were no predators until the Māori first came, around AD 700. Birdlife included the 12-foot flightless moa, which

the Māori hunted to extinction. This happened relatively quickly, because the birds had never needed to develop evasive behavior to stay alive. The Māori brought dogs and rats, and Europeans brought deer, possums, goats, trout, and other fauna, some of which were used for their pelts, others for sport. In almost all cases, the exotic fauna have done tremendous damage to the landscape. And, of course, the human presence itself has dramatically altered the land. Early Māori farming practices involved burning, which reduced a portion of the forests. When Europeans settled the country, they brought sheep, cattle, and the grasses that their livestock needed to eat. And they cut down the forests for, among other uses, ship masts. The kauri served this purpose better than any other wood in the world and paid in numbers for that virtue.

None of this makes the forests that cover New Zealand any less exotic, or any less fascinating. Some plants have adapted growth cycles in which the plant completely changes appearance—lancewood is an example—some of them two or three times until they reach maturity. As a result, botanists at one time believed there to be two or three species where in fact there was only one. If you have never been in a rain forest, the sheer density of vegetation in various subtropical areas will be dazzling. There are species here that exist nowhere else on earth. And keep in mind that one-fifth of the country is set aside as parkland. In those wild woods, you will still find no predators, and native species are alive and well, in many cases making comebacks very dramatic indeed.

Here is a short list of plants and animals that you might encounter in New Zealand.

The New Zealand forest has a sound that is different from any other, and it's the welcoming, chiming song of the **bell-**

bird, together with that of the *tūī,* that makes it unique.

It's a lot easier to get into the grips of a **bush lawyer** plant than out of them. It is a thorny, viney thing that grows in dense forest, climbing in and out of whatever it chooses.

The odd plant clumps fastened to the sides of trees throughout forests are **epiphytes,** not parasites. They grow on the trees but make their own living off water and other airborne particles. Some are orchids, a marvelous sight if you catch them in bloom.

The abundance of **ferns** may be what you most readily associate with the New Zealand bush. Two of the most magnificent are the *mamaku* and the *punga.* The former also goes by the English name black tree fern, and it is the one that grows as much as 60 feet tall and is found countrywide, with the exception of the east coast of the South Island. The Māori used to cook and eat parts of the plant that are said to taste a bit like applesauce. The punga is shorter than the mamaku, reaching a height of 30 feet. Its English name, silver tree fern, comes from the color of the undersides of the fronds. Their silvery whiteness illuminates darker parts of the bush. The punga is the ferny emblem of New Zealand's international sports teams and Air New Zealand.

The **Hector's dolphin** is rare and confined to New Zealand waters. You might have the luck of seeing one near Kaikoura or off the Banks Peninsula. They have an unusual rounded dorsal fin, along with the distinction of being the world's smallest dolphin.

The *horoeka* (also called lancewood) tree is one of the freakish New Zealand natives par excellence. In its youth, its long, serrated, almost woody leaves hardly look alive, hanging down from their scrawny trunk. Horoeka inch their way skyward like this for as many as 20 years before maturing, flowering profusely, and bearing black berries.

The towering **kahikatea** (ka-*hee*-ka-*tee*-ah) is the tallest tree in the country, reaching as high as 200 feet with its slender and elegant profile. A mature tree bears a tremendous amount of berries, which Māori climbers used to harvest by ascending 80 branchless feet and more to pluck. These days wood pigeons are the prime consumers of the fruit.

There are still **kauri** trees in Northland and the Coromandel Peninsula that are as much as 1,500 years old, with a girth of at least 30 feet and height upward of 150 feet. The lower trunks of the trees are branchless, and branches on an old tree begin some 50 feet above the ground. Lumberjacks in the 1800s spared some of these giants, and their presence is awesome. Like so many other native trees, kauri are slow growers—a mere 80-year-old will stand just 30 feet tall. Kauri were valued for their gum as well as their wood. The gum doesn't rot, so balls of gum of any age were usable to make varnish and paint. It is now illegal to cut down a kauri, and as a result the trees are making a solid comeback. Visitors with limited time can see impressive kauri trees in the Waitakere Ranges, just west of Auckland, but the oldest and largest examples are in the Waipoua Forest in Northland. The southernmost kauri trees are found just south of Katikati in the Bay of Plenty.

Much is said of the formidable South Island **kea** (*kee*-ah), a mountain parrot, which, because it has been accused of killing sheep, has in the last century barely escaped extinction. Its numbers are significant today, much to the dismay of campers and anyone who lives under a tin roof. Kea love to play, which means anything from ripping tents to shreds to clattering around on metal roofs at all hours to peeling out the rubber gaskets around car windows. They are smart birds, smart enough, perhaps, to delight in taking revenge on those who tried to wipe them out. Observe their behavior keenly; it may be the only way to maintain a sense of humor if harassed.

It takes effort and more than a fair share of luck to spot a **kiwi** in the wild. These nocturnal, bush-loving birds are scarce and shy, and their numbers had dwindled significantly with the felling of forests over the last 150 years. Predator eradication programs have helped them make a slight resurgence over the last few years. Along with the now-extinct giant moa and other species, the kiwi is one of the remarkable New Zealand natives that live (or lived) nowhere else on earth. If you're keen on seeing one in the feather, plan a trip to Stewart Island and hire a guide to take you on a search, or stop at a wildlife park. Your best chance of sighting one on the North Island is to pitch a tent in the Waipoua forest campground.

The **mohua,** or yellowhead, is a small insect-eating bird you'll find only in the forests of the South Island and Stewart Island. The bird is easily identifiable from the splash of bright yellow that covers its head and breast. The rest of the body is brown with varying tinges of yellow and olive.

The **manuka** is a small tree shrub found throughout the country in tough, impenetrable thickets. Early settlers made a tea from the plant until something tastier came along. The tea tree's white or rosy blossoms attract bees in profusion, and they in turn produce the popular, strong-tasting manuka honey that you can find in stores just about everywhere.

The **nikau palm** is one of the country's most exotic-looking trees, growing to a height of about 30 feet. The Māori used different parts of the leaves both for food and for thatch in shelters.

Phormium tenax, also called New Zealand flax—even though it isn't a true flax—has been used in traditional and contemporary weaving. It favors damp areas and hillsides. Its thick, spiky, dark green leaves originate from a central saddle and can grow to 6 feet. The telltale flower stalk can reach 15 feet and bears dark red flowers. A number of varieties are ornamental and are very popular in New Zealand gardens.

The **pohutukawa** (po-*hoo*-too-*ka*-wa) tree is a sight both for its gnarly roots that like watery places and its red blossoms, which burst forth toward the end of December—hence its Kiwi name: New Zealand's Christmas tree.

Currently about 80 million in number, **possums** are an introduced species that is gobbling up New Zealand forests. Try as they may to get rid of them, New Zealanders are having a rough go with the tree dwellers. Their nickname, "squash 'ems," comes from seeing so many splayed out on roads throughout the country.

The **pukeko** (poo-*keh*-ko) is a bird that kicks around on farms and roadsides often enough that you're likely to see plenty of them. They're blue, with a red bill, and they stand about 15 inches tall.

You'll get to know the **rangiora** (rang-ee-*ohr*-ah) plant better if you remember it as "bushman's friend"—its soft, silvery underside is the forest's best tissue for your underside.

There are a couple of species of **rata.** The northern rata is a parasite plant, climbing a host tree and eventually cutting off its light and water supplies. The rata and its host wage a long-term struggle, and the rata doesn't always win. The southern rata is a freestanding tree, yielding beautiful red lumber. Rata flowers are a pretty red themselves, resembling the pohutukawa tree's blooms but coming out about a month earlier, in November.

If you're in the country in November, you'll first see evidence of the **rewarewa** (*re*-wa-*re*-wa) tree in its fallen blossoms on the ground. They are tightly woven, magenta bottle-brush-like flowers, with touches of chartreuse and black, that are some of the most enchanting in the country, in part for their uniqueness.

One of those ingenious New Zealand plants that goes through three distinct stages on its way to maturity, the **rimu** red pine is a valuable source of timber. It spends its first stage in life as a delicate treelet, with pale green, weeping branches that look something like an upright moss. It then turns itself into a conical shape before finishing its growth as a soaring, 100-plus-foot wonder with a branchless trunk and a rounded head. Charcoal from rimu was used in traditional Māori tattooing.

Supplejack vines just hang about in the forest, so dense in places that they make passage next to impossible. You'll often find that their soft, edible tips have been nipped off by the teeth of wild goats that *Pākehā* (Europeans) introduced. Believe it or not, this is a member of the lily family.

New Zealand's living dinosaur, the **tuatara,** is an ancient reptile found on protected islands such as Stephens Island in Marlborough Sounds. It feeds on insects, small mammals, and birds' eggs and has a vestigial third eye. The combination of its nocturnal habits and its rarity means that the likelihood of seeing one in the wild is virtually nil. Your best bet is to see one in captivity at a zoo. Auckland Zoo has a particularly good tuatara display in its Kiwi House.

Along with the bellbird, the **tūī** is the chanteuse extraordinaire that fills Aotearoa's woods with its magically clear melodies. You may have never thought of birds as actually singing, but you certainly will when you hear a tūī.

Weka (*weh*-kah) are funny birds. They can appear to be oblivious to what's going on around them as they walk about pecking at this or that, looking bemused. They are flightless rails, and they'll steal your food if you're camping, so hide it away. Weka are also attracted to small, shiny things, so keep a careful eye on your car keys if you're camping or picnicking! Generally speaking, though, they're pleasant to have around, particularly if you're looking for some entertainment.

Weta are large insects, some species of which are topped in size only by the African goliath beetle. If you chance upon one, it is likely to throw its spiny back legs up in the air as a defense, giving it a particularly ferocious look. However, weta are not as fearsome as they look, and in the unlikely event that you do get nipped, it will result only in a slight stinging sensation. The largest species is found on Little Barrier Island near Auckland. You may well see specimens in the wild in forests such as the Waitakere Ranges near Auckland, but if you like your fierce-looking insects safely behind glass, they can be viewed at the Arataki Visitors Centre, west of Auckland, or the Karori Wildlife Sanctuary in Wellington.

You'll have no trouble figuring out that the **kereru,** or wood pigeon, is indeed a pigeon, but your jaw will drop at the size—they look like they've been inflated like balloons. They're beautiful birds.

–Stephen Wolf, Barbara Blechman,
and Stu Freeman

CHRONOLOGY

ca. AD 750   The first Polynesians arrive, settling mainly in the South Island, where they find the moa, a flightless bird and an important food source, in abundance.

950   Kupe, the Polynesian voyager, names the country Aotearoa, "land of the long white cloud." He returns to his native Hawaiki, believed to be present-day French Polynesia.

1300s   A population explosion in Hawaiki triggers a wave of immigrants.

1642   Abel Tasman of the Dutch East India Company becomes the first European to sight the land—he names his discovery Nieuw Zeeland. But after several of his crew are killed by Māori, he sails away without landing.

1769   Captain James Cook becomes the first European to set foot on New Zealand. He claims it in the name of the British crown.

1790   Sealers, whalers, and timber cutters arrive, plundering the natural wealth and introducing the Māori to the musket, liquor, and influenza.

1814   The Reverend Samuel Marsden establishes the first mission station, but 11 years pass before the first convert is made.

1832   James Busby is appointed British Resident, charged with protecting the Māori people and fostering British trade.

1840   Captain William Hobson, representing the crown, and Māori chiefs sign the Treaty of Waitangi. In return for the peaceful possession of their land and the rights and privileges of British citizens, the chiefs recognize British sovereignty.

1840–41   The New Zealand Company, an association of British entrepreneurs, establishes settlements at Wanganui, New Plymouth, Nelson, and Wellington.

1852   The British Parliament passes the New Zealand Constitution Act, establishing limited self-government. The country's first gold strike occurs in Coromandel town in the Coromandel Peninsula.

1860–72   Māori grievances over loss of land trigger the Land Wars in the North Island. The Māori win some notable victories, but lack of unity ensures their ultimate defeat. Vast tracts of ancestral land are confiscated from rebel tribes.

1861   Gold is discovered in the river valleys of central Otago, west of Dunedin.

1882   The first refrigerated cargo is dispatched to England, giving the country a new source of prosperity—sheep. A century later, there will be 20 sheep for every New Zealander.

1893   Under the Liberal government, New Zealand becomes the first country to give women the vote.

1914 New Zealand enters World War I.

1931 The Hawke's Bay earthquake kills 258 and levels the city of Napier.

1939 New Zealand enters World War II.

1950 New Zealand troops sail for Korea.

1965 Despite public disquiet, troops are sent to Vietnam.

1973 Britain joins the European Economic Community, and New Zealand's loss of this traditional export market is reflected in a crippling balance-of-payments deficit two years later.

1981 Violent antigovernment demonstrations erupt during a tour by a South African rugby team.

1984 David Lange's Labour Government wins a landslide majority in the general election, at least partly because of its pledge to ban nuclear-armed vessels from New Zealand waters.

1985 The Greenpeace ship *Rainbow Warrior* is sunk by a mine in Auckland Harbour, and a crewman is killed. Two of the French secret-service agents responsible are arrested, jailed, transferred to French custody—then soon released.

      Sir Paul Reeves is sworn in as the first Māori governor-general.

      Relations with the United States sour when the government bans visits by ships carrying nuclear weapons. The U.S. government responds by ejecting New Zealand from the ANZUS (Australia/New Zealand/United States) alliance.

1986 Goods and Services Tax is introduced at 10% (later to be raised to 12.5%). Tourists are not exempt from the tax, although many exports and foreign exchange earners are.

1989 David Lange resigns as prime minister.

1990 The National Party replaces the Labour Party in government.

1993 The country votes for a major constitutional change, replacing the "first past the post" electoral system inherited from Britain with a "mixed-member proportional" (MMP) system. The election sees the National Party clinging to power within a coalition.

1995 New Zealand's *Black Magic* wins the America's Cup yachting regatta. The country goes into party mode over the win, which signals both a sporting triumph and a coming-of-age technologically.

      Mt. Ruapehu in the North Island's Tongariro National Park bubbles and sputters, attracting interested onlookers from around the world.

      New Zealanders' abhorrence of all things nuclear comes to the fore again with major floating protests against France's resumed nuclear testing in the South Pacific.

1996 Noisy Ruapehu spews debris into the air, covering nearby towns with a few inches of ash.

New Zealand elects its first MMP government, having voted for constitutional change three years earlier. New Zealand First holds the balance of power and goes into government with the National Party.

1997 New Zealand starts to feel the effect of weakening Asian currencies, particularly as the number of Korean and Japanese tourists falls.

Jenny Shipley becomes the country's first woman PM.

1998 The government introduces a controversial "work for the dole" scheme, in which people on unemployment are required to work or train 20 hours a week or risk having their income slashed.

As the Asian economic crisis continues to bite, industrial strikes on Australia's waterfront also affect New Zealand's economy. The country's economic fundamentals remain strong, but these outside influences cause the N.Z. dollar to lose value against U.S. currency.

1999 The New Zealand cricketers record their first test-win over England at Lords, regarded as the spiritual home of the game. New Zealand goes on to win the series.

New Zealand contributes personnel and machinery to a United Nations peace-keeping force in Indonesia.

A Labour-Alliance coalition wins the general election, but a close vote means it still needs the support of the Green Party in matters of national importance. Helen Clark becomes New Zealand's second successive female prime minister.

2000 The airline Ansett New Zealand enters a franchise with Qantas Airways. The carrier operates as Qantas New Zealand, but the airline goes belly-up just months later.

New Zealand successfully defends the America's Cup, becoming the first country outside the United States to do so.

The lone, 125-year-old pine at the top of Auckland's One Tree Hill, one of the city's defining features, is removed.

2001 National carrier Air New Zealand runs into financial troubles and is bailed out by a $885 million taxpayer-financed rescue package.

Sir Peter Blake, a yachting champion who led New Zealand to win and retain the America's Cup, is murdered by pirates while on a conservation expedition in the Amazon.

2002 A simmering dispute over sponsorship and control of corporate facilities culminates with the International Rugby Board's dropping New Zealand as a subhost of the 2003 Rugby World Cup. Australia becomes the event's sole host, and the rugby-mad New Zealand public is left fuming.

Internal wrangling sees the minor government partner, the Alliance, split in half, though both sides continue to support Labour. After an early election, Labour has to rely on the support of several minor parties rather than a single coalition partner.

2003   Debate flares up as Māori request a legal inquiry into their precolonial customary ownership of the seabed and shore. Thousands of protesters march on Parliament in support of Māori claims.

2004   *The Return of the King,* the final film in Peter Jackson's *Lord of the Rings* trilogy, wins 11 Academy Awards. Keisha Castle-Hughes becomes the youngest nominee in the Academy Awards' Best Actress category for her work in *Whale Rider.*

Don Brash, leader of the National Party, ignites a furor with a speech at Orewa. He argues that the Crown should own the foreshore and the seabed, asserts that all claims based on the Treaty of Waitangi should be settled by 2010, and attacks the welfare system.

The Seabed and Foreshore Act is passed, ensuring that as of January 2005 any territory below the high-tide mark belongs to the Crown.

Labour MP Tariana Turia resigns after opposing the Labour Party's Seabed and Foreshore Act, going on to establish the Māori Party.

The Maori Television Service takes to the airwaves.

2005   Helen Clark's Labour Party wins a third term in Parliament, this time in coalition with Jim Anderton's Progressive Party, with support from Winston Peters's New Zealand First and Peter Dunne's United Future.

David Lange, 1984–1989 Labour leader of New Zealand, dies of complications associated with renal failure and blood disease on August 13, 2005. He was perhaps best known for implementing New Zealand's nuclear-free legislation.

The Lions, a British and Irish rugby team, tour New Zealand to play against regional rugby teams as well as longstanding rivals the All Blacks and the Māori All Blacks. The Lions are outstandingly beaten by both the All Blacks and the Māori All Blacks.

GLOSSARY

A Kiwi Glossary

Talking Kiwi is hardly a daunting prospect for people traveling abroad with the English language under their belt. You'll seldom be at a complete loss, and if a phrase does confuse you, the locals will delight in explaining its meaning. The word *kiwi* itself can be a source of confusion—it can mean the brown flightless bird that lives in New Zealand forests, the people of New Zealand, a furry fruit that is one of the country's best-known exports, a quick lottery ticket, or even a rugby league team. You'll have to figure it out in context. Despite being half a world away, New Zealanders are in many ways still fairly protective of the Queen's English and have resisted the Americanization of the language to a greater extent than their cousins in Australia. In newspapers and magazines you will read *colour* instead of *color, organise* instead of organize, and *programme* instead of *program*. New Zealanders are prone to shorten names and also to give nicknames, but this is not as prevalent as in Australia. And Kiwis have developed a few quirky terms of their own. Here are a few translations that will help:

Across the Ditch: Over the Tasman Sea in Australia

Aubergine: Eggplant

Aussie: An Australian

Bach: Vacation house (North Island) (pronounced *batch*)

Battle on: Try hard with limited success

Bludger: Someone who lives off other people's effort

Bush: The outdoors, wilderness

Capsicum: Bell pepper

Carpark: Parking lot

Chilly bin: A cooler

Chocka (or chocka block): Full

Courgette: Zucchini

Cuppa: Cup of tea or coffee

Crib: Vacation house (South Island)

Crook: Sick

Dag: Amusing person or happening

Dairy: Convenience or corner store

Devonshire tea: Cream tea with scones (served morning and afternoon)

En suite: Bathroom attached to your hotel room

Fair go: Fair chance

Fanny: Woman's privates (considered obscene)

Flat white: Coffee with milk (equivalent to a café au lait)

Footie: Rugby football

Footpath: Sidewalk

Give a wide berth: Leave alone

Greenie: Conservationist

Home and hosed: Successful

Jandal: Open-topped footwear

Jersey: Sweater

Loo: Toilet (*bathroom* is only for bathing)

Mainlander: Resident of the South Island

Metal road: Gravel road

Motorway: Freeway or highway

Mozzie: Mosquito

Mug: Good-hearted to the point of being foolish

Nappie: Diaper

Pavlova: A meringue cake

Pom or pommie: Native of England

Rubber: Eraser (also condom)

Sealed road: Paved road

Serviette: Napkin

Shout: Buy a round of drinks

Sink a few: Drink some beer

Smoko: Tea or coffee break

Sticking plaster: Adhesive bandage

Ta: Thanks

Take-away: Food to go, takeout

Tall poppy: One who excels and stands out in doing so (often used to describe someone disparagingly, rather than in admiration)

Take the piss: Ridicule (Kiwis have tons of slang words involving piss)

Tea: Dinner (also the beverage)

Togs: Swimsuit

Track: Hiking trail

Tramping: Hiking

Up with the play: Knows what is going on

Ute: Pickup truck

Whinger: Whiner or moaner

A Māori Glossary

The use of the *Te Reo Māori* (Māori language) is experiencing a resurgence in contemporary New Zealand, with nearly 90% of Māori children enrolled in some form of Māori language early-childhood education. This is a heartening outcome for a language that has stood for decades tenuously at the brink of extinction.

Though the language was never officially legislated against, the great-grandparents of today's generation were beaten at school for speaking Māori. Not until the 1980s was government funding made available for Māori language education.

The realms of Māori language use are slowly moving out of the *marae* (gathering place) and into schools, parliament, and broadcasting. The advent of Māori TV, the recently established Māori television channel, has meant that a range of programs, from news, talk shows, and documentaries to soap operas and kids' shows, are now produced and broadcast in the Māori language. In terms of daily use, however, unless you're involved in a specifically Māori activity or event, you won't be hearing it much (though expressions such as "kia ora" have made their way into general Kiwi speech).

Still, knowing how to pronounce Māori words can be important when trying to say place-names in New Zealand. Even if you have a natural facility for picking up languages, you'll find many Māori words to be quite baffling. The West Coast town of Punakaiki (pronounced poon-ah-*kye*-kee) is relatively straightforward, but when you get to places such as Whangamata, the going gets tricky—the opening *wh* is pronounced like an *f*, and the accent is placed on the last syllable: "fahng-ah-ma-*ta*." Sometimes it is the mere length of words that makes them difficult, as in the case of Waitakaruru (why-ta-ka-ru-ru) or Whakarewarewa (fa-ka-*re*-wa-*re*-wa). You'll notice that the ends of both of these have repeats—of "ru" and "rewa," which is something to look out for to make longer words more manageable. Town names like Waikanea (*why*-can-eye) you'll just have to repeat to yourself a few times before saying them without pause.

The Māori *r* is rolled so that it sounds a little like a *d*. Thus the Northland town of Whangarei is pronounced "fang-ah-day," and the word *Māori* is pronounced "mah-*aw*-dee," or sometimes "mo-dee," with the *o* sounding like it does in the word *mold*, and a rolled *r*. A macron indicates a lengthened vowel. In general, *a* is pronounced *ah* as in "car"; *e* is said as the *ea* in "weather." *O* is pronounced like "awe," rather than *oh*, and *u* sounds like the *u* of "June." *Ng*, meanwhile, has a soft, blunted sound, as the *ng* in "singing." All of this is a little too complicated for those who still choose not to bother with Māori pronunciations. So in some places, if you say you've just driven over from "fahng-ah-ma-*ta*," the reply might be: "You mean 'wang-ah-*ma*-tuh.' " "You can pronounce these words either way, but more and more people these days are pronouncing Māori words correctly.

Āe: Yes

Ahau: I, me

Aotearoa: Land of the long white cloud (New Zealand)

Atua: Spirit, god

Awa: River

Awhi: Help

Haere atu: Go away, farewell, depart

Haere mai: Welcome, come here

Haere rā: Farewell, good-bye

Haka: Fierce rhythmical dance made internationally famous by the country's rugby team, the All Blacks, and performed before each game

Hākari: Feast, gift

Hāngi: Earth oven, food from an earth oven

Hapū: Subtribe

Harakeke: Flax leaf (also used to refer to woven flax items)

Heitiki: Greenstone pendant

Hongi: Press noses in greeting

Hui: Gathering

Ika: Fish

Iwi: People, tribe

Kāhore: No

Kai: Food, eat, dine

Kai moana: Seafood

Karakia: Ritual chant, prayer, religious service

Kaumātua: Elder

Kete: Flax bag

Kino: Bad

Koha: Customary gift, donation

Kōhanga reo: Māori preschool

Kōtiro: Girl

Kūmara: Sweet potato

Kura kaupapa: Total immersion Māori-language school

Mana: Influence, prestige, power

Manu: Bird

Manuhiri: Guest, visitor

Māoritanga: Māori culture, perspective

Marae: Traditional gathering place

Maunga: Mountain

Mauri: Life principle, source of vitality and mana

Mihi: To greet, congratulate

Moana: Sea, lake

Moko: Tattoo

Motu: Island

Pā: Fortress

Pai: Good

Pākehā: Non-Māori, European, Caucasian

Poi: Light ball attached to string

Rangatira: Chief, person of rank

Reo: Language

Roto: Lake

Taiaha: Long, two-handed weapon, with blade at one end and point at the other

Tama: Boy

Tāne: Man

Tangata whenua: People of the land, local people

Taniwha: Spirit-monsters living in the sea and inland waters

Taonga: Treasure

Tapu: Sacred, under religious restriction, taboo

Tauiwi: Foreigner

Tino rangatiratanga: Chief's authority, self-determination

Toa: Warrior

Tohunga: Priest, expert

Tupuna: Ancestor

Wahine: Woman

Wai: Water, liquid

Waiata: Sing, song

Wairua: Soul, spirit

Waka: Canoe

Whai kōrero: Speech

Whakapapa: Genealogy, cultural identity

Whānau: Family

Whare: House

Whenua: Land, country

Greetings & Expressions
Kia ora: Hello, thank you

Tēnā koe (korua) (koutou): Hello to one person (to two people) (to three or more people)

Haere mai: Welcome

Haere rā: Good-bye (from the person staying to the one leaving)

E noho ra: Good-bye (from the person leaving to the person staying)

Ka pai: Good, excellent

Kei te pehea koe: How are you? (to one person)

Māori Place-Names
Kirikiriroa: Hamilton

Ōtautahi: Christchurch

Ōtepoti: Dunedin

Rakiura: Stewart Island

Tāmaki-makau-rau: Auckland

Te Ika-A-Māui: North Island

Te Waipounamu–Te-Waka-A-Aoraki: South Island

Whanganui-a-tara: Wellington

BOOKS & MOVIES

Books

Because of the limited availability of many first-rate books on New Zealand outside the country, there is only so much that you'll be able to read before you go. So leave room in your suitcase for pick-up reading once you arrive, and bring something home to make your trip linger longer. One caveat: because of economies of scale in the New Zealand publishing industry, books tend to be expensive. That's one reason to do some secondhand shopping; another is the stores' usually knowledgeable staff, who can make recommendations.

History & Observations. Michael King's *Penguin History of New Zealand* (2003) became a runaway best seller in New Zealand. It's hard to find in the United States, but if you're interested in this topic, it's well worth buying once you get to New Zealand.

If you're interested in issues around the Treaty of Waitangi, *Healing Our History* (2001) by Robert Consedine focuses on New Zealand Pākehā identity, racism within New Zealand, and its intersection with the Treaty of Waitangi. Written from (and for) a non-Māori perspective, it aims to provide a better understanding of New Zealand's colonial history and the effect it's had on the Māori.

The *Oxford Illustrated History of New Zealand,* edited by Keith Sinclair, provides a comprehensive and highly readable account of the country's social, political, cultural, and economic evolution from the earliest Māori settlements until 1989. James Belich's *Making Peoples* looks at New Zealand history from a 1990s perspective, with more emphasis on the Māori view than some earlier publications. His *Paradise Reforged: A History of the New Zealanders from the Beginning of the Twentieth Century* (2002) also pays particular attention to the Māori population.

The *Colonial New Zealand Wars,* by Tim Ryan and Bill Parham, is a vivid history of the Māori-British battles. Lavishly illustrated with photographs of colonial infantry and drawings of Māori hill forts, flags, and weapons, the book makes far more compelling reading than the dry military history suggested by the title. Another highly readable military-historical book is James Belich's *The New Zealand Wars.* J. C. Beaglehole's *The Discovery of New Zealand* is an authoritative and scholarly analysis of the voyages of discovery, from the first Polynesians to the Europeans of the late 18th century. *A Traveller's History of New Zealand,* by John Chambers, is a suitcase-friendly reference.

As the title suggests, *New Zealand's Top 100 History-Makers* profiles 100 New Zealand icons, from politicians and artists to explorers and inventors. Author Joseph Romanos stretches back into the far reaches of New Zealand history before leading up to the present day, covering people made of the stuff from which local legends are made.

The terrific *Slipping Into Paradise,* by Jeffrey Moussaieff Masson (2004), is both memoir and commentary on the Kiwi culture. It includes his personal favorite-trip itinerary and a fun glossary of Kiwi words and expressions.

Fiction. New Zealand's best-known short-story writer is Katherine Mansfield (1888–1923), whose early stories were set in and around the city of Wellington, her birthplace. *The Best of Katherine Mansfield* is a fine compilation of stories from five collections. Reading her journals will give you a sense of her passionate romantic side, and as much as she disliked the small-minded provincial qualities of New Zealand, she loved the country deeply.

One of New Zealand's most distinguished writers was Janet Frame (1924–2004). Her works are numerous, from novels such as her successful *The Carpathians* to a three-part autobiography, which is a lyrical evocation of growing up in small-town New Zealand in the 1920s and 1930s and of the gradual awakening of a writer of great courage. Kiwi filmmaker Jane Campion adapted part of it for the screenplay of *An Angel at My Table.* Maurice Gee is another acclaimed novelist. His *Plumb* won the James Tait Prize for the best novel in Britain when it was published. *Plumb* reaches back to the early 20th century for its story of a renegade parson and his battle with old-world moral pieties. One particularly compelling scene is set in a mining town, where Plumb happens to be the man to hear the last testament of a notorious murderer. A more recent volume is *Ellie and the Shadow Man.* Gee is also known for his young adult fiction, in which he often plays out a fantasy–science fiction story in a New Zealand setting. Best examples include *Half Men of O* and *Under the Mountain. In My Father's Den,* a suspenseful small-town drama that Gee wrote in 1972, was made into a movie in 2004.

Two of the finest and most exciting writers at work in the country today are Patricia Grace and Witi Ihimaera, both Māori whose story collections and novels are on a par with the best fiction in the United Kingdom and the States. Grace's stories are beautifully and fluidly related, very much from inside her characters. Look for *The Dream Sleepers and Other Stories* and her novel *Mutuwhenua.* Her newest book, *Tu,* is a historical novel that recounts the life of a young boy who runs away to join the Māori Battalion and fight in World War II. Ihimaera (ee-hee-may-ra) also uses very clear prose and Māori experience. His early novel *Tangi* opens with the death of a father and moves through the 22-year-old son's experience of loss and innocence to his acceptance of his role as a man. Māori elements of the story are fascinating both culturally and emotionally. Also look for his *Bulibasha* and *Nights in the Garden of Spain.*

Keri Hulme's internationally celebrated *The Bone People* won the Booker McConnell Prize in 1985. Set on the isolated West Coast of the South Island, this challenging, vital novel weaves Polynesian myth with Christian symbolism and the powerful sense of place that characterizes modern Māori writing. More recently, Alan Duff's *Once Were Warriors* is a frank, uncompromising, and ultimately transcendent look at urban Māori society. Both the novel and the film were real sensations in New Zealand. The sequel, *One Night Out Stealing,* as well as *What Becomes of the Broken Hearted* and *Both Sides of the Moon,* has also been hugely successful. In a move to nonfiction, Duff addresses Māori issues in *Maori: The Crisis and the Challenge.*

Lloyd Jones, a hot current novelist, focuses on New Zealand while also looking beyond the country's borders. In *The Book of Fame* (2001), for instance, he fictionalizes the true story of New Zealand's All Blacks rugby team, who set out by steamer in 1905 to tour Great Britain. In *Here at the End of the World We Learn to Dance,* he brings tango music to the rural West Coast.

Margaret Mahy is a prolific children's-book writer; her books for kids under 10 include *Bubble Trouble* and *Down the Dragon's Tongue.*

On a lighter note, cartoonist Murray Ball has created an amusing look at Kiwi country life with his *Footrot Flats* series.

Poetry. *100 New Zealand Poems by 100 New Zealand Poets,* edited by New Zealand's current poet laureate, Bill Manhire, ranges from the country's earliest poems to the new poets of the 1990s. Greg O'Brien and Jenny Bornholdt's *My Heart Goes Swimming* is a charming selection of New Zealand love poems. A more wide-ranging and weighty collection is *An Anthology of New Zealand Poetry in English,* edited by Mark Williams, Greg O'Brien, and Jenny Bornholdt. Hone Tuwhare (too-fah-dee) is perhaps New

Zealand's most distinguished Māori poet. With a background in trades-union organizations, Tuwhare's poetry highlights an ongoing commitment to working-class and Māori issues, combined with his lyrical love of the land. Born in 1922, Tuwhare is still writing. Look out for *Oooooo.!!!,* a collection of new poems and previously unpublished work.

Specialized Topics. *Wine Atlas of New Zealand,* by Michael Cooper, is the first such tome devoted to New Zealand. It discusses all the key wine regions, with illustrations, tasting notes, and maps. *The Wines and Vineyards of New Zealand,* also by Cooper, is an exhaustive evaluation in words and pictures of every vineyard in the country. For travelers who plan to make hiking a major component of their vacations, *Tramping in New Zealand,* published by Lonely Planet, is an invaluable guide. *A Field Guide to Auckland* is a wonderful introduction to the natural and historic attractions of the Auckland region. It includes an overview of natural and human history and details of more than 140 interesting places to visit within easy distance of the city. If you're interested in off-roading, *Classic New Zealand Mountain Bike Rides,* by Paul, Simon, and Jonathan Kennett, provides route information for more than 400 rides, ranging from as far north as Cape Reinga all the way to the deep south. The Kennett brothers have been mountain biking since the 1980s. They organize numerous mountain-biking events throughout the year, and manage the popular New Zealand Mountain Bike Web site, www.mtbnz.org.nz.

Published just days before his death, *David Lange: My Life,* is a memoir that chronicles the life of Lange, who became the country's youngest prime minister at age 41. His Labour government was responsible for groundbreaking legislation that established the world's first nuclear-free state, as well as for heralding many social and human rights reforms such as the New Zealand homosexual law reform and the bill of rights legislation.

Art Books. Greg O'Brien's *Hotere: Out the Black Window* covers the work of one of the country's most respected artists. *The Art of Robyn Kahukiwa* presents the art of another well-known and loved artist. Kahukiwa explores sociocultural issues particular to Māori in New Zealand, intersecting Māori culture and mythology with colonialism through her often vibrant, always powerful works. For a broad sampling of New Zealand art, *Icons Ngā Taonga: From the Collections of the Museum of New Zealand Te Papa Tongarewa* is a glossy showcase of photographs of almost 400 *taonga* (treasures) from Te Papa Tongarewa, New Zealand's national museum. The art in this book covers Māori painting, carving, sculpture, and other cultural artifacts. Accompanying text is written in Māori and English.

Movies

New Zealand director Peter Jackson dazzled moviegoers with the imagery and creativity of his home country with the *The Lord of the Rings* film trilogy. Each of the three movies was a knockout, winning Academy Awards and a huge following. The final film, *The Return of the King,* capped the accomplishment by sweeping the 2003 Academy Awards with 11 Oscars. Wellington-based Weta Workshop, which designed and achieved many of the film's effects, won several Academy Awards for its phenomenal work. But one of the strongest effects in the film was that of the scenery. By shooting in many of New Zealand's national parks and mountain ranges, Jackson introduced thousands of viewers to the stunning Kiwi landscape.

In 2006, Peter Jackson wrapped up another blockbuster, a $207 million remake of *King Kong.* Three hours long (as opposed to the 100-minute 1933 original), *Kong* was mostly shot in and around Wellington. Thanks once again to the Weta team, the movie is packed with the kind of special effects Jackson fans have grown accustomed to. The other major 2005 movie that was largely filmed in New Zealand (and worked on by the Weta Workshop) was *The Chronicles of Narnia: The Lion, the Witch & the Wardrobe* by New Zealand director Andrew Adamson (director of the *Shrek* movies).

But New Zealand films haven't always needed the Weta Workshop for success. *Whale Rider* (2002), a decidedly un-high-tech, grassroots film, also did tremendously well. Shot in rural eastern North Island and based on a novel by Witi Ihimaera, it's about a young Māori girl struggling to find a place in her family and society.

Until the past few years, New Zealand's film industry has had a relatively small output, but the quality of its films has been consistently high. Jane Campion's *The Piano* (1993) is a prime example, as are her earlier *An Angel at My Table* (1990) and *Sweetie* (1988), which was made in Australia. Roger Donaldson's 1977 thriller *Sleeping Dogs* was the first New Zealand film released in the United States, followed by the equally worthy *Smash Palace* (1982). The tough, urban portrayal of *Once Were Warriors* (1995) is one of the most recent to make it across the Pacific.

Its portrait of urban Māori life, unfortunately, makes New Zealand look a little too much like Los Angeles. *Scarfies,* a black comedy about Otago University students, received positive feedback at the 2000 Sundance Film Festival, after success in local cinemas. Christine Jeffs's haunting depiction of troubled family dynamics, *Rain* (2001), was filmed on the North Island coast. In *The Last Samurai* (2003), starring Tom Cruise, New Zealand stood in for Japan, with Mt. Taranaki doubling as Mt. Fuji.

Peter Jackson was having an effect on the industry long before *The Lord of the Rings.* His first foray into film was the splatter comedy *Bad Taste* (1987), followed by the intense murder drama *Heavenly Creatures* (1994), which introduced Kate Winslet to a worldwide audience. *The Frighteners* (1996), another dip into the horror pool, starred Michael J. Fox.

Hardly high culture, but still a major success for New Zealand's film and television industry, was the *Hercules* television series starring Kevin Sorbo. The show was axed in the United States in 1999, but its spin-off series, *Xena: Warrior Princess,* survived until 2001. Both series were filmed in West Auckland, doing its best to look like ancient Greece.

SMART TRAVEL TIPS

ADDRESSES

New Zealand uses postal codes, but this would be news to many New Zealanders—addresses are often listed without postal codes. Although the New Zealand postal service can process mail a bit faster with the postal code, it's not necessary and mail will arrive without it.

A street number with a slash in it indicates that there's more than one home or business at that address. Keep in mind that in New Zealand, "first floor" means the floor above the ground floor.

AIR TRAVEL

BOOKING

When you book look for nonstop flights and remember that "direct" flights stop at least once. Try to avoid connecting flights, which require a change of plane. Two airlines may operate a connecting flight jointly, so ask if your airline operates every segment of the trip; you may find that the carrier you prefer flies you only part of the way. To find more booking tips and to check prices and make on-line flight reservations, log on to ⊕ www.fodors.com

CARRIERS

Air New Zealand flies twice daily from Los Angeles to Auckland and is the only carrier that extends a nonstop flight from San Francisco to Auckland as well as a nonstop flight from Los Angeles to Christchurch. Qantas flies from Los Angeles to New Zealand, both nonstop and direct. United and Air Canada connect from points in North America with flights of their own out of Los Angeles.

British Airways, Cathay Pacific, Japan Airlines, Qantas, and Singapore Airlines operate between London and Auckland, with a stopover in Asia. Air New Zealand and United operate between London and Auckland by way of the United States.

Within New Zealand, Air New Zealand and Qantas compete on intercity trunk routes. Air New Zealand serves a wide network of provincial and tourist centers, while Qantas works with local airline Origin Pacific to cover a number of secondary routes. For more information about regional travel, *see* the A to Z sections within regional chapters.

Pacific Blue, the sister carrier to Australia's domestic airline Virgin Blue, launched flights between Australia and New Zealand, providing direct flights between Melbourne and Christchurch.

🚹 **To & from New Zealand Air Canada** ☎ 888/247-2262 in U.S. and Canada, 09/969-7470 or toll-free 0508/747-767 in New Zealand ⊕ www.aircanada.ca. **Air New Zealand** ☎ 310/615-1111, 800/262-1234 in U.S., 800/663-5494 in Canada, toll-free 0800/028-4149 in U.K. or toll-free 0800/737-000 in New Zealand ⊕ www.airnewzealand.co.nz. **British Airways** ☎ 800/247-9297 in U.S., 0870/850-9850 in the U.K., 09/966-9777 in New Zealand ⊕ www.britishairways.com. **Cathay Pacific** ☎ 020/8834-8888 in U.K., 0800/800-454 in New Zealand ⊕ www.cathaypacific.com. **Japan Airlines** ☎ 800/525-3663 in U.S., 845/774-7700 in U.K., 09/379-3202 in New Zealand ⊕ www.jal.com. **Qantas** ☎ 800/227-4500 in U.S. and Canada, 0845/774-7767 in U.K., 0800/808-767 in New Zealand ⊕ www.qantas.com.au. **Singapore Airlines** ☎ 800/742-3333 in U.S., 0870/608-8886 in U.K., 0800/808-909 in New Zealand ⊕ www.singaporeair.com. **United** ☎ 800/538-2929 in U.S., 845/8444-777 in U.K., 0800/508-648 in New Zealand ⊕ www.ual.com.

🚹 **Within New Zealand Origin Pacific** ☎ 0800/302-302 ⊕ www.originpacific.co.nz. **Pacific Blue** ☎ 0800/670-000 ⊕ www.flypacificblue.com. **Qantas** ☎ 0800/808-767 ⊕ www.qantas.com.au.

CHECK-IN & BOARDING

When taking your return flight from New Zealand, you will need to pay a departure tax. This tax is already factored into your airfare on your way to New Zealand, but must be paid separately when leaving. It's usually around NZ$25 and you pay it between checking in and going through the immigration checkpoint.

Always ask your carrier about its check-in policy. Plan to arrive at the airport about 1 hour before your scheduled departure time for domestic flights and 3 hours before international flights. For domestic flights within New Zealand, check in at least a half hour before departure. Assuming that not everyone with a ticket will show up, airlines routinely overbook planes. When everyone does, airlines ask for volunteers to give up their seats. In re-

turn, these volunteers usually get a certificate for a free flight and are rebooked on the next flight out. If there are not enough volunteers, the airline must choose who will be denied boarding. The first to get bumped are passengers who checked in late and those flying on discounted tickets, so get to the gate and check in as early as possible, especially during peak periods.

Always bring a government-issued photo ID to the airport; even when it's not required, a passport is best.

CUTTING COSTS

The least expensive airfares to New Zealand are priced for round-trip travel and must usually be purchased in advance. Airlines generally allow you to change your return date for a fee; most low-fare tickets, however, are nonrefundable. It's smart to call a number of airlines and check the Internet; when you are quoted a good price, book it on the spot—the same fare may not be available the next day. Always check different routings and look into using alternate airports. Also, price off-peak flights, which may be significantly less expensive than others. Travel agents, especially low-fare specialists (⇨ Discounts and Deals, *below*), are helpful.

To expedite an airline fare search on the Web, check travel search engines with meta-search technology, such as www.mobissimo.com. These search across a broad supplier base so you can compare rates offered by travel agents, consolidators, and airlines in one fell swoop.

Consolidators are another good source. They buy tickets for scheduled international flights at reduced rates from the airlines, then sell them at prices that beat the best fare available directly from the airlines. Sometimes you can even get your money back if you need to return the ticket. Carefully read the fine print detailing penalties for changes and cancellations, purchase the ticket with a credit card, and confirm your consolidator reservation with the airline.

When you fly as a courier, you trade your checked-luggage space for a ticket deeply subsidized by a courier service. There are restrictions on when you can book and how long you can stay. Some courier companies list with membership organizations, such as the Air Courier Association and the International Association of Air Travel Couriers; these require you to become a member before you can book a flight.

Many airlines, singly or in collaboration, offer discount air passes that allow foreigners to travel economically in a particular country or region. These visitor passes usually must be reserved and purchased before you leave home. Information about passes can be difficult to track down on airline Web sites, which tend to be geared to travelers departing from a given carrier's country rather than to those intending to visit that country. Try typing the name of the pass into a search engine, or search for "pass" within the carrier's Web site.

Although budget air travel within New Zealand is still expensive compared with the cost of bus or train travel, the one-way fare system does make it easy to get around, especially if you don't have a lot of time and don't want to spend it all on the road. These days, booking your domestic flights in conjunction with your international flight won't save you any money, but it will allow you to travel with the international luggage allowance (2 x 32 kg bags), significantly higher than domestic allowances (2 x 20 kg bags).

Some airlines give great deals if you **add stopovers to your flight itinerary.** You'll need to stop in at a Pacific destination like Tahiti or Fiji for a limited time before heading to New Zealand. Check with the airline and see what they're offering—make sure that New Zealand is included in Pacific deals—sometimes it's the one exception.

If you hold an international student identification card, you'll save even more (⇨ Students in New Zealand, *below*).

🎦 Consolidators AirlineConsolidator.com ☎ 888/468-5385 ⊕ www.airlineconsolidator.com, for international tickets. **Best Fares** ☎ 800/880-1234 ⊕ www.bestfares.com; $59.90 annual membership. **Cheap Tickets** ☎ 800/377-1000 or 800/652-4327 ⊕ www.cheaptickets.com. **Expedia** ☎ 800/397-3342 or 404/728-8787 ⊕ www.expedia.com. **Hotwire** ☎ 866/468-9473 or 920/330-9418 ⊕ www.hotwire.com. **Now Voyager Travel** ✉ 1717 Avenue M, Brooklyn, NY 11230 ☎ 212/459-1616

☎ 718/504-4762 ⊕ www.nowvoyagertravel.com. **Onetravel.com** ⊕ www.onetravel.com. **Orbitz** ☎ 888/656-4546 ⊕ www.orbitz.com. **Priceline. com** ⊕ www.priceline.com. **Travelocity** ☎ 888/709-5983, 877/282-2925 in Canada, 0870/111-7061 in U.K. ⊕ www.travelocity.com.

🎦 Courier Resources Air Courier Association/ Cheaptrips.com ☎ 800/211-5119 ⊕ www.aircourier. org or www.cheaptrips.com; $20 annual membership.

🎦 Discount Passes Pacific Explorer Airpass Hideaway Holidays ☎ 02/8799-2500 in Australia 🖷 02/9647-1267 in Australia, 530/325-4069 in U.S. ⊕ www.hideawayholidays.com.au. **Polypass** Polynesian Airlines ☎ 800/264-0823 in U.S., 1300/653-737 in Australia, 0800/800-993 or 04/472-2544 in New Zealand ⊕ www.polynesianairlines.com.

ENJOYING THE FLIGHT

State your seat preference when purchasing your ticket, and then repeat it when you confirm and when you check in. For more legroom, you can request one of the few emergency-aisle seats at check-in, if you are capable of lifting at least 50 pounds—a Federal Aviation Administration requirement of passengers in these seats. Seats behind a bulkhead also offer more legroom, but they don't have underseat storage. Don't sit in the row in front of the emergency aisle or in front of a bulkhead, where seats may not recline.

Ask the airline whether a snack or meal is served on the flight. If you have dietary concerns, request special meals when booking. These can be vegetarian, low-cholesterol, or kosher, for example. It's a good idea to pack some healthy snacks and a small (plastic) bottle of water in your carry-on bag. On long flights, try to maintain a normal routine, to help fight jet lag. At night, get some sleep. By day, eat light meals, drink water (not alcohol). For additional jet-lag tips consult *Fodor's FYI: Travel Fit & Healthy* (available at bookstores everywhere).

Long flights put you at a higher risk of deep vein thrombosis (DVT), otherwise known as "economy class syndrome." When you stay motionless for an extended period of time, blood can pool in your legs and clot; these clots can later lodge in a vital organ and cause major medical complications. So it's extremely important to

flex your feet and walk around the cabin regularly to keep your blood flowing.

All New Zealand domestic flights and flights between New Zealand and Australia are no-smoking. Air New Zealand has banned smoking on all of its flights worldwide.

FLYING TIMES

From New York to Auckland (via Los Angeles) flights take about 19 hours; from Chicago, about 17 hours; from Los Angeles to Auckland (nonstop), about 12 hours. From the United States and Canada, you will have to connect to a New Zealand–bound flight in L.A.

Flights from London to Auckland take about 24 hours, either via the United States or via Southeast Asia. Flights between Sydney and Auckland take about three hours. These are all actual air hours and do not include ground time.

HOW TO COMPLAIN

If your baggage goes astray or your flight goes awry, complain right away. Most carriers require that you **file a claim immediately.** The Aviation Consumer Protection Division of the Department of Transportation publishes *Fly-Rights,* which discusses airlines and consumer issues and is available online. At PassengerRights.com, a Web site where you can compose a letter of complaint and distribute it electronically.
🔀 Airline Complaints **Aviation Consumer Protection Division** ✉ U.S. Department of Transportation, Room 4107, C-75, Washington, DC 20590 ☎ 202/366-2220 ⊕ www.dot.gov/airconsumer. **Federal Aviation Administration Consumer Hotline** ☎ 800/322-7873.

RECONFIRMING

Check the status of your flight before you leave for the airport. You can do this on your carrier's Web site, by linking to a flight-status checker (many Web booking services offer these), or by calling your carrier or travel agent. Always confirm international flights at least 72 hours ahead of the scheduled departure time. It is not required that you reconfirm outbound flights from or within New Zealand.

AIRPORTS

The major airport is Auckland International Airport (AKL). It is usually a bit cheaper to fly into and out of this airport, but the supplemental fees for flights to Wellington (WLG) or Christchurch (CHC) are quite reasonable. New Zealand's airports in general are relatively compact and easy to negotiate. But if you're in Auckland's airport, **don't wait to hear your boarding announcement,** because it has adopted "the quiet airport" concept. There are usually no flight announcements made over a loudspeaker; instead, information on flight arrivals and departures appears on display boards and TV monitors.

Less quiet features of Auckland's airport are its children's play areas, such as the playground equipment on the top floor of the terminal. Complimentary showers are also available to all passengers; these are near Gate 5 and Gate 9. Towels and toiletries can be rented at the Collection Point, where duty-free goods, health care items, and crafts are also sold.

New Zealand has a dense network of domestic air routes, so hopping from one area to another is fairly easy, if not inexpensive. The regional airlines that service the smaller airports such as Picton and Kaikoura often partner with Air New Zealand or Qantas, so you can make these flight arrangements when booking your international flight. There are also numerous charter companies with planes carrying a dozen passengers or less. For details on local services, see this guide's destination chapters.
🔀 Airport Information **Auckland International Airport** ☎ 09/275-0789 ⊕ www.auckland-airport.co.nz. **Christchurch International Airport** ☎ 03/374-7100 ⊕ www.christchurch-airport.co.nz. **Wellington International Airport** ☎ 04/385-5123 ⊕ www.wlg-airport.co.nz.

DUTY-FREE SHOPPING

The international airports in Auckland and Christchurch have some of the best duty-free deals (on liquor, cigarettes, and cosmetics) in the South Pacific and even compare favorably with those in many Asian countries.

BIKE TRAVEL

New Zealand is a sensational place to take cycling tours. For information on multiday trips throughout the country, *see* Chapter 11. Major cities are increasing their biking facilities, such as cycling lanes in central areas.

Bike-rental shops can be found in all larger cities and other tourist centers. Pedaltours NZ, for instance, has bike-rental outlets in both Auckland and Christchurch. You can rent a bike for a day or for even weeks at a stretch, even picking up your bike at one end of the country and dropping it off at the other end. They can also customize tour itineraries for special-interest groups.

The Cycling Advocates' Network lists events and gives touring advice as well as links to different New Zealand bike-touring companies on their Web site. The New Zealand Mountain Bike Association is a good resource for travelers that like roughing it. On their Web site, you can exchange messages with fellow bikers and view listings of upcoming biking events. And whether your passion for peddling is fulfilled on the seat of a road bike, BMX bike, or even a unicycle, check out ⊕ www.cyclingnz.com for club lists, riders' reports, and more.

The New Zealand Cyclist Guide to Cycle Touring by J. B. Ringer has North Island and South Island editions and is available in some bike shops and major bookstores around the country or you can pick up a copy of either the North Island or South Island editions (or both!) of *Pedallers' Paradise*, another cycle touring guide by Nigel Rushton.

🄵 Bike Rentals **Cycling Advocates' Network** ⌂ Box 6491, Auckland ☎ 04/972-2552 ⊕ www. can.org.nz. **New Zealand Mountain Bike Association** ⌂ Box 4536, Christchurch ☎ 03/545-6512 ⊕ www.mtbnz.org.nz. **Pedaltours NZ** ⌂ Box 37575, Parnell, Auckland ☎ 888/222-9187 in U.S., 09/585-1338, or toll-free 0800/302-096 ⊕ www. pedaltours.co.nz.

BIKES IN FLIGHT

Most airlines accommodate bikes as luggage, provided they are dismantled and boxed; check with individual airlines about packing requirements. Airlines sell bike boxes, which are often free at bike shops, for about $15 (bike bags start at $100). International travelers often can substitute a bike for a piece of checked luggage at no charge; otherwise, the cost is about $100. Domestic and Canadian airlines charge $40–$80 each way.

BUSINESS HOURS

BANKS & OFFICES
Banks are open weekdays 9–4:30, but trading in foreign currencies ceases at 3.

GAS STATIONS
Gas stations are usually open, at the least, from 7 AM to 7 PM daily. Large stations on main highways are commonly open 24 hours.

MUSEUMS
Museums around the country do not have standard hours, but many are open daily from 10 AM to 5 PM. Larger museums and government-run collections are generally open daily, but the hours of small local museums vary, as many are run by volunteers. The Museums Aotearoa Web site, ⊕ www.museums-aotearoa.org.nz, can be a helpful info source.

PHARMACIES
Pharmacies are open from 9 AM to 5 PM. In larger cities, you will find basic nonprescription drugstore items in supermarkets, many of which are open until 10 PM. During off-hours there will usually be emergency-hour pharmacies in the major cities. Phone the local hospital for details.

SHOPS
Shops are generally open Monday through Thursday 9–5:30, Friday 9–9, and Saturday 9–noon (until 5 in main cities). Sunday trading is becoming more common but still varies greatly from place to place. In many rural areas, stores are closed on Sunday, but most Auckland shopping centers are at least open Sunday morning. Liquor stores are often open daily. In major cities supermarkets and convenience stores, called "dairies," are usually open from 7 AM to 10 PM; a few stay open 24 hours.

BUS TRAVEL
New Zealand is served by an extensive bus network; for many travelers, buses offer

566 < **Smart Travel Tips**

the optimal combination of cost and convenience. InterCity and Newmans are the main bus lines. They operate under a collective marketing umbrella and are part of a larger shareholder group. Newmans differentiates itself by offering newer, spiffier vehicles, which conform to a strict criteria based upon vehicle age and amenities.

Some Newmans and InterCity bus routes overlap, but Newmans tends to have fewer stops and stick to the key corridors, making travel times a bit shorter. InterCity buses, on the other hand, covers more remote areas. Nevertheless, both services stop at small towns along the way. After all, buses are the backbone of the country's long-distance passenger transport system (stopping at 600 towns and cities every day) and are used by locals as much as tourists.

Although Newmans and InterCity are the top national carriers, there are also many regional bus services. For instance, Bottom Bus runs around the Catlins and Southland; Atomic Travel also covers the majority of the South Island. *See the* A to Z sections in regional chapters for more details on local services.

Take a hop-on, hop-off bus if you prefer a more flexible itinerary. Although the buses run by companies like Kiwi Experience and Magic Travellers Network may not be quite as comfortable as Newmans and InterCity, they offer flexible coach passes, typically valid for 12 months. Some passes cover all of New Zealand, whereas others are limited to specific regions. Most of these backpacker buses have affiliations with hostels and hotels, and various combination packages are available. Stray Travel, operated by the people who founded Kiwi Experience, gives you the option of using the service as a tour or having unlimited stopovers for the validity of your chosen pass.

Putting a dent in even the most flexible schedule are unexpected road closings. Bus routes go through some tough terrain like mountain passes and river gorges, which can be closed in bad weather. It's always a good idea to **call ahead to confirm your itinerary.** Otherwise, the buses tend to run on schedule. So in terms of time, you'll be

smokin'—figuratively anyway, because there's no smoking on any bus lines.

Overall, bus fares vary greatly, depending on how much flexibility you have in terms of days and times traveled. A standard full fare between Auckland and Wellington is $103 but can be obtained for as low as $68. A certain number of seats are offered at a discounted rate, so it's advantageous to **book your tickets as early as possible.** This is especially true during the holidays. Individual company Web sites are the best way to find out about special fares; both Newmans and InterCity have online reservation systems.

🚌 Bus Information **Atomic Travel** ☎ 03/322-8883 ⊕ www.atomictravel.co.nz. **Bottom Bus** ☎ 03/434-7370 ⊕ www.bottombus.co.nz. **InterCity** ☎ 09/913-6100 or 0508/353-947 toll-free in New Zealand ⊕ www.intercitycoach.co.nz. **Kiwi Experience** ☎ 09/366-9830 ⊕ www.kiwiexperience.com. **Magic Travellers Network** ☎ 09/358-5600 ⊕ www.magicbus.co.nz. **Newmans** ☎ 09/913-6200 ⊕ www.newmanscoach.co.nz. **Stray Travel** ☎ 09/309-8772 or 03/377-6192 ⊕ www.straytravel.co.nz.

CUTTING COSTS

Look into the various flexible passes that allow coach travel over a set route in a given time frame, usually three or six months. You can travel whenever you like, without paying extra, as long as you stick to the stops covered by your pass. There is also the New Zealand Travelpass, which allows unlimited travel on buses and trains and on the Interislander ferries that link the North and South Islands (⇨ Discounts and Deals, *below*). Both Newmans and InterCity offer a 20% discount to students and 15% for Youth Hostel members. Identification cards are required. Discounts are given to senior citizens and children, too.

The Flexi-Pass, ⊕ www.flexipass.co.nz, is sold in blocks of time during which you're eligible to travel on regular InterCity bus routes or on any Newmans sightseeing packages, or both. This is such a good deal that locals even use this pass for their daily commute. Typically valid for a year, you can hop on and off, changing your plans without a penalty at least two hours prior to your departure. If you find you are running out of time, you can always buy more; as with classic economies of scale, the more time blocks you buy, the cheaper they are. You must schedule in advance, as independent bus ticketing windows don't track your Flexi-Pass hours.

Kiwi Experience and Magic Travellers Network offer packages that combine one-way domestic flights with bus passes to help you cover a little more ground for a little less money.

PAYING

Credit cards and traveler's checks are accepted by the major bus companies.

CAMERAS & PHOTOGRAPHY

If you are taking photos of mountains and lakes, avoid the glare of the afternoon—take your shots at dusk and dawn, the best times. In the North Island, the West Coast has some spectacular sunsets. In the South Island, particularly in Fiordland, thick fog wraps itself around moss-laden trees on winter mornings, providing for eerie-looking photographs. For a spectacular wide-angled photograph, be sure to travel to the top of Bob's Peak by the Skyline Gondola and take a shot of Queenstown and the Remarkables mountain range. For an evocative urban shot, head to the Auckland waterfront and take a picture of the joggers, skaters, and cyclists, with the Rangitoto Island in the background. The *Kodak Guide to Shooting Great Travel Pictures* (available at bookstores everywhere) is loaded with tips.

New Zealanders are usually happy to have their photograph taken, but if you're getting up close, it pays to ask permission first. Also ask first before taking any photos of Māori buildings or during traditional Māori ceremonies. If you're touring a Māori cultural center, photos are welcomed, but be especially considerate if you're extended a personal invitation to an event or *marae* (traditional gathering spot). 🔲 **Photo Help Kodak Information Center** ☎ 800/242-2424 ⊕ www.kodak.com.

EQUIPMENT PRECAUTIONS

Don't pack film and equipment in checked luggage, where it is much more susceptible to damage. X-ray machines used to view checked luggage are becoming much more

powerful and therefore are much more likely to ruin your film. Try to ask for hand inspection of film, which becomes clouded after repeated exposure to airport X-ray machines, and keep videotapes and computer disks away from metal detectors. Always keep film, tape, and computer disks out of the sun. Carry an extra supply of batteries, and be prepared to turn on your camera, camcorder, or laptop to prove to airport security personnel that the device is real.

FILM & DEVELOPING

Film is readily available in airport duty-free shops, pharmacies, department stores, tourist shops, and gas stations. Kodak and Fuji are widely available. A roll of 36-exposure film costs about $13. Twenty-four-hour film developing is available even in smaller towns, and some pharmacies and photo shops will develop in an hour or two.

VIDEOS, CDS, AND DVDS

The local standard for videotape is PAL; a three-hour tape will cost around $6. A DVD for your digital video camera will cost around $3, while a CD for burning photos won't cost more than about $2.

CAR RENTAL

Japanese brands dominate rental agencies in New Zealand. Cars in the "economy" ranges are likely to include Honda Logos, Honda Civics, Toyota Corollas, or similar types. They are suitable for two or three people. At the luxury end of the scale you will find Honda Legends. **For some local flavor, rent a Holden Commodore,** a popular car in New Zealand. Most major agencies will have this as a luxury option and some even offer Lexus convertibles and other high-end hot rods. Domestic agency Smart Cars specializes in luxury rentals such as Mercedes and Audi convertibles and BMW sport-utility vehicles. With exception to these performance models, stick shift proves to be the more economical choice. Stick also tends to be the norm, so **specify if you prefer an automatic.**

Renting from a domestic agency is sometimes cheaper, but if the car is damaged in an accident, it's easier to deal with an international company once you've returned home. Kiwi companies Maui Rentals and

Kea Rentals are best known for wide selections of campers, motorhomes, and 4x4 vehicles. Other reputable domestic agencies are Apex Car Rental and Auto Rentals NZ Wide, which have several branches throughout the country.

Rates in New Zealand begin at $40 a day and $320 a week for an economy car with unlimited mileage. This does not include tax on car rentals, which is 12.5%. **Reserve a vehicle well in advance** if renting during holiday peak seasons, especially Christmas, as renting a vehicle at the last minute can pose a challenge.

🏳 Major Agencies **Alamo** ☎ 800/522-9696 ⊕ www.alamo.com. **Avis** ☎ 800/331-1084, 800/879-2847 in Canada, 0870/606-0100 in U.K., 02/9353-9000 in Australia, 09/526-2847, 800/655-111 in New Zealand ⊕ www.avis.com. **Budget** ☎ 800/527-0700, 0870/156-5656 in U.K., 800/283-438 in New Zealand ⊕ www.budget.com. **Dollar** ☎ 800/800-6000, 0124/622-0111 in U.K. where it's affiliated with Sixt, 02/9223-1444 in Australia ⊕ www.dollar.com. **Hertz** ☎ 800/654-3001, 800/263-0600 in Canada, 020/8897-2072 in U.K., 02/9669-2444 in Australia, 09/256-8690,800/654-321 in New Zealand ⊕ www.hertz.com. **National Car Rental** ☎ 800/227-7368, 020/8680-4800 in U.K., 800/800-115 (operating as Europcar in New Zealand) ⊕ www.nationalcar.com. 🏳 Local Agencies **Apex Car Rental** ☎ 03/379-6897 or 0800/93-9597 toll-free in New Zealand ⊕ www.apexrentals.co.nz. **Auto Rentals NZ Wide, Ltd.** ☎ 03/3717-343 or 0800/736-893 toll-free in New Zealand, 800/905-8071 in U.S., 0800/904-7516 in U.K. ⊕ www.autorentals.co.nz. **Kea Campers** ☎ 09/441-7833 in New Zealand ⊕ www.keacampers.com. **Maui Rentals** ☎ 09/275-3013 or 0800/651-080 toll-free in New Zealand ⊕ www.maui-rentals.com. **Smart Cars** ☎ 09/307-3553 or 0800/458-987 in New Zealand, 866/626-3844 toll-free in U.S., 0871/733-1526 in U.K. ⊕ www.smartcars.co.nz.

CROSS-ISLAND RENTALS

Most major international companies have a convenient service if you are taking the ferry between North and South islands and want to continue your rental contract. You simply drop off the car in Wellington and on the same contract pick up a new car in Picton, or vice versa. It saves you from paying the considerable fare for taking a car across on the ferry (and it's easier

for the company to keep track of its rental fleet). Your rental contract is terminated only at the far end of your trip, wherever you end up. In this system, there is no drop-off charge for one-way rentals, making an Auckland–Queenstown rental as easy as it could be.

CUTTING COSTS

For a good deal, book through a travel agent who will shop around. If you're renting a car in New Zealand, **check for special rates based on a south-to-north itinerary**; it may be less expensive this way, as it's against the normal flow. Special rates should be available whether you book from abroad or within New Zealand.

INSURANCE

When driving a rented car you are generally responsible for any damage to or loss of the vehicle. You may also be liable for any property damage or personal injury that you may cause while driving. Before you rent, **see what coverage you already have** under the terms of your personal auto-insurance policy and credit cards.

In New Zealand, it is usual to have the insurance included in the rental price, but you will almost certainly be expected to pay what Kiwis call an "excess" if you badly damage the car. A deposit amount is placed on your credit card when making the reservation and then reimbursed if you return the car unscathed. The deposit will run you anywhere from NZ$750 to NZ$1,200.

Since deductibles are very high with the most basic coverage, you may want to opt for total coverage. Another thing to keep in mind is that standard "excess" coverage does not cover any water-related damage—the kind of damage that's usually incurred when crossing creeks, flooded plain areas, or on beaches. Some policies even specify places you're not supposed to drive the rental, such as Skippers Road in Queenstown, 90 Mile Beach in Northland, Ball Hut Road near Mt. Cook, and north of Colville Township on the Coromandel Peninsula. Be sure to **read the fine print on restricted areas** and get all of the details from the rental agent before you choose your coverage.

REQUIREMENTS & RESTRICTIONS

In New Zealand your own driver's license is acceptable. An International Driver's Permit is a good idea; it's available from the American or Canadian Automobile Association, and, in the United Kingdom, from the Automobile Association or Royal Automobile Club. These international permits are universally recognized, and having one in your wallet may save you a problem with the local authorities.

The minimum age for renting a car in New Zealand is 21. Even so, with some rental car companies, drivers under 25 years old may still be liable for an extra "underage driver's fee" of $25 plus the 12.5% general sales tax (GST) in addition to the quoted rates. Children's car seats are mandatory for kids under five years old. Car-rental companies may ask drivers not to take their cars onto certain roads, so be sure to ask about any such restrictions.

SURCHARGES

Before you pick up a car in one city and leave it in another, **ask about drop-off charges or one-way service fees,** which can be substantial. Note, too, that some rental agencies charge extra if you return the car before the time specified in your contract. To avoid a hefty refueling fee, **fill the tank just before you turn in the car,** but be aware that gas stations near the rental outlet may overcharge. It's almost never a deal to buy the tank of gas in the car when you rent it; the understanding is that you'll return it empty, but some fuel usually remains.

CAR TRAVEL

Nothing beats the freedom and mobility of a car for exploring. Even for those nervous about driving on the "wrong" side of the road, motoring here is relatively easy.

Remember this simple axiom: **drive left, look right.** That means keep to the left lane, and when turning right or left from a stop sign, the closest lane of traffic will be coming from the right, so look in that direction first. By the same token, pedestrians should **look right before crossing the street.** Americans and Canadians can blindly step into the path of an oncoming car by looking left as they do when crossing streets at home. So repeat this several times: drive left, look

right. You'll find yourself in a constant comedy of errors when you go to use directional signals and windshield wipers—in Kiwi cars it's the reverse of what you're used to. You won't be able to count how many times those wipers start flapping back and forth when you go to signal a turn (it'll happen in reverse when you get back home).

AUTO CLUBS

⚑ In Australia **Australian Automobile Association** ☎ 02/6247-7311.
⚑ In Canada **Canadian Automobile Association (CAA)** ☎ 613/247-0117.
⚑ In New Zealand **New Zealand Automobile Association** ☎ 09/302-1825, 800/500-333 or 800/500-222 ⊕ www.aa.co.nz.
⚑ In the U.K. **Automobile Association (AA)** ☎ 0990/500-600. **Royal Automobile Club (RAC)** ☎ 0990/722-722 for membership, 0345/121-345 for insurance.
⚑ In the U.S. **American Automobile Association** ☎ 800/564-6222.

EMERGENCY SERVICES

In the case of serious accident, immediately pull over to the side of the road and **phone 111.** Emergency phone boxes are not common; you may have to rely on a cellular phone. You will find New Zealanders quick to help if they are able to, particularly if you need to use a phone. Minor accidents are normally sorted out in a calm and collected manner at the side of the road. However, "road rage" is not unknown. If the driver of the other vehicle looks particularly angry or aggressive, you are within your rights to take note of the registration number and then report the accident at the local or nearest police station.

The New Zealand Automobile Association offers emergency road service and is associated with the American Automobile Association (AAA). If you are an AAA member, you will be covered by the service as long as you register in person with a NZAA office in New Zealand and present your membership card.

Should you find yourself at a panel beater (repair shop) after a prang (minor car accident), talking about your vehicle might end up sounding like more of an Abbott and Costello routine if you're not prepared with the appropriate vehicle vernacular.

For instance, you might hear the mechanic say, "Crickey dick! What are ya?! Doing the ton on loose metal when it was hosing down was two sammies short of a picnic. You have a chip in the windscreen, the fender has to be reattached under the boot, and your axle is puckeroo. Pop the bonnet and let's take a look." Translation: "Wow! Are you nuts?! Driving so fast on a gravel road in the rain was crazy (aka two sandwiches short of a picnic). You chipped the windshield, the bumper needs to be reattached under the trunk, and the axle is broken. Pop the hood."

🔝 **New Zealand Automobile Association** ✉ 99 Albert St., Auckland ☎ 09/302-1825, 0800/500-222 or 0800/500-333 toll-free or *222 toll-free from your cell phone ⊕ /www.aa.co.nz.

GASOLINE

On main routes you'll find stations at regular intervals. However, if you're traveling on back roads where the population is sparse **don't let your tank get very low**—it can be a long walk to the nearest helpful farmer if you run out of gas.

The price of gas (Kiwis say "petrol") in New Zealand is more volatile than the fuel itself. At press time prices had recently rocketed from 82¢ per liter to about $1.39 a liter. Credit cards are widely accepted, though not necessarily at small country gas stations, so ask before you fill up.

Unleaded gas is widely available and is often referred to as 91. High-octane unleaded gas is called 96. The 91 is usually a couple of cents cheaper than 96; most rental cars run on 91. Leaded fuel is no longer sold widely in New Zealand, and cars that still run on this require a special additive, available from gas stations. Virtually all gas stations will have staff on hand to pump gas or assist motorists in other ways; however, they tend to have self-service facilities for anyone in a hurry. These are simply operated by pushing numbers on a console to coincide with the dollar value of the gas required. When you pump the gas, the pump will automatically switch off when you have reached the stated amount. Pay at the counter inside the station after you fill your tank. For gas station opening hours, *see* Business Hours, *above*.

ROAD CONDITIONS

Roads are well maintained and generally uncrowded. In rural areas, you may still find some unpaved roads. Unfortunately, signposting, even on major highways, is often poor. On most highways, it's easier to **use the signposted names of upcoming towns to navigate** rather than route numbers. At this writing, there are no toll roads, although one new highway stretching north from Auckland was under consideration for a toll.

Due to the less than flat terrain, many New Zealand roads are "wonky," or crooked. So when mapping out your itinerary, don't plan on averaging 100 kph (62 mph) very often. Expect two or three lanes plus a common center lane on main highways. The common center lane is the passing lane; it's used country-road style, with cars passing while facing oncoming traffic in the opposite lane. There are no special multi-occupant lanes on the major highways. Rural areas still have some one-lane roads. One-lane bridges are common and are sometimes used by trains as well as cars; *see* Rules of the Road, *below*.

Most roads pass through knockout scenery so you may be sorely tempted to look at everything, but keep your eyes on the road. There are plenty of rest areas where you can catch the views; these are marked with a blue sign with a table icon and typically have rest rooms, too. Designated lookout points, marked by light brown signs, will give you even better views. **Keep an eye out for sheep or other animals in the road,** especially in rural areas. If some livestock is sharing the road with you, slow down but don't frighten them by honking the horn. If you injure an animal on the road, you must notify the owner of the animal or a police officer as soon as possible.

New Zealanders are seldom as good at driving as they think they are, so the best policy is just to **keep at a safe distance.** Dangerous overtaking, speeders, lack of indication, and slow drivers in passing lanes are all afflictions you will have to suffer on New Zealand highways. In saying that, driving has improved over recent years due to increased education about speeding and drunk driving and bad driving in general.

ROAD MAPS

Road maps are widely available in gas stations, at airports, and in bookshops around the country; AA maps are reliable bets. Car-rental companies will also hand you a road map on request. In the unlikely event you can't find what you want, contact the New Zealand Automobile Association (⇨ Auto Clubs, *above*).

RULES OF THE ROAD

The speed limit is 100 km per hour (62 mi per hour) on the open road and 50 kph (31 mph) in towns and cities. A circular sign with the letters LSZ (Limited Speed Zone) means speed should be governed by prevailing road conditions but still not exceed 100 kph. **Watch out for speed cameras,** particularly in city suburbs and on approaches to and exits from small towns. The police force (not to mention the money counters) has taken to them with relish. Fines start at about $60 for speeds 10 km (6 mi) over the speed limit.

Right turns are not permitted on red lights. The law states that you must **always wear a seat belt** in New Zealand, whether you are driving or a passenger in a car. You can be fined for any passenger under the age of 15 not wearing a seat belt or approved child restraint if under the age of 5. If you are caught without a seat belt and you are clearly not a New Zealander, the result is likely to be a friendly but firm warning. At this writing, a ban on using hand-held mobile phones while driving was under consideration.

Drunk drivers are not tolerated in New Zealand. The blood alcohol limit is 0.05 (80 milligrams of alcohol per 100 milliliters of blood for adults), and it's safest to **avoid driving altogether if you've had a drink.** If you are caught driving over the limit you will be taken to the nearest police station to dry out and required to pay a high fine. Repeat offences or instances of causing injury or death while under the influence of alcohol are likely to result in jail terms.

When driving in rural New Zealand, cross one-lane bridges with caution—there are plenty of them. A yellow sign on the left will usually warn you that you are approaching a one-lane bridge, and another sign will tell you whether you have the right-of-way. A rectangular blue sign means you have the right-of-way, and a circular sign with a red border means you must pull over to the left and wait to cross until oncoming traffic has passed. Even when you have the right-of-way, slow down and take care. Some one-lane bridges in South Island are used by trains as well as cars. Trains always have the right-of-way.

Roundabouts can be particularly confusing for newcomers. **When entering a roundabout, yield to all vehicles coming from the right.** A blue sign with a white arrow indicates that you should keep to the left of the traffic island as you come up to the roundabout. In a multilane roundabout, stay in the lane closest to the island until ready to exit the circle.

You can only pass on the left if there are two or more lanes on your side of the center line, if the vehicle you are passing has stopped, or if the vehicle ahead is signaling a right turn. At all other times, **you must pass on the right.**

When you encounter fog, remember to drive with low-beamed headlights, as high-beams refract light and decrease visibility. It is illegal to drive with only your parking lights on.

The usual fine for parking over the time limit on meters is $10–$15. In the last few years "pay-and-display" meters have been put up in cities. You'll need to drop a couple of dollars' worth of coins in the meter, take the dispensed ticket, and put it in view on the dashboard of your car. The fine for running over the time for these meters runs about $12, but if you don't display your ticket at all, the fine will be at least $40 and you may risk being towed. So **carry a few coins at all times**—any denomination will usually do. Make sure to observe all NO PARKING signs. If you don't, your car will almost certainly be towed away. It will cost about $100 to have the car released, and most tow companies won't accept anything but cash.

For more road rules and safety tips, check the Land Transport Safety Authority (LTSA) Web site, ⊕ www.ltsa.govt.nz.

TRAFFIC

The only city with a serious congestion problem during rush hour is Auckland, particularly on inner-city motorway on and off ramps. Avoid driving between 7:30 AM and 9 AM, and 5 PM and 6:30 PM. Traffic around other cities, such as Wellington and Christchurch, builds up at these times, too, and it is worth taking this into account if you have important appointments or a plane to catch. Give yourself a spare 15 or 20 minutes to be on the safe side.

CHILDREN IN NEW ZEALAND

New Zealand may not have the high-tech theme parks of many other destinations, but the big appeal for children here is the same as it is for adults: wide, open spaces. The forests are safe to explore (there are no poisonous snakes, spiders, or even poison ivy); remote beaches have secret coves to discover; and there are lakes to kayak on and cool, clear rivers to swim in. Visiting the bubbling geothermal mud pools near Rotorua or going whale-watching in Kaikoura are also perennial kid favorites. But some natural wonders may not be appropriate for your children. For example, the glowworm caves in Waitomo are popular, but some paths into the caves can be a bit treacherous, and small children may find the darkness scary. **Make sure the activities you choose are age-appropriate for your children.** Don't hesitate to ask a tour operator for advice.

Accompany children at all times, especially around water. Many New Zealand beaches are not always safe for swimming, so **watch for signs warning swimmers** of strong currents and undertows. For information on safety in parklands, check out the Department of Conservation's (DOC) pamphlet *Time in the Wild with Children. You can download this pamphlet from www.doc.govt.nz/Explore/Children.asp.*

If you are renting a car, don't forget to **arrange for a car seat** when you reserve. For general advice about traveling with children, consult *Fodor's FYI: Travel with Your Baby* (available in bookstores everywhere).

BABYSITTING

Most hotels and resorts have babysitters available at a charge of around $10–$15 per hour. Babysitting services are also listed in the yellow pages of city telephone directories.

DINING OUT

Children are welcome in all restaurants throughout the country; however, they are rarely seen in those restaurants that appear in Fodor's very expensive ($$$$) and expensive ($$$) price categories. These restaurants may not have high chairs or be prepared to make special children's meals. Besides the run-of-the-mill fast-food franchises such as McDonald's, there are few family chain restaurants in New Zealand. One option is Valentines, a chain of buffet-style restaurants. On the other hand, there are plenty of independently owned cafés that welcome children. Many coffee shops offer a yummy kids' treat called a "fluffy": a mug of steamed milk dusted with cocoa, sometimes served with marshmallows on the side.

Kids Friendly NZ, an excellent Web resource for families, lists many kid-tested, parent-approved dining options throughout the country. This online magazine is updated weekly and also includes information about special family-oriented events. Another family magazine called *Kidz Go!* provides lots of helpful information on travel within the Queenstown, Wanaka, and southern lakes regions.

🔝 Parent Resources Kids Friendly NZ ⊕ www. kidsfriendlynz.com. Kidz Go! ⊕ www.kidzgo.co.nz.

FLYING

If your children are two or older, **ask about children's airfares.** As a general rule, infants under two not occupying a seat fly at greatly reduced fares or even for free. When booking, **confirm carry-on allowances** if you're traveling with infants. In general, for babies charged 10% of the adult fare you are allowed one carry-on bag and a collapsible stroller; if the flight is full, the stroller may have to be checked or you may be limited to less.

Experts agree that it's a good idea to use safety seats aloft for children weighing less than 40 pounds. Airlines set their own policies: U.S. carriers usually require that the child be ticketed, even if he or she is young enough to ride free, since the seats must be strapped into regular seats. Do **check your** airline's policy about using safety seats during takeoff and landing. Safety seats are not allowed everywhere in the plane, so get your seat assignments as early as possible.

When reserving, **request children's meals or a freestanding bassinet** (not available at all airlines) if you need them. But note that bulkhead seats, where you must sit to use the bassinet, may lack an overhead bin or storage space on the floor.

LODGING

Most hotels in New Zealand allow children under a certain age to stay in their parents' room at no extra charge, but others charge for them as extra adults; be sure to **find out the cutoff age for children's discounts.**

In hotels, roll-away beds are usually free, but few hotels have other separate facilities for children.

Home hosting provides an ideal opportunity for visitors to stay with a local family, either in town or on a working farm. For information on home and farm stays, home exchange, and apartment rentals, *see* Lodging, *below.*

SIGHTS & ATTRACTIONS

Many city attractions are increasingly child-friendly, with museums adding "discovery" centers where young people can have hands-on learning experiences. These and other sights and attractions of special interest to children are highlighted in this book by a ☺ icon in the margin.

SUPPLIES & EQUIPMENT

Baby products such as disposable diapers (ask for napkins or nappies), formula, and baby food can be found in chemists' shops (pharmacies). They are less expensive in supermarkets. The Plunket Society, a non-profit organization, can direct you to health-care facilities in each region and provide you with contacts for renting or purchasing any supplies you might need for your child while traveling. Take note: a "crib" refers to a New Zealander's summer cottage, so if you ask for one you might be renting more than you bargained for! Instead, request a cot.

🔝 Stroller & Bassinet Rental **The Plunket Society** ✉ 5 Alexis Ave., Mt. Albert, Auckland ☎ 0800/ 933-922 or 09/849-5652 ⊕ www.plunket.org.nz.

COMPUTERS ON THE ROAD

Traveling with a laptop does not present any problems in New Zealand, where the electricity supply is reliable. However, you will need a converter and adapter as with other electronic equipment (⇨ Electricity, *below*). It pays to **carry a spare battery and adapter,** since they're expensive and can be hard to replace.

City hotels and even provincial hotels and motels are well equipped to handle computers and modems. You may get a little stuck in family-run bed-and-breakfasts and farm stays in remote areas, but even these places will probably be able to sort something out for you.

CONSULATES & EMBASSIES

In Auckland, the Australian and Canadian consulates are open from 8:30 until just before 5 on weekdays. The British and U.S. consulates are open only from 9:30 until around 12:30 on weekdays.

In Wellington, the Australian High Commission is open weekdays 8:45–12:15; the Canadian High Commission is open weekdays 8:30–4:30; the British High Commission is open weekdays 9:30–noon and 2–3:30; and the United States Embassy is open weekdays 10–noon and 2–4.

🏴 Australia **Australian Consulate** ✉ Level 7, PricewaterhouseCoopers Tower, 188 Quay St., city center ☎ 09/921-8800 **Australian High Commission** ✉ 72-78 Hobson St., Thorndon, Wellington ☎ 04/473-6411 ⊕ www.australia.org.nz

🏴 Canada **Canadian Consulate** ✉ Jetset Centre, 48 Emily Pl. ☎ 09/309-3690. **Canadian High Commission** ✉ 61 Molesworth St., Thorndon, Wellington ☎ 04/473-9577.

🏴 United Kingdom **British Consulate** ✉ Level 17, IAG House, 151 Queen St. ☎ 09/303-2973. **British High Commission** ✉ 44 Hill St., Thorndon, Wellington ☎ 04/924-2888.

🏴 United States **U.S. Consulate** ✉ Level 3, Citibank Centre, 23 Customs St. E ☎ 09/303-2724. **United States Embassy** ✉ 29 Fitzherbert Terr., Thorndon, Wellington ☎ 04/462-6000.

CONSUMER PROTECTION

Whether you're shopping for gifts or purchasing travel services, **pay with a major credit card** whenever possible, so you can cancel payment or get reimbursed if there's a problem (and you can provide documentation). If you're doing business with a particular company for the first time, **contact your local Better Business Bureau and the attorneys general offices** in your state and (for U.S. businesses) the company's home state as well. Have any complaints been filed? Finally, if you're buying a package or tour, always **consider travel insurance** that includes default coverage (⇨ Insurance, *below*).

🛂 BBBs **Council of Better Business Bureaus** ✉ 4200 Wilson Blvd., Suite 800, Arlington, VA 22203 ☎ 703/276-0100 🖷 703/525-8277 ⊕ www. bbb.org.

CRUISE TRAVEL

Auckland's bright cruise depot, opened in 2001, reflects the upswing in the cruising industry in recent years. Since the 1990s more companies have been drawn to Auckland's superb harbor, as well as to the gorgeous scenery in places such as the Bay of Islands and Marlborough Sounds. New Zealand is now included on world-cruise itineraries by vessels such as Cunard's *QEII,* Crystal Cruises' *Crystal Serenity,* Radisson Seven Seas Cruise's *Seven Seas Voyager,* and Norwegian Cruise Line's *The Amsterdam,* but some of the best cruising programs are those that concentrate entirely on the South Pacific and combine New Zealand with destinations such as Fiji, New Caledonia, Tonga, and Samoa. Generally, such cruises start and finish in Auckland and visit South Pacific islands in between.

The Princess Cruises vessels *Sapphire Princess,* and *Diamond Princess* are joining the scene. P&O Holidays operates *Pacific Sky,* which runs about six cruises out of Auckland from May to July, as well as fly-and-cruise packages out of Auckland with Sydney as the ship's departure point. The "Land of Legends" cruise covers New Zealand most thoroughly, visiting Auckland, Tauranga, Christchurch, Dunedin, and Milford Sound. Another choice is the Holland America Line vessel *Prinsendam,* with its 16-day cruises around New Zealand and Australia between late November and mid-February. The cruises visit eight or nine New Zealand ports, plus three or four in Australia.

Seabourn's *Seabourn Spirit* offers a series of cruises exploring both the North and South Island; in 2006 the port of Gisborne will be added to their route. Silversea Cruises sends the *Silver Cloud* through Milford Sound to Stewart Island, Dunedin, Christchurch, Picton, Napier, and Auckland. The Clipper Cruise Line sends smaller ships through Doubtful and Dusky sounds and hits Dunedin, Akaroa, Wellington, and Napier among other stops.

To learn how to plan, choose, and book a cruise-ship voyage, consult *Fodor's FYI: Plan & Enjoy Your Cruise* (available in bookstores everywhere).

🛂 Cruise Lines **Clipper Cruise Line** ☎ 800/325-0010 or 314/655-6700 ⊕ www.clippercruise.com. **Crystal Cruises** ☎ 800/804-1500 or 310/785-9300 ⊕ www.crystalcruises.com. **Cunard** ☎ 800/728-6273 ⊕ www.cunard.com. **Holland America Line** ☎ 877/724-5425 ⊕ www.hollandamerica.com. **Norwegian Cruise Line** ⊕ www.ncl.com. **P & O Cruises** ☎ 0800/441-766, or 0800/951-200 in New Zealand ⊕ www.pocruises.com.au. **Radisson Seven Seas Cruises** ☎ 800/774-6237 ⊕ www.princesscruises. com. **Silversea Cruises** ⊕ www.silversea.com. **Seabourn** ☎ 800/929-9391 ⊕ www.seabourn.com.

CUSTOMS & DUTIES

When shopping abroad, **keep receipts** for all purchases. Upon reentering the country, **be ready to show customs officials what you've bought.** If you feel a duty is incorrect, appeal the assessment. If you object to the way your clearance was handled, note the inspector's badge number. In either case, first ask to see a supervisor. If the problem isn't resolved, write to the appropriate authorities, beginning with the port director at your point of entry.

IN AUSTRALIA

Australian residents who are 18 or older may bring home A$900 worth of souvenirs and gifts (including jewelry), 250 cigarettes or 250 grams of cigars or other tobacco products, and 2.25 liters of alcohol (including wine, beer, and spirits). Residents under 18 may bring back A$450 worth of goods. If any of these individual allowances are exceeded, you must pay duty for the entire amount (of the group of products in which the allowance was exceeded). Members of the same family traveling together may pool their allowances. Prohibited items include meat products. Seeds, plants, and fruits need to be declared upon arrival.

🔳 **Australian Customs Service** ✏️ Locked Bag 3000, Sydney International Airport, Sydney, NSW 2020 ☎ 02/6275-6666 or 1300/363263, 02/8334-7444 or 1800/020-504 quarantine-inquiry line 🖷 02/8339-6714 🌐 www.customs.gov.au.

IN CANADA

Canadian residents who have been out of Canada for at least seven days may bring in C$750 worth of goods duty-free. If you've been away fewer than seven days but more than 48 hours, the duty-free allowance drops to C$200. If your trip lasts 24 to 48 hours, the allowance is C$50; if the goods are worth more than C$50, you must pay full duty on all of the goods. You may not pool allowances with family members. Goods claimed under the C$750 exemption may follow you by mail; those claimed under the lesser exemptions must accompany you. Alcohol and tobacco products may be included in the 7 -day and 48-hour exemptions but not in the 24-hour exemption. If you meet the age requirements of the province or territory through which you reenter Canada, you may bring in, duty-free, 1.5 liters of wine *or* 1.14 liters (40 imperial ounces) of liquor *or* 24 12-ounce cans or bottles of beer or ale. Also, if you meet the local age requirement for tobacco products, you may bring in, duty-free, 200 cigarettes, 50 cigars or cigarillos, and 200 grams of tobacco. You may have to pay a minimum duty on tobacco products, regardless of whether or not you exceed your personal exemption. Check ahead of time with the Canada Border Services Agency or the Department of Agriculture for policies regarding meat products, seeds, plants, and fruits.

You may send an unlimited number of gifts (only one gift per recipient, however) worth up to C$60 each duty-free to Canada. Label the package UNSOLICITED GIFT—VALUE UNDER $60. Alcohol and tobacco are excluded.

🔳 **Canada Customs and Revenue Agency** ✉ 2265 St. Laurent Blvd. S, Ottawa, Ontario K1G 4K3 ☎ 204/983-3500, 506/636-5064, or 800/461-9999 🌐 www.ccra-adrc.gc.ca/.

IN NEW ZEALAND

New Zealand has stringent regulations governing the import of weapons, foodstuffs, and certain plant and animal material. Anti-drug laws are strict and penalties severe. In addition to personal effects, nonresidents over 17 years of age may bring in, duty-free, 200 cigarettes or 250 grams of tobacco or 50 cigars, 4.5 liters of wine, one bottle containing not more than 1,125 ml of spirits or liqueur, and personal purchases and gifts up to the value of US$440 (NZ$700).

Don't stash any fruit in your carry-on to take into the country. The agricultural quarantine is serious business, and you'll be hit with an instant $250 fine if you're caught bringing in even an undeclared piece of fruit. So if you've been hiking recently and are bringing your boots with you, clean them before you pack. Since the foot-and-mouth-disease outbreak in the United Kingdom and Europe in 2000–2001, as well as terrorist attacks in the United States, airport officers have become even more vigilant and all bags coming into the country are X-rayed. The authorities for very good reason don't want any nonnative seeds haplessly transported into the country. It's a small and fragile ecosystem, and Kiwis rightfully want to protect it.

IN THE U.K.

From countries outside the European Union, including New Zealand, you may bring home, duty-free, 200 cigarettes or 50 cigars; 1 liter of spirits or 2 liters of fortified or sparkling wine or liqueurs; 2 liters of still table wine; 60 ml of perfume; 250 ml of toilet water; plus £145 worth of other goods, including gifts and souvenirs. Prohibited items include meat products, seeds, plants, and fruits.

🔳 **HM Customs and Excise** ✉ Portcullis House, 21 Cowbridge Rd. E, Cardiff CF11 9SS ☎ 029/2038-6423 or 0845/010-9000 🌐 www.hmce.gov.uk.

IN THE U.S.

U.S. residents who have been out of the country for at least 48 hours may bring home, for personal use, $400 worth of foreign goods duty-free, as long as they haven't used the $400 allowance or any part of it in the past 30 days. This exemption may include 1 liter of alcohol (for travelers 21 and older), 200 cigarettes, and 100 non-Cuban cigars. Family members from the same household who are traveling together may pool their $400 personal exemptions. For fewer than 48 hours, the duty-free allowance drops to $200, which may include 50 cigarettes, 10 non-Cuban cigars, and 150 ml of alcohol (or perfume containing alcohol). The $200 allowance cannot be combined with other individuals' exemptions, and if you exceed it, the full value of all the goods will be taxed. Antiques, which the U.S. Customs Service defines as objects more than 100 years old, enter duty-free, as do original works of art done entirely by hand, including paintings, drawings, and sculptures.

You may also send packages home duty-free, with a limit of one parcel per addressee per day (except alcohol or tobacco products or perfume worth more than $5). You can mail up to $200 worth of goods for personal use; label the package PERSONAL USE and attach a list of its contents and their retail value. If the package contains your used personal belongings, mark it PERSONAL GOODS RETURNED to avoid paying duties. You may send up to $100 worth of goods as a gift; mark the package UNSOLICITED GIFT. Mailed items do not affect your duty-free allowance on your return.

🛈 **U.S. Customs Service** for inquiries and complaints ✉ 1300 Pennsylvania Ave. NW, Washington, DC 20229 ⊕ www.customs.gov ☎ 877/227-5551, 202/354-1000.

DISABILITIES & ACCESSIBILITY

Mclaren Brown publishes *Accessible New Zealand*, listing accommodations, attractions, restaurants, and thermal pools with special facilities. Among the community organizations, a good contact is Enable New Zealand, which has some pertinent travel information for people with disabilities. The Disability Resource Centre (DRC) in Auckland has networking contacts and information on local services. These two organizations collaborated to create ⊕ www.weka.net.nz, a national resources Web site that covers news bulletins and community events.

🛈 Local Resources **Disability Resource Organization** ✉ 14 Erson Ave. Royal Oak ☎ 09/625-8069 or 0800/693-342 ⊕ www.disabilityresource.org.nz. **Enable New Zealand** ✉ 60 Bennett St. Palmerston North ☎ 06/952-0011 or 0800/362-253 ⊕ www.enable.co.nz. **New Zealand Tourism Board** ☎ 04/472-8860 ⊕ www.newzealand.com.

AIR TRAVEL

In addition to making arrangements for wheelchair-using passengers, Qantas accommodates trained dogs accompanying passengers with sight and hearing impairments. On Air New Zealand, wheelchairs for in-flight mobility are standard equipment; seat-belt extensions, quadriplegic harnesses, and padded leg rests are also available. To find out more about the services available for people requiring special assistance, go to www.airnz.co.nz/travelinfo/travelsupport/specialassistance/.

The U.S. Department of Transportation Aviation Consumer Protection Division's online publication *New Horizons: Information for the Air Traveler with a Disability* offers advice for travelers with a disability, and outlines basic rights. Visit DisabilityInfo.gov for general information.

🛈 Information and Complaints **Aviation Consumer Protection Division** (⇨ Air Travel) for airline-related problems; ⊕ airconsumer.ost.dot.gov/publications/horizons.htm for airline travel advice and rights. **Departmental Office of Civil Rights** ✉ For general inquiries, U.S. Department of Transportation, S-30, 400 7th St. SW, Room 10215, Washington, DC 20590 ☎ 202/366-4648, 202/366-8538 TTY 📠 202/366-9371 ⊕ www.dotcr.ost.dot.gov. **Disability Rights Section** ✉ NYAV, U.S. Department of Justice, Civil Rights Division, 950 Pennsylvania Ave. NW, Washington, DC 20530 ☎ ADA information line 202/514-0301, 800/514-0301, 202/514-0383 TTY, 800/514-0383 TTY ⊕ www.ada.gov. **U.S. Department of Transportation Hotline** ☎ For disability-related air-travel problems, 800/778-4838 or 800/455-9880 TTY.

CAR RENTAL

Budget offers cars fitted with hand controls, but these are limited. Hertz will fit hand-held controls onto standard cars in some cities. *See* Car Rental, *above.* New Zealand CCS (⊕ www.ccs.org.nz), a New Zealand–based service provider for people with physical disabilities, can supply the temporary disabled parking permits needed for using specified parking places.

LODGING

In New Zealand, all accommodations are required by law to provide at least one room with facilities for guests with disabilities. Even independent lodgings with more than eight rooms should provide at least one room with such facilities. The major hotel chains provide three or four rooms with facilities for guests with disabilities in most of their properties.

RESERVATIONS

When discussing accessibility with an operator or reservations agent, **ask hard questions.** Are there any stairs, inside *or* out? Are there grab bars next to the toilet *and* in the shower/tub? How wide is the doorway to the room? To the bathroom? For the most extensive facilities meeting the latest legal specifications, **opt for newer accommodations.** If you reserve through a toll-free number, consider also calling the hotel's local number to confirm the information from the central reservations office. Get confirmation in writing when you can.

TAXIS

Companies have recently introduced vans equipped with hoists and floor clamps, but these should be booked several hours in advance if possible; refer to the ⇨ Local Resources *above* for more information. As the Plunket Society (⇨ Children in New Zealand, *above*) organization specializes in providing families with health services in New Zealand, it can also be a useful resource for other information.

TRANSPORTATION

Passengers on mainline passenger trains in New Zealand can request collapsible wheelchairs to negotiate narrow interior corridors. However, compact toilet areas and platform-access problems make long-distance train travel difficult.

InterCity and Newmans bus lines are equipped to serve travelers with most disabilities. However, wheelchairs can only be accommodated if they're manual and you must have someone accompanying you. (Electric wheelchairs are not allowed because they cannot be lifted into a bus un-

aided.) There are some smaller operators who specialize in servicing wheelchair passengers. EasyRider Tours, for instance, can transport several travelers with wheelchairs for charter services.

Many buses in the main cities are wheelchair-accessible via ramps and a "kneeling" ability; they don't have lifts. The interisland ferries have gangways with gentle incline ramps, lifts, and staff to aid passengers with special needs once onboard.

⚑ Local Resource **EasyRider Tours** ☎ 07/ 829-8925 ⊕ www.easyrider.co.nz.

TRAVEL AGENCIES

In the United States, the Americans with Disabilities Act requires that travel firms serve the needs of all travelers. Some agencies specialize in working with people with disabilities.

⚑ Travelers with Mobility Problems **Access Adventures** ✉ 206 Chestnut Ridge Rd., Scottsville, NY 14624 ☎ 716/889-9096 ✉ dltravel@prodigy.net, run by a former physical-rehabilitation counselor. **Flying Wheels Travel** ✉ 143 W. Bridge St. ⌂ Box 382, Owatonna, MN 55060 ☎ 507/451-5005 🖷 507/451-1685 ⊕ www.flyingwheelstravel.com.

DISCOUNTS & DEALS

Be a smart shopper and **compare all your options** before making decisions. A plane ticket bought with a promotional coupon from travel clubs, coupon books, and direct-mail offers or purchased on the Internet may not be cheaper than the least expensive fare from a discount-ticket agency. And always keep in mind that what you get is just as important as what you save.

Look into the New Zealand Travelpass to save money by combining bus, ferry, and train costs. The Travelpass has no fixed itineraries and gives you 3,000 different stops to choose from. You choose from a certain number of days of travel and kinds of transportation; there's also an option to tack on air travel. Most Travelpasses are valid for one year, the bus-only version is valid for unlimited travel on InterCity and Newmans coaches over a one-, two- or three-month period, with an incremental-rate structure. You can purchase an open-ended pass from your travel agent prior to leaving and then call the Travelpass reservations center to make reservations.

The Tranz Scenic rail service also has a couple of deals worth checking out, including ThroughFares, which combine Tranz Scenic train trips with SoundsAir flights and the Interislander ferries.

If the outdoors are calling your name, you can save on over a 100 different activities as well as things like car rentals and hotels with the New Zealand Outdoors Card (NZO Card. The NZO card is a discount card which comes free with *New Zealand Outside Annual and Directory* an annually published directory of activities, accommodation, and wineries, along with articles about travel in New Zealand. You can buy the publication for $15 from most magazine and bookstores. You can also buy the discount card by itself from the NZO Web site (www.nzoutside.com/discount) for $10, although the card won't come with the list of places that offer discounts.

When hitting local visitor centers, be sure to **browse the display racks for brochures with discounts.** Visitor bureaus stock booklets with coupons for local restaurants and attractions throughout the region.

🖪 Discount Resources **New Zealand Travelpass** ☎ 09/638-5782 or 0800/339-966 🌐 www.travelpass.co.nz. **Tranz Scenic** ☎ 04/495-0775 or 0800/872-467 🌐 www.tranzscenic.co.nz.

DISCOUNT RESERVATIONS

To save money, **look into discount reservations services** with Web sites and toll-free numbers, which use their buying power to get a better price on hotels, airline tickets, even car rentals. When booking a room, always **call the hotel's local toll-free number** (if one is available) rather than the central reservations number—you'll often get a better price. Always ask about special packages or corporate rates.

When shopping for the best deal on hotels and car rentals, **look for guaranteed exchange rates,** which protect you against a falling dollar. With your rate locked in, you won't pay more, even if the price goes up in the local currency.

🖪 Hotel Rooms **Accommodations Express** ☎ 800/444-7666 or 800/277-1064. **Hotels.com**

☎ 800/246-8357 🌐 www.hotels.com. **Turbotrip. com** ☎ 800/473-7829 🌐 www.turbotrip.com.

PACKAGE DEALS

Don't confuse packages and guided tours. When you buy a package, you travel on your own, just as though you had planned the trip yourself. Fly-drive packages, which combine airfare and car rental, are often a good deal.

EATING & DRINKING

The restaurants we list are the cream of the crop in each price category. Properties indicated by an ✕🏠 are lodging establishments whose restaurant warrants a special trip and welcomes nonovernight guests.

Some restaurants offer a fixed-price dinner, but the majority are à la carte. Remember that "entrée" in Kiwi English is the equivalent of an appetizer. It's wise to make a reservation and inquire if the restaurant has a liquor license or is "BYOB" or "BYO" (Bring Your Own Bottle)—many places have both. By the way, this only pertains to wine, not bottles of beer or liquor. **Be prepared to pay a corkage fee,** which is usually a couple of dollars.

Many restaurants add a 15% surcharge on public holidays. Employers are required by law to pay staff a higher wage during these holidays, and the cost gets shared with the customer. This amount will be itemized separately on your bill.

New Zealand's *Cuisine* magazine has a special annual issue devoted to restaurants throughout the country; hit their Web site, 🌐 www.cuisine.co.nz, if you'd like to get a copy before your trip. There are also a few helpful New Zealand dining Web sites worth a look. Through some, you can make online reservations. These include 🌐 www.cup.co.nz, an independent nationwide café guide; 🌐 www.dineout.co.nz, a national database with customer reviews; and 🌐 www.menus.co.nz, which posts photos and menus of restaurants in Auckland and Wellington.

MEALS & SPECIALTIES

When in New Zealand, **have a little lamb.** No matter where you go in the country, it's sure to be there on the menu. Cervena, or farm-raised venison, is another local delicacy available all over New Zealand, and farmed ostrich is gaining popularity as well.

In New Zealand restaurants, many vegetables have two names, used interchangeably. Eggplants are often called aubergines, zucchini are also known as courgettes. The vegetable North Americans know as a bell pepper is a capsicum here.

Don't miss a Māori *hāngi*. This culinary experience can be loosely compared to a family barbecue (hosted by a family that likes to do a lot of dancing and singing). The traditional preparation involves steaming meat, seafood, and vegetables in a large underground pit, and the meal is accompanied by Māori performances. See the "Dinner on the Rocks" CloseUp box in Chapter 4. Also be sure to try *kūmara,* an indigenous sweet potato that's sacred to the Māori.

Of course, seafood is a specialty, and one of the tastiest fish around is snapper. Grouper (often listed by its Māori name of *hapuku*), flounder, and salmon are also menu toppers, as is whitebait, the juvenile of several fish species, in spring. As for shellfish: **try the Bluff oysters** (in season March–August), Greenshell mussels (also known as green-lipped or New Zealand green mussels), scallops, crayfish (spiny lobster), and local clamlike shellfish, *pipi* and *tuatua.* For more on native foods, see the "Something to Chew On" CloseUp box in Chapter 5.

Burgers are a staple for a quick bite. However, you'll find there's a whole lot more than two all-beef patties between your bun—one of the most popular toppings is beetroot. Another Kiwi snack staple, meat pies, are sold just about everywhere. The classic steak-and-mince fillings are getting gussied up these days with combinations like steak and cheese and steak and oysters. And who could forget good ol' fish-and-chips in this former British colony? Appropriately called "greasies," this mainstay is often made of shark but called lemon fish or flake.

Lemon & Paeroa, otherwise known as L&P, is New Zealand's most famous soft drink. If you've got a sweet tooth, **nibble a chocolate fish,** a chocolate-covered fish-shaped marshmallow. This treat has become so popular in New Zealand that it's now synonymous with success. You'll often hear someone say, "you deserve a chocolate fish!" in place of "job well done!" Hokey pokey, a lacy honey toffee, is another favorite candy. And if you're traveling in the heat of the summer, don't leave town until you've tried a hokey pokey ice cream, another New Zealand mainstay. If you want to try a truly unique bit of New Zealand grub, and we do mean grub, taste the larvae of the huhu beetle.

MEALTIMES

Restaurants serve breakfast roughly between 7 and 9:30. Lunch usually starts up at about noon and is over by 2. Dinners are usually served from 5 PM onward, but the most popular dining time is around 7. Restaurants in cities and resort areas will serve dinner well into the night, but some places in small towns or rural areas still shut their doors at around 9.

Unless otherwise noted, the restaurants listed in this guide are open daily for lunch and dinner.

PAYING

Credit cards are widely accepted in restaurants and even small cafés. You may find exceptions to this rule, so check first. In some areas, American Express and Diners Club cards are accepted far less frequently than MasterCard and Visa.

RESERVATIONS & DRESS

Reservations are always a good idea; we mention them only when they're essential or not accepted. Book as far ahead as you can, and reconfirm as soon as you arrive. (Large parties should always call ahead to check the reservations policy.)

Attire countrywide is pretty casual; unless you're planning to dine at the finest of places, men won't need to bring a jacket and tie. At the same time, the most common dinner attire is usually a notch above jeans and T shirts. We specify dress only when men are required to wear a jacket or a jacket and tie.

WINE, BEER & SPIRITS

New Zealand's wine industry has leaped forward over the last decade. Best known for its white wines, particularly sauvignon blanc, riesling, and chardonnay, the country is now gaining a reputation for red wines such as cabernet sauvignon, pinot noir, and merlot. The main wine-producing areas are West Auckland, Hawke's Bay, Martinborough, Marlborough, and Nelson. Emerging regions include Canterbury and central Otago. Restaurants almost without exception feature New Zealand products on their wine list. For a rundown on New Zealand's wine industry, *see* "News from the Grapevine" *in* Chapter 7.

When ordering a beer, you'll get either a handle (mug) or a one-liter jug (pitcher). To get beer served in a glass, you have to request it. Only 15 years ago people ordering a beer in New Zealand had a choice of two—Lion Red or DB Draught. Now those two breweries have substantially improved their range, and small microbreweries have added to the mix. Monteith Breweries and Macs are South Island–based breweries that distribute around the country and have a strong local following. Steinlager, probably the most famous of New Zealand beers, is brewed by Lion Breweries and is widely available. The boutique beers Loaded Hog and One Red Dog are on many restaurant menus, too. Most restaurants and liquor stores sell beers from Australia, the United States, Europe, and other parts of the world. Some of the beer in New Zealand is stronger than the 4% alcohol per volume brew that is the norm in the United States. Many go up to 7% or 8% alcohol per volume, so check that number before downing your usual number of drinks.

New Zealand only has a couple of spirits it can really call its own. One is Wilson's Whisky, distilled in Dunedin—a city with a strong Scottish heritage. Another popular drink is 42 Below. With its claim to fame as "the world's southernmost vodka," 42 Below incorporates local flavors: feijoa, manuka honey, passionfruit, and kiwifruit. Most inner-city bars will have it on the menu if you want to try before you buy a bottle; and having won a slew of gold and silver medals at international wine and spirit competitions around the world, it makes a cool duty-free gift to bring back to vodka connoisseurs back home. You'll also sometimes find sticky-sweet kiwifruit or feijoa liqueurs.

Since 1999 it has been possible to purchase beer and wine in supermarkets as well as specialized shops and to do so seven days a week. People under 18 are not permitted by law to purchase alcohol, and shops, bars, and restaurants strictly enforce this. If you look younger than you are, carry photo identification to prove your age.

ECOTOURISM

For anyone passionate about the natural world, a journey to New Zealand offers the chance to step back in time to a primeval era. Isolated from other landmasses for at least 80 million years, New Zealand has enormous biological diversity.

Learn about local flora and fauna with eco-sensitive tour operators from the 100% Pure Nature network, a group that works with Tourism New Zealand to promote nature tourism. These are knowledgeable tour operators who are actively involved in conservation.

When visiting national parks, remember that you will need to pack out your garbage.

🔲 100% Nature Eco-Tourism Operators **Akaroa Harbour Cruises** ✉ Akaroa ☎ 03/304–7641 ⊕ www.blackcat.co.nz. **Bush & Beach** ✉ Auckland ☎ 09/575–1458 ⊕ www.bushandbeach.co.nz. **Dolphin Discoveries** ✉ Bay of Islands ☎ 09/402–8234 ⊕ www.dolphinz.co.nz. **Guided Nature Walks** ✉ Queenstown ☎ 03/442–7126 ⊕ www.nzwalks. com. **Heritage Expeditions Ltd.** ✉ Christchurch ☎ 03/338–9944 ⊕ www.heritage-expeditions.com. **Kiwi Dundee Adventures** ✉ Coromandel ☎ 07/865–8809 ⊕ www.kiwidundee.co.nz. **Monarch Wildlife Cruises** ✉ Dunedin ☎ 03/477–4276 ⊕ www.wildlife.co.nz. **Mt. Bruce National Wildlife Center** ✉ Masterton ☎ 06/375–8004 ⊕ www.mtbruce.org.nz. **Nature Connection** ✉ Rotorua ☎ 07/347–1705. **Nature Guides Otago** ✉ Dunedin ☎ 03/454–5169 ⊕ www.natureguidesotago.co.nz. **100% Pure Nature Network** ⊕ www.purenz.com. **Otago Peninsula Trust** ✉ Dunedin ☎ 03/476–1775. **Penguin Place** ✉ Dunedin ☎ 03/478–0286 ⊕ www.penguin-place.co.nz. **Waimangu Valley** ✉ Rotorua ☎ 07/366–6137 ⊕ www.waimangu. com. **Whalewatch Kaikoura** ✉ Kaikoura ☎ 03/319–5045 ⊕ www.whalewatch.co.nz. **Wilderness Lodge Arthur's Pass** ✉ Canterbury ☎ 03/318–9246 ⊕ www.wildernesslodge.co.nz.

ELECTRICITY

To use your U.S.-purchased electric-powered equipment, **bring a converter and adapter.** If you forget to pack one, you'll find a selection on sale at duty-free shops in Auckland's airport and at electrical shops around the city. The electrical current in New Zealand is 240 volts, 50 cycles alternating current (AC); wall outlets take slanted three-prong plugs (but not the U.K. three-prong) and plugs with two flat prongs set at a "V" angle.

If your appliances are dual-voltage, you'll need only an adapter. Don't use 110-volt outlets, marked FOR SHAVERS ONLY, for high-wattage appliances such as blow-dryers. Most laptops operate equally well on 110 and 220 volts and therefore only require an adapter.

EMBASSIES

🛐 Australia ✉ 72-78 Hobson St., Wellington
☎ 04/473-6411.
🛐 Canada ✉ 61 Molesworth St., Wellington
☎ 04/473-9577.
🛐 U.K. ✉ 44 Hill St., Wellington ☎ 04/924-2888.
🛐 U.S. ✉ 29 Fitzherbert Terr., Wellington ☎ 04/462-6000.

EMERGENCIES

For either fire, police, or ambulance services, **dial 111.**
🛐 ☎ 111.

ETIQUETTE

In general, Kiwis are accommodating folk who are more likely to good-naturedly tease you about a cultural faux pas than to take offence, but there are a few etiquette points to keep in mind. First, the word "kiwi" refers to either people (New Zealanders) or to the protected kiwi bird, but not the kiwifruit. Also, don't lump New Zealanders in with Australians. A New Zealand accent does not sound just like an Australian one, or a British accent for that matter, and a Kiwi will be the first to point this out. For tips on how to distinguish between these accents, *see* Language, *below.*

Be considerate of Māori traditions. For instance, *marae,* the area in front of a meeting house, should not be entered unless you are invited, or unless it's in use as a cultural center. Also, it's best not to use *hongi* (touching foreheads and noses in greeting) unless someone initiates it. For more on Māori traditions, *see* the Understanding New Zealand chapter.

If you're visiting someone's house, take along a small gift. Among gestures, avoid the "V" symbol with the first two fingers with the palm facing in—an offensive vulgarity.

In the business world, people try to be right on time for meetings, and call ahead if they're running late. First-name usage is the norm.

FERRY TRAVEL

To travel between North Island and South Island take Tranz Scenic's Interislander ferry or the Bluebridge ferry between Wellington and Picton. Both ferries carry cars. They also connect with Tranz Scenic's trains, and a free shuttle is available between the railway station and ferry terminal in both Wellington and Picton. The Interislander travels five–six times a day; Bluebridge, twice daily. Standard one-way fare can be as much as $70, but there are off-peak deals to be had for as low as $39. The fare for a medium-size sedan costs around $200. Be sure to ask about specials, including ferry-train package deals through Tranz Scenic, when you book. For package ideas that include ferry travel, *see* Discounts & Deals, *above.*

FARES & SCHEDULES

Schedules are available at train stations and visitor-information centers around the country. Most will arrange Interislander ferry bookings. You can also check schedules and fares and book online via the Interislander Web site. Some fares allow you to make schedule changes up to the last minute and guarantee a full refund if you cancel prior to check-in. Discount fares can be booked once in New Zealand; these have some restrictions. No matter how you go about it, it's a good idea to reserve in advance, especially during holiday periods.
🛐 Ferry Information **Tranz Scenic Interislander**
☎ 04/498-3302, 0800/802-802 toll-free in New Zealand ⊕ www.interislander.co.nz.
Bluebridge ☎ 0800/844-844 toll-free in New Zealand ⊕ www.bluebridge.co.nz.

GAY & LESBIAN TRAVEL

In 1993, discrimination on the grounds of sexual orientation was deemed illegal in New Zealand, and in 2002, passage of the Property ("Relationships") Bill recognized gay relationships of three years or more in all property issues. In December 2004, by a margin of 65 votes to 55, the New Zealand Government passed the Civil Union Bill, which recognizes unions between same-sex couples (as well as women and men who don't wish to marry). The law, which came into effect in April 2005, provides unmarried couples with the same legal rights as married couples. Overall, Kiwis are as accepting and tolerant as their legislature.

Auckland is the hub of gay life; many gay-friendly spots are on and around Ponsonby Road. Other strong gay communities can be found in Wellington, Christchurch, and Dunedin. Even in smaller towns, though, people don't get too worked up about same-sex couples staying in a hotel room together.

Auckland hosts a major annual gay-pride event, Hero Festival, in February, with three weeks full of parties and social gatherings. Out Takes Lesbian & Gay Film Festival is also held in Auckland as well as Wellington, Dunedin, and Christchurch in late May and early June.

The New Zealand Gay & Lesbian Tourism Association (NZGLTA) has created a network of gay-, lesbian- and bisexual-friendly accommodations, tour operators, and other organizations in the tourism industry. Their Web site provides links to these establishments, and lists activities and events. The Gay Tourism New Zealand Web site also has helpful links, with everything from skiing events to a gay-friendly bus company. The popular daily news Web site, ⊕ www. gayNZ.com posts articles, nightlife listings, support group contacts, and more.

🗐 Local Resources **Gay Tourism New Zealand** ☎ 04/917-9176 ⊕ www.gaytourismnewzealand. com. **NZGLTA** ☎ 09/917-9184 ⊕ http://www. gaynewzealandvacations.com/nzglta.

🗐 Gay- & Lesbian-Friendly Travel Agencies **Different Roads Travel** ✉ 1017 N. LaCienega Blvd., Suite 308, West Hollywood, CA 90069 ☎ 310/289-6000 or 800/429-8747 (Ext. 14 for both) 🖷 310/855-

0323 ✍ lgernert@tzell.com. **Kennedy Travel** ✉ 130 W. 42nd St., Suite 401, New York, NY 10036 ☎ 800/237-7433 or 212/840-8659 🖷 212/730-2269 ⊕ www.kennedytravel.com. **Now, Voyager** ✉ 4406 18th St., San Francisco, CA 94114 ☎ 415/626-1169 or 800/255-6951 🖷 415/626-8626 ⊕ www. nowvoyager.com. **Skylink Travel and Tour/Flying Dutchmen Travel** ✉ 1455 N. Dutton Ave., Suite A, Santa Rosa, CA 95401 ☎ 707/546-9888 or 800/225-5759 🖷 707/636-0951; serving lesbian travelers.

HEALTH

General health standards in New Zealand are high, and it would be hard to find a more pristine natural environment.

The major health hazard in New Zealand is sunburn or sunstroke. Even people who are not normally bothered by strong sun should cover up with a long-sleeve shirt, a hat, and pants or a beach wrap. At higher altitudes you will burn more easily, so **apply sunscreen liberally** before you go out—even for a half hour—and wear a visor or sunglasses.

Dehydration is another serious danger that can be easily avoided, so be sure to carry water and drink often. **Limit the amount of time you spend in the sun** for the first few days until you are acclimatized, and avoid sunbathing in the middle of the day.

DIVERS' ALERT
Do not fly within 24 hours of scuba diving.

PESTS

There are no venomous snakes, and the only native poisonous spider, the *katipo*, is a rarity. The whitetail spider, an unwelcome and accidental import from Australia, packs a nasty bite and can cause discomfort but is also rarely encountered.

One New Zealander you will come to loathe is the tiny black sand fly, common to the western half of South Island, which inflicts a painful bite that can itch for several days (some call it the state bird). In other parts of the country, especially around rivers and lakes, you may be pestered by mosquitoes. Be sure to use insect repellent.

WATERBORNE HAZARDS

One of New Zealand's rare health hazards involves its pristine-looking bodies of water; **don't drink water from natural outdoor sources.** Although the country's alpine lakes might look like backdrops for mineral-water ads, some in the South Island harbor a tiny organism that can cause "duck itch," a temporary but intense skin irritation. The organism is found only on the shallow lake margins, so the chances of infection are greatly reduced if you stick to deeper water. Streams can be infected by giardia, a waterborne protozoal parasite that can cause gastrointestinal disorders, including acute diarrhea. Giardia is most likely contracted when drinking from streams that pass through an area inhabited by mammals (such as cattle or possums). There is no risk of infection if you drink from streams above the tree line.

Less common, but a risk nevertheless, is the possibility of contracting amoebic meningitis from the water in geothermal pools. The illness is caused by an organism that can enter the body when the water is forced up the nose. The organism is quite rare, but you should **avoid putting your head underwater in thermal pools** or jumping in them. Also remember not to drink geothermic water.

HOLIDAYS
On Christmas Day, Good Friday, Easter Sunday, and at least the morning of ANZAC Day, everything closes down in New Zealand except for a few gas stations, some shops selling essential food items, and emergency facilities. On other public holidays (often referred to as bank holidays) many museums and attractions will stay open, as will transportation systems, though on a reduced schedule. Local anniversary days, which vary from region to region, pop up as once-a-year three-day weekends in each particular area; some businesses close but hotels and restaurants stay open. Around Christmas and New Year's Kiwis pack up and go to the beach, so seaside resorts will be difficult to visit unless you have booked well in advance. You'll get plenty of sunshine and far fewer crowds if you visit from late January through to the colder period of late March. Cities such as Auckland and Wellington are quite pleasant over Christmas and New Year's. Fewer cars are on the road, and you'll get good prices from hotels trying to make up for the lack of corporate guests. *See* Festivals & Seasonal Events, *below,* for more information on public holidays.

INSURANCE
The most useful travel-insurance plan is a comprehensive policy that includes coverage for trip cancellation and interruption, default, trip delay, and medical expenses (with a waiver for preexisting conditions).

Without insurance you will lose all or most of your money if you cancel your trip, regardless of the reason. Default insurance covers you if your tour operator, airline, or cruise line goes out of business. Trip-delay covers expenses that arise because of bad weather or mechanical delays. Study the fine print when comparing policies.

If you're traveling internationally, a key component of travel insurance is coverage for medical bills incurred if you get sick on the road. Such expenses are not generally covered by Medicare or private policies. U.K. residents can buy a travel-insurance policy valid for most vacations taken during the year in which it's purchased (but check preexisting-condition coverage). British and Australian citizens need extra medical coverage when traveling overseas.

Always **buy travel policies directly from the insurance company**; if you buy them from a cruise line, airline, or tour operator that goes out of business you probably will not be covered for the agency or operator's default, a major risk. Before making any purchase, **review your existing health and home-owner's policies** to find what they cover away from home.

⚐ Travel Insurers In the U.S.: **Access America** ✉ 2805 N. Parham Rd., Richmond, VA 23294 ☎ 800/284-8300 🖷 804/673-1469 or 800/346-9265 ⊕ www.accessamerica.com. **Travel Guard International** ✉ 1145 Clark St., Stevens Point, WI 54481 ☎ 800/826-1300 or 715/345-1041 🖷 800/955-8785 or 715/345-1990 ⊕ www.travelguard.com. **⚐** In the U.K.: **Association of British Insurers** ✉ 51 Gresham St., London EC2V 7HQ ☎ 020/7600-3333 🖷 020/7696-8999 ⊕ www.abi.org.uk. In Canada: **RBC Insurance** ✉ 6880 Financial Dr., Mississauga, Ontario L5N 7Y5 ☎ 800/387-4357 or 905/816-2559 🖷 888/298-6458 ⊕ www.

rbcinsurance.com. In Australia: **Insurance Council of Australia** ✉ Level 3, 56 Pitt St. Sydney, NSW 2000 ☎ 02/9253-5100 🖶 02/9253-5111 ⊕ www.ica.com.au. In New Zealand: **Insurance Council of New Zealand** ✉ Level 7, 111–115 Customhouse Quay, Box 474, Wellington ☎ 04/472-5230 🖶 04/473-3011 ⊕ www.icnz.org.nz.

LANGUAGE

To an outsider's ear, Kiwi English can be mystifying. The colloquialisms alone can make things puzzling, not to mention rural slang. Otherwise known as "cow cockie" talk, this is what you'll hear when "girls" refers to someone's cows and gummies (galoshes) are the favored footwear.

The Māori language has added many commonly used words and phrases to the New Zealand lexicon. For instance, the Māori greeting is *kia ora,* which can also mean "thank you," "good-bye," "good health," or "good luck." You'll hear it from everyone, *Pākehā* (non-Māori) and Māori alike. Many place names are Māori as well, and can sometimes be so long as to seem unpronounceable. (A Māori word, after all, stands as the longest place name in the world.) Just take things slowly, syllable by syllable. *See* the Kiwi and Māori Glossaries *in* the Understanding New Zealand chapter for guidance on pronunciation.

Avoid the grave error of mistaking a Kiwi accent for an Australian one by listening for certain signature vowel pronunciations. For instance, New Zealanders often pronounce a short "e" as a short "i," making "pen" sound like "pin." And, vice versa, short "i" often sounds like a short "e." Both Aussies and Kiwis pronounce "day" as "die," although using more of an "oi" sound is an Australian twist. The easiest test to tell an Aussie from a Kiwi is to listen for the phrase "fish-and-chips." If it sounds like "feesh-and-cheeps," you're listening to an Australian but if it sounds like "fush-and-chups," you're with a Kiwi.

The biggest communication glitch between New Zealanders and visitors often involves the Kiwis' eloquent use of the understatement. This facet of Kiwi speech is both blessing and curse. Everything sounds relaxed and easy-going . . . but if you're trying to judge something like distance or

difficulty you may run into trouble. For instance, no matter how far away something is, people often say it's "just down the road" or "just over the hill." Ask specific questions to avoid a misunderstanding.

LODGING

The New Zealand Tourism Board (⇨ Visitor Information, *below*) publishes an annual "Where to Stay" directory listing more than 1,000 properties. This directory lists all properties who register for it, but it gives priority to those accredited by Qualmark, the national tourism–quality assurance organization.

The lodgings we list are the cream of the crop in each price category. We always list the facilities that are available but we don't specify whether they cost extra: when pricing accommodations, always ask what's included and what costs extra. Properties are assigned price categories based on the range from their least-expensive standard double room at high season (excluding holidays) to the most expensive. All rooms listed have an en suite or private bath unless otherwise noted. In New Zealand, the phrase "en-suite bathroom" means that the bathroom is connected directly with the bedroom, while a "private bath" often is outside the bedroom but is not shared with other guests.

Assume that hotels operate on the European Plan (EP, with no meals) unless we specify that they use the Continental Plan (CP, with a Continental breakfast), Breakfast Plan (BP, with a full breakfast), Modified American Plan (MAP, with breakfast and dinner), or the Full American Plan (FAP, with all meals).

Properties marked ✕🏠 are lodging establishments whose restaurants warrant a special trip and welcome nonovernight guests.

B&BS

There are some helpful resources on the Web for researching and booking B&B choices. On Web sites such as those maintained by SelectionsNZ and Jasons Travel Media, you'll find hundreds of listings and advertisements for B&Bs throughout the country. Heritage & Character Inns of New Zealand specializes in higher-end B&Bs.

Once in New Zealand you will find the *New Zealand Bed and Breakfast Book* in most major bookstores. It lists about 1,000 B&Bs, but be aware that the editorial copy in the book has been provided by the property owners themselves, rather than providing independent assessments as this Fodor's guide does.

🔢 **Heritage & Character Inns of New Zealand** ⊕ www.heritageinns.co.nz. **Jasons Travel Media** ⊕ www.jasons.com. **SelectionsNZ** ⊕ www. selections.co.nz.

CAMPING

There are more than 950 backcountry huts in New Zealand. They provide basic shelter but few frills. Huts are usually placed about four hours apart, although in isolated areas it can take a full day to get from one hut to the next. They are graded from "Basic," "Standard," and "Serviced," and the cost varies from free (for the basic hut) to $5 for the standard hut, to $10 for the serviced hut (per person per night), with some variations. The serviced hut shave cooking equipment and fuel, bunks or sleeping platforms with mattresses, toilets, washing facilities, and a supply of water. At the other end of the scale, Category 4 huts (the free ones) are simple shelters without a mattress or other facilities. You can camp next to a hut for half the price of staying in the hut itself, a good option if you're in a group that wants to share facilities. During high season, it can be difficult to find free huts available. Travelers can't reserve the huts in advance and can only stay in them for a couple of days. You can **purchase tickets for backcountry huts in advance** from Department of Conservation (DOC) offices, visitor centers, outdoor-recreation clubs. When you reach the hut, deposit one section of each ticket and keep the other section to show that you paid the fee. If you plan to make extensive use of huts, an annual pass giving access to all the back country huts for one year is available for $90. Also, be sure to also grab a copy of *Back Country Huts,* (or you can download it from the DOC Web site), which lists the locations of all of the national, maritime, forest-park, and scenic-reserve huts throughout the country.

In addition to the huts, the DOC runs more than 250 campsites on protected lands. These range from campgrounds with hot showers, flush toilets, and powered sites to bare-bones spots. Rates run between $2 and $10 a night. For more information on huts and campgrounds, contact the appropriate regional DOC bureau.

🔢 **Department of Conservation** ⊕ www.doc. govt.nz.

HOME & FARM STAYS

If you think green acres is the place to be, New Zealand has plenty of them. Home and farm stays offer not only comfortable accommodations but a chance to get to know the countryside and experience the renowned Kiwi hospitality. Most operate on a B&B basis, though some also offer an evening meal. Farm accommodations vary from modest shearers' cabins to elegant homesteads. Some hosts offer day trips, as well as horseback riding, hiking, and fishing. For two people, the average cost is $90–$150 per night, including meals.

Home stays, the urban equivalent of farm stays, are less expensive. Most New Zealanders seem to have vacation homes, called *baches* on North Island, *cribs* on South Island; these are frequently available for rent. New Zealand Vacation Homes lists houses and apartments for rent on both North and South Island. Baches and Holiday Homes to Rent Ltd. publishes an annual directory of rental homes throughout the country, with color photos for each listing.

Another accommodation option is a home exchange. Intervac, one of the largest international home-exchange services, has a New Zealand representative on hand.

🔢 **Baches and Holiday Homes to Rent Ltd.** ⌂ Box 3107, Richmond, Nelson ⊕ www. holidayhomes.co.nz. **Farm Helpers in New Zealand** ⌂ 16 Aspen Way, Palmerston North ⊕ www.fhinz. co.nz. **Intervac** ⌂ 54 McKinley Crescent, Wellington ⊕ www.intervac.com. **New Zealand Farm Holidays Ltd.** ⌂ Box 74, Auckland ☎ 09/412–9649 ⊕ www.nzaccom.co.nz. **New Zealand Vacation Homes Ltd.** ⌂ Box 76112, Auckland ☎ 09/268–2161 ⊕ www.nzvacationhomes.co.nz. **Rural Holidays NZ Ltd.** ⌂ Box 2155, Christchurch ☎ 03/355–6218 ⊕ www.ruralholidays.co.nz.

HOSTELS

No matter what your age, you can **save on lodging costs by staying at hostels.** In some 4,500 locations in more than 70 countries around the world, Hostelling International (HI), the umbrella group for a number of national youth-hostel associations, offers single-sex, dorm-style beds and, at many hostels, rooms for couples and family accommodations. Membership in any HI national hostel association, open to travelers of all ages, allows you to stay in HI-affiliated hostels at member rates; one-year membership is about $25 for adults (C$35 for a two-year minimum membership in Canada, £15 in the United Kingdom, A$52 in Australia, and NZ$40 in New Zealand); hostels run about $18–$65 per night. Members have priority if the hostel is full; they're also eligible for discounts around the world, even on rail and bus travel in some countries.

In addition to the International Youth Hostels, a network of low-cost, independent backpacker hostels operates in New Zealand. They can be found in nearly every city and tourist spot, and they offer clean, twin- and small-dormitory-style accommodations and self-catering kitchens, similar to those of the Youth Hostel Association (or YHA, the Australian version of IYH), with no membership required.

Qualmark, New Zealand's official tourism quality-assurance company, rates backpacker hostels on a one- to five-star system. You can check ratings on the company's Web site, ⊕ www.qualmark.co.nz

🚩 Organizations Hostelling International–USA ⊠ 8401 Colesville Rd., Suite 600, Silver Spring, MD 20910 ☎ 301/495-1240 🖷 301/495-6697 ⊕ www. hiusa.org. **Hostelling International–Canada** ⊠ 205 Catherine St., Suite 400, Ottawa, Ontario K2P 1C3 ☎ 613/237-7884 or 800/663-5777 🖷 613/237-7868 ⊕ www.hihostels.ca. **YHA England and Wales** ⊠ Trevelyan House, Dimple Rd., Matlock, Derbyshire DE4 3YH, U.K. ☎ 0870/870-8808, 0870/770-8868, or 0162/959-2600 🖷 0870/770-6127 ⊕ www.yha.org.uk. **YHA Australia** ⊠ 422 Kent St., Sydney, NSW 2001 ☎ 02/9261-1111 🖷 02/9261-1969 ⊕ www.yha.com.au. **YHA New Zealand** ⊠ Level 1, Moorhouse City, 166 Moorhouse Ave., Box 436, Christchurch ☎ 03/379-9970 or 0800/278-299 🖷 03/365-4476 ⊕ www.yha.org.nz.

HOTELS

When looking up hotel information, you'll often see a reference to Qualmark, New Zealand's official tourism quality-assurance agency. This nonprofit service grades hotels on a one- to five-star rating system and participation is voluntary. Each business applies and undergoes a strict assessment and licensing process to win Qualmark accreditation, shelling out some cash in the process. These ratings are generally fair gauges of each property's cleanliness and security. You can check a hotel's Qualmark rating on the Web site ⊕ www.qualmark.co.nz.

🚩 Toll-Free Numbers Best Western ☎ 800/528-1234 ⊕ www.bestwestern.com. **Choice** ☎ 800/424-6423 ⊕ www.choicehotels.com. **Holiday Inn** ☎ 800/465-4329 ⊕ www.sixcontinentshotels.com.

MOTELS

Motels are the most common accommodations, and most offer comfortable rooms for $70–$195 per night. They're usually open every day of the year. Unlike in the United States, motels in New Zealand are not always below the standard of hotels. For instance, "motel flats" are set up like apartments, with living areas as well as bedrooms. Accommodations with more basic facilities are called "serviced motels." All motel rooms come with tea- and coffee-making equipment; many have full kitchen facilities. Air-conditioning is rare in small-town or rural motels. The Motel Association of New Zealand (MANZ) is an independent company with nearly 1,000 members. Its Web site, ⊕ www.manz.co.nz, allows you to find properties by region or by motel name.

MOTOR CAMPS

The least expensive accommodations in the country are the tourist cabins and flats in most of the country's 400 motor camps. Tourist cabins offer basic accommodation and shared cooking, laundry, and bathroom facilities. Bedding and towels are not provided. A notch higher up the comfort scale, tourist flats usually provide bedding, fully equipped kitchens, and private bathrooms. Tent sites and caravan sites usually cost less than $10 and overnight rates for cabins range anywhere from $6 to $20. More fully equipped tourist flats will cost $25 to $70.

LUXURY LODGES

At the high end of the price scale, a growing number of luxury lodges offer the best of country life, fine dining, and superb accommodations. Fishing is a specialty at many of them, but there is usually a range of outdoor activities for nonanglers. Tariffs run about $350–$800 per day for two people; meals are generally included. For information, visit the New Zealand Lodge Association's Web site, ⊕ www.lodgesofnz.co.nz where you can even download an electronic catalog of lodges in New Zealand.

MAIL & SHIPPING

Airmail should take around six or seven days to reach the United Kingdom or the United States and two or three days to reach Australia.

OVERNIGHT SERVICES

Overnight services are available between New Zealand and Australia, but to destinations farther afield "overnight" will in reality be closer to 48 hours. Even to Australia, truly overnight service is only offered between major cities and can be subject to conditions, such as the time you call in. A number of major operators are represented in New Zealand and the services are reliable, particularly from cities.
📛 Major Services **DHL World Express** ☏ 09/976-2976 or 0800/800-020 ⊕ www.dhl.co.nz. **Federal Express** ☏ 0800/733-339 ⊕ www.fedex.com. **TNT International Express** ☏ 0800/275-868 or 09/255-0500 ⊕ www.tnt.com.

POSTAL RATES

Post offices are open weekdays 8:30–5, and in some areas on Saturdays from 10–12. The cost of mailing a letter within New Zealand is 45¢ standard post, 90¢ fast post. Sending a standard-size letter by airmail costs $2 to North America, $2 to Europe, and $1.50 to Australia. Aerograms and postcards are $1.50 to any overseas destination.
📛 Postal Service **New Zealand Post** ☏ 0800/501-501 ⊕ www.nzpost.co.nz.

RECEIVING MAIL

If you wish to receive correspondence, have mail sent to New Zealand held for you for up to one month at the central post office in any town or city if it is addressed to you "c/o Poste Restante, CPO," followed by the name of the town. This service is free; you may need to show ID.

SHIPPING PARCELS

You can use the major international overnight companies listed above or purchase packaging and prepaid mail services from the post office. Major duty-free stores and stores that deal frequently with travelers will be able to help with international shipping, but if you purchase from small shops, particularly in country areas, arrange shipping with a company in the nearest city.

MEDIA

New Zealand has its share of scandal sheets and gossip magazines, but in general the standard of journalism is high. Because it is a small and physically isolated country, you'll find the interest in international news greater than you may expect. Any major stories coming out of the United States and the United Kingdom—or major sports events around the world—are likely to receive full coverage.

NEWSPAPERS & MAGAZINES

There are daily metropolitan newspapers in all cities (two in Wellington), smaller local dailies in provincial towns, and many community and local papers. The Auckland-based *New Zealand Herald* is the daily with the country's largest circulation. The *Dominion Post* is Wellington's morning paper and is the best source for the nation's political events. In Christchurch, the *Press* is highly regarded. On Sunday the *Sunday Star Times* and the *Sunday News* vie for readership; both are available nationally.

The country has a massive array of locally published magazines—there are more local magazine titles per capita than in any other country in the world. *Cuisine* focuses on cooking and wine. *Women's Weekly, Women's Day,* and *New Idea* will keep you current with royal scandals from Britain and who's doing what to whom among the local celebrities. For more serious reading, pick up a copy of *North & South* (monthly) or *Listener* (weekly). Both have in-depth articles on issues facing

New Zealand. The monthly *Metro* magazine is slightly more lighthearted and concentrates on Auckland issues. *Pavement,* another monthly, pitches to the hip.

RADIO & TELEVISION
For news, views, and talk back (talk radio) try Newstalk ZB at AM 1080, and for sports coverage (including American sports events in the middle of the night New Zealand time) tune to AM 1332. There's a good array of music stations. For the latest hits, go to the ZM network (FM 91 in Auckland).

New Zealand has four main television channels: TV 1, 2, 3, and 4, plus other free channels (Prime and Triangle) that you'll find in main centers. Channels 1 and 3 have news at 6 PM. Channels 2 and 4 are targeted at the youth market, and this is where you'll find popular U.S. programs. In 2004, Māori Television was launched, with the aim of promoting and preserving Māori language and culture. Along with news, the mostly publicly funded channel screens soap operas, talk shows, documentaries, music, and shows for youth, either all in te reo (the Māori language), or in a combination of te reo and English. Most TVs are tuned in to Māori TV, but the channel number varies.

Most hotels have Sky TV, including the news channel that takes a feed from CNN.

MONEY MATTERS
For most travelers, New Zealand is not an expensive destination. The cost of meals, accommodation, and travel prove comparable to larger cities within the United States and somewhat less than in Western Europe. At about $1 per liter—equal to about US$2.10 per gallon—premium-grade gasoline costs about the same as it does in North America; prices are much cheaper than in Europe.

Prices quoted in this book are in New Zealand dollars. The following were sample costs in New Zealand at press time:

Cup of coffee, $3; glass of beer in a bar, $2.50–$4; take-out ham sandwich or meat pie, $2.50; hamburger in a café, $5–$8; room-service sandwich in a hotel, $12; a 2-km (1-mi) taxi ride, $5.

Prices throughout this guide are given for adults. Substantially reduced fees are almost always available for children, students, and senior citizens. For information on taxes, *see* Taxes, *below.*

ATMS
EFTPOS (Electronic Fund Transfer at Point of Sale) is widely used in New Zealand stores and gas stations. Needless to say, ATMs are easily found in city and town banks and in shopping malls. The number of ATMs in small rural communities continues to grow, but there are still areas where ATMs or banks are few and far between. For example, there are no ATMs on Stewart Island. All the major banks in New Zealand (Bank of New Zealand, Westpac, and Auckland Savings Bank) accept cards in the Cirrus and Plus networks. The norm for PINs in New Zealand is four digits. If the PIN for your account has a different number of digits, you must **change your PIN number before you leave for New Zealand.**

CREDIT CARDS
Throughout this guide, the following abbreviations are used: AE, American Express; DC, Diners Club; MC, MasterCard; and V, Visa. MasterCard and Visa are the most widely accepted cards throughout New Zealand. Discover Cards are not recognized.

🔁 Reporting Lost Cards **American Express** ☎ 09/367-4247 or 0800/656-660. **Diners Club** ☎ 09/359-7797 or 0800/657-373. **MasterCard** ☎ 0800/449-140 or call the U.S. collect at 636/722-7111. **Visa** ☎ 0508/600-300.

CURRENCY
New Zealand's unit of currency is the dollar, divided into 100 cents. Bills are in $100, $50, $10, and $5 denominations. Coins are $2, $1, 50¢, 20¢, 10¢, and 5¢. At press time the rate of exchange was NZ$1.40 to the U.S. dollar, NZ$1.20 to the Canadian dollar, NZ$2.50 to the pound sterling, and almost equal to the Australian dollar. Exchange rates change on a daily basis.

CURRENCY EXCHANGE
For the most favorable rates, **change money through banks.** Although ATM

transaction fees may be higher abroad than at home, ATM rates are excellent because they are based on wholesale rates offered only by major banks. You won't do as well as exchange booths in airports or rail and bus stations, in hotels, in restaurants, or in stores. To avoid lines at airport exchange booths, **get a bit of local currency before you leave home.**

🖪 Exchange Services **International Currency Express** ✉ 427 N. Camden Dr., Suite F, Beverly Hills, CA 90210 ☎ 888/278-6628 orders 🖷 310/278-6410 ⊕ www.foreignmoney.com. **Travel Ex Currency Services** ☎ 800/287-7362 orders and retail locations ⊕ www.travelex.com.

TRAVELER'S CHECKS

Do you need traveler's checks? It depends on where you're headed. If you're going to rural areas and small towns, go with cash; traveler's checks are best used in cities. Lost or stolen checks can usually be replaced within 24 hours. To ensure a speedy refund, buy your own traveler's checks—don't let someone else pay for them: irregularities like this can cause delays. The person who bought the checks should make the call to request a refund.

PACKING

In New Zealand, **be prepared for weather that can turn suddenly** and temperatures that vary greatly from day to night, particularly at the change of seasons. The wisest approach to dressing is to **wear layered outfits.** You'll appreciate being able to remove or put on a jacket. Take along a light raincoat and umbrella, but remember that plastic raincoats and nonbreathing polyester are uncomfortable in humid climates. Don't wear lotions or perfume in humid places like Southland either, since they attract mosquitoes and other bugs; carry insect repellent. Bring a hat with a brim to provide protection from the strong sunlight (⇨ Health, *above*) and sunglasses for either summer or winter; the glare on snow or glaciers can be intense. You'll need warm clothing for South Island; a windbreaker is a good idea wherever you plan to be.

Dress is casual in most cities, though top resorts and restaurants may require a jacket and tie. In autumn, a light wool sweater and/or a jacket will suffice for evenings in coastal cities, but winter demands a heavier coat—a raincoat with a zip-out wool lining is ideal. Comfortable walking shoes are a must. You should have a pair of running shoes or the equivalent if you're planning to trek, and rubber-sole sandals or canvas shoes for the beaches.

In your carry-on luggage, pack an extra pair of eyeglasses or contact lenses and enough of any medication you take to last a few days longer than the entire trip. You may also ask your doctor to write a spare prescription using the drug's generic name, as brand names may vary from country to country. **Never pack prescription drugs, valuables, or undeveloped film in luggage to be checked.** And don't forget to carry with you the addresses of offices that handle refunds of lost traveler's checks. Check *Fodor's How to Pack* (available at online retailers and bookstores everywhere) for more tips.

To avoid customs and security delays, carry medications in their original packaging. Don't pack any sharp objects in your carry-on luggage, including knives of any size or material, scissors, nail clippers, and corkscrews, or anything else that might arouse suspicion.

To avoid having your checked luggage chosen for hand inspection, don't cram bags full. The U.S. Transportation Security Administration suggests packing shoes on top and placing personal items you don't want touched in clear plastic bags.

CHECKING LUGGAGE

You're allowed to carry aboard one bag and one personal article, such as a purse or a laptop computer. Make sure what you carry on fits under your seat or in the overhead bin. Get to the gate early, so you can board as soon as possible, before the overhead bins fill up.

Baggage allowances vary by carrier, destination, and ticket class. On international flights, you're usually allowed to check two bags weighing up to 70 pounds (32 kilograms) each, although a few airlines allow checked bags of up to 88 pounds (40 kilograms) in first class. Some international carriers don't allow more than 66 pounds (30 kilograms) per bag in business class and 44 pounds (20 kilograms) in economy. If you're flying to or through the United Kingdom, your luggage cannot exceed 70 pounds (32 kilograms) per bag. On domestic flights, the limit is usually 50 to 70 pounds (23 to 32 kilograms) per bag. In general, carry-on bags shouldn't exceed 40 pounds (18 kilograms). Most airlines won't accept bags that weigh more than 100 pounds (45 kilograms) on domestic or international flights. Expect to pay a fee for baggage that exceeds weight limits. Check baggage restrictions with your carrier before you pack.

Airline liability for baggage is limited to $2,500 per person on flights within the United States. On international flights it amounts to $9.07 per pound or $20 per kilogram for checked baggage (roughly $640 per 70-pound bag), with a maximum of $634.90 per piece, and $400 per passenger for unchecked baggage. You can buy additional coverage at check-in for about $10 per $1,000 of coverage, but it often excludes a rather extensive list of items, shown on your airline ticket.

Before departure, itemize your bags' contents and their worth, and label the bags with your name, address, and phone number. (If you use your home address, cover it so potential thieves can't see it readily.) Include a label inside each bag and **pack a copy of your itinerary.** At check-in, make sure each bag is correctly tagged with the destination airport's three-letter code. Because some checked bags will be opened for hand inspection, the U.S. Transportation Security Administration recommends that you leave luggage unlocked or use the plastic locks offered at check-in. TSA screeners place an inspection notice inside searched bags, which are resealed with a special lock.

If your bag has been searched and contents are missing or damaged, file a claim with the TSA Consumer Response Center as soon as possible. If your bags arrive damaged or fail to arrive at all, file a written report with the airline before leaving the airport.

🔃 Complaints U.S. Transportation Security Administration Contact Center ☎ 866/289-9673 ⊕ www.tsa.gov.

PASSPORTS & VISAS

When traveling internationally, **carry your passport** even if you don't need one. Not only is it the best form of I.D., but it's also being required more and more. As of December 31, 2005, for instance, Americans need a passport to reenter the country from Bermuda, the Caribbean, and Panama. Such requirements also affect reentry from Canada and Mexico by air and sea (as of December 31, 2006) and land (as of December 31, 2007). **Make two photocopies of the data page** (one for someone at home and another for you, carried separately from your passport). If you lose your passport, promptly call the nearest embassy or consulate and the local police.

U.S. passport applications for children under age 14 require consent from both parents or legal guardians; both parents must appear together to sign the application. If only one parent appears, he or she must submit a written statement from the other parent authorizing passport issuance for the child. A parent with sole authority must present evidence of it when applying; acceptable documentation includes the child's certified birth certificate listing only the applying parent, a court order specifically permitting this parent's travel with the child, or a death certificate for the non-applying parent. Application forms and instructions are available on the Web site of the U.S. State Department's Bureau of Consular Affairs (⊕ www.travel.state.gov).

ENTERING NEW ZEALAND

U.S., Canadian, and U.K. citizens need only a valid passport to enter New Zealand for stays of up to 90 days.

PASSPORT OFFICES

The best time to apply for a passport or to renew is in fall and winter. Before any trip, **check your passport's expiration date,** and, if necessary, renew it as soon as possible.

🔃 Australian Citizens Passports Australia Australian Department of Foreign Affairs and Trade ☎ 131-232 ⊕ www.passports.gov.au.
🔃 Canadian Citizens Passport Office ⊠ To mail in applications: 70 Cremazie St., Gatineau, Québec J8Y 3P2 ☎ 819/994-3500 or 800/567-6868 ⊕ www.ppt.gc.ca.
🔃 U.K. Citizens U.K. Passport Service ☎ 0870/521-0410 ⊕ www.passport.gov.uk.

🛂 U.S. Citizens **National Passport Information Center** ☎ 877/487-2778, 888/874-7793 TDD/TTY ⊕ travel.state.gov.

RESTROOMS

Shopping malls in cities, major bus and train stations, gas stations, and many rest areas on main highways have public toilets. Look for a blue sign with white figures (ladies and gents) for directions to a public toilet. New Zealanders often use the word "loo," or better yet, "super loo."

Most New Zealand public restroom facilities are clean and tidy and often have a separate room for mothers with young children.

Some gas stations, shops, and hotels have signs stating that only customers can use the rest room. Kiwis are generally fair-minded folk, so if you're genuinely caught short and explain the situation you will probably not be turned away.

Most gas stations in New Zealand have toilet facilities, but their standard is variable. As a rule of thumb, the newer and more impressive the gas station, the cleaner and better the toilet facilities.

SAFETY

New Zealand is safe for travelers, but international visitors have been known to get into trouble when they take their safety for granted and let their guard down. **Use common sense,** particularly if walking around cities at night. Stick around other people and avoid deserted alleys. Although New Zealand is an affluent society by world standards, it has its share of poor and homeless (often referred to as "street kids" if they are young). Avoid bus and train stations or city squares late at night. The crowds in some pubs can get a bit rough late at night, so if you sense irritation, leave.

Hotels offer safes for guests' valuables, and it pays to use them. Don't flash your wealth, and remember to lock doors of hotel rooms and cars. Unfortunately, opportunist criminals stake out parking lots at some popular tourist attractions. **Put valuables out of sight under seats or lock them in your trunk** before you arrive at the destination.

Most visitors have no trouble and find New Zealanders among the friendliest people in the world. Nine times out of 10, offers of help or other friendly gestures will be genuine.

WOMEN IN NEW ZEALAND

Women will not attract more unwanted attention than in most other Western societies, nor will they be immune from the usual hassles. In cities at night, stick to well-lit areas and avoid being totally alone. Hotel staff will be happy to give tips on any areas to avoid, and the times to avoid them. New Zealand is relatively safe for women, but don't be complacent.

Many of the top Kiwi destinations have accommodation especially geared to women. Wellington, for instance, has a women-only guesthouse, and the Base Backpacker hostel chain (⊕ www.basebackpackers.com), with locations in major New Zealand cities, created Sanctuary Floors, secure women-only zones with special amenities.

Don't wear a money belt or a waist pack, both of which peg you as a tourist. If you carry a purse, choose one with a zipper and a thick strap that you can drape across your body; adjust the length so that the purse sits in front of you at or above hip level. Store only enough money in the purse to cover casual spending. Distribute the rest of your cash and any valuables (including credit cards and your passport) between a deep front pocket, an inside jacket or vest pocket, and a hidden money pouch. Do not reach for the money pouch once in public.

SENIOR-CITIZEN TRAVEL

To qualify for age-related discounts, mention your senior-citizen status up front when booking hotel reservations (not when checking out) and before you're seated in restaurants (not when paying the bill). Be sure to have identification on hand. When renting a car, ask about promotional car-rental discounts, which can be cheaper than senior-citizen rates.

🛂 **Educational Programs Elderhostel** ✉ 11 Ave. de Lafayette, Boston, MA 02111 ☎ 877/426-8056, 978/323-4141 international callers, 877/426-2167 TTY 📠 877/426-2166 ⊕ www.elderhostel.org.

SHOPPING

New Zealand is not widely regarded as a shopping destination for tourists. However, the state of the Kiwi dollar at press time means that visitors from the United States and Europe will find plenty of bargains. Duty-free shopping is particularly good, and at Auckland International Airport you'll find prices to rival anywhere else in the world. Most cities and towns have outdoor markets at least once a week. You'll often find local arts and crafts at these, as well as secondhand clothing and assorted knickknacks. Ask at local visitor-information centers for dates, times, and locations of markets.

If you have a car and want to meet Kiwis in a slightly unusual way, pick up a Friday-morning newspaper and look in the classified ads for weekend-morning garage sales. Sometimes you'll find five or six garage sales in the space of a few suburban miles—especially in places west and south of Auckland. Some of your fellow buyers will be "professionals" who pick up bargains and resell them in secondhand stores; others are just people out looking for a good deal.

New Zealand shops have set prices, but you'll be able to bargain a bit in antiques and secondhand stores, or markets. Don't expect to be able to knock more than a few dollars off the stated price though. A TOI IHO MĀORI MADE MARK label indicates that the product was made by Māori.

SMART SOUVENIRS

A **rugby jersey,** especially for the All Black team, can look more fashionable than it sounds. Expect to pay about $100.

A **bottle of wine,** like sauvignon blanc from the Marlborough District, a cabernet sauvignon or chardonnay from Hawke's Bay, or pinot noir from central Otago, is a tasty souvenir and will cost between $20 and $30. It's fun to buy from the vineyard, but you can also buy New Zealand wine at general stores and in city wine shops.

A great gift for young children is the **Buzzy Bee,** a brightly painted, wooden, pull-along toy which buzzes as its wings rotate. Crafted in the 1940s, this small children's toy has become an icon of New Zealand "Kiwiana." They usually cost around $40.

Tawari honey, called the "beaujolais of honey" comes from the lowland forests of New Zealand's Far North, where the tawari tree's waxy white flowers produce this light-colored, butterscotchy treat. Manuka honey, from an indigenous tea tree, is another unique sweet.

Pounamu or **greenstone** (jade) is available in tourist and souvenir shops. It's beautiful stone and is best when carved and polished. Prices vary greatly depending on the size and quality of the item. Tradition says that it should be given as a gift, not bought for oneself, but if you have to break with tradition, so be it.

Crafts made from **kauri and *rimu* wood** are prized Kiwi keepsakes. The wood from the kauri tree, New Zealand's largest and most famous native tree, must be recovered from swamps because it is illegal to chop the trees down. Kauri timber has a beautiful, distinctive grain which when polished is a deep golden color.

Woollen Swanndri jackets, shirts, and pullovers in the traditional plaid, called "Swannies," are the quintessential bush shirt. These were worn by New Zealand's pioneers as far back as the 1800s and are supposedly dipped in a secret waterproofing formula. Considering the Kiwi no-nonsense approach to fashion, it's no wonder they're still in.

Also keep an eye out for **possum fur** and possum wool. Possums have become quite a pest in New Zealand, especially as they threaten native forests, so possum-population control is a big point there. Spinning a fashion statement out of necessity, possum products came on the scene and you can now get anything from fur earmuffs to fur throw pillows.

WATCH OUT

Buy a sheepskin rug if you must, but don't do it from an inner-city souvenir shop unless you want to pay more than it's worth. Look at a few shops before making a decision. New Zealand tourist shops have taken to selling toy koalas. They're adorable, so buy one if it makes you happy, but they have absolutely nothing to do with New Zealand. You won't even find koalas in the zoos here because the leaves they eat grow widely only in Australia. A much more appropriate choice, if you are buying for kids, is a fluffy toy kiwi bird.

STUDENTS IN NEW ZEALAND

Many attractions and activities in New Zealand offer discounts to students holding a current academic identification card. Students holding a New Zealand Travelpass (⇨ Air Travel, *above*) can save 50% on the normal economy-class domestic airfare with Air New Zealand. The drawback is that such tickets are on a standby basis.

A couple of New Zealand's larger universities have good student Web sites with useful links. Check out Auckland University's student association site, ⊕ www. ausa.org.nz or University of Canterbury's ⊕ www.ucsa.org.nz.

🚩 **IDs & Services STA Travel** ✉ 10 Downing St., New York, NY 10014 ☎ 212/627-3111, 800/777-0112 24-hr service center 🖷 212/627-3387 ⊕ www.sta. com. **Travel Cuts** ✉ 187 College St., Toronto, Ontario M5T 1P7, Canada ☎ 800/592-2887 in U.S., 416/979-2406 or 866/246-9762 in Canada 🖷 416/ 979-8167 ⊕ www.travelcuts.com.

SMOKING

Smoking is not allowed indoors in New Zealand restaurants, bars, cafés, or clubs. If you light up inside, you can be asked to leave and the establishment risks a fine. Smoking is also not allowed on most transportation, including buses or Air New Zealand flights.

TAXES

Many restaurants add a 15% surcharge to your bill on public holidays, reflecting the need to pay staff a higher wage on holidays. This tax will be itemized separately on your bill when applicable.

AIRPORT

Visitors exiting New Zealand must pay a departure tax of $25. (*See* Air Travel, *above*.)

VALUE-ADDED TAX

A goods and services tax (GST) of 12.5% is levied throughout New Zealand. It's usually incorporated into the cost of an item, but in some hotels and some restaurants it is added to the bill.

TELEPHONES
AREA & COUNTRY CODES

The country code for New Zealand is 64. When dialing from abroad, drop the initial "0" from the local area code. Main area codes within New Zealand include 09 (Auckland and the North), 04 (Wellington), and 03 (South Island). Dialing from New Zealand to back home, the country code is 1 for the United States and Canada, 61 for Australia, and 44 for the United Kingdom. The prefixes 0800 and 0867 are used for toll-free numbers.

CELLULAR PHONE RENTALS

There are both analog and digital mobile-communications networks covering most of the country, which operate on the GSM system. If you have a tri-band GSM phone you can rent a SIM card for about $6 per week. Keep in mind, however, that the phone must be unlocked, so you should be sure to get that number from your provider prior to leaving.

Cell phones can be rented at Auckland, Wellington, Queenstown, and Christchurch airports, starting at $4 a day. Look for a Vodafone stand in the arrival area of each airport. Prior reservations are a good idea, though not absolutely necessary. Make phone-rental arrangements in advance so you can **give family and friends your number before you leave.**

🚩 **Vodafone** ☎ 09/275-8154 or 0800/800-021 ⊕ www.vodarent.co.nz.

DIRECTORY & OPERATOR ASSISTANCE

Dial 018 for New Zealand directory assistance. For international numbers, dial 0172. To call the operator, dial 010; for international operator assistance, dial 0170. To find phone numbers within New Zealand online go to ⊕ www.whitepages. co.nz.

INTERNATIONAL CALLS

To make international calls directly, dial 00, then the international access code, area code, and number required.

LONG-DISTANCE SERVICES

AT&T, MCI, and Sprint access codes make calling long-distance relatively convenient,

but you may find the local access number blocked in many hotel rooms. First ask the hotel operator to connect you. If the hotel operator balks, ask for an international operator, or dial the international operator yourself. One way to improve your odds of getting connected to your long-distance carrier is to travel with more than one company's calling card (a hotel may block Sprint, for example, but not MCI). If all else fails, call from a pay phone. If you are travelling for a longer period of time, consider renting a cell-phone from a local company.
Access Codes AT & T Direct ☎ 000–911. **MCI WorldPhone** ☎ 000–912. **Sprint International Access** ☎ 000–913.

PUBLIC PHONES

Most pay phones now accept PhoneCards or major credit cards rather than coins. PhoneCards, available in denominations of $5, $10, $20, or $50, are sold at post offices, dairies (convenience stores), tourist centers, and any other shops displaying the green PhoneCard symbol. To use a PhoneCard, lift the receiver, put the card in the slot in the front of the phone, and dial. The cost of the call is automatically deducted from your card; the display on the telephone tells you how much credit you have left at the end of the call. A local call from a public phone costs 70¢. Don't forget to take your PhoneCard with you when you finish your call or those minutes will be lost—or spent by a stranger.

Telecom offers a reliable card called YABBA, which covers minutes to the United States for as low as 29¢ per minute. You can add minutes to the card by using your credit card; unlike a PhoneCard, you don't need to purchase a new one when you're running out of time. You can buy YABBA cards at Telecom retailers, gas stations, and hostels.

The Net2Phone Direct Calling Card offers an affordable solution by utilizing local access numbers to make calls utilizing the Internet. This is used in the same manner as a regular calling card, but depending upon the area from which you are calling there is sometimes a slight voice delay. This type of technology has also made it possible to make phone calls right from your laptop computer. If you are going to have free access to Internet, this can prove to be the most affordable means of making International calls, with rates from New Zealand to the U.S. being approximately 4¢ per minute with Net2Phone's PC2Phone plan. It is advisable to use a headset for the best clarity.
Calling Cards Telecom YABBA ☎ 0800/922–2248.

TIME

Trying to figure out just what time it is in New Zealand can get dizzying, especially because of cross-hemisphere daylight-saving times and multi-time-zone countries. Without daylight-saving times, Auckland is 17 hours ahead of New York; 18 hours ahead of Chicago and Dallas; 20 hours ahead (or count back 4 hours and add a day) of Los Angeles; 12 hours ahead of London; and 2 hours ahead of Sydney.

From Canada and the States, **call New Zealand after 5 PM.** From the United Kingdom or Europe, it isn't quite as complicated: call early in the morning or very late at night. When faxing, it's usually not a problem to ring discreet fax numbers at any time of day.

TIPPING

Tipping is not as widely practiced in New Zealand as in the United States or Europe, but in city restaurants and hotels it's appreciated if you acknowledge good service with a 10% tip.

Taxi drivers will appreciate rounding up the fare to the nearest $5 amount, but don't feel you have to do this. Porters will be happy with a $1 or $2 coin. Most other people, like bartenders, theater attendants, gas-station attendants, or barbers, will probably wonder what you are doing if you try to give them a tip.

TOURS & PACKAGES

Because everything is prearranged on a prepackaged tour or independent vacation, you'll spend less time planning—and often get it all at a good price. Among companies that sell tours to New Zealand, the following are a selection of nationally known organizations with a proven reputation. The key difference between the categories listed below is usually in the accommodations, which run from budget to better, and better-yet to best.

BOOKING WITH AN AGENT

Travel agents are excellent resources. But it's a good idea to collect brochures from several agencies, as some agents' suggestions may be influenced by relationships with tour and package firms that reward them for volume sales. If you have a special interest, find an agent with expertise in that area. The American Society of Travel Agents (ASTA) has a database of specialists worldwide; you can log on to the group's Web site to find one near you.

Make sure your travel agent knows the accommodations and other services of the place being recommended. Ask about the hotel's location, room size, beds, and whether it has a pool, room service, or programs for children, if you care about these. Has your agent been there in person or sent others whom you can contact?

Do some homework on your own, too: local tourism boards can provide information about lesser-known and small-niche operators, some of which may sell only direct.

🛈 Tour-Operator Recommendations **American Society of Travel Agents** (⇨ Travel Agencies). **CrossSphere–The Global Association for Packaged Travel** ⊠ 546 E. Main St., Lexington, KY 40508 ☎ 859/226-4444 or 800/682-8886 🖷 859/226-4414 ⊕ www.CrossSphere.com. **United States Tour Operators Association (USTOA)** ⊠ 275 Madison Ave., Suite 2014, New York, NY 10016 ☎ 212/599-6599 🖷 212/599-6744 ⊕ www.ustoa.com.

LUXURY

Abercrombie & Kent, otherwise known as A&K, is the benchmark for pairing deluxe accommodations with soft adventure. Its itineraries can be combined with a visit to Australia or focus solely New Zealand. Sometimes better deals can be landed by booking a flight package with their affiliate airlines, Qantas. Tauck World Discovery offers trips with private chartered plane service. Antipodes Tours combed New Zealand for posh accommodations; one tour is devoted to the best of the lodges. The "Connoisseur Collection" tour series with Luxury Vacations New Zealand takes

small groups of just eight people to both the North and South islands.

🛈 Luxury Tour Companies **Abercrombie & Kent** ⊠ 1520 Kensington Rd., Oak Brook, IL 60523 ☎ 800/554-7016 or 630/954-2944 🖷 630-954-3324 ⊕ www.abercrombiekent.com. **Antipodes Tours** ⊠ 5933 W. Century Blvd., Suite 422, Los Angeles, CA 90045 ☎ 800/354-7471 or 310/410-9734 🖷 310/410-9451 ⊕ www.antipodestours.com. **Luxury Vacations New Zealand** ⊠ 121 Elliot St., 1st fl., Howick, Auckland ☎ 09/537-2325 🖷 09/532-8825 ⊕ www.luxuryvacationsnz.com. **Tauk World Discovery** ⊠ 10 Norden Pl., Norwalk, CT 06881 ☎ 800/788-7885 or 203/899-6500 🖷 203/221-6828 ⊕ www.tauck.com.

MODERATE

Scenic Tours of Auckland and Pacific Travel of Christchurch formed a joint marketing venture to promote North and South Island tours called Scenic Pacific Tours. Its wide range of tours depart daily from Auckland, Wellington, Picton, Nelson, Christchurch, Dunedin, and Queenstown. You can mix and match your tours and choose your level of accommodations to fit your budget. ATS Tours and Australian Pacific Touring (APT) both specialize in South Pacific vacations and can arrange everything from self-drive to fully escorted tours.

🛈 Moderate Tour Companies **ATS Tours** ⊠ 2381 Rosecrans Ave., Suite 325, El Segundo, CA 90245 ☎ 888/781-5170 or 310/643-0044 🖷 310/643-0032 ⊕ www.atstours.com. **Australian Pacific Touring (APT)** ⊠ 2 Sutton Crescent, Hunter's Corner, Auckland ☎ 0800/278-687, 800/290-8687 in U.S. 🖷 09/279-8813 ⊕ www.aptours.com. **Scenic Pacific Tours** ⊠ P.O. Box 14037, Christchurch ☎ 03/355-3999–or Toll-free in New Zealand, 0800/500-388 🖷 03/359-9058 ⊕ www.scenicpacific.co.nz.

BUDGET

Thrifty Tours New Zealand packaged holidays are flexible, combining regular bus, train, and ferry services with pre-booked accommodation. Flying Kiwi Wilderness Expeditions Ltd. helps tie up loose ends for those on a shoestring budget. It's geared to camping rather than hotels and sometimes the major means of transit are your two feet, but this tour company has been a longtime Kiwi favorite.

🛈 Budget Tour Companies **Flying Kiwi Wilderness Expeditions Ltd.** ⊠ 4B Forests Rd., Nelson ☎ 03/547-0171 or 0800/693-296 🖷 03/547-0173 ⊕ www.

flyingkiwi.com. **Thrifty Tours New Zealand** ✉ 3024 Gt North Rd., New Lynn, Auckland ☎ 09/359-8380 🖷 09/358-5408 ⊕ www.thriftytours.co.nz.

THEME TRIPS

Golf Wine New Zealand and Food and Wine Trails share astute insights on Hawke's Bay, Martinborough, and Marlborough vintages, the former with some time on the links as well. Homestay NZ Ltd. will arrange theme trips based upon your individual interests, be it wine or whale-watching. One of their more unique options includes having dinner at a local New Zealand family's home.

Serious outdoor enthusiasts can take a walk on the wild side, or bike, kayak, or bungee jump with Active New Zealand. For more New Zealand–based outfitters who organize multiday sports trips, *see* the Adventure Vacations chapter.

📶 Theme-Tour Companies **Active New Zealand** ✉ Box 972, Queenstown ☎ 800/661-9073 or 03/450-0414, or 800/500-3398 in U.S. 🖷 03/409-0119 or 603/251-1051 in U.S. ⊕ www.activenewzealand. com. **Food & Wine Trails** ✉ 707 Fourth St., Santa Rosa, CA 95404 ☎ 800/367-5348 or 707/526-2922 🖷 707/526-6949 ⊕ www.foodandwinetrails.com. **Golf Wine New Zealand** ✉ 7708 East Shea Blvd., Scottsdale, AZ 85260 ☎ 480/607-1717 🖷 480/607-1771 ⊕ www.golfwinenewzealand.com. **Homestay NZ Ltd.** ✉ Box 25-115, Auckland ☎ 09/411-9166.

TRAIN TRAVEL

New Zealand's Tranz Scenic trains travel, as a rule, north and south along the main trunk of New Zealand. If you want to crisscross the country, then you'll have to abandon the country's rail network. There are some exceptions, most notably the famous Tranz-Alpine Express, a spectacular scenic ride across Arthur's Pass and the mountainous spine of South Island between Greymouth and Christchurch.

Even the most popular services tend to run only once daily. They do leave and arrive on time as a rule. Trains have one class, and they have standard, comfortable seats, and a basic food service offering light meals, snacks, beer, wine, and spirits. Special meals (diabetic/wheat free/vegetarian) can be arranged, but you have to order at least 48 hours before you board the train. Most carriages have large windows from

which to view the spectacular passing scenery, and some routes have a commentary on points of interest. Most trains also have a viewing carriage at the rear.

CUTTING COSTS

To save money, **look into rail passes.** But be aware that if you don't plan to cover many miles you may come out ahead by buying individual tickets.

Travelers can purchase a New Zealand Travelpass for unlimited travel by train, bus, and Interislander ferry for a variety of periods. *See* Discounts & Deals, above, for more information. For Youth Hostel Association members, InterCity provides a 15% discount on most train service, all InterCity coach service, and on Interislander ferries. Students with an International Student Identity Card (ISIC) get a 20% discount. Senior citizens (over 60) get a 20% discount with proof of age.

📶 Buying Passes **ATS Tours** ☎ 310/643-0044, 888/781-5170 in U.S. ⊕ www.atstours.com. **InterCity Travel Centres** ☎ 09/623-1503 in Auckland, 03/365-1113 in Christchurch, 04/385-0520 in Wellington or 0508/353-947 toll-free in New Zealand.

FARES & SCHEDULES

You can obtain both schedules and tickets at visitor-information centers and at train stations.

📶 Train Information **Tranz Scenic** ☎ 04/495-0775 or 0800/872-467 for bookings, 0800/277-482 ⊕ www.tranzscenic.co.nz.

PAYING

Major credit cards are accepted, as are cash and traveler's checks.

RESERVATIONS

Reservations are advised, particularly in the summer months. **Book at least 48 hours in advance.**

TRAVEL AGENCIES

A good travel agent puts your needs first. Look for an agency that has been in business at least five years, emphasizes customer service, and has someone on staff who specializes in your destination. In addition, **make sure the agency belongs to a professional trade organization.** The American Society of Travel Agents (ASTA) has more than 10,000 members in some 140 countries, enforces a strict code of ethics, and will step in to mediate agent-client disputes involving ASTA members. ASTA also maintains a directory of agents on its Web site; ASTA's TravelSense.org, a trip planning and travel advice site, can also help to locate a travel agent who caters to your needs.

🇫 Local Agent Referrals American Society of Travel Agents (ASTA) ✉ 1101 King St., Suite 200, Alexandria, VA 22314 ☎ 703/739-2782, 800/965-2782 24-hr hotline 🖨 703/684-8319 ⊕ www.astanet. com and www.travelsense.org. **Association of British Travel Agents** ✉ 68-71 Newman St., London W1T 3AH ☎ 020/7637-2444 🖨 020/7637-0713 ⊕ www.abta.com. **Association of Canadian Travel Agencies** ✉ 130 Albert St., Suite 1705, Ottawa, Ontario K1P 5G4 ☎ 613/237-3657 🖨 613/237-7052 ⊕ www.acta.ca. **Australian Federation of Travel Agents** ✉ Level 3, 309 Pitt St., Sydney, NSW 2000 ☎ 02/9264-3299 or 1300/363-416 🖨 02/9264-1085 ⊕ www.afta.com.au. **Travel Agents' Association of New Zealand** ✉ Level 5, Tourism and Travel House, 79 Boulcott St., Box 1888, Wellington 6001 ☎ 04/499-0104 🖨 04/499-0786 ⊕ www.taanz.org.nz.

VISITOR INFORMATION

Tourism New Zealand is a government agency that serves as a hub for the 28 different Regional Tourism Organizations (RTOs) based throughout the country. These locally funded RTOs run most of the 90 i-SITE visitor centers. These centers are marked with blue signs and a white letter i. Please see the individual chapter A to Z sections for details on local visitor bureaus.

🇫 New Zealand Tourism Board In the United States ✉ 501 Santa Monica Blvd., Los Angeles, CA 90401 ☎ 310/395-7480 or 866/639-9325 🖨 310/395-5453 ⊕ www.newzealand.com. **In Canada** ✉ 888 Dunsmuir St., Suite 1200, Vancouver, BC V6C 3K4 ☎ 604/684-2117 or 800/888-5494 🖨 604/684-1265. **In the United Kingdom** ✉ New Zealand House, Haymarket, London SW1Y 4TQ ☎ 020/7930-1662 🖨 020/7839-8929.

🇫 U.S. Government Advisories U.S. Department of State ✉ Bureau of Consular Affairs, Overseas Citizens Services Office, 2201 C St. NW Washington, DC 20520 ☎ 202/647-5225or 888/407-4747, 317/472-2328 for interactive hotline ⊕ www.travel.state.gov.

WEB SITES

Do check out the World Wide Web when planning your trip. You'll find everything from weather forecasts to virtual tours of famous cities. Be sure to visit Fodors.com

(⊕ www.fodors.com), a complete travel-planning site. You can research prices and book plane tickets, hotel rooms, rental cars, vacation packages, and more. In addition, you can post your pressing questions in the Travel Talk section. Other planning tools include a currency converter and weather reports, and there are loads of links to travel resources.

Tourism New Zealand's site, ⊕ www. newzealand.com includes city and regional overviews as well as features such as travel journals, information on major events like the America's Cup, and cultural background. Stuff (⊕ www.stuff.co.nz) and NZ Pages (⊕ www.nzpages.co.nz) are also good catch-all sites for Kiwi news, links to local resources, and more.

For the latest on the grape, Wine OnLine (⊕ www.wineonline.co.nz) and the official Web site for the New Zealand Wine and Grape Industry, New Zealand Wine (⊕ www.nzwine.com), post updates on some of the country's top wineries. NZ Gardens Net (⊕ www.gardens.co.nz) cultivates information on New Zealand's public and private gardens. At ⊕ www.maori.org. nz of Māori Organisations of New Zealand, you can find answers to cultural FAQs.

For detailed information on New Zealand's wilderness areas, visit the Department of Conservation's site, ⊕ www.doc.govt.nz, which covers all the national parks, major walking tracks, campgrounds and huts, safety tips, and so forth. Snowco (⊕ www. snow.co.nz) provides countrywide snow reports; the New Zealand Alpine Club (⊕ www.alpineclub.org.nz) focuses on all kinds of climbing. To get up to speed on the all-consuming rugby news, check out the New Zealand Rugby Union's ⊕ www. allblacks.com or the comprehensive Planet Rugby at ⊕ www.planet-rugby.com

Cuisine magazine's online presence, ⊕ www.cuisine.co.nz, includes restaurant reviews and discussions of local wines. If you're inspired, look up recipes for Kiwi dishes. The New Zealand Historic Places Trust site, ⊕ www.historic.org.nz, will give you the latest on heritage sights throughout the country. And at ⊕ www. nzmusic.com you can get the scoop on New Zealand bands and shows.

INDEX

PHOTO CREDITS

ABOUT OUR WRITERS

Writing about travel and the people she meets along the way are what Nelson resident **Sue Farley** enjoys most about her work. She's keen on searching out wild, remote spots of Australia and New Zealand, and the territory she covered to update the chapters on the Upper South Island, Christchurch & Canterbury, The Southern Alps & Fiordland, and Otago, Invercargill, and Stewart Island certainly filled the bill.

Doug Johansen and **Jan Poole**, who updated the Adventure Vacations chapter, are owner-operators of Kiwi Dundee Adventures, Ltd., which offers a variety of tours and off-the-beaten-path hiking trips on the Coromandel Peninsula and around New Zealand. They are two nature-loving Kiwis who have a deep respect for the mountains, forests, and coastlines of their country. Doug is known as one of New Zealand's pioneers of nature tourism and in 1992 won the inaugural New Zealand Ecotourism Award. Both are recipients of Queens medals for their work in tourism.

Alia Levine moved from Aotearoa (New Zealand) to New York City in 1997 and spent several years working in publishing, education, and women's rights. In 2003, she headed back to the southern hemisphere's peaceful, green gateway to the world, where she's finishing up a Master of Arts degree in Development Studies, writing, and reacclimating to getting around without a subway. For this edition, she updated Coromandel & the Bay of Plenty, as well as the Smart Travel Tips and Understanding New Zealand chapters.

Bob Marriott was born in Nottingham, England, but has made his home in New Zealand since 1966. His travels have taken him all over the world, and his work has been widely published in New Zealand, Australia, the United States, Britain, Malaysia, and on the Web. His own photographs illustrate most of his feature articles. Bob contributed to Fodor's guide to Southeast Asia; for this book he revised the Wellington & the Wairarapa and East Coast & Volcanic Zone chapters. He'd like to thank his wife Linda for her understanding when the paper-chase is on.

Toni Mason is not a native Aucklander, but the city's combination of urban offerings and easy access to beaches makes it her favorite part of the country. For this edition, she didn't have to travel far, but rediscovered Auckland and Northland & The Bay of Islands from a traveler's perspective. In addition to writing, she's also a freelance editor, translator, and television researcher.

Kathy Ombler, who updated the Western North Island chapter, is a freelance writer whose interests lie in conservation, nature tourism, and the travel, tourism, and hospitality industries. She has written several outdoor recreation guides, including *National Parks and Other Wild Places of New Zealand* (part of an international series), *Walking Wellington*, and *A Visitor's Guide to New Zealand National Parks*. Kathy grew up on a Waikato farm, has lived in many places throughout New Zealand from big cities to small rural settlements in national parks, and is now based in Wellington.

Shortly after 9/11, American writer **Stephanie Stephens**, who updated the front section of this book, visited New Zealand on the QE2 World Cruise. The place, pace, and people captivated her, so she applied for and was granted her indefinite visa. She now divides her time between Orange County, California, and Cambridge, in New Zealand's lovely green Waikato region. She proudly owns and rides NZ show jumper Cheleken Ruanuku, "the wizard." When not riding, she writes for publications such as *Family Circle, (Delta) Sky, Continental, Ladies' Home Journal,* and more. She just stresses less in New Zealand.

You can rest assured that you're in good hands—and that no property mentioned in the book has paid to be included. Each has been selected strictly on its merits, as the best of its type in its price range.